PETERSON'S COLLEGES IN THE MIDWEST

24th Edition

About Peterson's

To succeed on your lifelong educational journey, you will need accurate, dependable, and practical tools and resources. That is why Peterson's is everywhere education happens. Because whenever and however you need education content delivered, you can rely on Peterson's to provide the information, know-how, and guidance to help you reach your goals. Tools to match the right students with the right school. It's here. Personalized resources and expert guidance. It's here. Comprehensive and dependable education content—delivered whenever and however you need it. It's all here.

For more information, contact Peterson's, 2000 Lenox Drive, Lawrenceville, NJ 08648; 800-338-3282; or find us on the World Wide Web at www.petersons.com/about.

Stephen Clemente, President; Bernadette Webster, Director of Publishing; Mark D. Snider, Editor; Ward Brigham, Research Project Manager; Cathleen Fee, Research Associate; Phyllis Johnson, Programmer; Ray Golaszewski, Manufacturing Manager; Linda M. Williams, Composition Manager; Janet Garwo, Mimi Kaufman, Karen Mount, Danielle Vreeland, Shannon White, Client Relations Representatives

ISSN pending
ISBN-13: 978-0-7689-2690-3
ISBN-10: 0-7689-2690-4

Printed in the United States of America

10 9 8 7 6 5 4 3 2 1 11 10 09

Twenty-fourth Edition

By producing this book on recycled paper (40% post consumer waste) 17 trees were saved.

CONTENTS

A Note from the Peterson's Editors

Welcome to the world of choosing a college. You are probably considering at least one college that is relatively near your home. It may surprise you to learn that the majority of all students go to college within a 300-mile radius of where they live. Because of that factor, we publish this series of college guides that focuses on the colleges in each of six regions of the country so that students can easily compare the colleges in their own area. (Two-year public and proprietary colleges are not included because their admission patterns are significantly different from other colleges.)

For advice and guidance in the college search and selection process, just turn the page. "Surviving Standardized Tests" describes the most frequently used tests. Of course, part of the college selection process involves visiting the schools themselves and "The Whys and Whats of College Visits" is just the planner you need to make those trips well worth your while. Next, "Applying 101" provides advice on how best to approach the application phase of the process. If you've got questions about transferring, "Successful Transfer" has got the answers you need. "Who's Paying for This? Financial Aid Basics" and the "Financial Aid Programs for Schools in the Midwest" articles provide you with the essential information on how to meet your education expenses. "Searching for Four-Year Colleges Online" gives you all the tips you'll need to augment your college search using the Internet. Lastly, you'll want to read through "How to Use This Guide" and learn how to use all the information presented in this volume.

Following these articles are the **Profiles of Colleges** sections. The **Profiles** are easy to read and should give you a good sense of whether a college meets your basic needs and warrants further consideration. This consistently formatted collection of data can provide a balance to the individual mailings you are likely to receive from colleges. The **Profiles** appear in geographical order by state.

In a number of the **Profiles** (those marked with a *Sponsor* icon), you will find helpful information about social life, academic life, campus visits, and interviews. These **Special Messages to Students** are written in each case by a college admissions office staff member. You will find valuable insights into what each writer considers special about his or her institution (both socially and academically), what is expected of you during your interview at that college, and how important the interview is there. You will also be alerted to outstanding attractions on campus or nearby so you can plan a productive visit. In many cases, travel information (nearest commercial airport and nearest interstate highway) that will be of help on your campus visit is included.

And if you still thirst for even more information, look for the two-page narrative descriptions appearing in the **Close-Ups of Colleges** sections of the book. These descriptions are written by admissions deans and provide great detail about each college. They are edited to provide a consistent format across entries for your ease of comparison.

The **Indexes** at the back of the book (Majors and Degrees, Athletic Programs and Scholarships, and ROTC Programs) enable you to pinpoint colleges listed in the **Profiles** according to their specific offerings. In addition, there is an Alphabetical Listing of Colleges and Universities to enable you to quickly find a school that you may have already determined meets your criteria.

We hope you will find this information helpful. Our advice is to relax, enjoy high school, and do as well as you can in your courses. Give yourself enough time during the early stages of your search to think about what kind of person you are and what you want to become so you can choose colleges for the right reasons. Read all college materials with an open mind, and visit as many campuses as you can. Plan ahead so you do not rush through your applications. Try to remember that admission directors are as interested in you and the possibility of you attending their college as you are in the possibility of applying. They spend most of their time reaching out to students, explaining their colleges' programs and policies, and simplifying the application process whenever they can. If you think of them as people who like students and if you can picture them taking the time to carefully provide the information in this book for you, it might help to lessen any anxiety you are feeling about applying. In fact, the admission people whose names you will find in this book hope to hear from you.

Peterson's publishes a full line of resources to help guide you and your family through the college admission process. Peterson's publications can be found at your local bookstore or library and at your high school guidance office;

you can access us online at **www.petersons.com.** Our Web-based resources for high school students can be found at **www.petersons.com/studentedge,** a personalized online resource center that helps you prepare for life after high school. It combines test preparation, college search, financial aid planning, and career exploration in one convenient location.

We welcome any comments or suggestions you may have about this publication and invite you to complete our online survey at **www.petersons.com/booksurvey**. Or you can fill out the survey at the back of this book, tear it out, and mail it to us at:

Publishing Department
Peterson's, a Nelnet company
2000 Lenox Drive
Lawrenceville, NJ 08648

Your feedback will help us make your education dreams possible. The editors at Peterson's wish you success and happiness wherever you enroll.

The College Admissions Process

Surviving Standardized Tests

WHAT ARE STANDARDIZED TESTS?

Colleges and universities in the United States use tests to help evaluate applicants' readiness for admission or to place them in appropriate courses. The tests that are most frequently used by colleges are the ACT of American College Testing, Inc., and the College Board's SAT. In addition, the Educational Testing Service (ETS) offers the TOEFL test, which evaluates the English-language proficiency of nonnative speakers. The tests are offered at designated testing centers located at high schools and colleges throughout the United States and U.S. territories and at testing centers in various countries throughout the world.

Upon request, special accommodations for students with documented visual, hearing, physical, or learning disabilities are available. Examples of special accommodations include tests in Braille or large print and such aids as a reader, recorder, magnifying glass, or sign language interpreter. Additional testing time may be allowed in some instances. Contact the appropriate testing program or your guidance counselor for details on how to request special accommodations.

THE ACT

The ACT is a standardized college entrance examination that measures knowledge and skills in English, mathematics, reading, and science reasoning and the application of these skills to future academic tasks. The ACT consists of four multiple-choice tests.

Test 1: English

- 75 questions, 45 minutes
- Usage and mechanics
- Rhetorical skills

Test 2: Mathematics

- 60 questions, 60 minutes
- Pre-algebra
- Elementary algebra
- Intermediate algebra
- Coordinate geometry
- Plane geometry
- Trigonometry

Test 3: Reading

- 40 questions, 35 minutes
- Prose fiction
- Humanities
- Social studies
- Natural sciences

Test 4: Science

- 40 questions, 35 minutes
- Data representation
- Research summary
- Conflicting viewpoints

Each section is scored from 1 to 36 and is scaled for slight variations in difficulty. Students are not penalized for incorrect responses. The composite score is the average of the four scaled scores. There is also a 30-minute Writing Test that is an optional component of the ACT.

To prepare for the ACT, ask your guidance counselor for a free guidebook called *Preparing for the ACT*. Besides providing general test-preparation information and additional test-taking strategies, this guidebook describes the content and format of the four ACT subject area tests, summarizes test administration procedures followed at ACT test centers, and includes a practice test. Peterson's publishes *The Real ACT Prep Guide* that includes three official ACT tests.

DON'T FORGET TO . . .

- Take the SAT or ACT before application deadlines.
- Note that test registration deadlines precede test dates by about six weeks.
- Register to take the TOEFL test if English is not your native language and you are planning on studying at a North American college.
- Practice your test-taking skills with *Peterson's Master the SAT, Peterson's Ultimate ACT Tool Kit, The Real ACT Prep Guide* (published by Peterson's), *Peterson's Master TOEFL Reading Skills, Peterson's Master TOEFL Vocabulary,* and *Peterson's Master TOEFL Writing Skills.*
- Contact the College Board or American College Testing, Inc., in advance if you need special accommodations when taking tests.

THE SAT

The SAT measures developed critical reading and mathematical reasoning abilities as they relate to successful performance in college. It is intended to supplement the secondary school record and other information about the student in assessing readiness for college. There is one unscored, experimental section on the exam, which is used for equating and/or pretesting purposes and can cover either the mathematics or critical reading area.

Critical Reading

- 67 questions, 70 minutes
- Sentence completion
- Passage-based reading

Mathematics

- 54 questions, 70 minutes
- Multiple-choice
- Student-produced response (grid-ins)

Writing

- 49 questions plus essay, 60 minutes
- Identifying sentence errors
- Improving paragraphs
- Improving sentences
- Essay

Students receive one point for each correct response and lose a fraction of a point for each incorrect response (except for student-produced responses). These points are totaled to produce the raw scores, which are then scaled to equalize the scores for slight variations in difficulty for various editions of the test. The critical reading, writing, and mathematics scaled scores range from 200–800 per section. The total scaled score range is from 600–2400.

SAT SUBJECT TESTS

Subject Tests are required by some institutions for admission and/or placement in freshman-level courses. Each Subject Test measures one's knowledge of a specific subject and the ability to apply that knowledge. Students should check with each institution for its specific requirements. In general, students are required to take three Subject Tests (one English, one mathematics, and one of their choice).

Subject Tests are given in the following areas: biology, chemistry, Chinese, French, German, Italian, Japanese, Korean, Latin, literature, mathematics, modern Hebrew, physics, Spanish, U.S. history, and world history. These tests are 1 hour long and are primarily multiple-choice tests. Three Subject Tests may be taken on one test date.

Scored like the SAT, students gain a point for each correct answer and lose a fraction of a point for each incorrect answer. The raw scores are then converted to scaled scores that range from 200 to 800.

THE TOEFL INTERNET-BASED TEST (IBT)

The Test of English as a Foreign Language Internet-Based Test (TOEFL iBT) is designed to help assess a student's grasp of English if it is not the student's first language. Performance on the TOEFL test may help interpret scores on the critical reading sections of the SAT. The test consists of four integrated sections: speaking, listening, reading, and writing. The TOEFL iBT emphasizes integrated skills. The paper-based versions of the TOEFL will continue to be administered in certain countries where the Internet-based version has not yet been introduced. For further information, visit www.toefl.org.

WHAT OTHER TESTS SHOULD I KNOW ABOUT?

The AP Program

This program allows high school students to try college-level work and build valuable skills and study habits in the process. Subject matter is explored in more depth in AP courses than in other high school classes. A qualifying score on an AP test—which varies from school to school—can earn you college credit or advanced placement. Getting qualifying grades on enough exams can even earn you a full year's credit and sophomore standing at more than 1,500 higher-education institutions. There are currently thirty-seven AP courses in twenty-two different subject areas, including art history, biology, and computer science. Speak to your guidance counselor for information about your school's offerings.

College-Level Examination Program (CLEP)

The CLEP enables students to earn college credit for what they already know, whether it was learned in school, through independent study, or through other experiences outside of the classroom. Approximately 2,900 colleges and universities now award credit for qualifying scores on one or more of the 34 CLEP exams. The exams, which are 90 minutes in length and are primarily multiple choice, are administered at participating colleges and universities. For more information, check out the Web site at www.collegeboard.com/clep.

TOP 10 WAYS NOT TO TAKE THE TEST

10. Cramming the night before the test.
9. Not becoming familiar with the directions before you take the test.
8. Not becoming familiar with the format of the test before you take it.
7. Not knowing how the test is graded.
6. Spending too much time on any one question.
5. Not checking spelling, grammar, and sentence structure in essays.
4. Second-guessing yourself.
3. Forgetting to take a deep breath to keep from—
2. Losing It!
1. Writing a one-paragraph essay.

WHAT CAN I DO TO PREPARE FOR THESE TESTS?

Know what to expect. Get familiar with how the tests are structured, how much time is allowed, and the directions for each type of question. Get plenty of rest the night before the test and eat breakfast that morning.

There are a variety of products, from books to software to videos, available to help you prepare for most standardized tests. Find the learning style that suits you best. As for which products to buy, there are two major categories—those created by the test makers and those created by private companies. The best approach is to talk to someone who has been through the process and find out which product or products he or she recommends.

Some students report significant increases in scores after participating in coaching programs. Longer-term programs (40 hours) seem to raise scores more than short-term programs (20 hours), but beyond 40 hours, score gains are minor. Math scores appear to benefit more from coaching than critical reading scores.

Resources

There is a variety of ways to prepare for standardized tests—find a method that fits your schedule and your budget. But you should definitely prepare. Far too many students walk into these tests cold, either because they find standardized tests frightening or annoying or they just haven't found the time to study. The key is that these exams are standardized. That means these tests are largely the same from administration to administration; they always test the same concepts. They have to, or else you couldn't compare the scores of people who took the tests on different dates. The numbers or words may change, but the underlying content doesn't.

So how do you prepare? At the very least, you should review relevant material, such as math formulas and commonly used vocabulary words, and know the directions for each question type or test section. You should take at least one practice test and review your mistakes so you don't make them again on the test day. Beyond that, you know best how much preparation you need. You'll also find lots of material in libraries or bookstores to help you: books and software from the test makers and from other publishers (including Peterson's) or live courses that range from national test-preparation companies to teachers at your high school who offer classes.

The Whys and Whats of College Visits

Dawn B. Sova, Ph.D.

The campus visit should not be a passive activity for you and your parents. Take the initiative and gather information beyond that provided in the official tour. You will see many important indicators during your visit that will tell you more about the true character of a college and its students than the tour guide will reveal. Know what to look for and how to assess the importance of such indicators.

WHAT SHOULD YOU ASK AND WHAT SHOULD YOU LOOK FOR?

Your first stop on a campus visit is the visitor center or admissions office, where you will probably have to wait to meet with a counselor. Colleges usually plan to greet visitors later than the appointed time in order to give them the opportunity to review some of the campus information that is liberally scattered throughout the visitor waiting room. Take advantage of the time to become even more familiar with the college by arriving 15 to 30 minutes before your appointment to observe the behavior of staff members and to browse through the yearbooks and student newspapers that will be available.

If you prepare in advance, you will have already reviewed the college catalog and map of the campus. These materials familiarize you with the academic offerings and the physical layout of the campus, but the true character of the college and its students emerges in other ways.

Begin your investigation with the visitor center staff members. As a student's first official contact with the college, they should make every effort to welcome prospective students and project a friendly image.

- How do they treat you and other prospective students who are waiting? Are they friendly and willing to speak with you, or do they try their hardest to avoid eye contact and conversation?
- Are they friendly with each other and with students who enter the office, or are they curt and unwilling to help?
- Does the waiting room have a friendly feeling or is it cold and sterile?

If the visitor center staff members seem indifferent to *prospective* students, there is little reason to believe that they will be warm and welcoming to current students. View such behavior as a warning to watch very carefully the interaction of others with you during the tour. An indifferent or unfriendly reception in the admissions office may be simply the first of many signs that attending this college will not be a pleasant experience.

Look through several yearbooks and see the types of activities that are actually photographed, as opposed to the activities that colleges promise in their promotional literature. Some questions are impossible to answer if the college is very large, but for small and moderately sized colleges the yearbook is a good indicator of campus activity.

- Has the number of clubs and organizations increased or decreased in the past five years?
- Do the same students appear repeatedly in activities?
- Do sororities and fraternities dominate campus activities?
- Are participants limited to one sex or one ethnic group, or is there diversity?
- Are all activities limited to the campus, or are students involved in activities in the community?

Use what you observe in the yearbooks as a means of forming a more complete understanding of the college, but don't base your entire impression on just one facet. If time permits, look through several copies of the school newspaper, which should reflect the major concerns and interests of the students. The paper is also a good way to learn about the campus social life.

- Does the paper contain a mix of national and local news?
- What products or services are advertised?
- How assertive are the editorials?
- With what topics are the columnists concerned?
- Are movies and concerts that meet your tastes advertised or reviewed?
- What types of ads appear in the classified section?

The newspaper should be a public forum for students, and, as such, should reflect the character of the campus and of the student body. A paper that deals only with seemingly safe and well-edited topics on the editorial page and in regular feature columns might indicate administrative censorship. A lack of ads for restaurants might indicate either a lack of good places to eat or that area restaurants do not welcome student business. A limited mention of movies, concerts, or other entertainment might reveal a severely limited campus social life. Even if ads and reviews are included, you should still balance how such activities reflect your tastes.

You will have only a limited amount of time to ask questions during your initial meeting with the admissions counselor, for very few schools include a formal interview in the initial campus visit or tour. Instead, this brief meeting is often just a nicety that allows the admissions office to begin a file for the student and to record some initial impressions. Save your questions for the tour guide and for students on campus you meet along the way.

HOW CAN YOU ASSESS THE TRUE CHARACTER OF A COLLEGE AND ITS STUDENTS?

Colleges do not train their tour guides to deceive prospective students, but they do caution guides to avoid unflattering topics and campus sites. Does this mean that you will see only a sugarcoated version of life on a particular college campus? Not at all, especially not if you are observant.

Most organized campus visits include such campus facilities as dormitories, dining halls, libraries, student activity and recreation centers, and the health and student services centers. Some may only be pointed out, while you will walk through others. Either way, you will find that many signs of the true character of the college emerge if you keep your eyes open.

Bulletin boards in dormitories and student centers contain a wealth of information about campus activities, student concerns, and campus groups. Read the posters, notices, and messages to learn what *really* interests students. Unlike ads in the school newspaper, posters put up by students advertise both on- and off-campus events, so they will give you an idea of what is also available in the surrounding community.

Review the notices, which may cover either campuswide events or events that concern only small groups of students. The catalog may not mention a performance group, but an individual dormitory with its own small theater may offer regular productions. Poetry readings, jam sessions, writers' groups, and other activities may be announced and show diversity of student interests.

Even the brief bulletin board messages offering objects for sale and noting objects that people want to purchase reveal a lot about a campus. Are most of the items computer related? Or do the messages specify CDs, audio equipment, or musical instruments? Are offers to trade goods or services posted? Don't ignore the "ride wanted" messages. Students who want to share rides home during a break may specify widely diverse geographical locations. If so, then you know that the student body is not limited to only the immediate area or one locale. Other messages can also enhance your knowledge of the true character of the campus and its students.

As you walk through various buildings, examine their condition carefully.

- Is the paint peeling, and do the exteriors look worn?
- Are the exteriors and interiors of the building clean?
- Is the equipment in the classrooms up-to-date or outdated?

Pay particular attention to the dormitories, especially to factors that might affect your safety. Observe the appearance of the structure, and ask about the security measures in and around the dormitories.

- Are the dormitories noisy or quiet?
- Do they seem crowded?
- How good is the lighting around each dormitory?
- Are the dormitories spread throughout the campus or are they clustered in one main area?
- Who has access to the dormitories in addition to students?
- How secure are the means by which students enter and leave the dormitory?

While you are on the subject of dormitory safety, you should also ask about campus safety. Don't expect that the guide will rattle off a list of crimes that have been committed in the past year. To obtain that information, access the recent year of issues of *The Chronicle of Higher Education* and locate its yearly report on campus crime. Also ask the guide about safety measures that the campus police take and those that students have initiated.

- Can students request escorts to their residences late at night?
- Do campus shuttle buses run at frequent intervals all night?
- Are "blue-light" telephones liberally placed throughout the campus for students to use to call for help?
- Do the campus police patrol the campus regularly?

If the guide does not answer your questions satisfactorily, wait until after the tour to contact the campus police or traffic office for answers.

Campus tours usually just point out the health services center without taking the time to walk through. Even if you don't see the inside of the building, you should take a close look at the location of the health services center and ask the guide questions about services.

- How far is the health center from the dormitories?
- Is a doctor always on call?
- Does the campus transport sick students from their dormitories or must they walk?
- What are the operating hours of the health center?
- Does the health center refer students to a nearby hospital?

If the guide can't answer your questions, visit the health center later and ask someone there.

Most campus tours take pride in showing students their activities centers, which may contain snack bars, game rooms, workout facilities, and other means of entertainment. Should you scrutinize this building as carefully as the rest? Of course. Outdated and poorly maintained activity equipment contributes to your total impression of the college. You should also ask about the hours, availability, and cost (no, the activities are usually *not* free) of using the bowling alleys, pool tables, air hockey tables, and other ammenities.

As you walk through campus with the tour, also look carefully at the appearance of the students who pass. The way in which both men and women groom themselves, the way they dress, and even their physical bearing communicate a lot more than any guidebook can. If everyone seems to conform to the same look, you might feel that you would be uncomfortable at the college, however nonconformist that look might be. On the other hand, you might not feel comfortable on a campus that stresses diversity of dress and behavior, and your observations now can save you discomfort later.

- Does every student seem to wear a sorority or fraternity t-shirt or jacket?
- Is everyone of your sex sporting the latest fad haircut?
- Do all of the men or the women seem to be wearing expensive name-brand clothes?
- Do most of the students seem to be working hard to look outrageous with regards to clothing, hair color, and body art?
- Would you feel uncomfortable in a room full of these students?

Is appearance important to you? If it is, then you should consider very seriously if you answer *yes* to any of the above questions. You don't have to be the same as everyone else on campus, but standing out too much may make you unhappy.

As you observe the physical appearance of the students, also listen to their conversations as you pass them. What are they talking about? How are they speaking? Are their voices and accents all the same, or do you hear diversity in their speech? Are you offended by their language? Think how you will feel if surrounded by the same speech habits and patterns for four years.

WHERE SHOULD YOU VISIT ON YOUR OWN?

Your campus visit is not over when the tour ends because you will probably have many questions yet to be answered and many places to still be seen. Where you go depends upon the extent to which the organized tour covers the campus. Your tour should take you to view residential halls, health and student services centers, the gymnasium or field house, dining halls, the library, and recreational centers. If any of the facilities on this list have been omitted, visit them on your own and ask questions of the students and staff members you meet. In addition, you should step off campus and gain an impression of the surrounding community. You will probably become bored with life on campus and spend at least some time off campus. Make certain that you know what the surrounding area is like.

The campus tour leaves little time to ask impromptu questions of current students, but you can do so after the tour. Eat lunch in one of the dining halls. Most will allow visitors to pay cash to experience a typical student meal. Food may not be important to you now while you are living at home and can simply take anything you want from the refrigerator at any time, but it will be when you are away at college with only a meal ticket to feed you.

- How clean is the dining hall? Consider serving tables, floors, and seating.
- What is the quality of the food?
- How big are the portions?
- How much variety do students have at each meal?
- How healthy are the food choices?

While you are eating, try to strike up a conversation with students and tell them that you are considering attending their college. Their reactions and advice can be eye-opening. Ask them questions about the academic atmosphere and the professors.

- Are the classes large or small?
- Do the majority of the professors only lecture or are tutorials and seminars common?
- Is the emphasis of the faculty career-oriented or abstract?
- Are the teaching methods innovative and stimulating or boring and dull?
- Is the academic atmosphere pressured, lax, or somewhere in between?
- Which are the strong majors? The weak majors?

- Is the emphasis on grades or social life or a mix of both at the college?
- How hard do students have to work to receive high grades?

Current students can also give you the inside line on the true nature of the college social life. You may gain some idea through looking in the yearbook, in the newspaper, and on the bulletin boards, but students will reveal the true highs and lows of campus life. Ask them about drug use, partying, dating, drinking, and anything else that may affect your life as a student.

- Which are the most popular club activities?
- What do students do on weekends? Do most go home?
- How frequently do concerts occur on campus? Who has recently performed?
- How can you become involved in specific activities (name them)?
- How strictly are campus rules enforced and how severe are penalties?
- What counseling services are available?
- Are academic tutoring services available?
- Do they feel that the faculty really cares about students, especially freshmen?

You will receive the most valuable information from current students, but you will only be able to speak with them after the tour is over. And you might have to risk rejection as you try to initiate conversations with students who might not want to reveal how they feel about the campus. Still, the value of this information is worth the chance.

If you have the time, you should also visit the library to see just how accessible research materials are and to observe the physical layout. The catalog usually specifies the days and hours of operation, as well as the number of volumes contained in the library and the number of periodicals to which it subscribes. A library also requires accessibility, good lighting, an adequate number of study carrels, and lounge areas for students. Many colleges have created 24-hour study lounges for students who find the residence halls too noisy for studying, although most colleges claim that they designate areas of the residences as "quiet study" areas. You may not be interested in any of this information, but when you are a student you will have to make frequent use of the campus library so you should know what is available. You should at least ask how extensive their holdings are in your proposed major area. If they have virtually nothing, you will have to spend a lot of time ordering items via interlibrary loan or making copies, which can become expensive. The ready answer of students that they will obtain their information from the Internet is unpleasantly countered by professors who demand journal articles with documentation.

Make a point of at least driving through the community surrounding the college because you will be spending time there shopping, dining, working in a part-time job, or attending events. Even the largest and best-stocked campus will not meet all of your social and personal needs. If you can spare the time, stop in several stores to see if they welcome college students.

- Is the surrounding community suburban, urban, or rural?
- Does the community offer stores of interest, such as bookstores, craft shops, and boutiques?
- Do the businesses employ college students?
- Does the community have a movie or stage theater?
- Are there several types of interesting restaurants?
- Do there seem to be any clubs that court a college clientele?
- Is the center of activity easy to walk to, or do you need other transportation?

You might feel that a day is not enough to answer all of your questions, but even answering some questions will provide you with a stronger basis for choosing a college. Many students visit a college campus several times before making their decision. Keep in mind that for the rest of your life you will be associated with the college that you attend. You will spend four years of your life at this college. The effort of spending several days to obtain the information to make your decision is worthwhile.

Dawn B. Sova, Ph.D., is a former newspaper reporter and columnist, as well as the author of more than eight books and numerous magazine articles. She teaches creative and research writing, as well as scientific and technical writing, newswriting, and journalism.

Applying 101

The words "applying yourself" have several important meanings in the college application process. One meaning refers to the fact that you need to keep focused during this important time in your life, keep your priorities straight, and know the dates that your applications are due so you can apply on time. The phrase might also refer to the person who is really responsible for your application—you.

You are the only person who should compile your college application. You need to take ownership of this process. The guidance counselor is not responsible for completing your applications, and neither are your parents. College applications must be completed in addition to your normal workload at school, college visits, and SAT, ACT, or TOEFL testing.

THE APPLICATION

The application is your way of introducing yourself to a college admissions office. As with any introduction, you want to make a good first impression. The first thing you should do in presenting your application is to find out what the college or university needs from you. Read the application carefully to find out the application fee and deadline, required standardized tests, number of essays, interview requirements, and anything else you can do or submit to help improve your chances for acceptance.

Completing college applications yourself helps you learn more about the schools to which you are applying. The information a college asks for in its application can tell you much about the school. State university applications often tell you how they are going to view their applicants. Usually, they select students based on GPAs and test scores. Colleges that request an interview, ask you to respond to a few open-ended questions, or require an essay are interested in a more personal approach to the application process and may be looking for different types of students than those sought by a state school.

In addition to submitting the actual application, there are several other items that are commonly required. You will be responsible for ensuring that your standardized test scores and your high school transcript arrive at the colleges to which you apply. Most colleges will ask that you submit teacher recommendations as well. Select teachers who know you and your abilities well and allow them plenty of time to complete the recommendations. When all portions of the application have been completed and sent in, whether electronically or by mail, make sure you follow up with the college to ensure their receipt.

FOLLOW THESE TIPS WHEN FILLING OUT YOUR APPLICATION

- **Follow the directions to the letter.** You don't want to be in a position to ask an admissions officer for exceptions due to your inattentiveness.
- **Proofread all parts of your application,** including your essay. Again, the final product indicates to the admissions staff how meticulous and careful you are in your work.
- **Submit your application as early as possible,** provided all of the pieces are available. If there is a problem with your application, this will allow you to work through it with the admissions staff in plenty of time. If you wait until the last minute, it not only takes away that cushion but also reflects poorly on your sense of priorities.
- **Keep a copy of the completed application,** whether it is a photocopy or a copy saved on your computer.

THE APPLICATION ESSAY

Whereas the other portions of your application—your transcript, test scores, and involvement in extracurricular activities—are a reflection of what you've accomplished up to this point, your application essay is an opportunity to present yourself in the here and now. The essay shows your originality and verbal skills and how you approach a topic or problem and express your opinion.

Some colleges may request one essay or a combination of essays and short-answer topics to learn more about who you are and how well you can communicate your thoughts. Common essay topics cover such simple themes as writing about yourself and your experiences or why you want to attend that particular school. Other colleges will ask that you show your imaginative or creative side by writing about a favorite author, for instance, or commenting on a hypothetical situation. In such cases, they will be looking at your thought processes and level of creativity.

Admissions officers, particularly those at small or mid-size colleges, use the essay to determine how you, as a student, will fit into life at that college. The essay, therefore, is a critical component of the application process. Here are some tips for writing a winning essay:

- Colleges are looking for an honest representation of who you are and what you think. Make sure that the tone of the essay reflects enthusiasm, maturity, creativity, the ability to communicate, talent, and your leadership skills.
- Be sure you set aside enough time to write the essay, revise it, and revise it *again.* Running "spell check" will only detect a fraction of the errors you probably made on your first pass at writing it. Take a break and then come back to it and reread it. You will probably notice other style, content, and grammar problems—and ways that you can improve the essay overall.
- Always answer the question that is being asked, making sure that you are specific, clear, and true to your personality.
- Enlist the help of reviewers who know you well—friends, parents, teachers—since they are likely to be the most honest and will keep you on track in the presentation of your true self.

THE PERSONAL INTERVIEW

Although it is relatively rare that a personal interview is required, many colleges recommend that you take this opportunity for a face-to-face discussion with a member of the admissions staff. Read through the application materials to determine whether or not a college places great emphasis on the interview. If they strongly recommend that you have one, it may work against you to forego it.

In contrast to a group interview and some alumni interviews, which are intended to provide information about a college, the personal interview is viewed both as an information session and as further evaluation of your skills and strengths. You will meet with a member of the admissions staff who will be assessing your personal qualities, high school preparation, and your capacity to contribute to undergraduate life at the institution. On average, these meetings last about 45 minutes—a relatively short amount of time in which to gather information and leave the desired impression—so here are some suggestions on how to make the most of it.

Scheduling Your Visit

Generally, students choose to visit campuses in the summer or fall of their senior year. Both times have their advantages. A summer visit, when the campus is not in session, generally allows for a less hectic visit and interview. Visiting in the fall, on the other hand, provides the opportunity to see what campus life is like in full swing. If you choose the fall, consider arranging an overnight trip so that you can stay in one of the college dormitories. At the very least, you should make your way around campus to take part in classes, athletic events, and social activities. Always make an appointment and avoid scheduling more than two college interviews on any given day. Multiple interviews in a single day hinder your chances of making a good impression, and your impressions of the colleges will blur into each other as you hurriedly make your way from place to place.

Preparation

Know the basics about the college before going for your interview. Read the college catalog and Web site in addition to this guide. You will be better prepared to ask questions that are not answered in the literature and that will give you a better understanding of what the college has to offer. You should also spend some time thinking about your strengths and weaknesses and, in particular, what you are looking for in a college education. You will find that as you get a few interviews under your belt, they will get easier. You might consider starting with a college that is not a top contender on your list, so that the stakes are not as high.

Asking Questions

Inevitably, your interviewer will ask you, "Do you have any questions?" Not having one may suggest that you're unprepared or, even worse, not interested. When you do ask questions, make sure that they are ones that matter to you and that have a bearing on your decision about whether or not to attend that college. The questions that you ask will give the interviewer some insight into your personality and priorities. Avoid asking questions that are answered in the college literature—again, a sign of unpreparedness. Although the interviewer will undoubtedly pose questions to you, the interview should not be viewed merely as a question-and-answer session. If a conversation evolves out of a particular question, so much the better. Your interviewer can learn a great deal about you from how you sustain a conversation. Similarly, you will be able to learn a great deal about the college in a conversational format.

Separate the Interview from the Interviewer

Many students base their feelings about a college solely on their impressions of the interviewer. Try not to characterize a college based only on your personal reaction, however, since your impressions can be skewed by whether you and your interviewer hit it off. Pay lots of attention to everything else that you see, hear, and learn about a college. Once on campus, you may never see your interviewer again.

In the end, remember to relax and be yourself. Your interviewer will expect you to be somewhat nervous, which will relieve some of the pressure. Don't drink jitters-producing caffeinated beverages prior to the interview, and suppress nervous fidgets like leg-wagging, finger-drumming, or bracelet-jangling. Consider your interview an opportunity to put forth your best effort and to enhance everything that the college knows about you up to this point.

THE FINAL DECISION

Once you have received your acceptance letters, it is time to go back and look at the whole picture. Provided you received more than one acceptance, you are now in a position to compare your options. The best way to do this is to compare your original list of important college-ranking criteria with what you've discovered about each college along the way. In addition, you and your family will need to factor in the financial aid component. You will need to look beyond these cost issues and the quantifiable pros and cons of each college, however, and know that you have a good feeling about your final choice. Before sending off your acceptance letter, you need to feel confident that the college will feel like home for the next four years. Once the choice is made, the only hard part will be waiting for an entire summer before heading off to college!

Successful Transfer

Adrienne Aaron Rulnick

Transfer students need and deserve detailed and accurate information but often lack direction as to where it can be obtained. Few general college guides offer information about transfer deadlines and required minimum grade point averages for transfer admission. College catalogs are not always clear about the specific requirements and procedures for transfer students who may be confused about whether they need to present high school records, SAT or ACT scores, or a guidance counselor's recommendation, particularly if they have been out of high school for several years. Transfer advisers are not available to those enrolled at a baccalaureate institution; at community and junior colleges, the transfer advising function may be performed by a designated transfer counselor or by a variety of college advisers who are less clearly identified.

The challenge for transfer students is to determine what they need to know in order to make good, informed decisions and identify the individuals and resources that can provide that information. An organized research process is at the heart of a successful transfer.

HOW TO BEGIN

Perhaps the most important first step in this process is one of self-analysis. Adopting a consumer approach is appropriate—higher education is a formidable purchase, no matter how it is financed. The reputation of the college from which you obtain your degree may open doors to future jobs and careers; friendships and contacts you make at college can provide a significant network for lifelong social and professional relationships. The environment of a transfer school may be the perfect opportunity for you to test out urban living or the joys of country life, explore a different area of the nation, experience college residential living for the first time, or move out of the family nest into your first apartment. Like any major purchase in your life, there are costs and benefits to be weighed. Trade-offs include cost, distance, rigor of academic work, extra time in school required by a cooperative education program, and specific requirements, such as foreign language competence at a liberal arts institution or courses in religion at an institution with a denominational affiliation.

USE EXPERIENCE AS A GUIDE

The wise consumer reflects on his or her own experience with a product (i.e., your initial college or colleges) and then seeks out people who have firsthand experience with the new product being considered. Talk to friends and family members who have attended the colleges you are considering. Ask college faculty members you know to tell you about the colleges they attended and how they view these schools. Talk to people engaged in the careers you are considering: What are their impressions of the best programs and schools in their field? Make sure you sample a variety of opinions, but beware of dated experiences. An engineering department considered top-notch when Uncle Joe attended college twenty years ago might be very different today!

THE NITTY-GRITTY

Once your list is reduced to a manageable number of schools, it is important to identify academic requirements, requisite grade point averages for admission, and deadline dates. Most schools admit for both the fall and spring semesters; those on a trimester system may have winter and summer admissions as well. Some schools have rolling admission policies and will process applications as they are received; others, particularly the more selective colleges, have firm deadlines because their admission process involves a committee review, and decisions are made on a competitive basis. It is helpful to know how many transfer students are typically accepted for the semester you wish to begin, whether the minimum grade point average is indicative of the actual average of accepted students (this can vary widely), and whether the major you are seeking has special prerequisites and admission procedures. For example, fine arts programs admission procedures usually require portfolios or auditions. For engineering, computer science, and some business majors, there are specific requirements in mathematics that must be met before a student is considered for admission. Many specialized health-care programs, including nursing, may only admit once a year. Some schools have different standards for sophomore and junior transfers or for in-state and out-of-state students.

Other criteria that you should identify include whether college housing and financial aid are available for transfer students. Some colleges have special transfer scholarships that require separate applications and references, while others simply award aid based on applications that indicate a high grade point average or membership in a nationally recognized junior and community college honor society, such as Phi Theta Kappa. There are also scholarships for transfer students who demonstrate accomplishment in specified academic and performance areas; the latter may be based on talent competitions or accomplishment evidenced in a portfolio or audition.

NONTRADITIONAL STUDENTS

For the nontraditional student, usually defined as anyone beyond the traditional college age range of 18 to 23, there may be additional aspects to investigate. Some colleges award credit based on demonstrated life experience; many colleges grant credit for qualifying scores on the CLEP exams or for participation in the DANTES program. Experience in industry may yield college credit as well. If you are ready and able to pursue further college work but are not in a position to attend regular classes, there are a variety of distance learning options at fully accredited colleges. Other colleges provide specialized support services for nontraditional students and may allow students the opportunity to attend part-time if they have family and work responsibilities. In some cases, usually at large universities, there may be married student housing or family housing available. More and more schools have established day-care facilities, although the waiting lists are often very long.

APPLYING

Once you have identified the schools that meet the needs you have established as priorities, it is time to begin the application process. Make sure you observe all the indicated deadlines. It never hurts to have everything in early, as there can be consequences, such as closed-out majors and the loss of housing and financial aid, if you submit your application late. Make appointments with faculty members and others who are providing references; make sure they understand what is required of them and when and where their references must be sent. It is your responsibility to follow through to make sure all of your credentials are received, including transcripts from all colleges previously attended, even if you only took one summer course or attended for less than a semester. If you have not yet had the opportunity to visit the schools to which you are applying, now is the time to do so. Arrange interviews wherever possible, and make sure to include a tour of the campus and visits to the department and career offices to gain a picture of the facilities and future opportunities. If you have questions about financial aid, schedule an appointment in the financial aid office, and make sure you are aware of all the deadlines and requirements and any scholarship opportunities for which you are eligible.

MAKING YOUR CHOICE

Congratulations! You have been accepted at the colleges of your choice. Now what? Carefully review the acceptance of your previous college credit and how it has been applied. You are entitled to know how many transfer credits you have received and your expected date of graduation. Compare financial aid packages and housing options. The best choice should emerge from this review process. Then, send a note to the schools you will not be attending. Acknowledge your acceptance, but indicate that you have chosen to attend elsewhere. Carefully read everything you have received from the college of your choice. Return required deposits within the deadline, reserve time to attend transfer orientation, arrange to have your final transcript sent from the college you currently attend, and review the financial picture. This is the time to finalize college loan applications and make sure you are in a position to meet all the costs entailed at your new college. Don't forget to include the costs of travel and housing.

You've done it! While many transfer students reflect on how much work was involved in the transfer admission process, those who took the time to follow all of the steps outlined report a sense of satisfaction with their choices and increased confidence in themselves.

Adrienne Aaron Rulnick was formerly a Transfer Counselor at Berkshire Community College.

Who's Paying for This? Financial Aid Basics

A college education can be expensive—costing more than $150,000 for four years at some of the higher priced private colleges and universities. Even at the lower cost state colleges and universities, the cost of a four-year education can approach $60,000. Determining how you and your family will come up with the necessary funds to pay for your education requires planning, perseverance, and learning as much as you can about the options that are available to you. But before you get discouraged, College Board statistics show that 56 percent of full-time students attend four-year public and private colleges with tuition and fees less than $9000, while 9 percent attend colleges that have tuition and fees more than $33,000. College costs tend to be less in the western states and higher in New England.

Paying for college should not be looked at as a four-year financial commitment. For many families, paying the total cost of a student's college education out of current income and savings is usually not realistic. For families that have planned ahead and have financial savings established for higher education, the burden is a lot easier. But for most, meeting the cost of college requires the pooling of current income and assets and investing in longer-term loan options. These family resources, together with financial assistance from state, federal, and institutional sources, enable millions of students each year to attend the institution of their choice.

FINANCIAL AID PROGRAMS

There are three types of financial aid:

1. Gift-aid—Scholarships and grants are funds that do not have to be repaid.
2. Loans—Loans must be repaid, usually after graduation; the amount you have to pay back is the total you've borrowed plus any accrued interest. This is considered a source of self-help aid.
3. Student employment—Student employment is a job arranged for you by the financial aid office. This is another source of self-help aid.

The federal government has four major grant programs—Federal Pell Grants, Federal Supplemental Educational Opportunity Grants, Academic Competitiveness Grants (ACG), and SMART grants. ACG and SMART grants are limited to students who qualify for a Pell grant and are awarded to a select group of students. Overall, these grants are targeted to low-to-moderate income families with significant financial need. The federal government also sponsors a student employment program called the Federal Work-Study Program, which offers jobs both on and off campus, and several loan programs, including those for students and for parents of undergraduate students.

There are two types of student loan programs: subsidized and unsubsidized. The subsidized Federal Stafford Student Loan and the Federal Perkins Loan are need-based, government-subsidized loans. Students who borrow through these programs do not have to pay interest on the loan until after they graduate or leave school. The unsubsidized Federal Stafford Student Loan and the Federal PLUS Loan Program are not based on need, and borrowers are responsible for the interest while the student is in school. These loans are administered by different methods. Once you choose your college, the financial aid office will guide you through this process.

After you've submitted your financial aid application and you've been accepted for admission, each college will send you a letter describing your financial aid award. Most award letters show estimated college costs, how much you and your family are expected to contribute, and the amount and types of aid you have been awarded. Most students are awarded aid from a combination of sources and programs. Hence, your award is often called a financial aid "package."

SOURCES OF FINANCIAL AID

Millions of students and families apply for financial aid each year. Financial aid from all sources exceeds $143 billion per year. The largest single source of aid is the federal government, which will award more than $100 billion this year.

The next largest source of financial aid is found in the college and university community. Most of this aid is awarded to students who have a demonstrated need based on the Federal Methodology. Some institutions use a different formula, the Institutional Methodology (IM), to award their own funds in conjunction with other forms of aid. Institutional aid may be either need-based or non-need based. Aid that is not based on need is usually awarded for a student's academic performance (merit awards), specific talents or abilities, or to attract the type of students a college seeks to enroll.

Another source of financial aid is from state government. All states offer grant and/or scholarship aid, most of which is need-based. However, more and more states are offering substantial merit-based aid programs. Most state programs award aid only to students attending college in their home state.

Other sources of financial aid include:

- Private agencies
- Foundations
- Corporations
- Clubs
- Fraternal and service organizations
- Civic associations
- Unions
- Religious groups that award grants, scholarships, and low-interest loans
- Employers that provide tuition reimbursement benefits for employees and their children

More information about these different sources of aid is available from high school guidance offices, public libraries, college financial aid offices, directly from the sponsoring organizations, and on the Web at www.petersons.com and www.finaid.org.

HOW NEED-BASED FINANCIAL AID IS AWARDED

When you apply for aid, your family's financial situation is analyzed using a government-approved formula called the Federal Methodology. This formula looks at five items:

1. Demographic information of the family
2. Income of the parents
3. Assets of the parents
4. Income of the student
5. Assets of the student

This analysis determines the amount you and your family are expected to contribute toward your college expenses, called your Expected Family Contribution or EFC. If the EFC is equal to or more than the cost of attendance at a particular college, then you do not demonstrate financial need. However, even if you don't have financial need, you may still qualify for aid, as there are grants, scholarships, and loan programs that are not need-based.

If the cost of your education is greater than your EFC, then you do demonstrate financial need and qualify for assistance. The amount of your financial need that can be met varies from school to school. Some are able to meet your full need, while others can only cover a certain percentage of need. Here's the formula:

Cost of Attendance
– Expected Family Contribution
= Financial Need

The EFC remains constant, but your need will vary according to the costs of attendance at a particular college. In general, the higher the tuition and fees at a particular college, the higher the cost of attendance will be. Expenses for books and supplies, room and board, transportation, and other miscellaneous items are included in the overall cost of attendance. It is important to remember that you do not have to be "needy" to qualify for financial aid. Many middle and upper-middle income families qualify for need-based financial aid.

APPLYING FOR FINANCIAL AID

Every student must complete the Free Application for Federal Student Aid (FAFSA) to be considered for financial aid. The FAFSA is available from your high school guidance office, many public libraries, colleges in your area, or directly from the U.S. Department of Education.

Students are encouraged to apply for federal student aid on the Web. The electronic version of the FAFSA can be accessed at http://www.fafsa.ed.gov. Both the student and at least one parent must apply for a federal PIN at http://www.pin.ed.gov. The PIN serves as your electronic signature when applying for aid on the Web.

To award their own funds, some colleges require an additional application, the CSS/Financial Aid PROFILE® application. The PROFILE asks supplemental questions that some colleges and awarding agencies feel provide a more accurate assessment of the family's ability to pay for college. It is up to the college to decide whether it will use only the FAFSA or both the FAFSA and the PROFILE. PROFILE applications are available from the high school guidance office and on the Web. Both the paper application and the Web site list those colleges and programs that require the PROFILE application.

If Every College You're Applying to for Fall 2010 Requires the FAFSA

. . . then it's pretty simple: Complete the FAFSA after January 1, 2010, being certain to send it in before any college-imposed deadlines. (You are not permitted to send in the 2010–11 FAFSA before January 1, 2010.) Most college FAFSA application deadlines are in February or early March. It is easier if you have all your financial records for the previous year available, but if that is not possible, you are strongly encouraged to use estimated figures.

After you send in your FAFSA, either with the paper application or electronically, you'll receive a Student Aid Report (SAR) that includes all of the information you reported and shows your EFC. If you provided an e-mail address, the SAR is sent to you electronically; otherwise, you will receive a paper copy in the mail. Be sure to review the SAR, checking to see if the information you reported is accurately represented. If you used estimated numbers to complete the FAFSA, you may have to resubmit the SAR with any corrections to the data. The college(s) you have designated on the FAFSA will receive the information you reported and will use that data to make their decision. In many instances, the colleges to which you've applied will ask you to send copies of your and your parents' federal income tax returns for 2009, plus any other documents needed to verify the information you reported.

If a College Requires the PROFILE

Step 1: Register for the PROFILE in the fall of your senior year in high school. You can apply for the PROFILE online at http://profileonline.collegeboard.com/prf/index.jsp. Registration information with a list of the colleges that require the PROFILE is available in most high school guidance offices. There is a fee for using the PROFILE application ($25 for the first college and $16 for each additional college). You must pay for the service by credit card when you register. If you do not have a credit card, you will be billed. A limited number of fee waivers are automatically granted to first-time applicants based on the financial information provided on the PROFILE.

Step 2: Fill out your customized PROFILE. Once you register, your application will be immediately available online and will have questions which all students must complete, questions which must be completed by the student's parents (unless the student is independent and the colleges or programs selected do not require parental information), and *may* have supplemental questions needed by one or more of your schools or programs. If required, those will be found in Section Q of the application.

In addition to the PROFILE application you complete online, you may also be required to complete a Business/Farm Supplement via traditional paper format. Completion of this form is not a part of the online process. If this form is required, instructions on how to download and print the supplemental form are provided. If your biological or adoptive parents are separated or divorced and your colleges and programs require it, your noncustodial parent may be asked to complete the Noncustodial PROFILE.

Once you complete and submit your PROFILE application, it will be processed and sent directly to your requested colleges and programs.

IF YOU DON'T QUALIFY FOR NEED-BASED AID

If you are not eligible for need-based aid, you can still find ways to lessen your burden.

Here are some suggestions:

- Search for merit scholarships. You can start at the initial stages of your application process. College merit awards are increasingly important as more and more colleges award these to students they especially want to attract. As a result, applying to a college at which your qualifications put you at the top of the entering class may give you a larger merit award. Another source of aid to look for is private scholarships that are given for special skills and talents. Additional information can be found at www.petersons.com and at www.finaid.org.
- Seek employment during the summer and the academic year. The student employment office at your college can help you locate a school-year job. Many colleges and local businesses have vacancies remaining after they have hired students who are receiving Federal Work-Study Program financial aid.
- Borrow through the unsubsidized Federal Stafford Student Loan programs. These are generally available to all students. The terms and conditions are similar to the subsidized loans. The biggest difference is that the borrower is responsible for the interest while still in college, although most lenders permit students to delay paying the interest right away and add the accrued interest to the total amount owed. You must file the FAFSA to be considered.
- After you've secured what you can through scholarships, working, and borrowing, you and your parents will be expected to meet your share of the college bill (the Expected Family Contribution). Many colleges offer monthly payment plans that spread the cost over the academic year. If the monthly payments are too high, parents can borrow through the Federal PLUS Loan Program, through one of the many private education loan programs available, or through home equity loans and lines of credit. Families seeking assistance in financing college expenses should inquire at the financial aid office about what programs are available at the college. Some families seek the advice of professional financial advisers and tax consultants.

[illegible] counselor and [illegible] PROFILE [illegible] it will be processed and sent [illegible] your [illegible] colleges and programs.

IF YOU DON'T QUALIFY FOR NEED-BASED AID

If you [illegible] not eligible for need-based aid, [illegible] you can still find ways to lessen your burden.

Here are some suggestions:

[illegible] search for merit-based awards. You can start at the [illegible] of your application process [illegible] or [illegible] to these opportunities as well [illegible] colleges award [illegible] students [illegible] especially [illegible] as a result of [illegible] to colleges [illegible] the top [illegible] percent [illegible] a large merit award. Another [illegible] of aid to look for [illegible] opportunities [illegible] talents and [illegible]. Additional information [illegible] professional or [illegible].

[illegible] employment during the [illegible] year. [illegible] student employment [illegible] colleges [illegible] [illegible] [illegible] their Federal Work-Study Program [illegible].

Borrow through the [illegible] Federal Stafford Student Loan programs. [illegible] available to all students. The terms [illegible] the [illegible] [illegible] responsible for the [illegible].

[illegible] accounts [illegible] [illegible] interest [illegible] and [illegible] to the [illegible] amount [illegible] can borrow is the [illegible].

[illegible] [illegible] pay the [illegible] [illegible] for [illegible] to the college bill [illegible] colleges [illegible] monthly [illegible] [illegible] [illegible] [illegible] through [illegible] [illegible] [illegible] [illegible] [illegible] [illegible] [illegible] [illegible] [illegible] [illegible] college expenses should [illegible] [illegible] [illegible] available [illegible] some families [illegible] [illegible] through the [illegible].

[illegible] corrections you [illegible] that it is [illegible] possible you [illegible] [illegible] to use estimated figures.

After you send in your FAFSA, either with the [illegible] application or electronically, you'll receive a Student Aid Report (SAR) that includes all of the information you reported [illegible] your EFC. [illegible] [illegible] [illegible] [illegible] [illegible] you will receive a paper [illegible] be sure to review the SAR [illegible] [illegible] [illegible] [illegible] [illegible] [illegible] [illegible] [illegible] you may have to resubmit [illegible] with any corrections [illegible] the college(s) you have designated on the FAFSA will receive the information you reported and will use that data to make their decision. [illegible] colleges to which you've applied will ask you to send [illegible] of your and your parents' [illegible] income tax returns for 2009, plus any other documents needed to verify the information you reported.

If a College Requires the PROFILE

Step 1: Register for the PROFILE in the fall of your senior year in high school. You can apply for the PROFILE online [illegible] [illegible] [illegible] with a list of the colleges that you [illegible] PROFILE [illegible] [illegible] [illegible]. There is a fee for the PROFILE [illegible] for the first college and [illegible] for each additional college. You must pay for the service [illegible] when you register. [illegible] [illegible] [illegible] billed. A limited number of fee waivers are [illegible] [illegible] based on the financial information provided on the PROFILE.

Step 2: Fill out your customized PROFILE. Once you [illegible] your [illegible] [illegible] [illegible] questions which all students must complete, questions which must be completed by the student's parents (unless the student is independent and the colleges or programs [illegible] do not require parental information), and [illegible] [illegible] questions required by one or more of your colleges or programs. Any [illegible] of these will be found in [illegible] of the application.

In addition to the PROFILE application, [illegible] [illegible] complete [illegible] [illegible] required to [illegible] [illegible] [illegible] [illegible] [illegible] [illegible] this form is [illegible] part of the [illegible]. If this form is [illegible] [illegible] [illegible] [illegible] [illegible] [illegible] [illegible] [illegible] [illegible] [illegible] [illegible] [illegible] [illegible] [illegible] [illegible] the [illegible] [illegible] to [illegible] [illegible] [illegible] [illegible] PROFILE.

Financial Aid Programs for Schools in the Midwest

Each state government has established one or more state-administered financial aid programs for qualified students. The state programs may be restricted to legal residents of the state, or they also may be available to out-of-state students who are attending public or private colleges or universities within the state. In addition, other qualifications may apply.

The program descriptions are arranged by state in alphabetical order, along with information about how to determine eligibility and apply. The information refers to awards for 2009–10, unless otherwise stated. Students should write to the address given for each program to request award details for 2010–11 be sent to them as soon as they are available.

ILLINOIS

Golden Apple Scholars of Illinois. Applicants must be between the ages of 16 and 21 and maintain a GPA of 2.5. Eligible applicants must be residents of Illinois studying in Illinois. Recipients must agree to teach in high-need Illinois schools. *Academic Fields/Career Goals:* Education. *Award:* Scholarship for use in freshman, sophomore, junior, or senior year; renewable. *Award amount:* $4500. *Number of awards:* 125. *Eligibility Requirements:* Applicant must be age 16-21; enrolled or expecting to enroll full-time at a four-year institution or university; resident of Illinois and studying in Illinois. Applicant must have 2.5 GPA or higher. Available to U.S. citizens. *Application Requirements:* Application, autobiography, essay, interview, photo, references, test scores, transcript. *Deadline:* December 1. **Contact:** Ms. Patricia Kilduff, Director of Recruitment and Placement, Golden Apple Foundation, 8 South Michigan Avenue, Suite 700, Chicago, IL 60603-3318. *E-mail:* kilduff@goldenapple.org. *Phone:* 312-407-0006 Ext. 105. *Fax:* 312-407-0344. *Web site:* www.goldenapple.org.

Grant Program for Dependents of Police, Fire, or Correctional Officers. Awards available to Illinois residents who are dependents of police, fire, and correctional officers killed or disabled in line of duty. Provides for tuition and fees at approved Illinois institutions. Number of grants and individual dollar amount awarded vary. *Award:* Grant for use in freshman, sophomore, junior, senior, graduate, or postgraduate years; renewable. *Award amount:* varies. *Number of awards:* varies. *Eligibility Requirements:* Applicant must be enrolled or expecting to enroll full- or part-time at a two-year, four-year, or technical institution or university; resident of Illinois and studying in Illinois. Applicant or parent of applicant must have employment or volunteer experience in police/firefighting. Available to U.S. citizens. *Application Requirements:* Application, proof of status. *Deadline:* varies. **Contact:** College Zone Counselor, Illinois Student Assistance Commission (ISAC), 1755 Lake Cook Road, Deerfield, IL 60015-5209. *E-mail:* collegezone@isac.org. *Phone:* 800-899-4722. *Web site:* www.collegezone.org.

Higher Education License Plate Program-HELP. Need-based grants for students who are Illinois residents and attend approved Illinois colleges. May be eligible to receive the grant for the equivalent of 10 semesters of full-time enrollment. Number of grants made through this program and the individual dollar amount awarded varies. *Award:* Grant for use in freshman, sophomore, junior, or senior year; not renewable. *Award amount:* varies. *Number of awards:* varies. *Eligibility Requirements:* Applicant must be enrolled or expecting to enroll full- or part-time at a two-year or four-year institution or university; resident of Illinois and studying in Illinois. Available to U.S. citizens. *Application Requirements:* Application, financial need analysis, FAFSA. *Deadline:* varies. **Contact:** College Zone Counselor, Illinois Student Assistance Commission (ISAC), 1755 Lake Cook Road, Deerfield, IL 60015-5209. *E-mail:* collegezone@isac.org. *Phone:* 800-899-4722. *Web site:* www.collegezone.org.

Illinois College Savings Bond Bonus Incentive Grant Program. Program offers Illinois college savings bond holders a grant for each year of bond maturity payable upon bond redemption if at least 70 percent of proceeds are used to attend college in Illinois. The amount of grant will depend on the amount of the bond, ranging from a $40 to $440 grant per $5000 of the bond. Applications are accepted between August 1 and May 30 of the academic year in which the bonds matured, or in the academic year immediately following maturity. *Award:* Grant for use in freshman, sophomore, junior, senior, graduate, or postgraduate years; not renewable. *Number of awards:* varies. *Eligibility Requirements:* Applicant must be enrolled or expecting to enroll full- or part-time at a two-year, four-year, or technical institution or university and studying in Illinois. Available to U.S. citizens. *Application Requirements:* Application. *Deadline:* varies. **Contact:** College Zone Counselor, Illinois Student Assistance Commission (ISAC), 1755 Lake Cook Road, Deerfield, IL 60015-5209. *E-mail:* collegezone@isac.org. *Phone:* 800-899-4722. *Web site:* www.collegezone.org.

Illinois Future Teachers Corps Program. Scholarships are available for students planning to become teachers in Illinois. Students must be Illinois residents, enrolled or accepted as a junior or above in a Teacher Education Program at an Illinois college or university. By receiving the award, students agree to teach for five years at either a public, private, or parochial Illinois preschool, or at a public elementary or secondary school. *Academic Fields/Career Goals:* Education. *Award:* Forgivable loan for use in junior, senior, or graduate year; renewable. *Award amount:* $5000–$15,000. *Number of awards:* 1150. *Eligibility Requirements:* Applicant must be enrolled or expecting to enroll full- or part-time at a four-year institution or university; resident of Illinois and studying in Illinois. Applicant must have 2.5 GPA or higher. Available to U.S. citizens. *Application Requirements:* Application, financial need analysis, FAFSA. *Deadline:* March 1. **Contact:** College Zone Counselor, Illinois Student Assistance Commission (ISAC), 1755 Lake Cook Road, Deerfield, IL 60015-5209. *E-mail:* collegezone@isac.org. *Phone:* 800-899-4722. *Web site:* www.collegezone.org.

Illinois General Assembly Scholarship. Scholarships available for Illinois students enrolled at an Illinois four-year state-supported college. Must contact the general assembly member for eligibility criteria. Deadline varies. *Award:* Scholarship for use in freshman, sophomore, junior, or senior year; not renewable. *Award amount:* varies. *Number of* *awards:* varies. *Eligibility Requirements:* Applicant must be enrolled or expecting to enroll full- or part-time at a four-year institution or university; resident of Illinois and studying in Illinois. Available to U.S. citizens. *Application Requirements:* Application. *Deadline:* varies. **Contact:** College Zone Counselor, Illinois Student Assistance Commission (ISAC), 1755 Lake Cook Road, Deerfield, IL 60015-5209. *E-mail:* collegezone@isac.org. *Phone:* 800-899-4722. *Web site:* www.collegezone.org.

Illinois Monetary Award Program. Awards to Illinois residents enrolled in a minimum of 3 hours per term in a degree program at an approved Illinois institution. See Web site for complete list of participating schools. Must demonstrate financial need, based on the information provided on the Free Application for Federal Student Aid. Number of grants and the individual dollar amount awarded vary. Deadlines: August 15 and September 30. *Award:* Grant for use in freshman, sophomore, junior, or senior year; renewable. *Award amount:* $2365. *Number of awards:* 146,853. *Eligibility Requirements:* Applicant must be enrolled or expecting to enroll full- or part-time at a two-year, four-year, or technical institution or university; resident of Illinois and studying in Illinois. Available to U.S. citizens. *Application Requirements:* Financial need analysis, FAFSA online. *Deadline:* varies. **Contact:** College Zone Counselor, Illinois Student Assistance Commission (ISAC), 1755 Lake Cook Road, Deerfield, IL 60015-5209. *E-mail:* collegezone@isac.org. *Phone:* 800-899-4722. *Web site:* www.collegezone.org.

Illinois National Guard Grant Program. Active duty members of the Illinois National Guard, or who are within 12 months of discharge, and who have completed one full year of service are eligible. May be used for study at Illinois two- or four-year public colleges for a maximum of the equivalent of four academic years of full-time enrollment. Deadlines: October 1 of the academic year for full year, March 1 for second/third term, or June 15 for the summer term. *Award:* Grant for use in freshman, sophomore, junior, senior, or graduate year; renewable. *Award amount:* varies. *Number of awards:* varies. *Eligibility Requirements:* Applicant must be enrolled or expecting to enroll full- or part-time at a two-year or four-year institution or university; resident of Illinois and studying in Illinois. Available to U.S. citizens. Applicant or parent must meet one or more of the following requirements: Air Force National Guard or Army National Guard experience; retired from active duty; disabled or killed as a result of military service; prisoner of war; or missing in action. *Application Requirements:* Application, documentation of service. *Deadline:* varies. **Contact:** College Zone Counselor, Illinois Student Assistance Commission (ISAC), 1755 Lake Cook Road, Deerfield, IL 60015-5209. *E-mail:* collegezone@isac.org. *Phone:* 800-899-4722. *Web site:* www.collegezone.org.

Illinois Special Education Teacher Tuition Waiver. Teachers or students who are pursuing a career in special education as public, private or parochial preschool, elementary or secondary school teachers in Illinois may be eligible for this program. This program will exempt such individuals from paying tuition and mandatory fees at an eligible institution, for up to four years. The individual dollar amount awarded are subject to sufficient annual appropriations by the Illinois General Assembly. *Academic Fields/Career Goals:* Special Education. *Award:* Forgivable loan for use in freshman, sophomore, junior, senior, or graduate year; renewable. *Award amount:* varies. *Number of awards:* up to 250. *Eligibility Requirements:* Applicant must be enrolled or expecting to enroll full- or part-time at a four-year institution or university; resident of Illinois and studying in Illinois. Available to U.S. citizens. *Application Requirements:* Application. *Deadline:* March 1. **Contact:** College Zone Counselor, Illinois Student Assistance Commission (ISAC), 1755 Lake Cook Road, Deerfield, IL 60015-5209. *E-mail:* collegezone@isac.org. *Phone:* 800-899-4722. *Web site:* www.collegezone.org.

Illinois Student-to-Student Program of Matching Grants. Grant is available to undergraduates at participating state-supported colleges. Number of grants and the individual dollar amount awarded vary. Contact financial aid office at the institution. *Award:* Grant for use in freshman, sophomore, junior, or senior year; not renewable. *Award amount:* $300–$1000. *Number of awards:* varies. *Eligibility Requirements:* Applicant must be enrolled or expecting to enroll full- or part-time at a two-year or four-year institution or university; resident of Illinois and studying in Illinois. Available to U.S. citizens. *Application Requirements:* Application, financial need analysis. *Deadline:* varies. **Contact:** College Zone Counselor, Illinois Student Assistance Commission (ISAC), 1755 Lake Cook Road, Deerfield, IL 60015-5209. *E-mail:* collegezone@isac.org. *Phone:* 800-899-4722. *Web site:* www.collegezone.org.

Illinois Veteran Grant Program-IVG. Awards qualified veterans and pays eligible tuition and fees for study in Illinois public universities or community colleges. Program eligibility units are based on the enrolled hours for a particular term, not the dollar amount of the benefits paid. Applications are available at college financial aid office and can be submitted any time during the academic year for which assistance is being requested. *Award:* Grant for use in freshman, sophomore, junior, senior, or graduate year; renewable. *Award amount:* $1400–$1600. *Number of awards:* 11,000–13,000. *Eligibility Requirements:* Applicant must be enrolled or expecting to enroll full- or part-time at a two-year or four-year institution or university; resident of Illinois and studying in Illinois. Available to U.S. citizens. Applicant or parent must meet one or more of the following requirements: general military experience; retired from active duty; disabled or killed as a result of military service; prisoner of war; or missing in action. *Application Requirements:* Application. *Deadline:* continuous. **Contact:** College Zone Counselor, Illinois Student Assistance Commission (ISAC), 1755 Lake Cook Road, Deerfield, IL 60015-5209. *E-mail:* collegezone@isac.org. *Phone:* 800-899-4722. *Web site:* www.collegezone.org.

Merit Recognition Scholarship (MRS) Program. One-time awards available to Illinois residents for use at Illinois institutions. Must be ranked in the top 5 percent of high school class or have scored among the top 5 percent on the ACT, SAT, or Prairie State Achievement Exam. Number of scholarships granted varies. *Award:* Scholarship for use in freshman year; not renewable. *Award amount:* up to $1000. *Number of awards:* varies. *Eligibility Requirements:* Applicant must be high school student; planning to enroll or expecting to enroll full- or part-time at a two-year or four-year institution or university; resident of Illinois and studying in Illinois. Applicant must have 3.5 GPA or higher. Available to U.S. citizens. *Application Requirements:* Application, transcript. *Deadline:* June 15. **Contact:** College Zone Counselor, Illinois Student Assistance Commission (ISAC), 1755 Lake Cook Road, Deerfield, IL 60015-5209. *E-mail:* collegezone@isac.org. *Phone:* 800-899-4722. *Web site:* www.collegezone.org.

MIA/POW Scholarships. One-time award for spouse, child, or step-child of veterans who are missing in action or were a prisoner of war. Must be enrolled at a state-supported school in Illinois. Candidate must be U.S. citizen. Must apply and be accepted before beginning of school. Also for children and spouses of veterans who are determined to be 100 percent disabled as established by the Veterans Administration. Scholarship value and the number of awards granted varies. *Award:* Scholarship for use in freshman, sophomore, junior, or senior year; renewable. *Award amount:* varies. *Number of awards:* varies. *Eligibility Requirements:* Applicant must be enrolled or expecting to enroll full- or part-time at a two-year or four-year institution or university; resident of Illinois and studying in Illinois. Available to U.S. citizens. Applicant or parent must meet one or more of the following requirements: general military experience; retired from active duty; disabled or killed as a result of military service; prisoner of war; or missing in action. *Application Requirements:* Application. *Deadline:* continuous. **Contact:** Ms. Tracy Smith, Grants Section, Illinois Department of Veterans' Affairs, 833 South Spring Street, Springfield, IL 62794-9432. *Phone:* 217-782-3564. *Fax:* 217-782-4161. *Web site:* www.state.il.us/agency/dva.

Minority Teachers of Illinois Scholarship Program. Award for minority students intending to become school teachers. Number of scholarships and the individual dollar amount awarded vary. *Academic Fields/Career Goals:* Education; Special Education. *Award:* Scholarship for use in freshman, sophomore, junior, senior, graduate, or postgraduate years; renewable. *Award amount:* up to $5000. *Number of awards:* 450–550. *Eligibility Requirements:* Applicant must be American Indian/ Alaska Native, Asian/Pacific Islander, Black (non-Hispanic), or Hispanic; enrolled or expecting to enroll full- or part-time at a two-year or four-year institution or university; resident of Illinois and studying in Illinois. Applicant must have 2.5 GPA or higher. Available to U.S. citizens. *Application Requirements:* Application, transcript. *Deadline:* March 1. **Contact:** College Zone Counselor, Illinois Student Assistance Commission (ISAC), 1755 Lake Cook Road, Deerfield, IL 60015-5209. *E-mail:* collegezone@isac.org. *Phone:* 800-899-4722. *Web site:* www.collegezone.org.

Robert C. Byrd Honors Scholarship-Illinois. Scholarship for Illinois residents and graduating high school seniors accepted on a full-time basis as an undergraduate student at an Illinois college or university. The award is up to $1500 per year, for a maximum of four years. Minimum 3.5 GPA required. Students are automatically considered for this scholarship if they meet the eligibility requirements. High school counselors submit information to selection process. *Award:* Scholarship for use in freshman year; renewable. *Award amount:* up to $1500. *Number of awards:* varies. *Eligibility Requirements:* Applicant must be high school student; planning to enroll or expecting to enroll full-time at a two-year or four-year institution or university; resident of Illinois and studying in Illinois. Applicant must have 3.5 GPA or higher. Available to U.S. citizens. *Application Requirements:* Application, test scores, transcript. *Deadline:* July 15. **Contact:** College Zone Counselor, Illinois Student Assistance Commission (ISAC), 1755 Lake Cook Road, Deerfield, IL 60015-5209. *E-mail:* collegezone@isac.org. *Phone:* 800-899-4722. *Fax:* 847-831-8549. *Web site:* www.collegezone.org.

Silas Purnell Illinois Incentive for Access Program. Students whose information provided on the FAFSA results in a calculated zero expected family contribution when they are college freshmen may be eligible to receive a grant of up to $500. Must be a U.S. citizen and an Illinois resident studying at a participating Illinois institution. See Web site for complete list of schools and additional requirements. *Award:* Grant for use in freshman year; not renewable. *Award amount:* up to $500. *Number of awards:* varies. *Eligibility Requirements:* Applicant must be high school student; planning to enroll or expecting to enroll full- or part-time at a two-year, four-year, or technical institution or university; resident of Illinois and studying in Illinois. Available to U.S. citizens. *Application Requirements:* Financial need analysis, FAFSA. *Deadline:* July 1. **Contact:** College Zone Counselor, Illinois Student Assistance Commission (ISAC), 1755 Lake Cook Road, Deerfield, IL 60015-5209. *E-mail:* collegezone@isac.org. *Phone:* 800-899-4722. *Web site:* www.collegezone.org.

Veterans' Children Educational Opportunities. $250 award for each child aged 10 to 18 of a veteran who died or became totally disabled as a result of service during World War I, World War II, Korean, or Vietnam War. Must be Illinois resident studying in Illinois. Death must be service-connected. Disability must be rated 100 percent for two or more years. *Award:* Grant for use in freshman year; not renewable. *Award amount:* $250. *Number of awards:* varies. *Eligibility Requirements:* Applicant must be age 10-18; enrolled or expecting to enroll full- or part-time at a two-year or four-year institution or university; resident of Illinois and studying in Illinois. Available to U.S. citizens. Applicant or parent must meet one or more of the following requirements: general military experience; retired from active duty; disabled or killed as a result of military service; prisoner of war; or missing in action. *Application Requirements:* Application. *Deadline:* June 30. **Contact:** Tracy Smith, Grants Section, Illinois Department of Veterans' Affairs, 833 South Spring Street, Springfield, IL 62794-9432. *Phone:* 217-782-3564. *Fax:* 217-782-4161. *Web site:* www.state.il.us/agency/dva.

INDIANA

Child of Disabled Veteran Grant or Purple Heart Recipient Grant. Free tuition at Indiana state-supported colleges or universities for children of disabled veterans or Purple Heart recipients. Must submit form DD214 or service record. Covers tuition and mandatory fees. *Award:* Grant for use in freshman, sophomore, junior, senior, graduate, or postgraduate years; renewable. *Award amount:* varies. *Number of awards:* varies. *Eligibility Requirements:* Applicant must be enrolled or expecting to enroll full- or part-time at a two-year or four-year institution or university; resident of Indiana and studying in Indiana. Available to U.S. citizens. Applicant or parent must meet one or more of the following requirements: general military experience; retired from active duty; disabled or killed as a result of military service; prisoner of war; or missing in action. *Application Requirements:* Application, FAFSA. *Deadline:* continuous. **Contact:** Jon Brinkley, State Service Officer, Indiana Department of Veterans Affairs, 302 West Washington Street, Room E-120, Indianapolis, IN 46204-2738. *E-mail:* jbrinkley@dva.in.gov. *Phone:* 317-232-3910. *Fax:* 317-232-7721. *Web site:* www.in.gov/dva.

Department of Veterans Affairs Free Tuition for Children of POW/MIA's in Vietnam. Renewable award for residents of Indiana who are the children of veterans declared missing in action or prisoner-of-war after January 1, 1960. Provides tuition at Indiana state-supported institutions for undergraduate study. *Award:* Grant for use in freshman, sophomore, junior, senior, graduate, or postgraduate years; renewable. *Award amount:* varies. *Number of awards:* varies. *Eligibility Requirements:* Applicant must be age 24 or under; enrolled or expecting to enroll full- or part-time at a two-year or four-year institution or university; resident of Indiana and studying in Indiana. Available to U.S. citizens. Applicant or parent must meet one or more of the following requirements: general military experience; retired from active duty; disabled or killed as a result of military service; prisoner of war; or missing in action. *Application Requirements:* Application. *Deadline:* continuous. **Contact:** Jon Brinkley, State Service Officer, Indiana Department of Veterans Affairs, 302 West Washington Street, Room E-120, Indianapolis, IN 46204-2738. *E-mail:* jbrinkley@dva.in.gov. *Phone:* 317-232-3910. *Fax:* 317-232-7721. *Web site:* www.in.gov/dva.

Frank O'Bannon Grant Program. A need-based, tuition-restricted program for students attending Indiana public, private, or proprietary institutions seeking a first undergraduate degree. Students (and parents of dependent students) who are U.S. citizens and Indiana residents must file the FAFSA yearly by the March 10 deadline. *Award:* Grant for use in freshman, sophomore, junior, or senior year; not renewable. *Award amount:* $200–$10,992. *Number of awards:* 48,408–70,239. *Eligibility Requirements:* Applicant must be enrolled or expecting to enroll full-time at a two-year, four-year, or technical institution or university; resident of Indiana and studying in Indiana. Available to U.S. citizens. *Application Requirements:* Application, financial need analysis, FAFSA. *Deadline:* March 10. **Contact:** Grants Counselor, State Student Assistance Commission of Indiana (SSACI), 150 West Market Street, Suite 500, Indianapolis, IN 46204-2805. *E-mail:* grants@ssaci.state.in.us. *Phone:* 317-232-2350. *Fax:* 317-232-3260. *Web site:* www.in.gov/ssaci.

Hoosier Scholar Award. A $500 nonrenewable award. Based on the size of the senior class, one to three scholars are selected by the guidance counselor's) of each accredited high school in Indiana. The award is based on academic merit and may be used for any educational expense at an eligible Indiana institution of higher education. *Award:* Scholarship for use in freshman year; not renewable. *Award amount:* $500. *Number of awards:* 666–840. *Eligibility Requirements:* Applicant must be high school student; planning to enroll or expecting to enroll full-time at a two-year or four-year institution or university; resident of Indiana and studying in Indiana. Applicant must have 3.5 GPA or higher. Available to U.S. citizens. *Application Requirements:* Application, references. *Deadline:* March 10. **Contact:** Ada Sparkman, Program Coordinator, State Student Assistance Commission of Indiana (SSACI), 150 West Market Street, Suite 500, Indianapolis, IN 46204-2805. *Phone:* 317-232-2350. *Fax:* 317-232-3260. *Web site:* www.in.gov/ssaci.

Indiana National Guard Supplemental Grant. The award is a supplement to the Indiana Higher Education Grant program. Applicants must be members of the Indiana National Guard. All Guard paperwork must be completed prior to the start of each semester. The FAFSA must be received by March 10. Award covers certain tuition and fees at select public colleges. *Award:* Grant for use in freshman, sophomore, junior, or senior year; not renewable. *Award amount:* $20–$7110. *Number of awards:* 503–925. *Eligibility Requirements:* Applicant must be enrolled or expecting to enroll full- or part-time at a two-year or four-year institution or university; resident of Indiana and studying in Indiana. Available to U.S. citizens. Applicant or parent must meet one or more of the following requirements: Air Force National Guard or Army National Guard experience; retired from active duty; disabled or killed as a result of military service; prisoner of war; or missing in action. *Application Requirements:* Application. *Deadline:* March 10. **Contact:** Kathryn Moore, Grants Counselor, State Student Assistance Commission of Indiana (SSACI), 150 West Market Street, Suite 500, Indianapolis, IN 46204-2805. *E-mail:* kmoore@ssaci.in.gov. *Phone:* 317-232-2350. *Fax:* 317-232-2360. *Web site:* www.in.gov/ssaci.

Indiana Nursing Scholarship Fund. Need-based tuition funding for nursing students enrolled full- or part-time at an eligible Indiana institution. Must be a U.S. citizen and an Indiana resident and have a minimum 2.0 GPA or meet the minimum requirements for the nursing program. Upon graduation, recipients must practice as a nurse in an Indiana health care setting for two years. *Academic Fields/Career Goals:* Nursing. *Award:* Scholarship for use in freshman, sophomore, junior, or senior year; not renewable. *Award amount:* $200–$5000. *Number of awards:* 490–690. *Eligibility Requirements:* Applicant must be enrolled or expecting to enroll full- or part-time at a two-year or four-year institution or university; resident of Indiana and studying in Indiana. Available to U.S. citizens. *Application Requirements:* Application, financial need analysis, FAFSA. *Deadline:* continuous. **Contact:** Yvonne Heflin, Director, Special Programs, State Student Assistance Commission of Indiana (SSACI), 150 West Market Street, Suite 500, Indianapolis, IN 46204-2805. *Phone:* 317-232-2350. *Fax:* 317-232-3260. *Web site:* www.in.gov/ssaci.

National Guard Scholarship Extension Program. A scholarship extension applicant is eligible for a tuition scholarship under Indiana Code 21-13-5-4 for a period not to exceed the period of scholarship extension the applicant served on active duty as a member of the National Guard (mobilized and deployed). Must apply not later than one year after the applicant ceases to be a member of the Indiana National Guard. Applicant should apply through the education officer of their last unit of assignment. *Award:* Grant for use in freshman, sophomore, junior, or senior year; renewable. *Award amount:* varies. *Number of awards:* varies. *Eligibility Requirements:* Applicant must be enrolled or expecting to enroll full- or part-time at a two-year, four-year, or technical institution or university and studying in Indiana. Available to U.S. citizens. Applicant must have served in the Air Force National Guard or Army National Guard. *Application Requirements:* Application. *Deadline:* continuous. **Contact:** Pamela Moody, National Guard Education Officer, Indiana Department of Veterans Affairs, 302 West Washington Street, Suite E120, Indianapolis, IN 46204. *E-mail:* pamela.moody@in.ngb.army.mil. *Phone:* 317-964-7017. *Fax:* 317-232-7721. *Web site:* www.in.gov/dva.

National Guard Tuition Supplement Program. Applicant must be a member of the Indiana National Guard, in active drilling status, who has not been AWOL during the last 12 months, does not possess a bachelor's degree, possesses the requisite academic qualifications, meets the requirements of the state-supported college or university, and meets all National Guard requirements. *Award:* Grant for use in freshman, sophomore, junior, or senior year; renewable. *Award amount:* varies. *Number of awards:* varies. *Eligibility Requirements:* Applicant must be enrolled or expecting to enroll full- or part-time at a two-year, four-year, or technical institution or university and studying in Indiana. Available to U.S. citizens. Applicant must have served in the Air Force National Guard or Army National Guard. *Application Requirements:* Application, FAFSA. *Deadline:* continuous. **Contact:** Jon Brinkley, State Service Officer, Indiana Department of Veterans Affairs, 302 West Washington Street, Room E-120, Indianapolis, IN 46204-2738. *E-mail:* jbrinkley@dva.in.gov. *Phone:* 317-232-3910. *Fax:* 317-232-7721. *Web site:* www.in.gov/dva.

Part-Time Grant Program. Program is designed to encourage part-time undergraduates to start and complete their associate or baccalaureate degrees or certificates by subsidizing part-time tuition costs. It is a term-based award that is based on need. State residency requirements must be met and a FAFSA must be filed. Eligibility is determined at the institutional level subject to approval by SSACI. *Award:* Grant for use in freshman, sophomore, junior, or senior year; not renewable. *Award amount:* $20–$4000. *Number of awards:* 4680–6700. *Eligibility Requirements:* Applicant must be enrolled or expecting to enroll part-time at a two-year, four-year, or technical institution or university; resident of Indiana and studying in Indiana. Available to U.S. citizens. *Application Requirements:* Application, financial need analysis. *Deadline:* continuous. **Contact:** Grants Counselor, State Student Assistance Commission of Indiana (SSACI), 150 West Market Street, Suite 500, Indianapolis, IN 46204-2805. *E-mail:* grants@ssaci.state.in.us. *Phone:* 317-232-2350. *Fax:* 317-232-3260. *Web site:* www.in.gov/ssaci.

Resident Tuition for Active Duty Military Personnel. Applicant must be a nonresident of Indiana serving on active duty and stationed in Indiana and attending any state-supported college or university. Dependents remain eligible for the duration of their enrollment, even if the active duty person is no longer in Indiana. Entitlement is to the resident tuition rate. *Award:* Grant for use in freshman, sophomore, junior, senior, graduate, or postgraduate years; renewable. *Award amount:* varies. *Number of awards:* varies. *Eligibility Requirements:* Applicant must be enrolled or expecting to enroll full- or part-time at a two-year, four-year, or technical institution or university and studying in Indiana. Available to U.S. citizens. Applicant or parent must meet one or more of the following requirements: Air Force, Army, Marine Corps, or Navy experience; retired from active duty; disabled or killed as a result of military service; prisoner of war; or missing in action. *Application Requirements:* Application. *Deadline:* continuous. **Contact:** Jon Brinkley, State Service Officer, Indiana Department of Veterans Affairs, 302 West Washington Street, Room E-120, Indianapolis, IN 46204-2738. *E-mail:* jbrinkley@dva.in.gov. *Phone:* 317-232-3910. *Fax:* 317-232-7721. *Web site:* www.in.gov/dva.

Tuition and Fee Remission for Children and Spouses of National Guard Members. Award to an individual whose father, mother or spouse was a member of the Indiana National Guard and suffered a service-connected death while serving on state active duty (which includes mobilized and deployed for federal active duty). The student must be eligible to pay the resident tuition rate at the state-supported college or university and must possess the requisite academic qualifications. *Award:* Grant for use in freshman, sophomore, junior, or senior year; renewable. *Award amount:* varies. *Number of awards:* varies. *Eligibility Requirements:* Applicant must be enrolled or expecting to enroll full- or part-time at a two-year, four-year, or technical institution or university and studying in Indiana. Available to U.S. citizens. Applicant or parent must meet one or more of the following requirements: Air Force National Guard or Army National Guard experience; retired from active duty; disabled or killed as a result of military service; prisoner of war; or missing in action. *Application Requirements:* Application, FAFSA. *Deadline:* continuous. **Contact:** R. Martin Umbarger, Adjutant General, Indiana Department of Veterans Affairs, 2002 South Holt Road, Indianapolis, IN 46241. *E-mail:* r.martin.umbarger@in.ngb.army.mil. *Phone:* 317-247-3559. *Fax:* 317-247-3540. *Web site:* www.in.gov/dva.

Twenty-first Century Scholars Gear Up Summer Scholarship. Grant of up to $3000 that pays for summer school tuition and regularly assessed course fees (does not cover other costs such as textbooks or room and board). *Award:* Scholarship for use in freshman, sophomore, junior, or senior year; not renewable. *Award amount:* up to $3000. *Number of awards:* 1. *Eligibility Requirements:* Applicant must be enrolled or expecting to enroll full-time at a two-year or four-year institution or university; resident of Indiana and studying in Indiana. Available to U.S. citizens. *Application Requirements:* Application, must be in twenty-first century scholars program, high school diploma. *Deadline:* varies. **Contact:** Coordinator, Office of Twenty-First Century Scholars, State Student Assistance Commission of Indiana (SSACI), 150 West Market

Street, Suite 500, Indianapolis, IN 46204. *E-mail:* 21stscholars@ssaci.in.gov. *Phone:* 317-234-1394. *Web site:* www.in.gov/ssaci.

IOWA

All Iowa Opportunity Scholarship. Students attending eligible Iowa colleges and universities may receive awards of up to $6420. Minimum 2.5 GPA. Priority will be given to students who participated in the Federal TRIO Programs, graduated from alternative high schools, and to homeless youth. Applicant must enroll within two academic years of graduating from high school. Maximum individual awards cannot exceed more than the resident tuition rate at Iowa Regent Universities. *Award:* Scholarship for use in freshman or sophomore year; renewable. *Award amount:* up to $6420. *Number of awards:* 179. *Eligibility Requirements:* Applicant must be enrolled or expecting to enroll full- or part-time at a two-year or four-year institution or university; resident of Iowa and studying in Iowa. Applicant must have 3.5 GPA or higher. Available to U.S. citizens. *Application Requirements:* Application, financial need analysis. *Deadline:* May 1. **Contact:** Todd Brown, Director, Scholarships, Grants, and Loan Forgiveness, Iowa College Student Aid Commission, 200 Tenth Street, Fourth Floor, Des Moines, IA 50309-3609. *E-mail:* todd.brown@iowa.gov. *Phone:* 515-725-3405. *Fax:* 515-725-3401. *Web site:* www.iowacollegeaid.gov.

Governor Terry E. Branstad Iowa State Fair Scholarship. Awards up to four scholarships ranging from $500 to $1000 to students graduating from an Iowa high school. Must actively participate at the Iowa State fair. For more details see Web site: http://www.iowacollegeaid.org. *Award:* Scholarship for use in freshman year; not renewable. *Award amount:* $500–$1000. *Number of awards:* up to 4. *Eligibility Requirements:* Applicant must be high school student; planning to enroll or expecting to enroll full- or part-time at a four-year institution or university; resident of Iowa and studying in Iowa. Available to U.S. citizens. *Application Requirements:* Application, essay, financial need analysis, references, transcript. *Deadline:* May 1. **Contact:** Misty Burke, Program Planner, Iowa College Student Aid Commission, 200 Tenth Street, Fourth Floor, Des Moines, IA 50309-3609. *E-mail:* misty.burke@iowa.gov. *Phone:* 515-725-3424. *Fax:* 515-725-3401. *Web site:* www.iowacollegeaid.gov.

Iowa Grants. Statewide need-based program to assist high-need Iowa residents. Recipients must demonstrate a high level of financial need to receive awards ranging from $100 to $1000. Awards are prorated for students enrolled for less than full-time. Awards must be used at Iowa postsecondary institutions. *Award:* Grant for use in freshman, sophomore, junior, or senior year; not renewable. *Award amount:* $100–$1000. *Number of awards:* 2100. *Eligibility Requirements:* Applicant must be enrolled or expecting to enroll full- or part-time at a two-year, four-year, or technical institution or university; resident of Iowa and studying in Iowa. Available to U.S. citizens. *Application Requirements:* Application, financial need analysis. *Deadline:* continuous. **Contact:** Todd Brown, Director, Scholarships, Grants, and Loan Forgiveness, Iowa College Student Aid Commission, 200 Tenth Street, Fourth Floor, Des Moines, IA 50309-3609. *E-mail:* todd.brown@iowa.gov. *Phone:* 515-725-3405. *Fax:* 515-725-3401. *Web site:* www.iowacollegeaid.gov.

Iowa National Guard Education Assistance Program. Program provides postsecondary tuition assistance to members of Iowa National Guard Units. Must study at a postsecondary institution in Iowa. Contact the office for additional information. *Award:* Grant for use in freshman, sophomore, junior, or senior year; not renewable. *Award amount:* $1200–$6420. *Number of awards:* varies. *Eligibility Requirements:* Applicant must be enrolled or expecting to enroll full- or part-time at a two-year, four-year, or technical institution or university; resident of Iowa and studying in Iowa. Available to U.S. citizens. Applicant or parent must meet one or more of the following requirements: Air Force National Guard or Army National Guard experience; retired from active duty; disabled or killed as a result of military service; prisoner of war; or missing in action. *Application Requirements:* Application. *Deadline:* continuous. **Contact:** Todd Brown, Director, Scholarships, Grants, and Loan Forgiveness, Iowa College Student Aid Commission, 200 Tenth Street, Fourth Floor, Des Moines, IA 50309-3609. *E-mail:* todd.brown@iowa.gov. *Phone:* 515-725-3405. *Fax:* 515-725-3401. *Web site:* www.iowacollegeaid.gov.

Iowa Tuition Grant Program. Program assists students who attend independent postsecondary institutions in Iowa. Iowa residents currently enrolled, or planning to enroll, for at least 3 semester hours at one of the eligible Iowa postsecondary institutions may apply. Awards currently range from $100 to $4000. Grants may not exceed the difference between independent college and university tuition fees and the average tuition fees at the three public Regent universities. *Award:* Grant for use in freshman, sophomore, junior, or senior year; not renewable. *Award amount:* $100–$4000. *Number of awards:* 17,200. *Eligibility Requirements:* Applicant must be enrolled or expecting to enroll full- or part-time at a four-year institution or university; resident of Iowa and studying in Iowa. Available to U.S. citizens. *Application Requirements:* Application, financial need analysis. *Deadline:* July 1. **Contact:** Todd Brown, Director, Scholarships, Grants, and Loan Forgiveness, Iowa College Student Aid Commission, 200 Tenth Street, Fourth Floor, Des Moines, IA 50309-3609. *E-mail:* todd.brown@iowa.gov. *Phone:* 515-725-3420. *Fax:* 515-725-3401. *Web site:* www.iowacollegeaid.gov.

Iowa Vocational-Technical Tuition Grant Program. Program provides need-based financial assistance to Iowa residents enrolled in career education (vocational-technical), and career option programs at Iowa area community colleges. Grants range from $150 to $1200, depending on the length of the program, financial need, and available funds. *Award:* Grant for use in freshman or sophomore year; not renewable. *Award amount:* $150–$1200. *Number of awards:* 2100. *Eligibility Requirements:* Applicant must be enrolled or expecting to enroll full- or part-time at a technical institution; resident of Iowa and studying in Iowa. Available to U.S. citizens. *Application Requirements:* Application, financial need analysis. *Deadline:* July 1. **Contact:** Todd Brown, Director, Program Administration, Iowa College Student Aid Commission, 200 Tenth Street, Fourth Floor, Des Moines, IA 50309-3609. *E-mail:* julie.leeper@iowa.gov. *Phone:* 515-725-3405. *Fax:* 515-725-3401. *Web site:* www.iowacollegeaid.gov.

KANSAS

Kansas Educational Benefits for Children of MIA, POW, and Deceased Veterans of the Vietnam War. Scholarship awarded to students who are children of veterans. Must show proof of parent's status as missing in action, prisoner of war, or killed in action in the Vietnam War. Kansas residence required of veteran at time of entry to service. Must attend a state-supported postsecondary school. *Award:* Scholarship for use in freshman, sophomore, junior, or senior year; not renewable. *Award amount:* varies. *Number of awards:* 1. *Eligibility Requirements:* Applicant must be enrolled or expecting to enroll full-time at a two-year, four-year, or technical institution or university and studying in Kansas. Available to U.S. citizens. Applicant or parent must meet one or more of the following requirements: general military experience; retired from active duty; disabled or killed as a result of military service; prisoner of war; or missing in action. *Application Requirements:* Application, birth certificate, school acceptance letter, military discharge of veteran. *Deadline:* varies. **Contact:** Wayne Bollig, Program Director, Kansas Commission on Veterans Affairs, 700 Jackson, SW, Suite 701, Topeka, KS 66603-3743. *E-mail:* wbollig@kcva.org. *Phone:* 785-296-3976. *Fax:* 785-296-1462. *Web site:* www.kcva.org.

Kansas Ethnic Minority Scholarship. Scholarship program designed to assist financially needy, academically competitive students who are identified as members of any of the following ethnic/racial groups: African American, American Indian or Alaskan Native, Asian or Pacific Islander, or Hispanic. Priority is given to applicants who are freshmen. For more details refer to Web site: http://www.kansasregents.org/financial_aid/minority.html. *Award:* Scholarship for use in freshman, sophomore, junior, or senior year; renewable. *Award amount:* up to $1850. *Number of awards:* varies. *Eligibility Requirements:* Applicant must be American Indian/Alaska Native, Asian/Pacific Islander, Black (non-Hispanic), or Hispanic; enrolled or expecting to enroll full-time at a two-year or four-year institution or university and studying in Kansas. Applicant must have 3.0 GPA or higher. Available to U.S. citizens. *Application Requirements:* Application, financial need analysis, test scores. *Fee:* $10. *Deadline:* May 1. **Contact:** Kansas Board of Regents. *Web site:* www.kansasregents.org.

Kansas Nurse Service Scholarship Program. This is a service scholarship loan program available to students attending two-year or four-year public and private postsecondary institutions as well as vocational technical schools with nursing education programs. Students can be pursuing either LPN or RN licensure. *Academic Fields/Career Goals:* Nursing. *Award:* Scholarship for use in freshman, sophomore, junior, or senior year; renewable. *Award amount:* $3500. *Number of awards:* varies. *Eligibility Requirements:* Applicant must be enrolled or expecting to enroll full-time at a two-year, four-year, or technical institution or university. Available to U.S. citizens. *Application Requirements:* Application, financial need analysis, test scores, transcript. *Fee:* $12. *Deadline:* May 1. **Contact:** Kansas Board of Regents. *Web site:* www.kansasregents.org.

Kansas Teacher Service Scholarship. Scholarship to encourage talented students to enter the teaching profession and teach in Kansas in specific curriculum areas or in underserved areas of Kansas. For more details, refer to Web site: http://www.kansasregents.org/financial_aid/teacher.html. *Academic Fields/Career Goals:* Education. *Award:* Scholarship for use in junior or senior year; renewable. *Award amount:* $5000. *Number of awards:* varies. *Eligibility Requirements:* Applicant must be enrolled or expecting to enroll full- or part-time at a four-year institution or university. Applicant must have 3.0 GPA or higher. Available to U.S. citizens. *Application Requirements:* Application, essay, financial need analysis, resume, references, test scores, transcript. *Fee:* $12. *Deadline:* May 1. **Contact:** Kansas Board of Regents. *Web site:* www.kansasregents.org.

Marsha's Angels Scholarship. Scholarship for students who have completed all prerequisites to enter their first year of an accredited nursing program. Applicants living in Sedgwick County, Kansas or one of the surrounding counties may attend an accredited nursing program anywhere in the U.S.; applicants from any other state in the U.S. may use the scholarship to attend a program in Sedgwick County, Kansas, one of the surrounding counties, or St. Luke's College in Missouri. *Academic Fields/Career Goals:* Nursing. *Award:* Scholarship for use in freshman year; not renewable. *Award amount:* $1600–$1800. *Number of awards:* varies. *Eligibility Requirements:* Applicant must be high school student and planning to enroll or expecting to enroll full- or part-time at a four-year institution or university. Available to U.S. citizens. *Application Requirements:* Application, transcript. *Deadline:* June 30. **Contact:** Scholarship Committee, Marsha's Angels Scholarship Fund, PO Box 401, Valley Center, KS 67147-0401. *E-mail:* marshasangels@gmail.com. *Web site:* www.marshasangels.org.

Ted and Nora Anderson Scholarships. Scholarship of $250 for each semester (one year only) given to the children of American Legion members or Auxiliary members who are holding membership for the past three consecutive years. Children of a deceased member can also apply. Parent of the applicant must be a veteran. Must be high school seniors or college freshmen or sophomores in a Kansas institution. Scholarship for use at an approved college, university, or trade school in Kansas. Must maintain a C average in college. *Award:* Scholarship for use in freshman or sophomore year; not renewable. *Award amount:* $250–$500. *Number of awards:* 4. *Eligibility Requirements:* Applicant must be enrolled or expecting to enroll full-time at a two-year, four-year, or technical institution or university; resident of Kansas and studying in Kansas. Applicant or parent of applicant must be member of American Legion or Auxiliary. Available to U.S. citizens. Applicant or parent must meet one or more of the following requirements: general military experience; retired from active duty; disabled or killed as a result of military service; prisoner of war; or missing in action. *Application Requirements:* Application, essay, financial need analysis, photo, references, transcript. *Deadline:* February 15. **Contact:** Jim Gravenstein, Chairman, Scholarship Committee, American Legion Department of Kansas, 1314 Topeka Boulevard, SW, Topeka, KS 66612. *Phone:* 785-232-9315. *Fax:* 785-232-1399. *Web site:* www.ksamlegion.org.

MICHIGAN

Children of Veterans Tuition Grant. Awards available for students who are children of a disabled or deceased Michigan veteran. Must be enrolled at least half time in a degree-granting Michigan public or private nonprofit institution. Must be a U.S. citizen or permanent resident and must be residing in Michigan. *Award:* Grant for use in freshman, sophomore, junior, or senior year; renewable. *Award amount:* up to $2800. *Number of awards:* varies. *Eligibility Requirements:* Applicant must be age 17-25; enrolled or expecting to enroll full- or part-time at a two-year or four-year institution or university; resident of Michigan and studying in Michigan. Available to U.S. citizens. Applicant or parent must meet one or more of the following requirements: general military experience; retired from active duty; disabled or killed as a result of military service; prisoner of war; or missing in action. *Application Requirements:* Application. *Deadline:* varies. **Contact:** Scholarship and Grant Director, Michigan Higher Education Assistance Authority, PO Box 30462, Lansing, MI 48909-7962. *E-mail:* osg@michigan.gov. *Phone:* 888-447-2687. *Web site:* www.michigan.gov/studentaid.

Children of Veterans Tuition Grant Program. Undergraduate tuition assistance to certain children older than 16 and less than 26 years of age who have been Michigan residents for the 12 months prior to application. To be eligible a student must be the natural or adopted child of a Michigan veteran. The veteran must have been a legal resident of Michigan immediately before entering military service and did not later reside outside of Michigan for more than two years; or the veteran must have established legal residency in Michigan after entering military service. *Award:* Grant for use in freshman, sophomore, junior, or senior year; renewable. *Award amount:* up to $2800. *Number of awards:* varies. *Eligibility Requirements:* Applicant must be age 16-26; enrolled or expecting to enroll full- or part-time at a two-year or four-year institution or university; resident of Michigan and studying in Michigan. Available to U.S. citizens. Applicant or parent must meet one or more of the following requirements: general military experience; retired from active duty; disabled or killed as a result of military service; prisoner of war; or missing in action. *Application Requirements:* Application. *Deadline:* continuous. **Contact:** Office of Scholarships and Grants. *Web site:* www.michigan.gov/osg.

Michigan Adult Part-Time Grant. Grant is intended for financially needy, independent undergraduates who have been out of high school for at least two years. Must be enrolled on a part-time basis. Must be Michigan resident. *Award:* Grant for use in freshman, sophomore, junior, or senior year; renewable. *Award amount:* up to $600. *Number of awards:* varies. *Eligibility Requirements:* Applicant must be enrolled or expecting to enroll part-time at a two-year or four-year institution or university; resident of Michigan and studying in Michigan. Available to U.S. citizens. *Application Requirements:* Financial need analysis. *Deadline:* March 1. **Contact:** Scholarship and Grant Director, Michigan Higher Education Assistance Authority, PO Box 30462, Lansing, MI 48909-7962. *E-mail:* osg@michigan.gov. *Phone:* 888-447-2687. *Web site:* www.michigan.gov/studentaid.

Michigan Competitive Scholarship. Renewable award of $1300 for Michigan resident to pursue undergraduate study at a Michigan institution. Awards limited to tuition. Must maintain at least a 2.0 grade point average and meet the college's academic progress requirements. Must file Free Application for Federal Student Aid. *Award:* Scholarship for use in freshman, sophomore, junior, or senior year; renewable. *Award amount:* $100–$1300. *Number of awards:* varies. *Eligibility Requirements:* Applicant must be enrolled or expecting to enroll full- or part-time at a two-year or four-year institution or university; resident of Michigan and studying in Michigan. Available to U.S. citizens. *Application Requirements:* Application, financial need analysis, test scores. *Deadline:* March 1. **Contact:** Scholarship and Grant Director, Michigan

Higher Education Assistance Authority, PO Box 30466, Lansing, MI 48909-7962. *E-mail:* osg@michigan.gov. *Phone:* 888-447-2687. *Web site:* www.michigan.gov/studentaid.

Michigan Educational Opportunity Grant. Need-based program for Michigan residents who are at least half-time undergraduates attending public Michigan college or university. Must maintain good academic standing. Award of up to $1000. *Award:* Grant for use in freshman, sophomore, junior, or senior year; renewable. *Award amount:* up to $1000. *Number of awards:* varies. *Eligibility Requirements:* Applicant must be enrolled or expecting to enroll full- or part-time at a two-year or four-year institution or university; resident of Michigan and studying in Michigan. Available to U.S. citizens. *Application Requirements:* Financial need analysis. *Deadline:* March 1. **Contact:** Scholarship and Grant Director, Michigan Higher Education Assistance Authority, PO Box 30462, Lansing, MI 48909-7962. *E-mail:* osg@michigan.gov. *Phone:* 888-447-2687. *Web site:* www.michigan.gov/studentaid.

Michigan Indian Tuition Waiver. Renewable award provides free tuition for Native-American of 1/4 or more blood degree who attend a Michigan public college or university. Must be a Michigan resident for at least one year. The tuition waiver program covers full-time, part-time or summer school student attending a public, state, community, junior college, public college, or public university. Deadline: continuous. *Award:* Scholarship for use in freshman, sophomore, junior, senior, graduate, or postgraduate years; renewable. *Award amount:* varies. *Number of awards:* varies. *Eligibility Requirements:* Applicant must be American Indian/Alaska Native; enrolled or expecting to enroll full- or part-time at a two-year, four-year, or technical institution or university; resident of Michigan and studying in Michigan. Available to U.S. citizens. *Application Requirements:* Application, driver's license, transcript, tribal certification, proof of residency. *Deadline:* continuous. **Contact:** Christin McKerchie, Executive Assistant to Programs, Inter-Tribal Council of Michigan Inc., 2956 Ashmun Street, Suite A, Sault Ste. Marie, MI 49783. *Phone:* 906-632-6896 Ext. 136. *Fax:* 906-632-6878. *Web site:* www.itcmi.org.

Michigan Nursing Scholarship. Scholarship for students enrolled in an LPN, associate degree in nursing, bachelor of science in nursing, or master of science in nursing programs. Colleges determine application procedure and select recipients. Recipients must fulfill in-state work commitment or repay scholarship. *Academic Fields/Career Goals:* Nursing. *Award:* Scholarship for use in freshman, sophomore, junior, or senior year; renewable. *Award amount:* up to $4000. *Number of awards:* varies. *Eligibility Requirements:* Applicant must be enrolled or expecting to enroll full- or part-time at a two-year or four-year institution or university; resident of Michigan and studying in Michigan. Available to U.S. citizens. *Application Requirements:* Recipients are selected by their college. *Deadline:* varies. **Contact:** Scholarship and Grant Director, Michigan Higher Education Assistance Authority, PO Box 30462, Lansing, MI 48909-7962. *E-mail:* osg@michigan.gov. *Phone:* 888-447-2687. *Web site:* www.michigan.gov/studentaid.

Michigan Promise Scholarship. Scholarship available for students who have taken the state's assessment test. Students who meet or exceed test standards may receive $1000 during each of their first two years of college and another $2000 after completing two years with at least a 2.5 GPA. Students who do not meet or exceed state standards may receive $4000 after completing two years of postsecondary study with at least a 2.5 GPA. Must be a Michigan resident enrolled at an approved Michigan postsecondary institution. *Award:* Scholarship for use in freshman, sophomore, or junior year; not renewable. *Award amount:* up to $4000. *Number of awards:* varies. *Eligibility Requirements:* Applicant must be enrolled or expecting to enroll full- or part-time at a two-year, four-year, or technical institution or university; resident of Michigan and studying in Michigan. Available to U.S. citizens. *Application Requirements:* Test scores. *Deadline:* continuous. **Contact:** Scholarship and Grant Director, Michigan Higher Education Assistance Authority, PO Box 30462, Lansing, MI 48909-7962. *E-mail:* osg@michigan.gov. *Phone:* 888-447-2687. *Web site:* www.michigan.gov/studentaid.

Michigan Tuition Grant. Need-based program. Students must be Michigan residents and attend a Michigan private, nonprofit, degree-granting college. Must file the Free Application for Federal Student Aid and meet the college's academic progress requirements. *Award:* Grant for use in freshman, sophomore, junior, or senior year; renewable. *Award amount:* $100–$2100. *Number of awards:* varies. *Eligibility Requirements:* Applicant must be enrolled or expecting to enroll full- or part-time at a four-year institution or university; resident of Michigan and studying in Michigan. Available to U.S. citizens. *Application Requirements:* Financial need analysis. *Deadline:* July 1. **Contact:** Scholarship and Grant Director, Michigan Higher Education Assistance Authority, PO Box 30462, Lansing, MI 48909-7962. *E-mail:* osg@michigan.gov. *Phone:* 888-447-2687. *Web site:* www.michigan.gov/studentaid.

Tuition Incentive Program. Award for Michigan residents who receive or have received Medicaid for required period of time through the Department of Human Services. Scholarship provides two years tuition towards an associate degree at a Michigan college or university and $2000 total assistance for third and fourth years. Must apply before graduating from high school or earning a general education development diploma. *Award:* Grant for use in freshman, sophomore, junior, or senior year; renewable. *Award amount:* varies. *Number of awards:* varies. *Eligibility Requirements:* Applicant must be high school student; planning to enroll or expecting to enroll full- or part-time at a two-year or four-year institution or university; resident of Michigan and studying in Michigan. Available to U.S. citizens. *Application Requirements:* Application, Medicaid eligibility for specified period of time. *Deadline:* continuous. **Contact:** Scholarship and Grant Director, Michigan Higher Education Assistance Authority, PO Box 30462, Lansing, MI 48909-7962. *E-mail:* osg@michigan.gov. *Phone:* 888-447-2687. *Web site:* www.michigan.gov/studentaid.

MINNESOTA

Leadership, Excellence and Dedicated Service Scholarship. Scholarship provides a maximum of thirty $1000 to selected high school seniors who become a member of the Minnesota National Guard and complete the application process. The award recognizes demonstrated leadership, community services and potential for success in the Minnesota National Guard. *Award:* Scholarship for use in freshman year; not renewable. *Award amount:* $1000. *Number of awards:* up to 30. *Eligibility Requirements:* Applicant must be high school student; planning to enroll or expecting to enroll full- or part-time at a two-year, four-year, or technical institution or university; resident of Minnesota and must have an interest in leadership. Applicant or parent of applicant must have employment or volunteer experience in community service. Available to U.S. citizens. Applicant or parent must meet one or more of the following requirements: Air Force National Guard or Army National Guard experience; retired from active duty; disabled or killed as a result of military service; prisoner of war; or missing in action. *Application Requirements:* Essay, resume, references, transcript. *Deadline:* March 15. **Contact:** Barbara O'Reilly, Education Services Officer, Minnesota Department of Military Affairs, 20 West 12th Street, Veterans Services Building, St. Paul, MN 55155-2098. *E-mail:* barbara.oreilly@mn.ngb.army.mil. *Phone:* 651-282-4508. *Web site:* www.minnesotanationalguard.org.

Minnesota Achieve Scholarship. Minnesota residents who complete one of four sets of rigorous programs of study while in high school or in a home-school setting may be eligible to receive a one-time scholarship of $1200. Student must have graduated from a Minnesota high school after January 1 and completed, with a grade of C or above, all of the required courses. Must have a household adjusted gross income of less than $75,000. Scholarships are available to eligible students up to 4 years after high school graduation. *Award:* Scholarship for use in freshman, sophomore, junior, or senior year; not renewable. *Award amount:* up to $1200. *Number of awards:* varies. *Eligibility Requirements:* Applicant must be enrolled or expecting to enroll full- or part-time at a two-year, four-year, or technical institution or university; resident of Minnesota and studying in Minnesota. Available to U.S. citizens.

Application Requirements: Application, financial need analysis, test scores, transcript. *Deadline:* varies. **Contact:** Scholarship Staff, Minnesota Office of Higher Education, 1450 Energy Park Drive, St. Paul, MN 55108. *Phone:* 651-642-0567. *Fax:* 651-642-0675. *Web site:* www.getreadyforcollege.org.

Minnesota GI Bill Program. Provides financial assistance to eligible Minnesota veterans and non-veterans who have served 5 or more years cumulatively as a member of the National Guard or Reserves, and served on or after September 11, 2001. Surviving spouses and children of service members who have died or have a total and permanent disability and who served on or after September 11, 2001, may also be eligible. Full-time students may receive up to $1000 per term, and part-time students up to $500 per term. Maximum lifetime benefit is $10,000. *Award:* Scholarship for use in freshman, sophomore, junior, or senior year; renewable. *Award amount:* up to $3000. *Number of awards:* varies. *Eligibility Requirements:* Applicant must be enrolled or expecting to enroll full- or part-time at a two-year, four-year, or technical institution or university; resident of Minnesota and studying in Minnesota. Available to U.S. citizens. Applicant or parent must meet one or more of the following requirements: general military experience; retired from active duty; disabled or killed as a result of military service; prisoner of war; or missing in action. *Application Requirements:* Application, financial need analysis, military records. *Deadline:* continuous. **Contact:** Scholarship Staff, Minnesota Office of Higher Education, 1450 Energy Park Drive, St. Paul, MN 55108. *Phone:* 651-642-0567. *Fax:* 651-642-0675. *Web site:* www.getreadyforcollege.org.

Minnesota Indian Scholarship. Scholarship for Minnesota residents who are one-fourth or more American Indian ancestry and attending an eligible Minnesota postsecondary institution. Maximum award is $4000 for undergraduate students and $6000 for graduate students. Scholarships are limited to 3 years for certificate or AA/AS programs, 5 years for bachelor's degree programs, and 5 years for graduate programs. Applicants must maintain satisfactory academic progress, not be in default on student loans, and be eligible to receive Pell or State Grant and have remaining need. *Award:* Scholarship for use in freshman, sophomore, junior, or senior year; renewable. *Award amount:* up to $6000. *Number of awards:* 500–600. *Eligibility Requirements:* Applicant must be American Indian/Alaska Native; enrolled or expecting to enroll full- or part-time at a two-year, four-year, or technical institution or university; resident of Minnesota and studying in Minnesota. Available to U.S. citizens. *Application Requirements:* Application, American Indian ancestry documentation. *Deadline:* varies. **Contact:** Scholarship Staff, Minnesota Office of Higher Education, 1450 Energy Park Drive, Suite 350, St. Paul, MN 55108. *E-mail:* sandy.bowes@state.mn.us. *Phone:* 651-642-0567 Ext. 1. *Fax:* 651-642-0675. *Web site:* www.getreadyforcollege.org.

Minnesota Nurses Loan Forgiveness Program. Program offering loan repayment to registered nurse and licensed practical nurse students who agree to practice in a Minnesota nursing home or an Intermediate Care Facility for persons with mental retardation for a minimum three-year/four-year service obligation after completion of training. Candidates must apply while still in school. *Academic Fields/Career Goals:* Health and Medical Sciences; Nursing. *Award:* Forgivable loan for use in freshman or sophomore year; not renewable. *Award amount:* $3750. *Eligibility Requirements:* Applicant must be enrolled or expecting to enroll full- or part-time at a two-year or four-year institution or university. Available to U.S. and non-U.S. citizens. *Application Requirements:* Application, essay, resume, references. *Deadline:* December 1. **Contact:** Minnesota Department of Health. *Web site:* www.health.state.mn.us.

Minnesota Reciprocal Agreement. Renewable tuition waiver for Minnesota residents. Waives all or part of non-resident tuition surcharge at public institutions in Iowa, Kansas, Michigan, Missouri, Nebraska, North Dakota, South Dakota, Wisconsin and Manitoba. Deadline: last day of academic term. *Award:* Scholarship for use in freshman, sophomore, junior, or senior year; renewable. *Award amount:* varies. *Number of awards:* varies. *Eligibility Requirements:* Applicant must be enrolled or expecting to enroll full- or part-time at a two-year, four-year, or technical institution or university; resident of Minnesota and studying in Iowa, Kansas, Manitoba, Michigan, Missouri, Nebraska, North Dakota, South Dakota, or Wisconsin. Available to U.S. citizens. *Application Requirements:* Application. *Deadline:* varies. **Contact:** Jodi Rouland, Program Assistant, Minnesota Office of Higher Education. *E-mail:* jodi.rouland@state.mn.us. *Phone:* 651-355-0614. *Fax:* 651-642-0675. *Web site:* www.getreadyforcollege.org.

Minnesota State Grant Program. Need-based grant program available for Minnesota residents attending Minnesota colleges. Student covers 46% of cost with remainder covered by Pell Grant, parent contribution and state grant. Students apply with FAFSA and college administers the program on campus. *Award:* Grant for use in freshman, sophomore, junior, or senior year; renewable. *Award amount:* $100–$8661. *Number of awards:* 71,000–81,000. *Eligibility Requirements:* Applicant must be age 17 and over; enrolled or expecting to enroll full- or part-time at a two-year, four-year, or technical institution or university; resident of Minnesota and studying in Minnesota. Available to U.S. citizens. *Application Requirements:* Application, financial need analysis. *Deadline:* varies. **Contact:** Grant Staff, Minnesota Office of Higher Education, 1450 Energy Park Drive, Suite 350, St. Paul, MN 55108. *Phone:* 651-642-0567 Ext. 1. *Web site:* www.getreadyforcollege.org.

Minnesota State Veterans' Dependents Assistance Program. Tuition assistance to dependents of persons considered to be prisoner-of-war or missing in action after August 1, 1958. Must be Minnesota resident attending Minnesota two- or four-year school. *Award:* Scholarship for use in freshman, sophomore, junior, or senior year; renewable. *Award amount:* varies. *Number of awards:* varies. *Eligibility Requirements:* Applicant must be enrolled or expecting to enroll full- or part-time at a two-year or four-year institution; resident of Minnesota and studying in Minnesota. Available to U.S. citizens. Applicant or parent must meet one or more of the following requirements: general military experience; retired from active duty; disabled or killed as a result of military service; prisoner of war; or missing in action. *Application Requirements:* Application. *Deadline:* continuous. **Contact:** Minnesota Office of Higher Education. *Web site:* www.getreadyforcollege.org.

Paul and Fern Yocum Scholarship. Scholarship to dependent children of full-time Yocum Oil employees. *Award:* Scholarship for use in freshman, sophomore, junior, senior, or graduate year; not renewable. *Award amount:* $1000. *Number of awards:* 3. *Eligibility Requirements:* Applicant must be enrolled or expecting to enroll full- or part-time at a four-year institution or university. Applicant or parent of applicant must be affiliated with Yocum Oil Company. Available to U.S. and non-Canadian citizens. *Application Requirements:* Application. *Deadline:* April 15. **Contact:** Donna Paulson, Administrative Assistant, Minnesota Community Foundation, 55 Fifth Street East, Suite 600, St. Paul, MN 55101-1797. *E-mail:* dkp@mncommunityfoundation.org. *Phone:* 651-325-4212. *Web site:* www.mncommunityfoundation.org.

Postsecondary Child Care Grant Program-Minnesota. Grant available for students not receiving MFIP. Based on financial need. Cannot exceed actual child care costs or maximum award chart (based on income). Must be Minnesota resident. For use at Minnesota two- or four-year school, including public technical colleges. *Award:* Grant for use in freshman, sophomore, junior, or senior year; renewable. *Award amount:* $100–$2600. *Number of awards:* varies. *Eligibility Requirements:* Applicant must be enrolled or expecting to enroll full- or part-time at a two-year, four-year, or technical institution or university; resident of Minnesota and studying in Minnesota. Available to U.S. citizens. *Application Requirements:* Application, financial need analysis. *Deadline:* continuous. **Contact:** Brenda Larter, Program Administrator, Minnesota Office of Higher Education, 1450 Energy Park Drive, Suite 350, St. Paul, MN 55108-5227. *E-mail:* brenda.larter@state.mn.us. *Phone:* 651-355-0612. *Fax:* 651-642-0675. *Web site:* www.getreadyforcollege.org.

Safety Officers' Survivor Grant Program. Grant for eligible survivors of Minnesota public safety officers killed in the line of duty. Safety officers who have been permanently or totally disabled in the line of duty are also eligible. Must be used at a Minnesota institution participating in State Grant Program. Write for details. Must submit proof of death or disability and Public Safety Officers Benefit Fund Certificate. Must apply for renewal each year for four years. *Award:* Grant for use in freshman, sophomore, junior, or senior year; not renewable. *Award amount:* up to $9438. *Number of awards:* 1. *Eligibility Requirements:* Applicant must be age 23 or under; enrolled or expecting to enroll full- or part-time at a two-year, four-year, or technical institution or university; resident of Minnesota and studying in Minnesota. Applicant or parent of applicant must have employment or volunteer experience in police/firefighting. Available to U.S. citizens. *Application Requirements:* Application, proof of death or disability. *Deadline:* continuous. **Contact:** Brenda Larter, Program Administrator, Minnesota Office of Higher Education. *E-mail:* brenda.larter@state.mn.us. *Phone:* 651-355-0612. *Fax:* 651-642-0675. *Web site:* www.getreadyforcollege.org.

MISSOURI

Access Missouri Financial Assistance Program. Need-based program that provides awards to students who are enrolled full time and have an expected family contribution (EFC) of $12,000 or less based on their Free Application for Federal Student Aid (FAFSA). Awards vary depending on EFC and the type of postsecondary school. *Award:* Grant for use in freshman, sophomore, junior, or senior year; not renewable. *Eligibility Requirements:* Applicant must be enrolled or expecting to enroll full-time at a two-year, four-year, or technical institution or university; resident of Missouri and studying in Missouri. Applicant must have 2.5 GPA or higher. Available to U.S. citizens. *Application Requirements:* FAFSA on file by April 1. **Contact:** Missouri Coordinating Board for Higher Education. *Web site:* www.dhe.mo.gov.

ACES/PRIMO Program. Program of the Missouri Area Health Education Centers (MAHEC) and the Primary Care Resource Initiative for Missouri students interested in Primary Care. Applicant should have a minimum GPA of 3.0. *Academic Fields/Career Goals:* Health and Medical Sciences. *Award:* Forgivable loan for use in freshman, sophomore, junior, or senior year; not renewable. *Award amount:* $3000–$5000. *Number of awards:* 100. *Eligibility Requirements:* Applicant must be enrolled or expecting to enroll full- or part-time at a four-year institution or university. Applicant must have 3.0 GPA or higher. Available to U.S. and non-U.S. citizens. *Application Requirements:* Application, proof of Missouri residency. *Deadline:* June 30. **Contact:** Cheryl Thomas, Management Analyst Specialist II, Missouri Department of Health, PO Box 570, Jefferson City, MO 65401-0570. *E-mail:* cheryl.thomas@dhss.mo.gov. *Phone:* 800-891-7415. *Fax:* 573-522-8146. *Web site:* www.dhss.mo.gov.

Environmental Education Scholarship Program (EESP). Scholarship to minority and other underrepresented students pursuing a bachelor's or master's degree in an environmental course of study. Must be a Missouri resident having a cumulative high school GPA of 3.0 or if enrolled in college, must have cumulative GPA of 2.5. *Academic Fields/Career Goals:* Environmental Science. *Award:* Scholarship for use in freshman, sophomore, junior, senior, or graduate year; renewable. *Award amount:* $2000. *Number of awards:* 16. *Eligibility Requirements:* Applicant must be American Indian/Alaska Native, Asian/Pacific Islander, Black (non-Hispanic), or Hispanic; enrolled or expecting to enroll full-time at a four-year institution or university and resident of Missouri. Applicant must have 3.0 GPA or higher. Available to U.S. citizens. *Application Requirements:* Application, essay, references, transcript. *Deadline:* June 1. **Contact:** Dana Muessig, Executive, Missouri Department of Natural Resources, PO Box 176, Jefferson City, MO 65102. *E-mail:* danamuessig@dnr.mo.gov. *Phone:* 800-361-4827. *Fax:* 573-526-3878. *Web site:* www.dnr.mo.gov.

Lillie Lois Ford Scholarship Fund. Two awards of $1000 each are given each year to one boy and one girl. Applicant must have attended a full session of Missouri Boys/Girls State or Missouri Cadet Patrol Academy. Must be a Missouri resident below age 21, attending an accredited college/university as a full-time student. Must be an unmarried descendant of a veteran having served at least 90 days on active duty in the Army, Air Force, Navy, Marine Corps or Coast Guard of the United States. *Award:* Scholarship for use in freshman year; not renewable. *Award amount:* $1000. *Number of awards:* 2. *Eligibility Requirements:* Applicant must be high school student; age 21 or under; planning to enroll or expecting to enroll full-time at a two-year or four-year institution or university; single and resident of Missouri. Available to U.S. citizens. Applicant or parent must meet one or more of the following requirements: general military experience; retired from active duty; disabled or killed as a result of military service; prisoner of war; or missing in action. *Application Requirements:* Application, financial need analysis, test scores, copy of the veteran's discharge certificate. *Deadline:* April 20. **Contact:** John Doane, Chairman, Education and Scholarship Committee, American Legion Department of Missouri, PO Box 179, Jefferson City, MO 65102-0179. *Phone:* 417-924-8186. *Web site:* www.missourilegion.org.

Marguerite Ross Barnett Memorial Scholarship. Scholarship was established for students who are employed while attending school part-time. Must be enrolled at least half-time but less than full-time at a participating Missouri postsecondary school, be employed and compensated for at least 20 hours per week, be 18 years of age, be a Missouri resident and a U.S. citizen or a permanent resident. *Award:* Scholarship for use in freshman, sophomore, junior, or senior year; renewable. *Award amount:* varies. *Number of awards:* varies. *Eligibility Requirements:* Applicant must be age 18 and over; enrolled or expecting to enroll part-time at a two-year, four-year, or technical institution or university; resident of Missouri and studying in Missouri. Applicant must have 2.5 GPA or higher. Available to U.S. citizens. *Application Requirements:* FAFSA on file by August 1. *Deadline:* August 1. **Contact:** Missouri Coordinating Board for Higher Education. *Web site:* www.dhe.mo.gov.

Missouri Higher Education Academic Scholarship (Bright Flight). Program encourages top-ranked high school seniors to attend approved Missouri postsecondary schools. Must be a Missouri resident and a U.S. citizen. Must have a composite score on the ACT or the SAT in the top three percent of all Missouri students taking those tests. Annual scholarship of $2000 is awarded in two payments of $1000 each semester. *Award:* Scholarship for use in freshman, sophomore, junior, or senior year; renewable. *Award amount:* $2000. *Number of awards:* varies. *Eligibility Requirements:* Applicant must be enrolled or expecting to enroll full-time at a two-year, four-year, or technical institution or university; resident of Missouri and studying in Missouri. Applicant must have 2.5 GPA or higher. Available to U.S. citizens. *Application Requirements:* Test scores. **Contact:** Missouri Coordinating Board for Higher Education. *Web site:* www.dhe.mo.gov.

Missouri Teacher Education Scholarship (General). Nonrenewable award for Missouri high school seniors or Missouri resident college students. Must attend approved teacher training program at a participating Missouri institution and rank in top 15 percent of high school class on ACT/SAT. Merit-based award. Recipients must commit to teach in Missouri for five years at a public elementary or secondary school or award must be repaid. *Academic Fields/Career Goals:* Education. *Award:* Scholarship for use in freshman, sophomore, junior, or senior year; not renewable. *Award amount:* up to $2000. *Number of awards:* 200–240. *Eligibility Requirements:* Applicant must be enrolled or expecting to enroll full-time at a two-year or four-year institution or university; resident of Missouri and studying in Missouri. Available to U.S. citizens. *Application Requirements:* Application, essay, resume, references, test scores, transcript. *Deadline:* February 15. **Contact:** Laura Harrison, Administrative Assistant II, Missouri Department of Elementary and Secondary Education, PO Box 480, Jefferson City, MO 65102-0480. *E-mail:* laura.harrison@dese.mo.gov. *Phone:* 573-751-1668. *Fax:* 573-526-3580. *Web site:* www.dese.mo.gov.

Primary Care Resource Initiative for Missouri Loan Program. Forgivable loans for Missouri residents attending Missouri institutions pursuing a degree as a primary care physician or dentist, dental hygienist, psychiatrist, psychologist, licensed professional counselor, licensed clinical social worker or dietitian . To be forgiven participant must work in a Missouri health professional shortage area. *Academic*

Fields/Career Goals: Dental Health/Services; Health and Medical Sciences; Nursing. *Award:* Forgivable loan for use in freshman, sophomore, junior, senior, or graduate year; not renewable. *Award amount:* $5000–$20,000. *Number of awards:* 100. *Eligibility Requirements:* Applicant must be enrolled or expecting to enroll full- or part-time at a four-year institution or university; resident of Missouri and studying in Missouri. Applicant must have 3.5 GPA or higher. Available to U.S. and non-U.S. citizens. *Application Requirements:* Application, proof of Missouri residency. *Deadline:* June 30. **Contact:** Cheryl Thomas, Management Analyst Specialist II, Missouri Department of Health, PO Box 570, Jefferson City, MO 65102-0570. *E-mail:* cheryl.thomas@dhss.mo.gov. *Phone:* 800-891-7415. *Fax:* 573-522-8146. *Web site:* www.dhss.mo.gov.

Robert C. Byrd Honors Scholarship-Missouri. Award for high school seniors who are residents of Missouri. Amount of the award each year depends on the amount the state is allotted by the U.S. Department of Education. Maximum amount awarded per student is $1500. Students must rank in top 10 percent of high school class and score in top 10 percent on ACT. *Award:* Scholarship for use in freshman year; renewable. *Award amount:* up to $1500. *Number of awards:* 100–150. *Eligibility Requirements:* Applicant must be high school student; planning to enroll or expecting to enroll full-time at a four-year institution or university and resident of Missouri. Available to U.S. citizens. *Application Requirements:* Application, test scores, transcript. *Deadline:* April 15. **Contact:** Laura Harrison, Administrative Assistant II, Missouri Department of Elementary and Secondary Education, PO Box 480, Jefferson City, MO 65102-0480. *E-mail:* laura.harrison@dese.mo.gov. *Phone:* 573-751-1668. *Fax:* 573-526-3580. *Web site:* www.dese.mo.gov.

Teacher Education Scholarship. The scholarship is a competitive, one-time, nonrenewable award of $2000 to be used in one academic year. Applicants must be a Missouri resident and a high school senior or student enrolled full-time at a community or four-year college or university in Missouri. *Award:* Scholarship for use in freshman, sophomore, junior, or senior year; not renewable. *Award amount:* up to $2000. *Number of awards:* up to 240. *Eligibility Requirements:* Applicant must be enrolled or expecting to enroll full-time at a two-year or four-year institution or university; resident of Missouri and studying in Missouri. Available to U.S. citizens. *Application Requirements:* Application, applicant must enter a contest, essay, resume, references, test scores, transcript. *Deadline:* February 15. **Contact:** Ms. Laura Harrison, Administrative Assistant, Missouri State Department of Elementary/Secondary Education, PO Box 480, Jefferson City, MO 65102-0480. *E-mail:* laura.harrison@dese.mo.gov. *Phone:* 573-751-1668. *Fax:* 573-526-3580. *Web site:* www.dese.mo.gov.

NEBRASKA

Nebraska State Grant. Available to undergraduates attending a participating postsecondary institution in Nebraska. Available to Pell Grant recipients only. Nebraska residency required. Awards determined by each participating institution. Contact financial aid office at institution for application and additional information. *Award:* Grant for use in freshman, sophomore, junior, or senior year; not renewable. *Award amount:* $100–$1600. *Number of awards:* varies. *Eligibility Requirements:* Applicant must be enrolled or expecting to enroll full- or part-time at a two-year, four-year, or technical institution or university; resident of Nebraska and studying in Nebraska. Available to U.S. citizens. *Application Requirements:* Application, financial need analysis. *Deadline:* continuous. **Contact:** Mr. J. Ritchie Morrow, Financial Aid Coordinator, State of Nebraska, 140 North Eighth Street, Suite 300, PO Box 95005, Lincoln, NE 68509-5005. *E-mail:* rmorrow@ccpe.st.ne.us. *Phone:* 402-471-2847. *Fax:* 402-471-2886. *Web site:* www.ccpe.state.ne.us.

NORTH DAKOTA

North Dakota Indian Scholarship Program. Award of $500 to $2000 per year to assist American Indian students who are North Dakota residents in obtaining a college education. Must have been accepted for admission at an institution of higher learning or state vocational education program within North Dakota. For full-time study only. Based upon scholastic ability and unmet financial need. Minimum 2.0 GPA required. *Award:* Scholarship for use in freshman, sophomore, junior, or senior year; renewable. *Award amount:* $800–$2000. *Number of awards:* 175–230. *Eligibility Requirements:* Applicant must be American Indian/Alaska Native; enrolled or expecting to enroll full-time at a two-year, four-year, or technical institution or university; resident of North Dakota and studying in North Dakota. Available to U.S. citizens. *Application Requirements:* Application, financial need analysis, transcript, proof of tribal enrollment, budget. *Deadline:* July 15. **Contact:** Rhonda Schauer, Coordinator of American Indian Higher Education, State of North Dakota, 919 South Seventh Street, Suite 300, Bismarck, ND 58504-5881. *E-mail:* rhonda.schauer@ndus.nodak.edu. *Phone:* 701-328-9661. *Web site:* www.ndus.edu.

North Dakota Scholars Program. Provides scholarships equal to cost of tuition at the public colleges in North Dakota for North Dakota residents. Must score at or above the 95th percentile on ACT and rank in top twenty percent of high school graduation class. Must take ACT in fall. For high school seniors with a minimum 3.5 GPA. Deadline: October or June ACT test date. *Award:* Scholarship for use in freshman year; renewable. *Award amount:* $5000. *Number of awards:* 45–50. *Eligibility Requirements:* Applicant must be high school student; planning to enroll or expecting to enroll full-time at a two-year or four-year institution or university; resident of North Dakota and studying in North Dakota. Available to U.S. citizens. *Application Requirements:* References, test scores. *Deadline:* varies. **Contact:** Peggy Wipf, Director of Financial Aid, State of North Dakota, 600 East Boulevard Avenue, Department 215, Bismarck, ND 58505-0230. *E-mail:* peggy.wipf@ndus.nodak.edu. *Phone:* 701-328-4114. *Web site:* www.ndus.edu.

North Dakota State Student Incentive Grant Program. Aids North Dakota residents attending an approved college or university in North Dakota. Must be enrolled in a program of at least nine months in length. Must be a U.S. citizen. *Award:* Grant for use in freshman, sophomore, junior, or senior year; renewable. *Award amount:* $800. *Number of awards:* 3500–3700. *Eligibility Requirements:* Applicant must be enrolled or expecting to enroll full-time at a two-year or four-year institution or university; resident of North Dakota and studying in North Dakota. Available to U.S. citizens. *Application Requirements:* Financial need analysis. *Deadline:* March 15. **Contact:** Peggy Wipf, Director of Financial Aid, State of North Dakota, 600 East Boulevard Avenue, Department 215, Bismarck, ND 58505-0230. *Phone:* 701-328-4114. *Web site:* www.ndus.edu.

OHIO

Ohio Environmental Science & Engineering Scholarships. Merit-based, non-renewable, tuition-only scholarships awarded to undergraduate students admitted to Ohio state or private colleges and universities. Must be able to demonstrate knowledge of, and commitment to, careers in environmental sciences or environmental engineering. *Academic Fields/Career Goals:* Environmental Science. *Award:* Scholarship for use in senior year; not renewable. *Award amount:* $1250–$2500. *Number of awards:* 18. *Eligibility Requirements:* Applicant must be enrolled or expecting to enroll full- or part-time at a two-year or four-year institution or university and studying in Ohio. Applicant must have 3.0 GPA or higher. Available to U.S. citizens. *Application Requirements:* Application, essay, resume, references, self-addressed stamped envelope, transcript. *Deadline:* June 1. **Contact:** Mr. Lynn E. Elfner, Chief Executive Officer, Ohio Academy of Science/Ohio Environmental Education Fund, 1500 West Third Avenue, Suite 228, Columbus, OH 43212-2817. *E-mail:* oas@iwaynet.net. *Phone:* 614-488-2228. *Fax:* 614-488-7629. *Web site:* www.ohiosci.org.

Ohio Instructional Grant. Award for low- and middle-income Ohio residents attending an approved college or school in Ohio or Pennsylvania. Must be enrolled full-time and have financial need. May be used for any course of study except theology. *Award:* Grant for use in freshman, sophomore, junior, or senior year; renewable. *Award* *amount:* $78–$5466. *Number of awards:* varies. *Eligibility Requirements:* Applicant must be enrolled or expecting to enroll full-time at a two-year or four-year institution or university; resident of Ohio and studying in Ohio or Pennsylvania. Available to U.S. citizens. *Application Requirements:* Application, financial need analysis. *Deadline:* October 1. **Contact:** Tamika Braswell, Program Administrator, Ohio Board of Regents, 30 East Broad Street, 36th Floor, Columbus, OH 43215-3414. *E-mail:* tbraswell@regents.state.oh.us. *Phone:* 614-728-8862. *Fax:* 614-752-5903. *Web site:* www.regents.ohio.gov.

Ohio Missing in Action and Prisoners of War Orphans Scholarship. Renewable award aids children of Vietnam conflict servicemen who have been classified as missing in action or prisoner of war. Applicants must be under the age of 25 and be enrolled full-time at an Ohio college. A percentage of tuition is awarded. Dollar value of each award varies. *Award:* Scholarship for use in freshman, sophomore, junior, or senior year; renewable. *Award amount:* varies. *Number of awards:* 1–5. *Eligibility Requirements:* Applicant must be age 25 or under; enrolled or expecting to enroll full-time at a four-year institution or university; resident of Ohio and studying in Ohio. Available to U.S. citizens. Applicant or parent must meet one or more of the following requirements: general military experience; retired from active duty; disabled or killed as a result of military service; prisoner of war; or missing in action. *Application Requirements:* Application. *Deadline:* July 1. **Contact:** Jathiya Abdullah-Simmons, Program Administrator, Ohio Board of Regents, 30 East Broad Street, 36th Floor, Columbus, OH 43215-3414. *E-mail:* jabdullah-simmons@regents.state.oh.us. *Phone:* 614-752-9528. *Fax:* 614-752-5903. *Web site:* www.regents.ohio.gov.

Ohio National Guard Scholarship Program. Scholarships are for undergraduate studies at an approved Ohio post-secondary institution. Applicants must enlist for six years of Selective Service Reserve Duty in the Ohio National Guard. Scholarship pays 100% instructional and general fees for public institutions and an average of cost of public schools is available for private schools. May reapply up to four years. Deadlines: July 1, November 1, February 1, April 1. *Award:* Scholarship for use in freshman, sophomore, junior, or senior year; not renewable. *Award amount:* up to $3911. *Number of awards:* up to 3500. *Eligibility Requirements:* Applicant must be enrolled or expecting to enroll full- or part-time at a two-year, four-year, or technical institution or university; resident of Ohio and studying in Ohio. Available to U.S. citizens. Applicant or parent must meet one or more of the following requirements: Air Force National Guard or Army National Guard experience; retired from active duty; disabled or killed as a result of military service; prisoner of war; or missing in action. *Application Requirements:* Application. *Deadline:* varies. **Contact:** Toni Davis, Grants Administrator, Ohio National Guard, 2825 West Dublin Granville Road, Columbus, OH 43235-2789. *E-mail:* toni.davis@tagoh.gov. *Phone:* 614-336-7143. *Fax:* 614-336-7318. *Web site:* www.ongsp.org.

Ohio Safety Officers College Memorial Fund. Renewable award covering up to full tuition is available to children and surviving spouses of peace officers, other safety officers and fire fighters killed in the line of duty in any state. Children must be under 26 years of age. Dollar value of each award varies. Must be an Ohio resident and enroll full-time or part-time at an Ohio college or university. Any spouse/child of a member of the armed services of the U.S., who has been killed in the line duty during Operation Enduring Freedom, Operation Iraqi Freedom or a combat zone designated by the President of the United States. Dollar value of each award varies. *Award:* Scholarship for use in freshman, sophomore, junior, or senior year; renewable. *Award amount:* varies. *Number of awards:* 50–65. *Eligibility Requirements:* Applicant must be age 26 or under; enrolled or expecting to enroll full- or part-time at a two-year or four-year institution or university; resident of Ohio and studying in Ohio. Applicant or parent of applicant must have employment or volunteer experience in police/firefighting. Available to U.S. citizens. *Application Requirements: Deadline:* continuous. **Contact:** Barbara Thoma, Program Administrator, Ohio Board of Regents, 30 East Broad Street, 36th Floor, Columbus, OH 43215-3414. *E-mail:* bthoma@regents.state.oh.us. *Phone:* 614-752-9535. *Fax:* 614-752-5903. *Web site:* www.regents.ohio.gov.

Ohio War Orphans Scholarship. Aids Ohio residents attending an eligible college in Ohio. Must be between the ages of 16 and 25, the child of a disabled or deceased veteran, and enrolled full-time. Renewable up to five years. Amount of award varies. Must include Form DD214. *Award:* Scholarship for use in freshman, sophomore, junior, or senior year; renewable. *Award amount:* varies. *Number of awards:* 300–450. *Eligibility Requirements:* Applicant must be age 16-25; enrolled or expecting to enroll full-time at a two-year or four-year institution or university; resident of Ohio and studying in Ohio. Available to U.S. citizens. Applicant or parent must meet one or more of the following requirements: general military experience; retired from active duty; disabled or killed as a result of military service; prisoner of war; or missing in action. *Application Requirements:* Application. *Deadline:* July 1. **Contact:** Jathiya Abdullah-Simmons, Program Administrator, Ohio Board of Regents, 30 East Broad Street, 36th Floor, Columbus, OH 43215-3414. *E-mail:* jabdullah-simmons@regents.state.oh.us. *Phone:* 614-752-9528. *Fax:* 614-752-5903. *Web site:* www.regents.ohio.gov.

OKLAHOMA

Academic Scholars Program. Awards for students of high academic ability to attend institutions in Oklahoma. Renewable up to four years. ACT or SAT scores must fall between 99.5 and 100th percentiles, or applicant must be designated as a National Merit scholar or finalist. Oklahoma public institutions can also select institutional nominees. *Award:* Scholarship for use in freshman year; renewable. *Award amount:* $1800–$5500. *Number of awards:* varies. *Eligibility Requirements:* Applicant must be high school student; planning to enroll or expecting to enroll full-time at a two-year or four-year institution or university and studying in Oklahoma. Available to U.S. citizens. *Application Requirements:* Application, test scores, transcript. *Deadline:* continuous. **Contact:** Scholarship Programs Coordinator, Oklahoma State Regents for Higher Education, PO Box 108850, Oklahoma City, OK 73101-8850. *E-mail:* studentinfo@osrhe.edu. *Phone:* 800-858-1840. *Fax:* 405-225-9230. *Web site:* www.okhighered.org.

Future Teacher Scholarship-Oklahoma. Open to outstanding Oklahoma high school graduates who agree to teach in shortage areas. Must rank in top 15 percent of graduating class or score above 85th percentile on ACT or similar test, or be accepted in an educational program. Students nominated by institution. Reapply to renew. Must attend college/university in Oklahoma. *Academic Fields/Career Goals:* Education. *Award:* Scholarship for use in freshman, sophomore, junior, senior, or graduate year; renewable. *Award amount:* $500–$1500. *Number of awards:* 85. *Eligibility Requirements:* Applicant must be enrolled or expecting to enroll full- or part-time at a two-year or four-year institution or university; resident of Oklahoma and studying in Oklahoma. Available to U.S. citizens. *Application Requirements:* Application, essay, test scores, transcript. *Deadline:* varies. **Contact:** Scholarship Programs Coordinator, Oklahoma State Regents for Higher Education, PO Box 108850, Oklahoma City, OK 73101-8850. *E-mail:* studentinfo@osrhe.edu. *Phone:* 800-858-1840. *Fax:* 405-225-9230. *Web site:* www.okhighered.org.

Oklahoma Tuition Aid Grant. Award for Oklahoma residents enrolled at an Oklahoma institution at least part time each semester in a degree program. May be enrolled in two- or four-year or approved vocational-technical institution. Award for students attending public institutions or private colleges. Application is made through FAFSA. *Award:* Grant for use in freshman, sophomore, junior, or senior year; renewable. *Award amount:* $1000–$1300. *Number of awards:* varies. *Eligibility Requirements:* Applicant must be enrolled or expecting to enroll full- or part-time at a two-year, four-year, or technical institution or university; resident of Oklahoma and studying in Oklahoma. Available to U.S. citizens. *Application Requirements:* Application, financial need analysis, FAFSA. *Deadline:* varies. **Contact:** Alicia Harris, Scholarship

Programs Coordinator, Oklahoma State Regents for Higher Education, PO Box 3020, Oklahoma City, OK 73101-3020. *E-mail:* aharris@osrhe.edu. *Phone:* 405-225-9131. *Fax:* 405-225-9230. *Web site:* www.okhighered.org.

Regional University Baccalaureate Scholarship. Renewable award for Oklahoma residents attending one of 11 participating Oklahoma public universities. Must have an ACT composite score of at least 30 or be a National Merit semifinalist or commended student. In addition to the award amount, each recipient will receive a resident tuition waiver from the institution. Must maintain a 3.25 GPA. Deadlines vary depending upon the institution attended. *Award:* Scholarship for use in freshman, sophomore, junior, or senior year; renewable. *Award amount:* $3000. *Number of awards:* varies. *Eligibility Requirements:* Applicant must be enrolled or expecting to enroll full-time at an institution or university; resident of Oklahoma and studying in Oklahoma. Available to U.S. citizens. *Application Requirements:* Application. *Deadline:* varies. **Contact:** Alicia Harris, Scholarship Programs Coordinator, Oklahoma State Regents for Higher Education, PO Box 108850, Oklahoma City, OK 73101-8850. *E-mail:* aharris@osrhe.edu. *Phone:* 405-225-9131. *Fax:* 405-225-9230. *Web site:* www.okhighered.org.

Robert C. Byrd Honors Scholarship-Oklahoma. Scholarships available to high school seniors. Applicants must be U.S. citizens or national, or be permanent residents of the United States. Must be legal residents of Oklahoma. Must have a minimum ACT composite score of 32 and/or a minimum SAT combined score of 1420 and/or 2130 or a minimum GED score of 700. Application URL: http://www.sde.state.ok.us/Finance/Scholarships/Byrd/Application.pdf. *Award:* Scholarship for use in freshman year; not renewable. *Award amount:* $1500. *Number of awards:* 10. *Eligibility Requirements:* Applicant must be high school student; planning to enroll or expecting to enroll full-time at a four-year institution or university and resident of Oklahoma. Available to U.S. citizens. *Application Requirements:* Application, essay, references, transcript. *Deadline:* April 11. **Contact:** Certification Specialist, Oklahoma State Department of Education, 2500 North Lincoln Boulevard, Suite 212, Oklahoma City, OK 73105-4599. *Phone:* 405-521-2808. *Web site:* www.sde.state.ok.us.

SOUTH DAKOTA

Haines Memorial Scholarship. One-time scholarship for South Dakota public university students who are sophomores, juniors, or seniors having at least a 2.5 GPA and majoring in a teacher education program. Must include resume with application. Must be South Dakota resident. *Academic Fields/Career Goals:* Education. *Award:* Scholarship for use in sophomore, junior, or senior year; not renewable. *Award amount:* $2150. *Number of awards:* 1. *Eligibility Requirements:* Applicant must be enrolled or expecting to enroll full-time at an institution or university; resident of South Dakota and studying in South Dakota. Applicant must have 3.5 GPA or higher. Available to U.S. citizens. *Application Requirements:* Application, driver's license, essay, resume, typed statement describing personal philosophy and philosophy of education. *Deadline:* February 8. **Contact:** South Dakota Board of Regents. *Web site:* www.sdbor.edu.

South Dakota Opportunity Scholarship. Renewable scholarship may be worth up to $5000 over four years to students who take a rigorous college-prep curriculum while in high school and stay in the state for their postsecondary education. *Award:* Scholarship for use in freshman year; renewable. *Award amount:* $1000. *Number of awards:* 1000. *Eligibility Requirements:* Applicant must be high school student; planning to enroll or expecting to enroll full-time at a two-year, four-year, or technical institution or university; resident of South Dakota and studying in South Dakota. Applicant must have 3.0 GPA or higher. Available to U.S. citizens. *Application Requirements:* Application, test scores, transcript. *Deadline:* September 1. **Contact:** Janelle Toman, Scholarship Committee, South Dakota Board of Regents, 306 East Capitol, Suite 200, Pierre, SD 57501-2545. *E-mail:* info@sdbor.edu. *Phone:* 605-773-3455. *Fax:* 605-773-2422. *Web site:* www.sdbor.edu.

WISCONSIN

Handicapped Student Grant-Wisconsin. One-time award available to residents of Wisconsin who have severe or profound hearing or visual impairment. Must be enrolled at least half-time at a nonprofit institution. If the handicap prevents the student from attending a Wisconsin school, the award may be used out-of-state in a specialized college. Refer to Web site for further details: http://www.heab.state.wi.us. *Award:* Grant for use in freshman, sophomore, junior, or senior year; not renewable. *Award amount:* $250–$1800. *Number of awards:* varies. *Eligibility Requirements:* Applicant must be enrolled or expecting to enroll full- or part-time at a four-year institution or university and resident of Wisconsin. Applicant must be hearing impaired or visually impaired. Available to U.S. citizens. *Application Requirements:* Application, financial need analysis. *Deadline:* continuous. **Contact:** Sandy Thomas, Program Coordinator, Wisconsin Higher Educational Aid Board, PO Box 7885, Madison, WI 53707-7885. *E-mail:* sandy.thomas@wi.gov. *Phone:* 608-266-0888. *Fax:* 608-267-2808. *Web site:* www.heab.wi.gov.

Menominee Indian Tribe Adult Vocational Training Program. Renewable award for enrolled Menominee tribal members to use at vocational or technical schools. Must be at least 1/4 Menominee and show proof of Indian blood. Must complete financial aid form. Deadlines: March 1 and November 1. *Award:* Grant for use in freshman or sophomore year; renewable. *Award amount:* $100–$2200. *Number of awards:* 50–70. *Eligibility Requirements:* Applicant must be American Indian/Alaska Native and enrolled or expecting to enroll full- or part-time at a technical institution. Available to U.S. citizens. *Application Requirements:* Application, financial need analysis, proof of Indian blood. *Deadline:* varies. **Contact:** Virginia Nuske, Education Director, Menominee Indian Tribe of Wisconsin, PO Box 910, Keshena, WI 54135. *E-mail:* vnuske@mitw.org. *Phone:* 715-799-5110. *Fax:* 715-799-5102. *Web site:* www.menominee-nsn.gov.

Menominee Indian Tribe of Wisconsin Higher Education Grants. Renewable award for enrolled Menominee tribal member to use at a two- or four-year college or university. Must be at least 1/4 Menominee and show proof of Indian blood. Must complete financial aid form. *Award:* Grant for use in freshman, sophomore, junior, or senior year; renewable. *Award amount:* $100–$2200. *Number of awards:* 136. *Eligibility Requirements:* Applicant must be American Indian/Alaska Native and enrolled or expecting to enroll full- or part-time at a two-year or four-year institution or university. Available to U.S. citizens. *Application Requirements:* Application, financial need analysis, proof of Indian blood. *Deadline:* continuous. **Contact:** Virginia Nuske, Education Director, Menominee Indian Tribe of Wisconsin, PO Box 910, Keshena, WI 54135. *E-mail:* vnuske@mitw.org. *Phone:* 715-799-5110. *Fax:* 715-799-5102. *Web site:* www.menominee-nsn.gov.

Minority Undergraduate Retention Grant-Wisconsin. The grant provides financial assistance to African-American, Native-American, Hispanic, and former citizens of Laos, Vietnam, and Cambodia, for study in Wisconsin. Must be Wisconsin resident, enrolled at least half-time in Wisconsin Technical College System schools, non-profit independent colleges and universities, and tribal colleges. Refer to Web site for further details: http://www.heab.state.wi.us. *Award:* Grant for use in sophomore, junior, or senior year; not renewable. *Award amount:* $250–$2500. *Number of awards:* varies. *Eligibility Requirements:* Applicant must be American Indian/Alaska Native, Asian/Pacific Islander, Black (non-Hispanic), or Hispanic; enrolled or expecting to enroll full- or part-time at a two-year, four-year, or technical institution or university; resident of Wisconsin and studying in Wisconsin. Available to U.S. and non-U.S. citizens. *Application Requirements:* Application, financial need analysis. *Deadline:* continuous. **Contact:** Mary Lou Kuzdas, Program Coordinator, Wisconsin Higher Educational Aid Board, PO Box 7885, Madison, WI 53707-7885. *E-mail:* mary.kuzdas@wi.gov. *Phone:* 608-267-2212. *Fax:* 608-267-2808. *Web site:* www.heab.wi.gov.

Talent Incentive Program Grant. Grant assists residents of Wisconsin who are attending a nonprofit institution in Wisconsin, and who have substantial financial need. Must meet income criteria, be considered economically and educationally disadvantaged, and be enrolled at least half-time. Refer to Web site for further details: http://www.heab.state.wi.us. *Award:* Grant for use in freshman, sophomore, junior, or senior year; renewable. *Award amount:* $250–$1800. *Number of awards:* varies. *Eligibility Requirements:* Applicant must be enrolled or expecting to enroll full- or part-time at a two-year, four-year, or technical institution or university; resident of Wisconsin and studying in Wisconsin. Available to U.S. citizens. *Application Requirements:* Application, financial need analysis, nomination by financial aid office. *Deadline:* continuous. **Contact:** Colette Brown, Program Coordinator, Wisconsin Higher Educational Aid Board, PO Box 7885, Madison, WI 53707-7885. *E-mail:* colette.brown@wi.gov. *Phone:* 608-266-1665. *Fax:* 608-267-2808. *Web site:* www.heab.wi.gov.

Veterans Education (VetEd) Reimbursement Grant. Open only to Wisconsin veterans enrolled at approved schools for undergraduate study. Benefit is based on length of time serving on active duty in the armed forces (active duty for training does not apply). Pre-application due no later than 180 days after the start of semester. Application deadline no later than 60 days after the course completion. Veterans may be reimbursed up to 100 percent of tuition and fees at UW—Madison rate for the same number of credits. *Award:* Grant for use in freshman, sophomore, junior, or senior year; renewable. *Award amount:* up to $3594. *Number of awards:* varies. *Eligibility Requirements:* Applicant must be enrolled or expecting to enroll full- or part-time at a two-year, four-year, or technical institution or university; resident of Wisconsin and studying in Minnesota or Wisconsin. Available to U.S. citizens. Applicant or parent must meet one or more of the following requirements: Air Force, Army, Coast Guard, Marine Corps, or Navy experience; retired from active duty; disabled or killed as a result of military service; prisoner of war; or missing in action. *Application Requirements:* Application, pre-application. *Deadline:* varies. **Contact:** Ms. Leslie Busby-Amegashie, Analyst, Wisconsin Department of Veterans Affairs, PO Box 7843, Madison, WI 53707-7843. *E-mail:* leslie.busby-amegashie@dva.state.wi.us. *Phone:* 800-947-8387. *Web site:* www.dva.state.wi.us.

Wisconsin Academic Excellence Scholarship. Renewable award for high school seniors with the highest GPA in graduating class. Must be a Wisconsin resident attending a nonprofit Wisconsin institution full-time. Scholarship value is $2250 toward tuition each year for up to four years. Must maintain 3.0 GPA for renewal. Refer to your high school counselor for more details. *Award:* Scholarship for use in freshman year; renewable. *Award amount:* up to $2250. *Number of awards:* varies. *Eligibility Requirements:* Applicant must be high school student; planning to enroll or expecting to enroll full-time at a two-year, four-year, or technical institution or university; resident of Wisconsin and studying in Wisconsin. Applicant must have 3.0 GPA or higher. Available to U.S. citizens. *Application Requirements:* Application, test scores, transcript. *Deadline:* continuous. **Contact:** Nancy Wilkison, Program Coordinator, Wisconsin Higher Educational Aid Board, PO Box 7885, Madison, WI 53707-7885. *E-mail:* nancy.wilkison@wi.gov. *Phone:* 608-267-2213. *Fax:* 608-267-2808. *Web site:* www.heab.wi.gov.

Wisconsin Higher Education Grants (WHEG). Grants for residents of Wisconsin enrolled at least half-time in degree or certificate programs at a University of Wisconsin Institution, Wisconsin Technical College or an approved Tribal College . Must show financial need. Refer to Web site for further details: http://www.heab.wi.gov. *Award:* Grant for use in freshman, sophomore, junior, or senior year; not renewable. *Award amount:* $250–$3000. *Number of awards:* varies. *Eligibility Requirements:* Applicant must be enrolled or expecting to enroll full- or part-time at a two-year, four-year, or technical institution or university; resident of Wisconsin and studying in Wisconsin. Available to U.S. citizens. *Application Requirements:* Application, financial need analysis. *Deadline:* continuous. **Contact:** Sandra Thomas, Program Coordinator, Wisconsin Higher Educational Aid Board, PO Box 7885, Madison, WI 53707-7885. *E-mail:* sandy.thomas@heab.state.wi.us. *Phone:* 608-266-0888. *Fax:* 608-267-2808. *Web site:* www.heab.wi.gov.

Wisconsin League for Nursing Inc., Scholarship. One-time award for Wisconsin residents who have completed half of an accredited Wisconsin school of nursing program. Financial need of student must be demonstrated. Scholarship applications are mailed by WLN office ONLY to Wisconsin nursing schools in January for distribution to students. Students interested in obtaining an application must contact their nursing school and submit completed applications to their school. Applications sent directly to WLN office will be returned to applicant. For further information visit Web site: http://www.wisconsinwln.org/Scholarships.htm. *Academic Fields/Career Goals:* Nursing. *Award:* Scholarship for use in junior or senior year; not renewable. *Award amount:* $500–$1000. *Number of awards:* 11–35. *Eligibility Requirements:* Applicant must be enrolled or expecting to enroll full-time at a two-year, four-year, or technical institution or university; resident of Wisconsin and studying in Wisconsin. Available to U.S. citizens. *Application Requirements:* Application, essay, financial need analysis. *Deadline:* March 1. **Contact:** Wisconsin League for Nursing, Inc. *Web site:* www.wisconsinwln.org.

Wisconsin Native American/Indian Student Assistance Grant. Grants for Wisconsin residents who are at least one-quarter American Indian. Must be attending a college or university within the state. Refer to Web site for further details: http://www.heab.state.wi.us. *Award:* Grant for use in freshman, sophomore, junior, or senior year; not renewable. *Award amount:* $250–$1100. *Number of awards:* varies. *Eligibility Requirements:* Applicant must be American Indian/Alaska Native; enrolled or expecting to enroll full- or part-time at a two-year, four-year, or technical institution or university; resident of Wisconsin and studying in Wisconsin. Available to U.S. citizens. *Application Requirements:* Application, financial need analysis. *Deadline:* continuous. **Contact:** Sandra Thomas, Program Coordinator, Wisconsin Higher Educational Aid Board, PO Box 7885, Madison, WI 53707-7885. *E-mail:* sandy.thomas@wi.gov. *Phone:* 608-266-0888. *Fax:* 608-267-2808. *Web site:* www.heab.wi.gov.

Searching for Four-Year Colleges Online

The Internet can be a great tool for gathering information about four-year colleges and universities. There are many worthwhile sites that are ready to help guide you through the various aspects of the selection process, including Peterson's College Search at www.petersons.com/ugchannel.

HOW PETERSON'S COLLEGE SEARCH CAN HELP

Peterson's College Search is a comprehensive information resource that will help you make sense of the college admissions process and is a great place to start your college search-and-selection journey—it's as easy as these three steps:

1. Decide what's important
2. Define your criteria
3. Get results

Decide What's Important

There's no such thing as a best college—there's only the best college *for you*! Peterson's College Search site is organized into various sections and offers you enhanced search criteria—and it's easy to use! You can find colleges by name or keyword for starters, or do a detailed search based on the following:

- The Basics (location, setting, size, cost, type, religious and ethnic affiliation)
- Student Body (male-female ratio, diversity, in-state vs. out-of-state)
- Getting In (selectivity, GPA)
- Academics (degree type, majors, special programs and services)
- Campus Life (sports, clubs, fraternities and sororities, housing)

Define Your Criteria

Now it's time to define your criteria by taking a closer look at some more specific details. Here you are able to answer questions about what is important to you, skip questions that aren't important, and click for instant results. You'll be prompted to think about criteria:

- Where do you want to study?
- What range of tuition are you willing to consider?
- How many people do you want to go to school with?

Get Results

Once you have gotten your results, simply click on any school to get information about the institution, including school type, setting, degrees offered, comprehensive cost, entrance difficulty, application deadline, undergraduate student population, minority breakdown, international population, housing info, freshman details, faculty, majors, academic programs, student life, athletics, facilities/endowments, costs, financial aid, and applying. If the schools you are interested in have provided Peterson's with a **Close-Up,** you will find that here too! Here, schools are given the opportunity to communicate unique features of their programs to prospective students.

Get Free Info

If, after looking at the information provided on Peterson's College Search, you still have questions, you can send an e-mail directly to the admissions department of the school. Just click on the "Get Free Info" button and send your message!

Visit School Site

For institutions that have provided information about their Web sites, simply click on any one of the links at the top of the page (e.g., School Web site, Apply Now, Online Tour) and you will be taken directly to that institution's Web page. Once you arrive at the school's Web site, look around and get a feel for the place. Often, schools offer virtual tours of the campus, complete with photos and commentary.

Add to My Saved Colleges

The "Add to My Saved Colleges" features help your college planning with management tools that create notes and track schools.

WRITE ADMISSIONS ESSAYS

This year, 500,000 college applicants will write 500,000 different admissions essays. Half will be rejected by their first-choice school, while only 11 percent will gain admission to the nation's most selective colleges. With acceptance rates at all-time lows, setting yourself apart requires more than just blockbuster SAT scores and impeccable transcripts—it requires the perfect application essay. Named "the world's premier application essay editing service" by the *New York Times* Learning Network and "one of the best essay services on the Internet" by the *Washington Post*, EssayEdge (www.essayedge.com) has helped more applicants write successful personal statements than any other company in the world. Learn more about EssayEdge and how it can give you an edge over hundreds of applicants with comparable academic credentials.

PRACTICE FOR YOUR TEST

At Peterson's, we understand that the college admissions process can be very stressful. With the stakes so high and the competition getting tighter every year, it's easy to feel like the process is out of your control. Fortunately, preparing for college admissions tests, like the PSAT, SAT, and ACT, helps you exert some control over the options you will have available to you. You can visit Peterson's Prep Central (click on the "Prepare for Tests" tab at the top of the screen) to learn more about how Peterson's can help you maximize your scores—and your options.

USE THE TOOLS TO YOUR ADVANTAGE

Choosing a college is an involved and complicated process. The tools available to you on www.petersons.com can help you to be more productive in this process. So, what are you waiting for? Fire up your computer; your future alma mater may be just a click away!

How to Use This Guide

This article provides an outline of the **Profile** format, describing the items covered. All college information presented was supplied to Peterson's by the colleges themselves. Any item that does not apply to a particular college or for which no current information was supplied may be omitted from that college's **Profile**. Colleges that were unable to supply usable data in time for publication are listed by name and, if available, Web address.

PROFILES OF COLLEGES IN THE MIDWEST

This section presents pertinent factual and statistical data for each college in a standard format for easy comparison.

General Information

The first paragraph gives a brief introduction to the college, covering the following elements.

Type of student body: The categories are *men's* (100 percent of the student body), *primarily men's*, *women's* (100 percent of the student body), *primarily women's*, and *coed*. A few schools are designated as *undergraduate: women only; graduate: coed* or *undergraduate: men only; graduate: coed*. A college may also be designated as coordinate with another institution, indicating that there are separate colleges or campuses for men and women, but facilities, courses, and institutional governance are shared.

Institutional control: A *public* college receives its funding wholly or primarily from the federal, state, and/or local government. The term *private* indicates an independent, nonprofit institution, that is, one whose funding comes primarily from private sources and tuition. This category includes independent, religious colleges, which may also specify a particular religious denomination or church affiliation. Profit-making institutions are designated as *proprietary*.

Institutional type: A *two-year college* awards associate degrees and/or offers the first two years of a bachelor's degree program. A *primarily two-year college* awards bachelor's degrees, but the vast majority of students are enrolled in two-year programs. A *four-year college* awards bachelor's degrees and may also award associate degrees, but it does not offer graduate (postbachelor's) degree programs. A *five-year college* offers a five-year bachelor's program in a professional field such as architecture or pharmacy but does not award graduate degrees. An *upper-level institution* awards bachelor's degrees, but entering students must have at least two years of previous college-level credit; it may also offer graduate degree programs. A *comprehensive institution* awards bachelor's degrees and may also award associate degrees; graduate degree programs are offered primarily at the master's, specialist's, or professional level, although one or two doctoral programs may also be offered. A *university* offers four years of undergraduate work plus graduate degrees through the doctorate in more than two academic and/or professional fields.

Founding date: This is the year the college came into existence or was chartered, reflecting the period during which it has existed as an educational institution, regardless of subsequent mergers or other organizational changes.

Degree levels: An *associate* degree program may consist of either a college-transfer program, equivalent to the first two years of a bachelor's degree, or a one- to three-year terminal program that provides training for a specific occupation. A *bachelor's* degree program represents a three- to five-year liberal arts, science, professional, or preprofessional program. A *master's* degree is the first graduate degree in the liberal arts and sciences and certain professional fields and usually requires one to two years of full-time study. A *doctoral* degree is the highest degree awarded in research-oriented academic disciplines and usually requires from three to six years of full-time graduate study; the *first professional* degrees in such fields as law and medicine are also at the doctoral level. For colleges that award degrees in one field only, such as art or music, the field of specialization is indicated.

Campus setting: This indicates the size of the campus in acres or hectares and its location.

Academic Information

This paragraph contains information on the following items.

Faculty: The number of full-time and part-time faculty members is given, followed by the percentage of the full-time faculty members who hold doctoral, first professional, or terminal degrees, and then the student-faculty ratio. (Not all colleges calculate the student-faculty ratio in the same way; Peterson's prints the ratio provided by the college.)

Library holdings: The numbers of books, serials, and audiovisual materials in the college's collections are listed.

Special programs: *Academic remediation for entering students* consists of instructional courses designed for students deficient in the general competencies necessary for a regular postsecondary curriculum and educational setting. *Services for LD students* include special help for learning-disabled students with resolvable difficulties, such as dyslexia. *Honors programs* are any special programs for very able students, offering the opportunity for educational enrichment, independent study, acceleration, or some combination of these. *Cooperative (co-op) education programs* are formal arrangements with off-campus employers, allowing students to combine work and study in order to gain degree-related experience, usually extending the time required to complete a degree. *Study abroad* is an arrangement by which a student completes part of the academic program studying in another country. A college may operate a campus abroad or it may have a cooperative agreement with other U.S. institutions or institutions in other countries. *Advanced placement* gives credit toward a degree awarded for acceptable scores on College Board Advanced Placement tests. *Accelerated degree programs* allow students to earn a bachelor's degree in three academic years. *Freshmen honors college* is a separate academic program for talented freshmen. *English as a second language (ESL)* is a course of study designed specifically for students whose native language is not English. *Double major* consists of a program of study in which a student concurrently completes the requirements of two majors. *Independent study* consists of academic work, usually undertaken outside the regular classroom structure, chosen or designed by the student with departmental approval and instructor supervision. *Distance learning* consists of credit courses that can be accessed off campus via cable television, the Internet, satellite, videotapes, correspondence courses, or other media. *Self-designed major* is a program of study based on individual interests, designed by the student with the assistance of an adviser. *Summer session for credit* includes summer courses through which students may make up degree work or accelerate their program. *Part-time degree programs* offer students the ability to earn a degree through part-time enrollment in regular session (daytime) classes or evening, weekend, or summer classes. *External degree programs* are programs of study in which students earn credits toward a degree through a combination of independent study, college courses, proficiency examinations, and personal experience. External degree programs require minimal or no classroom attendance. *Adult/continuing education programs* are courses offered for nontraditional students who are currently working or are returning to formal education. *Internships* are any short-term, supervised work experience, usually related to a student's major field, for which the student earns academic credit. The work can be full- or part-time, on or off campus, paid or unpaid. *Off-campus study* is a formal arrangement with one or more domestic institutions under which students may take courses at the other institution(s) for credit.

Most popular majors: The most popular field or fields of study at the college, in terms of the number of undergraduate degrees conferred in 2008, are listed.

Student Body Statistics

Enrollment: The total number of students, undergraduates, and freshmen (or entering students for an upper-level institution) enrolled in degree programs as of fall 2008 are given.

With reference to the undergraduate enrollment for fall 2008, the percentages of women and men and the number of states and countries from which students hail are listed. The following percentages are also provided: in-state students, international students, and the percentage of undergraduates who went on to graduate and professional schools.

Expenses

Costs are given in each profile according to the most up-to-date figures available from each college for the 2008–09 or 2009–10 academic year.

Annual expenses may be expressed as a comprehensive fee (the annual cost of attending, including full-time tuition, mandatory fees, and college room and board) or as separate figures for full-time tuition, fees, room and board, and/or room only. For public institutions where tuition differs according to residence, separate figures are given for area and/or state residents and for nonresidents. Part-time tuition and fees are expressed in terms of a per-unit rate (per credit, per semester hour, etc.) as specified by the college.

The tuition structure at some institutions is complex in that freshmen and sophomores may be charged a different rate from that of juniors and seniors; a professional or vocational division may have a different fee structure from the liberal arts division of the same institution; or part-time tuition may be prorated on a sliding scale according to the number of credit hours taken. In all of these cases, the average figures are given along with an explanation of the basis for the variable rate. For colleges that report that the room and board costs vary according to the type of accommodation and meal plan, the average costs are given. The phrase *no college housing* indicates that the college does not own or operate any housing facilities for its undergraduate students.

Financial Aid

This paragraph contains information on the following items.

Forms of financial aid: The categories of college-administered aid available to undergraduates are listed. College-administered means that the college itself determines the recipient and amount of each award. The types of aid covered are *non-need scholarships, need-based scholarships, athletic grants,* and *part-time jobs.*

Financial aid: This item pertains to undergraduates who enrolled full-time in a four-year college in 2007 or 2008. The figures given are the dollar amount of the average financial aid package, including scholarships, grants, loans, and part-time jobs, received by such undergraduates.

Financial aid application deadline: This deadline may be given as a specific date, as continuous processing up to a specific date or until all available aid has been awarded, or as a priority date rather than a strict deadline, meaning that students are encouraged to apply by that date in order to have the best chance of obtaining aid.

Freshman Admission

The supporting data that a student must submit when applying for freshman admission are grouped into three categories: *required for all*, *recommended*, and *required for some*. They may include an essay, a high school transcript, letters of recommendation, an interview on campus or with local alumni, standardized test scores, and, for certain types of schools or programs, special requirements such as a musical audition or an art portfolio.

The most commonly required standardized tests are the ACT and the College Board's SAT and SAT Subject Tests. TOEFL (Test of English as a Foreign Language) is for international students whose native language is not English.

The application deadline for admission is given as either a specific date or *rolling*. Rolling means that applications are processed as they are received, and qualified students are accepted as long as there are openings. The application deadline for out-of-state students is indicated if it differs from the date for state residents. *Early decision* and *early action* deadlines are also given when applicable. Early decision is a program whereby students may apply early, are notified of acceptance or rejection well in advance of the usual notification date, and agree to accept an offer of admission, the assumption being that only one early application has been made. Early action is the same as early decision except that applicants are not obligated to accept an offer of admission.

Transfer Admission

This paragraph gives the application requirements and application deadline for a student applying for admission as a transfer from another institution. In addition to the requirements previously listed for freshman applicants, requirements for transfers may also include a college transcript and a minimum college grade point average (expressed as a number on a scale of 0 to 4.0, where 4.0 equals A, 3.0 equals B, etc.). The name of the person to contact for additional transfer information is also given if it is different from the person listed in **For Further Information.**

Entrance Difficulty

This paragraph contains the college's own assessment of its *entrance difficulty* level, including notation of an *open admission policy* where applicable. Open admission means that virtually all applicants are accepted without regard to standardized test scores, grade average, or class rank. A college may indicate that open admission is limited to a certain category of applicants, such as state residents, or does not apply to certain selective programs, often those in the health professions.

The five levels of entrance difficulty are *most difficult*, *very difficult*, *moderately difficult*, *minimally difficult*, and *noncompetitive*.

The final item in this paragraph is the percentage of applicants accepted for the fall 2008 freshman (or entering) class.

For Further Information

The name, title, and mailing address of the person to contact for more information on application and admission procedures are given at the end of the **Profile.** A telephone number, fax number, e-mail address, and Web site are also included in this paragraph. Profiles with a *Sponsor* icon do not contain this information, since it is already available in the **Special Message to Students.**

SPECIAL MESSAGES TO STUDENTS

In addition, a number of college admissions office staff members, as part of a major information-dissemination effort, have supplemented their **Profile** with special descriptive information on four topics of particular interest to students.

Social Life: This paragraph conveys a feeling for life on campus by addressing such questions as the following: What are the most popular activities? Are there active fraternities and sororities? What is the role of student government? Do most students live on campus or commute? Does the college have a religious orientation?

Academic Highlights: This paragraph describes some of the special features and characteristics of the college's academic program, such as special degree programs and opportunities for study abroad or internships.

Interviews and Campus Visits: Colleges that conduct on-campus admission interviews describe the importance of an interview in their admission process and what they try to learn about a student through the interview. For those colleges that do not interview applicants individually, there is information on how a student interested in the college can visit the campus to meet administrators, faculty members, and currently enrolled students as well as on what the prospective applicant should try to accomplish through such a visit. This paragraph may also include a list of the most noteworthy places or things to see during a campus visit and the location, telephone number (including toll-free numbers if available), and business hours of the office to contact for information about appointments and campus visits. Also included, when available, is travel information, specifically the nearest commercial airport and the nearest interstate highway, with the appropriate exit.

For Further Information: The name and mailing address of the person and/or office to contact for more information on the school are included in this paragraph. A telephone number, fax number, e-mail address, and Web site may also be included.

CLOSE-UPS OF COLLEGES IN THE MIDWEST

Two-page narrative descriptions appear in this section, providing an inside look at colleges and universities, shifting the focus to a variety of other factors, some of them intangible, that should also be considered. The descriptions presented in this section provide a wealth of statistics that are crucial components in the college decision-making equation—components such as tuition, financial aid, and major fields of study. Prepared exclusively by college officials, the descriptions are designed to help give students a better sense of the individuality of each institution, in terms that include campus environment, student activities, and lifestyle. Such quality-of-life intangibles can be the deciding factors in the college selection process.

The absence from this section of any college or university does not constitute an editorial decision on the part of Peterson's. In essence, this section is an open forum for colleges and universities, on a voluntary basis, to communicate their particular message to prospective college students. The colleges included have paid a fee to Peterson's to provide this information. The descriptions are edited to provide a consistent format across entries for your ease of comparison and are presented alphabetically by the official name of the institution.

PROFILES AND CLOSE-UPS OF OTHER COLLEGES TO CONSIDER

Do you know that schools sometimes target specific areas of the country for student recruitment? In this section, you'll find **Profiles** and **Close-Ups** of schools outside the region of this guide looking to recruit students like you. The format of both the **Profiles** and the **Close-Ups** in this section matches the format in the previous sections.

INDEXES

Majors and Degrees

This index lists hundreds of undergraduate major fields of study that are currently offered most widely. The majors appear in alphabetical order, each followed by an alphabetical list of the colleges that report offering a program in that field and the degree levels (*A* for associate, *B* for bachelor's) available. The majors represented here are based on the National Center for Education Statistics (NCES) 2000 Classification of Instructional Programs (CIP). The CIP is a taxonomic coding scheme that contains titles and descriptions of instructional programs, primarily at the postsecondary level. CIP was originally developed to facilitate NCES's collection and reporting of postsecondary degree completions, by major field of study, using standard classifications that capture the majority of program activity. The CIP is the accepted federal government reporting standard for classifying instructional programs. However, although the term "major" is used in this guide, some colleges may use other terms, such as "concentration," "program of study," or "field."

Athletic Programs and Scholarships

This index lists the colleges that report offering intercollegiate athletic programs, listed alphabetically. An *M* or *W* following the college name indicates that the sport is offered for men or women, respectively. An *s* in parentheses following an *M* or *W* indicates that athletic scholarships (or grants-in-aid) are offered by the college for men or women, respectively, in that sport.

ROTC Programs

This index lists the colleges that report offering Reserve Officers' Training Corps programs in one or more branches of the armed services, as indicated by letter codes following the college name: *A* for Army, *N* for Navy, and *AF* for Air Force. A *c* in parentheses following the branch letter code indicates that the program is offered through a cooperative arrangement on another college's campus.

Alphabetical Listing of Colleges and Universities

This index gives the page locations of various entries for all the colleges and universities in this book. The page numbers for the **Profiles** are printed in regular type, those for **Profiles** with **Special Messages** in *italic* type, and those for **Close-Ups** in **boldface** type.

DATA COLLECTION PROCEDURES

The data contained in the **Profiles** and **Indexes** were researched between winter 2008 and spring 2009 through *Peterson's Annual Survey of Undergraduate Institutions* and *Peterson's Annual Survey of Undergraduate Financial Aid*. Questionnaires were sent to the more than 2,200 colleges and universities that met the outlined inclusion criteria. All data included in this edition have been submitted by officials (usually admissions and financial aid officers, registrars, or institutional research personnel) at the colleges. In addition, many of the institutions that submitted data were contacted directly by the Peterson's research staff to verify unusual figures, resolve discrepancies, or obtain additional data. All usable information received in time for publication has been included. The omission of any particular item from an index or profile listing signifies that the information is either not applicable to that institution or not available. Because of Peterson's comprehensive editorial review and because all material comes directly from college officials, we believe that the information presented in this guide is accurate. You should check with a specific college or university at the time of application to verify such figures as tuition and fees, which may have changed since the publication of this volume.

CRITERIA FOR INCLUSION IN THIS BOOK

The term "four-year college" is the commonly used designation for institutions that grant the baccalaureate degree. Four years is the expected amount of time required to earn this degree, although some bachelor's degree programs may be completed in three years, others require five years, and part-time programs may take considerably longer. Upper-level institutions offer only the junior and senior years and accept only students with two years of college-level credit. Therefore, "four-year college" is a conventional term that accurately describes most of the institutions included in this guide, but should not be taken literally in all cases. In addition, some two-year colleges granting associate degrees have been included in this publication. Private nonprofit and religious two-year colleges were selected for inclusion.

To be included in this guide, an institution must have full accreditation or be a candidate for accreditation (preaccreditation) status by an institutional or specialized accrediting body recognized by the U.S. Department of Education or the Council for Higher Education Accreditation (CHEA). Institutional accrediting bodies, which review each institution as a whole, include the six regional associations of schools and colleges (Middle States, New England, North Central, Northwest, Southern, and Western), each of which is responsible for a specified portion of the United States and its territories. Other institutional accrediting bodies are national in scope and accredit specific kinds of institutions (e.g., Bible colleges, independent colleges, and rabbinical and Talmudic schools). Program registration by the New York State Board of Regents is considered to be the equivalent of institutional accreditation, since the board requires that all programs offered by an institution meet its standards before recognition is granted. There are recognized specialized or professional accrediting bodies in more than forty different fields, each of which is authorized to accredit institutions or specific programs in its particular field. For specialized institutions that offer programs in one field only, we designate this to be the equivalent of institutional accreditation. A full explanation of the accrediting process and complete information on recognized, institutional (regional and national) and specialized accrediting bodies can be found online at www.chea.org or at www.ed.gov/admins/finaid/accred/index.html.

Profiles of Colleges in the Midwest

Map of the Midwest

This map provides a general perspective on the Midwest and shows the major metropolitan areas and capital of each state.

Illinois

AMERICAN ACADEMY OF ART

Chicago, Illinois

http://www.aaart.edu/

AMERICAN INTERCONTINENTAL UNIVERSITY ONLINE

Hoffman Estates, Illinois

American InterContinental University Online is a coed, proprietary, comprehensive institution, founded in 1970, offering degrees at the associate, bachelor's, and master's levels (offers online degree programs only). It has a 1-acre campus in Hoffman Estates.

Academic Information The faculty has 396 members. Special programs include academic remediation, advanced placement credit, accelerated degree programs, distance learning, part-time degree programs, and adult/continuing education programs. The most frequently chosen baccalaureate fields are business/marketing, computer and information sciences, security and protective services.
Student Body Statistics The student body totals 22,424, of whom 20,341 are undergraduates (10,304 freshmen). 67 percent are women and 33 percent are men.
Expenses for 2009–10 *Application fee:* $50. Contact campus for information. See: www.aiuniv.edu.
Freshman Admission American InterContinental University Online requires an essay, a high school transcript, and an interview. The application deadline for regular admission is rolling and for nonresidents it is rolling.
Transfer Admission The application deadline for admission is rolling.
Entrance Difficulty American InterContinental University Online assesses its entrance difficulty level as minimally difficult.
For Further Information Contact Jennifer Ziegenmier, Senior Vice President of Admissions and Marketing, American InterContinental University Online, 5550 Prairie Stone Parkway, Suite 400, Hoffman Estates, IL 60192. *Phone:* 877-564-6248 or 877-701-3800 (toll-free). *E-mail:* info@aiu-online.com. *Web site:* http://www.aiuniv.edu/.

ARGOSY UNIVERSITY, CHICAGO

Chicago, Illinois

Argosy University, Chicago is a coed, proprietary university, founded in 1976, offering degrees at the bachelor's, master's, and doctoral levels.

Expenses for 2009–10 Tuition varies by program. Students should contact Argosy University for tuition information.
For Further Information Contact Director of Admissions, Argosy University, Chicago, 225 North Michigan Avenue, Suite 1300, Chicago, IL 60601. *Phone:* 312-777-7600 or 800-626-4123 (toll-free). *Fax:* 312-777-7748. *Web site:* http://www.argosy.edu/chicago/.

ARGOSY UNIVERSITY, SCHAUMBURG

Schaumburg, Illinois

Argosy University, Schaumburg is a coed, proprietary university, founded in 1979, offering degrees at the bachelor's, master's, and doctoral levels and post-master's certificates.

Expenses for 2009–10 Tuition varies by program. Students should contact Argosy University for tuition information.
For Further Information Contact Director of Admissions, Argosy University, Schaumburg, 999 North Plaza Drive, Suite 111, Schaumburg, IL 60173-5403. *Phone:* 847-969-4900 or 866-290-2777 (toll-free). *Fax:* 847-969-4999. *Web site:* http://www.argosy.edu/schaumburg/.

AUGUSTANA COLLEGE

Rock Island, Illinois

Augustana College is a coed, private, four-year college, founded in 1860, affiliated with the Evangelical Lutheran Church in America, offering degrees at the bachelor's level. It has a 115-acre campus in Rock Island.

Academic Information The faculty has 265 members (68% full-time), 65% with terminal degrees. The student-faculty ratio is 12:1. The library holds 213,982 titles, 3,251 serial subscriptions, and 2,825 audiovisual materials. Special programs include services for learning-disabled students, an honors program, study abroad, advanced placement credit, double majors, independent study, self-designed majors, summer session for credit, part-time degree programs (daytime, evenings), and internships. The most frequently chosen baccalaureate fields are biological/life sciences, business/marketing, health professions and related sciences.
Student Body Statistics The student body is made up of 2,546 undergraduates (641 freshmen). 57 percent are women and 43 percent are men. Students come from 30 states and territories and 20 other countries. 87 percent are from Illinois. 1 percent are international students.
Expenses for 2008–09 *Application fee:* $35. *Comprehensive fee:* $37,800 includes full-time tuition ($30,150) and college room and board ($7650). *College room only:* $3870. Full-time tuition varies according to course load. Room and board charges vary according to board plan and housing facility. *Part-time tuition:* $1100 per credit hour.
Financial Aid Forms of aid include need-based and non-need-based scholarships and part-time jobs. The average aided 2007–08 undergraduate received an aid package worth $22,510. The priority application deadline for financial aid is April 1.
Freshman Admission Augustana College requires a high school transcript and TOEFL scores for international students. An essay and interview are required for some. The application deadline for regular admission is rolling.
Transfer Admission The application deadline for admission is rolling.
Entrance Difficulty Augustana College assesses its entrance difficulty level as moderately difficult. For the fall 2008 freshman class, 69 percent of the applicants were accepted.
For Further Information Contact Megan Cooley, Director of Admissions, Augustana College, 639 38th Street, Rock Island, IL 61201-2296. *Phone:* 309-794-7341 or 800-798-8100 (toll-free). *Fax:* 309-794-7422. *E-mail:* admissions@augustana.edu. *Web site:* http://www.augustana.edu/.

AURORA UNIVERSITY

Aurora, Illinois

Aurora University is a coed, private, comprehensive institution, founded in 1893, offering degrees at the bachelor's, master's, and doctoral levels and post-master's and postbachelor's certificates. It has a 30-acre campus in Aurora near Chicago.

Academic Information The faculty has 393 members (28% full-time), 36% with terminal degrees. The undergraduate student-faculty ratio is 14:1. The library holds 99,000 titles, 210 serial subscriptions, and 7,621 audiovisual materials. Special programs include academic remediation, services for learning-disabled students, an honors program, study abroad, advanced placement credit, accelerated degree programs, double majors, independent study, self-designed majors, summer session for credit, part-time degree programs (daytime, evenings, weekends, summer), adult/continuing education programs, internships, and arrangement for off-campus study with 3 members of the Council of West

Aurora University (continued)

Suburban Colleges. The most frequently chosen baccalaureate fields are business/marketing, education, health professions and related sciences.
Student Body Statistics The student body totals 4,291, of whom 2,202 are undergraduates (378 freshmen). 68 percent are women and 32 percent are men. Students come from 23 states and territories and 1 other country. 93 percent are from Illinois.
Expenses for 2009–10 *Application fee:* $25. *Comprehensive fee:* $25,950 includes full-time tuition ($18,000), mandatory fees ($100), and college room and board ($7850). *Part-time tuition:* $540 per semester hour.
Financial Aid Forms of aid include need-based and non-need-based scholarships and part-time jobs. The average aided 2008–09 undergraduate received an aid package worth an estimated $15,522. The priority application deadline for financial aid is April 15.
Freshman Admission Aurora University requires a high school transcript, a minimum 2.0 high school GPA, SAT or ACT scores, and TOEFL scores for international students. An essay and an interview are recommended. 2 recommendations and an interview are required for some. The application deadline for regular admission is May 1.
Transfer Admission The application deadline for admission is rolling.
Entrance Difficulty Aurora University assesses its entrance difficulty level as moderately difficult. For the fall 2008 freshman class, 79 percent of the applicants were accepted.

SPECIAL MESSAGE TO STUDENTS

Social Life Aurora University is a great place to get involved. Students may choose to participate in social clubs, theater, student government, service activities, Campus Ministries, the University Chorale, and intramural sports. Students may also take advantage of the various social activities that are offered in and near Aurora—the second-largest city in Illinois—and Chicago, 40 miles to the east. Aurora University combines a residential and commuter population.

Academic Highlights The curriculum ranges from traditional academic programs in arts, sciences, and business to the "helping" disciplines of athletic training, criminal justice, education, nursing, social work, and special education. There are three colleges: the College of Arts and Sciences, the College of Professional Studies, and the College of Education.

Interviews and Campus Visits Aurora University encourages campus visits. Fall, winter, and spring open houses are held. Individual visits are always welcome. Students can meet with an admission representative, faculty members, a financial aid counselor, and coaches as well as take a tour of campus and visit with current students. Campus tours include academic buildings such as Dunham and Stephens Halls, the Parolini Fine Arts Center, the Institute for Collaboration (AU's newest classroom building), and four residence halls. Housed in Dunham Hall is the Schingoethe Museum of Native American Culture, which is open to the public. The University is accessible by train and local bus lines. For more information about appointments and campus visits, students should call the Office of Admission and Financial Aid at 630-844-5533 or 800-742-5281 (toll-free).

For Further Information Write to the Office of Admission and Financial Aid, Aurora University, Aurora, IL 60506. *Web site:* http://www.aurora.edu.

See page 226 for the Close-Up.

BARAT COLLEGE

See DePaul University.

BENEDICTINE UNIVERSITY

Lisle, Illinois

Benedictine University is a coed, private, Roman Catholic, comprehensive institution, founded in 1887, offering degrees at the associate, bachelor's, master's, and doctoral levels and postbachelor's certificates. It has a 108-acre campus in Lisle near Chicago.

Academic Information The faculty has 661 members (15% full-time), 32% with terminal degrees. The undergraduate student-faculty ratio is 13:1. The library holds 138,000 titles, 23,906 serial subscriptions, and 3,007 audiovisual materials. Special programs include academic remediation, services for learning-disabled students, an honors program, study abroad, advanced placement credit, accelerated degree programs, ESL programs, double majors, independent study, distance learning, summer session for credit, part-time degree programs (evenings, weekends, summer), adult/continuing education programs, internships, and arrangement for off-campus study with 3 members of the Council of West Suburban Colleges. The most frequently chosen baccalaureate fields are business/marketing, health professions and related sciences, psychology.
Student Body Statistics The student body totals 5,279, of whom 3,282 are undergraduates (435 freshmen). 57 percent are women and 43 percent are men. Students come from 25 states and territories and 13 other countries. 100 percent are from Illinois. 1.2 percent are international students.
Expenses for 2008–09 *Application fee:* $40. *Comprehensive fee:* $29,610 includes full-time tuition ($21,600), mandatory fees ($710), and college room and board ($7300). Full-time tuition and fees vary according to class time, degree level, and location. Room and board charges vary according to board plan and housing facility. *Part-time tuition:* $720 per credit hour. *Part-time mandatory fees:* $15 per credit hour. Part-time tuition and fees vary according to class time and degree level.
Financial Aid Forms of aid include need-based and non-need-based scholarships and part-time jobs. The average aided 2007–08 undergraduate received an aid package worth $14,391. The application deadline for financial aid is continuous.
Freshman Admission Benedictine University requires an essay, a high school transcript, SAT or ACT scores, and TOEFL scores for international students. Rank in upper 50% of high school class is recommended. An interview is required for some. The application deadline for regular admission is rolling.
Transfer Admission The application deadline for admission is rolling.
Entrance Difficulty Benedictine University assesses its entrance difficulty level as moderately difficult. For the fall 2008 freshman class, 80 percent of the applicants were accepted.
For Further Information Contact Ms. Kari Gibbons, Dean of Enrollment, Benedictine University, 5700 College Road, Lisle, IL 60532-0900. *Phone:* 630-829-6300 or 888-829-6363 (toll-free out-of-state). *Fax:* 630-829-6301. *E-mail:* admissions@ben.edu. *Web site:* http://www.ben.edu/.

See page 230 for the Close-Up.

BLACKBURN COLLEGE

Carlinville, Illinois

Blackburn College is a coed, private, Presbyterian, four-year college, founded in 1837, offering degrees at the bachelor's level. It has an 80-acre campus in Carlinville near St. Louis.

Expenses for 2008–09 *Application fee:* $0. *Comprehensive fee:* $15,493 includes full-time tuition ($11,020), mandatory fees ($110), and college room and board ($4363). *College room only:* $2205. *Part-time tuition:* $450 per semester hour.
For Further Information Contact Ron Bryan, Director of Admission, Blackburn College, 700 College Avenue, Carlinville, IL 62626-1498. *Phone:* 217-854-3231 Ext. 4293 or 800-233-3550 (toll-free). *Fax:* 217-854-3713. *E-mail:* admit@mail.blackburn.edu. *Web site:* http://www.blackburn.edu/.

BLESSING-RIEMAN COLLEGE OF NURSING

Quincy, Illinois

Blessing-Rieman College of Nursing is a coed, primarily women's, private, comprehensive institution, founded in 1985, offering degrees at the bachelor's and master's levels. It has a 1-acre campus in Quincy.

Academic Information The faculty has 18 members (100% full-time), 28% with terminal degrees. The undergraduate student-faculty ratio is 12:1. The library holds 3,767 titles and 125 serial subscriptions. Special programs include academic remediation, an honors program, advanced placement credit, double majors, distance learning, summer session for credit, part-time degree programs (daytime, evenings), adult/continuing education programs, and internships. The most frequently chosen baccalaureate field is health professions and related sciences.
Student Body Statistics The student body totals 219, of whom 211 are undergraduates (20 freshmen). 92 percent are women and 8 percent are men. Students come from 8 states and territories. 53 percent are from Illinois.
Expenses for 2008–09 *Application fee:* $0. *Comprehensive fee:* $28,790 includes full-time tuition ($20,800), mandatory fees ($470), and college room and board ($7520). *College room only:* $3720. Full-time tuition and fees vary according to course load, location, and student level. Room and board charges vary according to board plan, location, and student level. *Part-time tuition:* $490 per credit hour. Part-time tuition varies according to course load, location, and student level.
Financial Aid Forms of aid include need-based scholarships. The application deadline for financial aid is continuous.
Freshman Admission Blessing-Rieman College of Nursing requires a high school transcript, a minimum 3.0 high school GPA, SAT or ACT scores, and TOEFL scores for international students. An essay and an interview are recommended. The application deadline for regular admission is rolling.
Transfer Admission The application deadline for admission is rolling.
Entrance Difficulty Blessing-Rieman College of Nursing assesses its entrance difficulty level as moderately difficult. For the fall 2008 freshman class, 77 percent of the applicants were accepted.
For Further Information Contact Ms. Heather Mutter or Ms. Kate Boster, Admissions Counselors, Blessing-Rieman College of Nursing, Broadway at 11th Street, POB 7005, Quincy, IL 62305-7005. *Phone:* 217-228-5520 Ext. 6979 or 800-877-9140 Ext. 6964 (toll-free). *Fax:* 217-223-4661. *E-mail:* admissions@brcn.edu. *Web site:* http://www.brcn.edu/.

BRADLEY UNIVERSITY

Peoria, Illinois

Bradley University is a coed, private, comprehensive institution, founded in 1897, offering degrees at the bachelor's, master's, and doctoral levels. It has an 85-acre campus in Peoria near Chicago and St. Louis.

Academic Information The faculty has 559 members (60% full-time), 50% with terminal degrees. The undergraduate student-faculty ratio is 13:1. The library holds 510,297 titles, 29,776 serial subscriptions, and 11,719 audiovisual materials. Special programs include academic remediation, an honors program, cooperative (work-study) education, study abroad, advanced placement credit, accelerated degree programs, double majors, independent study, distance learning, self-designed majors, summer session for credit, part-time degree programs (daytime, evenings, summer), adult/continuing education programs, internships, and arrangement for off-campus study with Georgetown University. The most frequently chosen baccalaureate fields are business/marketing, communications/journalism, engineering.
Student Body Statistics The student body totals 5,872, of whom 5,074 are undergraduates (1,032 freshmen). 54 percent are women and 46 percent are men. Students come from 39 states and territories and 30 other countries. 89 percent are from Illinois. 0.6 percent are international students.
Expenses for 2008–09 *Application fee:* $35. *Comprehensive fee:* $30,164 includes full-time tuition ($22,600), mandatory fees ($214), and college room and board ($7350). Full-time tuition and fees vary according to student level. Room and board charges vary according to board plan. *Part-time tuition:* varies with course load.
Financial Aid Forms of aid include need-based and non-need-based scholarships, athletic grants, and part-time jobs. The average aided 2008–09 undergraduate received an aid package worth an estimated $13,798. The priority application deadline for financial aid is March 1.
Freshman Admission Bradley University requires an essay, a high school transcript, 1 recommendation, SAT or ACT scores, and TOEFL scores for international students. A minimum 3.0 high school GPA, 3 recommendations, and an interview are recommended. The application deadline for regular admission is rolling.
Entrance Difficulty Bradley University assesses its entrance difficulty level as moderately difficult. For the fall 2008 freshman class, 64 percent of the applicants were accepted.
For Further Information Contact Mr. Rodney San Jose, Director of Admissions, Bradley University, 1501 West Bradley Avenue, 100 Swords Hall, Peoria, IL 61625-0002. *Phone:* 309-677-1000 or 800-447-6460 (toll-free). *Fax:* 309-677-2797. *E-mail:* admissions@bradley.edu. *Web site:* http://www.bradley.edu/.

See page 232 for the Close-Up.

CHICAGO STATE UNIVERSITY

Chicago, Illinois

Chicago State University is a coed, public, comprehensive institution, founded in 1867, offering degrees at the bachelor's, master's, and doctoral levels and postbachelor's certificates. It has a 161-acre campus in Chicago.

Expenses for 2008–09 *Application fee:* $25. *State resident tuition:* $6870 full-time, $229 per credit hour part-time. *Nonresident tuition:* $13,650 full-time, $455 per credit hour part-time. *Mandatory fees:* $2008 full-time, $375 per term part-time. *College room and board:* $7250.
For Further Information Contact Ms. Addie Epps, Director of Admissions, Chicago State University, 95th Street at King Drive, ADM 200, Chicago, IL 60628. *Phone:* 773-995-2513. *Fax:* 773-995-3820. *E-mail:* ug-admissions@csu.edu. *Web site:* http://www.csu.edu/.

CHRISTIAN LIFE COLLEGE

Mount Prospect, Illinois

Christian Life College is a coed, private, four-year college, founded in 1950, offering degrees at the associate and bachelor's levels.

Academic Information The faculty has 15 members (40% full-time), 27% with terminal degrees. The student-faculty ratio is 10:1.
Student Body Statistics The student body is made up of 40 undergraduates.
Expenses for 2008–09 *Application fee:* $35. *Tuition:* $9120 full-time, $365 per credit hour part-time. *Mandatory fees:* $850 full-time, $375 per term part-time. *College room only:* $3700.
Financial Aid Forms of aid include need-based and non-need-based scholarships and part-time jobs. The priority application deadline for financial aid is July 1.
Freshman Admission Christian Life College requires a high school transcript, recommendations, and TOEFL scores for international students.
For Further Information Contact Director of Admissions, Christian Life College, 400 East Gregory Street, Mount Prospect, IL 60056. *Phone:* 847-259-1840. *E-mail:* mail@christianlifecollege.edu. *Web site:* http://www.christianlifecollege.edu/.

COLLEGE OF ST. FRANCIS

See University of St. Francis.

COLUMBIA COLLEGE CHICAGO

Chicago, Illinois

Columbia College Chicago is a coed, private, comprehensive institution, founded in 1890, offering degrees at the bachelor's and master's levels and postbachelor's certificates.

SPECIAL MESSAGE TO STUDENTS

Social Life When Columbia students are not showing at campus galleries, publishing in award-winning magazines, performing on stage, or freestyling at poetry slams, they are taking an active role in the College's more than eighty-five social and academic clubs and organizations, and interacting with the larger Chicago community. The presence of Columbia's students can be felt in theaters, bookstores, nightclubs, and radio stations throughout the city, and every spring, Columbia returns the favor by inviting Chicago to their doorstep for Manifest, the city's largest student arts exhibition.

Academic Highlights Columbia College takes a pragmatic, hands-on approach to teaching in all major disciplines. Students are encouraged to "learn by doing," and all programs of study are grounded in a rigorous liberal arts core curriculum that not only inspires students' creative work and places it in a cultural context, but also requires them to think about their endeavors professionally. Intimate class settings facilitate personal attention and practical mentoring with a faculty of working professionals. Columbia's faculty and student body comprise a widely diverse mix of cultures and backgrounds, creating a stimulating environment ideally suited to the pursuit of creative innovation.

Interviews and Campus Visits Columbia College Chicago strongly encourages all prospective students to visit campus so they can get a sense of whether or not Columbia is the right college for them. Campus tours are offered Monday through Friday at 10:30 and 1:30 and Saturday at 11. To contact the school, prospective students should call 312-344-7130.

For Further Information Write to Undergraduate Admissions, Columbia College Chicago, 600 South Michigan Avenue, Chicago, IL 60647. *E-mail:* admissions@colum.edu. *Web site:* http:www.colum.edu.

See page 234 for the Close-Up.

CONCORDIA UNIVERSITY CHICAGO

River Forest, Illinois

Concordia University Chicago is a coed, private, comprehensive unit of Concordia University System, founded in 1864, affiliated with the Lutheran Church–Missouri Synod, offering degrees at the bachelor's, master's, and doctoral levels and post-master's and postbachelor's certificates. It has a 40-acre campus in River Forest near Chicago.

Academic Information The faculty has 287 members (38% full-time). The undergraduate student-faculty ratio is 17:1. The library holds 158,666 titles, 150 serial subscriptions, and 3,330 audiovisual materials. Special programs include academic remediation, services for learning-disabled students, an honors program, study abroad, advanced placement credit, accelerated degree programs, double majors, independent study, distance learning, summer session for credit, part-time degree programs (daytime, evenings, summer), adult/continuing education programs, internships, and arrangement for off-campus study with Chicago Consortium of Colleges and Universities, Dominican University. The most frequently chosen baccalaureate fields are business/marketing, education, psychology.
Student Body Statistics The student body totals 4,185, of whom 1,153 are undergraduates (249 freshmen). 60 percent are women and 40 percent are men. Students come from 24 states and territories and 1 other country. 63 percent are from Illinois. 0.4 percent are international students.
Expenses for 2009–10 *Comprehensive fee:* $31,158 includes full-time tuition ($22,998), mandatory fees ($460), and college room and board ($7700). *Part-time tuition:* $719 per semester hour.
Financial Aid Forms of aid include need-based and non-need-based scholarships and part-time jobs. The average aided 2008–09 undergraduate received an aid package worth an estimated $21,018. The application deadline for financial aid is August 15 with a priority deadline of April 1.
Freshman Admission Concordia University Chicago requires a high school transcript, a minimum 2.0 high school GPA, 1 recommendation, SAT or ACT scores, and TOEFL scores for international students. An essay and an interview are required for some. The application deadline for regular admission is rolling.
Transfer Admission The application deadline for admission is rolling.
Entrance Difficulty Concordia University Chicago assesses its entrance difficulty level as moderately difficult. For the fall 2008 freshman class, 83 percent of the applicants were accepted.
For Further Information Contact Dr. Evelyn Burdick, Vice President for Enrollment Services, Concordia University Chicago, 7400 Augusta Street, River Forest, IL 60305. *Phone:* 708-209-3100 or 800-285-2668 (toll-free). *Fax:* 708-209-3473. *E-mail:* crfadmis@cuchicago.edu. *Web site:* http://www.cuchicago.edu/.

DePAUL UNIVERSITY

Chicago, Illinois

DePaul University is a coed, private, Roman Catholic university, founded in 1898, offering degrees at the bachelor's, master's, doctoral, and first professional levels and post-master's, first professional, and postbachelor's certificates. It has a 36-acre campus in Chicago.

Academic Information The faculty has 1,842 members (49% full-time), 50% with terminal degrees. The undergraduate student-faculty ratio is 16:1. The library holds 897,564 titles, 28,514 serial subscriptions, and 27,242 audiovisual materials. Special programs include academic remediation, services for learning-disabled students, an honors program, cooperative (work-study) education, study abroad, advanced placement credit, accelerated degree programs, Freshman Honors College, ESL programs, double majors, independent study, distance learning, self-designed majors, summer session for credit, part-time degree programs, adult/continuing education programs, and internships. The most frequently chosen baccalaureate fields are business/marketing, communications/journalism, social sciences.
Student Body Statistics The student body totals 24,352, of whom 15,782 are undergraduates (2,555 freshmen). 55 percent are women and 45 percent are men. Students come from 50 states and territories and 66 other countries. 82 percent are from Illinois. 1.6 percent are international students.
Expenses for 2008–09 *Application fee:* $40. *Comprehensive fee:* $36,307 includes full-time tuition ($25,490), mandatory fees ($577), and college room and board ($10,240). *College room only:* $7600. *Part-time tuition:* $460 per quarter hour.
Financial Aid Forms of aid include need-based and non-need-based scholarships, athletic grants, and part-time jobs. The average aided 2008–09 undergraduate received an aid package worth an estimated $17,279. The priority application deadline for financial aid is March 1.
Freshman Admission DePaul University requires a minimum 2.0 high school GPA, SAT or ACT scores, and TOEFL scores for international students. A high school transcript and a minimum 2.5 high school GPA are recommended. A minimum 3.0 high school GPA and audition are required for some. The application deadline for regular admission is February 1 and for early action it is November 15.
Transfer Admission The application deadline for admission is rolling.
Entrance Difficulty DePaul University assesses its entrance difficulty level as moderately difficult. For the fall 2008 freshman class, 64 percent of the applicants were accepted.
For Further Information Contact Carlene Klaas, Undergraduate Admissions, DePaul University, 1 East Jackson Boulevard, Suite 9100, Chicago, IL 60604. *Phone:* 312-362-8300. *E-mail:* admitdpu@depaul.edu. *Web site:* http://www.depaul.edu/.

DeVry University
Addison, Illinois

DeVry University is a coed, proprietary, four-year college of DeVry University, founded in 1982, offering degrees at the associate and bachelor's levels. It has a 14-acre campus in Addison near Chicago.

Academic Information The faculty has 121 members (36% full-time). The student-faculty ratio is 16:1. The library holds 18,500 titles and 4,000 serial subscriptions. Special programs include academic remediation, advanced placement credit, accelerated degree programs, distance learning, summer session for credit, part-time degree programs (daytime, evenings, weekends, summer), and adult/continuing education programs. The most frequently chosen baccalaureate fields are business/marketing, computer and information sciences, engineering technologies.
Student Body Statistics The student body is made up of 1,403 undergraduates (225 freshmen). 27 percent are women and 73 percent are men. 98 percent are from Illinois. 2.8 percent are international students.
Expenses for 2009–10 *Application fee:* $50. *Tuition:* $14,080 full-time, $550 per credit hour part-time.
Financial Aid Forms of aid include need-based scholarships and part-time jobs. The average aided 2007–08 undergraduate received an aid package worth $13,134. The application deadline for financial aid is continuous.
Freshman Admission DeVry University requires a high school transcript, an interview, and TOEFL scores for international students. The application deadline for regular admission is rolling.
Transfer Admission The application deadline for admission is rolling.
Entrance Difficulty DeVry University assesses its entrance difficulty level as minimally difficult; moderately difficult for electronics engineering technology program.
For Further Information Contact Admissions Office, DeVry University, 1221 North Swift Road, Addison, IL 60101. *Phone:* 630-953-1300 or 800-346-5420 (toll-free). *Web site:* http://www.devry.edu/.

DeVry University
Chicago, Illinois

DeVry University is a coed, proprietary, four-year college of DeVry University, founded in 1931, offering degrees at the associate and bachelor's levels. It has a 17-acre campus in Chicago.

Academic Information The faculty has 159 members (25% full-time). The student-faculty ratio is 17:1. The library holds 16,573 titles and 79 serial subscriptions. Special programs include academic remediation, services for learning-disabled students, advanced placement credit, accelerated degree programs, distance learning, summer session for credit, part-time degree programs (daytime, evenings, weekends, summer), and adult/continuing education programs. The most frequently chosen baccalaureate fields are business/marketing, computer and information sciences, engineering technologies.
Student Body Statistics The student body is made up of 1,890 undergraduates (379 freshmen). 43 percent are women and 57 percent are men. 99 percent are from Illinois. 3.8 percent are international students.
Expenses for 2009–10 *Application fee:* $50. *Tuition:* $14,080 full-time, $550 per credit hour part-time.
Financial Aid Forms of aid include need-based scholarships and part-time jobs. The average aided 2007–08 undergraduate received an aid package worth $16,145. The application deadline for financial aid is continuous.
Freshman Admission DeVry University requires a high school transcript, an interview, and TOEFL scores for international students. The application deadline for regular admission is rolling.
Transfer Admission The application deadline for admission is rolling.
Entrance Difficulty DeVry University assesses its entrance difficulty level as minimally difficult; moderately difficult for electronics engineering technology program.
For Further Information Contact Admissions Office, DeVry University, 3300 North Campbell Avenue, Chicago, IL 60618-5994. *Phone:* 773-929-8500. *Web site:* http://www.devry.edu/.

DeVry University
Elgin, Illinois

http://www.devry.edu/

DeVry University
Gurnee, Illinois

http://www.devry.edu/

DeVry University
Naperville, Illinois

http://www.devry.edu/

DeVry University
Oakbrook Terrace, Illinois

http://www.devry.edu/

DeVry University
Tinley Park, Illinois

DeVry University is a coed, proprietary, comprehensive unit of DeVry University, founded in 2000, offering degrees at the associate, bachelor's, and master's levels. It has a 12-acre campus in Tinley Park.

Academic Information The faculty has 75 members (47% full-time). The undergraduate student-faculty ratio is 19:1. The library holds 17,500 titles and 82 serial subscriptions. Special programs include academic remediation, services for learning-disabled students, advanced placement credit, accelerated degree programs, distance learning, summer session for credit, part-time degree programs (daytime, evenings, weekends, summer), and adult/continuing education programs. The most frequently chosen baccalaureate fields are business/marketing, computer and information sciences, engineering technologies.
Student Body Statistics The student body totals 1,401, of whom 1,092 are undergraduates (203 freshmen). 32 percent are women and 68 percent are men. 88 percent are from Illinois. 0.2 percent are international students.
Expenses for 2009–10 *Application fee:* $50. *Tuition:* $14,080 full-time, $550 per credit hour part-time.
Financial Aid Forms of aid include need-based scholarships and part-time jobs. The average aided 2007–08 undergraduate received an aid package worth $12,346. The application deadline for financial aid is continuous.
Freshman Admission DeVry University requires a high school transcript, an interview, and TOEFL scores for international students. The application deadline for regular admission is rolling.
Transfer Admission The application deadline for admission is rolling.
Entrance Difficulty DeVry University assesses its entrance difficulty level as minimally difficult; moderately difficult for electronics engineering technology program.
For Further Information Contact Admissions Office, DeVry University, 18624 West Creek Drive, Tinley Park, IL 60477-6243. *Phone:* 708-342-3300. *Web site:* http://www.devry.edu/.

DeVry University Online
Oakbrook Terrace, Illinois

DeVry University Online is a coed, proprietary, comprehensive institution, founded in 2000, offering degrees at the associate, bachelor's, and master's levels.

DeVry University (continued)

Expenses for 2008–09 *Application fee:* $50. *Tuition:* $14,480 full-time, $540 per credit hour part-time. *Mandatory fees:* $80 full-time.

For Further Information Contact Admissions Office, DeVry University Online, One Tower Lane, Suite 1000, Oakbrook Terrace, IL 60181. *Phone:* 866-338-7934 (toll-free). *Web site:* http://www.online.devry.edu/.

DOMINICAN UNIVERSITY

River Forest, Illinois

Dominican University is a coed, private, Roman Catholic, comprehensive institution, founded in 1901, offering degrees at the bachelor's and master's levels and post-master's and postbachelor's certificates. It has a 30-acre campus in River Forest near Chicago.

Academic Information The faculty has 407 members (32% full-time), 46% with terminal degrees. The undergraduate student-faculty ratio is 11:1. The library holds 348,474 titles and 30,249 serial subscriptions. Special programs include services for learning-disabled students, an honors program, study abroad, advanced placement credit, accelerated degree programs, ESL programs, double majors, independent study, distance learning, self-designed majors, summer session for credit, part-time degree programs (daytime, evenings, weekends, summer), adult/continuing education programs, internships, and arrangement for off-campus study with Concordia University (IL), Illinois Institute of Technology. The most frequently chosen baccalaureate fields are business/marketing, psychology, social sciences.

Student Body Statistics The student body totals 3,413, of whom 1,709 are undergraduates (417 freshmen). 69 percent are women and 31 percent are men. Students come from 28 states and territories and 21 other countries. 92 percent are from Illinois. 2.3 percent are international students.

Expenses for 2008–09 *Application fee:* $25. *One-time mandatory fee:* $150. *Comprehensive fee:* $31,150 includes full-time tuition ($23,700), mandatory fees ($100), and college room and board ($7350). Full-time tuition and fees vary according to program. Room and board charges vary according to board plan and housing facility. *Part-time tuition:* $790 per semester hour. *Part-time mandatory fees:* $10 per course. Part-time tuition and fees vary according to location and program.

Financial Aid Forms of aid include need-based and non-need-based scholarships and part-time jobs. The average aided 2008–09 undergraduate received an aid package worth an estimated $17,524. The priority application deadline for financial aid is April 15.

Freshman Admission Dominican University requires an essay, a high school transcript, a minimum 2.75 high school GPA, SAT or ACT scores, and TOEFL scores for international students. An interview is recommended. 2 recommendations and an interview are required for some. The application deadline for regular admission is rolling.

Transfer Admission The application deadline for admission is rolling.

Entrance Difficulty Dominican University assesses its entrance difficulty level as moderately difficult. For the fall 2008 freshman class, 71 percent of the applicants were accepted.

For Further Information Contact Mr. Glenn Hamilton, Assistant Vice President, Enrollment Management, Dominican University, 7900 West Division Street, River Forest, IL 60305. *Phone:* 708-524-6800 or 800-828-8475 (toll-free). *Fax:* 708-524-6864. *E-mail:* domadmis@dom.edu. *Web site:* http://www.dom.edu/.

EASTERN ILLINOIS UNIVERSITY

Charleston, Illinois

Eastern Illinois University is a coed, public, comprehensive institution, founded in 1895, offering degrees at the bachelor's and master's levels and post-master's and postbachelor's certificates. It has a 320-acre campus in Charleston.

Academic Information The faculty has 807 members (81% full-time), 55% with terminal degrees. The undergraduate student-faculty ratio is 15:1. The library holds 950,188 titles, 32,860 serial subscriptions, and 32,183 audiovisual materials. Special programs include academic remediation, services for learning-disabled students, an honors program, study abroad, advanced placement credit, double majors, independent study, distance learning, summer session for credit, part-time degree programs (daytime, evenings, weekends, summer), external degree programs, adult/continuing education programs, internships, and arrangement for off-campus study with Olney Central College, Kaskaskia College, Parkland College, Danville Aea Community College, Richland Community College, Lakeland College. The most frequently chosen baccalaureate fields are business/marketing, education, English.

Student Body Statistics The student body totals 12,040, of whom 10,261 are undergraduates (1,780 freshmen). 58 percent are women and 42 percent are men. Students come from 31 states and territories and 24 other countries. 98 percent are from Illinois. 0.5 percent are international students.

Expenses for 2008–09 *Application fee:* $30. *State resident tuition:* $6540 full-time, $218 per credit hour part-time. *Nonresident tuition:* $19,620 full-time, $654 per credit hour part-time. *Mandatory fees:* $2243 full-time, $81 per credit hour part-time. Both full-time and part-time tuition and fees vary according to course load. *College room and board:* $7588. Room and board charges vary according to board plan and housing facility.

Financial Aid Forms of aid include need-based scholarships, athletic grants, and part-time jobs. The average aided 2008–09 undergraduate received an aid package worth an estimated $8727. The priority application deadline for financial aid is March 1.

Freshman Admission Eastern Illinois University requires a high school transcript, a minimum 2.25 high school GPA, audition for music program, SAT or ACT scores, and TOEFL scores for international students. An essay and 2 recommendations are recommended. 3 recommendations are required for some. The application deadline for regular admission is rolling.

Transfer Admission The application deadline for admission is rolling.

Entrance Difficulty Eastern Illinois University assesses its entrance difficulty level as moderately difficult. For the fall 2008 freshman class, 69 percent of the applicants were accepted.

For Further Information Contact Brenda Major, Director of Admissions, Eastern Illinois University, 600 Lincoln Avenue, Charleston, IL 61920-3099. *Phone:* 217-581-2223 or 800-252-5711 (toll-free). *Fax:* 217-581-7060. *E-mail:* admissions@eiu.edu. *Web site:* http://www.eiu.edu/.

EAST-WEST UNIVERSITY

Chicago, Illinois

East-West University is a coed, private, four-year college, founded in 1978, offering degrees at the associate and bachelor's levels.

Academic Information The faculty has 77 members (23% full-time). The student-faculty ratio is 15:1. The library holds 32,820 titles, 3,474 serial subscriptions, and 6 audiovisual materials. Special programs include academic remediation, an honors program, cooperative (work-study) education, advanced placement credit, Freshman Honors College, ESL programs, double majors, summer session for credit, part-time degree programs (daytime, evenings, summer), and internships.

Student Body Statistics The student body is made up of 1,170 undergraduates (358 freshmen). 63 percent are women and 37 percent are men. Students come from 7 states and territories and 14 other countries. 93 percent are from Illinois. 12 percent are international students.

Expenses for 2008–09 *Application fee:* $40. *Tuition:* $12,900 full-time, $430 per credit hour part-time. *Mandatory fees:* $675 full-time.

Financial Aid Forms of aid include need-based and non-need-based scholarships and part-time jobs. The average aided 2007–08 undergraduate received an aid package worth $9020. The priority application deadline for financial aid is June 30.

Freshman Admission East-West University requires an essay, a high school transcript, a minimum 2.0 high school GPA, an interview, and ACT scores. TOEFL scores for international students are recommended. 1 recommendation is required for some. The application deadline for regular admission is rolling and for early decision it is July 1.

Transfer Admission The application deadline for admission is rolling.

Entrance Difficulty East-West University assesses its entrance difficulty level as minimally difficult. For the fall 2008 freshman class, 89 percent of the applicants were accepted.
For Further Information Contact Mr. Ho Chung, Director of Admissions, East-West University, 819 South Wabash Avenue, Chicago, IL 60605-2103. *Phone:* 312-939-0111 Ext. 1830. *Fax:* 312-939-0083. *E-mail:* ho@eastwest.edu. *Web site:* http://www.eastwest.edu/.

ELMHURST COLLEGE

Elmhurst, Illinois

Elmhurst College is a coed, private, comprehensive institution, founded in 1871, affiliated with the United Church of Christ, offering degrees at the bachelor's and master's levels. It has a 38-acre campus in Elmhurst near Chicago.

Academic Information The faculty has 351 members (37% full-time), 45% with terminal degrees. The undergraduate student-faculty ratio is 14:1. The library holds 225,254 titles, 1,414 serial subscriptions, and 48,004 audiovisual materials. Special programs include academic remediation, services for learning-disabled students, an honors program, cooperative (work-study) education, study abroad, advanced placement credit, accelerated degree programs, double majors, independent study, summer session for credit, part-time degree programs (daytime, evenings, weekends, summer), adult/continuing education programs, internships, and arrangement for off-campus study. The most frequently chosen baccalaureate fields are business/marketing, education, health professions and related sciences.
Student Body Statistics The student body totals 3,316, of whom 3,045 are undergraduates (577 freshmen). 63 percent are women and 37 percent are men. Students come from 32 states and territories and 34 other countries. 92 percent are from Illinois. 1.1 percent are international students.
Expenses for 2009–10 *Application fee:* $0. *Comprehensive fee:* $35,204 includes full-time tuition ($27,270), mandatory fees ($60), and college room and board ($7874). *College room only:* $4720. *Part-time tuition:* $76 per semester hour.
Financial Aid Forms of aid include need-based and non-need-based scholarships and part-time jobs. The average aided 2008–09 undergraduate received an aid package worth an estimated $19,361. The priority application deadline for financial aid is April 15.
Freshman Admission Elmhurst College requires a high school transcript, SAT or ACT scores, and TOEFL scores for international students. An essay and an interview are recommended. An essay and an interview are required for some. The application deadline for regular admission is July 15.
Entrance Difficulty Elmhurst College assesses its entrance difficulty level as moderately difficult. For the fall 2008 freshman class, 69 percent of the applicants were accepted.
For Further Information Contact Mrs. Stephanie Levenson, Director of Admission, Elmhurst College, Elmhurst College Admission Office, 190 South Prospect Avenue, Elmhurst, IL 60126-3296. *Phone:* 630-617-3400 or 800-697-1871 (toll-free out-of-state). *Fax:* 630-617-5501. *E-mail:* admit@elmhurst.edu. *Web site:* http://www.elmhurst.edu/.

EUREKA COLLEGE

Eureka, Illinois

Eureka College is a coed, private, four-year college, founded in 1855, affiliated with the Christian Church (Disciples of Christ), offering degrees at the bachelor's level. It has a 112-acre campus in Eureka.

Academic Information The library holds 75,000 titles, 330 serial subscriptions, and 500 audiovisual materials. Special programs include an honors program, cooperative (work-study) education, study abroad, advanced placement credit, double majors, independent study, self-designed majors, summer session for credit, part-time degree programs (daytime, evenings, summer), and internships.
Student Body Statistics The student body is made up of 672 undergraduates.
Expenses for 2008–09 *Application fee:* $0. *Comprehensive fee:* $23,385 includes full-time tuition ($15,675), mandatory fees ($580), and college room and board ($7130). *College room only:* $3410. *Part-time tuition:* $450 per semester hour.
Financial Aid Forms of aid include need-based and non-need-based scholarships and part-time jobs. The average aided 2008–09 undergraduate received an aid package worth an estimated $12,717. The priority application deadline for financial aid is April 1.
Freshman Admission Eureka College requires a high school transcript, a minimum 2.3 high school GPA, 1 recommendation, SAT or ACT scores, and TOEFL scores for international students. An essay and an interview are recommended. An essay and 3 recommendations are required for some. The application deadline for regular admission is August 1.
Transfer Admission The application deadline for admission is August 15.
Entrance Difficulty Eureka College assesses its entrance difficulty level as moderately difficult.
For Further Information Contact Dr. Brian Sajko, Dean of Admissions and Financial Aid, Eureka College, 300 East College Avenue, Eureka, IL 61530-0128. *Phone:* 309-467-6350 or 888-4-EUREKA (toll-free). *Fax:* 309-467-6576. *E-mail:* admissions@eureka.edu. *Web site:* http://www.eureka.edu/.

GOVERNORS STATE UNIVERSITY

University Park, Illinois

http://www.govst.edu/

GREENVILLE COLLEGE

Greenville, Illinois

Greenville College is a coed, private, Free Methodist, comprehensive institution, founded in 1892, offering degrees at the bachelor's and master's levels. It has a 12-acre campus in Greenville near St. Louis.

Academic Information The faculty has 153 members (38% full-time), 26% with terminal degrees. The undergraduate student-faculty ratio is 17:1. The library holds 135,210 titles, 8,543 serial subscriptions, and 3,873 audiovisual materials. Special programs include academic remediation, an honors program, cooperative (work-study) education, study abroad, advanced placement credit, accelerated degree programs, double majors, independent study, self-designed majors, summer session for credit, part-time degree programs (daytime, evenings, summer), adult/continuing education programs, internships, and arrangement for off-campus study with 13 members of the Christian College Consortium; 100 members of the Council for Christian Colleges and Universities. The most frequently chosen baccalaureate fields are business/marketing, education, visual and performing arts.
Student Body Statistics The student body totals 1,618, of whom 1,435 are undergraduates (305 freshmen). 54 percent are women and 46 percent are men. Students come from 40 states and territories and 16 other countries. 69 percent are from Illinois. 1.5 percent are international students.
Expenses for 2009–10 *Application fee:* $25. *Comprehensive fee:* $27,012 includes full-time tuition ($20,064), mandatory fees ($152), and college room and board ($6796). *College room only:* $3260. *Part-time tuition:* $422 per credit hour.
Financial Aid Forms of aid include need-based and non-need-based scholarships and part-time jobs. The application deadline for financial aid is continuous.
Freshman Admission Greenville College requires an essay, a high school transcript, a minimum 2.5 high school GPA, 2 recommendations, agreement to code of conduct, and SAT or ACT scores. TOEFL scores for international students are recommended. An interview is required for some. The application deadline for regular admission is August 1.
Transfer Admission The application deadline for admission is August 1.

Greenville College (continued)

Entrance Difficulty Greenville College assesses its entrance difficulty level as moderately difficult. For the fall 2008 freshman class, 79 percent of the applicants were accepted.

For Further Information Contact Mr. Michael Ritter, Dean of Admissions, Greenville College, 315 East College Avenue, Greenville, IL 62246. *Phone:* 618-664-7100 or 800-345-4440 (toll-free). *Fax:* 618-664-9841. *E-mail:* admissions@greenville.edu. *Web site:* http://www.greenville.edu/.

HARRINGTON COLLEGE OF DESIGN

Chicago, Illinois

http://www.interiordesign.edu/

HEBREW THEOLOGICAL COLLEGE

Skokie, Illinois

Hebrew Theological College is private, Jewish, comprehensive institution, founded in 1922, offering degrees at the bachelor's and first professional levels. It has a 13-acre campus in Skokie near Chicago.

Academic Information The library holds 63,000 titles and 60 serial subscriptions. Special programs include academic remediation, study abroad, advanced placement credit, accelerated degree programs, double majors, independent study, summer session for credit, part-time degree programs (daytime), and internships.

Student Body Statistics The student body totals 422, of whom 415 are undergraduates.

Financial Aid Forms of aid include part-time jobs.

Freshman Admission Hebrew Theological College requires an essay, a high school transcript, 2 recommendations, an interview, SAT or ACT scores, and TOEFL scores for international students. The application deadline for regular admission is August 15.

Entrance Difficulty Hebrew Theological College assesses its entrance difficulty level as moderately difficult.

For Further Information Contact Rabbi Berish Cardash, Hebrew Theological College, 7135 North Carpenter Road, Skokie, IL 60077-3263. *Phone:* 847-982-2500. *Web site:* http://www.htc.edu/.

ILLINOIS COLLEGE

Jacksonville, Illinois

Illinois College is a coed, private, interdenominational, four-year college, founded in 1829, offering degrees at the bachelor's level. It has a 62-acre campus in Jacksonville near St. Louis.

Academic Information The faculty has 89 members (82% full-time), 72% with terminal degrees. The student-faculty ratio is 11:1. The library holds 163,810 titles and 10,234 serial subscriptions. Special programs include study abroad, advanced placement credit, accelerated degree programs, double majors, independent study, self-designed majors, summer session for credit, and internships. The most frequently chosen baccalaureate fields are biological/life sciences, interdisciplinary studies, social sciences.

Student Body Statistics The student body is made up of 898 undergraduates (166 freshmen). 52 percent are women and 48 percent are men. Students come from 22 states and territories and 15 other countries. 92 percent are from Illinois. 2.2 percent are international students.

Expenses for 2008–09 *Application fee:* $0. *Comprehensive fee:* $27,900 includes full-time tuition ($19,900), mandatory fees ($400), and college room and board ($7600). *College room only:* $3000. Full-time tuition and fees vary according to student level. Room and board charges vary according to board plan and housing facility.

Financial Aid Forms of aid include need-based and non-need-based scholarships and part-time jobs. The average aided 2008–09 undergraduate received an aid package worth an estimated $17,193. The priority application deadline for financial aid is March 1.

Freshman Admission Illinois College requires a high school transcript, 1 recommendation, SAT or ACT scores, and TOEFL scores for international students. An essay, a minimum 2.5 high school GPA, and an interview are recommended. An essay is required for some. The application deadline for regular admission is rolling.

Transfer Admission The application deadline for admission is July 31.

Entrance Difficulty Illinois College assesses its entrance difficulty level as moderately difficult. For the fall 2008 freshman class, 67 percent of the applicants were accepted.

For Further Information Contact Mr. Rick Bystry, Associate Director of Admission, Illinois College, 1101 West College, Jacksonville, IL 62650. *Phone:* 217-245-3030 or 866-464-5265 (toll-free). *Fax:* 217-245-3034. *E-mail:* admissions@ic.edu. *Web site:* http://www.ic.edu/.

THE ILLINOIS INSTITUTE OF ART–CHICAGO

Chicago, Illinois

The Illinois Institute of Art–Chicago is a coed, proprietary, four-year college of Education Management Corporation, founded in 1916, offering degrees at the associate and bachelor's levels.

Expenses for 2009–10 Tuition cost varies by program. Prospective students should contact the school for current tuition costs. Other charges include a starting kit for all first-quarter students. Kits vary in price, depending on the program of study.

For Further Information Contact Director of Admissions, The Illinois Institute of Art–Chicago, 350 N. Orleans Street, Chicago, IL 60654-1593. *Phone:* 312-280-3500 or 800-351-3450 (toll-free). *Fax:* 312-280-8562. *Web site:* http://www.artinstitutes.edu/chicago.

THE ILLINOIS INSTITUTE OF ART–SCHAUMBURG

Schaumburg, Illinois

The Illinois Institute of Art–Schaumburg is a coed, proprietary, four-year college of Education Management Corporation, offering degrees at the associate and bachelor's levels.

Expenses for 2009–10 Tuition cost varies by program. Prospective students should contact the school for current tuition costs. Other charges include a starting kit for all first-quarter students. Kits vary in price, depending on the program of study.

For Further Information Contact Director of Admissions, The Illinois Institute of Art–Schaumburg, 1000 Plaza Drive, Suite 100, Schaumburg, IL 60173. *Phone:* 847-619-3450 or 800-314-3450 (toll-free). *Fax:* 847-619-3064. *Web site:* http://www.artinstitutes.edu/schaumburg.

ILLINOIS INSTITUTE OF TECHNOLOGY

Chicago, Illinois

Illinois Institute of Technology is a coed, private university, founded in 1890, offering degrees at the bachelor's, master's, doctoral, and first professional levels. It has a 120-acre campus in Chicago.

Academic Information The faculty has 640 members (58% full-time), 77% with terminal degrees. The undergraduate student-faculty ratio is 9:1. The library holds 2 million titles, 33,535 serial subscriptions, and 1,071 audiovisual materials. Special programs include services for learning-disabled students, cooperative (work-study) education, study abroad, advanced placement credit, ESL programs, double majors, independent study, distance learning, summer session for credit, and part-time degree programs (daytime, evenings, summer). The most frequently chosen baccalaureate fields are architecture, computer and information sciences, engineering.

Student Body Statistics The student body totals 7,613, of whom 2,639 are undergraduates (530 freshmen). 28 percent are women and 72 percent

are men. Students come from 48 states and territories and 68 other countries. 68 percent are from Illinois. 16.5 percent are international students.
Expenses for 2008–09 *Application fee:* $0. *Comprehensive fee:* $36,746 includes full-time tuition ($26,709), mandatory fees ($804), and college room and board ($9233). *College room only:* $4921. Room and board charges vary according to board plan and housing facility. *Part-time tuition:* $832 per credit hour. *Part-time mandatory fees:* $7 per credit hour, $250 per term. Part-time tuition and fees vary according to course load.
Financial Aid Forms of aid include need-based and non-need-based scholarships, athletic grants, and part-time jobs. The average aided 2008–09 undergraduate received an aid package worth an estimated $21,674.
Freshman Admission Illinois Institute of Technology requires an essay, a high school transcript, 1 recommendation, and TOEFL scores for international students. An interview is recommended. SAT or ACT scores are required for some. The application deadline for regular admission is rolling.
Transfer Admission The application deadline for admission is rolling.
Entrance Difficulty Illinois Institute of Technology assesses its entrance difficulty level as very difficult. For the fall 2008 freshman class, 57 percent of the applicants were accepted.
For Further Information Contact Mr. Gerald Doyle, Vice Provost, Undergraduate Admissions and Financial Aid, Illinois Institute of Technology, Office of Undergraduate Admission, Perlstein 101, 10 West 33rd Street, Chicago, IL 60616. *Phone:* 312-567-3025 or 800-448-2329 (toll-free out-of-state). *Fax:* 312-567-6939. *E-mail:* admission@iit.edu. *Web site:* http://www.iit.edu/.

ILLINOIS STATE UNIVERSITY

Normal, Illinois

Illinois State University is a coed, public university, founded in 1857, offering degrees at the bachelor's, master's, and doctoral levels and post-master's and postbachelor's certificates. It has an 850-acre campus in Normal.

Academic Information The faculty has 1,183 members (73% full-time), 67% with terminal degrees. The undergraduate student-faculty ratio is 19:1. The library holds 2 million titles and 14,166 serial subscriptions. Special programs include academic remediation, services for learning-disabled students, an honors program, cooperative (work-study) education, study abroad, advanced placement credit, accelerated degree programs, ESL programs, double majors, independent study, distance learning, self-designed majors, summer session for credit, part-time degree programs (daytime, evenings, summer), adult/continuing education programs, internships, and arrangement for off-campus study with National Student Exchange. The most frequently chosen baccalaureate fields are business/marketing, education, social sciences.
Student Body Statistics The student body totals 20,799, of whom 18,065 are undergraduates (3,394 freshmen). 57 percent are women and 43 percent are men. Students come from 47 states and territories and 39 other countries. 99 percent are from Illinois. 0.5 percent are international students.
Expenses for 2008–09 *Application fee:* $40. *State resident tuition:* $7680 full-time, $256 per semester hour part-time. *Nonresident tuition:* $14,310 full-time, $477 per semester hour part-time. *Mandatory fees:* $2134 full-time, $60.40 per semester hour part-time, $906 per term part-time. Both full-time and part-time tuition and fees vary according to course load, degree level, and student level. *College room and board:* $7458. *College room only:* $3740. Room and board charges vary according to board plan, housing facility, and location.
Financial Aid Forms of aid include need-based and non-need-based scholarships, athletic grants, and part-time jobs. The average aided 2008–09 undergraduate received an aid package worth an estimated $10,898. The priority application deadline for financial aid is March 1.
Freshman Admission Illinois State University requires an essay, a high school transcript, SAT or ACT scores, and TOEFL scores for international students. The application deadline for regular admission is March 1.
Transfer Admission The application deadline for admission is rolling.
Entrance Difficulty Illinois State University assesses its entrance difficulty level as moderately difficult. For the fall 2008 freshman class, 64 percent of the applicants were accepted.
For Further Information Contact Ms. Molly Arnold, Director of Admissions, Illinois State University, Campus Box 2200, Normal, IL 61790-2200. *Phone:* 309-438-2478 or 800-366-2478 (toll-free in-state). *Fax:* 309-438-3932. *E-mail:* admissions@ilstu.edu. *Web site:* http://www.ilstu.edu/.

ILLINOIS WESLEYAN UNIVERSITY

Bloomington, Illinois

Illinois Wesleyan University is a coed, private, four-year college, founded in 1850, offering degrees at the bachelor's level. It has a 79-acre campus in Bloomington.

Academic Information The faculty has 233 members (69% full-time), 79% with terminal degrees. The student-faculty ratio is 11:1. The library holds 330,300 titles, 32,080 serial subscriptions, and 7,797 audiovisual materials. Special programs include services for learning-disabled students, an honors program, study abroad, advanced placement credit, double majors, independent study, self-designed majors, internships, and arrangement for off-campus study with Midwest College Arts program, Colleges of the Midwest Urban Education program, Washington semenster, United Nations semester. The most frequently chosen baccalaureate fields are business/marketing, social sciences, visual and performing arts.
Student Body Statistics The student body is made up of 2,125 undergraduates (562 freshmen). 59 percent are women and 41 percent are men. Students come from 39 states and territories and 22 other countries. 87 percent are from Illinois. 3.6 percent are international students.
Expenses for 2008–09 *Application fee:* $0. *Comprehensive fee:* $39,784 includes full-time tuition ($32,260), mandatory fees ($174), and college room and board ($7350). *College room only:* $4570. Room and board charges vary according to board plan and housing facility. *Part-time tuition:* $4032 per course.
Financial Aid Forms of aid include need-based and non-need-based scholarships and part-time jobs. The average aided 2008–09 undergraduate received an aid package worth an estimated $25,006. The application deadline for financial aid is March 1.
Freshman Admission Illinois Wesleyan University requires an essay, a high school transcript, a minimum 2.0 high school GPA, 1 recommendation, SAT or ACT scores, and TOEFL scores for international students. A minimum 3.0 high school GPA, 2 recommendations, and an interview are recommended. The application deadline for regular admission is rolling.
Transfer Admission The application deadline for admission is August 15.
Entrance Difficulty Illinois Wesleyan University assesses its entrance difficulty level as very difficult. For the fall 2008 freshman class, 52 percent of the applicants were accepted.
For Further Information Contact Mr. Tony Bankston, Dean of Admissions, Illinois Wesleyan University, PO Box 2900, Bloomington, IL 61702-2900. *Phone:* 309-556-3031 or 800-332-2498 (toll-free). *Fax:* 309-556-3820. *E-mail:* iwuadmit@iwu.edu. *Web site:* http://www.iwu.edu/.

INTERNATIONAL ACADEMY OF DESIGN & TECHNOLOGY

Chicago, Illinois

International Academy of Design & Technology is a coed, primarily women's, proprietary, four-year college of Career Education Corporation, founded in 1977, offering degrees at the associate and bachelor's levels. It has a 1-acre campus in Chicago.

International Academy of Design & Technology (continued)
Expenses for 2008–09 *Application fee:* $50. *Tuition:* $23,040 full-time, $360 per credit part-time. *Mandatory fees:* $600 full-time.
For Further Information Contact Suzanne Reichart, Director of Student Management, International Academy of Design & Technology, One North State Street, Suite 500, Chicago, IL 60602. *Phone:* 312-980-9200 or 877-ACADEMY (toll-free out-of-state). *Fax:* 312-541-3929. *E-mail:* sreichart@iadtchicago.edu. *Web site:* http://www.iadtchicago.edu/.

See page 240 for the Close-Up.

ITT TECHNICAL INSTITUTE

Burr Ridge, Illinois

ITT Technical Institute is a coed, proprietary, primarily two-year college of ITT Educational Services, Inc., founded in 1998, offering degrees at the associate and bachelor's levels.

Financial Aid Forms of aid include need-based scholarships and part-time jobs. The application deadline for financial aid is continuous.
Entrance Difficulty ITT Technical Institute assesses its entrance difficulty level as minimally difficult.
For Further Information Contact Director of Recruitment, ITT Technical Institute, 7040 High Grove Boulevard, Burr Ridge, IL 60527. *Phone:* 630-455-6470 or 877-488-0001 (toll-free in-state). *Fax:* 630-455-6476. *Web site:* http://www.itt-tech.edu/.

ITT TECHNICAL INSTITUTE

Mount Prospect, Illinois

ITT Technical Institute is a coed, proprietary, primarily two-year college of ITT Educational Services, Inc., founded in 1986, offering degrees at the associate and bachelor's levels. It has a 1-acre campus in Mount Prospect near Chicago.

Financial Aid Forms of aid include need-based scholarships and part-time jobs. The application deadline for financial aid is continuous.
Freshman Admission TOEFL scores for international students are recommended.
Entrance Difficulty ITT Technical Institute assesses its entrance difficulty level as minimally difficult.
For Further Information Contact Director of Recruitment, ITT Technical Institute, 1401 Feehanville Drive, Mount Prospect, IL 60056. *Phone:* 847-375-8800. *Fax:* 847-375-9022. *Web site:* http://www.itt-tech.edu/.

ITT TECHNICAL INSTITUTE

Orland Park, Illinois

ITT Technical Institute is a coed, proprietary, primarily two-year college of ITT Educational Services, Inc., founded in 1993, offering degrees at the associate and bachelor's levels. It is located in Orland Park near Chicago.

Financial Aid Forms of aid include need-based scholarships and part-time jobs. The application deadline for financial aid is continuous.
Entrance Difficulty ITT Technical Institute assesses its entrance difficulty level as minimally difficult.
For Further Information Contact Director of Recruitment, ITT Technical Institute, 11551 184th Place, Orland Park, IL 60467. *Phone:* 708-326-3200. *Fax:* 708-747-0023. *Web site:* http://www.itt-tech.edu/.

JUDSON UNIVERSITY

Elgin, Illinois

Judson University is a coed, private, Baptist, comprehensive institution, founded in 1963, offering degrees at the bachelor's and master's levels. It has an 80-acre campus in Elgin near Chicago.

Expenses for 2008–09 *Application fee:* $35. *Comprehensive fee:* $29,350 includes full-time tuition ($21,350), mandatory fees ($500), and college room and board ($7500). Room and board charges vary according to board plan. *Part-time tuition:* $750 per credit hour. *Part-time mandatory fees:* $250 per term. Part-time tuition and fees vary according to course load.
For Further Information Contact Mr. William W. Dean, Director of Enrollment Management, Judson University, 1151 North State Street, Elgin, IL 60123-1498. *Phone:* 847-695-2522 or 800-879-5376 (toll-free). *Fax:* 847-628-2526. *E-mail:* bdean@judsoncollege.edu. *Web site:* http://www.judsonu.edu/.

KENDALL COLLEGE

Chicago, Illinois

Kendall College is a coed, private, United Methodist, four-year college, founded in 1934, offering degrees at the associate and bachelor's levels. It has a 4-acre campus in Chicago.

Academic Information The faculty has 80 members (46% full-time). The student-faculty ratio is 19:1. Special programs include academic remediation, cooperative (work-study) education, advanced placement credit, accelerated degree programs, ESL programs, independent study, self-designed majors, summer session for credit, part-time degree programs (daytime, evenings, weekends, summer), and internships. The most frequently chosen baccalaureate fields are business/marketing, education, personal and culinary services.
Student Body Statistics The student body is made up of 1,913 undergraduates (173 freshmen). 71 percent are women and 29 percent are men. Students come from 36 states and territories and 19 other countries. 92 percent are from Illinois.
Expenses for 2008–09 *Application fee:* $50. Tuition varies by program.
Financial Aid Forms of aid include need-based and non-need-based scholarships and part-time jobs. The priority application deadline for financial aid is April 15.
Freshman Admission Kendall College requires an essay, a high school transcript, SAT or ACT scores, and TOEFL scores for international students. A minimum 2.0 high school GPA is recommended. An interview is required for some. The application deadline for regular admission is rolling.
Transfer Admission The application deadline for admission is rolling.
Entrance Difficulty Kendall College assesses its entrance difficulty level as moderately difficult.
For Further Information Contact Susanne Noel, Vice President of Admissions, Kendall College, 900 N North Branch Street, Chicago, IL 60622. *Phone:* 312-752-2020, 866-667-3344 (toll-free in-state), or 877-588-8860 (toll-free out-of-state). *Fax:* 312-752-2021. *E-mail:* admissions@kendall.edu. *Web site:* http://www.kendall.edu/.

KNOX COLLEGE

Galesburg, Illinois

Knox College is a coed, private, four-year college, founded in 1837, offering degrees at the bachelor's level. It has an 82-acre campus in Galesburg near Peoria.

Academic Information The faculty has 135 members (76% full-time), 81% with terminal degrees. The student-faculty ratio is 12:1. The library holds 324,807 titles, 1,556 serial subscriptions, and 9,179 audiovisual materials. Special programs include academic remediation, services for learning-disabled students, an honors program, study abroad, advanced placement credit, double majors, independent study, self-designed majors, part-time degree programs (daytime), internships, and arrangement for off-campus study with Associated Colleges of the Midwest, Great Lakes College Association. The most frequently chosen baccalaureate fields are English, biological/life sciences, social sciences.
Student Body Statistics The student body is made up of 1,379 undergraduates (367 freshmen). 58 percent are women and 42 percent are men. Students come from 47 states and territories and 35 other countries. 53 percent are from Illinois. 6.9 percent are international students.

Expenses for 2009–10 *Application fee:* $40. *Comprehensive fee:* $39,075 includes full-time tuition ($31,575), mandatory fees ($336), and college room and board ($7164). *College room only:* $3603.
Financial Aid Forms of aid include need-based and non-need-based scholarships and part-time jobs. The average aided 2008–09 undergraduate received an aid package worth an estimated $25,060. The priority application deadline for financial aid is February 15.
Freshman Admission Knox College requires an essay, a high school transcript, 2 recommendations, and TOEFL scores for international students. An interview and SAT or ACT scores are recommended. The application deadline for regular admission is February 1 and for early action it is December 1.
Transfer Admission The application deadline for admission is April 1.
Entrance Difficulty Knox College assesses its entrance difficulty level as very difficult. For the fall 2008 freshman class, 66 percent of the applicants were accepted.
For Further Information Contact Mr. Paul Steenis, Dean of Admissions, Knox College, Box K-148, Galesburg, IL 61401. *Phone:* 309-341-7100 or 800-678-KNOX (toll-free). *Fax:* 309-341-7070. *E-mail:* admission@knox.edu. *Web site:* http://www.knox.edu/.

LAKE FOREST COLLEGE

Lake Forest, Illinois

Lake Forest College is a coed, private, comprehensive institution, founded in 1857, offering degrees at the bachelor's and master's levels. It has a 110-acre campus in Lake Forest near Chicago.

Academic Information The faculty has 159 members (59% full-time), 77% with terminal degrees. The undergraduate student-faculty ratio is 12:1. The library holds 276,117 titles, 2,364 serial subscriptions, and 6,694 audiovisual materials. Special programs include services for learning-disabled students, study abroad, advanced placement credit, double majors, independent study, self-designed majors, summer session for credit, part-time degree programs, internships, and arrangement for off-campus study with 14 members of the Associated Colleges of the Midwest. The most frequently chosen baccalaureate fields are communications/journalism, social sciences, visual and performing arts.
Student Body Statistics The student body totals 1,400, of whom 1,381 are undergraduates (379 freshmen). 59 percent are women and 41 percent are men. Students come from 44 states and territories and 69 other countries. 48 percent are from Illinois. 9.9 percent are international students.
Expenses for 2008–09 *Application fee:* $40. *Comprehensive fee:* $40,244 includes full-time tuition ($32,130), mandatory fees ($390), and college room and board ($7724). *College room only:* $3826. Full-time tuition and fees vary according to course load. Room and board charges vary according to board plan and housing facility. *Part-time tuition:* $4016 per course. Part-time tuition varies according to course load.
Financial Aid Forms of aid include need-based and non-need-based scholarships and part-time jobs. The average aided 2008–09 undergraduate received an aid package worth an estimated $26,073. The priority application deadline for financial aid is March 1.
Freshman Admission Lake Forest College requires an essay, a high school transcript, 2 recommendations, graded paper, and TOEFL scores for international students. An interview is recommended. SAT or ACT scores are required for some. The application deadline for regular admission is rolling, for early decision it is December 1, and for early action it is December 1.
Transfer Admission The application deadline for admission is rolling.
Entrance Difficulty Lake Forest College assesses its entrance difficulty level as very difficult. For the fall 2008 freshman class, 59 percent of the applicants were accepted.
For Further Information Contact Mr. William Motzer, Vice President for Admissions and Career Services, Lake Forest College, 555 North Sheridan Road, Lake Forest, IL 60045-2338. *Phone:* 847-735-5000 or 800-828-4751 (toll-free). *Fax:* 847-735-6271. *E-mail:* admissions@lakeforest.edu. *Web site:* http://www.lakeforest.edu/.

LAKEVIEW COLLEGE OF NURSING

Danville, Illinois

http://www.lakeviewcol.edu/

LEWIS UNIVERSITY

Romeoville, Illinois

Lewis University is a coed, private, comprehensive institution, founded in 1932, affiliated with the Roman Catholic Church, offering degrees at the associate, bachelor's, master's, and doctoral levels and post-master's certificates. It has a 375-acre campus in Romeoville near Chicago.

Academic Information The faculty has 563 members (33% full-time), 29% with terminal degrees. The undergraduate student-faculty ratio is 13:1. The library holds 149,870 titles and 1,990 serial subscriptions. Special programs include academic remediation, services for learning-disabled students, an honors program, study abroad, advanced placement credit, accelerated degree programs, ESL programs, double majors, independent study, distance learning, self-designed majors, summer session for credit, part-time degree programs (daytime, evenings, weekends, summer), adult/continuing education programs, internships, and arrangement for off-campus study. The most frequently chosen baccalaureate fields are business/marketing, health professions and related sciences, security and protective services.
Student Body Statistics The student body totals 5,536, of whom 3,973 are undergraduates (655 freshmen). 59 percent are women and 41 percent are men. Students come from 30 states and territories and 20 other countries. 96 percent are from Illinois. 3 percent are international students.
Expenses for 2008–09 *Application fee:* $40. *Comprehensive fee:* $30,740 includes full-time tuition ($21,990) and college room and board ($8750). *College room only:* $6000. Full-time tuition varies according to course load and program. Room and board charges vary according to board plan and housing facility. *Part-time tuition:* $705 per credit hour. Part-time tuition varies according to course load and program.
Financial Aid Forms of aid include need-based and non-need-based scholarships, athletic grants, and part-time jobs. The average aided 2007–08 undergraduate received an aid package worth $15,095. The priority application deadline for financial aid is May 1.
Freshman Admission Lewis University requires a high school transcript, a minimum 2.0 high school GPA, SAT or ACT scores, and TOEFL scores for international students. An interview is required for some. The application deadline for regular admission is August 1.
Transfer Admission The application deadline for admission is rolling.
Entrance Difficulty Lewis University assesses its entrance difficulty level as moderately difficult; minimally difficult for applicants 24 or over. For the fall 2008 freshman class, 71 percent of the applicants were accepted.
For Further Information Contact Mr. Ryan Cockerill, Director of Freshman Admission, Lewis University, Box 297, One University Parkway, Romeoville, IL 60446. *Phone:* 815-838-0500 Ext. 5237 or 800-897-9000 (toll-free). *Fax:* 815-836-5002. *E-mail:* admissions@lewisu.edu. *Web site:* http://www.lewisu.edu/.

LEWIS UNIVERSITY AT HICKORY HILLS

Hickory Hills, Illinois

http://www.lewisu.edu/campuses/hickoryhills/index.htm

LEWIS UNIVERSITY AT OAK BROOK

Oak Brook, Illinois

http://www.lewisu.edu/campuses/oakbrook/index.htm

LEWIS UNIVERSITY AT SHOREWOOD

Shorewood, Illinois

http://www.lewisu.edu/campuses/shorewood/index.htm

LEWIS UNIVERSITY AT TINLEY PARK

Tinley Park, Illinois

http://www.lewisu.edu/campuses/tinleypark/index.htm

LEXINGTON COLLEGE

Chicago, Illinois

Lexington College is a women's, private, four-year college, founded in 1977, offering degrees at the associate and bachelor's levels.

Academic Information The faculty has 17 members (24% full-time), 29% with terminal degrees. The student-faculty ratio is 6:1. Special programs include academic remediation, cooperative (work-study) education, study abroad, advanced placement credit, independent study, part-time degree programs (daytime, evenings, weekends), and internships.
Student Body Statistics The student body is made up of 53 undergraduates (8 freshmen). Students come from 6 states and territories and 3 other countries. 77 percent are from Illinois. 3.8 percent are international students.
Expenses for 2009–10 *Application fee:* $30. *One-time mandatory fee:* $50. *Tuition:* $22,800 full-time, $760 per credit hour part-time. *Mandatory fees:* $1000 full-time.
Financial Aid Forms of aid include need-based scholarships and part-time jobs. The average aided 2007–08 undergraduate received an aid package worth $17,199. The application deadline for financial aid is October 1 with a priority deadline of May 15.
Freshman Admission Lexington College requires an essay, a high school transcript, and a minimum 2.0 high school GPA. An interview is recommended. 2 recommendations and SAT or ACT scores are required for some. The application deadline for regular admission is rolling.
Transfer Admission The application deadline for admission is rolling.
Entrance Difficulty Lexington College has an open admission policy. It assesses its entrance difficulty as minimally difficult for out-of-state applicants; minimally difficult for transfers.
For Further Information Contact Mrs. Laura Bromann, Admissions Representative, Lexington College, 310 South Peoria Street, Suite 512, Chicago, IL 60607-3534. *Phone:* 312-226-6294 Ext. 228. *Fax:* 312-226-6405. *E-mail:* admissions@lexingtoncollege.edu. *Web site:* http://www.lexingtoncollege.edu/.

LINCOLN CHRISTIAN COLLEGE

Lincoln, Illinois

http://www.lccs.edu/

LINCOLN COLLEGE

Lincoln, Illinois

http://www.lincolncollege.edu/

LINCOLN COLLEGE–NORMAL

Normal, Illinois

Lincoln College–Normal is a coed, private, four-year college, founded in 1865, offering degrees at the associate and bachelor's levels. It has a 10-acre campus in Normal.

For Further Information Contact Brian Smith, Admissions Counselor, Lincoln College–Normal, 715 West Raab Road, Normal, IL 61761. *Phone:* 309-454-0500 or 800-569-0558 (toll-free). *Fax:* 309-454-5652. *E-mail:* ncadmissionsinfo@lincolncollege.edu. *Web site:* http://www.lincolncollege.edu/normal/.

LOYOLA UNIVERSITY CHICAGO

Chicago, Illinois

Loyola University Chicago is a coed, private, Roman Catholic (Jesuit) university, founded in 1870, offering degrees at the bachelor's, master's, doctoral, and first professional levels and post-master's and postbachelor's certificates (also offers adult part-time program with significant enrollment not reflected in profile). It has a 105-acre campus in Chicago.

Academic Information The faculty has 1,365 members (44% full-time). The undergraduate student-faculty ratio is 15:1. The library holds 1 million titles, 13,939 serial subscriptions, and 15,174 audiovisual materials. Special programs include academic remediation, services for learning-disabled students, an honors program, study abroad, advanced placement credit, accelerated degree programs, ESL programs, double majors, independent study, distance learning, summer session for credit, part-time degree programs (evenings), adult/continuing education programs, internships, and arrangement for off-campus study with School of the Art Institute of Chicago. The most frequently chosen baccalaureate fields are business/marketing, health professions and related sciences, social sciences.
Student Body Statistics The student body totals 15,670, of whom 10,124 are undergraduates (2,176 freshmen). 65 percent are women and 35 percent are men. Students come from 50 states and territories and 96 other countries. 65 percent are from Illinois. 1 percent are international students.
Expenses for 2009–10 *Application fee:* $25. *Comprehensive fee:* $41,541 includes full-time tuition ($29,850), mandatory fees ($806), and college room and board ($10,885). *College room only:* $7160. *Part-time tuition:* $605 per semester hour.
Financial Aid Forms of aid include need-based and non-need-based scholarships, athletic grants, and part-time jobs. The average aided 2008–09 undergraduate received an aid package worth an estimated $25,490. The application deadline for financial aid is continuous.
Freshman Admission Loyola University Chicago requires an essay, a high school transcript, a minimum 2.0 high school GPA, SAT or ACT scores, and TOEFL scores for international students. An interview is recommended. The application deadline for regular admission is April 1.
Transfer Admission The application deadline for admission is July 1.
Entrance Difficulty Loyola University Chicago assesses its entrance difficulty level as moderately difficult. For the fall 2008 freshman class, 74 percent of the applicants were accepted.
For Further Information Contact Ms. Lori Greene, Director of Admissions, Loyola University Chicago, 820 North Michigan Avenue, Suite 613, Chicago, IL 60611-9810. *Phone:* 773-508-3075 or 800-262-2373 (toll-free). *Fax:* 312-915-7216. *E-mail:* admission@luc.edu. *Web site:* http://www.luc.edu/.

See page 246 for the Close-Up.

MACCORMAC COLLEGE

Chicago, Illinois

MacCormac College is a coed, primarily women's, private, two-year college, founded in 1904, offering degrees at the associate level.

Expenses for 2008–09 *Application fee:* $20. *Tuition:* $9960 full-time, $415 per credit hour part-time. *Mandatory fees:* $125 full-time, $10 per course part-time.
For Further Information Contact Mr. David Grassi, Director of Admissions, MacCormac College, 506 South Wabash Avenue, Chicago, IL 60605-1667. *Phone:* 312-922-1884 Ext. 102. *Fax:* 630-941-0937. *Web site:* http://www.maccormac.edu/.

MacMURRAY COLLEGE
Jacksonville, Illinois

MacMurray College is a coed, private, United Methodist, four-year college, founded in 1846, offering degrees at the associate and bachelor's levels. It has a 60-acre campus in Jacksonville.

Academic Information The faculty has 66 members (53% full-time), 36% with terminal degrees. The student-faculty ratio is 14:1. The library holds 2 million titles and 185 serial subscriptions. Special programs include academic remediation, services for learning-disabled students, cooperative (work-study) education, study abroad, advanced placement credit, double majors, independent study, self-designed majors, summer session for credit, part-time degree programs (daytime, evenings, summer), internships, and arrangement for off-campus study with 5 members of the Western Illinois Foreign Language Consortium. The most frequently chosen baccalaureate fields are personal and culinary services, psychology, social sciences.
Student Body Statistics The student body is made up of 602 undergraduates (90 freshmen). 66 percent are women and 34 percent are men. Students come from 21 states and territories and 1 other country. 88 percent are from Illinois. 0.2 percent are international students.
Expenses for 2008–09 *Application fee:* $0. *Comprehensive fee:* $24,620 includes full-time tuition ($17,000), mandatory fees ($330), and college room and board ($7290). *College room only:* $4450. Room and board charges vary according to board plan. *Part-time tuition:* $565 per credit hour. *Part-time mandatory fees:* $25 per credit. Part-time tuition and fees vary according to course load.
Financial Aid Forms of aid include need-based and non-need-based scholarships and part-time jobs. The average aided 2008–09 undergraduate received an aid package worth an estimated $20,992. The priority application deadline for financial aid is May 1.
Freshman Admission MacMurray College requires a high school transcript, SAT or ACT scores, and TOEFL scores for international students. An essay, a minimum 2.5 high school GPA, 1 recommendation, and an interview are required for some. The application deadline for regular admission is rolling.
Transfer Admission The application deadline for admission is rolling.
Entrance Difficulty MacMurray College assesses its entrance difficulty level as moderately difficult. For the fall 2008 freshman class, 60 percent of the applicants were accepted.
For Further Information Contact Ms. Alicia Zeone, Senior Admission Counselor, MacMurray College, 447 East College Avenue, Jacksonville, IL 62650. *Phone:* 217-479-7059 or 800-252-7485 (toll-free in-state). *Fax:* 217-291-0702. *E-mail:* alicia.zeone@mac.edu. *Web site:* http://www.mac.edu/.

McKENDREE UNIVERSITY
Lebanon, Illinois

McKendree University is a coed, private, comprehensive institution, founded in 1828, affiliated with the United Methodist Church, offering degrees at the bachelor's and master's levels. It has an 80-acre campus in Lebanon near St. Louis.

Academic Information The faculty has 144 members (65% full-time), 63% with terminal degrees. The undergraduate student-faculty ratio is 13:1. The library holds 109,000 titles, 450 serial subscriptions, and 6,637 audiovisual materials. Special programs include academic remediation, services for learning-disabled students, an honors program, study abroad, advanced placement credit, accelerated degree programs, double majors, independent study, self-designed majors, summer session for credit, part-time degree programs (daytime, evenings, summer), internships, and arrangement for off-campus study with University of Evansville. The most frequently chosen baccalaureate fields are business/marketing, education, health professions and related sciences.
Student Body Statistics The student body totals 3,327, of whom 2,308 are undergraduates (308 freshmen). 56 percent are women and 44 percent are men. Students come from 22 states and territories and 14 other countries. 75 percent are from Illinois. 1.8 percent are international students.
Expenses for 2008–09 *Application fee:* $40. *Comprehensive fee:* $29,120 includes full-time tuition ($20,570), mandatory fees ($700), and college room and board ($7850). *College room only:* $4180. Full-time tuition and fees vary according to course load and degree level. Room and board charges vary according to board plan and housing facility. *Part-time tuition:* $690 per hour. Part-time tuition varies according to course load and degree level.
Financial Aid Forms of aid include need-based and non-need-based scholarships, athletic grants, and part-time jobs. The average aided 2008–09 undergraduate received an aid package worth an estimated $16,988. The priority application deadline for financial aid is May 31.
Freshman Admission McKendree University requires an essay, a high school transcript, a minimum 2.5 high school GPA, 1 recommendation, rank in upper 50% of high school class, SAT or ACT scores, and TOEFL scores for international students. An interview is required for some. The application deadline for regular admission is rolling.
Transfer Admission The application deadline for admission is rolling.
Entrance Difficulty McKendree University assesses its entrance difficulty level as moderately difficult. For the fall 2008 freshman class, 67 percent of the applicants were accepted.
For Further Information Contact Chris Hall, Vice President for Admissions and Financial Aid, McKendree University, 701 College Road, Lebanon, IL 62254. *Phone:* 618-537-6833 or 800-232-7228 Ext. 6831 (toll-free). *Fax:* 618-537-6496. *E-mail:* inquiry@mckendree.edu. *Web site:* http://www.mckendree.edu/.

MENNONITE COLLEGE OF NURSING

See Illinois State University.

MIDSTATE COLLEGE
Peoria, Illinois

Midstate College is a coed, primarily women's, proprietary, four-year college, founded in 1888, offering degrees at the associate and bachelor's levels. It has a 1-acre campus in Peoria.

Academic Information The library holds 8,724 titles and 104 serial subscriptions. Special programs include academic remediation, an honors program, cooperative (work-study) education, Freshman Honors College, summer session for credit, part-time degree programs (daytime, evenings, summer), and internships.
Student Body Statistics The student body is made up of 641 undergraduates.
Expenses for 2008–09 *Application fee:* $25. *Tuition:* $11,985 full-time, $282.50 per quarter hour part-time.
Financial Aid Forms of aid include need-based scholarships and part-time jobs. The application deadline for financial aid is continuous.
Freshman Admission Midstate College requires a high school transcript, TOEFL scores for international students, and Wonderlic aptitude test. An interview is recommended. The application deadline for regular admission is rolling.
Transfer Admission The application deadline for admission is rolling.
Entrance Difficulty Midstate College assesses its entrance difficulty level as moderately difficult; minimally difficult for transfers.
For Further Information Contact Ms. Jessica Hancock, Director of Admissions, Midstate College, 411 West Northmoor Road, Peoria, IL 61614. *Phone:* 309-692-4092. *Fax:* 309-692-3893. *E-mail:* jhancock2@midstate.edu. *Web site:* http://www.midstate.edu/.

MILLIKIN UNIVERSITY

Decatur, Illinois

Millikin University is a coed, private, comprehensive institution, founded in 1901, affiliated with the Presbyterian Church (U.S.A.), offering degrees at the bachelor's and master's levels. It has a 70-acre campus in Decatur.

Academic Information The faculty has 291 members (54% full-time), 54% with terminal degrees. The undergraduate student-faculty ratio is 11:1. The library holds 216,883 titles, 430 serial subscriptions, and 2,734 audiovisual materials. Special programs include services for learning-disabled students, an honors program, cooperative (work-study) education, study abroad, advanced placement credit, accelerated degree programs, double majors, independent study, self-designed majors, summer session for credit, part-time degree programs (daytime, evenings, summer), adult/continuing education programs, internships, and arrangement for off-campus study with Drew University, American University, Urban Life Center. The most frequently chosen baccalaureate fields are business/marketing, education, visual and performing arts.
Student Body Statistics The student body totals 2,344, of whom 2,296 are undergraduates (484 freshmen). 62 percent are women and 38 percent are men. Students come from 35 states and territories and 10 other countries. 89 percent are from Illinois. 1.3 percent are international students.
Expenses for 2009–10 *Application fee:* $0. *Comprehensive fee:* $34,211 includes full-time tuition ($25,750), mandatory fees ($595), and college room and board ($7866). *College room only:* $4306. *Part-time tuition:* $860 per credit hour. *Part-time mandatory fees:* $75 per term.
Financial Aid Forms of aid include need-based and non-need-based scholarships and part-time jobs. The average aided 2007–08 undergraduate received an aid package worth $17,726.
Freshman Admission Millikin University requires a high school transcript, a minimum 2.0 high school GPA, 2 recommendations, SAT or ACT scores, and TOEFL scores for international students. An interview is recommended. Audition for school of music; portfolio review for art program; audition for theatre and musical/theatre program is required for some. The application deadline for regular admission is rolling.
Transfer Admission The application deadline for admission is rolling.
Entrance Difficulty Millikin University assesses its entrance difficulty level as moderately difficult; most difficult for James Millikin Scholars, Presidential Scholars programs. For the fall 2008 freshman class, 61 percent of the applicants were accepted.
For Further Information Contact Mr. Joe Havis, Assistant Director of Admission, Millikin University, 1184 West Main Street, Decatur, IL 62522-2084. *Phone:* 217-424-6210 or 800-373-7733 (toll-free). *Fax:* 217-425-4669. *E-mail:* admis@millikin.edu. *Web site:* http://www.millikin.edu/.

MONMOUTH COLLEGE

Monmouth, Illinois

Monmouth College is a coed, private, four-year college, founded in 1853, affiliated with the Presbyterian Church, offering degrees at the bachelor's level. It has an 80-acre campus in Monmouth near Peoria.

Academic Information The faculty has 126 members (63% full-time), 62% with terminal degrees. The student-faculty ratio is 14:1. The library holds 191,866 titles, 599 serial subscriptions, and 7,900 audiovisual materials. Special programs include services for learning-disabled students, an honors program, study abroad, advanced placement credit, ESL programs, double majors, independent study, self-designed majors, part-time degree programs (daytime), internships, and arrangement for off-campus study with members of the Associated Colleges of the Midwest, Great Lakes Colleges Association. The most frequently chosen baccalaureate fields are business/marketing, education, English.
Student Body Statistics The student body is made up of 1,328 undergraduates (383 freshmen). 52 percent are women and 48 percent are men. Students come from 11 states and territories and 12 other countries. 99 percent are from Illinois. 1.7 percent are international students.
Expenses for 2009–10 *Application fee:* $0. *Comprehensive fee:* $32,250 includes full-time tuition ($24,950) and college room and board ($7300). *College room only:* $4250.
Financial Aid Forms of aid include need-based and non-need-based scholarships and part-time jobs. The average aided 2008–09 undergraduate received an aid package worth an estimated $20,583. The priority application deadline for financial aid is March 1.
Freshman Admission Monmouth College requires a high school transcript, SAT or ACT scores, and TOEFL scores for international students. An essay and an interview are recommended. An essay, 2 recommendations, and an interview are required for some. The application deadline for regular admission is rolling.
Transfer Admission The application deadline for admission is rolling.
Entrance Difficulty Monmouth College assesses its entrance difficulty level as moderately difficult. For the fall 2008 freshman class, 74 percent of the applicants were accepted.
For Further Information Contact Ms. Christine Johnston, Dean of Admission, Monmouth College, 700 East Broadway, Monmouth, IL 61462-1988. *Phone:* 309-457-2210 or 800-747-2687 (toll-free). *Fax:* 309-457-2141. *E-mail:* admit@monm.edu. *Web site:* http://www.monm.edu/.

MOODY BIBLE INSTITUTE

Chicago, Illinois

Moody Bible Institute is a coed, private, nondenominational, comprehensive institution, founded in 1886, offering degrees at the bachelor's, master's, and first professional levels. It has a 25-acre campus in Chicago.

Academic Information The library holds 135,000 titles and 987 serial subscriptions. Special programs include study abroad, advanced placement credit, ESL programs, double majors, independent study, distance learning, summer session for credit, part-time degree programs (daytime, evenings, weekends, summer), external degree programs, adult/continuing education programs, internships, and arrangement for off-campus study with Roosevelt University, University of Illinois at Chicago, City Colleges of Chicago, Harold Washington College.
Financial Aid Forms of aid include need-based scholarships. The application deadline for financial aid is continuous.
Freshman Admission Moody Bible Institute requires an essay, a high school transcript, a minimum 2.3 high school GPA, 4 recommendations, Christian testimony, SAT and SAT Subject Test or ACT scores, and TOEFL scores for international students. An interview is required for some. The application deadline for regular admission is March 1 and for early decision it is December 1.
Transfer Admission The application deadline for admission is March 1.
Entrance Difficulty Moody Bible Institute assesses its entrance difficulty level as moderately difficult.
For Further Information Contact Mrs. Marthe Campa, Application Coordinator, Moody Bible Institute, 820 North LaSalle Boulevard, Chicago, IL 60610. *Phone:* 312-329-4266 or 800-967-4MBI (toll-free). *Fax:* 312-329-8987. *E-mail:* admissions@moody.edu. *Web site:* http://www.moody.edu/.

MORRISON INSTITUTE OF TECHNOLOGY

Morrison, Illinois

http://www.morrison.tec.il.us/

NATIONAL-LOUIS UNIVERSITY

Chicago, Illinois

National-Louis University is a coed, private university, founded in 1886, offering degrees at the bachelor's, master's, and doctoral levels and post-master's and postbachelor's certificates. It has a 12-acre campus in Chicago.

Academic Information The faculty has 726 members (35% full-time). The undergraduate student-faculty ratio is 9:1. The library holds 4,857 audiovisual materials. Special programs include academic remediation, services for learning-disabled students, an honors program, advanced placement credit, accelerated degree programs, ESL programs,

independent study, summer session for credit, part-time degree programs (daytime, evenings, weekends, summer), external degree programs, adult/continuing education programs, and internships. The most frequently chosen baccalaureate fields are business/marketing, interdisciplinary studies, liberal arts/general studies.
Student Body Statistics The student body totals 7,056, of whom 1,749 are undergraduates (5 freshmen). 77 percent are women and 23 percent are men. Students come from 14 states and territories. 99 percent are from Illinois.
Expenses for 2008–09 *Application fee:* $25. *Tuition:* $17,955 full-time, $399 per quarter hour part-time. *Mandatory fees:* $120 full-time, $20 per term part-time. Both full-time and part-time tuition and fees vary according to course level, course load, degree level, location, and program.
Financial Aid Forms of aid include need-based and non-need-based scholarships and part-time jobs. The average aided 2007–08 undergraduate received an aid package worth $8921. The application deadline for financial aid is continuous.
Freshman Admission National-Louis University requires a high school transcript and a minimum 2.0 high school GPA. An interview is recommended. 2 recommendations and SAT or ACT scores are required for some. The application deadline for regular admission is rolling.
Transfer Admission The application deadline for admission is rolling.
Entrance Difficulty National-Louis University assesses its entrance difficulty level as minimally difficult.
For Further Information Contact Dr. Larry Poselli, National-Louis University, 1000 Capitol Drive, Wheeling, IL 60090. *Phone:* 888-NLU-TODAY, 888-NLU-TODAY (toll-free in-state), or 800-443-5522 (toll-free out-of-state). *Web site:* http://www.nl.edu/.

NORTH CENTRAL COLLEGE

Naperville, Illinois

North Central College is a coed, private, United Methodist, comprehensive institution, founded in 1861, offering degrees at the bachelor's and master's levels and postbachelor's certificates. It has a 56-acre campus in Naperville near Chicago.

Academic Information The faculty has 228 members (52% full-time), 63% with terminal degrees. The undergraduate student-faculty ratio is 15.7:1. The library holds 152,785 titles, 3,092 serial subscriptions, and 4,004 audiovisual materials. Special programs include academic remediation, services for learning-disabled students, an honors program, study abroad, advanced placement credit, accelerated degree programs, ESL programs, double majors, independent study, self-designed majors, summer session for credit, part-time degree programs, internships, and arrangement for off-campus study with Aurora University, Benedictine University. The most frequently chosen baccalaureate fields are business/marketing, education, social sciences.
Student Body Statistics The student body totals 2,726, of whom 2,388 are undergraduates (528 freshmen). 55 percent are women and 45 percent are men. Students come from 28 states and territories and 28 other countries. 92 percent are from Illinois. 0.9 percent are international students.
Expenses for 2008–09 *Application fee:* $25. *Comprehensive fee:* $34,155 includes full-time tuition ($25,698), mandatory fees ($240), and college room and board ($8217). Room and board charges vary according to housing facility. *Part-time tuition:* $645 per term. *Part-time mandatory fees:* $20 per term. Part-time tuition and fees vary according to course load.
Financial Aid Forms of aid include need-based and non-need-based scholarships and part-time jobs. The average aided 2008–09 undergraduate received an aid package worth an estimated $18,739. The application deadline for financial aid is continuous.
Freshman Admission North Central College requires a high school transcript, a minimum 2.5 high school GPA, SAT or ACT scores, and TOEFL scores for international students. An essay, 1 recommendation, and ACT scores are recommended. An interview is required for some. The application deadline for regular admission is rolling.
Transfer Admission The application deadline for admission is rolling.
Entrance Difficulty North Central College assesses its entrance difficulty level as moderately difficult. For the fall 2008 freshman class, 68 percent of the applicants were accepted.
For Further Information Contact Ms. Martha Stolze, Director of Freshman Admission, North Central College, 30 North Brainard Street, PO Box 3063, Naperville, IL 60566-7063. *Phone:* 630-637-5800 or 800-411-1861 (toll-free). *Fax:* 630-637-5819. *E-mail:* admissions@noctrl.edu. *Web site:* http://www.noctrl.edu/.

NORTHEASTERN ILLINOIS UNIVERSITY

Chicago, Illinois

Northeastern Illinois University is a coed, public, comprehensive institution, founded in 1961, offering degrees at the bachelor's and master's levels. It has a 67-acre campus in Chicago.

Academic Information The faculty has 697 members (60% full-time), 52% with terminal degrees. The undergraduate student-faculty ratio is 15:1. The library holds 711,087 titles, 22,233 serial subscriptions, and 8,433 audiovisual materials. Special programs include academic remediation, services for learning-disabled students, an honors program, cooperative (work-study) education, study abroad, advanced placement credit, ESL programs, double majors, independent study, distance learning, summer session for credit, part-time degree programs (daytime, evenings, summer), external degree programs, adult/continuing education programs, internships, and arrangement for off-campus study with National Student Exchange. The most frequently chosen baccalaureate fields are business/marketing, education, liberal arts/general studies.
Student Body Statistics The student body totals 11,193, of whom 8,987 are undergraduates (1,017 freshmen). 59 percent are women and 41 percent are men. Students come from 18 states and territories and 45 other countries. 99 percent are from Illinois. 1 percent are international students.
Expenses for 2008–09 *Application fee:* $25. *State resident tuition:* $6600 full-time, $220 per credit hour part-time. *Nonresident tuition:* $13,200 full-time, $440 per credit hour part-time. *Mandatory fees:* $1416 full-time, $47 per credit hour part-time, $3 per term part-time. Full-time tuition and fees vary according to student level.
Financial Aid Forms of aid include need-based and non-need-based scholarships and part-time jobs. The average aided 2008–09 undergraduate received an aid package worth an estimated $8578.
Freshman Admission Northeastern Illinois University requires a high school transcript, ACT scores, and TOEFL scores for international students. The application deadline for regular admission is July 1.
Transfer Admission The application deadline for admission is July 1.
Entrance Difficulty Northeastern Illinois University assesses its entrance difficulty level as minimally difficult; moderately difficult for transfers. For the fall 2008 freshman class, 71 percent of the applicants were accepted.
For Further Information Contact Ms. Zarrin Kerwell, Admissions Counselor, Northeastern Illinois University, 5500 North St. Louis Avenue, Chicago, IL 60625. *Phone:* 773-442-4026. *Fax:* 773-794-6243. *E-mail:* admrec@neiu.edu. *Web site:* http://www.neiu.edu/.

NORTHERN ILLINOIS UNIVERSITY

De Kalb, Illinois

Northern Illinois University is a coed, public university, founded in 1895, offering degrees at the bachelor's, master's, doctoral, and first professional levels. It has a 589-acre campus in De Kalb near Chicago.

Expenses for 2008–09 *State resident tuition:* $6720 full-time, $249 per credit hour part-time. *Nonresident tuition:* $13,620 full-time, $454 per credit hour part-time. *Mandatory fees:* $1592 full-time, $66.35 per credit hour part-time. Both full-time and part-time tuition and fees vary according to course load and location. *College room and board:* $8230. Room and board charges vary according to board plan and housing facility.
For Further Information Contact Dr. Robert Burk, Director of Admissions, Northern Illinois University, Office of Admissions, DeKalb, IL 60115-2857. *Phone:* 815-753-0446 or 800-892-3050 (toll-free in-state). *E-mail:* admission-info@niu.edu. *Web site:* http://www.niu.edu/.

NORTH PARK UNIVERSITY

Chicago, Illinois

North Park University is a coed, private, comprehensive institution, founded in 1891, affiliated with the Evangelical Covenant Church, offering degrees at the bachelor's, master's, doctoral, and first professional levels. It has a 30-acre campus in Chicago.

Academic Information The library holds 260,685 titles and 1,178 serial subscriptions. Special programs include academic remediation, an honors program, study abroad, advanced placement credit, accelerated degree programs, Freshman Honors College, ESL programs, self-designed majors, summer session for credit, part-time degree programs, adult/continuing education programs, internships, and arrangement for off-campus study with Christian College Coalition.
Student Body Statistics The student body totals 2,181, of whom 1,573 are undergraduates (320 freshmen). 62 percent are women and 38 percent are men.
Expenses for 2008–09 *Application fee:* $40. *Comprehensive fee:* $25,180 includes full-time tuition ($17,600) and college room and board ($7580). *College room only:* $4180. Full-time tuition varies according to program. Room and board charges vary according to board plan, housing facility, and student level. *Part-time tuition:* $730 per credit. Part-time tuition varies according to program.
Financial Aid Forms of aid include need-based and non-need-based scholarships and part-time jobs. The priority application deadline for financial aid is May 1.
Freshman Admission North Park University requires an essay, a high school transcript, a minimum 2.0 high school GPA, 2 recommendations, SAT or ACT scores, and TOEFL scores for international students. A minimum 3.0 high school GPA is recommended. An interview is required for some. The application deadline for regular admission is rolling.
Transfer Admission The application deadline for admission is rolling.
Entrance Difficulty North Park University assesses its entrance difficulty level as moderately difficult.
For Further Information Contact Office of Admissions, North Park University, 3225 West Foster Avenue, Chicago, IL 60625-4895. *Phone:* 773-244-5500 or 800-888-NPC8 (toll-free). *Fax:* 773-583-0858. *E-mail:* afao@northpark.edu. *Web site:* http://www.northpark.edu/.

NORTHWESTERN UNIVERSITY

Evanston, Illinois

Northwestern University is a coed, private university, founded in 1851, offering degrees at the bachelor's, master's, doctoral, and first professional levels and post-master's certificates. It has a 250-acre campus in Evanston near Chicago.

Academic Information The faculty has 1,153 members (89% full-time), 100% with terminal degrees. The undergraduate student-faculty ratio is 7:1. The library holds 5 million titles and 77,933 serial subscriptions. Special programs include services for learning-disabled students, an honors program, cooperative (work-study) education, study abroad, advanced placement credit, accelerated degree programs, double majors, independent study, self-designed majors, summer session for credit, part-time degree programs (daytime, evenings, summer), adult/continuing education programs, and internships. The most frequently chosen baccalaureate fields are communications/journalism, engineering, social sciences.
Student Body Statistics The student body totals 18,431, of whom 8,476 are undergraduates (2,078 freshmen). 52 percent are women and 48 percent are men. Students come from 51 states and territories and 55 other countries. 25 percent are from Illinois. 5.4 percent are international students.
Expenses for 2009–10 *Application fee:* $65. *Comprehensive fee:* $50,164 includes full-time tuition ($38,088), mandatory fees ($373), and college room and board ($11,703). *College room only:* $6657.
Financial Aid Forms of aid include need-based and non-need-based scholarships, athletic grants, and part-time jobs. The average aided 2008–09 undergraduate received an aid package worth an estimated $29,411. The application deadline for financial aid is February 15.
Freshman Admission Northwestern University requires an essay, a high school transcript, 1 recommendation, SAT or ACT scores, and TOEFL scores for international students. SAT Subject Test scores are recommended. Audition for music program and SAT Subject Test scores are required for some. The application deadline for regular admission is January 1 and for early decision it is November 1.
Transfer Admission The application deadline for admission is May 1.
Entrance Difficulty Northwestern University assesses its entrance difficulty level as most difficult; very difficult for transfers. For the fall 2008 freshman class, 26 percent of the applicants were accepted.
For Further Information Contact Mr. Christopher Watson, Dean of Undergraduate Admission, Northwestern University, PO Box 3060, Evanston, IL 60204-3060. *Phone:* 847-491-7271. *E-mail:* ug-admission@northwestern.edu. *Web site:* http://www.northwestern.edu/.

OLIVET NAZARENE UNIVERSITY

Bourbonnais, Illinois

Olivet Nazarene University is a coed, private, comprehensive institution, founded in 1907, affiliated with the Church of the Nazarene, offering degrees at the associate, bachelor's, master's, and doctoral levels. It has a 200-acre campus in Bourbonnais near Chicago.

Academic Information The library holds 160,039 titles, 925 serial subscriptions, and 6,818 audiovisual materials. Special programs include academic remediation, study abroad, advanced placement credit, double majors, independent study, summer session for credit, part-time degree programs (daytime, evenings, summer), adult/continuing education programs, and internships.
Student Body Statistics The student body totals 4,636, of whom 3,190 are undergraduates.
Expenses for 2008–09 *Application fee:* $25. *Comprehensive fee:* $27,990 includes full-time tuition ($20,750), mandatory fees ($840), and college room and board ($6400). Full-time tuition and fees vary according to course load. Room and board charges vary according to board plan. *Part-time tuition:* varies with course load.
Financial Aid Forms of aid include need-based and non-need-based scholarships, athletic grants, and part-time jobs. The average aided 2008–09 undergraduate received an aid package worth an estimated $15,986. The priority application deadline for financial aid is March 1.
Freshman Admission Olivet Nazarene University requires a high school transcript, a minimum 2.0 high school GPA, 2 recommendations, ACT scores, and TOEFL scores for international students. An essay and an interview are recommended. The application deadline for regular admission is rolling.
Transfer Admission The application deadline for admission is rolling.
Entrance Difficulty Olivet Nazarene University assesses its entrance difficulty level as minimally difficult.
For Further Information Contact Susan Wolfe, Director of Admissions, Olivet Nazarene University, One University Avenue, Bourbonnais, IL 60914. *Phone:* 815-939-5203 or 800-648-1463 (toll-free). *Fax:* 815-935-4998. *E-mail:* admissions@olivet.edu. *Web site:* http://www.olivet.edu/.

See page 260 for the Close-Up.

PRINCIPIA COLLEGE

Elsah, Illinois

http://www.prin.edu/college/

QUINCY UNIVERSITY

Quincy, Illinois

Quincy University is a coed, private, Roman Catholic, comprehensive institution, founded in 1860, offering degrees at the associate, bachelor's, and master's levels. It has a 75-acre campus in Quincy.

Academic Information The faculty has 137 members (36% full-time), 40% with terminal degrees. The library holds 204,557 titles, 365 serial subscriptions, and 9,293 audiovisual materials. Special programs include academic remediation, an honors program, study abroad, advanced placement credit, accelerated degree programs, ESL programs, double

majors, independent study, distance learning, self-designed majors, summer session for credit, part-time degree programs (daytime, evenings, summer), adult/continuing education programs, and internships. The most frequently chosen baccalaureate fields are business/marketing, education, health professions and related sciences.
Student Body Statistics The student body totals 1,424, of whom 1,144 are undergraduates (246 freshmen). 55 percent are women and 45 percent are men. Students come from 26 states and territories and 3 other countries. 75 percent are from Illinois. 0.3 percent are international students.
Expenses for 2008–09 *Application fee:* $25. *One-time mandatory fee:* $150. *Comprehensive fee:* $28,690 includes full-time tuition ($20,100), mandatory fees ($690), and college room and board ($7900). *College room only:* $4240. Room and board charges vary according to board plan and housing facility. *Part-time tuition:* $480 per credit hour. *Part-time mandatory fees:* $15 per credit hour.
Financial Aid Forms of aid include need-based and non-need-based scholarships, athletic grants, and part-time jobs. The average aided 2007–08 undergraduate received an aid package worth $18,744. The priority application deadline for financial aid is March 15.
Freshman Admission Quincy University requires an essay, a high school transcript, a minimum 2.0 high school GPA, SAT or ACT scores, and TOEFL scores for international students. An interview is recommended. 1 recommendation is required for some. The application deadline for regular admission is rolling.
Transfer Admission The application deadline for admission is rolling.
Entrance Difficulty Quincy University assesses its entrance difficulty level as moderately difficult. For the fall 2008 freshman class, 90 percent of the applicants were accepted.
For Further Information Contact Mrs. Syndi Peck, Director of Admissions, Quincy University, Admissions Office, Quincy, IL 62301. *Phone:* 217-228-5210 or 800-688-4295 (toll-free). *E-mail:* admissions@quincy.edu. *Web site:* http://www.quincy.edu/.

ROBERT MORRIS COLLEGE

Chicago, Illinois

Robert Morris College is a coed, private, comprehensive institution, founded in 1913, offering degrees at the associate, bachelor's, and master's levels.

Academic Information The faculty has 317 members (41% full-time), 16% with terminal degrees. The undergraduate student-faculty ratio is 23:1. The library holds 145,170 titles and 40,684 audiovisual materials. Special programs include services for learning-disabled students, an honors program, cooperative (work-study) education, study abroad, advanced placement credit, accelerated degree programs, independent study, distance learning, summer session for credit, part-time degree programs (evenings), adult/continuing education programs, and internships. The most frequently chosen baccalaureate fields are business/marketing, computer and information sciences, visual and performing arts.
Student Body Statistics The student body totals 4,590, of whom 4,240 are undergraduates (995 freshmen). 62 percent are women and 38 percent are men. Students come from 29 states and territories and 20 other countries. 95 percent are from Illinois. 0.6 percent are international students.
Expenses for 2009–10 *Application fee:* $30. *Tuition:* $19,200 full-time, $2133 per term part-time.
Financial Aid Forms of aid include need-based and non-need-based scholarships, athletic grants, and part-time jobs. The average aided 2007–08 undergraduate received an aid package worth $12,071. The application deadline for financial aid is continuous.
Freshman Admission Robert Morris College requires a high school transcript and TOEFL scores for international students. A minimum 2.0 high school GPA, an interview, and SAT or ACT scores are recommended. The application deadline for regular admission is rolling.
Transfer Admission The application deadline for admission is rolling.
Entrance Difficulty Robert Morris College assesses its entrance difficulty level as minimally difficult. For the fall 2008 freshman class, 79 percent of the applicants were accepted.
For Further Information Contact Ms. Catherine Lockwood, Vice President for Undergraduate Admissions, Robert Morris College, 401 South State Street, Chicago, IL 60605. *Phone:* 312-935-6640 or 800-RMC-5960 (toll-free). *Fax:* 312-935-6819. *E-mail:* enroll@robertmorris.edu. *Web site:* http://www.robertmorris.edu/.

See page 262 for the Close-Up.

ROBERT MORRIS COLLEGE–DuPAGE

Aurora, Illinois

http://www.robertmorris.edu/

ROBERT MORRIS COLLEGE–ORLAND PARK

Orland Park, Illinois

http://www.robertmorris.edu/

ROCKFORD BUSINESS COLLEGE

Rockford, Illinois

http://www.rbcsuccess.com/

ROCKFORD COLLEGE

Rockford, Illinois

Rockford College is a coed, private, comprehensive institution, founded in 1847, offering degrees at the bachelor's and master's levels. It has a 130-acre campus in Rockford near Chicago.

Academic Information The faculty has 144 members (46% full-time). The undergraduate student-faculty ratio is 11:1. The library holds 140,000 titles and 831 serial subscriptions. Special programs include academic remediation, services for learning-disabled students, an honors program, study abroad, advanced placement credit, accelerated degree programs, ESL programs, double majors, independent study, summer session for credit, part-time degree programs (daytime, evenings, summer), adult/continuing education programs, internships, and arrangement for off-campus study with American University, Central College (IA), Drew University. The most frequently chosen baccalaureate fields are business/marketing, education, psychology.
Student Body Statistics The student body totals 1,391, of whom 874 are undergraduates (121 freshmen). 61 percent are women and 39 percent are men. Students come from 15 states and territories. 90 percent are from Illinois. 0.7 percent are international students.
Expenses for 2009–10 *Application fee:* $35. *Comprehensive fee:* $31,000 includes full-time tuition ($24,250) and college room and board ($6750). *College room only:* $3850. *Part-time tuition:* $650 per credit. *Part-time mandatory fees:* $30 per credit.
Financial Aid Forms of aid include need-based and non-need-based scholarships and part-time jobs. The average aided 2007–08 undergraduate received an aid package worth $17,351. The priority application deadline for financial aid is March 1.
Freshman Admission Rockford College requires a high school transcript, SAT or ACT scores, and TOEFL scores for international students. A minimum 2.65 high school GPA, an interview, and campus visit are recommended. An essay, a minimum 2.65 high school GPA, and 2 recommendations are required for some.

Rockford College (continued)

Entrance Difficulty Rockford College assesses its entrance difficulty level as moderately difficult. For the fall 2008 freshman class, 67 percent of the applicants were accepted.

For Further Information Contact Rebecca Miziniak, Assistant Director of Admission, Rockford College, Nelson Hall, Rockford, IL 61108-2393. *Phone:* 815-226-4050 or 800-892-2984 (toll-free). *Fax:* 815-226-2822. *E-mail:* rcadmissions@rockford.edu. *Web site:* http://www.rockford.edu/.

ROOSEVELT UNIVERSITY

Chicago, Illinois

Roosevelt University is a coed, private, comprehensive institution, founded in 1945, offering degrees at the bachelor's, master's, and doctoral levels and post-master's certificates.

Academic Information The faculty has 631 members (34% full-time). The undergraduate student-faculty ratio is 13:1. The library holds 202,000 titles and 1,300 serial subscriptions. Special programs include academic remediation, services for learning-disabled students, an honors program, study abroad, advanced placement credit, accelerated degree programs, ESL programs, double majors, independent study, distance learning, self-designed majors, summer session for credit, part-time degree programs (daytime, evenings, weekends, summer), external degree programs, adult/continuing education programs, internships, and arrangement for off-campus study with School of the Art Institute of Chicago. The most frequently chosen baccalaureate fields are business/marketing, psychology, visual and performing arts.

Student Body Statistics The student body totals 7,692, of whom 4,389 are undergraduates (502 freshmen). 67 percent are women and 33 percent are men. Students come from 47 states and territories and 41 other countries. 88 percent are from Illinois. 2.5 percent are international students.

Expenses for 2009–10 *Application fee:* $25. *Comprehensive fee:* $32,394 includes full-time tuition ($21,000), mandatory fees ($300), and college room and board ($11,094). *Part-time tuition:* $689 per semester hour. *Part-time mandatory fees:* $125 per term. Full-time tuition for College of Performing Arts is $28,000.

Financial Aid Forms of aid include need-based and non-need-based scholarships and part-time jobs. The priority application deadline for financial aid is April 1.

Freshman Admission Roosevelt University requires an essay, a high school transcript, a minimum 2.5 high school GPA, audition for music and theater programs, and SAT or ACT scores. TOEFL scores for international students are recommended. An interview is required for some. The application deadline for regular admission is August 1.

Transfer Admission The application deadline for admission is rolling.

Entrance Difficulty Roosevelt University assesses its entrance difficulty level as moderately difficult; very difficult for performing arts. For the fall 2008 freshman class, 24 percent of the applicants were accepted.

For Further Information Contact Ms. Beth Gierach, Assistant Vice President for Admission, Roosevelt University, 430 South Michigan Avenue, Room 104, Chicago, IL 60605-1394. *Phone:* 312-341-6733 or 877-APPLYRU (toll-free). *Fax:* 312-341-3523. *E-mail:* bgierach@roosevelt.edu. *Web site:* http://www.roosevelt.edu/.

RUSH UNIVERSITY

Chicago, Illinois

Rush University is a coed, private, upper-level institution, founded in 1969, offering degrees at the bachelor's, master's, doctoral, and first professional levels and post-master's certificates. It has a 35-acre campus in Chicago.

Academic Information The faculty has 796 members (100% full-time). The undergraduate student-faculty ratio is 8:1. The library holds 120,042 titles, 1,100 serial subscriptions, and 4,750 audiovisual materials. Special programs include distance learning. The most frequently chosen baccalaureate field is health professions and related sciences.

Student Body Statistics The student body totals 1,566, of whom 166 are undergraduates. 87 percent are women and 13 percent are men. Students come from 14 states and territories and 4 other countries. 81 percent are from Illinois. 4.2 percent are international students.

Expenses for 2008–09 *Application fee:* $40. *Comprehensive fee:* $30,312 includes full-time tuition ($20,352) and college room and board ($9960). *Part-time tuition:* $424 per credit hour.

Financial Aid Forms of aid include need-based and non-need-based scholarships and part-time jobs. The priority application deadline for financial aid is March 1.

Transfer Admission Rush University requires a college transcript. A minimum 2.75 college GPA is recommended. Standardized test scores are required for some. The application deadline for admission is rolling.

Entrance Difficulty Rush University assesses its entrance difficulty level as moderately difficult. For the fall 2008 entering class, 37 percent of the applicants were accepted.

For Further Information Contact Ms. Hicela Castruita Woods, Director of College Admission Services, Rush University, 600 South Paulina, Suite 440, College Admissions Services, Chicago, IL 60612-3878. *Phone:* 312-942-7100. *Fax:* 312-942-2219. *E-mail:* rush_admissions@rush.edu. *Web site:* http://www.rushu.rush.edu/.

SAINT ANTHONY COLLEGE OF NURSING

Rockford, Illinois

http://www.sacn.edu/

ST. AUGUSTINE COLLEGE

Chicago, Illinois

St. Augustine College is a coed, private, four-year college, founded in 1980, offering degrees at the associate and bachelor's levels (offers bilingual Spanish/English degree programs). It has a 4-acre campus in Chicago.

Academic Information The faculty has 134 members (16% full-time), 69% with terminal degrees. The student-faculty ratio is 9:1. The library holds 24,007 titles, 50 serial subscriptions, and 2,358 audiovisual materials. Special programs include academic remediation, services for learning-disabled students, cooperative (work-study) education, ESL programs, double majors, independent study, summer session for credit, part-time degree programs (daytime, evenings, summer), adult/continuing education programs, and internships.

Student Body Statistics The student body is made up of 1,248 undergraduates (391 freshmen). 76 percent are women and 24 percent are men. Students come from 2 states and territories.

Expenses for 2008–09 *Application fee:* $0. *Tuition:* $7680 full-time, $320 per credit hour part-time.

Financial Aid Forms of aid include need-based and non-need-based scholarships and part-time jobs. The application deadline for financial aid is continuous.

Entrance Difficulty St. Augustine College has an open admission policy.

For Further Information Contact Ms. Gloria Quiroz, Director of Recruitment, St. Augustine College, 1333-1345 West Argyle, Chicago, IL 60640-3501. *Phone:* 773-878-3256. *Fax:* 773-728-7067. *E-mail:* info@staugustine.edu. *Web site:* http://www.staugustinecollege.edu/.

SAINT FRANCIS MEDICAL CENTER COLLEGE OF NURSING

Peoria, Illinois

Saint Francis Medical Center College of Nursing is a coed, primarily women's, private, Roman Catholic, upper-level institution, founded in 1986, offering degrees at the bachelor's and master's levels.

Academic Information The faculty has 44 members (73% full-time). The undergraduate student-faculty ratio is 8:1. Special programs include advanced placement credit, independent study, distance learning, and summer session for credit. The most frequently chosen baccalaureate field is health professions and related sciences.

Student Body Statistics The student body totals 452, of whom 333 are undergraduates. 90 percent are women and 10 percent are men. Students come from 4 states and territories. 99 percent are from Illinois.
Expenses for 2009–10 *Application fee:* $50. *Tuition:* $14,160 full-time, $472 per semester hour part-time. *Mandatory fees:* $556 full-time, $130 per term part-time. *College room only:* $2400.
Financial Aid Forms of aid include need-based and non-need-based scholarships. The average aided 2008–09 undergraduate received an aid package worth an estimated $10,956. The priority application deadline for financial aid is March 1.
Transfer Admission Saint Francis Medical Center College of Nursing requires a college transcript and a minimum 2.5 college GPA.
Entrance Difficulty Saint Francis Medical Center College of Nursing assesses its entrance difficulty level as moderately difficult for transfers. For the fall 2008 entering class, 63 percent of the applicants were accepted.
For Further Information Contact Mrs. Janice Farquharson, Director of Admissions and Registrar, Saint Francis Medical Center College of Nursing, 511 Greenleaf Street, Peoria, IL 61603-3783. *Phone:* 309-624-8980. *Fax:* 309-624-8973. *E-mail:* janice.farquharson@osfhealthcare.org. *Web site:* http://www.sfmccon.edu/.

ST. JOHN'S COLLEGE

Springfield, Illinois

http://www.st-johns.org/education/schools/nursing/

SAINT JOSEPH COLLEGE OF NURSING

See University of St. Francis.

SAINT XAVIER UNIVERSITY

Chicago, Illinois

Saint Xavier University is a coed, private, Roman Catholic, comprehensive institution, founded in 1847, offering degrees at the bachelor's and master's levels and post-master's and postbachelor's certificates. It has a 70-acre campus in Chicago.

Academic Information The faculty has 419 members (42% full-time), 48% with terminal degrees. The undergraduate student-faculty ratio is 15:1. The library holds 170,753 titles and 717 serial subscriptions. Special programs include academic remediation, services for learning-disabled students, an honors program, cooperative (work-study) education, study abroad, advanced placement credit, accelerated degree programs, ESL programs, double majors, independent study, self-designed majors, summer session for credit, part-time degree programs (daytime, evenings, weekends, summer), adult/continuing education programs, and internships. The most frequently chosen baccalaureate fields are business/marketing, education, health professions and related sciences.
Student Body Statistics The student body totals 5,337, of whom 3,169 are undergraduates (553 freshmen). 70 percent are women and 30 percent are men. Students come from 28 states and territories and 2 other countries. 94 percent are from Illinois. 0.3 percent are international students.
Expenses for 2008–09 *Application fee:* $25. *Comprehensive fee:* $31,013 includes full-time tuition ($22,486), mandatory fees ($520), and college room and board ($8007). *College room only:* $4664. Full-time tuition and fees vary according to course load. Room and board charges vary according to board plan and housing facility. *Part-time tuition:* $753 per credit hour. *Part-time mandatory fees:* $350 per year. Part-time tuition and fees vary according to course load.
Financial Aid Forms of aid include need-based and non-need-based scholarships, athletic grants, and part-time jobs. The average aided 2008–09 undergraduate received an aid package worth an estimated $18,960. The priority application deadline for financial aid is March 1.
Freshman Admission Saint Xavier University requires a high school transcript, SAT or ACT scores, and TOEFL scores for international students. An essay, a minimum 2.5 high school GPA, and an interview are recommended. An interview is required for some. The application deadline for regular admission is rolling.
Transfer Admission The application deadline for admission is rolling.
Entrance Difficulty Saint Xavier University assesses its entrance difficulty level as moderately difficult. For the fall 2008 freshman class, 71 percent of the applicants were accepted.
For Further Information Contact Dr. Kathleen Carlson, Vice President, Saint Xavier University, 3700 West 103rd Street, Chicago, IL 60655-3105. *Phone:* 773-298-3305 or 800-462-9288 (toll-free). *Fax:* 773-298-3076. *E-mail:* carlson@sxu.edu. *Web site:* http://www.sxu.edu/.

SCHOOL OF THE ART INSTITUTE OF CHICAGO

Chicago, Illinois

School of the Art Institute of Chicago is a coed, private, comprehensive institution, founded in 1866, offering degrees at the bachelor's and master's levels. It has a 1-acre campus in Chicago.

For Further Information Contact Mr. Scott Ramon, Director, Undergraduate Admissions, School of the Art Institute of Chicago, 36 South Wabash, Chicago, IL 60603. *Phone:* 312-629-6100 or 800-232-SAIC (toll-free). *Fax:* 312-629-6101. *E-mail:* admiss@saic.edu. *Web site:* http://www.artic.edu/saic/.

SHIMER COLLEGE

Chicago, Illinois

Shimer College is a coed, private, four-year college, founded in 1853, offering degrees at the bachelor's level. It has a 3-acre campus in Chicago near Chicago and Milwaukee.

Academic Information The faculty has 12 members (75% full-time), 8% with terminal degrees. The student-faculty ratio is 8:1. The library holds 200,000 titles and 200 serial subscriptions. Special programs include cooperative (work-study) education, study abroad, double majors, independent study, self-designed majors, summer session for credit, part-time degree programs (daytime, weekends, summer), adult/continuing education programs, internships, and arrangement for off-campus study with Barat College, Northwestern University. The most frequently chosen baccalaureate fields are liberal arts/general studies, biological/life sciences, social sciences.
Student Body Statistics The student body is made up of 100 undergraduates (27 freshmen). 52 percent are women and 48 percent are men. Students come from 22 states and territories and 2 other countries. 63 percent are from Illinois. 2 percent are international students.
Expenses for 2008–09 *Application fee:* $25. *Comprehensive fee:* $34,950 includes full-time tuition ($23,750) and college room and board ($11,200). *College room only:* $6900. Full-time tuition varies according to class time and course load. Room and board charges vary according to housing facility. *Part-time tuition:* $850 per credit hour. *Part-time mandatory fees:* $1100 per year. Part-time tuition and fees vary according to class time and course load.
Financial Aid Forms of aid include need-based and non-need-based scholarships and part-time jobs. The average aided 2008–09 undergraduate received an aid package worth an estimated $11,993. The application deadline for financial aid is continuous.
Freshman Admission Shimer College requires an essay, a high school transcript, 1 recommendation, an interview, and TOEFL scores for international students. SAT or ACT scores are required for some. The application deadline for regular admission is July 31.
Transfer Admission The application deadline for admission is rolling.
Entrance Difficulty Shimer College assesses its entrance difficulty level as moderately difficult. For the fall 2008 freshman class, 90 percent of the applicants were accepted.
For Further Information Contact Ms. Elaine Vincent, Director of Admission, Shimer College, 3424 South State Street, Chicago, IL 60616. *Phone:* 312-235-3504 or 800-215-7173 (toll-free). *Fax:* 847-249-8798. *E-mail:* e.vincent@shimer.edu. *Web site:* http://www.shimer.edu/.

SOUTHERN ILLINOIS UNIVERSITY CARBONDALE

Carbondale, Illinois

Southern Illinois University Carbondale is a coed, public unit of Southern Illinois University, founded in 1869, offering degrees at the associate, bachelor's, master's, doctoral, and first professional levels and first professional and postbachelor's certificates. It has a 1,133-acre campus in Carbondale near St. Louis.

Academic Information The faculty has 1,073 members (87% full-time), 79% with terminal degrees. The undergraduate student-faculty ratio is 17:1. The library holds 4 million titles, 18,271 serial subscriptions, and 371,180 audiovisual materials. Special programs include academic remediation, services for learning-disabled students, an honors program, cooperative (work-study) education, study abroad, advanced placement credit, ESL programs, double majors, independent study, distance learning, summer session for credit, part-time degree programs, adult/continuing education programs, internships, and arrangement for off-campus study with Southern Illinois University School of Medicine; off campus courses offered at 34 Military bases across the U.S. The most frequently chosen baccalaureate fields are business/marketing, education, engineering technologies.
Student Body Statistics The student body totals 20,673, of whom 15,980 are undergraduates (2,686 freshmen). 43 percent are women and 57 percent are men. Students come from 50 states and territories and 98 other countries. 86 percent are from Illinois. 1.6 percent are international students.
Expenses for 2008–09 *Application fee:* $30. *State resident tuition:* $6975 full-time, $232 per semester hour part-time. *Nonresident tuition:* $17,437 full-time, $581 per semester hour part-time. *Mandatory fees:* $2838 full-time, $130 per semester hour part-time. Both full-time and part-time tuition and fees vary according to course load. *College room and board:* $7137. *College room only:* $4097. Room and board charges vary according to board plan and housing facility.
Financial Aid Forms of aid include need-based and non-need-based scholarships, athletic grants, and part-time jobs. The average aided 2008–09 undergraduate received an aid package worth an estimated $11,682.
Freshman Admission Southern Illinois University Carbondale requires a high school transcript, SAT or ACT scores, and TOEFL scores for international students. The application deadline for regular admission is rolling.
Transfer Admission The application deadline for admission is rolling.
Entrance Difficulty Southern Illinois University Carbondale assesses its entrance difficulty level as moderately difficult. For the fall 2008 freshman class, 69 percent of the applicants were accepted.
For Further Information Contact Patsy Reynolds, Director, Undergraduate Admissions, Southern Illinois University Carbondale, Mail Code 4710, Southern Illinois University Carbondale, Carbondale, IL 62901-4710. *Phone:* 618-536-4405. *Fax:* 618-453-4609. *E-mail:* pradmit@siu.edu. *Web site:* http://www.siuc.edu.

See page 270 for the Close-Up.

SOUTHERN ILLINOIS UNIVERSITY EDWARDSVILLE

Edwardsville, Illinois

Southern Illinois University Edwardsville is a coed, public, comprehensive unit of Southern Illinois University, founded in 1957, offering degrees at the bachelor's, master's, and first professional levels and post-master's, first professional, and postbachelor's certificates. It has a 2,660-acre campus in Edwardsville near St. Louis.

Academic Information The faculty has 880 members (68% full-time). The undergraduate student-faculty ratio is 17:1. The library holds 847,631 titles, 24,530 serial subscriptions, and 30,078 audiovisual materials. Special programs include academic remediation, services for learning-disabled students, an honors program, cooperative (work-study) education, study abroad, advanced placement credit, accelerated degree programs, ESL programs, double majors, independent study, distance learning, self-designed majors, summer session for credit, part-time degree programs (daytime, evenings, weekends, summer), internships, and arrangement for off-campus study with University of Missouri–St. Louis, International Student Exchange Program, MBA program at southwestern Illinois College. The most frequently chosen baccalaureate fields are business/marketing, education, health professions and related sciences.
Student Body Statistics The student body totals 13,602, of whom 10,977 are undergraduates (1,922 freshmen). 54 percent are women and 46 percent are men. Students come from 45 states and territories and 48 other countries. 91 percent are from Illinois. 0.7 percent are international students.
Expenses for 2008–09 *Application fee:* $30. *State resident tuition:* $5850 full-time, $195 per semester hour part-time. *Nonresident tuition:* $14,625 full-time, $487.50 per semester hour part-time. *Mandatory fees:* $1969 full-time. *College room and board:* $7040.
Financial Aid Forms of aid include need-based and non-need-based scholarships, athletic grants, and part-time jobs. The average aided 2008–09 undergraduate received an aid package worth an estimated $14,527. The priority application deadline for financial aid is March 1.
Freshman Admission Southern Illinois University Edwardsville requires a high school transcript, SAT or ACT scores, and TOEFL scores for international students. A minimum 2.5 high school GPA is recommended. The application deadline for regular admission is May 1.
Transfer Admission The application deadline for admission is July 24.
Entrance Difficulty Southern Illinois University Edwardsville assesses its entrance difficulty level as moderately difficult. For the fall 2008 freshman class, 84 percent of the applicants were accepted.
For Further Information Contact Mr. Todd Burrell, Director of Admissions, Southern Illinois University Edwardsville, Campus Box 1600, Rendleman Hall, Edwardsville, IL 62026-1600. *Phone:* 618-650-3705 or 800-447-SIUE (toll-free). *Fax:* 618-650-5013. *E-mail:* admissions@siue.edu. *Web site:* http://www.siue.edu/.

SPRINGFIELD COLLEGE IN ILLINOIS

Springfield, Illinois

Springfield College in Illinois is a coed, private, two-year college, founded in 1929, affiliated with the Roman Catholic Church, offering degrees at the associate level (the college partners with Benedictine University, offering baccalaureate and master degree programs at Springfield College's campus). It has an 8-acre campus in Springfield.

Expenses for 2008–09 *Application fee:* $20. *Comprehensive fee:* $16,900 includes full-time tuition ($8010), mandatory fees ($1990), and college room and board ($6900). *Part-time tuition:* $335 per hour.
For Further Information Contact Kevin Hinkle, Associate Director of Admissions, Springfield College in Illinois, 1500 North Fifth Street, Springfield, IL 62702. *Phone:* 217-525-1420 Ext. 321 or 800-635-7289 (toll-free). *Fax:* 217-525-1497. *E-mail:* khinkle@sci.edu. *Web site:* http://www.sci.edu/.

TELSHE YESHIVA–CHICAGO

Chicago, Illinois

Telshe Yeshiva–Chicago is a men's, private, Jewish, comprehensive institution, founded in 1960, offering degrees at the bachelor's and master's levels.

Academic Information Special programs include summer session for credit and part-time degree programs (daytime, summer).
Student Body Statistics The student body totals 77, of whom 61 are undergraduates.
Financial Aid Forms of aid include part-time jobs.
Freshman Admission Telshe Yeshiva–Chicago requires an interview. Recommendations are recommended.

Entrance Difficulty For the fall 2008 freshman class, 100 percent of the applicants were accepted.
For Further Information Contact Rosh Hayeshiva, Telshe Yeshiva–Chicago, 3535 West Foster Avenue, Chicago, IL 60625-5598. *Phone:* 773-463-7738.

TRINITY CHRISTIAN COLLEGE

Palos Heights, Illinois

Trinity Christian College is a coed, private, Christian Reformed, four-year college, founded in 1959, offering degrees at the bachelor's level and postbachelor's certificates. It has a 53-acre campus in Palos Heights near Chicago.

Academic Information The faculty has 154 members (52% full-time), 34% with terminal degrees. The student-faculty ratio is 12:1. The library holds 75,298 titles, 284 serial subscriptions, and 1,841 audiovisual materials. Special programs include academic remediation, services for learning-disabled students, an honors program, cooperative (work-study) education, study abroad, advanced placement credit, double majors, independent study, part-time degree programs (evenings), adult/continuing education programs, internships, and arrangement for off-campus study with Saint Xavier College, Moraine Valley Community College. The most frequently chosen baccalaureate fields are business/marketing, education, health professions and related sciences.
Student Body Statistics The student body is made up of 1,404 undergraduates (235 freshmen). 70 percent are women and 30 percent are men. Students come from 38 states and territories and 8 other countries. 28 percent are from Illinois. 2 percent are international students.
Expenses for 2008–09 *Application fee:* $20. *Comprehensive fee:* $27,466 includes full-time tuition ($19,936), mandatory fees ($110), and college room and board ($7420). *College room only:* $3970. Room and board charges vary according to board plan. *Part-time tuition:* $664 per semester hour. Part-time tuition varies according to course load.
Financial Aid Forms of aid include need-based and non-need-based scholarships, athletic grants, and part-time jobs. The average aided 2008–09 undergraduate received an aid package worth an estimated $6342. The priority application deadline for financial aid is February 15.
Freshman Admission Trinity Christian College requires an essay, a high school transcript, a minimum 2.0 high school GPA, an interview, SAT or ACT scores, and TOEFL scores for international students. ACT scores are recommended. 1 recommendation is required for some. The application deadline for regular admission is rolling.
Entrance Difficulty Trinity Christian College assesses its entrance difficulty level as moderately difficult. For the fall 2008 freshman class, 94 percent of the applicants were accepted.
For Further Information Contact Mr. Jeremy Klyn, Director of Admissions, Trinity Christian College, 6601 West College Drive, Palos Heights, IL 60463. *Phone:* 708-239-4708 or 800-748-0085 (toll-free). *Fax:* 708-239-4826. *E-mail:* admissions@trnty.edu. *Web site:* http://www.trnty.edu/.

TRINITY COLLEGE OF NURSING AND HEALTH SCIENCES

Rock Island, Illinois

http://www.trinitycollegeqc.edu/

TRINITY INTERNATIONAL UNIVERSITY

Deerfield, Illinois

Trinity International University is a coed, private university, founded in 1897, affiliated with the Evangelical Free Church of America, offering degrees at the bachelor's, master's, doctoral, and first professional levels and postbachelor's certificates. It has a 108-acre campus in Deerfield near Chicago.

Academic Information The faculty has 82 members (52% full-time), 50% with terminal degrees. The undergraduate student-faculty ratio is 12:1. The library holds 266,586 titles and 979 serial subscriptions. Special programs include academic remediation, an honors program, study abroad, advanced placement credit, double majors, independent study, part-time degree programs (daytime, evenings), adult/continuing education programs, internships, and arrangement for off-campus study with 13 members of the Christian College Consortium. The most frequently chosen baccalaureate fields are business/marketing, education, theology and religious vocations.
Student Body Statistics The student body totals 2,671, of whom 968 are undergraduates (134 freshmen). 57 percent are women and 43 percent are men. Students come from 38 states and territories and 19 other countries. 59 percent are from Illinois. 1.1 percent are international students.
Expenses for 2009–10 *Application fee:* $25. *Comprehensive fee:* $29,410 includes full-time tuition ($21,980) and college room and board ($7430). *College room only:* $4050.
Financial Aid Forms of aid include need-based and non-need-based scholarships, athletic grants, and part-time jobs. The average aided 2008–09 undergraduate received an aid package worth an estimated $18,908. The priority application deadline for financial aid is April 1.
Freshman Admission Trinity International University requires an essay, a high school transcript, a minimum 2.5 high school GPA, 1 recommendation, SAT or ACT scores, and TOEFL scores for international students. A minimum 3.0 high school GPA is recommended. An interview is required for some. The application deadline for regular admission is rolling.
Transfer Admission The application deadline for admission is rolling.
Entrance Difficulty Trinity International University assesses its entrance difficulty level as moderately difficult. For the fall 2008 freshman class, 63 percent of the applicants were accepted.
For Further Information Contact Mr. Aaron Mahl, Director of Undergraduate Admissions, Trinity International University, 2065 Half Day Road, Deerfield, IL 60015-1284. *Phone:* 847-317-7000 or 800-822-3225 (toll-free out-of-state). *Fax:* 847-317-8097. *E-mail:* tcadmissions@tiu.edu. *Web site:* http://www.tiu.edu/.

UNIVERSITY OF CHICAGO

Chicago, Illinois

University of Chicago is a coed, private university, founded in 1891, offering degrees at the bachelor's, master's, doctoral, and first professional levels. It has a 211-acre campus in Chicago.

Academic Information The faculty has 1,717 members (64% full-time), 89% with terminal degrees. The undergraduate student-faculty ratio is 6:1. The library holds 7 million titles and 47,000 serial subscriptions. Special programs include study abroad, advanced placement credit, accelerated degree programs, double majors, independent study, self-designed majors, summer session for credit, adult/continuing education programs, internships, and arrangement for off-campus study with Committee on Institutional Cooperation, Associated Colleges of the Midwest. The most frequently chosen baccalaureate fields are biological/life sciences, foreign languages and literature, social sciences.
Student Body Statistics The student body totals 12,787, of whom 5,065 are undergraduates (1,306 freshmen). 50 percent are women and 50 percent are men. Students come from 52 states and territories and 72 other countries. 22 percent are from Illinois. 8.8 percent are international students.
Expenses for 2008–09 *Application fee:* $65. *Comprehensive fee:* $49,329 includes full-time tuition ($36,891), mandatory fees ($741), and college room and board ($11,697). Room and board charges vary according to board plan and housing facility. *Part-time tuition:* varies with course load.
Financial Aid Forms of aid include need-based and non-need-based scholarships and part-time jobs. The priority application deadline for financial aid is February 1.
Freshman Admission University of Chicago requires an essay, a high school transcript, 3 recommendations, SAT or ACT scores, and TOEFL scores for international students. An interview is recommended. The application deadline for regular admission is January 2 and for early action it is November 1.
Transfer Admission The application deadline for admission is March 1.

University of Chicago (continued)

Entrance Difficulty University of Chicago assesses its entrance difficulty level as most difficult. For the fall 2008 freshman class, 28 percent of the applicants were accepted.

For Further Information Contact Mr. Theodore O'Neill, Dean of Admissions, University of Chicago, Rosenwald Hall, 1101 East 58th Street, Suite 105, Chicago, IL 60637-1513. *Phone:* 773-702-8650. *Fax:* 773-702-4199. *E-mail:* questions@phoenix.uchicago.edu. *Web site:* http://www.uchicago.edu/.

UNIVERSITY OF ILLINOIS AT CHICAGO

Chicago, Illinois

University of Illinois at Chicago is a coed, public unit of University of Illinois System, founded in 1946, offering degrees at the bachelor's, master's, doctoral, and first professional levels and post-master's, first professional, and postbachelor's certificates. It has a 240-acre campus in Chicago.

Academic Information The faculty has 1,566 members (77% full-time), 72% with terminal degrees. The undergraduate student-faculty ratio is 15.5:1. The library holds 3 million titles, 44,614 serial subscriptions, and 20,253 audiovisual materials. Special programs include academic remediation, services for learning-disabled students, an honors program, cooperative (work-study) education, study abroad, advanced placement credit, accelerated degree programs, ESL programs, double majors, independent study, distance learning, self-designed majors, summer session for credit, part-time degree programs (daytime, summer), internships, and arrangement for off-campus study with University Center of Lake County. The most frequently chosen baccalaureate fields are business/marketing, biological/life sciences, psychology.

Student Body Statistics The student body totals 25,835, of whom 15,665 are undergraduates (2,964 freshmen). 53 percent are women and 47 percent are men. Students come from 42 states and territories and 49 other countries. 98 percent are from Illinois. 1.5 percent are international students.

Expenses for 2008–09 *Application fee:* $40. *State resident tuition:* $8130 full-time. *Nonresident tuition:* $20,250 full-time. *Mandatory fees:* $3586 full-time. Full-time tuition and fees vary according to program. *College room and board:* $8744. *College room only:* $6144. Room and board charges vary according to board plan and housing facility.

Financial Aid Forms of aid include need-based and non-need-based scholarships, athletic grants, and part-time jobs. The average aided 2007–08 undergraduate received an aid package worth $11,136. The priority application deadline for financial aid is March 1.

Freshman Admission University of Illinois at Chicago requires a high school transcript, SAT or ACT scores, and TOEFL scores for international students. An essay is recommended. The application deadline for regular admission is January 31.

Transfer Admission The application deadline for admission is March 31.

Entrance Difficulty University of Illinois at Chicago assesses its entrance difficulty level as moderately difficult; very difficult for honors program, Guaranteed Professional Program. For the fall 2008 freshman class, 60 percent of the applicants were accepted.

For Further Information Contact Mr. Thomas Glenn, Executive Director of Admissions, University of Illinois at Chicago, 1100 SSB, m/c 018, Chicago, IL 60607-7128. *Phone:* 312-996-4350. *Fax:* 312-996-2953. *E-mail:* uic.admit@uic.edu. *Web site:* http://www.uic.edu/.

UNIVERSITY OF ILLINOIS AT SPRINGFIELD

Springfield, Illinois

University of Illinois at Springfield is a coed, public, comprehensive unit of University of Illinois System, founded in 1969, offering degrees at the bachelor's, master's, and doctoral levels and post-master's and postbachelor's certificates. It has a 746-acre campus in Springfield.

Academic Information The faculty has 352 members (59% full-time), 61% with terminal degrees. The undergraduate student-faculty ratio is 12:1. The library holds 554,122 titles, 46,131 serial subscriptions, and 42,511 audiovisual materials. Special programs include services for learning-disabled students, an honors program, cooperative (work-study) education, study abroad, advanced placement credit, ESL programs, double majors, independent study, distance learning, self-designed majors, summer session for credit, part-time degree programs (daytime, evenings, weekends, summer), internships, and arrangement for off-campus study. The most frequently chosen baccalaureate fields are business/marketing, psychology, security and protective services.

Student Body Statistics The student body totals 4,711, of whom 2,889 are undergraduates (309 freshmen). 56 percent are women and 44 percent are men. Students come from 43 states and territories and 12 other countries. 91 percent are from Illinois. 0.9 percent are international students.

Expenses for 2008–09 *Application fee:* $40. *State resident tuition:* $7215 full-time, $240.50 per credit hour part-time. *Nonresident tuition:* $16,365 full-time, $545.50 per credit hour part-time. *Mandatory fees:* $1854 full-time, $670 per term part-time. *College room and board:* $8840. *College room only:* $6140. Room and board charges vary according to board plan and housing facility.

Financial Aid Forms of aid include need-based scholarships, athletic grants, and part-time jobs. The average aided 2007–08 undergraduate received an aid package worth $9582. The application deadline for financial aid is November 15 with a priority deadline of April 1.

Freshman Admission University of Illinois at Springfield requires an essay, a high school transcript, SAT or ACT scores, and TOEFL scores for international students. The application deadline for regular admission is rolling.

Transfer Admission The application deadline for admission is rolling.

Entrance Difficulty University of Illinois at Springfield assesses its entrance difficulty level as moderately difficult. For the fall 2008 freshman class, 60 percent of the applicants were accepted.

For Further Information Contact Dr. Marya Leatherwood, Associate Vice Chancellor and Director of Enrollment Management, University of Illinois at Springfield, One University Plaza, Room 1015, Springfield, IL 62703. *Phone:* 217-206-6581 or 888-977-4847 (toll-free). *Fax:* 217-206-6048. *E-mail:* admissions@uis.edu. *Web site:* http://www.uis.edu/.

UNIVERSITY OF ILLINOIS AT URBANA–CHAMPAIGN

Champaign, Illinois

University of Illinois at Urbana–Champaign is a coed, public unit of University of Illinois System, founded in 1867, offering degrees at the bachelor's, master's, doctoral, and first professional levels and post-master's and postbachelor's certificates. It has a 1,470-acre campus in Champaign.

Academic Information The faculty has 2,039 members (97% full-time), 92% with terminal degrees. The undergraduate student-faculty ratio is 17:1. The library holds 10 million titles, 63,413 serial subscriptions, and 4,245 audiovisual materials. Special programs include academic remediation, services for learning-disabled students, an honors program, cooperative (work-study) education, study abroad, advanced placement credit, accelerated degree programs, ESL programs, double majors, independent study, distance learning, self-designed majors, summer session for credit, internships, and arrangement for off-campus study with members of the Committee on Institutional Cooperation, Midwest Universities Consortium for International Activities. The most frequently chosen baccalaureate fields are business/marketing, engineering, social sciences.

Student Body Statistics The student body totals 43,246, of whom 31,417 are undergraduates (7,287 freshmen). 46 percent are women and 54 percent are men. Students come from 52 states and territories and 69 other countries. 94 percent are from Illinois. 6.5 percent are international students.

Expenses for 2009–10 *Application fee:* $40. *State resident tuition:* $9242 full-time. *Nonresident tuition:* $23,026 full-time. *Mandatory fees:* $2864 full-time. *College room and board:* $8764.

Financial Aid Forms of aid include need-based and non-need-based scholarships, athletic grants, and part-time jobs. The average aided 2008–09 undergraduate received an aid package worth an estimated $11,029.
Freshman Admission University of Illinois at Urbana–Champaign requires an essay, a high school transcript, SAT or ACT scores, and TOEFL scores for international students. Audition, statement of professional interest is required for some. The application deadline for regular admission is January 2.
Transfer Admission The application deadline for admission is March 1.
Entrance Difficulty University of Illinois at Urbana–Champaign assesses its entrance difficulty level as very difficult. For the fall 2008 freshman class, 69 percent of the applicants were accepted.
For Further Information Contact Mrs. Stacey Kostell, Director of Admissions, University of Illinois at Urbana–Champaign, 901 West Illinois, Urbana, IL 61801. *Phone:* 217-333-0302. *Fax:* 217-244-4614. *E-mail:* ugradadmissions@uiuc.edu. *Web site:* http://www.uiuc.edu/.

UNIVERSITY OF PHOENIX–CHICAGO CAMPUS

Schaumburg, Illinois

University of Phoenix–Chicago Campus is a coed, proprietary, comprehensive institution, founded in 2002, offering degrees at the bachelor's and master's levels.

Academic Information The faculty has 191 members (8% full-time), 19% with terminal degrees. The library holds 16,781 serial subscriptions. Special programs include services for learning-disabled students, advanced placement credit, accelerated degree programs, independent study, distance learning, external degree programs, and adult/continuing education programs. The most frequently chosen baccalaureate fields are business/marketing, computer and information sciences, health professions and related sciences.
Student Body Statistics The student body totals 1,178, of whom 1,025 are undergraduates (164 freshmen). 64 percent are women and 36 percent are men. 3.4 percent are international students.
Expenses for 2008–09 *Application fee:* $0. *Tuition:* $12,000 full-time. Full-time tuition varies according to course level and course load.
Financial Aid Forms of aid include need-based and non-need-based scholarships. The average aided 2007–08 undergraduate received an aid package worth $6221. The application deadline for financial aid is continuous.
Freshman Admission University of Phoenix–Chicago Campus requires 1 recommendation and TOEFL scores for international students. A high school transcript is required for some. The application deadline for regular admission is rolling.
Transfer Admission The application deadline for admission is rolling.
Entrance Difficulty University of Phoenix–Chicago Campus has an open admission policy.
For Further Information Contact Ms. Audra McQuarie, Registrar/ Executive Director, University of Phoenix–Chicago Campus, 4035 South Riverpoint Parkway, Mail Stop CF-L101, Phoenix, AZ 85040-1958. *Phone:* 480-557-6151, 800-776-4867 (toll-free in-state), or 800-228-7240 (toll-free out-of-state). *Fax:* 480-643-3068. *E-mail:* audra.mcquarie@phoenix.edu. *Web site:* http://www.phoenix.edu/.

UNIVERSITY OF ST. FRANCIS

Joliet, Illinois

University of St. Francis is a coed, private, Roman Catholic, comprehensive institution, founded in 1920, offering degrees at the bachelor's and master's levels and post-master's certificates. It has a 22-acre campus in Joliet near Chicago.

Academic Information The faculty has 219 members (38% full-time), 37% with terminal degrees. The undergraduate student-faculty ratio is 13:1. The library holds 117,111 titles, 13,500 serial subscriptions, and 4,500 audiovisual materials. Special programs include academic remediation, services for learning-disabled students, an honors program, study abroad, advanced placement credit, accelerated degree programs, double majors, independent study, distance learning, self-designed majors, summer session for credit, part-time degree programs (daytime, evenings, weekends, summer), external degree programs, adult/continuing education programs, internships, and arrangement for off-campus study. The most frequently chosen baccalaureate fields are education, business/marketing, health professions and related sciences.
Student Body Statistics The student body totals 2,146, of whom 1,273 are undergraduates (203 freshmen). 69 percent are women and 31 percent are men. Students come from 16 states and territories. 96 percent are from Illinois. 1.4 percent are international students.
Expenses for 2008–09 *Application fee:* $30. *Comprehensive fee:* $29,604 includes full-time tuition ($21,450), mandatory fees ($410), and college room and board ($7744). Room and board charges vary according to board plan and housing facility. *Part-time tuition:* $715 per credit hour.
Financial Aid Forms of aid include need-based and non-need-based scholarships, athletic grants, and part-time jobs. The average aided 2008–09 undergraduate received an aid package worth an estimated $16,780. The priority application deadline for financial aid is April 1.
Freshman Admission University of St. Francis requires a high school transcript, a minimum 2.5 high school GPA, SAT or ACT scores, and TOEFL scores for international students. An essay, 2 recommendations, and an interview are required for some. The application deadline for regular admission is August 1.
Entrance Difficulty University of St. Francis assesses its entrance difficulty level as moderately difficult. For the fall 2008 freshman class, 60 percent of the applicants were accepted.
For Further Information Contact Ms. Julie Klinzing, Director of Undergraduate Admissions, University of St. Francis, 500 North Wilcox Street, Joliet, IL 60435-6188. *Phone:* 800-735-7500, 800-735-3500 (toll-free in-state), or 800-735-7500 (toll-free out-of-state). *Fax:* 815-740-5032. *E-mail:* jklinzing@stfrancis.edu. *Web site:* http://www.stfrancis.edu/.

VANDERCOOK COLLEGE OF MUSIC

Chicago, Illinois

VanderCook College of Music is a coed, private, comprehensive institution, founded in 1909, offering degrees at the bachelor's and master's levels. It has a 1-acre campus in Chicago.

For Further Information Contact Director of Undergraduate Admissions, VanderCook College of Music, 3140 South Federal Street, Chicago, IL 60616. *Phone:* 312-225-6288 or 800-448-2655 (toll-free). *Fax:* 312-225-5211. *E-mail:* admissions@vandercook.edu. *Web site:* http://www.vandercook.edu/.

WESTERN ILLINOIS UNIVERSITY

Macomb, Illinois

Western Illinois University is a coed, public, comprehensive institution, founded in 1899, offering degrees at the bachelor's, master's, and doctoral levels and postbachelor's certificates. It has a 1,050-acre campus in Macomb.

Academic Information The faculty has 750 members (89% full-time), 65% with terminal degrees. The undergraduate student-faculty ratio is 16:1. The library holds 998,041 titles and 3,200 serial subscriptions. Special programs include academic remediation, services for learning-disabled students, an honors program, study abroad, advanced placement credit, Freshman Honors College, ESL programs, double majors, independent study, distance learning, self-designed majors, summer session for credit, part-time degree programs (daytime, evenings, weekends, summer), external degree programs, adult/continuing education programs, internships, and arrangement for off-campus study with Western Illinois Education Consortium. The most frequently chosen baccalaureate fields are business/marketing, liberal arts/general studies, security and protective services.
Student Body Statistics The student body totals 13,175, of whom 10,735 are undergraduates (1,816 freshmen). 47 percent are women and 53

Western Illinois University (continued)

percent are men. Students come from 41 states and territories and 55 other countries. 95 percent are from Illinois. 1.3 percent are international students.

Expenses for 2008–09 *Application fee:* $30. *State resident tuition:* $6456 full-time, $215.20 per semester hour part-time. *Nonresident tuition:* $9684 full-time, $322.80 per semester hour part-time. *Mandatory fees:* $1816 full-time, $60.55 per semester hour part-time. Both full-time and part-time tuition and fees vary according to course load, location, and student level. *College room and board:* $7210. *College room only:* $4350. Room and board charges vary according to board plan, housing facility, and student level.

Financial Aid Forms of aid include need-based and non-need-based scholarships, athletic grants, and part-time jobs. The average aided 2008–09 undergraduate received an aid package worth an estimated $9423.

Freshman Admission Western Illinois University requires a high school transcript, a minimum 2.5 high school GPA, SAT or ACT scores, and TOEFL scores for international students. The application deadline for regular admission is May 15.

Transfer Admission The application deadline for admission is rolling.

Entrance Difficulty Western Illinois University assesses its entrance difficulty level as moderately difficult. For the fall 2008 freshman class, 68 percent of the applicants were accepted.

For Further Information Contact Mr. Eric Campbell, Director of Admissions, Western Illinois University, 1 University Circle, 115 Sherman Hall, Macomb, IL 61455-1390. *Phone:* 309-298-3157 or 877-742-5948 (toll-free). *Fax:* 309-298-3111. *E-mail:* admissions@wiu.edu. *Web site:* http://www.wiu.edu/.

WEST SUBURBAN COLLEGE OF NURSING

Oak Park, Illinois

West Suburban College of Nursing is a coed, primarily women's, private, upper-level institution, founded in 1982, offering degrees at the bachelor's and master's levels. It has a 10-acre campus in Oak Park near Chicago.

Academic Information The faculty has 24 members (71% full-time), 17% with terminal degrees. Special programs include academic remediation, advanced placement credit, accelerated degree programs, independent study, summer session for credit, and part-time degree programs (daytime, summer).

Student Body Statistics The student body totals 262, of whom 237 are undergraduates. 83 percent are women and 17 percent are men. Students come from 2 states and territories.

Expenses for 2008–09 *Application fee:* $30. *Tuition:* $20,360 full-time, $690 per credit hour part-time. *Mandatory fees:* $550 full-time, $135 per term part-time.

Transfer Admission The application deadline for admission is February 1.

Entrance Difficulty West Suburban College of Nursing assesses its entrance difficulty level as moderately difficult.

For Further Information Contact Ms. Cynthia Valdez, Director of Enrollment Management, West Suburban College of Nursing, 3 Erie Court, Oak Park, IL 60302. *Phone:* 708-763-6530. *Fax:* 708-763-1531. *Web site:* http://www.wscn.edu/.

WESTWOOD COLLEGE–CHICAGO DU PAGE

Woodridge, Illinois

Westwood College–Chicago Du Page is a coed, proprietary, four-year college, offering degrees at the associate and bachelor's levels. It is located in Woodridge near Chicago.

Student Body Statistics The student body is made up of 519 undergraduates.

Financial Aid Forms of aid include need-based scholarships and part-time jobs. The application deadline for financial aid is continuous.

Freshman Admission Westwood College–Chicago Du Page requires an interview.

For Further Information Contact Director of Admissions, Westwood College–Chicago Du Page, 7155 James Avenue, Woodridge, IL 60517-2321. *Phone:* 630-434-8244 or 888-721-7646 (toll-free in-state). *Fax:* 630-434-8255. *E-mail:* info@westwood.edu. *Web site:* http://www.westwood.edu/.

WESTWOOD COLLEGE–CHICAGO LOOP CAMPUS

Chicago, Illinois

http://www.westwood.edu/

WESTWOOD COLLEGE–CHICAGO O'HARE AIRPORT

Schiller Park, Illinois

http://www.westwood.edu/

WESTWOOD COLLEGE–CHICAGO RIVER OAKS

Calumet City, Illinois

http://www.westwood.edu/

WHEATON COLLEGE

Wheaton, Illinois

Wheaton College is a coed, private, nondenominational, comprehensive institution, founded in 1860, offering degrees at the bachelor's, master's, and doctoral levels and postbachelor's certificates. It has an 80-acre campus in Wheaton near Chicago.

Academic Information The faculty has 300 members (66% full-time), 75% with terminal degrees. The undergraduate student-faculty ratio is 12:1. The library holds 465,822 titles, 5,747 serial subscriptions, and 33,228 audiovisual materials. Special programs include services for learning-disabled students, study abroad, advanced placement credit, double majors, independent study, self-designed majors, summer session for credit, internships, and arrangement for off-campus study with members of the Christian College Consortium, Council for Christian Colleges and Universities. The most frequently chosen baccalaureate fields are social sciences, business/marketing, theology and religious vocations.

Student Body Statistics The student body totals 2,915, of whom 2,366 are undergraduates (581 freshmen). 50 percent are women and 50 percent are men. Students come from 52 states and territories and 18 other countries. 23 percent are from Illinois. 1.3 percent are international students.

Expenses for 2008–09 *Application fee:* $50. *Comprehensive fee:* $33,118 includes full-time tuition ($25,500) and college room and board ($7618). *College room only:* $4524. Full-time tuition varies according to degree level. Room and board charges vary according to board plan and housing facility. *Part-time tuition:* $1063 per credit hour. Part-time tuition varies according to course load and degree level.

Financial Aid Forms of aid include need-based and non-need-based scholarships and part-time jobs. The average aided 2008–09 undergraduate received an aid package worth an estimated $21,185. The priority application deadline for financial aid is February 15.

Freshman Admission Wheaton College requires an essay, a high school transcript, 2 recommendations, SAT or ACT scores, and TOEFL scores for international students. An interview is recommended. The application deadline for regular admission is January 10 and for early action it is November 1.

Transfer Admission The application deadline for admission is March 1.

Entrance Difficulty Wheaton College assesses its entrance difficulty level as very difficult. For the fall 2008 freshman class, 62 percent of the applicants were accepted.
For Further Information Contact Ms. Shawn Leftwich, Director of Admissions, Wheaton College, 501 College Avenue, Wheaton, IL 60187. *Phone:* 630-752-5011 or 800-222-2419 (toll-free out-of-state). *Fax:* 630-752-5285. *E-mail:* admissions@wheaton.edu. *Web site:* http://www.wheaton.edu/.

WORSHAM COLLEGE OF MORTUARY SCIENCE

Wheeling, Illinois

http://www.worshamcollege.com/

Indiana

ANCILLA COLLEGE

Donaldson, Indiana

Ancilla College is a coed, private, Roman Catholic, two-year college, founded in 1937, offering degrees at the associate level. It has a 63-acre campus in Donaldson near Chicago.

Expenses for 2008–09 *Application fee:* $0. *Tuition:* $11,850 full-time, $395 per credit hour part-time. *Mandatory fees:* $230 full-time, $55 per term part-time. Both full-time and part-time tuition and fees vary according to course load and program.
For Further Information Contact Erin Alonzo, Director of Admissions, Ancilla College, 9601 Union Road, Donaldson, IN 46513. *Phone:* 574-936-8898 Ext. 330 or 866-262-4552 Ext. 350 (toll-free in-state). *Fax:* 574-935-1773. *E-mail:* admissions@ancilla.edu. *Web site:* http://www.ancilla.edu/.

ANDERSON UNIVERSITY

Anderson, Indiana

Anderson University is a coed, private, comprehensive institution, founded in 1917, affiliated with the Church of God, offering degrees at the associate, bachelor's, master's, doctoral, and first professional levels. It has a 100-acre campus in Anderson near Indianapolis.

Academic Information The faculty has 315 members (43% full-time), 32% with terminal degrees. The undergraduate student-faculty ratio is 12:1. The library holds 325,133 titles, 698 serial subscriptions, and 5,029 audiovisual materials. Special programs include academic remediation, services for learning-disabled students, an honors program, study abroad, advanced placement credit, accelerated degree programs, double majors, independent study, self-designed majors, summer session for credit, part-time degree programs, adult/continuing education programs, internships, and arrangement for off-campus study. The most frequently chosen baccalaureate fields are business/marketing, education, health professions and related sciences.
Student Body Statistics The student body totals 2,737, of whom 2,154 are undergraduates (544 freshmen). 57 percent are women and 43 percent are men. Students come from 35 states and territories and 26 other countries. 67 percent are from Indiana. 1.8 percent are international students.
Expenses for 2009–10 *Application fee:* $25. *Comprehensive fee:* $30,890 includes full-time tuition ($22,910) and college room and board ($7980). *College room only:* $5100. *Part-time tuition:* $955 per semester hour.
Financial Aid Forms of aid include need-based and non-need-based scholarships and part-time jobs. The priority application deadline for financial aid is March 1.
Freshman Admission Anderson University requires a high school transcript, a minimum 2.0 high school GPA, 2 recommendations, lifestyle statement, and SAT or ACT scores. An essay and TOEFL scores for international students are recommended. An interview is required for some. The application deadline for regular admission is July 1.
Transfer Admission The application deadline for admission is rolling.
Entrance Difficulty Anderson University assesses its entrance difficulty level as moderately difficult. For the fall 2008 freshman class, 68 percent of the applicants were accepted.
For Further Information Contact Mr. Jim King, Director of Admissions, Anderson University, 1100 East 5th Street, Anderson, IN 46012-3495. *Phone:* 765-641-4080, 800-421-3014 (toll-free in-state), or 800-428-6414 (toll-free out-of-state). *Fax:* 765-641-3851. *E-mail:* info@anderson.edu. *Web site:* http://www.anderson.edu/.

THE ART INSTITUTE OF INDIANAPOLIS

Indianapolis, Indiana

The Art Institute of Indianapolis is a coed, proprietary, four-year college of Education Management Corporation, offering degrees at the associate and bachelor's levels.

Expenses for 2009–10 Tuition cost varies by program. Prospective students should contact the school for current tuition costs. Other charges include a starting kit for all first-quarter students. Kits vary in price, depending on the program of study.
For Further Information Contact Director of Admissions, The Art Institute of Indianapolis, 3500 Depauw Boulevard, Suite 1010, Indianapolis, IN 46268-6124. *Phone:* 317-613-4821. *Fax:* 317-613-4808. *Web site:* http://www.artinstitutes.edu/indianapolis/.

BALL STATE UNIVERSITY

Muncie, Indiana

Ball State University is a coed, public university, founded in 1918, offering degrees at the associate, bachelor's, master's, and doctoral levels and post-master's and postbachelor's certificates. It has a 955-acre campus in Muncie near Indianapolis.

Academic Information The faculty has 1,173 members (79% full-time), 64% with terminal degrees. The undergraduate student-faculty ratio is 16:1. The library holds 1 million titles, 3,243 serial subscriptions, and 456,126 audiovisual materials. Special programs include academic remediation, an honors program, cooperative (work-study) education, study abroad, advanced placement credit, accelerated degree programs, Freshman Honors College, ESL programs, double majors, independent study, distance learning, summer session for credit, part-time degree programs, external degree programs, adult/continuing education programs, and internships. The most frequently chosen baccalaureate fields are business/marketing, education, liberal arts/general studies.
Student Body Statistics The student body totals 20,243, of whom 16,832 are undergraduates (4,039 freshmen). 52 percent are women and 48 percent are men. Students come from 49 states and territories and 47 other countries. 93 percent are from Indiana.
Expenses for 2008–09 *Application fee:* $25. *State resident tuition:* $7000 full-time, $269 per credit hour part-time. *Nonresident tuition:* $18,804 full-time, $692 per credit hour part-time. *Mandatory fees:* $500 full-time. Full-time tuition and fees vary according to course level and reciprocity agreements. Part-time tuition varies according to course level and course load. *College room and board:* $7598. Room and board charges vary according to board plan and housing facility.
Financial Aid Forms of aid include need-based and non-need-based scholarships, athletic grants, and part-time jobs. The average aided 2008–09 undergraduate received an aid package worth an estimated $9346.
Freshman Admission Ball State University requires a high school transcript and TOEFL scores for international students. An essay, an interview, and SAT or ACT scores are required for some. The application deadline for regular admission is August 15.
Transfer Admission The application deadline for admission is rolling.

Ball State University (continued)

Entrance Difficulty Ball State University assesses its entrance difficulty level as moderately difficult; very difficult for architecture program. For the fall 2008 freshman class, 73 percent of the applicants were accepted.
For Further Information Contact Mr. Christopher Munchel, Associate Director of Admissions and Orientation, Ball State University, 2000 University Avenue, Muncie, IN 47306. *Phone:* 765-285-8300 or 800-482-4BSU (toll-free). *Fax:* 765-285-1632. *E-mail:* askus@bsu.edu. *Web site:* http://www.bsu.edu/.

BETHEL COLLEGE

Mishawaka, Indiana

Bethel College is a coed, private, comprehensive institution, founded in 1947, affiliated with the Missionary Church, offering degrees at the associate, bachelor's, and master's levels and postbachelor's certificates. It has a 70-acre campus in Mishawaka.

Academic Information The faculty has 220 members (43% full-time), 29% with terminal degrees. The undergraduate student-faculty ratio is 12:1. The library holds 118,393 titles, 1,496 serial subscriptions, and 2,962 audiovisual materials. Special programs include academic remediation, study abroad, advanced placement credit, accelerated degree programs, double majors, independent study, self-designed majors, summer session for credit, part-time degree programs (daytime, evenings, summer), adult/continuing education programs, internships, and arrangement for off-campus study with Northern Indiana Consortium for Education, Coalition for Christian Colleges and Universities. The most frequently chosen baccalaureate fields are business/marketing, education, health professions and related sciences.
Student Body Statistics The student body totals 2,075, of whom 1,862 are undergraduates (277 freshmen). 66 percent are women and 34 percent are men. Students come from 32 states and territories and 23 other countries. 76 percent are from Indiana. 2.1 percent are international students.
Expenses for 2009–10 *Application fee:* $25. *One-time mandatory fee:* $600. *Comprehensive fee:* $27,232 includes full-time tuition ($21,296) and college room and board ($5936). *College room only:* $3100. *Part-time tuition:* $480 per credit hour.
Financial Aid Forms of aid include need-based and non-need-based scholarships, athletic grants, and part-time jobs. The average aided 2008–09 undergraduate received an aid package worth an estimated $15,174. The priority application deadline for financial aid is March 1.
Freshman Admission Bethel College requires an essay, a high school transcript, a minimum 2.0 high school GPA, 1 recommendation, SAT or ACT scores, and TOEFL scores for international students. A minimum 2.5 high school GPA and an interview are recommended. The application deadline for regular admission is August 6.
Transfer Admission The application deadline for admission is August 6.
Entrance Difficulty Bethel College assesses its entrance difficulty level as minimally difficult. For the fall 2008 freshman class, 82 percent of the applicants were accepted.
For Further Information Contact Krista Wong, Director of Admission, Bethel College, 1001 Bethel Circle, Mishwawaka, IN 46545. *Phone:* 574-807-7600 or 800-422-4101 (toll-free). *Fax:* 574-807-7650. *E-mail:* admissions@bethelcollege.edu. *Web site:* http://www.bethelcollege.edu.

BROWN MACKIE COLLEGE–FORT WAYNE

Fort Wayne, Indiana

Brown Mackie College–Fort Wayne is a coed, proprietary, primarily two-year college of Education Management Corporation, offering degrees at the associate and bachelor's levels.

Expenses for 2009–10 Tuition varies by program. Students should contact Brown Mackie College for tuition information.
For Further Information Contact Director of Admissions, Brown Mackie College–Fort Wayne, 3000 East Coliseum Boulevard, Ft. Wayne, IN 46805. *Phone:* 260-484-4400 or 866-433-2289 (toll-free). *Fax:* 260-484-2678. *Web site:* http://www.brownmackie.edu/fortwayne.

BROWN MACKIE COLLEGE–INDIANAPOLIS

Indianapolis, Indiana

Brown Mackie College–Indianapolis is a coed, proprietary, primarily two-year college of Education Management Corporation, offering degrees at the associate and bachelor's levels.

Expenses for 2009–10 Tuition varies by program. Students should contact Brown Mackie College for tuition information.
For Further Information Contact Director of Admissions, Brown Mackie College–Indianapolis, 1200 North Meridian Street, Suite 100, Indianapolis, IN 46204. *Phone:* 317-554-8301 or 866-255-0279 (toll-free). *Fax:* 317-632-4557. *Web site:* http://www.brownmackie.edu/Indianapolis/.

BROWN MACKIE COLLEGE–MERRILLVILLE

Merrillville, Indiana

Brown Mackie College–Merrillville is a coed, proprietary, primarily two-year college of Education Management Corporation, founded in 1890, offering degrees at the associate and bachelor's levels.

Expenses for 2009–10 Tuition varies by program. Students should contact Brown Mackie College for tuition information.
For Further Information Contact Director of Admissions, Brown Mackie College–Merrillville, 1000 East 80th Place, Suite 101N, Merrillville, IN 46410. *Phone:* 219-769-3321 or 800-258-3321 (toll-free). *Fax:* 219-738-1076. *Web site:* http://www.brownmackie.edu/Merrillville.

BROWN MACKIE COLLEGE–MICHIGAN CITY

Michigan City, Indiana

Brown Mackie College–Michigan City is a coed, proprietary, primarily two-year college of Education Management Corporation, offering degrees at the associate and bachelor's levels.

Expenses for 2009–10 Tuition varies by program. Students should contact Brown Mackie College for tuition information.
For Further Information Contact Director of Admissions, Brown Mackie College–Michigan City, 325 East U.S. Highway 20, Michigan City, IN 46360. *Phone:* 219-877-3100 or 800-519-2416 (toll-free). *Fax:* 219-877-3110. *Web site:* http://www.brownmackie.edu/MichiganCity.

BROWN MACKIE COLLEGE–SOUTH BEND

South Bend, Indiana

Brown Mackie College–South Bend is a coed, proprietary, primarily two-year college of Education Management Corporation, founded in 1882, offering degrees at the associate and bachelor's levels.

Expenses for 2009–10 Tuition varies by program. Students should contact Brown Mackie College for tuition information.
For Further Information Contact Director of Admissions, Brown Mackie College–South Bend, 1030 East Jefferson Boulevard, South Bend, IN 46617. *Phone:* 574-237-0774 or 800-743-2447 (toll-free). *Fax:* 571-237-3585. *Web site:* http://www.brownmackie.edu/SouthBend.

BUTLER UNIVERSITY

Indianapolis, Indiana

Butler University is a coed, private, comprehensive institution, founded in 1855, offering degrees at the associate, bachelor's, master's, and first professional levels. It has a 290-acre campus in Indianapolis.

Academic Information The faculty has 461 members (66% full-time), 61% with terminal degrees. The undergraduate student-faculty ratio is

11:1. The library holds 361,690 titles, 25,965 serial subscriptions, and 16,359 audiovisual materials. Special programs include services for learning-disabled students, an honors program, cooperative (work-study) education, study abroad, advanced placement credit, double majors, independent study, self-designed majors, summer session for credit, part-time degree programs (daytime, evenings, summer), adult/continuing education programs, internships, and arrangement for off-campus study with 6 members of the Consortium for Urban Education. The most frequently chosen baccalaureate fields are business/marketing, education, health professions and related sciences.
Student Body Statistics The student body totals 4,438, of whom 3,639 are undergraduates (934 freshmen). 61 percent are women and 39 percent are men. Students come from 44 states and territories and 69 other countries. 59 percent are from Indiana. 3.2 percent are international students.
Expenses for 2008–09 *Application fee:* $35. *Comprehensive fee:* $37,676 includes full-time tuition ($27,500), mandatory fees ($766), and college room and board ($9410). *College room only:* $4610. Full-time tuition and fees vary according to course load, degree level, and program. Room and board charges vary according to housing facility. *Part-time tuition:* $1150 per credit. Part-time tuition varies according to course load, degree level, and program.
Financial Aid Forms of aid include need-based and non-need-based scholarships, athletic grants, and part-time jobs. The average aided 2008–09 undergraduate received an aid package worth an estimated $19,880. The priority application deadline for financial aid is March 1.
Freshman Admission Butler University requires an essay, a high school transcript, SAT or ACT scores, and TOEFL scores for international students. An interview and audition are required for some. The application deadline for regular admission is rolling and for early action it is December 1.
Transfer Admission The application deadline for admission is August 15.
Entrance Difficulty Butler University assesses its entrance difficulty level as moderately difficult. For the fall 2008 freshman class, 72 percent of the applicants were accepted.
For Further Information Contact Mr. Scott McIntyre, Director of Admissions, Butler University, 4600 Sunset Avenue, Indianapolis, IN 46208-3485. *Phone:* 317-940-8100 or 888-940-8100 (toll-free). *Fax:* 317-940-8150. *E-mail:* admission@butler.edu. *Web site:* http://www.butler.edu/.

CALUMET COLLEGE OF SAINT JOSEPH

Whiting, Indiana

Calumet College of Saint Joseph is a coed, private, Roman Catholic, comprehensive institution, founded in 1951, offering degrees at the associate, bachelor's, and master's levels and postbachelor's certificates. It has a 25-acre campus in Whiting near Chicago.

Academic Information The faculty has 116 members (25% full-time), 36% with terminal degrees. The undergraduate student-faculty ratio is 13:1. The library holds 110,000 titles, 4,000 serial subscriptions, and 1,000 audiovisual materials. Special programs include academic remediation, services for learning-disabled students, cooperative (work-study) education, advanced placement credit, accelerated degree programs, double majors, independent study, distance learning, summer session for credit, part-time degree programs (daytime, evenings, weekends), external degree programs, adult/continuing education programs, and internships. The most frequently chosen baccalaureate fields are business/marketing, education, security and protective services.
Student Body Statistics The student body totals 1,213, of whom 1,102 are undergraduates (147 freshmen). 52 percent are women and 48 percent are men. Students come from 2 states and territories. 0.2 percent are international students.
Expenses for 2008–09 *Application fee:* $0. *Tuition:* $12,300 full-time, $385 per credit hour part-time. *Mandatory fees:* $160 full-time, $80 per term part-time.
Financial Aid Forms of aid include need-based and non-need-based scholarships, athletic grants, and part-time jobs. The average aided 2008–09 undergraduate received an aid package worth an estimated $15,696. The priority application deadline for financial aid is March 1.
Freshman Admission Calumet College of Saint Joseph requires a high school transcript and TOEFL scores for international students. A minimum 2.0 high school GPA, an interview, and SAT or ACT scores are recommended. An essay, an interview, and ACT COMPASS are required for some. The application deadline for regular admission is rolling.
Transfer Admission The application deadline for admission is rolling.
Entrance Difficulty Calumet College of Saint Joseph assesses its entrance difficulty level as noncompetitive. For the fall 2008 freshman class, 63 percent of the applicants were accepted.
For Further Information Contact Mr. Chuck Walz, Director of Admissions, Calumet College of Saint Joseph, 2400 New York Avenue, Whiting, IN 46394. *Phone:* 219-473-4215 Ext. 379 or 877-700-9100 (toll-free). *Fax:* 219-473-4259. *E-mail:* admissions@ccsj.edu. *Web site:* http://www.ccsj.edu/.

CROSSROADS BIBLE COLLEGE

Indianapolis, Indiana

Crossroads Bible College is a coed, private, Baptist, four-year college, founded in 1980, offering degrees at the associate and bachelor's levels. It has a 6-acre campus in Indianapolis.

Academic Information Special programs include services for learning-disabled students, accelerated degree programs, double majors, independent study, distance learning, summer session for credit, part-time degree programs (daytime, evenings, summer), external degree programs, adult/continuing education programs, and internships.
Student Body Statistics The student body is made up of 228 undergraduates.
Financial Aid Forms of aid include need-based and non-need-based scholarships and part-time jobs. The average aided 2007–08 undergraduate received an aid package worth $1100. The application deadline for financial aid is June 30 with a priority deadline of May 31.
Freshman Admission Crossroads Bible College requires an essay, a high school transcript, and recommendations. SAT and SAT Subject Test or ACT scores are recommended. An interview is required for some. The application deadline for regular admission is August 8.
Transfer Admission The application deadline for admission is August 8.
Entrance Difficulty Crossroads Bible College has an open admission policy.
For Further Information Contact Tiffany Powell, Director of Admissions, Crossroads Bible College, 601 North Shortridge Road, Indianapolis, IN 46219. *Phone:* 317-352-8736 or 800-273-2224 Ext. 230 (toll-free). *Fax:* 317-352-9145. *E-mail:* admissions@crossroads.edu. *Web site:* http://www.crossroads.edu/.

DEPAUW UNIVERSITY

Greencastle, Indiana

DePauw University is a coed, private, four-year college, founded in 1837, affiliated with the United Methodist Church, offering degrees at the bachelor's level. It has a 655-acre campus in Greencastle near Indianapolis.

Academic Information The faculty has 281 members (77% full-time), 89% with terminal degrees. The student-faculty ratio is 10:1. The library holds 333,346 titles, 2,030 serial subscriptions, and 22,491 audiovisual materials. Special programs include services for learning-disabled students, an honors program, study abroad, advanced placement credit, double majors, independent study, self-designed majors, part-time degree programs (daytime, evenings), internships, and arrangement for off-campus study with Great Lakes Colleges Association.
Student Body Statistics The student body is made up of 2,298 undergraduates (600 freshmen). 57 percent are women and 43 percent are men. Students come from 43 states and territories and 32 other countries. 45 percent are from Indiana. 5.2 percent are international students.
Expenses for 2008–09 *Application fee:* $40. *Comprehensive fee:* $40,225 includes full-time tuition ($31,400), mandatory fees ($425), and college room and board ($8400). *College room only:* $4400. Room and board charges vary according to board plan. *Part-time tuition:* $3925 per credit hour.
Financial Aid Forms of aid include need-based and non-need-based scholarships and part-time jobs. The average aided 2008–09 undergraduate received an aid package worth an estimated $25,910. The application deadline for financial aid is February 15.

DePauw University (continued)

Freshman Admission DePauw University requires an essay, a high school transcript, 1 recommendation, and SAT or ACT scores. An interview and TOEFL scores for international students are recommended. The application deadline for regular admission is February 1, for early decision it is November 1, and for early action it is December 1.
Transfer Admission The application deadline for admission is March 1.
Entrance Difficulty DePauw University assesses its entrance difficulty level as moderately difficult. For the fall 2008 freshman class, 65 percent of the applicants were accepted.
For Further Information Contact Brett Kennedy, Senior Associate Director of Admission, DePauw University, 101 East Seminary Street, Greencastle, IN 46135-0037. *Phone:* 765-658-4006 or 800-447-2495 (toll-free). *Fax:* 765-658-4007. *E-mail:* admission@depauw.edu. *Web site:* http://www.depauw.edu/.

DeVRY UNIVERSITY

Indianapolis, Indiana

DeVry University is a coed, proprietary, comprehensive unit of DeVry University, offering degrees at the associate, bachelor's, and master's levels.

Academic Information The faculty has 31 members. The undergraduate student-faculty ratio is 14:1. Special programs include academic remediation, services for learning-disabled students, advanced placement credit, accelerated degree programs, distance learning, summer session for credit, part-time degree programs (daytime, evenings, weekends, summer), and adult/continuing education programs. The most frequently chosen baccalaureate fields are business/marketing, computer and information sciences.
Student Body Statistics The student body totals 302, of whom 184 are undergraduates (25 freshmen). 53 percent are women and 47 percent are men. 96 percent are from Indiana. 0.5 percent are international students.
Expenses for 2009–10 *Application fee:* $50. *Tuition:* $14,080 full-time, $550 per credit hour part-time.
Financial Aid Forms of aid include need-based scholarships and part-time jobs. The average aided 2007–08 undergraduate received an aid package worth $14,132.
Freshman Admission DeVry University requires a high school transcript and an interview. The application deadline for regular admission is rolling.
Transfer Admission The application deadline for admission is rolling.
Entrance Difficulty DeVry University assesses its entrance difficulty level as minimally difficult; moderately difficult for Electronics Engineering Technology Program.
For Further Information Contact Admissions Office, DeVry University, 9100 Keystone Crossing, Suite 350, Indianapolis, IN 46240-2158. *Phone:* 317-581-8854. *Web site:* http://www.devry.edu/.

DeVRY UNIVERSITY

Merrillville, Indiana

http://www.devry.edu/

EARLHAM COLLEGE

Richmond, Indiana

Earlham College is a coed, private, comprehensive institution, founded in 1847, affiliated with the Society of Friends, offering degrees at the bachelor's, master's, and first professional levels. It has an 800-acre campus in Richmond near Cincinnati, Indianapolis, and Dayton.

Academic Information The faculty has 104 members (90% full-time), 92% with terminal degrees. The undergraduate student-faculty ratio is 12:1. The library holds 406,316 titles, 22,439 serial subscriptions, and 7,951 audiovisual materials. Special programs include services for learning-disabled students, study abroad, advanced placement credit, accelerated degree programs, ESL programs, double majors, independent study, self-designed majors, internships, and arrangement for off-campus study with members of the Great Lakes Colleges Association. The most frequently chosen baccalaureate fields are biological/life sciences, interdisciplinary studies, social sciences.
Student Body Statistics The student body totals 1,308, of whom 1,184 are undergraduates (324 freshmen). 56 percent are women and 44 percent are men. Students come from 44 states and territories and 71 other countries. 32 percent are from Indiana. 12.7 percent are international students.
Expenses for 2008–09 *Application fee:* $0. *Comprehensive fee:* $40,844 includes full-time tuition ($33,274), mandatory fees ($756), and college room and board ($6814). *College room only:* $3424. Room and board charges vary according to board plan. *Part-time tuition:* $1109 per credit.
Financial Aid Forms of aid include need-based scholarships and part-time jobs. The average aided 2007–08 undergraduate received an aid package worth $24,146. The priority application deadline for financial aid is March 1.
Freshman Admission Earlham College requires an essay, a high school transcript, a minimum 3.0 high school GPA, 2 recommendations, SAT or ACT scores, and TOEFL scores for international students. An interview is recommended. The application deadline for regular admission is February 15, for early decision it is December 1, and for early action it is January 1.
Transfer Admission The application deadline for admission is April 1.
Entrance Difficulty Earlham College assesses its entrance difficulty level as very difficult. For the fall 2008 freshman class, 75 percent of the applicants were accepted.
For Further Information Contact Mr. Jeff Rickey, Dean of Admissions and Financial Aid, Earlham College, 801 National Road West, Richmond, IN 47374. *Phone:* 765-983-1600 or 800-327-5426 (toll-free). *Fax:* 765-983-1560. *E-mail:* admission@earlham.edu. *Web site:* http://www.earlham.edu/.

FRANKLIN COLLEGE

Franklin, Indiana

Franklin College is a coed, private, four-year college, founded in 1834, affiliated with the American Baptist Churches in the U.S.A., offering degrees at the bachelor's level. It has a 74-acre campus in Franklin near Indianapolis.

Academic Information The faculty has 105 members (66% full-time), 61% with terminal degrees. The student-faculty ratio is 12.4:1. The library holds 25,434 titles, 292 serial subscriptions, and 7,669 audiovisual materials. Special programs include academic remediation, services for learning-disabled students, cooperative (work-study) education, study abroad, advanced placement credit, double majors, independent study, summer session for credit, part-time degree programs (daytime, summer), internships, and arrangement for off-campus study with Marian College, University of Indianapolis, Indiana University-Purdue University at Indianapolis, Butler University, Martin University, Ivy Tech State College. The most frequently chosen baccalaureate fields are communications/journalism, biological/life sciences, education.
Student Body Statistics The student body is made up of 1,153 undergraduates (362 freshmen). 52 percent are women and 48 percent are men. Students come from 13 states and territories and 3 other countries. 97 percent are from Indiana.
Expenses for 2008–09 *Application fee:* $30. *Comprehensive fee:* $29,085 includes full-time tuition ($22,270), mandatory fees ($175), and college room and board ($6640). *College room only:* $3940. Room and board charges vary according to board plan and housing facility. *Part-time tuition:* $310 per credit hour. Part-time tuition varies according to course load.
Financial Aid Forms of aid include need-based and non-need-based scholarships and part-time jobs. The average aided 2007–08 undergraduate received an aid package worth $16,564. The application deadline for financial aid is March 1.
Freshman Admission Franklin College requires an essay, a high school transcript, SAT or ACT scores, and TOEFL scores for international students. An interview is required for some. The application deadline for regular admission is rolling.

Entrance Difficulty Franklin College assesses its entrance difficulty level as moderately difficult. For the fall 2008 freshman class, 66 percent of the applicants were accepted.
For Further Information Contact Ms. Jacqueline Acosta, Director of Admissions, Franklin College, 101 Branigin Boulevard, Franklin, IN 46131-2623. *Phone:* 317-738-8062 or 800-852-0232 (toll-free). *Fax:* 317-738-8274. *E-mail:* jacosta@franklincollege.edu. *Web site:* http://www.franklincollege.edu/.

GOSHEN COLLEGE

Goshen, Indiana

Goshen College is a coed, private, Mennonite, comprehensive institution, founded in 1894, offering degrees at the bachelor's and master's levels. It has a 135-acre campus in Goshen.

Academic Information The faculty has 114 members (59% full-time), 47% with terminal degrees. The undergraduate student-faculty ratio is 10.6:1. The library holds 137,000 titles, 350 serial subscriptions, and 2,948 audiovisual materials. Special programs include academic remediation, services for learning-disabled students, an honors program, advanced placement credit, accelerated degree programs, Freshman Honors College, double majors, independent study, self-designed majors, summer session for credit, part-time degree programs, internships, and arrangement for off-campus study with Northern Indiana Consortium for Education. The most frequently chosen baccalaureate fields are business/marketing, education, health professions and related sciences.
Student Body Statistics The student body totals 958, of whom 930 are undergraduates (174 freshmen). 60 percent are women and 40 percent are men. Students come from 34 states and territories and 27 other countries. 46 percent are from Indiana. 5.1 percent are international students.
Expenses for 2009–10 *Application fee:* $25. *Comprehensive fee:* $31,300 includes full-time tuition ($23,400) and college room and board ($7900). *College room only:* $4150. *Part-time tuition:* $890 per credit hour.
Financial Aid Forms of aid include need-based and non-need-based scholarships, athletic grants, and part-time jobs. The priority application deadline for financial aid is February 15.
Freshman Admission Goshen College requires an essay, a high school transcript, a minimum 2.0 high school GPA, 2 recommendations, SAT or ACT scores, and TOEFL scores for international students. A minimum 2.6 high school GPA, an interview, and rank in upper 50% of high school class are recommended. The application deadline for regular admission is August 15.
Transfer Admission The application deadline for admission is August 15.
Entrance Difficulty Goshen College assesses its entrance difficulty level as moderately difficult. For the fall 2008 freshman class, 63 percent of the applicants were accepted.
For Further Information Contact Ms. Lynn Jackson, Vice President for Enrollment Management, Goshen College, 1700 South Main Street, Goshen, IN 46526-4794. *Phone:* 574-535-7535 or 800-348-7422 (toll-free). *Fax:* 574-535-7609. *E-mail:* lynnj@goshen.edu. *Web site:* http://www.goshen.edu/.

GRACE COLLEGE

Winona Lake, Indiana

Grace College is a coed, private, comprehensive institution, founded in 1948, affiliated with the Fellowship of Grace Brethren Churches, offering degrees at the associate, bachelor's, master's, doctoral, and first professional levels. It has a 160-acre campus in Winona Lake.

Academic Information The faculty has 110 members (48% full-time), 40% with terminal degrees. The undergraduate student-faculty ratio is 17:1. The library holds 156,637 titles, 23,972 serial subscriptions, and 3,806 audiovisual materials. Special programs include academic remediation, services for learning-disabled students, an honors program, cooperative (work-study) education, study abroad, advanced placement credit, accelerated degree programs, double majors, independent study, distance learning, summer session for credit, part-time degree programs (daytime, evenings, summer), adult/continuing education programs, internships, and arrangement for off-campus study with Coalition for Christian Colleges and Universities. The most frequently chosen baccalaureate fields are business/marketing, education, psychology.
Student Body Statistics The student body totals 1,508, of whom 1,332 are undergraduates (327 freshmen). 50 percent are women and 50 percent are men. Students come from 34 states and territories and 5 other countries. 61 percent are from Indiana. 0.2 percent are international students.
Expenses for 2008–09 *Application fee:* $30. *Comprehensive fee:* $27,024 includes full-time tuition ($20,376) and college room and board ($6648). Room and board charges vary according to board plan and housing facility. *Part-time tuition:* $450 per credit hour. Part-time tuition varies according to course load.
Financial Aid Forms of aid include need-based and non-need-based scholarships, athletic grants, and part-time jobs. The average aided 2007–08 undergraduate received an aid package worth $14,540. The priority application deadline for financial aid is March 10.
Freshman Admission Grace College requires an essay, a high school transcript, a minimum 2.3 high school GPA, 2 recommendations, personal statement of faith, SAT or ACT scores, and TOEFL scores for international students. An interview is required for some. The application deadline for regular admission is August 1 and for early action it is December 1.
Transfer Admission The application deadline for admission is August 1.
Entrance Difficulty Grace College assesses its entrance difficulty level as moderately difficult. For the fall 2008 freshman class, 96 percent of the applicants were accepted.
For Further Information Contact Admissions Office, Grace College, 200 Seminary Drive, Winona Lake, IN 46590. *Phone:* 574-372-5100 Ext. 6008, 800-54-GRACE Ext. 6412 (toll-free in-state), or 800-54 GRACE Ext. 6412 (toll-free out-of-state). *Fax:* 574-372-5120. *E-mail:* enroll@grace.edu. *Web site:* http://www.grace.edu/.

HANOVER COLLEGE

Hanover, Indiana

Hanover College is a coed, private, Presbyterian, four-year college, founded in 1827, offering degrees at the bachelor's level. It has a 630-acre campus in Hanover near Louisville.

Academic Information The faculty has 95 members (96% full-time), 98% with terminal degrees. The student-faculty ratio is 10:1. The library holds 224,478 titles, 1,035 serial subscriptions, and 5,080 audiovisual materials. Special programs include services for learning-disabled students, study abroad, advanced placement credit, double majors, independent study, self-designed majors, internships, and arrangement for off-campus study with 8 members of the Spring Term Consortium. The most frequently chosen baccalaureate fields are psychology, social sciences, visual and performing arts.
Student Body Statistics The student body is made up of 926 undergraduates (328 freshmen). 55 percent are women and 45 percent are men. Students come from 25 states and territories and 13 other countries. 65 percent are from Indiana. 3 percent are international students.
Expenses for 2008–09 *Application fee:* $40. *One-time mandatory fee:* $250. *Comprehensive fee:* $32,720 includes full-time tuition ($24,700), mandatory fees ($520), and college room and board ($7500). *College room only:* $3650. Full-time tuition and fees vary according to reciprocity agreements. Room and board charges vary according to housing facility and location. *Part-time tuition:* $2740 per unit. Part-time tuition varies according to course load and reciprocity agreements.
Financial Aid Forms of aid include need-based and non-need-based scholarships. The average aided 2008–09 undergraduate received an aid package worth an estimated $20,946.
Freshman Admission Hanover College requires an essay, a high school transcript, 1 recommendation, SAT or ACT scores, and TOEFL scores for international students. An interview is recommended. The application deadline for regular admission is March 1 and for early action it is December 1.
Transfer Admission The application deadline for admission is rolling.

Hanover College (continued)

Entrance Difficulty Hanover College assesses its entrance difficulty level as moderately difficult. For the fall 2008 freshman class, 67 percent of the applicants were accepted.
For Further Information Contact Mr. Chris Gage, Director of Admission, Hanover College, PO Box 108, Hanover, IN 47243-0108. *Phone:* 812-866-7021 or 800-213-2178 (toll-free). *Fax:* 812-866-7098. *E-mail:* admission@hanover.edu. *Web site:* http://www.hanover.edu/.

HOLY CROSS COLLEGE

Notre Dame, Indiana

http://www.hcc-nd.edu/

HUNTINGTON UNIVERSITY

Huntington, Indiana

Huntington University is a coed, private, comprehensive institution, founded in 1897, affiliated with the Church of the United Brethren in Christ, offering degrees at the associate, bachelor's, and master's levels and postbachelor's certificates. It has a 170-acre campus in Huntington near Fort Wayne.

Academic Information The faculty has 92 members (64% full-time), 57% with terminal degrees. The undergraduate student-faculty ratio is 13:1. The library holds 176,744 titles. Special programs include academic remediation, services for learning-disabled students, study abroad, advanced placement credit, double majors, independent study, summer session for credit, part-time degree programs, adult/continuing education programs, internships, and arrangement for off-campus study with Saint Francis College (IN). The most frequently chosen baccalaureate fields are business/marketing, education, theology and religious vocations.
Student Body Statistics The student body totals 1,211, of whom 978 are undergraduates (277 freshmen). 55 percent are women and 45 percent are men. Students come from 37 states and territories and 17 other countries. 51 percent are from Indiana. 3.3 percent are international students.
Expenses for 2008–09 *Application fee:* $20. *Comprehensive fee:* $27,240 includes full-time tuition ($19,840), mandatory fees ($460), and college room and board ($6940). Full-time tuition and fees vary according to program. Room and board charges vary according to board plan. *Part-time tuition:* $590 per semester hour. *Part-time mandatory fees:* $160 per term. Part-time tuition and fees vary according to program.
Financial Aid Forms of aid include need-based and non-need-based scholarships, athletic grants, and part-time jobs. The average aided 2008–09 undergraduate received an aid package worth an estimated $15,322. The priority application deadline for financial aid is March 1.
Freshman Admission Huntington University requires an essay, a high school transcript, a minimum 2.3 high school GPA, SAT or ACT scores, and TOEFL scores for international students. An interview is recommended. The application deadline for regular admission is August 1.
Transfer Admission The application deadline for admission is rolling.
Entrance Difficulty Huntington University assesses its entrance difficulty level as moderately difficult. For the fall 2008 freshman class, 88 percent of the applicants were accepted.
For Further Information Contact Mr. Jeff Berggren, Vice President of Enrollment Management and Marketing, Huntington University, 2303 College Avenue, Huntington, IN 46750-1299. *Phone:* 260-356-6000 Ext. 4016 or 800-642-6493 (toll-free). *Fax:* 260-356-9448. *E-mail:* admissions@huntington.edu. *Web site:* http://www.huntington.edu/.

INDIANA BUSINESS COLLEGE

Evansville, Indiana

Indiana Business College is a coed, proprietary, primarily two-year college, offering degrees at the associate and bachelor's levels.

For Further Information Contact Ms. Starlet Gupton, Indiana Business College, 4601 Theater Drive, Evansville, IN 47715. *Phone:* 812-476-6000 or 800-IBC-GRAD (toll-free in-state). *Fax:* 812-471-8576. *E-mail:* starlet.gupton@ibcschools.edu. *Web site:* http://www.ibcschools.edu/.

INDIANA BUSINESS COLLEGE

Fort Wayne, Indiana

Indiana Business College is a coed, proprietary, primarily two-year college, offering degrees at the associate and bachelor's levels.

For Further Information Contact Mr. Matt Wallace, Associate Director of Admissions, Indiana Business College, 6413 North Clinton Street, Fort Wayne, IN 46825. *Phone:* 260-471-7667. *Fax:* 260-471-6918. *E-mail:* matt.wallace@ibcschools.edu. *Web site:* http://www.ibcschools.edu/.

INDIANA BUSINESS COLLEGE

Indianapolis, Indiana

Indiana Business College is a coed, proprietary, primarily two-year college, founded in 1902, offering degrees at the associate and bachelor's levels. It has a 1-acre campus in Indianapolis.

For Further Information Contact Mr. Ted Lukomski, Director of Admissions, Indiana Business College, 550 East Washington Street, Indianapolis, IN 46204. *Phone:* 317-264-5656 or 800-IBC-GRAD (toll-free in-state). *Fax:* 317-264-5650. *E-mail:* ted.lukomski@ibcschools.edu. *Web site:* http://www.ibcschools.edu/.

INDIANA BUSINESS COLLEGE

Muncie, Indiana

Indiana Business College is a coed, proprietary, primarily two-year college, offering degrees at the associate and bachelor's levels.

For Further Information Contact Mr. Jeremy Linder, Associate Director of Admissions, Indiana Business College, 411 West Riggin Road, Muncie, IN 47303. *Phone:* 765-288-8681 or 800-IBC-GRAD (toll-free in-state). *Fax:* 765-288-8797. *E-mail:* Jeremy.linder@ibcschools.edu. *Web site:* http://www.ibcschools.edu/.

INDIANA BUSINESS COLLEGE

Terre Haute, Indiana

Indiana Business College is a coed, proprietary, primarily two-year college, founded in 1902, offering degrees at the associate and bachelor's levels.

For Further Information Contact Sarah Stultz, Associate Director of Admissions, Indiana Business College, 1378 South State Road 46, Terre Haute, IN 47803. *Phone:* 812-877-2100 or 800-IBC-GRAD (toll-free in-state). *Fax:* 812-877-4440. *E-mail:* sarah.stultz@ibcschools.edu. *Web site:* http://www.ibcschools.edu/.

INDIANA STATE UNIVERSITY

Terre Haute, Indiana

Indiana State University is a coed, public university, founded in 1865, offering degrees at the associate, bachelor's, master's, doctoral, and first professional levels and post-master's and postbachelor's certificates. It has a 91-acre campus in Terre Haute near Indianapolis.

Academic Information The faculty has 627 members (70% full-time), 60% with terminal degrees. The undergraduate student-faculty ratio is 17.6:1. The library holds 1 million titles and 82,595 audiovisual materials. Special programs include academic remediation, services for learning-disabled students, an honors program, cooperative (work-study) education, study abroad, advanced placement credit, accelerated degree programs, ESL programs, double majors, independent study, distance learning, summer session for credit, part-time degree programs (daytime, evenings, summer), adult/continuing education programs, internships, and arrangement for off-campus study with Saint Mary-of-the-Woods College, Rose-Hulman Institute of Technology. The most frequently chosen baccalaureate fields are business/marketing, education, social sciences.
Student Body Statistics The student body totals 10,457, of whom 8,386 are undergraduates (1,940 freshmen). 52 percent are women and 48 percent are men. Students come from 47 states and territories and 37 other countries. 87 percent are from Indiana. 2.4 percent are international students.
Expenses for 2008–09 *Application fee:* $25. *State resident tuition:* $6792 full-time, $245 per credit hour part-time. *Nonresident tuition:* $15,046 full-time, $530 per credit hour part-time. *Mandatory fees:* $356 full-time, $178 per term part-time. Part-time tuition and fees vary according to course load. *College room and board:* $6672. *College room only:* $3578. Room and board charges vary according to board plan, housing facility, and student level.
Financial Aid Forms of aid include need-based and non-need-based scholarships, athletic grants, and part-time jobs. The average aided 2008–09 undergraduate received an aid package worth an estimated $9234. The application deadline for financial aid is March 1.
Freshman Admission Indiana State University requires a high school transcript, SAT or ACT scores, and TOEFL scores for international students. Recommendations and an interview are required for some. The application deadline for regular admission is August 15.
Entrance Difficulty Indiana State University assesses its entrance difficulty level as moderately difficult. For the fall 2008 freshman class, 66 percent of the applicants were accepted.
For Further Information Contact Mr. Richard Toomey, Director of Admissions, Indiana State University, 218 North Sixth Street, Erickson Hall, Terre Haute, IN 47809-9989. *Phone:* 812-237-2121 or 800-742-0891 (toll-free). *Fax:* 812-237-8023. *E-mail:* admisu@isugw.indstate.edu. *Web site:* http://www.indstate.edu/.

INDIANA TECH

Fort Wayne, Indiana

Indiana Tech is a coed, private, comprehensive institution, founded in 1930, offering degrees at the associate, bachelor's, and master's levels. It has a 25-acre campus in Fort Wayne.

Academic Information The faculty has 295 members (12% full-time), 7% with terminal degrees. The undergraduate student-faculty ratio is 20:1. The library holds 20,000 titles, 80 serial subscriptions, and 102 audiovisual materials. Special programs include academic remediation, services for learning-disabled students, cooperative (work-study) education, advanced placement credit, accelerated degree programs, double majors, independent study, distance learning, self-designed majors, summer session for credit, part-time degree programs (daytime, evenings, weekends, summer), external degree programs, adult/continuing education programs, and internships. The most frequently chosen baccalaureate fields are business/marketing, computer and information sciences, engineering.
Student Body Statistics The student body totals 3,512, of whom 3,184 are undergraduates (393 freshmen). 54 percent are women and 46 percent are men. Students come from 36 states and territories and 10 other countries. 65 percent are from Indiana. 0.7 percent are international students.
Expenses for 2009–10 *Application fee:* $50. *Comprehensive fee:* $29,440 includes full-time tuition ($21,080), mandatory fees ($320), and college room and board ($8040).
Financial Aid Forms of aid include need-based and non-need-based scholarships and part-time jobs. The priority application deadline for financial aid is March 1.
Freshman Admission Indiana Tech requires a high school transcript, SAT or ACT scores, and TOEFL scores for international students. A minimum 3.0 high school GPA, an interview, and 2 references are recommended.
Entrance Difficulty Indiana Tech assesses its entrance difficulty level as moderately difficult. For the fall 2008 freshman class, 74 percent of the applicants were accepted.
For Further Information Contact Ms. Monica Chamberlain, Director of Admissions for Day Division, Indiana Tech, 1600 East Washington Boulevard, Fort Wayne, IN 46803. *Phone:* 260-422-5561, 800-937-2448 (toll-free in-state), or 888-666-TECH (toll-free out-of-state). *Fax:* 260-422-7696. *E-mail:* admissions@indianatech.edu. *Web site:* http://www.indianatech.edu.

INDIANA UNIVERSITY BLOOMINGTON

Bloomington, Indiana

Indiana University Bloomington is a coed, public unit of Indiana University System, founded in 1820, offering degrees at the associate, bachelor's, master's, doctoral, and first professional levels and post-master's and postbachelor's certificates. It has a 1,933-acre campus in Bloomington near Indianapolis.

Academic Information The faculty has 2,361 members (85% full-time), 68% with terminal degrees. The undergraduate student-faculty ratio is 18:1. The library holds 7 million titles. Special programs include academic remediation, services for learning-disabled students, an honors program, cooperative (work-study) education, study abroad, advanced placement credit, accelerated degree programs, Freshman Honors College, ESL programs, double majors, independent study, distance learning, self-designed majors, summer session for credit, part-time degree programs (daytime, evenings, summer), external degree programs, adult/continuing education programs, internships, and arrangement for off-campus study. The most frequently chosen baccalaureate fields are business/marketing, communications/journalism, education.
Student Body Statistics The student body totals 40,354, of whom 31,626 are undergraduates (7,419 freshmen). 50 percent are women and 50 percent are men. Students come from 47 states and territories and 114 other countries. 66 percent are from Indiana. 5.1 percent are international students.
Expenses for 2008–09 *Application fee:* $50. *State resident tuition:* $7368 full-time, $230.05 per credit hour part-time. *Nonresident tuition:* $23,906 full-time, $747.15 per credit hour part-time. *Mandatory fees:* $863 full-time. Full-time tuition and fees vary according to location and program. Part-time tuition varies according to course load, location, and program. *College room and board:* $7138. *College room only:* $4338. Room and board charges vary according to board plan and housing facility.
Financial Aid Forms of aid include need-based scholarships, athletic grants, and part-time jobs. The average aided 2008–09 undergraduate received an aid package worth an estimated $10,206.
Freshman Admission Indiana University Bloomington requires a high school transcript and SAT or ACT scores. An interview, SAT Subject Test scores, and TOEFL scores for international students are recommended. The application deadline for regular admission is rolling.
Transfer Admission The application deadline for admission is rolling.
Entrance Difficulty Indiana University Bloomington assesses its entrance difficulty level as moderately difficult. For the fall 2008 freshman class, 71 percent of the applicants were accepted.
For Further Information Contact Ms. Mary Ellen Anderson, Director of Admissions, Indiana University Bloomington, 300 North Jordan Avenue, Bloomington, IN 47405-1106. *Phone:* 812-855-0661. *Fax:* 812-855-5102. *E-mail:* iuadmit@indiana.edu. *Web site:* http://www.iub.edu/.

INDIANA UNIVERSITY EAST

Richmond, Indiana

Indiana University East is a coed, public, comprehensive unit of Indiana University System, founded in 1971, offering degrees at the associate, bachelor's, and master's levels and postbachelor's certificates. It has a 174-acre campus in Richmond near Indianapolis.

Indiana University East (continued)

Academic Information The faculty has 186 members (44% full-time), 37% with terminal degrees. The undergraduate student-faculty ratio is 16:1. The library holds 67,036 titles and 435 serial subscriptions. Special programs include academic remediation, services for learning-disabled students, cooperative (work-study) education, advanced placement credit, double majors, independent study, distance learning, summer session for credit, part-time degree programs, external degree programs, adult/continuing education programs, internships, and arrangement for off-campus study with Earlham College. The most frequently chosen baccalaureate fields are business/marketing, education, health professions and related sciences.

Student Body Statistics The student body totals 2,447, of whom 2,388 are undergraduates (326 freshmen). 68 percent are women and 32 percent are men. Students come from 15 states and territories and 10 other countries. 86 percent are from Indiana. 0.2 percent are international students.

Expenses for 2008–09 *Application fee:* $25. *State resident tuition:* $5178 full-time, $172.60 per credit hour part-time. *Nonresident tuition:* $13,344 full-time, $444.80 per credit hour part-time. *Mandatory fees:* $378 full-time. Full-time tuition and fees vary according to course load, program, and reciprocity agreements. Part-time tuition varies according to course load, program, and reciprocity agreements.

Financial Aid Forms of aid include need-based scholarships, athletic grants, and part-time jobs. The average aided 2008–09 undergraduate received an aid package worth an estimated $7971.

Freshman Admission Indiana University East requires a high school transcript and SAT or ACT scores. A minimum 2.0 high school GPA is recommended. The application deadline for regular admission is rolling.

Transfer Admission The application deadline for admission is rolling.

Entrance Difficulty Indiana University East assesses its entrance difficulty level as moderately difficult. For the fall 2008 freshman class, 80 percent of the applicants were accepted.

For Further Information Contact Ms. Molly Vanderpool, Admissions Counselor, Indiana University East, 2325 Chester Boulevard, WZ 116, Richmond, IN 47374-1289. *Phone:* 765-973-8415 or 800-959-EAST (toll-free). *Fax:* 765-973-8288. *E-mail:* eaadmit@indiana.edu. *Web site:* http://www.iue.edu/.

INDIANA UNIVERSITY KOKOMO

Kokomo, Indiana

Indiana University Kokomo is a coed, public, comprehensive unit of Indiana University System, founded in 1945, offering degrees at the associate, bachelor's, and master's levels and postbachelor's certificates. It has a 51-acre campus in Kokomo near Indianapolis.

Academic Information The faculty has 168 members (54% full-time), 36% with terminal degrees. The undergraduate student-faculty ratio is 16:1. The library holds 132,424 titles and 1,513 serial subscriptions. Special programs include academic remediation, services for learning-disabled students, an honors program, study abroad, advanced placement credit, accelerated degree programs, Freshman Honors College, double majors, independent study, distance learning, summer session for credit, part-time degree programs, external degree programs, adult/continuing education programs, and internships. The most frequently chosen baccalaureate fields are health professions and related sciences, education, liberal arts/general studies.

Student Body Statistics The student body totals 2,690, of whom 2,540 are undergraduates (399 freshmen). 67 percent are women and 33 percent are men. Students come from 5 states and territories and 16 other countries. 0.5 percent are international students.

Expenses for 2008–09 *Application fee:* $30. *State resident tuition:* $5174 full-time, $172.45 per credit hour part-time. *Nonresident tuition:* $13,337 full-time, $444.55 per credit hour part-time. *Mandatory fees:* $417 full-time. Full-time tuition and fees vary according to course load and program. Part-time tuition varies according to course load and program.

Financial Aid Forms of aid include need-based scholarships and part-time jobs. The average aided 2008–09 undergraduate received an aid package worth an estimated $7271. The application deadline for financial aid is March 1.

Freshman Admission Indiana University Kokomo requires a high school transcript and SAT or ACT scores. The application deadline for regular admission is rolling.

Entrance Difficulty Indiana University Kokomo assesses its entrance difficulty level as minimally difficult. For the fall 2008 freshman class, 82 percent of the applicants were accepted.

For Further Information Contact Mr. David Campbell, Admissions Director, Indiana University Kokomo, PO Box 9003, Kelley Student Center 230A, Kokomo, IN 46904-9003. *Phone:* 765-455-9217 or 888-875-4485 (toll-free). *Fax:* 765-455-9537. *E-mail:* iuadmis@iuk.edu. *Web site:* http://www.iuk.edu/.

INDIANA UNIVERSITY NORTHWEST

Gary, Indiana

Indiana University Northwest is a coed, public, comprehensive unit of Indiana University System, founded in 1959, offering degrees at the associate, bachelor's, and master's levels and postbachelor's certificates. It has a 38-acre campus in Gary near Chicago.

Academic Information The faculty has 362 members (51% full-time), 46% with terminal degrees. The undergraduate student-faculty ratio is 15:1. The library holds 251,508 titles and 1,541 serial subscriptions. Special programs include academic remediation, services for learning-disabled students, an honors program, cooperative (work-study) education, study abroad, advanced placement credit, accelerated degree programs, double majors, independent study, distance learning, self-designed majors, summer session for credit, part-time degree programs, external degree programs, adult/continuing education programs, internships, and arrangement for off-campus study. The most frequently chosen baccalaureate fields are health professions and related sciences, business/marketing, liberal arts/general studies.

Student Body Statistics The student body totals 4,794, of whom 4,168 are undergraduates (768 freshmen). 70 percent are women and 30 percent are men. Students come from 7 states and territories and 35 other countries. 99 percent are from Indiana. 0.3 percent are international students.

Expenses for 2008–09 *Application fee:* $25. *State resident tuition:* $5228 full-time, $174.25 per credit hour part-time. *Nonresident tuition:* $13,343 full-time, $444.75 per credit hour part-time. *Mandatory fees:* $441 full-time. Full-time tuition and fees vary according to course load and program. Part-time tuition varies according to course load and program.

Financial Aid Forms of aid include need-based scholarships, athletic grants, and part-time jobs. The average aided 2008–09 undergraduate received an aid package worth an estimated $8070.

Freshman Admission Indiana University Northwest requires a high school transcript, a minimum 2.0 high school GPA, and SAT or ACT scores. TOEFL scores for international students are recommended. The application deadline for regular admission is rolling.

Transfer Admission The application deadline for admission is rolling.

Entrance Difficulty Indiana University Northwest assesses its entrance difficulty level as minimally difficult; moderately difficult for out-of-state applicants. For the fall 2008 freshman class, 80 percent of the applicants were accepted.

For Further Information Contact Dr. Linda B. Templeton, Director of Admissions, Indiana University Northwest, Hawthorne 100, 3400 Broadway, Gary, IN 46408-1197. *Phone:* 219-980-6767 or 800-968-7486 (toll-free). *Fax:* 219-981-4219. *E-mail:* admit@iun.edu. *Web site:* http://www.iun.edu/.

INDIANA UNIVERSITY–PURDUE UNIVERSITY FORT WAYNE

Fort Wayne, Indiana

Indiana University–Purdue University Fort Wayne is a coed, public, comprehensive unit of Indiana University System and Purdue University System, founded in 1917, offering degrees at the associate, bachelor's, and master's levels and postbachelor's certificates. It has a 643-acre campus in Fort Wayne.

Academic Information The faculty has 778 members (51% full-time), 49% with terminal degrees. The undergraduate student-faculty ratio is 17:1. The library holds 455,020 titles, 22,433 serial subscriptions, and 3,967 audiovisual materials. Special programs include academic remediation, services for learning-disabled students, an honors program, cooperative (work-study) education, study abroad, advanced placement credit, accelerated degree programs, ESL programs, double majors, independent study, distance learning, self-designed majors, summer session for credit, part-time degree programs (daytime, evenings, weekends, summer), adult/continuing education programs, internships, and arrangement for off-campus study with National Student Exchange. The most frequently chosen baccalaureate fields are business/marketing, education, liberal arts/general studies.
Student Body Statistics The student body totals 12,338, of whom 11,578 are undergraduates (2,094 freshmen). 56 percent are women and 44 percent are men. Students come from 44 states and territories and 66 other countries. 95 percent are from Indiana. 1.1 percent are international students.
Expenses for 2008–09 *Application fee:* $30. *State resident tuition:* $5181 full-time, $192 per credit hour part-time. *Nonresident tuition:* $13,235 full-time, $490 per credit hour part-time. *Mandatory fees:* $755 full-time, $28 per credit hour part-time. Both full-time and part-time tuition and fees vary according to course load and student level. *College room only:* $5400. Room charges vary according to housing facility.
Financial Aid Forms of aid include need-based scholarships, athletic grants, and part-time jobs. The average aided 2007–08 undergraduate received an aid package worth $8537.
Freshman Admission Indiana University–Purdue University Fort Wayne requires a high school transcript, SAT or ACT scores, and TOEFL scores for international students. Rank in upper 50% of high school class is recommended. The application deadline for regular admission is August 1.
Transfer Admission The application deadline for admission is August 1.
Entrance Difficulty Indiana University–Purdue University Fort Wayne assesses its entrance difficulty level as minimally difficult; moderately difficult for out-of-state applicants; noncompetitive for students graduating high school over 2 years ago. For the fall 2008 freshman class, 96 percent of the applicants were accepted.
For Further Information Contact Ms. Carol Isaacs, Director of Admissions, Indiana University–Purdue University Fort Wayne, 2101 East Coliseum Boulevard, Fort Wayne, IN 46805-1499. *Phone:* 260-481-6812 or 800-324-4739 (toll-free in-state). *Fax:* 260-481-6880. *E-mail:* ipfwadms@ipfw.edu. *Web site:* http://www.ipfw.edu/.

INDIANA UNIVERSITY–PURDUE UNIVERSITY INDIANAPOLIS

Indianapolis, Indiana

Indiana University–Purdue University Indianapolis is a coed, public unit of Indiana University System, founded in 1969, offering degrees at the associate, bachelor's, master's, doctoral, and first professional levels and postbachelor's certificates. It has a 509-acre campus in Indianapolis.

Academic Information The faculty has 3,252 members (70% full-time), 66% with terminal degrees. The undergraduate student-faculty ratio is 18:1. The library holds 1 million titles and 14,673 serial subscriptions. Special programs include academic remediation, services for learning-disabled students, an honors program, cooperative (work-study) education, study abroad, advanced placement credit, accelerated degree programs, ESL programs, double majors, independent study, distance learning, self-designed majors, summer session for credit, part-time degree programs, external degree programs, adult/continuing education programs, internships, and arrangement for off-campus study with 5 members of the Consortium for Urban Education. The most frequently chosen baccalaureate fields are business/marketing, health professions and related sciences, liberal arts/general studies.
Student Body Statistics The student body totals 30,300, of whom 21,423 are undergraduates (2,998 freshmen). 58 percent are women and 42 percent are men. Students come from 46 states and territories and 117 other countries. 98 percent are from Indiana. 2.9 percent are international students.
Expenses for 2008–09 *Application fee:* $50. *State resident tuition:* $6531 full-time, $217.70 per credit hour part-time. *Nonresident tuition:* $19,919 full-time, $663.95 per credit hour part-time. *Mandatory fees:* $660 full-time. Full-time tuition and fees vary according to course load and program. Part-time tuition varies according to course load and program. *College room only:* $3140. Room charges vary according to housing facility.
Financial Aid Forms of aid include need-based scholarships, athletic grants, and part-time jobs. The average aided 2008–09 undergraduate received an aid package worth an estimated $8816.
Freshman Admission Indiana University–Purdue University Indianapolis requires a high school transcript, SAT or ACT scores, and TOEFL scores for international students. Portfolio for art program is recommended. An interview is required for some. The application deadline for regular admission is June 1.
Transfer Admission The application deadline for admission is rolling.
Entrance Difficulty Indiana University–Purdue University Indianapolis assesses its entrance difficulty level as moderately difficult. For the fall 2008 freshman class, 70 percent of the applicants were accepted.
For Further Information Contact Mr. Chris J. Foley, Director of Admissions, Indiana University–Purdue University Indianapolis, Cavanaugh Hall 129, 425 University Boulevard, Indianapolis, IN 46202-5143. *Phone:* 317-274-4591. *Fax:* 317-278-1862. *E-mail:* apply@iupui.edu. *Web site:* http://www.iupui.edu/.

INDIANA UNIVERSITY SOUTH BEND

South Bend, Indiana

Indiana University South Bend is a coed, public, comprehensive unit of Indiana University System, founded in 1922, offering degrees at the associate, bachelor's, and master's levels and postbachelor's certificates. It has an 80-acre campus in South Bend near Chicago.

Academic Information The faculty has 525 members (54% full-time), 43% with terminal degrees. The undergraduate student-faculty ratio is 15:1. The library holds 300,202 titles and 1,937 serial subscriptions. Special programs include an honors program, study abroad, accelerated degree programs, ESL programs, double majors, distance learning, summer session for credit, part-time degree programs, external degree programs, adult/continuing education programs, internships, and arrangement for off-campus study with Bethel College, Saint Mary's College (IN), Holy Cross College, Goshen College. The most frequently chosen baccalaureate fields are business/marketing, education, liberal arts/general studies.
Student Body Statistics The student body totals 7,712, of whom 6,756 are undergraduates (1,130 freshmen). 63 percent are women and 37 percent are men. Students come from 22 states and territories and 70 other countries. 96 percent are from Indiana. 2 percent are international students.
Expenses for 2008–09 *Application fee:* $45. *State resident tuition:* $5324 full-time, $177.45 per credit hour part-time. *Nonresident tuition:* $14,441 full-time, $481.35 per credit hour part-time. *Mandatory fees:* $439 full-time. Full-time tuition and fees vary according to course load and program. Part-time tuition varies according to course load and program.
Financial Aid Forms of aid include need-based scholarships, athletic grants, and part-time jobs. The average aided 2008–09 undergraduate received an aid package worth an estimated $7495. The application deadline for financial aid is March 1.
Freshman Admission Indiana University South Bend requires a high school transcript, a minimum 2.0 high school GPA, SAT or ACT scores, and TOEFL scores for international students. An interview is required for some. The application deadline for regular admission is rolling.
Transfer Admission The application deadline for admission is rolling.
Entrance Difficulty Indiana University South Bend assesses its entrance difficulty level as moderately difficult. For the fall 2008 freshman class, 84 percent of the applicants were accepted.
For Further Information Contact Mr. Jeff Johnston, Director of Recruitment/Admissions, Indiana University South Bend, 1700 Mishawaka Avenue, Administration Building, Room 169, PO Box 7111, South Bend, IN 46634-7111. *Phone:* 574-237-4480 or 877-GO-2-IUSB (toll-free). *Fax:* 574-237-4834. *E-mail:* admissio@iusb.edu. *Web site:* http://www.iusb.edu/.

INDIANA UNIVERSITY SOUTHEAST

New Albany, Indiana

Indiana University Southeast is a coed, public, comprehensive unit of Indiana University System, founded in 1941, offering degrees at the associate, bachelor's, and master's levels and postbachelor's certificates. It has a 177-acre campus in New Albany near Louisville.

Academic Information The faculty has 453 members (44% full-time), 41% with terminal degrees. The undergraduate student-faculty ratio is 16:1. The library holds 215,429 titles and 962 serial subscriptions. Special programs include academic remediation, services for learning-disabled students, study abroad, advanced placement credit, accelerated degree programs, double majors, independent study, self-designed majors, summer session for credit, part-time degree programs, external degree programs, adult/continuing education programs, internships, and arrangement for off-campus study with 7 members of the Kentuckiana Metroversity. The most frequently chosen baccalaureate fields are business/marketing, education, liberal arts/general studies.
Student Body Statistics The student body totals 6,482, of whom 5,585 are undergraduates (1,065 freshmen). 61 percent are women and 39 percent are men. Students come from 13 states and territories and 44 other countries. 75 percent are from Indiana. 0.3 percent are international students.
Expenses for 2008–09 *Application fee:* $30. *State resident tuition:* $5184 full-time, $172.80 per credit hour part-time. *Nonresident tuition:* $13,344 full-time, $444.80 per credit hour part-time. *Mandatory fees:* $460 full-time. Full-time tuition and fees vary according to course load, program, and reciprocity agreements. Part-time tuition varies according to course load, program, and reciprocity agreements. *College room only:* $3276. Room charges vary according to housing facility.
Financial Aid Forms of aid include need-based scholarships, athletic grants, and part-time jobs. The average aided 2008–09 undergraduate received an aid package worth an estimated $7221. The priority application deadline for financial aid is March 1.
Freshman Admission Indiana University Southeast requires a high school transcript, SAT or ACT scores, and TOEFL scores for international students. An interview is required for some. The application deadline for regular admission is rolling.
Transfer Admission The application deadline for admission is rolling.
Entrance Difficulty Indiana University Southeast assesses its entrance difficulty level as minimally difficult; moderately difficult for out-of-state applicants; moderately difficult for transfers. For the fall 2008 freshman class, 87 percent of the applicants were accepted.
For Further Information Contact Ms. Anne Skuce, Director of Admissions, Indiana University Southeast, University Center Building, Room 100, 4201 Grant Line Road, New Albany, IN 47150. *Phone:* 812-941-2212 or 800-852-8835 (toll-free in-state). *Fax:* 812-941-2595. *E-mail:* admissions@ius.edu. *Web site:* http://www.ius.edu/.

INDIANA WESLEYAN UNIVERSITY

Marion, Indiana

Indiana Wesleyan University is a coed, private, Wesleyan, comprehensive institution, founded in 1920, offering degrees at the associate, bachelor's, master's, and doctoral levels and post-master's and postbachelor's certificates (also offers adult program with significant enrollment not reflected in profile). It has a 132-acre campus in Marion near Indianapolis.

Academic Information The faculty has 312 members (53% full-time), 36% with terminal degrees. The undergraduate student-faculty ratio is 16:1. The library holds 164,272 titles, 85,642 serial subscriptions, and 12,648 audiovisual materials. Special programs include academic remediation, services for learning-disabled students, an honors program, study abroad, advanced placement credit, accelerated degree programs, Freshman Honors College, double majors, independent study, distance learning, self-designed majors, summer session for credit, part-time degree programs (daytime, evenings, weekends, summer), adult/continuing education programs, internships, and arrangement for off-campus study with Taylor University, Council for Christian Colleges and Universities. The most frequently chosen baccalaureate fields are business/marketing, education, health professions and related sciences.
Student Body Statistics The student body is made up of 3,201 undergraduates (894 freshmen). 63 percent are women and 37 percent are men. Students come from 48 states and territories and 20 other countries. 55 percent are from Indiana. 0.3 percent are international students.
Expenses for 2009–10 *Application fee:* $25. *Comprehensive fee:* $27,266 includes full-time tuition ($20,496) and college room and board ($6770). *College room only:* $3260. *Part-time tuition:* $732 per credit hour.
Financial Aid Forms of aid include need-based and non-need-based scholarships and part-time jobs. The priority application deadline for financial aid is March 1.
Freshman Admission Indiana Wesleyan University requires an essay, a high school transcript, a minimum 2.0 high school GPA, 1 recommendation, SAT or ACT scores, and TOEFL scores for international students. An interview is required for some. The application deadline for regular admission is rolling.
Transfer Admission The application deadline for admission is rolling.
Entrance Difficulty Indiana Wesleyan University assesses its entrance difficulty level as moderately difficult. For the fall 2008 freshman class, 85 percent of the applicants were accepted.
For Further Information Contact Mr. Daniel Solms, Director of Admissions, Indiana Wesleyan University, 4201 South Washington Street, Marion, IN 46953. *Phone:* 866-468-6498 Ext. 2138 or 800-332-6901 (toll-free). *Fax:* 765-677-2333. *E-mail:* admissions@indwes.edu. *Web site:* http://www.indwes.edu/.

INTERNATIONAL BUSINESS COLLEGE

Fort Wayne, Indiana

http://www.ibcfortwayne.edu/

ITT TECHNICAL INSTITUTE

Fort Wayne, Indiana

ITT Technical Institute is a coed, proprietary, primarily two-year college of ITT Educational Services, Inc., founded in 1967, offering degrees at the associate and bachelor's levels.

Financial Aid Forms of aid include need-based scholarships and part-time jobs. The application deadline for financial aid is continuous.
Freshman Admission ITT Technical Institute requires TOEFL scores for international students.
Entrance Difficulty ITT Technical Institute assesses its entrance difficulty level as minimally difficult.
For Further Information Contact Director of Recruitment, ITT Technical Institute, 2810 Dupont Commerce Court, fort Wayne, IN 46825. *Phone:* 260-497-6200 or 800-866-4488 (toll-free). *Fax:* 260-497-6299. *Web site:* http://www.itt-tech.edu/.

ITT TECHNICAL INSTITUTE

Indianapolis, Indiana

ITT Technical Institute is a coed, proprietary, primarily two-year college of ITT Educational Services, Inc., founded in 1966, offering degrees at the associate and bachelor's levels. It has a 10-acre campus in Indianapolis.

Financial Aid Forms of aid include need-based scholarships and part-time jobs. The application deadline for financial aid is continuous.
Entrance Difficulty ITT Technical Institute assesses its entrance difficulty level as minimally difficult.
For Further Information Contact Director of Recruitment, ITT Technical Institute, 9511 Angola Court, Indianapolis, IN 46268. *Phone:* 317-875-8640 or 800-937-4488 (toll-free). *Fax:* 317-875-8641. *Web site:* http://www.itt-tech.edu/.

ITT TECHNICAL INSTITUTE

Newburgh, Indiana

ITT Technical Institute is a coed, proprietary, primarily two-year college of ITT Educational Services, Inc., founded in 1966, offering degrees at the associate and bachelor's levels.

Financial Aid Forms of aid include need-based scholarships and part-time jobs. The application deadline for financial aid is continuous.
Freshman Admission TOEFL scores for international students are recommended.
Entrance Difficulty ITT Technical Institute assesses its entrance difficulty level as minimally difficult.
For Further Information Contact Director of Recruitment, ITT Technical Institute, 10999 Stahl Road, Newburgh, IN 47630. *Phone:* 812-858-1600 or 800-832-4488 (toll-free in-state). *Fax:* 812-858-0646. *Web site:* http://www.itt-tech.edu/.

ITT TECHNICAL INSTITUTE

South Bend, Indiana

ITT Technical Institute is a coed, proprietary, four-year college of ITT Educational Services, Inc., offering degrees at the associate and bachelor's levels.

For Further Information Contact Director of Recruitment, ITT Technical Institute, 17390 Dugdale Drive, Suite 100, South Bend, IN 46635. *Phone:* 574-247-8300 or 877-474-1926 (toll-free). *Web site:* http://www.itt-tech.edu/.

LUTHERAN COLLEGE OF HEALTH PROFESSIONS

See University of Saint Francis.

MANCHESTER COLLEGE

North Manchester, Indiana

Manchester College is a coed, private, four-year college, founded in 1889, affiliated with the Church of the Brethren, offering degrees at the associate and bachelor's levels. It has a 125-acre campus in North Manchester.

Academic Information The faculty has 89 members (75% full-time), 71% with terminal degrees. The student-faculty ratio is 15:1. Special programs include services for learning-disabled students, an honors program, study abroad, advanced placement credit, accelerated degree programs, double majors, independent study, self-designed majors, summer session for credit, part-time degree programs, adult/continuing education programs, internships, and arrangement for off-campus study. The most frequently chosen baccalaureate fields are business/marketing, education, health professions and related sciences.
Student Body Statistics The student body is made up of 1,145 undergraduates (397 freshmen). 50 percent are women and 50 percent are men. Students come from 28 states and territories and 26 other countries. 90 percent are from Indiana. 3.4 percent are international students.
Expenses for 2008–09 *Application fee:* $25. *One-time mandatory fee:* $225. *Comprehensive fee:* $30,820 includes full-time tuition ($22,000), mandatory fees ($720), and college room and board ($8100). *College room only:* $5000. Room and board charges vary according to board plan and housing facility. *Part-time tuition:* varies with course load. *Part-time mandatory fees:* $350 per year. Part-time feesvary according to course load.
Financial Aid Forms of aid include need-based and non-need-based scholarships and part-time jobs. The average aided 2008–09 undergraduate received an aid package worth an estimated $21,380.
Freshman Admission Manchester College requires a high school transcript, 1 recommendation, rank in upper 50% of high school class, SAT or ACT scores, and TOEFL scores for international students. A minimum 2.3 high school GPA and an interview are recommended. An essay, a minimum 3.0 high school GPA, and an interview are required for some. The application deadline for regular admission is rolling.
Transfer Admission The application deadline for admission is rolling.
Entrance Difficulty Manchester College assesses its entrance difficulty level as moderately difficult. For the fall 2008 freshman class, 79 percent of the applicants were accepted.
For Further Information Contact Mr. Adam Hohman, Assistant Director of Admissions, Manchester College, 604 East College Avenue, North Manchester, IN 46962. *Phone:* 260-982-5055 or 800-852-3648 (toll-free). *Fax:* 260-982-5239. *E-mail:* admitinfo@manchester.edu. *Web site:* http://www.manchester.edu/.

See page 248 for the Close-Up.

MARIAN UNIVERSITY

Indianapolis, Indiana

Marian University is a coed, private, Roman Catholic, comprehensive institution, founded in 1851, offering degrees at the associate, bachelor's, and master's levels. It has a 114-acre campus in Indianapolis.

Academic Information The faculty has 185 members (46% full-time). The undergraduate student-faculty ratio is 12:1. The library holds 102,237 titles, 337 serial subscriptions, and 2,517 audiovisual materials. Special programs include academic remediation, services for learning-disabled students, an honors program, cooperative (work-study) education, study abroad, advanced placement credit, accelerated degree programs, double majors, independent study, summer session for credit, part-time degree programs (daytime, evenings, weekends, summer), adult/continuing education programs, internships, and arrangement for off-campus study with Franklin College of Indiana, Indiana University–Purdue University at Indianapolis, University of Indianapolis, Christian Theological Seminary, Butler University. The most frequently chosen baccalaureate fields are business/marketing, education, health professions and related sciences.
Student Body Statistics The student body totals 2,143, of whom 1,971 are undergraduates. Students come from 15 states and territories. 94 percent are from Indiana. 0.4 percent are international students.
Expenses for 2008–09 *Application fee:* $20. *Comprehensive fee:* $29,628 includes full-time tuition ($22,400) and college room and board ($7228). Full-time tuition varies according to course load. Room and board charges vary according to board plan and housing facility. *Part-time tuition:* $940 per credit hour. Part-time tuition varies according to course load.
Financial Aid Forms of aid include need-based and non-need-based scholarships, athletic grants, and part-time jobs. The average aided 2008–09 undergraduate received an aid package worth an estimated $19,509. The priority application deadline for financial aid is March 1.
Freshman Admission Marian University requires a minimum 2.3 high school GPA, college transcripts, SAT or ACT scores, and TOEFL scores for international students. An essay and an interview are required for some. The application deadline for regular admission is August 1.
Transfer Admission The application deadline for admission is August 1.
Entrance Difficulty Marian University assesses its entrance difficulty level as moderately difficult. For the fall 2008 freshman class, 54 percent of the applicants were accepted.
For Further Information Contact Ms. Luann Brames, Director of Enrollment, Marian University, 3200 Cold Spring Road, Indianapolis, IN 46222-1997. *Phone:* 317-955-6300 or 800-772-7264 (toll-free in-state). *Fax:* 317-955-6401. *E-mail:* admissions@marian.edu. *Web site:* http://www.marian.edu/.

MARTIN UNIVERSITY

Indianapolis, Indiana

Martin University is a coed, private, comprehensive institution, founded in 1977, offering degrees at the bachelor's and master's levels. It has a 5-acre campus in Indianapolis.

Academic Information The faculty has 43 members (60% full-time), 84% with terminal degrees. The undergraduate student-faculty ratio is 21:1. Special programs include academic remediation, an honors program, advanced placement credit, accelerated degree programs, double majors,

Martin University (continued)

independent study, self-designed majors, summer session for credit, part-time degree programs (daytime, evenings, weekends, summer), external degree programs, adult/continuing education programs, internships, and arrangement for off-campus study with Consortium for Urban Education (CUE). The most frequently chosen baccalaureate fields are liberal arts/general studies, business/marketing, psychology.
Student Body Statistics The student body totals 1,236, of whom 1,074 are undergraduates (234 freshmen). 68 percent are women and 32 percent are men. Students come from 1 state or territory and 2 other countries.
Expenses for 2009–10 *Application fee:* $25. *One-time mandatory fee:* $25. *Tuition:* $13,200 full-time, $440 per credit part-time. *Mandatory fees:* $320 full-time, $160 per term part-time.
Financial Aid Forms of aid include need-based scholarships and part-time jobs. The average aided 2008–09 undergraduate received an aid package worth an estimated $10,231. The application deadline for financial aid is continuous.
Freshman Admission Martin University requires an essay, a high school transcript, an interview, writing sample, and TOEFL scores for international students. The application deadline for regular admission is rolling.
Transfer Admission The application deadline for admission is rolling.
Entrance Difficulty Martin University has an open admission policy.
For Further Information Contact Ms. Brenda Shaheed, Director of Enrollment Management, Martin University, PO Box 18567, 2171 Avondale Place, Indianapolis, IN 46218-3867. *Phone:* 317-543-3237. *Fax:* 317-543-4790. *E-mail:* bshaheed@martin.edu. *Web site:* http://www.martin.edu/.

MICHIANA COLLEGE

See Brown Mackie College–Fort Wayne.

MICHIANA COLLEGE

See Brown Mackie College–South Bend.

MID-AMERICA COLLEGE OF FUNERAL SERVICE

Jeffersonville, Indiana

http://www.mid-america.edu/

OAKLAND CITY UNIVERSITY

Oakland City, Indiana

Oakland City University is a coed, private, General Baptist, comprehensive institution, founded in 1885, offering degrees at the associate, bachelor's, master's, doctoral, and first professional levels. It has a 20-acre campus in Oakland City.

Expenses for 2008–09 *Application fee:* $35. *Comprehensive fee:* $21,588 includes full-time tuition ($15,000), mandatory fees ($360), and college room and board ($6228). *College room only:* $2052. Room and board charges vary according to housing facility. *Part-time tuition:* $500 per semester hour.
For Further Information Contact Mr. Brian Baker, Director of Admissions, Oakland City University, 138 North Lucretia Street, Oakland City, IN 47660. *Phone:* 812-749-1222 or 800-737-5125 (toll-free). *Web site:* http://www.oak.edu/.

PURDUE UNIVERSITY

West Lafayette, Indiana

Purdue University is a coed, public unit of Purdue University System, founded in 1869, offering degrees at the associate, bachelor's, master's, doctoral, and first professional levels. It has a 2,307-acre campus in West Lafayette near Indianapolis.

Academic Information The faculty has 2,427 members (87% full-time), 96% with terminal degrees. The undergraduate student-faculty ratio is 14:1. The library holds 3 million titles and 40,073 serial subscriptions. Special programs include services for learning-disabled students, an honors program, cooperative (work-study) education, study abroad, advanced placement credit, accelerated degree programs, Freshman Honors College, ESL programs, double majors, independent study, distance learning, summer session for credit, part-time degree programs, adult/continuing education programs, and internships. The most frequently chosen baccalaureate fields are business/marketing, engineering, engineering technologies.
Student Body Statistics The student body totals 40,090, of whom 31,761 are undergraduates (6,840 freshmen). 42 percent are women and 58 percent are men. Students come from 54 states and territories and 128 other countries. 74 percent are from Indiana. 7.4 percent are international students.
Expenses for 2008–09 *Application fee:* $30. *State resident tuition:* $7317 full-time, $278 per credit hour part-time. *Nonresident tuition:* $22,791 full-time, $771 per credit hour part-time. *Mandatory fees:* $433 full-time. Full-time tuition and fees vary according to course load and program. Part-time tuition varies according to course load. *College room and board:* $7930. *College room only:* $3410. Room and board charges vary according to board plan and housing facility.
Financial Aid Forms of aid include need-based and non-need-based scholarships, athletic grants, and part-time jobs. The average aided 2008–09 undergraduate received an aid package worth an estimated $9734. The priority application deadline for financial aid is March 1.
Freshman Admission Purdue University requires a high school transcript, SAT or ACT scores, and TOEFL scores for international students. The application deadline for regular admission is March 1.
Transfer Admission The application deadline for admission is rolling.
Entrance Difficulty Purdue University assesses its entrance difficulty level as moderately difficult; most difficult for engineering, aviation flight, nursing, veterinary technology, computer related, health related programs, hospitality and tourism management. For the fall 2008 freshman class, 72 percent of the applicants were accepted.
For Further Information Contact Ms. Pamela T. Horne, Assistant Vice President for Enrollment Management and Dean of Admissions, Purdue University, 475 Stadium Mall Drive, Schleman Hall, West Lafayette, IN 47907-2050. *Phone:* 765-494-1776. *Fax:* 765-494-0544. *E-mail:* admissions@purdue.edu. *Web site:* http://www.purdue.edu/.

PURDUE UNIVERSITY CALUMET

Hammond, Indiana

Purdue University Calumet is a coed, public, comprehensive unit of Purdue University System, founded in 1951, offering degrees at the associate, bachelor's, and master's levels and postbachelor's certificates. It has a 167-acre campus in Hammond near Chicago.

Academic Information The faculty has 399 members (66% full-time), 50% with terminal degrees. The undergraduate student-faculty ratio is 22:1. The library holds 272,153 titles, 996 serial subscriptions, and 1,285 audiovisual materials. Special programs include academic remediation, services for learning-disabled students, an honors program, cooperative (work-study) education, advanced placement credit, accelerated degree programs, Freshman Honors College, ESL programs, double majors, independent study, distance learning, summer session for credit, part-time degree programs (daytime, evenings, weekends, summer), adult/continuing education programs, and internships.
Student Body Statistics The student body totals 9,325, of whom 8,353 are undergraduates (1,382 freshmen). 56 percent are women and 44

percent are men. Students come from 28 states and territories and 21 other countries. 89 percent are from Indiana. 3.7 percent are international students.

Expenses for 2008–09 *Application fee:* $0. *State resident tuition:* $5757 full-time, $192 per credit hour part-time. *Nonresident tuition:* $12,285 full-time, $425 per credit hour part-time. *Mandatory fees:* $17.20 per credit hour part-time. Full-time tuition varies according to program. Part-time tuition and fees vary according to course load and program. *College room and board:* $6155. *College room only:* $4270. Room and board charges vary according to housing facility.

Financial Aid Forms of aid include need-based and non-need-based scholarships, athletic grants, and part-time jobs. The average aided 2007–08 undergraduate received an aid package worth $6249. The priority application deadline for financial aid is March 10.

Freshman Admission Purdue University Calumet requires a high school transcript, a minimum 2.0 high school GPA, and SAT or ACT scores. The application deadline for regular admission is rolling.

Transfer Admission A minimum 2.0 college GPA is recommended. Standardized test scores and a college transcript are required for some. The application deadline for admission is rolling.

Entrance Difficulty Purdue University Calumet assesses its entrance difficulty level as moderately difficult. For the fall 2008 freshman class, 74 percent of the applicants were accepted.

For Further Information Contact Mr. Paul McGuinness, Director of Admissions, Purdue University Calumet, 2200-169th Street, Hammond, IN 46323-2094. *Phone:* 219-989-2213 or 800-447-8738 (toll-free in-state). *E-mail:* adms@calumet.purdue.edu. *Web site:* http://www.calumet.purdue.edu/.

PURDUE UNIVERSITY NORTH CENTRAL

Westville, Indiana

Purdue University North Central is a coed, public, comprehensive unit of Purdue University System, founded in 1967, offering degrees at the associate, bachelor's, and master's levels and postbachelor's certificates. It has a 305-acre campus in Westville near Chicago.

Academic Information The faculty has 289 members (41% full-time), 33% with terminal degrees. The undergraduate student-faculty ratio is 18:1. The library holds 87,307 titles, 222 serial subscriptions, and 395 audiovisual materials. Special programs include academic remediation, services for learning-disabled students, an honors program, cooperative (work-study) education, study abroad, advanced placement credit, double majors, independent study, distance learning, self-designed majors, summer session for credit, part-time degree programs (daytime, evenings, summer), adult/continuing education programs, internships, and arrangement for off-campus study. The most frequently chosen baccalaureate fields are business/marketing, engineering technologies, liberal arts/general studies.

Student Body Statistics The student body totals 4,245, of whom 4,142 are undergraduates (856 freshmen). 58 percent are women and 42 percent are men. Students come from 10 states and territories and 8 other countries. 99 percent are from Indiana.

Expenses for 2008–09 *State resident tuition:* $5447 full-time, $181.55 per credit hour part-time. *Nonresident tuition:* $8125 full-time, $452.40 per credit hour part-time. *Mandatory fees:* $633 full-time, $21.10 per credit hour part-time. Both full-time and part-time tuition and fees vary according to course load, location, and program.

Financial Aid Forms of aid include need-based and non-need-based scholarships, athletic grants, and part-time jobs. The average aided 2008–09 undergraduate received an aid package worth an estimated $6925. The application deadline for financial aid is June 30 with a priority deadline of March 10.

Freshman Admission Purdue University North Central requires a high school transcript and TOEFL scores for international students. SAT or ACT scores are recommended. An essay, a minimum 2.0 high school GPA, and an interview are required for some. The application deadline for regular admission is August 15.

Transfer Admission The application deadline for admission is August 15.

Entrance Difficulty Purdue University North Central assesses its entrance difficulty level as minimally difficult; moderately difficult for engineering, nursing programs. For the fall 2008 freshman class, 84 percent of the applicants were accepted.

For Further Information Contact Mr. Anthony Cardenas, Director of Admissions, Purdue University North Central, 1401 South U.S. Highway 421, Westville, IN 46391. *Phone:* 219-785-5283 or 800-872-1231 (toll-free in-state). *Fax:* 219-785-5538. *E-mail:* acardenas@pnc.edu. *Web site:* http://www.pnc.edu/.

ROSE-HULMAN INSTITUTE OF TECHNOLOGY

Terre Haute, Indiana

Rose-Hulman Institute of Technology is a coed, primarily men's, private, comprehensive institution, founded in 1874, offering degrees at the bachelor's and master's levels. It has a 200-acre campus in Terre Haute near Indianapolis.

Academic Information The faculty has 172 members (95% full-time), 99% with terminal degrees. The undergraduate student-faculty ratio is 11:1. The library holds 80,301 titles, 23,498 serial subscriptions, and 930 audiovisual materials. Special programs include services for learning-disabled students, cooperative (work-study) education, study abroad, advanced placement credit, accelerated degree programs, double majors, independent study, summer session for credit, adult/continuing education programs, internships, and arrangement for off-campus study with Indiana State University, St. Mary-of-the-Woods College. The most frequently chosen baccalaureate fields are computer and information sciences, biological/life sciences, engineering.

Student Body Statistics The student body totals 1,923, of whom 1,832 are undergraduates (482 freshmen). 20 percent are women and 80 percent are men. Students come from 50 states and territories and 20 other countries. 42 percent are from Indiana. 1.9 percent are international students.

Expenses for 2008–09 *Application fee:* $40. *Comprehensive fee:* $41,694 includes full-time tuition ($32,286), mandatory fees ($540), and college room and board ($8868). *College room only:* $5142. Full-time tuition and fees vary according to course load. Room and board charges vary according to board plan. *Part-time tuition:* $939 per credit. Part-time tuition varies according to course load.

Financial Aid Forms of aid include need-based scholarships and part-time jobs. The average aided 2008–09 undergraduate received an aid package worth an estimated $31,456.

Freshman Admission Rose-Hulman Institute of Technology requires a high school transcript, 1 recommendation, curricular, SAT or ACT scores, and TOEFL scores for international students. An essay and an interview are recommended. The application deadline for regular admission is March 1.

Entrance Difficulty Rose-Hulman Institute of Technology assesses its entrance difficulty level as very difficult. For the fall 2008 freshman class, 70 percent of the applicants were accepted.

For Further Information Contact Mr. James Goecker, Dean of Admissions and Financial Aid, Rose-Hulman Institute of Technology, 5500 Wabash Avenue, CM 1, Terre Haute, IN 47803-3920. *Phone:* 812-877-8894 or 800-248-7448 (toll-free). *Fax:* 812-877-8941. *E-mail:* admissions@rose-hulman.edu. *Web site:* http://www.rose-hulman.edu/.

SAINT FRANCIS COLLEGE

See University of Saint Francis.

SAINT JOSEPH'S COLLEGE

Rensselaer, Indiana

Saint Joseph's College is a coed, private, Roman Catholic, comprehensive institution, founded in 1889, offering degrees at the associate, bachelor's, and master's levels. It has a 180-acre campus in Rensselaer near Chicago.

Academic Information The faculty has 107 members (55% full-time), 79% with terminal degrees. The undergraduate student-faculty ratio is 15:1. The library holds 228,858 titles, 326 serial subscriptions, and 26,374 audiovisual materials. Special programs include academic remediation, services for learning-disabled students, an honors program, study abroad, advanced placement credit, accelerated degree programs, double majors, independent study, self-designed majors, summer session for credit, part-time degree programs (daytime), and internships. The most frequently chosen baccalaureate fields are business/marketing, education, health professions and related sciences.
Student Body Statistics The student body is made up of 1,076 undergraduates (298 freshmen). 57 percent are women and 43 percent are men. Students come from 23 states and territories and 5 other countries. 73 percent are from Indiana. 0.7 percent are international students.
Expenses for 2008–09 *Application fee:* $25. *Comprehensive fee:* $30,350 includes full-time tuition ($23,000), mandatory fees ($180), and college room and board ($7170). Full-time tuition and fees vary according to reciprocity agreements. Room and board charges vary according to housing facility. *Part-time tuition:* $770 per credit. Part-time tuition varies according to course load and reciprocity agreements.
Financial Aid Forms of aid include need-based and non-need-based scholarships, athletic grants, and part-time jobs. The average aided 2008–09 undergraduate received an aid package worth an estimated $22,877. The priority application deadline for financial aid is March 1.
Freshman Admission Saint Joseph's College requires a high school transcript, a minimum 2.0 high school GPA, SAT or ACT scores, and TOEFL scores for international students. An essay and an interview are required for some. The application deadline for regular admission is rolling.
Transfer Admission The application deadline for admission is rolling.
Entrance Difficulty Saint Joseph's College assesses its entrance difficulty level as moderately difficult. For the fall 2008 freshman class, 74 percent of the applicants were accepted.
For Further Information Contact Ms. Karen Raftus, Director of Admissions, Saint Joseph's College, PO Box 815, Rensselaer, IN 47978-0850. *Phone:* 219-866-6170 or 800-447-8781 (toll-free out-of-state). *Fax:* 219-866-6122. *E-mail:* admissions@saintjoe.edu. *Web site:* http://www.saintjoe.edu/.

SAINT MARY-OF-THE-WOODS COLLEGE

Saint Mary-of-the-Woods, Indiana

Saint Mary-of-the-Woods College is a coed, primarily women's, private, Roman Catholic, comprehensive institution, founded in 1840, offering degrees at the associate, bachelor's, and master's levels and post-master's and postbachelor's certificates (also offers external degree program with significant enrollment not reflected in profile). It has a 67-acre campus in Saint Mary-of-the-Woods near Indianapolis.

Academic Information The faculty has 133 members (50% full-time), 37% with terminal degrees. The undergraduate student-faculty ratio is 9:1. The library holds 55 serial subscriptions and 532 audiovisual materials. Special programs include academic remediation, an honors program, study abroad, advanced placement credit, accelerated degree programs, double majors, independent study, distance learning, self-designed majors, summer session for credit, part-time degree programs (evenings, weekends, summer), external degree programs, adult/continuing education programs, internships, and arrangement for off-campus study with Indiana State University, Rose-Hulman Institute of Technology, DePauw University, Wabash College. The most frequently chosen baccalaureate fields are agriculture, business/marketing, education.
Student Body Statistics The student body totals 1,572, of whom 1,414 are undergraduates (139 freshmen). 96 percent are women and 4 percent are men. Students come from 24 states and territories and 4 other countries. 81 percent are from Indiana. 1.1 percent are international students.
Expenses for 2009–10 *Application fee:* $30. *One-time mandatory fee:* $70. *Comprehensive fee:* $31,510 includes full-time tuition ($22,360), mandatory fees ($700), and college room and board ($8450). *College room only:* $3300. *Part-time tuition:* $424 per hour. *Part-time mandatory fees:* $150 per year.
Financial Aid Forms of aid include need-based and non-need-based scholarships and part-time jobs. The application deadline for financial aid is continuous.
Freshman Admission Saint Mary-of-the-Woods College requires an essay, a high school transcript, a minimum 2.5 high school GPA, 1 recommendation, SAT or ACT scores, and TOEFL scores for international students. An interview is recommended. The application deadline for regular admission is August 1.
Transfer Admission The application deadline for admission is August 1.
Entrance Difficulty Saint Mary-of-the-Woods College assesses its entrance difficulty level as moderately difficult.
For Further Information Contact Ms. Jill Blunk, Director of Admission, Saint Mary-of-the-Woods College, Guerin Hall, Saint Mary-of-the-Woods, IN 47876. *Phone:* 812-535-5107 or 800-926-SMWC (toll-free). *Fax:* 812-535-5010. *E-mail:* smwcadms@smwc.edu. *Web site:* http://www.smwc.edu/.

SAINT MARY'S COLLEGE

Notre Dame, Indiana

Saint Mary's College is a women's, private, Roman Catholic, four-year college, founded in 1844, offering degrees at the bachelor's level. It has a 75-acre campus in Notre Dame.

Academic Information The faculty has 203 members (67% full-time), 71% with terminal degrees. The student-faculty ratio is 10:1. The library holds 268,569 titles and 938 serial subscriptions. Special programs include academic remediation, services for learning-disabled students, cooperative (work-study) education, study abroad, advanced placement credit, accelerated degree programs, double majors, independent study, self-designed majors, summer session for credit, part-time degree programs (daytime), internships, and arrangement for off-campus study with University of Notre Dame, members of the Northern Indiana Consortium for Education. The most frequently chosen baccalaureate fields are business/marketing, communications/journalism, social sciences.
Student Body Statistics The student body is made up of 1,628 undergraduates (455 freshmen). Students come from 43 states and territories and 5 other countries. 27 percent are from Indiana. 0.4 percent are international students.
Expenses for 2008–09 *Application fee:* $30. *Comprehensive fee:* $37,150 includes full-time tuition ($27,600), mandatory fees ($612), and college room and board ($8938). *College room only:* $5506. Room and board charges vary according to board plan and housing facility. *Part-time tuition:* $1091 per credit hour. *Part-time mandatory fees:* $306 per term.
Financial Aid Forms of aid include need-based scholarships and part-time jobs. The average aided 2008–09 undergraduate received an aid package worth an estimated $20,936.
Freshman Admission Saint Mary's College requires an essay, a high school transcript, 1 recommendation, SAT or ACT scores, and TOEFL scores for international students. An interview is recommended. The application deadline for regular admission is February 15 and for early decision it is November 15.
Transfer Admission The application deadline for admission is rolling.
Entrance Difficulty Saint Mary's College assesses its entrance difficulty level as moderately difficult. For the fall 2008 freshman class, 80 percent of the applicants were accepted.
For Further Information Contact Mona Bowe, Director of Admission, Saint Mary's College, Notre Dame, IN 46556. *Phone:* 574-284-4587 or 800-551-7621 (toll-free). *Fax:* 574-284-4841. *E-mail:* admission@saintmarys.edu. *Web site:* http://www.saintmarys.edu/.

See page 264 for the Close-Up.

TAYLOR UNIVERSITY

Upland, Indiana

Taylor University is a coed, private, interdenominational, comprehensive institution, founded in 1846, offering degrees at the associate, bachelor's, and master's levels. It has a 950-acre campus in Upland near Indianapolis.

Academic Information The faculty has 197 members (64% full-time), 59% with terminal degrees. The undergraduate student-faculty ratio is 12.8:1. The library holds 188,986 titles, 30,449 serial subscriptions, and 9,837 audiovisual materials. Special programs include academic remediation, services for learning-disabled students, an honors program, cooperative (work-study) education, study abroad, advanced placement credit, ESL programs, double majors, independent study, distance learning, self-designed majors, summer session for credit, part-time degree programs, internships, and arrangement for off-campus study with members of the Christian College Coalition and the Christian College Consortium, Bowling Green University, Trinity Christian College. The most frequently chosen baccalaureate fields are business/marketing, education, psychology.

Student Body Statistics The student body is made up of 1,871 undergraduates (465 freshmen). 55 percent are women and 45 percent are men. Students come from 44 states and territories and 31 other countries. 31 percent are from Indiana. 2.2 percent are international students.

Expenses for 2008–09 *Application fee:* $25. *Comprehensive fee:* $30,898 includes full-time tuition ($24,314), mandatory fees ($232), and college room and board ($6352). *College room only:* $3144. Full-time tuition and fees vary according to course load. Room and board charges vary according to board plan and housing facility. *Part-time tuition:* $870 per credit hour. *Part-time mandatory fees:* $36 per term. Part-time tuition and fees vary according to course load.

Financial Aid Forms of aid include need-based and non-need-based scholarships, athletic grants, and part-time jobs. The average aided 2008–09 undergraduate received an aid package worth an estimated $16,444. The application deadline for financial aid is March 10.

Freshman Admission Taylor University requires an essay, a high school transcript, 2 recommendations, an interview, SAT or ACT scores, and TOEFL scores for international students. A minimum 2.8 high school GPA is recommended. The application deadline for regular admission is rolling and for early action it is December 1.

Transfer Admission The application deadline for admission is rolling.

Entrance Difficulty Taylor University assesses its entrance difficulty level as moderately difficult. For the fall 2008 freshman class, 84 percent of the applicants were accepted.

For Further Information Contact Ms. Amy Barnett, Visit Coordinator, Taylor University, 236 West Reade Avenue, Upland, IN 46989-1001. *Phone:* 765-998-5565 or 800-882-3456 (toll-free). *Fax:* 765-998-4925. *E-mail:* admissions@taylor.edu. *Web site:* http://www.taylor.edu/.

TRINE UNIVERSITY

Angola, Indiana

Trine University is a coed, private, comprehensive institution, founded in 1884, offering degrees at the associate, bachelor's, and master's levels. It has a 400-acre campus in Angola.

Academic Information The faculty has 99 members (70% full-time), 51% with terminal degrees. The undergraduate student-faculty ratio is 16:1. The library holds 57,990 titles, 32,725 serial subscriptions, and 1,862 audiovisual materials. Special programs include academic remediation, an honors program, cooperative (work-study) education, study abroad, advanced placement credit, double majors, distance learning, self-designed majors, summer session for credit, part-time degree programs (daytime, evenings, summer), adult/continuing education programs, and internships. The most frequently chosen baccalaureate fields are business/marketing, engineering, security and protective services.

Student Body Statistics The student body totals 1,451, of whom 1,441 are undergraduates (435 freshmen). 32 percent are women and 68 percent are men. Students come from 26 states and territories and 10 other countries. 58 percent are from Indiana. 2 percent are international students.

Expenses for 2009–10 *Application fee:* $0. *Comprehensive fee:* $32,500 includes full-time tuition ($24,100), mandatory fees ($100), and college room and board ($8300). *Part-time tuition:* $753 per credit hour.

Financial Aid Forms of aid include need-based and non-need-based scholarships and part-time jobs. The average aided 2008–09 undergraduate received an aid package worth an estimated $17,193. The priority application deadline for financial aid is March 10.

Freshman Admission Trine University requires a high school transcript, a minimum 2.5 high school GPA, and SAT or ACT scores. An essay, 2 recommendations, an interview, and TOEFL scores for international students are recommended. The application deadline for regular admission is August 1.

Transfer Admission The application deadline for admission is August 1.

Entrance Difficulty Trine University assesses its entrance difficulty level as moderately difficult. For the fall 2008 freshman class, 53 percent of the applicants were accepted.

For Further Information Contact Mr. Scott Goplin, Dean of Admission, Trine University, 1 University Avenue, Angola, IN 46703. *Phone:* 260-665-4365 or 800-347-4TSU (toll-free). *Fax:* 260-665-4578. *E-mail:* admit@trine.edu. *Web site:* http://www.trine.edu/.

See page 274 for the Close-Up.

UNIVERSITY OF EVANSVILLE

Evansville, Indiana

University of Evansville is a coed, private, comprehensive institution, founded in 1854, affiliated with the United Methodist Church, offering degrees at the associate, bachelor's, master's, and doctoral levels. It has a 75-acre campus in Evansville.

Academic Information The faculty has 231 members (76% full-time), 72% with terminal degrees. The undergraduate student-faculty ratio is 13:1. The library holds 274,174 titles, 845 serial subscriptions, and 12,710 audiovisual materials. Special programs include services for learning-disabled students, an honors program, cooperative (work-study) education, study abroad, advanced placement credit, accelerated degree programs, ESL programs, double majors, independent study, self-designed majors, summer session for credit, part-time degree programs (daytime, evenings, summer), external degree programs, adult/continuing education programs, and internships. The most frequently chosen baccalaureate fields are business/marketing, education, engineering.

Student Body Statistics The student body totals 2,789, of whom 2,632 are undergraduates (619 freshmen). 59 percent are women and 41 percent are men. Students come from 39 states and territories and 52 other countries. 60 percent are from Indiana. 6.5 percent are international students.

Expenses for 2008–09 *Application fee:* $35. *Comprehensive fee:* $34,075 includes full-time tuition ($25,130), mandatory fees ($715), and college room and board ($8230). *College room only:* $4250. Room and board charges vary according to board plan and housing facility. *Part-time tuition:* $690 per hour. *Part-time mandatory fees:* $45 per term. Part-time tuition and fees vary according to course load.

Financial Aid Forms of aid include need-based and non-need-based scholarships, athletic grants, and part-time jobs. The average aided 2008–09 undergraduate received an aid package worth an estimated $21,693. The priority application deadline for financial aid is March 10.

Freshman Admission University of Evansville requires a high school transcript, 1 recommendation, SAT or ACT scores, and TOEFL scores for international students. A minimum 3.0 high school GPA and an interview are recommended. An essay and an interview are required for some. The application deadline for regular admission is February 1 and for early action it is December 1.

Transfer Admission The application deadline for admission is rolling.

University of Evansville (continued)

Entrance Difficulty University of Evansville assesses its entrance difficulty level as moderately difficult; very difficult for engineering, physical therapy. For the fall 2008 freshman class, 88 percent of the applicants were accepted.

For Further Information Contact Don Vos, Dean of Admission, University of Evansville, 1800 Lincoln Avenue, Evansville, IN 47722. *Phone:* 812-488-2468 or 800-423-8633 Ext. 2468 (toll-free). *Fax:* 812-488-4076. *E-mail:* admission@evansville.edu. *Web site:* http://www.evansville.edu/.

UNIVERSITY OF INDIANAPOLIS

Indianapolis, Indiana

University of Indianapolis is a coed, private, comprehensive institution, founded in 1902, affiliated with the United Methodist Church, offering degrees at the associate, bachelor's, master's, and doctoral levels. It has a 65-acre campus in Indianapolis.

Academic Information The faculty has 433 members (46% full-time), 56% with terminal degrees. The undergraduate student-faculty ratio is 12:1. The library holds 173,363 titles and 1,015 serial subscriptions. Special programs include academic remediation, services for learning-disabled students, an honors program, cooperative (work-study) education, study abroad, advanced placement credit, accelerated degree programs, Freshman Honors College, ESL programs, double majors, independent study, self-designed majors, summer session for credit, part-time degree programs (evenings), adult/continuing education programs, internships, and arrangement for off-campus study with 7 members of the Consortium for Urban Education, 10 members of the May Term Consortium. The most frequently chosen baccalaureate fields are business/marketing, education, health professions and related sciences.

Student Body Statistics The student body totals 4,701, of whom 3,573 are undergraduates. 85 percent are from Indiana. 5.3 percent are international students.

Expenses for 2008–09 *Application fee:* $25. *Comprehensive fee:* $28,300 includes full-time tuition ($20,320), mandatory fees ($190), and college room and board ($7790). *College room only:* $3700. Room and board charges vary according to board plan and housing facility. *Part-time tuition:* varies with course load.

Financial Aid Forms of aid include need-based and non-need-based scholarships, athletic grants, and part-time jobs. The priority application deadline for financial aid is March 1.

Freshman Admission University of Indianapolis requires a high school transcript, a minimum 2.0 high school GPA, SAT or ACT scores, and TOEFL scores for international students. An interview is required for some. The application deadline for regular admission is rolling.

Transfer Admission The application deadline for admission is rolling.

Entrance Difficulty University of Indianapolis assesses its entrance difficulty level as moderately difficult. For the fall 2008 freshman class, 79 percent of the applicants were accepted.

For Further Information Contact Mr. Ronald Wilks, Director of Admissions, University of Indianapolis, 1400 East Hanna Avenue, Indianapolis, IN 46227-3697. *Phone:* 317-788-3216 or 800-232-8634 Ext. 3216 (toll-free). *Fax:* 317-788-3300. *E-mail:* admissions@uindy.edu. *Web site:* http://www.uindy.edu/.

UNIVERSITY OF NOTRE DAME

Notre Dame, Indiana

University of Notre Dame is a coed, private, Roman Catholic university, founded in 1842, offering degrees at the bachelor's, master's, doctoral, and first professional levels. It has a 1,250-acre campus in Notre Dame.

Academic Information The faculty has 813 full-time members. The undergraduate student-faculty ratio is 12:1. The library holds 3 million titles, 42,029 serial subscriptions, and 62,296 audiovisual materials. Special programs include services for learning-disabled students, an honors program, study abroad, advanced placement credit, accelerated degree programs, double majors, independent study, distance learning, self-designed majors, summer session for credit, internships, and arrangement for off-campus study with Saint Mary's College (IN), Xavier University of Louisiana, Clark Atlanta University, St. Mary's University of San Antonio. The most frequently chosen baccalaureate fields are business/marketing, engineering, social sciences.

Student Body Statistics The student body totals 11,731, of whom 8,363 are undergraduates (2,000 freshmen). 47 percent are women and 53 percent are men. Students come from 53 states and territories and 42 other countries. 8 percent are from Indiana. 2.7 percent are international students.

Expenses for 2008–09 *Application fee:* $65. *Comprehensive fee:* $46,675 includes full-time tuition ($36,340), mandatory fees ($507), and college room and board ($9828). *Part-time tuition:* $1514 per credit.

Financial Aid Forms of aid include need-based and non-need-based scholarships, athletic grants, and part-time jobs. The average aided 2008–09 undergraduate received an aid package worth an estimated $32,113. The application deadline for financial aid is February 15.

Freshman Admission University of Notre Dame requires an essay, a high school transcript, 1 recommendation, SAT or ACT scores, and TOEFL scores for international students. SAT Subject Test scores are required for some. The application deadline for regular admission is December 31 and for early action it is November 1.

Transfer Admission The application deadline for admission is April 15.

Entrance Difficulty University of Notre Dame assesses its entrance difficulty level as most difficult. For the fall 2008 freshman class, 27 percent of the applicants were accepted.

For Further Information Contact Office of Undergraduate Admissions, University of Notre Dame, 220 Main Building, Notre Dame, IN 46556-5612. *Phone:* 574-631-7505. *Fax:* 574-631-8865. *E-mail:* admissions@nd.edu. *Web site:* http://www.nd.edu/.

UNIVERSITY OF PHOENIX–INDIANAPOLIS CAMPUS

Indianapolis, Indiana

University of Phoenix–Indianapolis Campus is a coed, proprietary, comprehensive institution, founded in 2003, offering degrees at the associate, bachelor's, and master's levels.

Academic Information The faculty has 80 members (19% full-time), 18% with terminal degrees. Special programs include services for learning-disabled students, advanced placement credit, accelerated degree programs, independent study, and distance learning. The most frequently chosen baccalaureate fields are business/marketing, health professions and related sciences.

Student Body Statistics The student body totals 339, of whom 271 are undergraduates (34 freshmen). 73 percent are women and 27 percent are men. 1.8 percent are international students.

Expenses for 2008–09 *Application fee:* $0. *Tuition:* $11,025 full-time. Full-time tuition varies according to course level and course load.

Financial Aid Forms of aid include need-based and non-need-based scholarships. The average aided 2007–08 undergraduate received an aid package worth $7000. The application deadline for financial aid is continuous.

Freshman Admission University of Phoenix–Indianapolis Campus requires 1 recommendation. A high school transcript is required for some. The application deadline for regular admission is rolling.

Transfer Admission The application deadline for admission is rolling.

Entrance Difficulty University of Phoenix–Indianapolis Campus has an open admission policy.

For Further Information Contact Ms. Audra McQuarie, Registrar/ Executive Director, University of Phoenix–Indianapolis Campus, 4035 South Riverpoint Parkway, Mail Stop CF-L101, Phoenix, AZ 85040. *Phone:* 480-557-6151, 800-776-4867 (toll-free in-state), or 800-228-7240 (toll-free out-of-state). *Fax:* 480-643-3068. *E-mail:* audra.mcquarie@phoenix.edu. *Web site:* http://www.phoenix.edu/.

UNIVERSITY OF SAINT FRANCIS

Fort Wayne, Indiana

University of Saint Francis is a coed, private, Roman Catholic, comprehensive institution, founded in 1890, offering degrees at the associate, bachelor's, and master's levels and postbachelor's certificates. It has a 74-acre campus in Fort Wayne.

Academic Information The faculty has 222 members (48% full-time), 31% with terminal degrees. The undergraduate student-faculty ratio is 12:1. The library holds 95,991 titles and 567 serial subscriptions. Special programs include academic remediation, services for learning-disabled students, an honors program, cooperative (work-study) education, study abroad, advanced placement credit, Freshman Honors College, double majors, independent study, distance learning, summer session for credit, part-time degree programs (daytime, evenings, weekends, summer), internships, and arrangement for off-campus study. The most frequently chosen baccalaureate fields are education, business/marketing, health professions and related sciences.
Student Body Statistics The student body totals 2,112, of whom 1,800 are undergraduates (322 freshmen). 68 percent are women and 32 percent are men. Students come from 15 states and territories and 3 other countries. 89 percent are from Indiana. 0.3 percent are international students.
Financial Aid Forms of aid include need-based and non-need-based scholarships, athletic grants, and part-time jobs. The average aided 2008–09 undergraduate received an aid package worth an estimated $16,101. The application deadline for financial aid is June 30 with a priority deadline of March 10.
Freshman Admission University of Saint Francis requires a high school transcript, a minimum 2.3 high school GPA, SAT or ACT scores, and TOEFL scores for international students. An essay is recommended. An interview is required for some. The application deadline for regular admission is rolling.
Transfer Admission The application deadline for admission is rolling.
Entrance Difficulty University of Saint Francis assesses its entrance difficulty level as moderately difficult. For the fall 2008 freshman class, 47 percent of the applicants were accepted.
For Further Information Contact Mr. Ron Schumacher, Vice President for Enrollment Management, University of Saint Francis, 2701 Spring Street, Fort Wayne, IN 46808. *Phone:* 260-434-3279 or 800-729-4732 (toll-free). *Fax:* 260-434-7590. *E-mail:* admis@sf.edu. *Web site:* http://www.sf.edu/.

UNIVERSITY OF SOUTHERN INDIANA

Evansville, Indiana

University of Southern Indiana is a coed, public, comprehensive unit of Indiana Commission for Higher Education, founded in 1965, offering degrees at the associate, bachelor's, master's, and doctoral levels and postbachelor's certificates. It has a 330-acre campus in Evansville.

Academic Information The faculty has 624 members (52% full-time), 41% with terminal degrees. The undergraduate student-faculty ratio is 18:1. The library holds 336,457 titles, 22,135 serial subscriptions, and 5,744 audiovisual materials. Special programs include academic remediation, services for learning-disabled students, an honors program, cooperative (work-study) education, study abroad, advanced placement credit, ESL programs, double majors, independent study, distance learning, summer session for credit, part-time degree programs (daytime, evenings, weekends, summer), adult/continuing education programs, and internships. The most frequently chosen baccalaureate fields are business/marketing, education, health professions and related sciences.
Student Body Statistics The student body totals 10,126, of whom 9,320 are undergraduates (2,104 freshmen). 59 percent are women and 41 percent are men. Students come from 33 states and territories and 48 other countries. 90 percent are from Indiana. 2 percent are international students.
Expenses for 2009–10 *Application fee:* $25. *State resident tuition:* $5019 full-time, $167.30 per credit hour part-time. *Nonresident tuition:* $11,954 full-time, $398.45 per credit hour part-time. *Mandatory fees:* $200 full-time, $22.75 per term part-time. *College room and board:* $6648. *College room only:* $3350.
Financial Aid Forms of aid include need-based and non-need-based scholarships, athletic grants, and part-time jobs. The average aided 2008–09 undergraduate received an aid package worth an estimated $10,574. The application deadline for financial aid is March 1.
Freshman Admission University of Southern Indiana requires a high school transcript, SAT or ACT scores, and TOEFL scores for international students. An essay and a minimum 2.0 high school GPA are recommended. An interview is required for some. The application deadline for regular admission is August 15.
Entrance Difficulty University of Southern Indiana assesses its entrance difficulty level as moderately difficult. For the fall 2008 freshman class, 88 percent of the applicants were accepted.
For Further Information Contact Mr. Eric Otto, Director of Admission, University of Southern Indiana, 8600 University Boulevard, Evansville, IN 47712-3590. *Phone:* 812-464-1765 or 800-467-1965 (toll-free). *Fax:* 812-465-7154. *E-mail:* enroll@usi.edu. *Web site:* http://www.usi.edu/.

VALPARAISO UNIVERSITY

Valparaiso, Indiana

Valparaiso University is a coed, private, comprehensive institution, founded in 1859, affiliated with the Lutheran Church, offering degrees at the associate, bachelor's, master's, doctoral, and first professional levels and post-master's and postbachelor's certificates. It has a 310-acre campus in Valparaiso near Chicago.

Academic Information The faculty has 376 members (68% full-time), 73% with terminal degrees. The undergraduate student-faculty ratio is 12:1. The library holds 506,437 titles, 50,199 serial subscriptions, and 6,594 audiovisual materials. Special programs include services for learning-disabled students, an honors program, cooperative (work-study) education, study abroad, advanced placement credit, accelerated degree programs, Freshman Honors College, ESL programs, double majors, independent study, distance learning, self-designed majors, summer session for credit, part-time degree programs (daytime, evenings, summer), adult/continuing education programs, internships, and arrangement for off-campus study with Associated Colleges of the Midwest, American University, Lutheran College Washington Consortium, Drew University. The most frequently chosen baccalaureate fields are business/marketing, engineering, social sciences.
Student Body Statistics The student body totals 3,976, of whom 2,881 are undergraduates (657 freshmen). 52 percent are women and 48 percent are men. Students come from 42 states and territories and 35 other countries. 40 percent are from Indiana. 2.9 percent are international students.
Expenses for 2008–09 *Application fee:* $30. *Comprehensive fee:* $34,570 includes full-time tuition ($26,070), mandatory fees ($880), and college room and board ($7620). *College room only:* $4680. Room and board charges vary according to housing facility and student level. *Part-time tuition:* $1205 per credit hour. *Part-time mandatory fees:* $25 per credit hour. Part-time tuition and fees vary according to course load.
Financial Aid Forms of aid include need-based and non-need-based scholarships, athletic grants, and part-time jobs. The average aided 2007–08 undergraduate received an aid package worth $24,061. The priority application deadline for financial aid is March 1.
Freshman Admission Valparaiso University requires an essay, a high school transcript, and SAT or ACT scores. 2 recommendations, an interview, and TOEFL scores for international students are recommended. An interview is required for some. The application deadline for regular admission is August 15 and for early action it is November 1.
Entrance Difficulty Valparaiso University assesses its entrance difficulty level as moderately difficult. For the fall 2008 freshman class, 92 percent of the applicants were accepted.
For Further Information Contact Office of Admission, Valparaiso University, Kretzmann Hall, 1700 Chapel Drive, Valparaiso, IN 46383-6493. *Phone:* 219-464-5011 or 888-GO-VALPO (toll-free). *Fax:* 219-464-6898. *E-mail:* undergrad.admissions@valpo.edu. *Web site:* http://www.valpo.edu/.

See page 280 for the Close-Up.

WABASH COLLEGE

Crawfordsville, Indiana

Wabash College is a men's, private, four-year college, founded in 1832, offering degrees at the bachelor's level. It has a 50-acre campus in Crawfordsville near Indianapolis.

Academic Information The faculty has 91 members (98% full-time), 96% with terminal degrees. The student-faculty ratio is 10:1. The library holds 296,556 titles, 24,569 serial subscriptions, and 14,669 audiovisual materials. Special programs include services for learning-disabled students, study abroad, advanced placement credit, double majors, independent study, internships, and arrangement for off-campus study with members of the Great Lakes Colleges Association. The most frequently chosen baccalaureate fields are philosophy and religious studies, psychology, social sciences.
Student Body Statistics The student body is made up of 917 undergraduates (253 freshmen). Students come from 35 states and territories and 14 other countries. 76 percent are from Indiana. 5.3 percent are international students.
Expenses for 2008–09 *Application fee:* $40. *Comprehensive fee:* $35,350 includes full-time tuition ($27,500), mandatory fees ($450), and college room and board ($7400). *College room only:* $3300. Full-time tuition and fees vary according to reciprocity agreements. Room and board charges vary according to board plan and housing facility. *Part-time tuition:* $4583 per course. Part-time tuition varies according to course load and reciprocity agreements.
Financial Aid Forms of aid include need-based and non-need-based scholarships and part-time jobs. The average aided 2008–09 undergraduate received an aid package worth an estimated $25,732. The application deadline for financial aid is March 1 with a priority deadline of February 15.
Freshman Admission Wabash College requires a high school transcript, SAT or ACT scores, and TOEFL scores for international students. An essay, 1 recommendation, and an interview are recommended. The application deadline for regular admission is rolling, for early decision it is November 15, and for early action it is December 15.
Transfer Admission The application deadline for admission is March 15.
Entrance Difficulty Wabash College assesses its entrance difficulty level as moderately difficult. For the fall 2008 freshman class, 49 percent of the applicants were accepted.
For Further Information Contact Mr. Steve Klein, Dean of Admissions, Wabash College, PO Box 362, Crawfordsville, IN 47933-0352. *Phone:* 765-361-6225 or 800-345-5385 (toll-free). *Fax:* 765-361-6437. *E-mail:* admissions@wabash.edu. *Web site:* http://www.wabash.edu/.

Iowa

AIB COLLEGE OF BUSINESS

Des Moines, Iowa

AIB College of Business is a coed, private, four-year college, founded in 1921, offering degrees at the associate and bachelor's levels. It has a 20-acre campus in Des Moines.

Academic Information The faculty has 70 members (40% full-time), 7% with terminal degrees. The student-faculty ratio is 24:1. The library holds 5,400 titles and 185 serial subscriptions. Special programs include academic remediation, cooperative (work-study) education, double majors, independent study, distance learning, summer session for credit, part-time degree programs (daytime, evenings, summer), adult/continuing education programs, and internships. The most frequently chosen baccalaureate field is business/marketing.
Student Body Statistics The student body is made up of 965 undergraduates. 71 percent are women and 29 percent are men. Students come from 7 states and territories. 97 percent are from Iowa.
Expenses for 2009–10 *Application fee:* $25. *Tuition:* $12,900 full-time, $240 per quarter hour part-time. *Mandatory fees:* $315 full-time. *College room only:* $3855.
Financial Aid Forms of aid include need-based scholarships and part-time jobs. The priority application deadline for financial aid is April 1.
Freshman Admission AIB College of Business requires a high school transcript, a minimum 2.0 high school GPA, and TOEFL scores for international students. An interview and ACT scores are recommended. The application deadline for regular admission is rolling.
Transfer Admission The application deadline for admission is rolling.
Entrance Difficulty AIB College of Business assesses its entrance difficulty level as minimally difficult; moderately difficult for Real-time Reporting program. For the fall 2008 freshman class, 87 percent of the applicants were accepted.
For Further Information Contact Ms. Shirley Krouch, Director of Admissions, AIB College of Business, Keith Fenton Administration Building, 2500 Fleur Drive, Des Moines, IA 50321-1799. *Phone:* 515-244-4221 or 800-444-1921 (toll-free). *Fax:* 515-244-6773. *E-mail:* krouchs@aib.edu. *Web site:* http://www.aib.edu/.

ALLEN COLLEGE

Waterloo, Iowa

Allen College is a coed, primarily women's, private, comprehensive institution, founded in 1989, offering degrees at the associate, bachelor's, and master's levels (liberal arts and general education courses offered at either University of North Iowa or Wartburg College). It has a 20-acre campus in Waterloo.

Academic Information The faculty has 34 members (79% full-time), 21% with terminal degrees. The undergraduate student-faculty ratio is 12:1. The library holds 3,200 titles, 199 serial subscriptions, and 350 audiovisual materials. Special programs include cooperative (work-study) education, advanced placement credit, accelerated degree programs, independent study, distance learning, part-time degree programs (daytime, evenings), internships, and arrangement for off-campus study. The most frequently chosen baccalaureate field is health professions and related sciences.
Student Body Statistics The student body totals 416, of whom 308 are undergraduates (4 freshmen). 95 percent are women and 5 percent are men. Students come from 5 states and territories. 95 percent are from Iowa.
Expenses for 2008–09 *Application fee:* $50. *Comprehensive fee:* $21,395 includes full-time tuition ($13,119), mandatory fees ($1460), and college room and board ($6816). *College room only:* $3408. *Part-time tuition:* $481 per credit hour. *Part-time mandatory fees:* $65 per credit hour.
Financial Aid Forms of aid include need-based and non-need-based scholarships and part-time jobs. The average aided 2008–09 undergraduate received an aid package worth an estimated $9479. The application deadline for financial aid is continuous.
Freshman Admission Allen College requires an essay, a high school transcript, 1 recommendation, ACT scores, and TOEFL scores for international students. A minimum 2.7 high school GPA and rank in upper 50% of high school class are recommended. An interview is required for some. The application deadline for regular admission is July 1 and for early decision it is March 1.
Transfer Admission The application deadline for admission is July 1.
Entrance Difficulty Allen College assesses its entrance difficulty level as moderately difficult.
For Further Information Contact Dina Dowden, Education Secretary, Student Services, Allen College, Barrett Forum, 1825 Logan Avenue, Waterloo, IA 50703. *Phone:* 319-226-2000. *Fax:* 319-226-2051. *E-mail:* allencollegeadmissions@ihs.org. *Web site:* http://www.allencollege.edu/.

ASHFORD UNIVERSITY

Clinton, Iowa

Ashford University is a coed, proprietary, comprehensive institution, founded in 1918, offering degrees at the bachelor's and master's levels. It has a 24-acre campus in Clinton near Chicago.

Expenses for 2008–09 *Application fee:* $20. *Comprehensive fee:* $21,906 includes full-time tuition ($15,340), mandatory fees ($766), and college room and board ($5800). *College room only:* $2500. *Part-time tuition:* $447 per credit hour. *Part-time mandatory fees:* $6 per credit hour, $275 per term.
For Further Information Contact Ms. Waunita M. Sullivan, Director of Enrollment, Ashford University, 400 North Bluff Boulevard, PO Box 2967, Clinton, IA 52733-2967. *Phone:* 563-242-4153 or 800-242-4153 (toll-free). *Fax:* 563-243-6102. *E-mail:* admissions@ashford.edu. *Web site:* http://www.ashford.edu/.

BRIAR CLIFF UNIVERSITY

Sioux City, Iowa

Briar Cliff University is a coed, private, Roman Catholic, comprehensive institution, founded in 1930, offering degrees at the associate, bachelor's, and master's levels. It has a 75-acre campus in Sioux City.

Academic Information The faculty has 108 members (56% full-time), 43% with terminal degrees. The undergraduate student-faculty ratio is 12:1. The library holds 76,339 titles, 164 serial subscriptions, and 1,270 audiovisual materials. Special programs include academic remediation, services for learning-disabled students, an honors program, study abroad, advanced placement credit, accelerated degree programs, double majors, independent study, distance learning, self-designed majors, summer session for credit, part-time degree programs (daytime, evenings, weekends, summer), adult/continuing education programs, internships, and arrangement for off-campus study with Colleges of Mid-America. The most frequently chosen baccalaureate fields are business/marketing, education, health professions and related sciences.
Student Body Statistics The student body totals 1,114, of whom 1,030 are undergraduates (252 freshmen). 55 percent are women and 45 percent are men. Students come from 24 states and territories and 4 other countries. 64 percent are from Iowa. 0.5 percent are international students.
Expenses for 2008–09 *Application fee:* $20. *Comprehensive fee:* $27,921 includes full-time tuition ($20,886), mandatory fees ($624), and college room and board ($6411). *College room only:* $3153. Room and board charges vary according to board plan and housing facility. *Part-time tuition:* $696 per credit hour. *Part-time mandatory fees:* $21 per credit hour. Part-time tuition and fees vary according to class time and course load.
Financial Aid Forms of aid include need-based and non-need-based scholarships and part-time jobs. The application deadline for financial aid is March 15.
Freshman Admission Briar Cliff University requires a high school transcript, a minimum 2.0 high school GPA, and SAT or ACT scores. TOEFL scores for international students are recommended. An essay, 3 recommendations, and an interview are required for some. The application deadline for regular admission is rolling and for nonresidents it is rolling.
Transfer Admission The application deadline for admission is rolling.
Entrance Difficulty Briar Cliff University assesses its entrance difficulty level as moderately difficult. For the fall 2008 freshman class, 69 percent of the applicants were accepted.
For Further Information Contact Briar Cliff Admissions, Briar Cliff University, 3303 Rebecca Street, Sioux City, IA 51104-0100. *Phone:* 712-279-5200 or 800-662-3303 Ext. 5200 (toll-free). *Fax:* 712-279-1632. *E-mail:* admissions@briarcliff.edu. *Web site:* http://www.briarcliff.edu/.

BUENA VISTA UNIVERSITY

Storm Lake, Iowa

Buena Vista University is a coed, private, comprehensive institution, founded in 1891, affiliated with the Presbyterian Church (U.S.A.), offering degrees at the bachelor's and master's levels. It has a 60-acre campus in Storm Lake.

Academic Information The faculty has 111 members (74% full-time), 54% with terminal degrees. The undergraduate student-faculty ratio is 10:1. The library holds 144,000 titles, 632 serial subscriptions, and 5,648 audiovisual materials. Special programs include academic remediation, services for learning-disabled students, an honors program, study abroad, advanced placement credit, ESL programs, double majors, independent study, distance learning, self-designed majors, summer session for credit, part-time degree programs, external degree programs, adult/continuing education programs, internships, and arrangement for off-campus study with Washington University in St. Louis. The most frequently chosen baccalaureate fields are business/marketing, education, interdisciplinary studies.
Student Body Statistics The student body totals 1,070, of whom 968 are undergraduates (274 freshmen). 50 percent are women and 50 percent are men. Students come from 24 states and territories and 8 other countries. 77 percent are from Iowa. 3 percent are international students.
Expenses for 2008–09 *Application fee:* $0. *Comprehensive fee:* $31,810 includes full-time tuition ($24,796) and college room and board ($7014). Room and board charges vary according to board plan. *Part-time tuition:* $833 per credit hour.
Financial Aid Forms of aid include need-based and non-need-based scholarships and part-time jobs. The average aided 2008–09 undergraduate received an aid package worth an estimated $27,086.
Freshman Admission Buena Vista University requires a high school transcript, SAT or ACT scores, and TOEFL scores for international students. A minimum 3.0 high school GPA is recommended. An essay and an interview are required for some.
Entrance Difficulty Buena Vista University assesses its entrance difficulty level as moderately difficult. For the fall 2008 freshman class, 75 percent of the applicants were accepted.
For Further Information Contact Alan Coheley, Vice President for Enrollment Management, Buena Vista University, 610 West Fourth Street, Storm Lake, IA 50588. *Phone:* 712-749-2235 or 800-383-9600 (toll-free). *E-mail:* admissions@bvu.edu. *Web site:* http://www.bvu.edu/.

CENTRAL COLLEGE

Pella, Iowa

Central College is a coed, private, four-year college, founded in 1853, affiliated with the Reformed Church in America, offering degrees at the bachelor's level. It has a 133-acre campus in Pella near Des Moines.

Academic Information The faculty has 156 members (57% full-time), 62% with terminal degrees. The student-faculty ratio is 14:1. The library holds 197,672 titles and 634 serial subscriptions. Special programs include services for learning-disabled students, an honors program, study abroad, ESL programs, double majors, independent study, self-designed majors, summer session for credit, part-time degree programs (daytime, evenings), internships, and arrangement for off-campus study. The most frequently chosen baccalaureate fields are business/marketing, parks and recreation, social sciences.
Student Body Statistics The student body is made up of 1,558 undergraduates (405 freshmen). 54 percent are women and 46 percent are men. Students come from 35 states and territories and 5 other countries. 83 percent are from Iowa. 1.3 percent are international students.
Expenses for 2008–09 *Application fee:* $25. *Comprehensive fee:* $31,950 includes full-time tuition ($23,564), mandatory fees ($380), and college room and board ($8006). *College room only:* $3926. *Part-time tuition:* $818 per semester hour.
Financial Aid Forms of aid include need-based and non-need-based scholarships and part-time jobs. The average aided 2008–09 undergraduate received an aid package worth an estimated $20,712. The priority application deadline for financial aid is March 15.
Freshman Admission Central College requires a high school transcript, SAT or ACT scores, and TOEFL scores for international students. A minimum 2.5 high school GPA and an interview are recommended. An essay, 3 recommendations, and an interview are required for some. The application deadline for regular admission is rolling.
Transfer Admission The application deadline for admission is rolling.
Entrance Difficulty Central College assesses its entrance difficulty level as moderately difficult. For the fall 2008 freshman class, 77 percent of the applicants were accepted.
For Further Information Contact Ms. Carol Williamson, Dean of Admission and Student Enrollment Services, Central College, 812 University Street, Pella, IA 50219-1999. *Phone:* 641-628-7600, 877-462-3687 (toll-free in-state), or 877-462-3689 (toll-free out-of-state). *Fax:* 641-628-5316. *E-mail:* admissions@central.edu. *Web site:* http://www.central.edu/.

CLARKE COLLEGE

Dubuque, Iowa

Clarke College is a coed, private, Roman Catholic, comprehensive institution, founded in 1843, offering degrees at the associate, bachelor's, master's, and doctoral levels. It has a 55-acre campus in Dubuque.

Academic Information The faculty has 130 members (55% full-time), 38% with terminal degrees. The undergraduate student-faculty ratio is 11:1. The library holds 120,000 titles, 9,600 serial subscriptions, and 1,400 audiovisual materials. Special programs include an honors program, cooperative (work-study) education, study abroad, advanced placement credit, accelerated degree programs, ESL programs, double majors, independent study, distance learning, self-designed majors, summer session for credit, part-time degree programs (evenings), adult/continuing education programs, internships, and arrangement for off-campus study with Tri-College Cooperative Effort. The most frequently chosen baccalaureate fields are business/marketing, education, health professions and related sciences.
Student Body Statistics The student body totals 1,156, of whom 956 are undergraduates (136 freshmen). 69 percent are women and 31 percent are men. Students come from 30 states and territories and 5 other countries. 62 percent are from Iowa. 1.8 percent are international students.
Expenses for 2009–10 *Application fee:* $25. *Comprehensive fee:* $30,360 includes full-time tuition ($22,800), mandatory fees ($720), and college room and board ($6840). *College room only:* $3360. *Part-time tuition:* $578 per credit hour.
Financial Aid Forms of aid include need-based and non-need-based scholarships, athletic grants, and part-time jobs. The average aided 2007–08 undergraduate received an aid package worth $18,581. The priority application deadline for financial aid is April 15.
Freshman Admission Clarke College requires a high school transcript, a minimum 2.0 high school GPA, rank in upper 50% of high school class, SAT or ACT scores, and TOEFL scores for international students. An interview is required for some. The application deadline for regular admission is rolling.
Transfer Admission The application deadline for admission is rolling.
Entrance Difficulty Clarke College assesses its entrance difficulty level as moderately difficult; very difficult for physical therapy program. For the fall 2008 freshman class, 62 percent of the applicants were accepted.
For Further Information Contact Mr. Andy Shroeder, Director of Admissions, Clarke College, 1550 Clarke Drive, Dubuque, IA 52001-3198. *Phone:* 563-588-6316 or 800-383-2345 (toll-free). *Fax:* 563-588-6789. *E-mail:* admissions@clarke.edu. *Web site:* http://www.clarke.edu/.

COE COLLEGE

Cedar Rapids, Iowa

Coe College is a coed, private, comprehensive institution, founded in 1851, affiliated with the Presbyterian Church, offering degrees at the bachelor's and master's levels. It has a 53-acre campus in Cedar Rapids.

Academic Information The undergraduate student-faculty ratio is 11:1. Special programs include services for learning-disabled students, an honors program, study abroad, advanced placement credit, accelerated degree programs, ESL programs, double majors, independent study, self-designed majors, summer session for credit, part-time degree programs (daytime, evenings, summer), internships, and arrangement for off-campus study with University of Iowa, Mount Mercy College, Associated Colleges of the Midwest, Washington University in St. Louis. The most frequently chosen baccalaureate fields are business/marketing, social sciences, visual and performing arts.
Student Body Statistics The student body totals 1,326, of whom 1,310 are undergraduates (342 freshmen). 55 percent are women and 45 percent are men. Students come from 43 states and territories and 18 other countries. 61 percent are from Iowa. 4.4 percent are international students.
Expenses for 2009–10 *Application fee:* $30. *Comprehensive fee:* $36,420 includes full-time tuition ($28,950), mandatory fees ($320), and college room and board ($7150). *College room only:* $3210. *Part-time tuition:* $3620 per course.
Financial Aid Forms of aid include need-based and non-need-based scholarships and part-time jobs. The average aided 2008–09 undergraduate received an aid package worth an estimated $23,972. The priority application deadline for financial aid is March 1.
Freshman Admission Coe College requires an essay, a high school transcript, 1 recommendation, and TOEFL scores for international students. A minimum 3.0 high school GPA and an interview are recommended. The application deadline for regular admission is March 1 and for early action it is December 10.
Transfer Admission The application deadline for admission is rolling.
Entrance Difficulty Coe College assesses its entrance difficulty level as moderately difficult.
For Further Information Contact Mr. John Grundig, Dean of Admission, Coe College, 1220 1st Avenue, NE, Cedar Rapids, IA 52402-5070. *Phone:* 319-399-8500 or 877-225-5263 (toll-free). *Fax:* 319-399-8816. *E-mail:* admission@coe.edu. *Web site:* http://www.coe.edu/.

CORNELL COLLEGE

Mount Vernon, Iowa

Cornell College is a coed, private, Methodist, four-year college, founded in 1853, offering degrees at the bachelor's level. It has a 129-acre campus in Mount Vernon.

Academic Information The faculty has 97 members (86% full-time), 91% with terminal degrees. The student-faculty ratio is 11:1. The library holds 194,131 titles, 490 serial subscriptions, and 3,559 audiovisual materials. Special programs include services for learning-disabled students, study abroad, advanced placement credit, ESL programs, double majors, independent study, self-designed majors, internships, and arrangement for off-campus study with Associated Colleges of the Midwest, Fisk University, School for International Training. The most frequently chosen baccalaureate fields are biological/life sciences, social sciences, visual and performing arts.
Student Body Statistics The student body is made up of 1,083 undergraduates (316 freshmen). 51 percent are women and 49 percent are men. Students come from 46 states and territories and 20 other countries. 29 percent are from Iowa. 3.1 percent are international students.
Expenses for 2008–09 *Application fee:* $30. *Comprehensive fee:* $35,070 includes full-time tuition ($27,670), mandatory fees ($180), and college room and board ($7220). *College room only:* $3370. Room and board charges vary according to board plan and housing facility. *Part-time tuition:* varies with course load, reciprocity agreements.
Financial Aid Forms of aid include need-based and non-need-based scholarships and part-time jobs. The average aided 2008–09 undergraduate received an aid package worth an estimated $23,720. The application deadline for financial aid is March 1.
Freshman Admission Cornell College requires an essay, a high school transcript, 1 recommendation, SAT or ACT scores, and TOEFL scores for international students. An interview and SAT Subject Test scores are recommended. The application deadline for regular admission is February 1 and for early action it is December 1.
Transfer Admission The application deadline for admission is March 1.
Entrance Difficulty Cornell College assesses its entrance difficulty level as moderately difficult. For the fall 2008 freshman class, 45 percent of the applicants were accepted.
For Further Information Contact Todd White, Director of Admission, Cornell College, 600 First Street Southwest, Mount Vernon, IA 52314-1098. *Phone:* 319-895-4167 or 800-747-1112 (toll-free). *Fax:* 319-895-4451. *E-mail:* twhite@cornellcollege.edu. *Web site:* http://www.cornellcollege.edu/.

DIVINE WORD COLLEGE

Epworth, Iowa

Divine Word College is a coed, primarily men's, private, Roman Catholic, four-year college, founded in 1912, offering degrees at the associate and bachelor's levels. It has a 28-acre campus in Epworth.

Academic Information The library holds 94,583 titles and 372 serial subscriptions. Special programs include academic remediation, study abroad, advanced placement credit, ESL programs, double majors, and independent study.
Student Body Statistics The student body is made up of 59 undergraduates.
Expenses for 2008–09 *Application fee:* $25. *Comprehensive fee:* $13,140 includes full-time tuition ($10,400), mandatory fees ($40), and college room and board ($2700). *Part-time tuition:* $347 per credit hour. *Part-time mandatory fees:* $40 per term.
Freshman Admission Divine Word College requires an essay, a high school transcript, 3 recommendations, an interview, medical history, SAT or ACT scores, and TOEFL scores for international students. The application deadline for regular admission is July 15.
Transfer Admission The application deadline for admission is July 15.
Entrance Difficulty Divine Word College assesses its entrance difficulty level as minimally difficult.
For Further Information Contact Mr. Len Uhal, Vice President of Recruitment/Director of Admissions, Divine Word College, 102 Jacoby Drive SW, Epworth, IA 52045-0380. *Phone:* 563-876-3353 or 800-553-3321 (toll-free). *Fax:* 563-876-5515. *E-mail:* luhal@dwci.edu. *Web site:* http://www.dwci.edu/.

DORDT COLLEGE

Sioux Center, Iowa

Dordt College is a coed, private, Christian Reformed, comprehensive institution, founded in 1955, offering degrees at the associate, bachelor's, and master's levels. It has a 100-acre campus in Sioux Center.

Academic Information The faculty has 106 members (75% full-time), 49% with terminal degrees. The undergraduate student-faculty ratio is 15:1. The library holds 170,000 titles and 6,597 serial subscriptions. Special programs include academic remediation, services for learning-disabled students, an honors program, study abroad, advanced placement credit, ESL programs, double majors, independent study, distance learning, self-designed majors, part-time degree programs (daytime, evenings), internships, and arrangement for off-campus study with Christian College Coalition, Chicago Metro Program, American Studies Program, Los Angeles Film Studies Program. The most frequently chosen baccalaureate fields are business/marketing, education, engineering.
Student Body Statistics The student body totals 1,400, of whom 1,363 are undergraduates (396 freshmen). 49 percent are women and 51 percent are men. Students come from 38 states and territories and 16 other countries. 39 percent are from Iowa. 16.5 percent are international students.
Expenses for 2009–10 *Application fee:* $25. *Comprehensive fee:* $28,090 includes full-time tuition ($21,720), mandatory fees ($360), and college room and board ($6010). *College room only:* $3170. *Part-time tuition:* $880 per semester hour. *Part-time mandatory fees:* $160 per term.
Financial Aid Forms of aid include need-based and non-need-based scholarships, athletic grants, and part-time jobs. The average aided 2008–09 undergraduate received an aid package worth an estimated $19,467. The priority application deadline for financial aid is April 1.
Freshman Admission Dordt College requires a high school transcript, a minimum 2.25 high school GPA, SAT or ACT scores, and TOEFL scores for international students. An essay and an interview are required for some. The application deadline for regular admission is August 1.
Transfer Admission The application deadline for admission is August 1.
Entrance Difficulty Dordt College assesses its entrance difficulty level as moderately difficult. For the fall 2008 freshman class, 87 percent of the applicants were accepted.
For Further Information Contact Mr. Quentin Van Essen, Executive Director of Admissions, Dordt College, 498 4th Avenue, NE, Sioux Center, IA 51250-1697. *Phone:* 712-722-6080 or 800-343-6738 (toll-free). *Fax:* 712-722-6035. *E-mail:* admissions@dordt.edu. *Web site:* http://www.dordt.edu/.

DRAKE UNIVERSITY

Des Moines, Iowa

Drake University is a coed, private university, founded in 1881, offering degrees at the bachelor's, master's, doctoral, and first professional levels and post-master's, first professional, and postbachelor's certificates. It has a 120-acre campus in Des Moines.

Academic Information The faculty has 407 members (66% full-time). The undergraduate student-faculty ratio is 14:1. The library holds 525,093 titles, 28,499 serial subscriptions, and 2,123 audiovisual materials. Special programs include services for learning-disabled students, an honors program, cooperative (work-study) education, study abroad, advanced placement credit, accelerated degree programs, ESL programs, double majors, independent study, distance learning, self-designed majors, summer session for credit, part-time degree programs, internships, and arrangement for off-campus study with Des Moines Consortium. The most frequently chosen baccalaureate fields are business/marketing, communications/journalism, education.
Student Body Statistics The student body totals 5,668, of whom 3,516 are undergraduates (902 freshmen). 57 percent are women and 43 percent are men. Students come from 41 states and territories and 46 other countries. 38 percent are from Iowa. 7.2 percent are international students.
Expenses for 2009–10 *Application fee:* $25. *Comprehensive fee:* $34,422 includes full-time tuition ($26,160), mandatory fees ($462), and college room and board ($7800). *College room only:* $4100.
Financial Aid Forms of aid include need-based and non-need-based scholarships, athletic grants, and part-time jobs. The average aided 2007–08 undergraduate received an aid package worth $20,836. The priority application deadline for financial aid is March 1.
Freshman Admission Drake University requires an essay, a high school transcript, SAT or ACT scores, and TOEFL scores for international students. An interview is recommended. The application deadline for regular admission is March 1.
Transfer Admission The application deadline for admission is rolling.
Entrance Difficulty Drake University assesses its entrance difficulty level as moderately difficult; most difficult for transfer students to the College of Pharmacy. For the fall 2008 freshman class, 69 percent of the applicants were accepted.
For Further Information Contact Ms. Laura Linn, Director of Admission, Drake University, 2507 University Avenue, Des Moines, IA 50311. *Phone:* 515-271-3181 Ext. 3182 or 800-44DRAKE Ext. 3181 (toll-free). *Fax:* 515-271-2831. *E-mail:* admission@drake.edu. *Web site:* http://www.drake.edu/.

EMMAUS BIBLE COLLEGE

Dubuque, Iowa

Emmaus Bible College is a coed, private, nondenominational, four-year college, founded in 1941, offering degrees at the associate and bachelor's levels. It has a 22-acre campus in Dubuque.

Academic Information The library holds 86,000 titles and 330 serial subscriptions. Special programs include advanced placement credit, double majors, independent study, part-time degree programs (daytime, evenings), internships, and arrangement for off-campus study.
Student Body Statistics The student body is made up of 244 undergraduates.
Expenses for 2008–09 *Application fee:* $25. *Comprehensive fee:* $16,242 includes full-time tuition ($10,368), mandatory fees ($662), and college room and board ($5212).
Financial Aid Forms of aid include need-based and non-need-based scholarships.
Freshman Admission Emmaus Bible College requires an essay, a high school transcript, 3 recommendations, and TOEFL scores for international students. The application deadline for regular admission is June 1.
Transfer Admission The application deadline for admission is August 1.

Emmaus Bible College (continued)
Entrance Difficulty Emmaus Bible College has an open admission policy.
For Further Information Contact Israel Chavez, Enrollment Services Director, Emmaus Bible College, 2570 Asbury Road, Dubuque, IA 52001. *Phone:* 563-588-8000 Ext. 1310 or 800-397-2425 (toll-free). *Fax:* 563-557-0573. *E-mail:* admissions@emmaus.edu. *Web site:* http://www.emmaus.edu/.

FAITH BAPTIST BIBLE COLLEGE AND THEOLOGICAL SEMINARY

Ankeny, Iowa

Faith Baptist Bible College and Theological Seminary is a coed, private, comprehensive institution, founded in 1921, affiliated with the General Association of Regular Baptist Churches, offering degrees at the associate, bachelor's, master's, and first professional levels. It has a 52-acre campus in Ankeny.

Academic Information The faculty has 34 members (62% full-time), 59% with terminal degrees. The undergraduate student-faculty ratio is 15:1. The library holds 63,840 titles, 395 serial subscriptions, and 6,563 audiovisual materials. Special programs include academic remediation, advanced placement credit, double majors, independent study, summer session for credit, part-time degree programs (daytime, summer), adult/continuing education programs, and internships. The most frequently chosen baccalaureate fields are education, theology and religious vocations.
Student Body Statistics The student body totals 387, of whom 321 are undergraduates (93 freshmen). 54 percent are women and 46 percent are men. Students come from 30 states and territories and 7 other countries. 48 percent are from Iowa. 0.9 percent are international students.
Expenses for 2008–09 *Application fee:* $25. *One-time mandatory fee:* $50. *Comprehensive fee:* $17,716 includes full-time tuition ($12,306), mandatory fees ($400), and college room and board ($5010). *College room only:* $2288. Full-time tuition and fees vary according to course load. Room and board charges vary according to board plan. *Part-time tuition:* $450 per credit hour. *Part-time mandatory fees:* $200 per term. Part-time tuition and fees vary according to course load.
Financial Aid Forms of aid include need-based and non-need-based scholarships. The priority application deadline for financial aid is March 1.
Freshman Admission Faith Baptist Bible College and Theological Seminary requires an essay, a high school transcript, 2 recommendations, SAT or ACT scores, and TOEFL scores for international students. A minimum 2.0 high school GPA is recommended. An interview is required for some. The application deadline for regular admission is August 1.
Transfer Admission The application deadline for admission is August 1.
Entrance Difficulty Faith Baptist Bible College and Theological Seminary assesses its entrance difficulty level as minimally difficult; moderately difficult for international students. For the fall 2008 freshman class, 87 percent of the applicants were accepted.
For Further Information Contact Miss Carrie Johnson, Admissions Secretary, Faith Baptist Bible College and Theological Seminary, 1900 NW 4th Street, Ankeny, IA 50023. *Phone:* 515-964-0601 or 888-FAITH 4U (toll-free). *Fax:* 515-964-1638. *E-mail:* admissions@faith.edu. *Web site:* http://www.faith.edu/.

GRACELAND UNIVERSITY

Lamoni, Iowa

Graceland University is a coed, private, Community of Christ, comprehensive institution, founded in 1895, offering degrees at the bachelor's and master's levels and post-master's certificates. It has a 169-acre campus in Lamoni near Des Moines.

Academic Information The faculty has 97 members (100% full-time), 70% with terminal degrees. The undergraduate student-faculty ratio is 13.6:1. The library holds 124,399 titles and 559 serial subscriptions. Special programs include academic remediation, services for learning-disabled students, an honors program, cooperative (work-study) education, study abroad, advanced placement credit, accelerated degree programs, ESL programs, double majors, independent study, distance learning, self-designed majors, summer session for credit, part-time degree programs (daytime), external degree programs, adult/continuing education programs, internships, and arrangement for off-campus study with Indian Hills Community College, North Central Missouri College. The most frequently chosen baccalaureate fields are education, business/marketing, health professions and related sciences.
Student Body Statistics The student body totals 2,444, of whom 1,679 are undergraduates (197 freshmen). 62 percent are women and 38 percent are men. 62 percent are from Iowa. 10 percent are international students.
Expenses for 2009–10 *Application fee:* $50. *Comprehensive fee:* $26,870 includes full-time tuition ($19,890), mandatory fees ($200), and college room and board ($6780). *College room only:* $2710. *Part-time tuition:* $630 per semester hour.
Financial Aid Forms of aid include need-based and non-need-based scholarships, athletic grants, and part-time jobs. The average aided 2008–09 undergraduate received an aid package worth an estimated $17,708. The application deadline for financial aid is continuous.
Freshman Admission Graceland University requires a high school transcript, a minimum 2.5 high school GPA, SAT or ACT scores, and TOEFL scores for international students. An essay, 2 recommendations, and an interview are required for some. The application deadline for regular admission is rolling.
Transfer Admission The application deadline for admission is rolling.
Entrance Difficulty Graceland University assesses its entrance difficulty level as moderately difficult. For the fall 2008 freshman class, 55 percent of the applicants were accepted.
For Further Information Contact Mr. Greg Sutherland, Vice President for Enrollment and Dean of Admission, Graceland University, 1 University Place, Lamoni, IA 50140. *Phone:* 641-784-5110 or 866-GRACELAND (toll-free). *Fax:* 641-784-5480. *E-mail:* admissions@graceland.edu. *Web site:* http://www.graceland.edu/.

See page 238 for the Close-Up.

GRAND VIEW UNIVERSITY

Des Moines, Iowa

Grand View University is a coed, private, comprehensive institution, founded in 1896, affiliated with the Evangelical Lutheran Church in America, offering degrees at the associate, bachelor's, and master's levels and postbachelor's certificates. It has a 25-acre campus in Des Moines.

Academic Information The faculty has 188 members (46% full-time), 44% with terminal degrees. The undergraduate student-faculty ratio is 16:1. The library holds 109,386 titles, 25,431 serial subscriptions, and 4,064 audiovisual materials. Special programs include academic remediation, services for learning-disabled students, an honors program, cooperative (work-study) education, study abroad, advanced placement credit, accelerated degree programs, Freshman Honors College, double majors, independent study, distance learning, self-designed majors, summer session for credit, part-time degree programs (daytime, evenings, weekends, summer), adult/continuing education programs, internships, and arrangement for off-campus study with Drake University, Des Moines Area Community College. The most frequently chosen baccalaureate fields are business/marketing, health professions and related sciences, visual and performing arts.
Student Body Statistics The student body is made up of 1,936 undergraduates (345 freshmen). 63 percent are women and 37 percent are men. Students come from 26 states and territories and 12 other countries. 92 percent are from Iowa. 1 percent are international students.
Expenses for 2008–09 *Application fee:* $35. *Comprehensive fee:* $24,778 includes full-time tuition ($18,234), mandatory fees ($380), and college room and board ($6164). Full-time tuition and fees vary according to class time. Room and board charges vary according to board plan and housing facility. *Part-time tuition:* $475 per hour. Part-time tuition varies according to class time.
Financial Aid Forms of aid include need-based and non-need-based scholarships, athletic grants, and part-time jobs. The average aided 2008–09 undergraduate received an aid package worth an estimated $18,489. The priority application deadline for financial aid is March 1.
Freshman Admission Grand View University requires a high school transcript, SAT or ACT scores, and TOEFL scores for international

students. A minimum 2.0 high school GPA is recommended. The application deadline for regular admission is August 15.
Transfer Admission The application deadline for admission is August 15.
Entrance Difficulty Grand View University assesses its entrance difficulty level as minimally difficult; very difficult for honors program. For the fall 2008 freshman class, 95 percent of the applicants were accepted.
For Further Information Contact Ms. Diane Schaefer, Director of Admissions, Grand View University, 1200 Grandview Avenue, Des Moines, IA 50316-1599. *Phone:* 515-263-2810 or 800-444-6083 Ext. 2810 (toll-free). *Fax:* 515-263-2974. *E-mail:* admissions@grandview.edu. *Web site:* http://www.grandview.edu/.

GRINNELL COLLEGE

Grinnell, Iowa

Grinnell College is a coed, private, four-year college, founded in 1846, offering degrees at the bachelor's level. It has a 120-acre campus in Grinnell.

Academic Information The faculty has 207 members (76% full-time), 77% with terminal degrees. The student-faculty ratio is 9:1. The library holds 1 million titles, 26,692 serial subscriptions, and 33,066 audiovisual materials. Special programs include services for learning-disabled students, study abroad, advanced placement credit, accelerated degree programs, double majors, independent study, self-designed majors, internships, and arrangement for off-campus study. The most frequently chosen baccalaureate fields are foreign languages and literature, biological/life sciences, social sciences.
Student Body Statistics The student body is made up of 1,678 undergraduates (464 freshmen). 53 percent are women and 47 percent are men. Students come from 51 states and territories and 51 other countries. 12 percent are from Iowa. 10.9 percent are international students.
Expenses for 2008–09 *Application fee:* $30. *Comprehensive fee:* $43,700 includes full-time tuition ($34,932), mandatory fees ($496), and college room and board ($8272). *College room only:* $3838. Full-time tuition and fees vary according to student level. Room and board charges vary according to board plan and housing facility. *Part-time tuition:* $1092 per credit. Part-time tuition varies according to student level.
Financial Aid Forms of aid include need-based and non-need-based scholarships and part-time jobs. The average aided 2008–09 undergraduate received an aid package worth an estimated $30,751. The application deadline for financial aid is February 1.
Freshman Admission Grinnell College requires an essay, a high school transcript, 3 recommendations, SAT or ACT scores, and TOEFL scores for international students. An interview is recommended. The application deadline for regular admission is January 2 and for early decision it is November 15.
Transfer Admission The application deadline for admission is May 1.
Entrance Difficulty Grinnell College assesses its entrance difficulty level as very difficult. For the fall 2008 freshman class, 43 percent of the applicants were accepted.
For Further Information Contact Mr. Seth Allen, Dean for Admission and Financial Aid, Grinnell College, 1103 Park Street, Grinnell, IA 50112. *Phone:* 641-269-3600 or 800-247-0113 (toll-free). *Fax:* 641-269-4800. *E-mail:* askgrin@grinnell.edu. *Web site:* http://www.grinnell.edu/.

HAMILTON TECHNICAL COLLEGE

Davenport, Iowa

Hamilton Technical College is a coed, proprietary, four-year college, founded in 1969, offering degrees at the associate and bachelor's levels.

Academic Information The faculty has 12 members (92% full-time). The student-faculty ratio is 20:1. The library holds 4,500 titles and 30 serial subscriptions. The most frequently chosen baccalaureate field is engineering technologies.
Expenses for 2008–09 *Application fee:* $25. *Tuition:* $8926 full-time.
Financial Aid Forms of aid include need-based scholarships. The priority application deadline for financial aid is June 30.
Freshman Admission Hamilton Technical College requires a high school transcript and an interview. The application deadline for regular admission is rolling.
Transfer Admission The application deadline for admission is rolling.
Entrance Difficulty Hamilton Technical College has an open admission policy.
For Further Information Contact Mr. Scott Ervin, Director of Admissions, Hamilton Technical College, 1011 East 53rd Street, Davenport, IA 52807. *Phone:* 563-386-3570. *Fax:* 563-386-6756. *E-mail:* admissions@hamiltontechcollege.com. *Web site:* http://www.hamiltontechcollege.com/.

IOWA STATE UNIVERSITY OF SCIENCE AND TECHNOLOGY

Ames, Iowa

Iowa State University of Science and Technology is a coed, public university, founded in 1858, offering degrees at the bachelor's, master's, doctoral, and first professional levels and post-master's certificates. It has a 1,788-acre campus in Ames.

Academic Information The faculty has 1,641 members (86% full-time), 89% with terminal degrees. The undergraduate student-faculty ratio is 15.6:1. The library holds 3 million titles and 66,195 serial subscriptions. Special programs include academic remediation, services for learning-disabled students, an honors program, cooperative (work-study) education, study abroad, advanced placement credit, accelerated degree programs, Freshman Honors College, ESL programs, double majors, independent study, distance learning, self-designed majors, summer session for credit, part-time degree programs (daytime, evenings, weekends, summer), external degree programs, adult/continuing education programs, internships, and arrangement for off-campus study with Iowa Regents' Universities Student Exchange, National Student Exchange. The most frequently chosen baccalaureate fields are business/marketing, agriculture, engineering.
Student Body Statistics The student body totals 26,856, of whom 21,607 are undergraduates (4,546 freshmen). 44 percent are women and 56 percent are men. Students come from 55 states and territories and 107 other countries. 77 percent are from Iowa. 4.6 percent are international students.
Expenses for 2009–10 *Application fee:* $30. *State resident tuition:* $5756 full-time, $240 per semester hour part-time. *Nonresident tuition:* $16,976 full-time, $708 per semester hour part-time. *Mandatory fees:* $895 full-time. *College room and board:* $7277. *College room only:* $3750.
Financial Aid Forms of aid include need-based and non-need-based scholarships, athletic grants, and part-time jobs. The average aided 2008–09 undergraduate received an aid package worth an estimated $10,262. The priority application deadline for financial aid is March 1.
Freshman Admission Iowa State University of Science and Technology requires a high school transcript, rank in upper 50% of high school class, and SAT or ACT scores. TOEFL scores for international students are recommended. The application deadline for regular admission is July 1.
Transfer Admission The application deadline for admission is July 1.
Entrance Difficulty Iowa State University of Science and Technology assesses its entrance difficulty level as moderately difficult. For the fall 2008 freshman class, 87 percent of the applicants were accepted.
For Further Information Contact Mr. Phil Caffrey, Associate Director for Freshman Admissions, Iowa State University of Science and Technology, 100 Enrollment Services Center, Ames, IA 50011-2010. *Phone:* 515-294-5836 or 800-262-3810 (toll-free). *Fax:* 515-294-2592. *E-mail:* admissions@iastate.edu. *Web site:* http://www.iastate.edu/.

IOWA WESLEYAN COLLEGE

Mount Pleasant, Iowa

Iowa Wesleyan College is a coed, private, United Methodist, four-year college, founded in 1842, offering degrees at the bachelor's level. It has a 60-acre campus in Mount Pleasant.

Academic Information The faculty has 90 members (56% full-time), 32% with terminal degrees. The student-faculty ratio is 14:1. The library

Iowa Wesleyan College (continued)

holds 102,356 titles, 9,452 serial subscriptions, and 5,643 audiovisual materials. Special programs include academic remediation, services for learning-disabled students, study abroad, advanced placement credit, double majors, independent study, distance learning, self-designed majors, summer session for credit, part-time degree programs (daytime, evenings, summer), adult/continuing education programs, internships, and arrangement for off-campus study with Southeastern Community College, Muscatine Community College.

Student Body Statistics The student body is made up of 843 undergraduates (150 freshmen). 61 percent are women and 39 percent are men. Students come from 27 states and territories and 25 other countries. 59 percent are from Iowa. 5.9 percent are international students.

Expenses for 2008–09 *Application fee:* $20. *Comprehensive fee:* $26,240 includes full-time tuition ($20,000) and college room and board ($6240). *College room only:* $2580. *Part-time tuition:* $495 per credit hour.

Financial Aid Forms of aid include need-based and non-need-based scholarships, athletic grants, and part-time jobs. The average aided 2007–08 undergraduate received an aid package worth $14,000.

Freshman Admission Iowa Wesleyan College requires a high school transcript, a minimum 2.5 high school GPA, SAT or ACT scores, and TOEFL scores for international students. An essay is required for some. The application deadline for regular admission is August 15.

Transfer Admission The application deadline for admission is August 15.

Entrance Difficulty Iowa Wesleyan College assesses its entrance difficulty level as moderately difficult. For the fall 2008 freshman class, 67 percent of the applicants were accepted.

For Further Information Contact Mr. Mark T. Petty, Dean of Admissions, Iowa Wesleyan College, 601 North Main Street, Mount Pleasant, IA 52641-1398. *Phone:* 319-385-6230 or 800-582-2383 Ext. 6231 (toll-free). *Fax:* 319-385-6296. *E-mail:* admitrwl@iwc.edu. *Web site:* http://www.iwc.edu/.

ITT TECHNICAL INSTITUTE

Clive, Iowa

ITT Technical Institute is a coed, proprietary, primarily two-year college of ITT Educational Services, Inc., offering degrees at the associate and bachelor's levels.

For Further Information Contact Director of Recruitment, ITT Technical Institute, 1860 Northwest 118th Street, Suite 110, Clive, IA 50325. *Phone:* 515-327-5500 or 877-526-7312 (toll-free). *Web site:* http://www.itt-tech.edu/.

KAPLAN UNIVERSITY, CEDAR FALLS

Cedar Falls, Iowa

Kaplan University, Cedar Falls is proprietary, primarily two-year college, founded in 2000, offering degrees at the associate and bachelor's levels.

Expenses for 2008–09 Contact institution for current costs.

For Further Information Contact Director of Admissions, Kaplan University, Cedar Falls, 7009 Nordic Drive, Cedar Falls, IA 50613. *Phone:* 319-277-0220 or 800-728-1220 (toll-free out-of-state). *Web site:* http://www.cedarfalls.kaplanuniversity.edu.

KAPLAN UNIVERSITY, CEDAR RAPIDS

Cedar Rapids, Iowa

Kaplan University, Cedar Rapids is proprietary, primarily two-year college, founded in 1900, offering degrees at the associate and bachelor's levels (branch locations in Des Moines, Mason City, and Cedar Falls with significant enrollment not reflected in profile). It has a 4-acre campus in Cedar Rapids.

Expenses for 2008–09 Contact institution for current costs.

For Further Information Contact Director of Admissions, Kaplan University, Cedar Rapids, 3165 Edgewood Parkway, SW, Cedar Rapids, IA 52404. *Phone:* 319-363-0481 or 800-728-0481 (toll-free out-of-state). *Web site:* http://www.cedarrapids.kaplanuniversity.edu.

KAPLAN UNIVERSITY, COUNCIL BLUFFS

Council Bluffs, Iowa

Kaplan University, Council Bluffs is proprietary, primarily two-year college, founded in 2004, offering degrees at the associate and bachelor's levels.

Expenses for 2008–09 Contact institution for current costs.

For Further Information Contact Director of Admissions, Kaplan University, Council Bluffs, 1751 Madison Avenue, Council Bluffs, IA 51503. *Phone:* 712-328-4212 or 800-518-4212 (toll-free out-of-state). *Web site:* http://www.councilbluffs.kaplanuniversity.edu.

KAPLAN UNIVERSITY–DAVENPORT CAMPUS

Davenport, Iowa

Kaplan University–Davenport Campus is a coed, proprietary, four-year college, founded in 1937, offering degrees at the associate and bachelor's levels (profile includes both traditional and on-line students).

Academic Information Special programs include summer session for credit.

Expenses for 2008–09 Contact institution for current costs.

Financial Aid Forms of aid include need-based scholarships and part-time jobs. The application deadline for financial aid is continuous.

Freshman Admission Kaplan University–Davenport Campus requires TOEFL scores for international students and Wonderlic aptitude test. The application deadline for regular admission is rolling.

For Further Information Contact Director of Admissions, Kaplan University–Davenport Campus, 1801 East Kimberly Road, Suite 1, Davenport, IA 52807. *Phone:* 563-355-3500 or 800-747-1035 (toll-free in-state). *Fax:* 563-355-1320. *E-mail:* infoke@kaplancollege.edu. *Web site:* http://www.ku-davenport.edu.

KAPLAN UNIVERSITY, DES MOINES

Urbandale, Iowa

Kaplan University, Des Moines is proprietary, primarily two-year college of Kaplan University—branch of the Davenport Campus, offering degrees at the associate and bachelor's levels.

Expenses for 2008–09 Contact institution for current costs.

For Further Information Contact Director of Admissions, Kaplan University, Des Moines, 4655 121st Street, Urbandale, IA 50323. *Phone:* 515-727-2100. *Web site:* http://www.desmoines.kaplanuniversity.edu.

KAPLAN UNIVERSITY–MASON CITY CAMPUS

Mason City, Iowa

Kaplan University–Mason City Campus is a coed, proprietary, four-year college of Kaplan University—branch of the Davenport Campus, founded in 1900, offering degrees at the associate and bachelor's levels.

Expenses for 2008–09 Contact institution for current costs.

Freshman Admission Kaplan University–Mason City Campus requires Wonderlic aptitude test. The application deadline for regular admission is rolling.

Entrance Difficulty Kaplan University–Mason City Campus assesses its entrance difficulty level as noncompetitive.
For Further Information Contact Director of Admissions, Kaplan University–Mason City Campus, Plaza West, 2570 4th Street, SW, Mason City, IA 50401. *Phone:* 641-423-2530. *Web site:* http://www.ku-masoncity.edu.

LORAS COLLEGE

Dubuque, Iowa

Loras College is a coed, private, Roman Catholic, comprehensive institution, founded in 1839, offering degrees at the associate, bachelor's, and master's levels. It has a 60-acre campus in Dubuque.

Academic Information The faculty has 161 members (71% full-time). The undergraduate student-faculty ratio is 14:1. The library holds 392,859 titles, 18,552 serial subscriptions, and 4,502 audiovisual materials. Special programs include academic remediation, services for learning-disabled students, an honors program, cooperative (work-study) education, advanced placement credit, double majors, independent study, distance learning, self-designed majors, summer session for credit, part-time degree programs (daytime, evenings, summer), internships, and arrangement for off-campus study. The most frequently chosen baccalaureate fields are business/marketing, education, social sciences.
Student Body Statistics The student body totals 1,588, of whom 1,512 are undergraduates (382 freshmen). 49 percent are women and 51 percent are men. Students come from 17 states and territories and 7 other countries. 54 percent are from Iowa. 3.7 percent are international students.
Expenses for 2009–10 *Application fee:* $25. *Comprehensive fee:* $32,374 includes full-time tuition ($24,070), mandatory fees ($1278), and college room and board ($7026). *College room only:* $3520. *Part-time tuition:* $457 per credit. *Part-time mandatory fees:* $25 per credit.
Financial Aid Forms of aid include need-based and non-need-based scholarships and part-time jobs. The average aided 2008–09 undergraduate received an aid package worth an estimated $16,333. The priority application deadline for financial aid is April 15.
Freshman Admission Loras College requires a high school transcript, a minimum 2.5 high school GPA, SAT or ACT scores, and TOEFL scores for international students. An essay and 1 recommendation are recommended. An interview is required for some. The application deadline for regular admission is rolling.
Transfer Admission The application deadline for admission is rolling.
Entrance Difficulty Loras College assesses its entrance difficulty level as moderately difficult. For the fall 2008 freshman class, 86 percent of the applicants were accepted.
For Further Information Contact Ms. Sharon Lyons, Director of Admissions, Loras College, 1450 Alta Vista, Dubuque, IA 52004-0178. *Phone:* 563-588-7829 or 800-245-6727 (toll-free). *Fax:* 563-588-7119. *E-mail:* adms@loras.edu. *Web site:* http://www.loras.edu/.

LUTHER COLLEGE

Decorah, Iowa

Luther College is a coed, private, four-year college, founded in 1861, affiliated with the Evangelical Lutheran Church in America, offering degrees at the bachelor's level. It has a 200-acre campus in Decorah.

Academic Information The faculty has 248 members (72% full-time), 73% with terminal degrees. The student-faculty ratio is 12:1. The library holds 327,019 titles, 831 serial subscriptions, and 1,866 audiovisual materials. Special programs include academic remediation, services for learning-disabled students, an honors program, study abroad, advanced placement credit, double majors, independent study, self-designed majors, summer session for credit, part-time degree programs, internships, and arrangement for off-campus study. The most frequently chosen baccalaureate fields are business/marketing, social sciences, visual and performing arts.
Student Body Statistics The student body is made up of 2,423 undergraduates (630 freshmen). 58 percent are women and 42 percent are men. Students come from 40 states and territories and 44 other countries. 35 percent are from Iowa. 4.1 percent are international students.
Expenses for 2009–10 *Application fee:* $25. *One-time mandatory fee:* $150. *Comprehensive fee:* $37,670 includes full-time tuition ($32,140), mandatory fees ($150), and college room and board ($5380). *College room only:* $2800. *Part-time tuition:* $1148 per credit hour.
Financial Aid Forms of aid include need-based and non-need-based scholarships and part-time jobs. The average aided 2008–09 undergraduate received an aid package worth an estimated $23,487. The priority application deadline for financial aid is March 1.
Freshman Admission Luther College requires an essay, a high school transcript, 1 recommendation, SAT or ACT scores, and TOEFL scores for international students. An interview is recommended.
Entrance Difficulty Luther College assesses its entrance difficulty level as moderately difficult. For the fall 2008 freshman class, 80 percent of the applicants were accepted.
For Further Information Contact Kirk Neubauer, Director of Recruiting Services, Luther College, 700 College Drive, Decorah, IA 52101. *Phone:* 563-387-1287 or 800-458-8437 (toll-free). *Fax:* 563-387-2159. *E-mail:* admissions@luther.edu. *Web site:* http://www.luther.edu/.

MAHARISHI UNIVERSITY OF MANAGEMENT

Fairfield, Iowa

Maharishi University of Management is a coed, private university, founded in 1971, offering degrees at the bachelor's, master's, and doctoral levels and postbachelor's certificates. It has a 272-acre campus in Fairfield.

Expenses for 2008–09 *Application fee:* $30. *Comprehensive fee:* $30,430 includes full-time tuition ($24,000), mandatory fees ($430), and college room and board ($6000). *Part-time tuition:* $550 per unit.
For Further Information Contact Ms. Barbara Rainbow, Associate Dean of Admissions, Maharishi University of Management, Office of Admissions, Fairfield, IA 52557. *Phone:* 641-472-1110 or 800-369-6480 (toll-free). *Fax:* 641-472-1179. *E-mail:* admissions@mum.edu. *Web site:* http://www.mum.edu/.

MERCY COLLEGE OF HEALTH SCIENCES

Des Moines, Iowa

Mercy College of Health Sciences is a coed, primarily women's, private, four-year college, founded in 1995, affiliated with the Roman Catholic Church, offering degrees at the associate and bachelor's levels. It has a 5-acre campus in Des Moines.

Academic Information The faculty has 45 members (91% full-time), 13% with terminal degrees. The student-faculty ratio is 11:1. The library holds 15,964 titles, 165 serial subscriptions, and 1,465 audiovisual materials. Special programs include academic remediation, services for learning-disabled students, advanced placement credit, accelerated degree programs, double majors, distance learning, summer session for credit, part-time degree programs, and arrangement for off-campus study. The most frequently chosen baccalaureate field is health professions and related sciences.
Student Body Statistics The student body is made up of 669 undergraduates (40 freshmen). 89 percent are women and 11 percent are men. Students come from 1 state or territory.
Expenses for 2009–10 *Application fee:* $25. *Tuition:* $13,000 full-time, $440 per credit hour part-time.
Financial Aid Forms of aid include need-based and non-need-based scholarships and part-time jobs. The application deadline for financial aid is July 1.
Freshman Admission Mercy College of Health Sciences requires a high school transcript, a minimum 2.25 high school GPA, and TOEFL scores for international students. An interview and ACT scores are required for some. The application deadline for regular admission is rolling.

Mercy College of Health Sciences (continued)
Entrance Difficulty Mercy College of Health Sciences has an open admission policy.
For Further Information Contact Kara Scholten, Admissions Representative, Mercy College of Health Sciences, 928 Sixth Avenue, Des Moines, IA 50309-1239. *Phone:* 515-643-3180 or 800-637-2994 (toll-free). *Fax:* 515-643-6698. *E-mail:* kscholten@mercydesmoines.org. *Web site:* http://www.mchs.edu/.

MORNINGSIDE COLLEGE

Sioux City, Iowa

Morningside College is a coed, private, comprehensive institution, founded in 1894, affiliated with the United Methodist Church, offering degrees at the bachelor's and master's levels. It has a 68-acre campus in Sioux City.

Academic Information The faculty has 177 members (39% full-time), 30% with terminal degrees. The undergraduate student-faculty ratio is 17:1. The library holds 94,775 titles, 325 serial subscriptions, and 1,306 audiovisual materials. Special programs include academic remediation, services for learning-disabled students, an honors program, study abroad, advanced placement credit, ESL programs, double majors, independent study, distance learning, self-designed majors, summer session for credit, part-time degree programs (daytime, evenings, summer), adult/continuing education programs, internships, and arrangement for off-campus study with American University, Drew University. The most frequently chosen baccalaureate fields are business/marketing, education, visual and performing arts.
Student Body Statistics The student body totals 1,906, of whom 1,214 are undergraduates (302 freshmen). 54 percent are women and 46 percent are men. Students come from 18 states and territories and 4 other countries. 68 percent are from Iowa. 1.2 percent are international students.
Expenses for 2009–10 *Application fee:* $25. *Comprehensive fee:* $28,975 includes full-time tuition ($21,116), mandatory fees ($1130), and college room and board ($6729). *College room only:* $3465. *Part-time tuition:* $670 per credit hour.
Financial Aid Forms of aid include need-based and non-need-based scholarships, athletic grants, and part-time jobs. The average aided 2008–09 undergraduate received an aid package worth an estimated $17,217. The priority application deadline for financial aid is March 1.
Freshman Admission Morningside College requires a high school transcript, rank in top 50% of high school class or achieved GPA of 2.5 or better, SAT or ACT scores, and TOEFL scores for international students. An interview is recommended. 2 recommendations are required for some. The application deadline for regular admission is rolling.
Transfer Admission The application deadline for admission is rolling.
Entrance Difficulty Morningside College assesses its entrance difficulty level as moderately difficult. For the fall 2008 freshman class, 74 percent of the applicants were accepted.
For Further Information Contact Ms. Amy Williams, Co-Director of Admissions, Morningside College, 1501 Morningside Avenue, Sioux City, IA 51106. *Phone:* 712-274-5111 or 800-831-0806 Ext. 5111 (toll-free). *Fax:* 712-274-5101. *E-mail:* mscadm@morningside.edu. *Web site:* http://www.morningside.edu/.

See page 252 for the Close-Up.

MOUNT MERCY COLLEGE

Cedar Rapids, Iowa

Mount Mercy College is a coed, private, Roman Catholic, comprehensive institution, founded in 1928, offering degrees at the bachelor's and master's levels. It has a 40-acre campus in Cedar Rapids.

Academic Information The faculty has 150 members (50% full-time), 35% with terminal degrees. The undergraduate student-faculty ratio is 12:1. The library holds 138,043 titles, 10,900 serial subscriptions, and 5,437 audiovisual materials. Special programs include academic remediation, services for learning-disabled students, an honors program, study abroad, advanced placement credit, accelerated degree programs, double majors, independent study, summer session for credit, part-time degree programs (daytime, evenings, weekends, summer), adult/continuing education programs, internships, and arrangement for off-campus study with Coe College. The most frequently chosen baccalaureate fields are business/marketing, education, health professions and related sciences.
Student Body Statistics The student body totals 1,555, of whom 1,474 are undergraduates (172 freshmen). 71 percent are women and 29 percent are men. Students come from 14 states and territories and 15 other countries. 95 percent are from Iowa. 1.6 percent are international students.
Expenses for 2008–09 *Application fee:* $20. *Comprehensive fee:* $27,775 includes full-time tuition ($21,125) and college room and board ($6650). Full-time tuition varies according to course load. Room and board charges vary according to board plan and housing facility. *Part-time tuition:* $585 per credit hour. Part-time tuition varies according to course load.
Financial Aid Forms of aid include need-based and non-need-based scholarships, athletic grants, and part-time jobs. The average aided 2008–09 undergraduate received an aid package worth an estimated $16,977. The priority application deadline for financial aid is March 1.
Freshman Admission Mount Mercy College requires an essay, a high school transcript, a minimum 2.5 high school GPA, SAT or ACT scores, and TOEFL scores for international students. 1 recommendation is required for some. The application deadline for regular admission is August 15.
Transfer Admission The application deadline for admission is August 15.
Entrance Difficulty Mount Mercy College assesses its entrance difficulty level as moderately difficult. For the fall 2008 freshman class, 80 percent of the applicants were accepted.

SPECIAL MESSAGE TO STUDENTS

Social Life Mount Mercy students can choose to participate in more than thirty campus clubs and organizations. Other campus events and activities include those sponsored by the student programming board and student organizations, including entertainment activities like the Roommate Game, Spring Fling, visits by hypnotists and mentalists, coffee house performances, and Mount Mercy Idol. Because of its prime location in Cedar Rapids, Iowa, the "Jewel of the Midwest," Mount Mercy students take advantage of many of the events held in this city of 140,000. The Student Activities Office offers students a significant price reduction on tickets to events such as hockey, baseball, the theater, the movies, and ice skating. The Mount Mercy Cultural Affairs Committee also sponsors a variety of cultural events for students, faculty and staff members, and the greater community. Past speakers and presenters include civil rights leader Julian Bond, U.S. Poet Laureate Ted Kooser, internationally renowned filmmaker Gerry Straub, and an annual visit by a Holocaust survivor.

Academic Highlights With high academic quality and generous scholarships, Mount Mercy offers outstanding educational value. At Mount Mercy students prepare themselves for life and work in the twenty-first century, with a unique blend of career preparation and liberal arts learning strengthened by a strong emphasis on leadership and service. The Freshman Partnership program helps first-time freshmen make a smooth transition to college life; the Honors Program offers accomplished students unique classes that encourage exploration beyond traditional academic boundaries; and the Academic Center for Excellence provides academic counseling and assistance to all students. Classes are small (average size is 15), and faculty members are focused on teaching and are readily available and approachable outside of the classroom. The student-faculty ratio is 12:1, which allows and encourages direct interaction in the classroom. The campus atmosphere is friendly, relaxed, and generally informal, allowing students and faculty and staff members to interact frequently and get to know one another on a personal level. Faculty and staff members are available to students for face-to-face meetings and social interaction and are also easily accessible via e-mail and home or cell phone.

Interviews and Campus Visits The best way to learn about Mount Mercy is to tour the beautiful hilltop campus, sit in on a class, meet with students and faculty members, and learn about scholarships and other forms of financial assistance. Mount Mercy welcomes students on special visit days throughout the year, and the Admission Office is happy to arrange individual weekday or weekend appointments. For more information about campus visits, students should call the Mount Mercy College Office of Admission at 800-248-4504 (toll-free) Monday through Thursday 8 to 5 (CST), and Friday 8 to 4:30, or e-mail the College at admission@mtmercy.edu.

For Further Information Write to Admission Office, Mount Mercy College, 1330 Elmhurst Drive, NE, Cedar Rapids, IA 52402. *E-mail:* admission@mtmercy.edu. *Web site:* http://www.mtmercy.edu.

See page 256 for the Close-Up.

MOUNT ST. CLARE COLLEGE

See Ashford University.

NORTHWESTERN COLLEGE

Orange City, Iowa

Northwestern College is a coed, private, four-year college, founded in 1882, affiliated with the Reformed Church in America, offering degrees at the bachelor's level. It has a 45-acre campus in Orange City.

Expenses for 2008–09 *Application fee:* $25. *Comprehensive fee:* $29,530 includes full-time tuition ($22,950) and college room and board ($6580). Room and board charges vary according to housing facility. *Part-time tuition:* varies with course load.
For Further Information Contact Mr. Mark Bloemendaal, Director of Admissions, Northwestern College, 101 7th Street SW, Orange City, IA 51041-1996. *Phone:* 712-737-7130 or 800-747-4757 (toll-free). *Fax:* 712-707-7164. *E-mail:* admissions@nwciowa.edu. *Web site:* http://www.nwciowa.edu/.

PALMER COLLEGE OF CHIROPRACTIC

Davenport, Iowa

Palmer College of Chiropractic is a coed, private, comprehensive institution, founded in 1897, offering degrees at the associate, incidental bachelor's, master's, and first professional levels.

Academic Information The library holds 55,278 titles and 525 serial subscriptions. Special programs include academic remediation, services for learning-disabled students, summer session for credit, and internships. The most frequently chosen baccalaureate field is biological/life sciences.
Student Body Statistics The student body totals 1,284, of whom 60 are undergraduates (4 freshmen). 48 percent are women and 52 percent are men. Students come from 3 states and territories and 1 other country.
Expenses for 2008–09 *Application fee:* $50. *One-time mandatory fee:* $150. *Tuition:* $6870 full-time, $170 per credit part-time. *Mandatory fees:* $105 full-time, $35 per term part-time. Both full-time and part-time tuition and fees vary according to course load and degree level.
Financial Aid Forms of aid include need-based and non-need-based scholarships and part-time jobs. The application deadline for financial aid is continuous.
Freshman Admission Palmer College of Chiropractic requires a high school transcript, a minimum 2.0 high school GPA, minimum 2.0 in math, science, and English courses, and TOEFL scores for international students. An essay and an interview are required for some. The application deadline for regular admission is rolling.
Entrance Difficulty Palmer College of Chiropractic has an open admission policy.
For Further Information Contact Lisa Gisel, Undergraduate Admissions Representative, Palmer College of Chiropractic, 1000 Brady Street, Davenport, IA 52803-5287. *Phone:* 563-884-5743 or 800-722-3648 (toll-free). *Fax:* 563-884-5226. *E-mail:* lisa.gisel@palmer.edu. *Web site:* http://www.palmer.edu/.

QUEST COLLEGE

See Kaplan University–Davenport Campus.

ST. AMBROSE UNIVERSITY

Davenport, Iowa

St. Ambrose University is a coed, private, Roman Catholic, comprehensive institution, founded in 1882, offering degrees at the bachelor's, master's, and doctoral levels and post-master's and postbachelor's certificates. It has a 50-acre campus in Davenport.

Academic Information The faculty has 383 members (46% full-time), 45% with terminal degrees. The undergraduate student-faculty ratio is 13:1. The library holds 169,549 titles, 728 serial subscriptions, and 3,822 audiovisual materials. Special programs include academic remediation, services for learning-disabled students, cooperative (work-study) education, study abroad, advanced placement credit, accelerated degree programs, double majors, independent study, distance learning, self-designed majors, summer session for credit, part-time degree programs (daytime, evenings, weekends, summer), external degree programs, adult/continuing education programs, internships, and arrangement for off-campus study with Black Hawk College, Eastern Iowa Community Colleges. The most frequently chosen baccalaureate fields are business/marketing, education, psychology.
Student Body Statistics The student body totals 3,794, of whom 2,922 are undergraduates (574 freshmen). 61 percent are women and 39 percent are men. Students come from 33 states and territories and 11 other countries. 47 percent are from Iowa. 0.5 percent are international students.
Expenses for 2009–10 *Application fee:* $25. *Comprehensive fee:* $30,845 includes full-time tuition ($22,590) and college room and board ($8255). *College room only:* $4207. *Part-time tuition:* $702 per credit hour.
Financial Aid Forms of aid include need-based and non-need-based scholarships, athletic grants, and part-time jobs. The average aided 2008–09 undergraduate received an aid package worth an estimated $15,414. The priority application deadline for financial aid is March 15.
Freshman Admission St. Ambrose University requires a high school transcript, a minimum 2.5 high school GPA, rank in top 50% of high school class, SAT or ACT scores, and TOEFL scores for international students. An interview and ACT scores are recommended. An interview is required for some. The application deadline for regular admission is rolling.
Transfer Admission The application deadline for admission is rolling.
Entrance Difficulty St. Ambrose University assesses its entrance difficulty level as moderately difficult. For the fall 2008 freshman class, 82 percent of the applicants were accepted.
For Further Information Contact Ms. Meg Halligan, Director of Admissions, St. Ambrose University, 518 West Locust Street, Davenport, IA 52803-2898. *Phone:* 563-333-6300 Ext. 6311 or 800-383-2627 (toll-free). *Fax:* 563-333-6297. *E-mail:* halliganmegf@sau.edu. *Web site:* http://www.sau.edu/.

ST. LUKE'S COLLEGE

Sioux City, Iowa

St. Luke's College is a coed, private, two-year college of St. Luke's Regional Medical Center, founded in 1967, offering degrees at the associate level. It has a 3-acre campus in Sioux City.

Expenses for 2008–09 *Application fee:* $25. *One-time mandatory fee:* $20. *Tuition:* $13,500 full-time, $375 per credit part-time. *Mandatory fees:* $600

St. Luke's College (continued)
full-time. Full-time tuition and fees vary according to course load. Part-time tuition varies according to course load.
For Further Information Contact Ms. Sherry McCarthy, Admissions Coordinator, St. Luke's College, 2720 Stone Park Boulevard, Sioux City, IA 51104. *Phone:* 712-279-3149 or 800-352-4660 Ext. 3149 (toll-free). *Fax:* 712-233-8017. *E-mail:* mccartsj@stlukes.org. *Web site:* http://stlukescollege.edu/.

SIMPSON COLLEGE

Indianola, Iowa

Simpson College is a coed, private, United Methodist, comprehensive institution, founded in 1860, offering degrees at the bachelor's and master's levels and postbachelor's certificates. It has a 75-acre campus in Indianola.

Academic Information The faculty has 203 members (50% full-time), 63% with terminal degrees. The undergraduate student-faculty ratio is 13:1. The library holds 161,529 titles, 457 serial subscriptions, and 4,542 audiovisual materials. Special programs include services for learning-disabled students, an honors program, cooperative (work-study) education, study abroad, advanced placement credit, accelerated degree programs, double majors, independent study, summer session for credit, part-time degree programs (daytime, evenings, weekends, summer), adult/continuing education programs, internships, and arrangement for off-campus study with Drew University, American University, Washington Center Internships and Symposia, George Washington Carver Teacher Initiative Consortium agreement with Iowa State University and Des Moines Area Community College. The most frequently chosen baccalaureate fields are business/marketing, communications/journalism, social sciences.
Student Body Statistics The student body totals 2,054, of whom 2,035 are undergraduates (389 freshmen). 59 percent are women and 41 percent are men. Students come from 21 states and territories and 16 other countries. 90 percent are from Iowa. 0.8 percent are international students.
Expenses for 2008–09 *Application fee:* $0. *One-time mandatory fee:* $200. *Comprehensive fee:* $31,759 includes full-time tuition ($24,414), mandatory fees ($357), and college room and board ($6988). *College room only:* $3354. Room and board charges vary according to board plan and housing facility. *Part-time tuition:* $275 per credit hour. Part-time tuition varies according to class time and course load.
Financial Aid Forms of aid include need-based and non-need-based scholarships and part-time jobs. The average aided 2008–09 undergraduate received an aid package worth an estimated $23,774. The application deadline for financial aid is continuous.
Freshman Admission Simpson College requires a high school transcript, 1 recommendation, and SAT or ACT scores. An interview is recommended. The application deadline for regular admission is August 15.
Transfer Admission The application deadline for admission is August 15.
Entrance Difficulty Simpson College assesses its entrance difficulty level as moderately difficult. For the fall 2008 freshman class, 88 percent of the applicants were accepted.

SPECIAL MESSAGE TO STUDENTS

Social Life Simpson has numerous opportunities available on campus. Activities include vocal and instrumental music groups, Theatre Simpson, honor and professional societies, service groups, and Religious Life Community. Simpson competes in Division III NCAA athletics and offers eighteen intercollegiate teams. Simpson also has an extensive intramural program. Students annually elect a president and vice president of the Student Government. Each housing unit elects representatives to Student Senate, and the senate appoints student members to appropriate College committees. Simpson is a residential campus with five traditional residence halls, seven apartment-style residences, eight theme houses, three national fraternities, one local fraternity, and three national sororities.

Academic Highlights Simpson's academic program is based on the best traditions of the liberal arts, enhanced by a genuine respect for the career requirements of today. With a student-faculty ratio of 13:1, professors get to know students personally. More than forty different majors and career programs are available. Simpson offers a unique 4-4-1 calendar, with two 4-month semesters and one 3-week term of concentrated study in May. The May Term course offerings provide an in-depth exploration of a subject and include internships, study-abroad opportunities, and career observations. Simpson also has exchange programs with international and domestic universities and offers study-abroad programs on a regular basis.

Interviews and Campus Visits Simpson College strongly encourages all students to visit the campus. An interview is an excellent opportunity for students and their parents. During the visit, students tour the campus with a Student Ambassador, perhaps meet with a professor or attend a class, and interview with an admissions counselor. Students can attend music or theater productions, athletic events, or other activities during their visit. Buildings of interest include historic College Hall, built in 1869; Carver Science Center, named after George Washington Carver who attended Simpson College; McNeill Hall for Business, housing a seminar room, conference center, computer labs, and classrooms; Dunn Library; the Amy Robertson Music Center, housing a 250-seat recital hall, studios, and practice rooms; and Cowles Athletic Center, in which a 25-meter swimming pool, physical education facilities, weight room, racquetball courts, and a field house are located. For more information, prospective students should call the Office of Admissions at 515-961-1624 or 800-362-2454 Ext. 1624 (toll-free), Monday through Friday, 8 to 4:30, or on designated Saturdays, 9 to noon. Students may also schedule visits online. The fax number is 515-961-1870. The Office of Admissions is located on the first floor of College Hall.

For Further Information Write to Office of Admissions, Simpson College, 701 North C Street, Indianola, IA 50125. *E-mail:* admiss@simpson.edu. *Web site:* http://www.simpson.edu.

See page 268 for the Close-Up.

UNIVERSITY OF DUBUQUE

Dubuque, Iowa

http://www.dbq.edu/

THE UNIVERSITY OF IOWA

Iowa City, Iowa

The University of Iowa is a coed, public university, founded in 1847, offering degrees at the bachelor's, master's, doctoral, and first professional levels and post-master's and first professional certificates. It has a 1,900-acre campus in Iowa City.

Academic Information The faculty has 1,673 members (95% full-time), 97% with terminal degrees. The undergraduate student-faculty ratio is 15:1. The library holds 4 million titles, 49,279 serial subscriptions, and 62,205 audiovisual materials. Special programs include academic remediation, services for learning-disabled students, an honors program, cooperative (work-study) education, study abroad, advanced placement credit, accelerated degree programs, ESL programs, double majors, independent study, distance learning, self-designed majors, summer session for credit, part-time degree programs (daytime, evenings, weekends, summer), external degree programs, adult/continuing education programs, internships, and arrangement for off-campus study with Iowa State University of Science and Technology, University of Northern Iowa, Committee on Institutional Cooperation. The most frequently chosen baccalaureate fields are business/marketing, communications/journalism, social sciences.
Student Body Statistics The student body totals 29,747, of whom 20,823 are undergraduates (4,246 freshmen). 52 percent are women and 48

percent are men. Students come from 56 states and territories and 67 other countries. 66 percent are from Iowa. 2.2 percent are international students.
Expenses for 2009–10 *Application fee:* $40. *State resident tuition:* $5782 full-time, $241 per semester hour part-time. *Nonresident tuition:* $21,156 full-time, $882 per semester hour part-time. *Mandatory fees:* $1042 full-time, $69 per semester hour part-time.
Financial Aid Forms of aid include need-based and non-need-based scholarships, athletic grants, and part-time jobs. The average aided 2008–09 undergraduate received an aid package worth an estimated $7512. The application deadline for financial aid is continuous.
Freshman Admission The University of Iowa requires a high school transcript, must meet Regent Admission Index (RAI) requirement: residents 245 or above; nonresidents 255 or above, SAT or ACT scores, and TOEFL scores for international students. The application deadline for regular admission is April 1.
Transfer Admission The application deadline for admission is April 1.
Entrance Difficulty The University of Iowa assesses its entrance difficulty level as moderately difficult. For the fall 2008 freshman class, 82 percent of the applicants were accepted.
For Further Information Contact Mr. Michael Barron, Assistant Provost for Enrollment Services and Director of Admissions, The University of Iowa, 107 Calvin Hall, Iowa City, IA 52242. *Phone:* 319-335-3847 or 800-553-4692 (toll-free). *Fax:* 319-335-1535. *E-mail:* admissions@uiowa.edu. *Web site:* http://www.uiowa.edu/.

UNIVERSITY OF NORTHERN IOWA

Cedar Falls, Iowa

University of Northern Iowa is a coed, public, comprehensive unit of Board of Regents, State of Iowa, founded in 1876, offering degrees at the bachelor's, master's, and doctoral levels. It has a 916-acre campus in Cedar Falls.

Academic Information The faculty has 856 members (75% full-time), 59% with terminal degrees. The undergraduate student-faculty ratio is 16:1. The library holds 1 million titles, 6,841 serial subscriptions, and 29,730 audiovisual materials. Special programs include academic remediation, services for learning-disabled students, an honors program, cooperative (work-study) education, study abroad, advanced placement credit, accelerated degree programs, ESL programs, double majors, independent study, distance learning, self-designed majors, summer session for credit, part-time degree programs (daytime, evenings, summer), external degree programs, adult/continuing education programs, internships, and arrangement for off-campus study with Iowa Regents' Universities Student Exchange, National Student Exchange. The most frequently chosen baccalaureate fields are business/marketing, education, social sciences.
Student Body Statistics The student body totals 12,998, of whom 11,086 are undergraduates (2,015 freshmen). 56 percent are women and 44 percent are men. Students come from 39 states and territories and 47 other countries. 92 percent are from Iowa. 2.4 percent are international students.
Expenses for 2009–10 *Application fee:* $40. *State resident tuition:* $5756 full-time, $240 per hour part-time. *Nonresident tuition:* $14,020 full-time, $584 per hour part-time. *Mandatory fees:* $880 full-time. *College room and board:* $7082. *College room only:* $3380.
Financial Aid Forms of aid include need-based and non-need-based scholarships, athletic grants, and part-time jobs. The average aided 2008–09 undergraduate received an aid package worth an estimated $7597. The application deadline for financial aid is continuous.
Freshman Admission University of Northern Iowa requires a high school transcript, rank in upper 50% of high school class, SAT or ACT scores, and TOEFL scores for international students. Recommendations and an interview are required for some. The application deadline for regular admission is August 15.
Transfer Admission The application deadline for admission is August 15.
Entrance Difficulty University of Northern Iowa assesses its entrance difficulty level as moderately difficult. For the fall 2008 freshman class, 84 percent of the applicants were accepted.
For Further Information Contact Ms. Christie Kangas, Director of Admissions, University of Northern Iowa, 120 Gilchrist Hall, Cedar Falls, IA 50614-0018. *Phone:* 319-273-2281 or 800-772-2037 (toll-free). *Fax:* 319-273-2885. *E-mail:* admissions@uni.edu. *Web site:* http://www.uni.edu/.

UPPER IOWA UNIVERSITY

Fayette, Iowa

http://www.uiu.edu/

VATTEROTT COLLEGE

Des Moines, Iowa

http://www.vatterott-college.edu/

WALDORF COLLEGE

Forest City, Iowa

Waldorf College is a coed, private, Lutheran, four-year college, founded in 1903, offering degrees at the bachelor's level. It has a 29-acre campus in Forest City.

Academic Information The faculty has 70 members (57% full-time), 34% with terminal degrees. The student-faculty ratio is 14:1. The library holds 48,500 titles and 55,989 serial subscriptions. Special programs include academic remediation, services for learning-disabled students, an honors program, cooperative (work-study) education, study abroad, advanced placement credit, accelerated degree programs, Freshman Honors College, double majors, independent study, self-designed majors, summer session for credit, part-time degree programs, adult/continuing education programs, and internships. The most frequently chosen baccalaureate fields are business/marketing, communications/journalism, education.
Student Body Statistics The student body is made up of 582 undergraduates (118 freshmen). 49 percent are women and 51 percent are men. Students come from 27 states and territories and 14 other countries. 62 percent are from Iowa. 3.8 percent are international students.
Expenses for 2008–09 *Application fee:* $0. *Comprehensive fee:* $25,864 includes full-time tuition ($19,214), mandatory fees ($840), and college room and board ($5810). Full-time tuition and fees vary according to class time, course load, and program. Room and board charges vary according to board plan and housing facility.
Financial Aid Forms of aid include need-based and non-need-based scholarships, athletic grants, and part-time jobs. The priority application deadline for financial aid is March 1.
Freshman Admission Waldorf College requires a high school transcript, SAT or ACT scores, and TOEFL scores for international students. A minimum 2.0 high school GPA is recommended. An interview is required for some. The application deadline for regular admission is rolling.
Transfer Admission The application deadline for admission is rolling.
Entrance Difficulty Waldorf College assesses its entrance difficulty level as moderately difficult. For the fall 2008 freshman class, 64 percent of the applicants were accepted.
For Further Information Contact Dawn Johnson, Vice President for Admission, Waldorf College, 106 South 6th Street, Forest City, IA 50436. *Phone:* 641-585-8112 or 800-292-1903 (toll-free). *Fax:* 641-585-8125. *E-mail:* admissions@waldorf.edu. *Web site:* http://www.waldorf.edu/.

WARTBURG COLLEGE

Waverly, Iowa

Wartburg College is a coed, private, Lutheran, four-year college, founded in 1852, offering degrees at the bachelor's level. It has a 118-acre campus in Waverly.

Academic Information The faculty has 176 members (62% full-time), 59% with terminal degrees. The student-faculty ratio is 12:1. The library holds 198,978 titles, 32,009 serial subscriptions, and 6,012 audiovisual materials. Special programs include academic remediation, services for learning-disabled students, an honors program, study abroad, advanced placement credit, accelerated degree programs, double majors, independent study, self-designed majors, summer session for credit, part-time degree programs, internships, and arrangement for off-campus study with

Wartburg College (continued)
members of the May Term Consortium. The most frequently chosen baccalaureate fields are biological/life sciences, business/marketing, communications/journalism.
Student Body Statistics The student body is made up of 1,799 undergraduates (514 freshmen). 53 percent are women and 47 percent are men. Students come from 27 states and territories and 40 other countries. 74 percent are from Iowa. 5.2 percent are international students.
Expenses for 2008–09 *Comprehensive fee:* $33,415 includes full-time tuition ($25,360), mandatory fees ($800), and college room and board ($7255). *College room only:* $3435. Room and board charges vary according to board plan and housing facility. *Part-time tuition:* $910 per course. *Part-time mandatory fees:* $75 per term. Part-time tuition and fees vary according to course load.
Financial Aid Forms of aid include need-based and non-need-based scholarships and part-time jobs. The average aided 2007–08 undergraduate received an aid package worth $20,435. The priority application deadline for financial aid is March 1.
Freshman Admission Wartburg College requires a high school transcript, a minimum 2.0 high school GPA, SAT or ACT scores, and TOEFL scores for international students. Secondary school report is recommended. An interview is required for some. The application deadline for regular admission is rolling and for early action it is December 1.
Transfer Admission The application deadline for admission is rolling.
Entrance Difficulty Wartburg College assesses its entrance difficulty level as moderately difficult. For the fall 2008 freshman class, 74 percent of the applicants were accepted.
For Further Information Contact Mr. Todd Coleman, Assistant Vice President for Admissions, Wartburg College, 100 Wartburg Boulevard, PO Box 1003, Waverly, IA 50677-0903. *Phone:* 319-352-8264 or 800-772-2085 (toll-free). *Fax:* 319-352-8579. *E-mail:* admissions@wartburg.edu. *Web site:* http://www.wartburg.edu/.

WILLIAM PENN UNIVERSITY

Oskaloosa, Iowa

http://www.wmpenn.edu/

Kansas

THE ART INSTITUTES INTERNATIONAL–KANSAS CITY

Lexena, Kansas

The Art Institutes International–Kansas City is a coed, proprietary, four-year college of Education Management Corporation, founded in 2008, offering degrees at the associate and bachelor's levels.

Expenses for 2009–10 Tuition cost varies by program. Prospective students should contact the school for current tuition costs. Other charges include a starting kit for all first-quarter students. Kits vary in price, depending on the program of study.
For Further Information Contact Admissions Office, The Art Institutes International–Kansas City, 8208 Melrose Drive, Lenexa, KS 66214. *Phone:* 913-217-4600 or 866-530-8508 (toll-free). *Fax:* 913-217-4690. *Web site:* http://www.artinstitutes.edu/kansascity/.

BAKER UNIVERSITY

Baldwin City, Kansas

Baker University is a coed, private, United Methodist, four-year college, founded in 1858, offering degrees at the bachelor's level. It has a 26-acre campus in Baldwin City near Kansas City.

Academic Information The faculty has 114 members (56% full-time), 58% with terminal degrees. The student-faculty ratio is 12:1. The library holds 107,255 titles, 676 serial subscriptions, and 5,471 audiovisual materials. Special programs include services for learning-disabled students, an honors program, study abroad, advanced placement credit, double majors, independent study, self-designed majors, summer session for credit, and internships. The most frequently chosen baccalaureate fields are business/marketing, biological/life sciences, education.
Student Body Statistics The student body is made up of 998 undergraduates (239 freshmen). 56 percent are women and 44 percent are men. Students come from 25 states and territories and 7 other countries. 74 percent are from Kansas. 0.8 percent are international students.
Expenses for 2008–09 *Application fee:* $0. *One-time mandatory fee:* $80. *Comprehensive fee:* $26,250 includes full-time tuition ($19,880) and college room and board ($6370). *College room only:* $2950. Full-time tuition varies according to location and program. Room and board charges vary according to board plan and housing facility. *Part-time tuition:* $600 per credit hour. Part-time tuition varies according to course load.
Financial Aid Forms of aid include need-based and non-need-based scholarships, athletic grants, and part-time jobs. The average aided 2008–09 undergraduate received an aid package worth an estimated $13,600. The priority application deadline for financial aid is March 1.
Freshman Admission Baker University requires a high school transcript, a minimum 2.75 high school GPA, 1 recommendation, SAT or ACT scores, and TOEFL scores for international students. An essay and an interview are required for some. The application deadline for regular admission is rolling.
Transfer Admission The application deadline for admission is rolling.
Entrance Difficulty Baker University assesses its entrance difficulty level as moderately difficult. For the fall 2008 freshman class, 50 percent of the applicants were accepted.
For Further Information Contact Mr. Daniel McKinney, Director of Admissions, Baker University, PO Box 65, Baldwin City, KS 66006-0065. *Phone:* 785-594-8307 or 800-873-4282 (toll-free). *Fax:* 785-594-8372. *E-mail:* admissions@bakeru.edu. *Web site:* http://www.bakeru.edu/.

BARCLAY COLLEGE

Haviland, Kansas

Barclay College is a coed, private, four-year college, founded in 1917, affiliated with the Society of Friends, offering degrees at the associate and bachelor's levels. It has a 13-acre campus in Haviland.

Academic Information The faculty has 15 members (47% full-time), 27% with terminal degrees. The student-faculty ratio is 12:1. The library holds 63,759 titles, 22,194 serial subscriptions, and 705 audiovisual materials. Special programs include academic remediation, advanced placement credit, double majors, independent study, distance learning, part-time degree programs (daytime, evenings), external degree programs, adult/continuing education programs, and internships. The most frequently chosen baccalaureate fields are psychology, business/marketing, theology and religious vocations.
Student Body Statistics The student body is made up of 147 undergraduates (34 freshmen). 49 percent are women and 51 percent are men. Students come from 19 states and territories and 3 other countries. 39 percent are from Kansas. 2 percent are international students.
Expenses for 2009–10 *Application fee:* $15. *Comprehensive fee:* $19,990 includes full-time tuition ($11,000), mandatory fees ($2590), and college room and board ($6400).
Financial Aid Forms of aid include need-based and non-need-based scholarships and part-time jobs. The priority application deadline for financial aid is March 15.
Freshman Admission Barclay College requires an essay, a high school transcript, a minimum 2.3 high school GPA, 2 recommendations, an interview, SAT or ACT scores, and TOEFL scores for international students. The application deadline for regular admission is September 1.
Transfer Admission The application deadline for admission is September 1.

Entrance Difficulty Barclay College assesses its entrance difficulty level as minimally difficult. For the fall 2008 freshman class, 87 percent of the applicants were accepted.
For Further Information Contact Mr. Justin Kendall, Admissions Recruiter, Barclay College, 607 North Kingman, Haviland, KS 67059. *Phone:* 620-862-5252 Ext. 21 or 800-862-0226 (toll-free). *Fax:* 620-862-5242. *E-mail:* jkendall@barclaycollege.edu. *Web site:* http://www.barclaycollege.edu/.

BENEDICTINE COLLEGE

Atchison, Kansas

Benedictine College is a coed, private, Roman Catholic, comprehensive institution, founded in 1859, offering degrees at the associate, bachelor's, and master's levels. It has a 225-acre campus in Atchison near Kansas City.

Academic Information The faculty has 114 members (67% full-time), 59% with terminal degrees. The undergraduate student-faculty ratio is 14:1. The library holds 207,316 titles, 32,834 serial subscriptions, and 1,032 audiovisual materials. Special programs include academic remediation, services for learning-disabled students, cooperative (work-study) education, study abroad, advanced placement credit, ESL programs, double majors, independent study, self-designed majors, summer session for credit, part-time degree programs (daytime, evenings, summer), internships, and arrangement for off-campus study with 16 members of the Kansas City Regional Council for Higher Education, Kansas State University. The most frequently chosen baccalaureate fields are business/marketing, education, philosophy and religious studies.
Student Body Statistics The student body totals 2,033, of whom 1,978 are undergraduates (396 freshmen). 58 percent are women and 42 percent are men. Students come from 38 states and territories and 20 other countries. 30 percent are from Kansas. 2.1 percent are international students.
Expenses for 2008–09 *Application fee:* $25. *Comprehensive fee:* $25,100 includes full-time tuition ($18,800) and college room and board ($6300). *College room only:* $3260. Full-time tuition varies according to course load and degree level. Room and board charges vary according to board plan and housing facility. *Part-time tuition:* $530 per credit hour. Part-time tuition varies according to course load and degree level.
Financial Aid Forms of aid include need-based and non-need-based scholarships, athletic grants, and part-time jobs. The average aided 2008–09 undergraduate received an aid package worth an estimated $15,739. The priority application deadline for financial aid is March 15.
Freshman Admission Benedictine College requires a high school transcript, a minimum 2.0 high school GPA, SAT or ACT scores, and TOEFL scores for international students. An interview is required for some.
Entrance Difficulty Benedictine College assesses its entrance difficulty level as moderately difficult. For the fall 2008 freshman class, 20 percent of the applicants were accepted.
For Further Information Contact Mr. Pete Helgesen, Dean of Enrollment Management, Benedictine College, 1020 North 2nd Street, Atchison, KS 66002. *Phone:* 913-367-5340 Ext. 2476 or 800-467-5340 (toll-free). *Fax:* 913-367-5462. *E-mail:* bcadmiss@benedictine.edu. *Web site:* http://www.benedictine.edu/.

BETHANY COLLEGE

Lindsborg, Kansas

Bethany College is a coed, private, Lutheran, four-year college, founded in 1881, offering degrees at the bachelor's level. It has an 80-acre campus in Lindsborg.

Academic Information The faculty has 87 members (51% full-time), 37% with terminal degrees. The student-faculty ratio is 9:1. The library holds 90,230 titles, 709 serial subscriptions, and 1,232 audiovisual materials. Special programs include academic remediation, services for learning-disabled students, an honors program, study abroad, advanced placement credit, accelerated degree programs, double majors, independent study, self-designed majors, summer session for credit, internships, and arrangement for off-campus study with 6 members of the Associated Colleges of Central Kansas. The most frequently chosen baccalaureate fields are biological/life sciences, business/marketing, education.
Student Body Statistics The student body is made up of 587 undergraduates (178 freshmen). 49 percent are women and 51 percent are men. Students come from 29 states and territories and 29 other countries. 56 percent are from Kansas. 5.6 percent are international students.
Expenses for 2008–09 *Application fee:* $20. *Comprehensive fee:* $23,774 includes full-time tuition ($17,824), mandatory fees ($300), and college room and board ($5650). *College room only:* $3075. *Part-time tuition:* $330 per credit hour.
Financial Aid Forms of aid include need-based and non-need-based scholarships, athletic grants, and part-time jobs. The average aided 2008–09 undergraduate received an aid package worth an estimated $20,734. The application deadline for financial aid is continuous.
Freshman Admission Bethany College requires a high school transcript, a minimum 2.5 high school GPA, SAT or ACT scores, and TOEFL scores for international students. An essay and an interview are required for some. The application deadline for regular admission is rolling.
Transfer Admission The application deadline for admission is rolling.
Entrance Difficulty Bethany College assesses its entrance difficulty level as moderately difficult. For the fall 2008 freshman class, 65 percent of the applicants were accepted.
For Further Information Contact Mrs. Tricia Hawk, Dean of Admissions and Financial Aid, Bethany College, 421 North First Street, Lindsborg, KS 67456. *Phone:* 785-227-3311 Ext. 8344 or 800-826-2281 (toll-free). *Fax:* 785-227-8993. *E-mail:* admissions@bethanylb.edu. *Web site:* http://www.bethanylb.edu/.

BETHEL COLLEGE

North Newton, Kansas

Bethel College is a coed, private, four-year college, founded in 1887, affiliated with the Mennonite Church USA, offering degrees at the bachelor's level. It has a 60-acre campus in North Newton near Wichita.

Academic Information The faculty has 83 members (59% full-time), 43% with terminal degrees. The student-faculty ratio is 8:1. The library holds 176,002 titles, 33,498 serial subscriptions, and 6,891 audiovisual materials. Special programs include academic remediation, services for learning-disabled students, study abroad, advanced placement credit, double majors, independent study, summer session for credit, part-time degree programs (daytime, evenings, summer), internships, and arrangement for off-campus study with 6 members of the Associated Colleges of Central Kansas, Hesston College. The most frequently chosen baccalaureate fields are English, health professions and related sciences, visual and performing arts.
Student Body Statistics The student body is made up of 500 undergraduates (119 freshmen). 48 percent are women and 52 percent are men. Students come from 23 states and territories and 20 other countries. 76 percent are from Kansas. 9.8 percent are international students.
Expenses for 2008–09 *Application fee:* $20. *Comprehensive fee:* $24,950 includes full-time tuition ($18,900) and college room and board ($6050). *College room only:* $3050. Full-time tuition varies according to course load. Room and board charges vary according to board plan and housing facility. *Part-time tuition:* $680 per credit hour. Part-time tuition varies according to course load.
Financial Aid Forms of aid include need-based and non-need-based scholarships, athletic grants, and part-time jobs. The average aided 2008–09 undergraduate received an aid package worth an estimated $20,941. The priority application deadline for financial aid is April 1.
Freshman Admission Bethel College requires a high school transcript, a minimum 2.5 high school GPA, SAT or ACT scores, and TOEFL scores for international students. An interview is recommended. An essay and 2 recommendations are required for some. The application deadline for regular admission is rolling.
Transfer Admission The application deadline for admission is rolling.

Bethel College (continued)

Entrance Difficulty Bethel College assesses its entrance difficulty level as moderately difficult. For the fall 2008 freshman class, 72 percent of the applicants were accepted.

For Further Information Contact Mr. Allan Bartel, Vice President for Admissions, Bethel College, 300 East 27th Street, North Newton, KS 67117-0531. *Phone:* 316-284-5230 or 800-522-1887 Ext. 230 (toll-free). *Fax:* 316-284-5870. *E-mail:* admissions@bethelks.edu. *Web site:* http://www.bethelks.edu/.

CENTRAL CHRISTIAN COLLEGE OF KANSAS

McPherson, Kansas

Central Christian College of Kansas is a coed, private, Free Methodist, four-year college, founded in 1884, offering degrees at the associate and bachelor's levels. It has a 16-acre campus in McPherson.

Academic Information The faculty has 46 members (41% full-time), 13% with terminal degrees. The student-faculty ratio is 15:1. The library holds 40,652 titles, 134 serial subscriptions, and 1,460 audiovisual materials. Special programs include academic remediation, services for learning-disabled students, cooperative (work-study) education, study abroad, advanced placement credit, double majors, independent study, distance learning, self-designed majors, part-time degree programs (daytime, evenings), adult/continuing education programs, internships, and arrangement for off-campus study with McPherson College, Christian Center for Urban Studies, Focus on the Family Institute, CCCU. The most frequently chosen baccalaureate fields are business/marketing, liberal arts/general studies, philosophy and religious studies.

Student Body Statistics The student body is made up of 399 undergraduates (125 freshmen). 50 percent are women and 50 percent are men. Students come from 34 states and territories and 3 other countries. 31 percent are from Kansas. 1.6 percent are international students.

Expenses for 2009–10 *Application fee:* $20. *Comprehensive fee:* $22,900 includes full-time tuition ($16,800), mandatory fees ($200), and college room and board ($5900). *College room only:* $2700. *Part-time tuition:* $475 per hour.

Financial Aid Forms of aid include need-based and non-need-based scholarships, athletic grants, and part-time jobs. The average aided 2007–08 undergraduate received an aid package worth $13,423. The priority application deadline for financial aid is March 1.

Freshman Admission Central Christian College of Kansas requires a high school transcript, a minimum 2.5 high school GPA, 2 recommendations, SAT or ACT scores, and TOEFL scores for international students. An essay and an interview are recommended. The application deadline for regular admission is rolling.

Transfer Admission The application deadline for admission is rolling.

Entrance Difficulty Central Christian College of Kansas assesses its entrance difficulty level as minimally difficult. For the fall 2008 freshman class, 100 percent of the applicants were accepted.

For Further Information Contact Dr. David Ferrell, Dean of Admissions, Central Christian College of Kansas, PO Box 1403, McPherson, KS 67460. *Phone:* 620-241-0723 Ext. 380 or 800-835-0078 Ext. 337 (toll-free). *Fax:* 620-241-6032. *E-mail:* admissions@centralchristian.edu. *Web site:* http://www.centralchristian.edu/.

CLEVELAND CHIROPRACTIC COLLEGE–KANSAS CITY CAMPUS

Overland Park, Kansas

Cleveland Chiropractic College–Kansas City Campus is a coed, private, upper-level institution, founded in 1922, offering degrees at the bachelor's and first professional levels. It has a 10-acre campus in Overland Park.

For Further Information Contact Ms. Melissa Denton, Director of Admissions, Cleveland Chiropractic College–Kansas City Campus, 10850 Lowell Avenue, Overland Park, KS 66210. *Phone:* 913-234-0750 or 800-467-2252 (toll-free). *Fax:* 913-234-0912. *E-mail:* kc.admissions@cleveland.edu. *Web site:* http://www.cleveland.edu/.

DONNELLY COLLEGE

Kansas City, Kansas

Donnelly College is a coed, private, Roman Catholic, two-year college, founded in 1949, offering degrees at the associate level. It has a 4-acre campus in Kansas City.

Academic Information The library holds 33,752 titles, 114 serial subscriptions, and 1,020 audiovisual materials. Special programs include academic remediation, services for learning-disabled students, advanced placement credit, ESL programs, double majors, independent study, summer session for credit, part-time degree programs (daytime, evenings, weekends, summer), external degree programs, and internships.

Student Body Statistics The student body is made up of 572 undergraduates.

Financial Aid Forms of aid include need-based scholarships and part-time jobs. The priority application deadline for financial aid is April 1.

Freshman Admission Donnelly College requires TOEFL scores for international students. A high school transcript is recommended. The application deadline for regular admission is rolling.

Transfer Admission The application deadline for admission is rolling.

Entrance Difficulty Donnelly College has an open admission policy.

For Further Information Contact Mr. Kevin Kelley, Vice President of Enrollment Management, Donnelly College, 608 North 18th Street, Kansas City, MO 66101. *Phone:* 913-621-8769. *Fax:* 913-621-8719. *E-mail:* admissions@donnelly.edu. *Web site:* http://www.donnelly.edu/.

EMPORIA STATE UNIVERSITY

Emporia, Kansas

Emporia State University is a coed, public, comprehensive unit of Kansas State Board of Education, founded in 1863, offering degrees at the bachelor's, master's, and doctoral levels and post-master's and postbachelor's certificates. It has a 207-acre campus in Emporia near Wichita.

Academic Information The faculty has 293 members (89% full-time), 75% with terminal degrees. The undergraduate student-faculty ratio is 18:1. The library holds 2 million titles, 37,675 serial subscriptions, and 9,256 audiovisual materials. Special programs include academic remediation, services for learning-disabled students, an honors program, study abroad, advanced placement credit, accelerated degree programs, ESL programs, double majors, independent study, distance learning, summer session for credit, part-time degree programs (daytime, evenings, weekends, summer), adult/continuing education programs, internships, and arrangement for off-campus study. The most frequently chosen baccalaureate fields are business/marketing, education, social sciences.

Student Body Statistics The student body totals 6,404, of whom 4,288 are undergraduates (681 freshmen). 60 percent are women and 40 percent are men. Students come from 31 states and territories and 25 other countries. 92 percent are from Kansas. 5.9 percent are international students.

Expenses for 2008–09 *Application fee:* $30. *State resident tuition:* $3294 full-time, $110 per credit hour part-time. *Nonresident tuition:* $11,806 full-time, $394 per credit hour part-time. *Mandatory fees:* $842 full-time,

$51 per credit hour part-time. Both full-time and part-time tuition and fees vary according to course level, course load, degree level, and location. *College room and board:* $5858. *College room only:* $3027. Room and board charges vary according to board plan and housing facility.
Financial Aid Forms of aid include need-based and non-need-based scholarships, athletic grants, and part-time jobs. The average aided 2008–09 undergraduate received an aid package worth an estimated $7117. The priority application deadline for financial aid is March 15.
Freshman Admission Emporia State University requires a high school transcript, SAT or ACT scores, and TOEFL scores for international students. A minimum 2.0 high school GPA is recommended. The application deadline for regular admission is rolling.
Transfer Admission The application deadline for admission is rolling.
Entrance Difficulty Emporia State University assesses its entrance difficulty level as noncompetitive; minimally difficult for transfers. For the fall 2008 freshman class, 87 percent of the applicants were accepted.
For Further Information Contact Ms. Laura Eddy, Director of Admissions, Emporia State University, 1200 Commercial Street, Campus Box 4034, Emporia, KS 66801-5087. *Phone:* 620-341-5465, 877-GOTOESU (toll-free in-state), or 877-468-6378 (toll-free out-of-state). *Fax:* 620-341-5599. *E-mail:* go2esu@emporia.edu. *Web site:* http://www.emporia.edu/.

FORT HAYS STATE UNIVERSITY

Hays, Kansas

Fort Hays State University is a coed, public, comprehensive unit of Kansas State Board of Education, founded in 1902, offering degrees at the associate, bachelor's, and master's levels and post-master's certificates. It has a 200-acre campus in Hays.

Academic Information The faculty has 291 members (87% full-time), 66% with terminal degrees. The undergraduate student-faculty ratio is 17:1. The library holds 624,637 titles and 1,689 serial subscriptions. Special programs include academic remediation, services for learning-disabled students, study abroad, advanced placement credit, ESL programs, double majors, distance learning, self-designed majors, summer session for credit, part-time degree programs (daytime, evenings, weekends, summer), external degree programs, adult/continuing education programs, internships, and arrangement for off-campus study with members of the National Student Exchange.
Student Body Statistics The student body totals 7,403, of whom 5,920 are undergraduates (904 freshmen). 54 percent are women and 46 percent are men. Students come from 48 states and territories and 15 other countries. 90 percent are from Kansas. 16 percent are international students.
Expenses for 2008–09 *Application fee:* $30. *State resident tuition:* $3051 full-time, $101.75 per credit hour part-time. *Nonresident tuition:* $9575 full-time, $319.17 per credit hour part-time. Both full-time and part-time tuition varies according to course load and location. *College room and board:* $5450. *College room only:* $2710. Room and board charges vary according to board plan, housing facility, and student level.
Financial Aid Forms of aid include need-based scholarships, athletic grants, and part-time jobs. The average aided 2007–08 undergraduate received an aid package worth $5955.
Freshman Admission Fort Hays State University requires a high school transcript, ACT scores, SAT or ACT scores, and TOEFL scores for international students. The application deadline for regular admission is rolling.
Transfer Admission The application deadline for admission is rolling.
Entrance Difficulty Fort Hays State University assesses its entrance difficulty level as noncompetitive; minimally difficult for out-of-state applicants; minimally difficult for transfers; moderately difficult for radiological technology program, School of Nursing. For the fall 2008 freshman class, 94 percent of the applicants were accepted.
For Further Information Contact Ms. Susan Cochran, Office Manager/Campus Visit Coordinator, Office of Admissions, Fort Hays State University, 600 Park Street, Hays, KS 67601-4099. *Phone:* 785-628-5666 or 800-628-FHSU (toll-free). *Fax:* 800-432-0248. *E-mail:* tigers@fhsu.edu. *Web site:* http://www.fhsu.edu/.

FRIENDS UNIVERSITY

Wichita, Kansas

Friends University is a coed, private, comprehensive institution, founded in 1898, offering degrees at the associate, bachelor's, and master's levels. It has a 45-acre campus in Wichita.

Academic Information The library holds 105,989 titles and 857 serial subscriptions. Special programs include academic remediation, an honors program, cooperative (work-study) education, advanced placement credit, accelerated degree programs, self-designed majors, summer session for credit, part-time degree programs, external degree programs, adult/continuing education programs, internships, and arrangement for off-campus study with Newman University, Wichita Area Vocational/Technical Institute.
Student Body Statistics The student body totals 2,826, of whom 2,225 are undergraduates.
Expenses for 2008–09 *Application fee:* $35. *Comprehensive fee:* $14,625 includes full-time tuition ($9100), mandatory fees ($75), and college room and board ($5450). *Part-time tuition:* $607 per credit hour. *Part-time mandatory fees:* $5 per credit hour.
Financial Aid Forms of aid include need-based and non-need-based scholarships, athletic grants, and part-time jobs. The priority application deadline for financial aid is March 15.
Freshman Admission Friends University requires a high school transcript, SAT or ACT scores, and TOEFL scores for international students. An interview is recommended. An essay and 1 recommendation are required for some. The application deadline for regular admission is rolling.
Transfer Admission The application deadline for admission is rolling.
Entrance Difficulty Friends University assesses its entrance difficulty level as moderately difficult.
For Further Information Contact Marla Sexson, Director of Admissions, Friends University, 2100 West University Street, Wichita, KS 67213. *Phone:* 316-295-5512 or 800-577-2233 (toll-free). *Fax:* 316-262-5027. *E-mail:* tmyers@friends.edu. *Web site:* http://www.friends.edu/.

HASKELL INDIAN NATIONS UNIVERSITY

Lawrence, Kansas

Haskell Indian Nations University is a coed, public, four-year college, founded in 1884, offering degrees at the associate and bachelor's levels. It has a 320-acre campus in Lawrence.

Academic Information The library holds 50,000 titles and 400 serial subscriptions. Special programs include academic remediation, services for learning-disabled students, advanced placement credit, independent study, distance learning, self-designed majors, summer session for credit, part-time degree programs (daytime, summer), internships, and arrangement for off-campus study with members of the American Indian Higher Education Consortium, Kansas City Regional Council for Higher Education, University of Kansas.
Student Body Statistics The student body is made up of 894 undergraduates.
Financial Aid Forms of aid include need-based scholarships and part-time jobs. The application deadline for financial aid is continuous.
Freshman Admission Haskell Indian Nations University requires a high school transcript, a minimum 2.0 high school GPA, and ACT scores. 2 recommendations are required for some. The application deadline for regular admission is July 30.
Transfer Admission The application deadline for admission is July 30.
Entrance Difficulty Haskell Indian Nations University assesses its entrance difficulty level as minimally difficult.
For Further Information Contact Ms. Patty Grant, Recruitment Officer, Haskell Indian Nations University, 155 Indian Avenue #5031, Lawrence, KS 66046. *Phone:* 785-749-8437 Ext. 437. *Fax:* 785-749-8429. *E-mail:* admissions@haskell.edu. *Web site:* http://www.haskell.edu/.

HESSTON COLLEGE

Hesston, Kansas

Hesston College is a coed, private, Mennonite, two-year college, founded in 1909, offering degrees at the associate level. It has a 50-acre campus in Hesston near Wichita.

Expenses for 2008–09 *Application fee:* $15. *Comprehensive fee:* $25,000 includes full-time tuition ($18,500), mandatory fees ($280), and college room and board ($6220). *Part-time tuition:* $771 per hour. *Part-time mandatory fees:* $70 per term. Part-time tuition and fees vary according to course load.

For Further Information Contact Joel Kauffman, Vice President of Admissions, Hesston College, Box 3000, Hesston, KS 67062. *Phone:* 620-327-8222 or 800-995-2757 (toll-free). *Fax:* 620-327-8300. *E-mail:* admissions@hesston.edu. *Web site:* http://www.hesston.edu/.

ITT TECHNICAL INSTITUTE

Wichita, Kansas

ITT Technical Institute is a coed, proprietary, four-year college of ITT Educational Services, Inc., offering degrees at the associate and bachelor's levels.

For Further Information Contact Director of Recruitment, ITT Technical Institute, One Brittany Place, Suite 100, 2024 N. Woodlawn, Wichita, KS 67208. *Phone:* 316-681-8400 or 877-207-1047 (toll-free). *Web site:* http://www.itt-tech.edu/.

KANSAS NEWMAN COLLEGE

See Newman University.

KANSAS STATE UNIVERSITY

Manhattan, Kansas

Kansas State University is a coed, public unit of Kansas State Board of Education, founded in 1863, offering degrees at the associate, bachelor's, master's, doctoral, and first professional levels. It has a 668-acre campus in Manhattan near Kansas City.

Academic Information The faculty has 1,099 members (86% full-time), 80% with terminal degrees. The undergraduate student-faculty ratio is 19:1. The library holds 2 million titles and 18,718 serial subscriptions. Special programs include academic remediation, services for learning-disabled students, an honors program, cooperative (work-study) education, study abroad, advanced placement credit, accelerated degree programs, Freshman Honors College, ESL programs, double majors, independent study, distance learning, summer session for credit, part-time degree programs (daytime, evenings, summer), adult/continuing education programs, internships, and arrangement for off-campus study with Manhattan Christian College, University of Missouri-Kansas City, 19 Kansas community colleges. The most frequently chosen baccalaureate fields are agriculture, business/marketing, education.

Student Body Statistics The student body totals 23,520, of whom 18,491 are undergraduates (3,761 freshmen). 48 percent are women and 52 percent are men. Students come from 50 states and territories and 100 other countries. 87 percent are from Kansas. 3.4 percent are international students.

Expenses for 2008–09 *Application fee:* $30. *State resident tuition:* $5954 full-time, $198.47 per credit hour part-time. *Nonresident tuition:* $16,259 full-time, $542 per credit hour part-time. *Mandatory fees:* $673 full-time. Full-time tuition and fees vary according to course load, location, program, and reciprocity agreements. Part-time tuition varies according to course load, location, program, and reciprocity agreements. *College room and board:* $6448. Room and board charges vary according to board plan, housing facility, and location.

Financial Aid Forms of aid include need-based scholarships, athletic grants, and part-time jobs. The average aided 2007–08 undergraduate received an aid package worth $6892.

Freshman Admission Kansas State University requires a high school transcript, a minimum 2.0 high school GPA, SAT or ACT scores, and TOEFL scores for international students. The application deadline for regular admission is rolling.

Transfer Admission The application deadline for admission is rolling.

Entrance Difficulty Kansas State University assesses its entrance difficulty level as noncompetitive; moderately difficult for out-of-state applicants; moderately difficult for transfers; very difficult for architecture and design programs. For the fall 2008 freshman class, 84 percent of the applicants were accepted.

For Further Information Contact Ms. Christy Crenshaw, Associate Director of Admissions, Kansas State University, 119 Anderson Hall, Manhattan, KS 66506. *Phone:* 785-532-6250 or 800-432-8270 (toll-free in-state). *Fax:* 785-532-6393. *E-mail:* kstate@ksu.edu. *Web site:* http://www.ksu.edu/.

KANSAS WESLEYAN UNIVERSITY

Salina, Kansas

Kansas Wesleyan University is a coed, private, United Methodist, comprehensive institution, founded in 1886, offering degrees at the associate, bachelor's, and master's levels. It has a 28-acre campus in Salina.

Academic Information The faculty has 80 members (54% full-time), 34% with terminal degrees. The undergraduate student-faculty ratio is 14:1. The library holds 97,060 titles, 188 serial subscriptions, and 1,797 audiovisual materials. Special programs include academic remediation, study abroad, advanced placement credit, ESL programs, double majors, independent study, distance learning, self-designed majors, summer session for credit, part-time degree programs (daytime, evenings, summer), adult/continuing education programs, internships, and arrangement for off-campus study with Associated Colleges of Central Kansas. The most frequently chosen baccalaureate fields are business/marketing, health professions and related sciences, parks and recreation.

Student Body Statistics The student body totals 879, of whom 818 are undergraduates. Students come from 18 states and territories and 8 other countries. 70 percent are from Kansas.

Expenses for 2009–10 *Application fee:* $20. *Comprehensive fee:* $25,800 includes full-time tuition ($19,200) and college room and board ($6600). *College room only:* $2400. *Part-time tuition:* $220 per credit hour.

Financial Aid Forms of aid include need-based and non-need-based scholarships and part-time jobs. The priority application deadline for financial aid is March 15.

Freshman Admission Kansas Wesleyan University requires a high school transcript, a minimum 2.5 high school GPA, SAT or ACT scores, and TOEFL scores for international students. The application deadline for regular admission is rolling.

Transfer Admission The application deadline for admission is rolling.

Entrance Difficulty Kansas Wesleyan University assesses its entrance difficulty level as moderately difficult. For the fall 2008 freshman class, 63 percent of the applicants were accepted.

For Further Information Contact Mr. Jim Allen, Director of Admissions, Kansas Wesleyan University, 100 East Claflin Avenue, Salina, KS 67401-6196. *Phone:* 785-827-5541 Ext. 1283 or 800-874-1154 Ext. 1285 (toll-free). *Fax:* 785-827-0927. *E-mail:* admissions@kwu.edu. *Web site:* http://www.kwu.edu/.

MANHATTAN CHRISTIAN COLLEGE

Manhattan, Kansas

Manhattan Christian College is a coed, private, four-year college, founded in 1927, affiliated with the Christian Churches and Churches of Christ, offering degrees at the associate and bachelor's levels. It has a 10-acre campus in Manhattan.

Academic Information The library holds 3,300 titles, 3,000 serial subscriptions, and 2,200 audiovisual materials. Special programs include academic remediation, advanced placement credit, double majors, independent study, distance learning, summer session for credit, adult/continuing education programs, and internships.

Student Body Statistics The student body is made up of 388 undergraduates.
Expenses for 2008–09 *Application fee:* $25. *Comprehensive fee:* $18,094 includes full-time tuition ($10,932), mandatory fees ($442), and college room and board ($6720). *Part-time tuition:* $449 per hour. *Part-time mandatory fees:* $8 per hour, $150 per term.
Financial Aid Forms of aid include need-based and non-need-based scholarships and part-time jobs. The average aided 2008–09 undergraduate received an aid package worth an estimated $10,129. The priority application deadline for financial aid is April 1.
Freshman Admission Manhattan Christian College requires an essay, a high school transcript, a minimum 2.0 high school GPA, 3 recommendations, and SAT or ACT scores. An interview is required for some. The application deadline for regular admission is August 1.
Transfer Admission The application deadline for admission is August 1.
Entrance Difficulty Manhattan Christian College assesses its entrance difficulty level as minimally difficult.
For Further Information Contact Eric Ingmire, Director of Admissions, Manhattan Christian College, 1415 Anderson Avenue, Manhattan, KS 66502-4081. *Phone:* 785-539-3571 Ext. 324 or 877-246-4622 (toll-free). *Fax:* 785-776-9251. *E-mail:* admit@mccks.edu. *Web site:* http://www.mccks.edu/.

McPHERSON COLLEGE
McPherson, Kansas

McPherson College is a coed, private, four-year college, founded in 1887, affiliated with the Church of the Brethren, offering degrees at the associate and bachelor's levels. It has a 26-acre campus in McPherson.

Academic Information The library holds 89,946 titles, 345 serial subscriptions, and 4,465 audiovisual materials. Special programs include academic remediation, services for learning-disabled students, study abroad, advanced placement credit, double majors, independent study, self-designed majors, summer session for credit, part-time degree programs (daytime, evenings, summer), adult/continuing education programs, internships, and arrangement for off-campus study with 6 members of the Associated Colleges of Central Kansas.
Student Body Statistics The student body is made up of 544 undergraduates.
Expenses for 2008–09 *Application fee:* $25. *Comprehensive fee:* $23,700 includes full-time tuition ($16,900), mandatory fees ($300), and college room and board ($6500). *College room only:* $2600. Full-time tuition and fees vary according to course load and program. *Part-time tuition:* $250 per hour. *Part-time mandatory fees:* $30 per hour.
Financial Aid Forms of aid include need-based and non-need-based scholarships, athletic grants, and part-time jobs. The average aided 2007–08 undergraduate received an aid package worth $18,134. The priority application deadline for financial aid is March 1.
Freshman Admission McPherson College requires a high school transcript, a minimum 2.0 high school GPA, SAT or ACT scores, and TOEFL scores for international students. ACT scores are recommended. The application deadline for regular admission is rolling.
Transfer Admission The application deadline for admission is rolling.
Entrance Difficulty McPherson College assesses its entrance difficulty level as moderately difficult.
For Further Information Contact Ms. Carol L. Williams, Director of Admissions and Financial Aid, McPherson College, 1600 East Euclid, McPherson, KS 67460. *Phone:* 620-241-0731 Ext. 1270 or 800-365-7402 (toll-free). *Fax:* 620-241-8443. *E-mail:* admiss@mcpherson.edu. *Web site:* http://www.mcpherson.edu/.

MIDAMERICA NAZARENE UNIVERSITY
Olathe, Kansas

MidAmerica Nazarene University is a coed, private, comprehensive institution, founded in 1966, affiliated with the Church of the Nazarene, offering degrees at the associate, bachelor's, and master's levels and post-master's certificates. It has a 105-acre campus in Olathe near Kansas City.

Academic Information The faculty has 218 members (40% full-time), 29% with terminal degrees. The undergraduate student-faculty ratio is 16:1. The library holds 132,991 titles, 1,250 serial subscriptions, and 11,427 audiovisual materials. Special programs include academic remediation, services for learning-disabled students, study abroad, advanced placement credit, accelerated degree programs, double majors, independent study, distance learning, self-designed majors, summer session for credit, part-time degree programs (daytime, summer), adult/continuing education programs, internships, and arrangement for off-campus study with Coalition for Christian Colleges and Universities. The most frequently chosen baccalaureate fields are business/marketing, education, health professions and related sciences.
Student Body Statistics The student body totals 1,743, of whom 1,305 are undergraduates (204 freshmen). 57 percent are women and 43 percent are men. Students come from 40 states and territories and 3 other countries. 32 percent are from Kansas. 1.1 percent are international students.
Expenses for 2008–09 *Application fee:* $25. *Comprehensive fee:* $24,396 includes full-time tuition ($17,216), mandatory fees ($1000), and college room and board ($6180). Full-time tuition and fees vary according to course load. Room and board charges vary according to board plan and housing facility. *Part-time tuition:* $576 per hour. *Part-time mandatory fees:* $365 per term. Part-time tuition and fees vary according to course load.
Financial Aid Forms of aid include need-based scholarships, athletic grants, and part-time jobs. The average aided 2008–09 undergraduate received an aid package worth an estimated $13,686.
Freshman Admission MidAmerica Nazarene University requires a high school transcript, a minimum 2.0 high school GPA, 1 recommendation, SAT or ACT scores, and TOEFL scores for international students. The application deadline for regular admission is August 1.
Transfer Admission The application deadline for admission is August 1.
Entrance Difficulty MidAmerica Nazarene University assesses its entrance difficulty level as minimally difficult. For the fall 2008 freshman class, 73 percent of the applicants were accepted.
For Further Information Contact Ms. Brigit Mattix, Associate Director of Admissions, MidAmerica Nazarene University, 2030 East College Way, Olathe, KS 66062-1899. *Phone:* 913-791-3380 or 800-800-8887 (toll-free). *Fax:* 913-791-3481. *E-mail:* admissions@mnu.edu. *Web site:* http://www.mnu.edu/.

NATIONAL AMERICAN UNIVERSITY
Overland Park, Kansas

http://www.national.edu/

NEWMAN UNIVERSITY
Wichita, Kansas

Newman University is a coed, private, Roman Catholic, comprehensive institution, founded in 1933, offering degrees at the associate, bachelor's, and master's levels. It has a 61-acre campus in Wichita.

Academic Information The faculty has 190 members (42% full-time). The undergraduate student-faculty ratio is 14:1. The library holds 110,167 titles, 156 serial subscriptions, and 1,952 audiovisual materials. Special programs include academic remediation, services for learning-disabled students, an honors program, cooperative (work-study) education, study abroad, advanced placement credit, accelerated degree programs, double majors, independent study, distance learning, summer session for credit, part-time degree programs (daytime, evenings, weekends, summer), adult/continuing education programs, internships, and arrangement for off-campus study with Friends University. The most frequently chosen baccalaureate fields are business/marketing, education, health professions and related sciences.
Student Body Statistics The student body totals 2,435, of whom 1,815 are undergraduates (117 freshmen). 64 percent are women and 36 percent

Newman University (continued)

are men. Students come from 27 states and territories and 22 other countries. 89 percent are from Kansas. 4.8 percent are international students.

Expenses for 2009–10 *Application fee:* $20. *One-time mandatory fee:* $150. *Comprehensive fee:* $26,306 includes full-time tuition ($19,200), mandatory fees ($450), and college room and board ($6656). *Part-time tuition:* $640 per credit hour. *Part-time mandatory fees:* $10 per credit hour.

Financial Aid Forms of aid include need-based and non-need-based scholarships, athletic grants, and part-time jobs. The average aided 2008–09 undergraduate received an aid package worth an estimated $12,624. The priority application deadline for financial aid is March 1.

Freshman Admission Newman University requires a high school transcript, a minimum 2.0 high school GPA, SAT or ACT scores, and TOEFL scores for international students. An interview is recommended. The application deadline for regular admission is rolling.

Transfer Admission The application deadline for admission is rolling.

Entrance Difficulty Newman University assesses its entrance difficulty level as minimally difficult; moderately difficult for nursing, occupational therapy programs. For the fall 2008 freshman class, 44 percent of the applicants were accepted.

For Further Information Contact Mr. John Clayton, Dean of Admissions, Newman University, 3100 McCormick Avenue, Wichita, KS 67213. *Phone:* 316-942-4291 Ext. 2233 or 877-NEWMANU Ext. 2144 (toll-free). *Fax:* 316-942-4483. *E-mail:* admissions@newmanu.edu. *Web site:* http://www.newmanu.edu/.

OTTAWA UNIVERSITY

Ottawa, Kansas

http://www.ottawa.edu/

PITTSBURG STATE UNIVERSITY

Pittsburg, Kansas

Pittsburg State University is a coed, public, comprehensive unit of Kansas State Board of Education, founded in 1903, offering degrees at the associate, bachelor's, and master's levels (associate, specialist in education). It has a 233-acre campus in Pittsburg.

Academic Information The faculty has 312 members. The undergraduate student-faculty ratio is 18:1. The library holds 741,835 titles, 15,338 serial subscriptions, and 2,420 audiovisual materials. Special programs include academic remediation, services for learning-disabled students, an honors program, cooperative (work-study) education, study abroad, advanced placement credit, Freshman Honors College, ESL programs, double majors, independent study, distance learning, self-designed majors, summer session for credit, part-time degree programs (daytime, evenings, summer), adult/continuing education programs, internships, and arrangement for off-campus study with Southside Education Center, Wichita, KS, Kansas City Metro Center, Lenexa, KS. The most frequently chosen baccalaureate fields are business/marketing, education, health professions and related sciences.

Student Body Statistics The student body totals 7,127, of whom 5,863 are undergraduates (909 freshmen). 47 percent are women and 53 percent are men. Students come from 44 states and territories and 23 other countries. 77 percent are from Kansas. 5.6 percent are international students.

Expenses for 2008–09 *Application fee:* $30. *State resident tuition:* $3420 full-time, $114 per credit hour part-time. *Nonresident tuition:* $11,674 full-time, $389 per credit hour part-time. *Mandatory fees:* $902 full-time, $40 per credit hour part-time. *College room and board:* $5394. Room and board charges vary according to board plan and housing facility.

Financial Aid Forms of aid include need-based and non-need-based scholarships, athletic grants, and part-time jobs. The average aided 2008–09 undergraduate received an aid package worth an estimated $9390. The priority application deadline for financial aid is March 1.

Freshman Admission Pittsburg State University requires a high school transcript, ACT scores, and TOEFL scores for international students. A minimum 2.0 high school GPA is required for some. The application deadline for regular admission is rolling.

Transfer Admission The application deadline for admission is rolling.

Entrance Difficulty Pittsburg State University assesses its entrance difficulty level as minimally difficult; moderately difficult for international students. For the fall 2008 freshman class, 88 percent of the applicants were accepted.

For Further Information Contact Director of Admission, Pittsburg State University, 1701 S. Broadway, Pittsburg, KS 66762. *Phone:* 620-235-4251 or 800-854-7488 Ext. 1 (toll-free). *Fax:* 620-235-6003. *E-mail:* psuadmit@pittstate.edu. *Web site:* http://www.pittstate.edu/.

SOUTHWESTERN COLLEGE

Winfield, Kansas

Southwestern College is a coed, private, United Methodist, comprehensive institution, founded in 1885, offering degrees at the bachelor's and master's levels. It has a 70-acre campus in Winfield near Wichita.

Academic Information The faculty has 100 members (49% full-time), 34% with terminal degrees. The undergraduate student-faculty ratio is 9:1. The library holds 81,621 titles, 33,234 serial subscriptions, and 9,597 audiovisual materials. Special programs include an honors program, study abroad, advanced placement credit, double majors, independent study, distance learning, self-designed majors, part-time degree programs (daytime, evenings, weekends, summer), adult/continuing education programs, internships, and arrangement for off-campus study with Urban Life Center, Chicago. The most frequently chosen baccalaureate fields are business/marketing, computer and information sciences, security and protective services.

Student Body Statistics The student body totals 1,823, of whom 1,623 are undergraduates (159 freshmen). 43 percent are women and 57 percent are men. Students come from 46 states and territories and 16 other countries. 69 percent are from Kansas. 1.7 percent are international students.

Expenses for 2009–10 *Application fee:* $20. *Comprehensive fee:* $25,380 includes full-time tuition ($19,530), mandatory fees ($100), and college room and board ($5750). *College room only:* $2716. *Part-time tuition:* $814 per semester hour.

Financial Aid Forms of aid include need-based and non-need-based scholarships, athletic grants, and part-time jobs. The average aided 2008–09 undergraduate received an aid package worth an estimated $22,382. The application deadline for financial aid is August 15 with a priority deadline of April 1.

Freshman Admission Southwestern College requires a high school transcript, a minimum 2.5 high school GPA, SAT or ACT scores, and TOEFL scores for international students. An essay is recommended. 2 recommendations and an interview are required for some. The application deadline for regular admission is August 25.

Transfer Admission The application deadline for admission is August 25.

Entrance Difficulty Southwestern College assesses its entrance difficulty level as moderately difficult. For the fall 2008 freshman class, 90 percent of the applicants were accepted.

For Further Information Contact Mrs. Marla Sexson, Director of Admission, Southwestern College, 100 College Street, Winfield, KS 67156. *Phone:* 620-229-6364 or 800-846-1543 (toll-free). *Fax:* 620-229-6344. *E-mail:* scadmit@sckans.edu. *Web site:* http://www.sckans.edu/.

STERLING COLLEGE

Sterling, Kansas

Sterling College is a coed, private, Presbyterian, four-year college, founded in 1887, offering degrees at the bachelor's level. It has a 46-acre campus in Sterling.

Academic Information The faculty has 59 members (68% full-time), 37% with terminal degrees. The student-faculty ratio is 13:1. The library holds 76,637 titles and 350 serial subscriptions. Special programs include services for learning-disabled students, study abroad, advanced placement credit, double majors, independent study, distance learning, self-designed majors, internships, and arrangement for off-campus study with 6 members of the Associated Colleges of Central Kansas.

Student Body Statistics The student body is made up of 653 undergraduates (150 freshmen). 48 percent are women and 52 percent are men. Students come from 39 states and territories and 7 other countries. 55 percent are from Kansas. 1.1 percent are international students.
Expenses for 2008–09 *Application fee:* $25. *One-time mandatory fee:* $100. *Comprehensive fee:* $22,730 includes full-time tuition ($16,500) and college room and board ($6230). Room and board charges vary according to board plan and housing facility. *Part-time tuition:* $335 per credit hour.
Financial Aid Forms of aid include need-based and non-need-based scholarships, athletic grants, and part-time jobs. The priority application deadline for financial aid is April 1.
Freshman Admission Sterling College requires a high school transcript, a minimum 2.2 high school GPA, SAT or ACT scores, and TOEFL scores for international students. An essay and an interview are recommended. 2 recommendations and audition required for fine arts majors are required for some. The application deadline for regular admission is July 15 and for early action it is November 15.
Transfer Admission The application deadline for admission is rolling.
Entrance Difficulty Sterling College assesses its entrance difficulty level as minimally difficult. For the fall 2008 freshman class, 53 percent of the applicants were accepted.
For Further Information Contact Marge Jones, Admissions Office Manager, Sterling College, 125 W. Cooper, Sterling, KS 67579. *Phone:* 620-278-4275 or 800-346-1017 (toll-free). *Fax:* 620-278-4416. *E-mail:* admissions@sterling.edu. *Web site:* http://www.sterling.edu/.

TABOR COLLEGE

Hillsboro, Kansas

Tabor College is a coed, private, Mennonite Brethren, comprehensive institution, founded in 1908, offering degrees at the associate, bachelor's, and master's levels. It has a 26-acre campus in Hillsboro near Wichita.

Expenses for 2008–09 *Application fee:* $30. *One-time mandatory fee:* $100. *Comprehensive fee:* $25,460 includes full-time tuition ($18,300), mandatory fees ($410), and college room and board ($6750). *College room only:* $2600. *Part-time tuition:* $720 per credit hour. *Part-time mandatory fees:* $5 per credit hour.
For Further Information Contact Mr. Rusty Allen, Dean of Enrollment Management, Tabor College, 400 South Jefferson, Hillsboro, KS 67063. *Phone:* 620-947-3121 or 800-822-6799 (toll-free). *Fax:* 620-947-6276. *E-mail:* rustya@tabor.edu. *Web site:* http://www.tabor.edu/.

THE UNIVERSITY OF KANSAS

Lawrence, Kansas

The University of Kansas is a coed, public unit of Regents system, State of Kansas, founded in 1866, offering degrees at the bachelor's, master's, doctoral, and first professional levels and post-master's certificates (University of Kansas is a single institution with academic programs and facilities at two primary locations: Lawrence and Kansas City.). It has a 1,100-acre campus in Lawrence near Kansas City.

Academic Information The faculty has 1,301 members (94% full-time), 96% with terminal degrees. The undergraduate student-faculty ratio is 19:1. The library holds 4 million titles, 62,016 serial subscriptions, and 64,062 audiovisual materials. Special programs include academic remediation, services for learning-disabled students, an honors program, cooperative (work-study) education, study abroad, advanced placement credit, accelerated degree programs, ESL programs, double majors, independent study, distance learning, summer session for credit, part-time degree programs (daytime, evenings, summer), and internships. The most frequently chosen baccalaureate fields are business/marketing, health professions and related sciences, social sciences.
Student Body Statistics The student body totals 29,365, of whom 21,332 are undergraduates (4,483 freshmen). 50 percent are women and 50 percent are men. Students come from 54 states and territories and 82 other countries. 77 percent are from Kansas. 3.4 percent are international students.
Expenses for 2008–09 *Application fee:* $30. *State resident tuition:* $6878 full-time, $229.25 per credit hour part-time. *Nonresident tuition:* $18,062 full-time, $602.05 per credit hour part-time. *Mandatory fees:* $847 full-time, $70.56 per credit hour part-time. Both full-time and part-time tuition and fees vary according to program, reciprocity agreements, and student level. *College room and board:* $6474. *College room only:* $3386. Room and board charges vary according to board plan and housing facility.
Financial Aid Forms of aid include need-based and non-need-based scholarships, athletic grants, and part-time jobs. The average aided 2007–08 undergraduate received an aid package worth $9358. The priority application deadline for financial aid is March 1.
Freshman Admission The University of Kansas requires a high school transcript, a minimum 2.0 high school GPA, Kansas Board of Regents admissions criteria or upper third of high school class, and SAT or ACT scores. TOEFL scores for international students are recommended. A minimum 2.5 high school GPA is required for some. The application deadline for regular admission is April 1.
Transfer Admission The application deadline for admission is May 1.
Entrance Difficulty The University of Kansas assesses its entrance difficulty level as moderately difficult; very difficult for architecture, all engineering programs. For the fall 2008 freshman class, 92 percent of the applicants were accepted.
For Further Information Contact Ms. Lisa Pinamonti Kress, Director of Admissions and Scholarships, The University of Kansas, KU Visitor Center, 1502 Iowa Street, Lawrence, KS 66045-7576. *Phone:* 785-864-3911 or 888-686-7323 (toll-free in-state). *Fax:* 785-864-5006. *E-mail:* adm@ku.edu. *Web site:* http://www.ku.edu.

UNIVERSITY OF PHOENIX–WICHITA CAMPUS

Wichita, Kansas

University of Phoenix–Wichita Campus is a coed, proprietary, comprehensive institution, founded in 2003, offering degrees at the bachelor's and master's levels.

Academic Information The faculty has 49 members (8% full-time), 20% with terminal degrees. Special programs include services for learning-disabled students, advanced placement credit, accelerated degree programs, independent study, and distance learning. The most frequently chosen baccalaureate fields are business/marketing, computer and information sciences, health professions and related sciences.
Student Body Statistics The student body totals 135, of whom 125 are undergraduates. 57 percent are women and 43 percent are men. 99 percent are from Kansas. 4 percent are international students.
Expenses for 2008–09 *Application fee:* $0. *Tuition:* $11,400 full-time. Full-time tuition varies according to course level and course load.
Financial Aid Forms of aid include need-based and non-need-based scholarships. The average aided 2007–08 undergraduate received an aid package worth $7422. The application deadline for financial aid is continuous.
Freshman Admission University of Phoenix–Wichita Campus requires 1 recommendation. A high school transcript is required for some. The application deadline for regular admission is rolling.
Transfer Admission The application deadline for admission is rolling.
Entrance Difficulty University of Phoenix–Wichita Campus has an open admission policy.
For Further Information Contact Ms. Audra McQuarie, Registrar/Executive Director, University of Phoenix–Wichita Campus, 4035 South Riverpoint Parkway, Mail Stop CF-L101, Phoenix, AZ 85040. *Phone:* 480-557-6151, 800-776-4867 (toll-free in-state), or 800-228-7240 (toll-free out-of-state). *Fax:* 480-643-3068. *E-mail:* audra.mcquarie@phoenix.edu. *Web site:* http://www.phoenix.edu/.

UNIVERSITY OF SAINT MARY

Leavenworth, Kansas

University of Saint Mary is a coed, private, Roman Catholic, comprehensive institution, founded in 1923, offering degrees at the associate, bachelor's, and master's levels. It has a 240-acre campus in Leavenworth near Kansas City.

Academic Information The faculty has 102 members (39% full-time), 34% with terminal degrees. The undergraduate student-faculty ratio is 11:1. The library holds 120,753 titles, 157 serial subscriptions, and 2,098 audiovisual materials. Special programs include services for learning-disabled students, an honors program, cooperative (work-study) education, study abroad, advanced placement credit, double majors, independent study, distance learning, self-designed majors, summer session for credit, part-time degree programs (daytime, evenings, summer), adult/continuing education programs, internships, and arrangement for off-campus study with University of Kansas, members of the Council of Independent Colleges. The most frequently chosen baccalaureate fields are health professions and related sciences, business/marketing, psychology.
Student Body Statistics The student body totals 955, of whom 651 are undergraduates (113 freshmen). 63 percent are women and 37 percent are men. Students come from 21 states and territories and 1 other country. 59 percent are from Kansas. 0.2 percent are international students.
Expenses for 2009–10 *Application fee:* $25. *Comprehensive fee:* $24,800 includes full-time tuition ($18,500), mandatory fees ($400), and college room and board ($5900). *Part-time tuition:* $355 per hour. *Part-time mandatory fees:* $80 per term.
Financial Aid Forms of aid include need-based and non-need-based scholarships and part-time jobs. The application deadline for financial aid is continuous.
Freshman Admission University of Saint Mary requires a high school transcript, a minimum 2.5 high school GPA, SAT or ACT scores, and TOEFL scores for international students. 1 recommendation and an interview are recommended. The application deadline for regular admission is rolling.
Transfer Admission The application deadline for admission is rolling.
Entrance Difficulty University of Saint Mary assesses its entrance difficulty level as moderately difficult. For the fall 2008 freshman class, 69 percent of the applicants were accepted.
For Further Information Contact Mr. Brandon Johnson, Director of Admissions, University of Saint Mary, 4100 South Fourth Street, Leavenworth, KS 66048. *Phone:* 913-758-6118 or 800-752-7043 (toll-free out-of-state). *Fax:* 913-758-6140. *E-mail:* admiss@stmary.edu. *Web site:* http://www.stmary.edu/.

WASHBURN UNIVERSITY

Topeka, Kansas

Washburn University is a coed, public, comprehensive institution, founded in 1865, offering degrees at the associate, bachelor's, master's, and first professional levels and first professional and postbachelor's certificates. It has a 160-acre campus in Topeka near Kansas City.

Academic Information The faculty has 524 members (51% full-time), 63% with terminal degrees. The undergraduate student-faculty ratio is 15:1. The library holds 345,642 titles, 1,672 serial subscriptions, and 3,141 audiovisual materials. Special programs include academic remediation, services for learning-disabled students, an honors program, cooperative (work-study) education, study abroad, advanced placement credit, ESL programs, double majors, independent study, distance learning, self-designed majors, summer session for credit, part-time degree programs, adult/continuing education programs, internships, and arrangement for off-campus study with Kansas City Kansas Community College, Johnson County Community College. The most frequently chosen baccalaureate fields are business/marketing, health professions and related sciences, security and protective services.
Student Body Statistics The student body totals 6,545, of whom 5,702 are undergraduates (830 freshmen). 61 percent are women and 39 percent are men. Students come from 44 states and territories and 42 other countries. 93 percent are from Kansas.
Expenses for 2008–09 *Application fee:* $20. *State resident tuition:* $5910 full-time, $197 per credit hour part-time. *Nonresident tuition:* $13,410 full-time, $447 per credit hour part-time. *Mandatory fees:* $86 full-time, $21 per term part-time. Both full-time and part-time tuition and fees vary according to program. *College room and board:* $5602. *College room only:* $3177. Room and board charges vary according to board plan and housing facility.
Financial Aid Forms of aid include need-based and non-need-based scholarships and athletic grants. The priority application deadline for financial aid is March 1.
Freshman Admission Washburn University requires a high school transcript, ACT scores, and TOEFL scores for international students. The application deadline for regular admission is August 1.
Transfer Admission The application deadline for admission is August 1.
Entrance Difficulty Washburn University assesses its entrance difficulty level as noncompetitive; minimally difficult for out-of-state applicants; minimally difficult for transfers; moderately difficult for nursing program. For the fall 2008 freshman class, 100 percent of the applicants were accepted.
For Further Information Contact Mr. Kirk R. Haskins, Director of Admission, Washburn University, 1700 SW College, MO 114, Topeka, KS 66621. *Phone:* 785-670-1030 or 800-332-0291 (toll-free in-state). *Fax:* 785-670-1089. *E-mail:* admissions@washburn.edu. *Web site:* http://www.washburn.edu/.

WICHITA STATE UNIVERSITY

Wichita, Kansas

Wichita State University is a coed, public unit of Kansas State Board of Education, founded in 1895, offering degrees at the associate, bachelor's, master's, and doctoral levels and post-master's and postbachelor's certificates. It has a 335-acre campus in Wichita.

Academic Information The faculty has 516 members (91% full-time), 76% with terminal degrees. The undergraduate student-faculty ratio is 18:1. The library holds 2 million titles, 3,697 serial subscriptions, and 21,829 audiovisual materials. Special programs include academic remediation, services for learning-disabled students, an honors program, cooperative (work-study) education, study abroad, advanced placement credit, accelerated degree programs, Freshman Honors College, ESL programs, double majors, independent study, distance learning, summer session for credit, part-time degree programs (daytime, evenings, weekends, summer), internships, and arrangement for off-campus study with National Student Exchange, Midwest Student Exchange. The most frequently chosen baccalaureate fields are business/marketing, education, health professions and related sciences.
Student Body Statistics The student body totals 14,612, of whom 11,600 are undergraduates (1,420 freshmen). 54 percent are women and 46 percent are men. Students come from 46 states and territories and 95 other countries. 96 percent are from Kansas. 7 percent are international students.
Expenses for 2008–09 *Application fee:* $30. *State resident tuition:* $4144 full-time, $138.15 per credit hour part-time. *Nonresident tuition:* $11,821 full-time, $394.05 per credit hour part-time. *Mandatory fees:* $940 full-time, $30.20 per credit hour part-time, $17 per term part-time. Both full-time and part-time tuition and fees vary according to course load and degree level. *College room and board:* $5860. Room and board charges vary according to board plan and housing facility.
Financial Aid Forms of aid include need-based and non-need-based scholarships, athletic grants, and part-time jobs. The average aided 2007–08 undergraduate received an aid package worth $8788. The priority application deadline for financial aid is March 1.
Freshman Admission Wichita State University requires TOEFL scores for international students. A high school transcript is recommended. Rank in top 1/3 of high school class or minimum of 2.0 high school GPA, and SAT or ACT scores are required for some. The application deadline for regular admission is rolling.
Transfer Admission The application deadline for admission is rolling.
Entrance Difficulty Wichita State University has an open admission policy for state residents who graduated from a Kansas high school before May 2001 or already have a previous bachelor degree. It assesses its entrance difficulty as moderately difficult for out-of-state applicants;

moderately difficult for transfers; very difficult for physical therapy, dental hygiene, nursing, physician assistant programs.
For Further Information Contact Mr. Bobby Gandu, Director of Admissions, Wichita State University, 1845 Fairmount Street, Wichita, KS 67260-0124. *Phone:* 316-978-3085 or 800-362-2594 (toll-free). *Fax:* 316-978-3174. *E-mail:* admissions@wichita.edu. *Web site:* http://www.wichita.edu/.

Michigan

ADRIAN COLLEGE

Adrian, Michigan

Adrian College is a coed, private, four-year college, founded in 1859, affiliated with the United Methodist Church, offering degrees at the associate and bachelor's levels. It has a 100-acre campus in Adrian near Detroit and Toledo.

Academic Information The faculty has 177 members (45% full-time), 45% with terminal degrees. The student-faculty ratio is 13:1. The library holds 145,742 titles, 567 serial subscriptions, and 3,069 audiovisual materials. Special programs include academic remediation, services for learning-disabled students, an honors program, study abroad, advanced placement credit, ESL programs, double majors, independent study, self-designed majors, summer session for credit, part-time degree programs (daytime), adult/continuing education programs, internships, and arrangement for off-campus study with Urban Life Center (Chicago), The Washington Center. The most frequently chosen baccalaureate fields are business/marketing, parks and recreation, visual and performing arts.
Student Body Statistics The student body is made up of 1,469 undergraduates (500 freshmen). 47 percent are women and 53 percent are men. Students come from 29 states and territories and 3 other countries. 80 percent are from Michigan. 4.2 percent are international students.
Expenses for 2009–10 *Application fee:* $0. *Comprehensive fee:* $31,900 includes full-time tuition ($24,140), mandatory fees ($300), and college room and board ($7460). *College room only:* $3610. *Part-time tuition:* $685 per credit hour. *Part-time mandatory fees:* $75 per term.
Financial Aid Forms of aid include need-based and non-need-based scholarships and part-time jobs. The average aided 2008–09 undergraduate received an aid package worth an estimated $20,945. The priority application deadline for financial aid is March 1.
Freshman Admission Adrian College requires a high school transcript, SAT or ACT scores, and TOEFL scores for international students. An interview and ACT scores are recommended. An essay is required for some. The application deadline for regular admission is March 15.
Transfer Admission The application deadline for admission is March 15.
Entrance Difficulty Adrian College assesses its entrance difficulty level as moderately difficult. For the fall 2008 freshman class, 58 percent of the applicants were accepted.
For Further Information Contact Ms. Carolyn Quinlan, Director of Admissions, Adrian College, 110 South Madison Street, Adrian, MI 49221. *Phone:* 800-877-2246 or 800-877-2246 (toll-free). *Fax:* 517-264-3331. *E-mail:* admissions@adrian.edu. *Web site:* http://www.adrian.edu/.

ALBION COLLEGE

Albion, Michigan

Albion College is a coed, private, Methodist, four-year college, founded in 1835, offering degrees at the bachelor's level. It has a 565-acre campus in Albion near Detroit.

Academic Information The faculty has 171 members (81% full-time), 75% with terminal degrees. The student-faculty ratio is 12:1. The library holds 363,870 titles, 16,293 serial subscriptions, and 10,837 audiovisual materials. Special programs include services for learning-disabled students, an honors program, study abroad, advanced placement credit, double majors, independent study, self-designed majors, summer session for credit, part-time degree programs (daytime, evenings, summer), internships, and arrangement for off-campus study with Great Lakes Colleges Association. The most frequently chosen baccalaureate fields are biological/life sciences, psychology, social sciences.
Student Body Statistics The student body is made up of 1,860 undergraduates (485 freshmen). 54 percent are women and 46 percent are men. Students come from 28 states and territories and 18 other countries. 91 percent are from Michigan. 0.9 percent are international students.
Expenses for 2008–09 *Application fee:* $20. *One-time mandatory fee:* $160. *Comprehensive fee:* $37,070 includes full-time tuition ($28,380), mandatory fees ($500), and college room and board ($8190). *College room only:* $4006. Full-time tuition and fees vary according to course load. Room and board charges vary according to housing facility. *Part-time tuition:* $4824 per course. *Part-time mandatory fees:* $250 per term, $500 per year.
Financial Aid Forms of aid include need-based and non-need-based scholarships and part-time jobs. The average aided 2008–09 undergraduate received an aid package worth an estimated $23,332. The priority application deadline for financial aid is March 1.
Freshman Admission Albion College requires an essay, a high school transcript, 1 recommendation, SAT or ACT scores, and TOEFL scores for international students. A minimum 3.2 high school GPA is recommended. An interview is required for some. The application deadline for regular admission is May 1 and for early action it is December 1.
Transfer Admission The application deadline for admission is June 1.
Entrance Difficulty Albion College assesses its entrance difficulty level as moderately difficult. For the fall 2008 freshman class, 83 percent of the applicants were accepted.
For Further Information Contact Mr. Doug Kellar, Associate Vice President for Enrollment, Albion College, 611 East Porter Street, Albion, MI 49224. *Phone:* 517-629-0321 or 800-858-6770 (toll-free). *Fax:* 517-629-0569. *E-mail:* admissions@albion.edu. *Web site:* http://www.albion.edu/.

ALMA COLLEGE

Alma, Michigan

Alma College is a coed, private, Presbyterian, four-year college, founded in 1886, offering degrees at the bachelor's level. It has a 125-acre campus in Alma.

Academic Information The faculty has 138 members (62% full-time), 65% with terminal degrees. The student-faculty ratio is 13:1. The library holds 275,723 titles, 1,500 serial subscriptions, and 10,031 audiovisual materials. Special programs include academic remediation, services for learning-disabled students, an honors program, study abroad, advanced placement credit, double majors, independent study, self-designed majors, summer session for credit, internships, and arrangement for off-campus study with New York Arts program, Philadelphia Center Internship, Urban Life Center, Washington Semester. The most frequently chosen baccalaureate fields are biological/life sciences, business/marketing, health professions and related sciences.
Student Body Statistics The student body is made up of 1,384 undergraduates (429 freshmen). 56 percent are women and 44 percent are men. Students come from 24 states and territories and 15 other countries. 96 percent are from Michigan. 0.8 percent are international students.
Expenses for 2008–09 *Application fee:* $25. *Comprehensive fee:* $32,970 includes full-time tuition ($24,630), mandatory fees ($220), and college room and board ($8120). *College room only:* $4000. Room and board charges vary according to board plan and housing facility. *Part-time tuition:* $955 per credit. Part-time tuition varies according to course load.
Financial Aid Forms of aid include need-based and non-need-based scholarships and part-time jobs. The average aided 2008–09 undergraduate received an aid package worth an estimated $19,768. The priority application deadline for financial aid is March 1.
Freshman Admission Alma College requires a high school transcript, a minimum 3.0 high school GPA, SAT or ACT scores, and TOEFL scores for international students. An interview is recommended. An essay and 3 recommendations are required for some. The application deadline for regular admission is rolling.
Transfer Admission The application deadline for admission is rolling.

Alma College (continued)

Entrance Difficulty Alma College assesses its entrance difficulty level as moderately difficult. For the fall 2008 freshman class, 73 percent of the applicants were accepted.

For Further Information Contact Mr. Evan Montague, Director of Admissions, Alma College, Admissions Office, Alma, MI 48801-1599. *Phone:* 800-321-2562 or 800-321-ALMA (toll-free). *Fax:* 989-463-7057. *E-mail:* admissions@alma.edu. *Web site:* http://www.alma.edu/.

ANDREWS UNIVERSITY

Berrien Springs, Michigan

Andrews University is a coed, private, Seventh-day Adventist university, founded in 1874, offering degrees at the associate, bachelor's, master's, doctoral, and first professional levels and post-master's and postbachelor's certificates. It has a 1,650-acre campus in Berrien Springs.

Academic Information The faculty has 298 members (72% full-time), 64% with terminal degrees. The undergraduate student-faculty ratio is 10:1. The library holds 615,937 titles, 39,000 serial subscriptions, and 55,998 audiovisual materials. Special programs include academic remediation, an honors program, cooperative (work-study) education, study abroad, advanced placement credit, accelerated degree programs, Freshman Honors College, ESL programs, double majors, distance learning, self-designed majors, summer session for credit, part-time degree programs (daytime, evenings), adult/continuing education programs, internships, and arrangement for off-campus study. The most frequently chosen baccalaureate fields are foreign languages and literature, business/marketing, health professions and related sciences.

Student Body Statistics The student body totals 3,419, of whom 1,889 are undergraduates (396 freshmen). 56 percent are women and 44 percent are men. Students come from 49 states and territories and 51 other countries. 46 percent are from Michigan. 12.7 percent are international students.

Expenses for 2008–09 *Application fee:* $30. *Comprehensive fee:* $26,260 includes full-time tuition ($19,320), mandatory fees ($610), and college room and board ($6330). *College room only:* $3380. *Part-time tuition:* $805 per credit hour.

Financial Aid Forms of aid include need-based and non-need-based scholarships and part-time jobs. The average aided 2007–08 undergraduate received an aid package worth $22,441. The application deadline for financial aid is continuous.

Freshman Admission Andrews University requires an essay, a high school transcript, a minimum 2.25 high school GPA, 2 recommendations, and SAT or ACT scores. The application deadline for regular admission is rolling.

Transfer Admission The application deadline for admission is rolling.

Entrance Difficulty Andrews University assesses its entrance difficulty level as moderately difficult. For the fall 2008 freshman class, 56 percent of the applicants were accepted.

For Further Information Contact Shanna Leak, Undergraduate Admissions Coordinator, Andrews University, Berrien Springs, MI 49104. *Phone:* 800-253-2874 or 800-253-2874 (toll-free). *Fax:* 269-471-3228. *E-mail:* enroll@andrews.edu. *Web site:* http://www.andrews.edu/.

AQUINAS COLLEGE

Grand Rapids, Michigan

Aquinas College is a coed, private, Roman Catholic, comprehensive institution, founded in 1886, offering degrees at the associate, bachelor's, and master's levels. It has a 107-acre campus in Grand Rapids near Detroit.

Academic Information The faculty has 262 members (36% full-time), 52% with terminal degrees. The undergraduate student-faculty ratio is 13:1. The library holds 99,293 titles and 526 serial subscriptions. Special programs include academic remediation, services for learning-disabled students, an honors program, cooperative (work-study) education, study abroad, advanced placement credit, accelerated degree programs, double majors, independent study, distance learning, self-designed majors, summer session for credit, part-time degree programs, external degree programs, adult/continuing education programs, internships, and arrangement for off-campus study with members of the Dominican College Interchange. The most frequently chosen baccalaureate fields are business/marketing, education, social sciences.

Student Body Statistics The student body totals 2,159, of whom 1,872 are undergraduates (456 freshmen). 63 percent are women and 37 percent are men. Students come from 21 states and territories and 4 other countries. 95 percent are from Michigan. 0.2 percent are international students.

Expenses for 2008–09 *Application fee:* $0. *Comprehensive fee:* $29,328 includes full-time tuition ($22,314) and college room and board ($7014). *College room only:* $3238. Full-time tuition varies according to course load. Room and board charges vary according to board plan and housing facility. *Part-time tuition:* $452 per credit. Part-time tuition varies according to course load.

Financial Aid Forms of aid include need-based and non-need-based scholarships, athletic grants, and part-time jobs. The application deadline for financial aid is August 15 with a priority deadline of March 1.

Freshman Admission Aquinas College requires a high school transcript, a minimum 2.5 high school GPA, SAT or ACT scores, and TOEFL scores for international students. An essay and an interview are required for some. The application deadline for regular admission is rolling.

Transfer Admission The application deadline for admission is rolling.

Entrance Difficulty Aquinas College assesses its entrance difficulty level as moderately difficult. For the fall 2008 freshman class, 82 percent of the applicants were accepted.

SPECIAL MESSAGE TO STUDENTS

Social Life Aquinas College, located in Grand Rapids, Michigan, has the advantage of being the cultural, medical, business, and commercial center of western Michigan. Students involve themselves in the Community Senate, intramural and intercollegiate athletics, music performance groups, volunteer and service groups, and campus ministry. Some campus-sponsored events include white-water rafting, Spring Fling, Homecoming, dinner nightclubs, Murder Mystery Night, a cultural series, Welcome Week, movie nights, Winterfest, a film series, dances, and lectures. Off-campus events include theater, concerts, and musical performances by nationally known performers and a local IHL hockey team as well as minor league baseball.

Academic Highlights Aquinas offers more than sixty different majors. The College has three schools: the School of Education, the School of Liberal Arts and Sciences, and the School of Management. The study program in Ireland provides a semester abroad for 30 students during the second semester of each academic year. The curriculum centers on Irish studies and culture and provides independent travel opportunities to the British Isles and the continent. Other cultural immersion programs include Costa Rica, France, Germany, Japan, and Spain. A general education plan ensures that the student is equipped with the skills necessary for both life and a career. Aquinas also offers a semester of field experience in career-related employment through which the student earns college credit and a salary. More than 200 internships with leading firms and organizations are available.

Interviews and Campus Visits Campus visits are highly recommended. Aquinas hosts AQ Days throughout the year. There are four General Visit Days and Athletics, Science, Math, Nursing, Leadership, and Fine Arts Days. This program gives the student the opportunity to tour the campus, meet with faculty members, participate in financial aid workshops, and enjoy a complimentary lunch. Students are encouraged to see the Holmdene Mansion, part of the original estate on which Aquinas is built, and the Art and Music Center, which houses recital halls, an art gallery, a sculpture studio, a photography lab, and a darkroom. The Albertus Magnus Hall of Science houses laboratories, a greenhouse, and an observatory. Campus visitors should also tour the Performing Arts Center, a state-of-the-art, $7-million facility. Jarecki Center provides the latest in classroom technology, and the Grace Hauenstein Library opened in fall 2006. The Ravine Apartments give students a living option beyond the traditional. For more information, prospective students should call the Admissions Office at 616-732-4460 or 800-678-9593 (toll-free), Monday through Friday, 8:30 to 5, and Saturdays, 9 to 1. The office is located in Hruby Hall, 1760 Fulton Street, on the campus.

For Further Information Write to Paula Meehan, Dean of Admissions, Aquinas College, 1607 Robinson Road, SE, Grand Rapids, MI 49506-1799. *E-mail:* admissions@aquinas.edu. *Web site:* http://www.aquinas.edu.

THE ART INSTITUTE OF MICHIGAN

Novi, Michigan

The Art Institute of Michigan is a coed, proprietary, four-year college of Education Management Corporation, offering degrees at the associate and bachelor's levels.

Expenses for 2009–10 Tuition cost varies by program. Prospective students should contact the school for current tuition costs. Other charges include a starting kit for all first-quarter students. Kits vary in price, depending on the program of study.
For Further Information Contact Director of Admissions, The Art Institute of Michigan, 28125 Cabot Drive, Suite 120, Novi, MI 48377. *Phone:* 248-675-3800 or 800-479-0087 (toll-free). *Fax:* 248-675-3830. *Web site:* http://www.artinstitutes.edu/detroit/.

AVE MARIA COLLEGE

Ypsilanti, Michigan

http://www.avemaria.edu/

BAKER COLLEGE OF ALLEN PARK

Allen Park, Michigan

Baker College of Allen Park is a coed, primarily women's, private, four-year college of Baker College System, founded in 2003, offering degrees at the associate and bachelor's levels. It has a 13-acre campus in Allen Park near Detroit.

Academic Information The faculty has 88 members (2% full-time), 12% with terminal degrees. The student-faculty ratio is 34:1.
Student Body Statistics The student body is made up of 2,551 undergraduates. 74 percent are women and 26 percent are men. Students come from 1 state or territory.
Expenses for 2009–10 *Application fee:* $0. *Tuition:* $7020 full-time, $195 per quarter hour part-time.
Freshman Admission Baker College of Allen Park requires a high school transcript and an interview. The application deadline for regular admission is September 24.
Entrance Difficulty For the fall 2008 freshman class, 100 percent of the applicants were accepted.
For Further Information Contact Mr. Steve Peterson, Vice President of Admissions, Baker College of Allen Park, 4500 Enterprise Drive, Allen Park, MI 48101. *Phone:* 313-425-3700 or 800-767-4120 (toll-free in-state). *E-mail:* steve.peterson@baker.edu. *Web site:* http://www.baker.edu/.

BAKER COLLEGE OF AUBURN HILLS

Auburn Hills, Michigan

Baker College of Auburn Hills is a coed, private, four-year college of Baker College System, founded in 1911, offering degrees at the associate and bachelor's levels and postbachelor's certificates. It has a 7-acre campus in Auburn Hills near Detroit.

Academic Information The faculty has 155 members (7% full-time), 15% with terminal degrees. The student-faculty ratio is 41:1. The library holds 5,400 titles and 95 serial subscriptions. Special programs include academic remediation, services for learning-disabled students, cooperative (work-study) education, advanced placement credit, accelerated degree programs, double majors, independent study, distance learning, summer session for credit, part-time degree programs (daytime, evenings, summer), external degree programs, and internships.
Student Body Statistics The student body is made up of 3,824 undergraduates. 72 percent are women and 28 percent are men. Students come from 1 state or territory.
Expenses for 2009–10 *Application fee:* $20. *Tuition:* $7020 full-time, $195 per quarter hour part-time.
Freshman Admission Baker College of Auburn Hills requires a high school transcript and TOEFL scores for international students. The application deadline for regular admission is rolling.
Transfer Admission The application deadline for admission is rolling.
Entrance Difficulty Baker College of Auburn Hills has an open admission policy.
For Further Information Contact Ms. Jan Bohlen, Vice President for Admissions, Baker College of Auburn Hills, 1500 University Drive, Auburn Hills, MI 48326-1586. *Phone:* 248-340-0600 or 888-429-0410 (toll-free in-state). *Fax:* 248-340-0608. *E-mail:* jan.bohlen@baker.edu. *Web site:* http://www.baker.edu/.

BAKER COLLEGE OF CADILLAC

Cadillac, Michigan

Baker College of Cadillac is a coed, private, four-year college of Baker College System, founded in 1986, offering degrees at the associate and bachelor's levels. It has a 40-acre campus in Cadillac.

Academic Information The faculty has 105 members (4% full-time), 5% with terminal degrees. The student-faculty ratio is 42:1. The library holds 4,000 titles and 78 serial subscriptions. Special programs include academic remediation, services for learning-disabled students, cooperative (work-study) education, advanced placement credit, double majors, independent study, distance learning, summer session for credit, part-time degree programs (daytime, evenings, weekends, summer), external degree programs, and internships.
Student Body Statistics The student body is made up of 1,952 undergraduates. 74 percent are women and 26 percent are men. Students come from 4 states and territories.
Expenses for 2009–10 *Application fee:* $20. *Tuition:* $7020 full-time, $195 per quarter hour part-time.
Freshman Admission Baker College of Cadillac requires a high school transcript and TOEFL scores for international students. An interview is recommended. SAT or ACT scores are required for some. The application deadline for regular admission is rolling.
Transfer Admission The application deadline for admission is rolling.
Entrance Difficulty Baker College of Cadillac has an open admission policy.
For Further Information Contact Mr. Mike Tisdale, Director of Admissions, Baker College of Cadillac, 9600 East 13th Street, Cadillac, MI 49601. *Phone:* 231-876-3100 or 888-313-3463 (toll-free in-state). *Fax:* 231-775-8505. *E-mail:* mike.tisdale@baker.edu. *Web site:* http://www.baker.edu/.

BAKER COLLEGE OF CLINTON TOWNSHIP

Clinton Township, Michigan

Baker College of Clinton Township is a coed, private, four-year college of Baker College System, founded in 1990, offering degrees at the associate and bachelor's levels. It has a 25-acre campus in Clinton Township near Detroit.

Academic Information The faculty has 208 members (8% full-time), 12% with terminal degrees. The student-faculty ratio is 45:1. The library holds 8,000 titles and 97 serial subscriptions. Special programs include academic remediation, services for learning-disabled students, cooperative (work-study) education, advanced placement credit, summer session for

Baker College of Clinton Township (continued)

credit, part-time degree programs (daytime, evenings, weekends, summer), external degree programs, and internships.
Student Body Statistics The student body is made up of 5,637 undergraduates. 73 percent are women and 27 percent are men. Students come from 2 states and territories.
Expenses for 2009–10 *Application fee:* $20. *Tuition:* $7020 full-time, $195 per quarter hour part-time.
Freshman Admission Baker College of Clinton Township requires a high school transcript and TOEFL scores for international students. SAT or ACT scores are required for some. The application deadline for regular admission is rolling.
Transfer Admission The application deadline for admission is rolling.
Entrance Difficulty Baker College of Clinton Township has an open admission policy.
For Further Information Contact Ms. Annette Looser, Vice President for Admissions, Baker College of Clinton Township, 34401 South Gratiot Avenue, Clinton Township, MI 48035. *Phone:* 586-790-3000 or 888-272-2842 (toll-free). *Fax:* 586-791-6811. *E-mail:* annette.looser@baker.edu. *Web site:* http://www.baker.edu/.

BAKER COLLEGE OF FLINT

Flint, Michigan

Baker College of Flint is a coed, private, four-year college of Baker College System, founded in 1911, offering degrees at the associate and bachelor's levels. It has a 30-acre campus in Flint near Detroit.

Academic Information The faculty has 315 members (13% full-time), 12% with terminal degrees. The student-faculty ratio is 31:1. The library holds 168,700 titles. Special programs include academic remediation, services for learning-disabled students, cooperative (work-study) education, advanced placement credit, accelerated degree programs, double majors, independent study, distance learning, summer session for credit, part-time degree programs, external degree programs, and internships.
Student Body Statistics The student body is made up of 5,820 undergraduates. 70 percent are women and 30 percent are men. Students come from 5 states and territories. 99 percent are from Michigan.
Expenses for 2009–10 *Application fee:* $20. *Tuition:* $7020 full-time, $195 per quarter hour part-time. *College room only:* $2700.
Freshman Admission Baker College of Flint requires a high school transcript and TOEFL scores for international students. The application deadline for regular admission is September 20.
Transfer Admission The application deadline for admission is September 20.
Entrance Difficulty Baker College of Flint has an open admission policy.
For Further Information Contact Ms. Jodi Cunez, Director of Admissions, Baker College of Flint, 1050 West Bristol Road, Flint, MI 48507-5508. *Phone:* 810-766-4008 or 800-964-4299 (toll-free). *Fax:* 810-766-4049. *Web site:* http://www.baker.edu/.

BAKER COLLEGE OF JACKSON

Jackson, Michigan

Baker College of Jackson is a coed, private, four-year college of Baker College System, founded in 1994, offering degrees at the associate and bachelor's levels. It has a 42-acre campus in Jackson near Lansing.

Academic Information The faculty has 85 members (6% full-time), 13% with terminal degrees. The student-faculty ratio is 36:1. The library holds 7,000 titles and 150 serial subscriptions. Special programs include academic remediation, services for learning-disabled students, cooperative (work-study) education, advanced placement credit, accelerated degree programs, double majors, independent study, distance learning, summer session for credit, part-time degree programs (daytime, evenings, weekends, summer), external degree programs, and internships.
Student Body Statistics The student body is made up of 1,830 undergraduates. 75 percent are women and 25 percent are men. Students come from 2 states and territories. 99 percent are from Michigan.
Expenses for 2009–10 *Application fee:* $20. *Tuition:* $7020 full-time, $195 per quarter hour part-time.
Freshman Admission Baker College of Jackson requires a high school transcript. The application deadline for regular admission is September 19.
Transfer Admission The application deadline for admission is rolling.
Entrance Difficulty Baker College of Jackson has an open admission policy.
For Further Information Contact Mr. Kevin Pnacek, Vice President for Admissions, Baker College of Jackson, 2800 Springport Road, Jackson, MI 49202. *Phone:* 517-788-7800 or 888-343-3683 (toll-free). *Fax:* 517-789-7331. *E-mail:* kevin.pnacek@baker.edu. *Web site:* http://www.baker.edu/.

BAKER COLLEGE OF MUSKEGON

Muskegon, Michigan

Baker College of Muskegon is a coed, private, four-year college of Baker College System, founded in 1888, offering degrees at the associate and bachelor's levels. It has a 40-acre campus in Muskegon near Grand Rapids.

Academic Information The faculty has 177 members (10% full-time), 8% with terminal degrees. The student-faculty ratio is 55:1. The library holds 32,000 titles and 140 serial subscriptions. Special programs include academic remediation, services for learning-disabled students, cooperative (work-study) education, advanced placement credit, accelerated degree programs, double majors, independent study, distance learning, summer session for credit, part-time degree programs (daytime, evenings, weekends), external degree programs, adult/continuing education programs, and internships.
Student Body Statistics The student body is made up of 5,232 undergraduates. 71 percent are women and 29 percent are men. Students come from 13 states and territories. 99 percent are from Michigan.
Expenses for 2009–10 *Application fee:* $20. *Tuition:* $7020 full-time, $195 per quarter hour part-time. *College room only:* $2700.
Freshman Admission Baker College of Muskegon requires a high school transcript and TOEFL scores for international students. The application deadline for regular admission is September 24.
Transfer Admission The application deadline for admission is rolling.
Entrance Difficulty Baker College of Muskegon has an open admission policy.
For Further Information Contact Ms. Kathy Jacobson, Vice President of Admissions, Baker College of Muskegon, 1903 Marquette Avenue, Muskegon, MI 49442-3497. *Phone:* 231-777-5207 or 800-937-0337 (toll-free in-state). *Fax:* 231-777-5201. *E-mail:* kathy.jacobson@baker.edu. *Web site:* http://www.baker.edu/.

BAKER COLLEGE OF OWOSSO

Owosso, Michigan

Baker College of Owosso is a coed, private, four-year college of Baker College System, founded in 1984, offering degrees at the associate and bachelor's levels. It has a 32-acre campus in Owosso.

Academic Information The faculty has 144 members (6% full-time), 15% with terminal degrees. The student-faculty ratio is 40:1. The library holds 35,424 titles and 215 serial subscriptions. Special programs include academic remediation, services for learning-disabled students, cooperative (work-study) education, advanced placement credit, accelerated degree programs, summer session for credit, part-time degree programs, external degree programs, adult/continuing education programs, and internships.
Student Body Statistics The student body is made up of 2,926 undergraduates. 67 percent are women and 33 percent are men. Students come from 4 states and territories.
Expenses for 2009–10 *Application fee:* $20. *Tuition:* $7020 full-time, $195 per quarter hour part-time. *College room only:* $2700.
Freshman Admission Baker College of Owosso requires a high school transcript and TOEFL scores for international students. The application deadline for regular admission is rolling.
Transfer Admission The application deadline for admission is rolling.

Entrance Difficulty Baker College of Owosso has an open admission policy.
For Further Information Contact Mr. Michael Konopacke, Vice President for Admissions, Baker College of Owosso, 1020 South Washington Street, Owosso, MI 48867-4400. *Phone:* 989-729-3350 or 800-879-3797 (toll-free). *Fax:* 989-729-3441. *E-mail:* mike.konopacke@baker.edu. *Web site:* http://www.baker.edu/.

BAKER COLLEGE OF PORT HURON

Port Huron, Michigan

Baker College of Port Huron is a coed, private, four-year college of Baker College System, founded in 1990, offering degrees at the associate and bachelor's levels. It has a 10-acre campus in Port Huron near Detroit.

Academic Information The faculty has 126 members (10% full-time), 7% with terminal degrees. The student-faculty ratio is 28:1. The library holds 16,823 titles and 181 serial subscriptions. Special programs include academic remediation, services for learning-disabled students, cooperative (work-study) education, advanced placement credit, accelerated degree programs, double majors, independent study, distance learning, summer session for credit, part-time degree programs (daytime, evenings, weekends, summer), external degree programs, and internships.
Student Body Statistics The student body is made up of 1,716 undergraduates. Students come from 1 state or territory.
Expenses for 2009–10 *Application fee:* $20. *Tuition:* $7020 full-time, $195 per quarter hour part-time.
Freshman Admission Baker College of Port Huron requires a high school transcript, an interview, and TOEFL scores for international students. The application deadline for regular admission is September 24.
Transfer Admission The application deadline for admission is rolling.
Entrance Difficulty Baker College of Port Huron has an open admission policy.
For Further Information Contact Mr. Daniel Kenny, Vice President for Admissions, Baker College of Port Huron, 3403 Lapeer Road, Port Huron, MI 48060-2597. *Phone:* 810-985-7000 or 888-262-2442 (toll-free). *Fax:* 810-985-7066. *E-mail:* kenny_d@porthuron.baker.edu. *Web site:* http://www.baker.edu/.

CALVIN COLLEGE

Grand Rapids, Michigan

Calvin College is a coed, private, comprehensive institution, founded in 1876, affiliated with the Christian Reformed Church, offering degrees at the bachelor's and master's levels and postbachelor's certificates. It has a 370-acre campus in Grand Rapids.

Academic Information The faculty has 418 members (77% full-time), 67% with terminal degrees. The undergraduate student-faculty ratio is 11:1. The library holds 1 million titles, 15,697 serial subscriptions, and 25,557 audiovisual materials. Special programs include academic remediation, services for learning-disabled students, an honors program, study abroad, advanced placement credit, accelerated degree programs, double majors, independent study, self-designed majors, summer session for credit, part-time degree programs (daytime, evenings, summer), adult/continuing education programs, internships, and arrangement for off-campus study with Council for Christian Colleges and Universities, Central College, Trinity Christian College, Au Sable Institute. The most frequently chosen baccalaureate fields are business/marketing, education, health professions and related sciences.
Student Body Statistics The student body totals 4,171, of whom 4,104 are undergraduates (936 freshmen). 54 percent are women and 46 percent are men. Students come from 48 states and territories and 54 other countries. 57 percent are from Michigan. 7.5 percent are international students.
Expenses for 2008–09 *Application fee:* $35. *Comprehensive fee:* $31,135 includes full-time tuition ($22,940), mandatory fees ($225), and college room and board ($7970). Full-time tuition and fees vary according to program. Room and board charges vary according to board plan. *Part-time tuition:* $550 per credit hour. Part-time tuition varies according to course load.
Financial Aid Forms of aid include need-based and non-need-based scholarships and part-time jobs. The average aided 2008–09 undergraduate received an aid package worth an estimated $16,558.
Freshman Admission Calvin College requires an essay, a high school transcript, a minimum 2.5 high school GPA, 1 recommendation, SAT or ACT scores, and TOEFL scores for international students. An interview is recommended. The application deadline for regular admission is August 15.
Transfer Admission The application deadline for admission is rolling.
Entrance Difficulty Calvin College assesses its entrance difficulty level as moderately difficult. For the fall 2008 freshman class, 94 percent of the applicants were accepted.
For Further Information Contact Mr. Dale Kuiper, Director of Admissions and Financial Aid, Calvin College, 3201 Burton Street, SE, Grand Rapids, MI 49546. *Phone:* 616-526-6106 or 800-688-0122 (toll-free). *Fax:* 616-526-6777. *E-mail:* admissions@calvin.edu. *Web site:* http://www.calvin.edu/.

CENTER FOR CREATIVE STUDIES-COLLEGE OF ART AND DESIGN

See College for Creative Studies.

CENTRAL MICHIGAN UNIVERSITY

Mount Pleasant, Michigan

Central Michigan University is a coed, public university, founded in 1892, offering degrees at the bachelor's, master's, and doctoral levels and post-master's and postbachelor's certificates. It has an 854-acre campus in Mount Pleasant.

Academic Information The faculty has 1,190 members (62% full-time), 61% with terminal degrees. The undergraduate student-faculty ratio is 21.2:1. The library holds 1 million titles and 7,711 serial subscriptions. Special programs include academic remediation, an honors program, study abroad, advanced placement credit, accelerated degree programs, Freshman Honors College, ESL programs, double majors, independent study, distance learning, self-designed majors, summer session for credit, part-time degree programs (daytime, evenings, summer), external degree programs, adult/continuing education programs, internships, and arrangement for off-campus study. The most frequently chosen baccalaureate fields are business/marketing, education, parks and recreation.
Student Body Statistics The student body totals 27,225, of whom 20,540 are undergraduates (3,899 freshmen). 55 percent are women and 45 percent are men. Students come from 41 states and territories and 50 other countries. 98 percent are from Michigan. 2.4 percent are international students.
Expenses for 2008–09 *Application fee:* $35. *State resident tuition:* $9720 full-time, $324 per credit part-time. *Nonresident tuition:* $22,590 full-time, $753 per credit part-time. Both full-time and part-time tuition varies according to student level. *College room and board:* $7668. *College room only:* $3834. Room and board charges vary according to board plan, housing facility, location, and student level.
Financial Aid Forms of aid include need-based and non-need-based scholarships, athletic grants, and part-time jobs. The average aided 2007–08 undergraduate received an aid package worth $10,048.
Freshman Admission Central Michigan University requires a high school transcript, ACT scores, and TOEFL scores for international students. A minimum 3.0 high school GPA is recommended. An essay and an interview are required for some. The application deadline for regular admission is rolling.
Transfer Admission The application deadline for admission is rolling.

Central Michigan University (continued)

Entrance Difficulty Central Michigan University assesses its entrance difficulty level as moderately difficult. For the fall 2008 freshman class, 70 percent of the applicants were accepted.

For Further Information Contact Ms. Betty J. Wagner, Director of Admissions, Central Michigan University, Warriner Hall 102, Mt. Pleasant, MI 48859. *Phone:* 989-774-3076 or 888-292-5366 (toll-free). *Fax:* 989-774-7267. *E-mail:* cmuadmit@cmich.edu. *Web site:* http://www.cmich.edu/.

CLEARY UNIVERSITY

Ann Arbor, Michigan

Cleary University is a coed, private, comprehensive institution, founded in 1883, offering degrees at the associate, bachelor's, and master's levels. It has a 32-acre campus in Ann Arbor near Detroit and Lansing.

Academic Information The faculty has 165 members (4% full-time), 15% with terminal degrees. The undergraduate student-faculty ratio is 10:1. Special programs include cooperative (work-study) education, advanced placement credit, accelerated degree programs, independent study, distance learning, summer session for credit, part-time degree programs (daytime, evenings, summer), and internships. The most frequently chosen baccalaureate field is business/marketing.

Student Body Statistics The student body totals 855, of whom 739 are undergraduates. 52 percent are women and 48 percent are men. Students come from 4 states and territories and 10 other countries. 99 percent are from Michigan.

Expenses for 2009–10 *Application fee:* $25. *Tuition:* $15,600 full-time, $325 per quarter hour part-time.

Financial Aid Forms of aid include need-based and non-need-based scholarships and part-time jobs. The average aided 2007–08 undergraduate received an aid package worth $10,428. The priority application deadline for financial aid is March 1.

Freshman Admission Cleary University requires a high school transcript and a minimum 2.0 high school GPA. An interview is recommended. An essay, 2 recommendations, SAT or ACT scores, and SAT Subject Test scores are required for some. The application deadline for regular admission is August 15.

Transfer Admission The application deadline for admission is August 15.

Entrance Difficulty Cleary University assesses its entrance difficulty level as moderately difficult. For the fall 2008 freshman class, 80 percent of the applicants were accepted.

For Further Information Contact Ms. Charlotte Paquette, Admissions Representative, Cleary University, 3601 Plymouth Road, Ann Arbor, MI 48105-2659. *Phone:* 517-548-3670 Ext. 2249 or 888-5-CLEARY Ext. 2249 (toll-free). *Fax:* 517-552-7805. *E-mail:* admissions@cleary.edu. *Web site:* http://www.cleary.edu/.

COLLEGE FOR CREATIVE STUDIES

Detroit, Michigan

College for Creative Studies is a coed, private, comprehensive institution, founded in 1926, offering degrees at the bachelor's and master's levels and postbachelor's certificates. It has an 11-acre campus in Detroit.

Academic Information The faculty has 248 members (23% full-time). The undergraduate student-faculty ratio is 10:1. The library holds 24,000 titles and 75 serial subscriptions. Special programs include academic remediation, services for learning-disabled students, cooperative (work-study) education, study abroad, advanced placement credit, ESL programs, double majors, independent study, summer session for credit, part-time degree programs (daytime, evenings, weekends, summer), internships, and arrangement for off-campus study with Association of Independent Colleges of Art and Design. The most frequently chosen baccalaureate field is visual and performing arts.

Student Body Statistics The student body totals 1,369, of whom 1,365 are undergraduates (241 freshmen). 43 percent are women and 57 percent are men. Students come from 35 states and territories and 18 other countries. 81 percent are from Michigan. 5.5 percent are international students.

Expenses for 2009–10 *Application fee:* $35. *Comprehensive fee:* $38,485 includes full-time tuition ($28,650), mandatory fees ($1335), and college room and board ($8500). *College room only:* $4900. *Part-time tuition:* $955 per credit hour.

Financial Aid Forms of aid include need-based and non-need-based scholarships and part-time jobs.

Freshman Admission College for Creative Studies requires an essay, a high school transcript, a portfolio, SAT or ACT scores, and TOEFL scores for international students. A minimum 2.5 high school GPA is recommended. An essay, recommendations, and an interview are required for some. The application deadline for regular admission is August 1.

Transfer Admission The application deadline for admission is rolling.

Entrance Difficulty College for Creative Studies assesses its entrance difficulty level as moderately difficult. For the fall 2008 freshman class, 37 percent of the applicants were accepted.

For Further Information Contact Office of Admissions, College for Creative Studies, 201 East Kirby, Detroit, MI 48202-4034. *Phone:* 800-952-2787 or 800-872-2739 (toll-free). *Fax:* 313-872-2739. *E-mail:* admissions@ccscad.edu. *Web site:* http://www.collegeforcreativestudies.edu/.

CONCORDIA UNIVERSITY

Ann Arbor, Michigan

Concordia University is a coed, private, comprehensive unit of Concordia University System, founded in 1963, affiliated with the Lutheran Church–Missouri Synod, offering degrees at the associate, bachelor's, and master's levels and postbachelor's certificates. It has a 187-acre campus in Ann Arbor near Detroit.

Academic Information The faculty has 95 members (41% full-time). The undergraduate student-faculty ratio is 17:1. Special programs include academic remediation, services for learning-disabled students, cooperative (work-study) education, advanced placement credit, accelerated degree programs, double majors, independent study, distance learning, self-designed majors, summer session for credit, part-time degree programs (daytime, evenings, weekends, summer), internships, and arrangement for off-campus study with Concordia University System. The most frequently chosen baccalaureate fields are business/marketing, communications/journalism, education.

Student Body Statistics The student body totals 1,075, of whom 521 are undergraduates (94 freshmen). 54 percent are women and 46 percent are men. Students come from 22 states and territories and 6 other countries. 83 percent are from Michigan. 1.3 percent are international students.

Expenses for 2008–09 *Application fee:* $25. *One-time mandatory fee:* $100. *Comprehensive fee:* $27,050 includes full-time tuition ($19,700) and college room and board ($7350). *Part-time tuition:* $650 per credit. Part-time tuition varies according to course load.

Financial Aid Forms of aid include need-based and non-need-based scholarships, athletic grants, and part-time jobs. The priority application deadline for financial aid is March 1.

Freshman Admission Concordia University requires a high school transcript, SAT or ACT scores, and TOEFL scores for international students. A minimum 2.5 high school GPA, 1 recommendation, and ACT scores are recommended. An essay and an interview are required for some. The application deadline for regular admission is rolling.

Transfer Admission The application deadline for admission is rolling.

Entrance Difficulty Concordia University assesses its entrance difficulty level as moderately difficult. For the fall 2008 freshman class, 66 percent of the applicants were accepted.

For Further Information Contact Amy Becher, Executive Director of Enrollment Services, Concordia University, 4090 Geddes Road, Ann Arbor, MI 48105-2797. *Phone:* 734-995-7450 or 800-253-0680 (toll-free). *Fax:* 734-995-4610. *E-mail:* admissions@cuaa.edu or bechea@cuaa.edu. *Web site:* http://www.cuaa.edu/.

CORNERSTONE UNIVERSITY

Grand Rapids, Michigan

Cornerstone University is a coed, private, nondenominational, comprehensive institution, founded in 1941, offering degrees at the associate, bachelor's, master's, and first professional levels. It has a 132-acre campus in Grand Rapids.

Academic Information The faculty has 127 members (49% full-time), 28% with terminal degrees. The undergraduate student-faculty ratio is 12:1. The library holds 160,815 titles, 2,587 serial subscriptions, and 43,820 audiovisual materials. Special programs include academic remediation, services for learning-disabled students, an honors program, study abroad, advanced placement credit, accelerated degree programs, ESL programs, double majors, independent study, distance learning, summer session for credit, part-time degree programs, adult/continuing education programs, internships, and arrangement for off-campus study with Calvin College, Reformed Bible College, Grace Bible College. The most frequently chosen baccalaureate fields are business/marketing, education, theology and religious vocations.
Student Body Statistics The student body totals 2,440, of whom 1,797 are undergraduates (205 freshmen). 59 percent are women and 41 percent are men. Students come from 35 states and territories and 7 other countries. 88 percent are from Michigan. 0.6 percent are international students.
Expenses for 2008–09 *Application fee:* $25. *Comprehensive fee:* $26,030 includes full-time tuition ($19,190), mandatory fees ($340), and college room and board ($6500). Room and board charges vary according to board plan. *Part-time tuition:* varies with course load.
Financial Aid Forms of aid include need-based and non-need-based scholarships, athletic grants, and part-time jobs. The average aided 2007–08 undergraduate received an aid package worth $16,272. The application deadline for financial aid is March 1.
Freshman Admission Cornerstone University requires an essay, a high school transcript, a minimum 2.5 high school GPA, 1 recommendation, pastoral letter, SAT or ACT scores, and TOEFL scores for international students. An interview is recommended. The application deadline for regular admission is rolling.
Transfer Admission The application deadline for admission is rolling.
Entrance Difficulty Cornerstone University assesses its entrance difficulty level as minimally difficult. For the fall 2008 freshman class, 75 percent of the applicants were accepted.
For Further Information Contact Office of Admissions, Cornerstone University, 1001 East Beltline Avenue, NE, Grand Rapids, MI 49525. *Phone:* 616-222-1426 or 800-787-9778 (toll-free). *Fax:* 616-222-1400. *E-mail:* admissions@cornerstone.edu. *Web site:* http://www.cornerstone.edu/.

DAVENPORT UNIVERSITY

Grand Rapids, Michigan

Davenport University is a coed, private, comprehensive institution, founded in 1866, offering degrees at the associate, bachelor's, and master's levels and post-master's and postbachelor's certificates.

Academic Information The faculty has 1,089 members (14% full-time). The undergraduate student-faculty ratio is 13:1. Special programs include academic remediation, services for learning-disabled students, cooperative (work-study) education, study abroad, advanced placement credit, accelerated degree programs, ESL programs, independent study, distance learning, self-designed majors, summer session for credit, part-time degree programs (daytime, evenings, summer), adult/continuing education programs, and internships. The most frequently chosen baccalaureate fields are business/marketing, computer and information sciences, health professions and related sciences.
Student Body Statistics The student body totals 10,764, of whom 9,806 are undergraduates (922 freshmen). 69 percent are women and 31 percent are men. 98 percent are from Michigan.
Expenses for 2008–09 *Application fee:* $25. *Tuition:* $10,440 full-time, $435 per credit part-time. *Mandatory fees:* $200 full-time. Full-time tuition and fees vary according to location. Part-time tuition varies according to location. *College room only:* $4990.
Financial Aid Forms of aid include need-based and non-need-based scholarships and part-time jobs. The priority application deadline for financial aid is March 1.
Freshman Admission Davenport University requires a high school transcript. An interview, SAT or ACT scores, and TOEFL scores for international students are recommended. The application deadline for regular admission is rolling and for nonresidents it is rolling.
Transfer Admission The application deadline for admission is rolling.
Entrance Difficulty Davenport University assesses its entrance difficulty level as minimally difficult.
For Further Information Contact Ms. Heather Knechtel, Director of Admissions, Davenport University, 415 East Fulton Street, Grand Rapids, MI 49503. *Phone:* 616-451-3511 or 800-632-9569 (toll-free). *E-mail:* heather.knechtel@davenport.edu. *Web site:* http://www.davenport.edu/.

DEVRY UNIVERSITY SOUTHFIELD CENTER

Southfield, Michigan

DeVry University Southfield Center is a coed, proprietary, comprehensive institution, founded in 2008, offering degrees at the associate, bachelor's, and master's levels.

Academic Information The faculty has 11 members. The undergraduate student-faculty ratio is 6:1. Special programs include accelerated degree programs and distance learning.
Student Body Statistics The student body is made up of 41 undergraduates (4 freshmen). 49 percent are women and 51 percent are men.
Expenses for 2009–10 *Application fee:* $50. *Tuition:* $14,080 full-time, $550 per credit hour part-time.
Financial Aid Forms of aid include need-based scholarships. The average aided 2007–08 undergraduate received an aid package worth $8705. The application deadline for financial aid is continuous.
Freshman Admission The application deadline for regular admission is rolling.
Transfer Admission The application deadline for admission is rolling.
For Further Information Contact Admissions Office, DeVry University Southfield Center, 26999 Central Park Boulevard, Suite 125, Southfield, MI 48076. *Web site:* http://www.devry.edu/.

EASTERN MICHIGAN UNIVERSITY

Ypsilanti, Michigan

Eastern Michigan University is a coed, public, comprehensive institution, founded in 1849, offering degrees at the bachelor's, master's, and doctoral levels and post-master's and postbachelor's certificates. It has a 460-acre campus in Ypsilanti near Detroit.

Academic Information The faculty has 1,236 members (60% full-time). The undergraduate student-faculty ratio is 18:1. The library holds 970,268 titles, 2,375 serial subscriptions, and 16,314 audiovisual materials. Special programs include academic remediation, services for learning-disabled students, an honors program, cooperative (work-study) education, advanced placement credit, accelerated degree programs, ESL programs, double majors, independent study, distance learning, self-designed majors, summer session for credit, part-time degree programs (daytime, evenings, weekends, summer), external degree programs, and internships. The most frequently chosen baccalaureate fields are business/marketing, education, health professions and related sciences.
Student Body Statistics The student body totals 21,926, of whom 17,213 are undergraduates. Students come from 49 states and territories and 45 other countries. 93 percent are from Michigan.
Expenses for 2008–09 *Application fee:* $30. *One-time mandatory fee:* $88. *State resident tuition:* $6885 full-time, $229.50 per credit hour part-time. *Nonresident tuition:* $20,280 full-time, $676 per credit hour part-time. *Mandatory fees:* $1184 full-time, $36.60 per credit hour part-time, $43 per term part-time. Both full-time and part-time tuition and fees vary according to reciprocity agreements. *College room and board:* $7352. *College room only:* $3452. Room and board charges vary according to board plan, housing facility, and location.

Eastern Michigan University (continued)

Financial Aid Forms of aid include need-based and non-need-based scholarships, athletic grants, and part-time jobs. The average aided 2007–08 undergraduate received an aid package worth $7296. The application deadline for financial aid is continuous.

Freshman Admission Eastern Michigan University requires a high school transcript, a minimum 2.0 high school GPA, SAT or ACT scores, and TOEFL scores for international students. 1 recommendation and an interview are required for some. The application deadline for regular admission is rolling.

Transfer Admission The application deadline for admission is rolling.

Entrance Difficulty Eastern Michigan University assesses its entrance difficulty level as moderately difficult. For the fall 2008 freshman class, 73 percent of the applicants were accepted.

For Further Information Contact Kathy Orscheln, Director of Admissions, Eastern Michigan University, 400 Pierce Hall, Ypsilanti, MI 48197. *Phone:* 734-487-3060 or 800-GO TO EMU (toll-free). *Fax:* 734-487-1484. *E-mail:* admissions@emich.edu. *Web site:* http://www.emich.edu/.

FERRIS STATE UNIVERSITY

Big Rapids, Michigan

Ferris State University is a coed, public, comprehensive institution, founded in 1884, offering degrees at the associate, bachelor's, master's, and first professional levels and postbachelor's certificates (Associate). It has an 880-acre campus in Big Rapids near Grand Rapids.

Academic Information The faculty has 857 members (62% full-time). The undergraduate student-faculty ratio is 15:1. The library holds 410,536 titles, 36,563 serial subscriptions, and 47,761 audiovisual materials. Special programs include academic remediation, services for learning-disabled students, an honors program, cooperative (work-study) education, advanced placement credit, accelerated degree programs, Freshman Honors College, double majors, independent study, distance learning, self-designed majors, summer session for credit, part-time degree programs (daytime, evenings, summer), external degree programs, internships, and arrangement for off-campus study with Delta College, Henry Ford Community College (CC), Lansing CC, Mott CC, Macomb CC, Macomb CC, St. Clair County CC, North Central Michigan College, Northwestern Michigan College, University Center, Gaylord, Westshore Community College, Muskegon CC, Southwestern Michigan College. The most frequently chosen baccalaureate fields are business/marketing, engineering technologies, security and protective services.

Student Body Statistics The student body totals 13,537, of whom 12,250 are undergraduates (2,139 freshmen). 48 percent are women and 52 percent are men. Students come from 44 states and territories and 27 other countries. 95 percent are from Michigan. 0.7 percent are international students.

Expenses for 2008–09 *Application fee:* $30. *State resident tuition:* $9000 full-time, $300 per credit hour part-time. *Nonresident tuition:* $15,900 full-time, $530 per credit hour part-time. *Mandatory fees:* $162 full-time, $162 per year part-time. Full-time tuition and fees vary according to degree level and reciprocity agreements. Part-time tuition and fees vary according to degree level. *College room and board:* $7944. Room and board charges vary according to board plan and housing facility.

Financial Aid Forms of aid include need-based and non-need-based scholarships, athletic grants, and part-time jobs. The average aided 2007–08 undergraduate received an aid package worth $14,424.

Freshman Admission Ferris State University requires a high school transcript, a minimum 2.5 high school GPA, SAT or ACT scores, and TOEFL scores for international students. The application deadline for regular admission is August 1.

Transfer Admission The application deadline for admission is July 1.

Entrance Difficulty Ferris State University has an open admission policy. It assesses its entrance difficulty as moderately difficult for transfers; very difficult for pharmacy, optometry.

For Further Information Contact Troy Tissue, Associate Director of Admissions, Ferris State University, 1201 South State Street, CSS201, Big Rapids, MI 49307-2742. *Phone:* 231-591-2000 or 800-433-7747 (toll-free). *Fax:* 231-591-3944. *E-mail:* admissions@ferris.edu. *Web site:* http://www.ferris.edu/.

FINLANDIA UNIVERSITY

Hancock, Michigan

Finlandia University is a coed, private, four-year college, founded in 1896, affiliated with the Evangelical Lutheran Church in America, offering degrees at the associate and bachelor's levels. It has a 25-acre campus in Hancock.

Expenses for 2008–09 *Application fee:* $30. *Comprehensive fee:* $23,714 includes full-time tuition ($17,414), mandatory fees ($500), and college room and board ($5800). Full-time tuition and fees vary according to program. Room and board charges vary according to housing facility. *Part-time tuition:* $580 per credit. Part-time tuition varies according to course load and program.

For Further Information Contact Martin Kinard, Finlandia University, 601 Quincy Street, Hancock, MI 49930. *Phone:* 906-487-7352 or 877-202-5491 (toll-free). *Fax:* 906-487-7383. *E-mail:* admissions@finlandia.edu. *Web site:* http://www.finlandia.edu/.

GMI ENGINEERING & MANAGEMENT INSTITUTE

See Kettering University.

GRACE BIBLE COLLEGE

Grand Rapids, Michigan

Grace Bible College is a coed, private, four-year college, founded in 1945, affiliated with the Grace Gospel Fellowship, offering degrees at the associate and bachelor's levels. It has a 16-acre campus in Grand Rapids.

Academic Information The faculty has 21 members (38% full-time), 19% with terminal degrees. The student-faculty ratio is 13:1. The library holds 42,143 titles and 155 serial subscriptions. Special programs include academic remediation, advanced placement credit, ESL programs, independent study, internships, and arrangement for off-campus study with Grand Rapids Community College, Davenport University, Cornerstone University. The most frequently chosen baccalaureate fields are business/marketing, education, interdisciplinary studies.

Student Body Statistics The student body is made up of 179 undergraduates (53 freshmen). 44 percent are women and 56 percent are men. Students come from 16 states and territories. 81 percent are from Michigan.

Expenses for 2008–09 *Application fee:* $0. *Comprehensive fee:* $20,020 includes full-time tuition ($12,800), mandatory fees ($520), and college room and board ($6700). *College room only:* $3000. Room and board charges vary according to housing facility. *Part-time tuition:* $450 per semester hour. Part-time tuition varies according to course load.

Financial Aid Forms of aid include need-based and non-need-based scholarships and part-time jobs. The average aided 2007–08 undergraduate received an aid package worth $9070. The priority application deadline for financial aid is February 28.

Freshman Admission Grace Bible College requires a high school transcript, 2 recommendations, SAT and SAT Subject Test or ACT scores, and TOEFL scores for international students. A minimum 2.5 high school GPA is recommended. An interview is required for some. The application deadline for regular admission is July 15.

Entrance Difficulty Grace Bible College assesses its entrance difficulty level as minimally difficult. For the fall 2008 freshman class, 65 percent of the applicants were accepted.
For Further Information Contact Mr. Kevin Gilliam, Director of Enrollment, Grace Bible College, 1101 Aldon Street, SW, PO Box 910, Grand Rapids, MI 49509. *Phone:* 616-538-2330 Ext. 239 or 800-968-1887 (toll-free). *Fax:* 616-538-0599. *E-mail:* gbc@gbcol.edu. *Web site:* http://www.gbcol.edu/.

GRAND VALLEY STATE UNIVERSITY

Allendale, Michigan

Grand Valley State University is a coed, public, comprehensive institution, founded in 1960, offering degrees at the bachelor's, master's, and doctoral levels and post-master's and postbachelor's certificates. It has a 900-acre campus in Allendale near Grand Rapids.

Academic Information The faculty has 1,529 members (65% full-time), 41% with terminal degrees. The undergraduate student-faculty ratio is 18:1. The library holds 664,000 titles and 8,000 serial subscriptions. Special programs include academic remediation, services for learning-disabled students, an honors program, cooperative (work-study) education, study abroad, advanced placement credit, accelerated degree programs, Freshman Honors College, ESL programs, double majors, independent study, distance learning, summer session for credit, part-time degree programs (daytime, evenings, weekends, summer), adult/continuing education programs, and internships. The most frequently chosen baccalaureate fields are biological/life sciences, business/marketing, health professions and related sciences.
Student Body Statistics The student body totals 23,892, of whom 20,416 are undergraduates (3,890 freshmen). 60 percent are women and 40 percent are men. Students come from 42 states and territories and 74 other countries. 96 percent are from Michigan. 0.8 percent are international students.
Expenses for 2008–09 *Application fee:* $30. *State resident tuition:* $8196 full-time, $356 per credit hour part-time. *Nonresident tuition:* $12,510 full-time, $532 per credit hour part-time. Full-time tuition varies according to degree level, program, and student level. Part-time tuition varies according to course load, degree level, program, and student level. *College room and board:* $7224. *College room only:* $5174. Room and board charges vary according to board plan, housing facility, and location.
Financial Aid Forms of aid include need-based and non-need-based scholarships, athletic grants, and part-time jobs. The average aided 2008–09 undergraduate received an aid package worth an estimated $8112. The priority application deadline for financial aid is March 1.
Freshman Admission Grand Valley State University requires a high school transcript, SAT or ACT scores, and TOEFL scores for international students. An essay and an interview are required for some. The application deadline for regular admission is May 1.
Transfer Admission The application deadline for admission is July 24.
Entrance Difficulty Grand Valley State University assesses its entrance difficulty level as moderately difficult. For the fall 2008 freshman class, 78 percent of the applicants were accepted.
For Further Information Contact Ms. Jodi Chycinski, Director of Admissions, Grand Valley State University, 1 Campus Drive, Allendale, MI 49401. *Phone:* 616-331-2025 or 800-748-0246 (toll-free). *Fax:* 616-331-2000. *E-mail:* go2gvsu@gvsu.edu. *Web site:* http://www.gvsu.edu/.

GREAT LAKES CHRISTIAN COLLEGE

Lansing, Michigan

Great Lakes Christian College is a coed, private, four-year college, founded in 1949, affiliated with the Christian Churches and Churches of Christ, offering degrees at the associate and bachelor's levels. It has a 50-acre campus in Lansing.

Academic Information The faculty has 23 members (43% full-time), 30% with terminal degrees. The student-faculty ratio is 15.5:1. Special programs include academic remediation, services for learning-disabled students, advanced placement credit, double majors, independent study, part-time degree programs (daytime, evenings), internships, and arrangement for off-campus study with Cornerstone College, Davenport College of Business. The most frequently chosen baccalaureate field is theology and religious vocations.
Student Body Statistics The student body is made up of 258 undergraduates (71 freshmen). 48 percent are women and 52 percent are men. Students come from 4 states and territories and 3 other countries. 98 percent are from Michigan. 2.3 percent are international students.
Expenses for 2009–10 *Application fee:* $30. *One-time mandatory fee:* $200. *Comprehensive fee:* $19,600 includes full-time tuition ($11,520), mandatory fees ($1080), and college room and board ($7000). *Part-time tuition:* $360 per credit hour. *Part-time mandatory fees:* $360 per credit hour.
Financial Aid Forms of aid include non-need-based scholarships and part-time jobs.
Freshman Admission Great Lakes Christian College requires an essay, a high school transcript, a minimum 2.25 high school GPA, 3 recommendations, SAT or ACT scores, and TOEFL scores for international students. The application deadline for regular admission is August 1.
Transfer Admission The application deadline for admission is August 1.
Entrance Difficulty Great Lakes Christian College assesses its entrance difficulty level as moderately difficult.
For Further Information Contact Mr. Lloyd Scharer, Director of Admissions and College Relations, Great Lakes Christian College, 6211 West Willow Highway, Lansing, MI 48917-1299. *Phone:* 517-321-0242 or 800-YES-GLCC (toll-free). *Fax:* 517-321-5902. *E-mail:* lscharer@glcc.edu. *Web site:* http://www.glcc.edu/.

HILLSDALE COLLEGE

Hillsdale, Michigan

Hillsdale College is a coed, private, four-year college, founded in 1844, offering degrees at the bachelor's level. It has a 200-acre campus in Hillsdale.

Academic Information The faculty has 154 members (76% full-time), 71% with terminal degrees. The student-faculty ratio is 10:1. The library holds 240,000 titles, 1,650 serial subscriptions, and 8,000 audiovisual materials. Special programs include an honors program, study abroad, advanced placement credit, accelerated degree programs, double majors, independent study, summer session for credit, part-time degree programs (daytime, summer), internships, and arrangement for off-campus study. The most frequently chosen baccalaureate fields are business/marketing, history, social sciences.
Student Body Statistics The student body is made up of 1,378 undergraduates (385 freshmen). 52 percent are women and 48 percent are men. Students come from 48 states and territories and 7 other countries. 37 percent are from Michigan.
Expenses for 2008–09 *Application fee:* $35. *Comprehensive fee:* $27,670 includes full-time tuition ($19,380), mandatory fees ($540), and college room and board ($7750). *College room only:* $3850. Room and board charges vary according to board plan. *Part-time tuition:* $760 per credit hour.
Financial Aid Forms of aid include need-based and non-need-based scholarships and athletic grants. The application deadline for financial aid is April 1 with a priority deadline of February 1.
Freshman Admission Hillsdale College requires an essay, a high school transcript, 2 recommendations, SAT or ACT scores, and TOEFL scores for international students. A minimum 3.3 high school GPA, an interview, and SAT Subject Test scores are recommended. An interview is required for some. The application deadline for regular admission is February 15, for nonresidents it is February 15, for early decision it is November 15, and for early action it is January 1.
Transfer Admission The application deadline for admission is February 15.
Entrance Difficulty Hillsdale College assesses its entrance difficulty level as very difficult. For the fall 2008 freshman class, 64 percent of the applicants were accepted.
For Further Information Contact Mr. Jeffrey S. Lantis, Director of Admissions, Hillsdale College, 33 East College Street, Hillsdale, MI 49242-1298. *Phone:* 517-607-2327. *Fax:* 517-607-2223. *E-mail:* admissions@hillsdale.edu. *Web site:* http://www.hillsdale.edu/.

HOPE COLLEGE

Holland, Michigan

Hope College is a coed, private, four-year college, founded in 1866, affiliated with the Reformed Church in America, offering degrees at the bachelor's level. It has a 45-acre campus in Holland near Grand Rapids.

Academic Information The faculty has 328 members (70% full-time). The student-faculty ratio is 11:1. The library holds 368,864 titles, 5,771 serial subscriptions, and 15,846 audiovisual materials. Special programs include services for learning-disabled students, study abroad, advanced placement credit, ESL programs, double majors, independent study, self-designed majors, summer session for credit, part-time degree programs (daytime), internships, and arrangement for off-campus study with members of the Great Lakes Colleges Association, Associated Colleges of the Midwest, Institute of European Studies, Council for International Educational Exchange. The most frequently chosen baccalaureate fields are business/marketing, education, social sciences.

Student Body Statistics The student body is made up of 3,238 undergraduates (808 freshmen). 60 percent are women and 40 percent are men. Students come from 43 states and territories and 30 other countries. 70 percent are from Michigan. 1.5 percent are international students.

Expenses for 2008–09 *Application fee:* $35. *Comprehensive fee:* $32,570 includes full-time tuition ($24,780), mandatory fees ($140), and college room and board ($7650). *College room only:* $3490. Room and board charges vary according to board plan. *Part-time tuition:* varies with course load.

Financial Aid Forms of aid include need-based and non-need-based scholarships and part-time jobs. The average aided 2008–09 undergraduate received an aid package worth an estimated $21,514. The priority application deadline for financial aid is March 1.

Freshman Admission Hope College requires an essay, a high school transcript, SAT or ACT scores, and TOEFL scores for international students. An interview is recommended. 1 recommendation is required for some. The application deadline for regular admission is rolling.

Transfer Admission The application deadline for admission is rolling.

Entrance Difficulty Hope College assesses its entrance difficulty level as moderately difficult. For the fall 2008 freshman class, 82 percent of the applicants were accepted.

For Further Information Contact Hope College Admissions, Hope College, 69 East 10th Street, P.O. Box 9000, Holland, MI 49422-9000. *Phone:* 616-395-7850 or 800-968-7850 (toll-free). *Fax:* 616-395-7130. *E-mail:* admissions@hope.edu. *Web site:* http://www.hope.edu/.

ITT TECHNICAL INSTITUTE

Canton, Michigan

ITT Technical Institute is a coed, proprietary, primarily two-year college of ITT Educational Services, Inc., founded in 2002, offering degrees at the associate and bachelor's levels.

Financial Aid Forms of aid include need-based scholarships and part-time jobs. The application deadline for financial aid is continuous.

Entrance Difficulty ITT Technical Institute assesses its entrance difficulty level as minimally difficult.

For Further Information Contact Director of Recruitment, ITT Technical Institute, 1905 South Haggerty Road, Canton, OH 28217. *Phone:* 784-397-7800 or 800-247-4477 (toll-free). *Fax:* 734-397-1945. *Web site:* http://www.itt-tech.edu/.

ITT TECHNICAL INSTITUTE

Grand Rapids, Michigan

ITT Technical Institute is a coed, proprietary, primarily two-year college of ITT Educational Services, Inc., offering degrees at the associate and bachelor's levels.

Financial Aid Forms of aid include need-based scholarships and part-time jobs. The application deadline for financial aid is continuous.

Entrance Difficulty ITT Technical Institute assesses its entrance difficulty level as minimally difficult.

For Further Information Contact Director of Recruitment, ITT Technical Institute, 4020 Sparks Drive SE, Grand Rapids, MI 49546. *Phone:* 616-956-1060 or 800-632-4676 (toll-free in-state). *Fax:* 616-956-5606. *Web site:* http://www.itt-tech.edu/.

ITT TECHNICAL INSTITUTE

Troy, Michigan

ITT Technical Institute is a coed, proprietary, primarily two-year college of ITT Educational Services, Inc., founded in 1987, offering degrees at the associate and bachelor's levels.

Financial Aid Forms of aid include need-based scholarships and part-time jobs. The application deadline for financial aid is continuous.

Entrance Difficulty ITT Technical Institute assesses its entrance difficulty level as minimally difficult.

For Further Information Contact Director of Recruitment, ITT Technical Institute, 1522 East Big Beaver Road, Troy, MI 48083-1905. *Phone:* 248-524-1800 or 800-832-6817 (toll-free in-state). *Fax:* 248-524-1965. *Web site:* http://www.itt-tech.edu/.

KALAMAZOO COLLEGE

Kalamazoo, Michigan

Kalamazoo College is a coed, private, four-year college, founded in 1833, affiliated with the American Baptist Churches in the U.S.A., offering degrees at the bachelor's level. It has a 60-acre campus in Kalamazoo.

Academic Information The faculty has 111 members (84% full-time), 80% with terminal degrees. The student-faculty ratio is 14:1. The library holds 342,939 titles and 1,495 serial subscriptions. Special programs include services for learning-disabled students, study abroad, advanced placement credit, ESL programs, double majors, independent study, internships, and arrangement for off-campus study with Western Michigan University. The most frequently chosen baccalaureate fields are biological/life sciences, psychology, social sciences.

Student Body Statistics The student body is made up of 1,387 undergraduates (364 freshmen). 57 percent are women and 43 percent are men. Students come from 38 states and territories and 13 other countries. 69 percent are from Michigan. 1.8 percent are international students.

Expenses for 2008–09 *Application fee:* $35. *One-time mandatory fee:* $100. *Comprehensive fee:* $38,166 includes full-time tuition ($30,723) and college room and board ($7443). *College room only:* $3630.

Financial Aid Forms of aid include need-based scholarships and part-time jobs. The average aided 2008–09 undergraduate received an aid package worth an estimated $24,710.

Freshman Admission Kalamazoo College requires an essay, a high school transcript, 2 recommendations, SAT or ACT scores, and TOEFL scores for international students. A minimum 3.0 high school GPA and an interview are recommended. The application deadline for regular admission is February 1, for early decision it is November 10, and for early action it is November 20.

Transfer Admission The application deadline for admission is May 1.

Entrance Difficulty Kalamazoo College assesses its entrance difficulty level as very difficult. For the fall 2008 freshman class, 70 percent of the applicants were accepted.

For Further Information Contact Mrs. Linda Wirgau, Records Manager, Kalamazoo College, Mandelle Hall, 1200 Academy Street, Kalamazoo, MI 49006-3295. *Phone:* 269-337-7166 or 800-253-3602 (toll-free). *Fax:* 269-337-7190. *E-mail:* admissions@kzoo.edu. *Web site:* http://www.kzoo.edu/.

KETTERING UNIVERSITY

Flint, Michigan

Kettering University is a coed, primarily men's, private, comprehensive institution, founded in 1919, offering degrees at the bachelor's and master's levels. It has an 85-acre campus in Flint near Detroit.

Academic Information The faculty has 137 members (88% full-time), 76% with terminal degrees. The undergraduate student-faculty ratio is 10:1. The library holds 130,000 titles, 400 serial subscriptions, and 1,200 audiovisual materials. Special programs include services for learning-disabled students, cooperative (work-study) education, study abroad, advanced placement credit, accelerated degree programs, double majors, independent study, distance learning, and internships. The most frequently chosen baccalaureate fields are business/marketing, computer and information sciences, engineering.
Student Body Statistics The student body totals 2,600, of whom 2,134 are undergraduates (441 freshmen). 17 percent are women and 83 percent are men. Students come from 48 states and territories and 14 other countries. 70 percent are from Michigan. 1 percent are international students.
Expenses for 2008–09 *Application fee:* $35. *One-time mandatory fee:* $310. *Comprehensive fee:* $33,118 includes full-time tuition ($26,496), mandatory fees ($440), and college room and board ($6182). *College room only:* $3872. *Part-time tuition:* $828 per credit hour.
Financial Aid Forms of aid include need-based and non-need-based scholarships and part-time jobs. The average aided 2008–09 undergraduate received an aid package worth an estimated $16,476.
Freshman Admission Kettering University requires a high school transcript, SAT or ACT scores, and TOEFL scores for international students. A minimum 3.0 high school GPA and an interview are recommended. An essay is required for some. The application deadline for regular admission is rolling.
Transfer Admission The application deadline for admission is rolling.
Entrance Difficulty Kettering University assesses its entrance difficulty level as very difficult. For the fall 2008 freshman class, 67 percent of the applicants were accepted.
For Further Information Contact Ms. Barbara Sosin, Director of Admissions, Kettering University, 1700 West Third Avenue, Flint, MI 48504-4898. *Phone:* 810-762-7865, 800-955-4464 Ext. 7865 (toll-free in-state), or 800-955-4464 (toll-free out-of-state). *Fax:* 810-762-9837. *E-mail:* admissions@kettering.edu. *Web site:* http://www.kettering.edu/.

See page 244 for the Close-Up.

KUYPER COLLEGE

Grand Rapids, Michigan

Kuyper College is a coed, private, four-year college, founded in 1939, offering degrees at the associate and bachelor's levels and postbachelor's certificates. It has a 34-acre campus in Grand Rapids.

Academic Information The faculty has 33 members (42% full-time), 30% with terminal degrees. The student-faculty ratio is 19:1. The library holds 56,590 titles, 204 serial subscriptions, and 3,515 audiovisual materials. Special programs include academic remediation, services for learning-disabled students, cooperative (work-study) education, study abroad, advanced placement credit, ESL programs, double majors, independent study, distance learning, self-designed majors, summer session for credit, part-time degree programs (daytime, evenings), internships, and arrangement for off-campus study with Grand Rapids Community College, Cornerstone University, Calvin College. The most frequently chosen baccalaureate fields are public administration and social services, business/marketing, theology and religious vocations.
Student Body Statistics The student body totals 319, of whom 315 are undergraduates (63 freshmen). 50 percent are women and 50 percent are men. Students come from 17 states and territories and 12 other countries. 88 percent are from Michigan. 8.7 percent are international students.
Expenses for 2009–10 *Application fee:* $25. *Comprehensive fee:* $21,209 includes full-time tuition ($14,694), mandatory fees ($525), and college room and board ($5990). *Part-time tuition:* $705 per credit hour.
Financial Aid Forms of aid include need-based and non-need-based scholarships and part-time jobs. The average aided 2008–09 undergraduate received an aid package worth an estimated $11,857. The priority application deadline for financial aid is March 1.
Freshman Admission Kuyper College requires an essay, a high school transcript, a minimum 2.5 high school GPA, SAT or ACT scores, and TOEFL scores for international students. An interview is required for some. The application deadline for regular admission is rolling.
Transfer Admission The application deadline for admission is rolling.
Entrance Difficulty Kuyper College assesses its entrance difficulty level as moderately difficult. For the fall 2008 freshman class, 86 percent of the applicants were accepted.
For Further Information Contact Admissions Office, Kuyper College, 3333 East Beltline Avenue, NE, Grand Rapids, MI 49525. *Phone:* 616-222-3000 Ext. 632 or 800-511-3749 (toll-free). *Fax:* 616-222-3045. *E-mail:* admissions@kuyper.edu. *Web site:* http://www.kuyper.edu/.

LAKE SUPERIOR STATE UNIVERSITY

Sault Sainte Marie, Michigan

Lake Superior State University is a coed, public, comprehensive institution, founded in 1946, offering degrees at the associate, bachelor's, and master's levels. It has a 115-acre campus in Sault Sainte Marie.

Academic Information The faculty has 184 members (57% full-time). The undergraduate student-faculty ratio is 18:1. The library holds 200,449 titles, 850 serial subscriptions, and 592 audiovisual materials. Special programs include services for learning-disabled students, an honors program, cooperative (work-study) education, advanced placement credit, Freshman Honors College, double majors, independent study, distance learning, self-designed majors, summer session for credit, part-time degree programs, and internships. The most frequently chosen baccalaureate fields are business/marketing, education, security and protective services.
Student Body Statistics The student body totals 2,583, of whom 2,565 are undergraduates (512 freshmen). 52 percent are women and 48 percent are men. Students come from 23 states and territories and 4 other countries. 86 percent are from Michigan. 10.9 percent are international students.
Expenses for 2008–09 *Application fee:* $35. *One-time mandatory fee:* $125. *State resident tuition:* $7824 full-time, $326 per credit hour part-time. *Nonresident tuition:* $15,648 full-time, $652 per credit hour part-time. *Mandatory fees:* $70 full-time. Full-time tuition and fees vary according to reciprocity agreements. Part-time tuition varies according to course load and reciprocity agreements. *College room and board:* $7567. Room and board charges vary according to board plan and housing facility.
Financial Aid Forms of aid include need-based scholarships, athletic grants, and part-time jobs. The priority application deadline for financial aid is February 21.
Freshman Admission Lake Superior State University requires a high school transcript, SAT or ACT scores, and TOEFL scores for international students. A minimum 2.2 high school GPA is required for some. The application deadline for regular admission is August 15.
Transfer Admission The application deadline for admission is rolling.
Entrance Difficulty Lake Superior State University assesses its entrance difficulty level as moderately difficult. For the fall 2008 freshman class, 88 percent of the applicants were accepted.
For Further Information Contact Ms. Susan Camp, Director of Admissions, Lake Superior State University, 650 West Easterday Avenue, Sault Saint Marie, MI 49783-1699. *Phone:* 906-635-2231 or 888-800-LSSU Ext. 2231 (toll-free). *Fax:* 906-635-6669. *E-mail:* admissions@gw.lssu.edu. *Web site:* http://www.lssu.edu/.

LAWRENCE TECHNOLOGICAL UNIVERSITY

Southfield, Michigan

Lawrence Technological University is a coed, private university, founded in 1932, offering degrees at the associate, bachelor's, master's, and doctoral levels and postbachelor's certificates. It has a 115-acre campus in Southfield near Detroit.

Academic Information The faculty has 423 members (30% full-time), 47% with terminal degrees. The undergraduate student-faculty ratio is

Lawrence Technological University (continued)

11.6:1. The library holds 129,721 titles, 62,000 serial subscriptions, and 170 audiovisual materials. Special programs include academic remediation, services for learning-disabled students, an honors program, cooperative (work-study) education, study abroad, advanced placement credit, ESL programs, double majors, independent study, distance learning, summer session for credit, part-time degree programs (daytime, evenings, weekends, summer), adult/continuing education programs, internships, and arrangement for off-campus study with Macomb University Center, Oakland Technical Center. The most frequently chosen baccalaureate fields are architecture, computer and information sciences, engineering.

Student Body Statistics The student body totals 4,417, of whom 3,019 are undergraduates (308 freshmen). 20 percent are women and 80 percent are men. Students come from 27 states and territories and 11 other countries. 97 percent are from Michigan. 8.3 percent are international students.

Expenses for 2008–09 *Application fee:* $30. *Comprehensive fee:* $30,050 includes full-time tuition ($21,659), mandatory fees ($320), and college room and board ($8071). *College room only:* $5417. Full-time tuition and fees vary according to course level, degree level, location, program, and student level. Room and board charges vary according to board plan and housing facility. *Part-time tuition:* $722 per credit hour. *Part-time mandatory fees:* $160 per term. Part-time tuition and fees vary according to course level, degree level, location, program, and student level.

Financial Aid Forms of aid include need-based and non-need-based scholarships and part-time jobs. The average aided 2007–08 undergraduate received an aid package worth $17,201. The priority application deadline for financial aid is April 1.

Freshman Admission Lawrence Technological University requires a high school transcript, a minimum 2.5 high school GPA, and ACT (preferred). TOEFL scores for international students are recommended. An essay, a minimum 2.75 high school GPA, 1 recommendation, and an interview are required for some. The application deadline for regular admission is August 15.

Transfer Admission The application deadline for admission is August 15.

Entrance Difficulty Lawrence Technological University assesses its entrance difficulty level as moderately difficult. For the fall 2008 freshman class, 51 percent of the applicants were accepted.

For Further Information Contact Office of Admissions, Lawrence Technological University, 21000 West Ten Mile Road, Southfield, MI 48075. *Phone:* 248-204-3160 or 800-225-5588 (toll-free). *Fax:* 248-204-3188. *E-mail:* admissions@ltu.edu. *Web site:* http://www.ltu.edu/.

LEWIS COLLEGE OF BUSINESS

Detroit, Michigan

http://www.lewiscollege.edu/

MADONNA UNIVERSITY

Livonia, Michigan

Madonna University is a coed, private, Roman Catholic, comprehensive institution, founded in 1947, offering degrees at the associate, bachelor's, and master's levels and post-master's and postbachelor's certificates. It has a 49-acre campus in Livonia near Detroit.

Academic Information The faculty has 307 members (37% full-time), 94% with terminal degrees. The undergraduate student-faculty ratio is 13:1. The library holds 199,000 titles, 970 serial subscriptions, and 938 audiovisual materials. Special programs include academic remediation, services for learning-disabled students, cooperative (work-study) education, study abroad, advanced placement credit, accelerated degree programs, ESL programs, double majors, independent study, distance learning, self-designed majors, summer session for credit, part-time degree programs (daytime, evenings, weekends, summer), adult/continuing education programs, internships, and arrangement for off-campus study with 5 members of the Detroit Area Consortium of Catholic Colleges. The most frequently chosen baccalaureate fields are business/marketing, health professions and related sciences, security and protective services.

Student Body Statistics The student body totals 4,035, of whom 2,968 are undergraduates (204 freshmen). 76 percent are women and 24 percent are men. Students come from 16 states and territories and 39 other countries. 99 percent are from Michigan. 7 percent are international students.

Expenses for 2008–09 *Application fee:* $25. *Comprehensive fee:* $18,870 includes full-time tuition ($12,330), mandatory fees ($100), and college room and board ($6440). *College room only:* $2878. Room and board charges vary according to board plan. *Part-time tuition:* $411 per credit hour. *Part-time mandatory fees:* $50 per term.

Financial Aid Forms of aid include need-based and non-need-based scholarships, athletic grants, and part-time jobs. The average aided 2007–08 undergraduate received an aid package worth $7396. The priority application deadline for financial aid is February 15.

Freshman Admission Madonna University requires an essay, a high school transcript, a minimum 2.75 high school GPA, SAT or ACT scores, and TOEFL scores for international students. An interview is recommended. 2 recommendations are required for some. The application deadline for regular admission is rolling.

Transfer Admission The application deadline for admission is rolling.

Entrance Difficulty Madonna University assesses its entrance difficulty level as moderately difficult. For the fall 2008 freshman class, 76 percent of the applicants were accepted.

For Further Information Contact Mr. Mike Quattro, Director of Enrollment Management, Madonna University, 36600 Schoolcraft Road, Livonia, MI 48150-1173. *Phone:* 734-432-5341 or 800-852-4951 (toll-free). *Fax:* 734-432-5393. *E-mail:* muinfo@madonna.edu. *Web site:* http://www.madonna.edu/.

MARYGROVE COLLEGE

Detroit, Michigan

http://www.marygrove.edu/

MICHIGAN CHRISTIAN COLLEGE

See Rochester College.

MICHIGAN JEWISH INSTITUTE

Oak Park, Michigan

Michigan Jewish Institute is a coed, private, four-year college, founded in 1994, offering degrees at the associate and bachelor's levels.

Expenses for 2008–09 *Application fee:* $50. *One-time mandatory fee:* $50. *Tuition:* $10,500 full-time, $350 per credit hour part-time. *Mandatory fees:* $50 per term part-time.

For Further Information Contact Mr. Dov Stein, Michigan Jewish Institute, 25401 Coolidge Highway, Oak Park, MI 48237. *Phone:* 248-414-6900 Ext. 103. *Fax:* 248-414-6907. *E-mail:* dstein@mji.edu. *Web site:* http://www.mji.edu/.

MICHIGAN STATE UNIVERSITY

East Lansing, Michigan

Michigan State University is a coed, public university, founded in 1855, offering degrees at the bachelor's, master's, doctoral, and first professional levels and post-master's certificates. It has a 5,192-acre campus in East Lansing near Detroit.

Academic Information The faculty has 2,997 members (87% full-time), 88% with terminal degrees. The undergraduate student-faculty ratio is 16:1. The library holds 5 million titles, 74,177 serial subscriptions, and 71,316 audiovisual materials. Special programs include academic remediation, services for learning-disabled students, an honors program, cooperative (work-study) education, study abroad, advanced placement credit, accelerated degree programs, Freshman Honors College, ESL

programs, double majors, independent study, distance learning, self-designed majors, summer session for credit, part-time degree programs, adult/continuing education programs, internships, and arrangement for off-campus study with Committee on Institutional Cooperation. The most frequently chosen baccalaureate fields are business/marketing, communications/journalism, social sciences.
Student Body Statistics The student body totals 46,648, of whom 36,337 are undergraduates (7,555 freshmen). 53 percent are women and 47 percent are men. Students come from 55 states and territories and 89 other countries. 92 percent are from Michigan. 6 percent are international students.
Expenses for 2008–09 *Application fee:* $35. *State resident tuition:* $9330 full-time, $311 per credit hour part-time. *Nonresident tuition:* $24,788 full-time, $826.25 per credit hour part-time. *Mandatory fees:* $884 full-time, $312 per term part-time. Both full-time and part-time tuition and fees vary according to course load, degree level, program, and student level. *College room and board:* $7026. *College room only:* $2900. Room and board charges vary according to board plan, housing facility, and student level.
Financial Aid Forms of aid include need-based and non-need-based scholarships, athletic grants, and part-time jobs. The average aided 2008–09 undergraduate received an aid package worth an estimated $10,308. The application deadline for financial aid is continuous.
Freshman Admission Michigan State University requires an essay, a high school transcript, SAT or ACT scores, and TOEFL scores for international students. The application deadline for regular admission is rolling and for early action it is October 6.
Transfer Admission The application deadline for admission is rolling.
Entrance Difficulty Michigan State University assesses its entrance difficulty level as moderately difficult. For the fall 2008 freshman class, 70 percent of the applicants were accepted.
For Further Information Contact James Cotter, Acting Director of Admissions, Michigan State University, 250 Administration Building, East Lansing, MI 48824. *Phone:* 517-355-8332. *Fax:* 517-353-1647. *E-mail:* admis@msu.edu. *Web site:* http://www.msu.edu/.

MICHIGAN TECHNOLOGICAL UNIVERSITY

Houghton, Michigan

Michigan Technological University is a coed, public university, founded in 1885, offering degrees at the associate, bachelor's, master's, and doctoral levels and postbachelor's certificates. It has a 925-acre campus in Houghton.

Academic Information The faculty has 428 members (85% full-time), 80% with terminal degrees. The undergraduate student-faculty ratio is 11:1. The library holds 799,775 titles, 2,777 serial subscriptions, and 6,797 audiovisual materials. Special programs include services for learning-disabled students, an honors program, cooperative (work-study) education, study abroad, advanced placement credit, ESL programs, double majors, independent study, distance learning, self-designed majors, summer session for credit, part-time degree programs, internships, and arrangement for off-campus study with National Student Exchange. The most frequently chosen baccalaureate fields are business/marketing, computer and information sciences, engineering.
Student Body Statistics The student body totals 7,018, of whom 6,034 are undergraduates (1,365 freshmen). 23 percent are women and 77 percent are men. Students come from 47 states and territories and 73 other countries. 77 percent are from Michigan. 6.7 percent are international students.
Expenses for 2008–09 *Application fee:* $0. *State resident tuition:* $9930 full-time, $331 per credit hour part-time. *Nonresident tuition:* $21,690 full-time, $723 per credit hour part-time. *Mandatory fees:* $831 full-time, $415.74 per term part-time. Both full-time and part-time tuition and fees vary according to course load and program. *College room and board:* $7738. *College room only:* $4111. Room and board charges vary according to board plan and housing facility.
Financial Aid Forms of aid include need-based scholarships, athletic grants, and part-time jobs. The average aided 2008–09 undergraduate received an aid package worth an estimated $10,020.
Freshman Admission Michigan Technological University requires a high school transcript, SAT or ACT scores, and TOEFL scores for international students. A minimum 2.75 high school GPA and an interview are recommended. The application deadline for regular admission is rolling.
Transfer Admission The application deadline for admission is rolling.
Entrance Difficulty Michigan Technological University assesses its entrance difficulty level as moderately difficult. For the fall 2008 freshman class, 75 percent of the applicants were accepted.
For Further Information Contact Ms. Allison Carter, Director of Admissions, Michigan Technological University, 1400 Townsend Drive, Houghton, MI 49931-1295. *Phone:* 906-487-2335 or 888-MTU-1885 (toll-free). *Fax:* 906-487-2125. *E-mail:* mtu4u@mtu.edu. *Web site:* http://www.mtu.edu/.

NORTHERN MICHIGAN UNIVERSITY

Marquette, Michigan

Northern Michigan University is a coed, public, comprehensive institution, founded in 1899, offering degrees at the associate, bachelor's, and master's levels and post-master's and postbachelor's certificates. It has a 300-acre campus in Marquette.

Academic Information The faculty has 443 members (71% full-time), 55% with terminal degrees. The undergraduate student-faculty ratio is 23:1. The library holds 615,406 titles, 4,573 serial subscriptions, and 8,251 audiovisual materials. Special programs include academic remediation, services for learning-disabled students, an honors program, study abroad, advanced placement credit, double majors, independent study, distance learning, self-designed majors, summer session for credit, part-time degree programs (daytime, evenings, weekends, summer), adult/continuing education programs, internships, and arrangement for off-campus study with other public institutions in Michigan. The most frequently chosen baccalaureate fields are business/marketing, education, health professions and related sciences.
Student Body Statistics The student body totals 9,111, of whom 8,488 are undergraduates (1,394 freshmen). 53 percent are women and 47 percent are men. Students come from 52 states and territories and 17 other countries. 80 percent are from Michigan. 0.6 percent are international students.
Expenses for 2008–09 *Application fee:* $30. *One-time mandatory fee:* $200. *State resident tuition:* $6504 full-time, $271 per credit hour part-time. *Nonresident tuition:* $10,656 full-time, $444 per credit hour part-time. *Mandatory fees:* $572 full-time, $31.13 per term part-time. *College room and board:* $7636. *College room only:* $3842. Room and board charges vary according to board plan and housing facility.
Financial Aid Forms of aid include need-based and non-need-based scholarships, athletic grants, and part-time jobs. The average aided 2007–08 undergraduate received an aid package worth $7937. The priority application deadline for financial aid is March 1.
Freshman Admission Northern Michigan University requires a high school transcript, SAT or ACT scores, and TOEFL scores for international students. A minimum 2.25 high school GPA is required for some. The application deadline for regular admission is rolling.
Transfer Admission The application deadline for admission is rolling.
Entrance Difficulty Northern Michigan University assesses its entrance difficulty level as minimally difficult. For the fall 2008 freshman class, 78 percent of the applicants were accepted.
For Further Information Contact Ms. Gerri Daniels, Director of Admissions, Northern Michigan University, 1401 Preque Isle Avenue, Marquette, MI 49855. *Phone:* 906-227-2650 or 800-682-9797 (toll-free). *Fax:* 906-227-1747. *E-mail:* admiss@nmu.edu. *Web site:* http://www.nmu.edu/.

NORTHWOOD UNIVERSITY

Midland, Michigan

Northwood University is a coed, private, comprehensive institution, founded in 1959, offering degrees at the associate, bachelor's, and master's levels. It has a 434-acre campus in Midland.

Academic Information The faculty has 129 members (41% full-time), 22% with terminal degrees. The undergraduate student-faculty ratio is 26:1. The library holds 40,063 titles and 335 serial subscriptions. Special

Northwood University (continued)

programs include academic remediation, an honors program, cooperative (work-study) education, study abroad, advanced placement credit, accelerated degree programs, ESL programs, double majors, independent study, distance learning, summer session for credit, part-time degree programs (daytime, evenings, weekends, summer), external degree programs, adult/continuing education programs, internships, and arrangement for off-campus study. The most frequently chosen baccalaureate fields are business/marketing, communications/journalism, parks and recreation.

Student Body Statistics The student body totals 2,269, of whom 1,950 are undergraduates (442 freshmen). 38 percent are women and 62 percent are men. Students come from 31 states and territories and 32 other countries. 89 percent are from Michigan. 7.9 percent are international students.

Expenses for 2008–09 *Application fee:* $25. *Comprehensive fee:* $25,092 includes full-time tuition ($16,620), mandatory fees ($924), and college room and board ($7548). *College room only:* $3900. *Part-time tuition:* $346 per credit hour.

Financial Aid Forms of aid include need-based and non-need-based scholarships, athletic grants, and part-time jobs. The average aided 2008–09 undergraduate received an aid package worth an estimated $14,635. The application deadline for financial aid is continuous.

Freshman Admission Northwood University requires an essay, a high school transcript, SAT or ACT scores, and TOEFL scores for international students. 1 recommendation and an interview are recommended. The application deadline for regular admission is rolling.

Transfer Admission The application deadline for admission is rolling.

Entrance Difficulty Northwood University assesses its entrance difficulty level as moderately difficult. For the fall 2008 freshman class, 75 percent of the applicants were accepted.

For Further Information Contact Mr. Daniel F. Toland, Dean of Admission, Northwood University, 4000 Whiting Drive, Midland, MI 48640. *Phone:* 989-837-4273 or 800-457-7878 (toll-free). *Fax:* 989-837-4490. *E-mail:* miadmit@northwood.edu. *Web site:* http://www.northwood.edu/.

OAKLAND UNIVERSITY

Rochester, Michigan

Oakland University is a coed, public university, founded in 1957, offering degrees at the bachelor's, master's, and doctoral levels and post-master's and postbachelor's certificates. It has a 1,444-acre campus in Rochester near Detroit.

Academic Information The faculty has 976 members (51% full-time), 59% with terminal degrees. The undergraduate student-faculty ratio is 23:1. The library holds 856,760 titles, 20,490 serial subscriptions, and 21,323 audiovisual materials. Special programs include academic remediation, services for learning-disabled students, an honors program, cooperative (work-study) education, study abroad, advanced placement credit, accelerated degree programs, ESL programs, double majors, independent study, distance learning, self-designed majors, summer session for credit, part-time degree programs (daytime, evenings, weekends, summer), internships, and arrangement for off-campus study with Macomb Community College, Beaumont Hospital-Troy. The most frequently chosen baccalaureate fields are business/marketing, communications/journalism, health professions and related sciences.

Student Body Statistics The student body totals 18,169, of whom 14,397 are undergraduates (2,350 freshmen). 61 percent are women and 39 percent are men. Students come from 30 states and territories and 45 other countries. 99 percent are from Michigan. 0.9 percent are international students.

Expenses for 2008–09 *Application fee:* $0. *State resident tuition:* $8055 full-time, $268.50 per credit part-time. *Nonresident tuition:* $18,802 full-time, $626.75 per credit part-time. Both full-time and part-time tuition varies according to program and student level. *College room and board:* $7105. Room and board charges vary according to housing facility.

Financial Aid Forms of aid include need-based and non-need-based scholarships, athletic grants, and part-time jobs. The average aided 2007–08 undergraduate received an aid package worth $9607.

Freshman Admission Oakland University requires a high school transcript, a minimum 2.5 high school GPA, and TOEFL scores for international students. SAT or ACT scores are recommended. A minimum 3.0 high school GPA, an interview, and audition are required for some. The application deadline for regular admission is rolling.

Transfer Admission The application deadline for admission is rolling.

Entrance Difficulty Oakland University assesses its entrance difficulty level as moderately difficult. For the fall 2008 freshman class, 85 percent of the applicants were accepted.

For Further Information Contact Ms. Eleanor Reynolds, Interim Assistant Vice President, Student Affairs, Oakland University, 101 North Foundation Hall, Rochester, MI 48309-4401. *Phone:* 248-370-3364 or 800-OAK-UNIV (toll-free). *Fax:* 248-370-4462. *E-mail:* ouinfo@oakland.edu. *Web site:* http://www.oakland.edu/.

OLIVET COLLEGE

Olivet, Michigan

Olivet College is a coed, private, comprehensive institution, founded in 1844, affiliated with the Congregational Christian Church, offering degrees at the bachelor's and master's levels. It has a 92-acre campus in Olivet.

Academic Information The library holds 90,000 titles and 415 serial subscriptions. Special programs include services for learning-disabled students, an honors program, cooperative (work-study) education, study abroad, advanced placement credit, accelerated degree programs, double majors, independent study, self-designed majors, summer session for credit, part-time degree programs (daytime, evenings, summer), and internships.

Student Body Statistics The student body totals 1,049, of whom 1,004 are undergraduates.

Expenses for 2008–09 *Application fee:* $25. *Comprehensive fee:* $26,016 includes full-time tuition ($19,244) and college room and board ($6772). *College room only:* $3472. Full-time tuition varies according to reciprocity agreements. Room and board charges vary according to board plan and housing facility. *Part-time tuition:* varies with course load, reciprocity agreements.

Financial Aid Forms of aid include need-based and non-need-based scholarships and part-time jobs. The average aided 2008–09 undergraduate received an aid package worth an estimated $16,731. The application deadline for financial aid is continuous.

Freshman Admission Olivet College requires a high school transcript, SAT or ACT scores, and TOEFL scores for international students. A minimum 2.6 high school GPA is recommended. An essay, recommendations, and an interview are required for some. The application deadline for regular admission is rolling.

Transfer Admission The application deadline for admission is rolling.

Entrance Difficulty Olivet College assesses its entrance difficulty level as minimally difficult.

For Further Information Contact Mr. Larry Vallar, Vice President for Enrollment Management, Olivet College, 320 South Main Street, Olivet, MI 49076. *Phone:* 269-749-7635 or 800-456-7189 (toll-free). *Fax:* 269-749-6617. *E-mail:* admissions@olivetcollege.edu. *Web site:* http://www.olivetcollege.edu/.

ROCHESTER COLLEGE

Rochester Hills, Michigan

Rochester College is a coed, private, comprehensive institution, founded in 1959, affiliated with the Church of Christ, offering degrees at the associate, bachelor's, and master's levels. It has an 83-acre campus in Rochester Hills near Detroit.

Expenses for 2008–09 *Application fee:* $25. *Comprehensive fee:* $23,630 includes full-time tuition ($15,040), mandatory fees ($1570), and college room and board ($7020). *College room only:* $3780. Full-time tuition and fees vary according to course load. Room and board charges vary according to board plan and housing facility. *Part-time tuition:* $488 per credit hour. *Part-time mandatory fees:* $785 per term. Part-time tuition and fees vary according to course load.

For Further Information Contact Mr. Larry Norman, Dean of Admissions, Rochester College, 800 West Avon Road, Rochester Hills, MI 48307-2764. *Phone:* 248-218-2190 or 800-521-6010 (toll-free). *Fax:* 248-218-2035. *E-mail:* admissions@rc.edu. *Web site:* http://www.rc.edu/.

SACRED HEART MAJOR SEMINARY

Detroit, Michigan

Sacred Heart Major Seminary is a coed, private, Roman Catholic, comprehensive institution, founded in 1919, offering degrees at the associate, bachelor's, master's, and first professional levels and postbachelor's certificates. It has a 24-acre campus in Detroit.

For Further Information Contact Fr. Michael Byrnes, Vice Rector, Sacred Heart Major Seminary, 2701 Chicago Boulevard, Detroit, MI 48206. *Phone:* 313-883-8552. *Fax:* 313-868-6400. *Web site:* http://www.archdioceseofdetroit.org/shms/shms.htm.

SAGINAW CHIPPEWA TRIBAL COLLEGE

Mount Pleasant, Michigan

http://www.sagchip.org/tribalcollege/

SAGINAW VALLEY STATE UNIVERSITY

University Center, Michigan

Saginaw Valley State University is a coed, public, comprehensive institution, founded in 1963, offering degrees at the bachelor's and master's levels and post-master's certificates. It has a 782-acre campus in University Center.

Academic Information The faculty has 594 members (49% full-time). The undergraduate student-faculty ratio is 20:1. The library holds 241,661 titles, 23,741 serial subscriptions, and 25,099 audiovisual materials. Special programs include academic remediation, services for learning-disabled students, an honors program, cooperative (work-study) education, study abroad, advanced placement credit, accelerated degree programs, ESL programs, double majors, independent study, distance learning, self-designed majors, summer session for credit, part-time degree programs (daytime, evenings, summer), adult/continuing education programs, and internships. The most frequently chosen baccalaureate fields are business/marketing, education, health professions and related sciences.

Student Body Statistics The student body totals 9,837, of whom 8,190 are undergraduates (1,661 freshmen). 58 percent are women and 42 percent are men. Students come from 18 states and territories and 38 other countries. 99 percent are from Michigan. 2.7 percent are international students.

Expenses for 2008–09 *Application fee:* $25. *State resident tuition:* $6054 full-time, $201.80 per credit hour part-time. *Nonresident tuition:* $14,453 full-time, $481.75 per credit hour part-time. *Mandatory fees:* $438 full-time, $14.60 per credit hour part-time. Both full-time and part-time tuition and fees vary according to course level, course load, location, and program. *College room and board:* $6830. *College room only:* $4100. Room and board charges vary according to board plan, housing facility, and student level.

Financial Aid Forms of aid include need-based and non-need-based scholarships, athletic grants, and part-time jobs. The average aided 2007–08 undergraduate received an aid package worth $6880.

Freshman Admission Saginaw Valley State University requires a high school transcript, ACT scores, and TOEFL scores for international students. A minimum 2.5 high school GPA is recommended. The application deadline for regular admission is rolling.

Transfer Admission The application deadline for admission is rolling.

Entrance Difficulty Saginaw Valley State University assesses its entrance difficulty level as moderately difficult. For the fall 2008 freshman class, 88 percent of the applicants were accepted.

For Further Information Contact Jennfier Pahl, Director of Admissions, Saginaw Valley State University, 7400 Bay Road, University Center, MI 48710-0001. *Phone:* 989-964-4200 or 800-968-9500 (toll-free). *Fax:* 989-790-0180. *E-mail:* admissions@svsu.edu. *Web site:* http://www.svsu.edu/.

SIENA HEIGHTS UNIVERSITY

Adrian, Michigan

Siena Heights University is a coed, private, Roman Catholic, comprehensive institution, founded in 1919, offering degrees at the associate, bachelor's, and master's levels. It has a 140-acre campus in Adrian near Detroit.

Academic Information The faculty has 216 members (31% full-time). The undergraduate student-faculty ratio is 12:1. The library holds 142,000 titles, 300 serial subscriptions, and 400 audiovisual materials. Special programs include academic remediation, services for learning-disabled students, cooperative (work-study) education, study abroad, advanced placement credit, accelerated degree programs, ESL programs, double majors, independent study, distance learning, self-designed majors, summer session for credit, part-time degree programs, internships, and arrangement for off-campus study with Adrian College. The most frequently chosen baccalaureate fields are business/marketing, engineering technologies, health professions and related sciences.

Student Body Statistics The student body totals 2,307, of whom 1,954 are undergraduates (205 freshmen). 58 percent are women and 42 percent are men. Students come from 7 states and territories and 27 other countries. 91 percent are from Michigan. 1.2 percent are international students.

Expenses for 2009–10 *Application fee:* $25. *Comprehensive fee:* $26,280 includes full-time tuition ($18,610), mandatory fees ($600), and college room and board ($7070). *Part-time tuition:* $375 per semester hour. *Part-time mandatory fees:* $125 per term.

Financial Aid Forms of aid include need-based and non-need-based scholarships and part-time jobs. The priority application deadline for financial aid is March 15.

Freshman Admission Siena Heights University requires a high school transcript, transfer GPA 2.0, SAT or ACT scores, and TOEFL scores for international students. A minimum 2.5 high school GPA and an interview are recommended. An essay and an interview are required for some. The application deadline for regular admission is rolling.

Transfer Admission The application deadline for admission is rolling.

Entrance Difficulty Siena Heights University assesses its entrance difficulty level as moderately difficult; minimally difficult for transfers. For the fall 2008 freshman class, 75 percent of the applicants were accepted.

For Further Information Contact Ms. Sara Johnson, Director of Admissions, Siena Heights University, 1247 East Siena Heights Drive, Adrian, MI 49221-1796. *Phone:* 517-264-7185 or 800-521-0009 (toll-free). *Fax:* 517-264-7745. *E-mail:* admissions@sienahts.edu. *Web site:* http://www.sienaheights.edu/.

SPRING ARBOR UNIVERSITY

Spring Arbor, Michigan

Spring Arbor University is a coed, private, Free Methodist, comprehensive institution, founded in 1873, offering degrees at the bachelor's and master's levels and postbachelor's certificates. It has a 123-acre campus in Spring Arbor.

Academic Information The faculty has 129 members (64% full-time), 49% with terminal degrees. The undergraduate student-faculty ratio is 15:1. The library holds 111,736 titles, 665 serial subscriptions, and 3,775 audiovisual materials. Special programs include academic remediation, services for learning-disabled students, an honors program, study abroad, advanced placement credit, accelerated degree programs, ESL programs, double majors, independent study, distance learning, self-designed majors, summer session for credit, part-time degree programs (daytime, evenings, weekends, summer), external degree programs, adult/continuing education

Spring Arbor University (continued)

programs, internships, and arrangement for off-campus study with Christian College Consortium. The most frequently chosen baccalaureate fields are business/marketing, education, family and consumer sciences.

Student Body Statistics The student body totals 3,973, of whom 2,737 are undergraduates (381 freshmen). 67 percent are women and 33 percent are men. Students come from 31 states and territories and 7 other countries. 86 percent are from Michigan. 0.7 percent are international students.

Expenses for 2008–09 *Application fee:* $30. *Comprehensive fee:* $25,890 includes full-time tuition ($18,700), mandatory fees ($540), and college room and board ($6650). *College room only:* $3110. Full-time tuition and fees vary according to course load, degree level, and program. Room and board charges vary according to board plan and housing facility. *Part-time tuition:* $470 per credit hour. *Part-time mandatory fees:* $225 per term. Part-time tuition and fees vary according to course load, degree level, program, and reciprocity agreements.

Financial Aid Forms of aid include need-based and non-need-based scholarships and part-time jobs. The average aided 2008–09 undergraduate received an aid package worth an estimated $21,266. The priority application deadline for financial aid is March 1.

Freshman Admission Spring Arbor University requires a high school transcript, SAT or ACT scores, and TOEFL scores for international students. A minimum 2.6 high school GPA, guidance counselor's evaluation form, and ACT scores are recommended. An essay and an interview are required for some. The application deadline for regular admission is August 1.

Transfer Admission The application deadline for admission is rolling.

Entrance Difficulty Spring Arbor University assesses its entrance difficulty level as moderately difficult. For the fall 2008 freshman class, 78 percent of the applicants were accepted.

For Further Information Contact Director of, Spring Arbor University, 106 East Main Street, Spring Arbor, MI 49283-9799. *Phone:* 517-750-1200 Ext. 1468 or 800-968-0011 (toll-free). *Fax:* 517-750-6620. *E-mail:* admissions@arbor.edu. *Web site:* http://www.arbor.edu/.

UNIVERSITY OF DETROIT MERCY

Detroit, Michigan

http://www.udmercy.edu/

UNIVERSITY OF MICHIGAN

Ann Arbor, Michigan

University of Michigan is a coed, public university, founded in 1817, offering degrees at the bachelor's, master's, doctoral, and first professional levels and post-master's and postbachelor's certificates. It has an 8,070-acre campus in Ann Arbor near Detroit.

Academic Information The faculty has 3,005 members (81% full-time), 88% with terminal degrees. The undergraduate student-faculty ratio is 15:1. The library holds 8 million titles, 74,022 serial subscriptions, and 102,217 audiovisual materials. Special programs include services for learning-disabled students, an honors program, cooperative (work-study) education, study abroad, advanced placement credit, accelerated degree programs, ESL programs, double majors, independent study, distance learning, self-designed majors, summer session for credit, part-time degree programs, adult/continuing education programs, internships, and arrangement for off-campus study with Committee on Institutional Cooperation. The most frequently chosen baccalaureate fields are engineering, psychology, social sciences.

Student Body Statistics The student body totals 41,028, of whom 25,994 are undergraduates (5,783 freshmen). 50 percent are women and 50 percent are men. Students come from 55 states and territories and 109 other countries. 65 percent are from Michigan. 5.3 percent are international students.

Expenses for 2008–09 *Application fee:* $40. *State resident tuition:* $11,738 full-time, $423 per credit hour part-time. *Nonresident tuition:* $34,230 full-time, $1341 per credit hour part-time. *Mandatory fees:* $189 full-time, $95 per term part-time. Full-time tuition and fees vary according to program and student level. Part-time tuition and fees vary according to course load, program, and student level. *College room and board:* $8590. Room and board charges vary according to board plan and housing facility.

Financial Aid Forms of aid include need-based and non-need-based scholarships, athletic grants, and part-time jobs. The average aided 2007–08 undergraduate received an aid package worth $11,408. The application deadline for financial aid is May 30 with a priority deadline of April 30.

Freshman Admission University of Michigan requires an essay, a high school transcript, SAT or ACT scores, and TOEFL scores for international students. An interview and SAT Subject Test scores are required for some. The application deadline for regular admission is February 1 and for early action it is November 1.

Transfer Admission The application deadline for admission is February 1.

Entrance Difficulty University of Michigan assesses its entrance difficulty level as very difficult. For the fall 2008 freshman class, 42 percent of the applicants were accepted.

For Further Information Contact Mr. Ted Spencer, Director of Undergraduate Admissions, University of Michigan, 1220 Student Activities Building, 515 East Jefferson, Ann Arbor, MI 48109-1316. *Phone:* 734-764-7433. *Fax:* 734-936-0740. *E-mail:* ugadmiss@umich.edu. *Web site:* http://www.umich.edu/.

UNIVERSITY OF MICHIGAN–DEARBORN

Dearborn, Michigan

University of Michigan–Dearborn is a coed, public, comprehensive unit of University of Michigan System, founded in 1959, offering degrees at the bachelor's and master's levels and postbachelor's certificates. It has a 210-acre campus in Dearborn near Detroit.

Academic Information The faculty has 487 members (60% full-time), 66% with terminal degrees. The undergraduate student-faculty ratio is 17:1. The library holds 366,577 titles, 589 serial subscriptions, and 5,737 audiovisual materials. Special programs include academic remediation, services for learning-disabled students, an honors program, cooperative (work-study) education, study abroad, advanced placement credit, accelerated degree programs, double majors, independent study, distance learning, self-designed majors, summer session for credit, part-time degree programs (daytime, evenings, weekends, summer), adult/continuing education programs, internships, and arrangement for off-campus study with University of Michigan. The most frequently chosen baccalaureate fields are business/marketing, education, engineering.

Student Body Statistics The student body totals 8,311, of whom 6,588 are undergraduates (953 freshmen). 53 percent are women and 47 percent are men. Students come from 14 states and territories and 24 other countries. 100 percent are from Michigan. 1 percent are international students.

Expenses for 2008–09 *Application fee:* $30. *State resident tuition:* $8035 full-time, $317.95 per credit hour part-time. *Nonresident tuition:* $18,141 full-time, $722 per credit hour part-time. *Mandatory fees:* $494 full-time, $153 per term part-time. Both full-time and part-time tuition and fees vary according to course level, course load, program, and student level.

Financial Aid Forms of aid include need-based and non-need-based scholarships, athletic grants, and part-time jobs. The average aided 2008–09 undergraduate received an aid package worth an estimated $10,056.

Freshman Admission University of Michigan–Dearborn requires a high school transcript, a minimum 3.0 high school GPA, SAT or ACT scores, and TOEFL scores for international students. An interview is required for some. The application deadline for regular admission is rolling.

Transfer Admission The application deadline for admission is rolling.

Entrance Difficulty University of Michigan–Dearborn assesses its entrance difficulty level as moderately difficult. For the fall 2008 freshman class, 61 percent of the applicants were accepted.

For Further Information Contact Mr. Christopher Tremblay, Director of Admissions and Orientation, University of Michigan–Dearborn, 4901 Evergreen Road, Dearborn, MI 48128-1491. *Phone:* 313-593-5100. *Fax:* 313-436-9167. *E-mail:* admissions@umd.umich.edu. *Web site:* http://www.umd.umich.edu/.

UNIVERSITY OF MICHIGAN–FLINT

Flint, Michigan

University of Michigan–Flint is a coed, public, comprehensive unit of University of Michigan System, founded in 1956, offering degrees at the bachelor's, master's, and doctoral levels. It has a 72-acre campus in Flint near Detroit.

Academic Information The faculty has 469 members (52% full-time), 42% with terminal degrees. The undergraduate student-faculty ratio is 16:1. The library holds 266,696 titles, 907 serial subscriptions, and 23,039 audiovisual materials. Special programs include academic remediation, services for learning-disabled students, an honors program, cooperative (work-study) education, study abroad, advanced placement credit, accelerated degree programs, ESL programs, double majors, independent study, distance learning, self-designed majors, summer session for credit, part-time degree programs (daytime, evenings, weekends, summer), adult/continuing education programs, internships, and arrangement for off-campus study. The most frequently chosen baccalaureate fields are business/marketing, education, health professions and related sciences.
Student Body Statistics The student body totals 7,260, of whom 6,155 are undergraduates (909 freshmen). 62 percent are women and 38 percent are men. Students come from 32 states and territories and 25 other countries. 98 percent are from Michigan. 1.5 percent are international students.
Expenses for 2008–09 *Application fee:* $30. *One-time mandatory fee:* $30. *State resident tuition:* $7407 full-time, $292 per credit hour part-time. *Nonresident tuition:* $14,454 full-time, $584 per credit hour part-time. *Mandatory fees:* $368 full-time, $141 per term part-time. Both full-time and part-time tuition and fees vary according to course level, course load, degree level, program, reciprocity agreements, and student level. *College room and board:* $6800. *College room only:* $4200. Room and board charges vary according to board plan.
Financial Aid Forms of aid include need-based and non-need-based scholarships and part-time jobs. The average aided 2007–08 undergraduate received an aid package worth $7656. The priority application deadline for financial aid is March 1.
Freshman Admission University of Michigan–Flint requires a high school transcript, a minimum 2.0 high school GPA, SAT or ACT scores, and TOEFL scores for international students.
Transfer Admission The application deadline for admission is August 19.
Entrance Difficulty University of Michigan–Flint assesses its entrance difficulty level as moderately difficult. For the fall 2008 freshman class, 87 percent of the applicants were accepted.
For Further Information Contact Ms. Kimberley Buster-Williams, Director of Admissions, University of Michigan–Flint, 303 East Kearsley Street, 245 UPAV, Flint, MI 48502-1950. *Phone:* 810-762-3300 or 800-942-5636 (toll-free in-state). *Fax:* 810-762-3272. *E-mail:* admissions@umflint.edu. *Web site:* http://www.umflint.edu/.

UNIVERSITY OF PHOENIX–DETROIT CAMPUS

Southfield, Michigan

http://www.phoenix.edu/

UNIVERSITY OF PHOENIX–METRO DETROIT CAMPUS

Troy, Michigan

University of Phoenix–Metro Detroit Campus is a coed, proprietary, comprehensive institution, offering degrees at the bachelor's and master's levels.

Academic Information The faculty has 329 members (12% full-time), 25% with terminal degrees. The library holds 1,759 titles and 692 serial subscriptions. Special programs include services for learning-disabled students, advanced placement credit, accelerated degree programs, independent study, distance learning, external degree programs, and adult/continuing education programs. The most frequently chosen baccalaureate fields are business/marketing, computer and information sciences, security and protective services.
Student Body Statistics The student body totals 2,547, of whom 2,018 are undergraduates (221 freshmen). 67 percent are women and 33 percent are men. 2.2 percent are international students.
Expenses for 2008–09 *Application fee:* $0. *Tuition:* $12,690 full-time. Full-time tuition varies according to course level and course load.
Financial Aid Forms of aid include need-based and non-need-based scholarships. The application deadline for financial aid is continuous.
Freshman Admission University of Phoenix–Metro Detroit Campus requires 1 recommendation and TOEFL scores for international students. A high school transcript is required for some. The application deadline for regular admission is rolling.
Transfer Admission The application deadline for admission is rolling.
Entrance Difficulty University of Phoenix–Metro Detroit Campus has an open admission policy.
For Further Information Contact Ms. Audra McQuarie, Registrar/Executive Director, University of Phoenix–Metro Detroit Campus, 4035 South Riverpoint Parkway, Mail Stop CF-L101, Phoenix, AZ 85040. *Phone:* 480-557-6151, 800-776-4867 (toll-free in-state), or 800-228-7240 (toll-free out-of-state). *Fax:* 480-643-3068. *E-mail:* audra.mcquarie@phoenix.edu. *Web site:* http://www.phoenix.edu/.

UNIVERSITY OF PHOENIX–WEST MICHIGAN CAMPUS

Walker, Michigan

University of Phoenix–West Michigan Campus is a coed, proprietary, comprehensive institution, founded in 2000, offering degrees at the bachelor's and master's levels.

Academic Information The faculty has 149 members (9% full-time), 16% with terminal degrees. The library holds 16,781 serial subscriptions. Special programs include services for learning-disabled students, advanced placement credit, accelerated degree programs, independent study, distance learning, external degree programs, and adult/continuing education programs. The most frequently chosen baccalaureate fields are business/marketing, computer and information sciences, public administration and social services.
Student Body Statistics The student body totals 524, of whom 456 are undergraduates (69 freshmen). 65 percent are women and 35 percent are men. 2.4 percent are international students.
Expenses for 2008–09 *Tuition:* $12,000 full-time. Full-time tuition varies according to course level and course load.
Financial Aid Forms of aid include need-based and non-need-based scholarships. The average aided 2007–08 undergraduate received an aid package worth $6821. The application deadline for financial aid is continuous.
Freshman Admission University of Phoenix–West Michigan Campus requires 1 recommendation and TOEFL scores for international students. A high school transcript is required for some. The application deadline for regular admission is rolling.
Transfer Admission The application deadline for admission is rolling.
Entrance Difficulty University of Phoenix–West Michigan Campus has an open admission policy.
For Further Information Contact Ms. Audra McQuarie, Registrar/Executive Director, University of Phoenix–West Michigan Campus, 4035 South Riverpoint Parkway, Mail Stop CF-L101, Phoenix, AZ 85040. *Phone:* 480-557-6151, 800-776-4867 (toll-free in-state), or 800-228-7240 (toll-free out-of-state). *Fax:* 480-643-3068. *E-mail:* audra.mcquarie@phoenix.edu. *Web site:* http://www.phoenix.edu/.

WALSH COLLEGE OF ACCOUNTANCY AND BUSINESS ADMINISTRATION

Troy, Michigan

Walsh College of Accountancy and Business Administration is a coed, private, upper-level institution, founded in 1922, offering degrees at the bachelor's and master's levels. It has a 29-acre campus in Troy near Detroit.

Academic Information The faculty has 178 members (10% full-time), 33% with terminal degrees. The undergraduate student-faculty ratio is 17:1. The library holds 26,300 titles, 8,210 serial subscriptions, and 121 audiovisual materials. Special programs include services for learning-disabled students, advanced placement credit, double majors, independent study, distance learning, summer session for credit, part-time degree programs, adult/continuing education programs, internships, and arrangement for off-campus study. The most frequently chosen baccalaureate fields are business/marketing, computer and information sciences.

Student Body Statistics The student body totals 3,106, of whom 1,025 are undergraduates. 55 percent are women and 45 percent are men. Students come from 6 states and territories and 37 other countries. 100 percent are from Michigan. 3.9 percent are international students.

Expenses for 2008–09 *Application fee:* $25. *Tuition:* $10,584 full-time, $294 per semester hour part-time. *Mandatory fees:* $375 full-time, $125 per term part-time.

Financial Aid Forms of aid include need-based and non-need-based scholarships and part-time jobs. The application deadline for financial aid is continuous.

Transfer Admission Walsh College of Accountancy and Business Administration requires a college transcript and a minimum 2.0 college GPA. Standardized test scores are required for some. The application deadline for admission is rolling.

Entrance Difficulty Walsh College of Accountancy and Business Administration has an open admission policy.

For Further Information Contact Mr. Jeremy Guc, Director of Admissions and Advising, Walsh College of Accountancy and Business Administration, PO Box 7006, Troy, MI 48007-7006. *Phone:* 248-823-1344 or 800-925-7401 (toll-free in-state). *Fax:* 248-823-1611. *E-mail:* admissions@walshcollege.edu. *Web site:* http://www.walshcollege.edu/.

WAYNE STATE UNIVERSITY

Detroit, Michigan

Wayne State University is a coed, public university, founded in 1868, offering degrees at the bachelor's, master's, doctoral, and first professional levels and post-master's and postbachelor's certificates. It has a 203-acre campus in Detroit.

Academic Information The faculty has 1,971 members (52% full-time), 43% with terminal degrees. The undergraduate student-faculty ratio is 17:1. The library holds 3 million titles, 45,200 serial subscriptions, and 77,293 audiovisual materials. Special programs include academic remediation, services for learning-disabled students, an honors program, cooperative (work-study) education, study abroad, advanced placement credit, accelerated degree programs, Freshman Honors College, ESL programs, double majors, independent study, distance learning, summer session for credit, part-time degree programs (daytime, evenings, weekends, summer), adult/continuing education programs, internships, and arrangement for off-campus study with University of Michigan, University of Windsor. The most frequently chosen baccalaureate fields are business/marketing, education, health professions and related sciences.

Student Body Statistics The student body totals 31,016, of whom 20,122 are undergraduates (2,917 freshmen). 58 percent are women and 42 percent are men. Students come from 36 states and territories and 45 other countries. 98 percent are from Michigan. 3.6 percent are international students.

Expenses for 2008–09 *Application fee:* $30. *State resident tuition:* $7182 full-time, $239.40 per credit hour part-time. *Nonresident tuition:* $16,452 full-time, $548.40 per credit hour part-time. *Mandatory fees:* $927 full-time, $19.40 per credit hour part-time, $172.50 per term part-time. Both full-time and part-time tuition and fees vary according to course load and student level. *College room and board:* $6932. Room and board charges vary according to board plan and housing facility.

Financial Aid Forms of aid include need-based and non-need-based scholarships, athletic grants, and part-time jobs. The average aided 2007–08 undergraduate received an aid package worth $12,357. The application deadline for financial aid is April 30 with a priority deadline of February 15.

Freshman Admission Wayne State University requires a high school transcript, a minimum 2.0 high school GPA, SAT or ACT scores, and TOEFL scores for international students. An interview and a portfolio are required for some. The application deadline for regular admission is August 1.

Transfer Admission The application deadline for admission is August 1.

Entrance Difficulty Wayne State University assesses its entrance difficulty level as moderately difficult; minimally difficult for transfers. For the fall 2008 freshman class, 79 percent of the applicants were accepted.

For Further Information Contact Ms. Susan Zwieg, Director, Undergraduate Admissions, Wayne State University, 3E HNJ, Detroit, MI 48202. *Phone:* 313-577-3577 or 877-WSU-INFO (toll-free). *Fax:* 313-577-7536. *E-mail:* admissions@wayne.edu. *Web site:* http://www.wayne.edu/.

WESTERN MICHIGAN UNIVERSITY

Kalamazoo, Michigan

Western Michigan University is a coed, public university, founded in 1903, offering degrees at the bachelor's, master's, and doctoral levels and post-master's and postbachelor's certificates (specialist). It has a 1,200-acre campus in Kalamazoo.

Academic Information The faculty has 1,436 members (65% full-time). The undergraduate student-faculty ratio is 19:1. The library holds 3 million titles, 12,711 serial subscriptions, and 29,615 audiovisual materials. Special programs include academic remediation, services for learning-disabled students, an honors program, study abroad, advanced placement credit, accelerated degree programs, Freshman Honors College, ESL programs, double majors, independent study, distance learning, self-designed majors, summer session for credit, part-time degree programs (daytime, evenings, weekends, summer), adult/continuing education programs, internships, and arrangement for off-campus study with Kalamazoo College, Kalamazoo Valley Community College, Davenport College of Business. The most frequently chosen baccalaureate fields are business/marketing, communications/journalism, education.

Student Body Statistics The student body totals 24,818, of whom 19,854 are undergraduates (3,828 freshmen). 50 percent are women and 50 percent are men. Students come from 42 states and territories and 59 other countries. 95 percent are from Michigan. 2.7 percent are international students.

Expenses for 2008–09 *Application fee:* $35. *One-time mandatory fee:* $300. *State resident tuition:* $7220 full-time, $245.06 per credit part-time. *Nonresident tuition:* $17,712 full-time, $601.15 per credit part-time. *Mandatory fees:* $708 full-time, $190.25 per term part-time. Both full-time and part-time tuition and fees vary according to course load, location, and student level. *College room and board:* $7377. *College room only:* $3689. Room and board charges vary according to board plan.

Financial Aid Forms of aid include need-based and non-need-based scholarships, athletic grants, and part-time jobs. The average aided 2007–08 undergraduate received an aid package worth $13,000. The priority application deadline for financial aid is March 15.

Freshman Admission Western Michigan University requires a high school transcript, a minimum 2.0 high school GPA, SAT or ACT scores, and TOEFL scores for international students. An interview is required for some. The application deadline for regular admission is rolling.

Transfer Admission The application deadline for admission is August 1.

Entrance Difficulty Western Michigan University assesses its entrance difficulty level as moderately difficult. For the fall 2008 freshman class, 85 percent of the applicants were accepted.
For Further Information Contact Ms. Penny Bundy, Director, Office of Admissions and Orientation, Western Michigan University, 1903 West Michigan Avenue, Kalamazoo, MI 49008-5211. *Phone:* 269-387-2000. *Fax:* 269-387-2096. *E-mail:* ask-wmu@wmich.edu. *Web site:* http://www.wmich.edu/.

See page 282 for the Close-Up.

YESHIVA GEDOLAH OF GREATER DETROIT
Oak Park, Michigan

Yeshiva Gedolah of Greater Detroit is a men's, private, Jewish, comprehensive institution, founded in 1985, offering degrees at the bachelor's, master's, and doctoral levels. It has a 1-acre campus in Oak Park near Detroit.

Student Body Statistics The student body totals 64, of whom 57 are undergraduates.
Financial Aid Forms of aid include non-need-based scholarships and part-time jobs.
Entrance Difficulty For the fall 2008 freshman class, 100 percent of the applicants were accepted.
For Further Information Contact Rabbi P. Rushnawitz, Director, Yeshiva Gedolah of Greater Detroit, 24600 Greenfield, Oak Park, MI 48237-1544.

Minnesota

ACADEMY COLLEGE
Minneapolis, Minnesota

Academy College is a coed, proprietary, four-year college, founded in 1936, offering degrees at the associate and bachelor's levels.

For Further Information Contact Ms. Tracey Schantz, Director, Academy College, 1101 East 78th Street, Suite 100, Minneapolis, MN 55420. *Phone:* 952-851-0066 or 800-292-9149 (toll-free). *Fax:* 952-851-0094. *E-mail:* admissions@academycollege.edu. *Web site:* http://www.academycollege.edu/.

ARGOSY UNIVERSITY, TWIN CITIES
Eagan, Minnesota

Argosy University, Twin Cities is a coed, proprietary unit of Education Management Corporation, founded in 1961, offering degrees at the associate, bachelor's, master's, and doctoral levels and post-master's certificates.

Expenses for 2009–10 Tuition varies by program. Students should contact Argosy University for tuition information.
For Further Information Contact Admissions Director, Argosy University, Twin Cities, 1515 Central Parkway, Eagan, MN 55121. *Phone:* 651-846-2882 or 888-844-2004 (toll-free). *Fax:* 651-994-7956. *Web site:* http://www.argosy.edu/twincities.

THE ART INSTITUTES INTERNATIONAL MINNESOTA
Minneapolis, Minnesota

The Art Institutes International Minnesota is a coed, proprietary, four-year college of Education Management Corporation, founded in 1964, offering degrees at the associate and bachelor's levels.

Expenses for 2009–10 Tuition cost varies by program. Prospective students should contact the school for current tuition costs. Other charges include a starting kit for all first-quarter students. Kits vary in price, depending on the program of study.
For Further Information Contact Director of Admissions, The Art Institutes International Minnesota, 15 South 9th Street, Minneapolis, MN 55402. *Phone:* 612-332-3361 or 800-777-3643 (toll-free). *Fax:* 612-332-3934. *Web site:* http://www.artinstitutes.edu/minneapolis/.

AUGSBURG COLLEGE
Minneapolis, Minnesota

Augsburg College is a coed, private, Lutheran, comprehensive institution, founded in 1869, offering degrees at the bachelor's and master's levels and post-master's and postbachelor's certificates. It has a 23-acre campus in Minneapolis.

Academic Information The faculty has 418 members (45% full-time), 48% with terminal degrees. The undergraduate student-faculty ratio is 14:1. The library holds 146,166 titles and 754 serial subscriptions. Special programs include academic remediation, services for learning-disabled students, an honors program, cooperative (work-study) education, study abroad, advanced placement credit, Freshman Honors College, ESL programs, double majors, independent study, self-designed majors, summer session for credit, part-time degree programs (daytime, weekends, summer), adult/continuing education programs, internships, and arrangement for off-campus study with Associated Colleges of the Twin Cities. The most frequently chosen baccalaureate fields are business/marketing, education, health professions and related sciences.
Student Body Statistics The student body totals 3,891, of whom 3,049 are undergraduates (455 freshmen). 56 percent are women and 44 percent are men. Students come from 36 states and territories and 21 other countries. 90 percent are from Minnesota. 1.2 percent are international students.
Expenses for 2009–10 *Application fee:* $25. *Tuition:* $27,020 full-time. *Mandatory fees:* $493 full-time.
Financial Aid Forms of aid include need-based and non-need-based scholarships and part-time jobs. The average aided 2008–09 undergraduate received an aid package worth an estimated $17,449. The application deadline for financial aid is August 15 with a priority deadline of May 1.
Freshman Admission Augsburg College requires an essay, a high school transcript, a minimum 2.5 high school GPA, an interview, and TOEFL scores for international students. SAT or ACT scores are recommended. 2 recommendations are required for some. The application deadline for regular admission is August 15.
Transfer Admission The application deadline for admission is August 15.
Entrance Difficulty Augsburg College assesses its entrance difficulty level as moderately difficult. For the fall 2008 freshman class, 56 percent of the applicants were accepted.
For Further Information Contact Ms. Carrie Carroll, Director of Undergraduate Day Admissions, Augsburg College, 2211 Riverside Avenue, Minneapolis, MN 55454-1351. *Phone:* 612-330-1001 or 800-788-5678 (toll-free). *Fax:* 612-330-1590. *E-mail:* admissions@augsburg.edu. *Web site:* http://www.augsburg.edu/.

BEMIDJI STATE UNIVERSITY
Bemidji, Minnesota

Bemidji State University is a coed, public, comprehensive unit of Minnesota State Colleges and Universities System, founded in 1919, offering degrees at the associate, bachelor's, and master's levels. It has an 89-acre campus in Bemidji.

Academic Information The faculty has 254 members (76% full-time), 46% with terminal degrees. The undergraduate student-faculty ratio is 19:1. The library holds 554,087 titles and 991 serial subscriptions. Special programs include academic remediation, services for learning-disabled students, an honors program, cooperative (work-study) education, study abroad, advanced placement credit, ESL programs, double majors, independent study, distance learning, summer session for credit, part-time degree programs (daytime, evenings, summer), external degree programs,

Bemidji State University (continued)
adult/continuing education programs, internships, and arrangement for off-campus study with other colleges in MNSCU system. The most frequently chosen baccalaureate fields are business/marketing, education, engineering technologies.
Student Body Statistics The student body totals 5,009, of whom 4,500 are undergraduates (774 freshmen). 52 percent are women and 48 percent are men. Students come from 36 states and territories and 40 other countries. 93 percent are from Minnesota. 4.2 percent are international students.
Expenses for 2009–10 *Application fee:* $20. *State resident tuition:* $6410 full-time. *Nonresident tuition:* $6410 full-time. *Mandatory fees:* $950 full-time. *College room and board:* $6325.
Financial Aid Forms of aid include need-based and non-need-based scholarships, athletic grants, and part-time jobs. The average aided 2008–09 undergraduate received an aid package worth an estimated $8381. The priority application deadline for financial aid is May 15.
Freshman Admission Bemidji State University requires a high school transcript, ACT scores, and TOEFL scores for international students. An essay and an interview are required for some. The application deadline for regular admission is rolling.
Transfer Admission The application deadline for admission is rolling.
Entrance Difficulty Bemidji State University assesses its entrance difficulty level as moderately difficult. For the fall 2008 freshman class, 83 percent of the applicants were accepted.
For Further Information Contact Mr. Russ Kreager, Director of Admissions, Bemidji State University, Deputy 102, Bemidji State University, 1500 Birchmont Drive, NE, Bemidji, MN 56601. *Phone:* 218-755-2040, 800-475-2001 (toll-free in-state), or 800-652-9747 (toll-free out-of-state). *Fax:* 218-755-2074. *E-mail:* admissions@bemidjistate.edu. *Web site:* http://www.bemidjistate.edu/.

BETHANY LUTHERAN COLLEGE

Mankato, Minnesota

Bethany Lutheran College is a coed, private, Lutheran, four-year college, founded in 1927, offering degrees at the bachelor's level. It has a 50-acre campus in Mankato near Minneapolis–St. Paul.

Academic Information The faculty has 80 members (49% full-time), 32% with terminal degrees. The student-faculty ratio is 12:1. The library holds 67,093 titles, 18,465 serial subscriptions, and 3,888 audiovisual materials. Special programs include academic remediation, services for learning-disabled students, study abroad, advanced placement credit, double majors, independent study, and internships. The most frequently chosen baccalaureate fields are business/marketing, biological/life sciences, communications/journalism.
Student Body Statistics The student body is made up of 615 undergraduates (181 freshmen). 57 percent are women and 43 percent are men. Students come from 25 states and territories and 9 other countries. 70 percent are from Minnesota. 0.2 percent are international students.
Expenses for 2008–09 *Application fee:* $0. *One-time mandatory fee:* $130. *Comprehensive fee:* $24,510 includes full-time tuition ($18,450), mandatory fees ($260), and college room and board ($5800). *College room only:* $2190. Room and board charges vary according to board plan and housing facility. *Part-time tuition:* $780 per credit hour. *Part-time mandatory fees:* $130 per term.
Financial Aid Forms of aid include need-based and non-need-based scholarships and part-time jobs. The average aided 2007–08 undergraduate received an aid package worth $14,779. The priority application deadline for financial aid is April 15.
Freshman Admission Bethany Lutheran College requires an essay, a high school transcript, a minimum 2.4 high school GPA, SAT or ACT scores, and TOEFL scores for international students. A minimum 3.2 high school GPA and an interview are recommended. An interview is required for some. The application deadline for regular admission is July 1.
Entrance Difficulty Bethany Lutheran College assesses its entrance difficulty level as moderately difficult; minimally difficult for transfers. For the fall 2008 freshman class, 83 percent of the applicants were accepted.
For Further Information Contact Mr. Donald Westphal, Dean of Admissions, Bethany Lutheran College, 700 Luther Drive, Mankato, MN 56001. *Phone:* 507-344-7320 or 800-944-3066 Ext. 331 (toll-free). *Fax:* 507-344-7376. *E-mail:* dwestpha@blc.edu. *Web site:* http://www.blc.edu/.

BETHEL UNIVERSITY

St. Paul, Minnesota

Bethel University is a coed, private, comprehensive institution, founded in 1871, affiliated with the Baptist General Conference, offering degrees at the associate, bachelor's, master's, and doctoral levels and post-master's and postbachelor's certificates. It has a 248-acre campus in St. Paul near Twin Cities.

Academic Information The faculty has 463 members (45% full-time), 52% with terminal degrees. The undergraduate student-faculty ratio is 13:1. The library holds 194,000 titles, 38,080 serial subscriptions, and 15,503 audiovisual materials. Special programs include academic remediation, services for learning-disabled students, an honors program, study abroad, advanced placement credit, accelerated degree programs, double majors, independent study, distance learning, self-designed majors, summer session for credit, part-time degree programs (daytime, evenings, summer), adult/continuing education programs, internships, and arrangement for off-campus study with members of the Christian College Consortium, Au Sable Institute, Coalition for Christian Colleges and Universities. The most frequently chosen baccalaureate fields are business/marketing, education, health professions and related sciences.
Student Body Statistics The student body totals 4,335, of whom 3,392 are undergraduates (642 freshmen). 63 percent are women and 37 percent are men. Students come from 38 states and territories and 20 other countries. 75 percent are from Minnesota. 0.4 percent are international students.
Expenses for 2008–09 *Application fee:* $0. *Comprehensive fee:* $33,480 includes full-time tuition ($25,750), mandatory fees ($110), and college room and board ($7620). *College room only:* $4540. *Part-time tuition:* $1035 per credit hour.
Financial Aid Forms of aid include need-based and non-need-based scholarships and part-time jobs. The average aided 2007–08 undergraduate received an aid package worth $16,511.
Freshman Admission Bethel University requires an essay, a high school transcript, rank in upper 50% of high school class, SAT or ACT scores, and TOEFL scores for international students. An interview is recommended. 2 recommendations are required for some.
Entrance Difficulty Bethel University assesses its entrance difficulty level as moderately difficult; very difficult for nursing program. For the fall 2008 freshman class, 81 percent of the applicants were accepted.

SPECIAL MESSAGE TO STUDENTS

Social Life The social atmosphere at Bethel is alive and inviting, with many student-led campus activities. Bethel has excellent music performance groups, competitive varsity and intramural sports, active student government, high-quality theater productions, and a wide variety of student clubs and spiritual growth opportunities. Spiritual life is a priority at Bethel. Community chapel services, residence hall Bible studies, and discipleship programs offer opportunities for Christian growth. There are also many ways for students to get involved in ministry through leading worship as well as campus outreach events, including Habitat for Humanity, community service programs, inner-city projects, and missions trips.

Academic Highlights With sixty-seven majors within seventy-eight areas of study, Bethel ranks in the top Midwestern Universities category of *U.S. News & World Report*'s "America's Best Colleges." Bethel's general education curriculum has become a model for many other institutions nationwide. General education courses give students a broad view of the world and their role as Christians in it. The courses are grouped around the following themes: personal development; biblical foundations; math, science, and technology; and global perspectives. Bethel strongly encourages and provides students with the opportunity to participate in a number of off-campus study programs, including Australia Term, England Term, Europe Term, Guatemala Term, South Africa Term, Spain Term, Thailand Term, the American Studies Program in Washington, D.C., the Los Angeles Film Studies Center, and the New York Center for Art & Media Studies.

Interviews and Campus Visits On-campus interviews are strongly encouraged but not required. An interview gives the prospective student the opportunity to learn more about the University, ask questions, and better determine if Bethel is a good fit. A campus visit gives students opportunities to stay in a residence hall, attend classes and chapel, meet with professors and coaches, enjoy free meals with Bethel students, and attend on-campus events. Bethel's beautiful wooded campus is located on the shores of Lake Valentine in Arden Hills, Minnesota—just 15 minutes from downtown St. Paul and Minneapolis. The Bethel campus offers modern academic, housing, and recreation facilities. The Community Life Center houses the 1,700-seat Benson Great Hall, which serves as a chapel and is hailed as one of the best music performance halls in the upper Midwest. For more information about Bethel University or to arrange a campus visit, students can call the Office of Admissions at 651-638-6242 or 800-255-8706 (toll-free), Monday through Friday, 8:30 to 4:30. The fax number is 651-635-1490. The Office of Admissions is located on campus in RC 341, Robertson Center building.

For Further Information Write to Office of Admissions, Bethel University, 3900 Bethel Drive, St. Paul, MN 55112. *E-mail:* BUadmissions-cas@bethel.edu. *Web site:* http://www.bethel.edu.

BROWN COLLEGE

Mendota Heights, Minnesota

Brown College is a coed, primarily men's, proprietary, primarily two-year college of Career Education Corporation, founded in 1946, offering degrees at the associate and bachelor's levels. It has a 20-acre campus in Mendota Heights near Minneapolis–St. Paul.

For Further Information Contact Mr. Mark Fredrichs, Registrar, Brown College, 1440 Northland Drive, Mendota Heights, MN 55120. *Phone:* 651-905-3400 or 800-6BROWN6 (toll-free). *Fax:* 651-905-3550. *Web site:* http://www.browncollege.edu/.

CAPELLA UNIVERSITY

Minneapolis, Minnesota

http://www.capella.edu/

CARLETON COLLEGE

Northfield, Minnesota

Carleton College is a coed, private, four-year college, founded in 1866, offering degrees at the bachelor's level. It has a 955-acre campus in Northfield near Minneapolis–St. Paul.

Academic Information The faculty has 232 members (93% full-time), 94% with terminal degrees. The student-faculty ratio is 9:1. The library holds 1 million titles and 10,964 serial subscriptions. Special programs include services for learning-disabled students, study abroad, advanced placement credit, accelerated degree programs, double majors, independent study, self-designed majors, internships, and arrangement for off-campus study with Cooperative programs/St. Olaf College, memberships in Associated Colleges of the Midwest, Higher Education Consortium for Urban Affairs. The most frequently chosen baccalaureate fields are physical sciences, biological/life sciences, social sciences.

Student Body Statistics The student body is made up of 2,000 undergraduates (489 freshmen). 52 percent are women and 48 percent are men. Students come from 51 states and territories and 44 other countries. 26 percent are from Minnesota. 6.1 percent are international students.
Expenses for 2008–09 *Application fee:* $30. *Comprehensive fee:* $48,039 includes full-time tuition ($37,845), mandatory fees ($201), and college room and board ($9993). *College room only:* $4770.
Financial Aid Forms of aid include need-based and non-need-based scholarships and part-time jobs. The average aided 2007–08 undergraduate received an aid package worth $32,132. The application deadline for financial aid is February 15.
Freshman Admission Carleton College requires an essay, a high school transcript, 2 recommendations, common application supplement, SAT or ACT scores, and TOEFL scores for international students. An interview and SAT Subject Test scores are recommended. The application deadline for regular admission is January 15, for early decision plan 1 it is November 15, and for early decision plan 2 it is January 15.
Transfer Admission The application deadline for admission is March 31.
Entrance Difficulty Carleton College assesses its entrance difficulty level as very difficult; most difficult for transfers. For the fall 2008 freshman class, 27 percent of the applicants were accepted.
For Further Information Contact Office of Admissions, Carleton College, 100 South College Street, Northfield, MN 55057. *Phone:* 507-222-4190 or 800-995-2275 (toll-free). *Fax:* 507-646-4526. *E-mail:* admissions@acs.carleton.edu. *Web site:* http://www.carleton.edu/.

COLLEGE OF SAINT BENEDICT

Saint Joseph, Minnesota

College of Saint Benedict is a coed, primarily women's, private, Roman Catholic, four-year college, founded in 1887, offering degrees at the bachelor's level (coordinate with Saint John's University for men). It has a 315-acre campus in Saint Joseph near Minneapolis–St. Paul.

Academic Information The faculty has 191 members (82% full-time), 75% with terminal degrees. The student-faculty ratio is 12:1. The library holds 749,886 titles, 13,700 serial subscriptions, and 34,747 audiovisual materials. Special programs include services for learning-disabled students, an honors program, study abroad, advanced placement credit, ESL programs, double majors, independent study, self-designed majors, internships, and arrangement for off-campus study with Tri-College Exchange Program (MN), Saint John's University (MN). The most frequently chosen baccalaureate fields are English, business/marketing, psychology.
Student Body Statistics The student body is made up of 2,110 undergraduates (519 freshmen). 100 percent are women. Students come from 39 states and territories and 47 other countries. 87 percent are from Minnesota. 5.7 percent are international students.
Expenses for 2008–09 *Application fee:* $0. *One-time mandatory fee:* $40. *Comprehensive fee:* $36,627 includes full-time tuition ($28,122), mandatory fees ($546), and college room and board ($7959). *College room only:* $3832. Full-time tuition and fees vary according to student level. Room and board charges vary according to board plan and housing facility. *Part-time tuition:* $1171 per credit hour. Part-time tuition varies according to course load.
Financial Aid Forms of aid include need-based and non-need-based scholarships and part-time jobs. The average aided 2008–09 undergraduate received an aid package worth an estimated $21,156. The priority application deadline for financial aid is March 15.
Freshman Admission College of Saint Benedict requires an essay, a high school transcript, 1 recommendation, SAT or ACT scores, and TOEFL scores for international students. A minimum 3.0 high school GPA and an interview are recommended. The application deadline for regular admission is rolling and for early action it is December 15.
Transfer Admission The application deadline for admission is rolling.

College of Saint Benedict (continued)

Entrance Difficulty College of Saint Benedict assesses its entrance difficulty level as moderately difficult. For the fall 2008 freshman class, 75 percent of the applicants were accepted.

For Further Information Contact Ms. Karen Backes, Associate Dean of Admissions, College of Saint Benedict, 37 South College Avenue, St. Joseph, MN 56374. *Phone:* 320-363-2196 or 800-544-1489 (toll-free). *Fax:* 320-363-2750. *E-mail:* admissions@csbsju.edu. *Web site:* http://www.csbsju.edu/.

THE COLLEGE OF ST. SCHOLASTICA

Duluth, Minnesota

The College of St. Scholastica is a coed, private, comprehensive institution, founded in 1912, affiliated with the Roman Catholic Church, offering degrees at the bachelor's, master's, and doctoral levels and post-master's and postbachelor's certificates. It has a 186-acre campus in Duluth.

Academic Information The faculty has 281 members (57% full-time), 43% with terminal degrees. The undergraduate student-faculty ratio is 14:1. The library holds 114,769 titles, 21,656 serial subscriptions, and 5,884 audiovisual materials. Special programs include services for learning-disabled students, an honors program, study abroad, advanced placement credit, accelerated degree programs, double majors, independent study, distance learning, self-designed majors, summer session for credit, part-time degree programs (evenings), external degree programs, adult/continuing education programs, internships, and arrangement for off-campus study with University of Wisconsin-Superior, University of Minnesota, Duluth. The most frequently chosen baccalaureate fields are business/marketing, biological/life sciences, health professions and related sciences.

Student Body Statistics The student body totals 3,593, of whom 2,769 are undergraduates (537 freshmen). 70 percent are women and 30 percent are men. Students come from 28 states and territories and 34 other countries. 85 percent are from Minnesota. 3.5 percent are international students.

Expenses for 2008–09 *Application fee:* $25. *Comprehensive fee:* $33,461 includes full-time tuition ($26,324), mandatory fees ($165), and college room and board ($6972). *College room only:* $3960. Full-time tuition and fees vary according to class time. Room and board charges vary according to board plan and housing facility. *Part-time tuition:* $819 per credit hour. Part-time tuition varies according to class time and course load.

Financial Aid Forms of aid include need-based and non-need-based scholarships and part-time jobs. The average aided 2008–09 undergraduate received an aid package worth an estimated $19,940. The priority application deadline for financial aid is March 1.

Freshman Admission The College of St. Scholastica requires a high school transcript, SAT or ACT scores, and TOEFL scores for international students. An interview is recommended. A minimum 2.0 high school GPA and an interview are required for some. The application deadline for regular admission is rolling.

Transfer Admission The application deadline for admission is rolling.

Entrance Difficulty The College of St. Scholastica assesses its entrance difficulty level as moderately difficult. For the fall 2008 freshman class, 83 percent of the applicants were accepted.

For Further Information Contact Mr. Eric Berg, Vice President for Enrollment Management, The College of St. Scholastica, 1200 Kenwood Avenue, Duluth, MN 55811-4199. *Phone:* 218-723-6053 or 800-249-6412 (toll-free). *Fax:* 218-723-5991. *E-mail:* admissions@css.edu. *Web site:* http://www.css.edu/.

COLLEGE OF VISUAL ARTS

St. Paul, Minnesota

College of Visual Arts is a coed, private, four-year college, founded in 1924, offering degrees at the bachelor's level. It has a 2-acre campus in St. Paul near Minneapolis.

Academic Information The faculty has 46 members (15% full-time), 15% with terminal degrees. The student-faculty ratio is 9:1. Special programs include academic remediation, services for learning-disabled students, an honors program, study abroad, advanced placement credit, double majors, independent study, summer session for credit, part-time degree programs (daytime, evenings, summer), internships, and arrangement for off-campus study. The most frequently chosen baccalaureate field is visual and performing arts.

Student Body Statistics The student body is made up of 191 undergraduates (49 freshmen). 62 percent are women and 38 percent are men. Students come from 10 states and territories and 2 other countries. 90 percent are from Minnesota.

Expenses for 2009–10 *Application fee:* $40. *Tuition:* $22,694 full-time. *Mandatory fees:* $500 full-time.

Financial Aid Forms of aid include need-based and non-need-based scholarships and part-time jobs. The average aided 2008–09 undergraduate received an aid package worth an estimated $11,510. The application deadline for financial aid is June 1 with a priority deadline of April 1.

Freshman Admission College of Visual Arts requires an essay, a high school transcript, a portfolio, SAT or ACT scores, and TOEFL scores for international students. A minimum 3.0 high school GPA, 1 recommendation, and an interview are recommended. The application deadline for regular admission is rolling.

Transfer Admission The application deadline for admission is rolling.

Entrance Difficulty College of Visual Arts assesses its entrance difficulty level as moderately difficult. For the fall 2008 freshman class, 72 percent of the applicants were accepted.

For Further Information Contact Anne White, Director for Student Life, College of Visual Arts, 344 Summit Avenue, St. Paul, MN 55102-2124. *Phone:* 651-757-4010 or 800-224-1536 (toll-free). *Fax:* 651-757-4049. *E-mail:* awhite@cva.edu. *Web site:* http://www.cva.edu/.

CONCORDIA COLLEGE

Moorhead, Minnesota

Concordia College is a coed, private, comprehensive institution, founded in 1891, affiliated with the Evangelical Lutheran Church in America, offering degrees at the bachelor's and master's levels. It has a 120-acre campus in Moorhead.

Academic Information The faculty has 266 members (71% full-time), 57% with terminal degrees. The undergraduate student-faculty ratio is 13:1. The library holds 340,006 titles, 3,329 serial subscriptions, and 11,185 audiovisual materials. Special programs include services for learning-disabled students, an honors program, cooperative (work-study) education, study abroad, advanced placement credit, ESL programs, double majors, independent study, summer session for credit, part-time degree programs (daytime, evenings, summer), adult/continuing education programs, internships, and arrangement for off-campus study with Tri-College University. The most frequently chosen baccalaureate fields are business/marketing, communications/journalism, education.

Student Body Statistics The student body totals 2,823, of whom 2,810 are undergraduates (776 freshmen). 61 percent are women and 39 percent are men. Students come from 41 states and territories and 37 other countries. 3.8 percent are international students.

Expenses for 2009–10 *Application fee:* $20. *Comprehensive fee:* $32,535 includes full-time tuition ($25,500), mandatory fees ($210), and college room and board ($6825). *College room only:* $2800. *Part-time tuition:* $4015 per course.

Financial Aid Forms of aid include need-based and non-need-based scholarships and part-time jobs. The average aided 2008–09 undergraduate received an aid package worth an estimated $17,921. The application deadline for financial aid is continuous.

Freshman Admission Concordia College requires a high school transcript, 2 recommendations, references, SAT or ACT scores, and TOEFL scores for international students. The application deadline for regular admission is rolling.

Transfer Admission The application deadline for admission is rolling.

Entrance Difficulty Concordia College assesses its entrance difficulty level as moderately difficult. For the fall 2008 freshman class, 78 percent of the applicants were accepted.
For Further Information Contact Mr. Scott E. Ellingson, Director of Admissions, Concordia College, 901 8th Street South, Moorhead, MN 56562. *Phone:* 218-299-3004 or 800-699-9897 (toll-free). *Fax:* 218-299-3947. *E-mail:* admissions@cord.edu. *Web site:* http://www.concordiacollege.edu/.

CONCORDIA UNIVERSITY, ST. PAUL

St. Paul, Minnesota

Concordia University, St. Paul is a coed, private, comprehensive institution, founded in 1893, affiliated with the Lutheran Church–Missouri Synod, offering degrees at the associate, bachelor's, and master's levels and postbachelor's certificates. It has a 37-acre campus in St. Paul.

Academic Information The faculty has 265 members (29% full-time), 37% with terminal degrees. The undergraduate student-faculty ratio is 14:1. The library holds 151,912 titles, 21,950 serial subscriptions, and 3,227 audiovisual materials. Special programs include academic remediation, services for learning-disabled students, an honors program, study abroad, advanced placement credit, accelerated degree programs, double majors, independent study, distance learning, self-designed majors, summer session for credit, part-time degree programs (daytime, evenings, summer), adult/continuing education programs, internships, and arrangement for off-campus study with University of Minnesota–Twin Cities Campus, University of St. Thomas, Oak Hill College. The most frequently chosen baccalaureate fields are business/marketing, education, family and consumer sciences.
Student Body Statistics The student body totals 2,644, of whom 1,691 are undergraduates (211 freshmen). 60 percent are women and 40 percent are men. Students come from 39 states and territories and 5 other countries. 80 percent are from Minnesota. 0.4 percent are international students.
Expenses for 2009–10 *Application fee:* $30. *Comprehensive fee:* $33,650 includes full-time tuition ($26,400) and college room and board ($7250). *Part-time tuition:* $550 per credit.
Financial Aid Forms of aid include need-based and non-need-based scholarships, athletic grants, and part-time jobs. The average aided 2008–09 undergraduate received an aid package worth an estimated $15,674. The priority application deadline for financial aid is May 1.
Freshman Admission Concordia University, St. Paul requires a high school transcript, 2 recommendations, and ACT scores. A minimum 2.0 high school GPA is recommended. An essay is required for some. The application deadline for regular admission is August 1.
Transfer Admission The application deadline for admission is August 1.
Entrance Difficulty Concordia University, St. Paul assesses its entrance difficulty level as minimally difficult. For the fall 2008 freshman class, 59 percent of the applicants were accepted.
For Further Information Contact Kristin Schoon, Director of Undergraduate Admission, Concordia University, St. Paul, 275 Syndicate North, St. Paul, MN 55104-5494. *Phone:* 651-641-8230 or 800-333-4705 (toll-free). *Fax:* 651-603-6320. *E-mail:* admission@csp.edu. *Web site:* http://www.csp.edu/.

CROSSROADS COLLEGE

Rochester, Minnesota

Crossroads College is a coed, private, four-year college, founded in 1913, affiliated with the Christian Churches and Churches of Christ, offering degrees at the associate and bachelor's levels. It has a 40-acre campus in Rochester near Minneapolis–St. Paul.

Academic Information The faculty has 31 members (23% full-time), 23% with terminal degrees. The student-faculty ratio is 9:1. The library holds 33,697 titles and 300 serial subscriptions. Special programs include academic remediation, advanced placement credit, double majors, independent study, self-designed majors, external degree programs, adult/continuing education programs, and internships. The most frequently chosen baccalaureate field is theology and religious vocations.
Student Body Statistics The student body is made up of 160 undergraduates (24 freshmen). 47 percent are women and 53 percent are men. Students come from 9 states and territories and 2 other countries. 70 percent are from Minnesota. 1.3 percent are international students.
Expenses for 2008–09 *Application fee:* $30. *Tuition:* $12,850 full-time, $375 per semester hour part-time. *Mandatory fees:* $360 full-time, $50. *College room only:* $3900.
Financial Aid Forms of aid include need-based and non-need-based scholarships and part-time jobs. The average aided 2007–08 undergraduate received an aid package worth $4120.
Freshman Admission Crossroads College requires an essay, a high school transcript, 3 recommendations, SAT or ACT scores, and TOEFL scores for international students. An interview is recommended. The application deadline for regular admission is August 15.
Transfer Admission The application deadline for admission is August 15.
Entrance Difficulty Crossroads College assesses its entrance difficulty level as noncompetitive.
For Further Information Contact Mr. Scott Klaehn, Director of Admissions, Crossroads College, 920 Mayowood Road, SW, Rochester, MN 55902-2382. *Phone:* 507-288-4563 Ext. 304 or 800-456-7651 (toll-free). *Fax:* 507-288-9046. *E-mail:* admissions@crossroadscollege.edu. *Web site:* http://www.crossroadscollege.edu/.

CROWN COLLEGE

St. Bonifacius, Minnesota

Crown College is a coed, private, comprehensive institution, founded in 1916, affiliated with The Christian and Missionary Alliance, offering degrees at the associate, bachelor's, and master's levels. It has a 215-acre campus in St. Bonifacius near Minneapolis–St. Paul.

Academic Information The faculty has 159 members (21% full-time), 36% with terminal degrees. The undergraduate student-faculty ratio is 14:1. The library holds 101,468 titles, 28,000 serial subscriptions, and 1,503 audiovisual materials. Special programs include academic remediation, services for learning-disabled students, an honors program, study abroad, advanced placement credit, accelerated degree programs, ESL programs, double majors, independent study, distance learning, summer session for credit, part-time degree programs (daytime, evenings, weekends, summer), external degree programs, adult/continuing education programs, and internships. The most frequently chosen baccalaureate fields are business/marketing, education, theology and religious vocations.
Student Body Statistics The student body totals 1,229, of whom 1,106 are undergraduates (168 freshmen). 61 percent are women and 39 percent are men. Students come from 33 states and territories and 1 other country. 66 percent are from Minnesota.
Expenses for 2009–10 *Application fee:* $35. *Comprehensive fee:* $27,140 includes full-time tuition ($19,774) and college room and board ($7366). *College room only:* $3834. *Part-time tuition:* $823 per credit.
Financial Aid Forms of aid include need-based and non-need-based scholarships and part-time jobs. The average aided 2008–09 undergraduate received an aid package worth an estimated $14,632. The application deadline for financial aid is August 1 with a priority deadline of April 5.
Freshman Admission Crown College requires an essay, a high school transcript, a minimum 2.0 high school GPA, 2 recommendations, SAT or ACT scores, and TOEFL scores for international students. An interview is required for some. The application deadline for regular admission is rolling.
Transfer Admission The application deadline for admission is rolling.
Entrance Difficulty Crown College assesses its entrance difficulty level as minimally difficult. For the fall 2008 freshman class, 70 percent of the applicants were accepted.
For Further Information Contact Ms. Jill Pautz, Director of Admissions, Crown College, 8700 College View Drive, St. Bonifacius, MN 55375-9001. *Phone:* 952-446-4144 or 800-68-CROWN (toll-free). *Fax:* 952-446-4149. *E-mail:* info@crown.edu. *Web site:* http://www.crown.edu/.

DeVRY UNIVERSITY

Edina, Minnesota

DeVry University is a coed, proprietary, comprehensive institution, offering degrees at the associate, bachelor's, and master's levels.

Academic Information The faculty has 12 members. The undergraduate student-faculty ratio is 35:1. Special programs include accelerated degree programs and distance learning. The most frequently chosen baccalaureate fields are business/marketing, computer and information sciences.
Student Body Statistics The student body totals 252, of whom 190 are undergraduates (36 freshmen). 42 percent are women and 58 percent are men. 94 percent are from Minnesota.
Expenses for 2009–10 *Application fee:* $50. *Tuition:* $14,080 full-time, $550 per credit hour part-time.
Financial Aid Forms of aid include need-based scholarships. The average aided 2007–08 undergraduate received an aid package worth $10,797. The application deadline for financial aid is continuous.
Freshman Admission DeVry University requires a high school transcript and an interview. The application deadline for regular admission is rolling.
Transfer Admission The application deadline for admission is rolling.
For Further Information Contact Admissions Office, DeVry University, 7700 France Avenue South, Suite 575, Edina, MN 55435-5876. *Phone:* 952-838-1860. *Web site:* http://www.devry.edu/.

DUNWOODY COLLEGE OF TECHNOLOGY

Minneapolis, Minnesota

Dunwoody College of Technology is a coed, primarily men's, private, primarily two-year college, founded in 1914, offering degrees at the associate and bachelor's levels. It has a 12-acre campus in Minneapolis.

Expenses for 2008–09 *Application fee:* $50. *One-time mandatory fee:* $50. *Tuition:* $12,433 full-time. *Mandatory fees:* $1110 full-time.
For Further Information Contact Shaun Manning, Director of Admissions, Dunwoody College of Technology, 818 Dunwoody Boulevard, Minneapolis, MN 55403. *Phone:* 612-374-5800 Ext. 8110 or 800-292-4625 (toll-free). *Fax:* 612-374-4128. *E-mail:* smanning@dunwoody.edu. *Web site:* http://www.dunwoody.edu/.

GLOBE COLLEGE

Oakdale, Minnesota

http://www.globecollege.com/

GUSTAVUS ADOLPHUS COLLEGE

St. Peter, Minnesota

Gustavus Adolphus College is a coed, private, four-year college, founded in 1862, affiliated with the Evangelical Lutheran Church in America, offering degrees at the bachelor's level. It has a 340-acre campus in St. Peter near Minneapolis–St. Paul.

Academic Information The faculty has 251 members (80% full-time), 75% with terminal degrees. The student-faculty ratio is 13:1. The library holds 343,448 titles, 22,931 serial subscriptions, and 17,976 audiovisual materials. Special programs include services for learning-disabled students, an honors program, cooperative (work-study) education, study abroad, advanced placement credit, accelerated degree programs, double majors, independent study, self-designed majors, summer session for credit, internships, and arrangement for off-campus study with Minnesota State University, Mankato. The most frequently chosen baccalaureate fields are business/marketing, psychology, social sciences.
Student Body Statistics The student body is made up of 2,578 undergraduates (606 freshmen). 57 percent are women and 43 percent are men. Students come from 40 states and territories and 15 other countries. 83 percent are from Minnesota. 1.6 percent are international students.
Expenses for 2008–09 *Application fee:* $0. *One-time mandatory fee:* $290. *Comprehensive fee:* $37,450 includes full-time tuition ($29,990) and college room and board ($7460). *College room only:* $4710. *Part-time tuition:* $4080 per course.
Financial Aid Forms of aid include need-based and non-need-based scholarships and part-time jobs. The average aided 2008–09 undergraduate received an aid package worth an estimated $25,531. The application deadline for financial aid is April 1 with a priority deadline of February 15.
Freshman Admission Gustavus Adolphus College requires an essay, a high school transcript, 1 recommendation, and TOEFL scores for international students. An interview and SAT or ACT scores are recommended. The application deadline for regular admission is April 1 and for early action it is November 1.
Transfer Admission The application deadline for admission is rolling.
Entrance Difficulty Gustavus Adolphus College assesses its entrance difficulty level as very difficult. For the fall 2008 freshman class, 75 percent of the applicants were accepted.
For Further Information Contact Mr. Mark Anderson, Vice President for Admission and Student Financial Aid, Gustavus Adolphus College, 800 West College Avenue, St. Peter, MN 56082-1498. *Phone:* 507-933-7676 or 800-GUSTAVU(S) (toll-free). *Fax:* 507-933-7474. *E-mail:* admission@gac.edu. *Web site:* http://www.gustavus.edu/.

HAMLINE UNIVERSITY

St. Paul, Minnesota

Hamline University is a coed, private, comprehensive institution, founded in 1854, affiliated with the United Methodist Church, offering degrees at the bachelor's, master's, doctoral, and first professional levels and postbachelor's certificates. It has a 50-acre campus in St. Paul.

Academic Information The faculty has 551 members (35% full-time), 52% with terminal degrees. The undergraduate student-faculty ratio is 13:1. The library holds 239,643 titles, 1,738 serial subscriptions, and 5,547 audiovisual materials. Special programs include academic remediation, services for learning-disabled students, an honors program, study abroad, advanced placement credit, ESL programs, double majors, independent study, self-designed majors, summer session for credit, part-time degree programs (daytime, evenings, summer), internships, and arrangement for off-campus study with members of the Associated Colleges of the Twin Cities, American University, Southern College Student Exchange Program, Higher Education Consortium for Urban Affairs, Drew University. The most frequently chosen baccalaureate fields are business/marketing, psychology, social sciences.
Student Body Statistics The student body totals 4,876, of whom 2,053 are undergraduates (452 freshmen). 56 percent are women and 44 percent are men. Students come from 35 states and territories and 62 other countries. 84 percent are from Minnesota. 3.5 percent are international students.
Expenses for 2008–09 *Application fee:* $0. *One-time mandatory fee:* $250. *Comprehensive fee:* $35,936 includes full-time tuition ($27,620), mandatory fees ($532), and college room and board ($7784). *College room only:* $3976. Full-time tuition and fees vary according to student level. Room and board charges vary according to board plan and housing facility. *Part-time tuition:* $863 per credit. *Part-time mandatory fees:* $206 per term. Part-time tuition and fees vary according to course load and student level.
Financial Aid Forms of aid include need-based and non-need-based scholarships and part-time jobs. The average aided 2008–09 undergraduate received an aid package worth an estimated $21,285. The priority application deadline for financial aid is March 1.
Freshman Admission Hamline University requires an essay, a high school transcript, 1 recommendation, SAT or ACT scores, and TOEFL scores for international students. An interview and activity resume are recommended. The application deadline for regular admission is rolling and for early action it is December 1.
Transfer Admission The application deadline for admission is rolling.

Entrance Difficulty Hamline University assesses its entrance difficulty level as moderately difficult. For the fall 2008 freshman class, 80 percent of the applicants were accepted.
For Further Information Contact Mr. Milyon Trulove, Director of Admission, Hamline University, 1536 Hewitt Avenue, C1930, St. Paul, MN 55104-2458. *Phone:* 651-523-2207 or 800-753-9753 (toll-free). *Fax:* 651-523-2458. *E-mail:* cla-admis@hamline.edu. *Web site:* http://www.hamline.edu/.

HERZING COLLEGE

Minneapolis, Minnesota

http://www.herzing.edu/

ITT TECHNICAL INSTITUTE

Eden Prairie, Minnesota

ITT Technical Institute is a coed, proprietary, primarily two-year college of ITT Educational Services, Inc., founded in 2003, offering degrees at the associate and bachelor's levels.

For Further Information Contact Director of Recruitment, ITT Technical Institute, 8911 Columbine Road, Eden Prairie, MN 55347. *Phone:* 952-914-5300 or 888-488-9646 (toll-free in-state). *Web site:* http://www.itt-tech.edu/.

LEECH LAKE TRIBAL COLLEGE

Cass Lake, Minnesota

Leech Lake Tribal College is a coed, private, two-year college, founded in 1992, offering degrees at the associate level.

Expenses for 2008–09 *Application fee:* $15. *Tuition:* $3750 full-time. *Mandatory fees:* $230 full-time.
For Further Information Contact Ms. Liz Jenkins, Admissions Representative, Leech Lake Tribal College, PO Box 180, Cass Lake, MN 56633. *Phone:* 218-335-4247. *Fax:* 218-335-4209. *E-mail:* liz.jenkins@lltc.edu. *Web site:* http://www.lltc.org/.

LOWTHIAN COLLEGE

See The Art Institutes International Minnesota.

MACALESTER COLLEGE

St. Paul, Minnesota

Macalester College is a coed, private, Presbyterian, four-year college, founded in 1874, offering degrees at the bachelor's level. It has a 53-acre campus in St. Paul.

Academic Information The faculty has 225 members (73% full-time), 84% with terminal degrees. The student-faculty ratio is 10:1. The library holds 434,850 titles, 3,541 serial subscriptions, and 11,698 audiovisual materials. Special programs include an honors program, study abroad, double majors, independent study, self-designed majors, part-time degree programs (daytime), internships, and arrangement for off-campus study with College of St. Catherine, University of St. Thomas, Augsburg College, Hamline University, Minneapolis College of Art and Design. The most frequently chosen baccalaureate fields are foreign languages and literature, interdisciplinary studies, social sciences.
Student Body Statistics The student body is made up of 1,900 undergraduates (479 freshmen). 58 percent are women and 42 percent are men. Students come from 51 states and territories and 91 other countries. 22 percent are from Minnesota. 11.2 percent are international students.
Expenses for 2009–10 *Application fee:* $40. *Comprehensive fee:* $46,942 includes full-time tuition ($37,974), mandatory fees ($200), and college room and board ($8768). *College room only:* $4666.
Financial Aid Forms of aid include need-based and non-need-based scholarships and part-time jobs. The average aided 2008–09 undergraduate received an aid package worth an estimated $30,394. The application deadline for financial aid is March 1 with a priority deadline of February 8.
Freshman Admission Macalester College requires an essay, a high school transcript, 3 recommendations, SAT or ACT scores, and TOEFL scores for international students. An interview is recommended. The application deadline for regular admission is January 15, for early decision plan 1 it is November 15, and for early decision plan 2 it is January 2.
Transfer Admission The application deadline for admission is April 15.
Entrance Difficulty Macalester College assesses its entrance difficulty level as very difficult. For the fall 2008 freshman class, 41 percent of the applicants were accepted.
For Further Information Contact Mr. Lorne T. Robinson, Dean of Admissions and Financial Aid, Macalester College, 1600 Grand Avenue, St. Paul, MN 55105-1899. *Phone:* 651-696-6357 or 800-231-7974 (toll-free). *Fax:* 651-696-6724. *E-mail:* admissions@macalester.edu. *Web site:* http://www.macalester.edu/.

MANKATO STATE UNIVERSITY

See Minnesota State University Mankato.

MARTIN LUTHER COLLEGE

New Ulm, Minnesota

Martin Luther College is a coed, private, comprehensive institution, founded in 1995, affiliated with the Wisconsin Evangelical Lutheran Synod, offering degrees at the bachelor's and master's levels and postbachelor's certificates. It has a 50-acre campus in New Ulm.

Academic Information The faculty has 79 members (65% full-time), 41% with terminal degrees. The undergraduate student-faculty ratio is 12:1. The library holds 115,309 titles, 519 serial subscriptions, and 5,786 audiovisual materials. Special programs include academic remediation, advanced placement credit, double majors, distance learning, and summer session for credit. The most frequently chosen baccalaureate fields are education, theology and religious vocations.
Student Body Statistics The student body totals 842, of whom 780 are undergraduates (175 freshmen). 50 percent are women and 50 percent are men. Students come from 35 states and territories and 9 other countries. 15 percent are from Minnesota. 1.6 percent are international students.
Expenses for 2009–10 *Application fee:* $25. *Comprehensive fee:* $14,800 includes full-time tuition ($10,660) and college room and board ($4140).
Financial Aid Forms of aid include need-based and non-need-based scholarships and part-time jobs. The average aided 2007–08 undergraduate received an aid package worth $9921. The application deadline for financial aid is April 15.
Freshman Admission Martin Luther College requires a high school transcript, a minimum 2.0 high school GPA, recommendations, ACT scores, and TOEFL scores for international students. The application deadline for regular admission is April 15.
Transfer Admission The application deadline for admission is April 15.
Entrance Difficulty Martin Luther College assesses its entrance difficulty level as moderately difficult. For the fall 2008 freshman class, 97 percent of the applicants were accepted.
For Further Information Contact Prof. Ronald B. Brutlag, Associate Director of Admissions, Martin Luther College, 1995 Luther Court, New Ulm, MN 56073. *Phone:* 507-354-8221 Ext. 280. *Fax:* 507-354-8225. *E-mail:* brutlaro@mlc-wels.edu. *Web site:* http://www.mlc-wels.edu/.

McNALLY SMITH COLLEGE OF MUSIC

Saint Paul, Minnesota

McNally Smith College of Music is a coed, proprietary, four-year college, founded in 1985, offering degrees at the associate and bachelor's levels.

Academic Information The faculty has 90 members (48% full-time). The student-faculty ratio is 9:1. The library holds 4,500 titles, 50 serial subscriptions, and 4,000 audiovisual materials. Special programs include services for learning-disabled students, cooperative (work-study) education, study abroad, advanced placement credit, double majors, independent study, distance learning, summer session for credit, part-time degree programs (daytime), internships, and arrangement for off-campus study. The most frequently chosen baccalaureate fields are business/marketing, visual and performing arts.

Student Body Statistics The student body is made up of 570 undergraduates (186 freshmen). 19 percent are women and 81 percent are men. Students come from 28 states and territories and 7 other countries. 35 percent are from Minnesota. 1.6 percent are international students.

Expenses for 2009–10 *Application fee:* $75. *Tuition:* $19,500 full-time, $750 per credit part-time. *Mandatory fees:* $2500 full-time, $225 per term part-time.

Freshman Admission McNally Smith College of Music requires an essay, a high school transcript, a minimum 2.0 high school GPA, 2 recommendations, an interview, and TOEFL scores for international students. A minimum 2.5 high school GPA and ACT scores are recommended. Audition and ACT scores are required for some. The application deadline for regular admission is August 1.

Entrance Difficulty McNally Smith College of Music has an open admission policy.

For Further Information Contact Mrs. Kathy Hawks, Director of Admissions, McNally Smith College of Music, 19 Exchange Street East, St. Paul, MN 55101. *Phone:* 651-291-0177 Ext. 2373 or 800-594-9500 (toll-free). *Fax:* 651-291-0366. *E-mail:* khawks@mcnallysmith.edu. *Web site:* http://www.mcnallysmith.edu/.

MEDICAL INSTITUTE OF MINNESOTA

See Argosy University, Twin Cities.

METROPOLITAN STATE UNIVERSITY

St. Paul, Minnesota

Metropolitan State University is a coed, public, comprehensive unit of Minnesota State Colleges and Universities System, founded in 1971, offering degrees at the bachelor's, master's, and doctoral levels (offers primarily part-time evening degree programs).

Expenses for 2008–09 *Application fee:* $20. *State resident tuition:* $5160 full-time, $172 per credit part-time. *Nonresident tuition:* $10,320 full-time, $344 per credit part-time. *Mandatory fees:* $313 full-time, $10.43 per credit part-time.

For Further Information Contact Ms. Monir Johnson, Director, Metropolitan State University, 700 East 7th Street, St. Paul, MN 55106. *Phone:* 651-793-1303. *Fax:* 651-793-1310. *E-mail:* monir.johnson@metrostate.edu. *Web site:* http://www.metrostate.edu/.

MINNEAPOLIS COLLEGE OF ART AND DESIGN

Minneapolis, Minnesota

Minneapolis College of Art and Design is a coed, private, comprehensive institution, founded in 1886, offering degrees at the bachelor's and master's levels and postbachelor's certificates. It has a 7-acre campus in Minneapolis.

Academic Information The faculty has 105 members (36% full-time). The undergraduate student-faculty ratio is 13:1. The library holds 47,166 titles, 196 serial subscriptions, and 139,245 audiovisual materials. Special programs include services for learning-disabled students, cooperative (work-study) education, study abroad, advanced placement credit, independent study, distance learning, summer session for credit, part-time degree programs (daytime), adult/continuing education programs, internships, and arrangement for off-campus study with members of the Association of Independent Colleges of Art and Design, Macalester College. The most frequently chosen baccalaureate field is visual and performing arts.

Student Body Statistics The student body totals 772, of whom 709 are undergraduates (103 freshmen). 56 percent are women and 44 percent are men. Students come from 39 states and territories. 65 percent are from Minnesota.

Expenses for 2008–09 *Application fee:* $50. *Tuition:* $28,400 full-time, $940 per credit part-time. *Mandatory fees:* $200 full-time, $100 per term part-time. *College room only:* $4340.

Financial Aid Forms of aid include need-based and non-need-based scholarships and part-time jobs. The average aided 2007–08 undergraduate received an aid package worth $14,586. The application deadline for financial aid is April 1 with a priority deadline of March 15.

Freshman Admission Minneapolis College of Art and Design requires an essay, a high school transcript, 1 recommendation, SAT or ACT scores, and TOEFL scores for international students. A minimum 2.75 high school GPA and an interview are recommended. A portfolio is required for some. The application deadline for regular admission is May 1.

Transfer Admission The application deadline for admission is May 1.

Entrance Difficulty Minneapolis College of Art and Design assesses its entrance difficulty level as moderately difficult. For the fall 2008 freshman class, 56 percent of the applicants were accepted.

For Further Information Contact Mr. William Mullen, Director of Admissions, Minneapolis College of Art and Design, 2501 Stevens Avenue South, Minneapolis, MN 55404. *Phone:* 612-874-3762 or 800-874-6223 (toll-free). *E-mail:* admissions@mn.mcad.edu. *Web site:* http://www.mcad.edu/.

MINNESOTA BIBLE COLLEGE

See Crossroads College.

MINNESOTA SCHOOL OF BUSINESS–BLAINE

Blaine, Minnesota

Minnesota School of Business–Blaine is a coed, primarily women's, proprietary, four-year college of Globe University/Minnesota School of Business, offering degrees at the associate and bachelor's levels.

Academic Information The faculty has 37 members (22% full-time), 19% with terminal degrees. The student-faculty ratio is 22:1. Special programs include academic remediation, services for learning-disabled students, advanced placement credit, independent study, distance learning, part-time degree programs, external degree programs, adult/continuing education programs, and internships.

Student Body Statistics The student body is made up of 751 undergraduates (137 freshmen). 75 percent are women and 25 percent are men. Students come from 1 state or territory and 1 other country. 83 percent are from Minnesota.

Expenses for 2008–09 *Application fee:* $50. *Tuition:* $18,720 full-time, $390 per credit part-time. *Mandatory fees:* $1000 full-time. Full-time tuition and fees vary according to course load, program, and student level. Part-time tuition varies according to course load, program, and student level.

Freshman Admission Minnesota School of Business–Blaine requires 1 recommendation and an interview. A high school transcript and SAT or ACT or Accuplacer are required for some. The application deadline for regular admission is October 5.

Transfer Admission The application deadline for admission is October 5.

Entrance Difficulty Minnesota School of Business–Blaine assesses its entrance difficulty level as moderately difficult. For the fall 2008 freshman class, 100 percent of the applicants were accepted.
For Further Information Contact Ms. Kristen Swanson, Director of Admissions, Minnesota School of Business–Blaine, 3680 Pheasant Ridge Drive NE, Blaine, MN 55449. *Phone:* 763-225-8003. *Fax:* 763-225-8001. *E-mail:* kswanson@msbcollege.edu. *Web site:* http://www.msbcollege.edu/oncampus/blaine/.

MINNESOTA SCHOOL OF BUSINESS–BROOKLYN CENTER

Brooklyn Center, Minnesota

Minnesota School of Business–Brooklyn Center is a coed, proprietary, primarily two-year college, founded in 1989, offering degrees at the associate, bachelor's, and master's levels.

Expenses for 2008–09 *Application fee:* $50. *Tuition:* $16,650 full-time, $370 per credit hour part-time.
For Further Information Contact Mr. Bruce Christman, Director of Admissions, Minnesota School of Business–Brooklyn Center, 5910 Shingle Creek Parkway, Brooklyn Center, MN 55430. *Phone:* 763-585-7777. *Fax:* 763-566-7030. *Web site:* http://www.msbcollege.edu/.

MINNESOTA SCHOOL OF BUSINESS–PLYMOUTH

Minneapolis, Minnesota

Minnesota School of Business–Plymouth is a coed, proprietary, primarily two-year college, founded in 2002, offering degrees at the associate, bachelor's, and master's levels. It has a 3-acre campus in Minneapolis.

Expenses for 2008–09 *Application fee:* $50. *Tuition:* $16,650 full-time, $370 per credit hour part-time.
For Further Information Contact Director of Admissions, Minnesota School of Business–Plymouth, 1455 County Road 101 North, Plymouth, MN 55447. *Phone:* 763-476-2000. *Fax:* 763-476-1000. *Web site:* http://www.msbcollege.edu/.

MINNESOTA SCHOOL OF BUSINESS–RICHFIELD

Richfield, Minnesota

Minnesota School of Business–Richfield is a coed, proprietary, primarily two-year college, founded in 1877, offering degrees at the associate, bachelor's, and master's levels. It has a 3-acre campus in Richfield near Minneapolis–St. Paul.

Expenses for 2008–09 *Application fee:* $50. *Tuition:* $17,550 full-time, $390 per credit hour part-time. Both full-time and part-time tuition varies according to course load.
For Further Information Contact Ms. Patricia Murray, Director of Admissions, Minnesota School of Business–Richfield, 1401 West 76th Street, Richfield, MN 55430. *Phone:* 612-861-2000 Ext. 720 or 800-752-4223 (toll-free in-state). *Fax:* 612-861-5548. *E-mail:* pmurray@msbcollege.com. *Web site:* http://www.msbcollege.edu/.

MINNESOTA SCHOOL OF BUSINESS–ROCHESTER

Rochester, Minnesota

Minnesota School of Business–Rochester is a coed, proprietary, comprehensive institution, offering degrees at the associate, bachelor's, and master's levels.

Expenses for 2008–09 *Application fee:* $50. *Tuition:* $24,960 full-time, $390 per credit part-time. *Mandatory fees:* $400 full-time. Full-time tuition and fees vary according to course load and program. Part-time tuition varies according to course load and program.
For Further Information Contact Mr. Shan Pollitt, Director of Admissions, Minnesota School of Business–Rochester, 2521 Pennington Drive NW, Rochester, MN 55901. *Phone:* 507-536-9500 or 888-662-8772 (toll-free). *Fax:* 507-535-8011. *E-mail:* spollitt@msbcollege.edu. *Web site:* http://www.msbcollege.edu/.

MINNESOTA SCHOOL OF BUSINESS–ST. CLOUD

Waite Park, Minnesota

Minnesota School of Business–St. Cloud is a coed, proprietary, primarily two-year college, founded in 2004, offering degrees at the associate, bachelor's, and master's levels.

Expenses for 2008–09 *Application fee:* $50. *Tuition:* $16,650 full-time, $370 per credit hour part-time.
For Further Information Contact Ms. Candi Janssen, Director of Admissions, Minnesota School of Business–St. Cloud, 1201 2nd Street S, Waite Park, MN 56387. *Phone:* 320-257-2000 or 866-403-3333 (toll-free out-of-state). *Fax:* 320-257-0131. *E-mail:* cjanssen@msbcollege.edu. *Web site:* http://www.msbcollege.edu/.

MINNESOTA SCHOOL OF BUSINESS–SHAKOPEE

Shakopee, Minnesota

Minnesota School of Business–Shakopee is a coed, proprietary, primarily two-year college, founded in 2004, offering degrees at the associate, bachelor's, and master's levels.

Expenses for 2008–09 *Application fee:* $50. *Tuition:* $16,650 full-time, $370 per credit hour part-time.
For Further Information Contact Ms. Gretchen Seifert, Director of Admissions, Minnesota School of Business–Shakopee, 1200 Shakopee Town Square, Shakopee, MN 55379. *Phone:* 952-516-7015 or 866-766-1200 (toll-free out-of-state). *Fax:* 952-345-1201. *Web site:* http://www.msbcollege.edu/.

MINNESOTA STATE UNIVERSITY MANKATO

Mankato, Minnesota

Minnesota State University Mankato is a coed, public unit of Minnesota State Colleges and Universities System, founded in 1868, offering degrees at the associate, bachelor's, master's, and doctoral levels and post-master's certificates. It has a 303-acre campus in Mankato near Minneapolis–St. Paul.

Academic Information The faculty has 763 members (66% full-time), 57% with terminal degrees. The undergraduate student-faculty ratio is 22:1. The library holds 1 million titles and 20,000 serial subscriptions. Special programs include academic remediation, services for learning-disabled students, an honors program, cooperative (work-study) education,

Minnesota State University Mankato (continued)

study abroad, advanced placement credit, ESL programs, double majors, independent study, distance learning, self-designed majors, summer session for credit, part-time degree programs (daytime, evenings, weekends, summer), adult/continuing education programs, internships, and arrangement for off-campus study with other colleges in the Minnesota State College and University System. The most frequently chosen baccalaureate fields are business/marketing, education, health professions and related sciences.

Student Body Statistics The student body totals 14,515, of whom 12,815 are undergraduates (2,360 freshmen). 52 percent are women and 48 percent are men. Students come from 45 states and territories and 66 other countries. 2.7 percent are international students.

Expenses for 2008–09 *Application fee:* $20. *State resident tuition:* $5,467 full-time, $218.60 per credit part-time. *Nonresident tuition:* $11,712 full-time, $467.05 per credit part-time. *Mandatory fees:* $796 full-time, $33.04 per credit part-time. Both full-time and part-time tuition and fees vary according to course load and reciprocity agreements. *College room and board:* $5732. Room and board charges vary according to board plan.

Financial Aid Forms of aid include need-based scholarships, athletic grants, and part-time jobs. The average aided 2008–09 undergraduate received an aid package worth an estimated $7082. The priority application deadline for financial aid is March 15.

Freshman Admission Minnesota State University Mankato requires a high school transcript, SAT or ACT scores, and TOEFL scores for international students. An essay, 3 recommendations, and personal statement are required for some. The application deadline for regular admission is rolling.

Transfer Admission The application deadline for admission is rolling.

Entrance Difficulty Minnesota State University Mankato assesses its entrance difficulty level as moderately difficult. For the fall 2008 freshman class, 93 percent of the applicants were accepted.

For Further Information Contact Office of Admissions, Minnesota State University Mankato, 122 Taylor Center, Mankato, MN 56001. *Phone:* 507-389-1822 or 800-722-0544 (toll-free). *Fax:* 507-389-1511. *E-mail:* admissions@mnsu.edu. *Web site:* http://www.mnsu.edu/.

MINNESOTA STATE UNIVERSITY MOORHEAD

Moorhead, Minnesota

Minnesota State University Moorhead is a coed, public, comprehensive unit of Minnesota State Colleges and Universities System, founded in 1885, offering degrees at the associate, bachelor's, master's, and doctoral levels and post-master's and postbachelor's certificates. It has a 118-acre campus in Moorhead.

Academic Information The faculty has 484 members (63% full-time), 45% with terminal degrees. The undergraduate student-faculty ratio is 17:1. The library holds 634,509 titles, 164 serial subscriptions, and 20,824 audiovisual materials. Special programs include academic remediation, services for learning-disabled students, an honors program, study abroad, advanced placement credit, Freshman Honors College, double majors, independent study, distance learning, self-designed majors, summer session for credit, part-time degree programs (daytime, evenings, weekends, summer), external degree programs, adult/continuing education programs, internships, and arrangement for off-campus study with North Dakota State University, Concordia College (Moorhead, MN), other colleges of the Minnesota State Colleges and Universities System. The most frequently chosen baccalaureate fields are business/marketing, education, health professions and related sciences.

Student Body Statistics The student body totals 7,520, of whom 7,055 are undergraduates (1,219 freshmen). 57 percent are women and 43 percent are men. Students come from 38 states and territories and 56 other countries. 48 percent are from Minnesota. 5.5 percent are international students.

Expenses for 2008–09 *Application fee:* $20. *State resident tuition:* $5236 full-time, $174.54 per credit part-time. *Nonresident tuition:* $10,472 full-time, $349.08 per credit part-time. *Mandatory fees:* $908 full-time, $25.82 per credit part-time, $168.82 per term part-time. Both full-time and part-time tuition and fees vary according to reciprocity agreements. *College room and board:* $5936. *College room only:* $3632. Room and board charges vary according to board plan and housing facility.

Financial Aid Forms of aid include need-based and non-need-based scholarships, athletic grants, and part-time jobs. The average aided 2008–09 undergraduate received an aid package worth an estimated $7453.

Freshman Admission Minnesota State University Moorhead requires a high school transcript, SAT or ACT scores, and TOEFL scores for international students. The application deadline for regular admission is August 1 and for nonresidents it is August 1.

Transfer Admission The application deadline for admission is August 1.

Entrance Difficulty Minnesota State University Moorhead assesses its entrance difficulty level as moderately difficult. For the fall 2008 freshman class, 80 percent of the applicants were accepted.

For Further Information Contact Ms. Gina Monson, Director of Admissions, Minnesota State University Moorhead, Owens Hall, Moorhead, MN 56563-0002. *Phone:* 218-477-2161 or 800-593-7246 (toll-free). *Fax:* 218-477-4374. *E-mail:* dragon@mnstate.edu. *Web site:* http://www.mnstate.edu/.

MUSICTECH COLLEGE

See McNally Smith College of Music.

NATIONAL AMERICAN UNIVERSITY

Roseville, Minnesota

http://www.national.edu/

NORTH CENTRAL UNIVERSITY

Minneapolis, Minnesota

North Central University is a coed, private, four-year college, founded in 1930, affiliated with the Assemblies of God, offering degrees at the associate and bachelor's levels. It has a 9-acre campus in Minneapolis.

Academic Information The faculty has 102 members (39% full-time). The student-faculty ratio is 19:1. The library holds 80,000 titles and 915 audiovisual materials. Special programs include academic remediation, services for learning-disabled students, cooperative (work-study) education, advanced placement credit, double majors, independent study, self-designed majors, summer session for credit, part-time degree programs (daytime, evenings, weekends, summer), internships, and arrangement for off-campus study.

Student Body Statistics The student body is made up of 1,125 undergraduates. Students come from 42 states and territories and 6 other countries. 45 percent are from Minnesota.

Expenses for 2009–10 *Application fee:* $25. *Comprehensive fee:* $21,201 includes full-time tuition ($14,640), mandatory fees ($1061), and college room and board ($5500). *College room only:* $2450. *Part-time tuition:* $488 per credit hour.

Financial Aid Forms of aid include need-based and non-need-based scholarships and part-time jobs. The application deadline for financial aid is continuous.

Freshman Admission North Central University requires an essay, a high school transcript, a minimum 2.2 high school GPA, Christian testimony, SAT or ACT scores, and TOEFL scores for international students. An interview is required for some. The application deadline for regular admission is June 1.

Transfer Admission The application deadline for admission is June 1.

Entrance Difficulty North Central University has an open admission policy.

For Further Information Contact Ms. Sigi Shawa, Assistant Director, North Central University, 910 Elliot Avenue, Minneapolis, MN 55404. *Phone:* 612-343-4460 or 800-289-6222 (toll-free). *Fax:* 612-343-4146. *E-mail:* admissions@northcentral.edu. *Web site:* http://www.northcentral.edu/.

NORTHWESTERN COLLEGE

St. Paul, Minnesota

Northwestern College is a coed, private, nondenominational, comprehensive institution, founded in 1902, offering degrees at the associate, bachelor's, and master's levels and postbachelor's certificates. It has a 107-acre campus in St. Paul.

Academic Information The faculty has 181 members (55% full-time), 48% with terminal degrees. The undergraduate student-faculty ratio is 14:1. The library holds 124,574 titles, 1,263 serial subscriptions, and 5,092 audiovisual materials. Special programs include academic remediation, services for learning-disabled students, an honors program, study abroad, advanced placement credit, double majors, independent study, distance learning, self-designed majors, summer session for credit, part-time degree programs (evenings, weekends), adult/continuing education programs, internships, and arrangement for off-campus study with Council for Christian Colleges and Universities, Focus on the Family Institute, William Mitchell College of Law. The most frequently chosen baccalaureate fields are education, business/marketing, theology and religious vocations.

Student Body Statistics The student body totals 1,939, of whom 1,846 are undergraduates (437 freshmen). 59 percent are women and 41 percent are men. Students come from 36 states and territories and 25 other countries. 70 percent are from Minnesota. 0.4 percent are international students.

Expenses for 2009–10 *Application fee:* $30. *Comprehensive fee:* $30,606 includes full-time tuition ($22,990), mandatory fees ($190), and college room and board ($7426). *College room only:* $4266.

Financial Aid Forms of aid include need-based and non-need-based scholarships and part-time jobs. The average aided 2008–09 undergraduate received an aid package worth an estimated $15,620.

Freshman Admission Northwestern College requires an essay, a high school transcript, a minimum 2.0 high school GPA, 2 recommendations, lifestyle agreement, statement of Christian faith, SAT or ACT scores, and TOEFL scores for international students. A minimum 3.0 high school GPA is recommended. An interview is required for some. The application deadline for regular admission is August 1.

Transfer Admission The application deadline for admission is August 1.

Entrance Difficulty Northwestern College assesses its entrance difficulty level as moderately difficult. For the fall 2008 freshman class, 95 percent of the applicants were accepted.

For Further Information Contact Mr. Kenneth K. Faffler, Director of Admissions, Northwestern College, Officer of Admissions, 3003 Snelling Avenue North, 212 Nazareth Hall, St. Paul, MN 55113-1598. *Phone:* 651-631-5111 or 800-827-6827 (toll-free). *Fax:* 651-631-5680. *E-mail:* admissions@nwc.edu. *Web site:* http://www.nwc.edu/.

OAK HILLS CHRISTIAN COLLEGE

Bemidji, Minnesota

Oak Hills Christian College is a coed, private, interdenominational, four-year college, founded in 1946, offering degrees at the associate and bachelor's levels. It has a 180-acre campus in Bemidji.

Academic Information The faculty has 20 members (30% full-time), 40% with terminal degrees. The student-faculty ratio is 12.6:1. The library holds 24,210 titles and 64 serial subscriptions. Special programs include academic remediation, services for learning-disabled students, an honors program, advanced placement credit, double majors, independent study, part-time degree programs (daytime, evenings), internships, and arrangement for off-campus study. The most frequently chosen baccalaureate fields are liberal arts/general studies, theology and religious vocations.

Student Body Statistics The student body is made up of 144 undergraduates (24 freshmen). 51 percent are women and 49 percent are men. Students come from 17 states and territories and 1 other country. 71 percent are from Minnesota. 0.7 percent are international students.

Expenses for 2008–09 *Application fee:* $25. *Comprehensive fee:* $18,320 includes full-time tuition ($13,480) and college room and board ($4840). Room and board charges vary according to board plan, housing facility, and location. *Part-time tuition:* $395 per credit. Part-time tuition varies according to course load.

Financial Aid Forms of aid include need-based and non-need-based scholarships and part-time jobs. The application deadline for financial aid is continuous.

Freshman Admission Oak Hills Christian College requires an essay, a high school transcript, a minimum 2.0 high school GPA, 2 recommendations, and SAT or ACT scores. An interview is required for some. The application deadline for regular admission is rolling.

Transfer Admission The application deadline for admission is rolling.

Entrance Difficulty Oak Hills Christian College assesses its entrance difficulty level as minimally difficult. For the fall 2008 freshman class, 91 percent of the applicants were accepted.

For Further Information Contact Shelly Fast, Assistant Director of Admissions, Oak Hills Christian College, 1600 Oak Hills Rd. SW, Bemidji, MN 56601. *Phone:* 218-751-8670 Ext. 1285 or 888-751-8670 Ext. 285 (toll-free). *Fax:* 218-751-8825. *E-mail:* admissions@oakhills.edu. *Web site:* http://www.oakhills.edu/.

RASMUSSEN COLLEGE EAGAN

Eagan, Minnesota

Rasmussen College Eagan is a coed, primarily women's, proprietary, primarily two-year college of Rasmussen College System, founded in 1904, offering degrees at the associate and bachelor's levels. It has a 10-acre campus in Eagan near Minneapolis–St. Paul.

Academic Information The faculty has 40 members (25% full-time). The student-faculty ratio is 12:1. Special programs include academic remediation, part-time degree programs (evenings), adult/continuing education programs, and internships.

Student Body Statistics The student body is made up of 537 undergraduates.

Financial Aid Forms of aid include need-based scholarships. The application deadline for financial aid is continuous.

Freshman Admission Rasmussen College Eagan requires a high school transcript, a minimum 2.0 high school GPA, an interview, TOEFL scores for international students, and ACT COMPASS. The application deadline for regular admission is rolling.

Transfer Admission The application deadline for admission is rolling.

Entrance Difficulty Rasmussen College Eagan assesses its entrance difficulty level as moderately difficult.

For Further Information Contact Ms. Jacinda Miller, Admissions Coordinator, Rasmussen College Eagan, 3500 Federal Drive, Eagan, MN 55122-1346. *Phone:* 651-687-9000 or 800-852-6367 (toll-free). *E-mail:* admission@rasmussen.edu. *Web site:* http://www.rasmussen.edu/.

RASMUSSEN COLLEGE MANKATO

Mankato, Minnesota

Rasmussen College Mankato is a coed, primarily women's, proprietary, primarily two-year college of Rasmussen College System, founded in 1904, offering degrees at the associate and bachelor's levels. It is located in Mankato near Minneapolis–St. Paul.

For Further Information Contact Ms. Kathy Clifford, Director of Admissions, Rasmussen College Mankato, 501 Holly Lane, Mankato, MN 56001-6803. *Phone:* 507-625-6556 or 800-657-6767 (toll-free in-state). *Fax:* 507-625-6557. *E-mail:* rascoll@ic.mankato.mn.us. *Web site:* http://www.rasmussen.edu/.

RASMUSSEN COLLEGE MOORHEAD

Moorhead, Minnesota

http://www.rasmussen.edu/

RASMUSSEN COLLEGE ST. CLOUD

St. Cloud, Minnesota

Rasmussen College St. Cloud is a coed, primarily women's, proprietary, primarily two-year college of Rasmussen College System, founded in 1904, offering degrees at the associate and bachelor's levels. It is located in St. Cloud near Minneapolis–St. Paul.

Academic Information The library holds 689 titles, 31 serial subscriptions, and 173 audiovisual materials. Special programs include academic remediation, double majors, distance learning, summer session for credit, part-time degree programs (daytime, evenings, summer), adult/continuing education programs, and internships.
Student Body Statistics The student body is made up of 743 undergraduates.
Financial Aid Forms of aid include need-based scholarships and part-time jobs. The application deadline for financial aid is continuous.
Freshman Admission Rasmussen College St. Cloud requires a high school transcript, a minimum 2.0 high school GPA, an interview, and ACT COMPASS. The application deadline for regular admission is rolling.
Transfer Admission The application deadline for admission is rolling.
Entrance Difficulty Rasmussen College St. Cloud assesses its entrance difficulty level as minimally difficult.
For Further Information Contact Ms. Andrea Peters, Director of Admissions, Rasmussen College St. Cloud, 226 Park Avenue South, St. Cloud, MN 56301. *Phone:* 320-251-5600 or 800-852-0460 (toll-free in-state). *Fax:* 320-251-3702. *E-mail:* admstc@rasmussen.edu. *Web site:* http://www.rasmussen.edu/.

ROCHESTER COMMUNITY AND TECHNICAL COLLEGE

Rochester, Minnesota

Rochester Community and Technical College is a coed, public, primarily two-year college of Minnesota State Colleges and Universities System, founded in 1915, offering degrees at the associate and bachelor's levels (also offers 13 programs that lead to a bachelor's degree with Winona State University or University of Minnesota). It has a 460-acre campus in Rochester.

Academic Information The library holds 62,000 titles and 600 serial subscriptions. Special programs include academic remediation, services for learning-disabled students, an honors program, advanced placement credit, ESL programs, independent study, distance learning, summer session for credit, part-time degree programs (daytime, evenings, weekends, summer), internships, and arrangement for off-campus study with other colleges in the Minnesota State Colleges and Universities System, Winona State University–Rochester Center.
Student Body Statistics The student body is made up of 5,898 undergraduates.
Expenses for 2008–09 *Application fee:* $20. *State resident tuition:* $4151 full-time, $138.35 per credit hour part-time. *Nonresident tuition:* $4151 full-time, $138.35 per credit hour part-time. Both full-time and part-time tuition varies according to course load and reciprocity agreements.
Financial Aid Forms of aid include need-based scholarships and part-time jobs. The application deadline for financial aid is continuous.
Freshman Admission Rochester Community and Technical College requires a high school transcript and TOEFL scores for international students. The application deadline for regular admission is August 24.
Transfer Admission The application deadline for admission is August 24.
Entrance Difficulty Rochester Community and Technical College has an open admission policy except for allied health, technology programs. It assesses its entrance difficulty as moderately difficult for allied health programs.
For Further Information Contact Mr. Troy Tynsky, Director of Admissions, Rochester Community and Technical College, 851 30th Avenue, SE, Rochester, MN 55904-4999. *Phone:* 507-280-3509. *Fax:* 507-285-7496. *Web site:* http://www.rctc.edu/.

ST. CATHERINE UNIVERSITY

St. Paul, Minnesota

St. Catherine University is an undergraduate: women only; graduate: coed, private, Roman Catholic, comprehensive institution, founded in 1905, offering degrees at the associate, bachelor's, master's, and doctoral levels and post-master's and postbachelor's certificates. It has a 110-acre campus in St. Paul near Minneapolis.

Academic Information The faculty has 480 members (56% full-time). The undergraduate student-faculty ratio is 11:1. The library holds 263,495 titles and 1,141 serial subscriptions. Special programs include academic remediation, services for learning-disabled students, an honors program, study abroad, advanced placement credit, double majors, independent study, self-designed majors, summer session for credit, part-time degree programs (daytime, weekends, summer), external degree programs, adult/continuing education programs, internships, and arrangement for off-campus study with Associated Colleges of the Twin Cities, Sisters of St. Joseph College Consortium, Higher Education Consortium for Urban Affairs. The most frequently chosen baccalaureate fields are business/marketing, English, health professions and related sciences.
Student Body Statistics The student body totals 5,201, of whom 3,727 are undergraduates (449 freshmen). 97 percent are women and 3 percent are men. Students come from 37 states and territories and 16 other countries. 92 percent are from Minnesota. 1.4 percent are international students.
Expenses for 2008–09 *Application fee:* $0. *One-time mandatory fee:* $85. *Comprehensive fee:* $34,504 includes full-time tuition ($27,136), mandatory fees ($278), and college room and board ($7090). *College room only:* $3950. Full-time tuition and fees vary according to class time and degree level. Room and board charges vary according to board plan and housing facility. *Part-time tuition:* $848 per credit hour. *Part-time mandatory fees:* $139 per term. Part-time tuition and fees vary according to class time and degree level.
Financial Aid Forms of aid include need-based and non-need-based scholarships and part-time jobs. The average aided 2008–09 undergraduate received an aid package worth an estimated $28,471. The priority application deadline for financial aid is April 15.
Freshman Admission St. Catherine University requires a high school transcript, 1 recommendation, SAT or ACT scores, and TOEFL scores for international students. An interview is recommended. An essay and an interview are required for some. The application deadline for regular admission is rolling.
Transfer Admission The application deadline for admission is rolling.
Entrance Difficulty St. Catherine University assesses its entrance difficulty level as moderately difficult. For the fall 2008 freshman class, 77 percent of the applicants were accepted.
For Further Information Contact Ms. Cory Piper-Hauswirth, Associate Director of Admission and Financial Aid, St. Catherine University, 2004 Randolph Avenue, F-02, St. Paul, MN 55105. *Phone:* 651-690-6047 or 800-656-5283 (toll-free in-state). *Fax:* 651-690-8824. *E-mail:* stkate@stkate.edu. *Web site:* http://www.stkate.edu/.

ST. CLOUD STATE UNIVERSITY

St. Cloud, Minnesota

St. Cloud State University is a coed, public, comprehensive unit of Minnesota State Colleges and Universities System, founded in 1869, offering degrees at the associate, bachelor's, master's, and doctoral levels and postbachelor's certificates. It has a 922-acre campus in St. Cloud near Minneapolis–St. Paul.

Academic Information The faculty has 945 members (68% full-time), 52% with terminal degrees. The undergraduate student-faculty ratio is 19:1. The library holds 947,787 titles, 955 serial subscriptions, and 26,927 audiovisual materials. Special programs include academic remediation, services for learning-disabled students, an honors program, study abroad, advanced placement credit, accelerated degree programs, ESL programs, double majors, independent study, distance learning, self-designed majors, summer session for credit, part-time degree programs (daytime, evenings, weekends, summer), adult/continuing education programs, internships, and arrangement for off-campus study with members of the Tri-College

Exchange Program, other colleges in the Minnesota State Colleges and University System. The most frequently chosen baccalaureate fields are business/marketing, communications/journalism, education.
Student Body Statistics The student body totals 16,921, of whom 15,157 are undergraduates (2,403 freshmen). 52 percent are women and 48 percent are men. Students come from 46 states and territories and 81 other countries. 91 percent are from Minnesota.
Expenses for 2008–09 *Application fee:* $20. *State resident tuition:* $5405 full-time, $180 per credit part-time. *Nonresident tuition:* $11,732 full-time, $391 per credit part-time. *Mandatory fees:* $742 full-time, $29.58 per credit part-time. Both full-time and part-time tuition and fees vary according to course load and reciprocity agreements. *College room and board:* $5770. *College room only:* $3688. Room and board charges vary according to board plan and housing facility.
Financial Aid Forms of aid include need-based and non-need-based scholarships, athletic grants, and part-time jobs. The average aided 2008–09 undergraduate received an aid package worth an estimated $10,059. The application deadline for financial aid is continuous.
Freshman Admission St. Cloud State University requires a high school transcript, SAT or ACT scores, and TOEFL scores for international students. The application deadline for regular admission is June 1.
Transfer Admission The application deadline for admission is August 15.
Entrance Difficulty St. Cloud State University assesses its entrance difficulty level as moderately difficult; most difficult for honors program. For the fall 2008 freshman class, 86 percent of the applicants were accepted.
For Further Information Contact Mr. Richard Shearer, Director of Admissions, St. Cloud State University, 115 AS Building, 720 4th Avenue South, St. Cloud, MN 56301-4498. *Phone:* 320-308-2244 or 877-654-7278 (toll-free). *Fax:* 320-308-2243. *E-mail:* scsu4u@stcloudstate.edu. *Web site:* http://www.stcloudstate.edu/.

SAINT JOHN'S UNIVERSITY

Collegeville, Minnesota

Saint John's University is a coed, primarily men's, private, Roman Catholic, comprehensive institution, founded in 1857, offering degrees at the bachelor's, master's, and first professional levels (coordinate with College of Saint Benedict for women). It has a 2,400-acre campus in Collegeville near Minneapolis–St. Paul.

Academic Information The faculty has 176 members (82% full-time), 76% with terminal degrees. The undergraduate student-faculty ratio is 12:1. The library holds 749,886 titles, 13,700 serial subscriptions, and 34,747 audiovisual materials. Special programs include services for learning-disabled students, an honors program, study abroad, advanced placement credit, accelerated degree programs, ESL programs, double majors, independent study, self-designed majors, internships, and arrangement for off-campus study with College of Saint Benedict, Tri-College Exchange Program. The most frequently chosen baccalaureate fields are business/marketing, English, social sciences.
Student Body Statistics The student body totals 2,063, of whom 1,938 are undergraduates (461 freshmen). 100 percent are men. Students come from 39 states and territories and 47 other countries. 84 percent are from Minnesota. 6.3 percent are international students.
Expenses for 2008–09 *Application fee:* $0. *One-time mandatory fee:* $40. *Comprehensive fee:* $35,876 includes full-time tuition ($28,122), mandatory fees ($506), and college room and board ($7248). *College room only:* $3664. Full-time tuition and fees vary according to student level. Room and board charges vary according to board plan and housing facility. *Part-time tuition:* $1171 per credit hour. Part-time tuition varies according to course load.
Financial Aid Forms of aid include need-based and non-need-based scholarships and part-time jobs. The average aided 2008–09 undergraduate received an aid package worth an estimated $21,653. The priority application deadline for financial aid is March 15.
Freshman Admission Saint John's University requires an essay, a high school transcript, 1 recommendation, SAT or ACT scores, and TOEFL scores for international students. A minimum 3.0 high school GPA and an interview are recommended. The application deadline for regular admission is rolling and for early action it is November 15.
Transfer Admission The application deadline for admission is rolling.
Entrance Difficulty Saint John's University assesses its entrance difficulty level as moderately difficult. For the fall 2008 freshman class, 74 percent of the applicants were accepted.
For Further Information Contact Mr. Matt Beirne, Director of Admission, Saint John's University, PO Box 7155, Collegeville, MN 56321-7155. *Phone:* 320-363-2196 or 800-544-1489 (toll-free). *Fax:* 320-363-2750. *E-mail:* admissions@csbsju.edu. *Web site:* http://www.csbsju.edu/.

SAINT MARY'S UNIVERSITY OF MINNESOTA

Winona, Minnesota

Saint Mary's University of Minnesota is a coed, private, Roman Catholic, comprehensive institution, founded in 1912, offering degrees at the bachelor's, master's, and doctoral levels and post-master's and postbachelor's certificates. It has a 350-acre campus in Winona.

Academic Information The faculty has 576 members (19% full-time), 45% with terminal degrees. The undergraduate student-faculty ratio is 12:1. The library holds 241,470 titles, 39,650 serial subscriptions, and 10,087 audiovisual materials. Special programs include academic remediation, services for learning-disabled students, an honors program, cooperative (work-study) education, study abroad, advanced placement credit, accelerated degree programs, ESL programs, double majors, independent study, self-designed majors, summer session for credit, part-time degree programs (daytime, evenings, summer), external degree programs, adult/continuing education programs, internships, and arrangement for off-campus study with Winona State University. The most frequently chosen baccalaureate fields are business/marketing, computer and information sciences, security and protective services.
Student Body Statistics The student body totals 5,611, of whom 2,067 are undergraduates (404 freshmen). 53 percent are women and 47 percent are men. Students come from 24 states and territories and 15 other countries. 61 percent are from Minnesota. 3.8 percent are international students.
Expenses for 2009–10 *Application fee:* $25. *Comprehensive fee:* $32,330 includes full-time tuition ($25,090), mandatory fees ($480), and college room and board ($6760). *College room only:* $3780. *Part-time tuition:* $840 per credit. *Part-time mandatory fees:* $480 per year.
Financial Aid Forms of aid include need-based and non-need-based scholarships and part-time jobs. The average aided 2008–09 undergraduate received an aid package worth an estimated $17,541.
Freshman Admission Saint Mary's University of Minnesota requires an essay, a high school transcript, a minimum 2.5 high school GPA, SAT or ACT scores, and TOEFL scores for international students. 2 recommendations are recommended. An interview is required for some. The application deadline for regular admission is May 1.
Transfer Admission The application deadline for admission is rolling.
Entrance Difficulty Saint Mary's University of Minnesota assesses its entrance difficulty level as moderately difficult. For the fall 2008 freshman class, 74 percent of the applicants were accepted.
For Further Information Contact Mr. Anthony M. Piscitiello, Vice President for Admission, Saint Mary's University of Minnesota, 700 Terrace Heights, Winona, MN 55987-1399. *Phone:* 507-457-1700 or 800-635-5987 (toll-free). *Fax:* 507-457-1722. *E-mail:* admission@smumn.edu. *Web site:* http://www.smumn.edu/.

ST. OLAF COLLEGE

Northfield, Minnesota

St. Olaf College is a coed, private, Lutheran, four-year college, founded in 1874, offering degrees at the bachelor's level. It has a 300-acre campus in Northfield near Minneapolis–St. Paul.

Academic Information The faculty has 323 members (60% full-time), 78% with terminal degrees. The student-faculty ratio is 12.8:1. The library holds 741,478 titles, 5,935 serial subscriptions, and 24,208 audiovisual materials. Special programs include services for learning-disabled students, study abroad, advanced placement credit, double majors, independent study, self-designed majors, summer session for credit, part-time degree

St. Olaf College (continued)

programs (daytime), internships, and arrangement for off-campus study with Augsburg College, Minnesota Intercollegiate Nursing Consortium, Oak Ridge Science semester, Biosphere 2 Earth semester, HECUA programs, Environmental Science at Superior Studies site. The most frequently chosen baccalaureate fields are biological/life sciences, social sciences, visual and performing arts.

Student Body Statistics The student body is made up of 3,073 undergraduates (813 freshmen). 55 percent are women and 45 percent are men. Students come from 50 states and territories and 30 other countries. 55 percent are from Minnesota. 2 percent are international students.

Expenses for 2009–10 *Application fee:* $0. *Comprehensive fee:* $43,700 includes full-time tuition ($35,500) and college room and board ($8200). *College room only:* $3800.

Financial Aid Forms of aid include need-based and non-need-based scholarships and part-time jobs. The average aided 2008–09 undergraduate received an aid package worth an estimated $27,401. The application deadline for financial aid is April 15 with a priority deadline of January 15.

Freshman Admission St. Olaf College requires an essay, a high school transcript, 2 recommendations, SAT or ACT scores, and TOEFL scores for international students. An interview is recommended. The application deadline for regular admission is January 15, for early decision plan 1 it is November 15, and for early decision plan 2 it is January 15.

Transfer Admission The application deadline for admission is March 1.

Entrance Difficulty St. Olaf College assesses its entrance difficulty level as very difficult. For the fall 2008 freshman class, 59 percent of the applicants were accepted.

For Further Information Contact Derek Gueldenzoph, Dean of Admissions, St. Olaf College, 1520 St. Olaf Avenue, Northfield, MN 55057. *Phone:* 507-786-3025 or 800-800-3025 (toll-free). *Fax:* 507-786-3832. *E-mail:* admissions@stolaf.edu. *Web site:* http://www.stolaf.edu/.

SOUTHWEST MINNESOTA STATE UNIVERSITY

Marshall, Minnesota

Southwest Minnesota State University is a coed, public, comprehensive unit of Minnesota State Colleges and Universities System, founded in 1963, offering degrees at the associate, bachelor's, and master's levels. It has a 216-acre campus in Marshall.

Academic Information The faculty has 215 members (59% full-time), 57% with terminal degrees. The undergraduate student-faculty ratio is 23:1. The library holds 394,508 titles, 301 serial subscriptions, and 11,239 audiovisual materials. Special programs include academic remediation, services for learning-disabled students, an honors program, study abroad, advanced placement credit, accelerated degree programs, Freshman Honors College, ESL programs, double majors, independent study, distance learning, self-designed majors, summer session for credit, part-time degree programs (daytime, evenings, weekends, summer), external degree programs, adult/continuing education programs, internships, and arrangement for off-campus study with other colleges in the Minnesota State College and University System. The most frequently chosen baccalaureate fields are business/marketing, education, parks and recreation.

Student Body Statistics The student body totals 6,502, of whom 6,114 are undergraduates (506 freshmen). 56 percent are women and 44 percent are men. Students come from 30 states and territories and 24 other countries. 84 percent are from Minnesota. 10.2 percent are international students.

Expenses for 2008–09 *Application fee:* $20. *State resident tuition:* $5780 full-time, $186 per credit part-time. *Nonresident tuition:* $5780 full-time, $186 per credit part-time. *Mandatory fees:* $916 full-time, $35.56 per credit part-time. Full-time tuition and fees vary according to reciprocity agreements. Part-time tuition and fees vary according to class time, course load, and reciprocity agreements. *College room and board:* $5984. *College room only:* $3484. Room and board charges vary according to board plan and housing facility.

Financial Aid Forms of aid include need-based and non-need-based scholarships, athletic grants, and part-time jobs. The average aided 2008–09 undergraduate received an aid package worth an estimated $7810. The priority application deadline for financial aid is March 1.

Freshman Admission Southwest Minnesota State University requires an essay, a high school transcript, an interview, SAT or ACT scores, and TOEFL scores for international students. ACT scores are recommended. The application deadline for regular admission is rolling.

Transfer Admission The application deadline for admission is rolling.

Entrance Difficulty Southwest Minnesota State University assesses its entrance difficulty level as minimally difficult. For the fall 2008 freshman class, 72 percent of the applicants were accepted.

For Further Information Contact Ms. LeAnn Thooft, Director of Admissions (Interim), Southwest Minnesota State University, 1501 State Street, Marshall, MN 56258. *Phone:* 507-537-6286 or 800-642-0684 (toll-free). *Fax:* 507-537-7154. *E-mail:* shearerr@southwest.msus.edu. *Web site:* http://www.smsu.edu/.

UNIVERSITY OF MINNESOTA, CROOKSTON

Crookston, Minnesota

University of Minnesota, Crookston is a coed, public, four-year college of University of Minnesota System, founded in 1966, offering degrees at the bachelor's level. It has a 237-acre campus in Crookston.

Academic Information The faculty has 108 members (49% full-time), 39% with terminal degrees. The student-faculty ratio is 16:1. The library holds 55,303 titles, 31,507 serial subscriptions, and 1,544 audiovisual materials. Special programs include academic remediation, services for learning-disabled students, study abroad, advanced placement credit, ESL programs, double majors, independent study, distance learning, self-designed majors, summer session for credit, part-time degree programs (daytime, evenings, summer), external degree programs, adult/continuing education programs, and internships. The most frequently chosen baccalaureate fields are agriculture, business/marketing, natural resources/environmental science.

Student Body Statistics The student body is made up of 2,199 undergraduates (276 freshmen). 48 percent are women and 52 percent are men. Students come from 35 states and territories and 23 other countries. 68 percent are from Minnesota. 8.4 percent are international students.

Expenses for 2008–09 *Application fee:* $30. *State resident tuition:* $6888 full-time. *Nonresident tuition:* $6888 full-time. *Mandatory fees:* $2493 full-time. Full-time tuition and fees vary according to course load. *College room and board:* $5670. *College room only:* $2820. Room and board charges vary according to board plan and housing facility. The U of M, Crookston has restructured the tuition policy in favor of a flat-rate tuition strategy which makes all credits above 13 per semester tuition-free. Students taking 13 or more credits will pay a flat tuition rate of $3,444 per semester. Students taking 1 to 12 credits will be assessed $264.92 per credit.

Financial Aid Forms of aid include need-based scholarships, athletic grants, and part-time jobs. The average aided 2008–09 undergraduate received an aid package worth an estimated $11,043. The priority application deadline for financial aid is March 1.

Freshman Admission University of Minnesota, Crookston requires a high school transcript and SAT or ACT scores. ACT scores and TOEFL scores for international students are recommended. The application deadline for regular admission is rolling.

Transfer Admission The application deadline for admission is rolling.

Entrance Difficulty University of Minnesota, Crookston assesses its entrance difficulty level as moderately difficult. For the fall 2008 freshman class, 75 percent of the applicants were accepted.

For Further Information Contact Ms. Amber Evans-Dailey, Director of Admissions, University of Minnesota, Crookston, 2900 University Avenue, Crookston, MN 56716-5001. *Phone:* 218-281-8569 or 800-862-6466 (toll-free). *Fax:* 218-281-8575. *E-mail:* info@umcrookston.edu. *Web site:* http://www.umcrookston.edu/.

UNIVERSITY OF MINNESOTA, DULUTH

Duluth, Minnesota

University of Minnesota, Duluth is a coed, public, comprehensive unit of University of Minnesota System, founded in 1947, offering degrees at the bachelor's, master's, doctoral, and first professional levels and postbachelor's certificates. It has a 250-acre campus in Duluth.

Academic Information The faculty has 599 members (73% full-time). The undergraduate student-faculty ratio is 22:1. The library holds 587,547 titles, 36,935 serial subscriptions, and 18,265 audiovisual materials. Special programs include academic remediation, services for learning-disabled students, an honors program, study abroad, advanced placement credit, ESL programs, double majors, independent study, self-designed majors, summer session for credit, part-time degree programs (daytime, evenings, summer), adult/continuing education programs, internships, and arrangement for off-campus study with University of Wisconsin-Superior, College of St. Scholastica. The most frequently chosen baccalaureate fields are business/marketing, education, social sciences.
Student Body Statistics The student body totals 11,365, of whom 10,243 are undergraduates. 47 percent are women and 53 percent are men. Students come from 36 states and territories and 42 other countries. 86 percent are from Minnesota. 1.4 percent are international students.
Expenses for 2008–09 *Application fee:* $35. *State resident tuition:* $8230 full-time, $316.54 per credit part-time. *Nonresident tuition:* $10,230 full-time, $393.47 per credit part-time. *Mandatory fees:* $2030 full-time, $55 per credit part-time. Both full-time and part-time tuition and fees vary according to course load, degree level, program, and reciprocity agreements. *College room and board:* $6078.
Financial Aid Forms of aid include need-based scholarships, athletic grants, and part-time jobs. The average aided 2008–09 undergraduate received an aid package worth an estimated $9265. The priority application deadline for financial aid is March 1.
Freshman Admission University of Minnesota, Duluth requires a high school transcript, SAT or ACT scores, and TOEFL scores for international students. The application deadline for regular admission is December 15.
Transfer Admission The application deadline for admission is August 1.
Entrance Difficulty University of Minnesota, Duluth assesses its entrance difficulty level as moderately difficult. For the fall 2008 freshman class, 66 percent of the applicants were accepted.
For Further Information Contact Admissions, University of Minnesota, Duluth, 23 Solon Campus Center, 1117 University Drive, Duluth, MN 55812-3000. *Phone:* 218-726-7171 or 800-232-1339 (toll-free). *Fax:* 218-726-7040. *E-mail:* umdadmis@d.umn.edu. *Web site:* http://www.d.umn.edu/.

UNIVERSITY OF MINNESOTA, MORRIS

Morris, Minnesota

University of Minnesota, Morris is a coed, public, four-year college of University of Minnesota System, founded in 1959, offering degrees at the bachelor's level. It has a 130-acre campus in Morris.

Academic Information The faculty has 153 members (69% full-time), 76% with terminal degrees. The student-faculty ratio is 13:1. Special programs include services for learning-disabled students, an honors program, advanced placement credit, accelerated degree programs, Freshman Honors College, ESL programs, double majors, independent study, distance learning, self-designed majors, summer session for credit, part-time degree programs (daytime, summer), internships, and arrangement for off-campus study with other units of the University of Minnesota System, National Student Exchange. The most frequently chosen baccalaureate fields are English, biological/life sciences, social sciences.
Student Body Statistics The student body is made up of 1,607 undergraduates (492 freshmen). 58 percent are women and 42 percent are men. Students come from 30 states and territories and 11 other countries. 88 percent are from Minnesota.
Expenses for 2008–09 *Application fee:* $35. *State resident tuition:* $8230 full-time. *Nonresident tuition:* $8230 full-time. *Mandatory fees:* $1776 full-time. Full-time tuition and fees vary according to reciprocity agreements. *College room and board:* $6710. *College room only:* $3130. Room and board charges vary according to board plan and housing facility.
Financial Aid Forms of aid include need-based and non-need-based scholarships and part-time jobs. The average aided 2007–08 undergraduate received an aid package worth $10,923. The priority application deadline for financial aid is March 1.
Freshman Admission University of Minnesota, Morris requires a high school transcript, SAT or ACT scores, and TOEFL scores for international students. A minimum 3.0 high school GPA is recommended. An essay, 1 recommendation, and an interview are required for some. The application deadline for regular admission is March 15.
Transfer Admission The application deadline for admission is May 1.
Entrance Difficulty University of Minnesota, Morris assesses its entrance difficulty level as moderately difficult. For the fall 2008 freshman class, 71 percent of the applicants were accepted.
For Further Information Contact Bryan Herrmann, Director of Admissions, University of Minnesota, Morris, 600 East 4th Street, Morris, MN 56267-2134. *Phone:* 320-539-6035 or 800-992-8863 (toll-free). *Fax:* 320-589-1673. *E-mail:* admissions@morris.umn.edu. *Web site:* http://www.mrs.umn.edu/.

UNIVERSITY OF MINNESOTA, TWIN CITIES CAMPUS

Minneapolis, Minnesota

University of Minnesota, Twin Cities Campus is a coed, public unit of University of Minnesota System, founded in 1851, offering degrees at the bachelor's, master's, doctoral, and first professional levels and post-master's, first professional, and postbachelor's certificates. It has a 2,000-acre campus in Minneapolis.

Academic Information The faculty has 2,892 members (67% full-time), 68% with terminal degrees. The undergraduate student-faculty ratio is 20:1. The library holds 6 million titles, 45,000 serial subscriptions, and 1 million audiovisual materials. Special programs include academic remediation, services for learning-disabled students, an honors program, cooperative (work-study) education, study abroad, advanced placement credit, accelerated degree programs, Freshman Honors College, ESL programs, double majors, independent study, distance learning, self-designed majors, summer session for credit, part-time degree programs (daytime, evenings, weekends, summer), external degree programs, adult/continuing education programs, internships, and arrangement for off-campus study with National Student Exchange, Minnesota Community College System. The most frequently chosen baccalaureate fields are engineering, business/marketing, social sciences.
Student Body Statistics The student body totals 51,140, of whom 32,557 are undergraduates (5,106 freshmen). 53 percent are women and 47 percent are men. Students come from 51 states and territories and 77 other countries. 74 percent are from Minnesota. 3.1 percent are international students.
Expenses for 2008–09 *Application fee:* $45. *State resident tuition:* $8500 full-time, $326.92 per credit part-time. *Nonresident tuition:* $20,130 full-time, $774.23 per credit part-time. *Mandatory fees:* $1773 full-time. Full-time tuition and fees vary according to program and reciprocity agreements. Part-time tuition varies according to course load, program, and reciprocity agreements. *College room and board:* $7280. *College room only:* $4294. Room and board charges vary according to board plan, housing facility, and location.
Financial Aid Forms of aid include need-based and non-need-based scholarships and part-time jobs. The average aided 2008–09 undergraduate received an aid package worth an estimated $12,823. The application deadline for financial aid is continuous.
Freshman Admission University of Minnesota, Twin Cities Campus requires a high school transcript, SAT or ACT scores, and TOEFL scores for international students. A minimum 2.0 high school GPA is recommended. The application deadline for regular admission is rolling.
Transfer Admission The application deadline for admission is rolling.
Entrance Difficulty University of Minnesota, Twin Cities Campus assesses its entrance difficulty level as moderately difficult; very difficult for

University of Minnesota, Twin Cities Campus (continued)

Institute of Technology, management, biological science programs. For the fall 2008 freshman class, 53 percent of the applicants were accepted.

For Further Information Contact Rachelle Hernandez, Associate Director of Admissions, University of Minnesota, Twin Cities Campus, 240 Williamson, Minneapolis, MN 55455-0213. *Phone:* 612-625-2008 or 800-752-1000 (toll-free). *Fax:* 612-626-1693. *E-mail:* admissions@tc.umn.edu. *Web site:* http://www.umn.edu/tc/.

UNIVERSITY OF ST. THOMAS

St. Paul, Minnesota

University of St. Thomas is a coed, private, Roman Catholic university, founded in 1885, offering degrees at the bachelor's, master's, doctoral, and first professional levels and post-master's and postbachelor's certificates. It has a 78-acre campus in St. Paul near Minneapolis.

Expenses for 2008–09 *Application fee:* $0. *Comprehensive fee:* $35,436 includes full-time tuition ($27,328), mandatory fees ($494), and college room and board ($7614). *College room only:* $4872. *Part-time tuition:* $854 per credit hour.

For Further Information Contact Ms. Marla Friederichs, Associate Vice President of Enrollment Management, University of St. Thomas, 2115 Summit Avenue, Mail #32F-1, St. Paul, MN 55105-1096. *Phone:* 651-962-6150 or 800-328-6819 Ext. 26150 (toll-free). *Fax:* 651-962-6160. *E-mail:* admissions@stthomas.edu. *Web site:* http://www.stthomas.edu/.

WALDEN UNIVERSITY

Minneapolis, Minnesota

Walden University is a coed, proprietary, upper-level unit of Laureate International Universities Network, founded in 1970, offering degrees at the bachelor's, master's, and doctoral levels.

Expenses for 2008–09 *Tuition:* $11,276 full-time, $250 per credit part-time. *Mandatory fees:* $120 full-time, $30 per term part-time. Both full-time and part-time tuition and fees vary according to course level, course load, and program. Based on a 12-month continuous enrollment from September thru August.

For Further Information Contact Ms. Dawn Wolff, Director of Admissions, Walden University, 155 Fifth Avenue South, Minneapolis, MN 55401. *Phone:* 800-925-3368 or 866-492-5336 (toll-free out-of-state). *Fax:* 410-843-8780. *E-mail:* request@waldenu.edu. *Web site:* http://www.waldenu.edu/.

WINONA STATE UNIVERSITY

Winona, Minnesota

Winona State University is a coed, public, comprehensive unit of Minnesota State Colleges and Universities System, founded in 1858, offering degrees at the associate, bachelor's, and master's levels and post-master's certificates. It has a 40-acre campus in Winona.

Academic Information The faculty has 501 members (73% full-time), 57% with terminal degrees. The undergraduate student-faculty ratio is 21:1. The library holds 350,000 titles, 1,000 serial subscriptions, and 8,000 audiovisual materials. Special programs include academic remediation, services for learning-disabled students, an honors program, study abroad, advanced placement credit, accelerated degree programs, ESL programs, double majors, independent study, distance learning, self-designed majors, summer session for credit, part-time degree programs (daytime, evenings, weekends, summer), external degree programs, adult/continuing education programs, internships, and arrangement for off-campus study with Saint Mary's University of Minnesota, other colleges in the Minnesota State Colleges and Universities System.

Student Body Statistics The student body totals 8,220, of whom 7,608 are undergraduates (1,727 freshmen). 62 percent are women and 38 percent are men. Students come from 21 states and territories and 48 other countries. 66 percent are from Minnesota. 4 percent are international students.

Expenses for 2008–09 *Application fee:* $20. *State resident tuition:* $5768 full-time. *Nonresident tuition:* $10,372 full-time. *Mandatory fees:* $1859 full-time. *College room and board:* $6430. *College room only:* $4674.

Financial Aid Forms of aid include need-based and non-need-based scholarships, athletic grants, and part-time jobs. The average aided 2007–08 undergraduate received an aid package worth $6020. The application deadline for financial aid is continuous.

Freshman Admission Winona State University requires a high school transcript, class rank, SAT or ACT scores, and TOEFL scores for international students. An essay and an interview are required for some. The application deadline for regular admission is rolling.

Transfer Admission The application deadline for admission is July 15.

Entrance Difficulty Winona State University assesses its entrance difficulty level as moderately difficult; minimally difficult for adult students. For the fall 2008 freshman class, 79 percent of the applicants were accepted.

For Further Information Contact Carl Stange, Director of Admissions, Winona State University, PO Box 5838, Winona, MN 55987. *Phone:* 507-457-5100 or 800-DIAL WSU (toll-free). *Fax:* 507-457-5620. *E-mail:* admissions@winona.edu. *Web site:* http://www.winona.edu/.

Missouri

AVILA UNIVERSITY

Kansas City, Missouri

Avila University is a coed, private, Roman Catholic, comprehensive institution, founded in 1916, offering degrees at the bachelor's and master's levels and postbachelor's certificates. It has a 50-acre campus in Kansas City.

Academic Information The faculty has 193 members (33% full-time), 38% with terminal degrees. The undergraduate student-faculty ratio is 12:1. The library holds 80,845 titles and 22,464 serial subscriptions. Special programs include academic remediation, services for learning-disabled students, cooperative (work-study) education, study abroad, advanced placement credit, accelerated degree programs, ESL programs, double majors, independent study, distance learning, summer session for credit, part-time degree programs (daytime, evenings, weekends, summer), adult/continuing education programs, internships, and arrangement for off-campus study with Sisters of St. Joseph Consortium, Council of Independent Colleges Exchange Program. The most frequently chosen baccalaureate fields are business/marketing, education, health professions and related sciences.

Student Body Statistics The student body totals 1,939, of whom 1,213 are undergraduates (183 freshmen). 66 percent are women and 34 percent are men. Students come from 20 states and territories and 33 other countries. 68 percent are from Missouri. 7.9 percent are international students.

Expenses for 2009–10 *Application fee:* $25. *Comprehensive fee:* $26,500 includes full-time tuition ($20,300) and college room and board ($6200). *College room only:* $3000. *Part-time tuition:* $515 per credit hour. *Part-time mandatory fees:* $24 per credit hour.

Financial Aid Forms of aid include need-based and non-need-based scholarships, athletic grants, and part-time jobs. The average aided 2008–09 undergraduate received an aid package worth an estimated $12,976. The application deadline for financial aid is continuous.

Freshman Admission Avila University requires a high school transcript, a minimum 2.5 high school GPA, Secondary School Report, SAT or ACT scores, and TOEFL scores for international students. An interview is recommended. An essay is required for some. The application deadline for regular admission is August 15.

Transfer Admission Avila University requires a college transcript. Standardized test scores are required for some. The application deadline for admission is August 15.

Entrance Difficulty Avila University assesses its entrance difficulty level as minimally difficult. For the fall 2008 freshman class, 48 percent of the applicants were accepted.
For Further Information Contact Ms. Patricia Harper, Director of Admission, Avila University, 11901 Wornall Road, Kansas City, MO 64145. *Phone:* 816-501-2400 or 800-GO-AVILA (toll-free). *Fax:* 816-501-2453. *E-mail:* patti.harper@avila.edu. *Web site:* http://www.avila.edu/.

BAPTIST BIBLE COLLEGE

Springfield, Missouri

Baptist Bible College is a coed, private, Baptist, comprehensive institution, founded in 1950, offering degrees at the associate, bachelor's, master's, and first professional levels. It has a 38-acre campus in Springfield.

For Further Information Contact Mr. Terry Allcorn, Director of Admissions, Baptist Bible College, 628 East Kearney, Springfield, MO 65803-3498. *Phone:* 417-268-6000. *Fax:* 417-268-6694. *Web site:* http://www.baptist.edu/.

BARNES-JEWISH COLLEGE, GOLDFARB SCHOOL OF NURSING

See Goldfarb School of Nursing at Barnes-Jewish College.

CALVARY BIBLE COLLEGE AND THEOLOGICAL SEMINARY

Kansas City, Missouri

Calvary Bible College and Theological Seminary is a coed, private, nondenominational, comprehensive institution, founded in 1932, offering degrees at the associate, bachelor's, master's, and first professional levels. It has a 55-acre campus in Kansas City.

Academic Information The faculty has 27 members (48% full-time), 41% with terminal degrees. The undergraduate student-faculty ratio is 12:1. The library holds 61,188 titles, 12,965 serial subscriptions, and 492 audiovisual materials. Special programs include academic remediation, advanced placement credit, double majors, independent study, self-designed majors, summer session for credit, part-time degree programs (daytime, evenings, weekends, summer), adult/continuing education programs, and internships. The most frequently chosen baccalaureate fields are business/marketing, education, theology and religious vocations.
Student Body Statistics The student body totals 300, of whom 242 are undergraduates (42 freshmen). 52 percent are women and 48 percent are men. 0.4 percent are international students.
Expenses for 2009–10 *Application fee:* $25. *Comprehensive fee:* $13,272 includes full-time tuition ($8100), mandatory fees ($772), and college room and board ($4400). *College room only:* $2200. *Part-time tuition:* $270 per credit hour.
Financial Aid Forms of aid include need-based and non-need-based scholarships. The application deadline for financial aid is April 1 with a priority deadline of March 1.
Freshman Admission Calvary Bible College and Theological Seminary requires an essay, a high school transcript, 2 recommendations, statement of faith, SAT or ACT scores, and TOEFL scores for international students. An interview is required for some. The application deadline for regular admission is July 15.
Transfer Admission The application deadline for admission is July 15.
Entrance Difficulty Calvary Bible College and Theological Seminary assesses its entrance difficulty level as minimally difficult. For the fall 2008 freshman class, 79 percent of the applicants were accepted.
For Further Information Contact Rev. Robert Reinsch, Director of Admissions, Calvary Bible College and Theological Seminary, 15800 Calvary Road, Kansas City, MO 64147-1341. *Phone:* 816-322-0110 Ext. 1326 or 800-326-3960 (toll-free). *Fax:* 816-331-4474. *E-mail:* admissions@calvary.edu. *Web site:* http://www.calvary.edu/.

CENTRAL BIBLE COLLEGE

Springfield, Missouri

Central Bible College is a coed, private, Assemblies of God, four-year college, founded in 1922, offering degrees at the associate and bachelor's levels. It has a 108-acre campus in Springfield.

Academic Information The library holds 107,023 titles, 1,074 serial subscriptions, and 6,894 audiovisual materials. Special programs include academic remediation, services for learning-disabled students, advanced placement credit, double majors, independent study, distance learning, summer session for credit, part-time degree programs (daytime, evenings, summer), and internships.
Student Body Statistics The student body is made up of 673 undergraduates.
Expenses for 2008–09 *Application fee:* $25. *Comprehensive fee:* $15,662 includes full-time tuition ($9824), mandatory fees ($806), and college room and board ($5032). *Part-time tuition:* $380 per credit hour.
Financial Aid Forms of aid include need-based and non-need-based scholarships and part-time jobs. The priority application deadline for financial aid is March 1.
Freshman Admission Central Bible College requires an essay, a high school transcript, 3 recommendations, and TOEFL scores for international students. A minimum 2.0 high school GPA is recommended. An interview is required for some. The application deadline for regular admission is rolling.
Transfer Admission The application deadline for admission is rolling.
Entrance Difficulty Central Bible College assesses its entrance difficulty level as moderately difficult; noncompetitive for out-of-state applicants.
For Further Information Contact James Bell, Executive Director for Enrollment Services, Central Bible College, 3000 North Grant Avenue, Springfield, MO 65803-1096. *Phone:* 417-833-2551 Ext. 1290 or 800-831-4222 Ext. 1184 (toll-free). *Fax:* 417-833-5141. *E-mail:* info@cbcag.edu. *Web site:* http://www.cbcag.edu/.

CENTRAL CHRISTIAN COLLEGE OF THE BIBLE

Moberly, Missouri

http://www.cccb.edu/

CENTRAL METHODIST UNIVERSITY

Fayette, Missouri

Central Methodist University is a coed, private, Methodist, comprehensive institution, founded in 1854, offering degrees at the associate, bachelor's, and master's levels. It has an 80-acre campus in Fayette.

Academic Information The faculty has 88 members (67% full-time), 43% with terminal degrees. The undergraduate student-faculty ratio is 14:1. The library holds 97,793 titles, 316 serial subscriptions, and 379 audiovisual materials. Special programs include services for learning-disabled students, an honors program, study abroad, accelerated degree programs, double majors, independent study, distance learning, part-time degree programs (daytime, evenings, summer), internships, and arrangement for off-campus study with Mineral Area College, East Central College. The most frequently chosen baccalaureate fields are education, business/marketing, health professions and related sciences.

Central Methodist University (continued)

Student Body Statistics The student body is made up of 1,031 undergraduates (300 freshmen). 51 percent are women and 49 percent are men. Students come from 22 states and territories and 8 other countries. 90 percent are from Missouri. 2.6 percent are international students.
Expenses for 2008–09 *Application fee:* $20. *One-time mandatory fee:* $100. *Comprehensive fee:* $23,980 includes full-time tuition ($17,250), mandatory fees ($730), and college room and board ($6000). *College room only:* $2960. Room and board charges vary according to board plan and housing facility. *Part-time tuition:* $180 per semester hour. *Part-time mandatory fees:* $31.25 per credit hour. Part-time tuition and fees vary according to course load.
Financial Aid Forms of aid include need-based and non-need-based scholarships, athletic grants, and part-time jobs. The average aided 2008–09 undergraduate received an aid package worth an estimated $14,653.
Freshman Admission Central Methodist University requires a high school transcript, a minimum 2.5 high school GPA, SAT or ACT scores, and TOEFL scores for international students. ACT scores are recommended. 2 recommendations are required for some. The application deadline for regular admission is rolling.
Transfer Admission The application deadline for admission is rolling.
Entrance Difficulty Central Methodist University assesses its entrance difficulty level as moderately difficult. For the fall 2008 freshman class, 66 percent of the applicants were accepted.
For Further Information Contact Mr. Larry Anderson, Director of Admissions, Central Methodist University, 411 Central Methodist Square, Fayette, MO 65248-1198. *Phone:* 660-248-6247 or 888-CMU-1854 (toll-free in-state). *Fax:* 660-248-1872. *E-mail:* admissions@centralmethodist.edu. *Web site:* http://www.centralmethodist.edu/.

CENTRAL MISSOURI STATE UNIVERSITY

See University of Central Missouri.

CHAMBERLAIN COLLEGE OF NURSING

St. Louis, Missouri

Chamberlain College of Nursing is a coed, proprietary, four-year college of DeVry Inc., founded in 1889, offering degrees at the associate and bachelor's levels. It has a 15-acre campus in St. Louis.

Academic Information The library holds 8,700 titles and 233 serial subscriptions. Special programs include academic remediation, advanced placement credit, ESL programs, summer session for credit, part-time degree programs, and arrangement for off-campus study with Fontbonne College.
Student Body Statistics The student body is made up of 1,452 undergraduates.
Financial Aid Forms of aid include need-based and non-need-based scholarships and part-time jobs. The priority application deadline for financial aid is April 1.
Freshman Admission Chamberlain College of Nursing requires an essay, a high school transcript, SAT or ACT scores, and TOEFL scores for international students. A minimum 2.5 high school GPA is recommended. An interview is required for some. The application deadline for regular admission is rolling.
Transfer Admission The application deadline for admission is rolling.
Entrance Difficulty Chamberlain College of Nursing assesses its entrance difficulty level as moderately difficult.
For Further Information Contact Larry Veeneman, National Director of Admissions, Chamberlain College of Nursing, 6150 Oakland Avenue, St. Louis, MO 63139-3215. *Phone:* 630-953-3690 or 800-942-4310 (toll-free). *Fax:* 314-768-5673. *E-mail:* info@chamberlain.edu. *Web site:* http://www.chamberlain.edu/.

COLLEGE OF THE OZARKS

Point Lookout, Missouri

College of the Ozarks is a coed, private, Presbyterian, four-year college, founded in 1906, offering degrees at the bachelor's level. It has a 1,000-acre campus in Point Lookout.

Academic Information The faculty has 119 members (76% full-time), 46% with terminal degrees. The student-faculty ratio is 13:1. The library holds 116,649 titles, 549 serial subscriptions, and 4,799 audiovisual materials. Special programs include academic remediation, services for learning-disabled students, cooperative (work-study) education, advanced placement credit, accelerated degree programs, double majors, independent study, self-designed majors, and internships. The most frequently chosen baccalaureate fields are business/marketing, agriculture, education.
Student Body Statistics The student body is made up of 1,331 undergraduates (274 freshmen). 57 percent are women and 43 percent are men. Students come from 36 states and territories and 15 other countries. 69 percent are from Missouri. 1.7 percent are international students.
Expenses for 2009–10 *Application fee:* $0. *Comprehensive fee:* $5000 includes full-time tuition ($0) and college room and board ($5000). The college guarantees to meet all of the tuition cost for each full-time student by using earnings from its endowment, operation of its own mandatory student work program, accepting student aid grants, gifts and other sources. In effect, each full-time student's Cost of Education (tuition) is met 100 percent by participating in the work program and a combination of private, institutional and federal/state student aid.
Financial Aid Forms of aid include need-based scholarships, athletic grants, and part-time jobs. The average aided 2007–08 undergraduate received an aid package worth $15,330. The priority application deadline for financial aid is February 15.
Freshman Admission College of the Ozarks requires a high school transcript, 2 recommendations, an interview, medical history, financial statement, SAT or ACT scores, and TOEFL scores for international students. A minimum 3.0 high school GPA is recommended. The application deadline for regular admission is February 15.
Transfer Admission The application deadline for admission is February 15.
Entrance Difficulty College of the Ozarks assesses its entrance difficulty level as moderately difficult; very difficult for out-of-state applicants. For the fall 2008 freshman class, 12 percent of the applicants were accepted.
For Further Information Contact Mrs. Gayle Groves, Admissions Secretary, College of the Ozarks, PO Box 17, Point Lookout, MO 65726. *Phone:* 417-690-2637 or 800-222-0525 (toll-free). *Fax:* 417-335-2618. *E-mail:* admiss4@cofo.edu. *Web site:* http://www.cofo.edu/.

COLORADO TECHNICAL UNIVERSITY NORTH KANSAS CITY

North Kansas City, Missouri

Colorado Technical University North Kansas City is a coed, proprietary, four-year college, founded in 1992, offering degrees at the associate and bachelor's levels.

Academic Information The faculty has 110 members. Special programs include cooperative (work-study) education, advanced placement credit, accelerated degree programs, double majors, distance learning, part-time degree programs, adult/continuing education programs, and internships. The most frequently chosen baccalaureate fields are business/marketing, health professions and related sciences, security and protective services.
Student Body Statistics The student body is made up of 679 undergraduates (104 freshmen). 78 percent are women and 22 percent are men. 98 percent are from Missouri.
Expenses for 2009–10 *Application fee:* $50. Contact campus for cost.
Freshman Admission Colorado Technical University North Kansas City requires an interview and TOEFL scores for international students. The application deadline for regular admission is rolling.
Transfer Admission The application deadline for admission is rolling.

Entrance Difficulty Colorado Technical University North Kansas City assesses its entrance difficulty level as minimally difficult.
For Further Information Contact Angela Vietti, Director of Admissions, Colorado Technical University North Kansas City, 520 East 19th Avenue, North Kansas City, MO 80907. *Phone:* 888-404-7555. *E-mail:* avietti@kc.coloradotech.edu. *Web site:* http://kc.coloradotech.edu/.

COLUMBIA COLLEGE

Columbia, Missouri

Columbia College is a coed, private, comprehensive institution, founded in 1851, affiliated with the Christian Church (Disciples of Christ), offering degrees at the associate, bachelor's, and master's levels (offers continuing education program with significant enrollment not reflected in profile). It has a 29-acre campus in Columbia.

Academic Information The faculty has 99 members (64% full-time), 57% with terminal degrees. The undergraduate student-faculty ratio is 15:1. The library holds 73,862 titles, 239 serial subscriptions, and 1,986 audiovisual materials. Special programs include services for learning-disabled students, an honors program, study abroad, advanced placement credit, ESL programs, double majors, independent study, distance learning, summer session for credit, part-time degree programs (daytime, evenings, summer), adult/continuing education programs, internships, and arrangement for off-campus study with local institutions. The most frequently chosen baccalaureate fields are business/marketing, interdisciplinary studies, psychology.
Student Body Statistics The student body totals 1,353, of whom 1,169 are undergraduates (220 freshmen). 59 percent are women and 41 percent are men. Students come from 26 states and territories and 19 other countries. 89 percent are from Missouri. 7.2 percent are international students.
Expenses for 2009–10 *Application fee:* $25. *Comprehensive fee:* $20,474 includes full-time tuition ($14,576) and college room and board ($5898). *College room only:* $3670. *Part-time tuition:* $312 per credit hour.
Financial Aid Forms of aid include need-based and non-need-based scholarships, athletic grants, and part-time jobs. The average aided 2007–08 undergraduate received an aid package worth $12,510.
Freshman Admission Columbia College requires a high school transcript, a minimum 2.5 high school GPA, SAT or ACT scores, and TOEFL scores for international students. An essay and an interview are required for some. The application deadline for regular admission is August 1.
Transfer Admission The application deadline for admission is August 1.
Entrance Difficulty Columbia College assesses its entrance difficulty level as moderately difficult; minimally difficult for transfers. For the fall 2008 freshman class, 53 percent of the applicants were accepted.

SPECIAL MESSAGE TO STUDENTS

Social Life An influential Student Government Association plans and organizes social activities. There are more than forty clubs and organizations, ranging from academic associations to special interest groups, providing myriad choices for students to get involved and experience leadership opportunities. Strong athletics are a tradition at Columbia College with a history of nationally ranked NAIA Division I teams. One of three institutions of higher education in town, Columbia College provides a vibrant small campus environment within a larger college community.

Academic Highlights Columbia College is known for its excellence in teaching and learning. Among the nearly forty programs offered, those in criminal justice, forensic science, art, education, and business are quite distinctive and attract students from across the United States. The Writing and Math Centers build on high-quality teaching in the classroom to provide opportunities for students to enhance their learning experience. INCC 111 Introduction to Columbia College is a popular freshman orientation course team-taught by a full-time professor and an upperclass student. Study-abroad opportunities are available, and internships can be obtained for a more hands-on experience in any field.

Interviews and Campus Visits Located in a small city consistently recognized by national magazines as an exceptional place to live, Columbia College welcomes visitors to its beautiful historic campus. The campus dates from 1851 and has several distinct architectural features in its older buildings. Williams Hall is the oldest building west of the Mississippi still in continuous use for education purposes. The entire campus is wireless. Visitors have the opportunity to sit in on a class and meet faculty members and students as well as financial aid officials. Campus visits may be arranged weekdays from 8 to 5 by calling the Admissions Office at 573-875-7352 or 800-231-2391 Ext. 7352 (toll-free).

For Further Information Write to Mr. John Wilkerson, Interim Director of Admissions, Columbia College, 1001 Rogers Street, Columbia, MO 65216. *E-mail:* admissions@ccis.edu. *Web site:* http://www.ccis.edu.

CONCEPTION SEMINARY COLLEGE

Conception, Missouri

http://www.conceptionabbey.org/

COTTEY COLLEGE

Nevada, Missouri

Cottey College is a women's, private, two-year college, founded in 1884, offering degrees at the associate level. It has a 51-acre campus in Nevada.

Academic Information The faculty has 42 members (81% full-time), 74% with terminal degrees. The student-faculty ratio is 9:1. The library holds 54,200 titles and 246 serial subscriptions. Special programs include services for learning-disabled students, study abroad, advanced placement credit, independent study, distance learning, part-time degree programs (daytime), and internships.
Student Body Statistics The student body is made up of 331 undergraduates (173 freshmen). Students come from 40 states and territories and 21 other countries. 20 percent are from Missouri. 9.5 percent are international students. 95 percent of the 2008 graduating class went on to four-year colleges.
Expenses for 2009–10 *Application fee:* $20. *Comprehensive fee:* $20,300 includes full-time tuition ($13,800), mandatory fees ($700), and college room and board ($5800). *Part-time tuition:* $150 per credit hour. *Part-time mandatory fees:* $11 per credit hour.
Financial Aid Forms of aid include need-based scholarships and part-time jobs. The priority application deadline for financial aid is March 31.
Freshman Admission Cottey College requires an essay, a high school transcript, 1 recommendation, SAT or ACT scores, and TOEFL scores for international students. A minimum 2.6 high school GPA and an interview are recommended. The application deadline for regular admission is rolling and for nonresidents it is rolling.
Transfer Admission The application deadline for admission is rolling.
Entrance Difficulty Cottey College assesses its entrance difficulty level as moderately difficult. For the fall 2008 freshman class, 63 percent of the applicants were accepted.
For Further Information Contact Ms. Judi Steege, Director of Admission, Cottey College, 1000 West Austin Boulevard, Nevada, MO 64772. *Phone:* 417-667-8181 or 888-526-8839 (toll-free). *Fax:* 417-667-8103. *E-mail:* enrollmgt@cottey.edu. *Web site:* http://www.cottey.edu/.

COX COLLEGE OF NURSING AND HEALTH SCIENCES

Springfield, Missouri

http://www.coxcollege.edu/

CULVER-STOCKTON COLLEGE

Canton, Missouri

Culver-Stockton College is a coed, private, four-year college, founded in 1853, affiliated with the Christian Church (Disciples of Christ), offering degrees at the bachelor's level. It has a 143-acre campus in Canton.

Academic Information The faculty has 80 members (58% full-time), 48% with terminal degrees. The student-faculty ratio is 14:1. The library holds 170,793 titles, 25,601 serial subscriptions, and 5,369 audiovisual materials. Special programs include an honors program, study abroad, advanced placement credit, double majors, independent study, distance learning, self-designed majors, summer session for credit, part-time degree programs, internships, and arrangement for off-campus study with Central College. The most frequently chosen baccalaureate fields are business/marketing, education, health professions and related sciences.
Student Body Statistics The student body is made up of 810 undergraduates (227 freshmen). 56 percent are women and 44 percent are men. Students come from 11 states and territories and 10 other countries. 54 percent are from Missouri. 2.3 percent are international students.
Expenses for 2008–09 *Application fee:* $25. *One-time mandatory fee:* $125. *Comprehensive fee:* $28,950 includes full-time tuition ($21,500), mandatory fees ($250), and college room and board ($7200). *College room only:* $3200. Room and board charges vary according to board plan. *Part-time tuition:* $500 per credit hour. *Part-time mandatory fees:* $10.42 per credit hour.
Financial Aid Forms of aid include need-based and non-need-based scholarships, athletic grants, and part-time jobs. The average aided 2008–09 undergraduate received an aid package worth an estimated $19,016. The application deadline for financial aid is June 1 with a priority deadline of March 1.
Freshman Admission Culver-Stockton College requires an essay, a high school transcript, a minimum 2.0 high school GPA, rank in upper 50% of high school class, SAT or ACT scores, and TOEFL scores for international students. An interview is recommended. An interview is required for some. The application deadline for regular admission is rolling.
Transfer Admission The application deadline for admission is rolling.
Entrance Difficulty Culver-Stockton College assesses its entrance difficulty level as moderately difficult. For the fall 2008 freshman class, 68 percent of the applicants were accepted.
For Further Information Contact Mr. Jim Lynes, Director of Admissions, Culver-Stockton College, One College Hill, Canton, MO 63435-1299. *Phone:* 573-288-6467 or 800-537-1883 (toll-free). *Fax:* 573-288-6618. *E-mail:* jlynes@culver.edu. *Web site:* http://www.culver.edu/.

See page 236 for the Close-Up.

DEACONESS COLLEGE OF NURSING

See Chamberlain College of Nursing.

DeVRY UNIVERSITY

Kansas City, Missouri

DeVry University is a coed, proprietary, comprehensive unit of DeVry University, founded in 1931, offering degrees at the associate, bachelor's, and master's levels. It has a 12-acre campus in Kansas City.

Academic Information The faculty has 88 members (34% full-time). The undergraduate student-faculty ratio is 15:1. The library holds 15,000 titles and 68 serial subscriptions. Special programs include academic remediation, services for learning-disabled students, advanced placement credit, accelerated degree programs, distance learning, summer session for credit, part-time degree programs (daytime, evenings, weekends, summer), and adult/continuing education programs. The most frequently chosen baccalaureate fields are business/marketing, computer and information sciences, engineering technologies.
Student Body Statistics The student body totals 1,116, of whom 949 are undergraduates (155 freshmen). 29 percent are women and 71 percent are men. 65 percent are from Missouri. 0.5 percent are international students.
Expenses for 2009–10 *Application fee:* $50. *Tuition:* $14,080 full-time, $550 per credit hour part-time.
Financial Aid Forms of aid include need-based scholarships and part-time jobs. The average aided 2007–08 undergraduate received an aid package worth $11,948. The application deadline for financial aid is continuous.
Freshman Admission DeVry University requires a high school transcript, an interview, and TOEFL scores for international students. The application deadline for regular admission is rolling.
Transfer Admission The application deadline for admission is rolling.
Entrance Difficulty DeVry University assesses its entrance difficulty level as minimally difficult; moderately difficult for electronics engineering technology program.
For Further Information Contact Admissions Office, DeVry University, 11224 Holmes Road, Kansas City, MO 64131. *Phone:* 819-941-0430. *Web site:* http://www.devry.edu/.

DeVRY UNIVERSITY

Kansas City, Missouri

http://www.devry.edu/

DeVRY UNIVERSITY

St. Louis, Missouri

http://www.devry.edu/

DRURY UNIVERSITY

Springfield, Missouri

Drury University is a coed, private, comprehensive institution, founded in 1873, offering degrees at the bachelor's and master's levels (also offers evening program with significant enrollment not reflected in profile). It has an 80-acre campus in Springfield.

Academic Information The faculty has 172 members (74% full-time), 69% with terminal degrees. The undergraduate student-faculty ratio is 12:1. The library holds 169,968 titles, 690 serial subscriptions, and 4,774 audiovisual materials. Special programs include services for learning-disabled students, an honors program, cooperative (work-study) education, study abroad, advanced placement credit, accelerated degree programs, ESL programs, double majors, independent study, distance learning, self-designed majors, summer session for credit, part-time degree programs (daytime, evenings, summer), adult/continuing education programs, internships, and arrangement for off-campus study. The most frequently chosen baccalaureate fields are biological/life sciences, business/marketing, communications/journalism.
Student Body Statistics The student body totals 2,060, of whom 1,555 are undergraduates (334 freshmen). 53 percent are women and 47 percent are men. Students come from 30 states and territories and 29 other countries. 83 percent are from Missouri. 5.7 percent are international students.
Expenses for 2009–10 *Application fee:* $25. *One-time mandatory fee:* $145. *Comprehensive fee:* $25,716 includes full-time tuition ($18,598), mandatory fees ($415), and college room and board ($6703).
Financial Aid Forms of aid include need-based and non-need-based scholarships, athletic grants, and part-time jobs. The average aided 2008–09 undergraduate received an aid package worth an estimated $7750. The priority application deadline for financial aid is March 15.

Freshman Admission Drury University requires an essay, a high school transcript, a minimum 2.7 high school GPA, 1 recommendation, SAT or ACT scores, and TOEFL scores for international students. An interview is recommended. The application deadline for regular admission is August 1.
Transfer Admission The application deadline for admission is rolling.
Entrance Difficulty Drury University assesses its entrance difficulty level as moderately difficult. For the fall 2008 freshman class, 72 percent of the applicants were accepted.
For Further Information Contact Mr. Chip Parker, Director of Admission, Drury University, 900 North Benton, Bay Hall, Springfield, MO 65802. *Phone:* 417-873-7205 or 800-922-2274 (toll-free). *Fax:* 417-866-3873. *E-mail:* druryad@drury.edu. *Web site:* http://www.drury.edu/.

EVANGEL UNIVERSITY

Springfield, Missouri

Evangel University is a coed, private, comprehensive institution, founded in 1955, affiliated with the Assemblies of God, offering degrees at the associate, bachelor's, and master's levels. It has an 80-acre campus in Springfield.

Academic Information The faculty has 161 members (65% full-time), 43% with terminal degrees. The undergraduate student-faculty ratio is 14:1. The library holds 100,691 titles and 1,060 serial subscriptions. Special programs include academic remediation, services for learning-disabled students, advanced placement credit, accelerated degree programs, double majors, summer session for credit, part-time degree programs (daytime, summer), and internships. The most frequently chosen baccalaureate fields are business/marketing, education, philosophy and religious studies.
Student Body Statistics The student body totals 1,911, of whom 1,726 are undergraduates (338 freshmen). 58 percent are women and 42 percent are men. Students come from 50 states and territories and 8 other countries. 49 percent are from Missouri. 0.1 percent are international students.
Expenses for 2008–09 *Application fee:* $25. *Comprehensive fee:* $20,430 includes full-time tuition ($14,200), mandatory fees ($820), and college room and board ($5410). *College room only:* $2760. Full-time tuition and fees vary according to course load. Room and board charges vary according to board plan. *Part-time tuition:* $554 per credit hour.
Financial Aid Forms of aid include need-based and non-need-based scholarships, athletic grants, and part-time jobs. The average aided 2007–08 undergraduate received an aid package worth $9814.
Freshman Admission Evangel University requires an essay, a high school transcript, an interview, SAT or ACT scores, and TOEFL scores for international students. A minimum 2.0 high school GPA is recommended. The application deadline for regular admission is August 1.
Transfer Admission The application deadline for admission is August 1.
Entrance Difficulty Evangel University assesses its entrance difficulty level as moderately difficult. For the fall 2008 freshman class, 67 percent of the applicants were accepted.
For Further Information Contact Mr. Jeff Burnett, Director of Admissions, Evangel University, 1111 North Glenstone, Springfield, MO 65802. *Phone:* 417-865-2811 Ext. 7205 or 800-382-6435 (toll-free in-state). *Fax:* 417-865-9599. *E-mail:* admissions@evangel.edu. *Web site:* http://www.evangel.edu/.

EVEREST COLLEGE

Springfield, Missouri

http://www.everest.edu/campus/springfield

FONTBONNE UNIVERSITY

St. Louis, Missouri

Fontbonne University is a coed, primarily women's, private, Roman Catholic, comprehensive institution, founded in 1917, offering degrees at the bachelor's and master's levels and postbachelor's certificates. It has a 13-acre campus in St. Louis.

Academic Information The faculty has 347 members (24% full-time). The undergraduate student-faculty ratio is 14:1. The library holds 88,063 titles, 19,532 serial subscriptions, and 3,084 audiovisual materials. Special programs include academic remediation, services for learning-disabled students, an honors program, cooperative (work-study) education, study abroad, advanced placement credit, accelerated degree programs, ESL programs, double majors, independent study, distance learning, self-designed majors, summer session for credit, part-time degree programs, adult/continuing education programs, internships, and arrangement for off-campus study with Webster University, Maryville College, Lindenwood College, Missouri Baptist College. The most frequently chosen baccalaureate fields are business/marketing, education, health professions and related sciences.
Student Body Statistics The student body totals 2,967, of whom 2,084 are undergraduates (191 freshmen). 71 percent are women and 29 percent are men. Students come from 29 states and territories and 29 other countries. 86 percent are from Missouri. 1.1 percent are international students.
Expenses for 2009–10 *Application fee:* $25. *Comprehensive fee:* $27,206 includes full-time tuition ($19,475), mandatory fees ($320), and college room and board ($7411). *College room only:* $4184. *Part-time tuition:* $521 per credit hour. *Part-time mandatory fees:* $16 per credit hour.
Financial Aid Forms of aid include need-based and non-need-based scholarships and part-time jobs. The priority application deadline for financial aid is April 30.
Freshman Admission Fontbonne University requires a high school transcript, a minimum 2.5 high school GPA, SAT or ACT scores, and TOEFL scores for international students. 2 recommendations and an interview are recommended. An essay is required for some. The application deadline for regular admission is rolling.
Transfer Admission The application deadline for admission is rolling.
Entrance Difficulty Fontbonne University assesses its entrance difficulty level as moderately difficult. For the fall 2008 freshman class, 82 percent of the applicants were accepted.
For Further Information Contact Ms. Peggy Musen, Vice President for Enrollment Management, Fontbonne University, 6800 Wydown Boulevard, St. Louis, MO 63105-3098. *Phone:* 314-889-1400. *Fax:* 314-889-1451. *E-mail:* pmusen@fontbonne.edu. *Web site:* http://www.fontbonne.edu/.

GLOBAL UNIVERSITY

Springfield, Missouri

Global University is a coed, private, comprehensive institution, founded in 1948, affiliated with the Assemblies of God, offering degrees at the associate, bachelor's, master's, and first professional levels and postbachelor's certificates (offers only external degree programs).

Expenses for 2008–09 *Application fee:* $40. *Tuition:* $3168 full-time, $105 per hour part-time. Part-time tuition varies according to class time.
For Further Information Contact Rev. Todd Waggoner, Enrollment and International Student Services Director, Global University, 1211 South Glenstone Avenue, Springfield, MO 65804. *Phone:* 417-862-9533 Ext. 2335 or 800-443-1083 (toll-free). *Fax:* 417-863-9621. *E-mail:* twaggoner@globaluniversity.edu. *Web site:* http://www.globaluniversity.edu/.

GOLDFARB SCHOOL OF NURSING AT BARNES-JEWISH COLLEGE

St. Louis, Missouri

Goldfarb School of Nursing at Barnes-Jewish College is a coed, private, comprehensive institution, founded in 1902, offering degrees at the bachelor's and master's levels and post-master's certificates.

Academic Information The faculty has 35 members (100% full-time). The undergraduate student-faculty ratio is 10:1. The library holds 1,100 titles, 44 serial subscriptions, and 280 audiovisual materials. Special programs include services for learning-disabled students, advanced placement credit, accelerated degree programs, independent study, summer session for credit, part-time degree programs (daytime, evenings, weekends,

Goldfarb School of Nursing at Barnes-Jewish College (continued)

summer), and arrangement for off-campus study with Washington University in St. Louis. The most frequently chosen baccalaureate field is health professions and related sciences.

Student Body Statistics The student body totals 659, of whom 545 are undergraduates. Students come from 21 states and territories and 21 other countries. 35 percent are from Missouri.

Expenses for 2009–10 *Application fee:* $50. *Tuition:* $15,000 full-time, $500 per credit hour part-time. *Mandatory fees:* $230 full-time.

Financial Aid Forms of aid include need-based and non-need-based scholarships and part-time jobs. The priority application deadline for financial aid is April 1.

Freshman Admission Goldfarb School of Nursing at Barnes-Jewish College requires TOEFL scores for international students.

Transfer Admission The application deadline for admission is rolling.

For Further Information Contact Dr. Michael D. Ward, Associate Dean for Student Programs, Goldfarb School of Nursing at Barnes-Jewish College, 306 South Kings Highway Boulevard, St. Louis, MO 63110. *Phone:* 314-362-9155 or 800-832-9009 (toll-free in-state). *Fax:* 314-454-5239. *E-mail:* jhcollegeinquiry@bjc.org. *Web site:* http://www.barnesjewishcollege.edu/.

GRACELAND UNIVERSITY

Independence, Missouri

http://www.graceland.edu/undergraduate/independencecampus/

GRANTHAM UNIVERSITY

Kansas City, Missouri

Grantham University is a coed, proprietary, comprehensive institution, founded in 1951, offering degrees at the associate, bachelor's, and master's levels (offers only external degree programs).

Academic Information The faculty has 163 members (12% full-time), 32% with terminal degrees. Special programs include advanced placement credit, accelerated degree programs, independent study, distance learning, self-designed majors, part-time degree programs, external degree programs, and adult/continuing education programs.

Student Body Statistics The student body totals 6,423, of whom 5,935 are undergraduates.

Expenses for 2009–10 *Application fee:* $30. *Tuition:* $7950 full-time, $265 per credit hour part-time.

Freshman Admission Grantham University requires a high school transcript and TOEFL scores for international students. The application deadline for regular admission is rolling and for nonresidents it is rolling.

Transfer Admission The application deadline for admission is rolling.

Entrance Difficulty Grantham University has an open admission policy.

For Further Information Contact Ms. DeAnn Wandler, Vice President of Enrollment Management, Grantham University, 7200 NW 86th Street, Kansas City, MO 64153. *Phone:* 800-955-2527 or 800-955-2527 (toll-free). *Fax:* 816-595-5757. *E-mail:* admissions@grantham.edu. *Web site:* http://www.grantham.edu/.

HANNIBAL-LAGRANGE COLLEGE

Hannibal, Missouri

Hannibal-LaGrange College is a coed, private, Southern Baptist, comprehensive institution, founded in 1858, offering degrees at the associate, bachelor's, and master's levels. It has a 110-acre campus in Hannibal.

Academic Information The faculty has 96 members (65% full-time), 20% with terminal degrees. The undergraduate student-faculty ratio is 14:1. The library holds 112,378 titles, 395 serial subscriptions, and 6,026 audiovisual materials. Special programs include academic remediation, services for learning-disabled students, an honors program, study abroad, advanced placement credit, accelerated degree programs, ESL programs, double majors, independent study, distance learning, summer session for credit, part-time degree programs (daytime, evenings, weekends, summer), adult/continuing education programs, and internships. The most frequently chosen baccalaureate fields are business/marketing, education, social sciences.

Student Body Statistics The student body totals 1,127, of whom 1,084 are undergraduates. Students come from 20 states and territories and 25 other countries. 80 percent are from Missouri. 6.8 percent are international students.

Expenses for 2008–09 *Application fee:* $25. *One-time mandatory fee:* $100. *Comprehensive fee:* $19,776 includes full-time tuition ($13,978), mandatory fees ($528), and college room and board ($5270). Full-time tuition and fees vary according to class time, course load, and program. Room and board charges vary according to housing facility. *Part-time tuition:* $466 per credit hour. *Part-time mandatory fees:* $100 per year. Part-time tuition and fees vary according to class time, course load, and program.

Financial Aid Forms of aid include need-based and non-need-based scholarships, athletic grants, and part-time jobs. The average aided 2007–08 undergraduate received an aid package worth $11,379. The application deadline for financial aid is continuous.

Freshman Admission Hannibal-LaGrange College requires a high school transcript, a minimum 2.0 high school GPA, SAT or ACT scores, and TOEFL scores for international students. GED is required for some. The application deadline for regular admission is rolling.

Transfer Admission The application deadline for admission is rolling.

Entrance Difficulty Hannibal-LaGrange College assesses its entrance difficulty level as moderately difficult. For the fall 2008 freshman class, 90 percent of the applicants were accepted.

For Further Information Contact Dr. Raymond Carty, Vice President for Enrollment Management, Hannibal-LaGrange College, 2800 Palmyra Road, Hannibal, MO 63401-1999. *Phone:* 573-629-2278 or 800-HLG-1119 (toll-free). *E-mail:* admissio@hlg.edu. *Web site:* http://www.hlg.edu/.

HARRIS-STOWE STATE UNIVERSITY

St. Louis, Missouri

Harris-Stowe State University is a coed, public, four-year college of Missouri Coordinating Board for Higher Education, founded in 1857, offering degrees at the bachelor's level and postbachelor's certificates. It has a 22-acre campus in St. Louis.

Academic Information The faculty has 162 members (33% full-time). The student-faculty ratio is 26:1. The library holds 60,000 titles and 340 serial subscriptions. Special programs include academic remediation, services for learning-disabled students, cooperative (work-study) education, advanced placement credit, self-designed majors, summer session for credit, part-time degree programs (daytime, evenings, weekends, summer), internships, and arrangement for off-campus study with Saint Louis University, University of Missouri–St. Louis. The most frequently chosen baccalaureate fields are business/marketing, education, interdisciplinary studies.

Student Body Statistics The student body is made up of 1,852 undergraduates (443 freshmen). 67 percent are women and 33 percent are men. Students come from 14 states and territories and 10 other countries. 90 percent are from Missouri. 0.6 percent are international students.

Expenses for 2009–10 *Application fee:* $15. *State resident tuition:* $4920 full-time, $164 per hour part-time. *Nonresident tuition:* $9692 full-time, $323.08 per hour part-time. *Mandatory fees:* $400 full-time, $200 per term part-time.

Financial Aid Forms of aid include need-based and non-need-based scholarships, athletic grants, and part-time jobs. The average aided 2008–09 undergraduate received an aid package worth an estimated $9500. The priority application deadline for financial aid is April 1.

Freshman Admission Harris-Stowe State University requires a high school transcript and TOEFL scores for international students. SAT or ACT scores are recommended. Institutional placement test is required for some. The application deadline for regular admission is rolling.

Transfer Admission The application deadline for admission is rolling.

Entrance Difficulty Harris-Stowe State University has an open admission policy.
For Further Information Contact Meghan Sprung, Assistant Director of Admissions, Harris-Stowe State University, 3026 Laclede Avenue, St. Louis, MO 63103. *Phone:* 314-340-3300. *Fax:* 314-340-3555. *E-mail:* admissions@hssu.edu. *Web site:* http://www.hssu.edu/.

HICKEY COLLEGE

St. Louis, Missouri

http://www.hickeycollege.edu/

IHM HEALTH STUDIES CENTER

St. Louis, Missouri

http://www.ihmhealthstudies.com/

ITT TECHNICAL INSTITUTE

Arnold, Missouri

ITT Technical Institute is a coed, proprietary, primarily two-year college of ITT Educational Services, Inc., founded in 1997, offering degrees at the associate and bachelor's levels.

Financial Aid Forms of aid include need-based scholarships and part-time jobs. The application deadline for financial aid is continuous.
Entrance Difficulty ITT Technical Institute assesses its entrance difficulty level as minimally difficult.
For Further Information Contact Director of Recruitment, ITT Technical Institute, 1930 Meyer Drury Drive, Arnold, MO 63010. *Phone:* 636-464-6600 or 888-488-1082 (toll-free). *Fax:* 636-464-6611. *Web site:* http://www.itt-tech.edu/.

ITT TECHNICAL INSTITUTE

Earth City, Missouri

ITT Technical Institute is a coed, proprietary, primarily two-year college of ITT Educational Services, Inc., founded in 1936, offering degrees at the associate and bachelor's levels. It has a 2-acre campus in Earth City near St. Louis.

Financial Aid Forms of aid include need-based scholarships and part-time jobs. The application deadline for financial aid is continuous.
Freshman Admission ITT Technical Institute requires TOEFL scores for international students.
Entrance Difficulty ITT Technical Institute assesses its entrance difficulty level as minimally difficult.
For Further Information Contact Director of Recruitment, ITT Technical Institute, 3640 Corporate Trail Drive, Earth City, MO 63045. *Phone:* 314-298-7800 or 800-235-5488 (toll-free). *Fax:* 314-298-0559. *Web site:* http://www.itt-tech.edu/.

ITT TECHNICAL INSTITUTE

Kansas City, Missouri

ITT Technical Institute is a coed, proprietary, primarily two-year college of ITT Educational Services, Inc., founded in 2004, offering degrees at the associate and bachelor's levels.

For Further Information Contact Director of Recruitment, ITT Technical Institute, 9150 East 41st Terrace, Kansas City, MO 64133. *Phone:* 816-276-1400 or 877-488-1442 (toll-free). *Fax:* 816-276-1410. *Web site:* http://www.itt-tech.edu/.

ITT TECHNICAL INSTITUTE

Springfield, Missouri

ITT Technical Institute is a coed, proprietary, four-year college of ITT Educational Services, Inc., offering degrees at the associate and bachelor's levels.

For Further Information Contact Director of Recruitment, ITT Technical Institute, 3216 S. National Avenue, Springfield, MO 65807. *Phone:* 417-877-4800 or 877-219-4387 (toll-free). *Web site:* http://www.itt-tech.edu/.

KANSAS CITY ART INSTITUTE

Kansas City, Missouri

Kansas City Art Institute is a coed, private, four-year college, founded in 1885, offering degrees at the bachelor's level. It has an 18-acre campus in Kansas City.

Academic Information The faculty has 104 members (49% full-time), 81% with terminal degrees. The student-faculty ratio is 12:1. Special programs include academic remediation, services for learning-disabled students, cooperative (work-study) education, advanced placement credit, ESL programs, double majors, independent study, summer session for credit, internships, and arrangement for off-campus study with New York Studio Program, AICAD School Exchange. The most frequently chosen baccalaureate field is visual and performing arts.
Student Body Statistics The student body is made up of 676 undergraduates (152 freshmen). 55 percent are women and 45 percent are men. Students come from 37 states and territories and 6 other countries. 41 percent are from Missouri. 0.9 percent are international students.
Expenses for 2009–10 *Application fee:* $35. *Comprehensive fee:* $37,290 includes full-time tuition ($28,580) and college room and board ($8710). *Part-time tuition:* $1190 per credit hour.
Financial Aid Forms of aid include need-based and non-need-based scholarships and part-time jobs. The average aided 2008–09 undergraduate received an aid package worth an estimated $20,854. The priority application deadline for financial aid is March 1.
Freshman Admission Kansas City Art Institute requires an essay, a high school transcript, a minimum 2.5 high school GPA, 2 recommendations, portfolio, statement of purpose, SAT or ACT scores, and TOEFL scores for international students. An interview is recommended. The application deadline for regular admission is rolling.
Transfer Admission The application deadline for admission is rolling.
Entrance Difficulty Kansas City Art Institute assesses its entrance difficulty level as moderately difficult. For the fall 2008 freshman class, 63 percent of the applicants were accepted.
For Further Information Contact Mr. Gerald Valet, Director of Admission Technology, Kansas City Art Institute, 4415 Warwick Boulevard, Kansas City, MO 64111-1874. *Phone:* 816-474-5224 or 800-522-5224 (toll-free). *Fax:* 816-802-3309. *E-mail:* admiss@kcai.edu. *Web site:* http://www.kcai.edu/.

LINCOLN UNIVERSITY

Jefferson City, Missouri

Lincoln University is a coed, public, comprehensive unit of Missouri Coordinating Board for Higher Education, founded in 1866, offering degrees at the associate, bachelor's, and master's levels and post-master's certificates. It has a 165-acre campus in Jefferson City.

Academic Information The faculty has 242 members (50% full-time). The undergraduate student-faculty ratio is 15:1. The library holds 204,948 titles, 368 serial subscriptions, and 5,497 audiovisual materials. Special programs include academic remediation, services for learning-disabled students, an honors program, study abroad, advanced placement credit, accelerated degree programs, double majors, independent study, distance learning, summer session for credit, part-time degree programs (daytime, evenings, weekends, summer), adult/continuing education programs, internships, and arrangement for off-campus study. The most frequently chosen baccalaureate fields are business/marketing, education, liberal arts/general studies.

Lincoln University (continued)

Student Body Statistics The student body totals 3,109, of whom 2,941 are undergraduates (575 freshmen). 60 percent are women and 40 percent are men. Students come from 35 states and territories and 23 other countries. 83 percent are from Missouri. 4 percent are international students.

Expenses for 2009–10 *Application fee:* $20. *State resident tuition:* $5505 full-time, $183.50 per credit hour part-time. *Nonresident tuition:* $10,065 full-time, $335.50 per credit hour part-time. *Mandatory fees:* $490 full-time. *College room and board:* $4590. *College room only:* $2358.

Financial Aid Forms of aid include need-based and non-need-based scholarships and part-time jobs. The average aided 2008–09 undergraduate received an aid package worth an estimated $8652.

Freshman Admission Lincoln University requires a high school transcript, SAT or ACT scores, and TOEFL scores for international students. A minimum 2.0 high school GPA and audition for sacred music and music education are required for some. The application deadline for regular admission is July 15.

Transfer Admission The application deadline for admission is July 15.

Entrance Difficulty Lincoln University has an open admission policy for first-time freshmen who are Missouri residents. It assesses its entrance difficulty as minimally difficult for out-of-state applicants; minimally difficult for transfers.

For Further Information Contact Mr. Mike Kosher, Director of Admissions, Lincoln University, Office of Admissions, 820 Chestnut Street, B-7 Young Hall, Jefferson City, MO 65102-0029. *Phone:* 573-681-5599 or 800-521-5052 (toll-free). *Fax:* 573-681-5889. *E-mail:* enroll@lincolnu.edu. *Web site:* http://www.lincolnu.edu/.

LINDENWOOD UNIVERSITY

St. Charles, Missouri

Lindenwood University is a coed, private, Presbyterian, comprehensive institution, founded in 1827, offering degrees at the bachelor's, master's, and doctoral levels and post-master's and postbachelor's certificates (education specialist). It has a 420-acre campus in St. Charles near St. Louis.

Academic Information The faculty has 617 members (32% full-time), 40% with terminal degrees. The undergraduate student-faculty ratio is 13:1. The library holds 89,807 titles, 402 serial subscriptions, and 1,960 audiovisual materials. Special programs include academic remediation, services for learning-disabled students, an honors program, cooperative (work-study) education, study abroad, advanced placement credit, accelerated degree programs, Freshman Honors College, ESL programs, double majors, independent study, distance learning, self-designed majors, summer session for credit, part-time degree programs (daytime, evenings, weekends, summer), adult/continuing education programs, internships, and arrangement for off-campus study with St. Louis Private College Consortium, Washington University in St. Louis, University of Missouri–Columbia. The most frequently chosen baccalaureate fields are business/marketing, communications/journalism, education.

Student Body Statistics The student body totals 10,085, of whom 6,343 are undergraduates (1,106 freshmen). 56 percent are women and 44 percent are men. Students come from 45 states and territories and 69 other countries. 80 percent are from Missouri. 9.7 percent are international students.

Expenses for 2008–09 *Application fee:* $30. *Comprehensive fee:* $19,500 includes full-time tuition ($12,700), mandatory fees ($300), and college room and board ($6500). *College room only:* $3400. Full-time tuition and fees vary according to program. *Part-time tuition:* $360 per credit hour. Part-time tuition varies according to course load.

Financial Aid Forms of aid include need-based and non-need-based scholarships and part-time jobs. The average aided 2008–09 undergraduate received an aid package worth an estimated $5490. The priority application deadline for financial aid is March 15.

Freshman Admission Lindenwood University requires a high school transcript, SAT or ACT scores, and TOEFL scores for international students. A minimum 2.25 high school GPA and an interview are recommended. An essay, 2 recommendations, and an interview are required for some. The application deadline for regular admission is rolling.

Transfer Admission The application deadline for admission is rolling.

Entrance Difficulty Lindenwood University assesses its entrance difficulty level as moderately difficult. For the fall 2008 freshman class, 40 percent of the applicants were accepted.

For Further Information Contact Mr. Joseph Parisi, Dean of Undergraduate Day Admissions, Lindenwood University, 209 South Kings Highway, St. Charles, MO 63301-1695. *Phone:* 636-949-4949. *Fax:* 636-949-4989. *E-mail:* admissions@lindenwood.edu. *Web site:* http://www.lindenwood.edu/.

LOGAN UNIVERSITY–COLLEGE OF CHIROPRACTIC

Chesterfield, Missouri

Logan University–College of Chiropractic is a coed, private, upper-level institution, founded in 1935, offering degrees at the bachelor's, master's, and first professional levels. It has a 111-acre campus in Chesterfield near St. Louis.

Academic Information The faculty has 100 members (50% full-time). The library holds 14,281 titles, 18,178 serial subscriptions, and 1,577 audiovisual materials. Special programs include services for learning-disabled students, advanced placement credit, independent study, distance learning, part-time degree programs (daytime, summer), adult/continuing education programs, and internships. The most frequently chosen baccalaureate field is biological/life sciences.

Student Body Statistics The student body totals 1,143, of whom 74 are undergraduates. 46 percent are women and 54 percent are men. 4.1 percent are international students.

Expenses for 2008–09 *Application fee:* $40. *Tuition:* $4860 full-time, $135 per credit hour part-time. *Mandatory fees:* $330 full-time, $110 per term part-time. Both full-time and part-time tuition and fees vary according to program.

Financial Aid Forms of aid include need-based and non-need-based scholarships and part-time jobs. The priority application deadline for financial aid is April 30.

Transfer Admission Logan University–College of Chiropractic requires a minimum 2.5 college GPA and a college transcript. The application deadline for admission is rolling.

Entrance Difficulty Logan University–College of Chiropractic assesses its entrance difficulty level as moderately difficult.

For Further Information Contact Mr. Greg Thornburg, Vice President of Academic Affairs, Logan University–College of Chiropractic, 1851 Schoettler Road, Chesterfield, MO 63006-1065. *Phone:* 636-227-2100 or 800-533-9210 (toll-free). *Fax:* 636-207-2425. *E-mail:* loganadm@logan.edu. *Web site:* http://www.logan.edu/.

MARYVILLE UNIVERSITY OF SAINT LOUIS

St. Louis, Missouri

Maryville University of Saint Louis is a coed, private, comprehensive institution, founded in 1872, offering degrees at the bachelor's, master's, and doctoral levels. It has a 130-acre campus in St. Louis.

Academic Information The faculty has 359 members (31% full-time), 62% with terminal degrees. The undergraduate student-faculty ratio is 12:1. The library holds 156,073 titles, 15,923 serial subscriptions, and 10,779 audiovisual materials. Special programs include services for learning-disabled students, an honors program, cooperative (work-study) education, study abroad, advanced placement credit, accelerated degree programs, Freshman Honors College, double majors, independent study, distance learning, self-designed majors, summer session for credit, part-time degree programs (daytime, evenings, weekends, summer), adult/continuing education programs, internships, and arrangement for off-campus study with Fontbonne University, Lindenwood University, Webster University, Missouri Baptist University. The most frequently chosen baccalaureate fields are business/marketing, health professions and related sciences, psychology.

Student Body Statistics The student body totals 3,517, of whom 2,898 are undergraduates (355 freshmen). 76 percent are women and 24 percent

are men. Students come from 24 states and territories and 10 other countries. 87 percent are from Missouri. 0.5 percent are international students.
Expenses for 2009–10 *Application fee:* $35. *Comprehensive fee:* $29,445 includes full-time tuition ($20,495), mandatory fees ($650), and college room and board ($8300). *Part-time tuition:* $590 per credit hour. *Part-time mandatory fees:* $137.50 per term.
Financial Aid Forms of aid include need-based and non-need-based scholarships and part-time jobs. The average aided 2008–09 undergraduate received an aid package worth an estimated $15,736.
Freshman Admission Maryville University of Saint Louis requires a high school transcript, a minimum 2.5 high school GPA, SAT or ACT scores, and TOEFL scores for international students. An essay, an interview, and audition, portfolio are required for some. The application deadline for regular admission is August 15.
Transfer Admission The application deadline for admission is rolling.
Entrance Difficulty Maryville University of Saint Louis assesses its entrance difficulty level as moderately difficult; very difficult for physical therapy, occupational therapy, education, actuarial science. For the fall 2008 freshman class, 54 percent of the applicants were accepted.
For Further Information Contact Ms. Shani Lenore, Assistant Vice President of Enrollment, Maryville University of Saint Louis, 650 Maryville University Drive, St. Louis, MO 63141-7299. *Phone:* 314-529-9350 or 800-627-9855 (toll-free). *Fax:* 314-529-9927. *E-mail:* admissions@maryville.edu. *Web site:* http://www.maryville.edu/.

MESSENGER COLLEGE

Joplin, Missouri

Messenger College is a coed, private, Pentecostal, four-year college, founded in 1987, offering degrees at the associate and bachelor's levels. It has a 16-acre campus in Joplin near Springfield.

Academic Information The faculty has 14 members (43% full-time), 21% with terminal degrees. The library holds 36,278 titles and 114 serial subscriptions. Special programs include academic remediation, an honors program, cooperative (work-study) education, double majors, independent study, distance learning, part-time degree programs (daytime, evenings), external degree programs, and internships.
Student Body Statistics The student body is made up of 70 undergraduates (9 freshmen). 50 percent are women and 50 percent are men.
Expenses for 2008–09 *Application fee:* $35. *Comprehensive fee:* $11,495 includes full-time tuition ($6825), mandatory fees ($670), and college room and board ($4000). Full-time tuition and fees vary according to course load. Room and board charges vary according to housing facility. *Part-time tuition:* $195 per credit hour. Part-time tuition varies according to course load.
Financial Aid Forms of aid include need-based and non-need-based scholarships and part-time jobs. The application deadline for financial aid is continuous.
Freshman Admission Messenger College requires an essay, a high school transcript, a minimum 2.0 high school GPA, 3 recommendations, a health form, SAT or ACT scores, and TOEFL scores for international students. An interview is required for some. The application deadline for regular admission is August 14.
Transfer Admission The application deadline for admission is August 14.
Entrance Difficulty Messenger College assesses its entrance difficulty level as moderately difficult. For the fall 2008 freshman class, 77 percent of the applicants were accepted.
For Further Information Contact Ron Cannon, Vice President of Academic Affairs, Messenger College, 300 East 50th, Joplin, MO 64804. *Phone:* 417-624-7070 Ext. 108 or 800-385-8940 (toll-free in-state). *Fax:* 417-624-5070. *E-mail:* info@messengercollege.edu. *Web site:* http://www.messengercollege.edu/.

METRO BUSINESS COLLEGE

Cape Girardeau, Missouri

Metro Business College is a coed, proprietary, primarily two-year college, offering degrees at the associate and bachelor's levels.

Student Body Statistics The student body is made up of 396 undergraduates.
Financial Aid Forms of aid include need-based scholarships. The application deadline for financial aid is continuous.
Entrance Difficulty Metro Business College assesses its entrance difficulty level as minimally difficult.
For Further Information Contact Ms. Janis Reimann, Director and Placement Director, Metro Business College, 1732 North Kingshighway, Cape Girardeau, MO 63701. *Phone:* 573-334-9181. *Fax:* 573-334-0617. *Web site:* http://www.metrobusinesscollege.edu/.

MIDWEST UNIVERSITY

Wentzville, Missouri

http://www.midwest.edu/

MISSOURI BAPTIST UNIVERSITY

St. Louis, Missouri

Missouri Baptist University is a coed, private, Southern Baptist, comprehensive institution, founded in 1964, offering degrees at the associate, bachelor's, and master's levels and post-master's and postbachelor's certificates. It has a 65-acre campus in St. Louis.

Academic Information The faculty has 236 members (30% full-time), 28% with terminal degrees. The undergraduate student-faculty ratio is 15:1. The library holds 71,634 titles, 452 serial subscriptions, and 2,155 audiovisual materials. Special programs include services for learning-disabled students, study abroad, advanced placement credit, accelerated degree programs, double majors, independent study, distance learning, self-designed majors, summer session for credit, part-time degree programs (daytime, evenings, summer), adult/continuing education programs, internships, and arrangement for off-campus study with Maryville University of Saint Louis, Lindenwood University, Fontbonne College, Webster University. The most frequently chosen baccalaureate fields are business/marketing, education, psychology.
Student Body Statistics The student body totals 4,614, of whom 3,276 are undergraduates (204 freshmen). 59 percent are women and 41 percent are men. Students come from 29 states and territories and 20 other countries. 93 percent are from Missouri. 4.7 percent are international students.
Expenses for 2008–09 *Application fee:* $30. *Comprehensive fee:* $23,942 includes full-time tuition ($16,170), mandatory fees ($702), and college room and board ($7070). Full-time tuition and fees vary according to course load, degree level, and location. Room and board charges vary according to housing facility. *Part-time tuition:* $560 per credit. *Part-time mandatory fees:* $13 per credit, $25 per term. Part-time tuition and fees vary according to course load, degree level, and location.
Financial Aid Forms of aid include need-based and non-need-based scholarships, athletic grants, and part-time jobs. The average aided 2008–09 undergraduate received an aid package worth an estimated $8232. The priority application deadline for financial aid is April 1.
Freshman Admission Missouri Baptist University requires a high school transcript, a minimum 2.0 high school GPA, an interview, and TOEFL scores for international students. SAT or ACT scores are required for some. The application deadline for regular admission is rolling.
Transfer Admission The application deadline for admission is rolling.

Missouri Baptist University (continued)

Entrance Difficulty Missouri Baptist University assesses its entrance difficulty level as moderately difficult. For the fall 2008 freshman class, 67 percent of the applicants were accepted.

For Further Information Contact Mr. Terry Dale Cruse, Director of Admissions, Missouri Baptist University, One College Park Drive, St. Louis, MO 63141-8660. *Phone:* 877-434-1115 or 877-434-1115 Ext. 2290 (toll-free). *Fax:* 314-434-7596. *E-mail:* admissions@mobap.edu. *Web site:* http://www.mobap.edu/.

MISSOURI COLLEGE

St. Louis, Missouri

Missouri College is a coed, primarily women's, proprietary, primarily two-year college, founded in 1963, offering degrees at the associate and bachelor's levels.

Student Body Statistics The student body is made up of 508 undergraduates.

Financial Aid Forms of aid include need-based scholarships and part-time jobs. The application deadline for financial aid is continuous.

Freshman Admission Missouri College requires an essay and an interview. The application deadline for regular admission is rolling.

Entrance Difficulty Missouri College has an open admission policy.

For Further Information Contact Mr. Doug Brinker, Admissions Director, Missouri College, 10121 Manchester Road, St. Louis, MO 63122-1583. *Phone:* 314-821-7700. *Fax:* 314-821-0891. *Web site:* http://www.mocollege.com/.

MISSOURI SOUTHERN STATE UNIVERSITY

Joplin, Missouri

Missouri Southern State University is a coed, public, comprehensive institution, founded in 1937, offering degrees at the associate, bachelor's, and master's levels. It has a 350-acre campus in Joplin.

Academic Information The faculty has 304 members (71% full-time), 46% with terminal degrees. The undergraduate student-faculty ratio is 18:1. Special programs include academic remediation, services for learning-disabled students, an honors program, cooperative (work-study) education, study abroad, advanced placement credit, accelerated degree programs, ESL programs, double majors, independent study, distance learning, summer session for credit, part-time degree programs (daytime, evenings, weekends, summer), external degree programs, adult/continuing education programs, internships, and arrangement for off-campus study with Nevada Consortium. The most frequently chosen baccalaureate fields are business/marketing, education, security and protective services.

Student Body Statistics The student body totals 5,264, of whom 5,219 are undergraduates (771 freshmen). 60 percent are women and 40 percent are men. Students come from 28 states and territories and 30 other countries. 87 percent are from Missouri.

Expenses for 2008–09 *Application fee:* $15. *State resident tuition:* $4290 full-time, $143 per credit part-time. *Nonresident tuition:* $8580 full-time, $286 per credit part-time. *Mandatory fees:* $245 full-time. Full-time tuition and fees vary according to course load. *College room and board:* $5440. Room and board charges vary according to board plan and housing facility.

Financial Aid Forms of aid include need-based and non-need-based scholarships, athletic grants, and part-time jobs. The average aided 2008–09 undergraduate received an aid package worth an estimated $10,304. The priority application deadline for financial aid is February 15.

Freshman Admission Missouri Southern State University requires a high school transcript, standardized test scores, class rank, SAT or ACT scores, and TOEFL scores for international students. ACT scores are recommended. 2 recommendations and Michigan Test of English Language Proficiency are required for some. The application deadline for regular admission is August 1.

Transfer Admission The application deadline for admission is August 1.

Entrance Difficulty Missouri Southern State University assesses its entrance difficulty level as moderately difficult; noncompetitive for transfers. For the fall 2008 freshman class, 96 percent of the applicants were accepted.

For Further Information Contact Mr. Derek Skaggs, Director of Enrollment Services, Missouri Southern State University, 3950 East Newman Road, Joplin, MO 64801-1595. *Phone:* 417-625-9537 or 866-818-MSSU (toll-free). *Fax:* 417-659-4429. *E-mail:* admissions@mssu.edu. *Web site:* http://www.mssu.edu/.

MISSOURI STATE UNIVERSITY

Springfield, Missouri

Missouri State University is a coed, public, comprehensive institution, founded in 1905, offering degrees at the bachelor's, master's, and doctoral levels and post-master's and postbachelor's certificates. It has a 225-acre campus in Springfield.

Academic Information The faculty has 1,047 members (69% full-time), 59% with terminal degrees. The undergraduate student-faculty ratio is 19:1. The library holds 2 million titles, 4,238 serial subscriptions, and 33,547 audiovisual materials. Special programs include services for learning-disabled students, an honors program, cooperative (work-study) education, study abroad, advanced placement credit, accelerated degree programs, Freshman Honors College, ESL programs, double majors, independent study, distance learning, self-designed majors, summer session for credit, part-time degree programs, internships, and arrangement for off-campus study with National Student Exchange. The most frequently chosen baccalaureate fields are business/marketing, education, social sciences.

Student Body Statistics The student body totals 19,348, of whom 16,255 are undergraduates (2,649 freshmen). 56 percent are women and 44 percent are men. Students come from 47 states and territories and 81 other countries. 94 percent are from Missouri. 1.9 percent are international students.

Expenses for 2008–09 *Application fee:* $35. *State resident tuition:* $6256 full-time, $186 per credit hour part-time. *Nonresident tuition:* $11,536 full-time, $362 per credit hour part-time. Both full-time and part-time tuition varies according to course load, degree level, location, and program.

Financial Aid Forms of aid include need-based scholarships, athletic grants, and part-time jobs. The average aided 2007–08 undergraduate received an aid package worth $6906.

Freshman Admission Missouri State University requires a high school transcript, SAT or ACT scores, and TOEFL scores for international students. An essay and an interview are required for some. The application deadline for regular admission is July 20.

Transfer Admission The application deadline for admission is July 20.

Entrance Difficulty Missouri State University assesses its entrance difficulty level as moderately difficult. For the fall 2008 freshman class, 75 percent of the applicants were accepted.

For Further Information Contact Ms. Jill Duncan, Associate Director of Admissions, Missouri State University, 901 South National, Springfield, MO 65804. *Phone:* 417-836-5517 or 800-492-7900 (toll-free). *Fax:* 417-836-6334. *E-mail:* info@missouristate.edu. *Web site:* http://www.missouristate.edu/.

MISSOURI TECH

St. Louis, Missouri

Missouri Tech is a coed, primarily men's, proprietary, four-year college, founded in 1932, offering degrees at the associate and bachelor's levels.

Academic Information Special programs include advanced placement credit, accelerated degree programs, summer session for credit, part-time degree programs (daytime, evenings), adult/continuing education programs, and internships.

Student Body Statistics The student body is made up of 114 undergraduates.

Expenses for 2008–09 *Tuition:* $12,600 full-time, $525 per credit part-time. *Mandatory fees:* $190 full-time, $95 per term part-time.

Financial Aid Forms of aid include need-based and non-need-based scholarships. The application deadline for financial aid is continuous.
Freshman Admission Missouri Tech requires a high school transcript and TOEFL scores for international students. ACT scores are recommended. An interview is required for some. The application deadline for regular admission is rolling.
Entrance Difficulty Missouri Tech assesses its entrance difficulty level as moderately difficult.
For Further Information Contact Mr. Bob Honaker, Director of Admissions, Missouri Tech, 1167 Corporate Lake Drive, St. Louis, MO 63132. *Phone:* 314-569-3600. *Fax:* 314-569-1167. *Web site:* http://www.motech.edu/.

MISSOURI UNIVERSITY OF SCIENCE AND TECHNOLOGY

Rolla, Missouri

Missouri University of Science and Technology is a coed, primarily men's, public unit of University of Missouri System, founded in 1870, offering degrees at the bachelor's, master's, and doctoral levels and postbachelor's certificates. It has a 284-acre campus in Rolla.

Academic Information The faculty has 446 members (81% full-time), 80% with terminal degrees. The undergraduate student-faculty ratio is 15:1. The library holds 477,201 titles, 2,593 serial subscriptions, and 4,353 audiovisual materials. Special programs include academic remediation, services for learning-disabled students, an honors program, cooperative (work-study) education, study abroad, advanced placement credit, accelerated degree programs, Freshman Honors College, ESL programs, double majors, independent study, distance learning, summer session for credit, part-time degree programs, adult/continuing education programs, internships, and arrangement for off-campus study with University of Missouri–Columbia. The most frequently chosen baccalaureate fields are computer and information sciences, business/marketing, engineering.
Student Body Statistics The student body totals 6,371, of whom 4,912 are undergraduates (1,046 freshmen). 22 percent are women and 78 percent are men. Students come from 47 states and territories and 26 other countries. 80 percent are from Missouri. 2.9 percent are international students.
Expenses for 2008–09 *Application fee:* $35. *State resident tuition:* $7368 full-time, $246 per credit hour part-time. *Nonresident tuition:* $18,459 full-time, $615 per credit hour part-time. *Mandatory fees:* $1130 full-time, $120.52 per credit hour part-time. Both full-time and part-time tuition and fees vary according to course load, degree level, and program. *College room and board:* $7035. *College room only:* $4350. Room and board charges vary according to board plan, housing facility, and location.
Financial Aid Forms of aid include need-based and non-need-based scholarships and part-time jobs. The average aided 2008–09 undergraduate received an aid package worth an estimated $11,792. The priority application deadline for financial aid is March 1.
Freshman Admission Missouri University of Science and Technology requires a high school transcript and SAT or ACT scores. TOEFL scores for international students are recommended. The application deadline for regular admission is July 1.
Transfer Admission The application deadline for admission is July 1.
Entrance Difficulty Missouri University of Science and Technology assesses its entrance difficulty level as very difficult; moderately difficult for transfers. For the fall 2008 freshman class, 92 percent of the applicants were accepted.
For Further Information Contact Admissions Office, Missouri University of Science and Technology, 106 Parker Hall, Rolla, MO 65409. *Phone:* 573-341-4165 or 800-522-0938 (toll-free). *Fax:* 573-341-4082. *E-mail:* admissions@mst.edu. *Web site:* http://www.mst.edu/.

MISSOURI VALLEY COLLEGE

Marshall, Missouri

Missouri Valley College is a coed, private, four-year college, founded in 1889, affiliated with the Presbyterian Church, offering degrees at the associate and bachelor's levels. It has a 140-acre campus in Marshall near Kansas City.

Expenses for 2008–09 *Application fee:* $15. *Comprehensive fee:* $22,000 includes full-time tuition ($15,450), mandatory fees ($500), and college room and board ($6050). *College room only:* $3100. *Part-time tuition:* $350 per credit hour.
For Further Information Contact Ms. Debi Bultmann, Admissions Office Manager, Missouri Valley College, Admissions Office, 500 East College, Marshall, MO 65340. *Phone:* 660-831-4125. *Fax:* 660-831-4233. *E-mail:* admissions@moval.edu. *Web site:* http://www.moval.edu/.

MISSOURI WESTERN STATE UNIVERSITY

St. Joseph, Missouri

Missouri Western State University is a coed, public, four-year college, founded in 1915, offering degrees at the associate and bachelor's levels. It has a 744-acre campus in St. Joseph near Kansas City.

Academic Information The faculty has 308 members (58% full-time), 51% with terminal degrees. The student-faculty ratio is 19:1. The library holds 147,509 titles and 1,068 serial subscriptions. Special programs include academic remediation, an honors program, study abroad, advanced placement credit, accelerated degree programs, Freshman Honors College, double majors, distance learning, summer session for credit, part-time degree programs (daytime, evenings, weekends, summer), and internships. The most frequently chosen baccalaureate fields are business/marketing, education, security and protective services.
Student Body Statistics The student body is made up of 5,276 undergraduates (1,059 freshmen). 59 percent are women and 41 percent are men. Students come from 31 states and territories and 7 other countries. 93 percent are from Missouri. 0.3 percent are international students.
Expenses for 2008–09 *Application fee:* $15. *State resident tuition:* $4992 full-time, $166.40 per credit hour part-time. *Nonresident tuition:* $9120 full-time, $304 per credit hour part-time. *Mandatory fees:* $568 full-time, $19.10 per credit hour part-time, $30 per term part-time. *College room and board:* $5868. Room and board charges vary according to board plan and housing facility.
Financial Aid Forms of aid include need-based and non-need-based scholarships, athletic grants, and part-time jobs. The average aided 2008–09 undergraduate received an aid package worth an estimated $7438. The priority application deadline for financial aid is March 1.
Freshman Admission Missouri Western State University requires a high school transcript and TOEFL scores for international students. The application deadline for regular admission is June 1.
Transfer Admission The application deadline for admission is June 1.
Entrance Difficulty Missouri Western State University has an open admission policy. It assesses its entrance difficulty as moderately difficult for nursing, computer science, education, criminal justice, leisure management, math, history, political science, social work programs.
For Further Information Contact Mr. Howard McCauley, Director of Admissions, Missouri Western State University, 4525 Downs Drive, St. Joseph, MO 64507-2294. *Phone:* 816-271-4267 or 800-662-7041 Ext. 60 (toll-free). *Fax:* 816-271-5833. *E-mail:* admission@missouriwestern.edu. *Web site:* http://www.missouriwestern.edu/.

NATIONAL AMERICAN UNIVERSITY

Kansas City, Missouri

National American University is a coed, proprietary, four-year college of National College, founded in 1941, offering degrees at the associate and bachelor's levels. It has a 1-acre campus in Kansas City.

Academic Information The library holds 1,500 titles and 60 serial subscriptions. Special programs include cooperative (work-study) education,

National American University (continued)
study abroad, independent study, distance learning, summer session for credit, part-time degree programs (daytime, evenings, weekends, summer), and external degree programs.
Student Body Statistics The student body is made up of 315 undergraduates.
Financial Aid Forms of aid include need-based and non-need-based scholarships and part-time jobs. The application deadline for financial aid is continuous.
Freshman Admission National American University requires a high school transcript, an interview, and TOEFL scores for international students. The application deadline for regular admission is rolling.
Entrance Difficulty National American University has an open admission policy.
For Further Information Contact Admissions Office, National American University, 7490 NW 87th Street, Kansas City, MO 64153. *Phone:* 816-412-5500. *Fax:* 816-353-1176. *E-mail:* zradmissions@national.edu. *Web site:* http://www.national.edu/.

NORTHWEST MISSOURI STATE UNIVERSITY

Maryville, Missouri

Northwest Missouri State University is a coed, public, comprehensive unit of Missouri Coordinating Board for Higher Education, founded in 1905, offering degrees at the bachelor's and master's levels and post-master's and postbachelor's certificates. It has a 240-acre campus in Maryville near Kansas City.

Academic Information The faculty has 309 members (82% full-time), 62% with terminal degrees. The undergraduate student-faculty ratio is 20:1. The library holds 339,878 titles, 38,955 serial subscriptions, and 7,004 audiovisual materials. Special programs include academic remediation, services for learning-disabled students, an honors program, study abroad, advanced placement credit, accelerated degree programs, ESL programs, double majors, independent study, distance learning, summer session for credit, part-time degree programs (daytime, evenings, summer), internships, and arrangement for off-campus study with Missouri Western State College, Truman State University, North Central Missouri College. The most frequently chosen baccalaureate fields are business/marketing, communications/journalism, education.
Student Body Statistics The student body totals 6,903, of whom 5,782 are undergraduates (1,533 freshmen). 56 percent are women and 44 percent are men. Students come from 35 states and territories and 21 other countries. 74 percent are from Missouri. 2 percent are international students.
Expenses for 2009–10 *Application fee:* $25. *One-time mandatory fee:* $100. *State resident tuition:* $5145 full-time, $214 per credit hour part-time. *Nonresident tuition:* $8923 full-time, $372 per credit hour part-time. *Mandatory fees:* $384 full-time, $16 per credit hour part-time. *College room and board:* $6876. *College room only:* $3966.
Financial Aid Forms of aid include need-based and non-need-based scholarships, athletic grants, and part-time jobs. The average aided 2007–08 undergraduate received an aid package worth $8497. The application deadline for financial aid is continuous.
Freshman Admission Northwest Missouri State University requires a high school transcript, a minimum 2.0 high school GPA, SAT or ACT scores, and TOEFL scores for international students. An interview is required for some. The application deadline for regular admission is rolling and for nonresidents it is rolling.
Transfer Admission The application deadline for admission is rolling.
Entrance Difficulty Northwest Missouri State University assesses its entrance difficulty level as moderately difficult; minimally difficult for transfers. For the fall 2008 freshman class, 75 percent of the applicants were accepted.
For Further Information Contact Ms. Tammi Grow, Associate Director of Admission, Northwest Missouri State University, 800 University Drive, Maryville, MO 64468-6001. *Phone:* 660-562-1146 or 800-633-1175 (toll-free). *Fax:* 660-562-1146. *E-mail:* admissions@nwmissouri.edu. *Web site:* http://www.nwmissouri.edu/.

OZARK CHRISTIAN COLLEGE

Joplin, Missouri

Ozark Christian College is a coed, private, Christian, four-year college, founded in 1942, offering degrees at the associate and bachelor's levels. It has a 110-acre campus in Joplin.

Expenses for 2008–09 *Application fee:* $30. *Comprehensive fee:* $12,500 includes full-time tuition ($8160), mandatory fees ($480), and college room and board ($3860). *College room only:* $2120. Full-time tuition and fees vary according to course load and program. Room and board charges vary according to board plan. *Part-time tuition:* $255 per hour. Part-time tuition varies according to course load and program.
For Further Information Contact Mr. Troy B. Nelson, Executive Director of Admissions, Ozark Christian College, 1111 North Main Street, Joplin, MO 64801-4804. *Phone:* 417-624-2518 or 800-299-4622 (toll-free). *Fax:* 417-624-0090. *E-mail:* occadmin@occ.edu. *Web site:* http://www.occ.edu/.

PARK UNIVERSITY

Parkville, Missouri

Park University is a coed, private, comprehensive institution, founded in 1875, offering degrees at the associate, bachelor's, and master's levels and postbachelor's certificates. It has an 800-acre campus in Parkville near Kansas City.

Academic Information The faculty has 1,019 members (15% full-time). The undergraduate student-faculty ratio is 15:1. The library holds 150,503 titles and 591 serial subscriptions. Special programs include academic remediation, services for learning-disabled students, an honors program, advanced placement credit, ESL programs, double majors, independent study, distance learning, self-designed majors, summer session for credit, part-time degree programs, external degree programs, adult/continuing education programs, internships, and arrangement for off-campus study with members of the Kansas City Professional Development Council. The most frequently chosen baccalaureate fields are business/marketing, psychology, security and protective services.
Student Body Statistics The student body totals 12,457, of whom 11,865 are undergraduates (257 freshmen). 51 percent are women and 49 percent are men. Students come from 50 states and territories and 105 other countries. 18 percent are from Missouri. 3.6 percent are international students.
Expenses for 2008–09 *Application fee:* $25. *Comprehensive fee:* $13,449 includes full-time tuition ($7644) and college room and board ($5805). *Part-time tuition:* $273 per credit hour.
Financial Aid Forms of aid include need-based and non-need-based scholarships, athletic grants, and part-time jobs. The average aided 2007–08 undergraduate received an aid package worth $3811. The priority application deadline for financial aid is April 1.
Freshman Admission Park University requires a high school transcript, a minimum 2.0 high school GPA, and SAT or ACT scores. An essay is recommended. 2 recommendations and an interview are required for some. The application deadline for regular admission is August 1.
Transfer Admission The application deadline for admission is August 1.
Entrance Difficulty Park University assesses its entrance difficulty level as moderately difficult. For the fall 2008 freshman class, 78 percent of the applicants were accepted.
For Further Information Contact Cathy Colapietro, Director of Admissions and Student Financial Services, Park University, 8700 NW River Park Drive, Campus Box 1, Parkville, MO 64152. *Phone:* 816-584-6728 or 800-745-7275 (toll-free). *Fax:* 816-741-4462. *E-mail:* admissions@mail.park.edu. *Web site:* http://www.park.edu/.

PATRICIA STEVENS COLLEGE

St. Louis, Missouri

Patricia Stevens College is a coed, proprietary, four-year college, founded in 1947, offering degrees at the associate and bachelor's levels.

Expenses for 2008–09 *Application fee:* $15. *Tuition:* $15,120 full-time, $210 per quarter hour part-time.
For Further Information Contact Mr. John Willmon, Director of Admissions, Patricia Stevens College, 330 North Fourth Street, Suite 306, St. Louis, MO 63102. *Phone:* 314-421-0949 or 800-871-0949 (toll-free). *Fax:* 314-421-0304. *E-mail:* admission@patriciastevenscollege.com. *Web site:* http://www.patriciastevenscollege.edu/.

RANKEN TECHNICAL COLLEGE

St. Louis, Missouri

Ranken Technical College is a coed, primarily men's, private, primarily two-year college, founded in 1907, offering degrees at the associate and bachelor's levels. It has a 10-acre campus in St. Louis.

Academic Information The library holds 11,000 titles and 182 serial subscriptions. Special programs include academic remediation, services for learning-disabled students, cooperative (work-study) education, advanced placement credit, independent study, distance learning, summer session for credit, part-time degree programs (daytime, evenings, weekends, summer), adult/continuing education programs, and internships.
Student Body Statistics The student body is made up of 1,743 undergraduates.
Expenses for 2008–09 *Application fee:* $25. *Tuition:* $11,760 full-time.
Financial Aid Forms of aid include need-based scholarships and part-time jobs. The application deadline for financial aid is continuous.
Freshman Admission Ranken Technical College requires an essay, a high school transcript, and an interview. TOEFL scores for international students are recommended. The application deadline for regular admission is rolling.
Entrance Difficulty Ranken Technical College assesses its entrance difficulty level as moderately difficult.
For Further Information Contact Ms. Elizabeth Keserauskis, Director of Admissions, Ranken Technical College, 4431 Finney Avenue, St. Louis, MO 63113. *Phone:* 314-371-0233 Ext. 4811 or 866-4RANKEN (toll-free out-of-state). *Fax:* 314-371-0241. *E-mail:* admissions@ranken.edu. *Web site:* http://www.ranken.edu/.

RESEARCH COLLEGE OF NURSING

Kansas City, Missouri

Research College of Nursing is a coed, primarily women's, private, comprehensive unit of Rockhurst University, founded in 1980, offering degrees at the bachelor's and master's levels (bachelor's degree offered jointly with Rockhurst College). It has a 66-acre campus in Kansas City.

Academic Information The faculty has 29 members (90% full-time), 14% with terminal degrees. The undergraduate student-faculty ratio is 7:1. The library holds 150,000 titles and 675 serial subscriptions. Special programs include services for learning-disabled students, an honors program, study abroad, advanced placement credit, accelerated degree programs, double majors, independent study, and summer session for credit. The most frequently chosen baccalaureate field is health professions and related sciences.
Student Body Statistics The student body totals 382, of whom 302 are undergraduates (58 freshmen). 94 percent are women and 6 percent are men. Students come from 7 states and territories.
Expenses for 2008–09 *Application fee:* $20. *One-time mandatory fee:* $160. *Comprehensive fee:* $31,680 includes full-time tuition ($23,980), mandatory fees ($700), and college room and board ($7000). *College room only:* $3800. Room and board charges vary according to board plan, housing facility, and location. *Part-time tuition:* $792 per credit hour. *Part-time mandatory fees:* $10 per credit hour. Part-time tuition and fees vary according to class time.
Financial Aid Forms of aid include need-based and non-need-based scholarships. The priority application deadline for financial aid is March 15.
Freshman Admission Research College of Nursing requires a high school transcript, 1 recommendation, SAT or ACT scores, and TOEFL scores for international students. A minimum 2.8 high school GPA and an interview are recommended. The application deadline for regular admission is June 30.
Transfer Admission The application deadline for admission is February 15.
Entrance Difficulty Research College of Nursing assesses its entrance difficulty level as moderately difficult. For the fall 2008 freshman class, 68 percent of the applicants were accepted.
For Further Information Contact Mr. Lane Ramey, Director of Transfer Admission, Research College of Nursing, 1100 Rockhurst Road, Kansas City, MO 64110. *Phone:* 816-501-4102 or 800-842-6776 (toll-free). *Fax:* 816-501-4588. *E-mail:* lane.ramey@rockhurst.edu. *Web site:* http://www.researchcollege.edu/.

ROCKHURST UNIVERSITY

Kansas City, Missouri

Rockhurst University is a coed, private, Roman Catholic (Jesuit), comprehensive institution, founded in 1910, offering degrees at the bachelor's, master's, and doctoral levels and postbachelor's certificates. It has a 35-acre campus in Kansas City.

Academic Information The faculty has 223 members (56% full-time), 64% with terminal degrees. The undergraduate student-faculty ratio is 12:1. The library holds 189,527 titles, 42,563 serial subscriptions, and 1,663 audiovisual materials. Special programs include academic remediation, services for learning-disabled students, an honors program, cooperative (work-study) education, study abroad, advanced placement credit, accelerated degree programs, Freshman Honors College, double majors, independent study, distance learning, summer session for credit, part-time degree programs (daytime, evenings, weekends, summer), internships, and arrangement for off-campus study with Kansas City Area Student Exchange. The most frequently chosen baccalaureate fields are business/marketing, health professions and related sciences, psychology.
Student Body Statistics The student body totals 3,086, of whom 2,242 are undergraduates (350 freshmen). 61 percent are women and 39 percent are men. Students come from 30 states and territories and 5 other countries. 62 percent are from Missouri. 0.6 percent are international students.
Expenses for 2009–10 *Application fee:* $25. *Comprehensive fee:* $32,970 includes full-time tuition ($24,950), mandatory fees ($940), and college room and board ($7080). *College room only:* $4180. *Part-time tuition:* $832 per credit hour.
Financial Aid Forms of aid include need-based and non-need-based scholarships, athletic grants, and part-time jobs. The average aided 2008–09 undergraduate received an aid package worth an estimated $24,533.
Freshman Admission Rockhurst University requires a high school transcript, a minimum 2.0 high school GPA, 1 recommendation, SAT or ACT scores, and TOEFL scores for international students. An essay and an interview are required for some. The application deadline for regular admission is June 30.
Transfer Admission The application deadline for admission is rolling.
Entrance Difficulty Rockhurst University assesses its entrance difficulty level as moderately difficult. For the fall 2008 freshman class, 76 percent of the applicants were accepted.
For Further Information Contact Lane Ramey, Director of Freshman Admissions, Rockhurst University, 1100 Rockhurst Road, Kansas City, MO 64110-2561. *Phone:* 816-501-4100 or 800-842-6776 (toll-free). *Fax:* 816-501-4142. *E-mail:* admission@rockhurst.edu. *Web site:* http://www.rockhurst.edu/.

ST. LOUIS CHRISTIAN COLLEGE

Florissant, Missouri

St. Louis Christian College is a coed, private, Christian, four-year college, founded in 1956, offering degrees at the associate and bachelor's levels. It has a 20-acre campus in Florissant near St. Louis.

Academic Information The faculty has 33 members (27% full-time), 24% with terminal degrees. The student-faculty ratio is 12:1. The library

St. Louis Christian College (continued)

holds 39,728 titles and 144 serial subscriptions. Special programs include academic remediation, services for learning-disabled students, advanced placement credit, accelerated degree programs, part-time degree programs (daytime), adult/continuing education programs, and internships. The most frequently chosen baccalaureate field is theology and religious vocations.
Student Body Statistics The student body is made up of 321 undergraduates (54 freshmen). 39 percent are women and 61 percent are men. Students come from 17 states and territories and 3 other countries. 66 percent are from Missouri. 2.2 percent are international students.
Expenses for 2008–09 *Application fee:* $0. *Comprehensive fee:* $12,800 includes full-time tuition ($8850), mandatory fees ($650), and college room and board ($3300). Room and board charges vary according to housing facility. *Part-time tuition:* $295 per credit hour.
Financial Aid Forms of aid include need-based and non-need-based scholarships and part-time jobs. The average aided 2008–09 undergraduate received an aid package worth an estimated $13,586. The application deadline for financial aid is continuous.
Freshman Admission St. Louis Christian College requires an essay, a high school transcript, 2 recommendations, ACT scores, and TOEFL scores for international students. A minimum 2.0 high school GPA is recommended. An interview is required for some. The application deadline for regular admission is August 15.
Transfer Admission The application deadline for admission is August 15.
Entrance Difficulty St. Louis Christian College assesses its entrance difficulty level as minimally difficult.
For Further Information Contact Carrie Chapman, Admissions Director, St. Louis Christian College, 1360 Grandview Drive, Florissant, MO 63033. *Phone:* 314-837-6777 or 800-887-SLCC (toll-free). *Fax:* 314-837-8291. *E-mail:* cchapman@slcconline.edu. *Web site:* http://www.slcconline.edu/.

ST. LOUIS COLLEGE OF PHARMACY

St. Louis, Missouri

St. Louis College of Pharmacy is a coed, private, comprehensive institution, founded in 1864, offering degrees at the first professional level. It has a 5-acre campus in St. Louis.

Academic Information The faculty has 106 members (73% full-time), 75% with terminal degrees. The undergraduate student-faculty ratio is 18:1. The library holds 69,820 titles, 155 serial subscriptions, and 1,887 audiovisual materials. Special programs include academic remediation, advanced placement credit, summer session for credit, and internships. The most frequently chosen baccalaureate field is health professions and related sciences.
Student Body Statistics The student body totals 1,191, of whom 645 are undergraduates (237 freshmen). 58 percent are women and 42 percent are men. Students come from 23 states and territories and 3 other countries. 50 percent are from Missouri. 0.9 percent are international students.
Expenses for 2009–10 *Application fee:* $50. *Comprehensive fee:* $30,079 includes full-time tuition ($21,525), mandatory fees ($400), and college room and board ($8154). *College room only:* $4600. *Part-time tuition:* $800 per credit hour.
Financial Aid Forms of aid include need-based and non-need-based scholarships and part-time jobs. The average aided 2008–09 undergraduate received an aid package worth an estimated $12,986. The priority application deadline for financial aid is March 15.
Freshman Admission St. Louis College of Pharmacy requires an essay, a high school transcript, a minimum 3.0 high school GPA, 2 recommendations, SAT or ACT scores, and TOEFL scores for international students. An interview is required for some. The application deadline for regular admission is February 1 and for early decision it is December 15.
Transfer Admission The application deadline for admission is February 1.
Entrance Difficulty St. Louis College of Pharmacy assesses its entrance difficulty level as moderately difficult; most difficult for transfers. For the fall 2008 freshman class, 49 percent of the applicants were accepted.
For Further Information Contact Connie Horrall, Administrative Assistant, St. Louis College of Pharmacy, 4588 Parkview Place, St. Louis, MO 63110-1088. *Phone:* 314-446-8328 or 800-278-5267 (toll-free in-state). *Fax:* 314-446-8310. *E-mail:* chorrall@stlcop.edu. *Web site:* http://www.stlcop.edu/.

SAINT LOUIS UNIVERSITY

St. Louis, Missouri

Saint Louis University is a coed, private, Roman Catholic (Jesuit) university, founded in 1818, offering degrees at the bachelor's, master's, doctoral, and first professional levels and post-master's and postbachelor's certificates. It has a 244-acre campus in St. Louis.

Academic Information The faculty has 1,076 members (59% full-time), 59% with terminal degrees. The undergraduate student-faculty ratio is 12:1. The library holds 2 million titles, 16,067 serial subscriptions, and 174,702 audiovisual materials. Special programs include academic remediation, services for learning-disabled students, an honors program, cooperative (work-study) education, study abroad, advanced placement credit, accelerated degree programs, Freshman Honors College, ESL programs, double majors, independent study, distance learning, self-designed majors, summer session for credit, part-time degree programs (daytime, evenings, weekends, summer), adult/continuing education programs, internships, and arrangement for off-campus study with Washington University in St. Louis. The most frequently chosen baccalaureate fields are business/marketing, health professions and related sciences, social sciences.
Student Body Statistics The student body totals 12,733, of whom 7,814 are undergraduates (1,645 freshmen). 59 percent are women and 41 percent are men. Students come from 43 states and territories and 57 other countries. 43 percent are from Missouri. 5.2 percent are international students.
Expenses for 2008–09 *Application fee:* $25. *Comprehensive fee:* $39,488 includes full-time tuition ($30,330), mandatory fees ($398), and college room and board ($8760). *College room only:* $4900. Full-time tuition and fees vary according to location and program. Room and board charges vary according to board plan, housing facility, and location. *Part-time tuition:* $1060 per credit hour. *Part-time mandatory fees:* $120 per semester hour. Part-time tuition and fees vary according to location and program.
Financial Aid Forms of aid include need-based and non-need-based scholarships, athletic grants, and part-time jobs. The average aided 2007–08 undergraduate received an aid package worth $19,456.
Freshman Admission Saint Louis University requires an essay, a high school transcript, a minimum 2.5 high school GPA, secondary school report form, SAT or ACT scores, and TOEFL scores for international students. 2 recommendations and an interview are recommended. The application deadline for regular admission is August 1 and for nonresidents it is August 1.
Transfer Admission The application deadline for admission is rolling.
Entrance Difficulty Saint Louis University assesses its entrance difficulty level as moderately difficult. For the fall 2008 freshman class, 72 percent of the applicants were accepted.
For Further Information Contact Director, Saint Louis University, 221 North Grand Boulevard, DuBourg Hall, Room 100, St. Louis, MO 63103-2097. *Phone:* 314-977-2500 or 800-758-3678 (toll-free out-of-state). *Fax:* 314-977-7136. *E-mail:* admitme@slu.edu. *Web site:* http://www.slu.edu/.

SAINT LUKE'S COLLEGE

Kansas City, Missouri

Saint Luke's College is a coed, private, Episcopal, upper-level institution, founded in 1903, offering degrees at the bachelor's level. It has a 3-acre campus in Kansas City.

Expenses for 2008–09 *Application fee:* $35. *Tuition:* $8850 full-time. *Mandatory fees:* $670 full-time.
For Further Information Contact Assistant Director of Admissions, Saint Luke's College, 8320 Ward Parkway, Suite 300, Kansas City, MO 64114. *Phone:* 816-932-3372. *Fax:* 816-932-9064. *E-mail:* slc-admissions@saint-lukes.org. *Web site:* http://www.saintlukescollege.edu/.

SANFORD-BROWN COLLEGE

Fenton, Missouri

Sanford-Brown College is a coed, proprietary, primarily two-year college, founded in 1868, offering degrees at the associate and bachelor's levels. It has a 6-acre campus in Fenton near St. Louis.

Academic Information Special programs include services for learning-disabled students, independent study, adult/continuing education programs, and internships.
Student Body Statistics The student body is made up of 659 undergraduates.
Financial Aid Forms of aid include need-based scholarships and part-time jobs. The application deadline for financial aid is continuous.
Freshman Admission Sanford-Brown College requires a high school transcript, an interview, and CPAt.
Entrance Difficulty Sanford-Brown College has an open admission policy.
For Further Information Contact Ms. Judy Wilga, Director of Admissions, Sanford-Brown College, 1203 Smizer Mill Road, Fenton, MO 63026. *Phone:* 636-349-4900 Ext. 102 or 800-456-7222 (toll-free). *Fax:* 636-349-9170. *Web site:* http://www.sanford-brown.edu/.

SOUTHEAST MISSOURI HOSPITAL COLLEGE OF NURSING AND HEALTH SCIENCES

Cape Girardeau, Missouri

Southeast Missouri Hospital College of Nursing and Health Sciences is a coed, private, two-year college, founded in 1928, offering degrees at the associate level and postbachelor's certificates.

Expenses for 2008–09 *Application fee:* $40. *Tuition:* $11,500 full-time, $300 per credit hour part-time. Both full-time and part-time tuition varies according to course load and program.
For Further Information Contact Tonya L. Buttry, President, Southeast Missouri Hospital College of Nursing and Health Sciences, 2001 William Street, Cape Girardeau, MO 63701. *Phone:* 573-334-6825. *Fax:* 573-339-7805. *E-mail:* tbuttry@sehosp.org. *Web site:* http://www.southeastmissourihospital.com/college/.

SOUTHEAST MISSOURI STATE UNIVERSITY

Cape Girardeau, Missouri

Southeast Missouri State University is a coed, public, comprehensive unit of Missouri Coordinating Board for Higher Education, founded in 1873, offering degrees at the associate, bachelor's, and master's levels and post-master's certificates. It has a 400-acre campus in Cape Girardeau near St. Louis.

Academic Information The faculty has 604 members (70% full-time), 58% with terminal degrees. The undergraduate student-faculty ratio is 18:1. The library holds 503,242 titles, 49,866 serial subscriptions, and 15,554 audiovisual materials. Special programs include academic remediation, services for learning-disabled students, an honors program, study abroad, advanced placement credit, accelerated degree programs, ESL programs, double majors, independent study, distance learning, self-designed majors, summer session for credit, part-time degree programs (daytime, evenings, summer), adult/continuing education programs, and internships. The most frequently chosen baccalaureate fields are education, business/marketing, liberal arts/general studies.
Student Body Statistics The student body totals 10,814, of whom 9,381 are undergraduates (1,828 freshmen). 59 percent are women and 41 percent are men. Students come from 37 states and territories and 33 other countries. 87 percent are from Missouri. 2.9 percent are international students.
Expenses for 2008–09 *Application fee:* $25. *State resident tuition:* $5544 full-time, $184.80 per credit hour part-time. *Nonresident tuition:* $10,179 full-time, $339.30 per credit hour part-time. *Mandatory fees:* $711 full-time, $23.70 per credit hour part-time. Both full-time and part-time tuition and fees vary according to course load and location. *College room and board:* $5935. *College room only:* $3673. Room and board charges vary according to board plan and housing facility.
Financial Aid Forms of aid include need-based and non-need-based scholarships, athletic grants, and part-time jobs. The average aided 2007–08 undergraduate received an aid package worth $7490. The priority application deadline for financial aid is March 1.
Freshman Admission Southeast Missouri State University requires a high school transcript, a minimum 2.0 high school GPA, SAT or ACT scores, and TOEFL scores for international students. The application deadline for regular admission is May 1.
Transfer Admission The application deadline for admission is August 1.
Entrance Difficulty Southeast Missouri State University assesses its entrance difficulty level as moderately difficult; minimally difficult for transfers. For the fall 2008 freshman class, 88 percent of the applicants were accepted.
For Further Information Contact Dr. Deborah Below, Director of Admissions, Southeast Missouri State University, MS 3550, Cape Girardeau, MO 63701. *Phone:* 573-651-2590. *Fax:* 573-651-5936. *E-mail:* admissions@semo.edu. *Web site:* http://www.semo.edu/.

SOUTHWEST BAPTIST UNIVERSITY

Bolivar, Missouri

Southwest Baptist University is a coed, private, Southern Baptist, comprehensive institution, founded in 1878, offering degrees at the associate, bachelor's, master's, and doctoral levels and post-master's certificates. It has a 152-acre campus in Bolivar.

Academic Information The faculty has 245 members (47% full-time), 40% with terminal degrees. The undergraduate student-faculty ratio is 14:1. The library holds 185,703 titles, 22,388 serial subscriptions, and 11,553 audiovisual materials. Special programs include academic remediation, services for learning-disabled students, an honors program, cooperative (work-study) education, study abroad, advanced placement credit, double majors, independent study, distance learning, self-designed majors, summer session for credit, part-time degree programs (daytime, evenings, summer), internships, and arrangement for off-campus study with Mountain View Center, Salem Center, Springfield Center. The most frequently chosen baccalaureate fields are business/marketing, education, health professions and related sciences.
Student Body Statistics The student body totals 3,656, of whom 2,803 are undergraduates (516 freshmen). 65 percent are women and 35 percent are men. Students come from 37 states and territories and 16 other countries. 70 percent are from Missouri. 0.9 percent are international students.
Expenses for 2009–10 *Application fee:* $30. *Comprehensive fee:* $22,000 includes full-time tuition ($15,800), mandatory fees ($730), and college room and board ($5470). *College room only:* $2820. *Part-time mandatory fees:* $580 per hour.
Financial Aid Forms of aid include need-based and non-need-based scholarships, athletic grants, and part-time jobs. The average aided 2008–09 undergraduate received an aid package worth an estimated $13,657.
Freshman Admission Southwest Baptist University requires a high school transcript, a minimum 2.5 high school GPA, SAT or ACT scores, and TOEFL scores for international students. An essay and an interview are recommended. 3 recommendations are required for some. The application deadline for regular admission is rolling.
Transfer Admission The application deadline for admission is rolling.

Southwest Baptist University (continued)

Entrance Difficulty Southwest Baptist University assesses its entrance difficulty level as moderately difficult. For the fall 2008 freshman class, 74 percent of the applicants were accepted.

For Further Information Contact Mr. Darren Crowder, Director of Admissions, Southwest Baptist University, 1600 University Avenue, Bolivar, MO 65613-2597. *Phone:* 417-328-1817 or 800-526-5859 (toll-free). *Fax:* 417-328-1808. *E-mail:* dcrowder@sbuniv.edu. *Web site:* http://www.sbuniv.edu/.

SOUTHWEST MISSOURI STATE UNIVERSITY

See Missouri State University.

SPRINGFIELD COLLEGE

See Everest College.

STEPHENS COLLEGE

Columbia, Missouri

Stephens College is an undergraduate: women only; graduate: coed, private, comprehensive institution, founded in 1833, offering degrees at the associate, bachelor's, and master's levels and postbachelor's certificates. It has an 86-acre campus in Columbia.

Academic Information The faculty has 110 members (50% full-time), 36% with terminal degrees. The undergraduate student-faculty ratio is 12:1. The library holds 133,581 titles, 21,375 serial subscriptions, and 1,548 audiovisual materials. Special programs include academic remediation, services for learning-disabled students, an honors program, cooperative (work-study) education, study abroad, advanced placement credit, accelerated degree programs, Freshman Honors College, ESL programs, double majors, independent study, distance learning, self-designed majors, part-time degree programs (daytime, weekends), external degree programs, adult/continuing education programs, internships, and arrangement for off-campus study with University of Missouri, Columbia College (MO). The most frequently chosen baccalaureate fields are business/marketing, health professions and related sciences, visual and performing arts.

Student Body Statistics The student body totals 1,147, of whom 947 are undergraduates (223 freshmen). 97 percent are women and 3 percent are men. Students come from 44 states and territories and 3 other countries. 53 percent are from Missouri. 0.3 percent are international students.

Expenses for 2008–09 *Application fee:* $25. *Comprehensive fee:* $31,730 includes full-time tuition ($23,000) and college room and board ($8730). *College room only:* $5080. Full-time tuition varies according to program and reciprocity agreements. Room and board charges vary according to board plan and housing facility. *Part-time tuition:* $700 per credit. Part-time tuition varies according to program.

Financial Aid Forms of aid include need-based and non-need-based scholarships, athletic grants, and part-time jobs. The average aided 2008–09 undergraduate received an aid package worth an estimated $20,388. The priority application deadline for financial aid is March 15.

Freshman Admission Stephens College requires an essay, a high school transcript, a minimum 2.5 high school GPA, 1 recommendation, SAT or ACT scores, and TOEFL scores for international students. An interview is recommended. The application deadline for regular admission is August 1.

Entrance Difficulty Stephens College assesses its entrance difficulty level as moderately difficult. For the fall 2008 freshman class, 67 percent of the applicants were accepted.

For Further Information Contact Mr. David Adams, Director of Enrollment, Stephens College, 1200 East Broadway, Box 2121, Columbia, MO 65215-0002. *Phone:* 573-876-7207 or 800-876-7207 (toll-free). *Fax:* 573-876-7237. *E-mail:* apply@stephens.edu. *Web site:* http://www.stephens.edu/.

See page 272 for the Close-Up.

TRUMAN STATE UNIVERSITY

Kirksville, Missouri

Truman State University is a coed, public, comprehensive institution, founded in 1867, offering degrees at the bachelor's and master's levels. It has a 140-acre campus in Kirksville.

Academic Information The faculty has 384 members (93% full-time), 81% with terminal degrees. The undergraduate student-faculty ratio is 16:1. The library holds 497,022 titles, 3,942 serial subscriptions, and 32,818 audiovisual materials. Special programs include services for learning-disabled students, an honors program, study abroad, advanced placement credit, double majors, independent study, self-designed majors, summer session for credit, part-time degree programs (daytime, summer), internships, and arrangement for off-campus study with Gulf Coast Research Laboratory, Reis Biological Station. The most frequently chosen baccalaureate fields are business/marketing, English, psychology.

Student Body Statistics The student body totals 5,842, of whom 5,586 are undergraduates (1,334 freshmen). 58 percent are women and 42 percent are men. Students come from 44 states and territories and 46 other countries. 79 percent are from Missouri. 5.2 percent are international students.

Expenses for 2008–09 *Application fee:* $0. *One-time mandatory fee:* $305. *State resident tuition:* $6458 full-time, $269 per credit part-time. *Nonresident tuition:* $11,309 full-time, $471 per credit part-time. *Mandatory fees:* $234 full-time. Part-time tuition varies according to course load. *College room and board:* $6290. Room and board charges vary according to housing facility.

Financial Aid Forms of aid include need-based and non-need-based scholarships, athletic grants, and part-time jobs. The average aided 2007–08 undergraduate received an aid package worth $7358. The priority application deadline for financial aid is April 1.

Freshman Admission Truman State University requires an essay, a high school transcript, SAT or ACT scores, and TOEFL scores for international students. A minimum 3.0 high school GPA, an interview, and ACT scores are recommended. The application deadline for regular admission is rolling.

Transfer Admission The application deadline for admission is rolling.

Entrance Difficulty Truman State University assesses its entrance difficulty level as moderately difficult. For the fall 2008 freshman class, 79 percent of the applicants were accepted.

For Further Information Contact Melody Chambers, Director of Admissions, Truman State University, 205 McClain Hall, 100 East Normal Street, Kirksville, MO 63501-4221. *Phone:* 660-785-4114 or 800-892-7792 (toll-free in-state). *Fax:* 660-785-7456. *E-mail:* admissions@truman.edu. *Web site:* http://www.truman.edu/.

See page 276 for the Close-Up.

UNIVERSITY OF CENTRAL MISSOURI

Warrensburg, Missouri

University of Central Missouri is a coed, public, comprehensive institution, founded in 1871, offering degrees at the associate, bachelor's, and master's levels and post-master's and postbachelor's certificates. It has a 1,561-acre campus in Warrensburg near Kansas City.

Academic Information The faculty has 562 members (78% full-time). The undergraduate student-faculty ratio is 18:1. The library holds 1 million titles, 1,605 serial subscriptions, and 20,893 audiovisual materials. Special programs include academic remediation, services for learning-disabled students, an honors program, cooperative (work-study) education, study abroad, advanced placement credit, ESL programs, double majors, distance learning, self-designed majors, summer session for credit, part-time degree programs (daytime, evenings, weekends, summer), adult/continuing education programs, internships, and arrangement for off-campus study. The most frequently chosen baccalaureate fields are business/marketing, education, engineering technologies.

Student Body Statistics The student body totals 11,063, of whom 8,980 are undergraduates (1,613 freshmen). 54 percent are women and 46

percent are men. Students come from 40 states and territories and 52 other countries. 94 percent are from Missouri. 2.9 percent are international students.

Expenses for 2008–09 *Application fee:* $30. *State resident tuition:* $6585 full-time, $219.50 per credit part-time. *Nonresident tuition:* $12,444 full-time, $414.80 per credit part-time. *Mandatory fees:* $726 full-time, $24.20 per credit part-time. Both full-time and part-time tuition and fees vary according to course load and location. *College room and board:* $6320. *College room only:* $4120. Room and board charges vary according to board plan and housing facility.

Financial Aid Forms of aid include need-based and non-need-based scholarships, athletic grants, and part-time jobs. The average aided 2007–08 undergraduate received an aid package worth $8044. The priority application deadline for financial aid is April 1.

Freshman Admission University of Central Missouri requires a high school transcript, rank in upper two-thirds of high school class, ACT scores, and TOEFL scores for international students. The application deadline for regular admission is rolling.

Transfer Admission The application deadline for admission is rolling.

Entrance Difficulty University of Central Missouri assesses its entrance difficulty level as moderately difficult; very difficult for business, teacher education, nursing programs. For the fall 2008 freshman class, 86 percent of the applicants were accepted.

For Further Information Contact Ms. Ann Nordyke, Director of Admissions, University of Central Missouri, 1400 Ward Edwards, Warrensburg, MO 64093. *Phone:* 660-543-4170 or 800-729-8266 (toll-free in-state). *Fax:* 660-543-8517. *E-mail:* admit@ucmo.edu. *Web site:* http://www.ucmo.edu/.

UNIVERSITY OF MISSOURI–COLUMBIA

Columbia, Missouri

University of Missouri–Columbia is a coed, public unit of University of Missouri System, founded in 1839, offering degrees at the bachelor's, master's, doctoral, and first professional levels and post-master's and first professional certificates. It has a 1,358-acre campus in Columbia.

Academic Information The faculty has 1,337 members (95% full-time), 92% with terminal degrees. The undergraduate student-faculty ratio is 17:1. The library holds 3 million titles, 54,347 serial subscriptions, and 29,522 audiovisual materials. Special programs include services for learning-disabled students, an honors program, cooperative (work-study) education, study abroad, advanced placement credit, accelerated degree programs, Freshman Honors College, ESL programs, double majors, independent study, distance learning, self-designed majors, summer session for credit, part-time degree programs (daytime, evenings, summer), external degree programs, adult/continuing education programs, internships, and arrangement for off-campus study with Mid-Missouri Associated Colleges and Universities, National Student Exchange. The most frequently chosen baccalaureate fields are business/marketing, communications/journalism, social sciences.

Student Body Statistics The student body totals 30,200, of whom 23,042 are undergraduates (5,782 freshmen). 52 percent are women and 48 percent are men. Students come from 53 states and territories and 57 other countries. 85 percent are from Missouri. 1.8 percent are international students.

Expenses for 2008–09 *Application fee:* $45. *State resident tuition:* $7368 full-time, $245.60 per credit hour part-time. *Nonresident tuition:* $18,459 full-time, $615.30 per credit hour part-time. *Mandatory fees:* $1099 full-time. Full-time tuition and fees vary according to course load, program, and reciprocity agreements. Part-time tuition varies according to course load, program, and reciprocity agreements. *College room and board:* $8100. Room and board charges vary according to board plan and housing facility.

Financial Aid Forms of aid include need-based and non-need-based scholarships, athletic grants, and part-time jobs. The average aided 2008–09 undergraduate received an aid package worth an estimated $12,757. The priority application deadline for financial aid is March 1.

Freshman Admission University of Missouri–Columbia requires a high school transcript, specific high school curriculum, SAT or ACT scores, and TOEFL scores for international students. ACT scores are recommended. The application deadline for regular admission is rolling.

Transfer Admission The application deadline for admission is rolling.

Entrance Difficulty University of Missouri–Columbia assesses its entrance difficulty level as moderately difficult. For the fall 2008 freshman class, 85 percent of the applicants were accepted.

For Further Information Contact Ms. Barbara Rupp, Director of Admissions, University of Missouri–Columbia, 230 Jesse Hall, Columbia, MO 65211. *Phone:* 573-882-7786 or 800-225-6075 (toll-free in-state). *Fax:* 573-882-7887. *E-mail:* mu4u@missouri.edu. *Web site:* http://www.missouri.edu/.

UNIVERSITY OF MISSOURI–KANSAS CITY

Kansas City, Missouri

University of Missouri–Kansas City is a coed, public unit of University of Missouri System, founded in 1929, offering degrees at the bachelor's, master's, doctoral, and first professional levels and post-master's and first professional certificates. It has a 191-acre campus in Kansas City.

Academic Information The faculty has 1,165 members (60% full-time), 60% with terminal degrees. The undergraduate student-faculty ratio is 12:1. The library holds 2 million titles, 30,976 serial subscriptions, and 444,679 audiovisual materials. Special programs include services for learning-disabled students, an honors program, cooperative (work-study) education, study abroad, advanced placement credit, accelerated degree programs, ESL programs, double majors, independent study, distance learning, self-designed majors, summer session for credit, part-time degree programs (daytime, evenings, weekends, summer), adult/continuing education programs, internships, and arrangement for off-campus study with other campuses of the University of Missouri System. The most frequently chosen baccalaureate fields are business/marketing, health professions and related sciences, liberal arts/general studies.

Student Body Statistics The student body totals 14,499, of whom 9,274 are undergraduates (1,007 freshmen). 59 percent are women and 41 percent are men. Students come from 42 states and territories and 58 other countries. 74 percent are from Missouri. 2.7 percent are international students.

Expenses for 2008–09 *Application fee:* $45. *State resident tuition:* $7368 full-time, $245.60 per credit hour part-time. *Nonresident tuition:* $18,459 full-time, $615.30 per credit hour part-time. *Mandatory fees:* $905 full-time, $30.15 per credit hour part-time, $30 per term part-time. Both full-time and part-time tuition and fees vary according to course load and program. *College room and board:* $7881. *College room only:* $5269. Room and board charges vary according to board plan and housing facility.

Financial Aid Forms of aid include need-based and non-need-based scholarships, athletic grants, and part-time jobs. The average aided 2008–09 undergraduate received an aid package worth an estimated $9596. The priority application deadline for financial aid is March 1.

Freshman Admission University of Missouri–Kansas City requires a high school transcript, SAT or ACT scores, and TOEFL scores for international students. An essay and an interview are required for some. The application deadline for regular admission is rolling.

Transfer Admission The application deadline for admission is rolling.

Entrance Difficulty University of Missouri–Kansas City assesses its entrance difficulty level as moderately difficult. For the fall 2008 freshman class, 73 percent of the applicants were accepted.

For Further Information Contact Ms. Jennifer DeHaemers, Director of Admissions, University of Missouri–Kansas City, Office of Admissions, 5100 Rockhill Road, Kansas City, MO 64110-2499. *Phone:* 816-235-1111 or 800-775-8652 (toll-free out-of-state). *Fax:* 816-235-5544. *E-mail:* admit@umkc.edu. *Web site:* http://www.umkc.edu/.

UNIVERSITY OF MISSOURI–ROLLA

See Missouri University of Science and Technology.

UNIVERSITY OF MISSOURI–ST. LOUIS

St. Louis, Missouri

University of Missouri–St. Louis is a coed, public unit of University of Missouri System, founded in 1963, offering degrees at the bachelor's,

University of Missouri–St. Louis (continued)
master's, doctoral, and first professional levels and postbachelor's certificates. It has a 350-acre campus in St. Louis.

Academic Information The faculty has 900 members (54% full-time), 53% with terminal degrees. The undergraduate student-faculty ratio is 16:1. The library holds 1 million titles, 3,181 serial subscriptions, and 3,905 audiovisual materials. Special programs include services for learning-disabled students, an honors program, cooperative (work-study) education, study abroad, advanced placement credit, accelerated degree programs, Freshman Honors College, ESL programs, double majors, independent study, distance learning, self-designed majors, summer session for credit, part-time degree programs (daytime, evenings, weekends, summer), adult/continuing education programs, internships, and arrangement for off-campus study with Southern Illinois University, Saint Louis University, Washington University in St. Louis, St. Charles Community College, Mineral Area Community College, East Central Community College, Jefferson Community College. The most frequently chosen baccalaureate fields are business/marketing, education, social sciences.
Student Body Statistics The student body totals 15,617, of whom 12,245 are undergraduates (469 freshmen). 65 percent are women and 35 percent are men. Students come from 40 states and territories and 75 other countries. 93 percent are from Missouri. 2.6 percent are international students.
Expenses for 2008–09 *Application fee:* $35. *State resident tuition:* $7368 full-time, $245.60 per credit hour part-time. *Nonresident tuition:* $18,459 full-time, $615.30 per credit hour part-time. *Mandatory fees:* $1227 full-time, $47.09 per credit hour part-time. Both full-time and part-time tuition and fees vary according to course load, program, and reciprocity agreements. *College room and board:* $7782. *College room only:* $5610. Room and board charges vary according to board plan and housing facility.
Financial Aid Forms of aid include need-based and non-need-based scholarships, athletic grants, and part-time jobs. The average aided 2008–09 undergraduate received an aid package worth an estimated $7838. The priority application deadline for financial aid is April 1.
Freshman Admission University of Missouri–St. Louis requires a high school transcript, CBHE core requirements, SAT or ACT scores, and TOEFL scores for international students. The application deadline for regular admission is rolling and for nonresidents it is rolling.
Transfer Admission The application deadline for admission is rolling.
Entrance Difficulty University of Missouri–St. Louis assesses its entrance difficulty level as moderately difficult. For the fall 2008 freshman class, 58 percent of the applicants were accepted.
For Further Information Contact Mr. Dennis Saunders, Associate Director of Admissions, University of Missouri–St. Louis, 351 Millennium Student Center, One University Boulevard, St. Louis, MO 63121-4400. *Phone:* 314-516-5451 or 888-GO2-UMSL (toll-free in-state). *Fax:* 314-516-5310. *E-mail:* admissions@umsl.edu. *Web site:* http://www.umsl.edu/.

UNIVERSITY OF PHOENIX–KANSAS CITY CAMPUS

Kansas City, Missouri

University of Phoenix–Kansas City Campus is a coed, proprietary, comprehensive institution, founded in 2002, offering degrees at the bachelor's and master's levels.

Academic Information The faculty has 124 members (6% full-time). The library holds 16,781 serial subscriptions. Special programs include services for learning-disabled students, advanced placement credit, accelerated degree programs, independent study, distance learning, external degree programs, and adult/continuing education programs. The most frequently chosen baccalaureate fields are business/marketing, computer and information sciences, security and protective services.
Student Body Statistics The student body totals 770, of whom 617 are undergraduates (57 freshmen). 65 percent are women and 35 percent are men.
Expenses for 2008–09 *Application fee:* $0. *Tuition:* $12,000 full-time. Full-time tuition varies according to course level and course load.
Financial Aid Forms of aid include need-based and non-need-based scholarships. The average aided 2007–08 undergraduate received an aid package worth $6610. The application deadline for financial aid is continuous.
Freshman Admission University of Phoenix–Kansas City Campus requires 1 recommendation and TOEFL scores for international students. A high school transcript is required for some. The application deadline for regular admission is rolling.
Transfer Admission The application deadline for admission is rolling.
Entrance Difficulty University of Phoenix–Kansas City Campus has an open admission policy.
For Further Information Contact Ms. Audra McQuarie, Registrar/Executive Director, University of Phoenix–Kansas City Campus, 4035 South Riverpoint Parkway, Mail Stop CF-L101, Phoenix, AZ 85040. *Phone:* 480-557-6151, 800-776-4867 (toll-free in-state), or 800-228-7240 (toll-free out-of-state). *Fax:* 480-643-3068. *E-mail:* audra.mcquarie@phoenix.edu. *Web site:* http://www.phoenix.edu/.

UNIVERSITY OF PHOENIX–ST. LOUIS CAMPUS

St. Louis, Missouri

University of Phoenix–St. Louis Campus is a coed, proprietary, comprehensive institution, founded in 2000, offering degrees at the associate, bachelor's, and master's levels.

Academic Information The faculty has 104 members (7% full-time), 13% with terminal degrees. The library holds 16,781 serial subscriptions. Special programs include services for learning-disabled students, advanced placement credit, accelerated degree programs, independent study, distance learning, external degree programs, and adult/continuing education programs. The most frequently chosen baccalaureate fields are business/marketing, computer and information sciences, security and protective services.
Student Body Statistics The student body totals 445, of whom 401 are undergraduates (60 freshmen). 65 percent are women and 35 percent are men. 4 percent are international students.
Expenses for 2008–09 *Application fee:* $0. *Tuition:* $12,690 full-time. Full-time tuition varies according to course level and course load.
Financial Aid Forms of aid include need-based and non-need-based scholarships. The average aided 2007–08 undergraduate received an aid package worth $7014. The application deadline for financial aid is continuous.
Freshman Admission University of Phoenix–St. Louis Campus requires 1 recommendation and TOEFL scores for international students. A high school transcript is required for some. The application deadline for regular admission is rolling.
Transfer Admission The application deadline for admission is rolling.
Entrance Difficulty University of Phoenix–St. Louis Campus has an open admission policy.
For Further Information Contact Ms. Audra McQuarie, Registrar/Executive Director, University of Phoenix–St. Louis Campus, 4035 South Riverpoint Parkway, Mail Stop CF-L101, Phoenix, AZ 85040. *Phone:* 480-557-6151, 800-776-4867 (toll-free in-state), or 800-228-7240 (toll-free out-of-state). *Fax:* 480-643-3068. *E-mail:* audra.mcquarie@phoenix.edu. *Web site:* http://www.phoenix.edu/.

UNIVERSITY OF PHOENIX–SPRINGFIELD CAMPUS

Springfield, Missouri

University of Phoenix–Springfield Campus is a coed, proprietary, comprehensive institution, offering degrees at the associate, bachelor's, and master's levels.

Academic Information The faculty has 39 members (13% full-time), 13% with terminal degrees. The undergraduate student-faculty ratio is 9:1. The library holds 16,781 serial subscriptions. Special programs include services for learning-disabled students, advanced placement credit,

accelerated degree programs, independent study, and distance learning. The most frequently chosen baccalaureate fields are business/marketing, computer and information sciences, security and protective services.
Student Body Statistics The student body totals 119, of whom 104 are undergraduates (23 freshmen). 60 percent are women and 40 percent are men. 1 percent are international students.
Expenses for 2008–09 *Application fee:* $45. *Tuition:* $10,350 full-time. Full-time tuition varies according to course level and course load.
Financial Aid Forms of aid include need-based and non-need-based scholarships. The average aided 2007–08 undergraduate received an aid package worth $6613. The application deadline for financial aid is continuous.
Freshman Admission University of Phoenix–Springfield Campus requires 1 recommendation. A high school transcript is required for some. The application deadline for regular admission is rolling.
Transfer Admission The application deadline for admission is rolling.
Entrance Difficulty University of Phoenix–Springfield Campus has an open admission policy.
For Further Information Contact Ms. Audra McQuarie, Registrar/ Executive Director, University of Phoenix–Springfield Campus, 4035 South Riverpoint Parkway, Mail Stop CF-L101, Phoenix, AZ 85040. *Phone:* 480-557-6151, 800-776-4867 (toll-free in-state), or 800-228-7240 (toll-free out-of-state). *Fax:* 480-643-3068. *E-mail:* audra.mcquarie@ phoenix.edu. *Web site:* http://www.phoenix.edu/.

VATTEROTT COLLEGE

St. Ann, Missouri

http://www.vatterott-college.edu/

VATTEROTT COLLEGE

Sunset Hills, Missouri

http://www.vatterott-college.edu/

WASHINGTON UNIVERSITY IN ST. LOUIS

St. Louis, Missouri

Washington University in St. Louis is a coed, private university, founded in 1853, offering degrees at the bachelor's, master's, doctoral, and first professional levels and post-master's and postbachelor's certificates. It has a 169-acre campus in St. Louis.

Academic Information The faculty has 1,080 members (84% full-time), 83% with terminal degrees. The undergraduate student-faculty ratio is 7:1. The library holds 2 million titles, 67,057 serial subscriptions, and 67,230 audiovisual materials. Special programs include services for learning-disabled students, cooperative (work-study) education, study abroad, advanced placement credit, accelerated degree programs, ESL programs, double majors, independent study, self-designed majors, summer session for credit, part-time degree programs, adult/continuing education programs, internships, and arrangement for off-campus study with Consortium on Financing Higher Education. The most frequently chosen baccalaureate fields are engineering, business/marketing, social sciences.
Student Body Statistics The student body totals 13,339, of whom 6,985 are undergraduates (1,426 freshmen). 52 percent are women and 48 percent are men. Students come from 54 states and territories and 54 other countries. 10 percent are from Missouri. 4.5 percent are international students.
Expenses for 2009–10 *Application fee:* $55. *Comprehensive fee:* $51,329 includes full-time tuition ($37,800), mandatory fees ($1064), and college room and board ($12,465). *College room only:* $8061.
Financial Aid Forms of aid include need-based and non-need-based scholarships and part-time jobs. The average aided 2008–09 undergraduate received an aid package worth an estimated $31,093. The application deadline for financial aid is February 15.
Freshman Admission Washington University in St. Louis requires an essay, a high school transcript, 2 recommendations, SAT or ACT scores, and TOEFL scores for international students. A minimum 3.0 high school GPA and portfolio for art and architecture programs are recommended. The application deadline for regular admission is January 15 and for early decision it is November 15.
Transfer Admission The application deadline for admission is April 15.
Entrance Difficulty Washington University in St. Louis assesses its entrance difficulty level as most difficult. For the fall 2008 freshman class, 22 percent of the applicants were accepted.
For Further Information Contact Ms. Julie Shimabukuro, Director of Admissions, Washington University in St. Louis, Campus Box 1089, One Brookings Drive, St. Louis, MO 63130-4899. *Phone:* 314-935-6000 or 800-638-0700 (toll-free). *Fax:* 314-935-4290. *E-mail:* admissions@wustl.edu. *Web site:* http://www.wustl.edu/.

WEBSTER UNIVERSITY

St. Louis, Missouri

Webster University is a coed, private, comprehensive institution, founded in 1915, offering degrees at the bachelor's, master's, and doctoral levels and post-master's and postbachelor's certificates. It has a 47-acre campus in St. Louis.

Academic Information The faculty has 863 members (21% full-time). The undergraduate student-faculty ratio is 12:1. The library holds 286,655 titles, 1,821 serial subscriptions, and 19,135 audiovisual materials. Special programs include academic remediation, services for learning-disabled students, cooperative (work-study) education, study abroad, advanced placement credit, accelerated degree programs, ESL programs, double majors, independent study, distance learning, self-designed majors, summer session for credit, part-time degree programs (daytime, evenings, summer), adult/continuing education programs, internships, and arrangement for off-campus study with Fontbonne College, Lindenwood College, Maryville University of Saint Louis, Eden Theological Seminary, Missouri Baptist College. The most frequently chosen baccalaureate fields are business/ marketing, communications/journalism, visual and performing arts.
Student Body Statistics The student body totals 8,010, of whom 3,584 are undergraduates (419 freshmen). 58 percent are women and 42 percent are men. Students come from 36 states and territories and 37 other countries. 79 percent are from Missouri. 2 percent are international students.
Expenses for 2008–09 *Application fee:* $35. *Comprehensive fee:* $29,440 includes full-time tuition ($20,440) and college room and board ($9000). *College room only:* $4760. Full-time tuition varies according to program. Room and board charges vary according to board plan and housing facility. *Part-time tuition:* $525 per credit hour. Part-time tuition varies according to location.
Financial Aid Forms of aid include need-based and non-need-based scholarships and part-time jobs. The priority application deadline for financial aid is April 1.
Freshman Admission Webster University requires an essay, a high school transcript, a minimum 2.5 high school GPA, 1 recommendation, SAT or ACT scores, and TOEFL scores for international students. A minimum 3.0 high school GPA and an interview are recommended. A minimum 3.0 high school GPA and audition are required for some. The application deadline for regular admission is June 1.
Transfer Admission The application deadline for admission is August 1.
Entrance Difficulty Webster University assesses its entrance difficulty level as moderately difficult. For the fall 2008 freshman class, 57 percent of the applicants were accepted.
For Further Information Contact Mr. Andrew Laue, Associate Director of Undergraduate Admission, Webster University, 470 East Lockwood Avenue, St. Louis, MO 63119-3194. *Phone:* 314-961-2660 or 800-75-ENROL (toll-free). *Fax:* 314-968-7115. *E-mail:* admit@webster.edu. *Web site:* http://www.webster.edu/.

WENTWORTH MILITARY ACADEMY AND JUNIOR COLLEGE

Lexington, Missouri

http://www.wma1880.org/

WESTMINSTER COLLEGE

Fulton, Missouri

Westminster College is a coed, private, four-year college, founded in 1851, affiliated with the Presbyterian Church, offering degrees at the bachelor's level. It has an 80-acre campus in Fulton.

Academic Information The faculty has 79 members (75% full-time), 71% with terminal degrees. The student-faculty ratio is 15:1. The library holds 128,667 titles, 19,308 serial subscriptions, and 2,043 audiovisual materials. Special programs include academic remediation, services for learning-disabled students, an honors program, cooperative (work-study) education, study abroad, advanced placement credit, double majors, independent study, self-designed majors, summer session for credit, part-time degree programs (daytime), internships, and arrangement for off-campus study with Chicago Urban Studies Semester, American University. The most frequently chosen baccalaureate fields are business/marketing, English, social sciences.
Student Body Statistics The student body is made up of 1,000 undergraduates (244 freshmen). 45 percent are women and 55 percent are men. Students come from 28 states and territories and 63 other countries. 76 percent are from Missouri. 14.9 percent are international students.
Expenses for 2009–10 *Application fee:* $0. *Comprehensive fee:* $25,110 includes full-time tuition ($17,990) and college room and board ($7120). *College room only:* $3700. *Part-time tuition:* $750 per credit hour.
Financial Aid Forms of aid include need-based and non-need-based scholarships and part-time jobs. The average aided 2008–09 undergraduate received an aid package worth an estimated $16,188.
Freshman Admission Westminster College requires a high school transcript, 1 recommendation, SAT or ACT scores, and TOEFL scores for international students. An essay and a minimum 2.5 high school GPA are recommended. An interview is required for some.
Entrance Difficulty Westminster College assesses its entrance difficulty level as moderately difficult. For the fall 2008 freshman class, 77 percent of the applicants were accepted.
For Further Information Contact Mr. George Wolf, Vice President and Dean of Enrollment Services, Westminster College, 501 Westminster Avenue, Fulton, MO 65251-1299. *Phone:* 573-592-5251 or 800-475-3361 (toll-free). *Fax:* 573-592-5255. *E-mail:* admissions@westminster-mo.edu. *Web site:* http://www.westminster-mo.edu/.

WILLIAM JEWELL COLLEGE

Liberty, Missouri

William Jewell College is a coed, private, Baptist, four-year college, founded in 1849, offering degrees at the bachelor's level (also offers evening program with significant enrollment not reflected in profile). It has a 200-acre campus in Liberty near Kansas City.

Academic Information The faculty has 152 members (50% full-time), 51% with terminal degrees. The student-faculty ratio is 10:1. The library holds 236,241 titles, 527 serial subscriptions, and 20,010 audiovisual materials. Special programs include academic remediation, services for learning-disabled students, an honors program, cooperative (work-study) education, study abroad, advanced placement credit, double majors, independent study, self-designed majors, summer session for credit, part-time degree programs (daytime, evenings, weekends, summer), adult/continuing education programs, internships, and arrangement for off-campus study. The most frequently chosen baccalaureate fields are business/marketing, health professions and related sciences, psychology.
Student Body Statistics The student body is made up of 1,210 undergraduates (265 freshmen). 60 percent are women and 40 percent are men. Students come from 33 states and territories. 70 percent are from Missouri. 0.2 percent are international students.
Expenses for 2009–10 *Application fee:* $25. *Comprehensive fee:* $31,300 includes full-time tuition ($24,300), mandatory fees ($300), and college room and board ($6700). *Part-time tuition:* $750 per credit hour.
Financial Aid Forms of aid include need-based and non-need-based scholarships, athletic grants, and part-time jobs. The average aided 2008–09 undergraduate received an aid package worth an estimated $18,222. The priority application deadline for financial aid is March 1.
Freshman Admission William Jewell College requires an essay, a high school transcript, SAT or ACT scores, and TOEFL scores for international students. An interview is recommended. An interview is required for some. The application deadline for regular admission is August 15.
Transfer Admission The application deadline for admission is rolling.
Entrance Difficulty William Jewell College assesses its entrance difficulty level as moderately difficult. For the fall 2008 freshman class, 63 percent of the applicants were accepted.
For Further Information Contact Ms. Bridget Gramling, Dean of Admission, William Jewell College, 500 College Hill, Liberty, MO 64068. *Phone:* 816-415-7511 or 888-2JEWELL (toll-free). *Fax:* 816-415-5040. *E-mail:* gramblingb@william.jewell.edu. *Web site:* http://www.jewell.edu/.

WILLIAM WOODS UNIVERSITY

Fulton, Missouri

William Woods University is a coed, private, comprehensive institution, founded in 1870, affiliated with the Christian Church (Disciples of Christ), offering degrees at the associate, bachelor's, and master's levels and post-master's and first professional certificates. It has a 170-acre campus in Fulton near St. Louis.

Expenses for 2008–09 *Application fee:* $25. *Comprehensive fee:* $23,430 includes full-time tuition ($16,250), mandatory fees ($430), and college room and board ($6750). Full-time tuition and fees vary according to degree level and program. Room and board charges vary according to board plan and housing facility. *Part-time tuition:* $520 per credit hour. *Part-time mandatory fees:* $15 per term. Part-time tuition and fees vary according to course load, degree level, and program.
For Further Information Contact Ms. Sharon Horn, Admissions Data Analyst, William Woods University, One University Avenue, Fulton, MO 65251. *Phone:* 573-592-4221 or 800-995-3159 Ext. 4221 (toll-free). *Fax:* 573-592-1146. *E-mail:* admissions@williamwoods.edu. *Web site:* http://www.williamwoods.edu/.

Nebraska

BELLEVUE UNIVERSITY

Bellevue, Nebraska

http://www.bellevue.edu/

CHADRON STATE COLLEGE

Chadron, Nebraska

http://www.csc.edu/

CLARKSON COLLEGE

Omaha, Nebraska

Clarkson College is a coed, primarily women's, private, comprehensive institution, founded in 1888, offering degrees at the associate, bachelor's, and master's levels and post-master's certificates. It has a 3-acre campus in Omaha.

Academic Information The faculty has 101 members (48% full-time). The undergraduate student-faculty ratio is 8:1. The library holds 8,807 titles, 262 serial subscriptions, and 530 audiovisual materials. Special programs include cooperative (work-study) education, study abroad, advanced placement credit, accelerated degree programs, double majors, independent study, distance learning, summer session for credit, part-time degree programs (daytime, evenings, summer), external degree programs,

adult/continuing education programs, and internships. The most frequently chosen baccalaureate field is health professions and related sciences.
Student Body Statistics The student body totals 820, of whom 658 are undergraduates (39 freshmen). 95 percent are women and 5 percent are men. Students come from 33 states and territories. 67 percent are from Nebraska.
Expenses for 2008–09 *Application fee:* $35. *One-time mandatory fee:* $100. *Tuition:* $10,374 full-time, $399 per credit hour part-time. *Mandatory fees:* $650 full-time, $29 per credit hour part-time. *College room only:* $6200.
Financial Aid Forms of aid include need-based and non-need-based scholarships and part-time jobs. The priority application deadline for financial aid is April 1.
Freshman Admission Clarkson College requires an essay, a high school transcript, and a minimum 2.5 high school GPA. A minimum 3.0 high school GPA is recommended. A minimum 3.0 high school GPA, 2 recommendations, and SAT or ACT scores are required for some. The application deadline for regular admission is rolling and for nonresidents it is rolling.
Transfer Admission The application deadline for admission is rolling.
Entrance Difficulty Clarkson College assesses its entrance difficulty level as moderately difficult. For the fall 2008 freshman class, 55 percent of the applicants were accepted.
For Further Information Contact Ms. Denise Work, Director of Admissions, Clarkson College, 101 South 42nd Street, Omaha, NE 68131-2739. *Phone:* 402-552-3100 or 800-647-5500 (toll-free). *Fax:* 402-552-6057. *E-mail:* admiss@clarksoncollege.edu. *Web site:* http://www.clarksoncollege.edu/.

COLLEGE OF SAINT MARY

Omaha, Nebraska

College of Saint Mary is a women's, private, Roman Catholic, comprehensive institution, founded in 1923, offering degrees at the associate, bachelor's, master's, and doctoral levels and postbachelor's certificates. It has a 25-acre campus in Omaha.

Academic Information The faculty has 160 members (36% full-time), 32% with terminal degrees. The undergraduate student-faculty ratio is 9:1. The library holds 76,781 titles, 272 serial subscriptions, and 2,057 audiovisual materials. Special programs include academic remediation, services for learning-disabled students, an honors program, study abroad, advanced placement credit, accelerated degree programs, double majors, independent study, distance learning, summer session for credit, part-time degree programs, adult/continuing education programs, and internships. The most frequently chosen baccalaureate fields are business/marketing, education, health professions and related sciences.
Student Body Statistics The student body totals 953, of whom 748 are undergraduates (85 freshmen). Students come from 23 states and territories and 10 other countries. 88 percent are from Nebraska. 0.4 percent are international students.
Expenses for 2008–09 *Application fee:* $30. *Comprehensive fee:* $27,660 includes full-time tuition ($20,780), mandatory fees ($480), and college room and board ($6400). Full-time tuition and fees vary according to degree level and location. Room and board charges vary according to housing facility. *Part-time tuition:* $685 per credit. *Part-time mandatory fees:* $16 per credit hour. Part-time tuition and fees vary according to class time, degree level, and location.
Financial Aid Forms of aid include need-based and non-need-based scholarships, athletic grants, and part-time jobs. The average aided 2008–09 undergraduate received an aid package worth an estimated $14,958. The priority application deadline for financial aid is March 15.
Freshman Admission College of Saint Mary requires a high school transcript, a minimum 2.0 high school GPA, SAT or ACT scores, and TOEFL scores for international students. An essay, a minimum 3.0 high school GPA, 2 recommendations, and an interview are required for some. The application deadline for regular admission is rolling.
Transfer Admission The application deadline for admission is rolling.
Entrance Difficulty College of Saint Mary assesses its entrance difficulty level as minimally difficult. For the fall 2008 freshman class, 45 percent of the applicants were accepted.
For Further Information Contact Ms. Erika Pritchard, Admissions Officer, College of Saint Mary, 7000 Mercy Road, Omaha, NE 68106. *Phone:* 402-399-2406 or 800-926-5534 (toll-free). *Fax:* 402-399-2412. *E-mail:* enroll@csm.edu. *Web site:* http://www.csm.edu/.

CONCORDIA UNIVERSITY, NEBRASKA

Seward, Nebraska

Concordia University, Nebraska is a coed, private, comprehensive institution, founded in 1894, affiliated with the Lutheran Church–Missouri Synod, offering degrees at the bachelor's and master's levels and postbachelor's certificates. It has a 120-acre campus in Seward near Omaha.

Academic Information The faculty has 161 members (36% full-time), 50% with terminal degrees. The undergraduate student-faculty ratio is 14:1. The library holds 175,000 titles, 350 serial subscriptions, and 5,160 audiovisual materials. Special programs include academic remediation, services for learning-disabled students, study abroad, advanced placement credit, accelerated degree programs, ESL programs, double majors, independent study, distance learning, summer session for credit, part-time degree programs (daytime, evenings, summer), adult/continuing education programs, internships, and arrangement for off-campus study with University of Nebraska–Lincoln. The most frequently chosen baccalaureate fields are business/marketing, education, theology and religious vocations.
Student Body Statistics The student body totals 1,344, of whom 1,118 are undergraduates (273 freshmen). 52 percent are women and 48 percent are men. Students come from 40 states and territories and 5 other countries. 41 percent are from Nebraska. 0.4 percent are international students.
Expenses for 2009–10 *Application fee:* $0. *Comprehensive fee:* $26,770 includes full-time tuition ($21,100), mandatory fees ($150), and college room and board ($5520). *College room only:* $2340. *Part-time tuition:* $650 per credit.
Financial Aid Forms of aid include need-based and non-need-based scholarships, athletic grants, and part-time jobs. The average aided 2008–09 undergraduate received an aid package worth an estimated $15,815.
Freshman Admission Concordia University, Nebraska requires a high school transcript, a minimum 2.5 high school GPA, SAT or ACT scores, and TOEFL scores for international students. An interview is recommended. Recommendations are required for some. The application deadline for regular admission is August 1.
Transfer Admission The application deadline for admission is August 1.
Entrance Difficulty Concordia University, Nebraska assesses its entrance difficulty level as moderately difficult. For the fall 2008 freshman class, 68 percent of the applicants were accepted.
For Further Information Contact Mr. Aaron Roberts, Director of Undergraduate Recruitment, Concordia University, Nebraska, 800 North Columbia Avenue, Seward, NE 68434-1599. *Phone:* 800-535-5494 Ext. 7233 or 800-535-5494 (toll-free). *Fax:* 402-643-4073. *E-mail:* admiss@cune.edu. *Web site:* http://www.cune.edu/.

THE CREATIVE CENTER

Omaha, Nebraska

The Creative Center is a coed, proprietary, primarily two-year college, founded in 1993, offering degrees at the associate and bachelor's levels. It has a 1-acre campus in Omaha.

For Further Information Contact Admissions and Placement Coordinator, The Creative Center, 10850 Emmet Street, Omaha, NE 68164. *Phone:* 402-898-1000 or 888-898-1789 (toll-free). *Fax:* 402-898-1301. *E-mail:* admission@creativecenter.edu. *Web site:* http://www.thecreativecenter.com/.

CREIGHTON UNIVERSITY

Omaha, Nebraska

Creighton University is a coed, private, Roman Catholic (Jesuit) university, founded in 1878, offering degrees at the associate, bachelor's, master's, doctoral, and first professional levels and postbachelor's certificates. It has a 110-acre campus in Omaha.

Academic Information The faculty has 721 members (70% full-time), 72% with terminal degrees. The undergraduate student-faculty ratio is 11:1. The library holds 925,385 titles, 42,374 serial subscriptions, and 21,005 audiovisual materials. Special programs include academic remediation, services for learning-disabled students, an honors program, study abroad, advanced placement credit, accelerated degree programs, Freshman Honors College, ESL programs, double majors, independent study, distance learning, summer session for credit, part-time degree programs (daytime, evenings, summer), adult/continuing education programs, internships, and arrangement for off-campus study with Creighton University; West Omaha Campus. The most frequently chosen baccalaureate fields are business/marketing, biological/life sciences, health professions and related sciences.
Student Body Statistics The student body totals 7,051, of whom 4,087 are undergraduates (992 freshmen). 59 percent are women and 41 percent are men. Students come from 51 states and territories and 33 other countries. 35 percent are from Nebraska. 1.4 percent are international students.
Expenses for 2008–09 *Application fee:* $40. *Comprehensive fee:* $37,058 includes full-time tuition ($27,282), mandatory fees ($1260), and college room and board ($8516). *College room only:* $4816. Full-time tuition and fees vary according to degree level, program, and student level. Room and board charges vary according to board plan and housing facility. *Part-time tuition:* $853 per semester hour. *Part-time mandatory fees:* $242 per year. Part-time tuition and fees vary according to degree level, program, and student level.
Financial Aid Forms of aid include need-based and non-need-based scholarships, athletic grants, and part-time jobs. The average aided 2008–09 undergraduate received an aid package worth an estimated $23,916.
Freshman Admission Creighton University requires an essay, a high school transcript, a minimum 2.75 high school GPA, 1 recommendation, SAT or ACT scores, and TOEFL scores for international students. The application deadline for regular admission is February 15.
Transfer Admission The application deadline for admission is August 1.
Entrance Difficulty Creighton University assesses its entrance difficulty level as moderately difficult. For the fall 2008 freshman class, 82 percent of the applicants were accepted.
For Further Information Contact Ms. Mary Chase, Assistant Vice President for Enrollment Management and Director of Admissions and Scholarships, Creighton University, 2500 California Plaza, Omaha, NE 68178-0001. *Phone:* 402-280-3105 or 800-282-5835 (toll-free). *Fax:* 402-280-2685. *E-mail:* admissions@creighton.edu. *Web site:* http://www.creighton.edu/.

DANA COLLEGE

Blair, Nebraska

Dana College is a coed, private, four-year college, founded in 1884, affiliated with the Evangelical Lutheran Church in America, offering degrees at the bachelor's level. It has a 150-acre campus in Blair near Omaha.

Academic Information The faculty has 66 members (53% full-time), 45% with terminal degrees. The student-faculty ratio is 12:1. The library holds 177,680 titles and 5,025 serial subscriptions. Special programs include services for learning-disabled students, an honors program, study abroad, advanced placement credit, accelerated degree programs, ESL programs, double majors, independent study, distance learning, self-designed majors, summer session for credit, part-time degree programs (daytime), adult/continuing education programs, internships, and arrangement for off-campus study with Consortium of Eastern Nebraska Colleges. The most frequently chosen baccalaureate fields are business/marketing, education, psychology.
Student Body Statistics The student body is made up of 546 undergraduates (138 freshmen). 45 percent are women and 55 percent are men. Students come from 25 states and territories. 59 percent are from Nebraska. 0.2 percent are international students.
Expenses for 2008–09 *Application fee:* $0. *Comprehensive fee:* $26,020 includes full-time tuition ($19,320), mandatory fees ($800), and college room and board ($5900). *College room only:* $2320. Room and board charges vary according to board plan and housing facility. *Part-time tuition:* $550 per credit hour. *Part-time mandatory fees:* $45 per term. Part-time tuition and fees vary according to course load.
Financial Aid Forms of aid include need-based and non-need-based scholarships, athletic grants, and part-time jobs. The average aided 2008–09 undergraduate received an aid package worth an estimated $17,856. The priority application deadline for financial aid is March 15.
Freshman Admission Dana College requires a high school transcript, a minimum 2.0 high school GPA, SAT or ACT scores, and TOEFL scores for international students. ACT scores are recommended. An essay, 1 recommendation, and an interview are required for some. The application deadline for regular admission is rolling.
Entrance Difficulty Dana College assesses its entrance difficulty level as moderately difficult. For the fall 2008 freshman class, 71 percent of the applicants were accepted.
For Further Information Contact Tina Blair, Director of Admissions, Dana College, 2848 College Drive, Blair, NE 68008-1099. *Phone:* 402-426-7220 or 800-444-3262 (toll-free). *Fax:* 402-426-7386. *E-mail:* admissions@dana.edu. *Web site:* http://www.dana.edu/.

DOANE COLLEGE

Crete, Nebraska

Doane College is a coed, private, comprehensive institution, founded in 1872, affiliated with the United Church of Christ, offering degrees at the bachelor's and master's levels (non-traditional undergraduate programs and graduate programs offered at Lincoln campus). It has a 300-acre campus in Crete near Omaha.

Academic Information The faculty has 131 members (56% full-time), 49% with terminal degrees. The undergraduate student-faculty ratio is 10:1. The library holds 229,043 titles, 29,588 serial subscriptions, and 3,546 audiovisual materials. Special programs include an honors program, cooperative (work-study) education, study abroad, advanced placement credit, ESL programs, double majors, independent study, self-designed majors, summer session for credit, internships, and arrangement for off-campus study with Association of Nebraska Interterm Colleges. The most frequently chosen baccalaureate fields are business/marketing, biological/life sciences, education.
Student Body Statistics The student body is made up of 900 undergraduates (248 freshmen). 50 percent are women and 50 percent are men. Students come from 24 states and territories and 3 other countries. 79 percent are from Nebraska. 0.6 percent are international students.
Expenses for 2008–09 *Application fee:* $0. *Comprehensive fee:* $25,750 includes full-time tuition ($19,750), mandatory fees ($400), and college room and board ($5600). *College room only:* $2000. Full-time tuition and fees vary according to location. Room and board charges vary according to board plan, housing facility, and location. *Part-time tuition:* $660 per credit hour. Part-time tuition varies according to course load, degree level, and location.
Financial Aid Forms of aid include need-based and non-need-based scholarships, athletic grants, and part-time jobs. The average aided 2008–09 undergraduate received an aid package worth an estimated $17,428.
Freshman Admission Doane College requires a high school transcript, 2 recommendations, SAT or ACT scores, and TOEFL scores for international students. A minimum 2.0 high school GPA is recommended. An interview is required for some. The application deadline for regular admission is rolling.
Transfer Admission The application deadline for admission is rolling.

Entrance Difficulty Doane College assesses its entrance difficulty level as moderately difficult. For the fall 2008 freshman class, 76 percent of the applicants were accepted.
For Further Information Contact Mr. Cezar Mesquita, Director of Admission, Doane College, 1014 Boswell Avenue, Crete, NE 68333-2430. *Phone:* 402-826-8222 or 800-333-6263 (toll-free). *Fax:* 402-826-8600. *E-mail:* admissions@doane.edu. *Web site:* http://www.doane.edu/.

GRACE UNIVERSITY

Omaha, Nebraska

Grace University is a coed, private, interdenominational, comprehensive institution, founded in 1943, offering degrees at the associate, bachelor's, and master's levels. It has a 15-acre campus in Omaha.

Academic Information The faculty has 50 members (50% full-time), 90% with terminal degrees. The undergraduate student-faculty ratio is 18:1. The library holds 46,736 titles, 3,721 serial subscriptions, and 3,882 audiovisual materials. Special programs include academic remediation, services for learning-disabled students, cooperative (work-study) education, study abroad, advanced placement credit, accelerated degree programs, double majors, independent study, distance learning, self-designed majors, summer session for credit, part-time degree programs, external degree programs, adult/continuing education programs, internships, and arrangement for off-campus study with Iowa Western Community College, Metropolitan Community College (NE), University of Nebraska at Omaha, Bellevue University, Clarkson College. The most frequently chosen baccalaureate fields are psychology, business/marketing, theology and religious vocations.
Student Body Statistics The student body totals 434, of whom 366 are undergraduates (97 freshmen). 57 percent are women and 43 percent are men. Students come from 26 states and territories and 6 other countries. 61 percent are from Nebraska. 1.1 percent are international students.
Expenses for 2009–10 *Application fee:* $20. *Comprehensive fee:* $20,030 includes full-time tuition ($13,900), mandatory fees ($390), and college room and board ($5740). *College room only:* $2550. *Part-time tuition:* $390 per credit hour. *Part-time mandatory fees:* $165 per term.
Financial Aid Forms of aid include need-based and non-need-based scholarships and part-time jobs. The average aided 2008–09 undergraduate received an aid package worth an estimated $12,607. The priority application deadline for financial aid is April 1.
Freshman Admission Grace University requires an essay, a high school transcript, a minimum 2.75 high school GPA, SAT or ACT scores, and TOEFL scores for international students. An interview is required for some. The application deadline for regular admission is rolling.
Transfer Admission The application deadline for admission is rolling.
Entrance Difficulty Grace University assesses its entrance difficulty level as moderately difficult. For the fall 2008 freshman class, 64 percent of the applicants were accepted.
For Further Information Contact Angela Wayman, Director of Admissions, Grace University, 1311 South Ninth Street, Omaha, NE 68108. *Phone:* 402-449-2831 or 800-383-1422 (toll-free). *Fax:* 402-341-9587. *E-mail:* admissions@graceuniversity.com. *Web site:* http://www.graceuniversity.edu/.

HASTINGS COLLEGE

Hastings, Nebraska

Hastings College is a coed, private, Presbyterian, comprehensive institution, founded in 1882, offering degrees at the bachelor's and master's levels. It has a 109-acre campus in Hastings.

Expenses for 2008–09 *Application fee:* $20. *Comprehensive fee:* $26,484 includes full-time tuition ($19,952), mandatory fees ($830), and college room and board ($5702). *College room only:* $2436. Full-time tuition and fees vary according to course level and program. Room and board charges vary according to board plan and housing facility. *Part-time tuition:* varies with course level, course load, program.
For Further Information Contact Ms. Mary Molliconi, Director of Admissions, Hastings College, 710 North Turner Avenue, Hastings, NE 68901-7621. *Phone:* 402-461-7320 or 800-532-7642 (toll-free). *Fax:* 402-461-7490. *E-mail:* mmolliconi@hastings.edu. *Web site:* http://www.hastings.edu/.

ITT TECHNICAL INSTITUTE

Omaha, Nebraska

ITT Technical Institute is a coed, proprietary, primarily two-year college of ITT Educational Services, Inc., founded in 1991, offering degrees at the associate and bachelor's levels. It has a 1-acre campus in Omaha.

Financial Aid Forms of aid include need-based scholarships. The application deadline for financial aid is continuous.
Freshman Admission ITT Technical Institute requires TOEFL scores for international students.
Entrance Difficulty ITT Technical Institute assesses its entrance difficulty level as minimally difficult.
For Further Information Contact Director of Recruitment, ITT Technical Institute, 9814 M Street, Omaha, NE 68127. *Phone:* 402-331-2900 or 800-677-9260 (toll-free). *Fax:* 402-331-9495. *Web site:* http://www.itt-tech.edu/.

KAPLAN UNIVERSITY, LINCOLN

Lincoln, Nebraska

Kaplan University, Lincoln is proprietary, primarily two-year college of Kaplan University—branch of the Davenport Campus, founded in 1884, offering degrees at the associate and bachelor's levels. It has a 5-acre campus in Lincoln near Omaha.

Expenses for 2008–09 Contact institution for current costs.
For Further Information Contact Office of Admissions, Kaplan University, Lincoln, 1821 K Street, Lincoln, NE 68508. *Phone:* 402-474-5315. *Fax:* 402-474-5302. *E-mail:* lsc@ix.netcom.com. *Web site:* http://www.lincoln.kaplanuniversity.edu.

KAPLAN UNIVERSITY, OMAHA

Omaha, Nebraska

Kaplan University, Omaha is proprietary, primarily two-year college of Kaplan University—branch of the Davenport Campus, founded in 1891, offering degrees at the associate and bachelor's levels. It has a 3-acre campus in Omaha.

Expenses for 2008–09 Contact institution for current costs.
For Further Information Contact Director of Admissions, Kaplan University, Omaha, 5425 North 103rd Street, Omaha, NE 68134. *Phone:* 402-572-8500 or 800-642-1456 (toll-free). *Web site:* http://www.omaha.kaplanuniversity.edu.

LINCOLN SCHOOL OF COMMERCE

See Kaplan University, Lincoln.

LITTLE PRIEST TRIBAL COLLEGE

Winnebago, Nebraska

Little Priest Tribal College is private, two-year college, founded in 1996, offering degrees at the associate level.

Student Body Statistics The student body is made up of 120 undergraduates.

Little Priest Tribal College (continued)

Expenses for 2008–09 *Application fee:* $10. *Tuition:* $2400 full-time, $80 per credit hour part-time. *Mandatory fees:* $575 full-time, $18.50 per credit hour part-time, $10 per term part-time.

Financial Aid Forms of aid include need-based scholarships and part-time jobs. The application deadline for financial aid is continuous.

Freshman Admission Little Priest Tribal College requires TOEFL scores for international students.

Entrance Difficulty Little Priest Tribal College has an open admission policy.

For Further Information Contact Ms. Karen Kemling, Director of Admissions and Records, Little Priest Tribal College, PO Box 270, Winnebago, NE 68071. *Phone:* 402-878-2380. *Web site:* http://www.lptc.bia.edu/.

MIDLAND LUTHERAN COLLEGE

Fremont, Nebraska

Midland Lutheran College is a coed, private, Lutheran, four-year college, founded in 1883, offering degrees at the associate and bachelor's levels. It has a 27-acre campus in Fremont near Omaha.

Expenses for 2008–09 *Application fee:* $30. *Comprehensive fee:* $27,372 includes full-time tuition ($22,006) and college room and board ($5366). Full-time tuition varies according to class time, course load, and program. Room and board charges vary according to board plan and housing facility. *Part-time tuition:* varies with class time, course load, program.

For Further Information Contact Mr. Todd Hansen, Associate Director of Admissions, Midland Lutheran College, Admissions Office, Fremont, NE 68025-4200. *Phone:* 402-941-6504 or 800-642-8382 Ext. 6501 (toll-free). *Fax:* 402-941-6513. *E-mail:* admissions@mlc.edu. *Web site:* http://www.mlc.edu/.

NEBRASKA CHRISTIAN COLLEGE

Papillon, Nebraska

Nebraska Christian College is a coed, private, four-year college, founded in 1944, affiliated with the Christian Churches and Churches of Christ, offering degrees at the associate and bachelor's levels. It has an 85-acre campus in Papillon.

Expenses for 2008–09 *Application fee:* $25. *Tuition:* $275 per credit part-time.

For Further Information Contact Ms. Alisha Livengood, Associate Director of Admissions, Nebraska Christian College, 1800 Syracuse Avenue, Norfolk, NE 68701. *Phone:* 402-935-9407. *Fax:* 402-379-5100. *E-mail:* admissions@nechristian.edu. *Web site:* http://www.nechristian.edu/.

NEBRASKA COLLEGE OF BUSINESS

See Kaplan University, Omaha.

NEBRASKA METHODIST COLLEGE

Omaha, Nebraska

Nebraska Methodist College is a coed, primarily women's, private, comprehensive institution, founded in 1891, affiliated with the United Methodist Church, offering degrees at the associate, bachelor's, and master's levels and post-master's certificates. It has a 5-acre campus in Omaha.

Academic Information The faculty has 57 members (58% full-time), 23% with terminal degrees. The undergraduate student-faculty ratio is 9:1. Special programs include academic remediation, services for learning-disabled students, advanced placement credit, accelerated degree programs, independent study, distance learning, summer session for credit, and internships. The most frequently chosen baccalaureate field is health professions and related sciences.

Student Body Statistics The student body totals 589, of whom 506 are undergraduates (56 freshmen). 92 percent are women and 8 percent are men. Students come from 6 states and territories. 75 percent are from Nebraska.

Expenses for 2008–09 *Application fee:* $25. *Tuition:* $13,440 full-time, $428 per credit hour part-time. *Mandatory fees:* $600 full-time, $20 per credit hour part-time. *College room only:* $6150.

Financial Aid Forms of aid include need-based and non-need-based scholarships and part-time jobs. The average aided 2007–08 undergraduate received an aid package worth $7470. The priority application deadline for financial aid is April 1.

Freshman Admission Nebraska Methodist College requires an essay, a high school transcript, a minimum 2.5 high school GPA, SAT or ACT scores, and TOEFL scores for international students.

Entrance Difficulty Nebraska Methodist College assesses its entrance difficulty level as moderately difficult. For the fall 2008 freshman class, 50 percent of the applicants were accepted.

For Further Information Contact Sara Bonney, Director of Enrollment Services, Nebraska Methodist College, 720 North 87th Street, Omaha, NE 68114. *Phone:* 402-354-7111 or 800-335-5510 (toll-free). *Fax:* 402-354-7020. *E-mail:* sara.bonney@methodistcollege.edu. *Web site:* http://www.methodistcollege.edu/.

NEBRASKA WESLEYAN UNIVERSITY

Lincoln, Nebraska

Nebraska Wesleyan University is a coed, private, United Methodist, comprehensive institution, founded in 1887, offering degrees at the bachelor's and master's levels and post-master's and postbachelor's certificates. It has a 50-acre campus in Lincoln near Omaha.

Academic Information The faculty has 159 members (66% full-time), 64% with terminal degrees. The undergraduate student-faculty ratio is 13:1. The library holds 251,909 titles, 597 serial subscriptions, and 8,734 audiovisual materials. Special programs include services for learning-disabled students, study abroad, advanced placement credit, accelerated degree programs, double majors, independent study, summer session for credit, part-time degree programs (evenings, summer), adult/continuing education programs, internships, and arrangement for off-campus study with Chicago Urban Life Center, Capitol Hill Internship Program. The most frequently chosen baccalaureate fields are business/marketing, biological/life sciences, health professions and related sciences.

Student Body Statistics The student body totals 2,086, of whom 1,870 are undergraduates (383 freshmen). 58 percent are women and 42 percent are men. Students come from 25 states and territories and 14 other countries. 89 percent are from Nebraska. 0.2 percent are international students.

Expenses for 2008–09 *Application fee:* $20. *One-time mandatory fee:* $120. *Comprehensive fee:* $27,102 includes full-time tuition ($20,950), mandatory fees ($442), and college room and board ($5710). Full-time tuition and fees vary according to class time, course load, degree level, location, and program. Room and board charges vary according to board plan. *Part-time tuition:* varies with class time, course load, degree level, location, program.

Financial Aid Forms of aid include need-based and non-need-based scholarships and part-time jobs. The average aided 2008–09 undergraduate received an aid package worth an estimated $15,072. The application deadline for financial aid is continuous.

Freshman Admission Nebraska Wesleyan University requires a high school transcript, a minimum 2.0 high school GPA, SAT or ACT scores, and TOEFL scores for international students. An interview is recommended. An essay and resume of activities are required for some. The application deadline for regular admission is August 15 and for early action it is November 15.

Transfer Admission The application deadline for admission is August 15.

Entrance Difficulty Nebraska Wesleyan University assesses its entrance difficulty level as moderately difficult. For the fall 2008 freshman class, 80 percent of the applicants were accepted.

For Further Information Contact David Duzik, Director of Admissions, Nebraska Wesleyan University, 5000 Saint Paul Avenue, Lincoln, NE 68504. *Phone:* 402-465-2218 or 800-541-3818 (toll-free). *Fax:* 402-465-2177. *E-mail:* admissions@nebrwesleyan.edu. *Web site:* http://www.nebrwesleyan.edu/.

PERU STATE COLLEGE

Peru, Nebraska

Peru State College is a coed, public, comprehensive unit of Nebraska State College System, founded in 1867, offering degrees at the bachelor's and master's levels. It has a 104-acre campus in Peru.

Expenses for 2008–09 *Application fee:* $0. *State resident tuition:* $3495 full-time, $116.50 per credit hour part-time. *Nonresident tuition:* $6990 full-time, $233 per credit hour part-time. *Mandatory fees:* $848 full-time. Full-time tuition and fees vary according to course level, course load, and location. Part-time tuition varies according to course level, course load, and location. *College room and board:* $4816. Room and board charges vary according to housing facility.

For Further Information Contact Ms. Micki Willis, Director of Recruitment and Admissions, Peru State College, PO Box 10, Peru, NE 68421. *Phone:* 402-872-2221 or 800-742-4412 (toll-free in-state). *Fax:* 402-872-2296. *E-mail:* mwillis@oakmail.peru.edu. *Web site:* http://www.peru.edu/.

UNION COLLEGE

Lincoln, Nebraska

Union College is a coed, private, Seventh-day Adventist, comprehensive institution, founded in 1891, offering degrees at the associate, bachelor's, and master's levels. It has a 26-acre campus in Lincoln near Omaha.

Academic Information The faculty has 95 members (61% full-time), 31% with terminal degrees. The undergraduate student-faculty ratio is 13:1. The library holds 147,813 titles and 1,357 serial subscriptions. Special programs include services for learning-disabled students, an honors program, cooperative (work-study) education, study abroad, advanced placement credit, accelerated degree programs, ESL programs, double majors, independent study, self-designed majors, summer session for credit, part-time degree programs (daytime, summer), adult/continuing education programs, internships, and arrangement for off-campus study with University of Nebraska, Southeast Community College. The most frequently chosen baccalaureate fields are business/marketing, education, health professions and related sciences.

Student Body Statistics The student body totals 914, of whom 843 are undergraduates (169 freshmen). 57 percent are women and 43 percent are men. Students come from 46 states and territories and 23 other countries. 18 percent are from Nebraska.

Expenses for 2008–09 *Application fee:* $0. *Comprehensive fee:* $22,530 includes full-time tuition ($16,440), mandatory fees ($480), and college room and board ($5610). *College room only:* $3210. Full-time tuition and fees vary according to course load and degree level. Room and board charges vary according to housing facility. *Part-time tuition:* $690 per credit hour.

Financial Aid Forms of aid include non-need-based scholarships and part-time jobs.

Freshman Admission Union College requires a high school transcript, a minimum 2.5 high school GPA, 3 recommendations, and SAT or ACT scores. An essay and an interview are required for some. The application deadline for regular admission is rolling.

Transfer Admission The application deadline for admission is rolling.

Entrance Difficulty Union College assesses its entrance difficulty level as moderately difficult.

For Further Information Contact Huda McClelland, Director of Admissions, Union College, 3800 South 48th Street, Lincoln, NE 68506. *Phone:* 402-486-2504 or 800-228-4600 (toll-free out-of-state). *Fax:* 402-486-2895. *E-mail:* ucenroll@ucollege.edu. *Web site:* http://www.ucollege.edu/.

UNIVERSITY OF NEBRASKA AT KEARNEY

Kearney, Nebraska

University of Nebraska at Kearney is a coed, public, comprehensive unit of University of Nebraska System, founded in 1903, offering degrees at the bachelor's and master's levels and post-master's certificates. It has a 235-acre campus in Kearney.

Academic Information The faculty has 400 members (76% full-time), 59% with terminal degrees. The undergraduate student-faculty ratio is 16:1. The library holds 464,532 titles, 1,223 serial subscriptions, and 84,395 audiovisual materials. Special programs include academic remediation, services for learning-disabled students, an honors program, cooperative (work-study) education, study abroad, advanced placement credit, ESL programs, double majors, independent study, distance learning, summer session for credit, part-time degree programs (daytime, evenings, weekends, summer), internships, and arrangement for off-campus study with National Student Exchange. The most frequently chosen baccalaureate fields are business/marketing, education, parks and recreation.

Student Body Statistics The student body totals 6,543, of whom 5,104 are undergraduates (1,045 freshmen). 52 percent are women and 48 percent are men. Students come from 46 states and territories and 49 other countries. 94 percent are from Nebraska. 11.1 percent are international students.

Expenses for 2008–09 *Application fee:* $45. *State resident tuition:* $4365 full-time, $145.50 per hour part-time. *Nonresident tuition:* $8940 full-time, $298 per hour part-time. *Mandatory fees:* $1061 full-time, $21.25 per hour part-time, $73.50 per term part-time. Both full-time and part-time tuition and fees vary according to course level, course load, degree level, and location. *College room and board:* $6330. *College room only:* $3270. Room and board charges vary according to board plan and housing facility.

Financial Aid Forms of aid include need-based and non-need-based scholarships, athletic grants, and part-time jobs. The average aided 2008–09 undergraduate received an aid package worth an estimated $8494.

Freshman Admission University of Nebraska at Kearney requires a high school transcript, rank in upper 50% of high school class, SAT and SAT Subject Test or ACT scores, and TOEFL scores for international students. The application deadline for regular admission is rolling.

Transfer Admission The application deadline for admission is rolling.

Entrance Difficulty University of Nebraska at Kearney assesses its entrance difficulty level as moderately difficult. For the fall 2008 freshman class, 80 percent of the applicants were accepted.

For Further Information Contact Mr. Dusty Newton, Director of Admissions, University of Nebraska at Kearney, 905 West 25th Street, Kearney, NE 68849-0001. *Phone:* 308-865-8702 or 800-532-7639 (toll-free). *Fax:* 308-865-8987. *E-mail:* admissionsug@unk.edu. *Web site:* http://www.unk.edu/.

UNIVERSITY OF NEBRASKA AT OMAHA

Omaha, Nebraska

University of Nebraska at Omaha is a coed, public unit of University of Nebraska System, founded in 1908, offering degrees at the bachelor's, master's, and doctoral levels and post-master's and postbachelor's certificates. It has a 158-acre campus in Omaha.

Academic Information The faculty has 880 members (54% full-time), 55% with terminal degrees. The undergraduate student-faculty ratio is 18:1. The library holds 1 million titles and 37,557 serial subscriptions. Special programs include services for learning-disabled students, an honors program, cooperative (work-study) education, study abroad, advanced placement credit, ESL programs, double majors, independent study, distance learning, self-designed majors, summer session for credit, part-time degree programs (daytime, evenings, summer), adult/continuing education programs, internships, and arrangement for off-campus study with other units of the University of Nebraska System. The most frequently chosen baccalaureate fields are business/marketing, education, security and protective services.

Student Body Statistics The student body totals 14,213, of whom 11,327 are undergraduates (1,816 freshmen). 52 percent are women and 48 percent are men. Students come from 40 states and territories and 58 other countries. 91 percent are from Nebraska. 2.3 percent are international students.

Expenses for 2008–09 *Application fee:* $45. *State resident tuition:* $4920 full-time, $164 per credit hour part-time. *Nonresident tuition:* $14,498 full-time, $483.25 per credit hour part-time. *Mandatory fees:* $960 full-time. Full-time tuition and fees vary according to course load and reciprocity agreements. Part-time tuition varies according to course load and reciprocity agreements. *College room and board:* $6980. Room and board charges vary according to board plan.

University of Nebraska at Omaha (continued)

Financial Aid Forms of aid include need-based and non-need-based scholarships and part-time jobs. The average aided 2008–09 undergraduate received an aid package worth an estimated $2445. The priority application deadline for financial aid is March 1.

Freshman Admission University of Nebraska at Omaha requires a high school transcript, SAT or ACT scores, and TOEFL scores for international students. The application deadline for regular admission is August 1.

Transfer Admission The application deadline for admission is August 1.

Entrance Difficulty University of Nebraska at Omaha assesses its entrance difficulty level as minimally difficult; moderately difficult for engineering program; noncompetitive for nontraditional, adult applicants. For the fall 2008 freshman class, 83 percent of the applicants were accepted.

For Further Information Contact Ms. Jolene Adams, Associate Director of Admissions, University of Nebraska at Omaha, 6001 Dodge Street, Omaha, NE 68182. *Phone:* 402-554-2393 or 800-858-8648 (toll-free in-state). *Fax:* 402-554-3472. *E-mail:* jadams@mail.unomaha.edu. *Web site:* http://www.unomaha.edu/.

UNIVERSITY OF NEBRASKA–LINCOLN

Lincoln, Nebraska

University of Nebraska–Lincoln is a coed, public unit of University of Nebraska System, founded in 1869, offering degrees at the associate, bachelor's, master's, doctoral, and first professional levels and post-master's and postbachelor's certificates. It has a 623-acre campus in Lincoln near Omaha.

Academic Information The faculty has 1,081 members (99% full-time), 96% with terminal degrees. The undergraduate student-faculty ratio is 20:1. The library holds 3 million titles, 29,245 serial subscriptions, and 37,036 audiovisual materials. Special programs include services for learning-disabled students, an honors program, cooperative (work-study) education, study abroad, advanced placement credit, accelerated degree programs, ESL programs, double majors, independent study, distance learning, self-designed majors, summer session for credit, part-time degree programs (daytime, evenings, summer), adult/continuing education programs, internships, and arrangement for off-campus study with University of Missouri, Kansas State University, University of South Dakota. The most frequently chosen baccalaureate fields are business/marketing, education, engineering.

Student Body Statistics The student body totals 23,537, of whom 18,490 are undergraduates (4,164 freshmen). 46 percent are women and 54 percent are men. Students come from 51 states and territories and 82 other countries. 82 percent are from Nebraska.

Expenses for 2008–09 *Application fee:* $45. *State resident tuition:* $5393 full-time, $179.75 per semester hour part-time. *Nonresident tuition:* $16,013 full-time, $533.75 per semester hour part-time. *Mandatory fees:* $1192 full-time, $242 per term part-time. Both full-time and part-time tuition and fees vary according to course load, program, and reciprocity agreements. *College room and board:* $6882. *College room only:* $3629. Room and board charges vary according to board plan and housing facility.

Financial Aid Forms of aid include need-based and non-need-based scholarships, athletic grants, and part-time jobs. The average aided 2007–08 undergraduate received an aid package worth $9521.

Freshman Admission University of Nebraska–Lincoln requires a high school transcript, SAT or ACT scores, and TOEFL scores for international students. ACT scores are recommended. Rank in upper 50% of high school class is required for some. The application deadline for regular admission is May 1.

Transfer Admission The application deadline for admission is May 1.

Entrance Difficulty University of Nebraska–Lincoln assesses its entrance difficulty level as moderately difficult; very difficult for architecture, engineering programs. For the fall 2008 freshman class, 63 percent of the applicants were accepted.

For Further Information Contact Pat McBride, Director, New Student Enrollment, University of Nebraska–Lincoln, 1410 Q Street, Lincoln, NE 68588-0256. *Phone:* 402-472-2023 or 800-742-8800 (toll-free). *Fax:* 402-472-0670. *E-mail:* admissions@unl.edu. *Web site:* http://www.unl.edu/.

UNIVERSITY OF NEBRASKA MEDICAL CENTER

Omaha, Nebraska

University of Nebraska Medical Center is a coed, public, upper-level unit of University of Nebraska System, founded in 1869, offering degrees at the bachelor's, master's, doctoral, and first professional levels and post-master's, first professional, and postbachelor's certificates. It has a 51-acre campus in Omaha.

Academic Information The faculty has 1,097 members (83% full-time), 84% with terminal degrees. The undergraduate student-faculty ratio is 3:1. The library holds 238,074 titles and 6,403 serial subscriptions. Special programs include services for learning-disabled students, an honors program, accelerated degree programs, distance learning, summer session for credit, part-time degree programs (daytime, summer), internships, and arrangement for off-campus study with University of Nebraska–Lincoln, University of Nebraska at Omaha, University of Nebraska at Kearney. The most frequently chosen baccalaureate field is health professions and related sciences.

Student Body Statistics The student body totals 3,194, of whom 806 are undergraduates. 88 percent are women and 12 percent are men. Students come from 22 states and territories and 4 other countries. 89 percent are from Nebraska. 0.9 percent are international students.

Expenses for 2008–09 *Application fee:* $45. *State resident tuition:* $5400 full-time, $180 per semester hour part-time. *Nonresident tuition:* $16,020 full-time, $534 per semester hour part-time. *Mandatory fees:* $400 full-time, $3 per semester hour part-time, $52 per term part-time. Both full-time and part-time tuition and fees vary according to program.

Financial Aid Forms of aid include need-based scholarships and part-time jobs. The priority application deadline for financial aid is March 15.

Transfer Admission University of Nebraska Medical Center requires a college transcript and a minimum 2.0 college GPA. Standardized test scores and a minimum 3.0 college GPA are required for some. The application deadline for admission is rolling.

Entrance Difficulty University of Nebraska Medical Center assesses its entrance difficulty level as moderately difficult.

For Further Information Contact Ms. Tymaree Tonjes, Administrative Technician, University of Nebraska Medical Center, 984265 Nebraska Medical Center, Omaha, NE 68198-4230. *Phone:* 402-559-6468 or 800-626-8431 Ext. 6468 (toll-free). *Fax:* 402-559-6796. *E-mail:* mmcnamee@unmc.edu. *Web site:* http://www.unmc.edu/.

WAYNE STATE COLLEGE

Wayne, Nebraska

Wayne State College is a coed, public, comprehensive unit of Nebraska State College System, founded in 1910, offering degrees at the bachelor's and master's levels and post-master's certificates. It has a 128-acre campus in Wayne.

Academic Information The faculty has 210 members (60% full-time), 51% with terminal degrees. The undergraduate student-faculty ratio is 19:1. The library holds 267,980 titles, 473 serial subscriptions, and 7,493 audiovisual materials. Special programs include services for learning-disabled students, an honors program, cooperative (work-study) education, study abroad, advanced placement credit, double majors, independent study, distance learning, self-designed majors, summer session for credit, part-time degree programs (daytime, evenings, weekends, summer), adult/continuing education programs, internships, and arrangement for off-campus study with Northeast Community College, Central Community College. The most frequently chosen baccalaureate fields are business/marketing, education, security and protective services.

Student Body Statistics The student body totals 3,566, of whom 2,879 are undergraduates (660 freshmen). 54 percent are women and 46 percent are men. Students come from 27 states and territories and 21 other countries. 86 percent are from Nebraska. 0.8 percent are international students.

Expenses for 2008–09 *Application fee:* $30. *State resident tuition:* $3495 full-time, $116.50 per credit hour part-time. *Nonresident tuition:* $6990 full-time, $235 per credit hour part-time. *Mandatory fees:* $1076 full-time,

$42.50 per credit hour part-time. Both full-time and part-time tuition and fees vary according to course level and course load. *College room and board:* $5054. *College room only:* $2390. Room and board charges vary according to board plan and housing facility.
Financial Aid Forms of aid include need-based and non-need-based scholarships, athletic grants, and part-time jobs.
Freshman Admission Wayne State College requires a high school transcript and TOEFL scores for international students. The application deadline for regular admission is rolling and for nonresidents it is rolling.
Transfer Admission The application deadline for admission is rolling.
Entrance Difficulty Wayne State College has an open admission policy. It assesses its entrance difficulty as minimally difficult for transfers.
For Further Information Contact Ms. Tammy Young, Director of Admissions, Wayne State College, 1111 Main Street, Wayne, NE 68787. *Phone:* 402-375-7234 or 800-228-9972 (toll-free in-state). *Fax:* 402-375-7204. *E-mail:* admit1@wsc.edu. *Web site:* http://www.wsc.edu/.

YORK COLLEGE

York, Nebraska

York College is a coed, private, four-year college, founded in 1890, affiliated with the Church of Christ, offering degrees at the associate and bachelor's levels. It has a 44-acre campus in York.

Academic Information The faculty has 43 members (60% full-time), 28% with terminal degrees. The student-faculty ratio is 9:1. The library holds 134,738 titles, 292 serial subscriptions, and 2,566 audiovisual materials. Special programs include academic remediation, services for learning-disabled students, an honors program, cooperative (work-study) education, study abroad, advanced placement credit, double majors, independent study, summer session for credit, part-time degree programs (daytime, evenings, summer), and internships.
Student Body Statistics The student body is made up of 396 undergraduates (110 freshmen). 47 percent are women and 53 percent are men. Students come from 30 states and territories and 4 other countries. 34 percent are from Nebraska. 1.3 percent are international students.
Expenses for 2008–09 *Application fee:* $20. *Comprehensive fee:* $18,500 includes full-time tuition ($12,500), mandatory fees ($1500), and college room and board ($4500). Full-time tuition and fees vary according to course load. Room and board charges vary according to board plan and housing facility. *Part-time tuition:* $390 per credit hour. *Part-time mandatory fees:* $220 per credit hour. Part-time tuition and fees vary according to course load.
Financial Aid Forms of aid include need-based and non-need-based scholarships, athletic grants, and part-time jobs. The average aided 2008–09 undergraduate received an aid package worth an estimated $11,754. The priority application deadline for financial aid is June 15.
Freshman Admission York College requires a high school transcript, a minimum 2.0 high school GPA, SAT or ACT scores, and TOEFL scores for international students. 1 recommendation is required for some. The application deadline for regular admission is rolling.
Transfer Admission The application deadline for admission is rolling.
Entrance Difficulty York College assesses its entrance difficulty level as moderately difficult. For the fall 2008 freshman class, 64 percent of the applicants were accepted.
For Further Information Contact Ms. Judy Rinard, York College, 1125 East 8th Street, York, NE 68467-2699. *Phone:* 402-363-5627 or 800-950-9675 (toll-free). *Fax:* 402-363-5623. *E-mail:* enroll@york.edu. *Web site:* http://www.york.edu/.

North Dakota

DICKINSON STATE UNIVERSITY

Dickinson, North Dakota

Dickinson State University is a coed, public, four-year college of North Dakota University System, founded in 1918, offering degrees at the associate and bachelor's levels. It has a 100-acre campus in Dickinson.

Expenses for 2008–09 *Application fee:* $35. *State resident tuition:* $4019 full-time, $167.46 per credit part-time. *Nonresident tuition:* $10,732 full-time, $447.11 per credit part-time. *Mandatory fees:* $1064 full-time, $44.37 per credit part-time. Full-time tuition and fees vary according to location, program, and reciprocity agreements. Part-time tuition and fees vary according to course load, location, program, and reciprocity agreements. *College room and board:* $4280. Room and board charges vary according to board plan.
For Further Information Contact Mr. Steve Glasser, Director of Enrollment Services, Dickinson State University, Campus Box 169, Dickinson, ND 58601. *Phone:* 701-483-2175 or 800-279-4295 (toll-free). *Fax:* 701-483-2409. *E-mail:* dsu.hawks@dsu.nodak.edu. *Web site:* http://www.dsu.nodak.edu/.

FORT BERTHOLD COMMUNITY COLLEGE

New Town, North Dakota

http://www.fbcc.bia.edu/

JAMESTOWN COLLEGE

Jamestown, North Dakota

Jamestown College is a coed, private, Presbyterian, four-year college, founded in 1883, offering degrees at the bachelor's level.

Academic Information The faculty has 82 members (67% full-time), 40% with terminal degrees. The student-faculty ratio is 15:1. The library holds 113,572 titles and 630 serial subscriptions. Special programs include services for learning-disabled students, an honors program, cooperative (work-study) education, study abroad, advanced placement credit, double majors, independent study, distance learning, self-designed majors, summer session for credit, part-time degree programs (daytime, evenings, summer), internships, and arrangement for off-campus study. The most frequently chosen baccalaureate fields are business/marketing, education, health professions and related sciences.
Student Body Statistics The student body is made up of 1,025 undergraduates (271 freshmen). 52 percent are women and 48 percent are men. Students come from 27 states and territories and 12 other countries. 52 percent are from North Dakota. 4.9 percent are international students.
Expenses for 2009–10 *Application fee:* $20. *Comprehensive fee:* $20,740 includes full-time tuition ($15,585) and college room and board ($5155). *College room only:* $2195. *Part-time tuition:* $350 per credit. *Part-time mandatory fees:* $200 per year.
Financial Aid Forms of aid include need-based and non-need-based scholarships, athletic grants, and part-time jobs. The average aided 2008–09 undergraduate received an aid package worth an estimated $11,107. The priority application deadline for financial aid is March 15.
Freshman Admission Jamestown College requires a high school transcript, SAT or ACT scores, and TOEFL scores for international students. A minimum 2.5 high school GPA is recommended. The application deadline for regular admission is rolling and for nonresidents it is rolling.
Transfer Admission The application deadline for admission is rolling.

Jamestown College (continued)

Entrance Difficulty Jamestown College assesses its entrance difficulty level as minimally difficult. For the fall 2008 freshman class, 67 percent of the applicants were accepted.

For Further Information Contact Ms. Tena Lawrence, Dean of Enrollment Management, Jamestown College, 6081 College Lane, Jamestown, ND 58405. *Phone:* 701-252-3467 Ext. 5512 or 800-336-2554 (toll-free). *Fax:* 701-253-4318. *E-mail:* admissions@jc.edu. *Web site:* http://www.jc.edu/.

MAYVILLE STATE UNIVERSITY

Mayville, North Dakota

Mayville State University is a coed, public, four-year college of North Dakota University System, founded in 1889, offering degrees at the associate and bachelor's levels. It has a 60-acre campus in Mayville.

Academic Information The faculty has 67 members (54% full-time), 30% with terminal degrees. The student-faculty ratio is 12:1. The library holds 93,684 titles, 424 serial subscriptions, and 12,262 audiovisual materials. Special programs include academic remediation, services for learning-disabled students, cooperative (work-study) education, advanced placement credit, accelerated degree programs, double majors, distance learning, self-designed majors, summer session for credit, part-time degree programs (daytime, evenings, summer), adult/continuing education programs, and internships. The most frequently chosen baccalaureate fields are business/marketing, education, parks and recreation.

Student Body Statistics The student body is made up of 789 undergraduates (90 freshmen). 62 percent are women and 38 percent are men. Students come from 36 states and territories and 3 other countries. 68 percent are from North Dakota. 3.4 percent are international students.

Expenses for 2008–09 *Application fee:* $35. *State resident tuition:* $3985 full-time, $166 per hour part-time. *Nonresident tuition:* $5977 full-time, $249 per hour part-time. *Mandatory fees:* $1669 full-time, $70 per hour part-time. Both full-time and part-time tuition and fees vary according to course load and reciprocity agreements. *College room and board:* $4272. *College room only:* $1730. Room and board charges vary according to board plan and housing facility.

Financial Aid Forms of aid include need-based and non-need-based scholarships, athletic grants, and part-time jobs. The average aided 2008–09 undergraduate received an aid package worth an estimated $5679.

Freshman Admission Mayville State University requires a high school transcript, a minimum 2.0 high school GPA, SAT or ACT scores, and TOEFL scores for international students. An interview is recommended. The application deadline for regular admission is rolling.

Transfer Admission Mayville State University requires a minimum 2.00 college GPA. The application deadline for admission is rolling.

Entrance Difficulty Mayville State University assesses its entrance difficulty level as noncompetitive; minimally difficult for transfers. For the fall 2008 freshman class, 87 percent of the applicants were accepted.

For Further Information Contact Dr. Ray Gerszewski, Vice President, Student Affairs and International Research, Mayville State University, 330 3rd Street, NE, Mayville, ND 58257-1299. *Phone:* 701-788-4842 or 800-437-4104 (toll-free). *Fax:* 701-788-4748. *E-mail:* admit@mayvillestate.edu. *Web site:* http://www.mayvillestate.edu/.

MEDCENTER ONE COLLEGE OF NURSING

Bismarck, North Dakota

Medcenter One College of Nursing is a coed, primarily women's, private, upper-level institution, founded in 1988, offering degrees at the bachelor's level. It has a 15-acre campus in Bismarck.

Academic Information The faculty has 12 members (83% full-time), 8% with terminal degrees. The student-faculty ratio is 8:1. The library holds 26,078 titles, 446 serial subscriptions, and 962 audiovisual materials. Special programs include independent study and internships. The most frequently chosen baccalaureate field is health professions and related sciences.

Student Body Statistics The student body is made up of 91 undergraduates. 86 percent are women and 14 percent are men. Students come from 7 states and territories. 93 percent are from North Dakota.

Expenses for 2008–09 *Application fee:* $40. *Tuition:* $10,017 full-time, $386 per credit part-time. *Mandatory fees:* $15.01 per credit part-time, $199.50 per term part-time. Part-time tuition and fees vary according to course load.

Financial Aid Forms of aid include need-based and non-need-based scholarships and part-time jobs. The average aided 2008–09 undergraduate received an aid package worth an estimated $11,879. The priority application deadline for financial aid is March 15.

Transfer Admission Medcenter One College of Nursing requires a college transcript and a minimum 2.5 college GPA. The application deadline for admission is November 7.

Entrance Difficulty Medcenter One College of Nursing assesses its entrance difficulty level as moderately difficult. For the fall 2008 entering class, 59 percent of the applicants were accepted.

For Further Information Contact Ms. Mary Smith, Director of Student Services, Medcenter One College of Nursing, 512 North 7th Street, Bismarck, ND 58501-4494. *Phone:* 701-323-6271. *Fax:* 701-323-6289. *E-mail:* msmith@mohs.org. *Web site:* http://www.medcenterone.com/collegeofnursing/index.asp.

MINOT STATE UNIVERSITY

Minot, North Dakota

Minot State University is a coed, public, comprehensive unit of North Dakota University System-System Office, founded in 1913, offering degrees at the associate, bachelor's, and master's levels and post-master's certificates. It has a 103-acre campus in Minot.

Academic Information The faculty has 262 members (67% full-time), 35% with terminal degrees. The undergraduate student-faculty ratio is 13:1. Special programs include academic remediation, services for learning-disabled students, an honors program, cooperative (work-study) education, study abroad, advanced placement credit, accelerated degree programs, double majors, independent study, distance learning, self-designed majors, summer session for credit, part-time degree programs (daytime, evenings, summer), adult/continuing education programs, and internships. The most frequently chosen baccalaureate fields are business/marketing, education, health professions and related sciences.

Student Body Statistics The student body totals 3,432, of whom 3,172 are undergraduates (437 freshmen). 61 percent are women and 39 percent are men. Students come from 50 states and territories and 13 other countries. 90 percent are from North Dakota. 8.7 percent are international students.

Expenses for 2008–09 *Application fee:* $35. *State resident tuition:* $4179 full-time, $210.16 per credit part-time. *Nonresident tuition:* $11,158 full-time, $500.94 per credit part-time. *Mandatory fees:* $865 full-time, $37 per credit part-time. Full-time tuition and fees vary according to class time, course load, degree level, location, program, and reciprocity agreements. Part-time tuition and fees vary according to class time, degree level, location, program, and reciprocity agreements. *College room and board:* $5234. *College room only:* $2700. Room and board charges vary according to board plan and housing facility.

Financial Aid Forms of aid include need-based and non-need-based scholarships, athletic grants, and part-time jobs. The average aided 2008–09 undergraduate received an aid package worth an estimated $5415. The priority application deadline for financial aid is March 15.

Freshman Admission Minot State University requires a high school transcript, SAT or ACT scores, and TOEFL scores for international students. A minimum 2.75 high school GPA is required for some. The application deadline for regular admission is rolling.

Transfer Admission Minot State University requires standardized test scores and a college transcript. The application deadline for admission is rolling.

Entrance Difficulty Minot State University assesses its entrance difficulty level as minimally difficult. For the fall 2008 freshman class, 72 percent of the applicants were accepted.

For Further Information Contact Kevin Harmon, Dean of Enrollment Services, Minot State University, 500 University Avenue West, Minot, ND 58707-0002. *Phone:* 701-858-3126 or 800-777-0750 Ext. 3350 (toll-free). *Fax:* 701-858-3825. *E-mail:* askmsu@minotstateu.edu. *Web site:* http://www.minotstateu.edu/.

NORTH DAKOTA STATE UNIVERSITY

Fargo, North Dakota

North Dakota State University is a coed, public unit of North Dakota University System, founded in 1890, offering degrees at the bachelor's, master's, doctoral, and first professional levels and post-master's and postbachelor's certificates. It has a 2,100-acre campus in Fargo.

Academic Information The faculty has 740 members (83% full-time), 71% with terminal degrees. The undergraduate student-faculty ratio is 17.9:1. The library holds 136,912 titles, 2,499 serial subscriptions, and 3,767 audiovisual materials. Special programs include academic remediation, services for learning-disabled students, an honors program, cooperative (work-study) education, study abroad, advanced placement credit, ESL programs, double majors, independent study, distance learning, self-designed majors, summer session for credit, part-time degree programs (daytime, evenings, summer), internships, and arrangement for off-campus study with members of the Tri-College University-Concordia College, Moorhead, MN, Minnesota State University Moorhead. The most frequently chosen baccalaureate fields are business/marketing, engineering, health professions and related sciences.
Student Body Statistics The student body totals 13,229, of whom 11,061 are undergraduates (2,661 freshmen). 43 percent are women and 57 percent are men. Students come from 46 states and territories and 84 other countries. 55 percent are from North Dakota. 4.1 percent are international students.
Expenses for 2008–09 *Application fee:* $35. *One-time mandatory fee:* $45. *State resident tuition:* $5264 full-time, $219.33 per credit part-time. *Nonresident tuition:* $14,053 full-time, $585.54 per credit part-time. *Mandatory fees:* $40.09 per credit part-time. Full-time tuition varies according to reciprocity agreements. Part-time tuition and fees vary according to course load and reciprocity agreements. *College room and board:* $6220. *College room only:* $2656. Room and board charges vary according to board plan and housing facility.
Financial Aid Forms of aid include need-based and non-need-based scholarships, athletic grants, and part-time jobs. The average aided 2007–08 undergraduate received an aid package worth $7030. The priority application deadline for financial aid is March 15.
Freshman Admission North Dakota State University requires a high school transcript, a minimum 2.5 high school GPA, SAT or ACT scores, and TOEFL scores for international students. The application deadline for regular admission is August 15.
Transfer Admission The application deadline for admission is August 15.
Entrance Difficulty North Dakota State University assesses its entrance difficulty level as moderately difficult. For the fall 2008 freshman class, 80 percent of the applicants were accepted.
For Further Information Contact Jobey Lichtblau, Director of Admission, North Dakota State University, PO Box 5454, Fargo, ND 58105-5454. *Phone:* 701-231-8643 or 800-488-NDSU (toll-free). *Fax:* 701-231-8802. *E-mail:* ndsu.admission@ndsu.edu. *Web site:* http://www.ndsu.edu/.

RASMUSSEN COLLEGE FARGO

Fargo, North Dakota

http://www.rasmussen.edu/

SITTING BULL COLLEGE

Fort Yates, North Dakota

http://www.sittingbull.edu/

TRINITY BIBLE COLLEGE

Ellendale, North Dakota

Trinity Bible College is a coed, private, Assemblies of God, four-year college, founded in 1948, offering degrees at the associate and bachelor's levels. It has a 28-acre campus in Ellendale.

Academic Information The library holds 67,868 titles, 227 serial subscriptions, and 2,258 audiovisual materials. Special programs include academic remediation, advanced placement credit, accelerated degree programs, double majors, distance learning, summer session for credit, part-time degree programs (evenings), and internships.
Student Body Statistics The student body is made up of 292 undergraduates.
Expenses for 2008–09 *Application fee:* $25. *Comprehensive fee:* $17,530 includes full-time tuition ($11,550), mandatory fees ($1390), and college room and board ($4590). *Part-time tuition:* $385 per credit. *Part-time mandatory fees:* $13 per credit, $273 per term.
Financial Aid Forms of aid include need-based and non-need-based scholarships and part-time jobs. The application deadline for financial aid is September 1 with a priority deadline of March 1.
Freshman Admission Trinity Bible College requires an essay, a high school transcript, a minimum 2.0 high school GPA, 2 recommendations, health form, evidence of Christian conversion, and ACT scores. TOEFL scores for international students are recommended. An interview and SAT scores are required for some. The application deadline for regular admission is rolling.
Transfer Admission The application deadline for admission is rolling.
Entrance Difficulty Trinity Bible College has an open admission policy.
For Further Information Contact Rev. Steve Tvedt, Vice President of College Relations, Trinity Bible College, 50 South Sixth Avenue, Ellendale, ND 58436. *Phone:* 701-349-3621 or 888-TBC-2DAY (toll-free). *Fax:* 701-349-5443. *E-mail:* admissions@trinitybiblecollege.edu. *Web site:* http://www.trinitybiblecollege.edu/.

TURTLE MOUNTAIN COMMUNITY COLLEGE

Belcourt, North Dakota

http://www.turtle-mountain.cc.nd.us/

UNIVERSITY OF MARY

Bismarck, North Dakota

University of Mary is a coed, private, Roman Catholic, comprehensive institution, founded in 1959, offering degrees at the associate, bachelor's, master's, and doctoral levels. It has a 107-acre campus in Bismarck.

Academic Information The faculty has 278 members (35% full-time), 30% with terminal degrees. The undergraduate student-faculty ratio is 15:1. The library holds 63,259 titles, 222 serial subscriptions, and 6,708 audiovisual materials. Special programs include academic remediation, services for learning-disabled students, cooperative (work-study) education, advanced placement credit, accelerated degree programs, double majors, independent study, distance learning, summer session for credit, part-time degree programs (daytime, evenings, weekends, summer), external degree programs, adult/continuing education programs, internships, and arrangement for off-campus study. The most frequently chosen baccalaureate fields are business/marketing, education, health professions and related sciences.
Student Body Statistics The student body totals 2,863, of whom 2,092 are undergraduates (374 freshmen). 61 percent are women and 39 percent are men. Students come from 32 states and territories and 16 other countries. 64 percent are from North Dakota. 1.7 percent are international students.
Expenses for 2009–10 *Application fee:* $25. *Comprehensive fee:* $17,524 includes full-time tuition ($12,360), mandatory fees ($224), and college room and board ($4940). *College room only:* $2300. *Part-time tuition:* $390 per credit. *Part-time mandatory fees:* $7 per credit.
Financial Aid Forms of aid include need-based and non-need-based scholarships and part-time jobs. The average aided 2008–09 undergraduate received an aid package worth an estimated $10,801. The application deadline for financial aid is continuous.
Freshman Admission University of Mary requires a high school transcript, 1 recommendation, SAT or ACT scores, and TOEFL scores for

University of Mary (continued)

international students. A minimum 2.5 high school GPA is recommended. An essay and an interview are required for some. The application deadline for regular admission is rolling.
Transfer Admission The application deadline for admission is rolling.
Entrance Difficulty University of Mary assesses its entrance difficulty level as moderately difficult. For the fall 2008 freshman class, 81 percent of the applicants were accepted.
For Further Information Contact Cheryl Kalberer, Director of Admissions, University of Mary, 7500 University Drive, Bismarck, ND 58504-9652. *Phone:* 701-355-8191 or 800-288-6279 (toll-free). *Fax:* 701-255-7687. *E-mail:* marauder@umary.edu. *Web site:* http://www.umary.edu/.

UNIVERSITY OF NORTH DAKOTA

Grand Forks, North Dakota

University of North Dakota is a coed, public unit of North Dakota University System, founded in 1883, offering degrees at the bachelor's, master's, doctoral, and first professional levels and post-master's certificates. It has a 550-acre campus in Grand Forks.

Academic Information The faculty has 635 members (90% full-time), 74% with terminal degrees. The undergraduate student-faculty ratio is 18:1. The library holds 2 million titles and 27,970 audiovisual materials. Special programs include services for learning-disabled students, an honors program, cooperative (work-study) education, study abroad, advanced placement credit, accelerated degree programs, ESL programs, double majors, independent study, distance learning, self-designed majors, summer session for credit, part-time degree programs, adult/continuing education programs, internships, and arrangement for off-campus study. The most frequently chosen baccalaureate fields are business/marketing, health professions and related sciences, transportation and materials moving.
Student Body Statistics The student body totals 12,748, of whom 10,129 are undergraduates (1,942 freshmen). 45 percent are women and 55 percent are men. Students come from 58 states and territories and 33 other countries. 52 percent are from North Dakota.
Expenses for 2008–09 *Application fee:* $35. *State resident tuition:* $5276 full-time. *Nonresident tuition:* $14,088 full-time. *Mandatory fees:* $1237 full-time. Full-time tuition and fees vary according to degree level, program, and reciprocity agreements. *College room and board:* $5472. *College room only:* $2222. Room and board charges vary according to board plan and housing facility.
Financial Aid Forms of aid include need-based and non-need-based scholarships, athletic grants, and part-time jobs. The average aided 2007–08 undergraduate received an aid package worth $5492. The priority application deadline for financial aid is March 15.
Freshman Admission University of North Dakota requires a high school transcript, SAT or ACT scores, and TOEFL scores for international students. A minimum 2.5 high school GPA and ACT scores are recommended.
Transfer Admission Standardized test scores and a college transcript are required for some. The application deadline for admission is rolling.
Entrance Difficulty University of North Dakota assesses its entrance difficulty level as minimally difficult; moderately difficult for transfers. For the fall 2008 freshman class, 75 percent of the applicants were accepted.
For Further Information Contact Deborah Melby, Director of Admissions, University of North Dakota, Box 8382, Grand Forks, ND 58202. *Phone:* 701-777-3821 or 800-CALLUND (toll-free). *Fax:* 701-777-2721. *E-mail:* enrollmentservices@mail.und.nodak.edu. *Web site:* http://www.und.nodak.edu/.

VALLEY CITY STATE UNIVERSITY

Valley City, North Dakota

Valley City State University is a coed, public, comprehensive unit of North Dakota University System, founded in 1890, offering degrees at the bachelor's and master's levels. It has a 55-acre campus in Valley City.

Academic Information The faculty has 89 members (64% full-time), 47% with terminal degrees. The undergraduate student-faculty ratio is 11:1. The library holds 102,000 titles, 7,500 serial subscriptions, and 1,200 audiovisual materials. Special programs include academic remediation, services for learning-disabled students, cooperative (work-study) education, double majors, distance learning, self-designed majors, summer session for credit, part-time degree programs (daytime, evenings, summer), internships, and arrangement for off-campus study with North Dakota State University, Mayville State University. The most frequently chosen baccalaureate fields are business/marketing, education, parks and recreation.
Student Body Statistics The student body totals 1,019, of whom 900 are undergraduates (159 freshmen). 54 percent are women and 46 percent are men. Students come from 39 states and territories and 11 other countries. 71 percent are from North Dakota. 5.1 percent are international students.
Expenses for 2008–09 *Application fee:* $35. *State resident tuition:* $4138 full-time, $137.93 per semester hour part-time. *Nonresident tuition:* $11,048 full-time, $368.27 per semester hour part-time. *Mandatory fees:* $1643 full-time, $68.44 per semester hour part-time. Both full-time and part-time tuition and fees vary according to course load, location, program, and reciprocity agreements. *College room and board:* $4071. *College room only:* $1592. Room and board charges vary according to board plan and housing facility.
Financial Aid Forms of aid include need-based and non-need-based scholarships, athletic grants, and part-time jobs. The average aided 2008–09 undergraduate received an aid package worth an estimated $5831. The priority application deadline for financial aid is March 15.
Freshman Admission Valley City State University requires a high school transcript and TOEFL scores for international students. SAT or ACT scores are required for some. The application deadline for regular admission is rolling.
Transfer Admission The application deadline for admission is rolling.
Entrance Difficulty Valley City State University has an open admission policy.
For Further Information Contact Ms. Alison Kasowski, Admission Counselor, Valley City State University, 101 College Street Southwest, Valley City, ND 58072. *Phone:* 701-845-7204 or 800-532-8641 Ext. 37101 (toll-free). *Fax:* 701-845-7299. *E-mail:* alison.kasowski@vcsu.edu. *Web site:* http://www.vcsu.edu/.

Ohio

ALLEGHENY WESLEYAN COLLEGE

Salem, Ohio

Allegheny Wesleyan College is a coed, private, four-year college, offering degrees at the bachelor's level.

Student Body Statistics The student body is made up of 54 undergraduates.
Expenses for 2008–09 *Application fee:* $35. *Tuition:* $3840 full-time, $160 per credit hour part-time. *Mandatory fees:* $640 full-time.
Entrance Difficulty Allegheny Wesleyan College has an open admission policy.
For Further Information Contact Admissions Office, Allegheny Wesleyan College, 2161 Woodsdale Road, Salem, OH 44460. *Phone:* 330-337-6403 or 800-292-3153 (toll-free). *E-mail:* college@awc.edu. *Web site:* http://www.awc.edu/.

ANTIOCH UNIVERSITY McGREGOR

Yellow Springs, Ohio

Antioch University McGregor is a coed, private, upper-level unit of Antioch University, founded in 1988, offering degrees at the bachelor's and master's levels and post-master's certificates. It has a 100-acre campus in Yellow Springs near Dayton.

Academic Information The faculty has 61 members (30% full-time). The undergraduate student-faculty ratio is 14:1. The library holds 355,000 titles, 12,200 serial subscriptions, and 6,400 audiovisual materials. Special programs include cooperative (work-study) education, advanced placement credit, accelerated degree programs, double majors, independent study, distance learning, summer session for credit, part-time degree programs (evenings, weekends, summer), adult/continuing education programs, and internships. The most frequently chosen baccalaureate fields are business/marketing, liberal arts/general studies, psychology.
Student Body Statistics The student body totals 630, of whom 160 are undergraduates. 76 percent are women and 24 percent are men. Students come from 1 state or territory.
Expenses for 2009–10 *Application fee:* $45. *Tuition:* $15,120 full-time, $315 per credit hour part-time.
Financial Aid Forms of aid include need-based scholarships and part-time jobs. The average aided 2007–08 undergraduate received an aid package worth $6300. The application deadline for financial aid is continuous.
Transfer Admission Antioch University McGregor requires a college transcript and a minimum 2.0 college GPA. The application deadline for admission is rolling.
Entrance Difficulty Antioch University McGregor assesses its entrance difficulty level as noncompetitive.
For Further Information Contact Mr. Oscar Robinson, Director of Admissions, Antioch University McGregor, Student and Alumni Services Division, Enrollment Services, 800 Livermore Street, Yellow Springs, OH 45387. *Phone:* 937-769-1823. *Fax:* 937-769-1805. *E-mail:* sas@mcgregor.edu. *Web site:* http://www.mcgregor.edu/.

ART ACADEMY OF CINCINNATI

Cincinnati, Ohio

Art Academy of Cincinnati is a coed, private, comprehensive institution, founded in 1887, offering degrees at the associate, bachelor's, and master's levels. It has a 184-acre campus in Cincinnati.

Academic Information The faculty has 44 members (32% full-time). The undergraduate student-faculty ratio is 10:1. Special programs include services for learning-disabled students, an honors program, cooperative (work-study) education, study abroad, advanced placement credit, double majors, independent study, self-designed majors, summer session for credit, part-time degree programs (daytime, evenings, summer), adult/continuing education programs, internships, and arrangement for off-campus study with members of the Greater Cincinnati Consortium of Colleges and Universities, Association of Independent Colleges of Art and Design. The most frequently chosen baccalaureate field is visual and performing arts.
Student Body Statistics The student body totals 165, of whom 164 are undergraduates (47 freshmen). 63 percent are women and 37 percent are men. Students come from 12 states and territories and 2 other countries. 76 percent are from Ohio. 1.3 percent are international students.
Expenses for 2009–10 *Application fee:* $0. *Tuition:* $21,500 full-time, $900 per hour part-time. *Mandatory fees:* $380 full-time, $190 per term part-time. *College room only:* $6000.
Financial Aid Forms of aid include need-based and non-need-based scholarships and part-time jobs. The average aided 2007–08 undergraduate received an aid package worth $13,197. The application deadline for financial aid is continuous.
Freshman Admission Art Academy of Cincinnati requires an essay, a high school transcript, a minimum 2.0 high school GPA, 1 recommendation, a portfolio, SAT or ACT scores, and TOEFL scores for international students. An interview is recommended. The application deadline for regular admission is June 30.
Transfer Admission The application deadline for admission is June 30.
Entrance Difficulty Art Academy of Cincinnati assesses its entrance difficulty level as moderately difficult. For the fall 2008 freshman class, 21 percent of the applicants were accepted.
For Further Information Contact Mr. John J. Wadell, Director of Admissions, Art Academy of Cincinnati, 1212 Jackson Street, Cincinnati, OH 45202-7106. *Phone:* 513-562-8744 or 800-323-5692 (toll-free in-state). *Fax:* 513-562-8778. *E-mail:* admissions@artacademy.edu. *Web site:* http://www.artacademy.edu/.

ASHLAND UNIVERSITY

Ashland, Ohio

Ashland University is a coed, private, comprehensive institution, founded in 1878, affiliated with the Brethren Church, offering degrees at the associate, bachelor's, master's, doctoral, and first professional levels. It has a 98-acre campus in Ashland near Cleveland.

Academic Information The faculty has 581 members (40% full-time), 54% with terminal degrees. The undergraduate student-faculty ratio is 16:1. The library holds 205,200 titles, 1,625 serial subscriptions, and 3,550 audiovisual materials. Special programs include academic remediation, services for learning-disabled students, an honors program, study abroad, advanced placement credit, ESL programs, double majors, independent study, self-designed majors, summer session for credit, part-time degree programs (daytime, evenings, weekends, summer), adult/continuing education programs, internships, and arrangement for off-campus study with Case Western Reserve University, Art Institute of Pittsburgh, Purdue University, Drew University, American University, Merrill-Palmer Institute, Hunter College of the City University of New York. The most frequently chosen baccalaureate fields are business/marketing, education, visual and performing arts.
Student Body Statistics The student body totals 6,475, of whom 2,654 are undergraduates (576 freshmen). 52 percent are women and 48 percent are men. Students come from 31 states and territories and 19 other countries. 90 percent are from Ohio. 2 percent are international students.
Expenses for 2009–10 *Application fee:* $0. *Comprehensive fee:* $32,998 includes full-time tuition ($24,828), mandatory fees ($812), and college room and board ($7358). *College room only:* $5028. *Part-time tuition:* $762 per credit.
Financial Aid Forms of aid include need-based and non-need-based scholarships, athletic grants, and part-time jobs. The average aided 2008–09 undergraduate received an aid package worth an estimated $21,554. The application deadline for financial aid is continuous.
Freshman Admission Ashland University requires a high school transcript, a minimum 2.5 high school GPA, SAT or ACT scores, and TOEFL scores for international students. An interview is recommended. Recommendations and an interview are required for some. The application deadline for regular admission is rolling.
Transfer Admission The application deadline for admission is rolling.
Entrance Difficulty Ashland University assesses its entrance difficulty level as moderately difficult. For the fall 2008 freshman class, 82 percent of the applicants were accepted.
For Further Information Contact Mr. Thomas Mansperger, Director of Admission, Ashland University, 401 College Avenue, Ashland, OH 44805. *Phone:* 419-289-5052 or 800-882-1548 (toll-free). *Fax:* 419-289-5999. *E-mail:* enrollme@ashland.edu. *Web site:* http://www.exploreashland.com/.

BALDWIN-WALLACE COLLEGE

Berea, Ohio

Baldwin-Wallace College is a coed, private, Methodist, comprehensive institution, founded in 1845, offering degrees at the bachelor's and master's levels. It has a 100-acre campus in Berea near Cleveland.

Academic Information The faculty has 401 members (41% full-time), 43% with terminal degrees. The library holds 200,000 titles and 22,000 serial subscriptions. Special programs include academic remediation, services for learning-disabled students, an honors program, study abroad, advanced placement credit, accelerated degree programs, ESL programs, double majors, independent study, distance learning, self-designed majors, summer session for credit, part-time degree programs (daytime, evenings, weekends, summer), adult/continuing education programs, internships, and arrangement for off-campus study with Drew University, American University. The most frequently chosen baccalaureate fields are business/marketing, education, visual and performing arts.
Student Body Statistics The student body totals 4,382, of whom 3,681 are undergraduates (738 freshmen). 57 percent are women and 43 percent are men. Students come from 36 states and territories and 13 other countries. 88 percent are from Ohio. 1.3 percent are international students.
Expenses for 2008–09 *Application fee:* $25. *Comprehensive fee:* $31,252 includes full-time tuition ($23,524) and college room and board ($7728).

Baldwin-Wallace College (continued)

College room only: $3776. Full-time tuition varies according to class time and course load. *Part-time tuition:* $748 per semester hour. Part-time tuition varies according to class time and course load.
Financial Aid Forms of aid include need-based and non-need-based scholarships and part-time jobs. The average aided 2008–09 undergraduate received an aid package worth an estimated $20,220. The application deadline for financial aid is September 1 with a priority deadline of May 1.
Freshman Admission Baldwin-Wallace College requires an essay, a high school transcript, a minimum 2.75 high school GPA, 1 recommendation, and TOEFL scores for international students. A minimum 3.2 high school GPA and an interview are recommended. SAT or ACT scores are required for some. The application deadline for regular admission is March 1.
Transfer Admission The application deadline for admission is August 1.
Entrance Difficulty Baldwin-Wallace College assesses its entrance difficulty level as moderately difficult. For the fall 2008 freshman class, 67 percent of the applicants were accepted.
For Further Information Contact Patricia Skrha, Director of Undergraduate Admission, Baldwin-Wallace College, Bonds Administration Building, 275 Eastland Road, Berea, OH 44017. *Phone:* 440-826-2222 or 877-BWAPPLY (toll-free in-state). *Fax:* 440-826-3830. *E-mail:* admission@bw.edu. *Web site:* http://www.bw.edu/.

See page 228 for the Close-Up.

BLUFFTON UNIVERSITY

Bluffton, Ohio

Bluffton University is a coed, private, Mennonite, comprehensive institution, founded in 1899, offering degrees at the bachelor's and master's levels. It has a 65-acre campus in Bluffton near Toledo.

Academic Information The faculty has 113 members (57% full-time), 45% with terminal degrees. The undergraduate student-faculty ratio is 13:1. The library holds 168,888 titles and 263 serial subscriptions. Special programs include academic remediation, an honors program, study abroad, advanced placement credit, double majors, independent study, self-designed majors, summer session for credit, part-time degree programs (evenings), adult/continuing education programs, internships, and arrangement for off-campus study with Christian College Coalition, Council of Independent Colleges. The most frequently chosen baccalaureate fields are business/marketing, education, public administration and social services.
Student Body Statistics The student body totals 1,149, of whom 1,032 are undergraduates (272 freshmen). 54 percent are women and 46 percent are men. Students come from 16 states and territories and 11 other countries. 89 percent are from Ohio. 2.1 percent are international students.
Expenses for 2008–09 *Application fee:* $20. *Comprehensive fee:* $30,516 includes full-time tuition ($22,470), mandatory fees ($450), and college room and board ($7596). *College room only:* $3660. Full-time tuition and fees vary according to course load and program. Room and board charges vary according to board plan and housing facility. *Part-time tuition:* $936 per credit hour. Part-time tuition varies according to course load and program.
Financial Aid Forms of aid include need-based and non-need-based scholarships and part-time jobs. The average aided 2008–09 undergraduate received an aid package worth an estimated $21,716. The application deadline for financial aid is October 1 with a priority deadline of May 1.
Freshman Admission Bluffton University requires a high school transcript, 1 recommendation, rank in upper 50% of high school class or 2.3 high school GPA, SAT or ACT scores, and TOEFL scores for international students. A minimum 2.3 high school GPA and an interview are recommended. An essay is required for some. The application deadline for regular admission is August 15.
Transfer Admission The application deadline for admission is rolling.
Entrance Difficulty Bluffton University assesses its entrance difficulty level as moderately difficult. For the fall 2008 freshman class, 58 percent of the applicants were accepted.
For Further Information Contact Mr. Chris Jebsen, Director of Admissions, Bluffton University, 1 University Drive, Bluffton, OH 45817. *Phone:* 419-358-3254 or 800-488-3257 (toll-free). *Fax:* 419-358-3081. *E-mail:* admissions@bluffton.edu. *Web site:* http://www.bluffton.edu/.

BOHECKER'S BUSINESS COLLEGE

Ravenna, Ohio

Bohecker's Business College is a coed, private, two-year college, offering degrees at the associate level.

Student Body Statistics The student body is made up of 482 undergraduates.
Financial Aid Forms of aid include need-based scholarships and part-time jobs. The application deadline for financial aid is continuous.
For Further Information Contact Admissions Office, Bohecker's Business College, 653 Enterprise Parkway, Ravenna, OH 44266. *Phone:* 800-794-2856 (toll-free in-state). *Web site:* http://www.boheckercollege.edu/.

BOWLING GREEN STATE UNIVERSITY

Bowling Green, Ohio

Bowling Green State University is a coed, public university, founded in 1910, offering degrees at the bachelor's, master's, and doctoral levels and post-master's certificates. It has a 1,230-acre campus in Bowling Green near Toledo.

Academic Information The faculty has 1,022 members (83% full-time). The undergraduate student-faculty ratio is 18:1. Special programs include academic remediation, services for learning-disabled students, an honors program, cooperative (work-study) education, study abroad, advanced placement credit, accelerated degree programs, ESL programs, double majors, independent study, distance learning, self-designed majors, summer session for credit, part-time degree programs (daytime, evenings, summer), adult/continuing education programs, internships, and arrangement for off-campus study with University of Toledo, Medical College of Ohio. The most frequently chosen baccalaureate fields are business/marketing, education, visual and performing arts.
Student Body Statistics The student body totals 17,874, of whom 14,862 are undergraduates (3,098 freshmen). 54 percent are women and 46 percent are men. Students come from 52 states and territories and 49 other countries. 90 percent are from Ohio. 1.6 percent are international students.
Expenses for 2008–09 *Application fee:* $40. *State resident tuition:* $7778 full-time, $380 per credit hour part-time. *Nonresident tuition:* $15,086 full-time, $729 per credit hour part-time. *Mandatory fees:* $1282 full-time, $64 per credit hour part-time. Full-time tuition and fees vary according to location. Part-time tuition and fees vary according to course load and location. *College room and board:* $7220. *College room only:* $4420. Room and board charges vary according to board plan and housing facility.
Financial Aid Forms of aid include need-based and non-need-based scholarships, athletic grants, and part-time jobs. The average aided 2007–08 undergraduate received an aid package worth $12,114. The application deadline for financial aid is continuous.
Freshman Admission Bowling Green State University requires a high school transcript, a minimum 2.5 high school GPA, SAT and SAT Subject Test or ACT scores, and TOEFL scores for international students. An interview is recommended. The application deadline for regular admission is July 15.
Transfer Admission The application deadline for admission is July 15.
Entrance Difficulty Bowling Green State University assesses its entrance difficulty level as moderately difficult. For the fall 2008 freshman class, 87 percent of the applicants were accepted.
For Further Information Contact Mr. Gary Swegan, Assistant Vice Provost/Director of Admissions, Bowling Green State University, 110 McFall, Bowling Green, OH 43403. *Phone:* 419-372-2478. *Fax:* 419-372-6955. *E-mail:* admissions@bgsu.edu. *Web site:* http://www.bgsu.edu/.

BOWLING GREEN STATE UNIVERSITY–FIRELANDS COLLEGE

Huron, Ohio

http://www.firelands.bgsu.edu/

BRYANT & STRATTON COLLEGE

Cleveland, Ohio

http://www.bryantstratton.edu/

BRYANT & STRATTON COLLEGE

Parma, Ohio

Bryant & Stratton College is a coed, proprietary, primarily two-year college of Bryant and Stratton Business Institute, Inc., founded in 1981, offering degrees at the associate and bachelor's levels. It has a 4-acre campus in Parma near Cleveland.

Academic Information The faculty has 57 members (28% full-time). The student-faculty ratio is 12:1. The library holds 1,500 titles and 20 serial subscriptions. Special programs include academic remediation, cooperative (work-study) education, double majors, independent study, distance learning, summer session for credit, part-time degree programs (daytime, evenings, summer), and internships.

Student Body Statistics The student body is made up of 528 undergraduates (189 freshmen). 81 percent are women and 19 percent are men. Students come from 1 state or territory.

Expenses for 2008–09 *Tuition:* $14,430 full-time, $458 per credit hour part-time. Full-time tuition varies according to class time, course load, degree level, and program. Part-time tuition varies according to course load and degree level.

Financial Aid Forms of aid include need-based scholarships and part-time jobs. The application deadline for financial aid is continuous.

Freshman Admission Bryant & Stratton College requires a high school transcript, an interview, entrance evaluation and placement evaluation, and CPAt. SAT or ACT scores are recommended. Recommendations are required for some. The application deadline for regular admission is rolling.

Transfer Admission The application deadline for admission is rolling.

Entrance Difficulty Bryant & Stratton College assesses its entrance difficulty level as minimally difficult.

For Further Information Contact Mr. William Cassidy, Market Director of Admissions, Bryant & Stratton College, 12955 Snow Road, Parma, OH 44130. *Phone:* 216-265-3151 Ext. 225 or 800-327-3151 (toll-free in-state). *Fax:* 216-265-0325. *E-mail:* finelly@bryantstratton.edu. *Web site:* http://www.bryantstratton.edu/.

BRYANT & STRATTON COLLEGE

Willoughby Hills, Ohio

Bryant & Stratton College is a coed, proprietary, primarily two-year college of Bryant and Stratton College, founded in 1987, offering degrees at the associate and bachelor's levels. It is located in Willoughby Hills near Cleveland.

Academic Information The faculty has 63 members (38% full-time), 13% with terminal degrees. The student-faculty ratio is 12:1. The library holds 1,500 titles and 19 serial subscriptions. Special programs include academic remediation, advanced placement credit, independent study, distance learning, summer session for credit, part-time degree programs (daytime, evenings, summer), and internships.

Student Body Statistics The student body is made up of 762 undergraduates (378 freshmen). 88 percent are women and 12 percent are men. Students come from 1 state or territory.

Expenses for 2008–09 *Application fee:* $35. *Tuition:* $14,430 full-time, $458 per credit hour part-time. Full-time tuition varies according to class time, course load, degree level, and program. Part-time tuition varies according to course load and degree level.

Financial Aid Forms of aid include need-based scholarships and part-time jobs.

Freshman Admission Bryant & Stratton College requires a high school transcript, an interview, entrance evaluation and placement evaluation, TOEFL scores for international students, and CPAt. A minimum 2.0 high school GPA and SAT or ACT scores are recommended. An essay and recommendations are required for some. The application deadline for regular admission is rolling.

Transfer Admission The application deadline for admission is rolling.

Entrance Difficulty Bryant & Stratton College assesses its entrance difficulty level as minimally difficult.

For Further Information Contact Ms. Melanie Pettit, Director of Admissions, Bryant & Stratton College, 27557 Chardon Road, Willoughby Hills, OH 44092. *Phone:* 440-510-1112. *Fax:* 440-944-9260. *E-mail:* jwpettit@bryantstratton.edu. *Web site:* http://www.bryantstratton.edu/.

CAPITAL UNIVERSITY

Columbus, Ohio

Capital University is a coed, private, comprehensive institution, founded in 1830, affiliated with the Evangelical Lutheran Church in America, offering degrees at the bachelor's, master's, and first professional levels. It has a 48-acre campus in Columbus.

Academic Information The faculty has 407 members (49% full-time), 45% with terminal degrees. The undergraduate student-faculty ratio is 11:1. The library holds 199,011 titles, 6,995 serial subscriptions, and 6,892 audiovisual materials. Special programs include services for learning-disabled students, an honors program, cooperative (work-study) education, study abroad, advanced placement credit, accelerated degree programs, Freshman Honors College, ESL programs, double majors, independent study, self-designed majors, summer session for credit, part-time degree programs (evenings, weekends, summer), external degree programs, adult/continuing education programs, internships, and arrangement for off-campus study with members of the Higher Education Council of Columbus. The most frequently chosen baccalaureate fields are business/marketing, education, health professions and related sciences.

Student Body Statistics The student body totals 3,632, of whom 2,675 are undergraduates (644 freshmen). 62 percent are women and 38 percent are men. Students come from 28 states and territories and 26 other countries. 95 percent are from Ohio. 1.2 percent are international students.

Expenses for 2008–09 *Application fee:* $25. *Comprehensive fee:* $34,830 includes full-time tuition ($27,680) and college room and board ($7150). Full-time tuition varies according to course load, degree level, program, and student level. Room and board charges vary according to board plan and housing facility. *Part-time tuition:* $925 per credit hour. Part-time tuition varies according to course load, degree level, program, and student level.

Financial Aid Forms of aid include need-based and non-need-based scholarships and part-time jobs. The priority application deadline for financial aid is February 28.

Freshman Admission Capital University requires a high school transcript, a minimum 2.6 high school GPA, SAT or ACT scores, and TOEFL scores for international students. An interview is recommended. 1 recommendation and audition are required for some. The application deadline for regular admission is April 1.

Transfer Admission The application deadline for admission is rolling.

Entrance Difficulty Capital University assesses its entrance difficulty level as moderately difficult. For the fall 2008 freshman class, 77 percent of the applicants were accepted.

For Further Information Contact Ms. Amanda Steiner, Interim Director of Admissions, Capital University, 1 College and Main, Columbus, OH 43209. *Phone:* 614-236-6574 or 800-289-6289 (toll-free). *Fax:* 614-236-6926. *E-mail:* asteiner@capital.edu. *Web site:* http://www.capital.edu/.

CASE WESTERN RESERVE UNIVERSITY

Cleveland, Ohio

Case Western Reserve University is a coed, private university, founded in 1826, offering degrees at the bachelor's, master's, doctoral, and first professional levels and postbachelor's certificates. It has a 150-acre campus in Cleveland.

Academic Information The faculty has 900 members (82% full-time), 85% with terminal degrees. The undergraduate student-faculty ratio is 9.7:1. The library holds 3 million titles, 54,252 serial subscriptions, and 53,892 audiovisual materials. Special programs include services for learning-disabled students, an honors program, cooperative (work-study) education, study abroad, advanced placement credit, accelerated degree

Case Western Reserve University (continued)

programs, ESL programs, double majors, independent study, self-designed majors, summer session for credit, part-time degree programs (daytime, evenings), adult/continuing education programs, internships, and arrangement for off-campus study with Cleveland Institute of Art, Cleveland Institute of Music, 11 other Cleveland area institutions. The most frequently chosen baccalaureate fields are engineering, biological/life sciences, social sciences.

Student Body Statistics The student body totals 9,814, of whom 4,356 are undergraduates (1,026 freshmen). 43 percent are women and 57 percent are men. Students come from 50 states and territories and 24 other countries. 54 percent are from Ohio. 3.4 percent are international students.

Expenses for 2008–09 *Application fee:* $0. *One-time mandatory fee:* $370. *Comprehensive fee:* $45,652 includes full-time tuition ($34,450), mandatory fees ($752), and college room and board ($10,450). *College room only:* $6080. Full-time tuition and fees vary according to student level. Room and board charges vary according to board plan, housing facility, and student level. *Part-time tuition:* $1436 per credit hour. Part-time tuition varies according to course load and student level.

Financial Aid Forms of aid include need-based and non-need-based scholarships and part-time jobs. The average aided 2008–09 undergraduate received an aid package worth an estimated $34,927. The priority application deadline for financial aid is February 15.

Freshman Admission Case Western Reserve University requires an essay, a high school transcript, 1 recommendation, SAT or ACT scores, and TOEFL scores for international students. An interview is recommended. The application deadline for regular admission is January 15 and for early action it is November 1.

Transfer Admission The application deadline for admission is May 15.

Entrance Difficulty Case Western Reserve University assesses its entrance difficulty level as very difficult. For the fall 2008 freshman class, 73 percent of the applicants were accepted.

For Further Information Contact Ms. Rae Ann DiBaggio, Co-Director of Undergraduate Admission, Case Western Reserve University, 10900 Euclid Avenue, Cleveland, OH 44106. *Phone:* 216-368-4450. *Fax:* 216-368-5111. *E-mail:* admission@case.edu. *Web site:* http://www.case.edu/.

CEDARVILLE UNIVERSITY

Cedarville, Ohio

Cedarville University is a coed, private, Baptist, comprehensive institution, founded in 1887, offering degrees at the bachelor's and master's levels. It has a 400-acre campus in Cedarville near Columbus and Dayton.

Academic Information The faculty has 254 members (75% full-time), 48% with terminal degrees. The undergraduate student-faculty ratio is 15:1. The library holds 181,053 titles, 21,050 serial subscriptions, and 16,464 audiovisual materials. Special programs include academic remediation, services for learning-disabled students, an honors program, study abroad, advanced placement credit, accelerated degree programs, double majors, independent study, distance learning, summer session for credit, part-time degree programs (daytime), internships, and arrangement for off-campus study with Au Sable Institute. The most frequently chosen baccalaureate fields are business/marketing, education, health professions and related sciences.

Student Body Statistics The student body totals 3,077, of whom 2,996 are undergraduates (774 freshmen). 54 percent are women and 46 percent are men. Students come from 50 states and territories and 21 other countries. 36 percent are from Ohio. 0.7 percent are international students.

Expenses for 2009–10 *Application fee:* $30. *One-time mandatory fee:* $120. *Comprehensive fee:* $27,310 includes full-time tuition ($22,304) and college room and board ($5006). *College room only:* $2740. *Part-time tuition:* $697 per credit hour.

Financial Aid Forms of aid include need-based and non-need-based scholarships, athletic grants, and part-time jobs. The average aided 2007–08 undergraduate received an aid package worth $19,272. The priority application deadline for financial aid is March 1.

Freshman Admission Cedarville University requires an essay, a high school transcript, a minimum 3.0 high school GPA, 2 recommendations, clear testimony of faith in Jesus Christ and evidence of consistent Christian lifestyle, SAT or ACT scores, and TOEFL scores for international students. SAT and SAT Subject Test or ACT scores are recommended. An interview is required for some. The application deadline for regular admission is rolling.

Transfer Admission The application deadline for admission is rolling.

Entrance Difficulty Cedarville University assesses its entrance difficulty level as moderately difficult. For the fall 2008 freshman class, 74 percent of the applicants were accepted.

For Further Information Contact Mr. Scott Van Loo, Director of Admissions, Cedarville University, 251 North Main Street, Cedarville, OH 45314-0601. *Phone:* 937-766-7700 or 800-CEDARVILLE (toll-free). *Fax:* 937-766-7575. *E-mail:* admiss@cedarville.edu. *Web site:* http://www.cedarville.edu/.

CENTRAL STATE UNIVERSITY

Wilberforce, Ohio

Central State University is a coed, public, comprehensive unit of Ohio Board of Regents, founded in 1887, offering degrees at the bachelor's and master's levels. It has a 60-acre campus in Wilberforce near Dayton.

Academic Information The faculty has 196 members (54% full-time), 43% with terminal degrees. The undergraduate student-faculty ratio is 15:1. The library holds 301,514 titles, 40,723 serial subscriptions, and 2,938 audiovisual materials. Special programs include services for learning-disabled students, an honors program, cooperative (work-study) education, study abroad, double majors, independent study, summer session for credit, part-time degree programs (daytime, evenings, weekends, summer), adult/continuing education programs, internships, and arrangement for off-campus study with members of the Southwestern Ohio Council for Higher Education. The most frequently chosen baccalaureate fields are business/marketing, education, social sciences.

Student Body Statistics The student body totals 2,171, of whom 2,142 are undergraduates (654 freshmen). 50 percent are women and 50 percent are men. Students come from 32 states and territories and 8 other countries. 61 percent are from Ohio. 0.3 percent are international students.

Expenses for 2008–09 *Application fee:* $20. *State resident tuition:* $5294 full-time, $218 per credit hour part-time. *Nonresident tuition:* $11,462 full-time, $496 per credit hour part-time. Both full-time and part-time tuition varies according to course load. *College room and board:* $7402. *College room only:* $3978. Room and board charges vary according to board plan.

Financial Aid Forms of aid include need-based and non-need-based scholarships, athletic grants, and part-time jobs. The priority application deadline for financial aid is February 15.

Freshman Admission Central State University requires a high school transcript, SAT or ACT scores, and TOEFL scores for international students. An interview and ACT scores are recommended. An essay, a minimum 2.0 high school GPA, 2 recommendations, and 2.5 high school GPA for nonresidents are required for some. The application deadline for regular admission is June 15.

Transfer Admission The application deadline for admission is June 15.

Entrance Difficulty Central State University has an open admission policy for state residents. It assesses its entrance difficulty as moderately difficult for out-of-state applicants; moderately difficult for transfers.

For Further Information Contact Ms. Robin Rucker, Director, Admissions, Central State University, PO Box 1004, 1400 Blush Row Road, Wilberforce, OH 45384. *Phone:* 937-376-6580 or 800-388-CSU1 (toll-free in-state). *Fax:* 937-376-6648. *E-mail:* admissions@centralstate.edu. *Web site:* http://www.centralstate.edu/.

CHANCELLOR UNIVERSITY

Cleveland, Ohio

Chancellor University is a coed, private, comprehensive institution, founded in 1848, offering degrees at the associate, bachelor's, and master's levels. It has a 1-acre campus in Cleveland.

Academic Information The library holds 15,027 titles, 140 serial subscriptions, and 377 audiovisual materials. Special programs include academic remediation, cooperative (work-study) education, advanced

placement credit, accelerated degree programs, double majors, independent study, distance learning, self-designed majors, summer session for credit, part-time degree programs (daytime, evenings, weekends, summer), external degree programs, adult/continuing education programs, internships, and arrangement for off-campus study with members of the Northeast Ohio Commission on Higher Education.
Student Body Statistics The student body totals 570, of whom 500 are undergraduates.
Expenses for 2008–09 *Application fee:* $25. *Tuition:* $10,800 full-time, $360 per semester hour part-time. *Mandatory fees:* $100 full-time.
Financial Aid Forms of aid include need-based and non-need-based scholarships and part-time jobs. The priority application deadline for financial aid is March 15.
Freshman Admission Chancellor University requires a high school transcript, SAT or ACT scores, and TOEFL scores for international students. Recommendations are recommended. An essay and an interview are required for some. The application deadline for regular admission is rolling.
Transfer Admission The application deadline for admission is rolling.
Entrance Difficulty Chancellor University assesses its entrance difficulty level as minimally difficult; moderately difficult for transfers.
For Further Information Contact Vice President for Enrollment Management, Chancellor University, 3921 Chester Avenue, Cleveland, OH 44114-4624. *Phone:* 216-432-8992 or 877-366-9377 (toll-free). *Fax:* 216-696-6430. *E-mail:* cjohnson@myers.edu. *Web site:* http://www.myers.edu/.

CHATFIELD COLLEGE

St. Martin, Ohio

http://www.chatfield.edu/

CINCINNATI CHRISTIAN UNIVERSITY

Cincinnati, Ohio

Cincinnati Christian University is a coed, private, comprehensive institution, founded in 1924, affiliated with the Church of Christ, offering degrees at the associate, bachelor's, master's, and first professional levels. It has a 40-acre campus in Cincinnati.

Academic Information The faculty has 110 members (33% full-time), 36% with terminal degrees. The undergraduate student-faculty ratio is 15:1. The library holds 9,400 titles and 656 serial subscriptions. Special programs include academic remediation, services for learning-disabled students, advanced placement credit, double majors, independent study, summer session for credit, part-time degree programs (daytime, evenings, summer), adult/continuing education programs, internships, and arrangement for off-campus study with College of Mount St. Joseph, Greater Cincinnati Consortium of Colleges and Universities. The most frequently chosen baccalaureate fields are psychology, business/marketing, theology and religious vocations.
Student Body Statistics The student body totals 1,125, of whom 811 are undergraduates (132 freshmen). 47 percent are women and 53 percent are men. 0.9 percent are international students.
Expenses for 2008–09 *Application fee:* $40. *Comprehensive fee:* $18,370 includes full-time tuition ($11,040), mandatory fees ($860), and college room and board ($6470). *College room only:* $3210. Full-time tuition and fees vary according to course load and student level. Room and board charges vary according to board plan and housing facility. *Part-time tuition:* $368 per credit hour. *Part-time mandatory fees:* $115 per term. Part-time tuition and fees vary according to course load and student level.
Financial Aid Forms of aid include need-based and non-need-based scholarships and part-time jobs. The priority application deadline for financial aid is March 15.
Freshman Admission Cincinnati Christian University requires an essay, a high school transcript, 1 recommendation, SAT or ACT scores, and TOEFL scores for international students. A minimum 2.0 high school GPA and an interview are recommended. The application deadline for regular admission is July 1.
Transfer Admission The application deadline for admission is July 1.
Entrance Difficulty Cincinnati Christian University assesses its entrance difficulty level as minimally difficult. For the fall 2008 freshman class, 75 percent of the applicants were accepted.
For Further Information Contact Paul Presta, Director of Undergraduate Admissions, Cincinnati Christian University, 2700 Glenway Avenue, Cincinnati, OH 45204-1799. *Phone:* 800-949-4228 (toll-free in-state). *Fax:* 513-244-8140. *E-mail:* admissions@cincybible.edu. *Web site:* http://www.ccuniversity.edu/.

CINCINNATI COLLEGE OF MORTUARY SCIENCE

Cincinnati, Ohio

http://www.ccms.edu/

CIRCLEVILLE BIBLE COLLEGE

See Ohio Christian University.

CLEVELAND COLLEGE OF JEWISH STUDIES

See Laura and Alvin Siegal College of Judaic Studies.

THE CLEVELAND INSTITUTE OF ART

Cleveland, Ohio

The Cleveland Institute of Art is a coed, private, four-year college, founded in 1882, offering degrees at the bachelor's level. It has a 488-acre campus in Cleveland.

Academic Information The faculty has 96 members (47% full-time), 73% with terminal degrees. The student-faculty ratio is 8:1. The library holds 45,000 titles, 250 serial subscriptions, and 2,500 audiovisual materials. Special programs include academic remediation, services for learning-disabled students, an honors program, study abroad, advanced placement credit, independent study, part-time degree programs (daytime), internships, and arrangement for off-campus study with Case Western Reserve University, Northeast Ohio Commission on Higher Education, Association of Independent Colleges of Art and Design. The most frequently chosen baccalaureate field is visual and performing arts.
Student Body Statistics The student body is made up of 503 undergraduates (103 freshmen). 52 percent are women and 48 percent are men. Students come from 17 states and territories and 3 other countries. 68 percent are from Ohio. 2.4 percent are international students.
Expenses for 2008–09 *Application fee:* $30. *Comprehensive fee:* $40,158 includes full-time tuition ($29,000), mandatory fees ($2010), and college room and board ($9148). *College room only:* $4948. Full-time tuition and fees vary according to program. Room and board charges vary according to board plan. *Part-time tuition:* $1210 per credit hour. *Part-time mandatory fees:* $120 per credit hour. Part-time tuition and fees vary according to course load and program.
Financial Aid Forms of aid include need-based and non-need-based scholarships and part-time jobs. The average aided 2008–09 undergraduate received an aid package worth an estimated $19,422.
Freshman Admission The Cleveland Institute of Art requires an essay, a high school transcript, a minimum 2.0 high school GPA, 1 recommendation, a portfolio, SAT or ACT scores, and TOEFL scores for international students. An interview is recommended. The application deadline for regular admission is rolling.
Transfer Admission The application deadline for admission is rolling.

The Cleveland Institute of Art (continued)

Entrance Difficulty The Cleveland Institute of Art assesses its entrance difficulty level as moderately difficult. For the fall 2008 freshman class, 87 percent of the applicants were accepted.

For Further Information Contact Office of Admissions, The Cleveland Institute of Art, 11141 East Boulevard, Cleveland, OH 44106. *Phone:* 216-421-7418 or 800-223-4700 (toll-free). *Fax:* 216-754-3634. *E-mail:* admissions@cia.edu. *Web site:* http://www.cia.edu/.

CLEVELAND INSTITUTE OF MUSIC

Cleveland, Ohio

http://www.cim.edu/

CLEVELAND STATE UNIVERSITY

Cleveland, Ohio

Cleveland State University is a coed, public university, founded in 1964, offering degrees at the bachelor's, master's, doctoral, and first professional levels and post-master's, first professional, and postbachelor's certificates. It has a 70-acre campus in Cleveland near Akron.

Academic Information The faculty has 1,068 members (51% full-time), 56% with terminal degrees. The undergraduate student-faculty ratio is 16:1. The library holds 847,731 titles, 7,826 serial subscriptions, and 143,894 audiovisual materials. Special programs include academic remediation, services for learning-disabled students, an honors program, cooperative (work-study) education, study abroad, advanced placement credit, accelerated degree programs, Freshman Honors College, ESL programs, double majors, independent study, self-designed majors, summer session for credit, part-time degree programs, adult/continuing education programs, internships, and arrangement for off-campus study with 7 members of the Cleveland Commission on Higher Education, University of Akron, Baldwin-Wallace College, University of Toledo. The most frequently chosen baccalaureate fields are business/marketing, health professions and related sciences, social sciences.

Student Body Statistics The student body totals 15,809, of whom 10,161 are undergraduates (1,056 freshmen). 56 percent are women and 44 percent are men. Students come from 34 states and territories and 75 other countries. 97 percent are from Ohio. 2.3 percent are international students.

Expenses for 2009–10 *Application fee:* $30. *State resident tuition:* $7970 full-time, $330 per credit hour part-time. *Nonresident tuition:* $10,774 full-time, $444.30 per credit hour part-time. *College room and board:* $8700. *College room only:* $5410.

Financial Aid Forms of aid include need-based and non-need-based scholarships, athletic grants, and part-time jobs. The average aided 2008–09 undergraduate received an aid package worth an estimated $8136. The priority application deadline for financial aid is February 15.

Freshman Admission Cleveland State University requires a high school transcript, SAT or ACT scores, and TOEFL scores for international students. The application deadline for regular admission is August 15 and for early action it is May 1.

Transfer Admission The application deadline for admission is July 15.

Entrance Difficulty Cleveland State University assesses its entrance difficulty level as moderately difficult. For the fall 2008 freshman class, 65 percent of the applicants were accepted.

For Further Information Contact Undergraduate Admissions Office, Cleveland State University, 2121 Euclid Avenue, RW 204, Cleveland, OH 44115. *Phone:* 216-687-2100 or 888-CSU-OHIO (toll-free). *Fax:* 216-687-9210. *E-mail:* admissions@csuohio.edu. *Web site:* http://www.csuohio.edu/.

COLLEGE OF MOUNT ST. JOSEPH

Cincinnati, Ohio

College of Mount St. Joseph is a coed, private, Roman Catholic, comprehensive institution, founded in 1920, offering degrees at the associate, bachelor's, master's, and doctoral levels and postbachelor's certificates. It has a 92-acre campus in Cincinnati.

Academic Information The faculty has 240 members (50% full-time), 46% with terminal degrees. The undergraduate student-faculty ratio is 10:1. The library holds 97,141 titles, 9,394 serial subscriptions, and 4,047 audiovisual materials. Special programs include academic remediation, services for learning-disabled students, an honors program, cooperative (work-study) education, study abroad, advanced placement credit, accelerated degree programs, double majors, independent study, distance learning, summer session for credit, part-time degree programs (daytime, evenings, weekends, summer), and internships. The most frequently chosen baccalaureate fields are business/marketing, health professions and related sciences, visual and performing arts.

Student Body Statistics The student body totals 2,133, of whom 1,831 are undergraduates (308 freshmen). 65 percent are women and 35 percent are men. Students come from 23 states and territories and 3 other countries. 84 percent are from Ohio. 0.3 percent are international students.

Expenses for 2008–09 *Application fee:* $25. *One-time mandatory fee:* $150. *Comprehensive fee:* $28,900 includes full-time tuition ($21,200), mandatory fees ($800), and college room and board ($6900). *College room only:* $3400. *Part-time tuition:* $465 per semester hour. *Part-time mandatory fees:* $200 per term.

Financial Aid Forms of aid include need-based and non-need-based scholarships and part-time jobs. The average aided 2008–09 undergraduate received an aid package worth an estimated $15,984. The priority application deadline for financial aid is March 1.

Freshman Admission College of Mount St. Joseph requires a high school transcript, SAT or ACT scores, and TOEFL scores for international students. A minimum 2.5 high school GPA is recommended. An essay, 1 recommendation, and an interview are required for some. The application deadline for regular admission is August 15.

Transfer Admission The application deadline for admission is August 1.

Entrance Difficulty College of Mount St. Joseph assesses its entrance difficulty level as moderately difficult. For the fall 2008 freshman class, 70 percent of the applicants were accepted.

For Further Information Contact Ms. Peggy Minnich, Director of Admission, College of Mount St. Joseph, 5701 Delhi Road, Cincinnati, OH 45233-1670. *Phone:* 513-244-4531 or 800-654-9314 (toll-free). *Fax:* 513-244-4629. *E-mail:* admissions@mail.msj.edu. *Web site:* http://www.msj.edu/.

THE COLLEGE OF WOOSTER

Wooster, Ohio

The College of Wooster is a coed, private, four-year college, founded in 1866, affiliated with the Presbyterian Church (U.S.A.), offering degrees at the bachelor's level. It has a 240-acre campus in Wooster near Cleveland.

Academic Information The faculty has 200 members (81% full-time). The student-faculty ratio is 11.5:1. The library holds 581,518 titles and 12,416 audiovisual materials. Special programs include services for learning-disabled students, cooperative (work-study) education, study abroad, advanced placement credit, double majors, independent study, self-designed majors, summer session for credit, internships, and arrangement for off-campus study. The most frequently chosen baccalaureate fields are psychology, philosophy and religious studies, social sciences.

Student Body Statistics The student body is made up of 1,884 undergraduates (519 freshmen). 53 percent are women and 47 percent are men. Students come from 47 states and territories and 29 other countries. 40 percent are from Ohio. 5.3 percent are international students.

Expenses for 2009–10 *Application fee:* $40. *Comprehensive fee:* $43,900.

Financial Aid Forms of aid include need-based and non-need-based scholarships and part-time jobs. The average aided 2008–09 undergraduate received an aid package worth an estimated $27,950. The application deadline for financial aid is September 1 with a priority deadline of February 15.

Freshman Admission The College of Wooster requires an essay, a high school transcript, 2 recommendations, SAT or ACT scores, and TOEFL scores for international students. An interview is recommended. The

application deadline for regular admission is February 15, for early decision plan 1 it is December 1, and for early decision plan 2 it is January 15.
Transfer Admission The application deadline for admission is June 1.
Entrance Difficulty The College of Wooster assesses its entrance difficulty level as moderately difficult. For the fall 2008 freshman class, 81 percent of the applicants were accepted.
For Further Information Contact Ms. Mary Karen Vellines, Vice President for Enrollment, The College of Wooster, 847 College Avenue, Wooster, OH 44691. *Phone:* 330-263-2270 Ext. 2118 or 800-877-9905 (toll-free). *Fax:* 330-263-2621. *E-mail:* admissions@wooster.edu. *Web site:* http://www.wooster.edu/.

COLUMBUS COLLEGE OF ART & DESIGN

Columbus, Ohio

Columbus College of Art & Design is a coed, private, four-year college, founded in 1879, offering degrees at the bachelor's level. It has a 10-acre campus in Columbus.

Academic Information The faculty has 183 members (43% full-time), 43% with terminal degrees. The student-faculty ratio is 12:1. The library holds 54,671 titles, 260 serial subscriptions, and 2,128 audiovisual materials. Special programs include academic remediation, services for learning-disabled students, advanced placement credit, ESL programs, double majors, independent study, summer session for credit, part-time degree programs (daytime, evenings, summer), internships, and arrangement for off-campus study with members of the Higher Education Council of Columbus. The most frequently chosen baccalaureate field is visual and performing arts.
Student Body Statistics The student body is made up of 1,599 undergraduates (169 freshmen). 60 percent are women and 40 percent are men. Students come from 40 states and territories and 17 other countries. 80 percent are from Ohio. 4 percent are international students.
Expenses for 2008–09 *Application fee:* $25. *Comprehensive fee:* $30,314 includes full-time tuition ($22,920), mandatory fees ($644), and college room and board ($6750). *Part-time tuition:* $955 per credit hour. *Part-time mandatory fees:* $322 per term.
Financial Aid Forms of aid include need-based and non-need-based scholarships and part-time jobs. The average aided 2008–09 undergraduate received an aid package worth an estimated $16,723. The priority application deadline for financial aid is February 16.
Freshman Admission Columbus College of Art & Design requires an essay, a high school transcript, a minimum 2.0 high school GPA, 1 recommendation, a portfolio, SAT or ACT scores, and TOEFL scores for international students. An interview is recommended. The application deadline for regular admission is rolling.
Transfer Admission The application deadline for admission is rolling.
Entrance Difficulty Columbus College of Art & Design assesses its entrance difficulty level as moderately difficult. For the fall 2008 freshman class, 72 percent of the applicants were accepted.
For Further Information Contact Mr. Thomas E. Green, Director of Admissions, Columbus College of Art & Design, 107 North Ninth Street, Columbus, OH 43215-1758. *Phone:* 614-224-9101 or 877-997-2223 (toll-free). *Fax:* 614-232-8344. *E-mail:* admissions@ccad.edu. *Web site:* http://www.ccad.edu/.

DAVID N. MYERS UNIVERSITY

See Chancellor University.

DEFIANCE COLLEGE

Defiance, Ohio

Defiance College is a coed, private, comprehensive institution, founded in 1850, affiliated with the United Church of Christ, offering degrees at the associate, bachelor's, and master's levels. It has a 150-acre campus in Defiance near Toledo.

Academic Information The faculty has 101 members (44% full-time), 33% with terminal degrees. The undergraduate student-faculty ratio is 12:1. The library holds 182,812 titles, 7,673 serial subscriptions, and 3,336 audiovisual materials. Special programs include academic remediation, services for learning-disabled students, an honors program, cooperative (work-study) education, advanced placement credit, double majors, independent study, distance learning, self-designed majors, summer session for credit, part-time degree programs (daytime, evenings, weekends, summer), adult/continuing education programs, internships, and arrangement for off-campus study with Bowling Green State University. The most frequently chosen baccalaureate fields are business/marketing, education, security and protective services.
Student Body Statistics The student body totals 1,001, of whom 892 are undergraduates (221 freshmen). 53 percent are women and 47 percent are men. Students come from 14 states and territories and 2 other countries. 84 percent are from Ohio.
Expenses for 2009–10 *Application fee:* $25. *One-time mandatory fee:* $75. *Comprehensive fee:* $30,645 includes full-time tuition ($22,375), mandatory fees ($520), and college room and board ($7750). *College room only:* $4235. *Part-time tuition:* $360 per credit hour. *Part-time mandatory fees:* $70 per term.
Financial Aid Forms of aid include need-based and non-need-based scholarships and part-time jobs. The average aided 2008–09 undergraduate received an aid package worth an estimated $18,117.
Freshman Admission Defiance College requires a high school transcript, a minimum 2.25 high school GPA, SAT or ACT scores, and TOEFL scores for international students. Recommendations and an interview are recommended. An essay and an interview are required for some. The application deadline for regular admission is August 15.
Transfer Admission The application deadline for admission is August 15.
Entrance Difficulty Defiance College assesses its entrance difficulty level as moderately difficult. For the fall 2008 freshman class, 73 percent of the applicants were accepted.
For Further Information Contact Mr. Brad Harsha, Director of Admissions, Defiance College, 701 North Clinton Street, Defiance, OH 43512-1610. *Phone:* 419-783-2365 or 800-520-4632 Ext. 2359 (toll-free). *Fax:* 419-783-2468. *E-mail:* admissions@defiance.edu. *Web site:* http://www.defiance.edu/.

DENISON UNIVERSITY

Granville, Ohio

Denison University is a coed, private, four-year college, founded in 1831, offering degrees at the bachelor's level. It has a 900-acre campus in Granville near Columbus.

Academic Information The faculty has 218 members (89% full-time), 91% with terminal degrees. The student-faculty ratio is 10:1. The library holds 767,118 titles, 6,616 serial subscriptions, and 32,745 audiovisual materials. Special programs include services for learning-disabled students, an honors program, cooperative (work-study) education, study abroad, advanced placement credit, double majors, independent study, self-designed majors, part-time degree programs (daytime), internships, and arrangement for off-campus study with American University, Great Lakes Colleges Association, Marine Science Consortium. The most frequently chosen baccalaureate fields are biological/life sciences, communications/journalism, social sciences.
Student Body Statistics The student body is made up of 2,200 undergraduates (605 freshmen). 56 percent are women and 44 percent are men. Students come from 50 states and territories and 27 other countries. 65 percent are from Ohio. 4.7 percent are international students.
Expenses for 2008–09 *Application fee:* $40. *Comprehensive fee:* $43,910 includes full-time tuition ($34,410), mandatory fees ($890), and college room and board ($8610). *College room only:* $4890. Room and board charges vary according to housing facility. *Part-time tuition:* $1080 per semester hour. Part-time tuition varies according to course load.
Financial Aid Forms of aid include need-based scholarships and part-time jobs. The average aided 2008–09 undergraduate received an aid package worth an estimated $30,099. The priority application deadline for financial aid is February 15.
Freshman Admission Denison University requires an essay, a high school transcript, and 2 recommendations. An interview and TOEFL scores for international students are recommended. SAT or ACT scores are required for some. The application deadline for regular admission is January 15 and for early decision it is December 1.

Denison University (continued)

Transfer Admission The application deadline for admission is June 1.
Entrance Difficulty Denison University assesses its entrance difficulty level as very difficult; moderately difficult for transfers. For the fall 2008 freshman class, 38 percent of the applicants were accepted.
For Further Information Contact Mr. Perry Robinson, Director of Admissions, Denison University, Box H, Granville, OH 43023. *Phone:* 740-587-6276 or 800-DENISON (toll-free). *Fax:* 740-587-6306. *E-mail:* admissions@denison.edu. *Web site:* http://www.denison.edu/.

DeVry University

Cleveland, Ohio

http://www.devry.edu/

DeVry University

Columbus, Ohio

DeVry University is a coed, proprietary, comprehensive unit of DeVry University, founded in 1952, offering degrees at the associate, bachelor's, and master's levels. It has a 21-acre campus in Columbus.

Academic Information The faculty has 236 members (19% full-time). The undergraduate student-faculty ratio is 18:1. The library holds 30,000 titles and 5,892 serial subscriptions. Special programs include academic remediation, services for learning-disabled students, advanced placement credit, accelerated degree programs, distance learning, summer session for credit, part-time degree programs (daytime, evenings, weekends, summer), and adult/continuing education programs. The most frequently chosen baccalaureate fields are business/marketing, computer and information sciences, engineering technologies.
Student Body Statistics The student body totals 2,776, of whom 2,526 are undergraduates (462 freshmen). 41 percent are women and 59 percent are men. 98 percent are from Ohio. 0.1 percent are international students.
Expenses for 2009–10 *Application fee:* $50. *Tuition:* $14,080 full-time, $550 per credit hour part-time.
Financial Aid Forms of aid include need-based scholarships and part-time jobs. The average aided 2007–08 undergraduate received an aid package worth $14,130. The application deadline for financial aid is continuous.
Freshman Admission DeVry University requires a high school transcript, an interview, and TOEFL scores for international students. The application deadline for regular admission is rolling.
Transfer Admission The application deadline for admission is rolling.
Entrance Difficulty DeVry University assesses its entrance difficulty level as minimally difficult; moderately difficult for electronics engineering technology program.
For Further Information Contact Admissions Office, DeVry University, 1350 Alum Creek Drive, Columbus, OH 43209-2705. *Phone:* 614-253-7291. *Web site:* http://www.devry.edu/.

DeVry University

Seven Hills, Ohio

http://www.devry.edu/

Franciscan University of Steubenville

Steubenville, Ohio

Franciscan University of Steubenville is a coed, private, Roman Catholic, comprehensive institution, founded in 1946, offering degrees at the associate, bachelor's, and master's levels. It has a 124-acre campus in Steubenville near Pittsburgh.

Academic Information The faculty has 214 members (53% full-time), 54% with terminal degrees. The undergraduate student-faculty ratio is 15:1. The library holds 410 serial subscriptions. Special programs include services for learning-disabled students, an honors program, study abroad, advanced placement credit, accelerated degree programs, double majors, independent study, distance learning, summer session for credit, part-time degree programs (daytime, evenings, summer), and internships. The most frequently chosen baccalaureate fields are health professions and related sciences, business/marketing, theology and religious vocations.
Student Body Statistics The student body totals 2,449, of whom 2,049 are undergraduates (389 freshmen). 60 percent are women and 40 percent are men. Students come from 51 states and territories and 13 other countries. 22 percent are from Ohio. 0.8 percent are international students.
Expenses for 2009–10 *Application fee:* $20. *Comprehensive fee:* $26,400 includes full-time tuition ($19,250), mandatory fees ($400), and college room and board ($6750). *Part-time tuition:* $645 per credit hour. *Part-time mandatory fees:* $15 per credit hour.
Financial Aid Forms of aid include need-based and non-need-based scholarships and part-time jobs. The average aided 2008–09 undergraduate received an aid package worth an estimated $11,754. The priority application deadline for financial aid is April 15.
Freshman Admission Franciscan University of Steubenville requires an essay, a high school transcript, a minimum 2.4 high school GPA, SAT or ACT scores, and TOEFL scores for international students. An interview is recommended. The application deadline for regular admission is rolling.
Transfer Admission The application deadline for admission is rolling.
Entrance Difficulty Franciscan University of Steubenville assesses its entrance difficulty level as moderately difficult. For the fall 2008 freshman class, 72 percent of the applicants were accepted.
For Further Information Contact Mrs. Margaret Weber, Director of Admissions, Franciscan University of Steubenville, 1235 University Boulevard, Steubenville, OH 43952-1763. *Phone:* 740-283-6226 or 800-783-6220 (toll-free). *Fax:* 740-284-5456. *E-mail:* admissions@franciscan.edu. *Web site:* http://www.franciscan.edu/.

Franklin University

Columbus, Ohio

Franklin University is a coed, private, comprehensive institution, founded in 1902, offering degrees at the associate, bachelor's, and master's levels and post-master's certificates. It has a 14-acre campus in Columbus.

Academic Information The library holds 27,547 titles, 15,290 serial subscriptions, and 246 audiovisual materials. Special programs include academic remediation, services for learning-disabled students, cooperative (work-study) education, study abroad, advanced placement credit, accelerated degree programs, ESL programs, independent study, distance learning, self-designed majors, summer session for credit, part-time degree programs (daytime, evenings, weekends, summer), adult/continuing education programs, internships, and arrangement for off-campus study with members of the Higher Education Council of Columbus.
Student Body Statistics The student body totals 7,559, of whom 6,729 are undergraduates.
Expenses for 2008–09 *Application fee:* $0. *Tuition:* $8400 full-time, $280 per credit hour part-time. Both full-time and part-time tuition varies according to program.
Financial Aid Forms of aid include need-based and non-need-based scholarships and part-time jobs. The priority application deadline for financial aid is June 15.
Freshman Admission Franklin University requires TOEFL scores for international students. A high school transcript is required for some. The application deadline for regular admission is rolling.
Transfer Admission The application deadline for admission is rolling.
Entrance Difficulty Franklin University has an open admission policy except for international students. It assesses its entrance difficulty as moderately difficult for international students.
For Further Information Contact Mr. Tracy Austin, Chief Student Officer, Franklin University, 201 South Grant Avenue, Columbus, OH 43215. *Phone:* 614-797-4700 or 877-341-6300 (toll-free). *Fax:* 614-224-8027. *E-mail:* info@franklin.edu. *Web site:* http://www.franklin.edu/.

GALLIPOLIS CAREER COLLEGE

Gallipolis, Ohio

Gallipolis Career College is a coed, primarily women's, private, two-year college, founded in 1962, offering degrees at the associate level.

Expenses for 2008–09 *Application fee:* $50. *Tuition:* $9600 full-time, $200 per credit part-time. *Mandatory fees:* $100 full-time, $100 per year part-time.
For Further Information Contact Mr. Jack Henson, Director of Admissions, Gallipolis Career College, 1176 Jackson Pike, Suite 312, Gallipolis, OH 45631. *Phone:* 740-446-4367 or 800-214-0452 (toll-free). *Fax:* 740-446-4124. *E-mail:* admissions@gallipoliscareercollege.com. *Web site:* http://www.gallipoliscareercollege.com/.

GOD'S BIBLE SCHOOL AND COLLEGE

Cincinnati, Ohio

http://www.gbs.edu/

HEIDELBERG UNIVERSITY

Tiffin, Ohio

Heidelberg University is a coed, private, comprehensive institution, founded in 1850, affiliated with the United Church of Christ, offering degrees at the bachelor's and master's levels. It has a 115-acre campus in Tiffin.

Academic Information The faculty has 154 members (40% full-time), 49% with terminal degrees. The undergraduate student-faculty ratio is 14:1. Special programs include academic remediation, services for learning-disabled students, an honors program, study abroad, advanced placement credit, accelerated degree programs, ESL programs, double majors, independent study, summer session for credit, part-time degree programs (daytime, evenings, weekends, summer), adult/continuing education programs, internships, and arrangement for off-campus study with members of the East Central College Consortium. The most frequently chosen baccalaureate fields are business/marketing, education, parks and recreation.
Student Body Statistics The student body totals 1,519, of whom 1,371 are undergraduates (402 freshmen). 48 percent are women and 52 percent are men. Students come from 25 states and territories and 14 other countries. 90 percent are from Ohio. 2.9 percent are international students.
Expenses for 2009–10 *Application fee:* $25. *Comprehensive fee:* $29,714 includes full-time tuition ($20,826), mandatory fees ($504), and college room and board ($8384). *College room only:* $3968. *Part-time tuition:* $504 per semester hour.
Financial Aid Forms of aid include need-based and non-need-based scholarships and part-time jobs. The average aided 2008–09 undergraduate received an aid package worth an estimated $17,223. The priority application deadline for financial aid is March 1.
Freshman Admission Heidelberg University requires a high school transcript, a minimum 2.5 high school GPA, and SAT or ACT scores. An essay, an interview, and TOEFL scores for international students are recommended. The application deadline for regular admission is August 15 and for nonresidents it is August 15.
Transfer Admission The application deadline for admission is August 15.
Entrance Difficulty Heidelberg University assesses its entrance difficulty level as moderately difficult. For the fall 2008 freshman class, 73 percent of the applicants were accepted.
For Further Information Contact Ms. Lindsay Sooy, Director of Admission, Heidelberg University, 310 East Market Street, Tiffin, OH 44883. *Phone:* 419-448-2330 or 800-434-3352 (toll-free). *Fax:* 419-448-2334. *E-mail:* adminfo@heidelberg.edu. *Web site:* http://www.heidelberg.edu/.

HIRAM COLLEGE

Hiram, Ohio

Hiram College is a coed, private, comprehensive institution, founded in 1850, affiliated with the Christian Church (Disciples of Christ), offering degrees at the bachelor's and master's levels. It has a 110-acre campus in Hiram near Cleveland.

Academic Information The faculty has 127 members (58% full-time), 64% with terminal degrees. The undergraduate student-faculty ratio is 12:1. The library holds 187,451 titles, 3,993 serial subscriptions, and 10,351 audiovisual materials. Special programs include services for learning-disabled students, study abroad, advanced placement credit, ESL programs, double majors, independent study, self-designed majors, summer session for credit, part-time degree programs (weekends), adult/continuing education programs, internships, and arrangement for off-campus study. The most frequently chosen baccalaureate fields are business/marketing, biological/life sciences, social sciences.
Student Body Statistics The student body totals 1,360, of whom 1,335 are undergraduates (339 freshmen). 54 percent are women and 46 percent are men. Students come from 29 states and territories and 19 other countries. 87 percent are from Ohio. 5.4 percent are international students.
Expenses for 2008–09 *Application fee:* $0. *Comprehensive fee:* $33,540 includes full-time tuition ($24,490), mandatory fees ($670), and college room and board ($8380). *College room only:* $4190. Full-time tuition and fees vary according to student level. Room and board charges vary according to housing facility. *Part-time tuition:* $375 per credit hour.
Financial Aid Forms of aid include need-based and non-need-based scholarships and part-time jobs. The priority application deadline for financial aid is February 15.
Freshman Admission Hiram College requires an essay, a high school transcript, SAT or ACT scores, and TOEFL scores for international students. 3 recommendations and an interview are recommended. An interview is required for some. The application deadline for regular admission is April 1.
Transfer Admission The application deadline for admission is July 15.
Entrance Difficulty Hiram College assesses its entrance difficulty level as moderately difficult. For the fall 2008 freshman class, 75 percent of the applicants were accepted.
For Further Information Contact Mr. Sherman C. Dean II, Director of Admission, Hiram College, PO Box 96, Hiram, OH 44234. *Phone:* 330-569-5169 or 800-362-5280 (toll-free). *Fax:* 330-569-5944. *E-mail:* admission@hiram.edu. *Web site:* http://www.hiram.edu/.

JOHN CARROLL UNIVERSITY

University Heights, Ohio

John Carroll University is a coed, private, Roman Catholic (Jesuit), comprehensive institution, founded in 1886, offering degrees at the bachelor's and master's levels. It has a 60-acre campus in University Heights near Cleveland.

Academic Information The faculty has 385 members (55% full-time), 66% with terminal degrees. The undergraduate student-faculty ratio is 15:1. The library holds 620,000 titles, 2,198 serial subscriptions, and 5,820 audiovisual materials. Special programs include services for learning-disabled students, an honors program, cooperative (work-study) education, study abroad, advanced placement credit, accelerated degree programs, double majors, independent study, self-designed majors, summer session for credit, part-time degree programs, adult/continuing education programs, internships, and arrangement for off-campus study with Northeast Ohio Commission on Higher Education. The most frequently chosen baccalaureate fields are business/marketing, psychology, social sciences.
Student Body Statistics The student body totals 3,826, of whom 3,117 are undergraduates (792 freshmen). 51 percent are women and 49 percent are men. Students come from 34 states and territories and 7 other countries. 72 percent are from Ohio.
Expenses for 2009–10 *Application fee:* $0. *One-time mandatory fee:* $325. *Comprehensive fee:* $37,170 includes full-time tuition ($27,940), mandatory fees ($900), and college room and board ($8330). *College room only:* $4420. *Part-time tuition:* $873 per credit hour.

John Carroll University (continued)

Financial Aid Forms of aid include need-based and non-need-based scholarships and part-time jobs. The average aided 2008–09 undergraduate received an aid package worth an estimated $21,262. The application deadline for financial aid is March 15 with a priority deadline of February 15.
Freshman Admission John Carroll University requires an essay, a high school transcript, 1 recommendation, SAT or ACT scores, and TOEFL scores for international students. An interview is required for some. The application deadline for regular admission is February 1.
Transfer Admission The application deadline for admission is rolling.
Entrance Difficulty John Carroll University assesses its entrance difficulty level as moderately difficult. For the fall 2008 freshman class, 80 percent of the applicants were accepted.
For Further Information Contact Mr. Thomas P. Fanning, Director of Admission, John Carroll University, 20700 North Park Boulevard, University Heights, OH 44118. *Phone:* 216-397-4246. *Fax:* 216-397-4981. *E-mail:* tfanning@jcu.edu. *Web site:* http://www.jcu.edu/.

KENT STATE UNIVERSITY

Kent, Ohio

Kent State University is a coed, public unit of Kent State University System, founded in 1910, offering degrees at the bachelor's, master's, and doctoral levels and post-master's and postbachelor's certificates. It has a 1,347-acre campus in Kent near Cleveland.

Academic Information The faculty has 1,569 members (58% full-time). The undergraduate student-faculty ratio is 22:1. The library holds 2 million titles, 12,000 serial subscriptions, and 15,578 audiovisual materials. Special programs include academic remediation, services for learning-disabled students, an honors program, cooperative (work-study) education, study abroad, advanced placement credit, accelerated degree programs, Freshman Honors College, ESL programs, double majors, independent study, distance learning, self-designed majors, summer session for credit, part-time degree programs (daytime, evenings, weekends, summer), external degree programs, adult/continuing education programs, internships, and arrangement for off-campus study with Cuyahoga Community College, Lorain County Community College, Lakeland Community College. The most frequently chosen baccalaureate fields are business/marketing, education, health professions and related sciences.
Student Body Statistics The student body totals 22,923, of whom 18,131 are undergraduates (3,764 freshmen). 59 percent are women and 41 percent are men. Students come from 43 states and territories and 57 other countries. 90 percent are from Ohio.
Expenses for 2008–09 *Application fee:* $30. *State resident tuition:* $8430 full-time, $384 per credit hour part-time. *Nonresident tuition:* $15,862 full-time, $722 per credit hour part-time. Both full-time and part-time tuition varies according to course level, course load, degree level, program, and reciprocity agreements. *College room and board:* $7200. *College room only:* $4410. Room and board charges vary according to board plan and housing facility.
Financial Aid Forms of aid include need-based and non-need-based scholarships, athletic grants, and part-time jobs. The average aided 2008–09 undergraduate received an aid package worth an estimated $7895. The priority application deadline for financial aid is March 1.
Freshman Admission Kent State University requires a high school transcript, a minimum 2.5 high school GPA, SAT or ACT scores, and TOEFL scores for international students. The application deadline for regular admission is rolling.
Transfer Admission The application deadline for admission is rolling.
Entrance Difficulty Kent State University assesses its entrance difficulty level as moderately difficult; minimally difficult for transfers; very difficult for architecture, 6-year medical program. For the fall 2008 freshman class, 74 percent of the applicants were accepted.
For Further Information Contact Mr. Christopher Buttenschon, Assistant Director of Admissions, Kent State University, 161 Michael Schwartz Center, Kent, OH 44242-0001. *Phone:* 330-672-2444 or 800-988-KENT (toll-free). *Fax:* 330-672-2499. *E-mail:* admissions@kent.edu. *Web site:* http://www.kent.edu/.

See page 242 for the Close-Up.

KENT STATE UNIVERSITY, ASHTABULA CAMPUS

Ashtabula, Ohio

http://www.ashtabula.kent.edu/

KENT STATE UNIVERSITY, GEAUGA CAMPUS

Burton, Ohio

Kent State University, Geauga Campus is a coed, public, primarily two-year college of Kent State University System, founded in 1964, offering degrees at the associate, bachelor's, and master's levels. It has an 87-acre campus in Burton near Cleveland.

Expenses for 2008–09 *Application fee:* $30. *State resident tuition:* $4770 full-time, $217 per credit hour part-time. *Nonresident tuition:* $12,202 full-time, $555 per credit hour part-time. Both full-time and part-time tuition varies according to course level.
For Further Information Contact Carolyn O'Lenic, Kent State University, Geauga Campus, 14111 Claridon-Troy Road, Burton, OH 44021. *Phone:* 440-834-4187. *Fax:* 440-834-8846. *E-mail:* colenic@kent.edu. *Web site:* http://www.geauga.kent.edu/.

KENT STATE UNIVERSITY, SALEM CAMPUS

Salem, Ohio

Kent State University, Salem Campus is a coed, public, primarily two-year college of Kent State University System, founded in 1966, offering degrees at the associate and bachelor's levels (also offers some upper-level and graduate courses). It has a 98-acre campus in Salem.

Academic Information The library holds 19,000 titles, 163 serial subscriptions, and 158 audiovisual materials. Special programs include academic remediation, services for learning-disabled students, an honors program, advanced placement credit, Freshman Honors College, distance learning, summer session for credit, part-time degree programs (daytime, evenings, weekends), adult/continuing education programs, and internships.
Student Body Statistics The student body is made up of 1,268 undergraduates.
Expenses for 2008–09 *Application fee:* $30. *State resident tuition:* $4770 full-time, $217 per credit hour part-time. *Nonresident tuition:* $12,202 full-time, $555 per credit hour part-time.
Financial Aid Forms of aid include need-based scholarships and part-time jobs. The priority application deadline for financial aid is March 1.
Freshman Admission Kent State University, Salem Campus requires a high school transcript and TOEFL scores for international students. An essay, recommendations, and ACT scores are required for some. The application deadline for regular admission is rolling.
Transfer Admission The application deadline for admission is rolling.
Entrance Difficulty Kent State University, Salem Campus has an open admission policy except for radiological technology, human services programs, and honors program. It assesses its entrance difficulty as very difficult for radiological technology, human services programs.
For Further Information Contact Mrs. Judy Heisler, Admissions Secretary, Kent State University, Salem Campus, 2491 State Route 45 South, Salem, OH 44460-9412. *Phone:* 330-332-0361 Ext. 74201. *E-mail:* ask-us@salem.kent.edu. *Web site:* http://www.salem.kent.edu/.

KENT STATE UNIVERSITY, STARK CAMPUS

Canton, Ohio

Kent State University, Stark Campus is a coed, public, comprehensive unit of Kent State University System, founded in 1967, offering degrees at the associate, bachelor's, and master's levels (also offers some graduate courses). It has a 200-acre campus in Canton near Cleveland.

Academic Information The faculty has 213 members (46% full-time). The undergraduate student-faculty ratio is 29:1. The library holds 81,962 titles, 231 serial subscriptions, and 3,590 audiovisual materials. Special programs include academic remediation, services for learning-disabled students, an honors program, study abroad, advanced placement credit, Freshman Honors College, ESL programs, double majors, independent study, distance learning, self-designed majors, summer session for credit, part-time degree programs (daytime, evenings, weekends, summer), adult/continuing education programs, internships, and arrangement for off-campus study with Stark State College of Technology.
Student Body Statistics The student body totals 3,939, of whom 3,872 are undergraduates (695 freshmen). 61 percent are women and 39 percent are men.
Expenses for 2008–09 *Application fee:* $30. *State resident tuition:* $4770 full-time, $217 per credit hour part-time. *Nonresident tuition:* $12,202 full-time, $555 per credit hour part-time. Both full-time and part-time tuition varies according to course level and course load.
Financial Aid Forms of aid include need-based scholarships and part-time jobs. The priority application deadline for financial aid is March 1.
Freshman Admission Kent State University, Stark Campus requires a high school transcript and TOEFL scores for international students. SAT or ACT scores are required for some. The application deadline for regular admission is rolling.
Transfer Admission The application deadline for admission is rolling.
Entrance Difficulty Kent State University, Stark Campus has an open admission policy.
For Further Information Contact Ms. Deborah Ann Speck, Director of Admissions, Kent State University, Stark Campus, 6000 Frank Avenue NW, Canton, OH 44720-7599. *Phone:* 330-499-9600 Ext. 53259. *Fax:* 330-499-0301. *E-mail:* admit@stark.kent.edu. *Web site:* http://www.stark.kent.edu/.

KENT STATE UNIVERSITY, TRUMBULL CAMPUS

Warren, Ohio

Kent State University, Trumbull Campus is a coed, public, primarily two-year college of Kent State University System, founded in 1954, offering degrees at the associate and bachelor's levels (also offers some upper-level and graduate courses). It has a 200-acre campus in Warren near Cleveland.

Expenses for 2008–09 *Application fee:* $30. *State resident tuition:* $4770 full-time, $217 per credit hour part-time. *Nonresident tuition:* $12,202 full-time, $555 per credit hour part-time. Both full-time and part-time tuition varies according to course level.
For Further Information Contact Linda Collins, Clerical Specialist, Kent State University, Trumbull Campus, 4314 Mahoning Avenue NW, Warren, OH 44483. *Phone:* 330-675-8967. *Fax:* 330-675-8855. *E-mail:* lscollin@kent.edu. *Web site:* http://www.trumbull.kent.edu/.

KENT STATE UNIVERSITY, TUSCARAWAS CAMPUS

New Philadelphia, Ohio

http://www.tusc.kent.edu/

KENYON COLLEGE

Gambier, Ohio

Kenyon College is a coed, private, four-year college, founded in 1824, offering degrees at the bachelor's level. It has a 1,200-acre campus in Gambier near Columbus.

Academic Information The faculty has 188 members (81% full-time), 91% with terminal degrees. The student-faculty ratio is 10:1. The library holds 1 million titles, 10,958 serial subscriptions, and 20,308 audiovisual materials. Special programs include services for learning-disabled students, an honors program, study abroad, advanced placement credit, accelerated degree programs, double majors, independent study, self-designed majors, internships, and arrangement for off-campus study. The most frequently chosen baccalaureate fields are English, social sciences, visual and performing arts.
Student Body Statistics The student body is made up of 1,644 undergraduates (456 freshmen). 53 percent are women and 47 percent are men. Students come from 47 states and territories and 30 other countries. 18 percent are from Ohio. 4 percent are international students.
Expenses for 2009–10 *Application fee:* $50. *Comprehensive fee:* $48,240 includes full-time tuition ($39,810), mandatory fees ($1170), and college room and board ($7260).
Financial Aid Forms of aid include need-based and non-need-based scholarships and part-time jobs. The average aided 2008–09 undergraduate received an aid package worth an estimated $30,181. The priority application deadline for financial aid is February 15.
Freshman Admission Kenyon College requires an essay, a high school transcript, counselor recommendation, SAT or ACT scores, and TOEFL scores for international students. A minimum 3.5 high school GPA, 2 recommendations, and an interview are recommended. The application deadline for regular admission is January 15, for early decision plan 1 it is November 15, and for early decision plan 2 it is January 15.
Transfer Admission The application deadline for admission is April 1.
Entrance Difficulty Kenyon College assesses its entrance difficulty level as very difficult. For the fall 2008 freshman class, 31 percent of the applicants were accepted.
For Further Information Contact Ms. Jennifer Delahunty, Dean of Admissions, Kenyon College, Ransom Hall, Gambier, OH 43022. *Phone:* 740-427-5778 or 800-848-2468 (toll-free). *Fax:* 740-427-5770. *E-mail:* admissions@kenyon.edu. *Web site:* http://www.kenyon.edu/.

KETTERING COLLEGE OF MEDICAL ARTS

Kettering, Ohio

Kettering College of Medical Arts is a coed, primarily women's, private, Seventh-day Adventist, comprehensive institution, founded in 1967, offering degrees at the associate, bachelor's, and master's levels. It has a 35-acre campus in Kettering.

Expenses for 2008–09 *Application fee:* $25. *Comprehensive fee:* $15,810 includes full-time tuition ($9450), mandatory fees ($560), and college room and board ($5800). *College room only:* $2500. Full-time tuition and fees vary according to course load, degree level, and program. *Part-time tuition:* $315 per credit hour. *Part-time mandatory fees:* $240 per year. Part-time tuition and fees vary according to course load, degree level, and program.
For Further Information Contact Mrs. Becky McDonald, Director of Enrollment Services, Kettering College of Medical Arts, 3737 Southern Boulevard, Kettering, OH 45429-1299. *Phone:* 937-395-8628 or 800-433-5262 (toll-free). *Fax:* 937-296-4238. *Web site:* http://www.kcma.edu/.

LAKE ERIE COLLEGE

Painesville, Ohio

Lake Erie College is a coed, private, comprehensive institution, founded in 1856, offering degrees at the bachelor's and master's levels and postbachelor's certificates. It has a 57-acre campus in Painesville near Cleveland.

Academic Information The faculty has 95 members (48% full-time), 54% with terminal degrees. The undergraduate student-faculty ratio is

Lake Erie College (continued)

14:1. The library holds 80,000 titles, 10,000 serial subscriptions, and 1,230 audiovisual materials. Special programs include academic remediation, services for learning-disabled students, an honors program, cooperative (work-study) education, study abroad, advanced placement credit, accelerated degree programs, Freshman Honors College, double majors, independent study, self-designed majors, summer session for credit, part-time degree programs (daytime, evenings, weekends, summer), adult/continuing education programs, internships, and arrangement for off-campus study with Northeast Ohio Commission on Higher Education. The most frequently chosen baccalaureate fields are agriculture, business/marketing, education.

Student Body Statistics The student body totals 1,054, of whom 837 are undergraduates (251 freshmen). 56 percent are women and 44 percent are men. Students come from 34 states and territories and 5 other countries. 84 percent are from Ohio. 0.9 percent are international students.

Expenses for 2009–10 *Application fee:* $30. *Comprehensive fee:* $33,368 includes full-time tuition ($23,950), mandatory fees ($1346), and college room and board ($8072). *College room only:* $4052. *Part-time tuition:* $655 per credit hour. *Part-time mandatory fees:* $47 per credit hour.

Financial Aid Forms of aid include need-based and non-need-based scholarships and part-time jobs. The application deadline for financial aid is continuous.

Freshman Admission Lake Erie College requires an essay, a high school transcript, a minimum 2.5 high school GPA, SAT or ACT scores, and TOEFL scores for international students. An interview is recommended.

Entrance Difficulty Lake Erie College assesses its entrance difficulty level as moderately difficult. For the fall 2008 freshman class, 62 percent of the applicants were accepted.

For Further Information Contact Mr. Eric Felver, Dean of Admissions and Financial Aid, Lake Erie College, 391 West Washington Street, Painesville, OH 44077-3389. *Phone:* 440-375-7050 or 800-916-0904 (toll-free). *Fax:* 440-375-7005. *E-mail:* admissions@lec.edu. *Web site:* http://www.lec.edu/.

LAURA AND ALVIN SIEGAL COLLEGE OF JUDAIC STUDIES

Beachwood, Ohio

Laura and Alvin Siegal College of Judaic Studies is a coed, private, comprehensive institution, founded in 1963, offering degrees at the bachelor's and master's levels. It has a 2-acre campus in Beachwood near Cleveland.

Academic Information The library holds 28,000 titles and 100 serial subscriptions. Special programs include cooperative (work-study) education, double majors, independent study, distance learning, summer session for credit, part-time degree programs, external degree programs, adult/continuing education programs, internships, and arrangement for off-campus study with John Carroll University, Ursuline College, Case Western Reserve University, Cleveland State University.

Student Body Statistics The student body totals 121, of whom 13 are undergraduates.

Financial Aid Forms of aid include need-based and non-need-based scholarships. The application deadline for financial aid is continuous.

Freshman Admission Laura and Alvin Siegal College of Judaic Studies requires an essay, a high school transcript, 2 recommendations, and an interview. The application deadline for regular admission is rolling.

Transfer Admission The application deadline for admission is rolling.

Entrance Difficulty Laura and Alvin Siegal College of Judaic Studies has an open admission policy.

For Further Information Contact Ms. Ruth Kronick, Director of Student Services, Laura and Alvin Siegal College of Judaic Studies, 26500 Shaker Boulevard, Beachwood, OH 44122-7116. *Phone:* 216-464-4050 or 888-336-2257 (toll-free). *Fax:* 216-464-5827. *E-mail:* admissions@siegalcollege.edu. *Web site:* http://www.siegalcollege.edu/.

LOURDES COLLEGE

Sylvania, Ohio

Lourdes College is a coed, private, Roman Catholic, comprehensive institution, founded in 1958, offering degrees at the associate, bachelor's, and master's levels and postbachelor's certificates. It has a 90-acre campus in Sylvania near Toledo.

Academic Information The faculty has 224 members (36% full-time), 29% with terminal degrees. The undergraduate student-faculty ratio is 11:1. The library holds 64,889 titles, 226 serial subscriptions, and 1,200 audiovisual materials. Special programs include academic remediation, services for learning-disabled students, cooperative (work-study) education, study abroad, advanced placement credit, double majors, independent study, distance learning, self-designed majors, summer session for credit, part-time degree programs (daytime, evenings, weekends, summer), adult/continuing education programs, and internships. The most frequently chosen baccalaureate fields are business/marketing, education, health professions and related sciences.

Student Body Statistics The student body totals 2,087, of whom 1,862 are undergraduates (140 freshmen). 81 percent are women and 19 percent are men. Students come from 3 states and territories. 91 percent are from Ohio. 0.1 percent are international students.

Expenses for 2008–09 *Application fee:* $25. *Tuition:* $12,930 full-time, $431 per credit hour part-time. *Mandatory fees:* $1800 full-time, $60 per credit hour part-time. Both full-time and part-time tuition and fees vary according to course load and location.

Financial Aid Forms of aid include need-based and non-need-based scholarships and part-time jobs. The average aided 2008–09 undergraduate received an aid package worth an estimated $11,202. The priority application deadline for financial aid is March 1.

Freshman Admission Lourdes College requires a high school transcript and TOEFL scores for international students. The application deadline for regular admission is rolling.

Transfer Admission The application deadline for admission is rolling.

Entrance Difficulty For the fall 2008 freshman class, 84 percent of the applicants were accepted.

For Further Information Contact Ms. Amy Mergen, Office of Admissions, Lourdes College, 6832 Convent Boulevard, Sylvania, OH 43560. *Phone:* 419-885-5291 or 800-878-3210 Ext. 1299 (toll-free). *Fax:* 419-882-3987. *E-mail:* lcadmits@lourdes.edu. *Web site:* http://www.lourdes.edu/.

MALONE UNIVERSITY

Canton, Ohio

Malone University is a coed, private, comprehensive institution, founded in 1892, affiliated with the Evangelical Friends Church–Eastern Region, offering degrees at the bachelor's and master's levels and postbachelor's certificates. It has a 78-acre campus in Canton near Cleveland.

Academic Information The faculty has 208 members (53% full-time), 47% with terminal degrees. The undergraduate student-faculty ratio is 14:1. The library holds 178,992 titles, 47,942 serial subscriptions, and 10,710 audiovisual materials. Special programs include academic remediation, services for learning-disabled students, an honors program, study abroad, advanced placement credit, accelerated degree programs, double majors, independent study, distance learning, self-designed majors, summer session for credit, part-time degree programs (daytime, evenings, summer), adult/continuing education programs, internships, and arrangement for off-campus study with members of the Christian College Consortium, Council for Christian Colleges and Universities. The most frequently chosen baccalaureate fields are business/marketing, education, health professions and related sciences.

Student Body Statistics The student body totals 2,442, of whom 2,033 are undergraduates (391 freshmen). 60 percent are women and 40 percent are men. Students come from 33 states and territories and 15 other countries. 87 percent are from Ohio. 1 percent are international students.

Expenses for 2009–10 *Application fee:* $20. *Comprehensive fee:* $28,180 includes full-time tuition ($20,730), mandatory fees ($350), and college room and board ($7100). *College room only:* $3620. *Part-time tuition:* $370 per credit hour. *Part-time mandatory fees:* $87.50 per term.

Financial Aid Forms of aid include need-based and non-need-based scholarships, athletic grants, and part-time jobs. The average aided 2008–09 undergraduate received an aid package worth an estimated $14,963. The application deadline for financial aid is July 31 with a priority deadline of March 1.
Freshman Admission Malone University requires a high school transcript, a minimum 2.0 high school GPA, 2 recommendations, SAT or ACT scores, and TOEFL scores for international students. An interview is recommended. An essay is required for some. The application deadline for regular admission is July 1.
Transfer Admission The application deadline for admission is July 1.
Entrance Difficulty Malone University assesses its entrance difficulty level as moderately difficult. For the fall 2008 freshman class, 71 percent of the applicants were accepted.
For Further Information Contact Mr. John Russell, Director of Admissions, Malone University, 2600 Cleveland Avenue NW, Canton, OH 44709-3897. *Phone:* 330-471-8145 or 800-521-1146 (toll-free). *Fax:* 330-471-8149. *E-mail:* admissions@malone.edu. *Web site:* http://www.malone.edu/.

MARIETTA COLLEGE

Marietta, Ohio

Marietta College is a coed, private, comprehensive institution, founded in 1835, offering degrees at the associate, bachelor's, and master's levels. It has a 120-acre campus in Marietta.

Academic Information The faculty has 145 members (71% full-time), 66% with terminal degrees. The undergraduate student-faculty ratio is 13:1. The library holds 246,706 titles, 28,188 serial subscriptions, and 6,147 audiovisual materials. Special programs include academic remediation, services for learning-disabled students, an honors program, study abroad, advanced placement credit, accelerated degree programs, ESL programs, double majors, independent study, self-designed majors, summer session for credit, part-time degree programs (daytime, evenings, summer), adult/continuing education programs, internships, and arrangement for off-campus study with American University, Stillman College, Central College, Institute of European Studies, Institute of Asian Studies. The most frequently chosen baccalaureate fields are business/marketing, communications/journalism, visual and performing arts.
Student Body Statistics The student body totals 1,602, of whom 1,485 are undergraduates (385 freshmen). 50 percent are women and 50 percent are men. Students come from 29 states and territories and 18 other countries. 67 percent are from Ohio. 9.1 percent are international students.
Expenses for 2008–09 *Application fee:* $25. *Comprehensive fee:* $33,844 includes full-time tuition ($25,430), mandatory fees ($650), and college room and board ($7764). *College room only:* $4244. Full-time tuition and fees vary according to course load and degree level. Room and board charges vary according to housing facility. *Part-time tuition:* $845 per credit hour. Part-time tuition varies according to course load and degree level.
Financial Aid Forms of aid include need-based and non-need-based scholarships and part-time jobs. The average aided 2008–09 undergraduate received an aid package worth an estimated $20,605. The priority application deadline for financial aid is March 1.
Freshman Admission Marietta College requires an essay, a high school transcript, a minimum 2.0 high school GPA, 1 recommendation, SAT or ACT scores, and TOEFL scores for international students. A minimum 3.0 high school GPA, an interview, and SAT Subject Test scores are recommended. The application deadline for regular admission is May 1.
Transfer Admission The application deadline for admission is rolling.
Entrance Difficulty Marietta College assesses its entrance difficulty level as moderately difficult. For the fall 2008 freshman class, 77 percent of the applicants were accepted.
For Further Information Contact Mr. Jason Turley, Director of Admission, Marietta College, 215 Fifth Street, Marietta, OH 45750. *Phone:* 740-376-4600 or 800-331-7896 (toll-free). *Fax:* 740-376-8888. *E-mail:* admit@marietta.edu. *Web site:* http://www.marietta.edu/.

THE MCGREGOR SCHOOL OF ANTIOCH UNIVERSITY

See Antioch University McGregor.

MEDCENTRAL COLLEGE OF NURSING

Mansfield, Ohio

MedCentral College of Nursing is a coed, primarily women's, private, four-year college, founded in 1996, offering degrees at the bachelor's level. It is located in Mansfield near Cleveland.

Academic Information Special programs include advanced placement credit, accelerated degree programs, independent study, part-time degree programs (daytime, evenings, weekends, summer), and adult/continuing education programs.
Student Body Statistics The student body is made up of 416 undergraduates.
Expenses for 2008–09 *Application fee:* $50. *Tuition:* $10,920 full-time, $350 per credit hour part-time. *Mandatory fees:* $500 full-time. *College room only:* $5130.
Freshman Admission MedCentral College of Nursing requires a high school transcript, a minimum 2.8 high school GPA, and SAT or ACT scores. A minimum 3.0 high school GPA is recommended. An essay and an interview are required for some. The application deadline for regular admission is August 1.
Transfer Admission The application deadline for admission is August 1.
Entrance Difficulty MedCentral College of Nursing assesses its entrance difficulty level as moderately difficult.
For Further Information Contact Student Services, MedCentral College of Nursing, 335 Glessner Avenue, Mansfield, OH 44903. *Phone:* 419-520-2600 or 877-656-4360 (toll-free). *Fax:* 419-520-2610. *E-mail:* admissions@medcentral.edu. *Web site:* http://www.medcentral.edu/.

MERCY COLLEGE OF NORTHWEST OHIO

Toledo, Ohio

Mercy College of Northwest Ohio is a coed, primarily women's, private, four-year college, founded in 1993, affiliated with the Roman Catholic Church, offering degrees at the associate and bachelor's levels. It is located in Toledo near Detroit.

Academic Information The faculty has 111 members (52% full-time), 18% with terminal degrees. The student-faculty ratio is 12:1. The library holds 8,797 titles, 171 serial subscriptions, and 591 audiovisual materials. Special programs include academic remediation, services for learning-disabled students, advanced placement credit, double majors, independent study, distance learning, summer session for credit, part-time degree programs (daytime, evenings, summer), and internships. The most frequently chosen baccalaureate field is health professions and related sciences.
Student Body Statistics The student body is made up of 921 undergraduates (68 freshmen). 86 percent are women and 14 percent are men. Students come from 4 states and territories. 77 percent are from Ohio.
Expenses for 2009–10 *Application fee:* $25. *One-time mandatory fee:* $15. *Tuition:* $9440 full-time, $326 per credit hour part-time. *Mandatory fees:* $650 full-time, $5 per credit hour part-time.
Financial Aid Forms of aid include need-based and non-need-based scholarships and part-time jobs. The average aided 2007–08 undergraduate received an aid package worth $8076. The application deadline for financial aid is continuous.
Freshman Admission Mercy College of Northwest Ohio requires a high school transcript. SAT or ACT scores are recommended. SAT or ACT scores are required for some. The application deadline for regular admission is rolling.
Transfer Admission The application deadline for admission is rolling.

Mercy College of Northwest Ohio (continued)

Entrance Difficulty Mercy College of Northwest Ohio assesses its entrance difficulty level as moderately difficult. For the fall 2008 freshman class, 74 percent of the applicants were accepted.

For Further Information Contact Admissions Counselor, Mercy College of Northwest Ohio, 2221 Madison Avenue, Toledo, OH 43604. *Phone:* 419-251-1313 or 888-80-Mercy (toll-free). *Fax:* 419-251-1462. *E-mail:* admissions@mercycollege.edu. *Web site:* http://www.mercycollege.edu/.

MIAMI UNIVERSITY

Oxford, Ohio

Miami University is a coed, public unit of Miami University System, founded in 1809, offering degrees at the associate, bachelor's, master's, and doctoral levels and post-master's certificates. It has a 2,000-acre campus in Oxford near Cincinnati.

Academic Information The faculty has 1,261 members (69% full-time), 69% with terminal degrees. The undergraduate student-faculty ratio is 16:1. The library holds 3 million titles and 14,089 serial subscriptions. Special programs include services for learning-disabled students, an honors program, cooperative (work-study) education, study abroad, advanced placement credit, double majors, independent study, self-designed majors, summer session for credit, adult/continuing education programs, internships, and arrangement for off-campus study with Greater Cincinnati Consortium of Colleges and Universities. The most frequently chosen baccalaureate fields are business/marketing, education, social sciences.

Student Body Statistics The student body totals 17,191, of whom 14,785 are undergraduates (3,609 freshmen). 54 percent are women and 46 percent are men. Students come from 51 states and territories and 46 other countries. 70 percent are from Ohio. 2.3 percent are international students.

Expenses for 2008–09 *Application fee:* $45. *State resident tuition:* $9721 full-time. *Nonresident tuition:* $23,605 full-time. *Mandatory fees:* $2166 full-time. *College room and board:* $8998. *College room only:* $4602. Room and board charges vary according to board plan and housing facility.

Financial Aid Forms of aid include need-based and non-need-based scholarships, athletic grants, and part-time jobs. The average aided 2008–09 undergraduate received an aid package worth an estimated $10,137.

Freshman Admission Miami University requires an essay, a high school transcript, 1 recommendation, SAT or ACT scores, and TOEFL scores for international students. An essay is recommended. The application deadline for regular admission is February 1, for early decision it is November 1, and for early action it is December 1.

Transfer Admission The application deadline for admission is June 1.

Entrance Difficulty Miami University assesses its entrance difficulty level as moderately difficult. For the fall 2008 freshman class, 80 percent of the applicants were accepted.

For Further Information Contact Laurie Koehler, Director of Undergraduate Admissions, Miami University, 301 South Campus Avenue, Oxford, OH 45056. *Phone:* 513-529-2531. *Fax:* 513-529-1550. *E-mail:* admission@muohio.edu. *Web site:* http://www.muohio.edu/.

MIAMI UNIVERSITY HAMILTON

Hamilton, Ohio

Miami University Hamilton is a coed, public, comprehensive unit of Miami University System, founded in 1968, offering degrees at the associate, bachelor's, and master's levels (degrees awarded by Miami University main campus). It has a 78-acre campus in Hamilton near Cincinnati.

Academic Information The faculty has 224 members (38% full-time). The undergraduate student-faculty ratio is 21:1. The library holds 68,000 titles and 400 serial subscriptions. Special programs include academic remediation, services for learning-disabled students, an honors program, cooperative (work-study) education, study abroad, advanced placement credit, ESL programs, double majors, distance learning, self-designed majors, summer session for credit, part-time degree programs (daytime, evenings, weekends, summer), adult/continuing education programs, and internships.

Student Body Statistics The student body totals 3,645, of whom 3,572 are undergraduates (796 freshmen). 54 percent are women and 46 percent are men.

Expenses for 2008–09 *Application fee:* $35. *State resident tuition:* $3948 full-time. *Nonresident tuition:* $8589 full-time. *Mandatory fees:* $402 full-time.

Financial Aid Forms of aid include need-based scholarships and part-time jobs. The priority application deadline for financial aid is February 15.

Freshman Admission Miami University Hamilton requires a high school transcript and TOEFL scores for international students. The application deadline for regular admission is rolling.

Transfer Admission The application deadline for admission is rolling.

Entrance Difficulty Miami University Hamilton has an open admission policy except for nursing program, transfer students. It assesses its entrance difficulty as minimally difficult for transfers; moderately difficult for nursing program.

For Further Information Contact Mr. Archie Nelson, Director of Admission and Financial Aid, Miami University Hamilton, 1601 University Boulevard, Hamilton, OH 45011-3399. *Phone:* 513-785-3111. *Fax:* 513-785-1807. *E-mail:* nelsona3@muohio.edu. *Web site:* http://www.ham.muohio.edu/.

MIAMI UNIVERSITY–MIDDLETOWN CAMPUS

Middletown, Ohio

Miami University–Middletown Campus is a coed, public, primarily two-year college of Miami University System, founded in 1966, offering degrees at the associate and bachelor's levels (also offers up to 2 years of most bachelor's degree programs offered at Miami University main campus). It has a 141-acre campus in Middletown near Cincinnati and Dayton.

Expenses for 2008–09 *Application fee:* $35. *State resident tuition:* $3948 full-time, $164.50 per credit hour part-time. *Nonresident tuition:* $17,579 full-time, $732.47 per credit hour part-time. *Mandatory fees:* $402 full-time, $15.25 per credit hour part-time, $18 per term part-time.

For Further Information Contact Diane Cantonwine, Assistant Director of Admission and Financial Aid, Miami University–Middletown Campus, 4200 East University Boulevard, Middletown, OH 45042. *Phone:* 513-727-3346 or 866-426-4643 (toll-free). *Fax:* 513-727-3223. *E-mail:* cantondm@muohio.edu. *Web site:* http://www.mid.muohio.edu/.

MOUNT CARMEL COLLEGE OF NURSING

Columbus, Ohio

Mount Carmel College of Nursing is a coed, primarily women's, private, comprehensive institution, founded in 1903, offering degrees at the bachelor's and master's levels and post-master's certificates.

Expenses for 2008–09 *Application fee:* $30. *One-time mandatory fee:* $225. *Tuition:* $14,336 full-time, $305 per semester hour part-time. *Mandatory fees:* $312 full-time, $312 per year part-time. Both full-time and part-time tuition and fees vary according to course load. *College room only:* $4500.

For Further Information Contact Kim Campbell, Director, Admissions and Recruitment, Mount Carmel College of Nursing, 127 South Davis Avenue, Columbus, OH 43222. *Phone:* 614-234-1085. *Fax:* 614-234-5427. *E-mail:* mccnadmissions@mchs.com. *Web site:* http://www.mccn.edu/.

MOUNT UNION COLLEGE

Alliance, Ohio

Mount Union College is a coed, private, United Methodist, four-year college, founded in 1846, offering degrees at the bachelor's level. It has a 115-acre campus in Alliance near Cleveland.

Academic Information The faculty has 232 members (54% full-time), 46% with terminal degrees. The student-faculty ratio is 13:1. The library

holds 225,620 titles, 52,896 serial subscriptions, and 6,061 audiovisual materials. Special programs include services for learning-disabled students, an honors program, cooperative (work-study) education, study abroad, advanced placement credit, accelerated degree programs, ESL programs, double majors, independent study, self-designed majors, summer session for credit, part-time degree programs (daytime, evenings, summer), adult/continuing education programs, internships, and arrangement for off-campus study with 6 members of the East Central College Consortium. The most frequently chosen baccalaureate fields are business/marketing, education, parks and recreation.

Student Body Statistics The student body is made up of 2,204 undergraduates (663 freshmen). 50 percent are women and 50 percent are men. Students come from 27 states and territories and 18 other countries. 90 percent are from Ohio. 2.7 percent are international students.

Expenses for 2008–09 *Application fee:* $0. *Comprehensive fee:* $30,170 includes full-time tuition ($22,870), mandatory fees ($250), and college room and board ($7050). Room and board charges vary according to board plan and housing facility. *Part-time tuition:* $965 per credit hour. *Part-time mandatory fees:* $50 per term.

Financial Aid Forms of aid include need-based and non-need-based scholarships and part-time jobs. The average aided 2007–08 undergraduate received an aid package worth $17,712. The application deadline for financial aid is continuous.

Freshman Admission Mount Union College requires an essay, a high school transcript, a minimum 2.0 high school GPA, 1 recommendation, SAT or ACT scores, and TOEFL scores for international students. An interview is recommended. The application deadline for regular admission is rolling.

Transfer Admission The application deadline for admission is rolling.

Entrance Difficulty Mount Union College assesses its entrance difficulty level as moderately difficult. For the fall 2008 freshman class, 77 percent of the applicants were accepted.

For Further Information Contact Mr. Vincent Heslop, Director of Enrollment Technology, Mount Union College, 1972 Clark Avenue, Alliance, OH 44601. *Phone:* 330-823-2590, 800-334-6682 (toll-free in-state), or 800-992-6682 (toll-free out-of-state). *Fax:* 330-823-5097. *E-mail:* admission@muc.edu. *Web site:* http://www.muc.edu/.

MOUNT VERNON NAZARENE UNIVERSITY

Mount Vernon, Ohio

Mount Vernon Nazarene University is a coed, private, Nazarene, comprehensive institution, founded in 1964, offering degrees at the associate, bachelor's, and master's levels. It has a 401-acre campus in Mount Vernon near Columbus.

Academic Information The faculty has 271 members (44% full-time), 39% with terminal degrees. The undergraduate student-faculty ratio is 13.6:1. The library holds 140,093 titles, 7,541 serial subscriptions, and 6,397 audiovisual materials. Special programs include academic remediation, services for learning-disabled students, an honors program, study abroad, advanced placement credit, double majors, independent study, distance learning, summer session for credit, part-time degree programs (evenings), adult/continuing education programs, internships, and arrangement for off-campus study with Kenyon College, Capital University, Coalition for Christian Colleges and Universities. The most frequently chosen baccalaureate fields are business/marketing, education, visual and performing arts.

Student Body Statistics The student body totals 2,558, of whom 2,090 are undergraduates (368 freshmen). 60 percent are women and 40 percent are men. Students come from 26 states and territories and 5 other countries. 92 percent are from Ohio. 0.5 percent are international students.

Expenses for 2009–10 *Application fee:* $25. *Comprehensive fee:* $26,470 includes full-time tuition ($19,980), mandatory fees ($600), and college room and board ($5890). *College room only:* $3290. *Part-time tuition:* $713 per semester hour. *Part-time mandatory fees:* $20 per semester hour.

Financial Aid Forms of aid include need-based and non-need-based scholarships, athletic grants, and part-time jobs. The average aided 2008–09 undergraduate received an aid package worth an estimated $14,690.

Freshman Admission Mount Vernon Nazarene University requires an essay, a high school transcript, a minimum 2.5 high school GPA, 2 recommendations, SAT or ACT scores, and TOEFL scores for international students. The application deadline for regular admission is July 15.

Entrance Difficulty Mount Vernon Nazarene University assesses its entrance difficulty level as moderately difficult. For the fall 2008 freshman class, 79 percent of the applicants were accepted.

For Further Information Contact James Smith, Director of Admissions and Student Recruitment, Mount Vernon Nazarene University, 800 Martinsburg Road, Mount Vernon, OH 43050. *Phone:* 740-392-6868 Ext. 4516 or 866-462-6868 (toll-free). *Fax:* 740-393-0511. *E-mail:* admissions@mvnu.edu. *Web site:* http://www.mvnu.edu/.

MUSKINGUM COLLEGE

New Concord, Ohio

Muskingum College is a coed, private, comprehensive institution, founded in 1837, affiliated with the Presbyterian Church (U.S.A.), offering degrees at the bachelor's and master's levels. It has a 215-acre campus in New Concord near Columbus.

Academic Information The library holds 233,000 titles, 900 serial subscriptions, and 6,000 audiovisual materials. Special programs include services for learning-disabled students, study abroad, advanced placement credit, accelerated degree programs, ESL programs, double majors, independent study, self-designed majors, summer session for credit, part-time degree programs (daytime, evenings, summer), external degree programs, internships, and arrangement for off-campus study with Case Western Reserve University.

Student Body Statistics The student body totals 2,099, of whom 1,709 are undergraduates.

Expenses for 2008–09 *Application fee:* $0. *One-time mandatory fee:* $215. *Comprehensive fee:* $26,260 includes full-time tuition ($18,400), mandatory fees ($510), and college room and board ($7350). *College room only:* $3750.

Financial Aid Forms of aid include need-based and non-need-based scholarships and part-time jobs. The average aided 2008–09 undergraduate received an aid package worth an estimated $18,865. The priority application deadline for financial aid is March 15.

Freshman Admission Muskingum College requires a high school transcript, a minimum 2.0 high school GPA, 1 recommendation, SAT or ACT scores, and TOEFL scores for international students. An essay, a minimum 3.0 high school GPA, and an interview are recommended. The application deadline for regular admission is June 1.

Transfer Admission The application deadline for admission is August 1.

Entrance Difficulty Muskingum College assesses its entrance difficulty level as moderately difficult.

For Further Information Contact Mrs. Beth DaLonzo, Director of Admission, Muskingum College, 163 Stormont Street, New Concord, OH 43762. *Phone:* 740-826-8137 or 800-752-6082 (toll-free). *Fax:* 740-826-8100. *E-mail:* adminfo@muskingum.edu. *Web site:* http://www.muskingum.edu/.

NORTHWESTERN COLLEGE

See University of Northwestern Ohio.

NOTRE DAME COLLEGE

South Euclid, Ohio

http://www.notredamecollege.edu/

OBERLIN COLLEGE

Oberlin, Ohio

Oberlin College is a coed, private, comprehensive institution, founded in 1833, offering degrees at the bachelor's and master's levels and postbachelor's certificates. It has a 440-acre campus in Oberlin near Cleveland.

Oberlin College (continued)

Academic Information The faculty has 285 members, 96% with terminal degrees. The undergraduate student-faculty ratio is 9:1. The library holds 2 million titles and 4,560 serial subscriptions. Special programs include services for learning-disabled students, an honors program, study abroad, advanced placement credit, ESL programs, double majors, independent study, self-designed majors, part-time degree programs (daytime), internships, and arrangement for off-campus study with Great Lakes Colleges Association.
Student Body Statistics The student body totals 2,865, of whom 2,839 are undergraduates (766 freshmen). 55 percent are women and 45 percent are men. Students come from 50 states and territories and 44 other countries. 9 percent are from Ohio. 6 percent are international students.
Expenses for 2008–09 *Application fee:* $35. *Comprehensive fee:* $48,150 includes full-time tuition ($38,012), mandatory fees ($268), and college room and board ($9870). *College room only:* $5150. Full-time tuition and fees vary according to course load. Room and board charges vary according to board plan and housing facility. *Part-time tuition:* $1580 per credit hour. Part-time tuition varies according to course load.
Financial Aid Forms of aid include need-based and non-need-based scholarships and part-time jobs. The average aided 2008–09 undergraduate received an aid package worth an estimated $31,257. The priority application deadline for financial aid is February 15.
Freshman Admission Oberlin College requires an essay, a high school transcript, 2 recommendations, SAT or ACT scores, and TOEFL scores for international students. SAT Subject Test scores are recommended. An interview is required for some. The application deadline for regular admission is January 15, for early decision plan 1 it is November 15, and for early decision plan 2 it is January 2.
Transfer Admission The application deadline for admission is March 15.
Entrance Difficulty Oberlin College assesses its entrance difficulty level as very difficult. For the fall 2008 freshman class, 33 percent of the applicants were accepted.
For Further Information Contact Ms. Debra Chermonte, Dean of Admissions and Financial Aid, Oberlin College, Admissions Office, Carnegie Building, Oberlin, OH 44074-1090. *Phone:* 440-775-8411 or 800-622-OBIE (toll-free). *Fax:* 440-775-6905. *E-mail:* college.admissions@oberlin.edu. *Web site:* http://www.oberlin.edu/.

OHIO CHRISTIAN UNIVERSITY

Circleville, Ohio

Ohio Christian University is a coed, private, four-year college, founded in 1948, affiliated with the Churches of Christ in Christian Union, offering degrees at the associate and bachelor's levels. It has a 40-acre campus in Circleville near Columbus.

Academic Information The library holds 37,521 titles, 111 serial subscriptions, and 1,995 audiovisual materials. Special programs include academic remediation, services for learning-disabled students, an honors program, advanced placement credit, double majors, independent study, self-designed majors, summer session for credit, part-time degree programs (daytime, evenings), adult/continuing education programs, internships, and arrangement for off-campus study with Columbus State Community College.
Student Body Statistics The student body is made up of 636 undergraduates.
Expenses for 2008–09 *Application fee:* $25. *Comprehensive fee:* $19,950 includes full-time tuition ($12,950), mandatory fees ($1010), and college room and board ($5990). *Part-time tuition:* $550 per hour. *Part-time mandatory fees:* $505 per term.
Financial Aid Forms of aid include need-based and non-need-based scholarships and part-time jobs. The average aided 2007–08 undergraduate received an aid package worth $9500. The priority application deadline for financial aid is March 31.
Freshman Admission Ohio Christian University requires an essay, a high school transcript, 4 recommendations, medical form, and TOEFL scores for international students. SAT scores are recommended. An interview and ACT scores are required for some. The application deadline for regular admission is rolling.
Transfer Admission The application deadline for admission is rolling.
Entrance Difficulty Ohio Christian University assesses its entrance difficulty level as minimally difficult; noncompetitive for transfers.
For Further Information Contact Mike Egenreider, Associate Vice President for Enrollment, Ohio Christian University, PO Box 458, Circleville, OH 43113-9487. *Phone:* 740-477-7741 or 800-701-0222 (toll-free). *Fax:* 740-477-7755. *E-mail:* enroll@biblecollege.edu. *Web site:* http://www.ohiochristian.edu/.

OHIO COLLEGE OF MASSOTHERAPY

Akron, Ohio

http://www.ocm.edu/

OHIO DOMINICAN UNIVERSITY

Columbus, Ohio

Ohio Dominican University is a coed, private, Roman Catholic, comprehensive institution, founded in 1911, offering degrees at the associate, bachelor's, and master's levels. It has a 62-acre campus in Columbus.

Academic Information The faculty has 205 members (35% full-time), 48% with terminal degrees. The undergraduate student-faculty ratio is 14:1. The library holds 114,115 titles, 8,408 serial subscriptions, and 3,894 audiovisual materials. Special programs include academic remediation, an honors program, study abroad, advanced placement credit, independent study, distance learning, self-designed majors, summer session for credit, part-time degree programs (daytime, evenings, weekends, summer), internships, and arrangement for off-campus study with members of the Higher Education Council of Columbus. The most frequently chosen baccalaureate fields are business/marketing, education, social sciences.
Student Body Statistics The student body totals 3,117, of whom 2,430 are undergraduates (366 freshmen). 61 percent are women and 39 percent are men. Students come from 18 states and territories and 13 other countries. 97 percent are from Ohio.
Expenses for 2009–10 *Application fee:* $25. *Comprehensive fee:* $32,716 includes full-time tuition ($24,116), mandatory fees ($500), and college room and board ($8100). *Part-time tuition:* $488 per credit hour. *Part-time mandatory fees:* $135 per credit hour.
Financial Aid Forms of aid include need-based and non-need-based scholarships, athletic grants, and part-time jobs. The priority application deadline for financial aid is April 1.
Freshman Admission Ohio Dominican University requires a high school transcript, a minimum 2.0 high school GPA, an interview, SAT or ACT scores, and TOEFL scores for international students. An essay and recommendations are required for some. The application deadline for regular admission is rolling.
Transfer Admission The application deadline for admission is rolling.
Entrance Difficulty Ohio Dominican University assesses its entrance difficulty level as moderately difficult. For the fall 2008 freshman class, 68 percent of the applicants were accepted.
For Further Information Contact Ms. Nicole A. Evans, Director of Admissions, Ohio Dominican University, 1216 Sunbury Road, Columbus, OH 43219. *Phone:* 614-251-4500 or 800-854-2670 (toll-free). *Fax:* 614-251-0156. *E-mail:* admissions@ohiodominican.edu. *Web site:* http://www.ohiodominican.edu/.

OHIO NORTHERN UNIVERSITY

Ada, Ohio

Ohio Northern University is a coed, private, comprehensive institution, founded in 1871, affiliated with the United Methodist Church, offering degrees at the bachelor's, master's, doctoral, and first professional levels and postbachelor's certificates. It has a 300-acre campus in Ada.

Academic Information The faculty has 322 members (73% full-time), 63% with terminal degrees. The undergraduate student-faculty ratio is 13:1. Special programs include academic remediation, services for learning-disabled students, an honors program, cooperative (work-study) education, study abroad, advanced placement credit, ESL programs, double majors, independent study, summer session for credit, part-time degree programs (daytime, evenings), internships, and arrangement for off-campus study. The most frequently chosen baccalaureate fields are business/marketing, biological/life sciences, engineering.
Student Body Statistics The student body totals 3,721, of whom 2,744 are undergraduates (749 freshmen). 47 percent are women and 53 percent are men. Students come from 48 states and territories and 18 other countries. 86 percent are from Ohio. 2.5 percent are international students.
Expenses for 2009–10 *Application fee:* $30. *Comprehensive fee:* $40,146 includes full-time tuition ($31,626), mandatory fees ($240), and college room and board ($8280). *College room only:* $4140. *Part-time tuition:* $880 per quarter hour.
Financial Aid Forms of aid include need-based and non-need-based scholarships and part-time jobs. The average aided 2008–09 undergraduate received an aid package worth an estimated $25,084.
Freshman Admission Ohio Northern University requires a high school transcript, SAT or ACT scores, and TOEFL scores for international students. An essay, a minimum 2.5 high school GPA, 2 recommendations, and an interview are recommended. The application deadline for regular admission is August 15.
Transfer Admission The application deadline for admission is September 1.
Entrance Difficulty Ohio Northern University assesses its entrance difficulty level as moderately difficult; very difficult for pharmacy. For the fall 2008 freshman class, 88 percent of the applicants were accepted.

SPECIAL MESSAGE TO STUDENTS

Social Life With more than 200 campus clubs and organizations available, life outside of the classroom at Ohio Northern University (ONU) is an enriched, rewarding experience. Activities are geared toward the more than 3,600 students on the residential campus and include sporting events, concerts, plays, and many other varieties of entertainment. Northern students are also encouraged to become involved in their campus through Greek life, religious groups, theater, music ensembles, student government, multicultural organizations, community service groups, and other such organizations.

Academic Highlights Ohio Northern's distinctive, high-quality academic programs blend the liberal arts with professional and/or preprofessional training in its four undergraduate Colleges of Arts and Sciences, Business Administration, Engineering, and Pharmacy. Internships, cooperative education, and study-abroad programs are available in each of the four undergraduate colleges and provide invaluable hands-on experience to those entering the professional workplace after graduation. The beautiful and well-maintained nearly 300-acre campus includes many exceptional facilities, such as the Freed Center for the Performing Arts, a magnificent theater/concert hall; Dial-Robertson Stadium Outdoor All-Events Facility; and the James F. Dicke College of Business Administration, which is completely equipped with state-of-the-art technology. Another impressive facility is the ONU Sports Center. It has been the site of five NCAA Division III Indoor Track and Field Championships and three Division III Wrestling Championships. Students have recreational use of three gymnasiums, a wrestling room, a six-lane swimming pool, two racquetball courts, and gymnastics rooms. The center also includes a 200-meter indoor running track, two weight-training rooms, classrooms, athletic faculty/staff offices, and modern athletic training and fitness areas. In the spring of 2009, the Mathile Center for the Natural Sciences is scheduled to open. It will be a new student-centered academic research and learning facility that will blend trademark hands-on teaching excellence with advanced technology in a functional modern environment. The building will include twenty-one classrooms, five seminar/conference rooms, twenty-one laboratories, thirty-four offices, and four storage spaces. The 95,145-square-foot structure will connect the Meyer Hall of Science with the Robertson-Evans Pharmacy building.

Interviews and Campus Visits Although interviews are not required for admission to Ohio Northern, they are encouraged. Depending on a student's preference, there are opportunities to attend class, tour the campus, speak to a professor about a specific area of interest, meet an athletic coach, and meet with an admissions or financial aid representative. For information about appointments and campus visits, students should call the Office of Admissions at 888-408-4668 (toll-free) Monday through Friday, 8 to 4:30, or Saturday, 8 to noon. The fax number is 419-772-2821. The nearest commercial airport is Port Columbus International.

For Further Information Write to Karen P. Condeni, Vice President and Dean of Enrollment, Office of Admissions, Ohio Northern University, Ada, OH 45810. *E-mail:* admissions-ug@onu.edu. *Web site:* http://www.onu.edu.

THE OHIO STATE UNIVERSITY

Columbus, Ohio

The Ohio State University is a coed, public university, founded in 1870, offering degrees at the associate, bachelor's, master's, doctoral, and first professional levels and post-master's and postbachelor's certificates. It has a 6,191-acre campus in Columbus.

Academic Information The faculty has 4,402 members (73% full-time), 73% with terminal degrees. The undergraduate student-faculty ratio is 13:1. The library holds 6 million titles, 78,903 serial subscriptions, and 83,587 audiovisual materials. Special programs include academic remediation, services for learning-disabled students, an honors program, cooperative (work-study) education, study abroad, advanced placement credit, accelerated degree programs, Freshman Honors College, ESL programs, double majors, independent study, distance learning, self-designed majors, summer session for credit, part-time degree programs (daytime, evenings, weekends, summer), adult/continuing education programs, internships, and arrangement for off-campus study with Higher Education Council of Columbus.
Student Body Statistics The student body totals 53,715, of whom 40,212 are undergraduates (6,173 freshmen). 47 percent are women and 53 percent are men. Students come from 54 states and territories and 75 other countries. 89 percent are from Ohio. 3 percent are international students.
Expenses for 2008–09 *Application fee:* $40. *State resident tuition:* $8406 full-time. *Nonresident tuition:* $21,015 full-time. *Mandatory fees:* $270 full-time. Full-time tuition and fees vary according to course load, program, reciprocity agreements, and student level. *College room and board:* $7755. Room and board charges vary according to board plan and housing facility.
Financial Aid Forms of aid include need-based and non-need-based scholarships, athletic grants, and part-time jobs. The average aided 2008–09 undergraduate received an aid package worth an estimated $10,225. The priority application deadline for financial aid is February 15.
Freshman Admission The Ohio State University requires an essay, a high school transcript, SAT or ACT scores, and TOEFL scores for international students.
Entrance Difficulty The Ohio State University assesses its entrance difficulty level as moderately difficult. For the fall 2008 freshman class, 62 percent of the applicants were accepted.
For Further Information Contact Dr. Mabel Freeman, Assistant Vice President for Undergraduate Admissions and First Year Experience, The Ohio State University, 110 Enarson Hall, 154 West 12th Avenue, Columbus, OH 43210. *Phone:* 614-292-3980. *Fax:* 614-292-4818. *E-mail:* askabuckeye@osu.edu. *Web site:* http://www.osu.edu/.

THE OHIO STATE UNIVERSITY AT LIMA

Lima, Ohio

The Ohio State University at Lima is a coed, public, comprehensive unit of Ohio State University, founded in 1960, offering degrees at the associate, bachelor's, and master's levels. It has a 565-acre campus in Lima.

The Ohio State University at Lima (continued)

Academic Information The faculty has 82 members (45% full-time), 44% with terminal degrees. Special programs include services for learning-disabled students, an honors program, cooperative (work-study) education, study abroad, advanced placement credit, accelerated degree programs, Freshman Honors College, ESL programs, double majors, independent study, distance learning, self-designed majors, summer session for credit, part-time degree programs, adult/continuing education programs, internships, and arrangement for off-campus study.
Student Body Statistics The student body totals 1,409, of whom 1,351 are undergraduates (502 freshmen). 51 percent are women and 49 percent are men. Students come from 8 states and territories. 99 percent are from Ohio.
Expenses for 2008–09 *Application fee:* $40. *State resident tuition:* $5664 full-time. *Nonresident tuition:* $18,273 full-time. Full-time tuition varies according to course load and student level.
Freshman Admission The Ohio State University at Lima requires an essay, a high school transcript, and SAT or ACT scores.
Entrance Difficulty The Ohio State University at Lima has an open admission policy for state residents. It assesses its entrance difficulty as moderately difficult for out-of-state applicants; moderately difficult for transfers.
For Further Information Contact Ms. Garlene Smithson, Director of Admissions, The Ohio State University at Lima, 4240 Campus Drive, Lima, OH 45804. *Phone:* 419-995-8434. *Fax:* 419-995-8483. *E-mail:* admissions@lima.ohio-state.edu. *Web site:* http://www.lima.ohio-state.edu/.

THE OHIO STATE UNIVERSITY AT MARION

Marion, Ohio

The Ohio State University at Marion is a coed, public, comprehensive unit of Ohio State University, founded in 1958, offering degrees at the associate, bachelor's, and master's levels. It has a 180-acre campus in Marion near Columbus.

Academic Information The faculty has 109 members (34% full-time), 33% with terminal degrees. The library holds 56,323 titles, 12,646 serial subscriptions, and 1,607 audiovisual materials. Special programs include academic remediation, services for learning-disabled students, an honors program, cooperative (work-study) education, study abroad, advanced placement credit, accelerated degree programs, Freshman Honors College, ESL programs, double majors, independent study, distance learning, self-designed majors, summer session for credit, part-time degree programs (daytime, evenings, summer), adult/continuing education programs, internships, and arrangement for off-campus study.
Student Body Statistics The student body totals 1,673, of whom 1,594 are undergraduates (553 freshmen). 54 percent are women and 46 percent are men. Students come from 5 states and territories and 2 other countries. 0.1 percent are international students.
Expenses for 2008–09 *Application fee:* $40. *State resident tuition:* $5664 full-time. *Nonresident tuition:* $18,273 full-time. Full-time tuition varies according to course load and student level.
Freshman Admission The Ohio State University at Marion requires an essay, a high school transcript, and TOEFL scores for international students.
Entrance Difficulty The Ohio State University at Marion has an open admission policy for state residents. It assesses its entrance difficulty as minimally difficult for transfers.
For Further Information Contact Mr. Matthew Moreau, Admissions and Financial Aid Coordinator, The Ohio State University at Marion, 1465 Mount Vernon Avenue, Marion, OH 43302. *Phone:* 740-725-6337. *Fax:* 740-386-2439. *E-mail:* moreau.1@osu.edu. *Web site:* http://www.marion.ohio-state.edu/.

THE OHIO STATE UNIVERSITY–MANSFIELD CAMPUS

Mansfield, Ohio

The Ohio State University–Mansfield Campus is a coed, public, comprehensive unit of The Ohio State University, founded in 1958, offering degrees at the associate, bachelor's, and master's levels. It has a 644-acre campus in Mansfield near Columbus and Cleveland.

Academic Information The faculty has 103 members (43% full-time), 42% with terminal degrees. The library holds 46,603 titles and 119 serial subscriptions. Special programs include academic remediation, services for learning-disabled students, an honors program, cooperative (work-study) education, study abroad, advanced placement credit, accelerated degree programs, ESL programs, double majors, independent study, distance learning, self-designed majors, summer session for credit, part-time degree programs (daytime, evenings, summer), adult/continuing education programs, internships, and arrangement for off-campus study.
Student Body Statistics The student body totals 1,545, of whom 1,476 are undergraduates (506 freshmen). 59 percent are women and 41 percent are men. Students come from 5 states and territories and 2 other countries. 0.2 percent are international students.
Expenses for 2008–09 *Application fee:* $40. *State resident tuition:* $5664 full-time. *Nonresident tuition:* $18,273 full-time. Full-time tuition varies according to course load and student level.
Freshman Admission The Ohio State University–Mansfield Campus requires an essay and a high school transcript.
Entrance Difficulty The Ohio State University–Mansfield Campus has an open admission policy for state residents. It assesses its entrance difficulty as moderately difficult for out-of-state applicants; moderately difficult for transfers.
For Further Information Contact Mr. Henry D. Thomas, Coordinator of Admissions and Financial Aid, The Ohio State University–Mansfield Campus, 1760 University Drive, Mansfield, OH 44906. *Phone:* 419-755-4225. *Fax:* 419-755-4241. *E-mail:* admissions@mansfield.ohio-state.edu. *Web site:* http://www.mansfield.osu.edu/.

THE OHIO STATE UNIVERSITY–NEWARK CAMPUS

Newark, Ohio

The Ohio State University–Newark Campus is a coed, public, comprehensive unit of Ohio State University, founded in 1957, offering degrees at the associate, bachelor's, and master's levels. It has a 106-acre campus in Newark near Columbus.

Academic Information The faculty has 131 members (40% full-time), 39% with terminal degrees. Special programs include academic remediation, services for learning-disabled students, an honors program, cooperative (work-study) education, study abroad, advanced placement credit, accelerated degree programs, Freshman Honors College, ESL programs, double majors, independent study, distance learning, self-designed majors, summer session for credit, part-time degree programs (daytime, evenings, summer), adult/continuing education programs, internships, and arrangement for off-campus study.
Student Body Statistics The student body totals 2,462, of whom 2,354 are undergraduates (1,091 freshmen). 52 percent are women and 48 percent are men. Students come from 11 states and territories. 99 percent are from Ohio.
Expenses for 2008–09 *Application fee:* $40. *State resident tuition:* $5664 full-time. *Nonresident tuition:* $18,273 full-time. Full-time tuition varies according to course load and student level.
Freshman Admission The Ohio State University–Newark Campus requires an essay and a high school transcript.

Entrance Difficulty The Ohio State University–Newark Campus has an open admission policy for state residents. It assesses its entrance difficulty as moderately difficult for transfers.
For Further Information Contact Ms. Ann Donahue, Director of Enrollment, The Ohio State University–Newark Campus, 1179 University Drive, Newark, OH 43055. *Phone:* 740-366-9333. *Fax:* 740-364-9645. *E-mail:* barclay.3@osu.edu. *Web site:* http://www.newark.osu.edu/.

OHIO UNIVERSITY

Athens, Ohio

Ohio University is a coed, public unit of Ohio Board of Regents, University System of Ohio, founded in 1804, offering degrees at the associate, bachelor's, master's, doctoral, and first professional levels. It has a 1,700-acre campus in Athens.

Academic Information The faculty has 1,178 members (75% full-time), 79% with terminal degrees. The undergraduate student-faculty ratio is 19:1. The library holds 3 million titles, 39,297 serial subscriptions, and 102,498 audiovisual materials. Special programs include academic remediation, services for learning-disabled students, an honors program, cooperative (work-study) education, study abroad, advanced placement credit, accelerated degree programs, ESL programs, double majors, independent study, distance learning, self-designed majors, summer session for credit, part-time degree programs, external degree programs, adult/continuing education programs, internships, and arrangement for off-campus study. The most frequently chosen baccalaureate fields are business/marketing, communications/journalism, education.
Student Body Statistics The student body totals 20,960, of whom 17,228 are undergraduates (3,965 freshmen). 51 percent are women and 49 percent are men. Students come from 50 states and territories and 126 other countries. 92 percent are from Ohio. 2.5 percent are international students.
Expenses for 2008–09 *Application fee:* $45. *State resident tuition:* $8907 full-time, $283 per quarter hour part-time. *Nonresident tuition:* $17,871 full-time, $578 per quarter hour part-time. *College room and board:* $8946. *College room only:* $4857. Room and board charges vary according to board plan.
Financial Aid Forms of aid include need-based and non-need-based scholarships, athletic grants, and part-time jobs. The average aided 2008–09 undergraduate received an aid package worth an estimated $8247. The priority application deadline for financial aid is March 15.
Freshman Admission Ohio University requires a high school transcript and SAT or ACT scores. 2 recommendations are recommended. An essay and an interview are required for some. The application deadline for regular admission is February 1 and for nonresidents it is February 1.
Transfer Admission The application deadline for admission is May 15.
Entrance Difficulty Ohio University assesses its entrance difficulty level as moderately difficult; very difficult for transfers; very difficult for business, journalism, honors tutorial college. For the fall 2008 freshman class, 78 percent of the applicants were accepted.
For Further Information Contact Undergraduate Admissions, Ohio University, Athens, OH 45701-2979. *Phone:* 740-593-4100. *Fax:* 740-593-0560. *E-mail:* admissions@ohio.edu. *Web site:* http://www.ohio.edu/.

OHIO UNIVERSITY–CHILLICOTHE

Chillicothe, Ohio

Ohio University–Chillicothe is a coed, public, comprehensive unit of Ohio Board of Regents, founded in 1946, offering degrees at the associate, bachelor's, and master's levels (offers first 2 years of most bachelor's degree programs available at the main campus in Athens; also offers several bachelor's degree programs that can be completed at this campus and several programs exclusive to this campus; also offers some graduate programs). It has a 124-acre campus in Chillicothe near Columbus.

Academic Information The library holds 47,900 titles and 418 serial subscriptions. Special programs include academic remediation, services for learning-disabled students, advanced placement credit, accelerated degree programs, double majors, independent study, distance learning, self-designed majors, summer session for credit, part-time degree programs (daytime, evenings, summer), adult/continuing education programs, and internships.
Student Body Statistics The student body is made up of 1,836 undergraduates.
Expenses for 2008–09 *Application fee:* $20. *State resident tuition:* $4581 full-time, $139 per hour part-time. *Nonresident tuition:* $8904 full-time, $270 per hour part-time.
Financial Aid Forms of aid include need-based and non-need-based scholarships and part-time jobs. The average aided 2008–09 undergraduate received an aid package worth an estimated $8265. The priority application deadline for financial aid is March 15.
Freshman Admission Ohio University–Chillicothe requires a high school transcript. The application deadline for regular admission is September 1.
Transfer Admission The application deadline for admission is September 1.
Entrance Difficulty Ohio University–Chillicothe has an open admission policy for state residents. It assesses its entrance difficulty as minimally difficult for transfers.
For Further Information Contact TJ Eveland, Coordinator of Student Enrollment, Ohio University–Chillicothe, 571 West Fifth Street, Chillicothe, OH 45601. *Phone:* 740-774-7200 Ext. 242 or 877-462-6824 (toll-free in-state). *Fax:* 740-774-7295. *E-mail:* evelandt@ohio.edu. *Web site:* http://www.chillicothe.ohiou.edu/.

OHIO UNIVERSITY–EASTERN

St. Clairsville, Ohio

Ohio University–Eastern is a coed, public, comprehensive unit of Ohio Board of Regents, founded in 1957, offering degrees at the associate, bachelor's, and master's levels (also offers some graduate courses). It has a 300-acre campus in St. Clairsville.

Academic Information The library holds 50,000 titles and 625 serial subscriptions. Special programs include academic remediation, advanced placement credit, accelerated degree programs, self-designed majors, summer session for credit, part-time degree programs, external degree programs, and adult/continuing education programs.
Student Body Statistics The student body is made up of 751 undergraduates.
Expenses for 2008–09 *Application fee:* $20. *State resident tuition:* $4395 full-time, $134 per credit hour part-time. *Nonresident tuition:* $5715 full-time, $174 per credit hour part-time. Both full-time and part-time tuition varies according to student level.
Financial Aid Forms of aid include need-based and non-need-based scholarships and part-time jobs. The average aided 2008–09 undergraduate received an aid package worth an estimated $6810. The priority application deadline for financial aid is March 15.
Freshman Admission Ohio University–Eastern requires a high school transcript. The application deadline for regular admission is rolling.
Transfer Admission The application deadline for admission is rolling.
Entrance Difficulty Ohio University–Eastern has an open admission policy.
For Further Information Contact N. Kip Howard, Assistant Vice President for Enrollment Services/Director of Admissions, Ohio University–Eastern, 45425 National Road, St. Clairsville, OH 43950-9724. *Phone:* 740-593-4120 or 800-648-3331 (toll-free in-state). *E-mail:* chenowet@ohio.edu. *Web site:* http://www.eastern.ohiou.edu/.

OHIO UNIVERSITY–LANCASTER

Lancaster, Ohio

Ohio University–Lancaster is a coed, public, comprehensive unit of Ohio Board of Regents, founded in 1968, offering degrees at the associate, bachelor's, and master's levels. It has a 360-acre campus in Lancaster near Columbus.

Academic Information The library holds 94,688 titles, 399 serial subscriptions, and 2,759 audiovisual materials. Special programs include academic remediation, advanced placement credit, accelerated degree

Ohio University–Lancaster (continued)

programs, double majors, independent study, distance learning, self-designed majors, summer session for credit, part-time degree programs (daytime, evenings, weekends, summer), external degree programs, adult/continuing education programs, and internships.

Student Body Statistics The student body is made up of 1,728 undergraduates.

Expenses for 2008–09 *Application fee:* $20. *State resident tuition:* $4581 full-time, $139 per credit hour part-time. *Nonresident tuition:* $8904 full-time, $270 per credit hour part-time.

Financial Aid Forms of aid include need-based and non-need-based scholarships and part-time jobs. The average aided 2008–09 undergraduate received an aid package worth an estimated $7459. The priority application deadline for financial aid is March 15.

Freshman Admission Ohio University–Lancaster requires a high school transcript. An interview is recommended. The application deadline for regular admission is rolling.

Transfer Admission The application deadline for admission is rolling.

Entrance Difficulty Ohio University–Lancaster has an open admission policy.

For Further Information Contact Pat Fox, Enrollment Manager, Ohio University–Lancaster, 1570 Granville Pike, Lancaster, OH 43130-1097. *Phone:* 740-654-6711 Ext. 215 or 888-446-4468 Ext. 215 (toll-free). *Fax:* 740-687-9497. *E-mail:* fox@ohio.edu. *Web site:* http://www.ohiou.edu/lancaster/.

OHIO UNIVERSITY–SOUTHERN CAMPUS

Ironton, Ohio

Ohio University–Southern Campus is a coed, public, comprehensive unit of Ohio Board of Regents, founded in 1956, offering degrees at the associate, bachelor's, and master's levels. It has a 9-acre campus in Ironton.

Academic Information The library holds 26,000 titles, 275 serial subscriptions, and 524 audiovisual materials. Special programs include academic remediation, self-designed majors, summer session for credit, part-time degree programs (daytime, evenings, weekends, summer), and adult/continuing education programs.

Student Body Statistics The student body totals 1,836, of whom 1,699 are undergraduates. 51 percent are women and 49 percent are men. Students come from 3 states and territories. 50 percent are from Ohio.

Expenses for 2008–09 *Application fee:* $20. *State resident tuition:* $4395 full-time, $134 per credit hour part-time. *Nonresident tuition:* $5715 full-time, $174 per credit hour part-time.

Financial Aid Forms of aid include need-based and non-need-based scholarships and part-time jobs. The average aided 2008–09 undergraduate received an aid package worth an estimated $8456. The priority application deadline for financial aid is March 15.

Freshman Admission A high school transcript and ACT scores are required for some. The application deadline for regular admission is rolling.

Transfer Admission The application deadline for admission is rolling.

Entrance Difficulty Ohio University–Southern Campus has an open admission policy.

For Further Information Contact Linda Harlow, Admission, Registration and Records Coordinator, Ohio University–Southern Campus, 1804 Liberty Avenue, Ironton, OH 45638. *Phone:* 740-533-4632 or 800-626-0513 (toll-free). *Fax:* 740-593-4632. *E-mail:* harlow@ohio.edu. *Web site:* http://www.ohiou.edu/.

OHIO UNIVERSITY–ZANESVILLE

Zanesville, Ohio

Ohio University–Zanesville is a coed, public, comprehensive unit of Ohio Board of Regents, founded in 1946, offering degrees at the associate, bachelor's, and master's levels (offers first 2 years of most bachelor's degree programs available at the main campus in Athens; also offers several bachelor's degree programs that can be completed at this campus; also offers some graduate courses). It has a 179-acre campus in Zanesville near Columbus.

Academic Information The faculty has 130 members (24% full-time), 25% with terminal degrees. The undergraduate student-faculty ratio is 23:1. The library holds 64,227 titles and 489 serial subscriptions. Special programs include academic remediation, services for learning-disabled students, advanced placement credit, self-designed majors, summer session for credit, part-time degree programs, external degree programs, adult/continuing education programs, and arrangement for off-campus study with Muskingum Area Technical College.

Student Body Statistics The student body is made up of 1,873 undergraduates (300 freshmen). 74 percent are women and 26 percent are men. Students come from 2 states and territories and 1 other country. 99 percent are from Ohio. 0.6 percent are international students.

Expenses for 2008–09 *Application fee:* $20. *State resident tuition:* $4515 full-time, $137 per credit hour part-time. *Nonresident tuition:* $8838 full-time, $268 per credit hour part-time. *Mandatory fees:* $81 full-time, $2 per credit hour part-time, $5 per term part-time.

Financial Aid Forms of aid include need-based and non-need-based scholarships and part-time jobs. The average aided 2008–09 undergraduate received an aid package worth an estimated $7623. The priority application deadline for financial aid is March 15.

Freshman Admission Ohio University–Zanesville requires a high school transcript. SAT or ACT scores are required for some. The application deadline for regular admission is rolling.

Transfer Admission The application deadline for admission is rolling.

Entrance Difficulty Ohio University–Zanesville has an open admission policy except for nursing, engineering, business, communications programs, education. It assesses its entrance difficulty as moderately difficult for nursing, business, engineering, communications programs.

For Further Information Contact Mrs. Karen Ragsdale, Student Services Secretary, Ohio University–Zanesville, Office of Student Services, 1425 Newark Road, Zanesville, OH 43701. *Phone:* 740-588-1440. *Fax:* 740-588-1444. *E-mail:* ouzservices@ohio.edu. *Web site:* http://www.zanesville.ohiou.edu/.

OHIO WESLEYAN UNIVERSITY

Delaware, Ohio

Ohio Wesleyan University is a coed, private, United Methodist, four-year college, founded in 1842, offering degrees at the bachelor's level. It has a 200-acre campus in Delaware near Columbus.

Academic Information The faculty has 204 members (66% full-time), 78% with terminal degrees. The student-faculty ratio is 12:1. The library holds 441,912 titles and 1,073 serial subscriptions. Special programs include services for learning-disabled students, an honors program, study abroad, advanced placement credit, Freshman Honors College, double majors, independent study, self-designed majors, summer session for credit, part-time degree programs (daytime, summer), internships, and arrangement for off-campus study with Great Lakes Colleges Association, New York City Arts Program, Wesleyan in Washington, Philadelphia Center. The most frequently chosen baccalaureate fields are biological/life sciences, business/marketing, social sciences.

Student Body Statistics The student body is made up of 1,960 undergraduates (570 freshmen). 53 percent are women and 47 percent are men. Students come from 45 states and territories and 45 other countries. 55 percent are from Ohio. 9.2 percent are international students.

Expenses for 2008–09 *Application fee:* $35. *Comprehensive fee:* $41,970 includes full-time tuition ($33,240), mandatory fees ($460), and college room and board ($8270). *College room only:* $4120. Room and board charges vary according to board plan. *Part-time tuition:* $3620 per course.

Financial Aid Forms of aid include need-based scholarships and part-time jobs. The average aided 2008–09 undergraduate received an aid package worth an estimated $25,103. The application deadline for financial aid is May 1 with a priority deadline of March 1.

Freshman Admission Ohio Wesleyan University requires an essay, a high school transcript, a minimum 2.5 high school GPA, 1 recommendation, SAT or ACT scores, and TOEFL scores for international students. 2 recommendations and an interview are recommended. The application deadline for regular admission is March 1, for early decision it is December 1, and for early action it is December 15.

Transfer Admission The application deadline for admission is May 15.
Entrance Difficulty Ohio Wesleyan University assesses its entrance difficulty level as very difficult; most difficult for honors program. For the fall 2008 freshman class, 63 percent of the applicants were accepted.
For Further Information Contact Ms. Carol DelPropost, Assistant Vice President of Admission and Financial Aid, Ohio Wesleyan University, 61 South Sandusky Street, Delaware, OH 43015. *Phone:* 740-368-3059 or 800-922-8953 (toll-free). *Fax:* 740-368-3314. *E-mail:* cjdelpro@owu.edu. *Web site:* http://www.owu.edu/.

See page 258 for the Close-Up.

OTTERBEIN COLLEGE

Westerville, Ohio

Otterbein College is a coed, private, United Methodist, comprehensive institution, founded in 1847, offering degrees at the bachelor's and master's levels. It has a 142-acre campus in Westerville near Columbus.

Academic Information The faculty has 280 members (58% full-time). The undergraduate student-faculty ratio is 12:1. The library holds 182,629 titles and 1,012 serial subscriptions. Special programs include academic remediation, services for learning-disabled students, an honors program, study abroad, advanced placement credit, double majors, self-designed majors, summer session for credit, part-time degree programs (daytime, evenings, weekends, summer), adult/continuing education programs, internships, and arrangement for off-campus study with American University, University of Pittsburgh (Semester at Sea), members of the Higher Education Council of Columbus. The most frequently chosen baccalaureate fields are business/marketing, education, visual and performing arts.
Student Body Statistics The student body totals 3,131, of whom 2,746 are undergraduates (654 freshmen). 63 percent are women and 37 percent are men. Students come from 29 states and territories and 12 other countries. 91 percent are from Ohio.
Expenses for 2008–09 *Application fee:* $25. *Comprehensive fee:* $33,780 includes full-time tuition ($26,319) and college room and board ($7461). *College room only:* $3570. Full-time tuition varies according to course load and program. Room and board charges vary according to housing facility. *Part-time tuition:* $315 per credit hour. Part-time tuition varies according to course load and program.
Financial Aid Forms of aid include need-based and non-need-based scholarships and part-time jobs. The average aided 2008–09 undergraduate received an aid package worth an estimated $16,337. The priority application deadline for financial aid is April 1.
Freshman Admission Otterbein College requires a high school transcript, SAT or ACT scores, and TOEFL scores for international students. A minimum 2.5 high school GPA and an interview are recommended. The application deadline for regular admission is March 1.
Transfer Admission The application deadline for admission is rolling.
Entrance Difficulty Otterbein College assesses its entrance difficulty level as moderately difficult. For the fall 2008 freshman class, 82 percent of the applicants were accepted.

SPECIAL MESSAGE TO STUDENTS

Social Life Students participate in more than ninety campus organizations, from music performance groups, such as the marching band, concert choir, and orchestra, to student government to student-run radio and television studios to intramural sports. Twenty-eight percent join one of the seven fraternities and six sororities. Many students are involved in campus service organizations, such as Habitat for Humanity. Religious activities are also available for students in most denominations. Cultural activities on campus include a Professional Artist Series, the Otterbein College Theatre, and musical performances. Off-campus activities in nearby Columbus include many social, sports, and cultural offerings.

Academic Highlights The curriculum revolves around Otterbein's nationally recognized liberal arts curriculum, Integrative Studies, combined with professional and career preparation. Otterbein offers fifty-six majors, seven baccalaureate degrees, and four graduate degrees. Internships are encouraged in order to give students hands-on work experience to complement their course work. Programs in theater and equine science have each achieved national recognition.

Interviews and Campus Visits Individual interviews are not required of all applicants, but campus visits are strongly recommended for all interested and accepted students. The visit is structured so students can gain a thorough understanding of the campus from a variety of perspectives. Faculty conferences, student-conducted tours, admission and financial aid conferences, and classroom observation are possibilities at campus visits. Roush Hall, Battelle Fine Arts Center, the Rike Physical Education Building, the Science Hall–Observatory, the campus center, residence halls, Towers Hall, the computer center, Courtright Memorial Library, the Clements Recreation Center, and the Art and Communication Facility should not be missed. For information about appointments and campus visits, prospective students should call the Office of Admission at 614-823-1500 (collect) or 800-488-8144 (toll-free), Monday through Friday, 8:30 to 5, or Saturday, 9:30 to 1. Campus visits can also be scheduled by visiting the Web site at http://www.otterbein.edu. The office is located in the Clippinger Administration Building on the campus.

For Further Information Write to Dr. Cass Johnson, Director of Admission, Otterbein College, Westerville, OH 43081. *Web site:* http://www.otterbein.edu.

PONTIFICAL COLLEGE JOSEPHINUM

Columbus, Ohio

Pontifical College Josephinum is a men's, private, Roman Catholic, comprehensive institution, founded in 1888, offering degrees at the bachelor's, master's, and first professional levels. It has a 100-acre campus in Columbus.

Academic Information The faculty has 31 members (35% full-time), 39% with terminal degrees. The undergraduate student-faculty ratio is 7:1. The library holds 137,883 titles and 465 serial subscriptions. Special programs include academic remediation, services for learning-disabled students, an honors program, advanced placement credit, ESL programs, double majors, internships, and arrangement for off-campus study with 2 members of the Theological Cluster. The most frequently chosen baccalaureate fields are English, area and ethnic studies, philosophy and religious studies.
Student Body Statistics The student body totals 164, of whom 115 are undergraduates (11 freshmen). Students come from 20 states and territories and 6 other countries. 30 percent are from Ohio. 8.7 percent are international students.
Expenses for 2008–09 *Application fee:* $25. *Tuition:* $15,597 full-time, $630 per credit hour part-time. *Mandatory fees:* $100 full-time.
Financial Aid Forms of aid include need-based and non-need-based scholarships and part-time jobs. The average aided 2007–08 undergraduate received an aid package worth $13,730. The priority application deadline for financial aid is September 2.
Freshman Admission Pontifical College Josephinum requires an essay, a high school transcript, 3 recommendations, an interview, SAT and SAT Subject Test or ACT scores, and TOEFL scores for international students. The application deadline for regular admission is July 31.
Transfer Admission The application deadline for admission is rolling.
Entrance Difficulty Pontifical College Josephinum assesses its entrance difficulty level as minimally difficult. For the fall 2008 freshman class, 93 percent of the applicants were accepted.
For Further Information Contact Mrs. Arminda Crawford, Secretary for Admissions, Pontifical College Josephinum, 7825 North High Street, Columbus, OH 43235. *Phone:* 614-985-2241 or 888-252-5812 (toll-free). *Fax:* 614-885-2307. *E-mail:* acrawford@pcj.edu. *Web site:* http://www.pcj.edu/.

RABBINICAL COLLEGE OF TELSHE

Wickliffe, Ohio

For Information Write to Rabbinical College of Telshe, Wickliffe, OH 44092-2523.

ROSEDALE BIBLE COLLEGE

Irwin, Ohio

http://www.rosedalebible.org/

SHAWNEE STATE UNIVERSITY

Portsmouth, Ohio

Shawnee State University is a coed, public, comprehensive unit of University System of Ohio, founded in 1986, offering degrees at the associate, bachelor's, and master's levels. It has a 52-acre campus in Portsmouth.

Academic Information The faculty has 304 members (50% full-time). The undergraduate student-faculty ratio is 17:1. The library holds 175,534 titles, 39,373 serial subscriptions, and 8,440 audiovisual materials. Special programs include academic remediation, services for learning-disabled students, an honors program, study abroad, advanced placement credit, double majors, independent study, distance learning, summer session for credit, part-time degree programs (daytime, evenings, summer), adult/continuing education programs, internships, and arrangement for off-campus study. The most frequently chosen baccalaureate fields are business/marketing, education, social sciences.
Student Body Statistics The student body totals 3,976, of whom 3,935 are undergraduates (610 freshmen). 59 percent are women and 41 percent are men. Students come from 14 states and territories and 18 other countries. 91 percent are from Ohio. 1 percent are international students.
Expenses for 2008–09 *Application fee:* $0. *State resident tuition:* $5184 full-time, $216 per credit hour part-time. *Nonresident tuition:* $9528 full-time, $397 per credit hour part-time. *Mandatory fees:* $648 full-time, $27 per credit hour part-time. Both full-time and part-time tuition and fees vary according to course load, reciprocity agreements, and student level. *College room and board:* $7670. *College room only:* $4838. Room and board charges vary according to board plan and housing facility.
Financial Aid Forms of aid include need-based and non-need-based scholarships, athletic grants, and part-time jobs. The average aided 2007–08 undergraduate received an aid package worth $3972. The priority application deadline for financial aid is April 1.
Freshman Admission Shawnee State University requires a high school transcript and TOEFL scores for international students. ACT scores are recommended. An interview and ACT scores are required for some. The application deadline for regular admission is rolling.
Transfer Admission The application deadline for admission is rolling.
Entrance Difficulty Shawnee State University has an open admission policy except for allied health programs, nonresident aliens. It assesses its entrance difficulty as moderately difficult for allied health programs.
For Further Information Contact Mr. Bob Trusz, Director of Admission, Shawnee State University, 940 Second Street, Commons Building, Portsmouth, OH 45662. *Phone:* 740-351-3610 Ext. 610 or 800-959-2SSU (toll-free). *Fax:* 740-351-3111. *E-mail:* to_ssu@shawnee.edu. *Web site:* http://www.shawnee.edu/.

SOUTHEASTERN BUSINESS COLLEGE

See Gallipolis Career College.

STRAYER UNIVERSITY—COLUMBUS CAMPUS

Columbus, Ohio

http://www.strayer.edu/columbus

STRAYER UNIVERSITY—MASON CAMPUS

Mason, Ohio

http://www.strayer.edu/mason

TEMPLE BAPTIST COLLEGE

Cincinnati, Ohio

Temple Baptist College is a coed, private, four-year college, founded in 1972, offering degrees at the bachelor's level.

Student Body Statistics The student body is made up of 60 undergraduates.
Expenses for 2008–09 *Application fee:* $50. *Tuition:* $7920 full-time, $220 per credit part-time. *Mandatory fees:* $750 full-time.
Freshman Admission Temple Baptist College requires a high school transcript and recommendations.
For Further Information Contact Temple Baptist College, 11965 Kenn Road, Cincinnati, OH 45240. *Web site:* http://www.templebaptistcollege.com/.

TIFFIN UNIVERSITY

Tiffin, Ohio

Tiffin University is a coed, private, comprehensive institution, founded in 1888, offering degrees at the associate, bachelor's, and master's levels. It has a 110-acre campus in Tiffin near Toledo.

Academic Information The faculty has 260 members (24% full-time), 27% with terminal degrees. The undergraduate student-faculty ratio is 16:1. The library holds 39,519 titles, 6,003 serial subscriptions, and 578 audiovisual materials. Special programs include an honors program, study abroad, advanced placement credit, accelerated degree programs, Freshman Honors College, ESL programs, double majors, independent study, distance learning, summer session for credit, external degree programs, adult/continuing education programs, internships, and arrangement for off-campus study. The most frequently chosen baccalaureate fields are business/marketing, psychology, security and protective services.
Student Body Statistics The student body totals 2,674, of whom 1,810 are undergraduates (421 freshmen). 55 percent are women and 45 percent are men. Students come from 36 states and territories and 15 other countries. 76 percent are from Ohio. 5 percent are international students.
Expenses for 2009–10 *Application fee:* $20. *Comprehensive fee:* $25,715 includes full-time tuition ($17,730) and college room and board ($7985). *College room only:* $4145. *Part-time tuition:* $591 per credit hour.
Financial Aid Forms of aid include need-based and non-need-based scholarships and part-time jobs. The average aided 2008–09 undergraduate received an aid package worth an estimated $12,141. The priority application deadline for financial aid is January 1.
Freshman Admission Tiffin University requires a high school transcript, SAT or ACT scores, and TOEFL scores for international students. An essay, a minimum 3.0 high school GPA, and an interview are recommended. An essay and an interview are required for some. The application deadline for regular admission is rolling.
Entrance Difficulty Tiffin University assesses its entrance difficulty level as minimally difficult. For the fall 2008 freshman class, 66 percent of the applicants were accepted.
For Further Information Contact Mr. Jeremy Marinis, Director of Undergraduate Admissions, Tiffin University, 155 Miami Street, Tiffin, OH 44883. *Phone:* 419-448-3301 or 800-968-6446 (toll-free). *Fax:* 419-443-5006. *E-mail:* marinisjj@tiffin.edu. *Web site:* http://www.tiffin.edu/.

TRI-STATE BIBLE COLLEGE

South Point, Ohio

Tri-State Bible College is a coed, private, nondenominational, four-year college, founded in 1970, offering degrees at the associate and bachelor's levels.

Student Body Statistics The student body is made up of 41 undergraduates.
Expenses for 2008–09 *Application fee:* $25. *Tuition:* $6000 full-time, $200 per semester hour part-time. *Mandatory fees:* $190 full-time, $5 per semester hour part-time, $15 per term part-time.
Entrance Difficulty Tri-State Bible College has an open admission policy.
For Further Information Contact Admissions Director, Tri-State Bible College, 506 Margaret Street, PO Box 445, South Point, OH 45680-8402. *Phone:* 740-377-2520. *Fax:* 740-377-0001. *E-mail:* recruitment@tsbc.edu. *Web site:* http://www.tsbc.edu/.

UNION INSTITUTE & UNIVERSITY

Cincinnati, Ohio

Union Institute & University is a coed, private university, founded in 1969, offering degrees at the bachelor's, master's, and doctoral levels and post-master's and postbachelor's certificates. It has a 5-acre campus in Cincinnati.

Academic Information The faculty has 322 members (12% full-time), 40% with terminal degrees. The library holds 14 serial subscriptions. Special programs include services for learning-disabled students, advanced placement credit, accelerated degree programs, independent study, distance learning, self-designed majors, summer session for credit, part-time degree programs (daytime, evenings, weekends, summer), external degree programs, adult/continuing education programs, and arrangement for off-campus study. The most frequently chosen baccalaureate fields are liberal arts/general studies, education, security and protective services.
Student Body Statistics The student body totals 1,698, of whom 916 are undergraduates (29 freshmen). 58 percent are women and 42 percent are men. Students come from 41 states and territories and 2 other countries. 81 percent are from Ohio.
Expenses for 2008–09 *Application fee:* $35. *Tuition:* $10,416 full-time, $434 per credit hour part-time. *Mandatory fees:* $112 full-time, $28 per term part-time.
Financial Aid Forms of aid include need-based and non-need-based scholarships and part-time jobs. The priority application deadline for financial aid is April 15.
Freshman Admission Union Institute & University requires an essay, a high school transcript, 2 recommendations, and an interview. The application deadline for regular admission is rolling.
Entrance Difficulty Union Institute & University assesses its entrance difficulty level as moderately difficult; minimally difficult for transfers.
For Further Information Contact Dr. Gregory Stewart, Vice President, Enrollment Management, Union Institute & University, 440 East McMillan Street, Cincinnati, OH 45206. *Phone:* 800-486-3116 (toll-free). *E-mail:* admissions@tui.edu. *Web site:* http://www.tui.edu/.

THE UNIVERSITY OF AKRON

Akron, Ohio

The University of Akron is a coed, public university, founded in 1870, offering degrees at the associate, bachelor's, master's, doctoral, and first professional levels and post-master's, first professional, and postbachelor's certificates (associate). It has a 218-acre campus in Akron near Cleveland.

Academic Information The faculty has 1,616 members (47% full-time), 53% with terminal degrees. The undergraduate student-faculty ratio is 19.5:1. The library holds 1 million titles, 14,765 serial subscriptions, and 48,423 audiovisual materials. Special programs include academic remediation, services for learning-disabled students, an honors program, cooperative (work-study) education, study abroad, advanced placement credit, accelerated degree programs, Freshman Honors College, ESL programs, double majors, independent study, distance learning, self-designed majors, summer session for credit, part-time degree programs (daytime, evenings, weekends, summer), external degree programs, adult/continuing education programs, and internships.
Student Body Statistics The student body totals 24,119, of whom 19,817 are undergraduates (4,149 freshmen). 50 percent are women and 50 percent are men. Students come from 37 states and territories and 43 other countries. 98 percent are from Ohio. 0.9 percent are international students.
Expenses for 2008–09 *Application fee:* $30. *State resident tuition:* $7218 full-time, $301 per credit part-time. *Nonresident tuition:* $16,467 full-time, $609 per credit part-time. *Mandatory fees:* $1394 full-time, $49 per credit part-time. Both full-time and part-time tuition and fees vary according to course load, degree level, and location. *College room and board:* $8311. *College room only:* $5203. Room and board charges vary according to board plan and housing facility.
Financial Aid Forms of aid include need-based and non-need-based scholarships, athletic grants, and part-time jobs. The average aided 2008–09 undergraduate received an aid package worth an estimated $6961. The priority application deadline for financial aid is February 1.
Freshman Admission The University of Akron requires a high school transcript, SAT or ACT scores, and TOEFL scores for international students. An essay, 3 recommendations, and an interview are required for some. The application deadline for regular admission is August 11 and for early action it is November 1.
Transfer Admission The application deadline for admission is rolling.
Entrance Difficulty The University of Akron has an open admission policy for Summit College Student Success Program and Wayne College. It assesses its entrance difficulty as noncompetitive for Summit College.
For Further Information Contact Ms. Diane Raybuck, Director of Admissions, The University of Akron, Simone Hall, 277 East Buchtel Avenue, Akron, OH 44325-2001. *Phone:* 330-972-7100 or 800-655-4884 (toll-free). *Fax:* 330-972-7022. *E-mail:* admissions@uakron.edu. *Web site:* http://www.uakron.edu/.

UNIVERSITY OF CINCINNATI

Cincinnati, Ohio

University of Cincinnati is a coed, public university, founded in 1819, offering degrees at the associate, bachelor's, master's, doctoral, and first professional levels and post-master's and postbachelor's certificates. It has a 137-acre campus in Cincinnati.

Academic Information The faculty has 1,249 members (97% full-time), 57% with terminal degrees. The undergraduate student-faculty ratio is 15:1. The library holds 3 million titles and 16,560 serial subscriptions. Special programs include academic remediation, services for learning-disabled students, an honors program, cooperative (work-study) education, study abroad, advanced placement credit, accelerated degree programs, ESL programs, double majors, independent study, distance learning, summer session for credit, part-time degree programs, adult/continuing education programs, internships, and arrangement for off-campus study with Greater Cincinnati Consortium of Colleges and Universities. The most frequently chosen baccalaureate fields are business/marketing, engineering, health professions and related sciences.
Student Body Statistics The student body totals 29,617, of whom 20,914 are undergraduates (3,738 freshmen). 51 percent are women and 49 percent are men. Students come from 54 states and territories and 102 other countries. 90 percent are from Ohio. 1.5 percent are international students.
Expenses for 2008–09 *Application fee:* $40. *State resident tuition:* $7896 full-time, $262 per credit hour part-time. *Nonresident tuition:* $23,922 full-time, $665 per credit hour part-time. *Mandatory fees:* $1503 full-time, $42 per credit hour part-time. Both full-time and part-time tuition and fees vary according to course load, degree level, location, program, and reciprocity agreements. *College room and board:* $9240. *College room only:* $5523. Room and board charges vary according to board plan and housing facility.
Financial Aid Forms of aid include need-based scholarships, athletic grants, and part-time jobs. The average aided 2008–09 undergraduate received an aid package worth an estimated $8459. The application deadline for financial aid is continuous.
Freshman Admission University of Cincinnati requires a high school transcript and SAT or ACT scores. An interview is recommended.

University of Cincinnati (continued)

2 recommendations and audition are required for some. The application deadline for regular admission is September 1.
Transfer Admission The application deadline for admission is rolling.
Entrance Difficulty University of Cincinnati assesses its entrance difficulty level as moderately difficult; most difficult for engineering, architecture programs. For the fall 2008 freshman class, 61 percent of the applicants were accepted.
For Further Information Contact Mr. Thomas Canepa, Assistant Vice President, Admissions, University of Cincinnati, 340 University Pavillion, Cincinnati, OH 45221-0091. *Phone:* 513-556-1100. *Fax:* 513-556-1105. *E-mail:* admissions@uc.edu. *Web site:* http://www.uc.edu/.

UNIVERSITY OF DAYTON

Dayton, Ohio

University of Dayton is a coed, private, Roman Catholic university, founded in 1850, offering degrees at the bachelor's, master's, doctoral, and first professional levels and post-master's certificates. It has a 259-acre campus in Dayton near Cincinnati.

Academic Information The faculty has 816 members (57% full-time). The undergraduate student-faculty ratio is 16:1. The library holds 920,035 titles, 10,481 serial subscriptions, and 2,186 audiovisual materials. Special programs include academic remediation, services for learning-disabled students, an honors program, cooperative (work-study) education, study abroad, advanced placement credit, accelerated degree programs, ESL programs, double majors, independent study, distance learning, self-designed majors, summer session for credit, part-time degree programs (daytime, evenings, summer), adult/continuing education programs, internships, and arrangement for off-campus study with Southwestern Ohio Council for Higher Education, Chaminade University of Honolulu, St. Mary's University. The most frequently chosen baccalaureate fields are business/marketing, communications/journalism, engineering.
Student Body Statistics The student body totals 10,920, of whom 7,731 are undergraduates (1,984 freshmen). 50 percent are women and 50 percent are men. Students come from 50 states and territories and 50 other countries. 62 percent are from Ohio. 1.6 percent are international students.
Expenses for 2008–09 *Application fee:* $50. *Comprehensive fee:* $35,310 includes full-time tuition ($26,200), mandatory fees ($1130), and college room and board ($7980). *College room only:* $4780. Full-time tuition and fees vary according to program. Room and board charges vary according to board plan, housing facility, and student level. *Part-time tuition:* $873 per credit hour. *Part-time mandatory fees:* $25 per term. Part-time tuition and fees vary according to course load and program.
Financial Aid Forms of aid include need-based and non-need-based scholarships, athletic grants, and part-time jobs. The average aided 2007–08 undergraduate received an aid package worth $19,563. The priority application deadline for financial aid is March 31.
Freshman Admission University of Dayton requires an essay, a high school transcript, 1 recommendation, SAT or ACT scores, and TOEFL scores for international students. An interview is recommended. Audition required for music, music therapy, music education programs is required for some. The application deadline for regular admission is rolling.
Transfer Admission The application deadline for admission is June 15.
Entrance Difficulty University of Dayton assesses its entrance difficulty level as moderately difficult. For the fall 2008 freshman class, 74 percent of the applicants were accepted.
For Further Information Contact Mr. Robert Durkle, Assistant Vice President and Dean of Admission, University of Dayton, 300 College Park, Dayton, OH 45469-1300. *Phone:* 937-229-4411 or 800-837-7433 (toll-free). *Fax:* 937-229-4729. *E-mail:* admission@udayton.edu. *Web site:* http://www.udayton.edu/.

THE UNIVERSITY OF FINDLAY

Findlay, Ohio

The University of Findlay is a coed, private, comprehensive institution, founded in 1882, affiliated with the Church of God, offering degrees at the associate, bachelor's, master's, and first professional levels. It has a 200-acre campus in Findlay near Toledo.

Academic Information The faculty has 363 members (52% full-time), 34% with terminal degrees. The undergraduate student-faculty ratio is 17:1. The library holds 132,052 titles and 23,128 serial subscriptions. Special programs include academic remediation, services for learning-disabled students, an honors program, cooperative (work-study) education, study abroad, advanced placement credit, accelerated degree programs, ESL programs, double majors, independent study, distance learning, self-designed majors, summer session for credit, part-time degree programs (daytime, evenings, weekends, summer), adult/continuing education programs, internships, and arrangement for off-campus study. The most frequently chosen baccalaureate fields are business/marketing, education, health professions and related sciences.
Student Body Statistics The student body totals 5,761, of whom 4,210 are undergraduates (622 freshmen). 63 percent are women and 37 percent are men. Students come from 45 states and territories and 34 other countries. 81 percent are from Ohio. 6.9 percent are international students.
Expenses for 2008–09 *Application fee:* $0. *Comprehensive fee:* $32,976 includes full-time tuition ($23,938), mandatory fees ($732), and college room and board ($8306). *College room only:* $4144. Full-time tuition and fees vary according to course load and program. *Part-time tuition:* $528 per semester hour. *Part-time mandatory fees:* $632 per term. Part-time tuition and fees vary according to course load and program.
Financial Aid Forms of aid include need-based and non-need-based scholarships, athletic grants, and part-time jobs. The average aided 2008–09 undergraduate received an aid package worth an estimated $17,345. The application deadline for financial aid is continuous.
Freshman Admission The University of Findlay requires an essay, a high school transcript, a minimum 2.3 high school GPA, recommendations, and SAT or ACT scores. TOEFL scores for international students are recommended. An interview is required for some. The application deadline for regular admission is rolling.
Transfer Admission The application deadline for admission is rolling.
Entrance Difficulty The University of Findlay assesses its entrance difficulty level as moderately difficult. For the fall 2008 freshman class, 68 percent of the applicants were accepted.
For Further Information Contact Mr. Randall Langston, Executive Director of Enrollment Services, The University of Findlay, 1000 North Main Street, Findlay, OH 45840-3653. *Phone:* 419-434-4732 or 800-548-0932 (toll-free). *Fax:* 419-434-4898. *E-mail:* admissions@findlay.edu. *Web site:* http://www.findlay.edu/.

See page 278 for the Close-Up.

UNIVERSITY OF NORTHWESTERN OHIO

Lima, Ohio

http://www.unoh.edu/

UNIVERSITY OF PHOENIX–CINCINNATI CAMPUS

West Chester, Ohio

University of Phoenix–Cincinnati Campus is a coed, proprietary, comprehensive institution, founded in 2003, offering degrees at the bachelor's and master's levels.

Academic Information The faculty has 47 members (13% full-time), 15% with terminal degrees. The library holds 16,781 serial subscriptions. Special programs include services for learning-disabled students, advanced placement credit, accelerated degree programs, independent study, and distance learning. The most frequently chosen baccalaureate fields are business/marketing, computer and information sciences.
Student Body Statistics The student body totals 143, of whom 70 are undergraduates. 60 percent are women and 40 percent are men.
Expenses for 2008–09 *Application fee:* $45. *Tuition:* $12,690 full-time. Full-time tuition varies according to course level and course load.

Financial Aid Forms of aid include need-based and non-need-based scholarships. The average aided 2007–08 undergraduate received an aid package worth $6180. The application deadline for financial aid is continuous.
Freshman Admission University of Phoenix–Cincinnati Campus requires 1 recommendation and TOEFL scores for international students. A high school transcript is required for some. The application deadline for regular admission is rolling.
Transfer Admission The application deadline for admission is rolling.
Entrance Difficulty University of Phoenix–Cincinnati Campus has an open admission policy.
For Further Information Contact Ms. Audra McQuarie, Registrar/Executive Director, University of Phoenix–Cincinnati Campus, 4035 South Riverpoint Parkway, Mail Stop CF-L101, Phoenix, AZ 85040. *Phone:* 480-557-6151, 800-776-4867 (toll-free in-state), or 800-228-7240 (toll-free out-of-state). *Fax:* 480-643-3068. *E-mail:* audra.mcquarie@phoenix.edu. *Web site:* http://www.phoenix.edu/.

UNIVERSITY OF PHOENIX–CLEVELAND CAMPUS

Independence, Ohio

University of Phoenix–Cleveland Campus is a coed, proprietary, comprehensive institution, founded in 2000, offering degrees at the associate, bachelor's, and master's levels.

Academic Information The faculty has 123 members (8% full-time), 15% with terminal degrees. The library holds 16,781 serial subscriptions. Special programs include services for learning-disabled students, advanced placement credit, accelerated degree programs, independent study, distance learning, external degree programs, and adult/continuing education programs. The most frequently chosen baccalaureate fields are business/marketing, computer and information sciences, health professions and related sciences.
Student Body Statistics The student body totals 664, of whom 394 are undergraduates (44 freshmen). 73 percent are women and 27 percent are men. 3.3 percent are international students.
Expenses for 2008–09 *Application fee:* $0. *Tuition:* $12,690 full-time, $423 per credit part-time. Full-time tuition varies according to course level and course load.
Financial Aid Forms of aid include need-based and non-need-based scholarships. The average aided 2007–08 undergraduate received an aid package worth $6935. The application deadline for financial aid is continuous.
Freshman Admission University of Phoenix–Cleveland Campus requires 1 recommendation and TOEFL scores for international students. A high school transcript is required for some. The application deadline for regular admission is rolling.
Transfer Admission The application deadline for admission is rolling.
Entrance Difficulty University of Phoenix–Cleveland Campus has an open admission policy.
For Further Information Contact Ms. Audra McQuarie, Registrar/Executive Director, University of Phoenix–Cleveland Campus, 4035 South Riverpoint Parkway, Mail Stop CF-L101, Phoenix, AZ 85040. *Phone:* 480-557-6151, 800-776-4867 (toll-free in-state), or 800-228-7240 (toll-free out-of-state). *Fax:* 480-643-3068. *E-mail:* audra.mcquarie@phoenix.edu. *Web site:* http://www.phoenix.edu/.

UNIVERSITY OF PHOENIX–COLUMBUS OHIO CAMPUS

Columbus, Ohio

University of Phoenix–Columbus Ohio Campus is a coed, proprietary, comprehensive institution, founded in 2003, offering degrees at the associate, bachelor's, and master's levels.

Academic Information The faculty has 65 members (6% full-time), 31% with terminal degrees. The library holds 16,781 serial subscriptions. Special programs include services for learning-disabled students, advanced placement credit, accelerated degree programs, independent study, and distance learning. The most frequently chosen baccalaureate field is business/marketing.
Student Body Statistics The student body totals 208, of whom 128 are undergraduates (17 freshmen). 56 percent are women and 44 percent are men. 2.3 percent are international students.
Expenses for 2008–09 *Application fee:* $45. *Tuition:* $12,690 full-time. *Mandatory fees:* $750 full-time. Full-time tuition and fees vary according to course level and course load.
Financial Aid Forms of aid include need-based and non-need-based scholarships. The average aided 2007–08 undergraduate received an aid package worth $6181. The application deadline for financial aid is continuous.
Freshman Admission University of Phoenix–Columbus Ohio Campus requires 1 recommendation and TOEFL scores for international students. A high school transcript is required for some. The application deadline for regular admission is rolling.
Transfer Admission The application deadline for admission is rolling.
Entrance Difficulty University of Phoenix–Columbus Ohio Campus has an open admission policy.
For Further Information Contact Ms. Audra McQuarie, Registrar/Executive Director, University of Phoenix–Columbus Ohio Campus, 4035 South Riverpoint Parkway, Mail Stop CF-L101, Phoenix, AZ 85040. *Phone:* 480-557-6151, 800-776-4867 (toll-free in-state), or 800-228-7240 (toll-free out-of-state). *Fax:* 480-643-3068. *E-mail:* audra.mcquarie@phoenix.edu. *Web site:* http://www.phoenix.edu/.

UNIVERSITY OF RIO GRANDE

Rio Grande, Ohio

University of Rio Grande is a coed, private, comprehensive institution, founded in 1876, offering degrees at the associate, bachelor's, and master's levels. It has a 170-acre campus in Rio Grande.

Academic Information The faculty has 184 members (50% full-time), 24% with terminal degrees. The undergraduate student-faculty ratio is 15:1. The library holds 96,731 titles and 850 serial subscriptions. Special programs include academic remediation, services for learning-disabled students, an honors program, cooperative (work-study) education, study abroad, advanced placement credit, accelerated degree programs, Freshman Honors College, ESL programs, double majors, independent study, distance learning, self-designed majors, summer session for credit, part-time degree programs (daytime, evenings), adult/continuing education programs, and internships. The most frequently chosen baccalaureate fields are education, health professions and related sciences, natural resources/environmental science.
Student Body Statistics The student body totals 2,070, of whom 1,893 are undergraduates. 57 percent are women and 43 percent are men. Students come from 7 states and territories and 7 other countries. 98 percent are from Ohio. 0.4 percent are international students.
Expenses for 2008–09 *Application fee:* $25. *Comprehensive fee:* $25,260 includes full-time tuition ($18,260) and college room and board ($7000). Full-time tuition varies according to course level, course load, degree level, program, reciprocity agreements, and student level. Room and board charges vary according to board plan, housing facility, and student level.
Financial Aid Forms of aid include need-based and non-need-based scholarships, athletic grants, and part-time jobs. The application deadline for financial aid is continuous.
Freshman Admission University of Rio Grande requires a high school transcript, medical history, and TOEFL scores for international students. ACT scores are recommended. The application deadline for regular admission is rolling.
Transfer Admission The application deadline for admission is rolling.

University of Rio Grande (continued)

Entrance Difficulty University of Rio Grande has an open admission policy except for nursing, rad tech, education, social work.

For Further Information Contact Ms. Rebecca Long, Director of Admissions, University of Rio Grande, PO Box 500, Rio Grande, OH 45674. *Phone:* 740-245-7425 or 800-282-7201 (toll-free in-state). *Fax:* 740-245-7260. *E-mail:* admissions@rio.edu. *Web site:* http://www.rio.edu/.

THE UNIVERSITY OF TOLEDO

Toledo, Ohio

The University of Toledo is a coed, public unit of University System of Ohio, founded in 1872, offering degrees at the associate, bachelor's, master's, doctoral, and first professional levels and post-master's and postbachelor's certificates. It has a 407-acre campus in Toledo near Detroit.

Academic Information The faculty has 1,592 members (70% full-time). The undergraduate student-faculty ratio is 15:1. The library holds 2 million titles, 76,981 serial subscriptions, and 158,678 audiovisual materials. Special programs include academic remediation, services for learning-disabled students, an honors program, cooperative (work-study) education, study abroad, advanced placement credit, ESL programs, double majors, independent study, distance learning, self-designed majors, summer session for credit, part-time degree programs (daytime, evenings, weekends, summer), adult/continuing education programs, internships, and arrangement for off-campus study with Bowling Green State University, Medical College of Ohio, Consortium for Health Education, The Central States Universities, Inc. The most frequently chosen baccalaureate fields are business/marketing, education, health professions and related sciences.

Student Body Statistics The student body totals 22,336, of whom 17,591 are undergraduates (4,194 freshmen). 50 percent are women and 50 percent are men. Students come from 41 states and territories and 90 other countries. 90 percent are from Ohio. 2.8 percent are international students.

Expenses for 2009–10 *Application fee:* $40. *State resident tuition:* $6816 full-time, $284 per semester hour part-time. *Nonresident tuition:* $15,627 full-time, $651 per semester hour part-time. *Mandatory fees:* $1111 full-time, $46.30 per semester hour part-time. *College room and board:* $9019. *College room only:* $5889.

Financial Aid Forms of aid include need-based and non-need-based scholarships, athletic grants, and part-time jobs. The average aided 2008–09 undergraduate received an aid package worth an estimated $8139. The priority application deadline for financial aid is April 1.

Freshman Admission The University of Toledo requires a high school transcript and SAT or ACT scores. TOEFL scores for international students are recommended. A minimum 2.0 high school GPA and CORE high school curriculum are required for some. The application deadline for regular admission is rolling.

Transfer Admission The application deadline for admission is rolling.

Entrance Difficulty The University of Toledo has an open admission policy for state residents. It assesses its entrance difficulty as moderately difficult for out-of-state applicants; moderately difficult for transfers; very difficult for physical therapy, engineering, pharmacy, legal assisting technology, pre-medicine, pre-dentistry programs.

For Further Information Contact Mr. William Pierce, Director of Undergraduate Admissions, The University of Toledo, 2801 West Bancroft, Toledo, OH 43606-3398. *Phone:* 419-530-5705 or 800-5TOLEDO (toll-free in-state). *Fax:* 419-530-5713. *E-mail:* william.pierce@utoledo.edu. *Web site:* http://www.utoledo.edu/.

URBANA UNIVERSITY

Urbana, Ohio

http://www.urbana.edu/

URSULINE COLLEGE

Pepper Pike, Ohio

Ursuline College is an undergraduate: women only; graduate: coed, private, Roman Catholic, comprehensive institution, founded in 1871, offering degrees at the bachelor's and master's levels and post-master's and postbachelor's certificates (applications from men are also accepted). It has a 112-acre campus in Pepper Pike near Cleveland.

Academic Information The faculty has 216 members (34% full-time), 39% with terminal degrees. The undergraduate student-faculty ratio is 9:1. The library holds 163,617 titles, 7,806 serial subscriptions, and 10,518 audiovisual materials. Special programs include academic remediation, services for learning-disabled students, cooperative (work-study) education, advanced placement credit, accelerated degree programs, double majors, independent study, distance learning, summer session for credit, part-time degree programs (daytime, evenings, weekends, summer), adult/continuing education programs, internships, and arrangement for off-campus study with Baldwin-Wallace College, Case Western Reserve University, Cleveland State University, Cuyahoga Community College, David N. Myers College, Notre Dame College of Ohio, John Carroll University. The most frequently chosen baccalaureate fields are business/marketing, health professions and related sciences, visual and performing arts.

Student Body Statistics The student body totals 1,426, of whom 1,103 are undergraduates (113 freshmen). 93 percent are women and 7 percent are men. Students come from 6 states and territories and 4 other countries. 99 percent are from Ohio.

Expenses for 2008–09 *Application fee:* $25. *Comprehensive fee:* $29,410 includes full-time tuition ($21,840), mandatory fees ($220), and college room and board ($7350). *College room only:* $3756. Full-time tuition and fees vary according to location. Room and board charges vary according to board plan and housing facility. *Part-time tuition:* $728 per credit. *Part-time mandatory fees:* $140 per term. Part-time tuition and fees vary according to location.

Financial Aid Forms of aid include need-based and non-need-based scholarships, athletic grants, and part-time jobs. The average aided 2007–08 undergraduate received an aid package worth $15,758.

Freshman Admission Ursuline College requires an essay, a high school transcript, SAT or ACT scores, and TOEFL scores for international students. A minimum 2.0 high school GPA, 1 recommendation, and an interview are recommended. The application deadline for regular admission is rolling and for early action it is November 15.

Transfer Admission The application deadline for admission is rolling.

Entrance Difficulty Ursuline College assesses its entrance difficulty level as minimally difficult. For the fall 2008 freshman class, 43 percent of the applicants were accepted.

For Further Information Contact Kimberly Shepherd, Director, Graduate and Undergraduate Admission, Ursuline College, 2550 Lander Road, Pepper Pike, OH 44124. *Phone:* 440-449-4203 or 888-URSULINE (toll-free). *Fax:* 440-684-6138. *E-mail:* admission@ursuline.edu. *Web site:* http://www.ursuline.edu/.

WALSH UNIVERSITY

North Canton, Ohio

Walsh University is a coed, private, Roman Catholic, comprehensive institution, founded in 1958, offering degrees at the associate, bachelor's, master's, and doctoral levels. It has a 134-acre campus in North Canton near Cleveland.

Academic Information The faculty has 289 members (37% full-time), 39% with terminal degrees. The undergraduate student-faculty ratio is 15:1. The library holds 241,075 titles, 6,257 serial subscriptions, and 2,530 audiovisual materials. Special programs include academic remediation, services for learning-disabled students, an honors program, study abroad, advanced placement credit, accelerated degree programs, ESL programs, double majors, independent study, summer session for credit, part-time degree programs (daytime, evenings, weekends, summer), adult/continuing education programs, internships, and arrangement for off-campus study with University of Michigan, Case Western Reserve University, Stark State College of Technology, Cooperative Center for Study Abroad. The most

frequently chosen baccalaureate fields are business/marketing, education, health professions and related sciences.
Student Body Statistics The student body totals 2,738, of whom 2,291 are undergraduates (516 freshmen). 65 percent are women and 35 percent are men. Students come from 18 states and territories and 20 other countries. 98 percent are from Ohio. 0.9 percent are international students.
Expenses for 2008–09 *Application fee:* $25. *One-time mandatory fee:* $215. *Comprehensive fee:* $29,350 includes full-time tuition ($20,550), mandatory fees ($690), and college room and board ($8110). *College room only:* $4290. Full-time tuition and fees vary according to location. Room and board charges vary according to board plan and housing facility. *Part-time tuition:* $675 per credit hour. *Part-time mandatory fees:* $23 per credit hour. Part-time tuition and fees vary according to course load and location.
Financial Aid Forms of aid include need-based and non-need-based scholarships, athletic grants, and part-time jobs. The application deadline for financial aid is continuous.
Freshman Admission Walsh University requires a high school transcript, a minimum 2.4 high school GPA, SAT or ACT scores, and TOEFL scores for international students. An interview is recommended. An essay, a minimum 3.0 high school GPA, and 2 recommendations are required for some. The application deadline for regular admission is rolling.
Transfer Admission The application deadline for admission is rolling.
Entrance Difficulty Walsh University assesses its entrance difficulty level as moderately difficult. For the fall 2008 freshman class, 81 percent of the applicants were accepted.
For Further Information Contact Mr. Brett Freshour, Vice President for Enrollment Management, Walsh University, 2020 East Maple, North Canton, OH 44720. *Phone:* 330-490-7171, 800-362-9846 (toll-free in-state), or 800-362-8846 (toll-free out-of-state). *Fax:* 330-490-7165. *E-mail:* admissions@walsh.edu. *Web site:* http://www.walsh.edu/.

WILBERFORCE UNIVERSITY

Wilberforce, Ohio

Wilberforce University is a coed, private, comprehensive institution, founded in 1856, affiliated with the African Methodist Episcopal Church, offering degrees at the bachelor's and master's levels. It has a 125-acre campus in Wilberforce near Dayton.

Academic Information The library holds 63,000 titles, 650 serial subscriptions, and 500 audiovisual materials. Special programs include academic remediation, an honors program, cooperative (work-study) education, study abroad, advanced placement credit, Freshman Honors College, external degree programs, and arrangement for off-campus study with 18 members of the Southwestern Ohio Council for Higher Education.
Student Body Statistics The student body totals 834, of whom 826 are undergraduates.
Expenses for 2008–09 *Application fee:* $50. *Comprehensive fee:* $16,880 includes full-time tuition ($10,500), mandatory fees ($1060), and college room and board ($5320). *Part-time tuition:* $438 per credit hour.
Financial Aid Forms of aid include need-based and non-need-based scholarships and part-time jobs. The application deadline for financial aid is June 1 with a priority deadline of April 30.
Freshman Admission Wilberforce University requires an essay, a high school transcript, a minimum 2.0 high school GPA, 2 recommendations, SAT or ACT scores, and TOEFL scores for international students. An interview is recommended. The application deadline for regular admission is July 1.
Transfer Admission The application deadline for admission is July 1.
Entrance Difficulty Wilberforce University assesses its entrance difficulty level as minimally difficult.
For Further Information Contact Ms. Kenya LeNoir Messer, Vice President for Student Development and Enrollment Management/Dean of Admissions, Wilberforce University, PO Box 1001, Wilberforce, OH 45384-1001. *Phone:* 937-708-5789 or 800-367-8568 (toll-free). *Fax:* 937-376-4751. *E-mail:* kchristm@wilberforce.edu. *Web site:* http://www.wilberforce.edu/.

WILMINGTON COLLEGE

Wilmington, Ohio

Wilmington College is a coed, private, Friends, comprehensive institution, founded in 1870, offering degrees at the bachelor's and master's levels. It has a 1,465-acre campus in Wilmington near Cincinnati and Columbus.

Academic Information The faculty has 122 members (59% full-time), 41% with terminal degrees. The undergraduate student-faculty ratio is 14:1. The library holds 103,706 titles, 408 serial subscriptions, and 1,280 audiovisual materials. Special programs include academic remediation, services for learning-disabled students, an honors program, study abroad, advanced placement credit, double majors, independent study, self-designed majors, summer session for credit, part-time degree programs (daytime, evenings, summer), adult/continuing education programs, internships, and arrangement for off-campus study with members of the Southwestern Ohio Council for Higher Education, Greater Cincinnati Consortium of Colleges and Universities. The most frequently chosen baccalaureate fields are business/marketing, education, psychology.
Student Body Statistics The student body totals 1,501, of whom 1,455 are undergraduates (351 freshmen). 55 percent are women and 45 percent are men. Students come from 15 states and territories and 6 other countries. 95 percent are from Ohio. 0.6 percent are international students.
Expenses for 2008–09 *Application fee:* $25. *Comprehensive fee:* $31,382 includes full-time tuition ($22,872), mandatory fees ($500), and college room and board ($8010). Room and board charges vary according to board plan and housing facility. *Part-time tuition:* $910 per credit. Part-time tuition varies according to course load.
Financial Aid Forms of aid include need-based and non-need-based scholarships and part-time jobs. The average aided 2008–09 undergraduate received an aid package worth an estimated $21,500.
Freshman Admission Wilmington College requires a high school transcript, SAT or ACT scores, and TOEFL scores for international students. A minimum 2.5 high school GPA, 1 recommendation, and an interview are recommended. The application deadline for regular admission is August 1.
Transfer Admission The application deadline for admission is rolling.
Entrance Difficulty Wilmington College assesses its entrance difficulty level as moderately difficult. For the fall 2008 freshman class, 90 percent of the applicants were accepted.
For Further Information Contact Ms. Tina Garland, Director of Admission and Financial Aid, Wilmington College, Pyle Center Box 1325, 251 Ludovic Street, Wilmington, OH 45177. *Phone:* 937-382-6661 Ext. 426 or 800-341-9318 (toll-free). *Fax:* 937-383-8542. *E-mail:* admissions@wilmington.edu. *Web site:* http://www.wilmington.edu/.

WITTENBERG UNIVERSITY

Springfield, Ohio

Wittenberg University is a coed, private, comprehensive institution, founded in 1845, affiliated with the Evangelical Lutheran Church, offering degrees at the bachelor's and master's levels. It has a 71-acre campus in Springfield near Columbus and Dayton.

Academic Information The faculty has 196 members (72% full-time), 74% with terminal degrees. The undergraduate student-faculty ratio is 12:1. The library holds 423,930 titles, 14,551 serial subscriptions, and 21,215 audiovisual materials. Special programs include academic remediation, an honors program, cooperative (work-study) education, study abroad, advanced placement credit, Freshman Honors College, ESL programs, double majors, independent study, self-designed majors, summer session for credit, part-time degree programs (daytime, evenings, summer), adult/continuing education programs, internships, and arrangement for off-campus study with 21 members of the Southwestern Ohio Council for Higher Education. The most frequently chosen baccalaureate fields are biological/life sciences, business/marketing, social sciences.
Student Body Statistics The student body totals 1,976, of whom 1,967 are undergraduates (510 freshmen). 56 percent are women and 44 percent are men. Students come from 40 states and territories and 26 other countries. 69 percent are from Ohio. 2.5 percent are international students.

Wittenberg University (continued)

Expenses for 2009–10 *Application fee:* $40. *Comprehensive fee:* $42,662 includes full-time tuition ($33,890) and college room and board ($8772). *College room only:* $4554. *Part-time tuition:* $1130 per credit hour.
Financial Aid Forms of aid include need-based and non-need-based scholarships and part-time jobs. The average aided 2007–08 undergraduate received an aid package worth $26,618. The priority application deadline for financial aid is March 1.
Freshman Admission Wittenberg University requires an essay, a high school transcript, an interview, and TOEFL scores for international students. Tests optional is recommended. The application deadline for for early decision it is November 15 and for early action it is December 1.
Transfer Admission The application deadline for admission is rolling.
Entrance Difficulty Wittenberg University assesses its entrance difficulty level as moderately difficult; very difficult for International United Nations Scholars Program, Institute of International Education Program. For the fall 2008 freshman class, 69 percent of the applicants were accepted.
For Further Information Contact Ms. Karen Hunt, Director of Admission, Wittenberg University, PO Box 720, Springfield, OH 45501-0720. *Phone:* 877-206-0332 Ext. 6377 or 800-677-7558 Ext. 6314 (toll-free). *Fax:* 937-327-6379. *E-mail:* admission@wittenberg.edu. *Web site:* http://www.wittenberg.edu/.

WRIGHT STATE UNIVERSITY

Dayton, Ohio

Wright State University is a coed, public university, founded in 1964, offering degrees at the associate, bachelor's, master's, doctoral, and first professional levels and post-master's certificates. It has a 557-acre campus in Dayton near Cincinnati.

Academic Information The faculty has 863 members (97% full-time). The undergraduate student-faculty ratio is 17:1. The library holds 703,000 titles, 443,200 serial subscriptions, and 29,800 audiovisual materials. Special programs include academic remediation, services for learning-disabled students, an honors program, cooperative (work-study) education, study abroad, advanced placement credit, Freshman Honors College, ESL programs, double majors, independent study, distance learning, self-designed majors, summer session for credit, part-time degree programs, adult/continuing education programs, internships, and arrangement for off-campus study with members of the Southwestern Ohio Council for Higher Education. The most frequently chosen baccalaureate fields are business/marketing, education, health professions and related sciences.
Student Body Statistics The student body totals 16,672, of whom 12,772 are undergraduates (2,616 freshmen). 55 percent are women and 45 percent are men. Students come from 51 states and territories and 54 other countries. 97 percent are from Ohio. 1.5 percent are international students.
Expenses for 2008–09 *Application fee:* $30. *State resident tuition:* $7278 full-time, $219 per credit hour part-time. *Nonresident tuition:* $14,004 full-time, $425 per credit hour part-time. Both full-time and part-time tuition varies according to course load. *College room and board:* $7180. Room and board charges vary according to board plan and housing facility.
Financial Aid Forms of aid include need-based and non-need-based scholarships, athletic grants, and part-time jobs. The average aided 2008–09 undergraduate received an aid package worth an estimated $9040. The priority application deadline for financial aid is February 15.
Freshman Admission Wright State University requires a high school transcript, SAT or ACT scores, and TOEFL scores for international students. A minimum 2.0 high school GPA is recommended. The application deadline for regular admission is rolling.
Transfer Admission The application deadline for admission is rolling.
Entrance Difficulty Wright State University assesses its entrance difficulty level as minimally difficult; moderately difficult for out-of-state applicants. For the fall 2008 freshman class, 85 percent of the applicants were accepted.
For Further Information Contact Ms. Cathy Davis, Director of Undergraduate Admissions, Wright State University, 3640 Colonel Glenn Highway, Dayton, OH 45435. *Phone:* 937-775-5700 or 800-247-1770 (toll-free). *Fax:* 937-775-5795. *E-mail:* admissions@wright.edu. *Web site:* http://www.wright.edu/.

XAVIER UNIVERSITY

Cincinnati, Ohio

Xavier University is a coed, private, Roman Catholic, comprehensive institution, founded in 1831, offering degrees at the associate, bachelor's, master's, and doctoral levels and post-master's and postbachelor's certificates. It has a 140-acre campus in Cincinnati.

Academic Information The faculty has 630 members (49% full-time), 52% with terminal degrees. The undergraduate student-faculty ratio is 12:1. The library holds 363,140 titles, 55,934 serial subscriptions, and 11,029 audiovisual materials. Special programs include academic remediation, services for learning-disabled students, an honors program, cooperative (work-study) education, study abroad, advanced placement credit, ESL programs, double majors, independent study, summer session for credit, part-time degree programs (daytime, evenings, weekends, summer), adult/continuing education programs, internships, and arrangement for off-campus study with 13 members of the Greater Cincinnati Consortium of Colleges and Universities. The most frequently chosen baccalaureate fields are business/marketing, communications/journalism, liberal arts/general studies.
Student Body Statistics The student body totals 6,584, of whom 3,923 are undergraduates (860 freshmen). 56 percent are women and 44 percent are men. Students come from 47 states and territories and 34 other countries. 61 percent are from Ohio. 2.7 percent are international students.
Expenses for 2009–10 *Application fee:* $35. *One-time mandatory fee:* $190. *Comprehensive fee:* $38,100 includes full-time tuition ($27,900), mandatory fees ($670), and college room and board ($9530). *College room only:* $5250. *Part-time tuition:* $550 per credit hour.
Financial Aid Forms of aid include need-based and non-need-based scholarships, athletic grants, and part-time jobs. The average aided 2008–09 undergraduate received an aid package worth an estimated $16,838. The priority application deadline for financial aid is February 15.
Freshman Admission Xavier University requires an essay, a high school transcript, 1 recommendation, SAT or ACT scores, and TOEFL scores for international students. The application deadline for regular admission is February 1.
Transfer Admission The application deadline for admission is rolling.
Entrance Difficulty Xavier University assesses its entrance difficulty level as moderately difficult; very difficult for occupational therapy program; dual enrollment medical program with University of Cincinnati. For the fall 2008 freshman class, 76 percent of the applicants were accepted.
For Further Information Contact Mr. Aaron J. Meis, Dean of Undergraduate Admissions, Xavier University, 3800 Victory Parkway, Cincinnati, OH 45207-5311. *Phone:* 513-745-2941 or 800-344-4698 (toll-free). *Fax:* 513-745-4319. *E-mail:* xuadmit@xavier.edu. *Web site:* http://www.xu.edu/.

YOUNGSTOWN STATE UNIVERSITY

Youngstown, Ohio

Youngstown State University is a coed, public, comprehensive institution, founded in 1908, offering degrees at the associate, bachelor's, master's, doctoral, and first professional levels and postbachelor's certificates. It has a 200-acre campus in Youngstown near Cleveland and Pittsburgh.

Academic Information The faculty has 964 members (46% full-time). The undergraduate student-faculty ratio is 18.5:1. The library holds 873,074 titles, 41,370 serial subscriptions, and 25,702 audiovisual materials. Special programs include academic remediation, services for learning-disabled students, an honors program, cooperative (work-study) education, study abroad, advanced placement credit, accelerated degree programs, ESL programs, double majors, distance learning, self-designed majors, summer session for credit, part-time degree programs (daytime, evenings, weekends, summer), adult/continuing education programs, internships, and arrangement for off-campus study with Lorain County Community College, Cuyahoga Community College, North Central State. The most frequently chosen baccalaureate fields are business/marketing, education, health professions and related sciences.
Student Body Statistics The student body totals 13,704, of whom 12,405 are undergraduates (2,181 freshmen). 54 percent are women and 46

percent are men. Students come from 38 states and territories and 48 other countries. 91 percent are from Ohio. 0.5 percent are international students.
Expenses for 2008–09 *Application fee:* $30. *State resident tuition:* $6492 full-time, $280 per credit part-time. *Nonresident tuition:* $12,165 full-time, $516 per credit part-time. *Mandatory fees:* $229 full-time, $10 per credit part-time. Full-time tuition and fees vary according to course load and degree level. Part-time tuition and fees vary according to degree level. *College room and board:* $7090. Room and board charges vary according to board plan and housing facility.
Financial Aid Forms of aid include need-based and non-need-based scholarships, athletic grants, and part-time jobs. The priority application deadline for financial aid is February 15.
Freshman Admission Youngstown State University requires a high school transcript, SAT or ACT scores, and TOEFL scores for international students. An interview is required for some. The application deadline for regular admission is August 15 and for early action it is February 15.
Transfer Admission The application deadline for admission is August 15.
Entrance Difficulty Youngstown State University has an open admission policy for state residents, students from Mercer and Lawrence Counties in Pennsylvania. It assesses its entrance difficulty as minimally difficult for out-of-state applicants; minimally difficult for transfers; moderately difficult for nursing, engineering, engineering technology and health occupations.
For Further Information Contact Ms. Sue Davis, Director of Undergraduate Admissions, Youngstown State University, One University Plaza, Youngstown, OH 44555-0001. *Phone:* 330-941-2000 or 877-468-6978 (toll-free). *Fax:* 330-941-3674. *E-mail:* enroll@ysu.edu. *Web site:* http://www.ysu.edu/.

Oklahoma

BACONE COLLEGE

Muskogee, Oklahoma

Bacone College is a coed, private, four-year college, founded in 1880, affiliated with the American Baptist Churches in the U.S.A., offering degrees at the associate and bachelor's levels. It has a 220-acre campus in Muskogee near Tulsa.

Academic Information The library holds 34,564 titles, 121 serial subscriptions, and 185 audiovisual materials. Special programs include academic remediation, services for learning-disabled students, cooperative (work-study) education, advanced placement credit, accelerated degree programs, self-designed majors, summer session for credit, part-time degree programs (daytime, evenings, weekends, summer), adult/continuing education programs, and internships.
Student Body Statistics The student body is made up of 884 undergraduates.
Financial Aid Forms of aid include need-based scholarships and part-time jobs. The priority application deadline for financial aid is March 31.
Freshman Admission Bacone College requires a high school transcript, a minimum 2.0 high school GPA, SAT or ACT scores, and TOEFL scores for international students. ACT scores are recommended. An essay, recommendations, and an interview are required for some. The application deadline for regular admission is rolling.
Transfer Admission The application deadline for admission is rolling.
Entrance Difficulty Bacone College assesses its entrance difficulty level as minimally difficult; moderately difficult for nursing, radiological technology programs.
For Further Information Contact Office of Admissions, Bacone College, 2299 Old Bacone Road, Muskogee, OK 74403. *Phone:* 918-781-7340 or 888-682-5514 Ext. 7340 (toll-free). *Fax:* 918-781-7416. *E-mail:* admissions@bacone.edu. *Web site:* http://www.bacone.edu/.

BARTLESVILLE WESLEYAN COLLEGE

See Oklahoma Wesleyan University.

BROWN MACKIE COLLEGE–TULSA

Tulsa, Oklahoma

Brown Mackie College–Tulsa is a coed, proprietary, primarily two-year college, offering degrees at the associate and bachelor's levels.

Expenses for 2009–10 Tuition varies by program. Students should contact Brown Mackie College for tuition information.
For Further Information Contact Director of Admissions, Brown Mackie College–Tulsa, 4608 South Garnett, Suite 110, Tulsa, OK 74146. *Phone:* 918-628-3700 or 888-794-8411 (toll-free). *Fax:* 918-828-9083. *Web site:* http://www.brownmackie.edu/Tulsa.

CAMERON UNIVERSITY

Lawton, Oklahoma

Cameron University is a coed, public, comprehensive unit of Oklahoma State Regents for Higher Education, founded in 1908, offering degrees at the associate, bachelor's, and master's levels and postbachelor's certificates. It has a 160-acre campus in Lawton.

Academic Information The faculty has 321 members (57% full-time), 40% with terminal degrees. The undergraduate student-faculty ratio is 18:1. The library holds 189,872 titles, 18,639 serial subscriptions, and 8,808 audiovisual materials. Special programs include academic remediation, services for learning-disabled students, an honors program, advanced placement credit, accelerated degree programs, ESL programs, double majors, independent study, distance learning, summer session for credit, part-time degree programs (daytime, evenings, weekends, summer), adult/continuing education programs, internships, and arrangement for off-campus study with University of Oklahoma, East Central University, Oklahoma State University. The most frequently chosen baccalaureate fields are business/marketing, education, security and protective services.
Student Body Statistics The student body totals 5,454, of whom 4,892 are undergraduates (888 freshmen). 60 percent are women and 40 percent are men. Students come from 47 states and territories and 44 other countries. 86 percent are from Oklahoma. 5.1 percent are international students.
Expenses for 2008–09 *Application fee:* $15. *State resident tuition:* $4110 full-time, $137 per credit hour part-time. *Nonresident tuition:* $9974 full-time, $332.50 per credit hour part-time. *Mandatory fees:* $1305 full-time, $43.50 per credit hour part-time. Both full-time and part-time tuition and fees vary according to course load. *College room and board:* $3534. *College room only:* $2586. Room and board charges vary according to board plan.
Financial Aid Forms of aid include need-based and non-need-based scholarships, athletic grants, and part-time jobs. The average aided 2007–08 undergraduate received an aid package worth $8100. The application deadline for financial aid is continuous.
Freshman Admission Cameron University requires a high school transcript, a minimum 2.7 high school GPA, SAT or ACT scores, and TOEFL scores for international students. The application deadline for regular admission is rolling.
Transfer Admission The application deadline for admission is rolling.
Entrance Difficulty Cameron University has an open admission policy.
For Further Information Contact Mr. Frank Myers, Admissions Counselor Coordinator, Cameron University, Admissions, 2800 West Gore Boulevard, Lawton, OK 73505-6377. *Phone:* 580-581-5496 or 888-454-7600 (toll-free). *Fax:* 580-581-5514. *E-mail:* admiss@cua.cameron.edu. *Web site:* http://www.cameron.edu/.

DEVRY UNIVERSITY

Oklahoma City, Oklahoma

DeVry University is a coed, proprietary, comprehensive institution, offering degrees at the associate, bachelor's, and master's levels.

Academic Information The faculty has 8 members. The undergraduate student-faculty ratio is 20:1. Special programs include accelerated degree programs and distance learning. The most frequently chosen baccalaureate field is business/marketing.

DeVry University (continued)
Student Body Statistics The student body totals 81, of whom 59 are undergraduates (16 freshmen). 32 percent are women and 68 percent are men. 95 percent are from Oklahoma.
Expenses for 2009–10 *Application fee:* $50. *Tuition:* $14,080 full-time, $550 per credit hour part-time.
Financial Aid Forms of aid include need-based scholarships. The average aided 2007–08 undergraduate received an aid package worth $10,842. The application deadline for financial aid is continuous.
Freshman Admission The application deadline for regular admission is rolling.
Transfer Admission The application deadline for admission is rolling.
For Further Information Contact Admissions Office, DeVry University, 4013 NW Expressway Street, Suite 100, Oklahoma City, OK 73116. *Phone:* 405-767-9516. *Web site:* http://www.devry.edu/.

EAST CENTRAL UNIVERSITY

Ada, Oklahoma

East Central University is a coed, public, comprehensive unit of Oklahoma State Regents for Higher Education, founded in 1909, offering degrees at the bachelor's and master's levels. It has a 140-acre campus in Ada near Oklahoma City.

Expenses for 2008–09 *Application fee:* $20. *State resident tuition:* $2410 full-time, $100.40 per semester hour part-time. *Nonresident tuition:* $7222 full-time, $300.90 per semester hour part-time. *Mandatory fees:* $1026 full-time, $38.80 per semester hour part-time, $47.50 per term part-time. *College room and board:* $4080. *College room only:* $1600. Room and board charges vary according to board plan and housing facility.
For Further Information Contact Ms. Pam Denny, Freshman Admissions Officer, East Central University, PMBJ8, 1100 East 14th Street, Ada, OK 74820-6999. *Phone:* 580-310-5233 Ext. 233. *Fax:* 580-310-5432. *E-mail:* pdenny@ecok.edu. *Web site:* http://www.ecok.edu/.

HILLSDALE FREE WILL BAPTIST COLLEGE

Moore, Oklahoma

Hillsdale Free Will Baptist College is a coed, private, Free Will Baptist, comprehensive institution, founded in 1959, offering degrees at the associate, bachelor's, and master's levels. It has a 41-acre campus in Moore near Oklahoma City.

Expenses for 2008–09 *Application fee:* $20. *One-time mandatory fee:* $20. *Comprehensive fee:* $13,960 includes full-time tuition ($7700), mandatory fees ($1560), and college room and board ($4700). *College room only:* $2100. Full-time tuition and fees vary according to course load. Room and board charges vary according to board plan and housing facility. *Part-time tuition:* $280 per credit hour. *Part-time mandatory fees:* $20 per credit hour, $180 per term. Part-time tuition and fees vary according to course load.
For Further Information Contact Ryan Giles, Admission Officer, Hillsdale Free Will Baptist College, PO Box 7208, Moore, OK 73160. *Phone:* 405-912-9007. *Fax:* 405-912-9050. *E-mail:* recruitment@hc.edu. *Web site:* http://www.hc.edu/.

ITT TECHNICAL INSTITUTE

Oklahoma City, Oklahoma

ITT Technical Institute is a coed, proprietary, four-year college of ITT Educational Services, Inc., founded in 2006, offering degrees at the associate and bachelor's levels.

For Further Information Contact Director of Recruitment, ITT Technical Institute, 50 Penn Place—Suite 305, 1900 NW Expressway, Oklahoma City, OK 73118. *Phone:* 405-810-4100 or 800-518-1612 (toll-free). *Web site:* http://www2.itt-tech.edu/dnm/campus/.

ITT TECHNICAL INSTITUTE

Tulsa, Oklahoma

ITT Technical Institute is a coed, proprietary, primarily two-year college, founded in 2005, offering degrees at the associate and bachelor's levels.

For Further Information Contact Director of Recruitment, ITT Technical Institute, 4943 South 78th East Avenue, Tulsa, OK 74145. *Phone:* 918-619-8700 or 800-514-6535 (toll-free in-state). *Fax:* 918-619-8799. *Web site:* http://www.itt-tech.edu/.

LANGSTON UNIVERSITY

Langston, Oklahoma

http://www.lunet.edu/

MID-AMERICA CHRISTIAN UNIVERSITY

Oklahoma City, Oklahoma

Mid-America Christian University is a coed, private, comprehensive institution, founded in 1953, affiliated with the Church of God, offering degrees at the associate, bachelor's, and master's levels. It has a 145-acre campus in Oklahoma City.

Academic Information The library holds 60,000 titles and 3,906 audiovisual materials. Special programs include academic remediation, services for learning-disabled students, advanced placement credit, accelerated degree programs, double majors, distance learning, summer session for credit, part-time degree programs (summer), adult/continuing education programs, and internships.
Student Body Statistics The student body is made up of 869 undergraduates.
Financial Aid Forms of aid include need-based and non-need-based scholarships and part-time jobs. The priority application deadline for financial aid is April 1.
Freshman Admission Mid-America Christian University requires a high school transcript and TOEFL scores for international students. 2 recommendations and an interview are required for some. The application deadline for regular admission is rolling.
Transfer Admission The application deadline for admission is rolling.
Entrance Difficulty Mid-America Christian University has an open admission policy.
For Further Information Contact Jason Duda, Director of Admissions, Mid-America Christian University, 3500 Southwest 119th Street, Oklahoma City, OK 73170. *Phone:* 405-392-3180. *Fax:* 405-692-3165. *E-mail:* mbcinfo@mabc.edu. *Web site:* http://www.macu.edu/.

NORTHEASTERN STATE UNIVERSITY

Tahlequah, Oklahoma

Northeastern State University is a coed, public, comprehensive unit of Regional University System of Oklahoma, founded in 1846, offering degrees at the bachelor's, master's, and first professional levels and post-master's and postbachelor's certificates. It has a 160-acre campus in Tahlequah near Tulsa.

Academic Information The faculty has 453 members (69% full-time), 57% with terminal degrees. The undergraduate student-faculty ratio is 22:1. The library holds 415,000 titles, 19,785 serial subscriptions, and 8,306 audiovisual materials. Special programs include academic remediation, services for learning-disabled students, an honors program, cooperative (work-study) education, advanced placement credit, double majors, independent study, distance learning, self-designed majors, summer session for credit, part-time degree programs, adult/continuing education programs, and internships. The most frequently chosen baccalaureate fields are business/marketing, education, psychology.
Student Body Statistics The student body totals 8,833, of whom 7,740 are undergraduates (999 freshmen). 61 percent are women and 39 percent

are men. Students come from 27 states and territories and 49 other countries. 96 percent are from Oklahoma. 3.1 percent are international students.
Expenses for 2008–09 *Application fee:* $0. *State resident tuition:* $3210 full-time, $107 per credit hour part-time. *Nonresident tuition:* $9300 full-time, $310 per credit hour part-time. *Mandatory fees:* $945 full-time, $31.50 per credit hour part-time. Both full-time and part-time tuition and fees vary according to course load and program. *College room and board:* $4544. Room and board charges vary according to board plan and housing facility.
Financial Aid Forms of aid include need-based and non-need-based scholarships, athletic grants, and part-time jobs. The average aided 2008–09 undergraduate received an aid package worth an estimated $8624. The priority application deadline for financial aid is April 1.
Freshman Admission Northeastern State University requires a high school transcript, a minimum 2.7 high school GPA, ACT scores, and TOEFL scores for international students. An interview is required for some. The application deadline for regular admission is August 1.
Transfer Admission The application deadline for admission is August 1.
Entrance Difficulty Northeastern State University assesses its entrance difficulty level as moderately difficult; minimally difficult for transfers. For the fall 2008 freshman class, 70 percent of the applicants were accepted.
For Further Information Contact Ms. Dawn Cain, Director of Admissions, Northeastern State University, 600 North Grand Avenue, Tahlequah, OK 74464. *Phone:* 918-444-2211 or 800-722-9614 (toll-free in-state). *Fax:* 918-458-2342. *E-mail:* cain@nsuok.edu. *Web site:* http://www.nsuok.edu/.

NORTHWESTERN OKLAHOMA STATE UNIVERSITY

Alva, Oklahoma

Northwestern Oklahoma State University is a coed, public, comprehensive unit of Oklahoma State Regents for Higher Education, founded in 1897, offering degrees at the bachelor's and master's levels and post-master's and postbachelor's certificates. It has a 70-acre campus in Alva.

Expenses for 2008–09 *Application fee:* $15. *State resident tuition:* $3488 full-time, $116.25 per credit hour part-time. *Nonresident tuition:* $9518 full-time, $317.25 per credit hour part-time. *Mandatory fees:* $623 full-time, $20.75 per credit hour part-time. Both full-time and part-time tuition and fees vary according to course load, location, and program. *College room and board:* $3430. *College room only:* $1300. Room and board charges vary according to board plan.
For Further Information Contact Mr. Matt Adair, Director of Recruitment, Northwestern Oklahoma State University, 709 Oklahoma Boulevard, Alva, OK 73717-2799. *Phone:* 580-327-8545. *Fax:* 580-327-8699. *E-mail:* wmadair@nwosu.edu. *Web site:* http://www.nwosu.edu/.

OKLAHOMA BAPTIST UNIVERSITY

Shawnee, Oklahoma

Oklahoma Baptist University is a coed, private, Southern Baptist, comprehensive institution, founded in 1910, offering degrees at the bachelor's and master's levels. It has a 125-acre campus in Shawnee near Oklahoma City.

Academic Information The library holds 230,000 titles, 1,800 serial subscriptions, and 1,600 audiovisual materials. Special programs include academic remediation, services for learning-disabled students, an honors program, cooperative (work-study) education, study abroad, advanced placement credit, double majors, independent study, self-designed majors, summer session for credit, part-time degree programs (daytime, summer), internships, and arrangement for off-campus study with St. Gregory's University.
Student Body Statistics The student body totals 1,618, of whom 1,593 are undergraduates.
Expenses for 2008–09 *Application fee:* $25. *One-time mandatory fee:* $25. *Comprehensive fee:* $21,990 includes full-time tuition ($15,468), mandatory fees ($1322), and college room and board ($5200). *Part-time tuition:* $503 per hour. *Part-time mandatory fees:* $319 per term.
Financial Aid Forms of aid include need-based and non-need-based scholarships, athletic grants, and part-time jobs. The average aided 2008–09 undergraduate received an aid package worth an estimated $14,046. The application deadline for financial aid is continuous.
Freshman Admission Oklahoma Baptist University requires a high school transcript, a minimum 2.5 high school GPA, SAT or ACT scores, and TOEFL scores for international students. An essay and an interview are required for some. The application deadline for regular admission is rolling.
Transfer Admission The application deadline for admission is August 1.
Entrance Difficulty Oklahoma Baptist University assesses its entrance difficulty level as moderately difficult.
For Further Information Contact Mr. Trent Argo, Dean of Enrollment Management, Oklahoma Baptist University, Box 61174, Shawnee, OK 74804. *Phone:* 405-878-2033 or 800-654-3285 (toll-free). *Fax:* 405-878-2046. *E-mail:* admissions@mail.okbu.edu. *Web site:* http://www.okbu.edu/.

OKLAHOMA CHRISTIAN UNIVERSITY

Oklahoma City, Oklahoma

Oklahoma Christian University is a coed, private, comprehensive institution, founded in 1950, affiliated with the Church of Christ, offering degrees at the bachelor's and master's levels. It has a 200-acre campus in Oklahoma City.

Academic Information The faculty has 197 members (54% full-time), 54% with terminal degrees. The undergraduate student-faculty ratio is 14.3:1. The library holds 129,324 titles, 8,694 serial subscriptions, and 6,775 audiovisual materials. Special programs include academic remediation, services for learning-disabled students, an honors program, study abroad, advanced placement credit, accelerated degree programs, ESL programs, double majors, independent study, distance learning, summer session for credit, internships, and arrangement for off-campus study with University of Central Oklahoma. The most frequently chosen baccalaureate fields are business/marketing, education, interdisciplinary studies.
Student Body Statistics The student body totals 2,161, of whom 1,904 are undergraduates (436 freshmen). 49 percent are women and 51 percent are men. Students come from 47 states and territories and 30 other countries. 39 percent are from Oklahoma. 5.6 percent are international students.
Expenses for 2009–10 *Application fee:* $25. *Comprehensive fee:* $22,206 includes full-time tuition ($14,690), mandatory fees ($1576), and college room and board ($5940). *College room only:* $2840. *Part-time tuition:* $612 per credit hour. *Part-time mandatory fees:* $788 per term, $762 per term.
Financial Aid Forms of aid include need-based and non-need-based scholarships, athletic grants, and part-time jobs. The average aided 2008–09 undergraduate received an aid package worth an estimated $15,445. The application deadline for financial aid is August 31 with a priority deadline of March 15.
Freshman Admission Oklahoma Christian University requires a high school transcript, 1 recommendation, SAT or ACT scores, and TOEFL scores for international students. The application deadline for regular admission is rolling.
Transfer Admission The application deadline for admission is rolling.
Entrance Difficulty Oklahoma Christian University assesses its entrance difficulty level as noncompetitive. For the fall 2008 freshman class, 49 percent of the applicants were accepted.
For Further Information Contact Ms. Risa Forrester, Vice President for Admissions and Marketing, Oklahoma Christian University, Box 11000, Oklahoma City, OK 73136-1100. *Phone:* 405-425-5050 or 800-877-5010 (toll-free in-state). *Fax:* 405-425-5208. *E-mail:* info@oc.edu. *Web site:* http://www.oc.edu/.

OKLAHOMA CITY UNIVERSITY

Oklahoma City, Oklahoma

Oklahoma City University is a coed, private, United Methodist, comprehensive institution, founded in 1904, offering degrees at the bachelor's, master's, and first professional levels. It has a 75-acre campus in Oklahoma City.

Academic Information The faculty has 329 members (60% full-time), 72% with terminal degrees. The undergraduate student-faculty ratio is 11:1. The library holds 520,953 titles, 14,000 serial subscriptions, and 1,611 audiovisual materials. Special programs include academic remediation, services for learning-disabled students, an honors program, cooperative (work-study) education, study abroad, advanced placement credit, accelerated degree programs, ESL programs, double majors, independent study, self-designed majors, summer session for credit, part-time degree programs (daytime, evenings, summer), external degree programs, adult/continuing education programs, internships, and arrangement for off-campus study with American University. The most frequently chosen baccalaureate fields are liberal arts/general studies, health professions and related sciences, visual and performing arts.
Student Body Statistics The student body totals 3,897, of whom 2,190 are undergraduates (376 freshmen). 62 percent are women and 38 percent are men. Students come from 48 states and territories and 34 other countries. 61 percent are from Oklahoma. 16.1 percent are international students.
Expenses for 2008–09 *Application fee:* $30. *Comprehensive fee:* $32,600 includes full-time tuition ($21,400), mandatory fees ($2000), and college room and board ($9200). *College room only:* $5566. Full-time tuition and fees vary according to program. Room and board charges vary according to board plan and housing facility. *Part-time tuition:* $730 per semester hour. *Part-time mandatory fees:* $60 per semester hour. Part-time tuition and fees vary according to program.
Financial Aid Forms of aid include need-based and non-need-based scholarships, athletic grants, and part-time jobs. The average aided 2008–09 undergraduate received an aid package worth an estimated $21,685. The priority application deadline for financial aid is March 1.
Freshman Admission Oklahoma City University requires an essay, a high school transcript, a minimum 3.0 high school GPA, 2 recommendations, SAT or ACT scores, and TOEFL scores for international students. An interview is recommended. An interview and audition for music and dance programs are required for some. The application deadline for regular admission is August 21.
Transfer Admission The application deadline for admission is rolling.
Entrance Difficulty Oklahoma City University assesses its entrance difficulty level as moderately difficult. For the fall 2008 freshman class, 79 percent of the applicants were accepted.
For Further Information Contact Ms. Michelle Lockhart, Associate Director, Undergraduate Admissions, Oklahoma City University, 2501 North Blackwelder, Oklahoma City, OK 73106. *Phone:* 405-208-5340 or 800-633-7242 (toll-free). *Fax:* 405-208-5916. *E-mail:* mlockhart@okcu.edu. *Web site:* http://www.okcu.edu/.

OKLAHOMA PANHANDLE STATE UNIVERSITY

Goodwell, Oklahoma

Oklahoma Panhandle State University is a coed, public, four-year college of Oklahoma State Regents for Higher Education, founded in 1909, offering degrees at the associate and bachelor's levels. It has a 40-acre campus in Goodwell.

Academic Information The faculty has 93 members (72% full-time), 23% with terminal degrees. The student-faculty ratio is 14:1. Special programs include academic remediation, advanced placement credit, ESL programs, double majors, distance learning, summer session for credit, and internships.
Student Body Statistics The student body is made up of 1,223 undergraduates (288 freshmen). 51 percent are women and 49 percent are men. Students come from 34 states and territories and 16 other countries. 53 percent are from Oklahoma. 3.7 percent are international students.
Expenses for 2008–09 *Application fee:* $0. *State resident tuition:* $2738 full-time. *Nonresident tuition:* $5340 full-time. *Mandatory fees:* $1504 full-time. Full-time tuition and fees vary according to course level, program, and student level. *College room and board:* $3320. *College room only:* $900. Room and board charges vary according to board plan and housing facility.
Financial Aid Forms of aid include need-based and non-need-based scholarships and part-time jobs. The average aided 2008–09 undergraduate received an aid package worth an estimated $7890.
Freshman Admission Oklahoma Panhandle State University requires a high school transcript and TOEFL scores for international students. SAT or ACT scores are recommended. The application deadline for regular admission is rolling.
Transfer Admission The application deadline for admission is rolling.
Entrance Difficulty Oklahoma Panhandle State University assesses its entrance difficulty level as noncompetitive. For the fall 2008 freshman class, 91 percent of the applicants were accepted.
For Further Information Contact Mr. Bobby Jenkins, Registrar and Director of Admissions, Oklahoma Panhandle State University, PO Box 430, 323 Eagle Boulevard, Goodwell, OK 73939-0430. *Phone:* 580-349-1376 or 800-664-6778 (toll-free). *Fax:* 580-349-1371. *E-mail:* opsu@opsu.edu. *Web site:* http://www.opsu.edu/.

OKLAHOMA STATE UNIVERSITY

Stillwater, Oklahoma

Oklahoma State University is a coed, public unit of Oklahoma State University, founded in 1890, offering degrees at the bachelor's, master's, doctoral, and first professional levels and post-master's and postbachelor's certificates. It has an 840-acre campus in Stillwater near Oklahoma City and Tulsa.

Academic Information The faculty has 1,263 members (78% full-time), 78% with terminal degrees. The undergraduate student-faculty ratio is 18:1. Special programs include academic remediation, services for learning-disabled students, an honors program, study abroad, advanced placement credit, accelerated degree programs, Freshman Honors College, ESL programs, double majors, independent study, distance learning, self-designed majors, summer session for credit, part-time degree programs (daytime, evenings, weekends, summer), internships, and arrangement for off-campus study with National Student Exchange. The most frequently chosen baccalaureate fields are agriculture, business/marketing, family and consumer sciences.
Student Body Statistics The student body totals 22,768, of whom 17,986 are undergraduates (3,073 freshmen). 48 percent are women and 52 percent are men. Students come from 49 states and territories and 79 other countries. 84 percent are from Oklahoma. 2.5 percent are international students.
Expenses for 2008–09 *Application fee:* $40. *One-time mandatory fee:* $95. *State resident tuition:* $3941 full-time, $131.35 per credit hour part-time. *Nonresident tuition:* $14,295 full-time, $476.50 per credit hour part-time. *Mandatory fees:* $2261 full-time, $75.35 per credit hour part-time. Both full-time and part-time tuition and fees vary according to program and student level. *College room and board:* $7402. *College room only:* $3402. Room and board charges vary according to board plan and housing facility.
Financial Aid Forms of aid include need-based and non-need-based scholarships, athletic grants, and part-time jobs. The average aided 2008–09 undergraduate received an aid package worth an estimated $10,262. The application deadline for financial aid is continuous.
Freshman Admission Oklahoma State University requires a high school transcript, a minimum 3.0 high school GPA, class rank, SAT or ACT scores, and TOEFL scores for international students. An essay and an interview are required for some. The application deadline for regular admission is rolling.
Transfer Admission The application deadline for admission is rolling.

Entrance Difficulty Oklahoma State University assesses its entrance difficulty level as moderately difficult. For the fall 2008 freshman class, 89 percent of the applicants were accepted.
For Further Information Contact Karen Lucas, Director of Undergraduate Admissions, Oklahoma State University, 219 Student Union, Stillwater, OK 74078. *Phone:* 405-744-4371, 800-233-5019 Ext. 1 (toll-free in-state), or 800-852-1255 (toll-free out-of-state). *Fax:* 405-744-5285. *E-mail:* admit@okstate.edu. *Web site:* http://www.okstate.edu/.

OKLAHOMA STATE UNIVERSITY, OKLAHOMA CITY

Oklahoma City, Oklahoma

Oklahoma State University, Oklahoma City is a coed, public, primarily two-year college of Oklahoma State University, founded in 1961, offering degrees at the associate and bachelor's levels. It has an 80-acre campus in Oklahoma City.

Academic Information The faculty has 321 members (25% full-time). The student-faculty ratio is 18:1. The library holds 11,973 titles and 244 serial subscriptions. Special programs include academic remediation, services for learning-disabled students, an honors program, cooperative (work-study) education, study abroad, advanced placement credit, double majors, independent study, distance learning, summer session for credit, and part-time degree programs (daytime, evenings, weekends, summer).
Student Body Statistics The student body is made up of 5,871 undergraduates. Students come from 9 states and territories and 8 other countries. 99 percent are from Oklahoma. 1.5 percent are international students.
Expenses for 2009–10 *Application fee:* $0. *State resident tuition:* $2889 full-time, $96.30 per credit hour part-time. *Nonresident tuition:* $7749 full-time, $258.30 per credit hour part-time. *Mandatory fees:* $30 full-time, $10.50 per credit hour part-time.
Financial Aid Forms of aid include need-based scholarships and part-time jobs. The application deadline for financial aid is continuous.
Freshman Admission Oklahoma State University, Oklahoma City requires a high school transcript and TOEFL scores for international students. The application deadline for regular admission is rolling.
Transfer Admission The application deadline for admission is rolling.
Entrance Difficulty Oklahoma State University, Oklahoma City has an open admission policy except for nursing program. It assesses its entrance difficulty as moderately difficult for nursing program.
For Further Information Contact Kyle Williams, Director, Enrollment Management, Oklahoma State University, Oklahoma City, 900 North Portland, AD202, Oklahoma City, OK 73107. *Phone:* 405-945-9152. *Fax:* 405-945-3277. *E-mail:* wilkylw@osuokc.edu. *Web site:* http://www.osuokc.edu/.

OKLAHOMA WESLEYAN UNIVERSITY

Bartlesville, Oklahoma

Oklahoma Wesleyan University is a coed, private, comprehensive institution, founded in 1909, affiliated with the Wesleyan Church, offering degrees at the associate, bachelor's, and master's levels. It has a 127-acre campus in Bartlesville near Tulsa.

Expenses for 2008–09 *Application fee:* $25. *Comprehensive fee:* $22,635 includes full-time tuition ($15,685), mandatory fees ($900), and college room and board ($6050). *College room only:* $3200. Full-time tuition and fees vary according to course load. Room and board charges vary according to board plan and housing facility. *Part-time tuition:* $650 per credit hour. *Part-time mandatory fees:* $55 per credit hour.
For Further Information Contact Mark Molder, Assistant Director of Enrollment Services, Oklahoma Wesleyan University, 2201 Silver Lake Drive, Bartlesville, OK 74006. *Phone:* 866-222-8226 or 866-222-8226 (toll-free in-state). *Fax:* 918-335-6229. *E-mail:* admissions@okwu.edu. *Web site:* http://www.okwu.edu/.

ORAL ROBERTS UNIVERSITY

Tulsa, Oklahoma

Oral Roberts University is a coed, private, interdenominational, comprehensive institution, founded in 1963, offering degrees at the bachelor's, master's, doctoral, and first professional levels. It has a 263-acre campus in Tulsa.

Academic Information The faculty has 291 members (64% full-time), 47% with terminal degrees. The undergraduate student-faculty ratio is 12:1. The library holds 216,691 titles and 600 serial subscriptions. Special programs include academic remediation, services for learning-disabled students, an honors program, study abroad, advanced placement credit, accelerated degree programs, Freshman Honors College, ESL programs, double majors, independent study, distance learning, self-designed majors, summer session for credit, part-time degree programs, external degree programs, adult/continuing education programs, internships, and arrangement for off-campus study with Christian College Coalition. The most frequently chosen baccalaureate fields are business/marketing, communications/journalism, theology and religious vocations.
Student Body Statistics The student body totals 3,067, of whom 2,558 are undergraduates (358 freshmen). 58 percent are women and 42 percent are men. 36 percent are from Oklahoma. 7.8 percent are international students.
Expenses for 2008–09 *Application fee:* $35. *Comprehensive fee:* $25,806 includes full-time tuition ($17,766), mandatory fees ($430), and college room and board ($7610). *College room only:* $3710. Full-time tuition and fees vary according to course load, degree level, and program. Room and board charges vary according to board plan and housing facility. *Part-time tuition:* $742 per credit hour. Part-time tuition varies according to course load, degree level, and program.
Financial Aid Forms of aid include need-based and non-need-based scholarships, athletic grants, and part-time jobs. The average aided 2007–08 undergraduate received an aid package worth $18,229. The priority application deadline for financial aid is March 15.
Freshman Admission Oral Roberts University requires an essay, a high school transcript, a minimum 2.0 high school GPA, 1 recommendation, proof of immunization, SAT or ACT scores, and TOEFL scores for international students. An interview is recommended. An interview is required for some. The application deadline for regular admission is rolling.
Transfer Admission The application deadline for admission is rolling.
Entrance Difficulty Oral Roberts University assesses its entrance difficulty level as moderately difficult; noncompetitive for transfers. For the fall 2008 freshman class, 73 percent of the applicants were accepted.
For Further Information Contact Chris Belcher, Director of Admissions, Oral Roberts University, 7777 South Lewis Avenue, Tulsa, OK 74171. *Phone:* 918-495-6529 or 800-678-8876 (toll-free). *Fax:* 918-495-6222. *E-mail:* cbelcher@oru.edu. *Web site:* http://www.oru.edu/.

ROGERS STATE UNIVERSITY

Claremore, Oklahoma

Rogers State University is a coed, public, four-year college of Oklahoma State Regents for Higher Education, founded in 1909, offering degrees at the associate and bachelor's levels. It has a 40-acre campus in Claremore near Tulsa.

Academic Information The faculty has 222 members (44% full-time), 35% with terminal degrees. The student-faculty ratio is 20:1. The library holds 77,120 titles, 355 serial subscriptions, and 6,826 audiovisual materials. Special programs include academic remediation, services for learning-disabled students, an honors program, cooperative (work-study) education, study abroad, advanced placement credit, double majors, independent study, distance learning, summer session for credit, part-time degree programs (daytime, evenings, weekends, summer), external degree programs, adult/continuing education programs, internships, and arrangement for off-campus study with Northeast Technology Centers, Claremore and Pryor, OK; Tri-County Technology Center, Bartlesville, OK; University Learning Center of Northern Oklahoma; Central

Rogers State University (continued)

Technology Center, Drumright, OK. The most frequently chosen baccalaureate fields are biological/life sciences, business/marketing, engineering technologies.
Student Body Statistics The student body is made up of 3,858 undergraduates (750 freshmen). 63 percent are women and 37 percent are men. Students come from 32 states and territories and 16 other countries. 97 percent are from Oklahoma. 0.6 percent are international students.
Expenses for 2009–10 *Application fee:* $0. *State resident tuition:* $2729 full-time, $90.95 per credit hour part-time. *Nonresident tuition:* $8186 full-time, $272.85 per credit hour part-time. *Mandatory fees:* $1548 full-time, $51 per credit hour part-time, $15 per term part-time. *College room and board:* $6615. *College room only:* $4455.
Financial Aid Forms of aid include need-based scholarships, athletic grants, and part-time jobs. The average aided 2007–08 undergraduate received an aid package worth $5408. The application deadline for financial aid is continuous.
Freshman Admission Rogers State University requires a high school transcript, SAT or ACT scores, and TOEFL scores for international students. ACT scores are recommended. A minimum 2.7 high school GPA and ACT COMPASS (for students over 21) are required for some. The application deadline for regular admission is rolling.
Transfer Admission The application deadline for admission is rolling.
Entrance Difficulty Rogers State University has an open admission policy for Associate's degree program.
For Further Information Contact Ms. Julie Rampey, Director of Admissions, Rogers State University, 1701 W. Will Rogers Boulevard, Claremore, OK 74017. *Phone:* 918-343-7545 or 800-256-7511 (toll-free). *Fax:* 918-343-7595. *E-mail:* info@rsu.edu. *Web site:* http://www.rsu.edu/.

ST. GREGORY'S UNIVERSITY

Shawnee, Oklahoma

St. Gregory's University is a coed, private, Roman Catholic, comprehensive institution, founded in 1875, offering degrees at the associate, bachelor's, master's, and first professional levels. It has a 640-acre campus in Shawnee near Oklahoma City.

Academic Information The faculty has 96 members (33% full-time), 21% with terminal degrees. The undergraduate student-faculty ratio is 9:1. The library holds 85,622 titles, 2,060 serial subscriptions, and 1,009 audiovisual materials. Special programs include services for learning-disabled students, an honors program, study abroad, advanced placement credit, accelerated degree programs, ESL programs, double majors, independent study, distance learning, self-designed majors, summer session for credit, part-time degree programs (daytime, evenings, summer), external degree programs, adult/continuing education programs, internships, and arrangement for off-campus study.
Student Body Statistics The student body totals 743, of whom 699 are undergraduates (101 freshmen). 63 percent are women and 37 percent are men. Students come from 17 states and territories and 15 other countries. 90 percent are from Oklahoma. 5 percent are international students.
Expenses for 2009–10 *Application fee:* $25. *Comprehensive fee:* $22,490 includes full-time tuition ($15,394), mandatory fees ($900), and college room and board ($6196). *College room only:* $3400. *Part-time tuition:* $515 per hour. *Part-time mandatory fees:* $37.50 per hour.
Financial Aid Forms of aid include need-based and non-need-based scholarships, athletic grants, and part-time jobs. The application deadline for financial aid is continuous.
Freshman Admission St. Gregory's University requires a high school transcript, a minimum 2.75 high school GPA, SAT or ACT scores, and TOEFL scores for international students. An essay and an interview are required for some. The application deadline for regular admission is rolling.
Transfer Admission The application deadline for admission is rolling.
Entrance Difficulty St. Gregory's University assesses its entrance difficulty level as minimally difficult. For the fall 2008 freshman class, 97 percent of the applicants were accepted.
For Further Information Contact Director of Admissions, St. Gregory's University, 1900 West MacArthur Drive, Shawnee, OK 74804. *Phone:* 405-878-5447 or 888-STGREGS (toll-free). *Fax:* 405-878-5198. *E-mail:* admissions@stgregorys.edu. *Web site:* http://www.stgregorys.edu/.

SOUTHEASTERN OKLAHOMA STATE UNIVERSITY

Durant, Oklahoma

Southeastern Oklahoma State University is a coed, public, comprehensive unit of Oklahoma State Regents for Higher Education, founded in 1909, offering degrees at the bachelor's and master's levels and post-master's certificates. It has a 177-acre campus in Durant.

Academic Information The faculty has 252 members (57% full-time), 53% with terminal degrees. The undergraduate student-faculty ratio is 18:1. The library holds 307,939 titles, 730 serial subscriptions, and 9,895 audiovisual materials. Special programs include academic remediation, services for learning-disabled students, an honors program, advanced placement credit, accelerated degree programs, double majors, independent study, distance learning, summer session for credit, part-time degree programs (daytime, evenings), adult/continuing education programs, internships, and arrangement for off-campus study with Ardmore Higher Education Center, E.T. Dunlap Higher Education Center, Tinker AFB, OKCCC. The most frequently chosen baccalaureate fields are education, engineering technologies, liberal arts/general studies.
Student Body Statistics The student body totals 3,889, of whom 3,481 are undergraduates (609 freshmen). 55 percent are women and 45 percent are men. Students come from 32 states and territories and 28 other countries. 78 percent are from Oklahoma. 1.3 percent are international students.
Expenses for 2008–09 *Application fee:* $20. *State resident tuition:* $3639 full-time, $121.30 per credit hour part-time. *Nonresident tuition:* $10,009 full-time, $333.65 per credit hour part-time. *Mandatory fees:* $677 full-time, $22.55 per credit hour part-time. Full-time tuition and fees vary according to course level. Part-time tuition and fees vary according to course level and course load. *College room and board:* $4290. *College room only:* $1850. Room and board charges vary according to board plan and housing facility.
Financial Aid Forms of aid include need-based and non-need-based scholarships, athletic grants, and part-time jobs. The average aided 2007–08 undergraduate received an aid package worth $1190.
Freshman Admission Southeastern Oklahoma State University requires a high school transcript, SAT or ACT scores, and TOEFL scores for international students. An interview is required for some. The application deadline for regular admission is rolling.
Transfer Admission The application deadline for admission is rolling.
Entrance Difficulty Southeastern Oklahoma State University has an open admission policy for adults over 21. It assesses its entrance difficulty as minimally difficult for transfers; very difficult for honors program.
For Further Information Contact Ms. Kristie Luke, Associate Dean of Admissions and Records/Registrar, Southeastern Oklahoma State University, 1405 North 4th Avenue PMB 4225, Durant, OK 74701-0609. *Phone:* 580-745-2060 or 800-435-1327 (toll-free). *Fax:* 580-745-7502. *E-mail:* admissions@sosu.edu. *Web site:* http://www.sosu.edu/.

SOUTHERN NAZARENE UNIVERSITY

Bethany, Oklahoma

Southern Nazarene University is a coed, private, Nazarene, comprehensive institution, founded in 1899, offering degrees at the associate, bachelor's, and master's levels. It has a 40-acre campus in Bethany near Oklahoma City.

Academic Information The faculty has 198 members (37% full-time), 57% with terminal degrees. The undergraduate student-faculty ratio is 15:1. The library holds 95,535 titles, 225 serial subscriptions, and 4,257

audiovisual materials. Special programs include academic remediation, services for learning-disabled students, an honors program, study abroad, advanced placement credit, accelerated degree programs, double majors, self-designed majors, summer session for credit, part-time degree programs (daytime, evenings, summer), external degree programs, adult/continuing education programs, internships, and arrangement for off-campus study with Christian College Coalition Council for Christian Colleges and Universities. The most frequently chosen baccalaureate fields are business/marketing, family and consumer sciences, health professions and related sciences.
Student Body Statistics The student body totals 2,069, of whom 1,628 are undergraduates (270 freshmen). 53 percent are women and 47 percent are men. Students come from 36 states and territories and 28 other countries. 54 percent are from Oklahoma. 0.6 percent are international students.
Expenses for 2009–10 *Application fee:* $35. *Comprehensive fee:* $24,154 includes full-time tuition ($17,040), mandatory fees ($624), and college room and board ($6490). *College room only:* $3200. *Part-time tuition:* $568 per credit hour. *Part-time mandatory fees:* $23 per credit hour.
Financial Aid Forms of aid include need-based and non-need-based scholarships and part-time jobs. The priority application deadline for financial aid is March 1.
Freshman Admission Southern Nazarene University requires a high school transcript, 2 recommendations, SAT or ACT scores, and TOEFL scores for international students. An interview and ACT scores are recommended. The application deadline for regular admission is August 15.
Transfer Admission The application deadline for admission is August 15.
Entrance Difficulty Southern Nazarene University has an open admission policy.
For Further Information Contact Mr. Warren W. Rogers III, Director of Admissions, Southern Nazarene University, 6729 Northwest 39th Expressway, Bethany, OK 73008. *Phone:* 405-491-6324 or 800-648-9899 (toll-free). *Fax:* 405-491-6320. *E-mail:* admiss@snu.edu. *Web site:* http://www.snu.edu/.

SOUTHWESTERN CHRISTIAN UNIVERSITY

Bethany, Oklahoma

Southwestern Christian University is a coed, private, comprehensive institution, founded in 1946, affiliated with the Pentecostal Holiness Church, offering degrees at the associate, bachelor's, and master's levels. It has a 7-acre campus in Bethany near Oklahoma City.

Academic Information The library holds 38,900 titles and 100 serial subscriptions. Special programs include academic remediation, advanced placement credit, double majors, summer session for credit, part-time degree programs (daytime, evenings, summer), internships, and arrangement for off-campus study with Southern Nazarene University.
Student Body Statistics The student body totals 264, of whom 180 are undergraduates.
Expenses for 2008–09 *Comprehensive fee:* $14,400 includes full-time tuition ($9750), mandatory fees ($50), and college room and board ($4600). *Part-time tuition:* $345 per credit hour. *Part-time mandatory fees:* $25 per term.
Financial Aid Forms of aid include need-based and non-need-based scholarships and part-time jobs. The average aided 2008–09 undergraduate received an aid package worth an estimated $9000. The priority application deadline for financial aid is August 1.
Freshman Admission Southwestern Christian University requires an essay, a high school transcript, a minimum 2.0 high school GPA, recommendations, ACT scores, and TOEFL scores for international students. An interview is recommended. The application deadline for regular admission is rolling.
Transfer Admission The application deadline for admission is rolling.
Entrance Difficulty Southwestern Christian University assesses its entrance difficulty level as minimally difficult.
For Further Information Contact Jason Vaughn, Director of Admissions, Southwestern Christian University, PO Box 340, Bethany, OK 73008-0340. *Phone:* 405-789-7661. *Fax:* 405-495-0078. *E-mail:* admissions@swcu.edu. *Web site:* http://www.swcu.edu/.

SOUTHWESTERN OKLAHOMA STATE UNIVERSITY

Weatherford, Oklahoma

Southwestern Oklahoma State University is a coed, public, comprehensive unit of Southwestern Oklahoma State University, founded in 1901, offering degrees at the associate, bachelor's, master's, and first professional levels. It has a 73-acre campus in Weatherford near Oklahoma City.

Academic Information The faculty has 230 members (93% full-time). The undergraduate student-faculty ratio is 20:1. The library holds 217,051 titles, 1,230 serial subscriptions, and 6,718 audiovisual materials. Special programs include academic remediation, services for learning-disabled students, study abroad, advanced placement credit, accelerated degree programs, double majors, independent study, distance learning, self-designed majors, summer session for credit, part-time degree programs (daytime, evenings, summer), adult/continuing education programs, internships, and arrangement for off-campus study with Academic Common Market. The most frequently chosen baccalaureate fields are business/marketing, education, health professions and related sciences.
Student Body Statistics The student body totals 4,869, of whom 4,196 are undergraduates (908 freshmen). 58 percent are women and 42 percent are men. Students come from 32 states and territories and 32 other countries. 89 percent are from Oklahoma. 1.3 percent are international students.
Expenses for 2008–09 *Application fee:* $15. *State resident tuition:* $3360 full-time, $112 per credit hour part-time. *Nonresident tuition:* $8700 full-time, $290 per credit hour part-time. *Mandatory fees:* $750 full-time, $25 per credit hour part-time. Both full-time and part-time tuition and fees vary according to program. *College room and board:* $3900. *College room only:* $1500. Room and board charges vary according to board plan.
Financial Aid Forms of aid include need-based and non-need-based scholarships, athletic grants, and part-time jobs. The average aided 2008–09 undergraduate received an aid package worth an estimated $4788. The application deadline for financial aid is March 1.
Freshman Admission Southwestern Oklahoma State University requires a high school transcript, a minimum 2.0 high school GPA, SAT or ACT scores, and TOEFL scores for international students. The application deadline for regular admission is rolling.
Transfer Admission The application deadline for admission is rolling.
Entrance Difficulty Southwestern Oklahoma State University assesses its entrance difficulty level as minimally difficult. For the fall 2008 freshman class, 90 percent of the applicants were accepted.
For Further Information Contact Ms. Connie Phillips, Admission Counselor, Southwestern Oklahoma State University, 100 Campus Drive, Weatherford, OK 73096. *Phone:* 580-774-3009. *Fax:* 580-774-3795. *E-mail:* ropers@swosu.edu. *Web site:* http://www.swosu.edu/.

SPARTAN COLLEGE OF AERONAUTICS AND TECHNOLOGY

Tulsa, Oklahoma

http://www.spartan.edu/

UNIVERSITY OF CENTRAL OKLAHOMA

Edmond, Oklahoma

University of Central Oklahoma is a coed, public, comprehensive unit of Oklahoma State Regents for Higher Education, founded in 1890, offering degrees at the bachelor's and master's levels. It has a 200-acre campus in Edmond near Oklahoma City.

Academic Information The faculty has 871 members (51% full-time), 49% with terminal degrees. The undergraduate student-faculty ratio is 21:1. Special programs include services for learning-disabled students, an honors program, advanced placement credit, accelerated degree programs, ESL programs, double majors, independent study, distance learning, summer session for credit, part-time degree programs (daytime, evenings,

University of Central Oklahoma (continued)

weekends, summer), and internships. The most frequently chosen baccalaureate fields are business/marketing, education, liberal arts/general studies.

Student Body Statistics The student body totals 15,724, of whom 14,156 are undergraduates (2,131 freshmen). 58 percent are women and 42 percent are men. Students come from 46 states and territories and 75 other countries. 97 percent are from Oklahoma. 5.6 percent are international students.

Expenses for 2008–09 *Application fee:* $25. *State resident tuition:* $3681 full-time, $122.70 per credit hour part-time. *Nonresident tuition:* $10,110 full-time, $337 per credit hour part-time. *Mandatory fees:* $542 full-time, $18.05 per credit hour part-time. Both full-time and part-time tuition and fees vary according to course load, degree level, and program. *College room and board:* $7468. *College room only:* $4588. Room and board charges vary according to board plan and housing facility.

Financial Aid Forms of aid include need-based and non-need-based scholarships, athletic grants, and part-time jobs. The average aided 2007–08 undergraduate received an aid package worth $6885.

Freshman Admission University of Central Oklahoma requires a high school transcript, a minimum 2.7 high school GPA, rank in upper 50% of high school class, SAT or ACT scores, and TOEFL scores for international students. The application deadline for regular admission is rolling.

Transfer Admission The application deadline for admission is rolling.

Entrance Difficulty University of Central Oklahoma assesses its entrance difficulty level as minimally difficult. For the fall 2008 freshman class, 69 percent of the applicants were accepted.

For Further Information Contact Ms. Linda Lofton, Director, Admissions and Records Processing, University of Central Oklahoma, Office of Enrollment Services, 100 North University Drive, Box 151, Edmond, OK 73034-5209. *Phone:* 405-974-2338 Ext. 2338 or 800-254-4215 (toll-free). *Fax:* 405-341-4964. *E-mail:* admituco@uco.edu. *Web site:* http://www.uco.edu/.

UNIVERSITY OF OKLAHOMA

Norman, Oklahoma

University of Oklahoma is a coed, public university, founded in 1890, offering degrees at the bachelor's, master's, doctoral, and first professional levels and post-master's and postbachelor's certificates. It has a 3,762-acre campus in Norman near Oklahoma City.

Academic Information The faculty has 1,387 members (82% full-time), 77% with terminal degrees. The undergraduate student-faculty ratio is 18.5:1. The library holds 5 million titles, 51,585 serial subscriptions, and 6,695 audiovisual materials. Special programs include academic remediation, services for learning-disabled students, an honors program, cooperative (work-study) education, study abroad, advanced placement credit, accelerated degree programs, Freshman Honors College, ESL programs, double majors, independent study, distance learning, self-designed majors, summer session for credit, part-time degree programs (daytime, evenings, weekends, summer), external degree programs, adult/continuing education programs, internships, and arrangement for off-campus study with Oklahoma State University, Langston University, Northeastern State University, Rose State College, Oklahoma City Community College, Rogers University, Cameron University. The most frequently chosen baccalaureate fields are business/marketing, communications/journalism, social sciences.

Student Body Statistics The student body totals 26,185, of whom 19,592 are undergraduates (3,803 freshmen). 50 percent are women and 50 percent are men. Students come from 50 states and territories and 78 other countries. 74 percent are from Oklahoma. 2 percent are international students.

Expenses for 2008–09 *Application fee:* $40. *State resident tuition:* $2830 full-time, $117.90 per credit hour part-time. *Nonresident tuition:* $10,814 full-time, $450.60 per credit hour part-time. *Mandatory fees:* $2415 full-time, $90.10 per credit hour part-time, $126.50 per term part-time. Both full-time and part-time tuition and fees vary according to course load, location, program, and reciprocity agreements. *College room and board:* $7376. *College room only:* $4038. Room and board charges vary according to board plan and housing facility.

Financial Aid Forms of aid include need-based and non-need-based scholarships, athletic grants, and part-time jobs. The average aided 2007–08 undergraduate received an aid package worth $10,468. The application deadline for financial aid is continuous.

Freshman Admission University of Oklahoma requires 15 specified curricular units, SAT or ACT scores, and TOEFL scores for international students. An essay and a high school transcript are required for some. The application deadline for regular admission is April 1.

Transfer Admission The application deadline for admission is April 1.

Entrance Difficulty University of Oklahoma assesses its entrance difficulty level as moderately difficult; most difficult for honors college program. For the fall 2008 freshman class, 82 percent of the applicants were accepted.

For Further Information Contact Mr. Craig Hayes, Executive Director of Recruitment Services, University of Oklahoma, 550 Parrington Oval, L-1, Norman, OK 73019-3032. *Phone:* 405-325-2151 or 800-234-6868 (toll-free). *Fax:* 405-325-7478. *E-mail:* ou-pss@ou.edu. *Web site:* http://www.ou.edu/.

UNIVERSITY OF OKLAHOMA HEALTH SCIENCES CENTER

Oklahoma City, Oklahoma

University of Oklahoma Health Sciences Center is a coed, public, upper-level unit of University of Oklahoma, founded in 1890, offering degrees at the bachelor's, master's, doctoral, and first professional levels and post-master's and postbachelor's certificates. It has a 200-acre campus in Oklahoma City.

Academic Information The faculty has 463 members (65% full-time), 69% with terminal degrees. The undergraduate student-faculty ratio is 9:1. The library holds 300,260 titles and 4,028 serial subscriptions. Special programs include an honors program, advanced placement credit, distance learning, summer session for credit, part-time degree programs (daytime, evenings, summer), and internships. The most frequently chosen baccalaureate fields are health professions and related sciences, interdisciplinary studies.

Student Body Statistics The student body totals 3,913, of whom 1,171 are undergraduates. 86 percent are women and 14 percent are men. Students come from 20 states and territories and 19 other countries. 73 percent are from Oklahoma. 0.9 percent are international students.

Expenses for 2008–09 *State resident tuition:* $3537 full-time, $117.90 per credit hour part-time. *Nonresident tuition:* $13,518 full-time, $450.60 per credit hour part-time. *Mandatory fees:* $2020 full-time, $52.45 per credit hour part-time, $223.25 per term part-time. Both full-time and part-time tuition and fees vary according to program.

Financial Aid Forms of aid include non-need-based scholarships.

Transfer Admission The application deadline for admission is rolling.

For Further Information Contact Mr. Scott Boeh, Assistant Vice Provost for Academic Affairs, University of Oklahoma Health Sciences Center, BSE-200, PO Box 26901, 941 S. L. Young Boulevard, Oklahoma City, OK 73190. *Phone:* 405-271-2359 Ext. 48916. *Fax:* 405-271-2480. *E-mail:* admissions@ouhsc.edu. *Web site:* http://www.ouhsc.edu/.

UNIVERSITY OF OKLAHOMA—TULSA

Tulsa, Oklahoma

http://tulsa.ou.edu/

UNIVERSITY OF PHOENIX–OKLAHOMA CITY CAMPUS

Oklahoma City, Oklahoma

University of Phoenix–Oklahoma City Campus is a coed, proprietary, comprehensive institution, founded in 1976, offering degrees at the bachelor's and master's levels.

Academic Information The faculty has 135 members (12% full-time), 21% with terminal degrees. The undergraduate student-faculty ratio is 13:1. The library holds 16,781 serial subscriptions. Special programs include services for learning-disabled students, advanced placement credit, accelerated degree programs, independent study, distance learning, external degree programs, and adult/continuing education programs. The most frequently chosen baccalaureate fields are business/marketing, computer and information sciences, security and protective services.
Student Body Statistics The student body totals 801, of whom 732 are undergraduates. 2.3 percent are international students.
Expenses for 2008–09 *Application fee:* $0. *Tuition:* $10,590 full-time, $353 per credit part-time. Full-time tuition varies according to course level and course load.
Financial Aid Forms of aid include need-based and non-need-based scholarships. The average aided 2007–08 undergraduate received an aid package worth $7056. The application deadline for financial aid is continuous.
Freshman Admission University of Phoenix–Oklahoma City Campus requires 1 recommendation and TOEFL scores for international students. A high school transcript is required for some. The application deadline for regular admission is rolling.
Transfer Admission The application deadline for admission is rolling.
Entrance Difficulty University of Phoenix–Oklahoma City Campus has an open admission policy.
For Further Information Contact Ms. Audra McQuarie, Registrar/Executive Director, University of Phoenix–Oklahoma City Campus, 4035 South Riverpoint Parkway, Mail Stop CF-L101, Phoenix, AZ 85040-1958. *Phone:* 480-557-3303, 800-776-4867 (toll-free in-state), or 800-228-7240 (toll-free out-of-state). *Fax:* 480-643-1020. *E-mail:* audra.mcquarie@phoenix.edu. *Web site:* http://www.phoenix.edu/.

UNIVERSITY OF PHOENIX–TULSA CAMPUS

Tulsa, Oklahoma

University of Phoenix–Tulsa Campus is a coed, proprietary, comprehensive institution, founded in 1998, offering degrees at the bachelor's and master's levels.

Academic Information The faculty has 155 members (10% full-time), 21% with terminal degrees. The library holds 16,781 serial subscriptions. Special programs include services for learning-disabled students, advanced placement credit, accelerated degree programs, independent study, distance learning, external degree programs, and adult/continuing education programs. The most frequently chosen baccalaureate fields are business/marketing, computer and information sciences, security and protective services.
Student Body Statistics The student body totals 785, of whom 703 are undergraduates (48 freshmen). 66 percent are women and 34 percent are men. 5.4 percent are international students.
Expenses for 2008–09 *Application fee:* $45. *Tuition:* $10,590 full-time. Full-time tuition varies according to course level and course load.
Financial Aid Forms of aid include need-based and non-need-based scholarships. The average aided 2007–08 undergraduate received an aid package worth $6707. The application deadline for financial aid is continuous.
Freshman Admission University of Phoenix–Tulsa Campus requires 1 recommendation and TOEFL scores for international students. A high school transcript is required for some. The application deadline for regular admission is rolling.
Transfer Admission The application deadline for admission is rolling.
Entrance Difficulty University of Phoenix–Tulsa Campus has an open admission policy.
For Further Information Contact Ms. Evelyn Gaskin, Registrar/Executive Director, University of Phoenix–Tulsa Campus, 4615 East Elwood Street, Mail Stop AA-K101, Phoenix, AZ 85040-1958. *Phone:* 480-557-3303, 800-776-4867 (toll-free in-state), or 800-228-7240 (toll-free out-of-state). *Fax:* 480-643-1020. *E-mail:* evelyn.gaskin@phoenix.edu. *Web site:* http://www.phoenix.edu/.

UNIVERSITY OF SCIENCE AND ARTS OF OKLAHOMA

Chickasha, Oklahoma

University of Science and Arts of Oklahoma is a coed, public, four-year college of Oklahoma State Regents for Higher Education, founded in 1908, offering degrees at the bachelor's level. It has a 75-acre campus in Chickasha near Oklahoma City.

Academic Information The faculty has 89 members (58% full-time), 60% with terminal degrees. The student-faculty ratio is 16:1. The library holds 75,184 titles, 44,827 serial subscriptions, and 4,813 audiovisual materials. Special programs include academic remediation, services for learning-disabled students, advanced placement credit, accelerated degree programs, double majors, independent study, self-designed majors, summer session for credit, part-time degree programs (daytime, evenings, summer), adult/continuing education programs, internships, and arrangement for off-campus study. The most frequently chosen baccalaureate fields are business/marketing, education, psychology.
Student Body Statistics The student body is made up of 1,158 undergraduates (225 freshmen). 64 percent are women and 36 percent are men. Students come from 22 states and territories and 14 other countries. 94 percent are from Oklahoma. 5.4 percent are international students.
Expenses for 2008–09 *Application fee:* $15. *State resident tuition:* $3270 full-time, $109 per hour part-time. *Nonresident tuition:* $9390 full-time, $313 per hour part-time. *Mandatory fees:* $1170 full-time, $39 per hour part-time. *College room and board:* $4710. *College room only:* $2460. Room and board charges vary according to board plan and housing facility.
Financial Aid Forms of aid include need-based and non-need-based scholarships, athletic grants, and part-time jobs. The average aided 2008–09 undergraduate received an aid package worth an estimated $8334.
Freshman Admission University of Science and Arts of Oklahoma requires SAT or ACT scores and TOEFL scores for international students. Graduation in top half of high school class is recommended. A high school transcript, a minimum 3.0 high school GPA, and graduation in top half of high school class are required for some. The application deadline for regular admission is August 31.
Transfer Admission The application deadline for admission is August 31.
Entrance Difficulty University of Science and Arts of Oklahoma assesses its entrance difficulty level as moderately difficult. For the fall 2008 freshman class, 93 percent of the applicants were accepted.
For Further Information Contact Office of Admissions, University of Science and Arts of Oklahoma, 1727 West Alabama, Chickasha, OK 73018-5322. *Phone:* 405-574-1357 or 800-933-8726 Ext. 1212 (toll-free). *Fax:* 405-574-1220. *E-mail:* usao-admissions@usao.edu. *Web site:* http://www.usao.edu/.

UNIVERSITY OF TULSA

Tulsa, Oklahoma

University of Tulsa is a coed, private university, founded in 1894, affiliated with the Presbyterian Church (U.S.A.), offering degrees at the bachelor's, master's, doctoral, and first professional levels and first professional and postbachelor's certificates. It has a 2,090-acre campus in Tulsa.

Academic Information The faculty has 397 members (80% full-time), 96% with terminal degrees. The undergraduate student-faculty ratio is 10:1. The library holds 1 million titles, 27,905 serial subscriptions, and 20,362 audiovisual materials. Special programs include services for learning-disabled students, an honors program, study abroad, advanced placement credit, accelerated degree programs, ESL programs, double majors, independent study, self-designed majors, summer session for credit, part-time degree programs (daytime, evenings, summer), adult/continuing education programs, and internships. The most frequently chosen baccalaureate fields are business/marketing, engineering, visual and performing arts.
Student Body Statistics The student body totals 4,192, of whom 3,049 are undergraduates (695 freshmen). 48 percent are women and 52 percent

University of Tulsa (continued)
are men. Students come from 47 states and territories and 50 other countries. 59 percent are from Oklahoma. 11.7 percent are international students.
Expenses for 2008–09 *Application fee:* $35. *One-time mandatory fee:* $425. *Comprehensive fee:* $31,716 includes full-time tuition ($23,860), mandatory fees ($80), and college room and board ($7776). *College room only:* $4294. Room and board charges vary according to board plan and housing facility. *Part-time tuition:* $856 per credit hour.
Financial Aid Forms of aid include need-based and non-need-based scholarships, athletic grants, and part-time jobs. The average aided 2007–08 undergraduate received an aid package worth $23,285.
Freshman Admission University of Tulsa requires an essay, a high school transcript, 1 recommendation, an interview, SAT or ACT scores, and TOEFL scores for international students. A minimum 3.0 high school GPA is recommended. The application deadline for regular admission is rolling.
Transfer Admission The application deadline for admission is rolling.
Entrance Difficulty University of Tulsa assesses its entrance difficulty level as very difficult; moderately difficult for transfers. For the fall 2008 freshman class, 46 percent of the applicants were accepted.
For Further Information Contact Mr. Earl Johnson, Dean of Admission, University of Tulsa, 600 South College Avenue, Tulsa, OK 74104. *Phone:* 918-631-2307 or 800-331-3050 (toll-free). *Fax:* 918-631-5003. *E-mail:* admission@utulsa.edu. *Web site:* http://www.utulsa.edu/.

South Dakota

AUGUSTANA COLLEGE

Sioux Falls, South Dakota

Augustana College is a coed, private, comprehensive institution, founded in 1860, affiliated with the Evangelical Lutheran Church in America, offering degrees at the bachelor's and master's levels. It has a 100-acre campus in Sioux Falls.

Academic Information The faculty has 174 members (68% full-time), 59% with terminal degrees. The undergraduate student-faculty ratio is 12:1. The library holds 203,804 titles, 5,533 serial subscriptions, and 4,491 audiovisual materials. Special programs include academic remediation, services for learning-disabled students, an honors program, cooperative (work-study) education, study abroad, advanced placement credit, accelerated degree programs, Freshman Honors College, double majors, independent study, self-designed majors, summer session for credit, part-time degree programs (daytime, evenings, summer), internships, and arrangement for off-campus study with 10 other colleges in the upper Midwest. The most frequently chosen baccalaureate fields are business/marketing, education, health professions and related sciences.
Student Body Statistics The student body totals 1,754, of whom 1,733 are undergraduates (438 freshmen). 64 percent are women and 36 percent are men. Students come from 28 states and territories and 14 other countries. 48 percent are from South Dakota. 2.5 percent are international students.
Expenses for 2009–10 *Application fee:* $0. *Comprehensive fee:* $29,735 includes full-time tuition ($23,275), mandatory fees ($272), and college room and board ($6188).
Financial Aid Forms of aid include need-based and non-need-based scholarships, athletic grants, and part-time jobs. The average aided 2008–09 undergraduate received an aid package worth an estimated $18,539. The priority application deadline for financial aid is March 1.
Freshman Admission Augustana College requires an essay, a high school transcript, a minimum 2.75 high school GPA, 1 recommendation, SAT or ACT scores, and TOEFL scores for international students. An interview is recommended. The application deadline for regular admission is August 1.
Transfer Admission The application deadline for admission is rolling.
Entrance Difficulty Augustana College assesses its entrance difficulty level as moderately difficult; minimally difficult for transfers. For the fall 2008 freshman class, 81 percent of the applicants were accepted.
For Further Information Contact Ms. Nancy Davidson, Vice President for Enrollment, Augustana College, 2001 S. Summit Avenue, Sioux Falls, SD 57197. *Phone:* 605-274-5516, 800-727-2844 Ext. 5516 (toll-free in-state), or 800-727-2844 (toll-free out-of-state). *Fax:* 605-274-5518. *E-mail:* admission@augie.edu. *Web site:* http://www.augie.edu/.

BLACK HILLS STATE UNIVERSITY

Spearfish, South Dakota

Black Hills State University is a coed, public, comprehensive unit of South Dakota State University System, founded in 1883, offering degrees at the associate, bachelor's, and master's levels and post-master's and postbachelor's certificates. It has a 123-acre campus in Spearfish.

Academic Information The faculty has 201 members (67% full-time), 51% with terminal degrees. The undergraduate student-faculty ratio is 19:1. Special programs include academic remediation, services for learning-disabled students, an honors program, cooperative (work-study) education, advanced placement credit, accelerated degree programs, double majors, independent study, distance learning, summer session for credit, part-time degree programs (daytime, evenings, summer), internships, and arrangement for off-campus study with South Dakota State University. The most frequently chosen baccalaureate fields are business/marketing, education, public administration and social services.
Student Body Statistics The student body totals 4,017, of whom 3,687 are undergraduates (583 freshmen). 64 percent are women and 36 percent are men. Students come from 45 states and territories and 13 other countries. 80 percent are from South Dakota.
Expenses for 2009–10 *Application fee:* $20. *State resident tuition:* $2934 full-time, $91.70 per credit hour part-time. *Nonresident tuition:* $9320 full-time, $291.25 per credit hour part-time. *Mandatory fees:* $3656 full-time, $115.84 per credit hour part-time. *College room and board:* $5172. *College room only:* $2701.
Financial Aid Forms of aid include need-based and non-need-based scholarships, athletic grants, and part-time jobs. The average aided 2007–08 undergraduate received an aid package worth $4241. The priority application deadline for financial aid is March 1.
Freshman Admission Black Hills State University requires a high school transcript, minimum 2.0 high school GPA in core curriculum, SAT or ACT scores, and TOEFL scores for international students. The application deadline for regular admission is July 18.
Transfer Admission The application deadline for admission is July 18.
Entrance Difficulty Black Hills State University assesses its entrance difficulty level as minimally difficult. For the fall 2008 freshman class, 95 percent of the applicants were accepted.
For Further Information Contact Ms. Beth Azevedo, Director of Admissions, Black Hills State University, 1200 University ST USB 9502, Spearfish, SD 57799-9502. *Phone:* 605-642-6343 or 800-255-2478 (toll-free). *Fax:* 605-642-6254. *E-mail:* admissions@bhsu.edu. *Web site:* http://www.bhsu.edu/.

COLORADO TECHNICAL UNIVERSITY SIOUX FALLS

Sioux Falls, South Dakota

Colorado Technical University Sioux Falls is a coed, proprietary, comprehensive institution, founded in 1965, offering degrees at the associate, bachelor's, and master's levels. It has a 3-acre campus in Sioux Falls.

Academic Information The faculty has 82 members. Special programs include cooperative (work-study) education, advanced placement credit, accelerated degree programs, double majors, distance learning, summer session for credit, part-time degree programs (daytime, evenings, weekends, summer), adult/continuing education programs, and internships. The most

frequently chosen baccalaureate fields are business/marketing, computer and information sciences, security and protective services.
Student Body Statistics The student body totals 912, of whom 816 are undergraduates (105 freshmen). 64 percent are women and 36 percent are men. 98 percent are from South Dakota.
Expenses for 2009–10 *Application fee:* $50. Contact campus for cost.
Financial Aid Forms of aid include need-based scholarships and part-time jobs. The average aided 2007–08 undergraduate received an aid package worth $3500. The application deadline for financial aid is continuous.
Freshman Admission Colorado Technical University Sioux Falls requires an interview and TOEFL scores for international students. The application deadline for regular admission is rolling and for nonresidents it is rolling.
Transfer Admission The application deadline for admission is rolling.
Entrance Difficulty Colorado Technical University Sioux Falls assesses its entrance difficulty level as minimally difficult.
For Further Information Contact Catherine Taplett Allen, VP of Admissions, Colorado Technical University Sioux Falls, 3901 West 59th Street, Sioux Falls, SD 57108. *Phone:* 605-361-0200. *Fax:* 605-361-5954. *E-mail:* callen@sf.coloradotech.edu. *Web site:* http://www.ctu-siouxfalls.com/.

DAKOTA STATE UNIVERSITY

Madison, South Dakota

Dakota State University is a coed, public, comprehensive unit of South Dakota Board of Regents, founded in 1881, offering degrees at the associate, bachelor's, master's, and doctoral levels. It has a 40-acre campus in Madison near Sioux Falls.

Academic Information The faculty has 121 members (74% full-time), 59% with terminal degrees. The undergraduate student-faculty ratio is 17:1. The library holds 95,819 titles, 350 serial subscriptions, and 436 audiovisual materials. Special programs include academic remediation, services for learning-disabled students, an honors program, cooperative (work-study) education, advanced placement credit, ESL programs, double majors, independent study, distance learning, summer session for credit, part-time degree programs (daytime, evenings, summer), adult/continuing education programs, internships, and arrangement for off-campus study with South Dakota State University, University of Sioux Falls, University of South Dakota. The most frequently chosen baccalaureate fields are business/marketing, computer and information sciences, education.
Student Body Statistics The student body totals 2,675, of whom 2,296 are undergraduates (273 freshmen). 54 percent are women and 46 percent are men. Students come from 26 states and territories and 13 other countries. 80 percent are from South Dakota.
Expenses for 2008–09 *Application fee:* $20. *State resident tuition:* $2646 full-time, $88 per credit hour part-time. *Nonresident tuition:* $3966 full-time, $132 per credit hour part-time. *Mandatory fees:* $3852 full-time, $106 per credit hour part-time. Both full-time and part-time tuition and fees vary according to location and reciprocity agreements. *College room and board:* $4612. *College room only:* $2545. Room and board charges vary according to board plan and housing facility.
Financial Aid Forms of aid include need-based and non-need-based scholarships, athletic grants, and part-time jobs. The average aided 2008–09 undergraduate received an aid package worth an estimated $7269. The priority application deadline for financial aid is March 1.
Freshman Admission Dakota State University requires a high school transcript, a minimum 2.7 high school GPA, rank in upper two-thirds of high school class, and SAT or ACT scores. TOEFL scores for international students are recommended. The application deadline for regular admission is rolling.
Transfer Admission The application deadline for admission is rolling.
Entrance Difficulty Dakota State University assesses its entrance difficulty level as minimally difficult; moderately difficult for out-of-state applicants; moderately difficult for transfers. For the fall 2008 freshman class, 96 percent of the applicants were accepted.
For Further Information Contact Ms. Dana Hoff, Admissions Secretary, Dakota State University, 820 North Washington, Madison, SD 57042-1799. *Phone:* 605-256-5139 or 888-DSU-9988 (toll-free). *Fax:* 605-256-5020. *E-mail:* yourfuture@dsu.edu. *Web site:* http://www.dsu.edu/.

DAKOTA WESLEYAN UNIVERSITY

Mitchell, South Dakota

Dakota Wesleyan University is a coed, private, United Methodist, comprehensive institution, founded in 1885, offering degrees at the associate, bachelor's, and master's levels. It has a 50-acre campus in Mitchell.

Academic Information The faculty has 79 members (56% full-time), 48% with terminal degrees. The undergraduate student-faculty ratio is 13:1. The library holds 92,910 titles, 164 serial subscriptions, and 3,944 audiovisual materials. Special programs include academic remediation, services for learning-disabled students, an honors program, study abroad, advanced placement credit, double majors, independent study, distance learning, self-designed majors, summer session for credit, part-time degree programs (daytime, evenings, summer), internships, and arrangement for off-campus study. The most frequently chosen baccalaureate fields are business/marketing, education, health professions and related sciences.
Student Body Statistics The student body totals 711, of whom 683 are undergraduates (163 freshmen). 59 percent are women and 41 percent are men. Students come from 28 states and territories and 6 other countries. 67 percent are from South Dakota. 1.5 percent are international students.
Expenses for 2009–10 *Application fee:* $25. *Comprehensive fee:* $24,650 includes full-time tuition ($19,000) and college room and board ($5650). *College room only:* $2300. *Part-time tuition:* $410 per credit.
Financial Aid Forms of aid include athletic grants and part-time jobs. The average aided 2007–08 undergraduate received an aid package worth $12,000. The priority application deadline for financial aid is April 15.
Freshman Admission Dakota Wesleyan University requires a high school transcript, SAT or ACT scores, and TOEFL scores for international students. A minimum 2.0 high school GPA is recommended. The application deadline for regular admission is August 27.
Transfer Admission The application deadline for admission is August 27.
Entrance Difficulty Dakota Wesleyan University assesses its entrance difficulty level as moderately difficult. For the fall 2008 freshman class, 75 percent of the applicants were accepted.
For Further Information Contact Mrs. Melissa Herr-Valburg, Director of Admissions, Dakota Wesleyan University, 1200 West University Avenue, Mitchell, SD 57301-4398. *Phone:* 605-995-2600 Ext. 2652 or 800-333-8506 (toll-free). *Fax:* 605-995-2699. *E-mail:* admissions@dwu.edu. *Web site:* http://www.dwu.edu/.

KILIAN COMMUNITY COLLEGE

Sioux Falls, South Dakota

Kilian Community College is a coed, private, two-year college, founded in 1977, offering degrees at the associate level. It has a 2-acre campus in Sioux Falls.

Academic Information The faculty has 35 members (20% full-time), 3% with terminal degrees. The student-faculty ratio is 9:1. The library holds 78,000 titles and 395 serial subscriptions. Special programs include academic remediation, services for learning-disabled students, cooperative (work-study) education, ESL programs, double majors, independent study, distance learning, summer session for credit, part-time degree programs (daytime, evenings, summer), and arrangement for off-campus study with Students are allowed to take courses from Presentation College, Aberdeen, SD, to complete their program of study.
Student Body Statistics The student body is made up of 330 undergraduates (41 freshmen). 71 percent are women and 29 percent are men. Students come from 3 states and territories. 95 percent are from South Dakota.
Expenses for 2009–10 *Application fee:* $25. *Tuition:* $8820 full-time, $245 per credit hour part-time. *Mandatory fees:* $255 full-time, $85 per term part-time.
Financial Aid Forms of aid include need-based scholarships and part-time jobs. The application deadline for financial aid is continuous.
Freshman Admission Kilian Community College requires a high school transcript and TOEFL scores for international students. The application deadline for regular admission is rolling and for nonresidents it is rolling.
Transfer Admission The application deadline for admission is rolling.

Kilian Community College (continued)
Entrance Difficulty Kilian Community College has an open admission policy.
For Further Information Contact Ms. Mary Klockman, Director of Admissions, Kilian Community College, 300 East 6th Street, Sioux Falls, SD 57103. *Phone:* 605-221-3100 or 800-888-1147 (toll-free). *Fax:* 605-336-2606. *E-mail:* info@killian.edu. *Web site:* http://www.kilian.edu/.

MOUNT MARTY COLLEGE

Yankton, South Dakota

Mount Marty College is a coed, private, Roman Catholic, comprehensive institution, founded in 1936, offering degrees at the associate, bachelor's, and master's levels. It has an 80-acre campus in Yankton.

Academic Information The faculty has 102 members (53% full-time), 32% with terminal degrees. The undergraduate student-faculty ratio is 11:1. The library holds 76,571 titles and 424 serial subscriptions. Special programs include academic remediation, services for learning-disabled students, an honors program, cooperative (work-study) education, advanced placement credit, accelerated degree programs, double majors, independent study, distance learning, self-designed majors, summer session for credit, part-time degree programs (daytime, evenings), adult/continuing education programs, internships, and arrangement for off-campus study with members of the Colleges of Mid-America. The most frequently chosen baccalaureate fields are education, business/marketing, health professions and related sciences.
Student Body Statistics The student body totals 1,180, of whom 1,046 are undergraduates (184 freshmen). 62 percent are women and 38 percent are men. Students come from 14 states and territories. 65 percent are from South Dakota. 0.2 percent are international students.
Expenses for 2008–09 *Application fee:* $35. *Comprehensive fee:* $23,460 includes full-time tuition ($16,420), mandatory fees ($1830), and college room and board ($5210). Full-time tuition and fees vary according to course load and location. *Part-time tuition:* $190 per credit hour. *Part-time mandatory fees:* $25 per credit hour. Part-time tuition and fees vary according to course load and location.
Financial Aid Forms of aid include need-based and non-need-based scholarships, athletic grants, and part-time jobs. The average aided 2008–09 undergraduate received an aid package worth an estimated $26,937. The priority application deadline for financial aid is March 1.
Freshman Admission Mount Marty College requires a high school transcript, a minimum 2.0 high school GPA, SAT or ACT scores, and TOEFL scores for international students. An interview is recommended. The application deadline for regular admission is rolling.
Transfer Admission The application deadline for admission is rolling.
Entrance Difficulty Mount Marty College assesses its entrance difficulty level as minimally difficult. For the fall 2008 freshman class, 78 percent of the applicants were accepted.
For Further Information Contact Ms. Brandi DeFries, Vice President for Enrollment Management, Mount Marty College, 1105 West 8th Street, Yankton, SD 57078. *Phone:* 605-668-1545 or 800-658-4552 (toll-free). *Fax:* 605-668-1607. *E-mail:* mmcadmit@mtmc.edu. *Web site:* http://www.mtmc.edu/.

NATIONAL AMERICAN UNIVERSITY

Rapid City, South Dakota

National American University is a coed, proprietary, comprehensive unit of National College, founded in 1941, offering degrees at the associate, bachelor's, and master's levels. It has an 8-acre campus in Rapid City.

For Further Information Contact Ms. Angela Beck, Director of Enrollment Management, National American University, 321 Kansas City Street, Rapid City, SD 57701. *Phone:* 605-394-4902 or 800-843-8892 (toll-free). *Fax:* 605-394-4871. *E-mail:* abeck@national.edu. *Web site:* http://www.rapid.national.edu/.

NATIONAL AMERICAN UNIVERSITY–SIOUX FALLS BRANCH

Sioux Falls, South Dakota

National American University–Sioux Falls Branch is a coed, proprietary, comprehensive unit of National College, founded in 1941, offering degrees at the associate, bachelor's, and master's levels.

For Further Information Contact Ms. Lisa Houtsma, Director of Admissions, National American University–Sioux Falls Branch, 2801 South Kiwanis Avenue, Suite 100, Sioux Falls, SD 57105. *Phone:* 605-336-4600 or 800-388-5430 (toll-free out-of-state). *Fax:* 605-336-4605. *E-mail:* lhoutsma@national.edu. *Web site:* http://www.national.edu/.

NORTHERN STATE UNIVERSITY

Aberdeen, South Dakota

Northern State University is a coed, public, comprehensive unit of South Dakota Board of Regents, founded in 1901, offering degrees at the associate, bachelor's, and master's levels and postbachelor's certificates. It has a 52-acre campus in Aberdeen.

Academic Information The faculty has 115 members (79% full-time), 67% with terminal degrees. The undergraduate student-faculty ratio is 22:1. The library holds 192,007 titles and 882 serial subscriptions. Special programs include academic remediation, services for learning-disabled students, an honors program, cooperative (work-study) education, study abroad, advanced placement credit, accelerated degree programs, ESL programs, distance learning, self-designed majors, summer session for credit, part-time degree programs, adult/continuing education programs, internships, and arrangement for off-campus study with National Student Exchange. The most frequently chosen baccalaureate fields are business/marketing, education, social sciences.
Student Body Statistics The student body totals 2,927, of whom 2,412 are undergraduates (400 freshmen). 58 percent are women and 42 percent are men. Students come from 35 states and territories and 14 other countries. 75 percent are from South Dakota. 11.6 percent are international students.
Expenses for 2008–09 *Application fee:* $20. *State resident tuition:* $2646 full-time, $88.20 per credit hour part-time. *Nonresident tuition:* $8404 full-time, $280.15 per credit hour part-time. *Mandatory fees:* $3066 full-time, $102.20 per credit hour part-time. Both full-time and part-time tuition and fees vary according to course level, course load, and reciprocity agreements. *College room and board:* $4664. *College room only:* $2483. Room and board charges vary according to board plan.
Financial Aid Forms of aid include need-based and non-need-based scholarships, athletic grants, and part-time jobs. The average aided 2008–09 undergraduate received an aid package worth an estimated $6166. The priority application deadline for financial aid is March 1.
Freshman Admission Northern State University requires a high school transcript, a minimum 2.6 high school GPA, SAT or ACT scores, and TOEFL scores for international students. Recommendations are required for some. The application deadline for regular admission is September 1.
Transfer Admission The application deadline for admission is September 1.
Entrance Difficulty Northern State University assesses its entrance difficulty level as minimally difficult; moderately difficult for transfers. For the fall 2008 freshman class, 92 percent of the applicants were accepted.
For Further Information Contact Mr. Allan Vogel, Director of Admissions-Campus, Northern State University, 1200 South Jay Street, Aberdeen, SD 57401. *Phone:* 605-626-2544 or 800-678-5330 (toll-free). *Fax:* 605-626-2587. *E-mail:* admissions1@northern.edu. *Web site:* http://www.northern.edu/.

OGLALA LAKOTA COLLEGE

Kyle, South Dakota

Oglala Lakota College is a coed, public, comprehensive institution, founded in 1970, offering degrees at the associate, bachelor's, and master's levels.

Academic Information The library holds 15,000 titles and 150 serial subscriptions. Special programs include academic remediation, cooperative (work-study) education, accelerated degree programs, summer session for credit, part-time degree programs (daytime, evenings, summer), adult/continuing education programs, internships, and arrangement for off-campus study with American Indian Higher Education Consortium.
Student Body Statistics The student body totals 1,000. Students come from 2 states and territories.
Financial Aid Forms of aid include need-based and non-need-based scholarships and part-time jobs. The application deadline for financial aid is continuous.
Entrance Difficulty Oglala Lakota College has an open admission policy.
For Further Information Contact Director of Admissions, Oglala Lakota College, 490 Piya Wiconi Road, Kyle, SD 57752-0490. *Phone:* 605-455-2321 Ext. 236. *E-mail:* lmeseteth@olc.edu. *Web site:* http://www.olc.edu/.

PRESENTATION COLLEGE

Aberdeen, South Dakota

Presentation College is a coed, primarily women's, private, Roman Catholic, four-year college, founded in 1951, offering degrees at the associate and bachelor's levels. It has a 100-acre campus in Aberdeen.

Academic Information The faculty has 88 members (50% full-time). The student-faculty ratio is 10:1. The library holds 40,000 titles and 430 serial subscriptions. Special programs include academic remediation, cooperative (work-study) education, advanced placement credit, accelerated degree programs, double majors, distance learning, summer session for credit, part-time degree programs (daytime, evenings, summer), external degree programs, adult/continuing education programs, and internships. The most frequently chosen baccalaureate fields are business/marketing, biological/life sciences, health professions and related sciences.
Student Body Statistics The student body is made up of 733 undergraduates (83 freshmen). 82 percent are women and 18 percent are men. Students come from 16 states and territories and 1 other country. 61 percent are from South Dakota. 0.2 percent are international students.
Expenses for 2009–10 *Application fee:* $25. *Comprehensive fee:* $19,750 includes full-time tuition ($14,250) and college room and board ($5500). *College room only:* $4100. *Part-time tuition:* $525 per credit.
Financial Aid Forms of aid include need-based and non-need-based scholarships and part-time jobs. The average aided 2007–08 undergraduate received an aid package worth $8737. The priority application deadline for financial aid is March 1.
Freshman Admission Presentation College requires a high school transcript, SAT or ACT scores, and TOEFL scores for international students. A minimum 2.0 high school GPA is recommended.
2 recommendations and college transcripts are required for some. The application deadline for regular admission is rolling.
Transfer Admission The application deadline for admission is rolling.
Entrance Difficulty Presentation College has an open admission policy except for allied health programs, nursing. It assesses its entrance difficulty as minimally difficult for allied health programs.
For Further Information Contact Ms. Jo Ellen Lindner, Vice President for Enrollment and Student Retention Services, Presentation College, 1500 North Main Street, Aberdeen, SD 57401. *Phone:* 605-229-8492 or 800-437-6060 (toll-free). *Fax:* 605-229-8425. *E-mail:* admit@presentation.edu. *Web site:* http://www.presentation.edu/.

SINTE GLESKA UNIVERSITY

Mission, South Dakota

Sinte Gleska University is a coed, private, comprehensive institution, founded in 1970, offering degrees at the associate, bachelor's, and master's levels. It has a 52-acre campus in Mission.

Academic Information The library holds 25,000 titles and 80 serial subscriptions. Special programs include academic remediation, an honors program, double majors, distance learning, summer session for credit, part-time degree programs (daytime, evenings, summer), adult/continuing education programs, internships, and arrangement for off-campus study with American Indian Higher Education Consortium.
Student Body Statistics The student body totals 971, of whom 869 are undergraduates.
Financial Aid Forms of aid include need-based and non-need-based scholarships and part-time jobs. The application deadline for financial aid is continuous.
Freshman Admission Sinte Gleska University requires a high school transcript. The application deadline for regular admission is August 20.
Transfer Admission The application deadline for admission is August 20.
Entrance Difficulty Sinte Gleska University has an open admission policy. It assesses its entrance difficulty as minimally difficult for transfers.
For Further Information Contact Mr. Jack Herman, Registrar and Director of Admissions, Sinte Gleska University, PO Box 105, Mission, SD 57555-0105. *Phone:* 605-856-8100 Ext. 8479. *Fax:* 605-747-2098. *Web site:* http://www.sintegleska.edu/.

SOUTH DAKOTA SCHOOL OF MINES AND TECHNOLOGY

Rapid City, South Dakota

South Dakota School of Mines and Technology is a coed, public unit of South Dakota State University System, founded in 1885, offering degrees at the associate, bachelor's, master's, and doctoral levels. It has a 120-acre campus in Rapid City.

Academic Information The faculty has 145 members (93% full-time), 76% with terminal degrees. The undergraduate student-faculty ratio is 13:1. The library holds 278,803 titles, 11,798 serial subscriptions, and 18,542 audiovisual materials. Special programs include academic remediation, services for learning-disabled students, cooperative (work-study) education, study abroad, advanced placement credit, ESL programs, double majors, independent study, distance learning, summer session for credit, part-time degree programs (daytime, evenings), adult/continuing education programs, and internships. The most frequently chosen baccalaureate fields are engineering, interdisciplinary studies, physical sciences.
Student Body Statistics The student body totals 2,061, of whom 1,817 are undergraduates (317 freshmen). 30 percent are women and 70 percent are men. Students come from 38 states and territories and 20 other countries. 63 percent are from South Dakota. 2.1 percent are international students.
Expenses for 2008–09 *Application fee:* $20. *State resident tuition:* $2650 full-time, $88.20 per credit hour part-time. *Nonresident tuition:* $3970 full-time, $132.20 per credit hour part-time. *Mandatory fees:* $3830 full-time, $133.54 per credit hour part-time. Both full-time and part-time tuition and fees vary according to course load, program, and reciprocity agreements. *College room and board:* $4740. Room and board charges vary according to board plan and housing facility.
Financial Aid Forms of aid include need-based and non-need-based scholarships, athletic grants, and part-time jobs. The average aided 2008–09 undergraduate received an aid package worth an estimated $8260.
Freshman Admission South Dakota School of Mines and Technology requires a high school transcript and TOEFL scores for international students. A minimum 2.6 high school GPA and SAT or ACT scores are recommended. SAT or ACT scores are required for some. The application deadline for regular admission is rolling.
Transfer Admission The application deadline for admission is rolling.

South Dakota School of Mines and Technology (continued)

Entrance Difficulty South Dakota School of Mines and Technology assesses its entrance difficulty level as moderately difficult. For the fall 2008 freshman class, 83 percent of the applicants were accepted.

For Further Information Contact Mr. Tex Claymore, Associate Director of Admissions, South Dakota School of Mines and Technology, 501 East Saint Joseph, Rapid City, SD 57701-3995. *Phone:* 605-394-2414 Ext. 1266 or 800-544-8162 Ext. 2414 (toll-free). *Fax:* 605-394-1979. *E-mail:* admissions@sdsmt.edu. *Web site:* http://www.sdsmt.edu/.

SOUTH DAKOTA STATE UNIVERSITY

Brookings, South Dakota

South Dakota State University is a coed, public unit of South Dakota Board of Regents, founded in 1881, offering degrees at the associate, bachelor's, master's, doctoral, and first professional levels and post-master's and postbachelor's certificates. It has a 272-acre campus in Brookings.

Academic Information The faculty has 674 members (71% full-time), 52% with terminal degrees. The undergraduate student-faculty ratio is 18:1. The library holds 987,599 titles, 44,599 serial subscriptions, and 3,280 audiovisual materials. Special programs include academic remediation, services for learning-disabled students, an honors program, cooperative (work-study) education, study abroad, advanced placement credit, accelerated degree programs, Freshman Honors College, ESL programs, double majors, independent study, distance learning, summer session for credit, part-time degree programs (daytime, evenings, summer), adult/continuing education programs, internships, and arrangement for off-campus study with National Student Exchange. The most frequently chosen baccalaureate fields are agriculture, health professions and related sciences, social sciences.

Student Body Statistics The student body totals 11,995, of whom 10,532 are undergraduates (2,101 freshmen). 52 percent are women and 48 percent are men. Students come from 36 states and territories and 24 other countries. 67 percent are from South Dakota. 0.9 percent are international students.

Expenses for 2008–09 *Application fee:* $20. *State resident tuition:* $2646 full-time, $88.20 per credit hour part-time. *Nonresident tuition:* $3966 full-time, $132.20 per credit hour part-time. *Mandatory fees:* $3162 full-time, $105.40 per credit hour part-time. Both full-time and part-time tuition and fees vary according to course load, location, program, and reciprocity agreements. *College room and board:* $5423. *College room only:* $2450. Room and board charges vary according to board plan and housing facility.

Financial Aid Forms of aid include need-based and non-need-based scholarships, athletic grants, and part-time jobs. The average aided 2008–09 undergraduate received an aid package worth an estimated $8634. The priority application deadline for financial aid is March 11.

Freshman Admission South Dakota State University requires a high school transcript, a minimum 2.6 high school GPA, SAT or ACT scores, and TOEFL scores for international students. The application deadline for regular admission is rolling.

Transfer Admission The application deadline for admission is rolling.

Entrance Difficulty South Dakota State University assesses its entrance difficulty level as minimally difficult. For the fall 2008 freshman class, 93 percent of the applicants were accepted.

For Further Information Contact Ms. Michelle Kuebler, Assistant Director of Admissions, South Dakota State University, PO Box 2201, Brookings, SD 57007. *Phone:* 605-688-4121 or 800-952-3541 (toll-free). *Fax:* 605-688-6891. *E-mail:* sdsu.admissions@sdstate.edu. *Web site:* http://www.sdstate.edu/.

UNIVERSITY OF SIOUX FALLS

Sioux Falls, South Dakota

University of Sioux Falls is a coed, private, American Baptist Churches in the USA, comprehensive institution, founded in 1883, offering degrees at the associate, bachelor's, master's, and doctoral levels. It has a 22-acre campus in Sioux Falls.

Academic Information The faculty has 140 members (43% full-time). The undergraduate student-faculty ratio is 15:1. The library holds 85,713 titles and 378 serial subscriptions. Special programs include academic remediation, services for learning-disabled students, an honors program, study abroad, advanced placement credit, accelerated degree programs, double majors, independent study, distance learning, self-designed majors, summer session for credit, part-time degree programs (daytime, evenings, weekends, summer), adult/continuing education programs, internships, and arrangement for off-campus study with Colleges of Mid-America, Augustana College (SD), North American Baptist Seminary, Christian College Coalition. The most frequently chosen baccalaureate fields are business/marketing, biological/life sciences, health professions and related sciences.

Student Body Statistics The student body totals 1,564, of whom 1,243 are undergraduates (292 freshmen). 53 percent are women and 47 percent are men. Students come from 30 states and territories and 5 other countries. 68 percent are from South Dakota. 0.4 percent are international students.

Expenses for 2009–10 *Application fee:* $25. *Comprehensive fee:* $26,190 includes full-time tuition ($19,870), mandatory fees ($400), and college room and board ($5920). *College room only:* $2770. *Part-time tuition:* $280 per semester hour. *Part-time mandatory fees:* $150 per year.

Financial Aid Forms of aid include need-based and non-need-based scholarships, athletic grants, and part-time jobs. The priority application deadline for financial aid is March 1.

Freshman Admission University of Sioux Falls requires a high school transcript, SAT or ACT scores, and TOEFL scores for international students. An essay and a minimum 2.5 high school GPA are recommended. 2 recommendations and an interview are required for some. The application deadline for regular admission is rolling.

Transfer Admission The application deadline for admission is rolling.

Entrance Difficulty University of Sioux Falls assesses its entrance difficulty level as moderately difficult. For the fall 2008 freshman class, 97 percent of the applicants were accepted.

For Further Information Contact Ms. Amanda Anderson, Director of Admissions and Academic Advising, University of Sioux Falls, 1101 West 22nd Street, Sioux Falls, SD 57105. *Phone:* 605-331-6600 Ext. 6743 or 800-888-1047 (toll-free). *Fax:* 605-331-6615. *E-mail:* admissions@usiouxfalls.edu. *Web site:* http://www.usiouxfalls.edu/.

THE UNIVERSITY OF SOUTH DAKOTA

Vermillion, South Dakota

The University of South Dakota is a coed, public university, founded in 1862, offering degrees at the associate, bachelor's, master's, doctoral, and first professional levels and post-master's and postbachelor's certificates. It has a 216-acre campus in Vermillion.

Academic Information The faculty has 407 members (95% full-time), 75% with terminal degrees. The undergraduate student-faculty ratio is 15:1. The library holds 716,915 titles, 1,950 serial subscriptions, and 48,921 audiovisual materials. Special programs include academic remediation, services for learning-disabled students, an honors program, advanced placement credit, ESL programs, double majors, independent study, distance learning, summer session for credit, part-time degree programs, external degree programs, adult/continuing education programs, internships, and arrangement for off-campus study with National Student Exchange. The most frequently chosen baccalaureate fields are business/marketing, education, psychology.

Student Body Statistics The student body totals 9,291, of whom 6,958 are undergraduates (1,162 freshmen). 63 percent are women and 37 percent are men. Students come from 53 states and territories and 29 other countries. 75 percent are from South Dakota.

Expenses for 2009–10 *Application fee:* $20. *State resident tuition:* $2751 full-time, $91.70 per credit hour part-time. *Nonresident tuition:* $8405 full-time, $291.25 per credit hour part-time. *Mandatory fees:* $3717 full-time, $123.90 per credit hour part-time. *College room and board:* $5787. *College room only:* $2859.

Financial Aid Forms of aid include need-based and non-need-based scholarships, athletic grants, and part-time jobs. The average aided 2007–08 undergraduate received an aid package worth $5660. The priority application deadline for financial aid is March 15.

Freshman Admission The University of South Dakota requires a high school transcript, SAT or ACT scores, and TOEFL scores for international students. A minimum 2.0 high school GPA is recommended. Recommendations are required for some. The application deadline for regular admission is rolling.
Transfer Admission The application deadline for admission is rolling.
Entrance Difficulty The University of South Dakota assesses its entrance difficulty level as moderately difficult. For the fall 2008 freshman class, 83 percent of the applicants were accepted.
For Further Information Contact Ms. Stephanie Moser, Director of Admissions, The University of South Dakota, 414 East Clark Street, Vermillion, SD 57069-2390. *Phone:* 605-677-5434 or 877-269-6837 (toll-free). *Fax:* 605-677-6753. *E-mail:* admiss@usd.edu. *Web site:* http://www.usd.edu/.

Wisconsin

ALVERNO COLLEGE

Milwaukee, Wisconsin

http://www.alverno.edu/

BELLIN COLLEGE OF NURSING

Green Bay, Wisconsin

Bellin College of Nursing is a coed, primarily women's, private, comprehensive institution, founded in 1909, offering degrees at the bachelor's and master's levels.

Academic Information The library holds 7,000 titles, 225 serial subscriptions, and 600 audiovisual materials. Special programs include advanced placement credit, accelerated degree programs, independent study, distance learning, summer session for credit, part-time degree programs (evenings, weekends), and arrangement for off-campus study with University of Wisconsin-Green Bay.
Student Body Statistics The student body totals 304, of whom 259 are undergraduates.
Financial Aid Forms of aid include need-based and non-need-based scholarships and part-time jobs. The average aided 2008–09 undergraduate received an aid package worth an estimated $17,711. The priority application deadline for financial aid is March 1.
Freshman Admission Bellin College of Nursing requires a high school transcript, a minimum 3.25 high school GPA, 3 recommendations, an interview, and ACT scores. A minimum 3.25 high school GPA is recommended. The application deadline for regular admission is rolling.
Transfer Admission The application deadline for admission is rolling.
Entrance Difficulty Bellin College of Nursing assesses its entrance difficulty level as moderately difficult.
For Further Information Contact Dr. Penny Croghan, Admissions Director, Bellin College of Nursing, 725 South Webster Avenue, Green Bay, WI 54301. *Phone:* 920-433-5803 or 800-236-8707 (toll-free). *Fax:* 920-433-7416. *E-mail:* admissio@bcon.edu. *Web site:* http://www.bcon.edu/.

BELOIT COLLEGE

Beloit, Wisconsin

Beloit College is a coed, private, four-year college, founded in 1846, offering degrees at the bachelor's level. It has a 65-acre campus in Beloit near Chicago and Milwaukee.

Academic Information The faculty has 133 members (93% full-time), 92% with terminal degrees. The student-faculty ratio is 11:1. The library holds 673,771 titles, 25,352 serial subscriptions, and 8,048 audiovisual materials. Special programs include services for learning-disabled students, study abroad, advanced placement credit, ESL programs, double majors, independent study, self-designed majors, summer session for credit, adult/continuing education programs, internships, and arrangement for off-campus study with University of Wisconsin-Madison, University of Chicago, Spelman College, Morehouse College, Associated Colleges of the Midwest. The most frequently chosen baccalaureate fields are foreign languages and literature, English, social sciences.
Student Body Statistics The student body is made up of 1,388 undergraduates (339 freshmen). 57 percent are women and 43 percent are men. Students come from 49 states and territories and 32 other countries. 22 percent are from Wisconsin. 5.2 percent are international students.
Expenses for 2008–09 *Application fee:* $35. *Comprehensive fee:* $38,236 includes full-time tuition ($31,310), mandatory fees ($230), and college room and board ($6696). *College room only:* $3282. Room and board charges vary according to board plan. *Part-time tuition:* $3913 per course.
Financial Aid Forms of aid include need-based and non-need-based scholarships and part-time jobs. The average aided 2008–09 undergraduate received an aid package worth an estimated $24,601. The priority application deadline for financial aid is March 1.
Freshman Admission Beloit College requires an essay, a high school transcript, 1 recommendation, SAT or ACT scores, and TOEFL scores for international students. An interview is recommended. An interview is required for some. The application deadline for regular admission is January 15 and for early action it is December 15.
Transfer Admission The application deadline for admission is rolling.
Entrance Difficulty Beloit College assesses its entrance difficulty level as very difficult. For the fall 2008 freshman class, 63 percent of the applicants were accepted.
For Further Information Contact Mr. James S. Zielinski, Director of Admissions, Beloit College, 700 College Street, Beloit, WI 53511-5596. *Phone:* 608-363-2500 or 800-9-BELOIT (toll-free). *Fax:* 608-363-2075. *E-mail:* admiss@beloit.edu. *Web site:* http://www.beloit.edu/.

BRYANT & STRATTON COLLEGE

Milwaukee, Wisconsin

Bryant & Stratton College is a coed, proprietary, primarily two-year college of Bryant and Stratton Business Institute, Inc., founded in 1863, offering degrees at the associate and bachelor's levels.

Academic Information The faculty has 102 members (19% full-time). The student-faculty ratio is 13:1. The library holds 120 serial subscriptions and 100 audiovisual materials. Special programs include academic remediation, cooperative (work-study) education, advanced placement credit, double majors, independent study, distance learning, summer session for credit, part-time degree programs (daytime, evenings, summer), adult/continuing education programs, and internships.
Student Body Statistics The student body is made up of 828 undergraduates (385 freshmen). 84 percent are women and 16 percent are men. Students come from 1 state or territory.
Expenses for 2008–09 *Application fee:* $0. *Tuition:* $14,430 full-time, $458 per credit hour part-time. Full-time tuition varies according to class time, course load, degree level, and program. Part-time tuition varies according to course load and degree level.
Financial Aid Forms of aid include need-based scholarships and part-time jobs. The application deadline for financial aid is continuous.
Freshman Admission Bryant & Stratton College requires a high school transcript, an interview, entrance and placement evaluations, TOEFL scores for international students, CPAt, and ACCUPLACER. SAT or ACT scores are recommended. Recommendations are required for some. The application deadline for regular admission is rolling.
Transfer Admission The application deadline for admission is rolling.
Entrance Difficulty Bryant & Stratton College assesses its entrance difficulty level as minimally difficult. For the fall 2008 freshman class, 89 percent of the applicants were accepted.
For Further Information Contact Ms. Kristin Weiss, Director of Admissions, Bryant & Stratton College, 310 West Wisconsin Avenue, Milwaukee, WI 53203-2214. *Phone:* 414-276-5200. *Web site:* http://www.bryantstratton.edu/.

BRYANT & STRATTON COLLEGE—WAUWATOSA CAMPUS

Wauwatosa, Wisconsin

Bryant & Stratton College—Wauwatosa Campus is a coed, proprietary, four-year college, offering degrees at the associate and bachelor's levels.

Academic Information The student-faculty ratio is 10:1. Special programs include academic remediation, services for learning-disabled students, cooperative (work-study) education, advanced placement credit, double majors, independent study, distance learning, part-time degree programs, adult/continuing education programs, and internships.
Student Body Statistics The student body is made up of 1,264 undergraduates. 86 percent are women and 14 percent are men. Students come from 2 states and territories.
Freshman Admission Bryant & Stratton College—Wauwatosa Campus requires a high school transcript, an interview, entrance and placement evaluation, and TABE. SAT or ACT scores are recommended. The application deadline for regular admission is rolling.
Transfer Admission The application deadline for admission is rolling.
For Further Information Contact Tony Krocak, Director of Admissions, Bryant & Stratton College—Wauwatosa Campus, 10950 W. Potter Road, Wauwatosa, WI 53226. *Phone:* 414-302-7000 Ext. 502. *Web site:* http://www.bryantstratton.edu/.

CARDINAL STRITCH UNIVERSITY

Milwaukee, Wisconsin

Cardinal Stritch University is a coed, private, Roman Catholic, comprehensive institution, founded in 1937, offering degrees at the associate, bachelor's, master's, and doctoral levels and postbachelor's certificates. It has a 40-acre campus in Milwaukee.

Expenses for 2008–09 *Application fee:* $25. *Comprehensive fee:* $26,530 includes full-time tuition ($20,000), mandatory fees ($510), and college room and board ($6020). Full-time tuition and fees vary according to course load. Room and board charges vary according to board plan. *Part-time tuition:* $625 per credit. *Part-time mandatory fees:* $205 per term. Part-time tuition and fees vary according to course load.
For Further Information Contact Ms. Kristine Bueno, Associate Director of Admissions, Cardinal Stritch University, 6801 North Yates Road, Milwaukee, WI 53217. *Phone:* 414-410-4040 or 800-347-8822 Ext. 4040 (toll-free). *Fax:* 414-410-4058. *E-mail:* admityou@stritch.edu. *Web site:* http://www.stritch.edu/.

CARROLL UNIVERSITY

Waukesha, Wisconsin

Carroll University is a coed, private, Presbyterian, comprehensive institution, founded in 1846, offering degrees at the bachelor's, master's, and first professional levels. It has a 52-acre campus in Waukesha near Milwaukee.

Academic Information The faculty has 289 members (42% full-time), 36% with terminal degrees. The undergraduate student-faculty ratio is 16:1. The library holds 150,000 titles, 18,000 serial subscriptions, and 1,025 audiovisual materials. Special programs include academic remediation, services for learning-disabled students, an honors program, study abroad, advanced placement credit, double majors, independent study, distance learning, self-designed majors, summer session for credit, part-time degree programs (daytime, evenings, weekends, summer), adult/continuing education programs, and internships. The most frequently chosen baccalaureate fields are business/marketing, health professions and related sciences, psychology.
Student Body Statistics The student body totals 3,316, of whom 3,030 are undergraduates (690 freshmen). 67 percent are women and 33 percent are men. Students come from 25 states and territories and 33 other countries. 76 percent are from Wisconsin. 1 percent are international students.
Expenses for 2008–09 *Application fee:* $0. *Comprehensive fee:* $28,620 includes full-time tuition ($21,410), mandatory fees ($516), and college room and board ($6694). *College room only:* $3450. Full-time tuition and fees vary according to program. Room and board charges vary according to board plan and housing facility. *Part-time tuition:* $260 per credit. Part-time tuition varies according to course load and program.
Financial Aid Forms of aid include need-based and non-need-based scholarships and part-time jobs. The average aided 2008–09 undergraduate received an aid package worth an estimated $16,584. The application deadline for financial aid is continuous.
Freshman Admission Carroll University requires a high school transcript, a minimum 2.0 high school GPA, 1 recommendation, and SAT or ACT scores. An interview, ACT scores, and TOEFL scores for international students are recommended. An essay is required for some. The application deadline for regular admission is rolling.
Transfer Admission The application deadline for admission is rolling.
Entrance Difficulty Carroll University assesses its entrance difficulty level as moderately difficult. For the fall 2008 freshman class, 73 percent of the applicants were accepted.
For Further Information Contact Mr. James Wiseman, Vice President of Enrollment, Carroll University, 100 North East Avenue, Waukesha, WI 53186-5593. *Phone:* 262-524-7221 or 800-CARROLL (toll-free). *Fax:* 262-524-7139. *E-mail:* cc.info@ccadmin.cc.edu. *Web site:* http://www.cc.edu/.

CARTHAGE COLLEGE

Kenosha, Wisconsin

Carthage College is a coed, private, comprehensive institution, founded in 1847, affiliated with the Evangelical Lutheran Church in America, offering degrees at the bachelor's and master's levels. It has a 72-acre campus in Kenosha near Chicago and Milwaukee.

Expenses for 2008–09 *Application fee:* $25. *Comprehensive fee:* $34,000 includes full-time tuition ($26,500) and college room and board ($7500). Room and board charges vary according to board plan and housing facility. *Part-time tuition:* $380 per credit hour. Part-time tuition varies according to class time and course load.
For Further Information Contact Mr. Bradley J. Andrews, Vice President for Enrollment & Student Life, Carthage College, 2001 Alford Park Drive, Kenosha, WI 53140. *Phone:* 262-551-6000 or 800-351-4058 (toll-free). *Fax:* 262-551-5762. *E-mail:* admissions@carthage.edu. *Web site:* http://www.carthage.edu/.

COLLEGE OF MENOMINEE NATION

Keshena, Wisconsin

http://www.menominee.edu/

COLUMBIA COLLEGE OF NURSING

Milwaukee, Wisconsin

Columbia College of Nursing is a coed, private, four-year college, founded in 1901, offering degrees at the bachelor's level (nursing degree is awarded in conjunction with Mount Mary College).

Academic Information The faculty has 20 members (90% full-time), 5% with terminal degrees. The student-faculty ratio is 13:1. Special programs include an honors program, advanced placement credit, double majors, independent study, summer session for credit, part-time degree programs (daytime, evenings, summer), and arrangement for off-campus study with Mount Mary College, Milwaukee, WI.
Student Body Statistics The student body is made up of 260 undergraduates (30 freshmen). 97 percent are women and 3 percent are men. Students come from 2 states and territories. 95 percent are from Wisconsin.
Expenses for 2009–10 *Application fee:* $25. *Comprehensive fee:* $25,550 includes full-time tuition ($19,950), mandatory fees ($1000), and college room and board ($4600). *College room only:* $3600. *Part-time tuition:* $590 per credit. *Part-time mandatory fees:* $50 per credit.

Financial Aid Forms of aid include need-based and non-need-based scholarships and part-time jobs. The application deadline for financial aid is continuous.
Freshman Admission Columbia College of Nursing requires a high school transcript, SAT or ACT scores, and TOEFL scores for international students. An essay, 1 recommendation, and an interview are recommended. An essay is required for some. The application deadline for regular admission is August 1.
Transfer Admission The application deadline for admission is rolling.
Entrance Difficulty Columbia College of Nursing assesses its entrance difficulty level as moderately difficult. For the fall 2008 freshman class, 46 percent of the applicants were accepted.
For Further Information Contact Ms. Amy Dobson, Dean of Admissions, Columbia College of Nursing, 2121 East Newport Avenue, Milwaukee, WI 53211-2952. *Phone:* 414-256-1219 or 800-321-6265 (toll-free out-of-state). *Fax:* 414-256-0180. *E-mail:* admiss@mtmary.edu. *Web site:* http://www.ccon.edu/.

CONCORDIA UNIVERSITY WISCONSIN

Mequon, Wisconsin

Concordia University Wisconsin is a coed, private, comprehensive unit of Concordia University System, founded in 1881, affiliated with the Lutheran Church–Missouri Synod, offering degrees at the associate, bachelor's, master's, doctoral, and first professional levels and postbachelor's certificates. It has a 192-acre campus in Mequon near Milwaukee.

Academic Information The faculty has 245 members (40% full-time), 36% with terminal degrees. The undergraduate student-faculty ratio is 11:1. The library holds 79,341 titles, 4,440 serial subscriptions, and 4,352 audiovisual materials. Special programs include academic remediation, services for learning-disabled students, study abroad, advanced placement credit, accelerated degree programs, ESL programs, double majors, independent study, distance learning, self-designed majors, summer session for credit, part-time degree programs, adult/continuing education programs, internships, and arrangement for off-campus study with Milwaukee Area Technical College, Milwaukee Institute of Art and Design, Cardinal Stritch University, Mount Mary College. The most frequently chosen baccalaureate fields are business/marketing, education, health professions and related sciences.
Student Body Statistics The student body totals 6,549, of whom 3,786 are undergraduates (405 freshmen). 63 percent are women and 37 percent are men. Students come from 41 states and territories and 23 other countries. 70 percent are from Wisconsin. 0.8 percent are international students.
Expenses for 2008–09 *Application fee:* $35. *Comprehensive fee:* $27,700 includes full-time tuition ($19,900), mandatory fees ($100), and college room and board ($7700). Full-time tuition and fees vary according to program. Room and board charges vary according to board plan. *Part-time tuition:* $830 per credit hour. Part-time tuition varies according to program.
Financial Aid Forms of aid include need-based scholarships and part-time jobs. The average aided 2008–09 undergraduate received an aid package worth an estimated $20,534. The priority application deadline for financial aid is April 1.
Freshman Admission Concordia University Wisconsin requires a high school transcript, a minimum 2.0 high school GPA, ACT scores, and TOEFL scores for international students. An interview is recommended. An essay, a minimum 3.0 high school GPA, and 3 recommendations are required for some. The application deadline for regular admission is August 15.
Transfer Admission The application deadline for admission is rolling.
Entrance Difficulty Concordia University Wisconsin assesses its entrance difficulty level as moderately difficult; minimally difficult for transfers. For the fall 2008 freshman class, 64 percent of the applicants were accepted.
For Further Information Contact Ms. Julie Schroeder, Concordia University Wisconsin, Admissions Office, 12800 N. Lake Drive, Mequon, WI 53097. *Phone:* 262-243-5700 or 888-628-9472 (toll-free). *Fax:* 262-243-4351. *E-mail:* admission@cuw.edu. *Web site:* http://www.cuw.edu/.

DEVRY UNIVERSITY

Milwaukee, Wisconsin

DeVry University is a coed, proprietary, comprehensive unit of DeVry University, offering degrees at the associate, bachelor's, and master's levels.

Academic Information The faculty has 2 members (50% full-time). The undergraduate student-faculty ratio is 77:1. Special programs include academic remediation, services for learning-disabled students, advanced placement credit, accelerated degree programs, distance learning, summer session for credit, part-time degree programs (daytime, evenings, weekends, summer), and adult/continuing education programs. The most frequently chosen baccalaureate field is business/marketing.
Student Body Statistics The student body totals 215, of whom 119 are undergraduates (14 freshmen). 55 percent are women and 45 percent are men. 98 percent are from Wisconsin.
Expenses for 2009–10 *Application fee:* $50. *Tuition:* $14,080 full-time, $550 per credit hour part-time.
Financial Aid Forms of aid include need-based scholarships. The average aided 2007–08 undergraduate received an aid package worth $11,858. The application deadline for financial aid is continuous.
Freshman Admission DeVry University requires a high school transcript and an interview. The application deadline for regular admission is rolling.
Transfer Admission The application deadline for admission is rolling.
Entrance Difficulty DeVry University assesses its entrance difficulty level as minimally difficult.
For Further Information Contact Admissions Office, DeVry University, 100 East Wisconsin Avenue, Suite 2550, Milwaukee, WI 53202-4107. *Phone:* 414-278-7677. *Web site:* http://www.devry.edu/.

DEVRY UNIVERSITY

Waukesha, Wisconsin

http://www.devry.edu/

EDGEWOOD COLLEGE

Madison, Wisconsin

Edgewood College is a coed, primarily women's, private, Roman Catholic, comprehensive institution, founded in 1927, offering degrees at the associate, bachelor's, master's, and doctoral levels. It has a 55-acre campus in Madison.

Academic Information The faculty has 288 members (34% full-time). The undergraduate student-faculty ratio is 12:1. The library holds 107,873 titles, 164 serial subscriptions, and 6,197 audiovisual materials. Special programs include academic remediation, services for learning-disabled students, an honors program, study abroad, advanced placement credit, accelerated degree programs, double majors, independent study, distance learning, self-designed majors, summer session for credit, part-time degree programs (daytime, evenings, weekends, summer), adult/continuing education programs, and internships. The most frequently chosen baccalaureate fields are education, business/marketing, health professions and related sciences.
Student Body Statistics The student body totals 2,544, of whom 1,989 are undergraduates (300 freshmen). 70 percent are women and 30 percent are men. Students come from 18 states and territories and 21 other countries. 93 percent are from Wisconsin. 1.8 percent are international students.
Expenses for 2008–09 *Application fee:* $25. *Comprehensive fee:* $26,868 includes full-time tuition ($20,040) and college room and board ($6828). *College room only:* $3468. Full-time tuition varies according to degree level. Room and board charges vary according to housing facility. *Part-time tuition:* $630 per credit. Part-time tuition varies according to course load and degree level.
Financial Aid Forms of aid include need-based and non-need-based scholarships and part-time jobs. The average aided 2008–09 undergraduate received an aid package worth an estimated $15,659. The priority application deadline for financial aid is March 1.

Edgewood College (continued)

Freshman Admission Edgewood College requires a high school transcript, a minimum 2.5 high school GPA, SAT or ACT scores, and TOEFL scores for international students. An essay, recommendations, and an interview are required for some. The application deadline for regular admission is August 26.

Transfer Admission The application deadline for admission is August 26.

Entrance Difficulty Edgewood College assesses its entrance difficulty level as moderately difficult. For the fall 2008 freshman class, 79 percent of the applicants were accepted.

For Further Information Contact Ms. Christine Benedict, Director of Admission, Edgewood College, 1000 Edgewood College Drive, Madison, WI 53711-1997. *Phone:* 608-663-2294 or 800-444-4861 Ext. 2294 (toll-free). *Fax:* 608-663-2214. *E-mail:* admissions@edgewood.edu. *Web site:* http://www.edgewood.edu/.

HERZING COLLEGE

Madison, Wisconsin

Herzing College is a coed, primarily men's, proprietary, primarily two-year college of Herzing Institutes, Inc., founded in 1948, offering degrees at the associate and bachelor's levels. It is located in Madison near Milwaukee.

For Further Information Contact Mr. Matthew Schneider, Admissions Director, Herzing College, 5218 East Terrace Drive, Madison, WI 53718. *Phone:* 608-663-0806 or 800-582-1227 (toll-free). *Fax:* 608-249-8593. *E-mail:* info@msn.herzing.edu. *Web site:* http://www.herzing.edu/madison.

ITT TECHNICAL INSTITUTE

Green Bay, Wisconsin

ITT Technical Institute is a coed, proprietary, primarily two-year college of ITT Educational Services, Inc., founded in 2000, offering degrees at the associate and bachelor's levels.

Financial Aid Forms of aid include need-based scholarships and part-time jobs. The application deadline for financial aid is continuous.

Entrance Difficulty ITT Technical Institute assesses its entrance difficulty level as minimally difficult.

For Further Information Contact Director of Recruitment, ITT Technical Institute, 470 Security Boulevard, Green Bay, WI 54313. *Phone:* 920-662-9000 or 888-884-3626 (toll-free out-of-state). *Fax:* 920-662-9384. *Web site:* http://www.itt-tech.edu/.

ITT TECHNICAL INSTITUTE

Greenfield, Wisconsin

ITT Technical Institute is a coed, proprietary, primarily two-year college of ITT Educational Services, Inc., founded in 1968, offering degrees at the associate and bachelor's levels. It is located in Greenfield near Milwaukee.

Financial Aid Forms of aid include need-based scholarships and part-time jobs. The application deadline for financial aid is continuous.

Entrance Difficulty ITT Technical Institute assesses its entrance difficulty level as minimally difficult.

For Further Information Contact Director of Recruitment, ITT Technical Institute, 6300 West Layton avenue, Greenfield, WI 53220-4612. *Phone:* 414-282-9494. *Fax:* 414-282-9698. *Web site:* http://www.itt-tech.edu/.

ITT TECHNICAL INSTITUTE

Madison, Wisconsin

ITT Technical Institute is a coed, proprietary, primarily two-year college of ITT Educational Services, Inc., offering degrees at the associate and bachelor's levels.

For Further Information Contact Director of Recruitment, ITT Technical Institute, 2450 Rimrock Road, Suite 100, Madison, WI 53713. *Phone:* 608-288-6301 or 877-628-5960 (toll-free in-state). *Web site:* http://www.itt-tech.edu/.

LAKELAND COLLEGE

Sheboygan, Wisconsin

Lakeland College is a coed, private, comprehensive institution, founded in 1862, affiliated with the United Church of Christ, offering degrees at the bachelor's and master's levels. It has a 240-acre campus in Sheboygan near Milwaukee.

Academic Information The faculty has 70 members (80% full-time), 64% with terminal degrees. The undergraduate student-faculty ratio is 17:1. The library holds 56,439 titles and 282 serial subscriptions. Special programs include academic remediation, services for learning-disabled students, an honors program, study abroad, advanced placement credit, ESL programs, double majors, independent study, distance learning, summer session for credit, part-time degree programs (evenings, summer), adult/continuing education programs, internships, and arrangement for off-campus study. The most frequently chosen baccalaureate fields are business/marketing, computer and information sciences, education.

Student Body Statistics The student body totals 3,941, of whom 3,022 are undergraduates (236 freshmen). 62 percent are women and 38 percent are men. Students come from 40 states and territories and 29 other countries. 85 percent are from Wisconsin. 4.5 percent are international students.

Expenses for 2009–10 *Application fee:* $20. *Comprehensive fee:* $25,748 includes full-time tuition ($18,970) and college room and board ($6778). *Part-time tuition:* $635 per credit.

Financial Aid Forms of aid include need-based and non-need-based scholarships and part-time jobs. The application deadline for financial aid is July 1 with a priority deadline of March 31.

Freshman Admission Lakeland College requires an essay, a high school transcript, a minimum 2.0 high school GPA, SAT or ACT scores, and TOEFL scores for international students. An interview is required for some. The application deadline for regular admission is rolling.

Transfer Admission The application deadline for admission is rolling.

Entrance Difficulty Lakeland College assesses its entrance difficulty level as minimally difficult. For the fall 2008 freshman class, 89 percent of the applicants were accepted.

For Further Information Contact Mr. Nathan Dehne, Director of Admissions, Lakeland College, PO Box 359, Nash Visitors Center, Sheboygan, WI 53082-0359. *Phone:* 920-565-1588 or 800-242-3347 (toll-free in-state). *Fax:* 920-565-1206. *E-mail:* admissions@lakeland.edu. *Web site:* http://www.lakeland.edu/.

LAWRENCE UNIVERSITY

Appleton, Wisconsin

Lawrence University is a coed, private, four-year college, founded in 1847, offering degrees at the bachelor's level. It has an 84-acre campus in Appleton.

Academic Information The faculty has 186 members (83% full-time), 87% with terminal degrees. The student-faculty ratio is 9:1. The library holds 659,425 titles, 34,122 serial subscriptions, and 23,008 audiovisual materials. Special programs include services for learning-disabled students, study abroad, advanced placement credit, double majors, independent study, self-designed majors, internships, and arrangement for off-campus study with Associated Colleges of the Midwest, Great Lakes Colleges Association. The most frequently chosen baccalaureate fields are social sciences, interdisciplinary studies, visual and performing arts.

Student Body Statistics The student body is made up of 1,503 undergraduates (382 freshmen). 54 percent are women and 46 percent are men. Students come from 47 states and territories and 48 other countries. 36 percent are from Wisconsin. 7.6 percent are international students.
Expenses for 2008–09 *Application fee:* $40. *Comprehensive fee:* $40,239 includes full-time tuition ($33,006), mandatory fees ($258), and college room and board ($6975). Room and board charges vary according to board plan.
Financial Aid Forms of aid include need-based and non-need-based scholarships and part-time jobs. The average aided 2008–09 undergraduate received an aid package worth an estimated $26,800. The priority application deadline for financial aid is March 15.
Freshman Admission Lawrence University requires an essay, a high school transcript, 2 recommendations, and audition for music program. A minimum 3.0 high school GPA, an interview, SAT or ACT scores, and TOEFL scores for international students are recommended. The application deadline for regular admission is January 15, for early decision it is November 15, and for early action it is December 1.
Transfer Admission The application deadline for admission is May 1.
Entrance Difficulty Lawrence University assesses its entrance difficulty level as very difficult. For the fall 2008 freshman class, 59 percent of the applicants were accepted.
For Further Information Contact Mr. Steven T. Syverson, Vice President for Enrollment Management, Lawrence University, PO Box 599, Appleton, WI 54912-0599. *Phone:* 920-832-6500 or 800-227-0982 (toll-free). *Fax:* 920-832-6782. *E-mail:* excel@lawrence.edu. *Web site:* http://www.lawrence.edu/.

MARANATHA BAPTIST BIBLE COLLEGE

Watertown, Wisconsin

Maranatha Baptist Bible College is a coed, private, Baptist, comprehensive institution, founded in 1968, offering degrees at the associate, bachelor's, and master's levels. It has a 60-acre campus in Watertown near Milwaukee.

Academic Information The faculty has 78 members (59% full-time), 26% with terminal degrees. The undergraduate student-faculty ratio is 16:1. The library holds 122,251 titles and 502 serial subscriptions. Special programs include academic remediation, accelerated degree programs, double majors, independent study, distance learning, summer session for credit, part-time degree programs (daytime, evenings, summer), internships, and arrangement for off-campus study with Madison Area Technical College. The most frequently chosen baccalaureate fields are education, business/marketing, theology and religious vocations.
Student Body Statistics The student body totals 865, of whom 817 are undergraduates (193 freshmen). 55 percent are women and 45 percent are men. Students come from 44 states and territories and 10 other countries. 30 percent are from Wisconsin. 0.6 percent are international students.
Expenses for 2008–09 *Application fee:* $50. *Comprehensive fee:* $16,360 includes full-time tuition ($9600), mandatory fees ($960), and college room and board ($5800). *Part-time tuition:* $400 per credit hour. *Part-time mandatory fees:* $40 per credit hour.
Financial Aid Forms of aid include need-based and non-need-based scholarships and part-time jobs. The average aided 2008–09 undergraduate received an aid package worth an estimated $6462. The priority application deadline for financial aid is March 1.
Freshman Admission Maranatha Baptist Bible College requires an essay, a high school transcript, 4 recommendations, ACT scores, and TOEFL scores for international students. The application deadline for regular admission is rolling.
Transfer Admission The application deadline for admission is rolling.
Entrance Difficulty Maranatha Baptist Bible College assesses its entrance difficulty level as noncompetitive. For the fall 2008 freshman class, 65 percent of the applicants were accepted.
For Further Information Contact Dr. James Harrison, Director of Admissions, Maranatha Baptist Bible College, 745 West Main Street, Watertown, WI 53094. *Phone:* 920-206-2327 or 800-622-2947 (toll-free). *Fax:* 920-261-9109. *E-mail:* admissions@mbbc.edu. *Web site:* http://www.mbbc.edu/.

MARIAN UNIVERSITY

Fond du Lac, Wisconsin

Marian University is a coed, private, Roman Catholic, comprehensive institution, founded in 1936, offering degrees at the bachelor's, master's, and doctoral levels. It has a 77-acre campus in Fond du Lac near Milwaukee.

Academic Information The faculty has 304 members (27% full-time), 24% with terminal degrees. The undergraduate student-faculty ratio is 12:1. The library holds 105,015 titles, 1,357 serial subscriptions, and 1,512 audiovisual materials. Special programs include academic remediation, services for learning-disabled students, an honors program, cooperative (work-study) education, study abroad, advanced placement credit, accelerated degree programs, ESL programs, double majors, independent study, distance learning, self-designed majors, summer session for credit, part-time degree programs (daytime, evenings, weekends, summer), and internships. The most frequently chosen baccalaureate fields are business/marketing, health professions and related sciences, security and protective services.
Student Body Statistics The student body totals 2,891, of whom 1,996 are undergraduates (284 freshmen). 75 percent are women and 25 percent are men. Students come from 10 states and territories and 10 other countries. 95 percent are from Wisconsin. 1.1 percent are international students.
Expenses for 2008–09 *Application fee:* $20. *One-time mandatory fee:* $100. *Comprehensive fee:* $25,320 includes full-time tuition ($19,590), mandatory fees ($350), and college room and board ($5380). *College room only:* $3730. Full-time tuition and fees vary according to class time, course load, and program. Room and board charges vary according to board plan and housing facility. *Part-time tuition:* $300 per credit. *Part-time mandatory fees:* $80 per term. Part-time tuition and fees vary according to class time, course load, and program.
Financial Aid Forms of aid include need-based and non-need-based scholarships and part-time jobs. The average aided 2008–09 undergraduate received an aid package worth an estimated $20,237. The priority application deadline for financial aid is March 1.
Freshman Admission Marian University requires a high school transcript, SAT or ACT scores, and TOEFL scores for international students. A minimum 2.0 high school GPA is recommended. An interview is required for some. The application deadline for regular admission is rolling.
Transfer Admission The application deadline for admission is rolling.
Entrance Difficulty Marian University assesses its entrance difficulty level as moderately difficult. For the fall 2008 freshman class, 86 percent of the applicants were accepted.
For Further Information Contact Ms. Stacey Akey, Vice President for Enrollment and Marketing, Marian University, 45 South National Avenue, Fond du Lac, WI 54935-4699. *Phone:* 800-262-7426 or 800-2-MARIAN Ext. 7652 (toll-free in-state). *Fax:* 920-923-8755. *E-mail:* admit@marianuniversity.edu. *Web site:* http://www.mariancollege.edu/.

MARQUETTE UNIVERSITY

Milwaukee, Wisconsin

Marquette University is a coed, private, Roman Catholic (Jesuit) university, founded in 1881, offering degrees at the bachelor's, master's, doctoral, and first professional levels and post-master's, first professional, and postbachelor's certificates. It has an 80-acre campus in Milwaukee.

Academic Information The faculty has 1,096 members (57% full-time), 71% with terminal degrees. The undergraduate student-faculty ratio is 14.5:1. The library holds 2 million titles and 24,242 serial subscriptions. Special programs include services for learning-disabled students, an honors program, cooperative (work-study) education, study abroad, advanced placement credit, accelerated degree programs, ESL programs, double majors, summer session for credit, part-time degree programs (daytime, evenings, weekends, summer), adult/continuing education programs, internships, and arrangement for off-campus study with Milwaukee Institute of Art and Design, Les Aspin Center for Government,

Marquette University (continued)

Washington, DC. The most frequently chosen baccalaureate fields are business/marketing, communications/journalism, health professions and related sciences.

Student Body Statistics The student body totals 11,633, of whom 8,012 are undergraduates (1,950 freshmen). 53 percent are women and 47 percent are men. Students come from 51 states and territories and 42 other countries. 46 percent are from Wisconsin. 1.5 percent are international students.

Expenses for 2009–10 *Application fee:* $30. *Comprehensive fee:* $35,426 includes full-time tuition ($28,680), mandatory fees ($416), and college room and board ($6330). *College room only:* $3350. *Part-time tuition:* $835 per credit.

Financial Aid Forms of aid include need-based and non-need-based scholarships, athletic grants, and part-time jobs. The average aided 2008–09 undergraduate received an aid package worth an estimated $20,038. The application deadline for financial aid is continuous.

Freshman Admission Marquette University requires an essay, a high school transcript, a minimum 2.5 high school GPA, 1 recommendation, SAT or ACT scores, and TOEFL scores for international students. A minimum 3.4 high school GPA is recommended. The application deadline for regular admission is December 1.

Transfer Admission The application deadline for admission is December 1.

Entrance Difficulty Marquette University assesses its entrance difficulty level as moderately difficult; very difficult for physical therapy and athletic training. For the fall 2008 freshman class, 65 percent of the applicants were accepted.

For Further Information Contact Mr. Robert Blust, Dean of Undergraduate Admissions, Marquette University, PO Box 1881, Milwaukee, WI 53201-1881. *Phone:* 414-288-7004 or 800-222-6544 (toll-free). *Fax:* 414-288-3764. *E-mail:* admissions@marquette.edu. *Web site:* http://www.marquette.edu/.

MILWAUKEE INSTITUTE OF ART AND DESIGN

Milwaukee, Wisconsin

http://www.miad.edu/

MILWAUKEE SCHOOL OF ENGINEERING

Milwaukee, Wisconsin

Milwaukee School of Engineering is a coed, primarily men's, private, comprehensive institution, founded in 1903, offering degrees at the bachelor's and master's levels. It has a 15-acre campus in Milwaukee.

Academic Information The faculty has 259 members (50% full-time), 49% with terminal degrees. The undergraduate student-faculty ratio is 14:1. The library holds 79,275 titles, 378 serial subscriptions, and 1,538 audiovisual materials. Special programs include academic remediation, services for learning-disabled students, study abroad, advanced placement credit, ESL programs, double majors, independent study, distance learning, summer session for credit, part-time degree programs (daytime, evenings, weekends, summer), adult/continuing education programs, and internships. The most frequently chosen baccalaureate fields are business/marketing, engineering, health professions and related sciences.

Student Body Statistics The student body totals 2,622, of whom 2,418 are undergraduates (645 freshmen). 18 percent are women and 82 percent are men. Students come from 32 states and territories and 15 other countries. 73 percent are from Wisconsin. 2.4 percent are international students.

Expenses for 2009–10 *Application fee:* $25. *Comprehensive fee:* $35,829 includes full-time tuition ($28,665) and college room and board ($7164). *College room only:* $4599. *Part-time tuition:* $498 per quarter hour.

Financial Aid Forms of aid include need-based and non-need-based scholarships and part-time jobs. The average aided 2007–08 undergraduate received an aid package worth $17,277.

Freshman Admission Milwaukee School of Engineering requires a high school transcript, a minimum 2.5 high school GPA, SAT or ACT scores, and TOEFL scores for international students. An essay and an interview are required for some. The application deadline for regular admission is rolling.

Transfer Admission The application deadline for admission is rolling.

Entrance Difficulty Milwaukee School of Engineering assesses its entrance difficulty level as moderately difficult. For the fall 2008 freshman class, 70 percent of the applicants were accepted.

For Further Information Contact Dana-Marie Grennier, Director of Admissions, Milwaukee School of Engineering, 1025 North Broadway, Milwaukee, WI 53202-3109. *Phone:* 414-277-6761 or 800-332-6763 (toll-free). *Fax:* 414-277-7475. *E-mail:* grennier@msoe.edu. *Web site:* http://www.msoe.edu/.

See page 250 for the Close-Up.

MOUNT MARY COLLEGE

Milwaukee, Wisconsin

Mount Mary College is an undergraduate: women only; graduate: coed, private, Roman Catholic, comprehensive institution, founded in 1913, offering degrees at the bachelor's and master's levels and postbachelor's certificates. It has an 80-acre campus in Milwaukee.

Academic Information The faculty has 212 members (31% full-time), 35% with terminal degrees. The undergraduate student-faculty ratio is 12:1. The library holds 696,609 titles, 28,163 serial subscriptions, and 27,288 audiovisual materials. Special programs include academic remediation, services for learning-disabled students, an honors program, study abroad, advanced placement credit, accelerated degree programs, double majors, independent study, distance learning, self-designed majors, summer session for credit, part-time degree programs (daytime, evenings, weekends, summer), adult/continuing education programs, and internships. The most frequently chosen baccalaureate fields are business/marketing, health professions and related sciences, visual and performing arts.

Student Body Statistics The student body totals 1,862, of whom 1,428 are undergraduates (176 freshmen). 97 percent are women and 3 percent are men. Students come from 6 states and territories and 12 other countries. 97 percent are from Wisconsin. 1 percent are international students.

Expenses for 2009–10 *Application fee:* $25. *Comprehensive fee:* $28,446 includes full-time tuition ($20,736), mandatory fees ($430), and college room and board ($7280). *Part-time tuition:* $596 per credit. *Part-time mandatory fees:* $220 per year.

Financial Aid Forms of aid include need-based and non-need-based scholarships and part-time jobs. The average aided 2008–09 undergraduate received an aid package worth an estimated $14,607. The priority application deadline for financial aid is March 1.

Freshman Admission Mount Mary College requires a high school transcript, a minimum 2.5 high school GPA, SAT or ACT scores, and TOEFL scores for international students. An interview is recommended. An essay and 2 recommendations are required for some. The application deadline for regular admission is rolling.

Transfer Admission The application deadline for admission is rolling.

Entrance Difficulty Mount Mary College assesses its entrance difficulty level as moderately difficult. For the fall 2008 freshman class, 58 percent of the applicants were accepted.

For Further Information Contact Ms. Mary Ellen Strieter, Admission Counselor Assistant/Receptionist, Mount Mary College, 2900 North Menomonee River Parkway, Milwaukee, WI 53222-4597. *Phone:* 414-258-4810 Ext. 219. *Fax:* 414-256-0180. *E-mail:* admiss@mtmary.edu. *Web site:* http://www.mtmary.edu/.

See page 254 for the Close-Up.

NORTHLAND COLLEGE

Ashland, Wisconsin

Northland College is a coed, private, four-year college, founded in 1892, affiliated with the United Church of Christ, offering degrees at the bachelor's level. It has a 130-acre campus in Ashland.

Academic Information The faculty has 83 members (47% full-time), 52% with terminal degrees. The student-faculty ratio is 13:1. The library holds 75,000 titles and 260 serial subscriptions. Special programs include services for learning-disabled students, an honors program, cooperative (work-study) education, study abroad, advanced placement credit, accelerated degree programs, double majors, independent study, distance learning, self-designed majors, summer session for credit, part-time degree programs (daytime, evenings, summer), adult/continuing education programs, internships, and arrangement for off-campus study with members of the May Term Consortium, Allegheny College, Beloit College, Ecoleaglue. The most frequently chosen baccalaureate fields are biological/life sciences, education, interdisciplinary studies.
Student Body Statistics The student body is made up of 669 undergraduates (133 freshmen). 54 percent are women and 46 percent are men. Students come from 40 states and territories and 6 other countries. 43 percent are from Wisconsin.
Expenses for 2008–09 *Application fee:* $25. *Comprehensive fee:* $29,541 includes full-time tuition ($22,500), mandatory fees ($601), and college room and board ($6440). *College room only:* $2600. Full-time tuition and fees vary according to course level. Room and board charges vary according to board plan and housing facility. *Part-time tuition:* varies with course level.
Financial Aid Forms of aid include need-based and non-need-based scholarships and part-time jobs. The average aided 2008–09 undergraduate received an aid package worth an estimated $19,551. The priority application deadline for financial aid is April 15.
Freshman Admission Northland College requires an essay, a high school transcript, 1 recommendation, SAT or ACT scores, and TOEFL scores for international students. A minimum 2.0 high school GPA and an interview are recommended. The application deadline for regular admission is rolling.
Transfer Admission The application deadline for admission is rolling.
Entrance Difficulty Northland College assesses its entrance difficulty level as moderately difficult. For the fall 2008 freshman class, 74 percent of the applicants were accepted.
For Further Information Contact Susan Greenwald, Vice President of Enrollment, Northland College, 1411 Ellis Avenue, Ashland, WI 54806. *Phone:* 715-682-1224, 800-753-1840 (toll-free in-state), or 800-753-1040 (toll-free out-of-state). *Fax:* 715-682-1258. *E-mail:* admit@northland.edu. *Web site:* http://www.northland.edu/.

RIPON COLLEGE

Ripon, Wisconsin

Ripon College is a coed, private, four-year college, founded in 1851, offering degrees at the bachelor's level. It has a 250-acre campus in Ripon near Milwaukee.

Academic Information The faculty has 92 members (61% full-time), 74% with terminal degrees. The student-faculty ratio is 15:1. The library holds 173,355 titles, 372 serial subscriptions, and 391 audiovisual materials. Special programs include services for learning-disabled students, study abroad, advanced placement credit, accelerated degree programs, double majors, self-designed majors, part-time degree programs (daytime), internships, and arrangement for off-campus study with American University, Newberry Library, Oak Ridge National Laboratory, University of Chicago, Associated Colleges of the Midwest Wilderness Field Station. The most frequently chosen baccalaureate fields are business/marketing, history, social sciences.
Student Body Statistics The student body is made up of 1,057 undergraduates (283 freshmen). 52 percent are women and 48 percent are men. Students come from 32 states and territories and 14 other countries. 76 percent are from Wisconsin. 2.1 percent are international students.
Expenses for 2008–09 *Application fee:* $30. *Comprehensive fee:* $31,015 includes full-time tuition ($23,970), mandatory fees ($275), and college room and board ($6770). *College room only:* $3490. *Part-time tuition:* $890 per credit.
Financial Aid Forms of aid include need-based and non-need-based scholarships and part-time jobs. The average aided 2008–09 undergraduate received an aid package worth an estimated $20,981. The priority application deadline for financial aid is March 1.
Freshman Admission Ripon College requires an essay, a high school transcript, a minimum 2.0 high school GPA, 1 recommendation, SAT or ACT scores, and TOEFL scores for international students. An interview is recommended. An interview is required for some. The application deadline for regular admission is rolling.
Transfer Admission The application deadline for admission is rolling.
Entrance Difficulty Ripon College assesses its entrance difficulty level as moderately difficult. For the fall 2008 freshman class, 79 percent of the applicants were accepted.
For Further Information Contact Office of Admission, Ripon College, 300 Seward Street, PO Box 248, Ripon, WI 54971. *Phone:* 920-748-8114 or 800-947-4766 (toll-free). *Fax:* 920-748-8335. *E-mail:* adminfo@ripon.edu. *Web site:* http://www.ripon.edu/.

ST. NORBERT COLLEGE

De Pere, Wisconsin

St. Norbert College is a coed, private, Roman Catholic, comprehensive institution, founded in 1898, offering degrees at the bachelor's and master's levels. It has a 92-acre campus in De Pere.

Academic Information The faculty has 180 members (73% full-time), 72% with terminal degrees. The undergraduate student-faculty ratio is 14:1. The library holds 229,958 titles, 485 serial subscriptions, and 6,971 audiovisual materials. Special programs include academic remediation, services for learning-disabled students, an honors program, study abroad, advanced placement credit, ESL programs, double majors, independent study, self-designed majors, summer session for credit, part-time degree programs (daytime, summer), internships, and arrangement for off-campus study with Higher Education Consortium for Urban Affairs, American University. The most frequently chosen baccalaureate fields are business/marketing, education, social sciences.
Student Body Statistics The student body totals 2,137, of whom 2,084 are undergraduates (532 freshmen). 56 percent are women and 44 percent are men. Students come from 33 states and territories and 28 other countries. 71 percent are from Wisconsin. 3.2 percent are international students.
Expenses for 2008–09 *Application fee:* $25. *Comprehensive fee:* $32,707 includes full-time tuition ($25,526), mandatory fees ($400), and college room and board ($6781). *College room only:* $3552. Full-time tuition and fees vary according to course load. Room and board charges vary according to board plan, housing facility, and student level. *Part-time tuition:* $798 per credit. Part-time tuition varies according to course load.
Financial Aid Forms of aid include need-based and non-need-based scholarships and part-time jobs. The average aided 2007–08 undergraduate received an aid package worth $17,948. The priority application deadline for financial aid is March 1.
Freshman Admission St. Norbert College requires a high school transcript, 1 recommendation, SAT or ACT scores, and TOEFL scores for international students. An essay is recommended. An interview is required for some. The application deadline for regular admission is rolling.
Transfer Admission The application deadline for admission is rolling.
Entrance Difficulty St. Norbert College assesses its entrance difficulty level as moderately difficult. For the fall 2008 freshman class, 81 percent of the applicants were accepted.
For Further Information Contact Ms. Bridget O'Connor, Vice President for Enrollment Management and Communications, St. Norbert College, 100 Grant Street, De Pere, WI 54115-2099. *Phone:* 920-403-3005 or 800-236-4878 (toll-free). *Fax:* 920-403-4072. *E-mail:* admit@snc.edu. *Web site:* http://www.snc.edu/.

See page 266 for the Close-Up.

SILVER LAKE COLLEGE

Manitowoc, Wisconsin

Silver Lake College is a coed, primarily women's, private, Roman Catholic, comprehensive institution, founded in 1869, offering degrees at the associate, bachelor's, and master's levels and postbachelor's certificates. It has a 30-acre campus in Manitowoc near Milwaukee.

Academic Information The faculty has 122 members (34% full-time), 24% with terminal degrees. The undergraduate student-faculty ratio is 7:1. The library holds 62,465 titles, 250 serial subscriptions, and 7,112

Silver Lake College (continued)

audiovisual materials. Special programs include academic remediation, cooperative (work-study) education, advanced placement credit, accelerated degree programs, ESL programs, double majors, independent study, distance learning, self-designed majors, summer session for credit, part-time degree programs (daytime, evenings, weekends, summer), adult/continuing education programs, and internships. The most frequently chosen baccalaureate fields are business/marketing, education, psychology.
Student Body Statistics The student body totals 853, of whom 592 are undergraduates (33 freshmen). 70 percent are women and 30 percent are men. Students come from 5 states and territories and 5 other countries. 98 percent are from Wisconsin. 1.6 percent are international students.
Expenses for 2009–10 *Application fee:* $35. *Comprehensive fee:* $26,960 includes full-time tuition ($20,340), mandatory fees ($220), and college room and board ($6400). *College room only:* $4900. *Part-time tuition:* $625 per credit. *Part-time mandatory fees:* $60 per term.
Financial Aid Forms of aid include need-based and non-need-based scholarships, athletic grants, and part-time jobs. The average aided 2008–09 undergraduate received an aid package worth an estimated $16,855.
Freshman Admission Silver Lake College requires a high school transcript, a minimum 2.5 high school GPA, SAT or ACT scores, and TOEFL scores for international students. An interview and audition are required for some. The application deadline for regular admission is August 1.
Transfer Admission The application deadline for admission is August 1.
Entrance Difficulty Silver Lake College assesses its entrance difficulty level as minimally difficult. For the fall 2008 freshman class, 50 percent of the applicants were accepted.
For Further Information Contact Matthew Thielen, Vice President of Student Life and Dean of Students, Silver Lake College, 2406 South Alverno Road, Manitowoc, WI 54220. *Phone:* 920-686-6199 or 800-236-4752 Ext. 175 (toll-free in-state). *Fax:* 920-684-7082. *E-mail:* admslc@silver.sl.edu. *Web site:* http://www.sl.edu/.

STRATTON COLLEGE

See Bryant & Stratton College.

UNIVERSITY OF PHOENIX–WISCONSIN CAMPUS

Brookfield, Wisconsin

University of Phoenix–Wisconsin Campus is a coed, proprietary, comprehensive institution, founded in 2001, offering degrees at the bachelor's and master's levels.

Academic Information The faculty has 53 members (11% full-time), 17% with terminal degrees. Special programs include services for learning-disabled students, advanced placement credit, accelerated degree programs, independent study, and distance learning. The most frequently chosen baccalaureate field is business/marketing.
Student Body Statistics The student body totals 80, of whom 63 are undergraduates. 62 percent are women and 38 percent are men. 4.8 percent are international students.
Expenses for 2008–09 *Application fee:* $0. *Tuition:* $12,000 full-time. Full-time tuition varies according to course level and course load.
Financial Aid Forms of aid include need-based and non-need-based scholarships. The average aided 2007–08 undergraduate received an aid package worth $6392. The application deadline for financial aid is continuous.
Freshman Admission University of Phoenix–Wisconsin Campus requires 1 recommendation and TOEFL scores for international students. A high school transcript is required for some. The application deadline for regular admission is rolling.
Transfer Admission The application deadline for admission is rolling.
Entrance Difficulty University of Phoenix–Wisconsin Campus has an open admission policy.
For Further Information Contact Ms. Audra McQuarie, Registrar/Executive Director, University of Phoenix–Wisconsin Campus, 4035 South Riverpoint Parkway, Mail Stop CF-L101, Phoenix, AZ 85040. *Phone:* 480-557-6151, 800-776-4867 (toll-free in-state), or 800-228-7240 (toll-free out-of-state). *Fax:* 480-643-3068. *E-mail:* audra.mcquarie@phoenix.edu. *Web site:* http://www.phoenix.edu/.

UNIVERSITY OF WISCONSIN–EAU CLAIRE

Eau Claire, Wisconsin

University of Wisconsin–Eau Claire is a coed, public, comprehensive unit of University of Wisconsin System, founded in 1916, offering degrees at the associate, bachelor's, and master's levels and post-master's and postbachelor's certificates. It has a 333-acre campus in Eau Claire.

Academic Information The faculty has 524 members (79% full-time), 71% with terminal degrees. The undergraduate student-faculty ratio is 21:1. The library holds 744,695 titles, 24,360 serial subscriptions, and 10,297 audiovisual materials. Special programs include academic remediation, services for learning-disabled students, an honors program, cooperative (work-study) education, study abroad, advanced placement credit, accelerated degree programs, ESL programs, double majors, independent study, distance learning, summer session for credit, part-time degree programs (daytime, evenings, summer), adult/continuing education programs, internships, and arrangement for off-campus study with National Student Exchange. The most frequently chosen baccalaureate fields are business/marketing, communications/journalism, health professions and related sciences.
Student Body Statistics The student body totals 10,889, of whom 10,346 are undergraduates (2,058 freshmen). 58 percent are women and 42 percent are men. Students come from 29 states and territories and 29 other countries. 79 percent are from Wisconsin. 1.3 percent are international students.
Expenses for 2008–09 *Application fee:* $35. *State resident tuition:* $5240 full-time, $258 per credit part-time. *Nonresident tuition:* $12,814 full-time, $574 per credit part-time. *Mandatory fees:* $963 full-time, $40 per credit part-time, $2 per term part-time. Both full-time and part-time tuition and fees vary according to reciprocity agreements. *College room and board:* $5210. *College room only:* $2730. Room and board charges vary according to board plan and housing facility.
Financial Aid Forms of aid include need-based and non-need-based scholarships and part-time jobs. The average aided 2007–08 undergraduate received an aid package worth $8056. The priority application deadline for financial aid is April 15.
Freshman Admission University of Wisconsin–Eau Claire requires a high school transcript, rank in upper 50% of high school class, SAT or ACT scores, and TOEFL scores for international students. The application deadline for regular admission is rolling.
Transfer Admission The application deadline for admission is July 1.
Entrance Difficulty University of Wisconsin–Eau Claire assesses its entrance difficulty level as moderately difficult. For the fall 2008 freshman class, 64 percent of the applicants were accepted.
For Further Information Contact Ms. Kristina Anderson, Executive Director of Enrollment Management and Director of Admissions, University of Wisconsin–Eau Claire, PO Box 4004, Eau Claire, WI 54702-4004. *Phone:* 715-836-5415. *Fax:* 715-836-2409. *E-mail:* admissions@uwec.edu. *Web site:* http://www.uwec.edu/.

UNIVERSITY OF WISCONSIN–GREEN BAY

Green Bay, Wisconsin

University of Wisconsin–Green Bay is a coed, public, comprehensive unit of University of Wisconsin System, founded in 1968, offering degrees at the associate, bachelor's, and master's levels and postbachelor's certificates. It has a 700-acre campus in Green Bay.

Academic Information The faculty has 334 members (56% full-time), 56% with terminal degrees. The undergraduate student-faculty ratio is

23:1. The library holds 360,795 titles, 4,452 serial subscriptions, and 48,563 audiovisual materials. Special programs include academic remediation, services for learning-disabled students, study abroad, advanced placement credit, double majors, independent study, distance learning, self-designed majors, summer session for credit, part-time degree programs (daytime, evenings, weekends, summer), external degree programs, adult/continuing education programs, internships, and arrangement for off-campus study with National Student Exchange. The most frequently chosen baccalaureate fields are business/marketing, biological/life sciences, psychology.

Student Body Statistics The student body totals 6,275, of whom 6,059 are undergraduates (1,017 freshmen). 64 percent are women and 36 percent are men. Students come from 36 states and territories and 31 other countries. 95 percent are from Wisconsin. 0.8 percent are international students.

Expenses for 2008–09 *Application fee:* $44. *One-time mandatory fee:* $200. *State resident tuition:* $5084 full-time, $212 per credit part-time. *Nonresident tuition:* $12,657 full-time, $527 per credit part-time. *Mandatory fees:* $1224 full-time, $52 per credit part-time. Full-time tuition and fees vary according to reciprocity agreements. *College room and board:* $5400. *College room only:* $3100. Room and board charges vary according to housing facility.

Financial Aid Forms of aid include need-based and non-need-based scholarships, athletic grants, and part-time jobs. The average aided 2008–09 undergraduate received an aid package worth an estimated $9610. The priority application deadline for financial aid is April 15.

Freshman Admission University of Wisconsin–Green Bay requires an essay, a high school transcript, SAT or ACT scores, and TOEFL scores for international students. An interview is required for some.

Entrance Difficulty University of Wisconsin–Green Bay assesses its entrance difficulty level as moderately difficult. For the fall 2008 freshman class, 72 percent of the applicants were accepted.

For Further Information Contact Ms. Pam Harvey-Jacobs, Director of Admissions, University of Wisconsin–Green Bay, 2420 Nicolet Drive, Green Bay, WI 54311-7001. *Phone:* 920-465-2111 or 888-367-8942 (toll-free out-of-state). *Fax:* 920-465-5754. *E-mail:* uwgb@uwgb.edu. *Web site:* http://www.uwgb.edu/.

UNIVERSITY OF WISCONSIN–LA CROSSE

La Crosse, Wisconsin

University of Wisconsin–La Crosse is a coed, public, comprehensive unit of University of Wisconsin System, founded in 1909, offering degrees at the associate, bachelor's, master's, and first professional levels and postbachelor's certificates. It has a 121-acre campus in La Crosse.

Academic Information The faculty has 508 members (69% full-time), 63% with terminal degrees. The library holds 695,925 titles and 1,052 serial subscriptions. Special programs include academic remediation, services for learning-disabled students, an honors program, cooperative (work-study) education, study abroad, advanced placement credit, ESL programs, double majors, independent study, distance learning, summer session for credit, part-time degree programs (daytime, summer), adult/continuing education programs, internships, and arrangement for off-campus study with Viterbo College. The most frequently chosen baccalaureate fields are business/marketing, biological/life sciences, education.

Student Body Statistics The student body totals 9,900, of whom 8,634 are undergraduates (1,784 freshmen). 58 percent are women and 42 percent are men. Students come from 37 states and territories and 35 other countries. 84 percent are from Wisconsin. 2.7 percent are international students.

Expenses for 2008–09 *Application fee:* $44. *State resident tuition:* $5643 full-time, $235.13 per credit hour part-time. *Nonresident tuition:* $13,216 full-time, $550.68 per credit hour part-time. *Mandatory fees:* $1005 full-time. Full-time tuition and fees vary according to degree level, program, and reciprocity agreements. Part-time tuition varies according to course load, degree level, program, and reciprocity agreements. *College room and board:* $5420. *College room only:* $3130. Room and board charges vary according to board plan and housing facility.

Financial Aid Forms of aid include need-based and non-need-based scholarships and part-time jobs. The average aided 2007–08 undergraduate received an aid package worth $6092.

Freshman Admission University of Wisconsin–La Crosse requires a high school transcript and SAT or ACT scores. An essay, ACT scores, and TOEFL scores for international students are recommended. An interview is required for some. The application deadline for regular admission is rolling and for nonresidents it is rolling.

Transfer Admission The application deadline for admission is rolling.

Entrance Difficulty University of Wisconsin–La Crosse assesses its entrance difficulty level as moderately difficult. For the fall 2008 freshman class, 66 percent of the applicants were accepted.

For Further Information Contact Ms. Kathryn Kiefer, Director of Admissions, University of Wisconsin–La Crosse, 1725 State Street, LaCrosse, WI 54601. *Phone:* 608-785-8939. *Fax:* 608-785-8940. *E-mail:* admissions@uwlax.edu. *Web site:* http://www.uwlax.edu/.

UNIVERSITY OF WISCONSIN–MADISON

Madison, Wisconsin

University of Wisconsin–Madison is a coed, public unit of University of Wisconsin System, founded in 1848, offering degrees at the bachelor's, master's, doctoral, and first professional levels and post-master's and first professional certificates. It has a 1,050-acre campus in Madison near Milwaukee.

Academic Information The faculty has 2,848 members (84% full-time), 88% with terminal degrees. The undergraduate student-faculty ratio is 14:1. Special programs include services for learning-disabled students, an honors program, cooperative (work-study) education, study abroad, advanced placement credit, accelerated degree programs, ESL programs, double majors, independent study, distance learning, self-designed majors, summer session for credit, part-time degree programs (daytime, evenings), adult/continuing education programs, and internships. The most frequently chosen baccalaureate fields are biological/life sciences, business/marketing, social sciences.

Student Body Statistics The student body totals 42,030, of whom 30,750 are undergraduates (5,774 freshmen). 52 percent are women and 48 percent are men. 68 percent are from Wisconsin. 4.6 percent are international students.

Expenses for 2008–09 *Application fee:* $44. *State resident tuition:* $6678 full-time, $278.27 per credit hour part-time. *Nonresident tuition:* $20,928 full-time, $872.01 per credit hour part-time. *Mandatory fees:* $890 full-time, $38.92 per credit hour part-time. Full-time tuition and fees vary according to degree level, program, and reciprocity agreements. Part-time tuition and fees vary according to course load, degree level, program, and reciprocity agreements. *College room and board:* $7700. Room and board charges vary according to board plan, housing facility, and location.

Financial Aid Forms of aid include need-based and non-need-based scholarships, athletic grants, and part-time jobs. The average aided 2007–08 undergraduate received an aid package worth $9948. The application deadline for financial aid is continuous.

Freshman Admission University of Wisconsin–Madison requires an essay, a high school transcript, SAT or ACT scores, and TOEFL scores for international students. The application deadline for regular admission is February 1.

Transfer Admission The application deadline for admission is February 1.

Entrance Difficulty University of Wisconsin–Madison assesses its entrance difficulty level as very difficult. For the fall 2008 freshman class, 53 percent of the applicants were accepted.

For Further Information Contact Office of Undergraduate Admissions, University of Wisconsin–Madison, 716 Langdon Street, Madison, WI 53706-1481. *Phone:* 608-262-3961. *Fax:* 608-262-7706. *E-mail:* onwisconsin@admissions.wisc.edu. *Web site:* http://www.wisc.edu/.

UNIVERSITY OF WISCONSIN–MILWAUKEE

Milwaukee, Wisconsin

University of Wisconsin–Milwaukee is a coed, public unit of University of Wisconsin System, founded in 1956, offering degrees at the bachelor's, master's, and doctoral levels and post-master's and postbachelor's certificates. It has a 90-acre campus in Milwaukee.

Academic Information The faculty has 824 members (92% full-time). The undergraduate student-faculty ratio is 31:1. The library holds 1 million titles and 8,240 serial subscriptions. Special programs include academic remediation, services for learning-disabled students, an honors program, cooperative (work-study) education, study abroad, advanced placement credit, accelerated degree programs, ESL programs, double majors, independent study, distance learning, self-designed majors, summer session for credit, part-time degree programs, adult/continuing education programs, internships, and arrangement for off-campus study with University of Wisconsin-Parkside. The most frequently chosen baccalaureate fields are business/marketing, education, health professions and related sciences.
Student Body Statistics The student body totals 29,215, of whom 24,299 are undergraduates (4,118 freshmen). 52 percent are women and 48 percent are men. Students come from 51 states and territories and 57 other countries. 96 percent are from Wisconsin. 1 percent are international students.
Expenses for 2008–09 *Application fee:* $44. *State resident tuition:* $6531 full-time, $272.13 per credit part-time. *Nonresident tuition:* $16,260 full-time, $677.48 per credit part-time. *Mandatory fees:* $778 full-time. Full-time tuition and fees vary according to location, program, and reciprocity agreements. Part-time tuition varies according to course load, location, program, and reciprocity agreements. *College room only:* $3840. Room charges vary according to housing facility.
Financial Aid Forms of aid include need-based and non-need-based scholarships, athletic grants, and part-time jobs. The average aided 2008–09 undergraduate received an aid package worth an estimated $7311. The priority application deadline for financial aid is March 1.
Freshman Admission University of Wisconsin–Milwaukee requires a high school transcript, SAT or ACT scores, TOEFL scores for international students, and ACT for state residents. An essay is recommended. The application deadline for regular admission is July 1.
Transfer Admission The application deadline for admission is August 1.
Entrance Difficulty University of Wisconsin–Milwaukee assesses its entrance difficulty level as moderately difficult. For the fall 2008 freshman class, 79 percent of the applicants were accepted.
For Further Information Contact Ms. Jan Ford, Director, Recruitment and Outreach, University of Wisconsin–Milwaukee, PO Box 749, Milwaukee, WI 53201. *Phone:* 414-229-4397. *Fax:* 414-229-6940. *E-mail:* uwmlook@uwm.edu. *Web site:* http://www.uwm.edu/.

UNIVERSITY OF WISCONSIN–OSHKOSH

Oshkosh, Wisconsin

University of Wisconsin–Oshkosh is a coed, public, comprehensive unit of University of Wisconsin System, founded in 1871, offering degrees at the associate, bachelor's, and master's levels and postbachelor's certificates. It has a 192-acre campus in Oshkosh near Milwaukee.

Academic Information The faculty has 599 members (64% full-time), 61% with terminal degrees. The undergraduate student-faculty ratio is 20:1. The library holds 446,774 titles and 5,219 serial subscriptions. Special programs include academic remediation, services for learning-disabled students, an honors program, cooperative (work-study) education, study abroad, advanced placement credit, accelerated degree programs, ESL programs, double majors, independent study, distance learning, self-designed majors, summer session for credit, part-time degree programs (daytime, evenings, weekends, summer), adult/continuing education programs, and internships. The most frequently chosen baccalaureate fields are business/marketing, education, health professions and related sciences.
Student Body Statistics The student body totals 12,669, of whom 11,355 are undergraduates (1,842 freshmen). 59 percent are women and 41 percent are men. Students come from 30 states and territories and 32 other countries. 97 percent are from Wisconsin.
Expenses for 2008–09 *Application fee:* $35. *State resident tuition:* $6038 full-time, $252 per credit hour part-time. *Nonresident tuition:* $13,610 full-time, $567 per credit hour part-time. *College room and board:* $5898. *College room only:* $3378.
Financial Aid Forms of aid include need-based scholarships and part-time jobs. The average aided 2008–09 undergraduate received an aid package worth an estimated $4500. The priority application deadline for financial aid is March 15.
Freshman Admission University of Wisconsin–Oshkosh requires a high school transcript, SAT or ACT scores, TOEFL scores for international students, and ACT required for state residents. An essay is recommended. The application deadline for regular admission is rolling.
Transfer Admission The application deadline for admission is rolling.
Entrance Difficulty University of Wisconsin–Oshkosh assesses its entrance difficulty level as moderately difficult. For the fall 2008 freshman class, 81 percent of the applicants were accepted.
For Further Information Contact Mr. Richard Hillman, Associate Director of Admissions, University of Wisconsin–Oshkosh, 800 Algoma Boulevard, Oshkosh, WI 54901. *Phone:* 920-424-0202. *E-mail:* oshadmuw@uwosh.edu. *Web site:* http://www.uwosh.edu/.

UNIVERSITY OF WISCONSIN–PARKSIDE

Kenosha, Wisconsin

University of Wisconsin–Parkside is a coed, public, comprehensive unit of University of Wisconsin System, founded in 1968, offering degrees at the bachelor's and master's levels. It has a 700-acre campus in Kenosha near Chicago and Milwaukee.

Academic Information The faculty has 293 members (61% full-time), 55% with terminal degrees. The undergraduate student-faculty ratio is 19:1. The library holds 400,000 titles and 1,590 serial subscriptions. Special programs include academic remediation, services for learning-disabled students, an honors program, study abroad, advanced placement credit, accelerated degree programs, double majors, independent study, distance learning, summer session for credit, part-time degree programs (daytime, evenings, weekends, summer), external degree programs, internships, and arrangement for off-campus study with Carthage College. The most frequently chosen baccalaureate fields are business/marketing, psychology, public administration and social services.
Student Body Statistics The student body totals 5,167, of whom 5,045 are undergraduates (928 freshmen). 55 percent are women and 45 percent are men. Students come from 23 states and territories and 13 other countries. 92 percent are from Wisconsin. 0.3 percent are international students.
Expenses for 2008–09 *Application fee:* $44. *State resident tuition:* $5084 full-time, $212 per credit hour part-time. *Nonresident tuition:* $12,922 full-time, $538 per credit hour part-time. *Mandatory fees:* $986 full-time. Full-time tuition and fees vary according to course load and reciprocity agreements. Part-time tuition varies according to course load. *College room and board:* $5986. *College room only:* $3792. Room and board charges vary according to board plan and housing facility.
Financial Aid Forms of aid include need-based and non-need-based scholarships, athletic grants, and part-time jobs.
Freshman Admission University of Wisconsin–Parkside requires a high school transcript, minimum of 17 high school units distributed as specified in the UW-Parkside catalog, and TOEFL scores for international students. SAT or ACT scores are required for some. The application deadline for regular admission is August 1.
Transfer Admission The application deadline for admission is August 1.
Entrance Difficulty University of Wisconsin–Parkside assesses its entrance difficulty level as moderately difficult; very difficult for international students. For the fall 2008 freshman class, 79 percent of the applicants were accepted.
For Further Information Contact Mr. Matthew Jensen, Director of Admissions, University of Wisconsin–Parkside, PO Box 2000, 900 Wood Road, Kenosha, WI 53141-2000. *Phone:* 262-595-2784. *Fax:* 262-595-2008. *E-mail:* matthew.jensen@uwp.edu. *Web site:* http://www.uwp.edu/.

UNIVERSITY OF WISCONSIN–PLATTEVILLE

Platteville, Wisconsin

University of Wisconsin–Platteville is a coed, public, comprehensive unit of University of Wisconsin System, founded in 1866, offering degrees at the associate, bachelor's, and master's levels and postbachelor's certificates. It has a 380-acre campus in Platteville.

Academic Information The faculty has 367 members (78% full-time), 66% with terminal degrees. The undergraduate student-faculty ratio is 20:1. The library holds 362,247 titles and 2,116 serial subscriptions. Special programs include academic remediation, services for learning-disabled students, an honors program, cooperative (work-study) education, study abroad, advanced placement credit, ESL programs, double majors, independent study, distance learning, self-designed majors, summer session for credit, part-time degree programs (daytime, evenings, weekends, summer), external degree programs, adult/continuing education programs, internships, and arrangement for off-campus study with Westfield State College. The most frequently chosen baccalaureate fields are business/marketing, education, engineering.
Student Body Statistics The student body totals 7,379, of whom 6,537 are undergraduates (1,465 freshmen). 36 percent are women and 64 percent are men. Students come from 15 states and territories and 13 other countries. 82 percent are from Wisconsin. 0.2 percent are international students.
Expenses for 2008–09 *Application fee:* $44. *State resident tuition:* $5184 full-time, $248.66 per credit part-time. *Nonresident tuition:* $13,919 full-time, $579.19 per credit part-time. *Mandatory fees:* $963 full-time. Full-time tuition and fees vary according to course load, degree level, and reciprocity agreements. Part-time tuition varies according to course load, degree level, and reciprocity agreements. *College room and board:* $5550. *College room only:* $2950. Room and board charges vary according to board plan.
Financial Aid Forms of aid include need-based and non-need-based scholarships and part-time jobs. The priority application deadline for financial aid is March 15.
Freshman Admission University of Wisconsin–Platteville requires a high school transcript, SAT or ACT scores, and TOEFL scores for international students. An essay and ACT scores are recommended. Recommendations and an interview are required for some. The application deadline for regular admission is rolling.
Transfer Admission The application deadline for admission is rolling.
Entrance Difficulty University of Wisconsin–Platteville assesses its entrance difficulty level as moderately difficult. For the fall 2008 freshman class, 85 percent of the applicants were accepted.
For Further Information Contact Ms. Angela Udelhofen, Director of Admissions and Enrollment Management, University of Wisconsin–Platteville, 1 University Plaza, 120 Brigham Hall, Platteville, WI 53818-3099. *Phone:* 608-342-1125 or 800-362-5515 (toll-free). *Fax:* 608-342-1122. *E-mail:* admit@uwplatt.edu. *Web site:* http://www.uwplatt.edu/.

UNIVERSITY OF WISCONSIN–RIVER FALLS

River Falls, Wisconsin

http://www.uwrf.edu/

UNIVERSITY OF WISCONSIN–STEVENS POINT

Stevens Point, Wisconsin

University of Wisconsin–Stevens Point is a coed, public, comprehensive unit of University of Wisconsin System, founded in 1894, offering degrees at the associate, bachelor's, master's, and doctoral levels. It has a 335-acre campus in Stevens Point.

Academic Information The faculty has 452 members (88% full-time), 73% with terminal degrees. The undergraduate student-faculty ratio is 20:1. The library holds 1 million titles, 18,428 serial subscriptions, and 8,850 audiovisual materials. Special programs include academic remediation, services for learning-disabled students, study abroad, advanced placement credit, accelerated degree programs, ESL programs, double majors, independent study, distance learning, self-designed majors, summer session for credit, part-time degree programs (daytime, evenings, summer), adult/continuing education programs, internships, and arrangement for off-campus study with University of Wisconsin campuses at Oshkosh, Eau Claire, Fond du Lac, Marinette, Marshfield, and Marathon.
Student Body Statistics The student body totals 9,155, of whom 8,710 are undergraduates (1,618 freshmen). 53 percent are women and 47 percent are men. Students come from 27 states and territories and 25 other countries. 93 percent are from Wisconsin. 1.9 percent are international students.
Expenses for 2008–09 *Application fee:* $44. *State resident tuition:* $5084 full-time, $212 per credit part-time. *Nonresident tuition:* $12,657 full-time, $527 per credit part-time. *Mandatory fees:* $1116 full-time, $98 per credit part-time. Both full-time and part-time tuition and fees vary according to course load and reciprocity agreements. *College room and board:* $5180. *College room only:* $3148.
Financial Aid Forms of aid include need-based and non-need-based scholarships and part-time jobs. The average aided 2007–08 undergraduate received an aid package worth $7585. The priority application deadline for financial aid is May 15.
Freshman Admission University of Wisconsin–Stevens Point requires a high school transcript, SAT or ACT scores, and TOEFL scores for international students. An essay and 3 recommendations are recommended. The application deadline for regular admission is rolling.
Transfer Admission The application deadline for admission is rolling.
Entrance Difficulty University of Wisconsin–Stevens Point assesses its entrance difficulty level as moderately difficult. For the fall 2008 freshman class, 74 percent of the applicants were accepted.
For Further Information Contact Ms. Catherine Glennon, Director of Admissions, University of Wisconsin–Stevens Point, 2100 Main Street, Stevens Point, WI 54481. *Phone:* 715-346-2441. *Fax:* 715-346-3296. *E-mail:* admiss@uwsp.edu. *Web site:* http://www.uwsp.edu/.

UNIVERSITY OF WISCONSIN–STOUT

Menomonie, Wisconsin

University of Wisconsin–Stout is a coed, public, comprehensive unit of University of Wisconsin System, founded in 1891, offering degrees at the bachelor's and master's levels and post-master's certificates. It has a 120-acre campus in Menomonie near Minneapolis–St. Paul.

Academic Information The faculty has 420 members (80% full-time), 67% with terminal degrees. The undergraduate student-faculty ratio is 19:1. The library holds 229,986 titles, 1,784 serial subscriptions, and 16,142 audiovisual materials. Special programs include an honors program, cooperative (work-study) education, study abroad, accelerated degree programs, double majors, independent study, distance learning, part-time degree programs, external degree programs, adult/continuing education programs, internships, and arrangement for off-campus study with Fashion Institute of Technology, University of Wisconsin–Eau Claire. The most frequently chosen baccalaureate fields are business/marketing, education, visual and performing arts.
Student Body Statistics The student body totals 8,811, of whom 7,766 are undergraduates (1,631 freshmen). 48 percent are women and 52 percent are men. Students come from 26 states and territories. 68 percent are from Wisconsin. 1 percent are international students.
Expenses for 2008–09 *Application fee:* $44. *State resident tuition:* $5662 full-time, $189 per credit part-time. *Nonresident tuition:* $13,408 full-time, $447 per credit part-time. *Mandatory fees:* $1922 full-time, $64 per credit part-time. Both full-time and part-time tuition and fees vary according to reciprocity agreements. *College room and board:* $5170. *College room only:* $3200. Room and board charges vary according to board plan and housing facility.
Financial Aid Forms of aid include need-based and non-need-based scholarships and part-time jobs. The average aided 2008–09 undergraduate received an aid package worth an estimated $8710.
Freshman Admission University of Wisconsin–Stout requires a high school transcript, SAT or ACT scores, and TOEFL scores for international students. A minimum 2.5 high school GPA is recommended.

University of Wisconsin–Stout (continued)

A minimum 2.75 high school GPA is required for some. The application deadline for regular admission is rolling.
Transfer Admission The application deadline for admission is rolling.
Entrance Difficulty University of Wisconsin–Stout assesses its entrance difficulty level as moderately difficult. For the fall 2008 freshman class, 56 percent of the applicants were accepted.
For Further Information Contact Dr. Cynthia S. Gilberts, Executive Director of Enrollment Services, University of Wisconsin–Stout, Admissions UW-Stout, Bowman Hall, Menomonie, WI 54751. *Phone:* 715-232-2639 or 800-HI-STOUT (toll-free in-state). *Fax:* 715-232-2639. *E-mail:* admissions@uwstout.edu. *Web site:* http://www.uwstout.edu/.

UNIVERSITY OF WISCONSIN–SUPERIOR

Superior, Wisconsin

University of Wisconsin–Superior is a coed, public, comprehensive unit of University of Wisconsin System, founded in 1893, offering degrees at the bachelor's and master's levels (associate, educational specialist). It has a 230-acre campus in Superior.

Academic Information The faculty has 187 members (65% full-time), 58% with terminal degrees. The undergraduate student-faculty ratio is 16:1. The library holds 467,700 titles and 753 serial subscriptions. Special programs include academic remediation, services for learning-disabled students, an honors program, cooperative (work-study) education, study abroad, advanced placement credit, Freshman Honors College, ESL programs, double majors, independent study, distance learning, self-designed majors, summer session for credit, part-time degree programs (daytime, evenings, weekends, summer), external degree programs, adult/continuing education programs, internships, and arrangement for off-campus study with College of St. Scholastica, Northland College, University of Minnesota, Duluth. The most frequently chosen baccalaureate fields are business/marketing, education, interdisciplinary studies.
Student Body Statistics The student body totals 2,688, of whom 2,439 are undergraduates. Students come from 26 states and territories and 28 other countries. 54 percent are from Wisconsin. 4.4 percent are international students.
Expenses for 2008–09 *Application fee:* $44. *State resident tuition:* $5293 full-time, $386 per semester hour part-time. *Nonresident tuition:* $12,866 full-time, $702 per semester hour part-time. *Mandatory fees:* $1066 full-time. Full-time tuition and fees vary according to reciprocity agreements. Part-time tuition varies according to reciprocity agreements. *College room and board:* $5154. *College room only:* $2874. Room and board charges vary according to board plan and housing facility.
Financial Aid Forms of aid include need-based and non-need-based scholarships and part-time jobs. The average aided 2008–09 undergraduate received an aid package worth an estimated $7621. The priority application deadline for financial aid is April 1.
Freshman Admission University of Wisconsin–Superior requires a high school transcript, SAT or ACT scores, and TOEFL scores for international students. An interview is recommended. An essay and recommendations are required for some. The application deadline for regular admission is rolling.
Transfer Admission The application deadline for admission is rolling.
Entrance Difficulty University of Wisconsin–Superior assesses its entrance difficulty level as moderately difficult. For the fall 2008 freshman class, 70 percent of the applicants were accepted.
For Further Information Contact Ms. Tonya Roth, Director of Admission, University of Wisconsin–Superior, Belknap and Catlin, PO Box 2000, Superior, WI 54880-4500. *Phone:* 715-394-8217. *Fax:* 715-394-8407. *E-mail:* admissions@uwsuper.edu. *Web site:* http://www.uwsuper.edu/.

UNIVERSITY OF WISCONSIN–WHITEWATER

Whitewater, Wisconsin

University of Wisconsin–Whitewater is a coed, public, comprehensive unit of University of Wisconsin System, founded in 1868, offering degrees at the associate, bachelor's, and master's levels. It has a 385-acre campus in Whitewater near Milwaukee.

Academic Information The faculty has 501 members (78% full-time), 74% with terminal degrees. The undergraduate student-faculty ratio is 22:1. The library holds 701,086 titles, 4,589 serial subscriptions, and 19,427 audiovisual materials. Special programs include academic remediation, services for learning-disabled students, an honors program, cooperative (work-study) education, study abroad, advanced placement credit, accelerated degree programs, ESL programs, double majors, independent study, distance learning, self-designed majors, summer session for credit, part-time degree programs (daytime, evenings, weekends, summer), external degree programs, adult/continuing education programs, and internships. The most frequently chosen baccalaureate fields are business/marketing, communications/journalism, education.
Student Body Statistics The student body totals 10,962, of whom 9,621 are undergraduates (2,154 freshmen). 49 percent are women and 51 percent are men. Students come from 24 states and territories and 27 other countries. 94 percent are from Wisconsin. 0.9 percent are international students.
Expenses for 2008–09 *Application fee:* $44. *State resident tuition:* $6162 full-time, $219.26 per credit part-time. *Nonresident tuition:* $13,736 full-time, $534.80 per credit part-time. *Mandatory fees:* $900 full-time. Full-time tuition and fees vary according to degree level and reciprocity agreements. *College room and board:* $4740. Room and board charges vary according to board plan.
Financial Aid Forms of aid include need-based and non-need-based scholarships and part-time jobs. The average aided 2008–09 undergraduate received an aid package worth an estimated $7280. The priority application deadline for financial aid is March 15.
Freshman Admission University of Wisconsin–Whitewater requires a high school transcript and TOEFL scores for international students. SAT or ACT scores are recommended. ACT scores are required for some. The application deadline for regular admission is rolling.
Transfer Admission The application deadline for admission is rolling.
Entrance Difficulty University of Wisconsin–Whitewater assesses its entrance difficulty level as moderately difficult. For the fall 2008 freshman class, 73 percent of the applicants were accepted.
For Further Information Contact Mr. Stephen J. McKellips, Director of Admissions, University of Wisconsin–Whitewater, 800 West Main Street, Whitewater, WI 53190-1790. *Phone:* 262-472-1440 Ext. 1512. *Fax:* 262-472-1515. *E-mail:* uwwadmit@uww.edu. *Web site:* http://www.uww.edu/.

VITERBO UNIVERSITY

La Crosse, Wisconsin

Viterbo University is a coed, primarily women's, private, Roman Catholic, comprehensive institution, founded in 1890, offering degrees at the associate, bachelor's, and master's levels and postbachelor's certificates. It has a 72-acre campus in La Crosse.

Academic Information The faculty has 232 members (46% full-time), 41% with terminal degrees. The undergraduate student-faculty ratio is 12.3:1. The library holds 88,377 titles, 24,452 serial subscriptions, and 7,159 audiovisual materials. Special programs include academic remediation, services for learning-disabled students, an honors program, study abroad, advanced placement credit, accelerated degree programs, double majors, independent study, distance learning, self-designed majors, summer session for credit, part-time degree programs (daytime, evenings, weekends, summer), adult/continuing education programs, internships, and arrangement for off-campus study with University of Wisconsin-La Crosse, Western Wisconsin Technical College, Viterbo Centers: West Demoine, West Allis, WI. The most frequently chosen baccalaureate fields are business/marketing, education, health professions and related sciences.

Student Body Statistics The student body is made up of 2,093 undergraduates (365 freshmen). 71 percent are women and 29 percent are men. Students come from 24 states and territories and 17 other countries. 81 percent are from Wisconsin. 1.5 percent are international students.
Expenses for 2009–10 *Application fee:* $25. *Comprehensive fee:* $27,670 includes full-time tuition ($19,670), mandatory fees ($490), and college room and board ($7510). *College room only:* $3030. *Part-time tuition:* $580 per credit. *Part-time mandatory fees:* $15 per credit, $45 per term.
Financial Aid Forms of aid include need-based and non-need-based scholarships, athletic grants, and part-time jobs. The priority application deadline for financial aid is March 15.
Freshman Admission Viterbo University requires a high school transcript, a minimum 2.0 high school GPA, ACT scores, and TOEFL scores for international students. An essay, an interview, and audition for theater and music; portfolio for art are required for some. The application deadline for regular admission is rolling and for nonresidents it is rolling.
Transfer Admission The application deadline for admission is rolling.
Entrance Difficulty Viterbo University assesses its entrance difficulty level as moderately difficult; most difficult for nursing programs. For the fall 2008 freshman class, 86 percent of the applicants were accepted.
For Further Information Contact Mr. Wayne Wojciechowski, Assistant Academic Vice President, Viterbo University, 900 Viterbo Drive, LaCrosse, WI 54601. *Phone:* 608-796-3085 or 800-VITERBO Ext. 3010 (toll-free). *Fax:* 608-796-3020. *E-mail:* admission@viterbo.edu. *Web site:* http://www.viterbo.edu/.

WISCONSIN LUTHERAN COLLEGE

Milwaukee, Wisconsin

Wisconsin Lutheran College is a coed, private, four-year college, founded in 1973, affiliated with the Wisconsin Evangelical Lutheran Synod, offering degrees at the bachelor's level. It has a 48-acre campus in Milwaukee.

Expenses for 2009–10 *Application fee:* $20. *Comprehensive fee:* $28,880 includes full-time tuition ($21,040), mandatory fees ($140), and college room and board ($7700). *College room only:* $4200. *Part-time tuition:* $640 per credit.
For Further Information Contact Ms. Meghan Wieselmann, Admissions Office Manager, Wisconsin Lutheran College, 8800 West Bluemound Road, Milwaukee, WI 53226-9942. *Phone:* 414-443-8718 or 888-WIS LUTH (toll-free). *Fax:* 414-443-8547. *E-mail:* meg.wieselmann@wlc.edu. *Web site:* http://www.wlc.edu/.

Close-Ups of Colleges in the Midwest

AURORA UNIVERSITY

AURORA, ILLINOIS

The University

Aurora University was founded in 1893. The school has grown substantially over the years and has taken on many new challenges. In 1938, it was one of the first small colleges to achieve regional accreditation. In 1947, the college's evening program was instituted—one of the nation's first adult education programs at a liberal arts college. In 1985, Aurora College was reorganized as Aurora University, reflecting both the increased size of the institution and the needs associated with its many new programs. In addition to the College of Arts and Sciences, the University comprises the College of Education (including health and physical education) and the College of Professional Studies (social work, nursing, and business). Today, the University enrolls 4,000 students in more than forty undergraduate programs and eleven graduate degree programs in business, social work, and education. An Ed.D. degree is offered in educational leadership. Degree programs are also offered on the shores of Geneva Lake in Williams Bay, Wisconsin. Degree programs include the B.S. in communication, business leadership, and recreation administration; the RN to B.S.N.; the Master of Arts in Teaching; the M.A. in reading instruction; the M.A. in special education; the M.S. in recreation administration; the M.B.A.; a weekend M.S.W. program; and the Ed.D. degree.

The University's student body includes 600 on-campus, traditional-age students; 1,400 undergraduate commuters; 1,800 graduate students; and more than 300 students at the George Williams College campus. The majority of Aurora's students come from the upper-Midwest region, but twenty states are also represented.

Social life is based on campus, and most activities are campus-wide. Aurora has more than sixty musical, literary, religious, social, and service clubs and organizations. There are also opportunities to be involved in theater and the highly regarded University Chorale. Aurora University has a long history of excellence in both intercollegiate and intramural athletics. A member of the NCAA Division III, Aurora fields intercollegiate teams in baseball, basketball, cross-country, football, golf, indoor track, soccer, softball, tennis, track, and volleyball, often with championship results.

Aurora University is accredited at the bachelor's, master's, and doctoral degree levels by the Higher Learning Commission of the North Central Association of Colleges and Schools, and its programs are accredited by the Commission on Collegiate Nursing Education, National League for Nursing Accrediting Commission, Illinois Department of Professional Regulation, Council on Social Work Education, National Recreation and Park Association/American Association of Leisure and Recreation, and Association of Collegiate Business Schools and Programs.

Location

Aurora University is located in an attractive residential neighborhood on the southwest side of Aurora, Illinois, which has a population of more than 162,000 and is the state's second-largest city. The 32-acre main campus is located only minutes from the Illinois Research and Development Corridor, the site of dozens of nationally and internationally based businesses and industries. Located within an hour's drive or train ride is Chicago, one of the most vibrant cities in the world.

Majors and Degrees

The Bachelor of Arts degree is awarded in accounting, art, biology, business administration, business and commerce, coaching and youth sport development, communication, computer science, criminal justice, elementary education, English, finance, history, management information technology, marketing, organizational management, physical education (K–12 teacher certification), political science, psychology, religion, sociology, special education, Spanish, and theater. The Bachelor of Science degree is awarded in accounting, actuarial science, athletic training, biology, business administration, business and commerce, computer science, health science (allied health, predentistry, premedicine, pre–physical therapy, and pre–veterinary studies), management information technology, marketing, mathematics, organizational management, physical education (fitness and health promotion), and recreation administration. The Bachelor of Science in Nursing and the Bachelor of Science in social work are also offered. The University offers supplemental majors in prelaw and secondary education as well as the YMCA Senior Director Certificate Program.

Academic Programs

Aurora University prides itself on its first-year program, which ensures that entering students make a successful transition to college. The only private college in Illinois selected to be part of a national project to create a model of excellence for the first college year, Aurora University recognizes the unique needs of freshmen.

Aurora University offers academic programs combining a liberal arts foundation with majors emphasizing career preparation and selected concentrations. Graduates are educated to be purposeful, ethical, and proficient—equipped for worthwhile careers and productive lives and for venturing forth into a changing world.

To earn a bachelor's degree, students are required to fulfill the general education core curriculum of the University and the major requirements for an approved major; complete at least 120 semester hours with a GPA of at least 2.0 on a 4.0 scale, including at least 52 semester hours at a senior college; and complete at least 30 semester hours, including the last 24 for the degree and at least 18 in the major, at Aurora University.

Entering freshmen who qualify and are highly motivated are invited to join the Honors Program. Students with an ACT score of 25 or above and a high school GPA of at least 3.0 on a 4.0 scale are invited to join. Those in the program participate in innovative seminars, service learning, advanced course work, and other special and cultural events.

Aurora University accepts credits earned through the CLEP, DANTES, Excelsior College Examinations, and NLN Mobility testing programs. In addition, credit based on portfolio assessment is available to students who have significant prior learning from career experience or individual study.

The University observes a semester calendar (two 16-week semesters), with classes beginning in late August and concluding in early May. A three-week May Term offers exciting course work, including international study/travel and unique intensive courses.

Off-Campus Programs

Aurora University offers travel-study programs abroad and within the United States. Recent travel/study destinations included Costa

Rica, France, England, Italy, South Africa, Mexico, and Greece. The University also has off-campus classes in various locations in Illinois and Wisconsin and twelve degree programs at the University's George Williams campus near Lake Geneva, Wisconsin.

Academic Facilities

The major buildings at Aurora are marked by the distinctive, red-tiled roofs specified by Charles Eckhart in his donation for the original campus. Dunham Hall houses state-of-the-art computer facilities as well as the Schingoethe Center for Native American Cultures. The newest classroom building houses the Institute for Collaboration, which brings together education, health and human services, business, and government to facilitate the development of collaborative leadership. Other facilities include the fully equipped Perry Theatre, the Parolini Fine Arts Center, science labs, a flora-fauna complex, and the College Commons. Music practice rooms, piano labs, and a spacious art studio are housed in the Parolini Music Center. The Charles B. Phillips Library has more than 99,000 volumes, 7,000 multimedia materials, and approximately 518 current periodical subscriptions. In addition, the library provides access to approximately 3,700 journals in electronic full text and interfaces with sixty-four other universities.

Costs

Tuition for the 2008–09 school year is $17,400 for full-time students (24–34 semester hours per year), and yearly room and board costs average $7540.

Financial Aid

Aurora University's financial aid program has been designed to make it possible for any academically qualified student to afford the benefits of a private education. The University works with students to determine the amount of their costs and to identify all available resources so students can meet these expenses. Financial aid is awarded based on financial need as reported on the FAFSA. In addition to need-based financial aid, Aurora University offers academic scholarships, including the Board of Trustees Scholarship, Crimi Scholarship, Deans' Scholarship, Solon B. Cousins Scholarship, Aurora University Opportunity Grant, and transfer scholarships.

Faculty

The favorable student-faculty ratio of 15:1 ensures that students receive plenty of individual attention in class. Instructors also make time for students outside of class, acting as mentors and advisers, and they are eager to answer questions and join students in campus activities.

Student Government

The student body is represented by the Aurora University Student Association (AUSA), which provides funding for sixty-three student groups on campus. Students are also active members of committees ranging from faculty searches to ad hoc task forces and are provided with certain voting privileges.

Admission Requirements

The Aurora University Committee on Admission considers the complete record of a candidate for admission. The University seeks qualified students from varied geographical, cultural, economic, racial, and religious backgrounds. Admission requirements include an ACT score of 20 or above, a high school GPA of 2.5 or above, and a college-preparatory curriculum. Two general qualities are considered in each candidate: academic ability, enabling the student to benefit from a high-quality academic program, and a diversity of talents and interests that can contribute to making the campus community a better and more interesting place for learning. An application for admission to Aurora University is considered on the basis of the academic ability, achievements, activities, and motivation of the student. Candidates for the Honors Program must have an ACT score of 25 or higher and a high school GPA of at least 3.0 on a 4.0 scale. Transfer students with fewer than 30 semester hours of credit should apply in the same manner as freshman applicants. Transfer students with more than 15 semester hours may be admitted to Aurora University if they have a transferable overall GPA of 2.5 or higher. Aurora accepts a maximum of 90 semester hours of transfer credits from a combination of two- and four-year schools. A maximum of 68 semester hours may be transferred from two-year schools. For further information, students should contact a transfer counselor in the Office of Admission and Financial Aid.

Application and Information

To apply for admission to Aurora University, the following items should be sent to the Office of Admission and Financial Aid: a completed application form, an official transcript from the guidance counselor, and official ACT or SAT scores. Transfer students should submit official transcripts from each college or university attended, along with the completed application.

For applications and further information, students may contact:

Office of Admission and Financial Aid
Aurora University
347 South Gladstone Avenue
Aurora, Illinois 60506
Phone: 630-844-5533
800-742-5281 (toll-free)
E-mail: admission@aurora.edu
Web site: http://www.aurora.edu

A view of Eckhart Hall at Aurora University in Aurora, Illinois.

BALDWIN-WALLACE COLLEGE

BEREA, OHIO

The College

Founded in 1845, Baldwin-Wallace College (B-W) in Berea, Ohio, is an accredited institution affiliated with the United Methodist Church that blends the hallmarks of a traditional liberal arts education with an emphasis on professional preparation. Baldwin-Wallace celebrates a long history of diversity and prides itself as being one of the first colleges in Ohio to admit students without regard to race or gender. That spirit of inclusiveness has flourished and evolved into a personalized approach to education—one that stresses individual growth as students learn to learn, respond to new ideas, adapt to new situations, and prepare for the certainty of change.

B-W's reputation as one of the most respected independent colleges in Ohio has led to consistent growth over the past decade and enrollment of approximately 3,100 full-time undergraduate students. The student profile shows that 25 percent of incoming freshmen come from the top 10 percent of their high school classes, with more than 60 percent in the top quarter. In addition to the traditional-aged college student, Baldwin-Wallace has helped adult learners for more than fifty years to develop skills, redirect careers, and enhance lives. Today, 600 adult learners of all ages participate in evening and weekend classes in a variety of programs that are designed to accommodate the varying learning styles and schedules of busy adult learners. Another 700 students are enrolled in part-time graduate programs in education and business administration.

Baldwin-Wallace College is an academic community committed to the liberal arts and sciences as the foundation for lifelong learning. The College fulfills this mission through a rigorous academic program that is characterized by excellence in teaching and learning within a challenging, supportive environment that enhances students' intellectual and personal growth. Baldwin-Wallace College is committed to the success of its students. In addition to receiving a top-notch liberal arts education, students also enjoy numerous opportunities for internships, faculty-directed research, and service-learning programs. Moreover, students work with their faculty adviser to develop personal action plans that are designed to help each individual student prepare fully for life after college. These programs and approaches are enhanced by B-W's student-focused faculty, close-knit community, and rich College traditions. In all, Baldwin-Wallace College provides a truly unique place to study and prepare for future success.

More than 90 percent of Baldwin-Wallace graduates find employment or enter graduate or professional school within nine months of graduation. Recent Baldwin-Wallace graduates have been accepted at some of the finest graduate schools in the world, including Boston College, Boston University, Carnegie Mellon University, Case Western Reserve University, University of Leeds (England), Manhattan School of Music, University of North Carolina, University of Virginia, Vanderbilt University, and Washington University.

Location

B-W students enjoy the best of both worlds. Berea, Ohio, with its tree-lined streets, picturesque homes, and population of 19,000, is an ideal college town. At the same time, students are only 20 minutes from the heart of Cleveland, which is home to Fortune 500 companies as well as unique recreational and cultural opportunities. Cleveland is home to outstanding museums and galleries, professional sporting events, a world-class orchestra, exciting nightlife, and an extensive park system.

Majors and Degrees

Baldwin-Wallace offers the Bachelor of Arts (B.A.), Bachelor of Science (B.S.), Bachelor of Science in Education (B.S.E.), Bachelor of Music (B.M.), and Bachelor of Music in Education (B.M.E.) degrees. Majors include accounting, art history, art studio, athletic training, biology, broadcasting and mass communications, business, chemistry, communication disorders, communication studies, computer information systems, computer science, criminal justice, economics, education, English, English creative writing, exercise science, film studies, finance, French, German, health promotion and education, history, human resource management, international business, international studies, management, marketing, mathematical economics, mathematics, medical technology, neuroscience, philosophy, physical education, physics, political science, pre-engineering, pre–physical therapy, psychology, public relations, religion, sociology, Spanish, sport management, sustainability, and theater. The Conservatory of Music offers majors in arts management, music composition, music education, music history and literature, music in the liberal arts, music management, music performance, music theater, music theory, and music therapy.

Academic Programs

More than fifty majors and several 3-2 cooperative and preprofessional programs are available to traditional B-W undergraduates. Evening and weekend programs include thirteen majors and six certificate programs.

Off-Campus Programs

Baldwin-Wallace College has institutional partnerships with several other universities around the globe, some of which include Edge Hill College (England), University of the Sunshine Coast (Australia), Ewha University (Korea), Bohme Jesus (Brazil), University of Osnabrück (Germany), Kansai Gaidai University (Japan), Hong Kong Baptist University (China), University of Hull (England), Athlone Institute of Technology (Ireland), Galway Mayo Institute of Technology (Ireland), American Business School in Paris, York St John University (England), Washington Center, New York Media Institute at Marist College, Christ College (India), and American University (Washington, D.C.).

In addition to traditional study-abroad programs, with students studying and living on a particular campus for the semester, B-W features a series of focused-study tours that are led by B-W faculty and staff members and examine specific topics or geographic regions. Some programs involve homestays, while others use hostels and hotels. Quite literally, students learn while on the road. Study tours are offered in alternating academic years.

B-W often sponsors faculty-led two- to three-week seminars for credit in May, which are perfect for students who seek an international experience but do not want to be away for extended periods. Destinations have included Vienna, Prague, and Budapest. Spring trips in 2008 included India and Italy, and there was a Seminar in Europe as well as an environmental excursion to Ecuador. Most locations for study-abroad programs offered during the academic year—such as Australia, China, England, Korea, and Spain—are also offered during the summer term. The Semester at Sea program sends students to ten different countries—such as Brazil, Egypt, India, Japan, and Vietnam—aboard a 23,000-ton ship with 600 other college undergraduates.

Academic Facilities

The Ritter Library offers special programs, including instruction on how to use the library and a reference service to help students find specific information quickly. The library's 250 convenient online databases, 45 million OhioLINK books, and 20,000 electronic and print periodicals offer a wealth of information. The Jones Music Library is located on the lower level of Merner-Pfeiffer Hall. Jones is the only lending music library on campus, and its collection of nearly 40,000 items composes a significant portion of Baldwin-Wallace College's music holdings. The Riemenschneider Bach Institute, located on the floor above the Jones Music Library, is the other music library at B-W and functions primarily as a research library. The institute is a world-renowned Bach center—the guardian of priceless Bach-related manuscripts and first editions and the publisher of *BACH: Journal of the Riemenschneider Bach Institute,* an international journal. The institute's facilities include a research library and a vault for manuscripts and rare books. Other resources include twenty campus computer labs; a 4,000-watt campus radio station; a multimedia lab for video digitizing and editing, Web site development, computer animation, and more; an on-campus gallery showcasing the work of student, faculty, and area artists; and the Burrell Memorial Observatory. The neuroscience lab includes a two-room vivarium, a small-animal surgery room, a neurophysical laboratory, and several rooms dedicated to behavioral observation and computer analysis.

Costs

In 2008–09, full-time (12–18 credit hours) liberal arts students pay $31,252 per academic year in tuition, room, board, and fees. Conservatory students pay $33,212 per academic year.

Financial Aid

Baldwin-Wallace's tuition ranks among the lowest and most affordable of private colleges in Ohio. To help students and their families meet the cost of a high-quality education, B-W awards more than $50 million annually to students in the form of scholarships, grants, loans, and work-study opportunities. B-W is committed to working with students and their families to offer financial support in terms of scholarships, grants, loans from government and private sources, and an array of campus employment opportunities. More than 90 percent of Baldwin-Wallace students receive some sort of financial assistance.

Merit scholarships are offered in the amounts of $7500, $10,000, and $13,000 to academically exceptional incoming freshmen. The College also offers competitive awards, ranging from $1000 to $4000. Baldwin-Wallace provides scholarships for transfer students. More information is available from the Office of Financial Aid.

Faculty

Close relationships are at the heart of the B-W experience. Most classes average only 18 students, and the student-faculty ratio is 15:1. Professors share their wisdom and experience on a one-to-one basis, helping students choose classes or assisting students in their search for the perfect internship. Faculty members regularly give out their home phone numbers. From corporate executives and lifelong educators to environmentalists and practicing psychologists, B-W's more than 300 full-time and part-time faculty members bring impressive credentials from their fields. Nearly 80 percent have earned the highest degree in their field. They are dedicated and talented teachers who want to provide an educational experience that goes well beyond the textbook.

Student Government

Student Government consists of three branches—the legislative, the executive, and the judicial. The Student Senate is the official representative body of the students of Baldwin-Wallace College. All meetings are open, and all students are welcome to participate. Senators meet with College administrators and faculty members to express the opinions of the student body in matters affecting student life and to establish and fund official student organizations. The president and vice president of the student body lead the executive branch of Student Government and work closely with the Senate to express student body views to the College faculty and administration. The judicial branch of Student Government consists of the supreme court of the student body, which hears cases pertaining to Student Government and the clubs it funds. Elections for student body government occur each February. All class officers are elected by the student body and help in planning various events on campus, including Homecoming, April Reign, and senior class events.

Admission Requirements

Applicants must submit the completed application (electronic or paper), a high school transcript, a teacher recommendation, the Secondary School Record Request Form, and the $25 application fee (waived if applying online). SAT and ACT results are optional. (In lieu of standardized test results, students must submit a graded writing sample.) Transfer applicants also must submit college or university transcripts. Candidates applying to the Conservatory of Music also must complete the Conservatory Audition Portfolio.

Application and Information

The deadline for undergraduate admission is May 1. The priority admission deadline is March 1. Applicants are notified on a rolling basis within four to six weeks of receipt of a completed application.

Office of Admission
Baldwin-Wallace College
275 Eastland Road
Berea, Ohio 44017-2088
Phone: 440-826-2222
877-BW-APPLY (toll-free)
Fax: 440-826-3830
E-mail: info@bw.edu
Web site: http://www.bw.edu/admission

BENEDICTINE UNIVERSITY

LISLE, ILLINOIS

Benedictine University
Informing today—Transforming tomorrow

The University

Benedictine University was founded in 1887 as St. Procopius College. One hundred twenty-one years later, the University remains committed to providing a high-quality, Catholic, liberal education for men and women. The undergraduate enrollment is nearly 3,000 students. The student body comprises students of diverse ages, religions, races, and national origins. Twenty-five percent of the full-time students reside on campus.

Benedictine University is situated on a rolling, tree-covered 108-acre campus of twenty major buildings with air-conditioned classrooms and modern, well-equipped laboratories. A student athletic center features three full-size basketball courts, three tennis courts, and training facilities. All of the residence halls are comfortable and spacious and have access to the Internet. On-campus apartments offer one-, two-, and four-bedroom residences. Other features include a scenic lake; a student center with dining halls, lounges, a chapel, a bookstore, and meeting rooms; and the Village of Lisle–Benedictine University Sports Complex, featuring a lighted multipurpose football/soccer stadium with a nine-lane track and lighted baseball and softball fields.

Benedictine University is highly competitive in varsity sports, with a total of seventeen sports. Men's varsity sports are baseball, basketball, cross-country, football, golf, soccer, and track and field (indoor and outdoor). Women's varsity sports are basketball, cross-country, golf, soccer, softball, tennis, track and field (indoor and outdoor), and volleyball. Aside from varsity and intramural athletic programs, forty organizations and clubs exist on campus, including student government, a student newspaper, an orchestra, a jazz group, an African-American Student Union, a Muslim Student Association, the Association of Latin American Students, campus ministry, and various other extracurricular and academic organizations.

Partnerships support the University's growth in the twenty-first century. In 2003, Benedictine and Springfield College in Illinois partnered to bring Benedictine programs and services to the Springfield area, Illinois' state capital. Benedictine partnered in 2004 with Shenyang University of Technology and Shenyang Jianzhu University in China to bring Master of Business Administration and Master of Science in management information systems programs overseas, as demands are high for American business programs. Benedictine opened the Moser Center in Naperville in 2006 to meet the needs of adult students and area businesses.

At Benedictine University, the environment is strengthened by success, not size. Renowned faculty members know students by name and care as much about each student's progress as they do about their own research. Those personal relationships have produced superb results. Benedictine graduates are accepted into some of the most prestigious graduate programs in the country. Approximately two thirds of Benedictine graduates who apply to medical school are accepted, in addition to similar ratios for other health-related professional schools (optometry, pharmacy, physical therapy, and podiatry). The liberal arts curriculum has helped place the University among some of the finest small private schools in the nation.

U.S. News & World Report's 2009 rankings listed Benedictine University as a Top School in the Midwest and sixth in Illinois for campus diversity.

The graduate division offers the following graduate degrees in the business, education, and health areas: the Doctor of Philosophy (Ph.D.) in organization development; the Doctor of Education (Ed.D.) in higher education and organizational change; the Master of Business Administration (M.B.A.); the Master of Arts in Education (M.A.Ed.); the Master of Education (M.Ed.); the Master of Science (M.S.) in accountancy, clinical psychology, clinical exercise physiology, management and organizational behavior, management information systems, nutrition and wellness, and science content and process; and the Master of Public Health (M.P.H.).

Adult undergraduate accelerated programs, taught by distinguished faculty members, are available in the following areas: accounting (B.B.A.), business and economics (B.A.), computer information systems (B.S.), computer science (B.S.), finance (B.A.), health administration (B.B.A.), management (B.A.M.), management and organizational behavior (B.B.A.), marketing (B.A.), nursing (B.S.), organizational leadership (B.A.), and psychology (B.A.). The University also offers an Associate of Arts in business administration in an accelerated format.

Location

Benedictine University is 25 miles west of Chicago, in suburban Lisle near Naperville, and is easily accessible from the city and suburbs via the interstate highway system. Metra trains stop in Lisle, and O'Hare International Airport is only a 30-minute drive. In addition to the many social and cultural offerings of the Chicago metropolitan area, the University enjoys the proximity and use of Argonne National Laboratory, Fermi National Accelerator Laboratory, the Morton Arboretum, a ski hill, a riding stable, and several golf courses. The University's location in the high-tech East-West Tollway corridor gives students opportunities for internships and employment.

Majors and Degrees

Benedictine University offers programs leading to the Bachelor of Arts, Bachelor of Business Administration, Bachelor of Science, and Bachelor of Fine Arts. Programs are offered in accounting, bilingual journalism, biochemistry/molecular biology, biology, business and economics (concentration in sports management), chemistry, clinical laboratory science, communication arts (concentration in sports communication), computer information systems, computer science, diagnostic medical sonography, economics, elementary education, engineering science, English language and literature, environmental science, finance, fine arts, global studies, health science, history, international business and economics, international studies (concentration in business and political science), management and organizational behavior, marketing, mathematics (concentration in actuarial science), music (concentration in chamber music), nuclear medicine technology, nutrition (concentration in dietetics), philosophy, physical education, physics (concentration in biological physics, engineering physics and physics), political science (concentration in prelaw), prepharmacy, preprofessional health programs (concentration in chiropractic, dentistry, medicine, occupational therapy, optometry, physical therapy, podiatry, and veterinary medicine), psychology, radiation therapy, secondary education, social science, sociology (concentration in criminal justice), Spanish, special education, studio art, theology, and writing and publishing.

In many areas of study, students may opt for a double major. Preprofessional health programs include chiropractic, dentistry, medicine, occupational therapy, optometry, physical therapy, podiatry, and veterinary medicine. Combined professional programs are available with cooperating institutions in clinical laboratory science, nuclear medicine technology, and engineering. A joint engineering program is offered with the Illinois Institute of Technology. A registered nurse may earn a Bachelor of Science degree in nursing. Teacher certification is available in the following majors: biology, business and economics, chemistry, English language and literature, mathematics, physical education, physics, social science, and Spanish.

Academic Programs

For graduation, a student must earn at least 120 semester hours, 55 of which must be completed at a four-year regionally accredited college. At least the final 45 semester hours must be completed at Benedictine University. The University makes selective exceptions to the normal academic residency requirement of 45 semester hours for adults who are eligible for the Degree Completion Program. Eligibility is limited to those who have nearly completed their undergraduate studies but, for reasons of employment, career change, or family situation, found it necessary to interrupt their studies.

The Second Major Program is designed for people who already have a degree in one area and would like to gain expertise in another. This program allows the student to concentrate on courses that fulfill the requirements of a second major. The student receives a certificate upon completion.

Each year, a select number of talented and motivated prospective students are invited to participate in the Scholars Program. The program is designed to enhance the college experience by developing students' international awareness and strengthening their leadership ability.

Off-Campus Programs

Benedictine University is a member of a three-school consortium in the west suburban Chicago area through which students are able to take classes at the other member colleges. Study abroad and internships abroad are encouraged to complement a liberal education.

Academic Facilities

The Kindlon Hall of Learning and the Birck Hall of Science bring science and technology to new levels. The Birck Hall of Science houses state-of-the art computer labs, specialized science labs, a research center, and the Jurica Nature Museum.

The Kindlon Hall of Learning houses computer labs, classrooms, multimedia labs, offices, and student lounges. It is also home to the Benedictine Library, which houses more than 120,000 volumes and can be found in the building's impressive five-story tower. The library is also equipped with eleven group study rooms, a computer lab, and an instruction room.

Benedictine University has distance education classrooms that provide students with the capability to interact globally with other colleges and universities in a classroom setting. Scholl Hall houses classrooms and faculty and administrative offices.

Costs

The cost of tuition for the 2008–09 academic year is $21,600. The average cost of room and board is $6943. Mandatory fees total $710 and include health, technology, and student activity fees.

Financial Aid

In 2007–08, Benedictine University freshmen received approximately $6.1 million from financial aid sources that included loans, scholarship and grants, tuition remission, and employment opportunities. Ninety-eight percent of the freshman class received financial aid. The average package was $16,853. Benedictine University has dedicated more than $10 million of the annual budget to providing grants and scholarships to its students. Students who wish to apply for aid must complete the Free Application for Federal Student Aid (FAFSA) and the Benedictine University application for admission.

Faculty

The 13:1 student-faculty ratio allows for close interaction between students and faculty members. Of the 93 full-time faculty members, 80 percent hold a Ph.D. or the terminal professional degree in their respective fields. All students are assigned a faculty member as an adviser to help plan programs of study.

Student Government

All full-time enrolled students are automatically members of the student government. The Student Government Association (SGA) is a representative body elected annually by the students to represent their interests. The SGA is responsible for the annual allocation of the student activity fee.

Admission Requirements

The Benedictine University admission philosophy is to select students who are expected to perform successfully in the University's academic programs and become active members of the University community. Typically, Benedictine University's freshman students are in the top third of their high school graduating class, with about 50 percent in the top quarter, and report better-than-average ACT or SAT scores. A minimum of 16 units in academic subjects is required, including 4 units of English, 1 unit of algebra, 1 unit of geometry, 1 unit of history, 1 unit of laboratory science, and 2 units of foreign language. Benedictine University does admit some students who fall below these standards. These applicants receive individual consideration by the Academic Admissions Committee. When appropriate, the committee will place conditions and/or restrictions upon students to help them reach their academic potential.

Students interested in transferring to Benedictine University must have a minimum cumulative average of C (2.0 on a 4.0 scale) or better from all colleges previously attended. Official transcripts from all colleges attended must be submitted directly to the Enrollment Center for evaluation. If fewer than 20 semester hours of transfer credit are submitted, an official high school transcript and SAT or ACT scores are required, and the general admission high school curriculum requirements must also be satisfied. Credits transferred from other institutions are evaluated on the basis of their equivalent at Benedictine University. Grades of D are accepted as transfer credit but do not satisfy Benedictine University requirements, which demand a minimum grade of C.

Requests for admission are considered without regard to the applicant's race, religion, gender, age, or disability.

Application and Information

Applications are reviewed on a rolling basis. Students are encouraged to apply for admission at any time after completing their junior year of high school. Transfer students may apply for admission during their last semester or quarter before anticipated transfer to Benedictine University. Earlier applications are encouraged for scholarship and financial aid opportunities.

For further information, students should contact:

Enrollment Center
Benedictine University
5700 College Road
Lisle, Illinois 60532
Phone: 630-829-6300
888-829-6363 (toll-free outside Illinois)
Fax: 630-829-6301
E-mail: admissions@ben.edu
Web site: http://www.ben.edu

The Birck Hall of Science houses science labs, classrooms, offices, a lecture hall, and the Jurica Nature Museum.

BRADLEY UNIVERSITY

PEORIA, ILLINOIS

The University

Bradley University is a four-year, private, independent university in Peoria, Illinois, offering more than 100 academic programs to 6,000 students. Students enjoy extensive resources not available at most small colleges and personal attention not commonly found at large universities. In addition to the traditional liberal arts and sciences, academic programs include business, communications, education, engineering, fine and performing arts, and health sciences. Unique programs include entrepreneurship, multimedia, and a doctoral program in physical therapy.

Located on a 75-acre campus in the heart of Peoria's historic West Bluff neighborhoods, Bradley offers a traditional, residential environment just 1 mile from downtown and 8 miles from the Greater Peoria Regional Airport.

Founded in 1897 by Lydia Moss Bradley, the University has a long and distinguished tradition of academic excellence, a focus on practical skill development through internships and practicums, and a dynamic student life. For her part in establishing this reputation, along with her many other philanthropic and humanitarian achievements, Mrs. Bradley was inducted into the National Women's Hall of Fame.

Bradley's five academic colleges and graduate school are fully accredited by the North Central Association of Colleges and Universities. Students may pursue more than 100 undergraduate academic programs. In addition, the Graduate School offers master's degrees in more than thirty areas of study. Bradley students are encouraged to take advantage of a wealth of internships, co-ops, practicums, and other "real-world" experiences. Bradley's retention, graduation, and placement rates are among the highest in the nation.

In addition to modern academic facilities, there are ten residence halls, which house first-year students as well as upperclassmen; a residential apartment complex for students with junior standing through graduate school; a student center that includes a food court, a cafeteria, and a movie theater; two student cafeterias; and two performing arts facilities.

The new Markin Family Recreation Center includes four basketball courts for intramural and recreational games, a championship basketball court, a 1/8-mile running/walking track open to the entire campus population, a climbing wall, an indoor pool, a weight room, and exercise rooms.

Bradley's active cocurricular environment includes more than 240 student organizations, Greek life, a comprehensive student government system, and NCAA Division I athletic programs offering baseball, basketball, cross-country, golf, soccer, and tennis for men and basketball, cross-country, golf, softball, tennis, track, and volleyball for women.

Location

Bradley University is located in Peoria, Illinois, a diverse, metropolitan community of approximately 360,000 residents located along the Illinois River. Peoria is home to several multinational corporations, businesses, and research centers, which offer numerous internships and chances for practicums and cooperative education. The greater Peoria area is the largest metropolitan area in downstate Illinois. In addition, Peoria offers an abundance of fine and performing arts, cultural attractions, shopping, entertainment, and professional sports teams. Both Chicago and St. Louis are less than a 3-hour drive.

Majors and Degrees

The College of Education and Health Sciences awards bachelor's degrees in dietetics, early childhood education, elementary education, family and consumer sciences education, foods and nutrition, general family and consumer sciences, health science (leads to Bradley's doctoral degree in physical therapy), learning behavior specialist studies, learning behavior specialist studies with elementary education, nursing, retail merchandising, secondary education, and special education.

The College of Engineering and Technology awards the Bachelor of Science degree in civil engineering, civil engineering with environmental option, construction, electrical engineering, electrical engineering with computer option, engineering physics, industrial engineering, manufacturing engineering, manufacturing engineering technology (design and systems options are available), mechanical engineering, and mechanical engineering with biomedical option.

The Foster College of Business Administration awards bachelor's degrees in accounting (includes a 3-2 B.S./M.S. option), actuarial science–business, economics, entrepreneurship, finance (includes a 3-2 B.S./M.S. option), international business, management and administration (concentrations in human resource management and legal studies in business), management information systems, and marketing (a concentration in professional selling is available).

Bradley University's College of Liberal Arts and Sciences offers programs in actuarial science–mathematics, administration of criminal justice, biochemistry, biology, cell and molecular biology, chemistry, computer information systems, computer science, economics, English, environmental science, French, German, history, international studies, mathematics, medical technology, philosophy, physics, political science, prelaw, premedicine, psychology, religious studies, social work, sociology, and Spanish.

The Slane College of Communications and Fine Arts awards bachelor's degrees in art (concentrations in ceramics, drawing, graphic design, painting, photography, printmaking, and sculpture), art education, art history, communication (concentrations in advertising, electronic media (radio/TV), journalism, organizational communication, and public relations), multimedia, music, music business, music composition, music education, music performance, theater performance, and theater production.

Students may select minor areas of study from throughout the five colleges in African American studies, applied ergonomics, art history, Asian studies, biology, business administration, business studies, chemistry, computer science and information systems, decision analysis, economics, English (creative writing, literature, and professional writing), family and consumer sciences, fine arts, French, German, health, history, journalism, Latin American studies, leadership studies, management, management information systems, manufacturing, marketing, mathematics, multimedia, music, philosophy, physics, political science, professional selling, psychology, quality engineering, religious studies, Russian and East European studies, social informatics, sociology, Spanish, studio art, theater arts, Western European studies, and women's studies.

Academic Programs

Although Bradley is in session year-round, the traditional academic year consists of two semesters. All students complete a set of basic general education requirements that blend course work from throughout the University in order to provide each student with a well-rounded education. General education courses include English composition, speech, mathematics, Western and non-Western civilization, literature, art, philosophy, the social sciences, and physical sciences. Considerable freedom is permitted in the selection of this course work. All undergraduate programs are designed so that students can complete their degree in just four years.

Bradley also offers a dynamic honors program for selected recipients of Bradley's prestigious Presidential Scholarship.

The Academic Exploration Program (AEP) allows students who are undecided about a major to receive academic advisement to assist them in declaring a major during their first year of enrollment. There are also special programs for new students who are undecided about which area of study to choose in engineering, business, or communications.

Off-Campus Programs

Nearly 15 percent of Bradley students take advantage of a study-abroad experience. Bradley has established formal relationships with universities around the world, and students regularly study in Austria, Denmark, Egypt, Germany, Ireland, Mexico, and Spain as well as a variety of other countries. Most academic programs encourage international travel and assist students in scheduling international study.

Bradley students also enjoy collaborative learning opportunities in the city of Peoria, including laboratory research at Caterpillar, Inc.; the Downstate Medical Center of Illinois; and the USDA National Center for Agricultural Utilization Research. In addition, the Bradley men's basketball and baseball teams play in professional facilities located in downtown Peoria.

Academic Facilities

The Cullom-Davis Library supports all of the University's programs and offers extensive opportunities for print and computerized research, including online and wireless resources and a Learning Assistance Center. The Michel Student Center hosts conferences, camps, and a variety of entertainers throughout the year. Inside the Caterpillar Global Communications Center, students have access to multimedia classrooms and labs, television and radio studios, video and audio editing suites, and a world-class telecommunication facility. Olin Hall of Science is home to some of the finest undergraduate laboratory facilities in the nation, while Jobst Hall includes robotic and automotive labs and a wind tunnel for engineering students. Several advanced labs throughout the campus provide access to Internet2. Bradley is one of only three private, nondoctoral universities in the nation to be a member of the Internet2 research community. Historic facilities include Westlake Hall, Constance Hall, the Hartmann Center for the Performing Arts, Dingeldine Recital Hall, and the newly renovated Bradley Hall.

Costs

Tuition for the 2008–09 academic year was $22,600. Room and board for the year were $7350. Students also paid a $214 health and activity fee. Books and supplies vary by major and year in school, but they averaged approximately $900.

Financial Aid

The Office of Financial Assistance provides many resources to assist families in managing the cost of a Bradley education. Academic scholarships, which are competitive and renewable, are divided into three categories: the Presidential Scholarship, the Deans Scholarship, and the University Scholarship. Each of these awards is based on a comprehensive review of the student's high school academic record, standardized test scores, cocurricular involvement, letters of recommendation, and personal statement. Bradley also offers scholarships to encourage diversity, talent in the fine and performing arts, and athletic achievement. The University also participates in federally sponsored aid programs, such as the Pell Grant, Work-Study, and Stafford Student Loan. In order to be considered for these sources of financial assistance, students must submit the Free Application for Federal Student Aid (FAFSA).

Faculty

Bradley University is home to more than 375 teaching faculty members. The student-faculty ratio is 14:1, and the average class size is 23 students. Academic, career, and personal counseling is readily available to all students. Bradley University is nationally recognized for the excellence of its faculty members, who not only teach undergraduates but also are active researchers and consultants in the academic disciplines.

Student Government

Bradley's Student Senate is the principal body of student participation in University governance and is a visible contributor to the quality of student life on campus. Members of the senate are elected from the general student body and can serve as early as their first year. The Student Senate is an active influence on University policy, and members of the Senate have frequent interaction with University administrators and faculty members.

Admission Requirements

Bradley University encourages applications from qualified students of all backgrounds who feel that they can contribute to the University's diverse intellectual and social environment. Students who have demonstrated past academic achievement and show promise and aptitude for successful performance at Bradley are encouraged to apply for admission. First-time college students are considered for admission based on a review of their high school transcript, standardized test scores (ACT or SAT), cocurricular involvement, letters of recommendation, and personal statement or essay.

Transfer students in good academic standing are encouraged to apply for admission to Bradley. Transfer students must submit a completed application and official transcripts from all colleges or universities attended. Several majors include additional requirements unique to transfer students.

Application and Information

To be considered for admission, students must submit the Application for Undergraduate Admission during one of three application periods. Bradley strongly encourages students to apply as early as possible during fall of their senior year. The application-review process begins each September. Applications received prior to February 1 are given priority consideration.

An application and additional information may be submitted online or by contacting:

Office of Admissions
Bradley University
1501 West Bradley Avenue
Peoria, Illinois 61625
Phone: 309-677-1000
800-447-6460 (toll-free)
Web site: http://admissions.bradley.edu

COLUMBIA COLLEGE CHICAGO

CHICAGO, ILLINOIS

The College

Columbia College Chicago is the nation's largest and most diverse visual, performing, media, and communication arts college. The foundation of a Columbia education features small class sizes that ensure close interaction with a faculty of working professionals, abundant internship opportunities with major employers in the Chicago and national marketplaces, and outstanding professional facilities that foster learning by doing. All students are encouraged to begin course work in their chosen fields during their freshman year, allowing them to fully master their craft and build professional portfolios, audition tapes, resumes, and clip books. The College provides a strong liberal arts and sciences background for the developing artist or communicator and supports student employment goals through a full range of career services.

Columbia's enrollment of approximately 12,500 students is drawn from across the United States and more than forty-six other countries. The student body is almost equally divided between men and women. Creative students who enjoy a supportive but challenging environment thrive at Columbia.

Columbia College Chicago's five residence halls extend the supportive philosophy of the College and immerse students in a creative environment both in and out of the classroom. There are a variety of apartment and suite style housing options with a range of amenities that may include: computer and study rooms, drawing and painting studios, music practice space, fitness rooms, an indoor heated pool, lake views, and a laundry room. Apartments, suites, and rooms are fully furnished. All facilities are conveniently located steps from the main campus buildings and are close to public transportation. Students have access to student health and counseling centers.

Outside the classroom, students participate in activities that include Columbia's award-winning student newspaper, radio station, student magazines, cable television soap opera, theaters, dance center, photography and art museums, and a film and video festival. Many of the more than 85 student clubs on campus offer avenues to expand social and professional networking opportunities. Columbia's numerous student gallery and performance spaces allow students to extend their classroom experiences by hosting a variety of activities, including art exhibits, film screenings, lectures, readings, and live performances of music, comedy, and dance.

Location

Columbia's campus is located in Chicago's Educational Corridor in the dynamic South Loop neighborhood, near several other colleges and universities. Also close by are the Art Institute, Navy Pier, the Adler Planetarium, the Field Museum, the Chicago Symphony, and the Goodman Theatre. Convenient public transportation allows Columbia's faculty members and students to utilize the city of Chicago as a social, cultural, educational, and professional resource.

Majors and Degrees

Columbia College grants the Bachelor of Arts (B.A.) and the Bachelor of Fine Arts (B.F.A.) degrees and the Bachelor of Music (B.M.) degree in composition.

The School of Fine and Performing Arts offers majors in art and design (advertising art direction, art history, fashion design, fine arts, graphic design, illustration, interior architecture, and product design); arts, entertainment, and media management (arts entrepreneurship/ small business management, fashion/retail merchandising, media management, music business management, performing arts management, sports management, and visual arts management); dance (dance, dancemaking, dance studies, choreography, teaching); fiction writing (fiction writing, playwriting); music (composition; contemporary, urban, and popular music; instrumental performance; vocal jazz; and vocal performance); photography; and theater (acting, directing, musical theater performance, theater, technical theater, and theater design).

The School of Media Arts offers majors in audio arts and acoustics (acoustics, audio arts and acoustics, audio for visual media, audio design and production, sound contracting, and sound reinforcement); film and video (alternative forms, animation: computer, animation: traditional, audio for visual media, cinematography, critical studies, directing, documentary, editing, film/video, post-production, producing, screenwriting); interactive arts and media (game design, interactive arts and media); journalism (broadcast journalism, magazine writing/editing, news reporting and writing, and reporting on health, science, and the environment); marketing communication (advertising, marketing, and public relations); radio; television (Internet and mobile media, post-production/effects, production/directing, writing/producing).

The School of Liberal Arts and Sciences offers majors in American Sign Language–English interpretation (ASL-English); humanities, history, and social sciences (cultural studies); education (early childhood education, teacher certification); English (creative writing–poetry, creative writing–nonfiction).

At the graduate level, Columbia College Chicago awards the Master of Arts (M.A.) in dance/movement therapy and counseling (as well as the Graduate Laban Certificate in Movement Analysis, GLCMA), interdisciplinary arts, and journalism; the Master of Fine Arts (M.F.A.) in creative writing–fiction (with the opportunity to earn a combined M.A. in teaching of writing), creative writing–poetry, film and video, interdisciplinary arts and media, interdisciplinary book and paper arts, music composition for the screen, and photography; the Master of Arts in Teaching (M.A.T.) in art education and elementary education; the Master of Arts Management (M.A.M) in arts entrepreneurship and small business management, arts in youth and community development (AYCD), media management, music business management, performing arts management, and visual arts management.

Academic Programs

Columbia supports creative and integrated approaches to education and encourages interdisciplinary study. The B.A. degree is awarded to students who successfully complete 120 semester hours, and the B.F.A. degree is awarded to students who successfully complete 128 semester hours of study in designated programs. Of the required 120 hours toward the completion of the B.A., 48 (36 for B.F.A. candidates) are distributed among courses in the humanities and literature, science and mathematics, English composition, oral communications, social sciences, and computer applications.

Columbia has an extensive internship program that offers its students access to some of the most renowned corporations and institutions in the world. The College believes that exposing students to real-world working environments is an invaluable element of their education and provides them with the necessary professional balance they will need upon graduation.

Columbia College Chicago's Portfolio Center is uniquely geared to assist students with professional-grade portfolio development. The Portfolio Center links industry professionals and alumni with current students through workshops, portfolio development sessions, and networking events. The Center also maintains an online portfolio archive that serves as an invaluable resource and inspiration for students. Students are expected to graduate with a working portfolio suitable for professional presentation.

Open to all students, Columbia's Learning Studio is an academic support center designed to help students navigate Columbia's rigorous and creative curriculum by providing a comfortable space where students can find support for their individual learning needs and styles. Services include tutoring in math, science, and writing; peer study groups; and services for students with disabilities.

Off-Campus Programs

Columbia College offers several study-abroad opportunities through both student exchange and individual departmental programs. Among the countries in which students may have the opportunity to study are: Austria, the Czech Republic, England, France, Ireland, Italy, and Mexico.

Columbia also offers domestic off-campus training programs. Comedy studies is a full semester's worth of immersive study in comedic literature, history, writing, and performance under the experts in comedy at Chicago's Second City. Also, the semester in Los Angeles is a five-week immersion program open to all students in which they maintain full-time status while gaining invaluable real-world experience at Raleigh Studios in Hollywood, CA.

Academic Facilities

Columbia College consists of twenty-three campus buildings in the historic South Loop neighborhood of downtown Chicago that house advanced facilities for radio, television, art, computer graphics, photography, interactive arts and media, fashion design, and film. These facilities are state-of-the-industry and include professionally equipped color and black-and-white darkrooms, digital imaging resources, photography and film stages, film and video editing suites, and studios for painting, drawing, and 3-D design. The campus also includes the Museum of Contemporary Photography (one of only two such facilities in the United States), and the Audio Technology Center, a recording production and research facility. The dance, music, and theater departments have separate centers and each is designed for their program's individual rehearsal and performance needs. Additionally, Columbia has extensive computer facilities for use by students, as well as dedicated computer resources geared for specific departmental needs.

The College's library contains 258,000 volumes and provides open study spaces and group study rooms for collaborative research and study. The library houses the College Archives, Special Collections, and comprehensive collections in the visual, performing, media and communication arts. In addition, the library also subscribes to more than 1,000 journals and magazines and over 100 electronic databases. As a member of a statewide online computer catalog and resource-sharing network, the library provides students with access to the resources of seventy-six academic institutions and millions of books.

Costs

For the 2008–09 academic year, full tuition (12 to 16 credit hours) was $8975 for each fifteen-week semester, or $17,950 per year. Part-time tuition (up to 11 credit hours) is $621 per credit hour. Summer school tuition is $484 per credit hour. Some courses require additional service or laboratory fees.

To enroll at Columbia College Chicago, applicants are required to confirm their decision by submitting a $250 tuition deposit (nonrefundable after May 1, 2009). Required nonrefundable fees that are charged each semester include the registration fee, $50; the student activity fee, $75 ($40 for part-time students); the U-Pass, $95 (for unlimited access to the public transportation system); and a health center fee, $35 ($20 for part-time students). There is also a one-time $30 library deposit that is refunded when the student leaves the College.

Financial Aid

Columbia College makes every effort to help students obtain financial assistance, including grants, on-campus work, and loans. The Office of Student Financial Services administers federal and state grant and loan programs. The College also provides information for students seeking part-time employment both on and off campus. On-campus jobs are available in technical, clerical, secretarial, and food service areas.

Columbia College Chicago offers a variety of scholarships for current and prospective students. Scholarships offered are based on one or more of the following criteria: financial need, academic merit, field (area) of study and accomplishments. Information about scholarship opportunities, application forms, and general information about financial aid is available through the Office of Undergraduate Admissions.

Faculty

Many of the college's 1,540 full- and part-time faculty members are working professionals (artists, writers, filmmakers, marketers, journalists, etc.) with national reputations. They are gifted instructors and are able to share practical expertise with students in informal workshop settings and in the classroom. Interaction with faculty members who are practicing professionals provides students with invaluable access to the latest information in their fields. Students also begin developing their own professional network as faculty members share contacts and information on how to break into the market.

Student Government

Through the Student Government Association (SGA) and the Student Organization Council (SOC), students are able to address College-wide and departmental issues and sponsor services and activities. SGA and SOC work closely with the Office of Student Affairs and serve as liaisons to the administration and academic departments. The more than eighty-five campus clubs and organizations reflect the interests and the diversity of Columbia's student body.

Film screenings, student-produced television shows, dance recitals, poetry readings, plays, campus radio, music concerts, and a national award–winning newspaper are just some of the campus events and activities that are available to students.

Admission Requirements

Columbia College invites applications from all students interested in studying the arts, media, and communication disciplines. Columbia does not require portfolios or previous experience in any discipline to be considered for admission. To apply for admission, all students must submit high school transcripts, a letter of recommendation, a personal essay, and a $35 application fee. ACT or SAT scores are not required but are strongly encouraged. Graduation from high school or an earned GED certificate is a requirement for admission consideration. Transfer students must submit transcripts from all other colleges and universities attended. Freshman applicants whose application materials suggest they are likely to be underprepared to meet the College's standards are required to successfully complete the Bridge Program to be admitted to the College. Columbia has a liberal transfer policy.

Application and Information

Students are strongly advised to apply early. The priority date is May 1 for the fall semester, November 15 for the spring semester, and April 15 for the summer term. Applicants are notified of their admission decision within three to four weeks after the College receives all the required information and documents. Students who want to live in on-campus housing are strongly advised to apply early. Housing assignments are offered on a first-come, first-served basis until full occupancy is achieved.

All students are strongly encouraged to tour the College. To arrange for a tour, students should call the Office of Undergraduate Admissions or sign up online.

For more information, students should contact:

Office of Undergraduate Admissions
Columbia College Chicago
600 South Michigan Avenue
Chicago, Illinois 60605
Phone: 312-344-7130
Fax: 312-344-8024
E-mail: admissions@colum.edu
Web site: http://www.colum.edu

CULVER-STOCKTON COLLEGE

CANTON, MISSOURI

The College

Students at Culver-Stockton College (C-SC) receive a superb education that extends far beyond the classroom. The four-year experience at C-SC expands not only the student's academic knowledge but also an awareness of the world in which they live. Besides achieving their academic goals, students receive an opportunity to develop their leadership skills, gain experience in their field, discover new interests, and form lasting relationships with classmates and faculty and staff members. These opportunities are the primary features of the College's redesigned EXP@CSC curriculum.

C-SC was founded in 1853 as the first coeducational institution of higher learning west of the Mississippi River. Affiliated with the Christian Church (Disciples of Christ), the College is personal (about 850 students) and provides a strong liberal arts foundation with practical learning experiences.

Primarily residential in character, the College offers a full array of extracurricular activities, including course-related clubs and organizations, an active national fraternity and sorority system, an intramural program, and a strong intercollegiate athletics program featuring men's teams in baseball, basketball, cross-country, football, golf, soccer, and track and field and women's teams in basketball, cross-country, golf, soccer, softball, track and field, and volleyball. The College also features a coed spirit squad team and an award-winning dance team. Performance opportunities in the fine arts include outstanding choral and instrumental ensembles as well as several theater productions each year, which are open to nonmajors as well.

Culver-Stockton College has more than 10,000 living alumni, many of whom have achieved distinction in the arts, government, medicine, law, education, and other professional fields. With more than 150 years of history, Culver-Stockton College moves into the twenty-first century as one of the truly distinctive small comprehensive baccalaureate colleges in the Midwest. Culver-Stockton College is fully accredited by the Higher Learning Commission of the North Central Association of Colleges and Schools, the Missouri Department of Elementary and Secondary Education, the International Assembly for Collegiate Business Education, the National Association of Schools of Music, the Commission on Accreditation of Allied Health Education Programs, the National League for Nursing Accrediting Commission, and the Commission on Collegiate Nursing Education.

Location

Canton, Missouri, a town of 2,700 on the Mississippi River, sits in the rolling farmland of northeast Missouri. The College has close ties with Quincy, Illinois, a progressive, arts-oriented community of approximately 45,000. Canton is located on U.S. 61, the "Avenue of the Saints," 30 miles north of historic Hannibal, Missouri, the boyhood home of the famous American author Mark Twain. St. Louis is within a 2½-hour drive, and Chicago and Kansas City are close enough to be significant factors in the cultural life of the College. Culver-Stockton sits atop a hill that overlooks Canton and the Mississippi River. Canton exhibits a strong sense of community pride, civic involvement, and a very low crime rate. Canton and Culver-Stockton work closely together on common issues such as emergency preparedness and economic development.

Majors and Degrees

Culver-Stockton offers an array of bachelor's degrees: the Bachelor of Arts, the Bachelor of Science, the Bachelor of Fine Arts (in art, arts management, music, musical theater, and theater), the Bachelor of Music Education, and the Bachelor of Science in Nursing. Study areas include accountancy, art, art education, arts management, athletic training, biology, biological chemistry, business, communication, criminal justice, education, English, finance, history, mathematics, music, musical theater, nursing, physical education, political science, psychology, religion and philosophy, speech and theater education, sports management, and theater. As part of the EXP@CSC curriculum, the College has a program for students who are undecided and works closely with them to explore career options and select one of C-SC's majors or help them design a major of their own. Interdisciplinary degrees and preprofessional programs also are offered.

Academic Programs

The Culver-Stockton EXP@CSC curriculum emphasizes a comprehensive education, greater knowledge of the global community, and hands-on experience in a student's field. A First-Year Experience Course, required of every student, focuses on strengthening skills in writing, speaking, critical thinking, and problem solving. Building from that base, the Common Experience portion of EXP@CSC requires each student to complete 41 credit hours selected from three categories of courses: Foundations Courses (14 hours that emphasize writing, literature, speech, cultural events, and human values), Explorations Courses (18–24 hours that emphasize diverse populations, mathematics, natural sciences, creativity and the arts, and the individual and society), and the Connections Course (a 3-hour multidisciplinary writing-intensive seminar). Some students may be required to take 6 credits of a foreign language. Requirements for completing a major vary from 32 to 62 additional hours, but every major includes a requirement for hands-on experience in the student's chosen field through an internship, practicum, clinical experience, or other work-based opportunity. Since the Common Experience applies to all majors, the College strongly encourages double majors and minors. The College requires 120 credit hours for degree completion.

As part of EXP@CSC, the College offers a unique academic calendar. Each of the fifteen-week semesters is divided into a twelve-week long term and a three-week short term. During the twelve-week term, students follow the more traditional path of taking multiple courses. During the three-week term, each student takes only one course, pursuing in-depth study of a single topic. The course may include study abroad, domestic travel, work experience, or study on campus. The first semester concludes before Christmas, and the spring semester ends by mid-May. Summer sessions are available.

Culver-Stockton emphasizes small classrooms, with an average class size of 17 students and a 13:1 student-teacher ratio, in order to maximize the exchange of ideas and present every student with opportunities to express their views and hear a diversity of other viewpoints.

The College has committed itself to academic distinction. Students are challenged to achieve their maximum potential in learned skills, breadth and depth of knowledge, and understanding their own values. Students are assigned an academic adviser, who is prepared to assist students in achieving their educational goals. An individualized plan is developed and then updated each semester until graduation.

For highly motivated students, including freshmen, the Honors Scholars Program provides the opportunity to participate in certain specially designated courses and events, culminating in an opportunity for independent study or research in an area of the student's special interest. The program is especially helpful for students planning for graduate programs.

Work completed at other colleges and universities is usually transferable toward Culver-Stockton graduation requirements, and various testing procedures (e.g., CLEP, AP, PEP) allow credit for equivalent knowledge or experience. Individualized learning options are plentiful; they range from individually negotiated independent study to developing an individualized major.

In January 2006, the College began offering online courses for nontraditional students through the Connected Campus program. As of fall 2008, the degree-completion programs include a Bachelor of Science in criminal justice and a Bachelor of Science in business, with three specializations available (management information systems, accountancy and finance, or organizational management).

Off-Campus Programs

Students at Culver-Stockton College may pursue a variety of study-abroad opportunities. As part of EXP@CSC, students and faculty members travel together for study-abroad courses. Recent trips have included such destinations as Austria, Greece, Great Britain, Italy, and China. Coming up in 2008–2010 are courses in Turkey, the British

Isles, Egypt, and the Netherlands. C-SC also offers a more traditional Semester Study and International Program in London in association with the Missouri Consortium for International Programs and Studies and International Enrichment Inc. The College's wind ensemble and concert choir tour domestically each year.

Academic Facilities

C-SC is a wireless campus. Not only are all buildings and some green spaces accessible by wireless devices, there are also several computer labs and a cyber café. Culver-Stockton maintains four general computer labs as well as four specialized labs. Faculty members have integrated computers into the classroom in almost every field, using dedicated computer labs equipped with major-specific software. An increasing number of SMART classrooms are being added.

The computerized Johann Memorial Library has a collection of 151,979 volumes and also presents comprehensive collections of periodicals, journals, and other materials in both hard copy and microform. Extensive interlibrary loan and electronic bibliographical search capabilities are available to both students and the faculty. C-SC belongs to the MOBIUS Consortium, which provides open access to the holdings of every academic library in Missouri. Students also have access to more than 6 million volumes through the College's link to a statewide library database.

The Robert W. Brown Performing Arts Center and Mabee Art Gallery house professional-quality art and performance studios, computer laboratories, and three performance stages where 200 to nearly 1,000 guests can attend theater and music performances.

The five-year-old Science Center is home to the departments of biology, chemistry, clinical laboratory sciences, and mathematics. Students can benefit from its state-of-the-art labs and technology, classrooms with full multimedia capabilities, and facilities designed specifically for student research.

Costs

The 2008–09 school-year costs at Culver-Stockton College are $21,500 for tuition, $7200 for room and board, approximately $1000 for books and supplies, and a $250 unified student fee. With the exception of students who are married or living with parents, all students receiving financial aid from the College are required to participate in the College's room-and-board plan. Variable board plans are available for the dining hall and Cat's Pause, the campus snack bar and cyber café.

Financial Aid

Culver-Stockton College understands the financial needs of students and their families and works to make a C-SC education affordable. Through scholarships, grants, work-study opportunities, and loans, the College works to offset the cost of a college education for qualified students, providing a great value for a superb educational experience.

The College participates in all federal and state financial aid programs, presenting aid packages that are based on need and merit. Merit awards are based on academic achievement as well as performance—theater, music, art, leadership, and athletics. The College requires the Free Application for Federal Student Aid (FAFSA). Some full-tuition scholarships are available each year based on GPA and ACT criteria. The College awards Vision for Success scholarships to students of the highest academic excellence and invites some highly qualified students to compete for the Pillars of Excellence scholarships.

Faculty

The strength of the College's academic program is the outstanding faculty. Faculty members provide instruction of high quality and individualized attention to students. Faculty members are active in scholarship, professional activity, and service. Faculty members also take an active role in many aspects of College life, including the advising and sponsorship of student organizations. The majority of faculty members have earned the highest degree possible in their area, and many have practical experience in their field.

Student Government

An active Student Government Association deals with significant issues of student interest and communicates information about them to the faculty and administration. Students have voting representation on key faculty committees, such as the Academic Council, the Student Development Council, the Academic and Cultural Events Committee, and others that have a direct impact upon the nature and quality of student life. The Student Government Association president also serves as the student representative on the College's board of trustees. An active Campus Programming Council regularly plans student events.

Admission Requirements

Prospective students are expected to have completed a college-preparatory course of study of 15 units at an accredited secondary school. A proper foundation to facilitate success in college studies includes 4 units of English, 3 units of history, at least 2 units of mathematics (algebra and geometry), and 2 to 4 units of science. Students who intend to major in scientific disciplines may wish to select additional high school courses in science and mathematics, and those interested in the humanities and social studies areas typically present additional course work in literature, foreign language, and social studies. Applicants must submit ACT or SAT scores. To be accepted, first-year students must have an overall high school GPA of at least 2.5 and a minimum ACT score of 20. Each applicant for admission is given personal attention and is considered on the basis of academic performance, test scores, and personal attributes. An electronic application is available on the College's Web site at http://www.culver.edu. As of July 1, 2008, Culver-Stockton is a member of the Common Application group (http://www.commonapp.org). Applicants must submit an essay and a faculty reference. Most accepted students are asked to take a math placement test before registering for C-SC classes.

Application and Information

Early application is recommended, as residence halls and classroom space may be limited. For further information, students should contact:

Admissions Office
Culver-Stockton College
One College Hill
Canton, Missouri 63435
Phone: 800-537-1883 (toll-free)
E-mail: admissions@culver.edu
Web site: http://www.culver.edu

Students on the Culver-Stockton College campus.

GRACELAND UNIVERSITY

LAMONI, IOWA

The University

Graceland University (GU) offers a strong academic program firmly rooted in the liberal arts tradition with an emphasis on career preparation. Since its founding in 1895 as a private, coeducational university, Graceland has maintained a tradition of academic excellence based on a commitment to the Christian view of the wholeness, worth, and dignity of every person. The University, sponsored by Community of Christ, is nonsectarian and offers a varied religious life program for those who wish to participate. Of Graceland's fall 2007 freshman class on the Lamoni campus, 17 percent came from Iowa. The remaining 83 percent represent twenty-six states and seventeen countries.

Graceland believes that an important part of a student's learning experience is achieved through association with other students in residence hall living. This belief is supported by an on-campus housing system that provides students with the camaraderie of a fraternity or sorority without the competition. Within the residence halls, there are men's and women's "houses." Members of each house elect a house council to plan social, intramural athletic, religious, and academic support activities. Residence halls are equipped with voice mail, e-mail, Internet connections, and cable TV.

Graceland University is a member of the North Central Association of Colleges and Schools (NCA) and is accredited by the Higher Learning Commission (30 North LaSalle Street, Suite 2400, Chicago, Illinois 60602-2504; 800-621-7440 (toll-free); http://www.ncahigherlearningcommission.org). All teacher-education programs at GU are approved by the Iowa Department of Education. The Bachelor of Arts (B.A.) in education and Master of Education (M.Ed.) programs in collaborative teaching and learning, quality education, and special education are accredited by the National Council for Accreditation of Teacher Education (NCATE; 2010 Massachusetts Avenue NW, Suite 500, Washington, D.C. 20036; 202-466-7496; http://www.ncate.org). All GU nursing programs are accredited by the Iowa and Missouri Departments of Education and the Commission on Collegiate Nursing Education (CCNE; One Dupont Circle NW, Suite 530, Washington, D.C. 20036; http://www.aacn.nche.edu). The athletic training program is accredited by the Commission on Accreditation of Athletic Training Education Programs (CAATE; 2201 Double Creek Drive, Suite 5006, Round Rock, Texas 78664; 512-733-9700; http://www.caate.net). These academic standards ensure that a degree from Graceland University is recognized by educational, business, and professional communities.

Graduate programs include the Master of Arts in Christian Ministries, Master of Arts in Religion, Master of Education, and Master of Science in Nursing. Certificates are offered in American humanics nonprofit management, post-master's family nurse practitioner, post-master's nurse educator, and post-master's health-care administration.

In addition to its traditional programs Graceland offers many options for distance learners. Programs offered online by the School of Nursing include the Bachelor in Healthcare Management, RN-B.S.N., RN-M.S.N., and M.S.N. programs. The M.S.N. program has three tracks: family nurse practitioner, nurse educator, and health-care administrator. The Graceland University School of Education offers a Master of Education with an emphasis in collaborative learning and teaching and special education. The Community of Christ Seminary also offers master's programs in religion and Christian ministries at a distance. The Master of Education program is offered in Cedar Rapids, Des Moines, and Lamoni, Iowa; Independence, Missouri; and online.

The Community of Christ Seminary offers a Master of Arts in Religion and a Master of Arts in Christian Ministries in blended delivery systems. The Community of Christ Seminary also offers master's programs in religion and Christian ministries at a distance.

Location

Lamoni, in south-central Iowa, is on Interstate 35. It is 3 miles north of the Missouri border, 1 hour from Des Moines, 2 hours from Kansas City, and 3 hours from Omaha. Lamoni is the home of Liberty Hall Historic Center, a 6-mile bike trail, an annual Civil War Days Re-Enactment and Living History Event, numerous hometown eateries, and several unique gift and antique shops. A county lake, Slip Bluff County Park, and Nine Eagles State Park are within 10 miles.

Majors and Degrees

Graceland awards the degrees of Bachelor of Arts, Bachelor of Science, and Bachelor of Science in Nursing. These degrees represent study in liberal arts with a concentration of courses in a major.

The majors and concentrations offered in the Bachelor of Arts programs are accounting, art (studio or visual communication), athletic training, business administration (emphases in entrepreneurship and free enterprise, finance, management, marketing, and pre-M.B.A.), chemistry, communications, economics, elementary education, English (concentrations in cinema studies, literature, and writing), fitness leadership, health, health-care administration, history, information technology, international business, international studies, liberal studies, mathematics, modern foreign language, music, music education, philosophy and religion, physical education and health, psychology, publications writing and design, recreation, religion, social science, sociology (concentrations in criminology, general sociology, and human services), Spanish, theater, visual communications (see: art), and wellness program management.

Bachelor of Science programs and majors are basic science, biology (concentrations in animal biology, ecology/environmental biology, molecular/cellular biology, preprofessional, and secondary school teaching), chemistry, clinical laboratory science/medical technology, and computer science.

The first two years of the Bachelor of Science in Nursing program are offered on the Lamoni campus, while the junior and senior years are on the Independence, Missouri, campus.

Graceland also offers degree programs at extended campus locations. Through a partnership with North Central Missouri College, Graceland offers undergraduate degrees in liberal studies and elementary education. Through a partnership with Indian Hills Community College, Graceland offers an undergraduate degree in elementary education. The undergraduate elementary education program is offered at the Graceland Independence campus location.

Academic Programs

Graceland is committed to helping develop the lives of its students—intellectually, socially, physically, and ethically—through a curriculum that is strongly rooted in the liberal arts. General education requirements are based on ten core competencies and can be satisfied by course selections, internships, portfolios, proficiency exams, work experience, independent studies, performance, and achievement. Graceland programs foster conceptual thinking, encourage team building, develop communication skills, and accommodate growth and enrichment.

Two programs at Graceland give attention to the special needs of students. The Honors Program is designed for highly motivated students wanting to expand their learning beyond the regular academic curriculum by developing and completing an honors thesis or project. Chance is a program for bright students who have the aptitude for university education but have experienced learning difficulties. The Lindamood and Bell clinical models are used for remediation in reading, spelling, and language comprehension.

The University operates on a 4-1-4 academic calendar. The regular semesters are separated by a one-month winter term in January. Full tuition for either the fall or the spring semester includes the winter term. This program is geared toward innovative and exceptional approaches and action-oriented learning experiences. On-campus programs vary from dance basics to science fiction to philosophy, and off-campus experiences range from scuba diving in Grand Cayman to touring Italy. Winter term is also the ideal time to explore career interests through an internship.

Off-Campus Programs

Many students see the world during the winter term by visiting such places as Australia, China, England, France, Grand Cayman Island in the British West Indies, Hungary, Italy, India, Israel, Japan, and Mexico. Students who major in a foreign language may study abroad during their junior or senior year under the auspices of a recognized study program. Graceland sponsors an International Health Center that provides opportunities for students to interact with health workers in villages in Africa and Asia.

Academic Facilities

The Helene Center for the Visual Arts includes 29,000 square feet for classrooms, studios, and exhibits. The large north-facing windows, an important feature, provide optimum light for artists.

The Shaw Center for the Performing Arts includes an 800-seat auditorium, a 150-seat studio theater, a 40-foot proscenium stage with orchestra pit, a Casavant pipe organ, a full fly gallery, a spacious scene shop, an art gallery, classrooms, rehearsal rooms, and faculty offices.

Computer facilities include three primary microcomputer laboratories with Macintosh and IBM-compatible computers. Students have access to equipment of commercial quality for desktop publishing and graphics design and to a music laboratory that provides computer-assisted tutoring, synthesis, and composition as well as professional-quality manuscript printing. The centerpiece of this laboratory is the Kurzweil synthesizer. Graceland's Enter.Net.C@fe provides 24-hour Internet access for student research and recreation.

The Frederick Madison Smith Library uses the latest technologies to provide the information services that students need. Ten fully networked computer workstations offer access to the Internet and many research databases, including 7 reference databases and more than 45 periodical databases, many providing access to full-text articles. Access to LIBBIE, the library's online catalog, and to the online reference sources is available to all patrons who use the library on the campus network as well as off-campus users via the Internet. Articles and books may be ordered from a worldwide network of research libraries. Students log on to the library's home page to ask reference questions. Holdings include 113,018 books and bound journals, 3,545 audiovisual materials, 72,866 government documents, 575 magazine and newspaper subscriptions, and 4,533 items in the Teacher Curriculum Lab. Three microcomputer labs and the Iowa Communications Network (ICN) classroom are located in the library.

The Dr. Charles Grabske, Sr. Library on the Independence campus provides resources for both on-campus and distance students in the nursing, education, and business departments. The library contains more than 3,000 nursing, education, and medical books; 250 audiovisual items, and approximately 1,000 journal titles. Grabske Library has one of the largest collections of nursing journals in the Kansas City area, with current subscriptions to more than 1,000 journals online and in print. Books, journal articles, and interlibrary loan services are available to on-campus and online students. Grabske Library is a member of the Health Sciences Library Network of Kansas City and a member library of the National Network for Libraries of Medicine. In 2006, Grabske Library received the award for Outstanding Academic Health Science Library from Health Sciences Library Network of Kansas City.

Students have the opportunity to use the ABT 52 scanning electron microscope, nuclear magnetic resonance spectroscope, Fourier-transform infrared spectroscope, and a computer lab with PCs that provide access to a multiple-operating system environment in the Platz-Mortimore Science Hall.

The Eugene E. and Julia Travis Closson Physical Education Center includes an indoor junior Olympic-size pool; an indoor track; a weight room; basketball, tennis, and volleyball courts; and a racquetball court. The Bruce Jenner Sports Complex contains the outdoor track, the football stadium, three soccer fields, five intramural fields, and eight tennis courts. The campus borders a nine-hole golf course and two small ponds for fishing and canoeing. Disc golf courses are located throughout the community.

Costs

Full-time tuition for 2008–09 is $18,680. Freshmen and sophomores are required to live on campus.

Financial Aid

Graceland's financial aid program is designed to assist qualified students attending the University. More than 90 percent of Graceland's students receive financial aid such as academic scholarships, performance grants, work-study, federal and state grants, and government loans. Academic scholarships are based on the high school GPA and composite ACT or combined SAT scores for entering freshmen and on cumulative GPA for transfer and continuing students. Grants are available for achievement in athletics and performing arts and for international students. The University matches a grant up to $1500 annually for a contribution made by a congregation and designated for a student attending Graceland. Some financial aid is available for distance learning programs; interested students should contact the Graceland University Financial Aid Services Office for specific information.

Faculty

The majority of faculty members have earned a doctorate or the highest degree in their field. Faculty members are active in their professional fields but consider teaching their primary responsibility. The student-faculty ratio is 15:1.

Student Government

Students are actively involved in the decision-making process of the University. Student-elected executive members of the Graceland Student Government attend faculty meetings and participate with voice and vote. Each academic department has student representatives who participate in business sessions and serve on faculty search committees. Students provide leadership for the housing system and for the campus social program. These and many other avenues are available allowing students to gain practical leadership experience.

Admission Requirements

Admission to Graceland is selective. To be considered, high school graduates must qualify in two of the following three areas: (1) rank in the upper 50 percent of their class; (2) have a minimum 2.5 GPA, based on a 4.0 system; and (3) have either a minimum composite ACT score of 21 or a minimum SAT combined score (Critical Reading and Math) of 960. Applicants who do not meet the above criteria may be considered individually. If accepted, they will be required to take developmental courses. Some applicants may be requested to test for the Chance Program prior to being considered for acceptance. Transfer, international, and home-schooled students should refer to the requirements listed in the catalog on the University's Web site. No one is denied admission to the University on the basis of race, color, religion, age, sex, national origin, disability, or sexual orientation. Prospective students and their families are encouraged to visit the campus.

Application and Information

Students are encouraged to apply as early as possible.

Admissions Office
Graceland University
1 University Place
Lamoni, Iowa 50140
Phone: 641-784-5196
866-GRACELAND (toll-free in the U.S. and Canada)
Fax: 641-784-5480
E-mail: admissions@graceland.edu
Web site: http://www.admissions.graceland.edu

Higdon Administration Building on Graceland's Lamoni Campus.

INTERNATIONAL ACADEMY OF DESIGN & TECHNOLOGY

CHICAGO, ILLINOIS

The Academy

The International Academy of Design & Technology in Chicago and Schaumburg offers educational programs in a variety of unique, diverse, energetic, and professional environments. Here students find the real-world guidance they want with the hands-on experience they need. They gain support from outstanding faculty members and fellow students and have the opportunity to cultivate career-building connections that may last a lifetime. The institution is filled with inspiration in the heart of Chicagoland's fashion, interior design, and advertising industries.

The Academy is a postsecondary degree-granting institution with career-based curricula and professional staff members who contribute to students' development in their chosen fields. The Academy provides a high-quality education, prepares students for positions in fields related to their area of study, and provides students with a professional environment that fosters cultural enrichment and personal development. The Academic Department at the Academy maintains high-quality curricula that are sensitive to industry needs, as defined by the Academy's Advisory Boards. The Career Services department offers career-planning services leading to employment opportunities for graduates to allow them to utilize their knowledge, skills, and talents.

The International Academy of Design & Technology in Chicago was founded in 1977 by Clem Stein Jr. as a private institution located in the Merchandise Mart of Chicago. In 1983, the Academy opened a campus in Toronto, Canada. The Tampa, Florida, campus was opened in 1984, and today there are ten campuses nationwide, including the Schaumburg campus, which opened in 2004. In 1997, Career Education Corporation acquired the Academy. Career Education Corporation operates postsecondary institutions throughout the U.S. and abroad. In 2001, the Academy changed its name from the International Academy of Merchandising & Design to the International Academy of Design & Technology, which better reflects the infusion of technology into all of the program curricula.

There are various associations and clubs for Academy students. These clubs include the Fashion Council (fashion design), Behind the Scene (merchandising management), the Information Technology Organization (IT), the Interior Design Student Association (interior design), Gamers Anonymous (game design), Anime Student Alliance, the Green Academy, the Book Club, and the American Institute of Graphic Arts (graphic design). GLBT@IADT Community is the Academy's outreach to gay, lesbian, bisexual, and transgender students. All of these clubs are organized by the students and for the students.

The Academy is incorporated under the laws of the state of Illinois and accredited by the Accrediting Council for Independent Colleges and Schools (ACICS). The interior design program is accredited by the Council for Interior Design Accreditation.

Location

The Academy is located in Chicago's Loop at historic One North State Street. The campus is close to some of Chicago's famous and world-renowned landmarks. Within walking distance of the campus are the Merchandise Mart and the Apparel Center complex in historic River North and the retail shops of North Michigan Avenue. Along the revitalized State Street are Macy's, Sears, and a multitude of nationally advertised retail outlets. More importantly, the Academy in Chicago is conveniently located in a region known for its internationally prominent advertising, graphic design, and interior design firms.

Nearby cultural and educational resources include the Art Institute of Chicago, the Harold Washington Library, the Chicago Cultural Center, the Athenaeum Museum of Architecture and Design, the Chicago Architecture Foundation, and the Goodman Theatre.

The natural beauty of Grant Park, Millennium Park, and the numerous public art works located throughout the Loop are the ideal complement to the Academy's exciting urban location.

Majors and Degrees

The Academy is authorized by the Illinois Board of Higher Education to grant a Bachelor of Arts degree in merchandising management (tracks in fashion merchandising and retail operations management), a Bachelor of Applied Science degree in information technology, a Bachelor of Science degree in computer forensics, and a Bachelor of Fine Arts degree in fashion design, interior design, and visual communications (tracks in advertising communication, advertising design, game design, graphic design, multimedia and Web design, and video and animation production). The Academy is also authorized to grant Associate of Applied Science degrees in fashion design, merchandising management (tracks in fashion merchandising and retail operations management), information technology, and visual communication (tracks in advertising communication, advertising design, graphic design, multimedia and Web design, and video and animation production).

All degree programs provide students with the opportunity for in-depth career preparation and a firm foundation in general education studies. In the bachelor's degree programs, students benefit from advanced career courses and have the option of choosing elective courses to complete their general education requirements.

Academic Programs

The programs of the Academy involve both classroom education and supervised activities off campus that are designed to prepare students for entry-level positions in their chosen field. Students must take a minimum of 180 quarter hours of study to earn the baccalaureate degree. Transfer credits are acceptable in all programs. Students must take a minimum of 96 quarter hours to earn the Associate of Applied Science degree and must complete all prescribed courses satisfactorily with a minimum grade point average of 2.0.

The curriculum for each program is reviewed periodically by faculty members, program chairs, and members of the program Advisory Boards. Members of the Advisory Boards are experienced professionals in their fields. The Advisory Boards provide the Academy with input on a variety of subjects related to their specific industry. These successful practitioners form an essential link between the academic world and the world that students enter upon graduation.

The Academy's programs are arranged into four quarters of eleven weeks each in a calendar year. A normal full-time load is 12 credit hours per quarter. As a result of the career-oriented emphasis of the Academy, course work is highly specialized and prepares students for entry into a career field. From the point at which they begin their studies at the Academy and continue through to graduation, students are given personal one-on-one academic guidance. Students are regularly advised by the Academy's academic advisers regarding their progress in classes.

Academic Facilities

Classrooms are designed to facilitate learning and consist of lecture rooms, textile labs, drafting labs, design studios, and sewing and pattern-making rooms. Computer labs equipped with Macintosh and IBM-compatible personal computers are used for instruction and practice.

The CECybrary is an Internet-accessible information center committed to facilitating the lifelong learning and achievement of the Career Education Corporation community. This virtual library contains a collection of full-text journals, books, and reference materials, links to Web sites relevant to each curricular area, instructional guides for using electronic library resources, and much more.

The virtual collection is carefully selected to support students as they advance through their programs of study and includes quality, full-text, peer-reviewed articles from scholarly journals and full-text electronic books. Instructional materials for students and faculty are designed to enhance information literacy skills.

A full-time librarian located at corporate headquarters manages the CECybrary. The librarians at the various CEC colleges participate in selecting the electronic resources and Web site links, and help prepare the instructional materials that are on the Web site.

Students at all CEC colleges have access to the CECybrary from their campus location and from home, if they have an Internet service provider. Access to the Cybrary is password-controlled. The password is easily obtained from the campus library.

The bookstore sells books and supplies used in the courses taught at the Academy. The bookstore attempts to keep a balance of inventory between new and used books whenever possible. School-specific merchandise and clothing are also available for purchase. The bookstore coordinates book buy-back periods at the end of each quarter.

Costs

Tuition for the 2008–09 academic year for all programs was $420 per credit hour for students enrolled in up to 12 credit hours and $370 per credit hour for students enrolled in 13 or more credit hours per term. Books and supplies are additional.

Financial Aid

The Academy helps students find the financial resources they need to achieve their educational goals. The Academy participates in the Federal Pell Grant, Federal Supplemental Educational Opportunity Grant (FSEOG), Federal Stafford Student Loan, Federal Parent PLUS programs, Academic Competitiveness Grant, and the National Science and Mathematics Access to Retain Talent Grant. In addition to state and federal aid, the Academy has its own scholarship programs.

Faculty

Faculty members of the Academy possess extensive academic and professional credentials. Their experience enables them to teach theoretical principles while emphasizing current practices in the field. Faculty members are sought and retained because they are committed to teaching at the undergraduate level. In and out of the classroom, the faculty is an integral part of the students' career preparation.

Admission Requirements

Pursuant to the mission of the institution, the Academy desires to admit students who possess appropriate credentials and have demonstrated the capacity or potential for successfully completing the educational programs offered by the institution. To that end, the institution evaluates all students and makes admission decisions on an individual basis. To assist the admissions personnel in making informed decisions, an admissions interview is required.

Transfer students meeting admission requirements are accepted. Students must have an official transcript from postsecondary institutions previously attended forwarded to the Academy. Credit may be given for a course taken at the previous institution if it is comparable in scope and length to an International Academy course, as stated in the Academy's Transfer Credit Guidelines.

Application and Information

Prospective students should apply for admission as soon as possible in order to be officially accepted for a specific program and its starting date. Prospective students must have an admissions interview, during which they are given an opportunity to tour the Academy with their families to see its equipment and facilities. At this time, there is also an opportunity to ask questions relating to the Academy's curricula and a student's possible career goals.

At the time of application, the student must complete an enrollment agreement, pay a $50 application fee, and complete an attestation of high school graduation or its equivalency or provide proof of high school graduation or its equivalency. Once an applicant has completed and submitted the enrollment agreement, the school reviews the information and informs the applicant of its decision.

For further information, students should contact:

Ernest Cochran III, Vice President of Admissions
International Academy of Design & Technology
One North State Street, Suite 500
Chicago, Illinois 60602-3300
Phone: 888-704-2111 (toll-free)
Fax: 312-541-3929
E-mail: info@iadtchicago.com
Web site: http://www.iadtchicago.edu

KENT STATE UNIVERSITY

KENT, OHIO

The University

Kent State University has experienced tremendous growth since its founding in 1910. Today, Kent State is a multicampus network serving more than 34,000 students at eight locations throughout northeastern Ohio. The eight-campus network is anchored by a classic residential campus in Kent, Ohio. Throughout the network, students can pursue certificate, associate, bachelor's, master's, and doctoral degrees. The Kent Campus, serving 18,163 undergraduates and 4,561 graduates, offers 281 undergraduate study areas and numerous graduate degrees. Kent State's seven regional campuses are located in Ashtabula, Geauga, Stark, Trumbull, and Tuscarawas counties and the cities of Salem and East Liverpool.

As a residential campus, Kent State requires students to reside in more than thirty residence halls until junior academic standing is achieved. Exceptions include commuting and nontraditional students. Students can easily walk to any of the more than 100 academic, residential, administrative, and recreational buildings. The University has an eighteen-hole golf course, a 291-acre airport, a two-rink indoor ice arena, three on-campus theaters, and a student recreation and wellness center. There are more than 230 student organizations, nineteen fraternities, ten sororities, and eighteen varsity sports. The Career Service Center provides career counseling and job placement assistance for students and alumni.

Location

Kent, Ohio, a city with a population of 28,000, is within easy traveling distance of the major metropolitan areas of northeastern Ohio. Within a 20-mile radius are concerts, cultural events, numerous amusement parks, museums, nature preserves, recreational areas, and year-round sports.

Majors and Degrees

The College of Architecture and Environmental Design offers the Bachelor of Science and Master of Architecture degrees. The School of Interior Design offers a Bachelor of Arts in interior design.

The College of the Arts offers the degrees of B.A., B.F.A., Bachelor of Music, and B.S. The college also offers multiple-degree programs. The academic divisions are the Schools of Art, Fashion Design and Merchandising, Music, and Theatre and Dance.

The College of Arts and Sciences awards Bachelor of Arts (B.A.), Bachelor of Science (B.S.), and Bachelor of General Studies degrees. Major fields of concentration are American Sign Language, American studies, anthropology, applied conflict management, applied mathematics, biology, biological chemistry, biology, biotechnology, botany, chemistry, classics, computer science, conservation, criminal justice studies, earth science, economics, English, French, French translation, geography, geology, German, German translation, history, international relations, Latin, Latin American studies, mathematics, medical technology, Pan-African studies, paralegal studies, philosophy, physics, political science, psychology, Russian, Russian translation, sociology, Soviet and East European studies, Spanish, Spanish translation, and zoology. Numerous interdisciplinary and preprofessional programs are available, including general studies, integrated life sciences, pre-dentistry, pre-engineering, prelaw, premedicine, pre-osteopathy, pre-pharmacy, and pre–veterinary medicine. Students may also design their own individualized major.

The College of Business Administration awards the Bachelor of Business Administration degree. Major fields of concentration are accounting, business management, computer information systems, economics, finance, marketing, and operations management. Students can choose a minor in any of these programs as well as international business.

The College of Communication and Information offers the B.A., Bachelor of Fine Arts (B.F.A.), and the B.S. degrees. Major fields of concentration are advertising, communication studies, electronic media, news, photo illustration, public relations, radio-television, visual communication design, and visual journalism.

The College of Education, Health, and Human Services offers the Bachelor of Science in Education, B.A. and B.S. degrees, and Master of Arts degrees, with licensure programs available in adolescence/young adult education, early childhood education, intervention specialist studies (majors include deaf education, educational interpreter studies, gifted education, mild/moderate educational needs, and moderate/intensive educational needs), middle childhood education, multiage education, and career technical teacher education (vocational education). In addition, separate degree programs are offered in the Schools of Exercise, Leisure, and Sport; Family and Consumer Studies; Integrated Health Studies; and Speech Pathology and Audiology.

The College of Nursing awards the Bachelor of Science in Nursing degree. The four-year program includes clinical practicums in the Cleveland-Akron-Warren-Youngstown areas.

The College of Technology offers associate, bachelor's, and master's degree programs throughout Kent State's eight-campus system. Students can select from a number of specialized academic programs in aeronautics, industrial, electrical, manufacturing, or educational technologies.

Academic Programs

Kent State's colleges and schools all maintain separate academic programs; completion of 36 to 37 credits of liberal education course work is a University requirement for all students. The number of credit hours required for graduation varies but is generally 121 semester hours. Credits can be transferred from previous college work satisfactorily completed or earned through courses taken at one of Kent State's regional campuses. Credit by examination is available. Generally, to earn a degree, students must earn at least 30 semester hours in residence.

The Honors College provides opportunities for students and faculty members to develop and implement special learning experiences. It offers four-year programs of undergraduate study with concurrent enrollment in one of the University's degree-granting programs. In addition, the Honors College awards Advanced Placement and International Baccalaureate credit, early admission to high school students, and specialized academic advising. Its Experimental and Integrative Studies Division offers nontraditional learning experiences for students and faculty members of the entire University community.

Support services are available for students needing assistance to ensure a successful college experience. The Academic Success Center program offers tutoring, and Student Accessibility Services provides assistance to students with various physical disabilities and specific learning disabilities.

Army and Air Force ROTC programs are offered on campus.

Off-Campus Programs

Through the Office of International Affairs, Kent State offers students a variety of overseas academic programs that provide a balance of academic, linguistic, and cross-cultural experiences and learning opportunities. Credit is granted toward degrees.

Academic Facilities

The collections of the University libraries total more than 2.7 million bound volumes, 14,560 periodicals, and 1.36 million microform pieces. The Honors Center is a living-learning residential complex that houses undergraduate students as well as staff offices, a library-seminar room, a student computer facility, and an audiovisual center. The Center for Applied Conflict Management is an academic unit offering programs of study, research, and service activities that focus on the dynamics of change in human systems. The Instructional Television Service operates a closed-circuit, campuswide network and a production center for NETO, Inc., Channels 45 and 49, northeastern Ohio's public television stations. Audiovisual services support regularly scheduled classes with films and other educational materials. The Instructional Resources Center assists students in the production of educational media materials. The Language Laboratory provides tapes and other tools to assist students in foreign language studies. The Academic Testing Services Office offers test administration, test scoring, and research activities. The School of Fashion Design and Merchandising sponsors a working museum of fashion for students and the general public. This school houses classrooms, labs, a library, and a collection of costumes donated from the Silverman-Rogers estate for hands-on study.

As a recognized leader in liquid crystal technology, Kent State's Glenn H. Brown Liquid Crystal Institute is the nation's only center devoted solely to liquid crystal research. With a recent grant from the National Science Foundation, Kent State became the home of Ohio's first Science and Technology Research Center for the Study of Advanced Liquid Crystalline Optical Materials.

Costs

Instructional and other fees for Ohio residents for 2008–09 were $8430 per year. For students residing outside Ohio, instructional and other fees were $15,862 per year. Although room rates vary, costs for board and a double room averaged $7500 per year. The average student spends $1030 per year for books and supplies and should budget extra money for personal needs and expenses. All fees and charges are subject to change.

Financial Aid

More than 80 percent of Kent State's freshmen receive assistance through scholarships, grants, loans, or employment opportunities. To be considered for financial aid awards, students must be admitted to the University and must submit the Free Application for Federal Student Aid (FAFSA). Ohio students should also check the Ohio College Opportunity Grant (OCOG) box on the FAFSA if they are interested in being considered. Students planning to attend the fall semester as freshmen should apply for financial aid after January 1 and before March 1 of the same year. In order to meet the March 1 priority deadline, it is recommended that all financial aid forms be completed and mailed no later than February 1. Applications received after March 1 are considered, but sufficient funds to assist all late applicants may be lacking. Additional information is available from the Student Financial Aid Office at http://www.sfa.kent.edu.

First-time freshmen and incoming transfer students from forty-nine states outside of Ohio are eligible for a $3700 University Award. For eligibility requirements, students should visit http://www.sfa.kent.edu.

Kent State's Honors College awards merit scholarships to selected individuals who have the potential for superior scholarly and creative work at the University as determined by academic performance and creative artist competitions. For additional information, students should visit the Honors College Web site at http://www.kent.edu/honors.

The Student Financial Aid Office also administers numerous scholarships, including the Founder's Scholarship, the Trustee Scholarship, the Oscar Ritchie Memorial Scholarship, the President's Scholarship for out-of-state students, the President's Grant for out-of-state students who are children of alumni, and various departmental scholarships.

To be considered for freshman scholarships at the Kent Campus, students must complete an application for admission by January 15 for priority consideration. Scholarships range from $1000 to full tuition and fees. Freshmen applying after this date are considered for scholarships if funds are available.

Faculty

The University's commitment to scholarship and teaching excellence is enhanced by a full-time faculty of approximately 2,100 members. Some of the faculty members are research oriented, and others publish widely.

Student Government

Students have leadership opportunities through residence hall and Greek organizations and the Undergraduate Student Senate. The senate is responsible for allocating student activity fees to registered undergraduate organizations, appointing undergraduates to all University committees and to other positions, conducting elections, and polling student opinion. Two students serve on Kent State's Board of Trustees.

Admission Requirements

Kent State's freshman admission policy differs for students with varying degrees of preparation for college studies. The students most likely to be admitted and to succeed at the Kent campus are those who have graduated with at least 16 units of the recommended college-preparatory curriculum in high school, achieved a high school grade point average of 2.5 or higher, and acquired an ACT score of 21 or better (or a combined SAT critical reading and math score of 980 or better).

For freshmen, selective admission requirements apply to aeronautics flight technology, architecture, dance, education, fashion design and merchandising, interior design, journalism and mass communication, music, nursing, sports administration, theater, and the six-year B.S./M.D. medical program with the Northeastern Ohio Universities College of Medicine (NEOUCOM). For transfer students, selective requirements apply to all of the preceding and to art and business. Students should refer to http://www.admissions.kent.edu for information.

Application and Information

Students are strongly encouraged to apply for admission online at http://www.admissions.kent.edu/apply. A $30 nonrefundable application fee is required. Application early in the senior year helps ensure priority consideration for fall registration, residence hall preference, and financial aid. Applications are processed on a rolling basis.

Nancy J. DellaVecchia
Director, Admissions Office
Kent State University
P.O. Box 5190
Kent, Ohio 44242-0001
Phone: 330-672-2444
800-988-KENT (toll-free)
E-mail: kentadm@kent.edu
Web site: http://www.kent.edu
http://www.kent.edu/admissions

KETTERING UNIVERSITY

FLINT, MICHIGAN

The University

Founded in 1919, Kettering University is a private university specializing in technical degrees. The school enrolls about 2,300 undergraduate students and offers a 9:1 student-faculty ratio. Most classes have fewer than 20 students and are taught by Ph.D.-level professors, not teaching assistants. This combination of small class size and highly qualified teaching staff ensures students of a much more personalized learning experience.

Kettering is a highly acclaimed university with the one of the country's most modern cooperative education programs. Whatever major is chosen, students alternate between study terms and full-time work terms—otherwise known as co-op. During study terms, students learn material in small, intense classes taught by University professors. During co-op terms, students work as paid professionals at corporations related to their studies and interests. Kettering co-op students have done everything from testing ballistic systems for the U.S. government to reengineering crowd management at Disney World. Kettering has the only cooperative program of its kind where students begin working as early as their freshman year. By graduation from Kettering, students have up to 2½ years of professional experience and an impressive resume. Ninety-eight percent of Kettering's students graduate with job offers or grad school acceptances in hand.

Kettering University's cooperative education program pairs hands-on education with real-world experience—all undergraduate students alternate between on-campus study terms and full-time terms of cooperative employment with one of more than 600 corporate partners. This unique system of education prepares students to be technology innovators—professionals with cutting-edge skills who are ready to compete in tomorrow's business environment.

Kettering University is accredited by the North Central Association of Colleges and Schools, the Accreditation Board for Engineering and Technology (ABET), and the Association of Collegiate Business Schools and Programs (ACBSP). Kettering is also a member of the National Commission of Cooperative Education (NCCE) and the Association of Independent Technological Universities.

Besides being academically ahead of the game, Kettering students bring a wide range of skills and interests with them to campus. To make sure that students get a life along with an education, Kettering offers more than fifty student organizations, including fourteen fraternities and six sororities, an active student government, a state-of-the-art recreation and fitness facility, and very competitive intramural sports. Recreation facilities include athletic fields, tennis courts, and a recreation center with an Olympic-size, six-lane swimming pool; aerobic fitness rooms; a full line of Nautilus equipment; and basketball, tennis, and racquetball courts. A public golf course is adjacent to the campus.

Professional counseling, support services, and health-care services are available.

Kettering also offers Master of Science degree programs in engineering, engineering management, information technology, manufacturing management, manufacturing operations, and operations management, in addition to an M.B.A. program.

Location

Kettering University is located in Flint, Michigan, which is 60 miles west of Lake Huron and 60 miles north of Detroit. Flint has approximately 115,000 residents and a metropolitan area population of 450,000.

Flint is particularly proud of its Cultural Center, which is only 10 minutes from Kettering's campus. Built and endowed entirely by the gifts of private citizens, the Cultural Center includes the Alfred P. Sloan Museum, the Whiting Auditorium (home of the Flint Symphony and host to leading stage shows and entertainers), the Robert T. Longway Planetarium (Michigan's largest and best-equipped sky show facility), the Flint Institute of Arts, the F. A. Bower Theater, the Dort Institute of Music, Mott Community College, and the Flint Public Library. Nearby is the University of Michigan–Flint campus.

The area also offers numerous outdoor and indoor recreational opportunities. Within a few minutes' drive are downhill and cross-country skiing facilities, lakes for the entire range of water sports, a wide selection of good public golf courses, excellent indoor and outdoor skating rinks, and plentiful shopping facilities and restaurants

Majors and Degrees

Kettering University offers a 4½-year, professional, cooperative education program with Bachelor of Science degrees in applied mathematics, applied physics, biochemistry, business administration, chemical engineering, chemistry, computer engineering, computer science, electrical engineering, engineering physics, industrial engineering, and mechanical engineering.

Kettering also offers a variety of dual-degree programs and enough minors, specialties, and concentrations to ensure that students' degrees are custom-fit to their interests and career goals.

Academic Programs

Although each program at Kettering University has its own requirements, 160 credit hours are generally required for graduation. The program involves nine academic terms and nine co-op terms, two of which are focused on the capstone thesis project, which is a major work project assigned by the co-op employer. Students alternate between eleven-week periods of academic study on the campus in Flint and twelve-week periods of related work experience with their corporate employer. The academic year consists of two 3-month academic terms on campus and two 3-month terms of paid work experience.

Academic Facilities

Kettering University offers some of the best facilities, labs, and educational resources in the world, and students start using them as early as their freshman year. The Crash Safety Center, for example, is the only one of its kind in the nation used in an undergraduate program. The University also offers labs in areas such as fuel-cell research, polymer optimization, machining, acoustics, and more.

Kettering is fully networked and allows 24-hour access to computer resources and the Internet from dorms and labs. A 445-student residence hall and an apartment complex are located on the campus for student housing. The library offers more than 94,000 cataloged volumes and 540 periodicals. And through online resources like Co-op Navigator and Blackboard, students can always be in touch with professors and University staff members.

Costs

For 2008–09, tuition costs are $26,496, and room and board cost $6182.

Financial Aid

Kettering University wants to invest in its students, so it does what it takes to help finance education through scholarships, loans, and work-study opportunities. In fact, more than 92 percent of the students receive some sort of financial aid. Pair that with co-op earnings—between $40,000 and $65,000 over the course of the college career—and students are looking at one of the best values in education today. In addition, Kettering's Merit Scholarship program awards students with scholarships up to $76,500 for 4½ years.

Students should fill out the Free Application for Federal Student Aid (FAFSA) and request a copy of the analysis to be sent to Kettering University. The University works to create a financial aid package for based on those results.

Faculty

Kettering University's 144 full-time faculty members have teaching as their main responsibility. Most professors have industrial experience in addition to academic credentials and maintain contact with industry through consulting, sponsored research, and advising on student thesis projects. More than 80 percent of faculty members hold a doctorate. Because only half of the students are on campus at any one time, class sizes are small, and opportunities for enrichment and extra help are readily available.

Admission Requirements

Admission to Kettering University is competitive and based on scholastic achievement and extracurricular interests, activities, and achievements. Applicants are required to have earned the following: 3 years of English, 2 years algebra, 1 year of geometry, 1 semester of trigonometry, 2 years of lab science (1 must be physics or chemistry; both are recommended). Applicants must submit results of the SAT or ACT (Kettering's ACT code number is 1998 and the SAT code number is 1246).

Most Kettering University students are in the top 10 percent of their graduating class. Kettering University also welcomes students wishing to transfer from other colleges and universities. The transfer alternative is an excellent way to gain admission for students who do not enroll as freshmen.

Application and Information

There is more than one way to apply to Kettering. Students can apply online (free) at http://www.admissions.kettering.edu or print an application and send it by mail. Students should call 800-955-4464 Ext. 7865 for assistance.

Kettering officials review applications and let students know if they have been accepted. Although Kettering accepts and processes applications throughout the year, it is best to apply as early as possible. Once accepted, students receive information on programs and the professional co-op program, which are only available to admitted students. Students should complete the co-op registration (resume) online and pay a $300 tuition deposit (to be credited to the first-semester tuition). The deposit shows that a student is as serious about Kettering as Kettering is about the student and ensures a place in the entering class and eligibility to begin the co-op employment search process.

Admissions Office
Kettering University
1700 West Third Avenue (now University Avenue)
Flint, Michigan 48504-4898
Phone: 810-762-7865
800-955-4464 (toll-free in the United States and Canada)
E-mail: admissions@kettering.edu
Web site: http://www.admissions.kettering.edu

Kettering has the experts, the labs, and the programs that bring theory and practice together.

LOYOLA UNIVERSITY CHICAGO

CHICAGO, ILLINOIS

The University

Consistently ranked a top national university and a best value by U.S. News & World Report, Loyola University Chicago is the largest of the twenty-eight Jesuit Catholic universities in the United States, with a total enrollment of 15,545 students from fifty states and eighty-two countries. Loyola offers more than seventy undergraduate majors and more than 140 graduate, professional, and graduate-level certificate programs. Loyola prepares people to lead extraordinary lives by building upon its Jesuit tradition with an innovative Core Curriculum, which equips students with lifelong skills for success, and a strong commitment to develop the whole person—intellectually, socially, physically, and spiritually.

Loyola gives students the best of campus and city life with diverse living and learning opportunities in world-class Chicago. Located off North Michigan Avenue, Chicago's Magnificent Mile, Loyola's dynamic Water Tower Campus is home to the Schools of Business Administration, Communication, Continuing and Professional Studies, Education, Law, and Social Work, and connects students to the heart of the city for myriad internship, job, and service opportunities. Loyola's Lake Shore Campus, home to the College of Arts and Sciences, the Graduate School, and the Marcella Niehoff School of Nursing, is located on the picturesque shores of Lake Michigan and offers students a traditional residential campus.

Loyola's student-faculty ratio of 13:1, well below the national average, ensures personal attention. Nearly all of Loyola's 940 full-time faculty members hold Ph.D.'s, and they are routinely called upon as experts in their fields.

Loyola students annually receive more than $180 million in financial assistance from numerous sources, including more than $45 million in Loyola-funded scholarships. Students gain practical experience and leadership, organizational, and life skills by participating in internships, engaging in service opportunities, and joining any of the school's more than 130 academic, social, cultural, and professional student organizations.

For information about admission, academics, housing, financial assistance, student life and more, students should visit http://www.LUC.edu/undergrad.

Location

Loyola's tranquil, residential Lake Shore Campus sits on the shores of Lake Michigan, just 8 miles north of downtown Chicago. The dynamic Water Tower Campus is located just off North Michigan Avenue, Chicago's Magnificent Mile in the heart of the city near theaters, museums, major corporate and financial institutions, and Chicago's most elegant shops and boutiques. A University-operated shuttle bus and convenient public transportation help students easily get back and forth between the two campuses.

Majors and Degrees

Loyola students may choose from more than seventy undergraduate majors and over seventy minors. Undergraduate degrees offered include the Bachelor of Arts (B.A.), B.A. Classics, Bachelor of Science (B.S.), Bachelor of Business Administration (B.B.A.), Bachelor of Science in Education (B.S.Ed.), Bachelor of Science in Nursing (B.S.N.), and Bachelor of Social Work (B.S.W.) degrees.

The College of Arts and Sciences offers undergraduate majors in anthropology, biochemistry, bioinformatics, biology, black world studies, chemistry, classical civilization, communications networks and security, computer science, criminal justice, ecology, economics, English, environmental sciences (chemistry), environmental studies, fine arts, forensic science, French, Greek (ancient), history, human services, information technology, international film and media studies, international studies, Italian, Latin, mathematics, mathematics and computer science, molecular biology, music, philosophy, philosophy–social justice, physics, physics and computer science, physics and engineering, political science, psychology, religious studies, sociology, sociology and anthropology, software development, Spanish, statistical science, theater, theology, theoretical physics and applied mathematics, and women's and gender studies (as a second major only).

The School of Business Administration offers majors in accounting, economics, entrepreneurship, finance, human resource management, information systems, international business, management, marketing, operations management, and sport management.

The School of Communication offers majors in advertising/public relations, communication studies, and journalism.

The School of Education offers majors in bilingual/bicultural education, elementary education, mathematics education, science education, and special education, along with an expanded secondary education dual-degree program.

The Marcella Niehoff School of Nursing offers the Bachelor of Science in Nursing, a health systems management major, and an accelerated B.S.N. program, which is available to students who have already completed a baccalaureate degree.

The School of Social Work offers an undergraduate major in social work and a combined bachelor's and master's degree in social work, which may be completed in five years.

Other special academic opportunities include preprofessional programs for law and health professions, more than fifteen 5-year (bachelor's/master's) degree programs, interdisciplinary programs, six-year early admission to Loyola's School of Law, early assurance to Loyola's Stritch School of Medicine, and the Loyola/Midwestern University Dual-Acceptance Pharmacy Program.

Academic Programs

Loyola's Core Curriculum sets goals for undergraduate education that focus on skills, values, and knowledge that prepare students for the realities of living and working in today's world. The Core Curriculum gives students who have not yet selected an academic major the opportunity to explore many courses before deciding on a field of study.

Most degrees require 128 credit hours for graduation. Exceptionally well-qualified students may apply to the Interdisciplinary Honors Program. Students may receive credit through the Advanced Placement Program (AP) tests and the International Baccalaureate (I.B.). Certain College-Level Examination Program (CLEP) tests are accepted. Loyola students may participate in Army and Navy ROTC programs through neighboring universities.

Off-Campus Programs

Loyola's John Felice Rome Center in Italy is both one of the largest American university programs in Western Europe and the most popular study-abroad destination for Loyola students.

Students may attend The Beijing Center for Chinese Studies or one of sixty other study-abroad programs in twenty-nine countries.

Academic Facilities

Loyola's state-of-the-art Michael R. and Marilyn C. Quinlan Life Sciences Education and Research Center houses laboratories used for biology, bioinformatics, chemistry, ecology, and other life science courses. It also provides numerous opportunities for undergraduates to engage in scientific research alongside their professors. The Sullivan Center for Student Services, which opened in 2006, consolidates a dozen student services offices into one convenient location.

Loyola's Department of Fine and Performing Arts recently moved into a renovated building that offers state-of-the-art studios for ceramics, metalworking/jewelry, and sculpture. The facility also features a dance studio and art gallery. The newly renovated Mundelein Center for the Fine and Performing Arts, which opened in fall 2007, contains a theater resource center and reading room, music resource center and listening lab, art history resource center, music classrooms, offices, and an auditorium theater. The tenth floor is home to eight fully equipped private practice rooms plus a deluxe music lab.

The University's library system, including the Cudahy Library at the Lake Shore Campus and the Lewis Library at the Water Tower Campus, contains more than 1 million books, 1,400 periodical subscriptions, and access to 30,000 online periodicals. The Loyola University Museum of Art, which recently opened at the Water Tower Campus, displays the University's Medieval and Renaissance collection, along with other permanent collections and rotating exhibitions of professional and student work. The Information Commons, which opened in spring 2008, is a new four-story lakeside research facility that provides individual study space for students, state-of-the-art technology with more than 220 computers, wireless Internet connections, and a lakefront café.

The Medical Center Campus in Maywood, a suburb of Chicago, consists of the Foster G. McGaw Hospital and the Stritch School of Medicine as well as the Mulcahy Outpatient Center, the Russo Surgical Pavilion, and the Cardinal Bernardin Cancer Center.

Costs

Undergraduate tuition in 2008–09 is $28,700. Room and board costs are dependent on a student's selection of residence hall and meal plan.

Financial Aid

Loyola attempts to meet the financial need of as many students as possible. Ninety-four percent of Loyola freshmen receive some form of aid, including University-funded scholarships and grants, federal and state grants, work-study, and loans. Students are encouraged to file the Free Application for Federal Student Aid (FAFSA) before Loyola's March 1 priority date to be considered for as many sources of aid as possible.

Merit scholarships are awarded to entering freshmen who have outstanding academic records. Presidential, Damen, Loyola, and Trustee Scholarships are awarded to students who rank at the top of their high school graduating class and score well on the ACT or SAT. Scholarship amounts for these programs range from $6000 to half-tuition per year. Transfer students who have completed 30 hours of college credit with an outstanding record of academic achievement may receive a Transfer Academic Scholarship. These awards are all renewable for up to three years. Students must be admitted to Loyola prior to February 1 to be considered for scholarships that are automatically awarded with admission.

Students may also look for additional scholarships, which require separate applications. A great place to start is Loyola's list of more than seventy-five types of additional scholarships, twenty of which are awarded without considering financial need. For more information, students should visit http://www.LUC.edu/finaid/scholarships.

Faculty

Nearly all of Loyola's full-time faculty members hold the Ph.D. or the highest degree in their field. Faculty members teach both graduate and undergraduate students, and senior faculty members often teach Core Curriculum courses. With a student-faculty ratio of 13:1, far below the national average, Loyola students have access to faculty members both as teachers and as advisers.

Student Government

Student government at Loyola provides a liaison between students and the administration, emphasizes concerns for student rights, and provides a forum for debate, recommendation, and action on issues that pertain to students. Students also take an active role in University policy and advisory committees and as elected representatives in the residence halls.

Admission Requirements

Students seeking admission to Loyola University Chicago are evaluated on their overall academic record, including ACT or SAT scores. For the freshman class entering in fall 2007, the middle 50 percent of ACT scores ranged between 23 and 28, the middle 50 percent of SAT critical reading scores ranged between 530 and 640, the middle 50 percent of SAT math scores ranged between 520 and 640, and the average GPA was 3.68. Most Loyola students rank in the upper quarter of their graduating class, but consideration is given to students in the upper half. Candidates should be graduating from an accredited secondary school with a college-preparatory curriculum, including courses in English, math, social studies, and science. Study of a foreign language is strongly recommended. Students must submit the application for admission along with high school transcripts, test scores, a writing sample, and a secondary school counselor recommendation. Admission counselors are available to meet and talk with students individually either before or after the application is submitted.

Transfer students with 20 semester hours or more of acceptable credit are evaluated on the basis of their college work only.

Application and Information

Applicants are notified of the admission decision three to four weeks after the application, supporting credentials, secondary school counselor recommendation, and $25 application fee are received. The application fee is waived for students who apply online.

Prospective students are encouraged to visit the campus. Undergraduate Admission encourages students to schedule individual appointments and campus tours up to two weeks in advance or to participate in one of the many campus programs offered throughout the year.

To obtain an application and further information and to arrange a visit, students should contact:

Undergraduate Admission Office
Loyola University Chicago
820 North Michigan Avenue
Chicago, Illinois 60611
Phone: 312-915-6500
800-262-2373 (toll-free)
E-mail: admission@luc.edu
Web site: http://www.LUC.edu/undergrad

MANCHESTER COLLEGE

NORTH MANCHESTER, INDIANA

The College

At Manchester College, students find academics that matter. They find their place among students who are motivated to learn and faculty members with top degrees who know what it takes to succeed.

With a rich social life, students become part of the Manchester family that covers the globe. With lasting relationships, their college years will last a lifetime.

Manchester students learn how to give meaning to success. They get the most from their college experience so they can get the most out of life.

Tim Polakowski, a recent graduate from Illinois, now teaching English in South Korea as a Fulbright scholar, says he found success at Manchester College. "In high school, I knew I wanted to make a difference. Today, I feel that Manchester College has not only prepared me to make that difference, but also made a difference in me. The professors want you to succeed and the challenges in and out of the classroom prepare you for a life outside the norm. After a year studying in Spain, a semester south of the border, and working with on-campus groups like Habitat for Humanity, I'm more convinced than ever that Manchester was the right place for me."

The undergraduate enrollment is 1,145. Most students are between the ages of 18 and 22. Approximately 85 percent of the full-time students are from Indiana. Students from twenty-five states and twenty-five countries are being enrolled during 2008–09. Six percent of the students are members of the Church of the Brethren. Many different religious backgrounds are represented, and all are welcomed.

Manchester is a member of the National Collegiate Athletic Association Division III and offers nine men's and eight women's sports. The Physical Education and Recreation Center houses physical education classes, a fitness center, intercollegiate and intramural sports, and recreational activities. The College has a very strong intramural program that involves about 80 percent of its students.

Location

Located in the heart of Indiana's beautiful lake country, North Manchester is a thriving community of 6,000 people. It is within a half hour's drive of Indiana's second-largest city, Fort Wayne, and is only 3½ hours from Chicago. Wide streets with large shade trees, graceful homes, and a beautiful park combine to provide a classic setting for college living.

Majors and Degrees

Manchester College grants Bachelor of Arts and Bachelor of Science degrees. Areas of study include accounting, adapted physical education, art, athletic training, biochemistry, biology, biotechnology, business, chemistry, coaching, communication studies, computer science, corporate finance, criminal justice, early childhood education, economics, elementary education, engineering science, English, environmental studies, exercise science, finance, fitness and sport management, French, gender studies, gerontology, history, journalism, management, marketing, mathematics, media studies, medical technology, music, peace studies, philosophy, physical education, physics, political science, prelaw, premedicine, prenursing, pre–occupational therapy, pre–physical therapy, psychology, public relations, religion, secondary education, social work, sociology, Spanish, and sports management. Individualized interdisciplinary majors can also be arranged to meet a student's particular goals.

Academic Programs

The curriculum reflects a commitment to sound training in a specific area of study, the major, and broad development of skills and understanding through the liberal arts. In addition, students may explore interests different from specific career or professional areas through elective courses. This combination prepares students for careers or graduate school immediately after graduation and equips them for the challenges and changes of the future.

Manchester College operates on a 4-1-4 calendar and offers online courses during two summer sessions. The College's innovative Fast Forward program allows students to complete a four-year degree in three years on campus and two summers online. Students save as much as $25,000 and enter graduate school or their careers a year earlier than classmates.

Off-Campus Programs

Manchester College students may study abroad for a semester or year in ten countries: Philipps-Universität Marburg in Marburg/Lahn (Germany), the Institut International d'Études Françaises of the University of Strasbourg (France), the University of Nancy (France), the University of Barcelona (Spain), St. Mary's College in Cheltenham (England), Hokkai Gakuen University in Sapporo (Japan), the Dalian Institute of Foreign Languages in Dalian (People's Republic of China), the Athens Center (Greece), the Catholic University of Ecuador, Cochin (India), and Universidad Veracruzana (Mexico).

During January session, numerous classes are held off campus. In recent years, professors have taken classes to India, Kenya, England, Mexico, Russia, France, Jamaica, Ghana, Vietnam, Nicaragua, Haiti, Germany, Costa Rica, Cuba, and Hawaii as well as destinations in the continental United States.

Field experiences and internships are offered for credit in accounting, broadcasting, business, criminal justice, early childhood education, elementary education, forensic chemistry, gerontology, health sciences practicum, journalism, peace studies, physical education, political science, psychology, secondary education, and social work.

Academic Facilities

Manchester College has more than 160 personal computers in student labs, one for every 6 students. In addition, the Clark Computer Center houses file servers, three computer labs, and an AS400 for student use. PC labs tied to the network are located in each residence hall and the library. A 45-Mbs DS3 line provides high-speed Internet access.

The $17-million Science Center, opened in fall 2005, provides extraordinary laboratories and fully wired classrooms. Students in astronomy use the 10-inch Newtonian reflector telescope in the Charles S. Morris Observatory.

The College Union, which was completely renovated in 2007, houses the Success Center, campus store, art gallery, dining facilities, and Oaks coffee bar.

The Funderburg Library is a recently renovated, three-story building that houses more than 170,000 books, 800 periodicals, and 4,500 audio recordings available for student use. Computer connections and interlibrary loan allow access to major library collections across the country.

Costs

Tuition and fees for 2008–09 are $22,720 for full-time students. Room and board costs for the residence halls (double occupancy) are $8100. The total charges with fees are $30,820 for the academic year.

Financial Aid

Manchester offers extensive scholarship and grant assistance through institutional resources. Academic awards include Honors, Trustee, Presidential, and Dean's Scholarships. Special scholarships based on academic merit and interest are awarded in music and entrepreneurship. International students can receive scholarships based on academic accomplishments and financial need. Manchester awards significant need-based grants. More than $11 million in College funds have been awarded in 2008–09.

Ninety-eight percent of Manchester's students have some type of financial assistance, whether it is a scholarship, a grant, a loan, or campus employment. Questions about financial aid should be referred to the Office of Admissions.

Faculty

Manchester's faculty consists of 71 full-time and 32 part-time members. Nearly 90 percent of full-time faculty members hold the highest degree in their field, and 94 percent of all courses are taught by full-time faculty members. The primary emphasis of the faculty members is teaching, but many are actively engaged in research as well. Faculty members serve as academic advisers, with a specially trained group of faculty members acting as primary advisers for new students. There is a 13.3:1 student-faculty ratio.

Student Government

Students at Manchester assume responsibility for the governmental and judicial activities of the College. The Student Government Association provides a forum for discussion and investigation of community concerns and a channel for evaluating and solving community problems.

Each of the College's five residence halls elects a governing body, which is responsible for providing leadership.

The Manchester Activities Council organizes programming of student events. Students are offered a wide variety of leadership and participation opportunities as part of the College's student development program.

Admission Requirements

Manchester College seeks to enroll students whose scholastic record, test scores, and personality give promise of success in college. Graduation from an accredited high school or its equivalent is required.

The College recommends that students take 4 years of English, 3 years of laboratory science, 3 years of mathematics, 2 years of foreign language, and 2 years of social studies in high school. Students may take either the ACT or the SAT, and personal recommendations from a high school principal or guidance counselor are required.

For transfer students, transcripts of all previous college work are required.

Application and Information

Students may apply for admission prior to each term. Applications are accepted on a rolling basis. There is a nonrefundable $25 application fee. Online applications are free.

Interested students and their parents are encouraged to visit Manchester College and meet faculty members, coaches, and current students; sit in on classes; and take a campus tour. Arrangements can be made by writing or calling the Office of Admissions.

For application forms and further information, students may contact:

Office of Admissions
Manchester College
North Manchester, Indiana 46962-0365
Phone: 800-852-3648 (toll-free)
E-mail: admitinfo@manchester.edu
Web site: http://www.manchester.edu

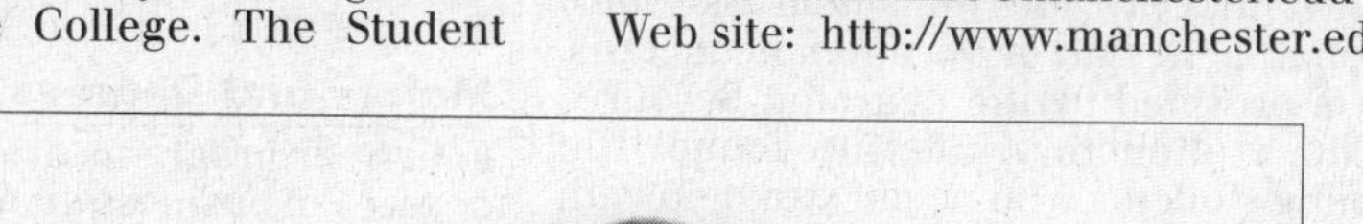

Students on the campus of Manchester College.

MILWAUKEE SCHOOL OF ENGINEERING

MILWAUKEE, WISCONSIN

The School

Ambitious students who want personal and professional success find a home at Milwaukee School of Engineering (MSOE). For more than 105 years, top students choose a rigorous and collaborative education and the supportive guidance of expert faculty members who are dedicated to student success. The university is fully dedicated to every student who is willing to be challenged and work hard to become a better person as a successful MSOE graduate. The campus has a close community feel because it is nestled in a vibrant downtown Milwaukee neighborhood, and offers students an engaging learning and living environment.

Advancing beyond acquisition to the highly sophisticated application of knowledge is the foundation of MSOE's educational philosophy. This approach, which is the university's educational niche, produces graduates who are well-rounded, technologically experienced, and highly productive professionals and leaders. Graduates begin their careers as work-ready problem solvers and develop into leaders: creating new products, starting or heading companies, and working to better their communities.

MSOE has a 98 percent graduate placement rate and an average starting salary of more than $52,500. Representatives from hundreds of firms from throughout the country, including Fortune 500 companies, visit MSOE during the academic year to interview graduating students for employment and discuss career opportunities. MSOE's longstanding ties with business, industry, and health care are represented by the Board of Regents, with more than 50 members, and the MSOE Corporation, with more than 200 members, who are elected from leaders in business and industry nationwide.

The student body of more than 2,600 men and women comes from throughout the United States and numerous countries. Since its founding, the university has encouraged the enrollment of students of any race, color, creed, or gender. Approximately half of the full-time students live in three high-rise residence halls.

MSOE's Counseling Services Office provides individual assistance for students with educational, personal, or vocational concerns. Free on-campus tutoring is provided by the Learning Resource Center and Tau Omega Mu, an honorary fraternity founded in 1953 for the purpose of aiding students who need extra help with their studies.

The Student Life and Campus Center provides on-campus recreational activities. This facility houses student activity rooms, student organization offices, a TV viewing area, a marketplace eatery, and a game room. Additional recreation areas can be found in the residence halls. The Kern Center is a 210,000-square-foot health, wellness, and fitness facility that houses a 1,600-seat ice arena, a fitness center, a 1,200-seat basketball arena, a field house, a recreational running track, and a wrestling area.

More than seventy professional societies, fraternities, and other special-interest groups serve the campus. MSOE's students tend to be participants, so many participate in intramural sports programs. MSOE is a member of the National Collegiate Athletic Association (NCAA) Division III and the Northern Athletics Conference (NAC). The Athletic Department sponsors NCAA varsity teams in men's baseball, basketball, cross-country, golf, ice hockey, indoor and outdoor track and field, lacrosse, rowing, soccer, tennis, volleyball, and wrestling and women's basketball, cross-country, golf, indoor and outdoor track and field, soccer, softball, tennis, and volleyball that compete with teams from other private colleges and universities in the Midwest.

MSOE's (and one of Milwaukee's) newest attraction and home to the world's most comprehensive art collection dedicated to the evolution of human work opened in October 2007. The Grohmann Museum welcomes visitors to three floors of galleries where the Eckhart G. Grohmann Collection "Man at Work" is housed. The collection comprises more than 700 paintings and sculptures from 1580 to today, reflecting a variety of artistic styles and subjects that depict organized work from farming to mining to trades to more unusual occupations such as seaweed gathering.

In addition to its seventeen undergraduate degree programs in the fields of engineering, architectural engineering and building construction, engineering technology, computers, business, and health-related areas, MSOE offers nine Master of Science degree programs: cardiovascular studies, engineering, engineering management (accelerated option available), environmental engineering, marketing and export management, medical informatics (jointly offered with the Medical College of Wisconsin), new-product management, perfusion, and structural engineering.

Milwaukee School of Engineering (MSOE) is a member of, and accredited by, the North Central Association of Colleges and Schools. Program-specific accrediting agencies are identified in the MSOE academic catalogs.

Location

The MSOE campus is located in the vibrant neighborhood of East Town in downtown Milwaukee. Nearby are the Bradley Center sports arena, the Midwest Airlines Center, the Marcus Center for the Performing Arts, the theater district, churches of most denominations, major hotels and office buildings, restaurants, and department stores. Famous for its friendly atmosphere, Milwaukee offers students many opportunities for educational, cultural, and professional growth as well as ample employment opportunities. The metropolitan area has more than 15,000 acres of parks and river parkways and miles of bike trails. A few blocks east of the MSOE campus is Lake Michigan, which offers year-round natural beauty. MSOE also offers classes in other locations in Wisconsin for students who wish to pursue select programs in the evening on a part-time basis.

Majors and Degrees

Four-year programs are offered that lead to Bachelor of Science degrees in business management, construction management, engineering, and specific areas of engineering (architectural, biomedical, biomolecular, computer, electrical, industrial, mechanical, and software), engineering technology—transfer programs only (electrical and mechanical), international business, management information systems, and nursing. A Bachelor of Science or Bachelor of Arts degree is offered in technical communication. A five-year, double-major option is available in a combination of business, construction management, engineering, and technical communication programs. An engineering/environmental or structural engineering dual degree (B.S./M.S. combination) also is available. An RN-to-B.S.N. program is available through the MSOE School of Nursing. Study-abroad opportunities and many double majors also exist.

Academic Programs

MSOE guarantees that the classes needed to graduate in four years will be available for full-time undergraduate students who start and stay on track and meet academic requirements.

The degree programs at MSOE combine study in degree specialty courses with basic study in sciences, communication, mathematics, and humanities in a high-technology, applications-oriented atmosphere. Students who are admitted with advanced credit to a program leading to a bachelor's degree must complete at least 50 percent of the curriculum in residence at MSOE. MSOE operates on a quarter system. Students average between 16 and 19 credits per quarter, which represent a combination of lecture and laboratory courses. Undergraduate students average 600 hours of laboratory experience.

MSOE offers students the opportunity to participate in the Air Force Reserve Officer Training Corps (AFROTC) program, the Army ROTC program, or the Navy ROTC program.

Academic Facilities

The Fred Loock Engineering Center adjoins the Allen-Bradley Hall of Science, forming a prime technical education and applied research complex. Rosenberg Hall houses the Rader School of Business faculty and technology-integrated classrooms and the U.S. Export Service Center for Milwaukee.

The Walter Schroeder Library is a popular meeting place on campus that houses more than 60,000 volumes, with collections that represent the specialized curricula of the university. The library offers Web-based access to more than 40,000 e-journals, 25,000 e-books, hundreds of specialized databases, unique collections, government agencies, and other sources of information throughout the world.

All students participate in a Technology Package program that includes a notebook computer and affiliated services. A full range of software is available on these systems and via the local area network linked by a fiber-optic ring around the campus. Most areas also have wireless capability for laptop use. State-of-the-art architectural, computer, electrical, mechanical, industrial, nursing, science, and software laboratories complement the respective areas of study.

The Applied Technology Center™ (ATC) utilizes faculty and student expertise to solve technological problems confronting business and industry. The ATC is heavily involved in the transferring of new technologies into real business practice through the Rapid Prototyping Center (MSOE is the only university in the world to possess the five leading rapid prototyping technologies), the Fluid Power Institute™, the NanoEngineering Laboratory, the Photonics and Applied Optics Center, the Construction Science and Engineering Center, and the Center for BioMolecular Modeling.

There are more laboratories than classrooms at MSOE, many with industrial sponsorship from such companies as Johnson Controls, Harley-Davidson, Rockwell Automation/Allen-Bradley, Master Lock, Snap-on, General Electric and Outboard Marine Corp. Undergraduates average an amazing 600 hours of laboratory experience.

Costs

For 2008–09, tuition was $27,300 per year plus $1140 for the Technology Package (notebook computer, software, insurance, maintenance, Internet access, and user services). The cost of room and board in the residence halls was approximately $7164 per year. Books and supplies average $400 per quarter but may be somewhat higher for the first quarter.

Financial Aid

Qualified students are assisted by a comprehensive financial aid program, including MSOE and industry-supported scholarships, student loans, and part-time employment; Federal Perkins Loan, Federal Stafford Student Loan, Federal Work-Study, Federal Pell Grant, and Federal Supplemental Educational Opportunity Grant Programs; and state-supported grant programs. Ninety-nine percent of full-time students receive financial aid. Students can also visit MSOE's Web site for a financial aid estimate.

Faculty

MSOE faculty members engage and challenge students, with individual attention and practical perspectives gained from an average of seven years of professional employment experience in their area of expertise. They are at MSOE because they love to teach—there is no "publish or perish" tenure system. There are more than 200 men and women on the MSOE faculty (full-time and part-time). Many are registered professional engineers, architects, and/or nurses. They and their colleagues in nontechnical academic areas are active in related professional societies. The student-faculty ratio is 12:1. MSOE does not use teaching assistants.

Student Government

The MSOE Student Government Association (SGA) represents clubs and fraternities as well as residence halls and commuting students. SGA appoints representatives to the Campus Security and Disciplinary Hearing committees, the Executive Educational Council, and the Alumni Association's Board of Directors.

Admission Requirements

Each applicant to MSOE is reviewed individually on the basis of potential for success as determined by academic preparation. Admission may be gained by submitting an application for admission and the appropriate transcripts. High school students are encouraged to complete math through precalculus (including algebra and geometry), chemistry, biology (nursing), physics, and four years of English. All entering freshmen are also required to provide results from the ACT or the SAT.

Transfer opportunities exist into the junior year of the Bachelor of Science in business management, electrical engineering technology, mechanical engineering technology, and technical communication programs with the appropriate associate degree or equivalent credits.

Application and Information

Classes start in September, November, March, and late May. Freshman and transfer students may enter at the beginning of any quarter; however, entry in the fall quarter is recommended. An application for admission may be obtained by contacting the address below or by visiting MSOE's Web site. Applicants are encouraged to visit MSOE and have a preadmission counseling interview. Transfer students are required to submit transcripts from all prior institutions attended. An applicant's prior course work is reviewed to determine eligibility for admission. Required course work varies depending on the desired course of study.

Admission Office
Milwaukee School of Engineering
1025 North Broadway
Milwaukee, Wisconsin 53202-3109
Phone: 414-277-6763
800-332-6763 (toll-free)
E-mail: explore@msoe.edu
Web site: http://www.msoe.edu

MSOE's undergraduate students average 600 hours of laboratory experience—just one more advantage to an MSOE education.

MORNINGSIDE COLLEGE

SIOUX CITY, IOWA

The College

The Morningside College experience cultivates a passion for lifelong learning and a dedication to ethical leadership and civic responsibility. For more than 110 years, the goal of Morningside College has been to provide students with an education of the highest quality. Morningside is rooted in a strong church-related, liberal arts tradition, and its challenge is to prepare students to be flexible in thought, open in attitude, and confident in themselves.

Founded in 1894, Morningside College is a private, four-year, coeducational, liberal arts institution affiliated with the United Methodist Church. The College seeks both students and faculty members representing diverse social, cultural, ethnic, racial, and national backgrounds.

At the graduate level, Morningside confers a Master of Arts in Teaching, with professional educator or special education tracks.

Morningside College's approximately 1,100 full-time students are encouraged to participate in a wide variety of activities, including departmental, professional, and religious organizations; honor societies; and sororities and fraternities. A newspaper, literary magazine, and campus radio station are all student directed. These activities provide students with many opportunities to develop leadership, interpersonal, and social skills. Since nearly all activities on campus are student initiated and student directed, ample opportunities for leadership development exist. Music recitals and concerts, theater productions, and an academic and cultural arts and lecture series are held each semester. Intercollegiate athletics are available for men in baseball, basketball, cross-country, football, golf, soccer, swimming, tennis, track and field, and wrestling and for women in basketball, cross-country, golf, soccer, softball, swimming, tennis, track, and volleyball. A variety of intramural activities are available.

The Hindman-Hobbs Center includes a pool, saunas, racquetball courts, a weight room, basketball courts, a wrestling room, and a jogging track as well as classroom facilities and offices.

Location

Morningside College is located on a 68-acre campus in Sioux City, the fourth-largest city in Iowa. The campus is based in a residential section of the community, adjacent to a city park, swimming pool, and tennis courts and within 5 minutes of a major regional shopping mall and a new shopping center. The Sioux City metropolitan area offers a blend of urban shopping, commerce, and recreation in a scenic setting. Students find Morningside's Sioux City location to be advantageous in seeking internship opportunities and full- or part-time employment.

Majors and Degrees

The five undergraduate degrees conferred by Morningside College are the Bachelor of Arts, Bachelor of Science, Bachelor of Science in Nursing, Bachelor of Music, and Bachelor of Music Education. Career programs consist of accounting, advertising, art, biology, business administration, chemistry, computer science, corporate communications, elementary education, engineering physics, English, graphic arts, history, interdisciplinary studies, marketing, mass communications, mathematics, music, nursing, philosophy, photography, political science, psychology, religious studies, Spanish, special education, and theater. Students choosing to teach in secondary school may be certified in most academic majors.

In cooperation with other institutions, Morningside offers preprofessional programs in dentistry, engineering, law, medical technology, medicine, the ministry, optometry, pharmacy, physical therapy, physician assistant studies, and veterinary medicine.

Academic Programs

Morningside operates on a two-semester system; sessions are held from late August to December and from January to early May. Evening classes are offered each semester. A three-week May Term and a six-week summer session are also available.

The Morningside College experience provides an education that develops the whole person through an emphasis on critical thinking, effective communication, cultural understanding, practical wisdom, spiritual discernment, and ethical action. By working with talented faculty members in a large number of majors, caring college staff members who provide numerous opportunities for valuable cocurricular experiences, and other exceptional and interesting students with whom they will form lifelong connections, Morningside students gain the knowledge, skills, and personal dispositions that will ensure their success.

Special opportunities include a voluntary Interdepartmental Honors Program, in which students meet weekly to discuss ideas that have shaped history from the ancient world into the future. Friday Is Writing Day, offered in a weekly discussion format, allows students and faculty members to read aloud and react to one another's writing.

Every entering full-time student is provided with a notebook computer that is used in classroom work. Student technology services include high-speed Internet connection, ports in all residence halls and classrooms, Web-accessible personal e-mail accounts, a digital library accessible day and night, specialized computer labs to support academic programs, and wireless network access points across campus.

Off-Campus Programs

Morningside students who qualify have the opportunity to take advantage of special programs for off-campus study. Programs are available for a semester or the entire school year. The College has agreements with schools in England, Japan, and Northern Ireland.

Students participate in exchange programs with Kansai Gaidai University in Japan; Queen's University, the University of Ulster, Belfast Institute for Further and Higher Education, Stranmillis University College, and St. Mary's University College in Northern Ireland; and Edge Hill University and the Centre for Medieval and Renaissance Studies in England.

In addition, Morningside has opportunities for students to enroll for a semester at American University in Washington, D.C., to study the U.S. government in action. Students may also be nominated for a semester at Drew University in New Jersey to study the United Nations. Students who participate in these programs maintain their enrollment at Morningside College.

Academic Facilities

The Hickman-Johnson-Furrow Learning Center is the home of the library and the Academic Support Services Center. The library has more than 99,000 volumes, nearly 3,000 audio recordings and video materials, and nearly 440 current print periodical subscriptions. Online accessibility includes student/faculty access to more than 18,000 full-text journals. The library's Web-based, integrated online system allows seamless access to numerous subscription databases as well as other online catalogs and Web sites. The library building also houses the Spoonholder Café, classrooms, the Mass Communication Department, and a computer lab.

Charles City College Hall is listed individually on the National Register of Historic Places and houses classrooms and offices for the History and Political Science, Philosophy, Religious Studies, and Theatre Departments.

The Eugene C. Eppley Fine Arts Building is one of the finest music and art facilities in the Midwest. The auditorium seats 1,400 and is noted for its acoustical qualities and the majestic Sanford Memorial Organ. The MacCollin Classroom Building, adjoining the auditorium, houses offices, art studios, practice rooms, and classrooms for music and art students.

The Helen Levitt Art Gallery adjoins the Eppley Auditorium and is home to the Levitt art collection, which includes work by internationally famous artists.

Lewis Hall, the second-oldest building on campus, is the site of the Education, English, Modern Languages, and Nursing Departments as well as administrative offices and Student Services.

The Robert M. Lincoln Center houses the College's division of business administration and economics and contains a library, auditorium, a conference room, several classrooms, and the newly remodeled Center for Entrepreneurship Education.

The James and Sharon Walker Science Center, completely renovated in 2001, features up-to-date laboratories and classrooms and houses offices for the Natural Sciences and Mathematics Division.

Costs

Tuition and fees for 2008–09 were $21,240, and room and board were $6410. These figures do not include books and personal expenses.

Financial Aid

In 2007–08, more than $26.3 million was awarded in financial aid to Morningside students, with an average financial aid package of $21,800. The financial aid resources of federal, state, and College programs are available to Morningside students through a combination of scholarships, grants, loans, and work-study employment. Morningside values students who achieve both in and out of the classroom—people who are thinkers and doers. Morningside Celebration of Excellence Scholarships recognize academic excellence and outstanding service, and awards of up to $10,000 per year are renewable for four years. Morningside also values its ties with alumni and the United Methodist Church, and those awards are also renewable for four years.

Students are encouraged to submit the Free Application for Federal Student Aid (FAFSA) as early as possible. The College's code number is 001879. The annual priority deadline for need-based financial aid is March 1.

Faculty

Seventy-nine percent of Morningside College's 70 full-time faculty members have earned the terminal degree in their chosen field. The College also employs 80 part-time instructors and has a 17:1 student-faculty ratio.

Student Government

Student government is directly responsible for regulation, supervision, and coordination of student campus activities. The president of the student body is a voting member of the Board of Directors, allowing for student input in decisions facing the Board.

Admission Requirements

Morningside College selects students for admission whose scholastic achievement and personal abilities provide a foundation for success at the college level. While the College seeks students who rank in the upper half of their graduating class, each application is considered on an individual basis. The student's academic record, class rank, and test scores are considered. Transfer students must have earned 24 transferable semester hours of a 2.25 or better cumulative GPA on previous college work to qualify for automatic admission. It is the policy and practice of Morningside College to not discriminate against persons on the basis of age, sex, religion, creed, race, color, national or ethnic origin, sexual orientation, or physical or mental disability.

Application and Information

Rolling admission allows for flexibility; however, prospective students are encouraged to apply as early as possible before the semester in which they wish to enroll. Transfer and international students are welcome. Catalogs, application forms, and financial aid forms are available from the Office of Admissions.

For further information, students should contact:

Office of Admissions
Morningside College
1501 Morningside Avenue
Sioux City, Iowa 51106
Phone: 712-274-5111
800-831-0806 (toll-free)
E-mail: mscadm@morningside.edu
Web site: http://www.morningside.edu

Morningside College offers students one-on-one interaction with instructors.

MOUNT MARY COLLEGE

MILWAUKEE, WISCONSIN

The College

Mount Mary College, one of only 50 all-women's colleges in the nation, is home nearly 1,900 undergraduate and graduate students. Located on a beautiful 80-acre wooded campus, only 15 minutes from downtown Milwaukee, students at Mount Mary are fully engaged in and outside of the classroom, learning not just the subject matter but also how to express opinions and develop leadership skills. Through exciting internships, club activities, community service, and campus ministry programs, students explore their interests and discover their skills. Special and professional interests are served by affiliates of national societies.

Caroline Hall, the student residence hall, provides accommodations for private occupancy and single and double suites. Over 90% of the rooms feature walk in closets and over two thirds have private bathrooms. Every floor in Caroline Hall has a kitchen, lounge area and a mini–computer lab. All residence hall rooms are wired for cable, telephone, and Internet connections. Mount Mary College sponsors many social activities including performances by comedians, holiday dances and campus picnics. Mount Mary students also attend social functions at other area colleges, and those students are also invited to Mount Mary events.

Physical fitness and an interest in athletics are fostered through various activities, fitness programs, health and dance courses, and intramural and intercollegiate athletics. Mount Mary College is a provisional member of the NCAA Division III. The Blue Angels compete in basketball, cross-country, soccer, softball, tennis, and volleyball. Facilities on campus and in the Bloechl Recreation Center, which opened in 2006, include a gymnasium, an indoor swimming pool, outdoor soccer fields and a fitness center. Bordering the campus is Menomonee River Parkway, ideal for biking, jogging, cross-country skiing, and much more.

Academic and professional student services are available to all Mount Mary students, including free tutoring and assistance with tests through the Academic Resource Center, advising, resume writing, career planning through the Advising and Career Development Center, and personal counseling through the Counseling Center.

Location

Mount Mary College is located in a residential area in northwestern Milwaukee, just 15 minutes from downtown and less than 5 minutes from a major shopping mall. Students can access public transportation right in front of the campus. Several other private and public universities call Milwaukee home, making it a great environment to meet students from other colleges.

Majors and Degrees

Mount Mary offers more than sixty areas of academic study including accounting, art, art therapy, behavioral science, biology, business administration, business/professional communication, chemistry, communication, dietetics, English, English professional writing, fashion: apparel product development, fashion: merchandise management, French, graphic design, history, interior design, international studies, justice, liberal studies, mathematics, occupational therapy, philosophy, psychology/behavioral science, public relations, radiologic technology ,social work, sonography, Spanish, student designed, teacher education, and theology. Columbia College of Nursing and Mount Mary College jointly offer a Bachelor of Science in Nursing (B.S.N.) degree. Special services for undeclared students help them find and focus on a major suited to their interests and talents.

In addition to undergraduate programs, Mount Mary also offers graduate programs in art therapy, business administration (MBA), community counseling, dietetics, English professional writing, occupational therapy and education.

Academic Programs

Mount Mary's curriculum integrates leadership skills into each student's educational experience, developing leaders who take individual responsibility for social justice. The curriculum and co-curricular activities promote self-knowledge and competence, an entrepreneurial sense of vision, effective oral and written communication skills, and the ability to strengthen leadership in others. In their professions, churches, and communities, Mount Mary students model collaborative leadership, enabling them to work effectively both in leadership positions and as supportive team members.

Many academic programs at Mount Mary College offer internships, which allow students to relate theory to practice and interact with professionals while learning life skills. The process encourages students to reflect on the skills and knowledge they hope to gain and allows them to tailor their practical experience to the career goals they have set for the future. Many of the programs incorporate a work experience into the curriculum. Work experience includes student teaching, clinicals, fieldwork, practicum, and internships. Several majors also offer study abroad components allowing students to gain hands on experience in their major along with learning about another culture.

Off-Campus Programs

Mount Mary encourages its students to take advantage of a variety of study abroad opportunities. Accordingly, Mount Mary College sponsors trips to China, England, France, Guatemala, Ireland, Italy, Nicaragua, and Peru. In addition to these study-abroad programs, the College maintains affiliate relationships with numerous international colleges and universities, including the American College, Dublin, Ireland; the American Intercontinental University, London and Dubai; Nanzan College, Japan; Universidad Cathólica de Santa Maria (UCSM), Arequipa, Peru; and Notre Dame College, Kyoto, Japan. Mount Mary College is part of a consortium directed by the Wisconsin Association of Independent Colleges and Universities that enables member institutions to share study-abroad opportunities.

The Office of International Studies also aids students in finding an accredited program that meets their individual needs.

Academic Facilities

Located on 80 beautiful acres, Mount Mary offers students unlimited space to grow.

Costs

For the 2008–09 academic year, undergraduate tuition was $19,950 for full-time students and $575 per credit for part-time students. The undergraduate fee (including matriculation, student activities, library, computer lab, parking, and health services) for full-time students was $400 per year; part-time students paid $200 per year. Room and board costs averaged $7124. All costs are subject to change.

Financial Aid

The financial aid office at Mount Mary College develops a financial package on an individual basis for qualified students. All students are automatically awarded an academic scholarship upon acceptance ranging from $ 5000 to $9000 per year. Additional scholarships are available. More than 90 percent of Mount Mary's full-time students receive some form of financial assistance. Students filing for financial aid should complete the Free Application for Federal Student Aid (FAFSA) by March 1.

Faculty

Faculty members holding advanced degrees do all the teaching; no classes are taught by teaching assistants. In addition, every student is assigned a faculty advisor with whom they meet with prior to registering each semester. With a total enrollment of nearly 1,900, Mount Mary offers a low faculty-to-student ratio with an average of 25 students per class and no large lecture halls.

Student Government

Students are encouraged to participate in the governance of the College. Student Government makes recommendations about College policies and other matters of importance to students and serves as a liaison to the Mount Mary administration, faculty, and staff.

Admission Requirements

Candidates for admission are considered on the basis of academic preparation, scholarship, and evidence of the ability to do college work and benefit from it. Sixteen secondary school units are required; of these, 11 must be academic (3 in English, 2 in college-preparatory mathematics, 2 in science, 4 in history, language, or social science) and 4 in electives. Students must have achieved a minimum composite score of 18 on the ACT (870 on the SAT) and rank in the top 40 percent of their high school graduating class or have a minimum GPA of 2.5 (on a 4.0 scale). Students who do not meet the admission requirements are reviewed by an admission committee. International students must take the Test of English as a Foreign Language (TOEFL) and achieve a minimum score of 500. Mount Mary does not discriminate against any individual for reasons of race, color, religion, age, national or ethnic origin, or disability.

Application and Information

Mount Mary has a rolling admission policy. Early acceptance is available, and advanced placement and IB credits are honored. Interested students should submit an admission application, official high school transcripts, ACT or SAT scores and a $25 application fee. After notification of acceptance, students wishing to enroll need to submit the $200 nonrefundable tuition deposit.

For further information, students should contact:

The Admission Office
Mount Mary College
2900 North Menomonee River Parkway
Milwaukee, Wisconsin 53222-4597
Phone: 414-256-1219
800-321-6265 (toll-free)
Fax: 414-256-0180
E-mail: admiss@mtmary.edu
Web site: http://www.mtmary.edu

Mount Mary College is located on 80 acres in a convenient Milwaukee neighborhood. Students have a safe, secure environment in which to live and learn.

MOUNT MERCY COLLEGE

CEDAR RAPIDS, IOWA

The College

Mount Mercy College is a Catholic institution offering baccalaureate and graduate education to more than 1,500 enrolled students. Founded by the Sisters of Mercy, Mount Mercy uniquely blends liberal arts learning and professional training, with an emphasis on leadership and service. Mount Mercy works to promote in its students reflective judgment, purposeful living, strategic communication, and service to the common good. Mount Mercy's distinct student populations—traditional residential, transfer, adult-accelerated, and graduate—participate in a variety of service-learning opportunities and immersion experiences.

Mount Mercy is fully accredited by the North Central Association of Colleges and Schools. Through its Emerging Leaders and Campus Ministry programs and Office of Volunteerism, Mount Mercy supports and encourages the concept of servant leadership and service to the common good. An unwavering tradition of service is a legacy of the Sisters of Mercy, who founded the College in 1928. This spirit of service provides students with a relevant foundation for leading practical, successful, and meaningful lives.

Mount Mercy's high academic quality and strong financial aid programs make it one of the best values in Midwest higher education. Under the direction of President Christopher R. L. Blake, Ph.D., who joined Mount Mercy in July 2006, the institution has begun to offer graduate education programs in business and education, as well as continuing to provide thirty-five major areas of study for baccalaureate programs.

Mount Mercy's recent graduate offerings include a Master of Business Administration (M.B.A.) and two Master of Arts in Education programs: special education and reading. The master's programs are offered in an accelerated format, giving students the unique opportunity to complete their degrees in less than two years while also maintaining full-time employment.

Student activities span more than thirty clubs and organizations, including a student newspaper, the Green Club, an active Student Government Association, a public relations club, and multiple community service clubs. Other campus events and activities include those sponsored by the student programming board and student organizations. The Student Activities Office offers students a significant price reduction on tickets to community events such as hockey, baseball, the theater, the movies, and ice skating. The Mount Mercy Cultural Affairs Committee also sponsors a variety of cultural events for the College community and surrounding area. Each May, commencement exercises are followed by a celebration for graduates and their families on Mount Mercy's beautiful hilltop campus. During the school year, many student activities take place in Lundy Commons, the student union that houses a game room, fitness center, conference rooms, student organization offices, the *Mount Mercy Times* office, lounge areas, and the campus bookstore.

Mount Mercy College is a member of the National Association of Intercollegiate Athletics (NAIA) and the Midwest Collegiate Conference. Mount Mercy offers intercollegiate competition in men's baseball, basketball, cross-country, golf, soccer, and track and field. In women's sports, the College offers basketball, cross-country, golf, soccer, softball, track and field, and volleyball. These programs have combined for more than thirty conference championships. Mount Mercy teams and individuals regularly qualify for regional and national championship events, and Mount Mercy student-athletes are annually recognized as NAIA academic all-Americans. Athletic scholarships are also available. Some intramural activities offered are basketball, cross-country, flag football, golf, softball, and volleyball.

Mount Mercy is committed to providing its traditional residential students a total college experience. Freshman and sophomore students are required to live on campus to fully integrate, both academically and socially, to Mount Mercy. Through the Freshman Partnership Program, professors are paired with first-year students to support their transition to college life and to enhance the intellectual growth needed to ensure future personal and academic success. Mount Mercy offers a variety of living arrangements, including Andreas House, which provides homey, four-bedroom suites, and the Lower Campus Apartments, which offer upperclassmen the opportunity to live in apartments while enjoying proximity to campus. A network of tunnels connects nearly all campus buildings; many students wear shorts and flip-flops all winter.

Location

Located in the heart of Cedar Rapids, Iowa, Mount Mercy is just minutes from a variety of museums, malls, movie theaters, and restaurants. The 40-acre, tree-lined campus is tucked into a safe and friendly residential neighborhood. Mount Mercy's hilltop, with its sweeping view of the city skyline, is the highest point in Linn County, Iowa. The city bus stops at the College's "front door," providing convenient in-town transportation. Mount Mercy is a 4-hour drive from Chicago, Minneapolis, St. Paul, Omaha, Kansas City, and St. Louis.

Mount Mercy's location in a thriving Midwestern city helps students explore career opportunities close to home. Mount Mercy provides a wide range of internship opportunities for students, including hands-on work at international corporations such as General Mills, Pillsbury, Quaker Oats, Rockwell Collins, AEGON, and Archer Daniels Midland. Many internships result in full-time employment after graduation, and each year, Mount Mercy hosts a career fair that introduces upcoming graduates to local employers. More than 96 percent of students report that they are employed or in graduate school within six months of graduation from Mount Mercy. Mount Mercy alumni also serve as resources for current students and assist with networking opportunities, since 73 percent of Mount Mercy's graduates reside in Iowa. Both economically and culturally, Cedar Rapids offers an outstanding quality of life.

Majors and Degrees

Mount Mercy awards the Bachelor of Arts, Bachelor of Science, Bachelor of Business Administration, Bachelor of Applied Science, Bachelor of Applied Arts, and Bachelor of Science in Nursing degrees.

The Bachelor of Arts degree is awarded to graduates who major in applied philosophy; art; biology; outdoor conservation; communication, including journalism and public relations; criminal justice; criminal justice/business administration–interdisciplinary; English; English/business administration–interdisciplinary; English–language arts (teacher education program); history; international studies; mathematics; music; music education (teacher education program); political science; political science/business administration–interdisciplinary; psychology; psychology/business administration–interdisciplinary; religious studies; secondary education; social science–American government (teacher education program); social science–psychology (teacher education program); social work; sociology; sociology/business administration–interdisciplinary; speech/drama; and visual arts/business administration–interdisciplinary.

The Bachelor of Science degree is awarded to graduates who major in biology, biology–education (teacher education program), business, computer information systems, computer science, elementary education, health services administration, mathematics, mathematics–education (teacher education program), medical technology, and secondary education. The Bachelor of Science in Nursing degree is awarded to graduates who major in nursing.

The Bachelor of Business Administration is awarded to graduates who major in accounting, administrative management, business–general (teacher education program), human resources, marketing, and secondary education.

The Bachelor of Applied Science and Bachelor of Applied Arts degree programs are designed for students with technical training who wish to broaden their specialized background to include a liberal arts education. The Bachelor of Applied Science degree is awarded to graduates who major in accounting, administrative management, biology, business, computer information systems, computer science, health services administration, marketing, and mathematics. The Bachelor of Applied Arts degree is awarded to graduates who major in art, biology, criminal justice, history, mathematics, music, political science, psychology, religious studies, sociology, and speech/drama.

Elementary education majors may choose from a range of subject-area endorsements, such as reading, early childhood, and special education. Original endorsements, coupled with a secondary education major, may also be completed in a number of subject-area endorsements, ranging from art to speech-communication.

Academic Programs

Mount Mercy requires 123 semester hours for graduation, with a cumulative GPA of at least 2.0. General education requirements include a total of twelve courses in philosophy, religious studies, English, speech, arts, social sciences, natural sciences, history, and multicultural studies. Students apply for admission to their major program in the spring of the sophomore year. Mount Mercy gives credit for related experience based on portfolio presentations and for independent study arranged by the student and the instructor. Graduation requirements may vary according to the major field of study.

Special academic opportunities are offered to outstanding students through special honors sections of general education courses. Students graduating in the honors program receive special recognition at commencement.

Mount Mercy's academic year consists of fall and spring semesters, plus a winter term. This four-week term offers required courses as well as exploratory electives and international travel, allowing students to make more rapid progress toward their degrees or participate in overseas learning trips. In addition, two 5-week summer sessions are also held.

Off-Campus Programs

Mount Mercy College has an exchange program with the University of Palacky in Olomouc, Czech Republic, and is exploring further partnerships with international institutions.

Academic Facilities

The Busse Library provides an inviting study and research environment and access to numerous online databases. The library houses the computer center; a computer classroom for instruction in writing, accounting, and computer skills; a media center; individual study carrels; group study rooms; and a variety of other comfortable study areas.

Basile Hall is a state-of-the-art business and biology building that opened in 2003, providing thirteen technology-ready classrooms and teaching labs, four seminar rooms, and a computer teaching laboratory.

All on-campus student rooms and faculty/staff offices are connected to a campus network, and all have wireless Internet capacity. Mount Mercy also has an ICN fiber-optics classroom, making it possible for students in more than one location to take the same course, interacting with other students and the instructor.

Costs

Full-time tuition for the 2007–08 academic year was $20,070. Major fees are included in this figure. Room and board costs average $6270.

Financial Aid

All of Mount Mercy's new, full-time freshmen receive some form of financial aid, including Mount Mercy scholarships or grants, federal or state grants, loans, on-campus employment, or a combination of these sources. Mount Mercy awards a number of academic scholarships based on academic achievement, including Presidential Scholarships, Distinguished Honor Scholarships, and Honor Scholarships. Each year, students who have been admitted to Mount Mercy and identified as Presidential Scholars are invited to the campus to compete for the Holland Scholarship, a full-tuition award named for the first president of Mount Mercy. Students may also apply for the Heritage Award, which is given to entering freshman and transfer students on the basis of their demonstrated leadership in school and community activities. In addition to these scholarships, other awards are available to students with records of achievement. Transfer students also qualify for academic awards, including Presidential Scholarships, Distinguished Honor Scholarships, and Honor Scholarships. Transfer students may qualify for an additional Phi Theta Kappa Scholarship. In 2007–08, the College awarded more than $6.2 million in institutional scholarships and grants to qualified students.

Students who show financial need may be eligible for the Federal Pell Grant, Iowa Tuition Grant, Federal Stafford Student Loan, and on-campus employment. Students in work-study positions typically earn from $1000 to $2000 per year. To apply for Mount Mercy scholarships and grants, students must first be admitted to the College. Early application is advised. The priority deadline for filing the FAFSA is March 1. Students should check other deadlines with their high school counselors or call the Mount Mercy financial aid office.

Faculty

Most of Mount Mercy's faculty members hold a terminal degree in their field. Many have been recognized for their achievements, and several faculty members have been Fulbright Fellows or have received grants from the National Endowment for the Humanities and the National Endowment for the Arts. With a student-faculty ratio of 13:1, Mount Mercy offers students unique one-on-one attention and the opportunity to know their teachers and to learn from them in an informal, friendly, and supportive environment. The faculty members offer an education that is deeply personal, while also providing academically challenging courses and vibrant programs.

Student Government

The official voice of students at Mount Mercy is the Student Government Association (SGA). Its officers serve on College committees, and SGA is represented at regular faculty meetings. SGA is the body through which all other campus organizations are formed and funded, and the group unanimously supported an amendment to mandate that all campus organizations include a service component each year, reflecting Mount Mercy's commitment to community outreach.

Admission Requirements

Mount Mercy admits students whose academic preparation, abilities, interests, and personal qualities give promise of success in college. Applicants are considered on the basis of academic record, class rank, test scores, and recommendations. An Admission Committee reviews the applications of students with minimum qualifications. To apply, freshman students must submit an application for admission, a transcript of high school credits, ACT or SAT scores, and a $20 application fee. Transfer students must submit an application for admission, official transcripts from all colleges attended, official transcripts from their high school (if not possessing an associate degree), and a $20 application fee. Mount Mercy College has an agreement with several two-year colleges in Iowa through which degree graduates of these colleges may be admitted to Mount Mercy with junior standing.

Prospective students are encouraged to visit the campus, sit in on classes, and meet students and faculty. Special campus visit days are scheduled each year, and individual appointments also may be made. Overnight accommodations in residence halls can be arranged.

Application and Information

Students who wish to be considered for Mount Mercy scholarships and grants should submit their applications for admission as early as possible after their junior year in high school. Admission decisions are made on a rolling basis. Application forms are available online at http://www.mtmercy.edu and may be completed online or printed.

Office of Admissions
Mount Mercy College
1330 Elmhurst Drive, NE
Cedar Rapids, Iowa 52402
Phone: 319-368-6460
800-248-4504 (toll-free)
E-mail: admission@mtmercy.edu
Web site: http://www.mtmercy.edu

Students at Mount Mercy College.

OHIO WESLEYAN UNIVERSITY

DELAWARE, OHIO

The University

"We inspire you. You change the world." These words are Ohio Wesleyan's charge to its students, and the University provides the tools to help them achieve that goal. A unique blend of liberal arts learning and preprofessional preparation sets Ohio Wesleyan University (OWU) apart. Founded by the United Methodist Church in 1842, the University is strongly committed to education for leadership and service, to fusing theory and practice, and to confronting specific issues of long-range public importance.

A selective, residential institution, Ohio Wesleyan is home to approximately 1,850 undergraduates, with a nearly equal number of men and women. Students come to Ohio Wesleyan from forty-seven states and fifty countries; most live on the attractive 200-acre campus. Housing options include six large residence halls; several small living units (SLUs), such as the Creative Arts House, the Modern Foreign Languages House, and the Peace and Justice House; and seven fraternity houses. The five sorority houses are nonresidential.

There is a wide range of cocurricular activities. Students initiate discussion groups, service projects, and intramural athletics. Other activities include the nation's oldest independent student newspaper; cultural- and ethnic-interest groups such as the Student Union on Black Awareness (SUBA) and SANGAM and VIVA (which promote an understanding of the cultures of South Asia and Latin America, respectively); the College Republicans and College Democrats; and prelaw and premed clubs. In the course of a year, students may enjoy more than 100 concerts, plays, dance programs, films, exhibits, and speakers. The Department of Theatre and Dance stages four major productions and much additional studio work each year, while the Music Department sponsors four large performance groups and a variety of smaller ensembles. The impressive Hamilton-Williams Campus Center is the hub of cocurricular life on campus.

There are twenty-three Division III varsity athletic teams—eleven for men and eleven for women; sailing is a coed sport. In 2007–08, the University won the North Coast Athletic Conference (NACA) All-Sports Trophy for the second consecutive time and the eighth time overall, posting top-3 finishes in seven of the nine spring sports and winning championships in baseball, golf, women's lacrosse, men's outdoor track and field, and men's and women's indoor track and field. The Bishops finished in the top 5 in nineteen of the twenty-two sports in which the NCAC offers championships.

Intramural programs are extensive, and all students have access to racquet sports, swimming, and weight-lifting facilities in the Branch Rickey Physical Education Center. Fitness equipment and health services are housed in the 7,000-square-foot Health and Wellness Center, conveniently located in Stuyvesant Hall. Off-campus opportunities for backpacking, boating, camping, golf, skiing, and swimming are abundant.

Location

Delaware combines the small-town pace and maple-lined streets of the county seat (population 31,000) with easy access to the state capital, Columbus, the fifteenth-largest city in America. Thirty minutes south of the campus, Columbus provides rich internship opportunities, international research centers, fine dining and shopping, and cultural events that complement those on campus.

Majors and Degrees

With ninety-three different courses of study, Ohio Wesleyan offers the Bachelor of Arts in accounting; ancient, medieval, and Renaissance studies; astronomy; biological sciences (botany, genetics, microbiology, and zoology); chemistry; computer science; economics (including accounting, international business, and management); education (elementary and secondary licensure in seventeen areas); English literature and writing; fine arts; French; geography; geology; German; history; humanities-classics; journalism; mathematics; music (applied or history/literature); philosophy; physical education; physics; politics and government; psychology; religion; sociology/anthropology; Spanish; and theater and dance. Interdisciplinary majors include Black world studies, East Asian studies, environmental studies, international studies, Latin American studies, neuroscience, urban studies, and women's and gender studies, as well as prelaw and premedicine. Students also may design majors in topical, period, or regional studies.

Two professional degrees are awarded: the Bachelor of Fine Arts in art history, arts education, and studio art, and the Bachelor of Music in music education and performance. Combined-degree (generally 3-2) programs are offered in engineering, medical technology, optometry, and physical therapy. Ohio Wesleyan is one of only eleven colleges in the United States that has a 3-2 engineering program with the California Institute of Technology.

Academic Programs

Ohio Wesleyan provides opportunities for students to acquire not only depth in a major area but also knowledge about their cultural past through the insight provided by a broad liberal arts curriculum. At Ohio Wesleyan, education is placed in a context of values, and students are encouraged to develop the intellectual skills of effective communication, independent and logical thought, and creative problem solving. To these ends, students are required to demonstrate competence in English composition and a foreign language (often through placement testing) and to complete distributional study in the natural and social sciences, the humanities, and the arts. With few exceptions, the major requires the completion of eight to fifteen courses. Many students double major or take more than one minor in addition to their major, and self-designed majors are not uncommon. Thirty-four courses are required for graduation.

Advanced placement is available with or without credit. Under the four-year honors program, even first-year students may be named Merit Scholars and work individually with faculty mentors on research, directed readings, or original creative work. Undergraduate students frequently present their research to prestigious societies such as the American Society for Microbiology, the American Microscopy Society, and the American Ornithologists' Union and many other nationally recognized professional organizations. Upperclass students also are encouraged to participate in independent study. Phi Beta Kappa is only one of the twenty-six scholastic honorary societies with chapters on campus.

The objectives of an Ohio Wesleyan education are crystallized in the distinctive Sagan National Colloquium, a program focused annually on one issue of compelling public importance. The 2008 Colloquium is titled "Cultivating a Green Campus: Promoting sustainability and environmental understanding on the OWU campus and the Delaware community." Through speakers, seminars, and student-led initiatives, the colloquium stimulates campuswide dialogue and encourages students to discover not only what they think about the issue but also why they think as they do and how to make important decisions based on their beliefs.

Off-Campus Programs

Full-semester internships and apprenticeships, as well as programs of advanced research, are available to students. Many are approved by the Great Lakes Colleges Association, Inc. (GLCA), a highly regarded academic consortium of twelve independent institutions. Programs include the Philadelphia Center, the GLCA New York Arts Program, and the Oak Ridge Science Semester. Other cooperative arrangements include the Newberry Library Program, Wesleyan in Washington, and the Drew University United Nations Semester. Students also conduct research locally at the U.S. Department of Agriculture (USDA) Laboratories in Delaware, the nearby Columbus Zoo, The Wilds, and several other sites. The Summer Science Research Program offers selected students the opportunity for an intensive, ten-week one-to-one research experience with a faculty member. The program concludes with a symposium at which research results are presented to the entire campus.

Ohio Wesleyan has been long committed to education for a global society. The curriculum has an international perspective, and a significant portion of the student body is drawn from other countries. In fact, OWU has the highest percentage of international students among undergraduate, bachelor's-degree-granting colleges in the state of Ohio and the fourteenth-highest percentage among similar colleges in the United States. Domestic students are offered a wide variety of opportunities to study abroad. Students can arrange individual projects, but formal programs are offered in more than twenty countries. These include Ohio Wesleyan's affiliation with the University of Salamanca in Spain as well as programs in Mexico, Ireland, Central Europe, Turkey, Africa, China, England, India/Nepal, Japan, Russia, and others.

Academic Facilities

The Beeghly Library houses more than 550,000 holdings, one of the largest collections in the country for a private university of Ohio Wesleyan's size. The library's federal documents depository is among the nation's oldest and largest, providing an additional 200,000 reference publications. Beeghly Library also offers the Online Computer Library Center's most advanced cataloging system. The collection is enhanced by OhioLINK and CONSORT membership. An Internet Café within the Beeghly Library provides students with a 24-hour study area. The café has eight computer workstations and wireless capabilities and serves Starbucks coffee and other assorted sandwiches and snacks.

The comprehensive academic computing system is accessible to students 24 hours per day, and all residence hall rooms are wired for campus network and global Internet access. The latest generation of wireless communication allows students to work online anywhere on the campus.

The Conrades-Wetherell Science Center includes a 145,000-square-foot three-level building that houses a wide variety of state-of-the-art instrumentation, including a scanning electron microscope and scanning and transmission electron microscopes, all for undergraduate use. Located in the Science Center is the Hobson Science Library, which consolidates all of OWU's science holdings. The University has a state-of-the-art Geographic Information Systems Computer Laboratory.

The R.W. Corns Building houses the Woltemade Center for Economics, Business, and Entrepreneurship; the Department of Economics; the Sagan Academic Resource Center, which includes the Writing Resource Center, the Academic Skills Center, and the Quantitative Skills Center; and Information Systems.

Perkins Observatory features a 32-inch reflecting telescope and two smaller instruments, while an on-campus student observatory includes a 9.5-in refracting telescope. Two University wilderness preserves cover a total of 100 acres. Other special facilities include the multi-stage Chappelear Drama Center; Sanborn Hall, home to the Music Department, Jemison Auditorium, and the Kinnison Music Library; and the 1,100-seat Gray Chapel, which houses the largest of only six Klais concert organs in the United States.

Costs

The general fee for 2008–09 is $41,970. This amount covers tuition and fees ($33,700) and room and board ($8270). Books and personal expenses average $1100. Nominal fees are charged for some studio art courses, off-campus study, private music lessons for students who are not majoring in music, and student teaching.

Financial Aid

Nearly all first-year students who demonstrate need are awarded aid packages that include grant, loan, and employment assistance from Ohio Wesleyan and the standard federal and state programs (such as Federal Pell Grant, Federal Stafford Student Loan, Federal Perkins Loan, and Federal Work-Study). More than two thirds of the students receive some form of need-based aid, and another quarter receive merit- or non-need-based aid. More than 75 percent of all aid is provided by grants and scholarships. On the average, students on financial aid at Ohio Wesleyan receive more scholarship and grant assistance and rely less on loan support than do students at most other institutions.

Several merit scholarship programs, some worth as much as full tuition per year; private loan programs; and flexible payment plans are available without regard to financial need. This year, more than 140 enrolling first-year students received merit awards.

Faculty

The full-time faculty numbers 137, providing a student-faculty ratio of approximately 12:1. Nearly 100 percent of the full-time faculty members hold the highest degree in their fields. Although committed first to teaching and advising, most faculty members maintain active research programs and publish important articles and books. Some members of the faculty are practicing artists whose contributions include the creation and exhibition of original works of art and theater.

Student Government

Students have a significant voice in the government of campus life. The Wesleyan Council on Student Affairs formulates basic policy. Students also sit on judicial boards and nine faculty committees and are represented at all meetings of the Board of Trustees.

Admission Requirements

The admission process is competitive. Each prospective student's application is individually reviewed. Although the applicant's academic record is the most important factor, followed closely by teacher and counselor evaluations and SAT or ACT scores, many other aspects are considered, such as evidence of creativity, community service, and leadership. A sixteen-course preparatory program is required. Four units of English and 3 each of mathematics, social studies, science, and foreign language are recommended, but variations of this program are considered. SAT Subject Tests are not required but may qualify students for advanced placement. Candidates for the Bachelor of Music degree must audition (tapes are accepted). Early action, early decision, and transfer admission are offered. Campus interviews are strongly recommended but not required. For the 2008–09 school year, approximately 4,200 applications were received; about 65 percent of the applicants gained admission.

Application and Information

Students are urged to complete the application process as early as possible in the senior year of secondary school, especially if they are applying for financial aid. Once complete credentials (application, transcript, recommendations, and SAT or ACT scores) are received, decisions are made on a rolling basis after January 1. The student's response is required by May 1. The deadline for early decision application is December 1; the deadline for early action application is December 15. Notification is given within four weeks. After April 1, students are admitted on a space-available, rolling admission basis.

For further information, students should contact:

Office of Admission
Ohio Wesleyan University
Delaware, Ohio 43015
Phone: 740-368-3020
800-922-8953 (toll-free)
Fax: 740-368-3314
E-mail: owuadmit@owu.edu
Web site: http://www.owu.edu

The Hamilton-Williams Campus Center is a magnificent meeting place for the campus community.

OLIVET NAZARENE UNIVERSITY

BOURBONNAIS, ILLINOIS

The University

Olivet Nazarene University (ONU) is a private, Christian liberal arts university with a strong emphasis on both academic excellence and Christ-centered living. ONU offers one of the finest liberal arts educations in the Midwest, world-class facilities for learning and entertainment, and an atmosphere that promotes fun, relationship building, and spiritual growth.

Olivet's high retention, graduation, and employment/placement rates demonstrate the University's commitment to students' success. The members of the faculty, staff, and administration are dedicated to teaching, encouraging, and mentoring each student as a whole person—academically, socially, and spiritually.

With 4,600 students (2,600 undergraduates), Olivet offers an ideal student population for a private institution, maintaining diversity without sacrificing personalized attention. Nearly half of the student body comes from the Nazarene denomination, and the rest come from some thirty other denominations. Most U.S. states are represented, as are more than twenty countries.

The campus offers a championship-caliber athletics department (seventeen intercollegiate men's and women's sports in all) and a large intramural sports program. Music and drama groups involve hundreds of students, and many clubs are organized for a wide variety of interests. Olivet students are also heavily involved in dozens of ministry groups and volunteer efforts, small-group Bible studies, and weekly student-led services.

The University recently completed a number of campus improvements, including the renovation of the lower level of Ludwig Center, the student union, to include a glass-enclosed gaming room featuring plasma TV screens, a convenience store, and new student leadership offices. In addition, the first floor of Nesbitt Hall, a residence hall, was converted into a fourth dining option for students, and the Department of Communication moved to a new, technologically advanced facility in Benner Library, which also houses some of the University's art programs, representing a partnership between the Departments of Communication and Art. Future plans call for a new chapel/performing arts center.

The University is home to the Chicago Bears' summer training camp and Shine.fm, a 35,000-watt station ranked among the top stations in the nation and staffed by Olivet's broadcasting students.

In addition to its traditional undergraduate programs, Olivet offers six degree-completion and continuing-studies programs, nearly twenty master's degrees, and a Doctor of Education in ethical leadership. The School of Graduate and Continuing Studies strives to meet the needs of the ever-expanding number of adults returning to school. Adult degree-completion programs are designed to assist working adults so they can complete their degree requirements without an interruption to their employment. The school serves as a resource for adults striving to enhance their personal and professional lives in a constantly changing world.

In addition to the classes held on the main campus, the School of Graduate and Continuing Studies offers courses for students throughout the Chicago area. Numerous students gather with other working adults for classes in churches, schools, hospitals, and other convenient locations near their home or workplace.

Location

The main University campus is located just 50 minutes south of Chicago's Loop in the historic village of Bourbonnais. The area includes malls, restaurants, entertainment, and natural recreation centered on the Kankakee River State Park system. Olivet students enjoy many activities nearby and often make the quick trip north for the limitless offerings of Chicago and its surroundings.

In addition to recreation, students find numerous opportunities for employment and internships in the area, which is ranked as one of the top locations in the nation for small businesses and the vast professional resources of Chicago. Students, faculty members, and staff members also find themselves working side by side in local and regional ministry projects. Olivet students are recognized professionally and ministerially as a valuable commodity by area businesses, churches, and parachurch organizations.

Majors and Degrees

Olivet confers Bachelor of Arts (B.A.) and/or Bachelor of Science (B.S.) degrees in the following fields of study (includes all majors, minors, and concentrations): accounting, art, art (education), athletic coaching, athletic training, biblical languages, biblical studies, biochemistry, biology, biology (education), business administration, chemistry, chemistry (education), child development, children's ministry, Christian education, church music, communication studies, computer science, corporate communication, criminal justice, dietetics, digital media (graphics), digital media (photography), digital production, drawing/illustration, early childhood education, economics/finance, electrical engineering, elementary education, engineering, English, English (education), environmental science, exercise science, family and consumer sciences, family and consumer sciences (education), fashion merchandising, film studies, finance, French, general science, general science (education), general studies, geological sciences, Greek, health education, history, history (education), hospitality, housing and environmental design, information systems, intercultural studies, international business, journalism, literature, management, marketing, mass communication, mathematics, mathematics (education), mechanical engineering, military science, missions, music, music composition, music education, music performance, nursing, painting, philosophy, physical education/health, physical science, physical science (education), political science, practical ministries, predentistry, prelaw, premedicine, preoptometry, prepharmacy, pre–physical therapy, pre–physician's assistant studies, pre–veterinarian studies, psychology, psychology (education), public policy, radio, religion, religion and philosophy, science (education), secondary education, social science, social science (education), social work, sociology, Spanish, Spanish (education), sports management, television/video production, theater, writing, youth ministry, and zoology.

Academic Programs

Olivet seeks to offer an "Education with a Christian Purpose." The University believes that this commitment to Christ mandates nothing less than the highest-quality academic programs. Olivet's liberal arts curriculum requires that students complete 45 to 58 hours of general education courses. With the addition of major and minor programs of study, students must complete a minimum of 128 credit hours to obtain a bachelor's degree. Credit may be earned through AP and CLEP tests. Students may also participate in ROTC.

Olivet operates on a two-semester schedule, from August to May. Two summer sessions are also available.

Off-Campus Programs

Olivet students are encouraged to participate in the various off-campus study programs offered each semester. International locations include Xiamen, China; San José, Costa Rica; Cairo, Egypt; Drummoyne, Australia; Oxford, England; Nizhni Novgorod and St. Petersburg, Russia; Mukono, Uganda; Sighisoara, Transylvania (Romania); and Quito, Ecuador. Domestic opportunities include the American Studies Program in Washington, D.C.; the Los Angeles Film Studies Program in Los Angeles, California; the Focus on the Family Institute in Colorado Springs, Colorado; the Contemporary Music Center on Martha's Vineyard; and the AuSable Institute (environmental science) in northern Michigan. Costs are usually comparable to a semester at Olivet, and credit is given for these programs. In addition, some sources of financial aid are applicable.

Many Olivet students participate in numerous educational and missions-oriented short-term trips that are available during the Christmas, spring, and summer breaks.

Academic Facilities

Olivet's 250-acre campus offers leading-edge academic facilities. These include high-quality performance halls and athletic venues; excellent natural science, engineering, and nursing laboratories; smart classrooms; and an observatory. It is one of only a handful of small college campuses in the nation to have a planetarium, which was completely renovated in 2008 with the same technology used in Chicago's Adler Planetarium. Each department uses the top software in its field. More than a dozen campus computer labs are available for student use, and two network ports in each dorm room and the campuswide wireless network give students access to e-mail, the Internet, and classroom applications 24 hours a day.

Benner Library and Resource Center provides unlimited access to any material a student needs, either on-site or through the interlibrary loan system. Benner Library offers more than 170,000 books, 350,000 other items in various formats, 700 periodicals, over 15,000 full-text electronic journals, and more than 30,410 electronic books.

Costs

Tuition, based on 12 to 18 credit hours, will be $22,750 per year in 2009–10. Room and board, based on double occupancy and the fourteen-meals-per-week plan, will cost $6400 per year. Additional fees will be $840 per year.

Financial Aid

Approximately 96 percent of traditional undergraduates receive a total of $24.9 million in scholarships and grants, of which $15.5 million comes from Olivet scholarships and grants.

Olivet's cost is below average for private colleges nationwide. The University also participates in all federal and state financial aid programs. The priority deadline for filing the Free Application for Federal Student Aid (FAFSA) is March 1. To apply for aid, students must fill out the FAFSA as well as Olivet's application for financial aid. The student must be an accepted applicant before a financial aid package can be created. Olivet offers a monthly installment plan in addition to the traditional three-payment plan. Olivet believes funding a student's education is a partnership between each family, Olivet, and the state and federal governments. The friendly staff is committed to making an Olivet education affordable to every young person.

Faculty

Olivet's more than 100 full-time faculty members are the key to excellence in and out of the classroom. Teaching is a ministry for these dedicated Christian individuals, and Olivet's student-faculty ratio gives them an opportunity to teach, mentor, and encourage students on a personal level. To that end, the faculty is heavily involved in campus life, whether sponsoring social organizations or participating in talent shows.

Within the traditional liberal arts curriculum, more than 75 percent of Olivet's faculty members have earned a Ph.D. or other terminal degree in their fields.

Student Government

The Associated Student Council is the student government organization on campus. Its Executive Council consists of a president, vice president of finance, vice president of spiritual life, vice president of social affairs, vice president of women's residential life, vice president of men's residential life, vice president of office management, the *GlimmerGlass* (student newspaper) editor, and the *Aurora* (yearbook) editor. They work alongside the University's administrative team to ensure the health and promotion of campus activities and organizations.

Admission Requirements

Admission to the University is moderately difficult. Students are considered for admission on the basis of their high school GPA and ACT or SAT scores. An ACT score is required for placement in courses. For international students, TOEFL results are an additional factor in the admission decision. Students with low test scores and GPAs may be admitted on a provisional basis. A campus visit and interview are strongly recommended for all prospective students.

Application and Information

Admission is on a rolling basis until the application deadline of May 1. An early decision is required for some scholarships. Students may apply via Olivet's home page online or in print. The application process includes the written (or electronic) application, high school transcripts, ACT or SAT scores, and a health form. There is a $25 application fee, and an Enrollment Deposit is collected to prioritize both student housing and class registration.

For more information or to arrange a campus visit, students should contact:

Office of Admissions
Olivet Nazarene University
One University Avenue
Bourbonnais, Illinois 60914
Phone: 800-648-1463 (toll-free)
E-mail: admissions@olivet.edu
Web site: http://www.olivet.edu

Students on the campus of Olivet Nazarene University.

ROBERT MORRIS COLLEGE

CHICAGO, BENSENVILLE, DUPAGE, ORLAND PARK, LAKE COUNTY, PEORIA, SCHAUMBURG, AND SPRINGFIELD, ILLINOIS

The College

As an accredited, private, not-for-profit institution, Robert Morris College (RMC) grants associate, bachelor's, and master's degrees to more than 3,000 students each year. Its mission is to offer professional, career-focused education in a collegiate setting to diverse communities. Associate degrees in twelve different fields of study; the Bachelor of Business Administration degree, with concentrations in accounting, health/fitness management, hospitality management, and management; the Bachelor of Applied Science degree in graphic design; the Bachelor of Applied Science degree in computer studies; the Bachelor of Professional Studies degree, with concentrations in architectural technology and law office administration; the Master of Business Administration degree, with concentrations in accounting, human resources, and management; and the Master of Information degree are awarded. RMC is accredited by the Higher Learning Commission and is a member of the North Central Association of Colleges and Schools (30 North LaSalle Street, Suite 2400, Chicago, Illinois 60602; 312-263-0456; http://www.ncahigherlearningcommission.org).

The history of Robert Morris College dates back to the founding of the Moser School, one of the outstanding independent business schools in Chicago, in 1913. Robert Morris College also has origins in Illinois at the site of the former Carthage College. Here, Robert Morris College was chartered and offered associate degrees in both liberal and vocational arts from 1965 to 1974. With the acquisition of the Moser School in 1975, RMC expanded to include business and allied health programs. The College now provides students with a choice of eight locations: Chicago, Bensenville, DuPage, Orland Park, Lake County, Peoria, Schaumburg, and Springfield, Illinois.

RMC offers programs in the School of Business Administration, the School of Nursing & Health Studies, the School of Computer Studies, the Institute of Culinary Arts, the Institute of Art & Design, and the Morris Graduate School of Management. Each of these divisions uses the most modern computer technology. Acquisition of such technology is imperative to providing real-world educational experiences that are relevant to the evolving workplace.

RMC's unique five-quarter system is designed for continuous learning. It enables students to accelerate their education, completing a bachelor's degree in less than four years and an associate degree in eighteen months. In addition, Robert Morris College is the fifth-largest private undergraduate college in Illinois, and its tuition rate is among the lowest of Illinois' private colleges and universities.

The student body of approximately 7,120 is a cross-cultural, ethnic, and racial mix representative of the communities served. Each student works with a team of program directors, instructors, and placement specialists in an effort to achieve educational and career goals. The records of the College's students and graduates are the best indicators of what a prospective student can expect. More than 90 percent of RMC students graduate from the bachelor's degree program they begin, compared to significantly lower percentages at other private and public colleges and universities.

Robert Morris College is a member of the National Association of Intercollegiate Athletics (NAIA) and the Chicagoland Collegiate Athletic Conference (CCAC), Division II. RMC athletic teams compete in top-level facilities located near each campus. The College offers men's and women's basketball, club hockey, cross-country, golf, soccer, and swimming. It also offers men's baseball and women's bowling, dance, lacrosse, softball, tennis, and volleyball.

Housing options are available within a short distance of the main campus at 320 North Michigan Street and at Automatic Lofts at 410 South Morgan Street, which provides a wealth of amenities, shopping, entertainment, and events that bring the community together in apartment-style student living.

Location

Located in the heart of Chicago's bustling cultural and financial districts, the College's main campus is minutes from all that Chicago offers, including the Chicago Board of Trade, Art Institute, Field Museum, Merchandise Mart, lakefront, sports arenas, theaters, and all forms of public transportation. The Chicago campus is readily accessible from all parts of the city and suburbs by bus lines and trains. Parking is available in the immediate vicinity. Robert Morris College is across the street from the renowned Harold Washington Public Library.

The Bensenville campus opened to better serve the residents of western Cook and DuPage Counties and to meet the demands of employers in the area. The recently expanded Orland Park campus now includes a technology center with the latest computer facilities available to industry and education. The campus is adjacent to the Orland Square Mall, approximately 30 miles southwest of Chicago. It is accessible via public transportation and I-80 and I-55, which run parallel on the south and north ends of the campus, respectively. Orland Park is becoming a corporate center of the southwest Chicago suburbs, offering students opportunity for professional growth through internships and employment.

The DuPage campus opened on the border between Naperville and Aurora and serves students as well as employers along the East-West High Tech Corridor—the heart of rapid technological development and close to a wide range of employers. The RMC Institute of Culinary Arts started at the DuPage campus and grew so significantly so quickly, the program expanded to the main campus in downtown Chicago and Orland Park.

The Springfield campus—initiated as the first step of the College's commitment to serve central Illinois—is located just east of White Oaks Mall and is accessible by bus; ample parking is also available. This campus has also expanded to a second building at the same location due to expansion of programs and increases in enrollment. The RMC presence in Illinois has further extended to a campus in Peoria, with a busy downtown location, and Waukegan, serving the northern region of Illinois. The most recent addition includes a graduate studies center in Schaumburg.

All RMC campuses provide students with access to the unlimited variety of business services and enhance the students' understanding of the world of work, the employment process, and an appreciation for the attributes of each community.

Majors and Degrees

The Bachelor of Business Administration degree at Robert Morris College offers concentrations in accounting, health/fitness management, hospitality management, and management. The Bachelor of Applied Science degree in graphic design offers a concentration in graphic arts, the Bachelor of Professional Studies degree offers concentrations in architectural technology and law office management, and the Bachelor of Applied Science degree in computer studies offers concentrations in systems integration and networking. The Associate of Applied Science degree is also awarded in accounting, business administration, CADD (architectural/mechanical), computer networking, culinary arts, fitness and exercise, graphic design, interior space planning and design, medical assisting, nursing, paralegal studies, pharmacy technology, and surgical technology.

More than twenty-six transfer agreements have been established between RMC and community colleges, allowing students who have earned associate degrees at community colleges in the state of Illinois to complete their bachelor's degrees at RMC by transferring in as a junior.

Academic Programs

The College's academic calendar consists of five quarters, each of which is ten weeks long. The program of study is designed so that students can complete their course work and enter their careers in the shortest time possible.

By concentrating on the specialized subjects related to the student's chosen career field, the College's curricula provide students with the skills and knowledge necessary to enter the job market. Each major consists of courses prescribed by the College to lead to this objective. An associate degree requires at least 92 quarter hours of credit, with a minimum of 36 hours of credit in general education in the areas of communications, humanities, math and science, and social and behavioral science. A minimum of 52 quarter hours of credit are required in career courses, and the remaining hours are electives split between general education and career courses. A bachelor's degree requires a minimum of 188 quarter hours of credit.

Robert Morris College offers students the opportunity to gain experience in their majors and improve their skills through internships and externships. Career services personnel work closely with students to secure positions related to their field of study. Internships offer many educational and professional benefits and provide students with the opportunity to earn academic credit for participating in a career-specific work experience.

Off-Campus Programs

Robert Morris College offers students the opportunity to study abroad in Vienna, Austria; London, England; Florence, Italy; Hamburg, Germany; and Madrid, Spain.

Academic Facilities

General-purpose classrooms are Internet and multimedia ready. Students have ample study, practice, and leisure space on campus. The Student Center at RMC's Chicago Campus has been recognized by *American School & University* as an outstanding design. Specialized laboratories are available for the systems integration, surgical technology, interior space planning and design, and culinary arts programs. The technology-based library has online capabilities that connect the College's various campuses. Students have access via the Internet to advanced research tools, sizable collections of reference and resource volumes, and periodical subscriptions.

Costs

Robert Morris College has one of the lowest tuition rates of any baccalaureate degree–granting private college in the state. Tuition for 2008–09 was $6000 per quarter. Book and supply costs vary by major from $400 to $600 per quarter. Housing and program fees are also applicable.

Financial Aid

Robert Morris College participates in the following federal and state financial aid programs: the Federal Pell Grant, Illinois Monetary Award (SSIG/IMA), Federal Supplemental Educational Opportunity Grant (FSEOG), Federal Stafford Student Loan, Federal Perkins Loan, Federal PLUS loan, and Federal Work-Study (FWS) Program. In addition, the College awards institutional grants on the basis of need, scholarship, residence, academic major, or a combination of these factors. All students must complete a financial planning interview with their admissions counselor, and all are urged to complete the Free Application for Federal Student Aid (FAFSA). Approximately 92 percent of the student body receives some financial assistance. In the 2007–08 academic year, the College awarded more than $17 million in institutional aid.

Faculty

The faculty members at Robert Morris College are selected on the basis of their academic credentials, career experiences in their field, and dedication to giving individual attention to every student. All faculty members possess a master's degree in their chosen field, and many possess a Ph.D. in their area of specialization. In addition to teaching courses, faculty members promote the progress of their students through the individualized academic, employment, and personal development counseling they provide.

Student Government

Robert Morris College has no formal student government. Student representatives serve on committees that make recommendations about campus issues. Student organizations and activities are available.

Admission Requirements

All graduates of accredited high schools or the equivalent (GED) are eligible for admission to the College. All candidates are encouraged to have a personal interview with an admissions representative and take a tour of the campus.

A variety of materials are considered for various applicants. Freshman applicants just graduating from high school must submit their high school record or GED score and test results from the ACT, SAT, Applied Education Skills Assessment (AESA), Advanced Placement, and SAT Subject Area tests.

Those enrolling as an adult must submit their high school record or GED score; test results from the ACT, SAT, AESA, College-Level Examination Program (CLEP), and DANTES; and evidence of a successful employment experience.

Transfer students must present a minimum of 12 transferable credit hours from an accredited institution and their academic records from any high schools and colleges previously attended.

International students must forward their official education records, the results from either the TOEFL or AESA, and an affidavit of financial support.

Homeschooled students must submit a complete transcript of all classes they have taken, curriculum documentation and its state certification, and results from any standardized exams they have taken.

Application and Information

Applications can be obtained by contacting the Admissions Office at any of the College's campuses. The completed application and the $30 nonrefundable application fee ($100 nonrefundable application fee for international students) should be sent to the Admissions Office. The College operates on a rolling admissions basis, and students can enroll during any of the five times offered during the year. For further information, prospective students should visit the Web site or contact:

Robert Morris College
Chicago–Main Campus
401 South State Street
Chicago, Illinois 60605

Phone: 800-RMC-5960 (toll-free)
Web site: http://www.robertmorris.edu

Robert Morris College
Bensenville Campus
1000 Tower Lane
Bensenville, Illinois 60106

Robert Morris College
DuPage Campus
905 Meridian Lake Drive
Aurora, Illinois 60504

Robert Morris College
Orland Park Campus
82 Orland Square
Orland Park, Illinois 60462

Robert Morris College
Lake County Campus
1507 South Waukegan Road
Waukegan, Illinois 60085

Robert Morris College
Peoria Campus
211 Fulton Street
Peoria, Illinois 61602

Morris Graduate School of Management
A Division of Robert Morris College
Schaumburg Campus
1000 East Woodfield Road
Schaumburg, Illinois 60173

Robert Morris College
Springfield Campus
3101 Montvale Drive
Springfield, Illinois 62704

SAINT MARY'S COLLEGE

NOTRE DAME, INDIANA

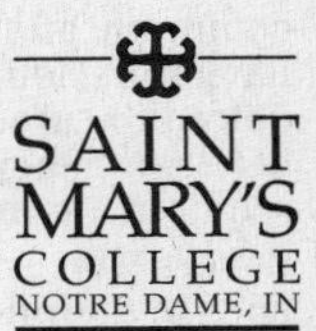

The College

One of the oldest Catholic colleges for women in the United States, Saint Mary's College was founded in 1844 and continues to be sponsored by the Sisters of the Holy Cross. The College has long been recognized as a pioneer in exploring with integrity and imagination the roles of women in society. Today, Saint Mary's enjoys a national reputation for academic excellence and vitality of campus life.

With more than 1,600 students from forty-two states and seven countries, Saint Mary's brings together women from a wide range of geographical areas, social backgrounds, and educational experiences. International and minority students compose 10 percent of the student body.

Saint Mary's College's liberal arts emphasis enhances a comprehensive curriculum. Strong programs in the humanities and sciences are complemented by professional programs in business administration, education, nursing, and social work; majors in the fine and performing arts; and courses of preprofessional study that prepare students for law school, medical school, or advanced study in other health professions.

Small classes (average class size: 16) and a low student-faculty ratio (11:1) encourage student participation in class discussions, collaboration with faculty members, and preparation for real-world challenges. The College enjoys a unique co-exchange program with the University of Notre Dame.

Approximately 80 percent of Saint Mary's students live on campus in five residence halls, each with its own distinctive character. Seniors may choose to live in Opus Hall, which offers apartment-style living on campus. Residence halls offer a full calendar of activities, from twice-yearly dances to discussions with professors. The College has a new student center, a dining hall, and a clubhouse for extracurricular activities. All residence halls have chapels, and the Church of Loretto is on campus.

As an NCAA Division III school and a member of the Michigan Intercollegiate Athletic Association, Saint Mary's sponsors varsity teams in basketball, cross-country, golf, soccer, softball, swimming and diving, tennis, and volleyball. Club sports, cosponsored with Notre Dame, include equestrian, gymnastics, lacrosse, and figure ice skating. In addition, Saint Mary's offers many intramural sports.

The College's Angela Athletic Facility contains multipurpose courts for tennis, volleyball, and basketball; a training and fitness center; and racquetball courts. The campus has tennis courts and athletic fields for both soccer and softball.

Location

Saint Mary's 75-acre campus, set alongside the Saint Joseph River, has great natural beauty. The College is located just across the street from the University of Notre Dame, minutes north of the city of South Bend, and only 90 miles from Chicago. Students from Saint Mary's and Notre Dame form a dynamic intercollegiate community. South Bend provides sites for internships and practicums and opportunities for volunteer service. Seventy-five percent of Saint Mary's students annually contribute their time to a variety of community service efforts.

Majors and Degrees

Saint Mary's College offers programs leading to the Bachelor of Arts, Bachelor of Science, Bachelor of Fine Arts, Bachelor of Business Administration, and Bachelor of Music degrees.

For a Bachelor of Arts degree, students may choose majors in art, biology, chemistry, communication studies, economics, elementary education, English literature, English writing, French, history, humanistic studies, Italian, mathematics, music, philosophy, political science, psychology, religious studies, social work, sociology, Spanish, statistics and actuarial mathematics, and theater.

A Bachelor of Science degree may be obtained in biology (with concentrations in cellular/molecular biology, environmental biology, and general biology), chemistry, computational mathematics, mathematics, nursing, and statistics and actuarial mathematics.

The Bachelor of Music degree program, which is a member of the National Association of Schools of Music, offers concentrations in music education and music performance. For talented art students, Saint Mary's offers a Bachelor of Fine Arts degree with concentrations in several media.

The Bachelor of Business Administration degree program offers majors in accounting, business administration (with concentrations in accounting, finance, international business, management, and marketing), and management information systems.

Superior students who are candidates for either a Bachelor of Arts or a Bachelor of Science degree may design a program of study outside the traditional department structure, called a Student Designed Major.

For women interested in engineering fields, a five-year, dual-degree program offered in cooperation with the University of Notre Dame leads to a bachelor's degree from Saint Mary's College and a Bachelor of Science in Engineering degree from Notre Dame in one of seven areas.

Saint Mary's education department, accredited by the National Council for Accreditation of Teacher Education, offers certification in elementary and secondary education.

In addition, the College offers more than forty minors in a variety of fields, including American history, communicative disorders, information science, justice studies, Latin American studies, and women's studies.

Academic Programs

Graduation from Saint Mary's College requires successful completion of at least 128 semester hours of credit. Every student must also complete a comprehensive examination in her major, which may take the form of a thesis, a research or creative project, or a written or oral examination, depending on the discipline. All students must demonstrate writing proficiency by satisfactorily completing a writing-intensive "W" course, usually in the first year, and an advanced portfolio of writings in the major discipline, usually in the senior year.

Students spend approximately one third of their time in general education courses in humanities, fine arts, foreign language, natural and social sciences, theology, and philosophy. Remaining course hours are devoted to their major and electives or minors. The College assists those students interested in pursuing independent study or research and internships.

Off-Campus Programs

Through Saint Mary's international study programs, students can study with Irish students at the National University of Ireland Maynooth, just outside Dublin. They can absorb Italian art and culture on Saint Mary's campus in the center of Rome or experience Southeast Asia with the India-based program in Mumbai.

Saint Mary's students may also enroll in the Spanish language programs of the Center for Cross-Cultural Study in Seville, Spain, or in the French language and culture study in Dijon, France. A new exchange program with the Australian University of Notre

Dame based in Freemantle is also available, as is a program based in Pietermaritzburg, South Africa. A summer study program in China was recently added.

Saint Mary's students may study in Austria and other countries through a cooperative program with the University of Notre Dame.

A student majoring in political science has the opportunity to spend a semester at the American University in Washington, D.C. Saint Mary's also participates in student and faculty member exchange programs with the University of Notre Dame and members of the Northern Indiana Consortium for Education.

Academic Facilities

Students have abundant access to technology systems, software, and services. Residence halls are wired for network access, and secure wireless network access is available in many public areas on campus, including many classrooms in the new Spes Unica academic building. Computer labs for students are available in several campus buildings as well as computer "collaboratories," where students and faculty members can conduct online research in groups in classroom settings. Extensive support services are available to students and faculty and staff members for instructional, administrative, and network systems. Faculty members make significant use of information technology resources for teaching, research, and scholarship.

The modern Cushwa-Leighton Library houses an outstanding collection of more than 228,000 volumes, and it includes the Trumper Computer Center, the Instructional Technology Resource Center, the College archives, and a rare book room.

In addition to extensive biology, chemistry, and physics lab facilities, laboratories for psychology research and for foreign language study and practice are available to students. Art studios, music practice rooms, the O'Laughlin Auditorium, and Moreau's Little Theatre provide ample space for fine arts creation, practice, and performance. The new Spes Unica academic building opened in August 2008, providing students with state-of-the-art classrooms and gathering places.

The professionally staffed Early Childhood Development Center provides education and psychology majors with an unusual on-campus opportunity to work with young children. Other facilities include the Madeleva classroom building, Science Hall, Havican nursing facility, and Moreau Art Galleries.

Costs

Expenses for the 2008–09 academic year include tuition and fees, $28,212; room and board, $8675 (double occupancy); and miscellaneous expenses (books, transportation, and living costs), $2625.

Financial Aid

The College strives to make a Saint Mary's education available for every admitted student by offering eligible students financial aid packages that may include grants, scholarships, work-study, and loans. Competitive scholarships, awarded solely on academic merit, as well as grants determined by financial need are available. Last year, more than 90 percent of Saint Mary's students received more than $25 million in financial assistance, more than $13 million from the College alone.

All applicants for financial assistance must complete the College Board PROFILE and the Free Application for Federal Student Aid (FAFSA) each year that they desire assistance. Applications for assistance must be received at the processing center by March 1 to be given priority consideration. Decisions concerning financial aid are made as soon as possible after a student has been accepted and upon receipt of the College Board PROFILE form.

Faculty

Saint Mary's has 129 full-time and 76 part-time faculty members. About 96 percent of the faculty members hold earned doctorates or other terminal degrees; of these, most teach first-year students as well as upper-division students. Faculty members work with students in all phases of college life, including academic counseling. All classes are taught by faculty members, not by teaching assistants.

Student Government

Students are active at every level of campus governance and share in community decision making. There are voting representatives on the president's two highest advisory boards, the Student Affairs Council and the Academic Affairs Council. A student is also a voting member of the College Board of Trustees. Student government sponsors many extracurricular and cocurricular activities.

Admission Requirements

Applicants for admission to Saint Mary's College should be graduates of an accredited high school and have completed a four-year program of 16 or more academic units. These academic units must include 4 units of English, 3 units of college-preparatory mathematics, 2 units of the same foreign language, 2 units of social science, and 2 units of laboratory science. The remaining units should be completed in college-preparatory courses in the previously mentioned areas. An applicant's credentials should include an academic transcript showing current rank and senior-year subjects, a counselor/administrator recommendation, SAT or ACT scores (at least one test should include the writing exam), and an essay. There is no application fee for students who apply online at http://www.saintmarys.edu or by completing the Common Application.

Home-schooled students are encouraged to apply for admission and should contact the Office of Admission for specific details.

An interview with an admission officer is recommended. Saint Mary's encourages students to visit the campus. The Office of Admission can make arrangements for students who wish to attend classes or stay overnight.

Mature, well-qualified students who graduated from high school after three years and who wish to enter college immediately upon graduation may apply for early admission. Saint Mary's College also grants deferred admission upon request to candidates who are accepted in the normal application process.

Application and Information

Saint Mary's has two application and notification programs: Early Decision and modified rolling admission. Highly qualified students who have selected Saint Mary's as their first choice for admission may apply under the Early Decision program. The application deadline is November 15, and the notification date is December 15. Students who apply for modified rolling admission and whose application files are complete on or before December 1 are notified of the admission decision in mid-January. Candidates are encouraged to apply by early fall of their senior year. The priority application deadline for regular admission is February 15. Applications are accepted, however, as long as space is available.

Interested students are encouraged to contact:

Director of Admission
Saint Mary's College
Notre Dame, Indiana 46556-5001
Phone: 574-284-4587
800-551-7621 (toll-free)
Fax: 574-284-4841
E-mail: admission@saintmarys.edu
Web site: http://www.saintmarys.edu

ST. NORBERT COLLEGE

DE PERE, WISCONSIN

The College

St. Norbert College (SNC) is the only college in the world sponsored by the Norbertines, a Catholic order devoted to community, education, and serving the needs of others. Father Bernard Pennings, a Norbertine priest, founded St. Norbert College in 1898 with the mission of providing a superior education that provides academic, social, and spiritual nourishment. St. Norbert prides itself in sustaining an environment that encourages students from all religions to develop their full potential inside as well as outside the classroom.

The student body is made up of 2,100 students, hailing from twenty-eight states and thirty-one countries; more than half of the population comes from distances of more than 100 miles. Ninety percent of the students are between the ages of 18 and 22. Nearly all of the students live on or near the campus, which creates a strong sense of community and a wide range of opportunities for involvement.

About sixty student activities and organizations—academic honor societies, independent social organizations, community service organizations, academic clubs, local and national fraternities and sororities, and special-interest activities—await the St. Norbert student. Students who want to write for a newspaper, get involved in community service, work for political candidates, or gain other leadership experiences find them at St. Norbert. Students who like physical activities should know that St. Norbert maintains membership in the Midwest Conference for men and women, offers NCAA Division III teams in twenty sports, and is a member of the Northern Collegiate Hockey Association. Successful men's and women's teams have acquired fifty-five conference championships since St. Norbert joined the Midwest Conference in 1983–84. An extensive intramural program, including club teams in crew, lacrosse, and rugby, complements the activities program and helps guarantee that St. Norbert does not become a suitcase college.

An innovative Career Services Office provides four years of service to help students toward a lifetime of productive, satisfying employment. Counseling, aptitude and interest assessments, career shadowing, career exploration workshops, resume-writing workshops, on-campus recruitment interviews, and job-search strategies are among the services available. St. Norbert pioneered the Career Network, in which professionals—many of whom are alumni of the College—conduct interviews with St. Norbert students. Students learn about their chosen profession from people in the field and develop leads to future employment. Extensive on- and off-campus internships complement classroom learning and ease the transition to the professional world. The goal is to achieve near-perfect placement for St. Norbert graduates. Twenty-seven percent of a typical graduating class immediately attends graduate or professional schools; seventy-two percent of new graduates seeking employment are employed within six months following graduation.

Location

The St. Norbert campus—approximately 86 acres—is located on the banks of the Fox River in De Pere, Wisconsin, just minutes south of Green Bay, a metropolitan area of about 250,000 people and home to the world-famous Green Bay Packers football team. Wisconsin's oldest community, today De Pere is a charming blend of old and new. The community of 20,000 has recently redeveloped its business district, which is within walking distance of the campus. Motels of the major chains are within a few miles, and Door County, Wisconsin's favorite vacation spot, is less than an hour away. Greater Green Bay serves St. Norbert students as an internship laboratory. Students are found in financial, industrial, and retail organizations and as reporters and writers at newspapers and television stations within the community.

Majors and Degrees

St. Norbert offers programs leading to the Bachelor of Arts, Bachelor of Science, Bachelor of Music, and Bachelor of Business Administration degrees. The Bachelor of Arts can be earned in art; communication, media, and theater; economics; education; English; graphic communication; history; international economics; international studies; mathematics; modern foreign languages (French, German, and Spanish); music education; philosophy; political science; psychology; religious studies; and sociology. Bachelor of Science degrees are conferred in biology, chemistry, computer information systems, computer science, environmental policy, environmental science, geology, natural sciences, and physics. In addition, a Bachelor of Science in natural sciences is awarded to students bound for professional schools (dentistry, medicine, and veterinary medicine). The Bachelor of Music is awarded in applied music. The Bachelor of Business Administration degree is offered to majors in accounting, business administration, and international business and language area studies.

In 2007, St. Norbert College entered into a collaborative agreement with the Bellin College of Nursing. The St. Norbert College and Bellin College of Nursing partnership provides more choices and more opportunities for students interested in health sciences, especially those who value a liberal arts foundation and a residential environment. Nursing students live and take half of their classes on St. Norbert College's beautiful riverfront campus; have labs and clinicals in local hospitals, community health centers, and outpatient settings; and earn a Bellin College of Nursing Bachelor of Science in Nursing degree within four years. This unique arrangement brings an added advantage for nursing students seeking to make a difference.

Academic Programs

Degrees are awarded upon the successful completion of thirty-two courses (128 semester hours) that include an approved major sequence, course work in general education, and either an academic minor or electives. Academic majors can be begun as early as the first semester of the freshman year. Early selection of a major is encouraged but not required in most majors. Students are not required to officially declare a major until the end of the sophomore year. The College offers a four-year graduation guarantee in all but two academic programs.

The General Education Program spans nine areas. The goal is to educate students broadly, regardless of major. Competence in writing and quantitative skills is required of all graduates. Other areas include study of philosophy, religion, the sciences, fine arts, American heritage, international heritage, and social science areas, e.g., sociology and psychology. The academic minor option provides flexibility for students planning graduate or professional study or those who seek career-related course work prior to entering the job market. An Honors Program offers additional challenge in areas of general education to those of superior ability, and an honors degree is awarded to those who successfully complete the program.

The accounting program is accredited by the Wisconsin Accounting Examination Board. The education programs lead to certification at elementary and secondary levels. A nursery school option is included in the elementary program. Student teaching can be completed in the greater Green Bay area or in Australia, Belize, England, Kenya, New Zealand, Scotland, Ireland, the Virgin Islands, and Wales. A program leading to certification for K–12 teaching in music is also available.

Army ROTC is available at St. Norbert through a collaborative program with the University of Wisconsin–Oshkosh. Several SNC students are recipients of full Army ROTC scholarships each year.

Among the College's alumni are 11 Army generals who completed ROTC at the College—the highest total of any college (with the exception of West Point).

Off-Campus Programs

St. Norbert students, regardless of major, can spend a summer, a semester, or a year abroad. Students completing liberal arts majors are encouraged to spend at least a semester abroad. An international study component is a part of majors in French, Spanish, and German and both the international business program and the international studies major. All approved international study carries regular academic credit. St. Norbert scholarship assistance and other financial aid are available to students studying overseas. Study-abroad opportunities include a Third World science field trip; exchange programs in Australia, France, Japan, Germany, the Philippines, Spain, and Ukraine; student teaching in Europe, Africa, Australia, and Latin America; and other study sites throughout Europe, South America, and Egypt. Programs run by the International Center help students, faculty members, and others discover new and exciting ways to explore and broaden their global horizons. St. Norbert's international curriculum, taught by a faculty committed to global learning, prepares students to live in a global society. The international experience that St. Norbert considers vital to today's graduates is a key component of the College's educational mission. A Washington semester is also available through American University.

Academic Facilities

The John Minahan Science Hall houses the science programs and thirty-eight laboratories, including the Center for Adaptive Education. Austin E. Cofrin Hall houses the business administration, computer science, mathematics, and economics programs. It also contains computing resources for the campus, which include minicomputers and 350 microcomputers. The Todd Wehr Library's open concept provides easy access to the College's 274,000 books, periodicals, and manuscripts. The College's archives are located in the library. The College's art collection can be viewed throughout the campus. The F. K. Bemis International Center provides students with opportunities to prepare for careers with greater international emphasis. It is also a culture and language resource to K–12 schools and Wisconsin businesses. Campus improvements in the past six years include the $6.8-million Bush Family Art Center, which was dedicated in 2002. Funding is currently under way for a new $23-million library and an extensive renovation of athletic and science facilities. Global links via multifaceted telecommunications technology, including compressed video, two-way interactive video, and satellite downlinks, bring world news to student residence halls, classrooms, and conference and seminar rooms. Seven computer labs are available for student use at no charge.

Costs

For 2008–09, tuition and required fees for full-time students totaled $25,526. Room costs averaged $3200 per year, and the average meal plan for full-time students cost $3395 per year.

Financial Aid

Students share in more than $21 million of financial aid each year, including scholarships and grants, campus jobs, and educational loans. SNC awards $14 million of its own scholarships and grants annually. Awards are based on need and merit. No-need scholarships available for freshmen include the Trustees Distinguished Scholarship (special consideration for National Merit and National Achievement commended students, semifinalists, and winners), the Presidential Scholarship, and the John F. Kennedy Scholarship.

Wisconsin residents who show need can qualify for assistance provided by the state through the Wisconsin Tuition Grant Program, which pays up to $2700 of tuition each year. Students also utilize Federal Pell Grants and Federal Stafford Student Loans. The College participates in the Federal Supplemental Educational Opportunity Grant, Federal Perkins Loan, and Federal Work-Study programs. Each year, nearly 1,300 SNC students are employed on campus. The typical job involves about 10 hours of work per week and produces about $1600 in annual wages. A number of students are hired through the College's own $1.7-million-per-year employment program. Qualified students, regardless of financial need, fill positions.

Need-based awards are made on the basis of the Free Application for Federal Student Aid (FAFSA) and the St. Norbert College institutional application for financial aid. Freshman applicants should submit these forms by March of their senior year of high school.

Faculty

The St. Norbert faculty is composed of 170 men and women, 126 of whom are full-time. Ninety-two percent of the full-time faculty members hold the doctoral or other terminal degree in their field. The faculty-student ratio is approximately 1:14. Faculty members work closely with students in their major area of study, help students prepare for graduate school, and work with those who seek independent study and research opportunities. Faculty members also work with Career Services in its professional practice program.

Student Government

Leadership is a key component of community life at St. Norbert. As one of the few institutions to offer a leadership studies minor, St. Norbert includes cocurricular involvement in its description of a rewarding college experience. Students may take advantage of numerous opportunities, including Emerging Leaders, a program providing guidance for students interested in leadership roles on campus. The Office of Leadership, Service, and Involvement coordinates a variety of clubs and service organizations, adventure trip programming, and recreation tournaments. A student-elected Campus Ministry Council sponsors various community outreach activities, both local and in the inner-city areas of major cities. Other social action activities are offered through the Peace and Justice Center, and students with an interest in College government can contribute through such activities as serving on the student-run College Activities Board, being a student representative on College Committees, and taking a decision-making role on the Residence Hall Association.

Living and learning are linked at St. Norbert through programs in the residence halls. Some residence halls focus on community service or feature campus programs, such as the Women's Center in Sensenbrenner Hall or Freshman Seminar in Bergstrom Hall. Many halls have chapels for students to use to reflect and pray.

Admission Requirements

The student's high school record is the single most important element in the admission decision. Students who have taken an academic or college-preparatory program are considered best qualified. Nearly 80 percent of the freshman class ranked in the top two fifths of their high school senior class. The middle 50 percent of ACT composite scores range from 22 to 27. Students with superior scores and grades may enroll in the honors program.

The College seeks a diversified student body. Because St. Norbert is residential in nature, emphasis in admission decisions is placed on how a student used his or her spare time during the high school years. The College seeks students who have participated in, or are interested in participating in, a variety of athletic, social, cultural, and intellectual activities. Transfer students are encouraged to apply. The minimum acceptable GPA for transfers is 2.0 (C) on a 4.0 scale.

Application and Information

Early application for the freshman class is encouraged in order for students to benefit from the College's practice of registering students and assigning housing in the order in which they enroll. Notification of the admission decision is made on a rolling basis beginning in late September. A $350 deposit is required to confirm enrollment. For more information about St. Norbert, students should contact:

Director of Admission
St. Norbert College
100 Grant Street
De Pere, Wisconsin 54115
Phone: 920-403-3005
800-236-4878 (toll-free)
Web site: http://www.snc.edu

SIMPSON COLLEGE

INDIANOLA, IOWA

The College

Founded in 1860, Simpson College is a private liberal arts college affiliated with the United Methodist Church. Simpson combines the best of a liberal arts education with outstanding career preparation and extracurricular programs. With a student to faculty ratio of 13:1, students have the opportunity to work closely with their professors. Simpson professors are dedicated to their fields of study and equally dedicated to teaching—and it shows in the classroom. When this type of dedication and passion is combined with well-prepared and motivated students, the potential for success is virtually unlimited.

Extracurricular activities at Simpson are designed to supplement and reinforce the academic program and contribute toward a total learning experience. Activities range from an award-winning music program to nationally recognized NCAA Division III teams. Students may participate in student government, campus publications, religious life, music, theater, residence hall organizations, departmental clubs, and various other organizations. Simpson has seven Greek chapters on campus, including three national fraternities, one local fraternity, and three national sororities. Simpson competes in eighteen intercollegiate sports and has an extensive intramural program.

Outstanding facilities are continually enhanced and updated, including the state-of-the-art Carver Science Center, named after Simpson's most distinguished alumnus, George Washington Carver. The 4-4-1 academic calendar includes a May Term that provides students with unique learning opportunities in the classroom, in internship settings, or studying abroad. Simpson's beautiful 85-acre, tree-lined campus provides a setting that nurtures creativity, energy, and productivity.

Location

Simpson is located in Indianola, a residential community with a population of 14,400. Indianola is just 12 miles south of Des Moines, Iowa's capital city, with easy access to Interstates 35 and 80. The Des Moines International Airport is 20 minutes from campus. Indianola is host to nationally-known events including the Des Moines Metropolitan Opera and the National Balloon Classic. The vibrant, small-town community has many choices for entertainment and recreation including Lake Ahquabi State Park, Summerset Trail, and unique restaurants and shops within walking distance of campus on the town square. Indianola's proximity to Des Moines gives students plenty of distinct advantages. Within minutes, students are right in the heart of some of the best entertainment and employment options Iowa and the Midwest have to offer.

Majors and Degrees

Simpson College grants Bachelor of Arts and Bachelor of Music degrees. Major and career programs include accounting, applied philosophy, art, athletic training, biochemistry, biology, chemistry, communication and media studies, computer information systems, computer science, criminal justice, early childhood education, economics, education (elementary and secondary), English, environmental science, ethics, exercise science, forensic science/biochemistry, French, German, history, human resources management, international management, international relations, Latin American studies, management, marketing, mathematics, music, music education, music performance, philosophy, physical education/coaching endorsements, physics, political science, psychology, religion, social work, sociology, Spanish, sports administration, theater arts, and women's studies.

Simpson also offers preprofessional programs in dentistry, engineering, law, medicine, optometry, pharmacy, physical therapy, theology/ministry, and veterinary medicine.

Academic Programs

Simpson College operates on a 4-4-1 academic calendar. The first semester starts in late August and ends in mid-December; the second semester starts in mid-January and ends in late April. A three-week session takes place during the month of May. During this period, students have the opportunity to take one class that focuses on a single subject, to study abroad, or to participate in a field experience or internship.

The First Year Program is a broadly inclusive program of orientation, group-building, mentoring, community service, advising, and classroom work structured to help new students adapt to their first year of college. The program begins with summer registration and extends throughout the full year. College and Character, a national initiative of the John Templeton Foundation, named Simpson College one of the 60 colleges in the nation that offer students an exemplary program in the first year to develop moral character.

The academic component of the First Year Program is the Liberal Arts Seminar, a joint classroom and advising concept that is unique among first-year programs. The seminars are small in size—no more than 18 first-year students each—and all are taught by students' faculty advisers.

All students must complete the requirements of the cornerstone studies in liberal arts and competencies in foreign language, math, and writing. To earn the Bachelor of Arts degree, students may take a maximum of 42 hours in the major department, excluding May Term programs, and 84 hours in the division of the major, including May Term programs. At least 128 semester hours of course work must be accumulated with a grade point average of C (2.0) or better.

For a Bachelor of Music degree, the same requirements apply, except that 84 hours must be earned in the major, excluding May Terms, and the candidate is limited to 12 additional hours in the division of fine arts. A minimum of 132 hours of course work must be completed with a cumulative grade point average of C (2.0) or better.

Off-Campus Programs

Simpson provides many opportunities for studying abroad, whether students want to participate in a semester-long program or a three-week May Term. Simpson's semester-long, faculty-led study-abroad programs include London, England; Schorndorf, Germany; Thailand; and French Polynesia. Students also have the opportunity to study abroad in semester-long programs in, but not limited to, France, Spain, Italy, and Australia.

Additional international travel courses are offered on a regular basis during May Term, including such destinations as Africa, Central America, Great Britain, France, Greece, Ireland, New Zealand, the Galapagos Islands, Brazil, Argentina, and Scandinavia. This three-week long faculty-led course gives students the opportunity to experience a different culture while gaining a stronger global perspective. Simpson has been recognized as one of the top 100 colleges in the nation for the highest percentage of students who study abroad—43 percent of Simpson students will have traveled abroad by the time they graduate.

The Capitol Hill Internship Program (CHIP) provides students with the opportunity to spend either the fall or spring semester in Washington, D.C. Past participants have held various internships; recent experiences include interning for members of Congress, and at the Smithsonian Institution, the Republican National Committee, the Justice Department, CNN, the Australian Embassy, and FOX News. In addition, students participate in two seminars for credit.

Academic Facilities

The George Washington Carver Science Center provides state-of-the-art research facilities, computer labs, a cadaver lab, and classrooms.

Simpson has a campuswide network and high-speed Internet access as well as wireless access in many areas. There are numerous computer labs distributed across the campus where students can use standard office suite applications or specialized, discipline-specific applications.

The Henry H. and Thomas H. McNeill Hall houses classrooms for management, accounting, economics, and communication studies. In addition, the hall houses a seminar room and the Pioneer Hi-Bred International Conference Center.

The Amy Robertson Music Center houses the music department and contains the Sven and Mildred Lekberg Recital Hall, ten studios, twenty-two practice rooms, a music computer lab, and the band rehearsal room. The Salsbury Wing includes a choral rehearsal room, a classroom, and studios.

Dunn Library, a contemporary academic learning resource center, contains approximately 154,000 volumes, 450 current periodicals, 22,230 electronic journals, 2,910 DVDs and videotapes, 1,125 music CDs, and access to more than 7,480 e-books. Additional materials for research can be obtained through a national interlibrary loan network. The library also provides media equipment and services to classrooms and the campus as a whole.

The A. H. and Theo Blank Performing Arts Center accommodates Simpson's well-known programs in theater arts and opera and includes the magnificent 500-seat Pote Theatre, with both proscenium and hydraulically controlled thrust stages; a studio theater; the Barborka Gallery; technical facilities and shops; and classrooms.

Wallace Hall, named to the National Register of Historic Places in 1991, contains facilities for education, sociology, and applied social science.Mary Berry Hall, renovated during the summer of 2008, houses the psychology department including faculty offices, six new labs, a control room for observation and data processing, and an animal care space.

Costs

Tuition and fees for 2008-09 were $24,771; room charges were $3354; and board was $3634. These figures did not include books, music fees, or personal expenses.

Financial Aid

Simpson College seeks to make it financially possible for qualified students to experience the advantages of a Simpson education. Generous gifts from alumni, trustees, and friends of the College—in addition to state and federal student aid programs—make this opportunity possible. Simpson offers financial aid on both a need and non-need basis. Need is determined by filing the Free Application for Federal Student Aid.

Financial aid granted on a non-need basis includes academic scholarships (awarded on the basis of prior academic records) and talent scholarships (available in theater, music, and art). The talent scholarships are determined by audition/portfolio.

Faculty

Ninety-one percent of Simpson's 90 full-time faculty members have earned their terminal degrees. At Simpson, faculty members serve as academic advisers as well as teachers and often attend College plays, operas, and athletic events, reinforcing their sincere interest in students. The student-faculty ratio is 13:1.

Student Government

Students annually elect a president and vice president of the Student Government. In addition, students elect representatives to the Student Senate. The Student Senate appoints student members to all College committees in which students hold membership. The senate also appoints 3 students-at-large who attend plenary sessions of the Board of Trustees.

Admission Requirements

Admission to Simpson College is selective and competitive. A strong academic record is essential. Applications are acted upon by an admissions committee, which is elected by the faculty and represents the five academic divisions of the College. These faculty members consider the college-preparatory courses taken, the grades received in those courses, rank in class, and standardized test scores (ACT and/or SAT), including test subscores.

Transfer applicants are accepted on the basis of successful completion of academic work at an accredited college or university. In addition, transfer applicants are required to submit official high school transcripts and ACT/SAT results.

Application and Information

Simpson's rolling admission policy allows flexibility; however, early application is recommended. Transfer and international students are welcome. Students are strongly encouraged to visit the campus.

For additional information or to obtain application materials, students should contact:

Office of Admissions
Simpson College
701 North C Street
Indianola, Iowa 50125
Phone: 515-961-1624
800-362-2454 Ext. 1624 (toll-free)
E-mail: admiss@simpson.edu
Web site: http://www.simpson.edu

The George Washington Carver Science Center provides Simpson students with state-of-the-art labs and research facilities.

SOUTHERN ILLINOIS UNIVERSITY CARBONDALE

CARBONDALE, ILLINOIS

The University

Southern Illinois University Carbondale (SIUC), chartered in 1869, is a comprehensive state-supported institution with nationally and internationally recognized instructional, research, and service programs. SIUC is fully accredited by the North Central Association of Colleges and Schools.

SIUC offers more than 150 undergraduate majors, specializations, and minors; two associate degree programs; ninety baccalaureate degree programs; sixty master's degree programs; thirty-two doctoral programs; and professional degrees in law and medicine. SIUC is a multicampus university and includes the Carbondale campus as well as the SIUC School of Medicine at Springfield.

During the 2008 academic year, SIUC's enrollment reached 20,673, which included 15,980 undergraduate students, 4,034 graduate students, and 659 professional students. The average age of undergraduates is 24. Five and one half percent of SIUC's enrolled students are international students. Of U.S. students, 16 percent are African American, .5 percent are American Indian/Alaskan, 2 percent are Asian or Pacific Islander, and 4 percent are Hispanic.

Students who are ready to start college but not ready to commit to a specific major can enroll in SIUC's Pre-Major Program. Premajor advisers and career counselors help premajor students plan their education and careers. SIUC faculty members, staff members, and alumni help students arrange internships, cooperative education programs, and work-study programs.

All single freshmen under the age of 21 are required to live on campus unless they are living at home. SIUC University Housing offers four on-campus residential areas for single students. Each area includes a dining hall, post office, and laundry facilities. Learning Resource Centers are available on both sides of campus and offer writing centers, computer labs, and student lounges. University Housing Residence Hall Dining provides a variety of meal plans, with all-you-care-to-eat meals and late night dining. Residence Hall Dining offers a variety of menus, vegetarian and light entrees, display cooking, and a full-time dietitian to help students who have special dietary needs.

Apartment housing is available for upperclass undergraduates, graduate students, and students with families.

SIUC intercollegiate sports teams compete at the NCAA Division I level (football is Division I-FCS). Conference affiliations include the Missouri Valley Conference and the Missouri Valley Football Conference. Intercollegiate sports teams include men's and women's basketball, cross-country, diving, golf, swimming, tennis, and track and field; men's baseball and football; and women's softball and volleyball. The campus holds various playfields, several tennis courts, and a campus lake with a beach and a boat dock. SIUC's Student Recreation Center houses an Olympic-size pool; indoor tracks; handball/racquetball and squash courts; a climbing wall; weight rooms; and basketball, volleyball, and tennis courts. It also offers outdoor equipment rental, an aerobic area, walleyball, martial arts, and dance and cardio studios.

The Student Center is one of the largest student centers in the U.S. without a hotel. It contains a bookstore, several restaurants, a craft shop, a bakery, and facilities for bowling and billiards. It is headquarters for 400 active student organizations and the student government office. It holds four ballrooms and an auditorium. On-campus events throughout the year include concerts, plays, festivals, guest speakers, and musicals.

Location

Carbondale is 6 hours south of Chicago, 2 hours southeast of St. Louis, and 3 hours north of Nashville. Four large recreational lakes, the two great rivers (the Mississippi and the Ohio), and the spectacular 270,000-acre Shawnee National Forest are within minutes of the campus. The mid-South climate is ideal for year-round outdoor activities.

Carbondale is a small city of 26,000 people that supports one large enclosed mall, several mini-malls, theaters, and restaurants. Students frequent the shops and restaurants that line Illinois and Grand Avenues.

Majors and Degrees

The University offers associate in applied science degree programs at the College of Applied Sciences and Arts in aviation flight and physical therapist assistant studies.

The College of Applied Sciences and Arts offers bachelor's degree programs in architectural studies, automotive technology, aviation management, aviation technologies, dental hygiene, electronics systems technologies, fashion design and merchandising, fire service management (off campus only), health care management, information systems technologies, interior design, mortuary science and funeral service, radiologic sciences, and technical resources management.

The College of Agriculture offers bachelor's degree programs in agribusiness economics, agricultural systems, animal science, forestry, hospitality and tourism administration, human nutrition and dietetics, and plant and soil science.

The College of Business and Administration offers bachelor's degree programs in accounting, business and administration, business economics, finance, management, and marketing.

The College of Education and Human Services offers bachelor's degree programs in athletic training, communication disorders and sciences, early childhood education, elementary education, exercise science, health education, physical education teacher education, recreation, rehabilitation services, social work, special education, and workforce education and development. Teacher preparation is available in art, biological sciences, English, French, German, health education, mathematics, music, physical education, secondary education, social sciences with designations in history and social studies, Spanish, and special education.

The College of Engineering offers bachelor's degree programs in civil engineering, computer engineering, electrical engineering, engineering technology, industrial technology, mechanical engineering, and mining engineering.

The College of Liberal Arts offers bachelor's degrees in administration of justice, anthropology, art, classics, design, economics, English, foreign language and international trade, French, geography and environmental resources, German, history, linguistics, mathematics, music, paralegal studies, philosophy, political science, psychology, sociology, Spanish, speech communication, theater, and university studies.

The College of Mass Communication and Media Arts offers bachelor's degrees in cinema and photography, journalism, and radio-television.

The College of Science offers bachelor's degree programs in biological sciences, chemistry and biochemistry, computer science, environmental studies, geology, mathematics, microbiology, physics, physiology, plant biology, zoology, and preprofessional programs in dentistry, medicine, nursing, optometry, pharmacy, physical therapy, physician assistant studies, podiatry, and veterinary medicine.

In addition to many majors offered at SIUC, specializations are offered in all colleges in many areas.

Academic Programs

Each bachelor's degree candidate must earn a minimum of 120 semester hours of credit, including at least 60 at a senior-level institution and the last 30 at SIUC. Each student must maintain at least a C average in all course work at SIUC. Each student must fulfill the University core curriculum and the specific requirements of their degree programs. SIUC awards credit through qualifying extension and correspondence programs, military experience, the High School Advanced Placement Program, the College-Level Examination Program (CLEP), SIUC's proficiency examination program, and work experience.

SIUC offers honors course work and special recognition for students who demonstrate exceptional academic achievement. The Air Force and Army offer ROTC programs at SIUC. SIUC offers fall and spring semesters, and a summer term.

Off-Campus Programs

At Southern Illinois University Carbondale, distance education courses are offered in interactive, print-based and Web-based formats. Print-based (correspondence) and Web-based courses are offered by the Individualized Learning Program (ILP). Web-based courses and Two-Way Interactive Video courses are offered through the Office of Distance Education. Many of the courses offered through the ILP and other distance education courses can be taken to complete the University Studies Degree (B.A.) in the College of Liberal Arts.

Off-campus credit programs are designed to meet the educational needs of adults wishing to pursue a degree but who are unable to travel to the Carbondale campus. Faculty members who teach off-campus courses travel to distant sites to teach SIUC courses.

Contractual services are provided and include specialized educational services to groups, organizations, governmental agencies, and businesses on a cost-recovery basis. These services are provided regionally, nationally, and internationally.

All credit courses offered through these programs carry full SIUC academic credit and are taught by faculty members appointed by the academic departments of the University. Additional information can be found on the Web (http://www.dce.siu.edu/siuconnected).

Academic Facilities

In addition to the 2.5 million volumes, 3.6 million microfilms, and more than 12,500 periodicals currently available in Morris Library, students and faculty members have access to more than 27,000 full-text electronic journals. SIUC students have access to several computer learning centers that are equipped, in all, with more than 1,600 microcomputers. Additional information can be found on the Web (http://www.lib.siu.edu).

Students learn and practice in the Southern Illinois Airport, outdoor laboratories, the student-run *Daily Egyptian* newspaper, WSIU-TV, WSIU-FM, art and natural history museums, a literary magazine, McCleod Theater, Memorial Hospital, a vivarium, the plant biology greenhouses, the University Farms, and the Touch of Nature Environmental Center.

Costs

Tuition and fee charges for the 2008–09 academic year (fall and spring) for students enrolled in 15 or more semester hours were $9813 for Illinois residents and $20,275 for out-of-state residents, including international students. Room and board were $7516. All costs are subject to change. Beginning fall 2009, new freshman, transfer, and graduate students from Arkansas, Indiana, Kentucky, Missouri, and Tennessee will qualify for a reduced tuition rate equal to the Illinois in-state rate. The cost of books and school supplies varies among programs. The average cost is $900 per academic year. Some courses require that students purchase special materials.

Financial Aid

More than $208 million in financial aid was distributed to more than 79 percent of SIUC students in fiscal year 2009 through federal, state, and institutionally funded financial aid programs.

To apply for financial aid at SIUC, students should complete a Free Application for Federal Student Aid (FAFSA). Applications that are filed before April 1 receive priority consideration for campus-based aid. The FAFSA can be completed electronically at the U.S. Department of Education's Web site (http://www.fafsa.ed.gov). When completing the FAFSA, students should list Southern Illinois University Carbondale (Federal School Code 001758) as a school of choice.

SIUC has one of the largest student employment programs in the country, with approximately 5,400 students employed each year in a wide variety of job classifications. SIUC offers competitive scholarships based on talent and academic achievement.

Faculty

Faculty members are dedicated to excellence in teaching and to their advancement of knowledge in a wide variety of disciplines and professions. Many faculty members are well-known both nationally and internationally for their varied research contributions. The undergraduate student-faculty ratio is 17:1. There are 1,333 full-time and 220 part-time instructional faculty members.

Teaching assistants at SIUC are graduate students who assist faculty members in teaching. While some teach introductory undergraduate classes, others provide support to faculty members by assisting in laboratories, monitoring tests, and helping students.

Student Government

The undergraduate student government consists of a president, vice president, executive assistant, and chief of staff. Under the vice president, there are 43 senators: 1 senator per 388 students. Each student has at least 2 represehtatives: 1–6 for their residential area, and 1–6 for the college in which they are enrolled. Under the 6 commissioners are a list of committees on which a varying number of students sit to represent the student body. The student government writes and passes legislation on University policies, funding, student organizations, and other matters that affect the students and the University.

Admission Requirements

Freshman applicants whose ACT or SAT scores are at or above the 66th percentile and class rank is in the upper three quarters are admitted. Applicants can also be admitted with an ACT or SAT score at or above the 50th percentile and class rank in the upper half. Finally, applicants can be admitted with an ACT or SAT score at or above the 33rd percentile and class rank in the top quarter. Admission standards are subject to change. Freshman applicants must meet course pattern requirements: 4 years of English, 3 years of mathematics, 3 years of laboratory science, 3 years of social science, and 2 years of electives.

Transfer applicants must have an overall grade point average of at least 2.0 on a 4.0 scale, based on work attempted at all institutions and calculated by SIUC grading policies. Transfer applicants must also be eligible to continue at the last institution attended.

Some programs have higher admission requirements or require additional screening for admission. Undergraduates can apply online (http://salukinet.siu.edu/admit/).

Application and Information

Admission is granted on a rolling basis. Application priority deadlines for freshmen are: June 1 for the summer 2009 term; May 1 for the fall 2009 semester; and December 1, 2009, for the spring 2010 semester. Application priority deadlines for transfer students are: June 1 for the summer 2009 term; July 1 for the fall 2009 semester; and December 1, 2009, for the spring 2010 semester. The application fee is $30.

Undergraduate Admissions MC 4710
425 Clocktower Drive
Southern Illinois University Carbondale
Carbondale, Illinois 62901
Phone: 618-536-4405
Fax: 618-453-3250
E-mail: joinsiuc@siu.edu
Web site: http://www.siuc.edu

SIUC's Pulliam Hall.

STEPHENS COLLEGE

COLUMBIA, MISSOURI

The College

Stephens College was founded in 1833 as the nation's second-oldest women's college. Stephens is ranked nationally in *U.S. News & World Report* and has repeatedly been selected to the *Princeton Review*'s list of the best colleges in the country (listed one of the Best in the Midwest, 2009, and seventh on the list of best college theater programs in the nation).

Students from around the globe enrich Stephens with their varied talents, interests, and backgrounds. Stephens students may choose to join one of ten honorary societies on campus, including Psi Chi, Alpha Epsilon Rho, and Mortar Board, or become involved in student government. Leadership experience is emphasized in all aspects of life at Stephens.

Stephens' residence halls provide much of the focus for campus activity. The Honors House Plan offers a living/learning environment in the humanities to a select group of freshmen each year. Since it began in the 1960s as an experiment funded by the Ford Foundation, the program has served as a model for similar living/learning communities in colleges and universities across the nation.

In addition to undergraduate degrees, Stephens offers master's degrees.

Location

Stephens College is located in Columbia, Missouri. Situated halfway between Kansas City and St. Louis, Columbia is the cultural, medical, and business center of mid-Missouri. Often called "College Town, USA," Columbia is also the home of Columbia College and the University of Missouri. Stephens students have easy access to Columbia's shopping, dining, and entertainment offerings.

Majors and Degrees

Stephens College awards the Associate in Arts, Bachelor of Arts, Bachelor of Fine Arts, and Bachelor of Science. Majors include accounting; biology; creative writing; dance; digital filmmaking; education; English; entrepreneurship and business management; equestrian business management; equestrian instruction and training; fashion communication; fashion design and product development; fashion marketing and management; graphic design; human development; interior design; legal studies; liberal studies; marketing: public relations and advertising; mass media (journalism, public relations, or TV and radio); psychology; student-initiated majors; theater arts; theater management; and theatrical costume design. The B.F.A. program includes professional-level work in the fine or performing arts plus a strong component in liberal arts.

Academic Programs

The bachelor's degree is generally completed in four years. Students pursue depth of study in an academic area, breadth in liberal arts study, and elective course work with guidance from faculty advisers. Academic departments require relevant internships and often provide opportunities for research projects in field settings. Stephens has introduced many innovative educational concepts into its programs. Stephens emphasizes personalized teaching and development of the individual. Small classes are offered, and most departments offer tutorial projects and readings.

Students in the bachelor's degree programs—B.A., B.F.A., or B.S.—must complete the residency requirement of seven semesters. Students take a total of 30 hours in the liberal arts program throughout their three or four years at the College. These courses provide an interdisciplinary platform of study with a global focus in behavioral/social sciences, literature, cultural studies, history, natural science, math, and ethics. All liberal arts courses, regardless of the topics they cover, provide opportunities for students to sharpen their critical thinking and communication skills.

Degree requirements for the Bachelor of Arts include completion of at least 24 semester hours in a department. At least 15 of these hours must be at or above the 300 level. As many as 45 semester hours may be required in the major, but no more than 45 may count toward a 120-semester-hour degree program. Students also may elect to design an interdisciplinary student-initiated Bachelor of Arts major.

The Bachelor of Science degree program requires completion of 45 to 57 hours, including a minimum of 15 hours at or above the 300 level. Bachelor of Science candidates may elect additional courses in the major, but no more than 60 hours may count toward a 120-semester-hour degree program. Students also may elect to design an interdisciplinary student-initiated Bachelor of Science major.

Degree requirements for the Bachelor of Fine Arts include completion of 60 to 75 semester hours, including at least 15 hours at or above the 300 level. B.F.A. candidates may elect additional courses in their major, up to a maximum of 78 hours within a 120-semester-hour degree program. The B.F.A. degree programs in theater and in dance are completed in three years and two summers. Students also may elect to design an interdisciplinary student-initiated Bachelor of Fine Arts major.

Through the Stephens College Division of Graduate & Continuing Studies, nontraditional students have the opportunity to earn degrees through programs that build on prior and current learning. The Division of Graduate & Continuing Studies offers an online-based degree completion program with several options for concentrations; an undergraduate program in health information administration (the first accredited external degree program in medical record administration in the country); and postbachelor's certificate programs in health information administration, business, event planning, human behavioral studies, and nonprofit management.

In addition, Stephens offers a Master of Business Administration (M.B.A.); a Master of Education (M.Ed.) in counseling, with three emphasis areas; and a Master of Education in curriculum and instruction. Undergraduates in entrepreneurship and business management, creative writing, education, equestrian business management, equestrian instruction and training, fashion marketing man management, filmmaking, and marketing: public relations and advertising, psycholody, and theater management may continue immediately into a master's program through the College's "Plus One" master's program. Students earn a bachelor's degree followed by a M.B.A. or M.Ed. in as little as one additional year. Certain requirements apply.

Stephens also offers numerous partnerships with other institutions wherein students may earn a bachelor's degree from

Stephens in three years and a master's degree from another college or university after two or three additional years. Partnerships currently exist in occupational therapy, physical therapy, physician assistant studies, accounting, and law. Training in Avid and Final Cut Pro is available to film students in a cross-training agreement with the University of Missouri-Columbia.

Off-Campus Programs

Stephens sponsors summer seminars in several countries, including France, Italy, and Japan, as extensions of courses that are regularly offered at the College. Summer-study programs include drama and musical theater at Okoboji Summer Theatre in Spirit Lake, Iowa. Stephens also offers international study opportunities in Korea, India, South America, and Spain.

Many other study opportunities are available through global partnerships with other universities.

Academic Facilities

The Hugh Stephens Resources Library contains more than 135,000 volumes. The library is the central building of a quadrangle that includes the Helis Communication Center and the Patricia Barry Television Studio. The E. S. Pillsbury Science Center houses science and mathematics classrooms and laboratories. Other working laboratories include the digital film G5 Mac lab, student-run Warehouse Theatre, the Johnson Plant Laboratory, and the Audrey Webb Child Study Center, which has an enrollment of approximately 100 children in preschool through fifth grade who interact with Stephens' college students.

Costs

For 2008–09, tuition was $23,000; room and board were $8730. Costs for room and board are subject to change. Students should also plan for indirect costs such as books, supplies, and personal expenses. The enrollment deposit is $100.

Financial Aid

More than 95 percent students receive some form of assistance through scholarships, grants, loans, or employment. Stephens participates in the Federal Pell Grant, Federal Supplemental Educational Opportunity Grant, Federal Perkins Loan, Federal Stafford Student Loan, and Federal Work-Study programs. Missouri residents are encouraged to apply for aid under the Missouri Student Grant Program. The Free Application for Federal Student Aid (FAFSA) is required for financial aid consideration. Applications for financial aid should be received by March 15. Stephens also offers an early financial aid estimate service.

Faculty

Though most faculty members have come to college teaching via the recognized route of graduate study and scholarship, some have prepared for teaching through work experience, particularly those in applied and performing arts with careers as actors, dancers, musicians, and artists. The faculty is primarily a teaching faculty, and many of the instructors include students in independent scholarly research. Men and women join the Stephens faculty with a commitment to individualized education. They are actively engaged in academic advising and tutorial relationships and frequently spend many more hours working with students outside the classroom than in formal teaching situations. The student-faculty ratio is 12:1.

Student Government

Each student is a member of the Student Government Association (SGA). Working in the SGA provides women with experience in planning and administering cultural, social, and recreational activities and in dealing with academic, residential, and community concerns. SGA recently founded an environmental awareness initiative, Stephens College Going Green (SCG^2), to encourage recycling and energy conservation by the entire campus community. The association has executive and legislative powers to govern student activities and to develop and maintain group-living standards. Students also serve as voting members of established faculty committees and in advisory capacities to committees of the Board of Trustees. Stephens has been nationally recognized for the many leadership opportunities it provides students.

Admission Requirements

Applicants are considered by the Admissions Committee on an individual basis without regard to race, religion, geographic origin, or handicap. Major factors for admission consideration are the recommendations and academic record, including rank in class, subjects studied, grade point average, proficiency in English, and test scores (SAT and ACT).

Application and Information

Candidates for admission should submit the application with the $25 application fee and arrange to have transcripts and recommendations mailed to the Office of Admissions. Students who visit campus or apply online at http://www.stephens.edu/admission/apply can waive the application fee. Upon receipt of the application, any additional material is mailed to the student. Qualified students are accepted on a rolling admissions basis upon receipt of all necessary credentials.

Office of Admission
Campus Box 2121
Stephens College
Columbia, Missouri 65215
Phone: 573-876-7207
800-876-7207 (toll-free)
Fax: 573-876-7237
E-mail: apply@stephens.edu
Web site: http://www.stephens.edu

On the Stephens College campus.

TRINE UNIVERSITY

ANGOLA, INDIANA

The University

Trine University is a private, independent, coeducational institution offering associate and baccalaureate degrees in more than thirty-five programs to students in engineering, mathematics, science, computer science, business administration, teacher education, communications, and criminal justice. In 2002, Trine was elevated to a graduate-degree-granting institution and now offers five-year Bachelor of Science/Master of Engineering dual-degree programs. In fall 2006, Trine introduced an interdisciplinary major in entrepreneurship. Majors in informatics and hospitality and tourism management have since been added.

Since its founding in 1884, Trine has focused on providing an affordable, comprehensive, career-oriented, hands-on education. With a worldwide reputation for being "job-ready," Trine graduates are in demand. That is why each year more than 90 percent of Trine graduates are employed in major-related positions within six months of graduation.

Trine's current undergraduate enrollment is approximately 1,300. Over 900 of these students live on campus in one of sixteen residence halls, apartment buildings, or villas. The University's 485-acre campus includes an eighteen-hole championship golf course. In August 2007, Trine opened its new $15.5-million University Center and Center for Technology and Online Resources, which houses a new dining hall, deli, bakery, bookstore, climbing wall, sports and wellness center, movie theater, post office, radio station, and library. Three new fully furnished student apartment buildings also opened in August 2007, providing new housing options to freshmen and upperclassmen.

The University's campus offers an informal and friendly atmosphere, which complements the seriousness and determination with which Trine students pursue their academic goals. While exploring ways to pursue their goals, Trine students enjoy many opportunities to develop friendships and to build leadership and teamwork skills through their participation in athletics and a range of campus organizations.

Men's intercollegiate sports include baseball, basketball, cross-country, football, golf, lacrosse, soccer, tennis, track, and wrestling. Women's sports include basketball, cross-country, golf, lacrosse, soccer, softball, tennis, track, and volleyball. Intramural sports are also a big part of recreational life at Trine.

Student organizations that offer opportunities for participation include the student senate, honor societies, professional organizations, the campus newspaper, the FM radio station, the yearbook, the drama club, and more. In addition, there are a total of fourteen social fraternities and sororities on campus, in which approximately 20 percent of the student body participate after their freshman year.

Trine is accredited by the Higher Learning Commission and a member of the North Central Association of Colleges and Schools (Web site: http://www.ncahigherlearningcommission.org; phone: 312-263-0456). Trine's programs in chemical engineering, civil engineering, electrical engineering, and mechanical engineering are accredited by the Engineering Accreditation Commission of the Accreditation Board for Engineering and Technology, Inc. (ABET). ABET's national office is located at 111 Market Place, Suite 1050, Baltimore, Maryland, 21202-4012; phone: 410-347-7700. All teacher preparation programs are accredited by the National Council for Accreditation of Teacher Education (NCATE) and the Indiana Professional Standards Board.

In addition to its undergraduate programs, Trine offers the Master of Engineering degree with majors in civil and mechanical engineering.

Location

Trine is located in Angola, Indiana, the heart of northeast Indiana's scenic lake resort region and about halfway between the metropolitan areas of Chicago, Illinois, and Cleveland, Ohio. Just a 45-minute drive from Fort Wayne, Indiana, Trine offers the safety and ease of a small-town environment while being in proximity to some of the nation's most vital cities. Pokagon State Park provides year-round recreational opportunities for the community and is just 5 miles from Trine's campus.

Majors and Degrees

The Allen School of Engineering & Technology awards Bachelor of Science degrees in chemical, civil, computer, electrical, and mechanical engineering; computer science; and design engineering technology (CADD).

Well-qualified high school graduates may be admitted directly into a five-year mechanical or civil engineering program. Mechanical and civil engineers with the skills necessary to lead the designing of a complex system are highly sought by industry professionals; therefore, the degree is a practice-oriented degree with a heavy design emphasis, as opposed to the research emphasis of a traditional Master of Science degree. On completion of this program, both the Bachelor of Science in mechanical or civil engineering and the Master of Engineering degree are awarded.

The Ketner School of Business awards the Bachelor of Science in Business Administration degree in accounting, entrepreneurship, finance, golf management, hospitality and tourism management, management, marketing, and sport management and the Bachelor of Science degree in fitness and recreational programming. Associate degrees are awarded in accounting and business administration.

The Franks School of Education awards Bachelor of Science degrees in elementary education, health and physical education, mathematics education, science education, and social studies education.

The Jannen School of Arts and Sciences awards Bachelor of Arts degrees with majors in communication, general studies, and psychology; Bachelor of Science degrees in biology, chemistry, criminal justice, forensic science, informatics, mathematics, premedicine, and psychology; and a Bachelor of Science degree in criminal justice. Associate degrees are awarded in arts, criminal justice, and science.

Academic Programs

The graduation requirements for a bachelor's degree are a cumulative grade point average of not less than 2.0 (on a 4.0 scale) and the completion of 120 to 132 semester hours, depending upon the major.

Trine's engineering programs concentrate on providing a fundamental, application-oriented engineering education. In addition to concentrated studies in a specialized area, students are required to complete courses in communication skills, sociohumanistic studies, and analysis and design.

The University's business programs include a broad range of hands-on practical experience to acquaint the student with the practices, procedures, and problems of the contemporary business professional. Guest lecturers are frequent visitors to the campus, and field trips are considered vital to the total educational experience.

Off-Campus Programs

Co-op and internship opportunities are available. Semesters of classroom study are alternated with professional work experience, giving students the opportunity to integrate theory with practice and gain a competitive edge in the job market. The length of a co-op program depends upon the student's class status when entering the program. Work-study schedules require from three to six semesters on work assignments. During the semesters worked, students are paid directly by the employer.

Academic Facilities

Fawick Hall of Engineering reopened in 1997 after a yearlong $5-million full renovation to house the University's Departments of Chemical Engineering, Civil and Environmental Engineering, Electrical and Computer Engineering, Mechanical and Aerospace Engineering, and Technology. Because of the University's commitment to a high-quality education, Trine students use sophisticated equipment such as a scanning electron microscope in their cast metals laboratories and in projects related to industrial consulting. Each department has a computer lab with pertinent software for their students.

Named in honor of John G. Best, a distinguished alumnus and former member of the Board of Trustees, the John G. Best Hall of Science contains classrooms and science laboratories. Best Hall also houses the Fairfield Lecture Room, the Department of Mathematics, the Department of Science, the science laboratories, and the Department of Criminal Justice, Psychology and Social Sciences.

Planned renovations to the Ketner School of Business and Franks School of Education include new infrastructure and technology, including a fiber-optic network, a wireless environment, and shared multimedia access to resources for teaching (SMART) classrooms. The new T. Furth Center for Performing Arts will preserve a landmark church while providing classrooms for a new music major and an auditorium for drama and music productions.

The University has recently channeled $2 million into campus-wide technology upgrades, creating a fully wireless environment. The University Center's Center for Technology and Online Resources houses a digital classroom with thirty desktop computers, a "my office" area with another twenty computers, and a global workspace with three videoconferencing stations to facilitate learning.

There are more than 200 computers dedicated to student access in labs across the campus. Every room in the student residences is wired to the University network and the Internet, and residential common areas are fitted with wireless Internet access.

Costs

Tuition for the academic year (two semesters) in 2008–09 was $23,350. Room and board for the academic year were $6700.

Financial Aid

Financial aid may be awarded in the form of scholarships, grants, loans, or employment. Any of these aids or any combination may be necessary to supplement family and student resources to meet basic educational expenses. Trine requires the Free Application for Federal Student Aid (FAFSA) and recommends its submission by March 10.

Faculty

Trine has a full-time faculty of 75 members. Most have doctoral degrees and/or are registered professional engineers. The central mission of the faculty members is teaching. The student-faculty ratio is 15:1.

Student Government

The student senate is organized for the purpose of promoting and coordinating campus activities for students. Representatives elected from campus organizations form the senate, which sponsors social activities and campus projects and aids in formulating policies for student organizations.

Admission Requirements

Graduation from an approved high school or equivalent preparation is required for admission. Trine gives careful consideration to the caliber of the academic records. Selection is made without regard to race, religion, or gender. The University requires that applicants for admission take the ACT or SAT prior to approval for admission (writing sections are optional).

Admission requirements for engineering include 4 years of English, 1 year of chemistry, 1 year of physics, 1 year of social studies, 2 years of algebra, 1 year of geometry, and ½ year of trigonometry. All other applicants must have the following high school credits: 4 years of English, 3 years of mathematics, 3 years of science, and 3 years of social studies.

Graduates of preprofessional or college-parallel programs at approved community or junior colleges are eligible for transfer into Trine's baccalaureate programs. Qualified graduates of these programs may be granted junior standing upon transfer. In general, credit may be allowed in subjects that parallel Trine programs, provided the student earned a grade of C or better in the course.

Application and Information

Trine admits applicants on the basis of scholastic achievement and academic potential. Admission decisions are made on a rolling basis, without regard to race, religion, color, gender, sexual orientation, or age. Applicants are notified of their status within two weeks after the online application and high school record have been received. Transfer students must also submit an official copy of their college transcript(s).

Interested students and their parents are encouraged to visit the campus. Arrangements can be made by writing or calling the Office of Admission.

For additional information, students should call or write:

Office of Admission
Trine University
One University Avenue
Angola, Indiana 46703-1764
Phone: 260-665-4100
800-347-4878 (toll-free within continental U.S.)
E-mail: admit@trine.edu
Internet: http://trine.edu

TRUMAN STATE UNIVERSITY

KIRKSVILLE, MISSOURI

The University

Truman has forged a national reputation for offering an exceptionally high-quality undergraduate education at a competitive price. For the eleventh consecutive year, *U.S. News & World Report* has ranked Truman as the number one master's-level public institution in the Midwest offering bachelor's and master's degrees. In addition, Truman is ranked as the second-best public college value in the nation by Princeton Review's 2008 edition of *America's Best Value Colleges.*

A commitment to student achievement and learning is at the core of everything Truman does. This commitment is evidenced by faculty and staff members who recognize the importance of providing students with the opportunity to interact with their professors both in and out of the classroom. With class sizes averaging only 24 students and 93 percent of freshman-level academic courses being taught by instructional faculty members, students find ample opportunity to ask questions of professors as well as interact with their multitalented peers. Truman's academic environment is enhanced by a student body that achieves at remarkable levels. The 2007 freshman class had an ACT midrange of 25 to 30 and an average GPA of 3.75 on a 4.0 scale. In addition, numerous opportunities exist for students to engage in undergraduate research. Each year, approximately 1,200 students work side by side with professors on University research projects, gaining greater confidence, knowledge, and skill in their chosen disciplines. The University offers these students the opportunity to present the results of their research at the annual Student Research Conference. In addition, selected students travel to the National Undergraduate Research Symposium to present their research findings. Undergraduate research stipends are also available.

The teaching degree at Truman is the Master of Arts in Education (M.A.E.). Students wishing to pursue a teaching career first complete a bachelor's degree in an academic discipline and then apply for admission into professional study at the master's level. Through this program, certification can be achieved for early childhood education, middle school education, special education, elementary education, and secondary education.

With more than 250 University organizations available to students, encompassing service, Greek, honorary, professional, religious, social, political, and recreational influences, Truman students have tremendous opportunities to become involved while enrolled at the University. Truman's Student Activities Board provides special events such as CSI Writers, comic acts such as Demetri Martin and Jen Koper, and musical artists like Cake, Dashboard Confessional, and hellogoodbye. In addition, admission to all varsity athletic events, Truman theater productions, and Lyceum Series events is free to Truman students. Recent theater productions have included *Bat Boy: The Musical*, *See How They Run*, and *Enchanted April.*

Location

Truman is located in Kirksville, a town of approximately 17,000 nestled in the northeast corner of Missouri. The town square, located within walking distance of the Truman campus, provides a connection to Kirksville's past. A multiplex movie theater is located on the town square; local merchants operate specialized gift, book, and clothing stores; and several restaurants offer a wide selection of American and international cuisine.

The Kirksville Aquatic Center is a great place to have fun and get fit. This indoor/outdoor pool complex offers a variety of activities, classes, and programs designed to appeal to people of all ages. Inside the complex is a six-lane indoor swimming pool, perfect for swimming, relaxing, or playing a game of water-basketball. The outdoor pool is designed with a zero-depth entry, a 1-meter diving board, and four 25-yard outdoor lap lanes as well as a 20-foot water slide.

The northeast region of Missouri is also home to Thousand Hills State Park. A 3,252-acre state park and 573-acre lake for camping, hiking, biking, fishing, swimming, boating, and waterskiing is located within 10 minutes of the Truman campus.

Majors and Degrees

Undergraduate degrees offered by Truman include the Bachelor of Arts (B.A.), Bachelor of Science (B.S.), Bachelor of Music: Performance (B.M.), Bachelor of Fine Arts (B.F.A.), and Bachelor of Science in Nursing (B.S.N.). Truman offers more than forty areas of study in the following disciplines: accounting, agricultural science, athletic training, art, art history, biology, business administration, chemistry, classics, communication, communication disorders, computer science, economics, English, exercise science, French, German, health science, history, interdisciplinary studies, justice systems, linguistics, mathematics, music, music: performance, nursing, philosophy and religion, physics, political science, psychology, Romance languages, Russian, sociology/anthropology, Spanish, and theater.

Professional paths include but are not limited to dentistry, engineering, law, medicine, optometry, pharmacy, physical therapy, and veterinary medicine.

Academic Programs

Truman is Missouri's premier liberal arts and sciences university and the only highly selective public institution in the state. The Liberal Studies Program is the heart of Truman's curriculum and is intended to serve as a foundation for all major programs of study offered by the University. Truman's mission is to "offer an exemplary undergraduate education, grounded in the liberal arts and sciences, in the context of a public institution of higher learning." Therefore, Truman is providing the kind of education in the liberal arts and sciences that has historically been offered only at private colleges. The program is a blend of two intellectual traditions in higher education, one that emphasizes the traditional thought and learning of the culture, as reflected in the classical works produced by it, and the other that emphasizes personal investigation and freedom of discovery. The philosophy behind the Liberal Studies Program is based upon a commitment that Truman has made to provide students with essential skills needed for lifelong learning, breadth across the traditional liberal arts and sciences through exposure to various discipline-based modes of inquiry, and interconnecting perspectives that stress interdisciplinary thinking and integration as well as linkage to other cultures and experiences. All students graduating from Truman must complete 63 or more credit hours in liberal arts and sciences courses.

Truman's Residential College Program brings the University learning community inside the student residence halls. Historically, residential colleges have been places where faculty members and students join together as "friends of learning." At Truman, this living/learning tradition is honored as one means of furthering its specific goals as a public liberal arts university. The Residential College Program seeks to make liberal arts education personally vital and engaging to the whole person.

Truman also offers an especially challenging General Honors Program. This program provides students with the opportunity to select the most rigorous honors courses to satisfy the liberal arts component of their respective programs. Students who successfully complete this program not only benefit from an even richer academic experience at Truman but also receive special recognition at graduation. Departmental honors are also available in several disciplines.

Off-Campus Programs

Each year, approximately 500 Truman students participate in enriching and life-changing study-abroad experiences. Truman's own study-abroad programs, combined with programs offered through Truman's membership in the College Consortium for International Studies, International Student Exchange Program, Australearn, and the Council on International Educational Exchange, provide students with study-abroad opportunities in more than forty countries worldwide, including Australia, China, England, Finland, France, Italy, Russia, Spain, and Thailand.

In addition, there are two cooperative programs affiliated with biology. Truman is affiliated with the Gulf Coast Research Laboratory at Ocean Springs, Mississippi. Marine biology courses may be taken at the laboratory during the summer, with credit awarded at Truman. In-depth study of the Ozark habitats is also available through Truman's affiliation with Reis Biological Station located near Steelville, Missouri.

In cooperation with the Washington Center for Internships and Academic Seminars, Truman offers a wide variety of experiential internships in Washington, D.C. Included are work-experience opportunities in such areas as public administration, the fine and performing arts, foreign affairs/diplomacy, government affairs, criminal justice, international relations, health and human services, environmental policy, business administration, and communications as well as other areas. Placement sites include nonprofit groups, media organizations, the State Department, Congress, museums, and much more.

Truman requires internships in education, health science, and exercise science and annually offers internship opportunities with the Missouri State Legislature. In recent years, students have completed internships with United States senators, the governor of Missouri, business and industry managers, zoos, broadcast and print media professionals, accountants, advertising agencies, physical therapists, musicians, artists, and the United States Supreme Court.

Academic Facilities

The Truman campus is beautifully situated on an expanse of 140 acres near downtown Kirksville. Featured among the forty facilities on campus is Pickler Memorial Library. This 460,116-volume facility provides a state-of-the-art library resource for students and faculty members alike. Materials not available in Pickler Memorial Library can be obtained through the Interlibrary Loan Office and MOBIUS.

Recent improvements to campus facilities include the $20-million renovation and expansion of Truman's science facility, Magruder Hall, which was completed for the spring 2006 semester and included new research labs, a greenhouse, classrooms, meeting areas, and a cyber café. The brand-new West Campus Suites opened to students in fall 2006. Each suite is equipped with a living room, two bedrooms housing 2 students each, closet space, a large bathroom, and central air conditioning. Renovations have been completed on Missouri Hall. Improvements included a 2,500-square-foot addition, laundry facilities on every floor, and individually controlled heating and cooling in each room. Renovations have begun on Blanton/Nason/Brewer and are expected to be completed for the fall 2008 semester. The renovations of the Student Union Building are also expected to be completed for the fall 2008 semester.

Additional facilities include a student media center with a TV studio, a radio station, print media production facilities, a speech-and-hearing clinic for students in communication disorders, a biofeedback laboratory, an organic chemistry lab, an analytical chemistry lab, an independent learning center for nursing students, an observatory, a greenhouse, a 5,000-seat football stadium, a soccer field, tennis and racquetball courts, softball and baseball diamonds, a 3,000-seat arena with three basketball courts, an Olympic-size swimming pool, a multicultural affairs center, a writing center, and a career center.

Costs

Tuition for Missouri residents for the 2008–09 academic year is $6458; out-of-state tuition is $11,309. Room and board totals for both Missouri residents and nonresidents start at $6290. Additional fees include a $305 freshman orientation fee, an annual $71 activities fee, a $4 student government fee, a $52 Student Health Center fee, an annual $100 athletic fee, a $50 parking fee for those with a vehicle, and the costs of books and personal expenses.

Financial Aid

Truman offers automatic scholarships ranging from $1000 to $2000. Competitive scholarship awards vary from $500 up to full tuition, room, and board plus a $4000 study-abroad stipend. The application for admission also serves as the application for the automatic and competitive scholarship programs.

Several scholarships are awarded to students for excellence in music, theater, or art. These scholarships are available for instrumental, strings, or vocal music; acting or dramatic production; and studio art or art history. Of special interest to piano students is the Truman Piano Fellowship Competition.

The National Collegiate Athletic Association and the University authorize a limited number of grants to outstanding athletes. The value of this aid may vary with each individual recipient.

Truman accepts the Free Application for Federal Student Aid (FAFSA) and participates in all Federal Title IV financial aid programs. Financial aid estimates are available upon request.

Faculty

Truman State University is committed to teaching the academically talented undergraduate student. The University has 344 full-time faculty members and 27 part-time faculty members. Of these, 98 percent teach undergraduates and 80 percent hold a doctoral degree or the highest terminal degree in their discipline. Most major graduate institutions are represented among the Truman faculty, including Harvard, Princeton, Yale, Berkeley, Oxford, and the Sorbonne. The student-faculty ratio at Truman is 16:1.

Student Government

Student Senate is the official elected governing body of the Student Association, representing approximately 5,800 students. Its mission is to represent the views of the Student Association in the formulation of the University policy through legislation and membership on all University committees; to facilitate communication and mutual understanding among the Student Association, faculty and staff members, and administration; to maintain a cohesive vision for the future of the University; and to actively participate in the fulfillment of the University's mission as an exemplary public liberal arts and sciences university.

Admission Requirements

Admission to Truman is competitive. Each applicant is evaluated for admission based upon academic and cocurricular record, ACT or SAT results, and the admission essay. Truman requires the following high school core: 4 units of English, 3 units of mathematics (4 recommended), 3 units of social studies/history, 3 units of natural science, 1 unit of fine arts, and 2 units of the same foreign language.

Application and Information

The priority deadline for admission is December 15. Students who have applied by this date are considered for all applicable competitive scholarships. Applications are processed on a rolling basis. There is no application fee. Students may apply online at the University's Web site. For further information or to schedule a campus visit, students should contact:

Admission Office
205 McClain Hall
Truman State University
100 East Normal
Kirksville, Missouri 63501
Phone: 660-785-4114
800-892-7792 (toll-free, Missouri only)
Fax: 660-785-7456
E-mail: admissions@truman.edu
Web site: http://admissions.truman.edu

THE UNIVERSITY OF FINDLAY

FINDLAY, OHIO

The University

The University of Findlay (UF) is a private coeducational institution with more than 4,400 full- and part-time students. Founded in 1882 by the Churches of God, General Conference, and the citizens of Findlay, it emphasizes preparation for careers and professions in an educational program that blends liberal arts and career education. Students of many denominations attend Findlay, and religious participation is a matter of personal choice.

Bachelor's degree programs are available in more than sixty different majors. Master's degrees are offered in athletic training; business administration; education; environmental, safety, and health management; liberal studies; occupational therapy; physical therapy; and teaching English to speakers of other languages (TESOL) and bilingual education. A Doctor of Pharmacy (Pharm.D.) degree program is expected to graduate its first class in 2010, and a Doctor of Physical Therapy program will graduate its first students in 2011.

The largest programs at Findlay are business, education, equestrian studies, pharmacy, and pre-veterinary medicine. Majors in the sciences and health professions include athletic training, chemistry, computer science, equestrian studies (English, Western, and equine management), nuclear medicine, occupational therapy, physical therapy, premedicine, and pre–veterinary medicine. Business degrees are founded in a comprehensive core program with eleven different majors.

Opportunities for internships and work-related experiences are available in most major fields.

Most of Findlay's students come from Ohio and the surrounding states of Michigan, Indiana, and Pennsylvania. More than thirty other states are also represented. UF also has a strong international-student population, with nearly 700 international students from thirty countries and territories.

Resident students live in eight modern residence halls and several town-house-style apartments. Social life at Findlay centers on student organizations, fraternities, and sororities. Findlay has three officially recognized fraternities: Alpha Sigma Phi, Tau Kappa Epsilon, and Theta Chi; there are two sororities: Phi Sigma Sigma and Sigma Kappa. Organizations include department and special interest clubs, the newspaper, musical groups, a radio and TV station, Circle K, and Aristos Eklektos (honors).

Athletic programs are affiliated with NCAA Division II and the Great Lakes Intercollegiate Athletic Conference, with the exception of the equestrian teams, which have won national championships in the Intercollegiate Horse Show Association. Findlay offers twelve intercollegiate sports for men: baseball, basketball, cross-country, equestrian, football, golf, indoor track and field, outdoor track and field, soccer, swimming and diving, tennis, and wrestling. It has eleven varsity sports for women: basketball, cross-country, equestrian, golf, indoor track and field, outdoor track and field, soccer, softball, swimming and diving, tennis, and volleyball. Athletic scholarships are available.

Croy Physical Education Center has a 25-meter swimming pool, exercise areas, a gymnasium, offices, and classrooms. The Gardner Fitness Center is a state-of-the-art facility. The 130,000-square-foot Koehler Recreation and Fitness Complex, opened in 1999, contains the Malcolm Athletic Center, with a six-lane, NCAA-regulation track and four multipurpose courts; the Clauss Ice Arena; locker rooms; a cardio center; and offices for the athletic department.

Student services include career and placement counseling, the Cosiano Health Center, academic tutoring and personal counseling, and study skills assistance through the Academic Support Center.

Location

Findlay was voted the most livable micropolitan city in Ohio and scored among the top twelve in the United States. It is within easy driving distance of Toledo, Columbus, Detroit, and Fort Wayne. Interstate 75 and the Ohio Turnpike (Interstates 80 and 90) are major highways serving the area. Airports in Toledo, Columbus, and Detroit are convenient. The town of Findlay has more than 37,000 residents and is home to Marathon Oil Corporation and Cooper Tire and Rubber Company. The Findlay campus consists of more than 200 acres on several sites. A 72-acre campus-owned farm houses the pre–veterinary medicine and Western equestrian studies programs. A second 32-acre facility houses the English riding program. Many opportunities exist for students who want business-related and social service agency experience. The University has established strong relationships with the community, which supports athletic and cultural events on the campus. Besides the full program of on-campus activities, off-campus trips to cultural and entertainment events are scheduled. The city of Findlay, which has an excellent business climate, offers part-time job opportunities, volunteer service organizations, and the chance to be involved with the larger civic community. Findlay's campus is attractive, safe, comfortable, and friendly.

Majors and Degrees

The Bachelor of Arts (B.A.) degree is awarded in the following majors: adolescent/young adult/integrated English/language arts, adolescent/young adult/integrated social studies, art, children's book illustration, criminal justice administration, digital media, English, English as an international language, graphic communication, health communication, history, interpersonal communication, Japanese, journalism, law and the liberal arts, middle childhood/language arts and social studies, multiage/drama/theater, multiage/Japanese, multiage/Spanish, multiage/visual arts, philosophy/applied philosophy, political science, psychology, public relations, religious studies, social work, sociology, Spanish, studio art, teaching English to speakers of other languages, and theater. Minors are offered in numerous areas.

The Bachelor of Science (B.S.) degree is granted in accounting; adolescent/young adult/earth science; adolescent/young adult/integrated mathematics; adolescent/young adult/life science; animal science; biology; business administration; business management; chemistry; computer science; early childhood; economics; entrepreneurship; environmental, safety, and occupational health management; equestrian studies (English and Western emphases); equine business management; finance; forensic science; health education; health studies; hospitality management; human resource management; international business; intervention specialist/mild to moderate disabilities; marketing; mathematics; medical technology; middle childhood/language arts/math; middle childhood/language arts/science; middle childhood/math/science; middle childhood/math/social studies; middle childhood/science/social studies; multiage/health education; multiage/physical education; nuclear medicine technology; occupational therapy; operations and logistics; physical education; physician assistant; physical therapy; recreation therapy; and strength and conditioning.

The Associate of Arts degree is available in accounting, computer science, criminal justice administration (corrections or law enforcement emphases), English as an international language, equestrian studies (English and Western riding), financial management, general social studies, human resource management, humanities, management information systems, massage therapy, nuclear medicine technology, personal training, religious studies, sales/retail management, and small business/entrepreneurship. Certificate programs are available in a variety of areas.

Academic Programs

Findlay operates on the semester system. Students must complete at least 124 semester hours with a minimum overall grade point average of 2.0 to earn a bachelor's degree. General education requirements and competency requirements in English, computer literacy, and speech must be fulfilled. The Oiler Experience is intended to introduce all freshmen to college life at UF. The course is designed and taught by a cadre of student services professionals whose educational backgrounds and specialized training are focused on assisting students to succeed, both in and out of the classroom. The Foundations Program offers students the chance to develop those skills in writing, reading, and thinking needed for their success as college students. Study skills, time management, and academic advising are included. Students are selected for this program at the time of admission. The Honors Program provides additional challenge to those students who qualify on the basis of academic credentials. Study- and travel-abroad programs are offered by various departments. Credit and/or placement can be earned through Advanced Placement (AP) exams.

The Equestrian Program is a well-recognized program of its kind and serves approximately 280 students from throughout the United States and abroad. Majors in equine business management and in English and Western riding are offered. The instruction, both in the classroom and on horseback, makes use of the expertise of recognized national equestrian champions. The pre–veterinary medicine program, using the farm facilities, offers the advantages of hands-on experience with livestock and an internship program in a distinctive curriculum. Graduates of the pre–veterinary program have been accepted to all twenty-eight veterinary schools in the United States, and several internationally.

The Nuclear Medicine Institute provides the training necessary to qualify students for careers in nuclear medicine technology, a growing health-related career field.

Academic Facilities

The focal point of the Findlay campus is Old Main, which houses classrooms, faculty and administrative offices, the computer center, facilities for various student activities, and the Ritz Auditorium. Shafer Library is a member of a consortium that provides extensive resources to students. The Gardner Fine Arts Pavilion, dedicated in 1994, houses the Mazza Museum of International Art from Children's Books, the first and largest teaching museum in the world dedicated to literacy and children's book art. The University has numerous computer labs. In 2006, the University acquired and renovated the former Findlay campus of Owens Community College at 300 Davis St., with its 62,000 square feet comprising the largest addition of academic space since the construction of Old Main. Other academic buildings include the Frost Science Center, with the Newhard Planetarium, and the Egner Center for the Performing Arts, which houses a 200-seat theater. A 101,000-square-foot athletic complex was completed in 1999. This facility houses a six-lane indoor track, sand pits for long jump, a state-of-the-art timing system, and a wrestling room. Also under the same roof is an ice arena with a seating capacity of 1,200 and a cardio center. Approximately 450 horses are stabled and trained at the equestrian facilities, which offer barns and indoor and outdoor riding arenas.

Costs

Tuition for the 2008–09 academic year totaled $23,938 for most programs. Room and board cost $8306. The estimated cost for transportation, books, fees, and supplies was $2482. There are additional program surcharges for equestrian studies and pre–veterinary medicine.

Financial Aid

Assistance is based on need as well as scholastic achievement. In 2008–09, 95 percent of UF students received institutional financial aid from the University. The average financial aid award for students with need in fall 2007 was $19,080. Merit scholarships at UF range from $9000 to $14,000 a year. Notification of aid awards is made on a rolling basis. Work-study jobs are available. Scholarships for high-achieving students and student athletes are offered.

Faculty

The 17:1 student-faculty ratio results in small classes—with an average class size of 20 students. Professors know their students, and every student has a faculty adviser.

Student Government

The Student Government Association (SGA) and the Campus Program Board are involved in planning and implementing student activities. SGA provides leadership experience for students and enhances cooperation among faculty members, the administration, and students. A representative from SGA sits on the Board of Trustees. The Campus Program Board plans activities for recreation and cultural enrichment.

Admission Requirements

The University of Findlay considers each applicant on an individualized basis. The University accepts applications on a rolling basis, but it encourages students to complete applications by January 15, as the class fills rapidly. Application deadlines are August 1 for the fall semester and December 15 for the spring semester. Major factors associated with rendering a decision include GPA, standardized test scores, and strength of curriculum. Although it is not required, a campus admission visit is encouraged. Applicants to Findlay should have a college-preparatory high school background, including 4 years of English, 3 to 4 years of mathematics, 2 to 3 years of social studies, and 2 years of sciences. A foreign language is recommended but not required. Results of the ACT or SAT should be submitted with the application for admission. Transfer students must be eligible to return to the institution last attended and must submit transcripts of all college work. For students not meeting regular minimum admission requirements, Findlay has a Foundations Program, which provides skill building and academic support during the first semester of the freshman year. Findlay is an equal opportunity institution in admission and employment.

Application and Information

For application forms and other information, students may contact:

Office of Undergraduate Admissions
The University of Findlay
1000 North Main Street
Findlay, Ohio 45840
Phone: 419-434-4732
800-548-0932 (toll-free)
E-mail: admissions@findlay.edu
Web site: http://www.findlay.edu

Old Main.

VALPARAISO UNIVERSITY

VALPARAISO, INDIANA

The University

Valparaiso University (Valpo) was founded in 1859 by the citizens of Valparaiso, Indiana, but its recent history dates from 1925, when it was purchased by the Lutheran University Association. Valpo is one of the nation's largest Lutheran-affiliated universities, yet it remains independent and is open to individuals of all faiths. The University's 4,000 students represent most states and more than forty countries; 63 percent come from outside of Indiana. Valparaiso University is a residential community in which activities outside the classroom form an important part of campus life; more than 70 percent of its students live on campus. Nearly 100 extracurricular and cocurricular programs are open to all, including various NCAA Division I intercollegiate and intramural sports teams for men and women. Approximately 35 percent of the students are members of the University's nine national fraternities and six national sororities. Both in and out of the classroom, students and professors operate a student-initiated honor code in which integrity is assumed to be the norm. If violations occur, they are handled by peers through a student-composed Honor Council. Because of these structures and the University philosophy as a whole, relationships among students, faculty, and administration are remarkably collaborative.

Major divisions at Valparaiso University include the Colleges of Arts and Sciences, Business Administration, Engineering, and Nursing; Christ College (the Honors College); the School of Law; and the Graduate Division. Graduates earned a 95 percent job placement rate last year.

Location

Valparaiso University is located in Valparaiso, a safe community of 31,000 in Indiana. Only 1 hour west, Chicago and its theaters, museums, restaurants, and cultural and sports offerings are accessible by auto, train, or bus. The campus is within walking distance of a vibrant town square and commercial/entertainment center with national chain stores and restaurants. Just 15 miles north is the Indiana Dunes National Lakeshore on Lake Michigan, a famous recreational area and home of the finest ecological laboratory in the nation. Air service is available nearby from Chicago's O'Hare and Midway International Airports and South Bend's Michiana Regional Airport.

Majors and Degrees

Valparaiso University offers the following undergraduate degrees: Associate of Arts, Associate of Science, Bachelor of Arts (B.A.), Bachelor of Music, Bachelor of Music Education, Bachelor of Science (B.S.), Bachelor of Science in Accounting, Bachelor of Science in Business Administration, Bachelor of Science in Civil Engineering, Bachelor of Science in Computer Engineering, Bachelor of Science in Education, Bachelor of Science in Electrical Engineering, Bachelor of Science in Fine Arts, Bachelor of Science in Mechanical Engineering, Bachelor of Science in Nursing, Bachelor of Science in Physical Education, and Bachelor of Social Work. The B.A. or B.S. degree may be earned in accounting, actuarial science, American studies, art, athletic training, biochemistry, biology, business administration, chemistry, Chinese and Japanese studies, church music, civil engineering, classics, communication, communication law, computer engineering, computer science, creative writing, economics, economics and computer analysis, education (elementary, middle, or secondary), electrical engineering, engineering, English, environmental science, exercise science, finance, French, geography, geoscience, German, history, information and decision sciences, international business, international economics and cultural affairs, international service, management, marketing, mathematics, mechanical engineering, meteorology, modern European studies, music, music composition, music education, music performance, new media–journalism, nursing, philosophy, physical education, physics, political science, professional writing, psychology, public and corporate communication, public relations, social work, sociology, Spanish, sports management, television-radio, theater, theology, and youth, family, and education ministry.

Academic Programs

Valparaiso University has a long tradition of combining professional colleges with a strong commitment to the values and broadening experiences of the liberal arts. The University helps students of varied interests and objectives to clarify their goals and explore new possibilities. Connections between students' lives and the classroom are encouraged through an emphasis on hands-on learning programs, including the Valpo Core. Programs are structured to provide a solid base for exploration in various fields, while offering students the freedom to develop depth in a specific interest. This philosophy is extended through the upper division, where students have three options when completing a degree: an individual plan of study involving the major and complementary courses from related fields of study, the election of a second academic major in addition to the first, or a special minor in connection with the major. Career planning is aided through the professional programs and the University's Career Center. Many students also gain professional work experience in their chosen field before graduation by participating in the cooperative education program and internships.

Valparaiso operates on the semester system; the fall semester begins in late August and ends before Christmas, and the spring semester starts in early January and ends during the second week in May. Valpo also has two summer terms that further extend opportunities for study on campus or at various off-campus locations.

The University participates in the Advanced Placement Program, the College-Level Examination Program, and the International Baccalaureate Program. In addition, Valparaiso provides its own placement testing in several academic areas.

All departments of the University offer opportunities for honors work through independent study, seminars, and research. Christ College, the Honors College of Valparaiso, has a well-established but continuously evolving program designed to challenge gifted students. Christ College students enroll concurrently in any other Valpo college.

Off-Campus Programs

Valparaiso University sponsors study-abroad programs in Reutlingen and Tübingen, Germany; Puebla, Mexico; Paris, France; Hangzhou, China; Granada, Spain; and Cambridge, England. Valparaiso also sponsors semester-long study opportunities at two universities in Japan, one in Namibia, and another in Greece. Valpo students may study at other overseas locations through Valparaiso's membership in the Central States College Association. In addition, Valpo grants credit for the following cooperative programs: Urban Studies Semester (Chicago), Urban Affairs Semester and Washington Semester (Washington, D.C.), and Semester on the United Nations (Madison, New Jersey).

Academic Facilities

Opened in 2004, the 115,000-square-foot Christopher Center for Library Information Services is a state-of-the-art facility, which offers a robotic book-retrieval system. In addition to library resources, the four-story structure houses a ninety-one-seat tiered classroom; three fireplace lounges; a sixty-seat computer lab; a snack bar; twenty-four stations for listening to, viewing, and developing multimedia projects; reading rooms; a writing center; electronic information services; and much more. The Neils Science Center houses an astronomical observatory, a greenhouse, and other facilities that have earned the University a citation from the Atomic Energy Commission for having a model undergraduate physics laboratory. The Kade-Duesenberg German House and Cultural Center, Virtual Nursing Learning Center, weather station (which includes Doppler radar), Center for the Arts, VisBox 3-D scientific learning system, and nonlinear (digital) video editing lab are state-of-the-art facilities. A new 202,000-square-foot Union is currently under construction and scheduled to open in the 2008–09 academic year.

Costs

Tuition for the 2008–09 academic year at Valparaiso University is $26,070, room is $4680, and board is $2940. General fees are $880. The total cost of tuition, room, board, and fees is $34,570. Students spend approximately $2840 per year for books, supplies, and such miscellaneous expenses as laundry and travel.

Financial Aid

Ninety-two percent of Valparaiso's undergraduate students receive financial aid, totaling more than $58 million. Many scholarships and awards are determined by the admissions application. Students are also encouraged to file the Free Application for Federal Student Aid (FAFSA) to apply for need-based grants, loans, and employment. Valpo awards federal, state, and University need-based aid based on FAFSA results, attempting to make up the difference between the cost of attending Valpo and the amount a family can afford. Early application is recommended for Valpo assistance, since the awarding of aid begins in January of the year of enrollment.

Faculty

Valparaiso's 254 full-time faculty members share a common interest—teaching in ways that encourage students and faculty members to get to know one another. The majority of the faculty members are full-time, and a considerable number serve as advisers to the various academic and social organizations on campus. Classes are led by professors, not teaching assistants. Almost 91 percent of the full-time professors have terminal degrees, and this figure reaches 100 percent in many departments. Each department has a full advising system to help students with course and program selection.

Student Government

Students and faculty members alike are involved in the internal governance of the institution. House Councils in each of the residence halls are composed of representatives elected by the residents. Each council makes decisions and sets standards within the guidelines established by the University. Students in the living units and off-campus students elect representatives to the Student Senate (composed entirely of students) and the University Senate (made up of an equal number of representatives from the student body, faculty, and administration). The functions of these two separate bodies cover most phases of student life.

Admission Requirements

Valparaiso admits candidates who exhibit the potential for academic success at the University. The freshman retention rate averaged 86 percent over the past five years, reflecting in part the high quality of the admission program. Qualified students are admitted without regard to race, color, gender, disability, national origin, or ancestry. The credentials of each applicant are individually and personally evaluated, and consideration is given not only to ACT or SAT scores, but also to grades and trends in the student's record, the nature of the high school and the program followed, outside interests, and recommendations. A campus visit and an interview with an admission counselor are recommended but not required. Students who have taken the ACT or SAT in their junior year and have submitted their high school transcripts, complete through the eleventh grade, may be considered for admission.

Application and Information

An applicant must complete a formal University admission application or the Common Application to be considered for admission. In addition, Valpo requires a high school transcript (complete through the junior year), ACT or SAT scores, a counselor evaluation form, and college transcripts (when applicable). Valpo's nonbinding early action option requires applicants to submit their applications no later than November 1. Regular admission notification begins on a rolling basis after December 1. First priority for scholarship consideration is given to those who apply for admission by the early action deadline; preference is then given to those who apply by January 15.

Information and application forms for admission and financial aid may be obtained from:

Office of Admission
Kretzmann Hall
1700 Chapel Drive
Valparaiso University
Valparaiso, Indiana 46383-6493
Phone: 219-464-5011
888-GO-VALPO (toll-free)
Fax: 219-464-6898
E-mail: undergrad.admissions@valpo.edu
Web site: http://www.valpo.edu

Students on the campus of Valparaiso University.

WESTERN MICHIGAN UNIVERSITY

KALAMAZOO, MICHIGAN

The University

Western Michigan University (WMU) is one of the country's top public universities and enjoys global recognition for its outstanding programs in aviation, fine arts, communications, and business marketing. WMU is also home to Lee Honors College, which has been in continuous operation longer than almost any other honors program in the country. More than 1,100 undergraduates are currently enrolled in Lee Honors College. With an increasing student demand for honors programs, the University plans to continue to enlarge Lee Honors College over the coming years.

Western Michigan University is focused on preparing its graduates for the competitive world of work as well as graduate and professional school. WMU is one of only 100 public universities in the United States to have a chapter of Phi Beta Kappa, the nation's premier honor society. In addition, *U.S. News & World Report* has ranked WMU among America's top 100 public universities for the past ten years.

With 24,818 students, WMU is Michigan's fourth-largest university. Even though it is a large university with a broad range of program offerings at both the undergraduate and graduate levels, WMU maintains a comfortable student-faculty ratio, and two thirds of all undergraduate classes have 30 or fewer students. Despite its size, complexity, and variety of offerings, WMU is one of the most affordable of Michigan's fifteen public universities, ranking eleventh from the top in tuition and required fees.

Founded in 1903, WMU has seven degree-granting colleges: Arts and Sciences, Aviation, the Haworth College of Business, Education, Engineering and Applied Sciences, Fine Arts, and Health and Human Services as well as the Graduate College, to assist students pursuing advanced degrees, and the Lee Honors College. Students have 237 academic programs from which to choose, 140 of them at the undergraduate level. Because it has a vibrant graduate component that includes twenty-nine doctoral programs, the University attracts faculty members who not only enjoy teaching at the undergraduate level but have distinguished themselves nationally through their research.

WMU has focused on enhancing its out-of-class opportunities by expanding its internship opportunities and student engagement in research and service. The Haenicke Institute for Global Education provides access to study-abroad programs all over the world and supports international students coming to study at WMU.

The University is home to a diverse student body that includes students from nearly every state across the United States as well as 1,114 international students from eighty-eight countries. Minority students also are well represented and make up 12 percent of the student population. The University's main campus enrollment of over 24,000 includes approximately 5,000 students who live in twenty-two campus residence halls that offer a variety of living arrangements.

There are more than 300 registered student organizations, including a wide range of Greek, academic honorary, and professional organizations. In addition, the University has nationally recognized arts programs, a lively cultural calendar, and NCAA Division I-A Mid-American and Central Collegiate Hockey Association sports teams. Its six men's and ten women's varsity sports, intramural teams, and club sports add vitality to campus life.

Location

For more than 100 years, Kalamazoo has been home to WMU. From the dedication of East Hall—the first building on campus—the community has supported Western's growth. Kalamazoo is an ideal college town, where business leaders recognize Western as their second-largest employer and where students and employees contribute more than $500 million annually to the economy of the region. Located just 40 miles from the beautiful eastern shoreline of Lake Michigan, the area embraces all four seasons with cool, sunny summers and moderate winters. Outdoor recreation abounds, from downhill skiing in winter months to every imaginable water sport available from late spring through early fall. Unlike much of eastern Michigan, southwest Michigan is composed of gently rolling hills, small recreational lakes, and dense woodlands. Fall is a particularly beautiful time to enjoy the variety of color while hiking or riding a bike on the Kal-Haven trail that connects Kalamazoo to the Lake Michigan resort town of South Haven. Nearly every weekend throughout the year Kalamazoo has something to offer its students and local residents. It is not unusual on a Saturday afternoon to find faculty members rubbing elbows with students at the annual Art Hop, Blues Festival, or Taste of Kalamazoo.

Kalamazoo, a city of more than 75,000, offers a wide array of lively entertainment including sports, such as professional baseball, hockey, and soccer; music, from jazz to heavy metal; intimate coffee houses and comedy clubs; and dining, from fast food to international cuisine. West Michigan is also home to numerous prosperous businesses, industries, and Fortune 500 companies including Haworth Inc., the Whirlpool Corporation, and the Kellogg Company. Many of these companies offer internships to WMU students.

Majors and Degrees

WMU offers a range of academic majors and programs to meet nearly everyone's needs. The College of Arts and Sciences offers undergraduate degrees in Africana studies; anthropology; biochemistry; biology; biomedical sciences; business-oriented chemistry; chemistry; communication studies; criminal justice; earth science; economics; English; film, video, and media studies; French; geochemistry; geography; geology; geophysics; German; global and international studies; history; hydrogeology; interpersonal communication; journalism; Latin; mathematics; organizational communication; philosophy; physics; political science; psychology; public history; public relations; religion; sociology; Spanish; statistics; student-planned major; telecommunications and information management; tourism and travel; preprofessional programs (dentistry, law, medicine); and coordinate majors (environmental studies, women's studies).

The College of Aviation offers programs in aviation flight science, aviation maintenance technology, and aviation science and administration.

The Haworth College of Business offers programs in accountancy, advertising and promotion, computer information systems, economics, electronic business design, finance, food and consumer package goods marketing, human resource management, integrated supply matrix management, management, marketing, personal financial planning, sales and business marketing, and telecommunications and information management.

The College of Education offers programs in elementary education that emphasize language arts, mathematics, science, and social science. Secondary education students may major in art, biology, business, chemistry, earth science, English, family and consumer science, French, geography, German, health education, history, industrial technology, Latin, marketing, mathematics, music, physical education, physics, political science, school health education, social studies, Spanish, and technology and design. Other programs include athletic training, community health education, dietetics, exercise science, family studies, food service administration, industrial technology, interior design, recreation, special education, and textile and apparel studies.

The College of Engineering and Applied Sciences offers programs in aeronautical engineering, chemical engineering, civil engineering, computer engineering, computer science, construction engineering, electrical engineering, engineering graphics and design technology, engineering management technology, entrepreneurial engineering, manufacturing engineering, manufacturing engineering technology, mechanical engineering, paper engineering, and paper science.

The College of Fine Arts offers programs in art, art education, art history, dance, graphic design, jazz studies, music, music composition, music education, music performance, music theater performance, music therapy, theater design and technical production, theater performance, and theater stage management.

The College of Health and Human Services offers programs in interdisciplinary health services, occupational therapy, nursing, nursing (RN), social work, and speech pathology and audiology.

Academic Programs

WMU is committed to student academic success, beginning with the new First-Year Experience program, which utilizes small-group seminars led by senior faculty members and upperclass student mentors. The University's college advisers help students plan their courses of study and consider program options, while advisers in University Curriculum assist undecided students in exploring academic programs and their relationships to various careers and professions. A comprehensive general education program provides the foundation for all fields of study. The Lee Honors College provides an atmosphere of small seminar classes, opportunities for research alongside faculty members, and the chance to explore new horizons through independent study. Student academic success is recognized through University, college, and department honor societies and through the prestigious Presidential Scholar Award given to outstanding graduating seniors.

Off-Campus Programs

WMU has seven branch campuses and a full complement of online courses. A host of U.S. business-industry partnerships and exchange agreements with universities and other organizations around the world provide training, research, and study-abroad opportunities for graduate and undergraduate students. In addition, the University actively assists students seeking internships in their chosen fields of study.

Academic Facilities

Western Michigan University is on Intel's list of the nation's 100 most wireless college campuses. WMU's network provides access to the University libraries, the Internet, and extensive campus information services. Computer labs are available across the campus, including many residence halls. Specialized labs support the work of students in engineering, graphic arts, teacher education, business, and other fields. Western Michigan University's new chemistry building opened in January 2007, and the new James W. and Lois I. Richmond Center for Visual Arts opened in April 2007. New construction is continuously transforming the campus while giving students access to acclaimed fine arts performance spaces, world-class aviation facilities, a leading-edge building for the College of Health and Human Services, and an innovative College of Engineering and Applied Sciences building that is located in a thriving business and research park.

Costs

A college education is one of the best investments a person can make, and, best of all, it never depreciates over time. Over a lifetime of work, WMU's graduates can expect to earn nearly twice that of someone with a high school diploma. WMU is committed to keeping costs as low as possible to ensure that all qualified students have access to the University. WMU's tuition and fees are among the lowest in the state. For 2008–09, tuition and fee costs were $7928, and room and board costs were $7377. Books and supplies and personal and travel expenses vary based on individual factors.

Financial Aid

The University annually awards more than $200 million in financial assistance to undergraduate students. Students who are qualified for need-based aid usually receive assistance through a combination of gift-aid (grants and scholarships), self-help (student loans), and employment (work-study).

A variety of academic achievement scholarships are available to students who have demonstrated academic success while in high school. A combination of awards can be sufficient to cover nearly all direct costs of attendance at WMU. Most merit awards are renewable by enrolling full-time and earning a minimum 3.0 cumulative grade point average while at WMU. The two most recognized awards are the Medallion Scholarship and the Dean's Scholarship. The Dean's Scholarship is awarded to the top academic students (based on high school grades and standardized test scores) who apply for admission in early December, compete in the Medallion competition in January, and enroll the following fall semester as new, first-time students. Medallion recipients receive $10,000 annually, and the scholarship is renewable for up to four years of full-time enrollment.

There are also scholarships for students who have earned associate degrees from state and regional community colleges and who have earned high grade point averages while completing degree requirements.

Faculty

WMU's commitment to academic excellence means that many of its 935 full-time and 501 part-time faculty members conduct research. Tenured professors teach freshman-level courses, and full-time faculty members teach the majority of all courses. Plus, hundreds of these scholars have academic or research experience outside of the United States, bringing a global perspective into the classroom.

Student Government

Governance structures include the Western Student Association and its Student Senate and the Residence Hall Association. Each provides students with a wide variety of opportunities for leadership.

Admission Requirements

Admission to the University is based primarily on a combination of high school cumulative grade point average and standardized test scores (either ACT or SAT). When admission is not conclusive or admission is sought to selective or highly competitive programs, consideration is given to academic rigor of courses taken and counselor/principal recommendations, in addition to grade point averages and test scores.

To ensure academic success at WMU, all students should have completed a minimum of 4 years of English, 3 years of mathematics (through intermediate algebra), 3 years of social sciences, 2 years of natural sciences, and 2 years of the same foreign language.

Offers of admission made to students still in high school are conditional, pending graduation from high school and the University's review of final senior-year grades.

Transfer students with a minimum of 26 transferable hours (39 quarter hours) at the time of application and a grade point average of at least 2.0 (C average) are considered for admission. The trend of the most recent grades is also taken into account. Applicants with fewer than 26 transferable hours (39 quarter hours) at the time of application also must submit a high school transcript. In such cases, admission is based on both college and high school records.

Application and Information

For an application or more information, students should contact:

Office of Admissions and Orientation
Western Michigan University
1903 West Michigan Avenue
Kalamazoo, Michigan 49008-5211
Phone: 269-387-2000
Web site: http://www.wmich.edu/admissions

This impressive Stewart Clock Tower joins Waldo Library, on the right, with the high-tech University Computing Center.

Profiles and Close-Ups of Other Colleges to Consider

Kentucky

TRANSYLVANIA UNIVERSITY

Lexington, Kentucky

Transylvania University is a coed, private, four-year college, founded in 1780, affiliated with the Christian Church (Disciples of Christ), offering degrees at the bachelor's level. It has a 40-acre campus in Lexington near Cincinnati and Louisville.

Academic Information The faculty has 109 members (78% full-time), 77% with terminal degrees. The student-faculty ratio is 12.6:1. The library holds 137,000 titles, 500 serial subscriptions, and 2,056 audiovisual materials. Special programs include study abroad, advanced placement credit, double majors, independent study, self-designed majors, summer session for credit, part-time degree programs (daytime), internships, and arrangement for off-campus study with Washington Center for Internships and Academic Seminars, Kentucky Institute for International Studies. The most frequently chosen baccalaureate fields are business/marketing, foreign languages and literature, social sciences.

Student Body Statistics The student body is made up of 1,158 undergraduates (317 freshmen). 60 percent are women and 40 percent are men. Students come from 27 states and territories and 2 other countries. 84 percent are from Kentucky. 0.2 percent are international students.

Expenses for 2008–09 *Application fee:* $30. *Comprehensive fee:* $31,260 includes full-time tuition ($22,840), mandatory fees ($970), and college room and board ($7450). *Part-time tuition:* $2465 per course.

Financial Aid Forms of aid include need-based and non-need-based scholarships and part-time jobs. The average aided 2008–09 undergraduate received an aid package worth an estimated $20,082. The priority application deadline for financial aid is March 1.

Freshman Admission Transylvania University requires an essay, a high school transcript, a minimum 2.75 high school GPA, 2 recommendations, SAT or ACT scores, and TOEFL scores for international students. An interview is recommended. An interview is required for some. The application deadline for regular admission is February 1 and for early action it is December 1.

Transfer Admission The application deadline for admission is rolling.

Entrance Difficulty Transylvania University assesses its entrance difficulty level as very difficult. For the fall 2008 freshman class, 80 percent of the applicants were accepted.

For Further Information Contact Mr. Bradley Goan, Director of Admissions, Transylvania University, 300 North Broadway, Lexington, KY 40508-1797. *Phone:* 859-233-4242 or 800-872-6798 (toll-free). *Fax:* 859-281-3642. *E-mail:* admissions@transy.edu. *Web site:* http://www.transy.edu/.

See page 294 for the Close-Up.

Louisiana

UNIVERSITY OF NEW ORLEANS

New Orleans, Louisiana

University of New Orleans is a coed, public unit of Louisiana State University System, founded in 1958, offering degrees at the bachelor's, master's, and doctoral levels and postbachelor's certificates. It has a 345-acre campus in New Orleans.

Academic Information The faculty has 604 members (74% full-time), 61% with terminal degrees. The undergraduate student-faculty ratio is 18:1. The library holds 957,096 titles, 12,998 serial subscriptions, and 39,768 audiovisual materials. Special programs include academic remediation, services for learning-disabled students, an honors program, cooperative (work-study) education, study abroad, advanced placement credit, ESL programs, double majors, independent study, distance learning, self-designed majors, summer session for credit, part-time degree programs, adult/continuing education programs, internships, and arrangement for off-campus study with Southern University at New Orleans, Delgado Community College, Nunez Community College. The most frequently chosen baccalaureate fields are business/marketing, engineering, liberal arts/general studies.

Student Body Statistics The student body totals 11,428, of whom 8,628 are undergraduates (1,267 freshmen). 52 percent are women and 48 percent are men. Students come from 49 states and territories and 74 other countries. 95 percent are from Louisiana. 4.3 percent are international students.

Expenses for 2008–09 *Application fee:* $40. *State resident tuition:* $3488 full-time, $116.27 per credit hour part-time. *Nonresident tuition:* $10,884 full-time, $362.80 per credit hour part-time. Both full-time and part-time tuition varies according to course load. *College room and board:* $6130. Room and board charges vary according to board plan and housing facility.

Financial Aid Forms of aid include need-based and non-need-based scholarships, athletic grants, and part-time jobs. The average aided 2008–09 undergraduate received an aid package worth an estimated $9312. The priority application deadline for financial aid is May 15.

Freshman Admission University of New Orleans requires a high school transcript, SAT or ACT scores, and TOEFL scores for international students. An essay and a minimum 2.5 high school GPA are required for some. The application deadline for regular admission is rolling and for nonresidents it is July 1.

Transfer Admission The application deadline for admission is July 1.

Entrance Difficulty University of New Orleans assesses its entrance difficulty level as moderately difficult. For the fall 2008 freshman class, 55 percent of the applicants were accepted.

For Further Information Contact Mr. Andy Benoit, Director of Admissions, University of New Orleans, Lake Front, New Orleans, LA 70148. *Phone:* 504-280-7013 or 800-256-5866 (toll-free out-of-state). *Fax:* 504-280-5522. *E-mail:* admissions@uno.edu. *Web site:* http://www.uno.edu/.

See page 300 for the Close-Up.

New York

CLARKSON UNIVERSITY

Potsdam, New York

Clarkson University is a coed, private university, founded in 1896, offering degrees at the bachelor's, master's, doctoral, and first professional levels. It has a 640-acre campus in Potsdam.

Academic Information The faculty has 217 members (86% full-time), 84% with terminal degrees. The undergraduate student-faculty ratio is 15.3:1. The library holds 309,235 titles, 3,396 serial subscriptions, and 2,095 audiovisual materials. Special programs include services for learning-disabled students, an honors program, cooperative (work-study) education, study abroad, advanced placement credit, accelerated degree programs, ESL programs, double majors, independent study, self-designed majors, summer session for credit, part-time degree programs (daytime, summer), internships, and arrangement for off-campus study with Associated Colleges of the St. Lawrence Valley. The most frequently chosen baccalaureate fields are business/marketing, biological/life sciences, engineering.

Student Body Statistics The student body totals 3,045, of whom 2,593 are undergraduates (735 freshmen). 27 percent are women and 73 percent are men. Students come from 42 states and territories and 25 other countries. 81 percent are from New York. 3.6 percent are international students.

Expenses for 2009–10 *Application fee:* $50. *Comprehensive fee:* $44,028 includes full-time tuition ($32,220), mandatory fees ($690), and college room and board ($11,118). *College room only:* $5890. *Part-time tuition:* $1074 per credit.

Financial Aid Forms of aid include need-based and non-need-based scholarships, athletic grants, and part-time jobs. The average aided

Clarkson University (continued)
2007–08 undergraduate received an aid package worth $23,189. The priority application deadline for financial aid is February 15.
Freshman Admission Clarkson University requires a high school transcript, 2 recommendations, SAT or ACT scores, and TOEFL scores for international students. An interview and SAT Subject Test scores are recommended. The application deadline for regular admission is January 15 and for early decision it is December 1.
Entrance Difficulty Clarkson University assesses its entrance difficulty level as very difficult. For the fall 2008 freshman class, 79 percent of the applicants were accepted.

SPECIAL MESSAGE TO STUDENTS

Social Life Clarkson's 640-acre wooded campus, more than eighty active clubs and organizations, and major cultural and educational events afford enormous extracurricular opportunities for students. The 6-million-acre Adirondack Park is only minutes away, and within 2 hours of campus are Lake Placid and the cosmopolitan Canadian cities of Montreal and Ottawa.

Academic Highlights Academics at Clarkson emphasize rigorous professional preparation; dynamic, real-world learning; flexibility and adaptability; and teamwork that spans disciplines. Clarkson's award-winning programs in engineering, arts, sciences, business, and health sciences also develop communication and collaboration skills, with a focus on practical application of knowledge and creative, open-ended problem solving. Undergraduates customize programs through specialized concentrations and minors that broaden career options. Clarkson's relatively small size encourages personal attention and interactions between students and faculty members, and Clarkson students enjoy extraordinary opportunities to pursue faculty-mentored research. They gain professional experience through internships and co-ops with corporations and government organizations and can broaden their perspectives through a wide range of study-abroad opportunities. The University offers an honors program and an accelerated three-year bachelor's degree.

Interviews and Campus Visits Clarkson strongly recommends that students visit the campus for a tour and a meeting with representatives. Students who visit the campus for an interview with an admission counselor receive a fee-waived voucher for a Clarkson application. Clarkson is located in the friendly community of Potsdam, between the beautiful Adirondack Mountains and the St. Lawrence River. The scenic, open campus features several new buildings, including a state-of-the-art building for business and liberal arts, which features fully networked classrooms and collaborative centers with wireless network access and videoconferencing capabilities and state-of-the-art laboratories, and the centrally located Cheel Student Center, which is a combination student union and multipurpose arena facility. In 2008, the 16,000-square-foot Technology Advancement Center was opened to provide critical laboratory and collaboration space for accelerating the development of research, especially in the fields of renewable energy and clean manufacturing technology. For information about appointments and campus visits, prospective students should call the Office of Undergraduate Admission at 315-268-6480 or 800-527-6577 (toll-free), Monday through Friday 8 to 4:30 or Saturday by appointment. The office is located in Holcroft House on the campus.

For Further Information Write to Mr. Brian Grant, Director of Admission, Clarkson University, P.O. Box 5605, Potsdam, NY 13699-5605. *E-mail:* admission@clarkson.edu. *Web site:* http://www.clarkson.edu.

See page 290 for the Close-Up.

Texas

SOUTHERN METHODIST UNIVERSITY

Dallas, Texas

Southern Methodist University is a coed, private university, founded in 1911, affiliated with the United Methodist Church, offering degrees at the bachelor's, master's, doctoral, and first professional levels and postbachelor's certificates. It has a 210-acre campus in Dallas.

Academic Information The faculty has 1,034 members (63% full-time), 71% with terminal degrees. The undergraduate student-faculty ratio is 12:1. The library holds 3 million titles, 11,701 serial subscriptions, and 45,168 audiovisual materials. Special programs include academic remediation, services for learning-disabled students, an honors program, cooperative (work-study) education, study abroad, advanced placement credit, accelerated degree programs, ESL programs, double majors, independent study, distance learning, self-designed majors, summer session for credit, part-time degree programs, adult/continuing education programs, and internships. The most frequently chosen baccalaureate fields are business/marketing, communications/journalism, social sciences.
Student Body Statistics The student body totals 10,965, of whom 6,240 are undergraduates (1,398 freshmen). 54 percent are women and 46 percent are men. Students come from 50 states and territories and 65 other countries. 58 percent are from Texas. 5.6 percent are international students.
Expenses for 2009–10 *Application fee:* $60. *Comprehensive fee:* $47,605 includes full-time tuition ($31,200), mandatory fees ($3960), and college room and board ($12,445). *Part-time tuition:* $1304 per credit hour. *Part-time mandatory fees:* $166 per credit hour.
Financial Aid Forms of aid include need-based scholarships, athletic grants, and part-time jobs. The average aided 2007–08 undergraduate received an aid package worth $26,276. The priority application deadline for financial aid is March 1.
Freshman Admission Southern Methodist University requires an essay, a high school transcript, 1 recommendation, SAT or ACT scores, and TOEFL scores for international students. SAT Subject Test scores are required for some. The application deadline for regular admission is January 15 and for early action it is November 1.
Transfer Admission The application deadline for admission is July 1.
Entrance Difficulty Southern Methodist University assesses its entrance difficulty level as moderately difficult. For the fall 2008 freshman class, 50 percent of the applicants were accepted.
For Further Information Contact Mr. Ron Moss, Director of Admission and Enrollment Management, Southern Methodist University, PO Box 750181, Dallas, TX 75275-0181. *Phone:* 214-768-3417 or 800-323-0672 (toll-free). *Fax:* 214-768-0202. *E-mail:* enrol_serv@smu.edu. *Web site:* http://www.smu.edu/.

See page 292 for the Close-Up.

UNIVERSITY OF DALLAS

Irving, Texas

University of Dallas is a coed, private, Roman Catholic university, founded in 1955, offering degrees at the bachelor's, master's, and doctoral levels and post-master's and postbachelor's certificates. It has a 750-acre campus in Irving near Dallas–Fort Worth.

Academic Information The faculty has 244 members (51% full-time), 64% with terminal degrees. The undergraduate student-faculty ratio is 13:1. The library holds 245,228 titles, 1,310 serial subscriptions, and 1,317 audiovisual materials. Special programs include services for learning-disabled students, study abroad, advanced placement credit, double majors, independent study, self-designed majors, summer session for credit, part-time degree programs (daytime, summer), internships, and arrangement for off-campus study.
Student Body Statistics The student body totals 2,977, of whom 1,299 are undergraduates (342 freshmen). 52 percent are women and 48 percent

are men. Students come from 55 states and territories and 20 other countries. 50 percent are from Texas. 2.2 percent are international students.

Expenses for 2009–10 *Application fee:* $40. *Comprehensive fee:* $34,514 includes full-time tuition ($24,646), mandatory fees ($1648), and college room and board ($8220). *College room only:* $4570. *Part-time tuition:* $1034 per credit hour. *Part-time mandatory fees:* $1648 per year.

Financial Aid Forms of aid include need-based and non-need-based scholarships and part-time jobs. The average aided 2008–09 undergraduate received an aid package worth an estimated $20,520. The priority application deadline for financial aid is March 1.

Freshman Admission University of Dallas requires an essay, a high school transcript, 2 recommendations, SAT or ACT scores, and TOEFL scores for international students. An interview is required for some. The application deadline for regular admission is August 1 and for early action it is November 1.

Transfer Admission The application deadline for admission is July 1.

Entrance Difficulty University of Dallas assesses its entrance difficulty level as moderately difficult. For the fall 2008 freshman class, 91 percent of the applicants were accepted.

For Further Information Contact Lucas Sifuentes, Associate Director Admissions, University of Dallas, 1845 East Northgate Drive, Irving, TX 75062-4736. *Phone:* 972-721-5266 or 800-628-6999 (toll-free). *Fax:* 972-721-5017. *E-mail:* ugadmis@udallas.edu. *Web site:* http://www.udallas.edu/.

See page 298 for the Close-Up.

West Virginia

UNIVERSITY OF CHARLESTON

Charleston, West Virginia

University of Charleston is a coed, private, comprehensive institution, founded in 1888, offering degrees at the associate, bachelor's, master's, and doctoral levels. It has a 40-acre campus in Charleston.

Academic Information The faculty has 143 members (62% full-time), 41% with terminal degrees. The undergraduate student-faculty ratio is 13:1. The library holds 164,457 titles, 14,192 serial subscriptions, and 3,759 audiovisual materials. Special programs include academic remediation, services for learning-disabled students, study abroad, advanced placement credit, accelerated degree programs, ESL programs, double majors, independent study, distance learning, self-designed majors, summer session for credit, part-time degree programs (daytime, evenings, summer), adult/continuing education programs, and internships. The most frequently chosen baccalaureate fields are business/marketing, health professions and related sciences, visual and performing arts.

Student Body Statistics The student body totals 1,398, of whom 1,171 are undergraduates (328 freshmen). 60 percent are women and 40 percent are men. Students come from 35 states and territories and 17 other countries. 69 percent are from West Virginia. 9.2 percent are international students.

Expenses for 2008–09 *Application fee:* $25. *Comprehensive fee:* $31,475 includes full-time tuition ($23,150) and college room and board ($8325). *College room only:* $4550. Room and board charges vary according to board plan and housing facility. *Part-time tuition:* $400 per credit. *Part-time mandatory fees:* $75 per term. Part-time tuition and fees vary according to program.

Financial Aid Forms of aid include need-based and non-need-based scholarships, athletic grants, and part-time jobs. The average aided 2007–08 undergraduate received an aid package worth $20,030.

Freshman Admission University of Charleston requires a high school transcript, a minimum 2.25 high school GPA, SAT or ACT scores, and TOEFL scores for international students. An essay and 3 recommendations are recommended. An interview is required for some. The application deadline for regular admission is rolling.

Transfer Admission The application deadline for admission is rolling.

Entrance Difficulty University of Charleston assesses its entrance difficulty level as moderately difficult. For the fall 2008 freshman class, 67 percent of the applicants were accepted.

For Further Information Contact Mr. Brad Parrish, Vice President for Enrollment, University of Charleston, 2300 MacCorkle Avenue, SE, Charleston, WV 25304. *Phone:* 304-357-4750 or 800-995-GOUC (toll-free). *Fax:* 304-357-4781. *E-mail:* admissions@ucwv.edu. *Web site:* http://www.ucwv.edu/.

See page 296 for the Close-Up.

CLARKSON UNIVERSITY

POTSDAM, NEW YORK

The University

Founded in 1896, Clarkson stands out among America's private, nationally ranked research institutions because of its dynamic collaborative learning environment, innovative degree and research programs, and unmatched track record for producing leaders and innovators.

The University attracts 3,000 enterprising students from diverse backgrounds (including some 400 graduate students) who thrive in rigorous programs in engineering, arts, sciences, business, and health sciences and in the University's close-knit, residential learning/living community. Clarkson defies convention in the classroom, in its laboratories, and by the impact its graduates have in the world. The University is New York State's highest-ranked small research institution. However, size is Clarkson's advantage—fostering leadership and problem-solving skills and readily affording students and faculty members the flexibility to span the boundaries of traditional academic areas.

Clarkson students also enjoy extraordinary opportunities to pursue faculty-mentored research. They gain professional experience through internships and co-ops with corporations and government organizations and can broaden their perspectives through a wide range of study-abroad opportunities.

Top graduate schools welcome Clarkson graduates to study medicine, law, and other professions. Johns Hopkins, MIT, Princeton, Yale, Caltech, Rice, and Stanford are just some of the schools chosen by Clarkson students.

Clarkson's 98 percent placement rate is among the nation's highest, with the most recent starting salaries averaging more than $52,000. Clarkson is a key recruitment source for many of America's industry leaders, including General Electric, Alcoa, Xerox, Accenture, IBM, and Procter & Gamble. In fact, 1 in 6 Clarkson alumni is already a CEO, president, vice president, or company owner.

Clarkson's active campus also offers a wide variety of extracurricular activities, including more than eighty clubs and interest groups. Students publish a lively campus newspaper and run campus radio and television stations. Active professional and honor societies enrich the campus experience.

There are Division I men's and women's hockey teams, as well as, seventeen Division III intercollegiate athletic teams for women and men. Recreational facilities include a field house and gym with racquetball, basketball, and indoor tennis courts; a state-of-the-art fitness center; and a swimming pool.

Location

Clarkson is located in Potsdam, the quintessential "college town," nestled in the foothills of the northern Adirondack region of New York. The beautiful Northeast corner of the state is the home of the 6-million-acre Adirondack Park. Within 2 hours of the campus are Lake Placid and the cosmopolitan Canadian cities of Montreal and Ottawa.

Majors and Degrees

Undergraduate degree programs offered are aeronautical engineering, American studies, applied mathematics and statistics, Areté (liberal arts/business), biology, biomolecular engineering, biomolecular science, management, chemical engineering, chemistry, civil engineering, communication, computer engineering, computer science, digital arts and sciences, electrical engineering, engineering and management, environmental engineering, environmental health science, environmental science and policy, financial information and analysis, global supply chain management, history, humanities, information systems and business processes, innovation and entrepreneurship, liberal studies, mathematics, mechanical engineering, physical therapy (pre–physical therapy leading to a doctorate), physics, political science, psychology, social sciences, and software engineering.

First-year students who are still deciding on a major may begin in a general program in business studies, engineering studies, science studies, or university studies.

Clarkson offers a University honors program, a three-year bachelor's degree option, a five-year B.S./M.S. in chemistry/biochemistry, a five-year B.S./M.B.A., and preprofessional programs in dentistry, law, medicine, physical therapy, and veterinary science.

Academic Programs

Clarkson's historic strengths in business, engineering, liberal arts, and science remain at the core of the curriculum. These programs have also been combined into cutting-edge, cross-disciplinary majors: biomolecular science, digital arts and sciences, environmental science and policy, information technology, interdisciplinary engineering and management, and software engineering.

A dynamic, hands-on approach to learning is one of the hallmarks of a Clarkson education. Clarkson students learn about business by actually starting a business. They conduct scientific research alongside distinguished faculty mentors in state-of-the-art laboratories. The University's undergraduate research program has produced 19 Goldwater Scholars since the highly competitive national scholarship program was launched in 1986.

National rankings and honors include the following: among the 125 "Best National Universities–Doctoral," *U.S. News & World Report,* 2009; among the "Best Undergraduate Engineering Programs," *U.S. News & World Report,* 2009; among the "Top 20 Wired Campuses," in *PC Magazine* and the *Princeton Review* 2007; the Supply Chain Management Program ranks thirteenth in the nation, *U.S. News & World Report,* 2009; and among the best business schools in the nation, the *Princeton Review's Best 282 Business Schools,* 2007 edition. The undergraduate program in innovation and entrepreneurship is ranked number twenty-two among 700 U.S. higher educational institutions by the *Princeton Review* and *Entrepreneur* magazine, 2006.

Clarkson was also ranked among the top 100 graduate schools in environmental engineering and civil engineering by *U.S. News & World Report's* "Best Graduate Programs," 2009.

In addition, Clarkson's award-winning Student Projects for Engineering Experience and Design (SPEED) program promotes multidisciplinary, project-based extracurricular learning opportunities for more than 400 undergraduates annually. Some fifteen design teams compete in national and regional collegiate competitions that involve design and analysis, teamwork, and communication skills.

Off-Campus Programs

Students benefit from the resources of the Associated Colleges of the St. Lawrence Valley, which comprises Clarkson University, St. Lawrence University, SUNY Canton, and SUNY Potsdam. Benefits for students include opportunities to participate in activities ranging from clubs to concerts, interlibrary exchange, and cross-registration that allows students to pursue two courses per year at member colleges at no extra cost.

Academic Facilities

The University's 640-acre wooded campus is the site of forty-six buildings that comprise more than 1.2-million square feet of assignable space. Dedicated exclusively to instructional programs are more than 375,000 square feet, including some 54,000 square feet of traditional classrooms and more than 168,000 square feet assigned as laboratory areas. In the Center for Advanced Materials Processing (a New York State Center for Advanced Technology), there are seventy state-of-the-art research labs, including many related to nanotechnology and environmental research. Others include a multidisciplinary engineering and project laboratory for team-based projects, such as the mini-Baja and Formulae SAE racers, a robotics laboratory, a high-voltage lab, electron microscopy, a Class 10 clean room, a polymer fabrication lab, crystal growth labs, and a structural testing lab. School of Arts and Sciences facilities include a virtual-reality laboratory, the Clarkson Open Source Institute, a molecular design laboratory, a human brain electrophysiology laboratory, and other specialized facilities. In 2008, a 16,000-square-foot Technology Advancement Center was opened.

Bertrand H. Snell Hall houses the School of Business and the School of Arts and Sciences administrative offices as well as fully networked classrooms and study spaces and collaborative centers that feature wireless network access and videoconferencing capabilities. The facility includes three academic centers, which are available to all students: the Shipley Center for Innovation, the Center for Global Competitiveness, and the Eastman Kodak Center for Excellence in Communication. The Center for Health Sciences at Clarkson is a regional center of excellence for education, treatment, and research in physical rehabilitation and other health sciences.

Costs

Tuition was $30,320 for the 2008–09 year, room (2-person) was $5586, and the meal plan was $4026. Student fees totaled $690. In addition, students usually spend about $2000 annually on books, supplies, travel, and personal expenses.

Financial Aid

The University offers a variety of scholarships and loans, including state and federal student loans, state scholarships and awards, individual scholarships, federal grants, and federal work-study programs.

Faculty

Clarkson's 190 full-time faculty members teach undergraduate and graduate classes, with graduate students assisting only in undergraduate lab sciences. With an excellent student-faculty ratio of 15:1, undergraduates benefit from regular interaction with the school's faculty members and small class sizes (especially at the upper levels). The University attracts teacher/scholars who are also highly regarded scholars in their fields. 96 percent hold a doctorate.

Student Government

The Student Senate and the Interfraternity Council combine to form the student government at Clarkson University. The former supervises all extracurricular activities (except athletics) and has responsibility for the allocation of student activity funds and for other appropriate business. The latter prescribes standards and rules for fraternities. Students are involved in the formation of University policies through membership, with faculty and staff representatives, on all important committees.

Admission Requirements

Clarkson recommends that prospective students follow a challenging secondary school curriculum that includes mathematics, science, and English. Candidates for entrance to the Wallace H. Coulter School of Engineering or students pursuing a degree in the sciences or an interdisciplinary engineering and management degree should have successfully completed secondary school courses in physics and chemistry. All candidates for admission are required to take the SAT or ACT. SAT Subject Tests are optional. The high school record is the most important factor in an admission decision. International students for whom English is a second language must submit a minimum TOEFL score of 550 (paper-based) or 212 (computer-based). All applicants must include a personal statement of 250 to 500 words describing a special interest, experience, or achievement.

Students achieving scores of 4 or better on the College Board's Advanced Placement examinations are considered for advanced placement and credit in virtually all academic areas. Advanced standing is most common in English, mathematics, and science.

An early decision plan is offered on a "first-choice" basis; this plan does not prohibit the student from making other applications, but it does commit the student to withdrawing other applications if accepted at Clarkson.

Although not required, a personal interview with a member of the Office of Admission is highly recommended, especially for early decision candidates. Interviews on campus should be arranged by letter or telephone at least one week prior to the intended visit. The Office of Admission is open Monday through Friday, from 8 a.m. to 4:30 p.m., and Saturday by appointment. The University welcomes visitors to the campus and makes arrangements, as requested, for families to tour and meet with academic and other departments on campus.

Application and Information

Office of Undergraduate Admission
Holcroft House
Clarkson University
P.O. Box 5605
Potsdam, New York 13699-5605
Phone: 315-268-6480
800-527-6577 (toll-free)
Fax: 315-268-7647
E-mail: admission@clarkson.edu
Web site: http://www.clarkson.edu

Clarkson is a leader in project-based learning, providing students with strong communication skills, leadership ability, and technological skill in their fields.

SOUTHERN METHODIST UNIVERSITY

DALLAS, TEXAS

The University

Southern Methodist University (SMU) is a small, caring academic community in the heart of a vibrant city, where excellence is the standard and the goal is helping students succeed. SMU prepares students for life and leadership in the twenty-first century by educating them to meet the challenges of a rapidly changing world, intellectually equipping them for lifelong learning, and preparing them for successful careers. The broad-based curriculum provides a strong foundation in the humanities and sciences. SMU's four undergraduate schools offer nearly eighty majors in business, engineering, the arts, and humanities and sciences. Learning at SMU includes opportunities for mentoring relationships, internships, leadership development, research experience, international study, and community service.

Founded in 1911, SMU welcomes students of every religion, race, color, ethnic origin, and economic status. Students come from all fifty states and more than ninety countries. Total University enrollment is 10,829; 6,176 are undergraduates. Sixty percent of all undergraduate lecture sections have fewer than 25 students. Academically promising students are invited into the University Honors Program.

The life of a student's education is enriched at SMU, where there are nearly 180 student activities and organizations. From debate club to intramural sports, campus events to marching band, academic interests to community service, students have many options. There are also a large number of academic honorary societies.

SMU hosts more than 400 public arts events each year. The world-renowned Willis M. Tate Distinguished Lecture Series brings guests, such as Secretary of State Colin Powell, actor Julie Andrews, and former President George Bush to campus. SMU is a member of the National Collegiate Athletic Association and participates in Conference USA, Division I-A. Seventeen Division I-A teams include basketball, football, golf, soccer, swimming/diving, and tennis and women's cross-country, equestrian, rowing, track and field, and volleyball.

SMU offers fourteen residence halls and living communities, including an honors hall, a fine arts community, and a service-learning house. First-year students are required to live on campus, except in special circumstances. Residence halls have local phone service, voice mail, Ethernet computer connections, Internet and e-mail, air conditioning, and community computer and lounge areas. Main campus, including the residence halls, also offers students free wireless Internet access.

Location

SMU's parklike campus, located north of downtown Dallas in a traditional and upscale residential neighborhood, features Georgian-style architecture and enjoys a pleasant Sun Belt climate. Dallas, often ranked as one of the world's most livable cities, is home to more than 6,000 corporate headquarters and offers outstanding opportunities for internships and future employment. A convenient light rail and bus system is located near the campus.

Majors and Degrees

SMU offers nearly eighty degrees through its four undergraduate schools, with flexible options such as double majors, minors, and dual degrees. Dedman College offers a Bachelor of Arts (B.A.) degree with a major in a department of the College and a Bachelor of Science (B.S.) degree with a major in mathematics, a natural science, or selected social sciences. The College also offers two part-time multidisciplinary evening degrees: the Bachelor of Humanities (B.Hum.) and the Bachelor of Social Science (B.Soc.Sci.). The Cox School of Business awards the Bachelor of Business Administration (B.B.A.) degree. The Meadows School of Arts awards the Bachelor of Fine Arts (B.F.A.) in art, art history, dance, and theater; the Bachelor of Arts (B.A.) in advertising, art history, cinema-television, journalism, music, corporate communications and public affairs; and the Bachelor of Music (B.M.) degrees. The School of Engineering offers the Bachelor of Arts (B.A.) degree in computer science and the Bachelor of Science (B.S.) degree in the fields of computer engineering, computer science, electrical engineering, environmental engineering, management science, and mechanical engineering, with specializations and biomedical and premed options.

Academic Programs

All undergraduates enter SMU through Dedman College. The College provides the University's general education curriculum, which is designed to help students develop analytical and communication skills, the ability to explore ethical issues, and a broad understanding of the world. The curriculum includes courses in such categories as cultural formation, perspectives, human diversity, and information technology. Students who know their career interest can select courses in their planned major while in Dedman College. Students majoring in the humanities, mathematics, the natural sciences, and the social or behavioral sciences remain in Dedman College. Requirements for graduation vary according to the major program.

SMU grants both credit and advanced placement for satisfactory completion of Advanced Placement (AP) courses in high school. Credit up to 6 semester hours is given for each course in which a score of 4 or 5 was earned; 12 to 14 hours of credit can be granted for foreign languages with a score of 4 or 5. SMU also gives credit for departmental examination. Credit also is awarded for scores from 5 to 7 on higher-level exams in transferable subjects for the International Baccalaureate. Credit is not awarded for subsidiary-level exams. High school students may earn dual credit by attending off-campus colleges. A maximum of 32 advanced credits can be awarded. The academic year at SMU is composed of two semesters, plus an optional summer session that comprises two 5-week terms. A May term is also available.

Off-Campus Programs

SMU Study Abroad offers thirty-three programs in Australia, China, Denmark, Egypt, France, Germany, Great Britain, Italy, Japan, Mexico, Russia, South Africa, Southeast Asia, Spain, and Taiwan. SMU-in-Taos is the University's summer campus in northern New Mexico.

Academic Facilities

Newer facilities include the Meadows Museum of Art, which houses one of the world's largest collections of Spanish art; an addition to the Fondren Library Center; the Dedman Life Sciences Building; the Lindsey Embrey Engineering Building; and the Gerald R. Ford Stadium and Paul B. Loyd Jr. All-Sports Center. SMU's Dedman Center for Lifetime Sports recently expanded to offer students more new and renovated indoor and outdoor facilities.

SMU libraries contain more than 3 million volumes. Fondren Library contains a catalog of all holdings and major works of a general nature. Other collections are located in the Science Information Center, the Underwood Law Library, the Bridwell Library (a component of Perkins School of Theology), Hamon Arts Library, DeGolyer Library, and the Business Information Center. The Altshuler Learning Enhancement Center, known as the A-LEC, offers students individual tutoring, study groups, and techniques to enhance study and time management skills and test-taking strategies.

SMU has high-quality facilities campuswide, including specialized laboratories in the Dallas Seismological Observatory and the electron microscopy laboratory. The Institute for the Study of Earth and Man houses specialized laboratories for archeology, ethnology, geology, and physical anthropology. The Dedman Life Sciences Building and the Junkins Electrical Engineering Building feature state-of-the-art research, teaching, and computer labs.

Costs

The comprehensive fee for full-time undergraduate students for the 2008–09 academic year was $43,295. This amount included tuition and fees totaling $33,170 and a room and board charge of $10,125. SMU offers a monthly payment plan and other resources and plans to help students manage their investment in a college education.

Financial Aid

About 78 percent of first-year students receive some form of financial assistance. The SMU financial aid program includes University, state, and federal scholarships; merit- and need-based scholarships; grants; part-time jobs; payment plans; and/or low-interest loans. Most students who demonstrate financial need are awarded an aid package that combines SMU funds with government resources. The University assists all qualified students who cannot afford an SMU education. Financial aid decisions are based on academic performance and financial need. Accepted students interested in federal or state financial aid must file the Free Application for Federal Student Aid (FAFSA). SMU's code is 003136. Students may file online at http://www.fafsa.ed.gov. Students should complete the FAFSA by February 15 to receive primary consideration.

Students who also wish to be considered for SMU need-based assistance must complete the College Scholarship Service Financial Aid PROFILE (CSS PROFILE) in addition to the FAFSA. The PROFILE is available online at http://profileonline.collegeboard.com.

Financial aid, such as grants, low-interest loans, and campus employment, is also available to transfer students who demonstrate financial need based on the FAFSA and the CSS PROFILE, both of which should be filed each year. SMU offers transfer students a range of merit scholarships. For details, students should contact a transfer admission counselor at the phone number listed in this description.

SMU's merit-based scholarships have been named among the best in the United States by *America's Best College Scholarships 2001*. SMU's most prestigious scholarship programs include the President's Scholars, the Nancy Ann and Ray L. Hunt Leadership Scholars, SMU Distinguished Scholars, University Scholars, and International Baccalaureate (IB) Scholars. National Merit Scholarships are available only to finalists who name SMU as their first college choice. Students must apply for merit scholarships by January 15.

Faculty

The undergraduate student-faculty ratio is 12:1, which allows students to interact closely with faculty members. Sixty percent of all undergraduate lecture sections have fewer than 25 students. Almost 90 percent of the full-time faculty members hold a Ph.D. or the highest degrees in their field. Regular, full-time faculty members teach most undergraduate classes (74 percent). SMU has more than 500 full-time faculty members.

Student Government

The SMU Student Senate is a comprehensive governing body that meets weekly to initiate and facilitate action on student affairs. The Senate is composed of 4 student body officers, 40 senators, and ten committees.

Admission Requirements

The Office of Admission bases selection of applicants on several criteria: the strength of the high school program and the grades received, SAT or ACT scores, teacher and counselor recommendations, an essay, and optional input from parents and peers. Applicants should present a college-preparatory program and are expected to complete a minimum of 4 years of English, 3 of mathematics (including algebra I and II and plane geometry), 3 of a natural science (including two lab sciences), 3 of social studies, and 2 of a foreign language. SMU places value on personal accomplishment, and an attempt is made to get to know the individual and the academic record beyond standardized scores.

Although the average GPA of successful transfer applicants who have completed 30 or more transferable hours is considerably higher than a 2.7 GPA (on a 4.0 scale), applicants with a GPA below this threshold are not typically successful in gaining admission. Candidates with a transferable GPA below 2.0 are not admitted to the University. For all candidates who have completed 30 or more college hours, the Admission Committee considers the rigorous nature of the courses attempted; in particular, applicants should have completed at least one course in English composition, a lab science, a math course beyond college algebra, and a course pertaining to the intended major. The committee weighs overall academic performance as well as evidence of recent improvement. For some applicants, the high school performance is also a factor. Candidates with fewer than 30 hours are considered on an individual basis and may be required to submit additional information, including high school records.

As a privately endowed institution, SMU has no limits on enrollment based solely on geography, and it makes no distinctions in tuition, fees, or other costs based on the home state of the student. Southern Methodist University does not discriminate on the basis of race, color, religion, national origin, sex, age, disability, or veteran status. SMU's commitment to equal opportunity includes nondiscrimination on the basis of sexual orientation.

Application and Information

Students should apply soon after completing the junior year of high school. Online applications are available at http://www.smu.edu/apply. The nonbinding early action deadline is November 1, with notification by December 31. For regular decision and priority merit scholarship application consideration, the deadline is January 15, with notification by March 15. SMU offers a spring decision deadline of March 15 on a space-available basis.

Transfer application deadlines are April 1 for the summer term entry, June 1 for fall term and merit scholarship consideration, and November 1 for spring term (including scholarship applicants).

For admission information, students should contact:

Division of Enrollment Services
Southern Methodist University
P.O. Box 750181
Dallas, Texas 75275-0181
Phone: 214-768-2058
800-323-0672 (toll-free)
E-mail: ugadmission@smu.edu
Web site: http://www.smu.edu/admission/

Dallas Hall is the landmark building of SMU, reflecting the neo-Georgian architecture of the campus.

TRANSYLVANIA UNIVERSITY

LEXINGTON, KENTUCKY

The University

Transylvania, a small, private liberal arts college of about 1,150 men and women, is consistently ranked among the best small colleges in the nation. The name, from the Latin that means "across the woods", refers to the heavily forested Transylvania settlement in which the University was founded in 1780. Transylvania was the first college west of the Allegheny Mountains and the sixteenth in the nation. The University established the first schools of medicine and law in what was then the West and educated the doctors, lawyers, ministers, political leaders, and others who helped shape the young nation. Transylvania also founded the first college literary magazine in the West, *The Transylvanian*, still published by students today.

Transylvania continues as a pioneer in higher education, preparing future leaders in business, government, education, the sciences, and the arts. While professors engage in research and other scholarly activities, they never lose sight of their primary role, being great teachers. With their dedication to students, it is not surprising that Transylvania faculty members have dominated Kentucky Professor of the Year awards, winning six times in the last nine years. Students work closely with professors in small classes, many with fewer than 10 students. Due in large part to these close collaborations with faculty members, a high percentage of graduates attend selective medical, law, and other graduate and professional programs.

Transylvania students are an active and involved group, and they benefit from tremendous opportunities for learning outside the classroom and off-campus. Transylvania has over sixty active student organizations, covering a range of student interests. Over two thirds of students study abroad, and many participate in internships, research projects, and volunteer activities.

Location

Transylvania is located in Lexington, Kentucky, a city of 270,000 and a growing center of commerce, culture, research, and education. Known as the horse capital of the world, Lexington is surrounded by the rolling green pastures of the famous Bluegrass region of central Kentucky. The area is home to over 30,000 college students, and Transylvania's parklike campus is just a 5-minute walk from downtown, with easy access to restaurants, shops, and entertainment. The proximity to downtown is an advantage for students who want convenient part-time jobs and internship opportunities in law offices, accounting firms, hospitals, and other organizations. Transylvania offers its students a shuttle service between the Transylvania library and the University of Kentucky libraries, and the main branch of the Lexington Public Library is only a few blocks from campus. Lexington is served by major airlines, and is only 80 miles away from both Louisville and Cincinnati.

Majors and Degrees

The Bachelor of Arts degree is awarded in the following majors: accounting, anthropology, art history, art studio, biology, business administration (concentrations in finance, hospitality management, management, and marketing), chemistry (concentrations in chemistry and biochemistry), classics, computer science, drama, economics, education, English, exercise science, French, history, mathematics, music, music technology, philosophy, physical education, physics, political science, psychology, religion, sociology, and Spanish. Individually designed majors also may be arranged. Minors are available in most majors and in classical studies, communication, environmental studies, German, hospitality management, international affairs, multicultural studies, and women's studies. Advising and undergraduate preparation are provided for preprofessional programs in dentistry, engineering, law, medicine, ministry, pharmacy, physical therapy, and veterinary medicine. A cooperative program in engineering allows students to earn a B.A. in physics or math from Transylvania in three years and a B.S. in engineering from the University of Kentucky or Vanderbilt University in two years. A cooperative program in accounting allows students to earn a B.A. in accounting from Transylvania in four years and an M.S. in accounting from the University of Kentucky in one year; graduates qualify to take the CPA exam.

Academic Programs

The academic year is based on a 4-4-1 academic calendar, with two 14-week terms (fall and winter) and a one-month May term. The fall term begins in early September and ends in mid-December. The winter term begins in mid-January and ends in late April. During the May term, students may participate in a variety of programs on or off campus. Students normally take four courses in each of the fall and winter terms and one course in the May term. Thirty-six courses are required to graduate. First-year students participate in a two-term program called Foundations of the Liberal Arts, which features small-group discussions with a faculty leader; lectures, films, concerts, and other presentations; and a tutorial program in basic communication, critical thinking, and study skills. Special study-skills clinics and workshops are offered on an optional basis. Students must complete requirements designed to ensure broad familiarity with the major areas of learning and human endeavor in the humanities and fine arts, social sciences, natural sciences and mathematics, logic, and languages.

Transylvania grants credit for scores of 4 or 5 on the Advanced Placement examinations of the College Board and at least 5 on the International Baccalaureate program. Detailed information may be obtained from the Office of the Registrar.

Off-Campus Programs

Experiencing diverse cultures through international study is a vital part of a Transylvania education, with over two thirds of students participating in study abroad. It is common for Transylvania students to study abroad for a summer, a semester, or during May Term. A program at Regent's College, London, allows students to study there for the same cost and course credit as a semester at Transylvania. Scholarships are available for both semester-long and summer study abroad. Summer study programs, including those in Austria, Brazil, China, Costa Rica, Ecuador, France, Germany, Italy, Japan, Mexico, and Spain, are available through Transylvania's affiliation with the Kentucky Institute for International Studies. Transylvania also cooperates with the English-Speaking Union to offer advanced students scholarships for summer study at Cambridge and Oxford Universities. Students may participate in seminars or internships in Washington, D.C., through the Washington Center and in the Canadian Parliamentary Internship Program in Ottawa. Internships with congressional offices, Kentucky state government, city government, and local firms are easily arranged. Participation in Reserve Officers' Training Corps (Air Force and Army ROTC) is offered in cooperation with the University of Kentucky.

Academic Facilities

Two Georgian-style buildings combine elegance with high-tech facilities to offer the latest advances in teaching and learning. The Cowgill Center for Business, Economics, and Education includes a multimedia classroom where professors from any discipline can use a large display screen to show the entire class information from one of the twenty-five networked student computers or from a TV, video, CD-ROM, or satellite. A specialized area for education majors includes a laboratory classroom for teacher training. The Lucille C. Little Theater, used for faculty- and student-directed productions and drama classes, is a technically innovative facility that includes computerized lighting and sound, flexible staging options, and movable seating. The Frances Carrick Thomas/J. Douglas Gay, Jr. Library offers sophisticated computerized databases, which are invaluable for research and can be accessed from any computer connected to Transylvania's server, including PCs in dorm rooms. The Mitchell Fine Arts Center provides music program facilities, including practice rooms, a recital hall, and an auditorium. It also houses the Career Development Center, which helps students explore career options, improve job search skills, arrange internships and part-time jobs, and apply to graduate schools and to professional positions. The new, state-of-the-art fine arts technology lab can also be found in Mitchell. The Shearer Art Building is dedicated to instructional space, student and faculty studios, and a student gallery. Other modern facilities include the newly renovated L. A. Brown Science Center, the Haupt Humanities Building, and the Clive M. Beck Athletic and Recreation Center, which includes a state-of-the-art fitness center. About 80 percent of students live on campus in seven residence halls—two for men, one for women, and four for men and women. These include traditional-style accommodations, apartment-style living for upperclass students, and suite-style rooms. All rooms are air-conditioned and offer access to Transylvania's free cable television and computer networks. Thomson Hall, a new suite-style hall, opened in fall 2008. Each residence hall has ample lounge and study space and easy access to computer labs and recreational facilities. The William T. Young Campus Center offers a competition-size indoor pool, a gymnasium, and other meeting and recreational facilities.

Costs

Transylvania charges an annual tuition that covers fall, winter, and May terms for a normal full-time schedule of courses. Special instruction fees are charged in addition for certain designated courses, such as applied music and May Term travel courses. For 2008–09, tuition and fees were $23,810 and room and board (double occupancy) were $7450.

Financial Aid

Transylvania is committed to providing financial aid to students and their families. Four types of financial assistance are available. Scholarships are based on academic performance, and leadership. Grants, loans, and work-study are based on financial need. About 90 percent of Transylvania students receive some form of financial assistance, and many receive more than one type of aid. Outstanding entering freshmen may qualify for one of twenty William T. Young Scholarships—each worth more than $90,000 over four years—that cover tuition and fees. Submission of Transylvania's Application for Admission and Scholarships by the appropriate deadline is all that is necessary to be considered for academic scholarships at Transylvania. Students who are interested in need-based aid must file the Free Application for Federal Student Aid (FAFSA).

Faculty

Transylvania's relatively small size and low student-faculty ratio of 13:1 allow for close, personal attention in teaching and advising. Ninety-seven percent of full-time faculty members hold a doctorate or the highest degree in their fields, and they have come to Transylvania from a variety of graduate and professional schools. Many faculty members are recognized for their scholarship and professional activities, but their central concern is teaching and advising students. Transylvania professors have won six top professor awards over the past nine years from the Carnegie Foundation for the Advancement of Teaching and the Council for Advancement and Support of Education and from the Kentucky Advocates for Higher Education.

Transylvania's commitment to outstanding teaching is also reflected in its nationally recognized Bingham Program for Excellence in Teaching, the first of its type in the nation to attract and retain gifted teachers through an external evaluation process and financial incentives.

Student Government

Students at Transylvania have a high degree of access to the administration and governing board of the University. The Student Government Association serves as a representative government, and students also hold positions on standing committees of the faculty and the Board of Trustees.

Admission Requirements

Each applicant is considered individually on the basis of academic records, SAT scores and/or ACT scores, activities, interests, essays, and recommendations. Admission is also offered to transfer students, international students, and nontraditional students.

Transylvania enrolled 329 new students for the 2008–09 academic year. The middle 50 percent composite ACT score for the freshman class was 24 to 29. Fifty percent were in the top 10 percent of their high school class.

Application and Information

Submission of a Transylvania Application for Admission and Scholarships or submission of the Common Application is all that is necessary to be considered for admission and most merit scholarships at Transylvania.

The early action deadline is December 1 for applicants who wish to learn of their admission by January 15 and who want to be considered for all Transylvania scholarships. February 1 is the regular admission and scholarships deadline for applicants who wish to be considered for all Transylvania scholarships except the William T. Young Scholarship. Applicants who apply after February 1 are considered on a space-available basis. The deadline for applications for the winter term, which begins in January, is December 1. The same deadlines apply to electronic applications, which may be submitted on the Internet at the Web address listed below.

Students considering Transylvania are urged to visit the campus, and high school seniors are encouraged to stay overnight in a dorm with a student admissions assistant.

Weekday visits may include a customized campus tour and opportunities to attend classes; talk with professors, coaches, students, and admissions and financial aid counselors; and enjoy meals on campus.

Visits should be arranged through the Office of Admissions, preferably one to two weeks in advance. Open houses are held in the fall and winter, and a college planning workshop for high school juniors and sophomores is held in the spring.

For more information and application materials, students should contact:

Office of Admissions
Transylvania University
300 North Broadway
Lexington, Kentucky 40508-1797
Phone: 859-233-8242
800-872-6798 (toll-free)
E-mail: admissions@transy.edu
Web site: http://www.transy.edu

Small class sizes at Transylvania give professors and students the opportunity to work closely together, and many are directly involved in student research projects.

UNIVERSITY OF CHARLESTON

CHARLESTON, WEST VIRGINIA

The University

The University of Charleston (UC) strives to educate each student for a life of productive work, enlightened living, and community involvement. The University is very serious about its responsibility to provide students with the knowledge, abilities, and character necessary for them to have successful careers and to be productive and active citizens.

Founded in 1888 and formerly known as Morris Harvey College, the University of Charleston acquired its new name in 1979 to signify its importance as the leading higher education opportunity in the capital. Today, UC proudly represents the capital city of Charleston and the surrounding Kanawha Valley. Currently, approximately 1,400 students representing thirty-five states and twenty countries enjoy the University's 40-acre riverfront campus overlooking the State Capitol Complex and the beautiful city of Charleston.

The University has received numerous national accolades for its outstanding quality and educational approach. In September 2007, the University of Charleston was recognized as the national leader in outcomes-based learning and student assessment by the *New York Times Magazine.* The University also was ranked number 1 in the nation for 2007 by the Collegiate Learning Assessment (CLA), which also showed that UC students show the largest learning gain from freshman to sophomore year among all schools in the CLA report. The University of Charleston has been recognized as a national model for the Freshman-Year Experience, which includes faculty mentoring, university transitions, and living/learning communities. In addition, *U.S. News & World Report* placed UC in the top 20 in the Baccalaureate Colleges in the South category and as the Top Ranked Comprehensive College in West Virginia in its "Best Colleges for 2007" rankings. Students at UC also score among the highest in the country on the National Survey of Student Engagement.

The UC educational program focuses on "Learning Your Way." Students are the focus at UC. The academic program allows them to demonstrate what they have learned in order to earn the credits necessary for graduation. Students are expected to demonstrate knowledge and skills in the areas of communication, critical thinking, citizenship, ethical practice, science, and creativity. These attributes are integrated with knowledge and skills in a chosen field of study. Future employers and graduate schools consistently seek and employ college graduates with these abilities, and it is imperative that all University graduates have a strong foundation in these skills. Therefore, the University of Charleston has designed this program to help students master the knowledge and skills that are necessary for success.

Students are also encouraged to demonstrate mastery and earn credits at their own pace. Many students earn more than the traditional 15–18 credits per semester and graduate within three years, double major, or earn a master's degree quicker than at other schools.

Housing facilities for residential students are very modern and student friendly. Brotherton Hall was built in 2000 and houses 220 students; New Hall, built in 2003, houses 183 students; and Middle Hall, built in 2005 and 2006, houses 240 students. An expansion was completed for Middle Hall in August 2006 to accommodate increased student housing numbers, allowing the campus to house approximately 700 students.

Because the University believes that students learn from their involvement in community and campus activities, students are strongly encouraged to participate in one or more of the forty cocurricular organizations found at the University. There are academic clubs, publications, fraternities, sororities, religious organizations, intramural sports, honorary societies, drama clubs, cheerleading, chorus and band programs, and many student leadership organizations. The new Morrison Fitness Center opened in January 2007 and houses modern exercise equipment, weight systems, and classrooms for dance, yoga, Tae Kwon Do, or other activities. The University's Welch Colleague program integrates student involvement, the academic curriculum, community service, and leadership. The Community Service program provides opportunities for students to participate both on campus and in the Charleston area through opportunities like Habitat for Humanity. In addition, there are numerous civic, political, social, and charitable organizations easily accessible in the community.

The varsity sports program for men and women has become one of the University's most valuable assets. Men and women may participate in basketball, cheerleading, soccer, and tennis. Men may also participate in baseball, football, and golf and women in crew, cross-country, softball, track and field, and volleyball. The University's athletic teams compete in Division II of the NCAA. In recent years, men's and women's teams have been contenders in the WVIAC tournaments, with several teams winning conference championships and attending national championship tournaments. The women's basketball team participated in the Elite 8 in 2005 and 2006, and the men's football team had the largest one-season turnaround in conference history in 2005. UC athletics won the President's and Commissioner's Cups in 2006–07, signifying the top athletic teams in the WVIAC Conference.

The University of Charleston is accredited by the North Central Association of Colleges and Schools, National Council for Accreditation of Teacher Education, National Athletic Trainers Association, Commission on the Accreditation of Allied Health Education Programs–Athletic Training, Joint Review Committee on Education in Radiological Technology, and the National League for Nursing Accrediting Commission. The University holds a variety of professional recognitions, approvals, and memberships, including the International Assembly of Collegiate Business Education, West Virginia Academy of Sciences, Interior Design Educator's Council, and the American Council on Education.

The University offers master's degrees in business administration: an Executive M.B.A. and a plus-one M.B.A. for full-time study, one year beyond the bachelor's degree. A new Graduate School of Business is scheduled to open in fall 2008 with an emphasis on experiential learning and an enhanced master's program for outstanding students. The University of Charleston School of Pharmacy, which offers the University's first doctoral-level program, opened in fall 2006.

Location

Charleston, West Virginia's vibrant state capital, is a cultural, social, political, and economic hub. Located in the Kanawha Valley near the foothills of the Appalachian Mountains, it offers scenic tranquility as well as the convenience and excitement of a modern city. With a metropolitan population of 200,000, Charleston has grown to be West Virginia's finest city. Accessibility to the city is quite easy via plane, car, bus, and train. A large civic center, historic sites, libraries, movie theaters, shopping malls, and a symphony orchestra are all highlights of the Charleston business district. The rapport between the University and the community is excellent, and many events are cosponsored annually.

Downtown Charleston, just a short ride from the campus by campus shuttle or city bus, offers the kind of social and cultural opportunities that can be found only in a large city. In addition, fishing, hunting, horseback riding, waterskiing, snow skiing, mountain biking, and white-water rafting are just a few of the many recreational activities to be found within a short distance of the campus.

Majors and Degrees

The University of Charleston offers undergraduate degree programs through its various divisions: the Morris Harvey Division of Arts and Sciences, the Herbert Jones Division of Business, and the Bert Bradford Division of Health Sciences.

The Morris Harvey Division of Arts and Sciences offers the Bachelor of Arts degree with the following majors: art, communications, education (various certifications), general studies, interior design, political science, and psychology. The Bachelor of Science degree is offered with majors in biology, chemistry, and a biology/chemistry preprofessional program focused on the health sciences. The Division of Arts and Sciences is also home to the popular Pre-Pharmacy program. This program is segmented into the Pre-Pharmacy Scholars track and the Traditional Pre-Pharmacy track. Students who excel in this unique program have preferential entry into the Pharm.D. program.

The Jones Division of Business offers Bachelor of Science degree programs in accounting, sports administration, business administration, and finance.

The Division of Health Sciences offers the Bachelor of Science degree in athletic training, nursing, and radiologic science. An Associate of Arts degree in nursing is also offered at the University.

Students may pursue directed independent study and internships in most majors. Army ROTC is offered to interested men and women.

Academic Programs

Candidates for a bachelor's degree from UC are required to complete a minimum of 120 semester hours and have a cumulative grade point average of at least 2.0 on all college work attempted. This must include 30 hours in upper division courses; demonstration of learning in the required outcomes of communication, critical thinking, ethical practice, creativity, science, and citizenship; and advanced work leading to a major in a department or a division. The minimum requirement for an associate degree is 60 semester hours and a cumulative grade point average of at least a 2.0 on all college work attempted, including completion of a prescribed program of general education and specialized work in a department.

The University follows a semester academic calendar and offers summer terms for students who wish to accelerate their college program.

Academic Facilities

A large number of support facilities and programs supplement the various academic opportunities at the University of Charleston. The Schoenbaum Library serves as the center of the learning experience. Located in the technologically advanced Clay Tower Building, the library has a collection of more than 120,000 books, 200,000 microforms, and 3,600 audiovisual items. More than 8,000 journal titles are available either in print or electronically and are accessible from any Web-enabled computer, on or off campus. In addition, numerous specialized collections, CD-ROM-based electronic indexes, and online electronic search services are at the students' disposal for specialized research and study. The library also offers wireless technology and laptop computer check-out.

The University has numerous computer labs for student and faculty use: the Cabot Apple Lab, the IBM-PC combination classroom labs, an IBM-PC network lab, and an IBM-PC open lab. Wireless access is also available on much of the campus, including the scenic riverbank. The Learning Support Center provides a variety of services and classes to help students achieve academic, personal, and professional success. The Communication Resource Center provides support for students and faculty members through consultation services, workshops, and electronic access to a variety of writing resources.

The Clay Tower Building houses state-of-the-art science, technology, and information resource facilities. Riggleman Hall, the main college building, houses classrooms, a 976-seat auditorium and stage, education and language laboratories, the Carleton Varney Department of Art and Design, and administrative offices.

Costs

For the 2007–08 academic year, tuition was $22,050, and room (double occupancy) and board were $7930, for a total of $29,980. This does not include the cost of books, supplies, or other incidental charges.

Financial Aid

The University of Charleston provides generous financial assistance that may include a combination of scholarships, grants, loans, and work-study. In 2007–08, more than 90 percent of full-time students received some form of financial aid. Special academic scholarships and grants are awarded to outstanding full-time students. The University also offers grants to qualified athletes and to students who are involved in leadership, community service, band, school newspaper, or vocal music.

Faculty

The University has 61 full-time and 38 part-time undergraduate faculty members. At the University of Charleston, faculty members provide academic, career, and in some cases, personal advice to students. They encourage active learning through collaborative projects and faculty/student research. Small classes through a 13:1 faculty-student ratio allow for individual attention for students.

Student Government

The Student Government Association is a policymaking body composed of students representing most campus organizations and student classes. Both the Student Government Association and the University believe that students should have the privilege, along with the faculty and administration, of participating in the governance of the University.

Admission Requirements

Admission to the University of Charleston is based on the academic records and potential for leadership and involvement. A qualified applicant's credentials must strongly suggest ability and motivation to succeed in higher education and in the University community. Candidates for admission must present a transcript of work from an accredited secondary school showing at least 16 academic units, grades indicating intellectual ability and promise, and proof of graduation or a GED. The pattern of courses should show purpose and continuity and furnish a background for the liberal learning outcomes curriculum offered by the University.

Since the unique and student-friendly curriculum emphasizes communication, critical thinking, and citizenship, secondary school courses should emphasize courses in English, mathematics, sciences, and social sciences. Candidates are also required to submit scores on the ACT or SAT. Students must have an above-average academic profile that includes a minimum 2.25 academic grade point average and a minimum ACT composite score of 19 or SAT score (combined math and critical reading) of 900. Applicants for admission are considered on an individual basis without regard to race, religion, geographic origin, or handicap. Letters of recommendation and a personal visit to the campus scheduled with the Office of Admissions are highly recommended.

Application and Information

For more information, interested students should contact:

Office of Admissions
University of Charleston
2300 MacCorkle Avenue, SE
Charleston, West Virginia 25304
Phone: 304-357-4750
800-995-GO UC (4682) (toll-free)
Fax: 304-357-4781
E-mail: admissions@ucwv.edu
Web site: http://www.ucwv.edu

The Clay Tower Building houses state-of-the-art science facilities and a library with lounges overlooking the Kanawha River. The campus is directly across the river from the State Capitol.

UNIVERSITY OF DALLAS

IRVING, TEXAS, AND ROME, ITALY

The University

In 1955, the Roman Catholic Diocese of Dallas/Fort Worth purchased land for a university on a 1,000-acre tract of rolling hills northwest of Dallas, and in 1956, the University of Dallas (UD) opened. His Excellency Bishop Thomas K. Gorman, Chancellor of the new university, announced that it would be a coeducational institution, welcoming students of all faiths and ethnic backgrounds. Headed by a lay president and a lay academic dean, the faculty was composed of laymen, diocesan and Cistercian priests, and sisters of the Order of St. Mary of Namur.

Current undergraduate enrollment is about 1,300 men and women. Undergraduates come from all fifty states and thirty-three other countries. Although approximately 75 percent are Catholic, twenty faiths are represented on campus.

The University of Dallas was the first Catholic institution to have a board of trustees made up of both lay and religious members. Since its founding, many other universities and colleges have followed its example. The first class, a group of individuals who won significant honors, such as Fulbright and Woodrow Wilson fellowships, graduated in 1960. There is a Phi Beta Kappa chapter on campus. In fact, UD is the youngest university in the twentieth century to have been awarded a Phi Beta Kappa chapter.

Through a $6-million endowment provided by the Blakley-Braniff Foundation, the Braniff Graduate School was established in 1966. Twelve graduate programs are now in existence, including doctoral programs in philosophy, politics, and literature and the M.F.A. program in art. The College of Business houses the Graduate School of Management, which is distinguished by its practice-oriented education, close ties with leading companies and professionals, and a global student body. In addition to its undergraduate programs, the College of Business offers Master of Business Administration (M.B.A.) and Master of Management degrees. The M.B.A. includes sixteen concentrations in the areas of finance, health care, information technology, management, marketing, and telecommunications.

The University of Dallas is a center of learning, and the experience on campus is intensive and highly directed. People choose to come to the University because they are serious students. While they engage in a full complement of extracurricular activities and independent study, it is the act of learning in association with their professors that shapes their college years. Because the undergraduate college is small and largely residential, it forms a close-knit community. Over 60 percent of UD's students come from outside of the state of Texas, a statistic shared by only one other Texas university; so UD is a constant bustle of activities, rarely emptying on the weekends. The University sponsors a number of lectures, concerts, and art exhibits, ranging from the old masters to the UD international printmaking invitational. The Student Government sponsors weekly events and current and classic films. The *University News* has consistently won awards for excellence in writing and design. Collegium Cantorum, the a cappella liturgical choir, performs both nationally and internationally. Intercollegiate NCAA Division III sports include baseball, basketball, cross-country, golf, lacrosse, soccer, softball, track, and volleyball. Rugby is very popular at the club level. Eighty-five percent of the on-campus students are involved in intramurals: basketball, flag football, soccer, softball, paintball, and other sports. Traditional events include coffeehouses featuring student entertainment, Charity Week, Mallapalooza, Oktoberfest, Spring Olympics, and Groundhog. UD boasts the second largest Groundhog Day celebration outside of Punxsutawney, Pennsylvania.

For Catholic students, daily and weekly Mass, Reconciliation, and rosary are held in the 500-seat Church of the Incarnation. Transportation is arranged for students of other faiths to attend services nearby. Campus Ministry provides numerous volunteer opportunities, including annual service projects in Appalachia and Ecuador.

Location

Irving, Texas, a city of 195,000 on the northwest side of the city of Dallas, is about 15 minutes from downtown Dallas, 10 minutes from Love Field airport, and 15 minutes from DFW airport. The Dallas–Fort Worth Metroplex, the fourth largest metroplex in the country, offers a diverse mix of cultural and entertainment attractions, including the Dallas Museum of Modern Art, the new Nasher Sculpture Center, and the Kimbell Museum in Fort Worth. The Dallas Theater Center and Stage One have built reputations as top-notch theaters and as proving grounds for Broadway-bound productions. Texas Stadium, home of the Dallas Cowboys, is just three blocks from the University. Dallas is home to professional sports teams in hockey, soccer, and basketball. Nearby Arlington is home to the Texas Rangers.

Majors and Degrees

The Constantin College of Liberal Arts offers programs leading to the Bachelor of Arts (B.A.) degree in art and art history, biology, business, chemistry, classics, drama, economics, economics and finance, education, English, history, mathematics, modern languages (French, German, and Spanish), philosophy, physics, politics, psychology, and theology. The Bachelor of Science degree is awarded in biochemistry, biology, chemistry, mathematics, and physics.

The College of Business offers Bachelor of Arts degrees in business leadership.

The University offers twenty-seven concentrations, or minors, including applied math, applied physics, art history, business, Christian contemplative studies, computer science, entrepreneurship, environmental science, international studies, journalism, math, medieval and Renaissance studies, modern language, music, and pure math.

Preprofessional programs in architecture, business, dentistry, engineering, law, medicine, and physical therapy are carefully integrated with the undergraduate Core Curriculum. The rate of acceptance and enrollment of the college's students by professional schools is exceptional. More than 80 percent eventually go on to graduate school, and the rate of acceptance to first-choice programs for medical and law school applicants is more than 90 percent.

Academic Programs

The undergraduate Core Curriculum is a shared series of specific courses, based on the great books of Western civilization that outline the development of Western thought and culture from classical to modern times. Every student becomes familiar with the same works of literature and the same great books and concepts, fostering a natural understanding and exchange of ideas. All students then go on to pursue their chosen major discipline, reaching a level of maturity and competence in the discipline that they could not have attained in the absence of a strong foundation shared among all students entering the major. The student body has an active and personal involvement with the Core Curriculum.

The University observes a two-semester calendar, with the semester examinations occurring before the monthlong Christmas break. An interterm session and three summer sessions are also offered.

Off-Campus Programs

All undergraduates, regardless of major, are encouraged to spend one semester on the University's campus in Rome. While not compulsory, the Rome experience is an important part of the undergraduate education; to seek one's heritage in the liberal arts and to be a student of the Western world is, in a sense, to be a citizen of Rome. Courses offered in Rome are from the Core Curriculum and are taught by professors from the Texas campus. The Rome campus is located just outside of downtown Rome. Transfer students who need courses offered on the Rome campus may participate after one semester on the main campus. The cost for tuition, room, and board for all participants is roughly equivalent to that on the main campus. More than 85 percent of University of Dallas graduates have participated in the Rome program.

Academic Facilities

The Science Center, a $6-million, state-of-the-art facility, houses some of the most advanced tools for scientific research available, including a working observatory. The Haggerty Arts Village has established the University as a leading center for ceramics and fine arts in the Southwest. Drama productions are staged in the Margaret Jonsson Theater. Blakely Library holds more than 275,000 volumes, including the personal library of the late political philosopher Wilmoore Kendall.

Costs

Annual tuition and fees for 2008–09 are $24,770; room and board costs average $7885. Costs are the same for in-state and out-of-state students.

Financial Aid

Tuition, fees, room, and board are substantially lower at the University of Dallas than at many other nationally recognized universities. In addition, all high school seniors who apply for admission by the freshman scholarship priority deadline of January 15 receive priority consideration for all of the University's achievement-based awards. The University currently offers three types of achievement-based awards: academic achievements, cocurricular achievements, and departmental awards. Departments currently offering awards include art, chemistry, classics (Latin and Greek), German, French, math, physics, and Spanish. Students who apply for admission between January 16 and March 1 receive regular consideration for achievement-based awards. Those who apply for admission after March 1 are considered for achievement-based awards dependent on the availability of funding.

All students who submit a Free Application for Federal Student Aid (FAFSA) are considered for all forms of financial assistance based on their family's finances. These forms of assistance include scholarships, grants, loans, and work-study programs. Priority is given to applicants whose FAFSA is received by the University of Dallas on or before March 1. The school code for sending a FAFSA to the University of Dallas is 003651.

Faculty

The University prides itself on its teaching faculty. Ninety-two percent hold terminal degrees. With a faculty-student ratio of 1:14, extensive consultation and direction are possible. The average class size is 17. The faculty is characterized by authority in the various disciplines, and its members have published more than 1,000 books and articles and secured major research grants.

Student Government

The Student Government Association and various departmental and special clubs, such as the social, film, lecture, and fine arts committees, encourage an extracurricular life created by the students themselves.

Admission Requirements

Although no rigid cutoff point is adhered to in admission, 52 percent of the students who enter as freshmen rank in the top 10 percent of their high school class. General admission requirements include SAT or ACT scores, rank in the upper third of the high school class, and 16 college-preparatory units, including 4 in English, 3 in mathematics, 2 in the same foreign language, 2 in social science, and 2 in a laboratory science. Interviews are not required but are strongly recommended. Through the Office of Undergraduate Admission, counseling appointments, tours, and overnight accommodations on campus may be arranged. Transfer students are welcome.

Application and Information

A transcript and SAT or ACT scores must be submitted along with letters of recommendation from a teacher and a counselor. A completed application and completed supplement, both of which are obtainable online or via mail or phone from the Office of Admission, must be submitted as well. Transfer students should submit all transcripts from colleges previously attended. A $40 application fee should accompany the application; the other material may follow as ready. The Early Action I deadline is November 1; the Early Action II deadline is December 1. The freshman priority scholarship deadline is January 15. The regular admission deadline is March 1. Rolling admission is March 2–August 1.

Transfer students should apply by December 1 for spring entry and by July 1 for fall entry.

For applications or further information, students should contact:

Office of Undergraduate Admission and Financial Aid
University of Dallas
1845 East Northgate Drive
Irving, Texas 75062
Phone: 972-721-5266
800-628-6999 (toll-free)
Web site: http://www.udallas.edu

University of Dallas students learning on-site at Sicily, Italy.

UNIVERSITY OF NEW ORLEANS

NEW ORLEANS, LOUISIANA

The University

The University of New Orleans (UNO) is part of the rich cultural tapestry of its hometown, which is one of the most extraordinary cities in the world. Established in 1958 to bring publicly supported higher education to the New Orleans area, UNO is fully accredited by the Commission on Colleges of the Southern Association of Colleges and Schools. With an enrollment of nearly 12,000 students (9,000 undergraduates and 3,000 graduate students) in fall 2008, UNO offers both undergraduate and graduate degrees through the doctoral level.

UNO derives its strength from its urban setting and strives to enhance the economic, social, and cultural amenities of New Orleans through its numerous research projects, outreach programs, and special cooperative agreements. The University of New Orleans attracts students from forty-eight states (approximately 12 percent) and 102 countries; a majority of the students are Louisiana residents (approximately 88 percent). The diverse student population (42 percent of students are members of ethnic minorities) provides an excellent opportunity for personal growth and understanding.

For students who are interested in on-campus housing, UNO offers two unique styles of living. Privateer Place overlooks beautiful Lake Pontchartrain and includes a swimming pool and Jacuzzi. Privateer Place contains seventy-two 2-person unfurnished efficiency apartments, 216 furnished two-bedroom apartments, and sixty furnished four-bedroom apartments. In fall 2007, UNO opened a new $38.5-million residence hall complex (Pontchartrain Hall), composed of two 4-story buildings totaling about 220,000 square feet. The facility includes 236 suite-style units that can accommodate 749 students, as well as TV and recreation rooms, study lounges, laundry facilities, and a convenience store. All complexes have disability-accessible rooms available.

Campus dining facilities are conveniently located near all on-campus housing facilities and heavily populated student areas, with various hours of operation. Other student services include six on-campus computer labs that provide free Internet access, a learning resource center that offers additional tutoring services, student counseling services, an on-campus medical office and pharmacy, student legal counseling, and religious centers.

UNO has more than 125 active student organizations on campus, including academic, professional, Greek, social, political, and religious organizations. UNO's newest addition is the University pep band, the UNO Blue Zoo, which performs at all UNO home basketball games and other University-related events. *Bayou* is UNO's annual national literary magazine that collects submissions from writers worldwide. UNO's student newspaper, *Driftwood,* is published weekly, and *Ellipsis,* a literary magazine, is published annually.

As a Division I member of the National Collegiate Athletic Association (NCAA), UNO fields men's teams in basketball, baseball, and tennis and women's teams in basketball, volleyball, and tennis. UNO students can also participate in many recreational and intramural sports. Students have access to a new 85,000-square-foot Recreation and Fitness Center, which features a 12,000-square-foot cardiovascular, circuit, and free-weight-training room; an indoor track; a lap pool; racquetball courts; an outdoor sundeck; a juice bar; and a social lounge. UNO also offers a variety of Intercollegiate Club Sports like football (Midwest Conference), rugby, soccer, sailing, cricket, karate, and hockey. Recreational sports have intramural activities for individuals and groups throughout the year.

Location

The University's 195-acre main campus is set in one of the most beautiful residential areas on the south shore of Lake Pontchartrain, only minutes from the fun and excitement of downtown New Orleans and the French Quarter. New Orleans is a cosmopolitan city, known for its great Southern hospitality and its unique tourist attractions. Renowned for Creole and Cajun cuisine, Mardi Gras, and jazz music festivals, New Orleans culture offers a unique environment for students to grow, both socially and academically. Whether exploring the art galleries of the Warehouse District or strolling down stately St. Charles Avenue, New Orleans has something for everyone, and the University of New Orleans is a part of it all.

Many of UNO's hotel, restaurant, and tourism administration majors find internships in the city's best hotels and restaurants. Film students have the opportunity to work at the Nims Center film studio complex as New Orleans becomes the "Hollywood of the South." Naval architecture students have access to the nation's largest undergraduate program in naval architecture and marine engineering as well as to the UNO–Avondale Maritime Center. As New Orleans continues to attract computer technology–based businesses to what has been called "the Silicon Bayou," the UNO Research and Technology Park continues to expand, producing more than 8,000 new jobs. Computer science majors are able to network with potential employers in one of the fastest-growing computer technology markets in the country.

Majors and Degrees

Bachelor of Science degrees are offered in accounting; biological sciences; chemistry; civil and environmental engineering; computer science; earth and environmental science; electrical engineering; entrepreneurship; finance; general business administration; hotel, restaurant, and tourism administration; management; marketing; mathematics; mechanical engineering; naval architecture and marine engineering; physics; psychology; transportation studies; urban studies and planning; and preprofessional programs in dentistry, medicine (with biology, chemistry, and psychology tracks), nursing, pharmacy, physical therapy studies, and veterinary medicine.

Bachelor of Arts degrees are offered in anthropology; early childhood education; elementary education; English; English education; film, theater, and communication arts; fine arts–history; fine arts–studio (with options that include digital media, painting, photography, and sculpture); French; geography; history; international studies; mathematics education; music (with options such as instrumental, jazz studies, theory and composition, and vocal); music education; philosophy; political science; secondary education; social science education; sociology; Spanish; and women's studies.

A four-year Bachelor of General Studies degree program is available for students who wish to design individual curricula. Credit programs in paralegal studies, medical coding, and medical transcripts are also offered. Additional interdisciplinary minors are offered in interdisciplinary studies in African studies, Asian studies, entrepreneurship, environmental studies, Latin American and Caribbean studies, medical coding, Native American studies, paralegal studies, and print journalism.

Academic Programs

All baccalaureate degree programs require a minimum of 128 semester hours with a minimum grade point average of 2.0 (C) in all work attempted in the college major. Also, all students must successfully complete an approved course demonstrating computer literacy. Other course requirements vary according to program. Programs leading to degrees with honors are offered in most academic majors. Credit for selected courses may be earned either through advanced-standing exams administered by the academic departments or through the College Board's Advanced Placement and College-Level Examination Program tests. College credit may also be gained for certain armed services and other nonacademic training. The academic year is composed of sixteen-week fall and spring semesters and three summer sessions.

Off-Campus Programs

The University of New Orleans Metropolitan College coordinates international study programs in Austria, Costa Rica, the Czech Republic, Ecuador, France, Greece, Honduras, and Italy. UNO's partnership with the University of Innsbruck, Austria, affords students an opportunity to participate in the largest international summer school of any American university in Europe. UNO offers college-credit exchange programs in Brazil and Canada. Students may also attend another school within the continental United States via the National Student Exchange (NSE) for one semester or one year.

UNO offers several off-campus facilities throughout the metropolitan New Orleans area, demonstrating UNO's commitment to community outreach. Off-campus locations offer both credit and noncredit courses, with hours varying from sunrise to evening and weekend classes.

Academic Facilities

The Earl K. Long Library's 1.5-million-volume collection includes approximately 12,000 journals, of which 3,800 are current subscriptions. Microform holdings include microfilm, microcard, and microfiche formats; microtext readers and reader-printers are also available. Other facilities include individual study carrels, a music listening room, computer terminals connected to the Computer Research Center, a Kurzweil reader for the visually impaired, and photocopy services. The Office of Educational Support Services includes a media resources center, which provides important media aids for the instructional staff in classroom presentations, and Television Resources, which coordinates a closed-circuit cable system and TV production studio. WWNO, the first public radio station in Louisiana, is located on the UNO campus.

All enrolled students and faculty and staff members receive a LAN and e-mail account. The University's computer network provides connections to approximately 5,000 locations campuswide as well as wireless connections in select buildings. High-speed ResNet service is available to students living in Privateer Place, and a free dial-up Internet modem pool provides access for all off-campus enrolled students and faculty and staff members.

The UNO Lee Circle Center for the Arts includes the Ogden Museum, which houses the largest collection of Southern art in the world. The center also houses the National D-Day Museum, which includes the world's largest collection of World War II color film. The 70,000-square-foot Nims Center, located 20 minutes from the main campus, houses a professional-quality sound stage, including a 10,000-square-foot studio for University film projects. The Nims Center is also available for professional film projects.

Costs

In 2008–09, combined undergraduate fees for full-time students for the fall and spring semesters were $3488 for Louisiana residents and $10,884 for nonresidents; summer session fees for full-time students were $965 for Louisiana residents and $1515 for nonresidents. Residence hall and board fees totaled $4420 (double occupancy) for the fall and spring semesters. Costs of books and supplies total approximately $1000 per year. Additional charges include a $40 application fee, a $10 registration fee, field service and laboratory fees (usually $10 to $35) for some courses, an $80 car registration fee (includes parking pass), a $30 late application fee, a $30 late registration fee, a $5 per credit hour (maximum $75) technology fee, and a $10 per credit hour (maximum $120) academic enhancement fee. All fees are subject to change and can be confirmed by calling the Office of Admissions.

Financial Aid

The Office of Student Financial Aid develops financial aid packages to assist students with their educational expenses. This package is usually a combination of grants, loans, student employment, and/or scholarships, which, along with family contribution, help to finance the student's education. To be eligible for most federal financial aid programs, students must enroll for at least 6 credit hours (half-time) in an eligible program (one that leads to a degree or certificate). More than three quarters of all freshmen in fall 2008 who showed financial need and took at least 6 credit hours were offered some form of financial aid. The priority date for the financial aid application is May 1. All applications postmarked on or before January 15 are considered for UNO's numerous academic scholarships, including those of international students. The University of New Orleans also offers scholarships in jazz studies; classical music; fine arts; film, theater, and communication arts; and creative writing. These scholarships require either an audition or the submission of a portfolio or manuscript along with the scholarship application.

Faculty

UNO has 525 full-time and 175 part-time faculty members, most of whom participate in both graduate and undergraduate instruction and research activity. Graduate students serve as teaching assistants in laboratory courses under the close supervision of the faculty. Approximately 80 percent of the faculty members hold doctorates. Most full-time faculty members devote themselves exclusively to University-related pursuits and are integrally involved in student affairs through counseling, teaching, research, and social activities. The student-faculty ratio is 18:1.

Student Government

Every student enrolled at UNO is a member of the Student Government (SG). SG offers students a way to create effective change, express opinions and concerns, and utilize resources to enhance their educational experiences. Some of the programs SG currently offers and/or sponsors are Student Legal Services, the Academic Travel Fund, 24-hour study hall during finals week, UNO pep band (the Blue Zoo), the Mechanical Engineering Mini Baja Competition, UNO Jazz Night at the University Center, musical excursions, the UNO student literary magazine *(Ellipsis)*, recreation and intramural sports, cheerleaders, and the Privateer dance team.

Admission Requirements

Students seeking admission to the University of New Orleans should submit their application as early as possible in their senior year. Admission requirements for Louisiana residents and nonresidents for fall 2009 include the completion of the Board of Regents core curriculum (in years): English (4), mathematics (3), science (3), social studies (3), foreign language (2), fine arts (1), mathematics/science elective (1), and computer science (½). Residents must also have either a high school cumulative GPA of at least 2.5 or an ACT composite score of at least 23 (1060 SAT) or rank in the top 25 percent of their high school graduating class, and students must not require more than one developmental/remedial course. Out-of-state students who do not meet the GPA, test score, and rank requirements must have a minimum ACT composite score of 26 (SAT 1170) for automatic admission.

Transfer requirements include the completion of 18 semester hours of nondevelopmental work, a minimum 2.25 cumulative GPA, and completion of all developmental course work before transferring. Students with fewer than 18 semester hours must meet both freshman and transfer requirements.

Application and Information

The University of New Orleans has a rolling admissions policy. The application fee is $40. Priority deadlines for application are as follows: July 1 for the fall semester, November 15 for the spring semester, and May 1 for the summer semester. Deadlines for international students are June 1, October 1, and March 1, respectively.

Office of Admissions
103 Administration Building
University of New Orleans
2000 Lakeshore Drive
New Orleans, Louisiana 70148
Phone: 504-280-6595
800-256-5-UNO (toll-free)
Fax: 504-280-5522
Web site: http://www.uno.edu

Indexes

Majors and Degrees

Accounting

Adrian Coll, MI B
AIB Coll of Business, IA A,B
Alma Coll, MI B
Anderson U, IN B
Andrews U, MI B
Aquinas Coll, MI B
Ashland U, OH B
Augsburg Coll, MN B
Augustana Coll, IL B
Augustana Coll, SD B
Aurora U, IL B
Avila U, MO B
Bacone Coll, OK A,B
Baker Coll of Allen Park, MI A
Baker Coll of Auburn Hills, MI A,B
Baker Coll of Clinton Township, MI A
Baker Coll of Owosso, MI A,B
Baker U, KS B
Baldwin-Wallace Coll, OH B
Ball State U, IN B
Bemidji State U, MN B
Benedictine Coll, KS B
Benedictine U, IL B
Bethany Coll, KS B
Bethel Coll, IN B
Black Hills State U, SD B
Bluffton U, OH B
Bohecker's Business Coll, OH A
Bowling Green State U, OH B
Bradley U, IL B
Briar Cliff U, IA B
Bryant & Stratton Coll, Parma, OH A
Bryant & Stratton Coll, Willoughby Hills, OH A
Bryant & Stratton Coll, WI A
Bryant & Stratton Coll—Wauwatosa Campus, WI A
Buena Vista U, IA B
Butler U, IN B
Calumet Coll of Saint Joseph, IN A,B
Calvin Coll, MI B
Cameron U, OK B
Capital U, OH B
Carroll U, WI B
Case Western Reserve U, OH B
Cedarville U, OH B
Central Christian Coll of Kansas, KS B
Central Coll, IA B
Central Methodist U, MO B
Central Michigan U, MI B
Central State U, OH B
Chancellor U, OH A,B
Clarke Coll, IA B
Clarkson U, NY B
Cleary U, MI B
Cleveland State U, OH B
Coe Coll, IA B
Coll of Mount St. Joseph, OH A,B
Coll of Saint Benedict, MN B
Coll of Saint Mary, NE A
The Coll of St. Scholastica, MN B
Coll of the Ozarks, MO B
Colorado Tech U North Kansas City, MO A,B
Colorado Tech U Sioux Falls, SD A,B
Columbia Coll, MO B
Concordia Coll, MN B
Concordia U Chicago, IL B
Concordia U, Nebraska, NE B
Concordia U, St. Paul, MN B
Concordia U Wisconsin, WI B
Cornerstone U, MI B
Creighton U, NE B
Culver-Stockton Coll, MO B
Dakota State U, SD B
Dakota Wesleyan U, SD B
Dana Coll, NE B
Davenport U, Grand Rapids, MI A,B
Defiance Coll, OH B
DePaul U, IL B
Doane Coll, NE B
Dominican U, IL B
Dordt Coll, IA B
Drake U, IA B
Drury U, MO B
Eastern Illinois U, IL B
Eastern Michigan U, MI B
East-West U, IL B
Edgewood Coll, WI B
Elmhurst Coll, IL B
Emporia State U, KS B
Eureka Coll, IL B
Ferris State U, MI B
Fort Hays State U, KS B
Franciscan U of Steubenville, OH A,B
Franklin Coll, IN B
Franklin U, OH A,B
Friends U, KS B
Goshen Coll, IN B
Grace Bible Coll, MI B
Grace Coll, IN B
Graceland U, IA B
Grace U, NE B
Grand Valley State U, MI B
Grand View U, IA B
Greenville Coll, IL B
Gustavus Adolphus Coll, MN B
Hannibal-LaGrange Coll, MO B
Harris-Stowe State U, MO B
Heidelberg U, OH B
Hillsdale Coll, MI B
Hope Coll, MI B
Huntington U, IN B
Illinois Coll, IL B
Illinois State U, IL B
Illinois Wesleyan U, IL B
Indiana State U, IN B
Indiana Tech, IN A,B
Indiana U–Purdue U Fort Wayne, IN B
Indiana Wesleyan U, IN A,B
Iowa State U of Science and Technology, IA B
Iowa Wesleyan Coll, IA B
Jamestown Coll, ND B
John Carroll U, OH B
Kansas State U, KS B
Kansas Wesleyan U, KS B
Kaplan U–Davenport Campus, IA A
Kaplan U–Mason City Campus, IA A
Kent State U, OH B
Kilian Comm Coll, SD A
Kuyper Coll, MI B
Lake Erie Coll, OH B
Lakeland Coll, WI B
Lake Superior State U, MI A,B
Lewis U, IL B
Lincoln U, MO B
Lindenwood U, MO B
Loras Coll, IA B
Lourdes Coll, OH B
Loyola U Chicago, IL B
Luther Coll, IA B
MacMurray Coll, IL B
Madonna U, MI B
Malone U, OH B
Manchester Coll, IN A,B
Marian U, WI B
Marian U, IN B
Marietta Coll, OH B
Marquette U, WI B
Martin U, IN B
Maryville U of Saint Louis, MO B
McKendree U, IL B
McPherson Coll, KS B
Miami U, OH B
Miami U Hamilton, OH B
Michigan State U, MI B
Michigan Technological U, MI B
MidAmerica Nazarene U, KS B
Midstate Coll, IL B
Millikin U, IL B
Minnesota School of Business–Blaine, MN A,B
Minnesota State U Mankato, MN B
Minnesota State U Moorhead, MN B
Minot State U, ND B
Missouri Baptist U, MO B
Missouri Southern State U, MO A
Missouri State U, MO B
Missouri Western State U, MO B
Monmouth Coll, IL B
Morningside Coll, IA B
Mount Marty Coll, SD A,B
Mount Mary Coll, WI B
Mount Mercy Coll, IA B
Mount Union Coll, OH B
Mount Vernon Nazarene U, OH B
Muskingum Coll, OH B
National-Louis U, IL B
Nebraska Wesleyan U, NE B
Newman U, KS B
North Central Coll, IL B
North Dakota State U, ND B
Northeastern Illinois U, IL B
Northeastern State U, OK B
Northern Michigan U, MI B
Northern State U, SD B
North Park U, IL B
Northwestern Coll, MN B
Northwest Missouri State U, MO B
Northwood U, MI B
Oakland U, MI B
Oglala Lakota Coll, SD A
Ohio Dominican U, OH B
Ohio Northern U, OH B
The Ohio State U, OH B
Ohio Wesleyan U, OH B
Oklahoma Baptist U, OK B
Oklahoma Christian U, OK B
Oklahoma City U, OK B
Oklahoma Panhandle State U, OK B
Oklahoma State U, OK B
Oklahoma State U, Oklahoma City, OK A
Olivet Nazarene U, IL B
Oral Roberts U, OK B
Otterbein Coll, OH B
Park U, MO B
Pittsburg State U, KS B
Purdue U, IN B
Purdue U Calumet, IN B
Quincy U, IL B
Rasmussen Coll Eagan, MN A
Rasmussen Coll St. Cloud, MN A
Rochester Comm and Tech Coll, MN A
Rockford Coll, IL B
Rogers State U, OK A
Roosevelt U, IL B
Saginaw Valley State U, MI B
St. Ambrose U, IA B
St. Catherine U, MN B
St. Cloud State U, MN B
Saint John's U, MN B

A—associate degree; B—bachelor's degree

Saint Joseph's Coll, IN B
Saint Mary-of-the-Woods Coll, IN B
Saint Mary's Coll, IN B
Saint Mary's U of Minnesota, MN B
St. Norbert Coll, WI B
Saint Xavier U, IL B
Shawnee State U, OH A
Siena Heights U, MI B
Silver Lake Coll, WI B
Simpson Coll, IA B
Southeastern Oklahoma State U, OK B
Southeast Missouri State U, MO B
Southern Illinois U Carbondale, IL B
Southern Illinois U Edwardsville, IL B
Southern Methodist U, TX B
Southern Nazarene U, OK B
Southwest Baptist U, MO B
Southwestern Oklahoma State U, OK B
Southwest Minnesota State U, MN A,B
Spring Arbor U, MI B
Stephens Coll, MO B
Taylor U, IN B
Tiffin U, OH A,B
Transylvania U, KY B
Trine U, IN A,B
Trinity Christian Coll, IL B
Trinity International U, IL B
Truman State U, MO B
Union Coll, NE A,B
U of Central Oklahoma, OK B
U of Charleston, WV A,B
U of Cincinnati, OH A,B
U of Dayton, OH B
U of Evansville, IN B
The U of Findlay, OH A,B
U of Illinois at Chicago, IL B
U of Illinois at Springfield, IL B
U of Illinois at Urbana–Champaign, IL B
U of Indianapolis, IN B
The U of Iowa, IA B
The U of Kansas, KS B
U of Mary, ND A,B
U of Michigan–Dearborn, MI B
U of Michigan–Flint, MI B
U of Minnesota, Crookston, MN B
U of Minnesota, Duluth, MN B
U of Minnesota, Twin Cities Campus, MN B
U of Missouri–Columbia, MO B
U of Missouri–Kansas City, MO B
U of Missouri–St. Louis, MO B
U of Nebraska at Omaha, NE B
U of Nebraska–Lincoln, NE B
U of New Orleans, LA B
U of North Dakota, ND B
U of Northern Iowa, IA B
U of Notre Dame, IN B
U of Oklahoma, OK B
U of Phoenix–Chicago Campus, IL B
U of Phoenix–Cleveland Campus, OH A,B
U of Phoenix–Indianapolis Campus, IN A,B
U of Phoenix–Kansas City Campus, MO B
U of Phoenix–Metro Detroit Campus, MI B
U of Phoenix–Oklahoma City Campus, OK B
U of Phoenix–St. Louis Campus, MO A,B
U of Phoenix–Springfield Campus, MO B
U of Phoenix–Tulsa Campus, OK B
U of Phoenix–West Michigan Campus, MI B
U of Phoenix–Wisconsin Campus, WI B
U of Rio Grande, OH A,B
U of St. Francis, IL B
U of Saint Francis, IN B
U of Saint Mary, KS B
U of Sioux Falls, SD B
The U of South Dakota, SD B
U of Southern Indiana, IN B
The U of Toledo, OH A,B
U of Tulsa, OK B
U of Wisconsin–Eau Claire, WI B
U of Wisconsin–Green Bay, WI B
U of Wisconsin–La Crosse, WI B
U of Wisconsin–Madison, WI B
U of Wisconsin–Milwaukee, WI B
U of Wisconsin–Oshkosh, WI B
U of Wisconsin–Parkside, WI B
U of Wisconsin–Platteville, WI B
U of Wisconsin–Stevens Point, WI B
U of Wisconsin–Superior, WI B
U of Wisconsin–Whitewater, WI B
Ursuline Coll, OH B
Valparaiso U, IN B
Viterbo U, WI B
Walsh Coll of Accountancy and Business Administration, MI B
Walsh U, OH A,B
Wartburg Coll, IA B
Washburn U, KS B
Washington U in St. Louis, MO B
Wayne State U, MI B
Webster U, MO B
Western Illinois U, IL B
Western Michigan U, MI B
Westminster Coll, MO B
Westwood Coll–Chicago Du Page, IL B
Wichita State U, KS B
Wilberforce U, OH B
William Jewell Coll, MO B
Wilmington Coll, OH B
Winona State U, MN B
Wright State U, OH B
Xavier U, OH B
York Coll, NE B
Youngstown State U, OH A,B

Accounting and Business/ Management

Illinois State U, IL B
ITT Tech Inst, Fort Wayne, IN B
ITT Tech Inst, Arnold, MO B
Kansas State U, KS A
Maranatha Baptist Bible Coll, WI B
Minnesota School of Business–Blaine, MN A
U of Illinois at Urbana–Champaign, IL B
Westwood Coll–Chicago Du Page, IL B

Accounting and Finance

Bethel U, MN B
Central Christian Coll of Kansas, KS A,B
Colorado Tech U Sioux Falls, SD B
Drake U, IA B
Ferris State U, MI B
Hiram Coll, OH B
Lourdes Coll, OH B
Northern Michigan U, MI B
U of North Dakota, ND B

Accounting Related

Central Michigan U, MI B
Franklin U, OH A,B
Maryville U of Saint Louis, MO B
North Dakota State U, ND B
Northern Michigan U, MI B
Rasmussen Coll Eagan, MN A
Saint Mary-of-the-Woods Coll, IN B

Accounting Technology and Bookkeeping

Baker Coll of Flint, MI A
Brown Mackie Coll–Fort Wayne, IN A
Brown Mackie Coll–Merrillville, IN A
Brown Mackie Coll–Michigan City, IN A
Brown Mackie Coll–South Bend, IN A
Brown Mackie Coll–Tulsa, OK A
Cleary U, MI A
DeVry U, Edina, MN A
DeVry U Southfield Center, MI A
Ferris State U, MI A,B
Miami U, OH A
Midstate Coll, IL A
Ohio U, OH A
Ohio U–Lancaster, OH A
Ohio U–Southern Campus, OH A
Robert Morris Coll, IL A
St. Augustine Coll, IL A
Sinte Gleska U, SD A
The U of Akron, OH A
U of Rio Grande, OH A
Wright State U, OH A

Acting

Bowling Green State U, OH B
Bradley U, IL B
Central Christian Coll of Kansas, KS A,B
Central Michigan U, MI B
Coe Coll, IA B
DePaul U, IL B
Drake U, IA B
Illinois Wesleyan U, IL B
Kent State U, OH B
Oakland U, MI B
Ohio U, OH B
Oral Roberts U, OK B
Roosevelt U, IL B
St. Cloud State U, MN B
U of Northern Iowa, IA B

Acting/Directing

Bradley U, IL B

Actuarial Science

Aurora U, IL B
Ball State U, IN B
Bradley U, IL B
Butler U, IN B
Carroll U, WI B
Central Coll, IA B
Central Michigan U, MI B
Drake U, IA B
Eastern Michigan U, MI B
Elmhurst Coll, IL B
Indiana U Northwest, IN B
Indiana U South Bend, IN B
Maryville U of Saint Louis, MO B
Michigan Technological U, MI B
North Central Coll, IL B
The Ohio State U, OH B
Pittsburg State U, KS B
Purdue U, IN B
Roosevelt U, IL B
Spring Arbor U, MI B
U of Central Oklahoma, OK B
U of Illinois at Urbana–Champaign, IL B
The U of Iowa, IA B
U of Michigan–Flint, MI B
U of Minnesota, Duluth, MN B
U of Minnesota, Twin Cities Campus, MN B
U of Nebraska–Lincoln, NE B
U of Northern Iowa, IA B
U of Wisconsin–Madison, WI B
U of Wisconsin–Stevens Point, WI B
Valparaiso U, IN B

Administrative Assistant and Secretarial Science

AIB Coll of Business, IA A
Baker Coll of Auburn Hills, MI A
Baker Coll of Cadillac, MI A
Baker Coll of Clinton Township, MI A
Baker Coll of Jackson, MI A
Baker Coll of Muskegon, MI A,B

Baker Coll of Owosso, MI	A,B
Ball State U, IN	A
Black Hills State U, SD	A
Bryant & Stratton Coll, Parma, OH	A
Bryant & Stratton Coll, Willoughby Hills, OH	A
Bryant & Stratton Coll, WI	A
Dordt Coll, IA	A
East-West U, IL	B
Faith Baptist Bible Coll and Theological Seminary, IA	A
Fort Hays State U, KS	A,B
Grace Coll, IN	A,B
Kent State U, Salem Campus, OH	A
Kilian Comm Coll, SD	A
Kuyper Coll, MI	A
Maranatha Baptist Bible Coll, WI	A,B
Mayville State U, ND	A
Midstate Coll, IL	A
Northern Michigan U, MI	A
Northwest Missouri State U, MO	B
Oglala Lakota Coll, SD	A
Ohio U, OH	A
Ohio U–Chillicothe, OH	A
Rasmussen Coll Eagan, MN	A
Rasmussen Coll St. Cloud, MN	A
Rochester Comm and Tech Coll, MN	A
St. Augustine Coll, IL	A
Sinte Gleska U, SD	A
Southeast Missouri State U, MO	B
The U of Akron, OH	A
U of Central Missouri, MO	A
U of Cincinnati, OH	A
The U of Findlay, OH	A
U of Rio Grande, OH	A
The U of Toledo, OH	A
Washburn U, KS	A
Wright State U, OH	A

Adult and Continuing Education

Dakota Wesleyan U, SD	B
Iowa Wesleyan Coll, IA	B
Lourdes Coll, OH	B
U of Central Oklahoma, OK	B
The U of Toledo, OH	B

Adult Development and Aging

Bowling Green State U, OH	B
Madonna U, MI	A,B
The U of Toledo, OH	A

Adult Health Nursing

Wright State U, OH	B

Advertising

The Art Inst of Michigan, MI	B
The Art Insts International–Kansas City, KS	B
The Art Insts International Minnesota, MN	B
Bradley U, IL	B
Central Michigan U, MI	B
Clarke Coll, IA	B
Concordia Coll, MN	B
Drake U, IA	B
Drury U, MO	B
Ferris State U, MI	B
Fontbonne U, MO	B
Grand Valley State U, MI	B
The Illinois Inst of Art–Chicago, IL	B
The Illinois Inst of Art–Schaumburg, IL	B
Iowa State U of Science and Technology, IA	B
Kent State U, OH	B
Loyola U Chicago, IL	B
Marquette U, WI	B
Michigan State U, MI	B
Minneapolis Coll of Art and Design, MN	B
Minnesota State U Moorhead, MN	B
Northeastern State U, OK	B
North Park U, IL	B
Northwest Missouri State U, MO	B
Ohio U, OH	B
Oklahoma Christian U, OK	B
Oklahoma City U, OK	B
Pittsburg State U, KS	B
St. Ambrose U, IA	B
St. Cloud State U, MN	B
Southern Methodist U, TX	B
Stephens Coll, MO	B
U of Central Oklahoma, OK	B
U of Illinois at Urbana–Champaign, IL	B
U of Missouri–Columbia, MO	B
U of Nebraska–Lincoln, NE	B
U of Oklahoma, OK	B
U of Southern Indiana, IN	B
U of Wisconsin–Madison, WI	B
Washington U in St. Louis, MO	B
Webster U, MO	B
Western Michigan U, MI	B
Winona State U, MN	B
Xavier U, OH	A,B
Youngstown State U, OH	B

Aeronautical/Aerospace Engineering Technology

Bowling Green State U, OH	B
Ohio U, OH	B
Purdue U, IN	A
Saint Louis U, MO	B
U of Central Missouri, MO	B

Aeronautics/Aviation/Aerospace Science and Technology

Augsburg Coll, MN	B
Indiana State U, IN	A
Kansas State U, KS	B
Kent State U, OH	B
Ohio U, OH	B
Oklahoma State U, OK	B
Purdue U, IN	B
South Dakota State U, SD	B
Southern Nazarene U, OK	A,B
U of Minnesota, Crookston, MN	B
U of Oklahoma, OK	B

Aerospace, Aeronautical and Astronautical Engineering

Case Western Reserve U, OH	B
Clarkson U, NY	B
Illinois Inst of Technology, IL	B
Iowa State U of Science and Technology, IA	B
Missouri U of Science and Technology, MO	B
The Ohio State U, OH	B
Oklahoma State U, OK	B
Purdue U, IN	B
Saint Louis U, MO	B
U of Cincinnati, OH	B
U of Illinois at Urbana–Champaign, IL	B
The U of Kansas, KS	B
U of Michigan, MI	B
U of Minnesota, Twin Cities Campus, MN	B
U of Notre Dame, IN	B
U of Oklahoma, OK	B
Western Michigan U, MI	B
Wichita State U, KS	B

African American/Black Studies

Coe Coll, IA	B
The Coll of Wooster, OH	B
Denison U, OH	B
DePaul U, IL	B
DePauw U, IN	B
Earlham Coll, IN	B
Eastern Illinois U, IL	B
Eastern Michigan U, MI	B
Indiana State U, IN	B
Indiana U Bloomington, IN	B
Indiana U Northwest, IN	B
Kent State U, OH	B
Knox Coll, IL	B
Loyola U Chicago, IL	B
Luther Coll, IA	B
Miami U, OH	B
Northwestern U, IL	B
Oberlin Coll, OH	B
The Ohio State U, OH	B
Ohio U, OH	B
Ohio Wesleyan U, OH	B
Purdue U, IN	B
Roosevelt U, IL	B
Southern Methodist U, TX	B
U of Chicago, IL	B
U of Cincinnati, OH	B
U of Illinois at Chicago, IL	B
The U of Iowa, IA	B
The U of Kansas, KS	B
U of Michigan, MI	B
U of Michigan–Flint, MI	B
U of Minnesota, Twin Cities Campus, MN	B
U of Nebraska at Omaha, NE	B
U of Notre Dame, IN	B
U of Oklahoma, OK	B
The U of Toledo, OH	B
U of Wisconsin–Madison, WI	B
U of Wisconsin–Milwaukee, WI	B
Washington U in St. Louis, MO	B
Wayne State U, MI	B
Western Illinois U, IL	B
Western Michigan U, MI	B
Wright State U, OH	B
Youngstown State U, OH	B

African Languages

Ohio U, OH	B
U of Wisconsin–Madison, WI	B

African Studies

Bowling Green State U, OH	B
Carleton Coll, MN	B
Illinois Wesleyan U, IL	B
Indiana U Bloomington, IN	B
North Park U, IL	B
Northwestern U, IL	B
Oakland U, MI	B
The Ohio State U, OH	B
Ohio U, OH	B
U of Chicago, IL	B
The U of Iowa, IA	B
The U of Kansas, KS	B
U of Minnesota, Twin Cities Campus, MN	B
Washington U in St. Louis, MO	B

Agribusiness

Andrews U, MI	B
Coll of the Ozarks, MO	B
Illinois State U, IL	B
Kent State U, Stark Campus, OH	B
Missouri State U, MO	B
North Dakota State U, ND	B
South Dakota State U, SD	B
Southeast Missouri State U, MO	B
Southwest Minnesota State U, MN	A,B
U of Central Missouri, MO	B
U of Minnesota, Crookston, MN	B

Agricultural and Extension Education

U of Illinois at Urbana–Champaign, IL	B

Agricultural and Food Products Processing

Kansas State U, KS	B
U of Nebraska–Lincoln, NE	B

Agricultural/Biological Engineering and Bioengineering

Dordt Coll, IA	B
Iowa State U of Science and Technology, IA	B
Kansas State U, KS	B
Michigan State U, MI	B
Missouri U of Science and Technology, MO	B
North Dakota State U, ND	B
The Ohio State U, OH	B
Oklahoma State U, OK	B
Purdue U, IN	B
South Dakota State U, SD	B

A—associate degree; B—bachelor's degree

U of Illinois at Urbana–Champaign, IL B
U of Minnesota, Twin Cities Campus, MN B
U of Nebraska–Lincoln, NE B
U of Wisconsin–Madison, WI B

Agricultural Business and Management
Fort Hays State U, KS B
Grace U, NE B
Iowa State U of Science and Technology, IA B
Kansas State U, KS B
Lincoln U, MO B
Michigan State U, MI B
Northwest Missouri State U, MO B
The Ohio State U, OH B
Oklahoma Panhandle State U, OK B
Oklahoma State U, OK B
Southwest Minnesota State U, MN B
Truman State U, MO B
U of Central Missouri, MO B
U of Illinois at Urbana–Champaign, IL B
U of Minnesota, Crookston, MN B
U of Minnesota, Twin Cities Campus, MN B
U of Missouri–Columbia, MO B
U of Nebraska at Kearney, NE B
U of Nebraska–Lincoln, NE B
U of Wisconsin–Platteville, WI B
Wilmington Coll, OH B

Agricultural Communication/ Journalism
Kansas State U, KS B
North Dakota State U, ND B
The Ohio State U, OH B
Oklahoma State U, OK B
Purdue U, IN B
U of Illinois at Urbana–Champaign, IL B
U of Nebraska–Lincoln, NE B

Agricultural Economics
Kansas State U, KS B
Michigan State U, MI B
North Dakota State U, ND B
Northwest Missouri State U, MO B
The Ohio State U, OH B
Oklahoma State U, OK B
Purdue U, IN B
South Dakota State U, SD B
Southern Illinois U Carbondale, IL B
U of Central Missouri, MO B
U of Illinois at Urbana–Champaign, IL B
U of Missouri–Columbia, MO B
U of Nebraska–Lincoln, NE B

Agricultural Mechanization
Coll of the Ozarks, MO B
Iowa State U of Science and Technology, IA B
Kansas State U, KS B
North Dakota State U, ND B
Northwest Missouri State U, MO B
Purdue U, IN B
South Dakota State U, SD B
U of Illinois at Urbana–Champaign, IL B
U of Missouri–Columbia, MO B
U of Nebraska–Lincoln, NE B

Agricultural Public Services Related
Oklahoma State U, OK B
U of Illinois at Urbana–Champaign, IL B

Agricultural Sciences
Cameron U, OK B

Agricultural Teacher Education
Coll of the Ozarks, MO B
Dordt Coll, IA B
Iowa State U of Science and Technology, IA B
Kansas State U, KS B
Missouri State U, MO B
North Dakota State U, ND B
Northwest Missouri State U, MO B
The Ohio State U, OH B
Oklahoma Panhandle State U, OK B
Oklahoma State U, OK B
Purdue U, IN B
South Dakota State U, SD B
U of Illinois at Urbana–Champaign, IL B
U of Minnesota, Crookston, MN B
U of Minnesota, Twin Cities Campus, MN B
U of Missouri–Columbia, MO B
U of Nebraska–Lincoln, NE B
U of Wisconsin–Madison, WI B
U of Wisconsin–Platteville, WI B
Wilmington Coll, OH B

Agriculture
Dordt Coll, IA B
Fort Hays State U, KS B
Illinois State U, IL B
Iowa State U of Science and Technology, IA B
Lincoln U, MO B
Missouri State U, MO B
North Dakota State U, ND B
Northwest Missouri State U, MO B
Oglala Lakota Coll, SD A
Oklahoma Panhandle State U, OK A
Purdue U, IN B
South Dakota State U, SD A,B
Southeast Missouri State U, MO B
Southern Illinois U Carbondale, IL B
Southern Nazarene U, OK A
Truman State U, MO B
U of Minnesota, Twin Cities Campus, MN B
U of Missouri–Columbia, MO B
U of Nebraska–Lincoln, NE B
Western Illinois U, IL B
Wilmington Coll, OH B

Agriculture and Agriculture Operations Related
Michigan State U, MI B

Agronomy and Crop Science
Coll of the Ozarks, MO B
Fort Hays State U, KS B
Iowa State U of Science and Technology, IA B
Kansas State U, KS B
Missouri State U, MO B
Northwest Missouri State U, MO B
The Ohio State U, OH B
Oklahoma Panhandle State U, OK B
Purdue U, IN B
South Dakota State U, SD B
Truman State U, MO B
U of Illinois at Urbana–Champaign, IL B
U of Minnesota, Crookston, MN B
U of Minnesota, Twin Cities Campus, MN B
U of Nebraska–Lincoln, NE B
U of Wisconsin–Platteville, WI B

Aircraft Powerplant Technology
Northern Michigan U, MI A

Air Force ROTC/Air Science
The U of Iowa, IA B

Airframe Mechanics and Aircraft Maintenance Technology
Kansas State U, KS A
Lewis U, IL A,B

Airline Pilot and Flight Crew
Baker Coll of Flint, MI A
Baker Coll of Muskegon, MI A
Central Christian Coll of Kansas, KS A
Eastern Michigan U, MI B
Indiana State U, IN B
Kansas State U, KS A,B
St. Cloud State U, MN B
Saint Louis U, MO B
Southeastern Oklahoma State U, OK B
Southern Illinois U Carbondale, IL A
U of Illinois at Urbana–Champaign, IL B
U of North Dakota, ND B
Western Michigan U, MI B

Air Traffic Control
Lewis U, IL B
St. Cloud State U, MN B
U of North Dakota, ND B

Allied Health and Medical Assisting Services Related
National American U, MO A

Allied Health Diagnostic, Intervention, and Treatment Professions Related
Ball State U, IN A
Cameron U, OK A
Kent State U, Salem Campus, OH A
Lewis U, IL B
Mercy Coll of Health Sciences, IA A
The U of Toledo, OH B

American Government and Politics
Oklahoma Christian U, OK B
Southern Nazarene U, OK B
The U of Akron, OH B

American Indian/Native American Studies
Bacone Coll, OK A
Bemidji State U, MN B
Black Hills State U, SD B
Creighton U, NE B
Haskell Indian Nations U, KS B
Little Priest Tribal Coll, NE A
Northeastern State U, OK B
Northland Coll, WI B
Oglala Lakota Coll, SD A,B
Sinte Gleska U, SD A,B
The U of Iowa, IA B
U of Minnesota, Duluth, MN B
U of Minnesota, Twin Cities Campus, MN B
U of North Dakota, ND B
U of Oklahoma, OK B
U of Science and Arts of Oklahoma, OK B
The U of South Dakota, SD B
U of Wisconsin–Eau Claire, WI B
U of Wisconsin–Green Bay, WI B
U of Wisconsin–Milwaukee, WI B

American Literature
Clarkson U, NY B
Washington U in St. Louis, MO B

American Native/Native American Education
The Coll of St. Scholastica, MN B
Northeastern State U, OK B

American Native/Native American Languages
Bemidji State U, MN B

American Sign Language (ASL)
Augustana Coll, SD B
Bethel Coll, IN A,B
Madonna U, MI A,B
North Central U, MN A,B
Oklahoma State U, Oklahoma City, OK A
St. Catherine U, MN B

American Studies
Albion Coll, MI B
Ashland U, OH B
Bowling Green State U, OH B
Carleton Coll, MN B
Case Western Reserve U, OH B
Cedarville U, OH B
Clarkson U, NY B
Coe Coll, IA B
Columbia Coll, MO B
Creighton U, NE B
DePaul U, IL B
Dominican U, IL B
Elmhurst Coll, IL B
Franklin Coll, IN B
Hillsdale Coll, MI B
Illinois Wesleyan U, IL B
Indiana U Bloomington, IN B
Kent State U, OH B
Kenyon Coll, OH B
Knox Coll, IL B
Lake Forest Coll, IL B
Lewis U, IL B
Miami U, OH B
Miami U Hamilton, OH B
Minnesota State U Moorhead, MN B
Mount Union Coll, OH B
Muskingum Coll, OH B
Northwestern U, IL B
Oklahoma City U, OK B
Oklahoma State U, OK B
St. Cloud State U, MN B
Saint Louis U, MO B
St. Olaf Coll, MN B
Southern Nazarene U, OK B
U of Chicago, IL B
U of Dayton, OH B
The U of Iowa, IA B
The U of Kansas, KS B
U of Michigan, MI B
U of Michigan–Dearborn, MI B
U of Minnesota, Twin Cities Campus, MN B
U of Missouri–Kansas City, MO B
U of Northern Iowa, IA B
U of Notre Dame, IN B
U of Rio Grande, OH B
U of Saint Francis, IN B
The U of Toledo, OH B
Ursuline Coll, OH B
Valparaiso U, IN B
Washington U in St. Louis, MO B
Wayne State U, MI B
Wittenberg U, OH B
Youngstown State U, OH B

Anatomy
Andrews U, MI B
Minnesota State U Mankato, MN B
Wright State U, OH B

Ancient/Classical Greek
Carleton Coll, MN B
Concordia U, MI B
Creighton U, NE B
DePauw U, IN B
Kenyon Coll, OH B
Lawrence U, WI B
Loyola U Chicago, IL B
Monmouth Coll, IL B
Ohio U, OH B
Rockford Coll, IL B
St. Olaf Coll, MN B
U of Chicago, IL B
U of Nebraska–Lincoln, NE B
U of Notre Dame, IN B
Washington U in St. Louis, MO B

Ancient Near Eastern and Biblical Languages
Central Bible Coll, MO B
Concordia U, MI B
Concordia U Chicago, IL B
Concordia U Wisconsin, WI B
Hope Coll, MI B
Indiana Wesleyan U, IN A,B
Luther Coll, IA B
North Central U, MN A
Olivet Nazarene U, IL B
U of Chicago, IL B
York Coll, NE B

Ancient Studies
Missouri State U, MO B
Ohio Wesleyan U, OH B
Rockford Coll, IL B
St. Olaf Coll, MN B
The U of Kansas, KS B
U of Michigan, MI B
U of Nebraska–Lincoln, NE B
Washington U in St. Louis, MO B

Animal Behavior and Ethology
Carroll U, WI B

Animal Genetics
Ohio Wesleyan U, OH B
U of Minnesota, Twin Cities Campus, MN B
U of Wisconsin–Madison, WI B

Animal/Livestock Husbandry and Production
Dordt Coll, IA B
U of Illinois at Urbana–Champaign, IL B

Animal Physiology
Minnesota State U Mankato, MN B
The U of Akron, OH B
U of Minnesota, Twin Cities Campus, MN B

Animal Sciences
Coll of the Ozarks, MO B
Dordt Coll, IA B
Fort Hays State U, KS B
Iowa State U of Science and Technology, IA B
Kansas State U, KS B
Michigan State U, MI B
Missouri State U, MO B
North Dakota State U, ND B
Northwest Missouri State U, MO B
The Ohio State U, OH B
Oklahoma Panhandle State U, OK B
Oklahoma State U, OK B
Purdue U, IN B
South Dakota State U, SD B
Southeast Missouri State U, MO B
Southern Illinois U Carbondale, IL B
Truman State U, MO B
U of Illinois at Urbana–Champaign, IL B
U of Minnesota, Crookston, MN B
U of Minnesota, Twin Cities Campus, MN B
U of Missouri–Columbia, MO B
U of Nebraska–Lincoln, NE B
U of Wisconsin–Platteville, WI B

Animal Sciences Related
U of Illinois at Urbana–Champaign, IL B
U of Minnesota, Crookston, MN B

Animation, Interactive Technology, Video Graphics and Special Effects
The Art Inst of Indianapolis, IN B
The Art Insts International Minnesota, MN B
Bradley U, IL B
Coll for Creative Studies, MI B
Davenport U, Grand Rapids, MI B
Ferris State U, MI B
The Illinois Inst of Art–Chicago, IL B
The Illinois Inst of Art–Schaumburg, IL B
ITT Tech Inst, Mount Prospect, IL B
ITT Tech Inst, Fort Wayne, IN B
ITT Tech Inst, Indianapolis, IN B
ITT Tech Inst, Newburgh, IN B
ITT Tech Inst, Canton, MI B
ITT Tech Inst, Grand Rapids, MI B
ITT Tech Inst, Troy, MI B
ITT Tech Inst, MN B
ITT Tech Inst, Arnold, MO B
ITT Tech Inst, Earth City, MO B
ITT Tech Inst, NE B
ITT Tech Inst, Green Bay, WI B
ITT Tech Inst, Greenfield, WI B
Kansas City Art Inst, MO B
Northwestern Coll, MN B

Anthropology
Albion Coll, MI B
Alma Coll, MI B
Augustana Coll, IL B
Ball State U, IN B
Beloit Coll, WI B
Butler U, IN B
Carleton Coll, MN B
Case Western Reserve U, OH B
Central Michigan U, MI B
Cleveland State U, OH B
Cornell Coll, IA B
Creighton U, NE B
Denison U, OH B
DePaul U, IL B
DePauw U, IN B
Drake U, IA B
Earlham Coll, IN B
Eastern Michigan U, MI B
Franciscan U of Steubenville, OH B
Grand Valley State U, MI B
Grinnell Coll, IA B
Gustavus Adolphus Coll, MN B
Hamline U, MN B
Hanover Coll, IN B
Heidelberg U, OH B
Illinois State U, IL B
Illinois Wesleyan U, IL B
Indiana State U, IN B
Indiana U Bloomington, IN B
Indiana U–Purdue U Fort Wayne, IN B
Indiana U–Purdue U Indianapolis, IN B
Iowa State U of Science and Technology, IA B
Kalamazoo Coll, MI B
Kansas State U, KS B
Kent State U, OH B
Kenyon Coll, OH B
Knox Coll, IL B
Lake Forest Coll, IL B
Lawrence U, WI B
Loyola U Chicago, IL B
Luther Coll, IA B
Macalester Coll, MN B
Marquette U, WI B
Miami U, OH B
Miami U Hamilton, OH B
Michigan State U, MI B
Minnesota State U Mankato, MN B
Minnesota State U Moorhead, MN B
Missouri State U, MO B
Monmouth Coll, IL B
Muskingum Coll, OH B
National-Louis U, IL B
North Dakota State U, ND B
Northeastern Illinois U, IL B
Northwestern U, IL B
Oakland U, MI B
Oberlin Coll, OH B
The Ohio State U, OH B
Ohio U, OH B
Ohio Wesleyan U, OH B
Oklahoma Baptist U, OK B
Purdue U, IN B
Ripon Coll, WI B
Rockford Coll, IL B
St. Cloud State U, MN B
Southeast Missouri State U, MO B

A—associate degree; B—bachelor's degree

Southern Illinois U Carbondale, IL B
Southern Illinois U Edwardsville, IL B
Southern Methodist U, TX B
Transylvania U, KY B
U of Chicago, IL B
U of Cincinnati, OH B
U of Illinois at Chicago, IL B
U of Illinois at Urbana–Champaign, IL B
U of Indianapolis, IN B
The U of Iowa, IA B
The U of Kansas, KS B
U of Michigan, MI B
U of Michigan–Dearborn, MI B
U of Michigan–Flint, MI B
U of Minnesota, Duluth, MN B
U of Minnesota, Morris, MN B
U of Minnesota, Twin Cities Campus, MN B
U of Missouri–Columbia, MO B
U of Missouri–St. Louis, MO B
U of Nebraska–Lincoln, NE B
U of New Orleans, LA B
U of North Dakota, ND B
U of Northern Iowa, IA B
U of Notre Dame, IN B
U of Oklahoma, OK B
The U of South Dakota, SD B
The U of Toledo, OH B
U of Tulsa, OK B
U of Wisconsin–Madison, WI B
U of Wisconsin–Milwaukee, WI B
U of Wisconsin–Oshkosh, WI B
Washburn U, KS B
Washington U in St. Louis, MO B
Wayne State U, MI B
Webster U, MO B
Western Michigan U, MI B
Westminster Coll, MO B
Wheaton Coll, IL B
Wichita State U, KS B
Wright State U, OH B
Youngstown State U, OH B

Anthropology Related
U of Michigan, MI B

Apparel and Accessories Marketing
Bluffton U, OH B

Apparel and Textile Marketing Management
The Art Inst of Michigan, MI B
South Dakota State U, SD B
Wayne State U, MI B

Apparel and Textiles
Indiana State U, IN B
Iowa State U of Science and Technology, IA B
Kansas State U, KS B
Michigan State U, MI B
Missouri State U, MO B
North Dakota State U, ND B
The Ohio State U, OH B
Ohio U, OH B
Purdue U, IN B
Southern Illinois U Carbondale, IL B
The U of Akron, OH B
U of Central Missouri, MO B
U of Missouri–Columbia, MO B
U of Nebraska–Lincoln, NE B
U of Northern Iowa, IA B
U of Wisconsin–Stout, WI B
Western Michigan U, MI B

Applied Art
Bemidji State U, MN B
Cleveland State U, OH B
Minnesota State U Mankato, MN B
Minnesota State U Moorhead, MN B
St. Cloud State U, MN B
Truman State U, MO B
U of Dayton, OH B
The U of Toledo, OH B
U of Wisconsin–Madison, WI B
Washington U in St. Louis, MO B
Winona State U, MN B

Applied Economics
Bowling Green State U, OH B
The Coll of St. Scholastica, MN B
Michigan State U, MI B
Southern Methodist U, TX B
U of Northern Iowa, IA B

Applied Horticulture
Coll of the Ozarks, MO B
Iowa State U of Science and Technology, IA B
Kent State U, Salem Campus, OH A
South Dakota State U, SD B
U of Illinois at Urbana–Champaign, IL B

Applied Mathematics
Bowling Green State U, OH B
Carroll U, WI B
Case Western Reserve U, OH B
Central Methodist U, MO A
Clarkson U, NY B
Creighton U, NE B
DePaul U, IL B
Ferris State U, MI B
Grand View U, IA B
Illinois Inst of Technology, IL B
Indiana U South Bend, IN B
Jamestown Coll, ND B
Kent State U, OH B
Kettering U, MI B
Maryville U of Saint Louis, MO B
Michigan State U, MI B
Michigan Technological U, MI B
Millikin U, IL B
Missouri U of Science and Technology, MO B
North Central Coll, IL B
Northwestern U, IL B
Ohio U, OH B
Purdue U, IN B
Saginaw Valley State U, MI B
Shawnee State U, OH B
Siena Heights U, MI B
Taylor U, IN B
The U of Akron, OH B
U of Central Oklahoma, OK B
U of Chicago, IL B
U of Michigan, MI B
U of Missouri–St. Louis, MO B
U of Northern Iowa, IA B
U of Sioux Falls, SD B
U of Tulsa, OK B
U of Wisconsin–Madison, WI B
U of Wisconsin–Milwaukee, WI B
U of Wisconsin–Stout, WI B
Washington U in St. Louis, MO B
Winona State U, MN B
Wright State U, OH B

Applied Mathematics Related
Carroll U, WI B
DePaul U, IL B
Saint Mary's Coll, IN B
U of Dayton, OH B

Arabic
The Ohio State U, OH B
U of Chicago, IL B
U of Notre Dame, IN B
Washington U in St. Louis, MO B

Archeology
The Coll of Wooster, OH B
Lawrence U, WI B
Minnesota State U Moorhead, MN B
Oberlin Coll, OH B
U of Evansville, IN B
U of Indianapolis, IN B
U of Missouri–Columbia, MO B
U of Wisconsin–La Crosse, WI B
Washington U in St. Louis, MO B
Wheaton Coll, IL B

Architectural Drafting and CAD/CADD
Baker Coll of Flint, MI A
Baker Coll of Muskegon, MI A
Indiana U–Purdue U Indianapolis, IN A
Purdue U Calumet, IN A
Purdue U North Central, IN A
The U of Toledo, OH A
Westwood Coll–Chicago Du Page, IL A

Architectural Engineering
Andrews U, MI B
Illinois Inst of Technology, IL B
Kansas State U, KS B
Milwaukee School of Engineering, WI B
Missouri U of Science and Technology, MO B
Oklahoma State U, OK B
U of Cincinnati, OH B
The U of Kansas, KS B
U of Nebraska–Lincoln, NE B
U of Oklahoma, OK B

Architectural Engineering Technology
Baker Coll of Clinton Township, MI A
Baker Coll of Owosso, MI A
Baker Coll of Port Huron, MI A
Ferris State U, MI A
Indiana State U, IN B
Indiana U–Purdue U Fort Wayne, IN A
Indiana U–Purdue U Indianapolis, IN B
Oklahoma State U, Oklahoma City, OK A
Purdue U, IN B
Purdue U North Central, IN A,B
Ranken Tech Coll, MO A,B
U of Cincinnati, OH A,B
Washington U in St. Louis, MO B

Architectural History and Criticism
Miami U, OH B
Miami U Hamilton, OH B
The U of Kansas, KS B

Architectural Technology
Washington U in St. Louis, MO B

Architecture
Andrews U, MI B
Ball State U, IN B
Coe Coll, IA B
Cornell Coll, IA B
Drury U, MO B
Illinois Inst of Technology, IL B
Iowa State U of Science and Technology, IA B
Kent State U, OH B
Lawrence Technological U, MI B
Miami U Hamilton, OH B
The Ohio State U, OH B
Oklahoma State U, OK B
Southern Illinois U Carbondale, IL B
U of Cincinnati, OH B
U of Illinois at Urbana–Champaign, IL B
The U of Kansas, KS B
U of Michigan, MI B
U of Minnesota, Twin Cities Campus, MN B
U of Nebraska–Lincoln, NE B
U of Notre Dame, IN B
U of Oklahoma, OK B
U of Wisconsin–Milwaukee, WI B
Washington U in St. Louis, MO B

Architecture Related
Northern Michigan U, MI B
U of Illinois at Chicago, IL B
U of Illinois at Urbana–Champaign, IL B
Washington U in St. Louis, MO B

Area, Ethnic, Cultural, and Gender Studies Related

Bethel U, MN B
Coe Coll, IA B
The Coll of Wooster, OH B
Kent State U, OH B
U of Chicago, IL B
Washington U in St. Louis, MO B

Area Studies

Denison U, OH B
Lake Forest Coll, IL B

Area Studies Related

Eastern Michigan U, MI B
Illinois Wesleyan U, IL B
Kent State U, OH B
Lewis U, IL B
Northwestern U, IL B
U of Illinois at Urbana–Champaign, IL B
U of Michigan–Dearborn, MI B
Washington U in St. Louis, MO B
Wayne State U, MI B
Wright State U, OH B

Army ROTC/Military Science

Minnesota State U Mankato, MN B
Northwest Missouri State U, MO B
The U of Iowa, IA B

Art

Adrian Coll, MI B
Albion Coll, MI B
Alma Coll, MI B
Andrews U, MI B
Aquinas Coll, MI B
Augsburg Coll, MN B
Augustana Coll, IL B
Augustana Coll, SD B
Aurora U, IL B
Avila U, MO B
Bacone Coll, OK A
Baldwin-Wallace Coll, OH B
Ball State U, IN B
Bemidji State U, MN B
Benedictine Coll, KS B
Bethany Coll, KS B
Bethany Lutheran Coll, MN B
Bethel Coll, IN B
Bethel U, MN B
Black Hills State U, SD B
Bluffton U, OH B
Bowling Green State U, OH B
Bradley U, IL B
Briar Cliff U, IA B
Buena Vista U, IA B
Calvin Coll, MI B
Cameron U, OK B
Capital U, OH B
Carroll U, WI B
Central Christian Coll of Kansas, KS A,B
Central Coll, IA B
Central Michigan U, MI B
Central State U, OH B
Clarke Coll, IA B
Cleveland State U, OH B
Coe Coll, IA B
Coll of Mount St. Joseph, OH A,B
Coll of Saint Benedict, MN B
Coll of Saint Mary, NE B
The Coll of St. Scholastica, MN B
Coll of the Ozarks, MO B
Columbia Coll, MO B
Concordia Coll, MN B
Concordia U, MI B
Concordia U Chicago, IL B
Concordia U, Nebraska, NE B
Concordia U Wisconsin, WI B
Cornell Coll, IA B
Creighton U, NE B
Culver-Stockton Coll, MO B
Dakota Wesleyan U, SD B
Dana Coll, NE B
Denison U, OH B
DePaul U, IL B
Doane Coll, NE B
Drake U, IA B
Earlham Coll, IN B
Eastern Illinois U, IL B
Eastern Michigan U, MI B
Edgewood Coll, WI B
Elmhurst Coll, IL B
Emporia State U, KS B
Eureka Coll, IL B
Evangel U, MO B
Fontbonne U, MO B
Fort Hays State U, KS B
Friends U, KS B
Goshen Coll, IN B
Graceland U, IA B
Grand View U, IA B
Greenville Coll, IL B
Grinnell Coll, IA B
Gustavus Adolphus Coll, MN B
Hamline U, MN B
Hannibal-LaGrange Coll, MO B
Hanover Coll, IN B
Haskell Indian Nations U, KS A
Hillsdale Coll, MI B
Hiram Coll, OH B
Huntington U, IN B
Illinois Coll, IL B
Illinois State U, IL B
Illinois Wesleyan U, IL B
Indiana State U, IN B
Indiana U Bloomington, IN B
Indiana U East, IN B
Indiana U Northwest, IN B
Indiana U South Bend, IN B
Indiana U Southeast, IN B
Indiana Wesleyan U, IN A,B
Iowa State U of Science and Technology, IA B
Iowa Wesleyan Coll, IA B
Jamestown Coll, ND B
Kalamazoo Coll, MI B
Kansas State U, KS B
Kansas Wesleyan U, KS B
Kent State U, Stark Campus, OH A
Kenyon Coll, OH B
Knox Coll, IL B
Lake Erie Coll, OH B
Lakeland Coll, WI B
Lindenwood U, MO B
Lourdes Coll, OH A,B
Luther Coll, IA B
MacMurray Coll, IL B
Manchester Coll, IN A,B
Marietta Coll, OH B
McKendree U, IL B
McPherson Coll, KS B
Miami U Hamilton, OH B
Michigan State U, MI B
Minnesota State U Mankato, MN B
Minnesota State U Moorhead, MN B
Minot State U, ND B
Missouri Southern State U, MO B
Missouri State U, MO B
Missouri Western State U, MO B
Monmouth Coll, IL B
Morningside Coll, IA B
Mount Mary Coll, WI B
Mount Mercy Coll, IA B
Mount Vernon Nazarene U, OH B
Muskingum Coll, OH B
National-Louis U, IL B
Nebraska Wesleyan U, NE B
Newman U, KS B
North Central Coll, IL B
North Dakota State U, ND B
Northeastern Illinois U, IL B
Northeastern State U, OK B
Northern Michigan U, MI B
Northern State U, SD B
Northland Coll, WI B
North Park U, IL B
Northwestern U, IL B
Northwest Missouri State U, MO B
Oberlin Coll, OH B
Ohio Northern U, OH B
The Ohio State U, OH B
Oklahoma Baptist U, OK B
Oklahoma Christian U, OK B
Oklahoma Panhandle State U, OK B
Oklahoma State U, OK B
Oklahoma State U, Oklahoma City, OK A
Olivet Coll, MI B
Olivet Nazarene U, IL B
Otterbein Coll, OH B
Pittsburg State U, KS B
Purdue U, IN B
Ripon Coll, WI B
Saginaw Valley State U, MI B
St. Ambrose U, IA B
St. Catherine U, MN B
St. Cloud State U, MN B
St. Gregory's U, Shawnee, OK A
Saint John's U, MN B
Saint Mary-of-the-Woods Coll, IN B
Saint Mary's Coll, IN B
St. Norbert Coll, WI B
St. Olaf Coll, MN B
Saint Xavier U, IL B
Shawnee State U, OH A,B
Siena Heights U, MI B
Silver Lake Coll, WI B
Simpson Coll, IA B
Southeastern Oklahoma State U, OK B
Southeast Missouri State U, MO B
Southern Illinois U Carbondale, IL B
Southern Illinois U Edwardsville, IL B
Southwest Baptist U, MO B
Southwest Minnesota State U, MN B
Spring Arbor U, MI B
Sterling Coll, KS B
Taylor U, IN B
Transylvania U, KY B
Trinity Christian Coll, IL B
Truman State U, MO B
Union Coll, NE A
U of Central Oklahoma, OK B
U of Charleston, WV B
U of Chicago, IL B
U of Cincinnati, OH B
U of Dallas, TX B
U of Evansville, IN B
The U of Findlay, OH B
U of Indianapolis, IN B
The U of Iowa, IA B
U of Minnesota, Duluth, MN B
U of Minnesota, Twin Cities Campus, MN B
U of Missouri–Columbia, MO B
U of Missouri–Kansas City, MO B
U of Nebraska at Kearney, NE B
U of Nebraska at Omaha, NE B
U of North Dakota, ND B
U of Northern Iowa, IA B
U of Oklahoma, OK B
U of Rio Grande, OH A,B
U of Saint Francis, IN B
U of Saint Mary, KS B
U of Science and Arts of Oklahoma, OK B
U of Sioux Falls, SD B
The U of South Dakota, SD B
U of Southern Indiana, IN B
The U of Toledo, OH A,B
U of Wisconsin–Eau Claire, WI B
U of Wisconsin–Green Bay, WI B
U of Wisconsin–Madison, WI B
U of Wisconsin–Milwaukee, WI B
U of Wisconsin–Oshkosh, WI B
U of Wisconsin–Parkside, WI B
U of Wisconsin–Platteville, WI B
U of Wisconsin–Whitewater, WI B
Valley City State U, ND B
Valparaiso U, IN B
Viterbo U, WI B

A—associate degree; B—bachelor's degree

Wabash Coll, IN B
Wartburg Coll, IA B
Washburn U, KS B
Washington U in St. Louis, MO B
Wayne State Coll, NE B
Wayne State U, MI B
Webster U, MO B
Western Illinois U, IL B
Western Michigan U, MI B
Wheaton Coll, IL B
Wichita State U, KS B
William Jewell Coll, MO B
Winona State U, MN B
Wittenberg U, OH B
Wright State U, OH B
Xavier U, OH B
Youngstown State U, OH B

Art History, Criticism and Conservation

Aquinas Coll, MI B
Art Academy of Cincinnati, OH B
Augsburg Coll, MN B
Augustana Coll, IL B
Baker U, KS B
Baldwin-Wallace Coll, OH B
Beloit Coll, WI B
Bethel U, MN B
Bowling Green State U, OH B
Bradley U, IL B
Calvin Coll, MI B
Carleton Coll, MN B
Case Western Reserve U, OH B
Clarke Coll, IA B
The Coll of Wooster, OH B
Concordia Coll, MN B
Cornell Coll, IA B
Denison U, OH B
DePaul U, IL B
DePauw U, IN B
Dominican U, IL B
Drake U, IA B
Drury U, MO B
Eastern Michigan U, MI B
Ferris State U, MI B
Grand Valley State U, MI B
Gustavus Adolphus Coll, MN B
Hamline U, MN B
Hanover Coll, IN B
Hope Coll, MI B
Indiana U Bloomington, IN B
Indiana U–Purdue U Indianapolis, IN B
John Carroll U, OH B
Kalamazoo Coll, MI B
Kansas City Art Inst, MO B
Kent State U, OH B
Kenyon Coll, OH B
Knox Coll, IL B
Lake Forest Coll, IL B
Lawrence U, WI B
Lindenwood U, MO B
Lourdes Coll, OH B
Loyola U Chicago, IL B
Macalester Coll, MN B
MacMurray Coll, IL B
Madonna U, MI B
Marian U, IN B
Miami U, OH B
Michigan State U, MI B
Minnesota State U Mankato, MN B
Minnesota State U Moorhead, MN B
Missouri State U, MO B
Northwestern U, IL B
Oakland U, MI B
Oberlin Coll, OH B
The Ohio State U, OH B
Ohio U, OH B
Ohio Wesleyan U, OH B
Oklahoma City U, OK B
Rockford Coll, IL B
St. Catherine U, MN B
St. Cloud State U, MN B
Saint Louis U, MO B
St. Olaf Coll, MN B
Siena Heights U, MI B
Southern Methodist U, TX B
Transylvania U, KY B
Truman State U, MO B
The U of Akron, OH B
U of Chicago, IL B
U of Cincinnati, OH B
U of Dallas, TX B
U of Dayton, OH B
U of Evansville, IN B
U of Illinois at Chicago, IL B
U of Illinois at Urbana–Champaign, IL B
The U of Iowa, IA B
The U of Kansas, KS B
U of Michigan, MI B
U of Michigan–Dearborn, MI B
U of Minnesota, Duluth, MN B
U of Minnesota, Morris, MN B
U of Minnesota, Twin Cities Campus, MN B
U of Missouri–Columbia, MO B
U of Missouri–Kansas City, MO B
U of Missouri–St. Louis, MO B
U of Nebraska at Omaha, NE B
U of Nebraska–Lincoln, NE B
U of New Orleans, LA B
U of Northern Iowa, IA B
U of Notre Dame, IN B
U of Oklahoma, OK B
U of Saint Francis, IN A
The U of Toledo, OH B
U of Tulsa, OK B
U of Wisconsin–Madison, WI B
U of Wisconsin–Milwaukee, WI B
U of Wisconsin–Superior, WI B
U of Wisconsin–Whitewater, WI B
Ursuline Coll, OH B
Washburn U, KS B
Washington U in St. Louis, MO B
Wayne State U, MI B
Webster U, MO B
Western Michigan U, MI B
Wichita State U, KS B
Wright State U, OH B
Youngstown State U, OH B

Artificial Intelligence and Robotics

U of Cincinnati, OH A

Arts Management

Adrian Coll, MI B
Aquinas Coll, MI B
Benedictine Coll, KS B
Benedictine U, IL B
Bethany Coll, KS B
Buena Vista U, IA B
Butler U, IN B
Culver-Stockton Coll, MO B
DePaul U, IL B
Drury U, MO B
Eastern Michigan U, MI B
Fontbonne U, MO B
Indiana U Bloomington, IN B
Kansas Wesleyan U, KS B
Marian U, IN B
Oklahoma City U, OK B
Tiffin U, OH B
The U of Iowa, IA B
U of Tulsa, OK B
U of Wisconsin–Stevens Point, WI B
Viterbo U, WI B
Wartburg Coll, IA B
Wright State U, OH B

Art Teacher Education

Adrian Coll, MI B
Alma Coll, MI B
Anderson U, IN B
Andrews U, MI B
Aquinas Coll, MI B
Ashland U, OH B
Augsburg Coll, MN B
Augustana Coll, IL B
Augustana Coll, SD B
Baker U, KS B
Beloit Coll, WI B
Bemidji State U, MN B
Bethany Coll, KS B
Bethel U, MN B
Bowling Green State U, OH B
Buena Vista U, IA B
Calumet Coll of Saint Joseph, IN B
Calvin Coll, MI B
Capital U, OH B
Carroll U, WI B
Case Western Reserve U, OH B
Central Christian Coll of Kansas, KS A,B
Central Michigan U, MI B
Clarke Coll, IA B
Coe Coll, IA B
Coll for Creative Studies, MI B
Coll of Mount St. Joseph, OH B
Coll of the Ozarks, MO B
Concordia Coll, MN B
Concordia U, MI B
Concordia U Chicago, IL B
Concordia U, Nebraska, NE B
Concordia U, St. Paul, MN B
Concordia U Wisconsin, WI B
Culver-Stockton Coll, MO B
Dakota Wesleyan U, SD B
Dana Coll, NE B
Defiance Coll, OH B
DePaul U, IL B
Eastern Michigan U, MI B
Edgewood Coll, WI B
Elmhurst Coll, IL B
Evangel U, MO B
Ferris State U, MI B
Fontbonne U, MO B
Fort Hays State U, KS B
Friends U, KS B
Grace Coll, IN B
Graceland U, IA B
Grand Valley State U, MI B
Gustavus Adolphus Coll, MN B
Hannibal-LaGrange Coll, MO B
Hope Coll, MI B
Huntington U, IN B
Indiana State U, IN B
Indiana U Bloomington, IN B
Indiana U–Purdue U Fort Wayne, IN B
Indiana U–Purdue U Indianapolis, IN B
Indiana Wesleyan U, IN B
Iowa Wesleyan Coll, IA B
Kansas Wesleyan U, KS B
Kent State U, OH B
Lawrence U, WI B
Lincoln U, MO B
Lindenwood U, MO B
Loras Coll, IA B
Malone U, OH B
Manchester Coll, IN B
Marian U, WI B
Marian U, IN B
Maryville U of Saint Louis, MO B
McKendree U, IL B
Miami U, OH B
Miami U Hamilton, OH B
Michigan State U, MI B
Millikin U, IL B
Minnesota State U Mankato, MN B
Minnesota State U Moorhead, MN B
Minot State U, ND B
Missouri State U, MO B
Missouri Western State U, MO B
Morningside Coll, IA B
Mount Mary Coll, WI B
Mount Mercy Coll, IA B
Mount Vernon Nazarene U, OH B
Muskingum Coll, OH B
North Central Coll, IL B
Northeastern State U, OK B
Northern Michigan U, MI B
Northern State U, SD B
Northwestern Coll, MN B
Northwest Missouri State U, MO B
Ohio Dominican U, OH B
Ohio Northern U, OH B
The Ohio State U, OH B
Ohio U, OH B
Ohio Wesleyan U, OH B
Oklahoma Baptist U, OK B
Oklahoma City U, OK B
Olivet Coll, MI B
Oral Roberts U, OK B

Otterbein Coll, OH B
Pittsburg State U, KS B
Saginaw Valley State U, MI B
St. Ambrose U, IA B
St. Catherine U, MN B
St. Cloud State U, MN B
Saint Joseph's Coll, IN B
Saint Mary-of-the-Woods Coll, IN B
Saint Mary's Coll, IN B
Saint Xavier U, IL B
Shawnee State U, OH B
Siena Heights U, MI B
Silver Lake Coll, WI B
Sinte Gleska U, SD B
Southeastern Oklahoma State U, OK B
Southeast Missouri State U, MO B
Southwest Baptist U, MO B
Southwestern Oklahoma State U, OK B
Southwest Minnesota State U, MN B
Taylor U, IN B
Transylvania U, KY B
Trinity Christian Coll, IL B
Union Coll, NE B
The U of Akron, OH B
U of Central Missouri, MO B
U of Central Oklahoma, OK B
U of Dayton, OH B
U of Evansville, IN B
The U of Findlay, OH B
U of Illinois at Chicago, IL B
U of Illinois at Urbana–Champaign, IL B
U of Indianapolis, IN B
The U of Iowa, IA B
The U of Kansas, KS B
U of Michigan–Flint, MI B
U of Minnesota, Duluth, MN B
U of Minnesota, Twin Cities Campus, MN B
U of Missouri–Columbia, MO B
U of Nebraska–Lincoln, NE B
U of Northern Iowa, IA B
U of Rio Grande, OH B
U of Saint Francis, IN B
U of Sioux Falls, SD B
The U of South Dakota, SD B
The U of Toledo, OH B
U of Wisconsin–La Crosse, WI B
U of Wisconsin–Madison, WI B
U of Wisconsin–Milwaukee, WI B
U of Wisconsin–Oshkosh, WI B
U of Wisconsin–Stout, WI B
U of Wisconsin–Superior, WI B
U of Wisconsin–Whitewater, WI B
Ursuline Coll, OH B
Valley City State U, ND B
Valparaiso U, IN B
Viterbo U, WI B
Waldorf Coll, IA B
Wartburg Coll, IA B
Washburn U, KS B
Washington U in St. Louis, MO B
Wayne State Coll, NE B
Wayne State U, MI B
Wichita State U, KS B
William Jewell Coll, MO B
Wilmington Coll, OH B
Winona State U, MN B
Wright State U, OH B
York Coll, NE B
Youngstown State U, OH B

Art Therapy

Capital U, OH B
DePaul U, IL B
Edgewood Coll, WI B
Millikin U, IL B
Mount Mary Coll, WI B
Ohio Wesleyan U, OH B
U of Indianapolis, IN B
U of Wisconsin–Superior, WI B
Webster U, MO B
Wright State U, OH B

Asian Studies

Augustana Coll, IL B
Beloit Coll, WI B
Bowling Green State U, OH B
Calvin Coll, MI B
Carleton Coll, MN B
Case Western Reserve U, OH B
Coe Coll, IA B
Illinois Wesleyan U, IL B
Indiana U Bloomington, IN B
John Carroll U, OH B
Knox Coll, IL B
Lake Forest Coll, IL B
Macalester Coll, MN B
Mount Union Coll, OH B
Northwestern U, IL B
Ohio U, OH B
Purdue U, IN B
St. Olaf Coll, MN B
U of Chicago, IL B
U of Cincinnati, OH B
The U of Iowa, IA B
U of Michigan, MI B
U of Northern Iowa, IA B
The U of Toledo, OH B
Washington U in St. Louis, MO B

Asian Studies (East)

Augsburg Coll, MN B
Denison U, OH B
DePaul U, IL B
DePauw U, IN B
Grand Valley State U, MI B
Hamline U, MN B
Indiana U Bloomington, IN B
John Carroll U, OH B
Lawrence U, WI B
Minnesota State U Moorhead, MN B
North Central Coll, IL B
Oakland U, MI B
Oberlin Coll, OH B
Ohio Wesleyan U, OH B
U of Chicago, IL B
U of Illinois at Urbana–Champaign, IL B
U of Minnesota, Twin Cities Campus, MN B
U of Missouri–Columbia, MO B
Valparaiso U, IN B
Washington U in St. Louis, MO B
Wayne State U, MI B
Wittenberg U, OH B

Asian Studies (South)

Indiana U Bloomington, IN B
Oakland U, MI B
U of Chicago, IL B
U of Minnesota, Twin Cities Campus, MN B
U of Missouri–Columbia, MO B

Asian Studies (Southeast)

Ohio U, OH B
U of Chicago, IL B

Astronomy

Benedictine Coll, KS B
Case Western Reserve U, OH B
Central Michigan U, MI B
Drake U, IA B
Minnesota State U Mankato, MN B
Northwestern U, IL B
The Ohio State U, OH B
Ohio Wesleyan U, OH B
U of Illinois at Urbana–Champaign, IL B
The U of Iowa, IA B
The U of Kansas, KS B
U of Michigan, MI B
U of Minnesota, Twin Cities Campus, MN B
U of Oklahoma, OK B
The U of Toledo, OH B
U of Wisconsin–Madison, WI B
Youngstown State U, OH B

Astrophysics

Augsburg Coll, MN B
Michigan State U, MI B
Ohio U, OH B
Ohio Wesleyan U, OH B
U of Minnesota, Twin Cities Campus, MN B
U of Oklahoma, OK B

Athletic Training

Anderson U, IN B
Aquinas Coll, MI B
Ashland U, OH B
Augsburg Coll, MN B
Augustana Coll, SD B
Baldwin-Wallace Coll, OH B
Benedictine Coll, KS B
Bethany Coll, KS B
Bethel Coll, KS B
Bethel U, MN B
Bowling Green State U, OH B
Buena Vista U, IA B
Capital U, OH B
Carroll U, WI B
Cedarville U, OH B
Central Christian Coll of Kansas, KS A
Central Coll, IA B
Central Methodist U, MO B
Central Michigan U, MI B
Clarke Coll, IA B
Coe Coll, IA B
Coll of Mount St. Joseph, OH B
Concordia U Wisconsin, WI B
Creighton U, NE B
Culver-Stockton Coll, MO B
Dakota Wesleyan U, SD B
Defiance Coll, OH B
DePauw U, IN B
Eastern Michigan U, MI B
Emporia State U, KS B
Eureka Coll, IL B
Franklin Coll, IN B
Graceland U, IA B
Grand Valley State U, MI B
Gustavus Adolphus Coll, MN B
Hamline U, MN B
Heidelberg U, OH B
Hope Coll, MI B
Illinois State U, IL B
Indiana State U, IN B
Indiana Wesleyan U, IN B
Kansas State U, KS B
Kent State U, OH B
Lake Superior State U, MI B
Lewis U, IL B
Lindenwood U, MO B
Loras Coll, IA B
Luther Coll, IA B
Manchester Coll, IN B
Marietta Coll, OH B
Marquette U, WI B
McKendree U, IL B
Miami U, OH B
Miami U Hamilton, OH B
MidAmerica Nazarene U, KS B
Millikin U, IL B
Minnesota State U Mankato, MN B
Missouri State U, MO B
Mount Union Coll, OH B
Nebraska Wesleyan U, NE B
North Central Coll, IL B
Northern Michigan U, MI B
North Park U, IL B
Ohio Northern U, OH B
The Ohio State U, OH B
Oklahoma Baptist U, OK B
Oklahoma State U, OK B
Olivet Coll, MI B
Olivet Nazarene U, IL B
Otterbein Coll, OH B
Park U, MO B
Purdue U, IN B
Saginaw Valley State U, MI B
Saint Louis U, MO B
Shawnee State U, OH B
Simpson Coll, IA B
South Dakota State U, SD B
Southern Nazarene U, OK B
Southwest Baptist U, MO B
Southwestern Coll, KS B
Sterling Coll, KS B
Trinity International U, IL B

A—associate degree; B—bachelor's degree

Truman State U, MO B
The U of Akron, OH B
U of Charleston, WV B
U of Evansville, IN B
The U of Findlay, OH B
U of Illinois at Urbana–Champaign, IL B
U of Indianapolis, IN B
The U of Iowa, IA B
The U of Kansas, KS B
U of Mary, ND B
U of Michigan, MI B
U of Nebraska–Lincoln, NE B
U of North Dakota, ND B
U of Northern Iowa, IA B
U of Tulsa, OK B
U of Wisconsin–Eau Claire, WI B
U of Wisconsin–La Crosse, WI B
U of Wisconsin–Stevens Point, WI B
Washburn U, KS B
Wayne State Coll, NE B
Wilmington Coll, OH B
Winona State U, MN B
Xavier U, OH B
Youngstown State U, OH B

Atmospheric Sciences and Meteorology

Creighton U, NE B
Iowa State U of Science and Technology, IA B
Northland Coll, WI B
Ohio U, OH B
Purdue U, IN B
St. Cloud State U, MN B
Saint Louis U, MO B
U of Illinois at Urbana–Champaign, IL B
The U of Kansas, KS B
U of Michigan, MI B
U of Missouri–Columbia, MO B
U of Nebraska–Lincoln, NE B
U of North Dakota, ND B
U of Wisconsin–Milwaukee, WI B
Valparaiso U, IN B

Atomic/Molecular Physics

Ohio U, OH B

Audio Engineering

Michigan Technological U, MI B

Audiology and Hearing Sciences

Cleveland State U, OH B
Indiana U–Purdue U Fort Wayne, IN B
Northwestern U, IL B
Ohio U, OH A
U of Illinois at Urbana–Champaign, IL B
U of Nebraska–Lincoln, NE B
U of Oklahoma Health Sciences Center, OK B

Audiology and Speech-Language Pathology

Andrews U, MI B
Augustana Coll, SD B
Ball State U, IN B
Calvin Coll, MI B
Elmhurst Coll, IL B
Fontbonne U, MO B
Fort Hays State U, KS B
Illinois State U, IL B
Indiana State U, IN B
Indiana U Bloomington, IN B
Kent State U, OH B
Marquette U, WI B
Miami U Hamilton, OH B
Michigan State U, MI B
Minnesota State U Mankato, MN B
Minnesota State U Moorhead, MN B
Missouri State U, MO B
Northeastern State U, OK B
Northern State U, SD B
Northwestern U, IL B
The Ohio State U, OH B
Ohio U, OH B
Otterbein Coll, OH B
Purdue U, IN B
St. Cloud State U, MN B
Saint Louis U, MO B
Southern Illinois U Edwardsville, IL B
U of Central Oklahoma, OK B
U of Cincinnati, OH B
U of Illinois at Urbana–Champaign, IL B
U of Minnesota, Duluth, MN B
U of Minnesota, Twin Cities Campus, MN B
U of Oklahoma Health Sciences Center, OK B
The U of Toledo, OH B
U of Tulsa, OK B
U of Wisconsin–Milwaukee, WI B
U of Wisconsin–Oshkosh, WI B
U of Wisconsin–Stevens Point, WI B
Western Michigan U, MI B
Wichita State U, KS B

Audiovisual Communications Technologies Related

Greenville Coll, IL B

Auditing

Pittsburg State U, KS B
U of Illinois at Urbana–Champaign, IL B

Autobody/Collision and Repair Technology

Pittsburg State U, KS B
Ranken Tech Coll, MO A

Automobile/Automotive Mechanics Technology

Baker Coll of Flint, MI A
Ferris State U, MI A
McPherson Coll, KS A
Northern Michigan U, MI A
Pittsburg State U, KS A,B
Ranken Tech Coll, MO A

Automotive Engineering Technology

Central Michigan U, MI B
Ferris State U, MI B
Indiana State U, IN B
Minnesota State U Mankato, MN B
Pittsburg State U, KS B
Southern Illinois U Carbondale, IL B

Aviation/Airway Management

Baker Coll of Muskegon, MI B
Bowling Green State U, OH B
Eastern Michigan U, MI B
Indiana State U, IN B
Kent State U, OH B
Lewis U, IL B
Minnesota State U Mankato, MN B
The Ohio State U, OH B
Ohio U, OH B
Quincy U, IL B
St. Cloud State U, MN B
Saint Louis U, MO B
South Dakota State U, SD B
Southeastern Oklahoma State U, OK B
Southern Illinois U Carbondale, IL B
U of Illinois at Urbana–Champaign, IL B
U of Nebraska at Kearney, NE B
U of Nebraska at Omaha, NE B
U of North Dakota, ND B
Winona State U, MN B

Avionics Maintenance Technology

Baker Coll of Flint, MI A
Southern Illinois U Carbondale, IL B

Baking and Pastry Arts

The Art Insts International Minnesota, MN A
Kendall Coll, IL A

Ballet

Friends U, KS B
Indiana U Bloomington, IN B

Banking and Financial Support Services

Buena Vista U, IA B
U of Illinois at Urbana–Champaign, IL B
U of Nebraska at Omaha, NE B
Washburn U, KS A

Behavioral Sciences

Andrews U, MI B
Augsburg Coll, MN B
Bemidji State U, MN B
Concordia U, Nebraska, NE B
Dakota Wesleyan U, SD B
East-West U, IL B
Evangel U, MO B
Indiana U Kokomo, IN B
Loyola U Chicago, IL B
Mid-America Christian U, OK B
Minnesota State U Mankato, MN B
Missouri Baptist U, MO B
Mount Mary Coll, WI B
National-Louis U, IL B
Northern Michigan U, MI B
Northwest Missouri State U, MO B
Purdue U North Central, IN B
St. Cloud State U, MN B
Sterling Coll, KS B
U of Chicago, IL B
The U of Kansas, KS B
U of Missouri–Columbia, MO B
Walsh U, OH B

Bengali

U of Chicago, IL B

Biblical Languages/Literatures

Oklahoma Baptist U, OK B

Biblical Studies

Anderson U, IN B
Andrews U, MI B
Barclay Coll, KS A,B
Bethel Coll, IN A,B
Bethel U, MN B
Calvary Bible Coll and Theological Seminary, MO A,B
Calvin Coll, MI B
Cedarville U, OH B
Central Bible Coll, MO A,B
Central Christian Coll of Kansas, KS B
Cincinnati Christian U, OH A,B
Cornerstone U, MI B
Crossroads Bible Coll, IN B
Crossroads Coll, MN B
Crown Coll, MN A,B
Emmaus Bible Coll, IA A,B
Evangel U, MO B
Faith Baptist Bible Coll and Theological Seminary, IA A,B
Goshen Coll, IN B
Grace Bible Coll, MI B
Grace Coll, IN B
Grace U, NE A,B
Great Lakes Christian Coll, MI B
Hannibal-LaGrange Coll, MO B
Huntington U, IN B
Indiana Wesleyan U, IN B
Kuyper Coll, MI A,B
Laura and Alvin Siegal Coll of Judaic Studies, OH B
Malone U, OH B
Manhattan Christian Coll, KS A,B
Maranatha Baptist Bible Coll, WI B
Messenger Coll, MO B
Moody Bible Inst, IL B
Mount Vernon Nazarene U, OH B
North Central U, MN A,B
North Park U, IL B
Northwestern Coll, MN B
Oklahoma Baptist U, OK B
Oklahoma Christian U, OK B
Oral Roberts U, OK B
St. Louis Christian Coll, MO B
Southwest Baptist U, MO B
Southwestern Christian U, OK B
Spring Arbor U, MI B

Taylor U, IN B
Trinity Bible Coll, ND A,B
Trinity International U, IL B
Tri-State Bible Coll, OH A,B
U of Evansville, IN B
Wheaton Coll, IL B
York Coll, NE B

Bilingual and Multilingual Education

Calvin Coll, MI B
Goshen Coll, IN B
Indiana U Bloomington, IN B
Loyola U Chicago, IL B
Mount Mary Coll, WI B
Northeastern Illinois U, IL B
Oglala Lakota Coll, SD B
The U of Findlay, OH B
U of Nebraska at Omaha, NE B
U of Wisconsin–Milwaukee, WI B
Western Illinois U, IL B

Biochemistry

Alma Coll, MI B
Anderson U, IN B
Andrews U, MI B
Augustana Coll, IL B
Beloit Coll, WI B
Benedictine Coll, KS B
Benedictine U, IL B
Bradley U, IL B
Calvin Coll, MI B
Capital U, OH B
Carroll U, WI B
Case Western Reserve U, OH B
Central Michigan U, MI B
Clarkson U, NY B
Coe Coll, IA B
Coll of Mount St. Joseph, OH B
Coll of Saint Benedict, MN B
The Coll of St. Scholastica, MN B
The Coll of Wooster, OH B
Cornell Coll, IA B
Dakota Wesleyan U, SD B
Denison U, OH B
DePauw U, IN B
Doane Coll, NE B
Dominican U, IL B
Drake U, IA B
Earlham Coll, IN B
Eastern Michigan U, MI B
Ferris State U, MI B
Grinnell Coll, IA B
Gustavus Adolphus Coll, MN B
Hamline U, MN B
Hiram Coll, OH B
Illinois Inst of Technology, IL B
Illinois State U, IL B
Indiana U Bloomington, IN B
Indiana U South Bend, IN B
Iowa State U of Science and Technology, IA B
Jamestown Coll, ND B
Kansas State U, KS B
Kenyon Coll, OH B
Kettering U, MI B
Knox Coll, IL B
Lakeland Coll, WI B
Lawrence Technological U, MI B
Lawrence U, WI B
Lewis U, IL B
Loras Coll, IA B
Loyola U Chicago, IL B
Madonna U, MI B
Marietta Coll, OH B
Marquette U, WI B
Maryville U of Saint Louis, MO B
McPherson Coll, KS B
Miami U, OH B
Miami U Hamilton, OH B
Michigan State U, MI B
Michigan Technological U, MI B
Minnesota State U Mankato, MN B
Missouri Southern State U, MO B
Missouri Western State U, MO B
Monmouth Coll, IL B
Mount Union Coll, OH B
Nebraska Wesleyan U, NE B
North Central Coll, IL B
Northern Michigan U, MI B
Northwestern U, IL B
Oakland U, MI B
Oberlin Coll, OH B
Ohio Northern U, OH B
The Ohio State U, OH B
Oklahoma Baptist U, OK B
Oklahoma Christian U, OK B
Oklahoma City U, OK B
Oklahoma State U, OK B
Olivet Coll, MI B
Otterbein Coll, OH B
Pittsburg State U, KS B
Purdue U, IN B
Ripon Coll, WI B
Rockford Coll, IL B
Rockhurst U, MO B
Saginaw Valley State U, MI B
St. Catherine U, MN B
Saint John's U, MN B
Saint Joseph's Coll, IN A,B
Saint Louis U, MO B
Saint Mary's U of Minnesota, MN B
Simpson Coll, IA B
South Dakota State U, SD B
Southern Methodist U, TX B
Southern Nazarene U, OK B
Southwestern Coll, KS B
Spring Arbor U, MI B
Union Coll, NE B
The U of Akron, OH B
U of Chicago, IL B
U of Cincinnati, OH B
U of Dallas, TX B
U of Dayton, OH B
U of Evansville, IN B
U of Illinois at Chicago, IL B
U of Illinois at Urbana–Champaign, IL B
The U of Iowa, IA B
The U of Kansas, KS B
U of Michigan, MI B
U of Michigan–Dearborn, MI B
U of Minnesota, Duluth, MN B
U of Minnesota, Twin Cities Campus, MN B
U of Missouri–Columbia, MO B
U of Missouri–St. Louis, MO B
U of Nebraska–Lincoln, NE B
U of Northern Iowa, IA B
U of Notre Dame, IN B
U of Oklahoma, OK B
U of Tulsa, OK B
U of Wisconsin–Madison, WI B
U of Wisconsin–Milwaukee, WI B
Valparaiso U, IN B
Viterbo U, WI B
Wartburg Coll, IA B
Washburn U, KS B
Washington U in St. Louis, MO B
Western Michigan U, MI B
Westminster Coll, MO B
William Jewell Coll, MO B
Wright State U, OH B

Biochemistry/Biophysics and Molecular Biology

Illinois Inst of Technology, IL B
Michigan State U, MI B
Nebraska Wesleyan U, NE B
North Dakota State U, ND B
U of Michigan–Flint, MI B
Wittenberg U, OH B

Bioethics/Medical Ethics

Cleveland State U, OH B
William Jewell Coll, MO B

Bioinformatics

Davenport U, Grand Rapids, MI B
Iowa State U of Science and Technology, IA B
Loyola U Chicago, IL B
Michigan Technological U, MI B
Rockhurst U, MO B
U of Nebraska at Omaha, NE B
U of Northern Iowa, IA B

Biological and Biomedical Sciences Related

Bethel U, MN B
Central Michigan U, MI B
Dakota State U, SD B
Grand Valley State U, MI B
Hiram Coll, OH B
Indiana U Bloomington, IN B
Kent State U, OH B
Logan U–Coll of Chiropractic, MO B
Park U, MO B
Sinte Gleska U, SD A
U of Illinois at Urbana–Champaign, IL B
The U of Kansas, KS B
U of Michigan, MI B
U of North Dakota, ND B
U of Wisconsin–Parkside, WI B
Ursuline Coll, OH B
Washington U in St. Louis, MO B

Biological and Physical Sciences

Alma Coll, MI B
Augsburg Coll, MN B
Bemidji State U, MN B
Buena Vista U, IA B
Calvin Coll, MI B
Central Christian Coll of Kansas, KS A
Coe Coll, IA B
Coll of Saint Benedict, MN B
Concordia U, MI B
Concordia U Chicago, IL B
Crown Coll, MN A
DePaul U, IL B
Eastern Michigan U, MI B
Eureka Coll, IL B
Ferris State U, MI A
Fort Hays State U, KS B
Grand Valley State U, MI B
Huntington U, IN B
Indiana U Kokomo, IN B
Indiana U–Purdue U Indianapolis, IN B
Iowa Wesleyan Coll, IA B
John Carroll U, OH B
Kent State U, Stark Campus, OH A
Maryville U of Saint Louis, MO B
Michigan State U, MI B
Minnesota State U Mankato, MN B
Mount Vernon Nazarene U, OH B
National-Louis U, IL B
North Central Coll, IL B
Northern State U, SD B
Northwestern U, IL B
Northwest Missouri State U, MO B
Ohio U, OH A
Ohio U–Lancaster, OH A
Ohio U–Southern Campus, OH A
Ohio U–Zanesville, OH A
Oklahoma City U, OK B
Oklahoma Panhandle State U, OK B
Olivet Coll, MI B
Palmer Coll of Chiropractic, IA B
Purdue U, IN B
Rockford Coll, IL B
St. Norbert Coll, WI B
Saint Xavier U, IL B
Shawnee State U, OH B
Trine U, IN A
U of Cincinnati, OH A
The U of Findlay, OH B
U of Northern Iowa, IA B
U of Notre Dame, IN B
U of Saint Francis, IN B
U of Southern Indiana, IN B
The U of Toledo, OH B
U of Wisconsin–Platteville, WI B

A—associate degree; B—bachelor's degree

U of Wisconsin–Superior, WI B
U of Wisconsin–Whitewater, WI B
Valparaiso U, IN A
Walsh U, OH B
Washington U in St. Louis, MO B
Wilmington Coll, OH B
Winona State U, MN B
Wright State U, OH B
Xavier U, OH B
York Coll, NE B

Biology/Biological Sciences

Adrian Coll, MI B
Albion Coll, MI B
Alma Coll, MI B
Anderson U, IN B
Andrews U, MI B
Aquinas Coll, MI B
Ashland U, OH B
Augsburg Coll, MN B
Augustana Coll, IL B
Augustana Coll, SD B
Aurora U, IL B
Avila U, MO B
Baker U, KS B
Baldwin-Wallace Coll, OH B
Ball State U, IN B
Beloit Coll, WI B
Bemidji State U, MN B
Benedictine Coll, KS B
Benedictine U, IL B
Bethany Coll, KS B
Bethany Lutheran Coll, MN B
Bethel Coll, IN B
Bethel Coll, KS B
Bethel U, MN B
Black Hills State U, SD B
Bluffton U, OH B
Bowling Green State U, OH B
Bradley U, IL B
Briar Cliff U, IA B
Buena Vista U, IA B
Butler U, IN B
Calvin Coll, MI B
Cameron U, OK B
Capital U, OH B
Carleton Coll, MN B
Carroll U, WI B
Case Western Reserve U, OH B
Cedarville U, OH B
Central Coll, IA B
Central Methodist U, MO B
Central Michigan U, MI B
Central State U, OH B
Clarke Coll, IA B
Clarkson U, NY B
Cleveland State U, OH B
Coe Coll, IA B
Coll of Mount St. Joseph, OH B
Coll of Saint Benedict, MN B
Coll of Saint Mary, NE B
The Coll of St. Scholastica, MN B
Coll of the Ozarks, MO B
The Coll of Wooster, OH B
Columbia Coll, MO B
Concordia Coll, MN B
Concordia U, MI B
Concordia U Chicago, IL B
Concordia U, Nebraska, NE B
Concordia U, St. Paul, MN B
Concordia U Wisconsin, WI B
Cornell Coll, IA B
Cornerstone U, MI B
Creighton U, NE B
Culver-Stockton Coll, MO B
Dakota Wesleyan U, SD B
Dana Coll, NE B
Defiance Coll, OH B
Denison U, OH B
DePaul U, IL B
DePauw U, IN B
Doane Coll, NE B
Dominican U, IL B
Dordt Coll, IA B
Drake U, IA B
Drury U, MO B
Earlham Coll, IN B
Eastern Illinois U, IL B
Eastern Michigan U, MI B
East-West U, IL B
Edgewood Coll, WI B
Elmhurst Coll, IL B
Emporia State U, KS B
Eureka Coll, IL B
Evangel U, MO B
Ferris State U, MI B
Fontbonne U, MO B
Fort Hays State U, KS B
Franciscan U of Steubenville, OH B
Franklin Coll, IN B
Friends U, KS B
Goshen Coll, IN B
Grace Coll, IN B
Graceland U, IA B
Grand Valley State U, MI B
Grand View U, IA B
Greenville Coll, IL B
Grinnell Coll, IA B
Gustavus Adolphus Coll, MN B
Hamline U, MN B
Hannibal-LaGrange Coll, MO B
Hanover Coll, IN B
Heidelberg U, OH B
Hillsdale Coll, MI B
Hiram Coll, OH B
Hope Coll, MI B
Huntington U, IN B
Illinois Coll, IL B
Illinois Inst of Technology, IL B
Illinois State U, IL B
Illinois Wesleyan U, IL B
Indiana State U, IN B
Indiana U Bloomington, IN B
Indiana U East, IN B
Indiana U Kokomo, IN B
Indiana U Northwest, IN B
Indiana U–Purdue U Fort Wayne, IN A,B
Indiana U–Purdue U Indianapolis, IN B
Indiana U South Bend, IN A,B
Indiana U Southeast, IN B
Indiana Wesleyan U, IN A,B
Iowa State U of Science and Technology, IA B
Iowa Wesleyan Coll, IA B
Jamestown Coll, ND B
John Carroll U, OH B
Kalamazoo Coll, MI B
Kansas State U, KS B
Kansas Wesleyan U, KS B
Kent State U, OH B
Kenyon Coll, OH B
Knox Coll, IL B
Lake Erie Coll, OH B
Lake Forest Coll, IL B
Lakeland Coll, WI B
Lawrence U, WI B
Lewis U, IL B
Lincoln U, MO B
Lindenwood U, MO B
Logan U–Coll of Chiropractic, MO B
Loras Coll, IA B
Lourdes Coll, OH A,B
Loyola U Chicago, IL B
Luther Coll, IA B
Macalester Coll, MN B
MacMurray Coll, IL B
Madonna U, MI B
Malone U, OH B
Manchester Coll, IN B
Maranatha Baptist Bible Coll, WI B
Marian U, WI B
Marian U, IN B
Marietta Coll, OH B
Marquette U, WI B
Martin U, IN B
Maryville U of Saint Louis, MO B
Mayville State U, ND B
McKendree U, IL B
McPherson Coll, KS B
Michigan State U, MI B
Michigan Technological U, MI B
MidAmerica Nazarene U, KS B
Millikin U, IL B
Minnesota State U Mankato, MN B
Minnesota State U Moorhead, MN B
Minot State U, ND B
Missouri Baptist U, MO B
Missouri Southern State U, MO B
Missouri State U, MO B
Missouri U of Science and Technology, MO B
Missouri Western State U, MO B
Monmouth Coll, IL B
Morningside Coll, IA B
Mount Marty Coll, SD B
Mount Mary Coll, WI B
Mount Mercy Coll, IA B
Mount Union Coll, OH B
Mount Vernon Nazarene U, OH B
Muskingum Coll, OH B
National-Louis U, IL B
Nebraska Wesleyan U, NE B
Newman U, KS B
North Central Coll, IL B
North Dakota State U, ND B
Northeastern Illinois U, IL B
Northeastern State U, OK B
Northern Michigan U, MI B
Northern State U, SD B
Northland Coll, WI B
North Park U, IL B
Northwestern Coll, MN B
Northwestern U, IL B
Northwest Missouri State U, MO B
Oakland U, MI B
Oberlin Coll, OH B
Ohio Dominican U, OH B
Ohio Northern U, OH B
The Ohio State U, OH B
The Ohio State U at Lima, OH B
The Ohio State U at Marion, OH B
Ohio U, OH B
Ohio Wesleyan U, OH B
Oklahoma Baptist U, OK B
Oklahoma Christian U, OK B
Oklahoma City U, OK B
Oklahoma Panhandle State U, OK B
Oklahoma State U, OK B
Olivet Coll, MI B
Olivet Nazarene U, IL B
Oral Roberts U, OK B
Otterbein Coll, OH B
Park U, MO B
Pittsburg State U, KS B
Presentation Coll, SD A,B
Purdue U, IN B
Purdue U Calumet, IN B
Purdue U North Central, IN A,B
Quincy U, IL B
Ripon Coll, WI B
Rockford Coll, IL B
Rockhurst U, MO B
Rogers State U, OK A,B
Roosevelt U, IL B
Rose-Hulman Inst of Technology, IN B
Saginaw Valley State U, MI B
St. Ambrose U, IA B
St. Catherine U, MN B
St. Cloud State U, MN B
St. Gregory's U, Shawnee, OK B
Saint John's U, MN B
Saint Joseph's Coll, IN B
Saint Louis U, MO B
Saint Mary-of-the-Woods Coll, IN B
Saint Mary's Coll, IN B
Saint Mary's U of Minnesota, MN B
St. Norbert Coll, WI B
St. Olaf Coll, MN B
Saint Xavier U, IL B
Shawnee State U, OH A,B
Siena Heights U, MI B
Silver Lake Coll, WI B
Simpson Coll, IA B
South Dakota State U, SD B
Southeastern Oklahoma State U, OK B
Southeast Missouri State U, MO B
Southern Illinois U Carbondale, IL B
Southern Illinois U Edwardsville, IL B

Southern Methodist U, TX B
Southern Nazarene U, OK B
Southwest Baptist U, MO B
Southwestern Coll, KS B
Southwestern Oklahoma State U, OK B
Southwest Minnesota State U, MN B
Spring Arbor U, MI B
Stephens Coll, MO B
Sterling Coll, KS B
Taylor U, IN B
Transylvania U, KY B
Trine U, IN B
Trinity Christian Coll, IL B
Trinity International U, IL B
Truman State U, MO B
Union Coll, NE B
The U of Akron, OH B
U of Central Missouri, MO B
U of Central Oklahoma, OK B
U of Charleston, WV B
U of Chicago, IL B
U of Cincinnati, OH B
U of Dallas, TX B
U of Dayton, OH B
U of Evansville, IN B
The U of Findlay, OH B
U of Illinois at Chicago, IL B
U of Illinois at Springfield, IL B
U of Illinois at Urbana–Champaign, IL B
U of Indianapolis, IN B
The U of Iowa, IA B
The U of Kansas, KS B
U of Mary, ND B
U of Michigan, MI B
U of Michigan–Dearborn, MI B
U of Michigan–Flint, MI B
U of Minnesota, Crookston, MN B
U of Minnesota, Duluth, MN B
U of Minnesota, Morris, MN B
U of Minnesota, Twin Cities Campus, MN B
U of Missouri–Columbia, MO B
U of Missouri–Kansas City, MO B
U of Missouri–St. Louis, MO B
U of Nebraska at Kearney, NE B
U of Nebraska at Omaha, NE B
U of Nebraska–Lincoln, NE B
U of New Orleans, LA B
U of North Dakota, ND B
U of Northern Iowa, IA B
U of Notre Dame, IN B
U of Rio Grande, OH A,B
U of St. Francis, IL B
U of Saint Mary, KS B
U of Science and Arts of Oklahoma, OK B
U of Sioux Falls, SD B
The U of South Dakota, SD B
U of Southern Indiana, IN B
The U of Toledo, OH A,B
U of Tulsa, OK B
U of Wisconsin–Eau Claire, WI B
U of Wisconsin–Green Bay, WI B
U of Wisconsin–La Crosse, WI B
U of Wisconsin–Madison, WI B
U of Wisconsin–Milwaukee, WI B
U of Wisconsin–Oshkosh, WI B
U of Wisconsin–Platteville, WI B
U of Wisconsin–Stevens Point, WI B
U of Wisconsin–Superior, WI B
U of Wisconsin–Whitewater, WI B
Ursuline Coll, OH B
Valley City State U, ND B
Valparaiso U, IN B
Viterbo U, WI B
Wabash Coll, IN B
Walsh U, OH B
Wartburg Coll, IA B
Washburn U, KS B
Washington U in St. Louis, MO B
Wayne State Coll, NE B
Wayne State U, MI B
Webster U, MO B
Western Illinois U, IL B
Western Michigan U, MI B
Westminster Coll, MO B
Wheaton Coll, IL B
Wichita State U, KS B
Wilberforce U, OH B
William Jewell Coll, MO B
Wilmington Coll, OH B
Winona State U, MN B
Wittenberg U, OH B
Wright State U, OH A,B
Xavier U, OH B
York Coll, NE B
Youngstown State U, OH B

Biology/Biotechnology Laboratory Technician
Cleveland State U, OH B
Michigan Technological U, MI B
Minnesota State U Mankato, MN B
Purdue U Calumet, IN B
St. Cloud State U, MN B
Washburn U, KS B

Biology Teacher Education
Alma Coll, MI B
Bethany Coll, KS B
Bethel U, MN B
Bowling Green State U, OH B
Buena Vista U, IA B
Carroll U, WI B
Cedarville U, OH B
Central Christian Coll of Kansas, KS A
Central Methodist U, MO B
Central Michigan U, MI B
Coll of the Ozarks, MO B
Concordia Coll, MN B
Concordia U, MI B
Concordia U Chicago, IL B
Concordia U, Nebraska, NE B
Concordia U, St. Paul, MN B
Cornerstone U, MI B
Dakota State U, SD B
Dakota Wesleyan U, SD B
DePaul U, IL B
Dordt Coll, IA B
Eastern Illinois U, IL B
Eastern Michigan U, MI B
Edgewood Coll, WI B
Elmhurst Coll, IL B
Evangel U, MO B
Ferris State U, MI B
Franklin Coll, IN B
Grand Valley State U, MI B
Greenville Coll, IL B
Gustavus Adolphus Coll, MN B
Hope Coll, MI B
Indiana U Bloomington, IN B
Indiana U–Purdue U Fort Wayne, IN B
Indiana U South Bend, IN B
Jamestown Coll, ND B
Lincoln U, MO B
Lindenwood U, MO B
Marian U, WI B
Maryville U of Saint Louis, MO B
Mayville State U, ND B
McKendree U, IL B
Miami U, OH B
Michigan Technological U, MI B
Millikin U, IL B
Minnesota State U Moorhead, MN B
Minot State U, ND B
Missouri State U, MO B
Mount Mary Coll, WI B
Mount Vernon Nazarene U, OH B
North Dakota State U, ND B
Northeastern State U, OK B
Northern Michigan U, MI B
Ohio Northern U, OH B
Ohio U, OH B
Ohio Wesleyan U, OH B
Pittsburg State U, KS B
Purdue U, IN B
Saginaw Valley State U, MI B
St. Ambrose U, IA B
St. Catherine U, MN B
Saint Mary's U of Minnesota, MN B
Saint Xavier U, IL B
Southwest Baptist U, MO B
Southwest Minnesota State U, MN B
Trinity Christian Coll, IL B
Union Coll, NE B
U of Charleston, WV B
U of Evansville, IN B
U of Illinois at Chicago, IL B
The U of Iowa, IA B
U of Mary, ND B
U of Michigan–Flint, MI B
U of Missouri–Columbia, MO B
U of Missouri–St. Louis, MO B
U of Nebraska–Lincoln, NE B
U of New Orleans, LA B
U of Rio Grande, OH B
U of Saint Francis, IN B
The U of South Dakota, SD B
U of Wisconsin–Superior, WI B
Valley City State U, ND B
Valparaiso U, IN B
Viterbo U, WI B
Washington U in St. Louis, MO B
Wayne State Coll, NE B
Xavier U, OH B
York Coll, NE B

Biomathematics and Bioinformatics Related
Case Western Reserve U, OH B

Biomedical/Medical Engineering
Case Western Reserve U, OH B
Illinois Inst of Technology, IL B
Indiana Tech, IN B
Indiana U–Purdue U Indianapolis, IN B
Lawrence Technological U, MI B
Marquette U, WI B
Michigan State U, MI B
Michigan Technological U, MI B
Milwaukee School of Engineering, WI B
Northwestern U, IL B
Oral Roberts U, OK B
Purdue U, IN B
Rose-Hulman Inst of Technology, IN B
Saint Louis U, MO B
The U of Akron, OH B
U of Central Oklahoma, OK B
U of Illinois at Chicago, IL B
U of Illinois at Urbana–Champaign, IL B
The U of Iowa, IA B
U of Michigan, MI B
U of Nebraska–Lincoln, NE B
The U of Toledo, OH B
U of Wisconsin–Madison, WI B
Washington U in St. Louis, MO B
Wright State U, OH B

Biomedical Science
Rochester Comm and Tech Coll, MN A

Biomedical Sciences
Central Michigan U, MI B
Marquette U, WI B
Maryville U of Saint Louis, MO B
St. Cloud State U, MN B
Stephens Coll, MO B
U of Michigan, MI B
U of Michigan–Flint, MI B
U of Wisconsin–Green Bay, WI B
Western Michigan U, MI B

A—associate degree; B—bachelor's degree

Biomedical Technology
Andrews U, MI B
Baker Coll of Flint, MI A
DeVry U, Addison, IL B
DeVry U, Chicago, IL B
DeVry U, Tinley Park, IL B
DeVry U, Kansas City, MO B
DeVry U, Columbus, OH B
Indiana U–Purdue U Indianapolis, IN A
Northwest Missouri State U, MO B
Wright State U, OH B

Biophysics
Andrews U, MI B
Clarkson U, NY B
Illinois Inst of Technology, IL B
Iowa State U of Science and Technology, IA B
Oakland U, MI B
Oklahoma City U, OK B
Saint Mary's U of Minnesota, MN B
Southern Nazarene U, OK B
Southwestern Oklahoma State U, OK B
U of Illinois at Urbana–Champaign, IL B
U of Michigan, MI B
U of Southern Indiana, IN B
Washington U in St. Louis, MO B

Biopsychology
Grand Valley State U, MI B
Morningside Coll, IA B
Nebraska Wesleyan U, NE B
Viterbo U, WI B
Washington U in St. Louis, MO B

Biotechnology
Calvin Coll, MI B
Clarkson U, NY B
Ferris State U, MI B
Indiana U Bloomington, IN B
Indiana U East, IN B
Indiana U–Purdue U Indianapolis, IN A,B
Kent State U, OH B
Missouri Baptist U, MO B
North Dakota State U, ND B
Roosevelt U, IL B
Southeastern Oklahoma State U, OK B
U of Illinois at Urbana–Champaign, IL B
U of Nebraska at Omaha, NE B
U of Northern Iowa, IA B
Ursuline Coll, OH B

Biotechnology Research
Missouri Western State U, MO B

Botany/Plant Biology
Andrews U, MI B
Eastern Illinois U, IL B
Iowa State U of Science and Technology, IA B
Kent State U, OH B
Miami U, OH B
Michigan State U, MI B
Minnesota State U Mankato, MN B
North Dakota State U, ND B
Northwest Missouri State U, MO B
The Ohio State U, OH B
Ohio U, OH B
Ohio Wesleyan U, OH B
Oklahoma State U, OK B
Purdue U, IN B
St. Cloud State U, MN B
Saint Xavier U, IL B
Southern Illinois U Carbondale, IL B
The U of Akron, OH B
U of Illinois at Urbana–Champaign, IL B
U of Minnesota, Twin Cities Campus, MN B
U of Nebraska–Lincoln, NE B
U of Oklahoma, OK B
U of Wisconsin–Madison, WI B

Botany/Plant Biology Related
Miami U Hamilton, OH B

Broadcast Journalism
Bemidji State U, MN B
Bowling Green State U, OH B
Calvary Bible Coll and Theological Seminary, MO B
Central State U, OH B
Coll of the Ozarks, MO B
Cornerstone U, MI A
Drake U, IA B
Evangel U, MO A,B
Goshen Coll, IN B
Grace U, NE B
Huntington U, IN B
Kuyper Coll, MI B
Lewis U, IL B
Lindenwood U, MO B
Manchester Coll, IN A
Marquette U, WI B
Minnesota State U Moorhead, MN B
Mount Vernon Nazarene U, OH B
Northwest Missouri State U, MO B
Ohio U, OH B
Ohio U–Zanesville, OH A
Ohio Wesleyan U, OH B
Oklahoma Christian U, OK B
Oklahoma City U, OK B
St. Cloud State U, MN B
Stephens Coll, MO B
U of Central Oklahoma, OK B
U of Cincinnati, OH B
U of Dayton, OH B
The U of Findlay, OH B
U of Illinois at Urbana–Champaign, IL B
U of Missouri–Columbia, MO B
U of Nebraska at Omaha, NE B
U of Nebraska–Lincoln, NE B
U of Northern Iowa, IA B
U of Oklahoma, OK B
U of Wisconsin–Madison, WI B
U of Wisconsin–Milwaukee, WI B
U of Wisconsin–Oshkosh, WI B
U of Wisconsin–Platteville, WI B
U of Wisconsin–Superior, WI B
Waldorf Coll, IA B
Wartburg Coll, IA B
Webster U, MO B
Winona State U, MN B

Building/Home/Construction Inspection
Oklahoma State U, Oklahoma City, OK A

Building/Property Maintenance and Management
Northern Michigan U, MI A
Park U, MO A
Rochester Comm and Tech Coll, MN A

Business Administration and Management
Adrian Coll, MI B
AIB Coll of Business, IA A
Albion Coll, MI B
Alma Coll, MI B
American InterContinental U Online, IL A,B
Anderson U, IN A,B
Antioch U McGregor, OH B
Aquinas Coll, MI B
Argosy U, Chicago, IL B
Argosy U, Schaumburg, IL B
Argosy U, Twin Cities, MN B
Ashland U, OH B
Augsburg Coll, MN B
Augustana Coll, IL B
Augustana Coll, SD B
Aurora U, IL B
Avila U, MO B
Bacone Coll, OK A,B
Baker Coll of Allen Park, MI A
Baker Coll of Auburn Hills, MI A,B
Baker Coll of Flint, MI A
Baker Coll of Owosso, MI A,B
Baldwin-Wallace Coll, OH B
Ball State U, IN A,B
Barclay Coll, KS B
Beloit Coll, WI B
Bemidji State U, MN B
Benedictine Coll, KS A,B
Benedictine U, IL A
Bethany Coll, KS B
Bethany Lutheran Coll, MN B
Bethel Coll, IN A,B
Bethel U, MN B
Black Hills State U, SD B
Bluffton U, OH B
Bohecker's Business Coll, OH A
Bradley U, IL B
Briar Cliff U, IA B
Brown Mackie Coll–Fort Wayne, IN A,B
Brown Mackie Coll–Indianapolis, IN A,B
Brown Mackie Coll–Merrillville, IN A,B
Brown Mackie Coll–Michigan City, IN A,B
Brown Mackie Coll–South Bend, IN A,B
Brown Mackie Coll–Tulsa, OK A,B
Bryant & Stratton Coll, Parma, OH B
Bryant & Stratton Coll, Willoughby Hills, OH A,B
Bryant & Stratton Coll—Wauwatosa Campus, WI B
Buena Vista U, IA B
Calumet Coll of Saint Joseph, IN A,B
Calvin Coll, MI B
Cameron U, OK A,B
Capital U, OH B
Carroll U, WI B
Case Western Reserve U, OH B
Cedarville U, OH B
Central Coll, IA B
Central Methodist U, MO B
Central Michigan U, MI B
Chancellor U, OH A,B
Clarke Coll, IA B
Clarkson Coll, NE B
Clarkson U, NY B
Cleary U, MI A,B
Cleveland State U, OH B
Coe Coll, IA B
Coll of Mount St. Joseph, OH A,B
Coll of Saint Benedict, MN B
Coll of Saint Mary, NE A,B
The Coll of St. Scholastica, MN B
Coll of the Ozarks, MO B
Colorado Tech U North Kansas City, MO A,B
Colorado Tech U Sioux Falls, SD A,B
Columbia Coll, MO A,B
Concordia Coll, MN B
Concordia U, MI B
Concordia U Chicago, IL B
Concordia U, Nebraska, NE B
Concordia U, St. Paul, MN B
Concordia U Wisconsin, WI B
Cornerstone U, MI B
Crossroads Coll, MN B
Crown Coll, MN B
Culver-Stockton Coll, MO B
Dakota State U, SD B
Dakota Wesleyan U, SD A,B
Dana Coll, NE B
Davenport U, Grand Rapids, MI A,B
DePaul U, IL B
DeVry U, Addison, IL B
DeVry U, Chicago, IL B
DeVry U, Tinley Park, IL B
DeVry U, Indianapolis, IN B
DeVry U, Edina, MN B
DeVry U, Kansas City, MO B
DeVry U, Columbus, OH B
DeVry U, OK B
DeVry U, Milwaukee, WI B
Doane Coll, NE B
Dominican U, IL B
Dordt Coll, IA B

College	Degree
Drake U, IA	B
Drury U, MO	B
Earlham Coll, IN	B
Eastern Illinois U, IL	B
Eastern Michigan U, MI	B
East-West U, IL	A,B
Edgewood Coll, WI	B
Elmhurst Coll, IL	B
Emporia State U, KS	B
Eureka Coll, IL	B
Evangel U, MO	B
Ferris State U, MI	A,B
Fontbonne U, MO	B
Fort Hays State U, KS	B
Franciscan U of Steubenville, OH	A,B
Franklin U, OH	A,B
Friends U, KS	B
Goshen Coll, IN	B
Grace Bible Coll, MI	A,B
Grace Coll, IN	B
Graceland U, IA	B
Grace U, NE	B
Grand View U, IA	B
Grantham U, MO	A,B
Greenville Coll, IL	B
Gustavus Adolphus Coll, MN	B
Hamline U, MN	B
Hannibal-LaGrange Coll, MO	B
Hanover Coll, IN	B
Harris-Stowe State U, MO	B
Haskell Indian Nations U, KS	A,B
Heidelberg U, OH	B
Hillsdale Coll, MI	B
Hiram Coll, OH	B
Hope Coll, MI	B
Huntington U, IN	A,B
Illinois Coll, IL	B
Illinois Inst of Technology, IL	B
Illinois State U, IL	B
Illinois Wesleyan U, IL	B
Indiana State U, IN	B
Indiana Tech, IN	A,B
Indiana U Bloomington, IN	B
Indiana U–Purdue U Fort Wayne, IN	A,B
Indiana Wesleyan U, IN	A,B
Iowa State U of Science and Technology, IA	B
Iowa Wesleyan Coll, IA	B
ITT Tech Inst, Fort Wayne, IN	B
ITT Tech Inst, Indianapolis, IN	B
ITT Tech Inst, Canton, MI	A
ITT Tech Inst, Grand Rapids, MI	A
ITT Tech Inst, Troy, MI	A
ITT Tech Inst, Arnold, MO	B
ITT Tech Inst, Green Bay, WI	B
ITT Tech Inst, Greenfield, WI	B
Jamestown Coll, ND	B
John Carroll U, OH	B
Kansas State U, KS	B
Kansas Wesleyan U, KS	A,B
Kaplan U–Davenport Campus, IA	A,B
Kaplan U–Mason City Campus, IA	A,B
Kendall Coll, IL	B
Kent State U, OH	A,B
Kent State U, Stark Campus, OH	A
Kilian Comm Coll, SD	A
Kuyper Coll, MI	B
Lake Erie Coll, OH	B
Lakeland Coll, WI	B
Lake Superior State U, MI	A,B
Lawrence Technological U, MI	B
Lewis U, IL	B
Lincoln U, MO	B
Lindenwood U, MO	B
Loras Coll, IA	B
Lourdes Coll, OH	A,B
Loyola U Chicago, IL	B
Luther Coll, IA	B
MacMurray Coll, IL	A,B
Madonna U, MI	A,B
Malone U, OH	B
Manchester Coll, IN	A,B
Maranatha Baptist Bible Coll, WI	B
Marian U, WI	B
Marian U, IN	B
Marietta Coll, OH	A,B
Marquette U, WI	B
Martin U, IN	B
Maryville U of Saint Louis, MO	B
Mayville State U, ND	B
McKendree U, IL	B
McPherson Coll, KS	B
Messenger Coll, MO	B
Miami U, OH	B
Miami U Hamilton, OH	A
Michigan State U, MI	B
Michigan Technological U, MI	B
Mid-America Christian U, OK	B
MidAmerica Nazarene U, KS	A,B
Midstate Coll, IL	A,B
Milwaukee School of Engineering, WI	B
Minnesota School of Business–Blaine, MN	A,B
Minnesota State U Mankato, MN	B
Minnesota State U Moorhead, MN	B
Minot State U, ND	B
Missouri Baptist U, MO	A,B
Missouri State U, MO	B
Missouri U of Science and Technology, MO	B
Missouri Western State U, MO	A,B
Monmouth Coll, IL	B
Morningside Coll, IA	B
Mount Marty Coll, SD	A,B
Mount Mary Coll, WI	B
Mount Mercy Coll, IA	B
Mount Union Coll, OH	B
Mount Vernon Nazarene U, OH	B
Muskingum Coll, OH	B
National American U, MO	A,B
National-Louis U, IL	B
Nebraska Wesleyan U, NE	B
Newman U, KS	A,B
North Central Coll, IL	B
North Central U, MN	A,B
North Dakota State U, ND	B
Northeastern Illinois U, IL	B
Northeastern State U, OK	B
Northern Michigan U, MI	B
Northland Coll, WI	B
North Park U, IL	B
Northwestern Coll, MN	B
Northwest Missouri State U, MO	B
Northwood U, MI	B
Oglala Lakota Coll, SD	A,B
Ohio Christian U, OH	A,B
Ohio Dominican U, OH	A,B
Ohio Northern U, OH	B
The Ohio State U, OH	B
Ohio U, OH	A,B
Ohio U–Chillicothe, OH	A,B
Ohio U–Eastern, OH	B
Ohio U–Lancaster, OH	A,B
Ohio Wesleyan U, OH	B
Oklahoma Christian U, OK	B
Oklahoma City U, OK	B
Oklahoma Panhandle State U, OK	A,B
Oklahoma State U, OK	B
Oklahoma State U, Oklahoma City, OK	A
Olivet Coll, MI	B
Olivet Nazarene U, IL	B
Oral Roberts U, OK	B
Otterbein Coll, OH	B
Park U, MO	B
Pittsburg State U, KS	B
Purdue U, IN	B
Purdue U Calumet, IN	B
Quincy U, IL	B
Ranken Tech Coll, MO	B
Rasmussen Coll Eagan, MN	A,B
Rasmussen Coll St. Cloud, MN	A,B
Ripon Coll, WI	B
Robert Morris Coll, IL	A,B
Rochester Comm and Tech Coll, MN	A
Rockford Coll, IL	B
Rockhurst U, MO	B
Rogers State U, OK	A,B
Roosevelt U, IL	B
Saginaw Valley State U, MI	B
St. Ambrose U, IA	B
St. Augustine Coll, IL	A
St. Catherine U, MN	B
St. Cloud State U, MN	B
St. Gregory's U, Shawnee, OK	A,B
Saint John's U, MN	B
Saint Louis U, MO	B
Saint Mary-of-the-Woods Coll, IN	B
Saint Mary's Coll, IN	B
Saint Mary's U of Minnesota, MN	B
St. Norbert Coll, WI	B
Sanford-Brown Coll, Fenton, MO	A,B
Shawnee State U, OH	A,B
Siena Heights U, MI	A,B
Silver Lake Coll, WI	B
Simpson Coll, IA	B
Sinte Gleska U, SD	A,B
Southeastern Oklahoma State U, OK	B
Southeast Missouri State U, MO	B
Southern Illinois U Carbondale, IL	B
Southern Illinois U Edwardsville, IL	B
Southern Methodist U, TX	B
Southern Nazarene U, OK	B
Southwest Baptist U, MO	B
Southwestern Christian U, OK	B
Southwestern Coll, KS	B
Southwestern Oklahoma State U, OK	B
Southwest Minnesota State U, MN	A,B
Spring Arbor U, MI	B
Stephens Coll, MO	B
Sterling Coll, KS	B
Taylor U, IN	A,B
Temple Baptist Coll, OH	B
Tiffin U, OH	A,B
Transylvania U, KY	B
Trine U, IN	A,B
Trinity Bible Coll, ND	A,B
Trinity Christian Coll, IL	B
Trinity International U, IL	B
Truman State U, MO	B
Union Coll, NE	A,B
Union Inst & U, OH	B
The U of Akron, OH	A,B
U of Central Missouri, MO	B
U of Central Oklahoma, OK	B
U of Charleston, WV	A,B
U of Cincinnati, OH	A,B
U of Dallas, TX	B
U of Dayton, OH	B
U of Evansville, IN	B
The U of Findlay, OH	A,B
U of Illinois at Chicago, IL	B
U of Illinois at Springfield, IL	B
U of Illinois at Urbana–Champaign, IL	B
The U of Iowa, IA	B
The U of Kansas, KS	B
U of Mary, ND	A,B
U of Michigan, MI	B
U of Michigan–Dearborn, MI	B
U of Michigan–Flint, MI	B
U of Minnesota, Crookston, MN	B
U of Minnesota, Duluth, MN	B
U of Minnesota, Morris, MN	B
U of Missouri–Columbia, MO	B
U of Missouri–Kansas City, MO	B
U of Missouri–St. Louis, MO	B
U of Nebraska at Kearney, NE	B
U of Nebraska at Omaha, NE	B
U of Nebraska–Lincoln, NE	B
U of New Orleans, LA	B

A—associate degree; B—bachelor's degree

U of North Dakota, ND	B
U of Northern Iowa, IA	B
U of Oklahoma, OK	B
U of Phoenix–Chicago Campus, IL	B
U of Phoenix–Cincinnati Campus, OH	B
U of Phoenix–Cleveland Campus, OH	B
U of Phoenix–Columbus Ohio Campus, OH	B
U of Phoenix–Indianapolis Campus, IN	B
U of Phoenix–Kansas City Campus, MO	B
U of Phoenix–Metro Detroit Campus, MI	B
U of Phoenix–Oklahoma City Campus, OK	B
U of Phoenix–St. Louis Campus, MO	B
U of Phoenix–Springfield Campus, MO	B
U of Phoenix–Tulsa Campus, OK	B
U of Phoenix–West Michigan Campus, MI	B
U of Phoenix–Wichita Campus, KS	B
U of Phoenix–Wisconsin Campus, WI	B
U of Rio Grande, OH	A,B
U of St. Francis, IL	B
U of Saint Francis, IN	A,B
U of Saint Mary, KS	B
U of Sioux Falls, SD	A
The U of South Dakota, SD	B
U of Southern Indiana, IN	B
The U of Toledo, OH	A,B
U of Tulsa, OK	B
U of Wisconsin–Eau Claire, WI	B
U of Wisconsin–Green Bay, WI	B
U of Wisconsin–La Crosse, WI	B
U of Wisconsin–Madison, WI	B
U of Wisconsin–Milwaukee, WI	B
U of Wisconsin–Oshkosh, WI	B
U of Wisconsin–Parkside, WI	B
U of Wisconsin–Platteville, WI	B
U of Wisconsin–Stevens Point, WI	B
U of Wisconsin–Stout, WI	B
U of Wisconsin–Superior, WI	B
U of Wisconsin–Whitewater, WI	B
Ursuline Coll, OH	B
Valley City State U, ND	B
Viterbo U, WI	B
Waldorf Coll, IA	B
Walsh Coll of Accountancy and Business Administration, MI	B
Walsh U, OH	A,B
Wartburg Coll, IA	B
Washburn U, KS	B
Washington U in St. Louis, MO	B
Wayne State Coll, NE	B
Webster U, MO	B
Western Illinois U, IL	B
Westminster Coll, MO	B
Wichita State U, KS	B
Wilberforce U, OH	B
William Jewell Coll, MO	B
Wilmington Coll, OH	B
Winona State U, MN	B
Wittenberg U, OH	B
Wright State U, OH	B
Xavier U, OH	A,B
York Coll, NE	B
Youngstown State U, OH	A,B

Business Administration, Management and Operations Related

AIB Coll of Business, IA	A
Benedictine U, IL	B
Capital U, OH	B
Central Michigan U, MI	B
Chancellor U, OH	B
Cleveland State U, OH	B
Cornerstone U, MI	B
Crossroads Coll, MN	B
Culver-Stockton Coll, MO	B
Davenport U, Grand Rapids, MI	B
DePaul U, IL	B
DeVry U, Addison, IL	B
DeVry U, Chicago, IL	B
DeVry U, Tinley Park, IL	B
DeVry U, Indianapolis, IN	B
DeVry U, Edina, MN	B
DeVry U, Kansas City, MO	B
DeVry U, Columbus, OH	B
DeVry U, OK	B
DeVry U, Milwaukee, WI	B
DeVry U Southfield Center, MI	B
Franklin U, OH	B
Indiana Tech, IN	B
Kettering U, MI	B
Malone U, OH	B
Mayville State U, ND	B
Miami U Hamilton, OH	B
Millikin U, IL	B
Missouri Baptist U, MO	B
Missouri Coll, MO	B
Missouri State U, MO	B
North Dakota State U, ND	B
Olivet Nazarene U, IL	B
St. Augustine Coll, IL	A
Saint Mary-of-the-Woods Coll, IN	B
Sinte Gleska U, SD	A,B
Southern Nazarene U, OK	B
Trinity Christian Coll, IL	B
U of Charleston, WV	B
U of Illinois at Springfield, IL	B
U of Michigan–Dearborn, MI	B
The U of Toledo, OH	B
Ursuline Coll, OH	B
Viterbo U, WI	B
Washington U in St. Louis, MO	B

Business Automation/Technology/Data Entry

Baker Coll of Clinton Township, MI	A
Metro Business Coll, Cape Girardeau, MO	A
Northern Michigan U, MI	A
U of Rio Grande, OH	A
The U of Toledo, OH	A

Business/Commerce

AIB Coll of Business, IA	A,B
Aurora U, IL	B
Avila U, MO	B
Baker Coll of Flint, MI	A
Baker Coll of Jackson, MI	B
Baker U, KS	B
Ball State U, IN	B
Benedictine U, IL	B
Bethel Coll, KS	B
Bowling Green State U, OH	B
Bryant & Stratton Coll, Parma, OH	A
Bryant & Stratton Coll, WI	A,B
Bryant & Stratton Coll—Wauwatosa Campus, WI	A
Central Christian Coll of Kansas, KS	B
Central State U, OH	B
Concordia Coll, MN	B
Concordia U, Nebraska, NE	B
Crown Coll, MN	A
Davenport U, Grand Rapids, MI	B
Drake U, IA	B
Earlham Coll, IN	B
Eastern Michigan U, MI	B
Ferris State U, MI	A
Franklin Coll, IN	B
Franklin U, OH	A,B
Grace Coll, IN	B
Grand Valley State U, MI	B
Harris-Stowe State U, MO	B
Indiana U Bloomington, IN	B
Indiana U East, IN	A,B
Indiana U Kokomo, IN	A,B
Indiana U Northwest, IN	A,B
Indiana U–Purdue U Indianapolis, IN	B
Indiana U South Bend, IN	A,B
Indiana U Southeast, IN	A,B
Kansas State U, KS	B
Kendall Coll, IL	A,B
Kent State U, Salem Campus, OH	A
Little Priest Tribal Coll, NE	A
Loras Coll, IA	B
Manchester Coll, IN	B
Marian U, WI	B
Maryville U of Saint Louis, MO	B
Mayville State U, ND	A
Miami U Hamilton, OH	B
Milwaukee School of Engineering, WI	B
Missouri Southern State U, MO	A,B
Missouri State U, MO	B
Mount Vernon Nazarene U, OH	A,B
Northeastern Illinois U, IL	B
Northern Michigan U, MI	A,B
Oakland U, MI	B
Ohio Northern U, OH	B
The Ohio State U at Lima, OH	B
The Ohio State U at Marion, OH	B
The Ohio State U–Mansfield Campus, OH	B
The Ohio State U–Newark Campus, OH	B
Ohio U, OH	B
Oklahoma Christian U, OK	B
Oklahoma City U, OK	B
Olivet Nazarene U, IL	A
Roosevelt U, IL	B
Saginaw Valley State U, MI	B
St. Ambrose U, IA	B
Saint Joseph's Coll, IN	B
Saint Mary-of-the-Woods Coll, IN	A
Saint Xavier U, IL	B
Sinte Gleska U, SD	A
Southern Methodist U, TX	B
Southern Nazarene U, OK	A
Southwest Baptist U, MO	A
Transylvania U, KY	B
Trinity Christian Coll, IL	B
Union Inst & U, OH	B
U of Central Oklahoma, OK	B
U of Illinois at Urbana–Champaign, IL	B
The U of Kansas, KS	B
U of Missouri–St. Louis, MO	B
U of Nebraska at Omaha, NE	B
U of Notre Dame, IN	B
U of Phoenix–Cleveland Campus, OH	A
U of Phoenix–Indianapolis Campus, IN	A
U of Phoenix–St. Louis Campus, MO	A
U of Science and Arts of Oklahoma, OK	B
U of Southern Indiana, IN	B
The U of Toledo, OH	A,B
U of Tulsa, OK	B
U of Wisconsin–Whitewater, WI	B
Washburn U, KS	B
Washington U in St. Louis, MO	B
Webster U, MO	B
Western Michigan U, MI	B
Wright State U, OH	B
Youngstown State U, OH	A,B

Business/Corporate Communications

Aquinas Coll, MI	B
Augustana Coll, SD	B
Calvin Coll, MI	B
Central Christian Coll of Kansas, KS	A
Dana Coll, NE	B
Marietta Coll, OH	B
Morningside Coll, IA	B
North Dakota State U, ND	B
Ohio Dominican U, OH	B
Rockhurst U, MO	B
Southwestern Coll, KS	B
The U of Findlay, OH	B

U of Mary, ND B
U of Phoenix–Cleveland Campus, OH B
U of Phoenix–Indianapolis Campus, IN B
U of Phoenix–Oklahoma City Campus, OK B
U of Phoenix–Springfield Campus, MO B
U of Phoenix–Tulsa Campus, OK B
U of Rio Grande, OH B

Business Family and Consumer Sciences/Human Sciences

The Ohio State U, OH B

Business, Management, and Marketing Related

Benedictine U, IL B
Bowling Green State U, OH B
Greenville Coll, IL B
Indiana Tech, IN A,B
Missouri U of Science and Technology, MO B
Mount Vernon Nazarene U, OH B
Nebraska Wesleyan U, NE B
Ohio U, OH B
Park U, MO B
Presentation Coll, SD B
Purdue U North Central, IN A,B
Union Inst & U, OH B
U of Phoenix–Kansas City Campus, MO B
U of Southern Indiana, IN A
The U of Toledo, OH B
U of Wisconsin–Stout, WI B

Business/Managerial Economics

Anderson U, IN B
Andrews U, MI B
Augsburg Coll, MN B
Ball State U, IN B
Beloit Coll, WI B
Benedictine U, IL B
Bethany Coll, KS B
Bowling Green State U, OH B
Bradley U, IL B
Buena Vista U, IA B
Capital U, OH B
Central Christian Coll of Kansas, KS A
Cleveland State U, OH B
Coll of the Ozarks, MO B
The Coll of Wooster, OH B
DePaul U, IL B
Eastern Michigan U, MI B
Ferris State U, MI B
Fort Hays State U, KS B
Grand Valley State U, MI B
Gustavus Adolphus Coll, MN B
Hope Coll, MI B
Huntington U, IN B
Illinois Coll, IL B
Indiana U–Purdue U Fort Wayne, IN B
Jamestown Coll, ND B
Kalamazoo Coll, MI B
Kent State U, OH B
Lake Forest Coll, IL B
Lake Superior State U, MI B
Lewis U, IL B
Loyola U Chicago, IL B
Marquette U, WI B
Miami U, OH B
Miami U Hamilton, OH B
Michigan Technological U, MI B
Northern State U, SD B
Northland Coll, WI B
Northwest Missouri State U, MO B
Oakland U, MI B
Ohio Wesleyan U, OH B
Oklahoma City U, OK B
Oklahoma State U, OK B
Olivet Coll, MI B
Otterbein Coll, OH B
Park U, MO B
Saginaw Valley State U, MI B
Southern Illinois U Carbondale, IL B
Southern Illinois U Edwardsville, IL B
U of Central Oklahoma, OK B
U of Dayton, OH B
U of Evansville, IN B
U of Indianapolis, IN B
The U of Iowa, IA B
U of Missouri–Columbia, MO B
U of Nebraska at Omaha, NE B
U of Nebraska–Lincoln, NE B
U of New Orleans, LA B
U of North Dakota, ND B
U of Oklahoma, OK B
The U of South Dakota, SD B
The U of Toledo, OH B
U of Wisconsin–Platteville, WI B
U of Wisconsin–Superior, WI B
U of Wisconsin–Whitewater, WI B
Washburn U, KS B
Washington U in St. Louis, MO B
Western Illinois U, IL B
Wheaton Coll, IL B
William Jewell Coll, MO B
Wilmington Coll, OH B
Winona State U, MN B
Wright State U, OH B
Xavier U, OH B
Youngstown State U, OH B

Business Operations Support and Secretarial Services Related

Sanford-Brown Coll, Fenton, MO A

Business Statistics

Cleveland State U, OH B
U of Central Missouri, MO B

Business Teacher Education

Ball State U, IN B
Bethany Coll, KS B
Bethel Coll, IN B
Bethel U, MN B
Black Hills State U, SD B
Bowling Green State U, OH B
Buena Vista U, IA B
Calumet Coll of Saint Joseph, IN B
Central Christian Coll of Kansas, KS A
Central Michigan U, MI B
Coll of the Ozarks, MO B
Concordia U, Nebraska, NE B
Concordia U Wisconsin, WI B
Dakota State U, SD B
Dakota Wesleyan U, SD B
Dana Coll, NE B
Defiance Coll, OH B
Doane Coll, NE B
Dordt Coll, IA B
Eastern Illinois U, IL B
Eastern Michigan U, MI B
Edgewood Coll, WI B
Evangel U, MO B
Ferris State U, MI B
Fort Hays State U, KS B
Friends U, KS B
Grace Coll, IN B
Grace U, NE B
Hannibal-LaGrange Coll, MO B
Huntington U, IN B
Illinois State U, IL B
Indiana State U, IN B
Kent State U, OH B
Lakeland Coll, WI B
Lincoln U, MO B
Lindenwood U, MO B
Maranatha Baptist Bible Coll, WI B
McKendree U, IL B
Michigan Technological U, MI B
MidAmerica Nazarene U, KS B
Minot State U, ND B
Missouri Baptist U, MO B
Missouri State U, MO B
Morningside Coll, IA B
Mount Mary Coll, WI B
Mount Vernon Nazarene U, OH B
Northern State U, SD B
Northwest Missouri State U, MO B
Ohio Wesleyan U, OH B
Oklahoma Panhandle State U, OK B
Oral Roberts U, OK B
St. Ambrose U, IA B
Saint Mary's Coll, IN B
Southeast Missouri State U, MO B
Trinity Christian Coll, IL B
Union Coll, NE B
U of Central Missouri, MO B
U of Central Oklahoma, OK B
The U of Findlay, OH B
U of Illinois at Urbana–Champaign, IL B
U of Indianapolis, IN B
U of Mary, ND B
U of Minnesota, Twin Cities Campus, MN B
U of Missouri–Columbia, MO B
U of Missouri–St. Louis, MO B
U of Nebraska at Kearney, NE B
U of Nebraska–Lincoln, NE B
U of North Dakota, ND B
U of Northern Iowa, IA B
U of Rio Grande, OH B
U of Saint Francis, IN B
U of Southern Indiana, IN B
The U of Toledo, OH B
U of Wisconsin–Superior, WI B
U of Wisconsin–Whitewater, WI B
Valley City State U, ND B
Viterbo U, WI B
Wayne State Coll, NE B
Western Michigan U, MI B
Wilmington Coll, OH B
Winona State U, MN B
Wright State U, OH B
York Coll, NE B
Youngstown State U, OH B

CAD/CADD Drafting/Design Technology

The Art Insts International Minnesota, MN A
Cameron U, OK B
Eastern Michigan U, MI B
Ferris State U, MI A
ITT Tech Inst, Burr Ridge, IL A
ITT Tech Inst, Mount Prospect, IL A
ITT Tech Inst, Orland Park, IL A
ITT Tech Inst, Fort Wayne, IN A
ITT Tech Inst, Indianapolis, IN A
ITT Tech Inst, Newburgh, IN A
ITT Tech Inst, South Bend, IN A
ITT Tech Inst, IA A
ITT Tech Inst, Canton, MI A
ITT Tech Inst, Grand Rapids, MI A
ITT Tech Inst, Troy, MI A
ITT Tech Inst, MN A
ITT Tech Inst, Arnold, MO A
ITT Tech Inst, Earth City, MO A
ITT Tech Inst, Kansas City, MO A
ITT Tech Inst, Springfield, MO A
ITT Tech Inst, NE A
ITT Tech Inst, Oklahoma City, OK A
ITT Tech Inst, Tulsa, OK A
ITT Tech Inst, Green Bay, WI A
ITT Tech Inst, Greenfield, WI A
ITT Tech Inst, Madison, WI A
Northern Michigan U, MI A

A—associate degree; B—bachelor's degree

Rochester Comm and Tech Coll, MN A
Shawnee State U, OH A

Canadian Studies
Franklin Coll, IN B

Cardiopulmonary Technology
Bacone Coll, OK A

Cardiovascular Technology
Nebraska Methodist Coll, NE A,B
Rochester Comm and Tech Coll, MN A
The U of Toledo, OH A

Caribbean Studies
Northwestern U, IL B

Carpentry
Oglala Lakota Coll, SD A
Ranken Tech Coll, MO A

Cartography
Missouri State U, MO B
Northern Michigan U, MI B
The U of Akron, OH A,B
U of Wisconsin–Madison, WI B
U of Wisconsin–Platteville, WI B

Cell and Molecular Biology
Bradley U, IL B
Cedarville U, OH B
Grand Valley State U, MI B
Missouri State U, MO B
Pittsburg State U, KS B
Purdue U, IN B
U of Illinois at Urbana–Champaign, IL B

Cell Biology and Histology
Beloit Coll, WI B
Clarkson U, NY B
Lindenwood U, MO B
Northeastern State U, OK B
Northwestern U, IL B
Ohio U, OH B
U of Illinois at Urbana–Champaign, IL B
U of Minnesota, Duluth, MN B
U of Minnesota, Twin Cities Campus, MN B
U of Wisconsin–Madison, WI B
William Jewell Coll, MO B

Ceramic Arts and Ceramics
Aquinas Coll, MI B
Bethany Coll, KS B
Bradley U, IL B
The Cleveland Inst of Art, OH B
Coe Coll, IA B
Columbia Coll, MO B
Indiana Wesleyan U, IN B
Kansas City Art Inst, MO B
Kent State U, OH B
Minnesota State U Mankato, MN B
Minnesota State U Moorhead, MN B
Northern Michigan U, MI B
Ohio Northern U, OH B
Ohio U, OH B
Pittsburg State U, KS B
St. Cloud State U, MN B
Shawnee State U, OH B
Trinity Christian Coll, IL B
U of Dallas, TX B
The U of Iowa, IA B
The U of Kansas, KS B
U of Michigan, MI B
U of Wisconsin–Milwaukee, WI B
Washington U in St. Louis, MO B

Ceramic Sciences and Engineering
Missouri U of Science and Technology, MO B
U of Illinois at Urbana–Champaign, IL B

Chemical Engineering
Ball State U, IN A
Calvin Coll, MI B
Case Western Reserve U, OH B
Clarkson U, NY B
Cleveland State U, OH B
Ferris State U, MI A
Illinois Inst of Technology, IL B
Iowa State U of Science and Technology, IA B
Kansas State U, KS B
Miami U, OH B
Michigan State U, MI B
Michigan Technological U, MI B
Missouri U of Science and Technology, MO B
Northwestern U, IL B
The Ohio State U, OH B
Ohio U, OH B
Oklahoma State U, OK B
Purdue U, IN B
Rose-Hulman Inst of Technology, IN B
South Dakota School of Mines and Technology, SD B
Trine U, IN B
The U of Akron, OH B
U of Cincinnati, OH B
U of Dayton, OH B
U of Illinois at Chicago, IL B
U of Illinois at Urbana–Champaign, IL B
The U of Iowa, IA B
The U of Kansas, KS B
U of Michigan, MI B
U of Minnesota, Duluth, MN B
U of Minnesota, Twin Cities Campus, MN B
U of Missouri–Columbia, MO B
U of Nebraska–Lincoln, NE B
U of North Dakota, ND B
U of Notre Dame, IN B
U of Oklahoma, OK B
The U of Toledo, OH B
U of Tulsa, OK B
U of Wisconsin–Madison, WI B
Waldorf Coll, IA B
Washington U in St. Louis, MO B
Wayne State U, MI B
Western Michigan U, MI B
Winona State U, MN B
Xavier U, OH B
Youngstown State U, OH B

Chemical Physics
Augustana Coll, SD B
Michigan State U, MI B
Michigan Technological U, MI B
Saginaw Valley State U, MI B

Chemical Technology
Dakota State U, SD B
Ferris State U, MI A
Indiana U–Purdue U Fort Wayne, IN A
Lawrence Technological U, MI A
Miami U, OH A
The U of Toledo, OH A

Chemistry
Adrian Coll, MI B
Albion Coll, MI B
Alma Coll, MI B
Anderson U, IN B
Andrews U, MI B
Aquinas Coll, MI B
Ashland U, OH B
Augsburg Coll, MN B
Augustana Coll, IL B
Augustana Coll, SD B
Baker U, KS B
Baldwin-Wallace Coll, OH B
Ball State U, IN B
Beloit Coll, WI B
Bemidji State U, MN B
Benedictine Coll, KS B
Benedictine U, IL B
Bethany Coll, KS B
Bethany Lutheran Coll, MN B
Bethel Coll, IN B
Bethel Coll, KS B
Bethel U, MN B
Black Hills State U, SD B
Bluffton U, OH B
Bowling Green State U, OH B
Bradley U, IL B
Briar Cliff U, IA B
Buena Vista U, IA B
Butler U, IN B
Calvin Coll, MI B
Cameron U, OK B
Capital U, OH B
Carleton Coll, MN B
Carroll U, WI B
Case Western Reserve U, OH B
Cedarville U, OH B
Central Coll, IA B
Central Methodist U, MO A,B
Central Michigan U, MI B
Central State U, OH B
Clarke Coll, IA B
Clarkson U, NY B
Cleveland State U, OH B
Coe Coll, IA B
Coll of Mount St. Joseph, OH B
Coll of Saint Benedict, MN B
Coll of Saint Mary, NE B
The Coll of St. Scholastica, MN B
Coll of the Ozarks, MO B
The Coll of Wooster, OH B
Columbia Coll, MO B
Concordia Coll, MN B
Concordia U, MI B
Concordia U Chicago, IL B
Concordia U, Nebraska, NE B
Cornell Coll, IA B
Creighton U, NE B
Dana Coll, NE B
Denison U, OH B
DePaul U, IL B
DePauw U, IN B
Doane Coll, NE B
Dominican U, IL B
Dordt Coll, IA B
Drake U, IA B
Drury U, MO B
Earlham Coll, IN B
Eastern Illinois U, IL B
Eastern Michigan U, MI B
Edgewood Coll, WI B
Elmhurst Coll, IL B
Emporia State U, KS B
Eureka Coll, IL B
Evangel U, MO B
Ferris State U, MI B
Fort Hays State U, KS B
Franciscan U of Steubenville, OH B
Franklin Coll, IN B
Friends U, KS B
Goshen Coll, IN B
Graceland U, IA B
Grand Valley State U, MI B
Greenville Coll, IL B
Grinnell Coll, IA B
Gustavus Adolphus Coll, MN B
Hamline U, MN B
Hanover Coll, IN B
Heidelberg U, OH B
Hillsdale Coll, MI B
Hiram Coll, OH B
Hope Coll, MI B
Huntington U, IN B
Illinois Coll, IL B
Illinois Inst of Technology, IL B
Illinois State U, IL B
Illinois Wesleyan U, IL B
Indiana State U, IN B
Indiana U Bloomington, IN B
Indiana U Kokomo, IN B
Indiana U Northwest, IN B
Indiana U–Purdue U Fort Wayne, IN A,B
Indiana U–Purdue U Indianapolis, IN B
Indiana U South Bend, IN B
Indiana U Southeast, IN B
Indiana Wesleyan U, IN A,B
Iowa State U of Science and Technology, IA B
Iowa Wesleyan Coll, IA B
Jamestown Coll, ND B
John Carroll U, OH B
Kalamazoo Coll, MI B
Kansas State U, KS B
Kansas Wesleyan U, KS B
Kent State U, OH B
Kenyon Coll, OH B

- Kettering U, MI B
- Knox Coll, IL B
- Lake Erie Coll, OH B
- Lake Forest Coll, IL B
- Lakeland Coll, WI B
- Lake Superior State U, MI A
- Lawrence Technological U, MI B
- Lawrence U, WI B
- Lewis U, IL B
- Lincoln U, MO B
- Lindenwood U, MO B
- Loras Coll, IA B
- Loyola U Chicago, IL B
- Luther Coll, IA B
- Macalester Coll, MN B
- MacMurray Coll, IL B
- Madonna U, MI A,B
- Malone U, OH B
- Manchester Coll, IN B
- Marian U, WI B
- Marian U, IN B
- Marietta Coll, OH B
- Marquette U, WI B
- Martin U, IN B
- Maryville U of Saint Louis, MO B
- Mayville State U, ND B
- McKendree U, IL B
- McPherson Coll, KS B
- Miami U, OH B
- Miami U Hamilton, OH B
- Michigan State U, MI B
- Michigan Technological U, MI B
- MidAmerica Nazarene U, KS B
- Millikin U, IL B
- Minnesota State U Mankato, MN B
- Minnesota State U Moorhead, MN B
- Minot State U, ND B
- Missouri Baptist U, MO B
- Missouri Southern State U, MO B
- Missouri State U, MO B
- Missouri U of Science and Technology, MO B
- Missouri Western State U, MO B
- Monmouth Coll, IL B
- Morningside Coll, IA B
- Mount Marty Coll, SD B
- Mount Mary Coll, WI B
- Mount Union Coll, OH B
- Mount Vernon Nazarene U, OH B
- Muskingum Coll, OH B
- Nebraska Wesleyan U, NE B
- Newman U, KS B
- North Central Coll, IL B
- North Dakota State U, ND B
- Northeastern Illinois U, IL B
- Northeastern State U, OK B
- Northern Michigan U, MI B
- Northern State U, SD B
- Northland Coll, WI B
- North Park U, IL B
- Northwestern U, IL B
- Northwest Missouri State U, MO B
- Oakland U, MI B
- Oberlin Coll, OH B
- Ohio Dominican U, OH A,B
- Ohio Northern U, OH B
- The Ohio State U, OH B
- Ohio U, OH B
- Ohio Wesleyan U, OH B
- Oklahoma Baptist U, OK B
- Oklahoma Christian U, OK B
- Oklahoma City U, OK B
- Oklahoma Panhandle State U, OK B
- Oklahoma State U, OK B
- Olivet Coll, MI B
- Olivet Nazarene U, IL B
- Oral Roberts U, OK B
- Otterbein Coll, OH B
- Park U, MO B
- Pittsburg State U, KS B
- Presentation Coll, SD A
- Purdue U, IN B
- Purdue U Calumet, IN B
- Purdue U North Central, IN A
- Quincy U, IL B
- Ripon Coll, WI B
- Rockford Coll, IL B
- Rockhurst U, MO B
- Roosevelt U, IL B
- Rose-Hulman Inst of Technology, IN B
- Saginaw Valley State U, MI B
- St. Ambrose U, IA B
- St. Catherine U, MN B
- St. Cloud State U, MN B
- Saint John's U, MN B
- Saint Joseph's Coll, IN B
- Saint Louis U, MO B
- Saint Mary's Coll, IN B
- Saint Mary's U of Minnesota, MN B
- St. Norbert Coll, WI B
- St. Olaf Coll, MN B
- Saint Xavier U, IL B
- Shawnee State U, OH B
- Siena Heights U, MI B
- Simpson Coll, IA B
- South Dakota School of Mines and Technology, SD B
- South Dakota State U, SD B
- Southeastern Oklahoma State U, OK B
- Southeast Missouri State U, MO B
- Southern Illinois U Carbondale, IL B
- Southern Illinois U Edwardsville, IL B
- Southern Methodist U, TX B
- Southern Nazarene U, OK B
- Southwest Baptist U, MO B
- Southwestern Coll, KS B
- Southwestern Oklahoma State U, OK B
- Southwest Minnesota State U, MN B
- Spring Arbor U, MI B
- Taylor U, IN B
- Transylvania U, KY B
- Trine U, IN B
- Trinity Christian Coll, IL B
- Trinity International U, IL B
- Truman State U, MO B
- Union Coll, NE B
- The U of Akron, OH B
- U of Central Missouri, MO B
- U of Central Oklahoma, OK B
- U of Charleston, WV B
- U of Chicago, IL B
- U of Cincinnati, OH B
- U of Dallas, TX B
- U of Dayton, OH B
- U of Evansville, IN B
- U of Illinois at Chicago, IL B
- U of Illinois at Springfield, IL B
- U of Illinois at Urbana–Champaign, IL B
- The U of Iowa, IA B
- The U of Kansas, KS B
- U of Michigan, MI B
- U of Michigan–Dearborn, MI B
- U of Michigan–Flint, MI B
- U of Minnesota, Duluth, MN B
- U of Minnesota, Morris, MN B
- U of Minnesota, Twin Cities Campus, MN B
- U of Missouri–Columbia, MO B
- U of Missouri–Kansas City, MO B
- U of Missouri–St. Louis, MO B
- U of Nebraska at Kearney, NE B
- U of Nebraska at Omaha, NE B
- U of Nebraska–Lincoln, NE B
- U of New Orleans, LA B
- U of North Dakota, ND B
- U of Northern Iowa, IA B
- U of Notre Dame, IN B
- U of Oklahoma, OK B
- U of Rio Grande, OH A,B
- U of Saint Francis, IN B
- U of Saint Mary, KS B
- U of Science and Arts of Oklahoma, OK B
- U of Sioux Falls, SD B
- The U of South Dakota, SD B
- U of Southern Indiana, IN B
- The U of Toledo, OH B
- U of Tulsa, OK B
- U of Wisconsin–Eau Claire, WI B
- U of Wisconsin–Green Bay, WI B
- U of Wisconsin–La Crosse, WI B
- U of Wisconsin–Madison, WI B
- U of Wisconsin–Milwaukee, WI B
- U of Wisconsin–Oshkosh, WI B
- U of Wisconsin–Parkside, WI B
- U of Wisconsin–Stevens Point, WI B
- U of Wisconsin–Superior, WI B
- U of Wisconsin–Whitewater, WI B
- Valley City State U, ND B
- Valparaiso U, IN B
- Viterbo U, WI B
- Wabash Coll, IN B
- Walsh U, OH B
- Wartburg Coll, IA B
- Washburn U, KS B
- Washington U in St. Louis, MO B
- Wayne State Coll, NE B
- Wayne State U, MI B
- Western Illinois U, IL B
- Western Michigan U, MI B
- Westminster Coll, MO B
- Wheaton Coll, IL B
- Wichita State U, KS B
- William Jewell Coll, MO B
- Wilmington Coll, OH B
- Winona State U, MN B
- Wittenberg U, OH B
- Wright State U, OH A,B
- Xavier U, OH B
- Youngstown State U, OH B

Chemistry Related

- Kettering U, MI B
- Lawrence Technological U, MI B
- Northern Michigan U, MI B
- Ohio Northern U, OH B
- Saginaw Valley State U, MI B
- Taylor U, IN B
- U of Northern Iowa, IA B
- U of Notre Dame, IN B
- U of Wisconsin–Eau Claire, WI B
- U of Wisconsin–Whitewater, WI B
- Washington U in St. Louis, MO B
- Western Illinois U, IL B
- Western Michigan U, MI B

Chemistry Teacher Education

- Alma Coll, MI B
- Bethany Coll, KS B
- Bethel U, MN B
- Buena Vista U, IA B
- Cameron U, OK B
- Carroll U, WI B
- Cedarville U, OH B
- Central Christian Coll of Kansas, KS A
- Central Methodist U, MO B
- Central Michigan U, MI B
- Coll of the Ozarks, MO B
- Concordia Coll, MN B
- Concordia U, MI B
- Concordia U, Nebraska, NE B
- Concordia U, St. Paul, MN B
- DePaul U, IL B
- Dordt Coll, IA B
- Eastern Michigan U, MI B
- Edgewood Coll, WI B
- Elmhurst Coll, IL B
- Evangel U, MO B
- Ferris State U, MI B
- Franklin Coll, IN B
- Grand Valley State U, MI B
- Greenville Coll, IL B
- Gustavus Adolphus Coll, MN B
- Hope Coll, MI B
- Indiana U Bloomington, IN B
- Indiana U–Purdue U Fort Wayne, IN B

A—associate degree; B—bachelor's degree

Indiana U South Bend, IN B
Indiana U Southeast, IN B
Jamestown Coll, ND B
Kent State U, OH B
Lincoln U, MO B
Lindenwood U, MO B
Marian U, WI B
Maryville U of Saint Louis, MO B
Mayville State U, ND B
Miami U, OH B
Miami U Hamilton, OH B
Michigan State U, MI B
Millikin U, IL B
Minnesota State U Moorhead, MN B
Minot State U, ND B
Missouri State U, MO B
Mount Marty Coll, SD B
Mount Mary Coll, WI B
Mount Vernon Nazarene U, OH B
North Dakota State U, ND B
Northeastern State U, OK B
Northern Michigan U, MI B
Ohio Dominican U, OH B
Ohio Northern U, OH B
Ohio Wesleyan U, OH B
Pittsburg State U, KS B
Purdue U, IN B
Saginaw Valley State U, MI B
St. Ambrose U, IA B
St. Catherine U, MN B
St. Cloud State U, MN B
Saint Mary's U of Minnesota, MN B
Southwest Baptist U, MO B
Southwest Minnesota State U, MN B
Transylvania U, KY B
Trinity Christian Coll, IL B
Union Coll, NE B
U of Evansville, IN B
U of Illinois at Chicago, IL B
U of Illinois at Urbana–Champaign, IL B
The U of Iowa, IA B
U of Michigan–Dearborn, MI B
U of Michigan–Flint, MI B
U of Missouri–Columbia, MO B
U of Missouri–St. Louis, MO B
U of Nebraska–Lincoln, NE B
U of New Orleans, LA B
U of Saint Francis, IN B
U of Wisconsin–Superior, WI B
Valley City State U, ND B
Valparaiso U, IN B
Viterbo U, WI B
Washington U in St. Louis, MO B
Wayne State Coll, NE B
Western Michigan U, MI B
William Jewell Coll, MO B
Xavier U, OH B

Child-Care and Support Services Management
Cameron U, OK A
Ferris State U, MI A,B
Mount Vernon Nazarene U, OH A
Purdue U Calumet, IN A
Rasmussen Coll Eagan, MN A
Rasmussen Coll St. Cloud, MN A
Saint Mary-of-the-Woods Coll, IN B
Siena Heights U, MI B
Southeast Missouri State U, MO A
Youngstown State U, OH A

Child-Care Provision
Mayville State U, ND A
Saint Mary-of-the-Woods Coll, IN A
Wayne State Coll, NE B

Child-Care Services Management
Rochester Comm and Tech Coll, MN A

Child Development
Ashland U, OH B
Bacone Coll, OK A
Bowling Green State U, OH B
Central Michigan U, MI B
Coll of the Ozarks, MO B
Concordia U, St. Paul, MN B
Evangel U, MO A
Franciscan U of Steubenville, OH A
Hannibal-LaGrange Coll, MO A
Kansas State U, KS B
Kuyper Coll, MI A,B
Madonna U, MI A,B
Minnesota State U Mankato, MN B
Missouri Baptist U, MO B
North Central U, MN B
Northern Michigan U, MI A
Northwest Missouri State U, MO B
Ohio U, OH A,B
Ohio U–Chillicothe, OH A
Ohio U–Lancaster, OH A
Oklahoma Christian U, OK B
Olivet Nazarene U, IL B
Pittsburg State U, KS B
St. Cloud State U, MN B
Union Inst & U, OH B
The U of Akron, OH B
U of Central Oklahoma, OK B
U of Cincinnati, OH A
U of Illinois at Urbana–Champaign, IL B
U of Saint Mary, KS B
U of Wisconsin–Madison, WI B
Youngstown State U, OH A,B

Child Guidance
U of Central Oklahoma, OK B

Chinese
Augustana Coll, IL B
Grinnell Coll, IA B
Lawrence U, WI B
The Ohio State U, OH B
U of Chicago, IL B
The U of Iowa, IA B
U of Minnesota, Twin Cities Campus, MN B
U of Notre Dame, IN B
U of Oklahoma, OK B
U of Wisconsin–Madison, WI B
Washington U in St. Louis, MO B

Chinese Studies
U of North Dakota, ND B

Christian Studies
Bethany Coll, KS B
Bethel Coll, IN B
The Coll of St. Scholastica, MN B
Crown Coll, MN B
Hillsdale Coll, MI B
Lindenwood U, MO B
Marian U, IN B
Missouri Baptist U, MO B
Oklahoma Baptist U, OK A
Ursuline Coll, OH B

Cinematography and Film/Video Production
The Art Insts International–Kansas City, KS B
Bowling Green State U, OH B
The Illinois Inst of Art–Chicago, IL B
The Illinois Inst of Art–Schaumburg, IL B
Minneapolis Coll of Art and Design, MN B
Northern Michigan U, MI B
Ohio U, OH B
Oklahoma City U, OK B
Southern Illinois U Carbondale, IL B
U of Illinois at Chicago, IL B
The U of Iowa, IA B
U of Oklahoma, OK B
Waldorf Coll, IA B
Wayne State U, MI B
Webster U, MO B

City/Urban, Community and Regional Planning
Ball State U, IN B
Iowa State U of Science and Technology, IA B
Miami U, OH B
Miami U Hamilton, OH B
Michigan State U, MI B
Minnesota State U Mankato, MN B
Missouri State U, MO B
St. Cloud State U, MN B
The U of Akron, OH B
U of Cincinnati, OH B
U of Illinois at Urbana–Champaign, IL B
Wright State U, OH B

Civil Engineering
Bradley U, IL B
Calvin Coll, MI B
Case Western Reserve U, OH B
Clarkson U, NY B
Cleveland State U, OH B
Dordt Coll, IA B
Illinois Inst of Technology, IL B
Indiana U–Purdue U Fort Wayne, IN B
Iowa State U of Science and Technology, IA B
Kansas State U, KS B
Lawrence Technological U, MI B
Lincoln U, MO B
Marquette U, WI B
Michigan State U, MI B
Michigan Technological U, MI B
Minnesota State U Mankato, MN B
Missouri U of Science and Technology, MO B
North Dakota State U, ND B
Northwestern U, IL B
Ohio Northern U, OH B
The Ohio State U, OH B
Ohio U, OH B
Oklahoma State U, OK B
Purdue U, IN B
Purdue U Calumet, IN B
Rose-Hulman Inst of Technology, IN B
South Dakota School of Mines and Technology, SD B
South Dakota State U, SD B
Southern Illinois U Carbondale, IL B
Southern Illinois U Edwardsville, IL B
Southern Methodist U, TX B
Trine U, IN B
The U of Akron, OH B
U of Cincinnati, OH B
U of Dayton, OH B
U of Evansville, IN B
U of Illinois at Chicago, IL B
U of Illinois at Urbana–Champaign, IL B
The U of Iowa, IA B
The U of Kansas, KS B
U of Michigan, MI B
U of Minnesota, Twin Cities Campus, MN B
U of Missouri–Columbia, MO B
U of Missouri–Kansas City, MO B
U of Missouri–St. Louis, MO B
U of Nebraska–Lincoln, NE B
U of New Orleans, LA B
U of North Dakota, ND B
U of Oklahoma, OK B
The U of Toledo, OH B
U of Wisconsin–Madison, WI B
U of Wisconsin–Milwaukee, WI B
U of Wisconsin–Platteville, WI B
Valparaiso U, IN B
Wayne State U, MI B
Western Michigan U, MI B
Youngstown State U, OH B

Civil Engineering Related
Bradley U, IL B
Ohio Northern U, OH B

Civil Engineering Technology
Ferris State U, MI A

Indiana U–Purdue U Fort Wayne, IN A
Indiana U–Purdue U Indianapolis, IN A
Michigan Technological U, MI A
Missouri Western State U, MO A,B
Oklahoma State U, Oklahoma City, OK A
Purdue U Calumet, IN A
Purdue U North Central, IN A
Rochester Comm and Tech Coll, MN A
U of Cincinnati, OH A,B
The U of Toledo, OH A,B
Youngstown State U, OH A,B

Classical, Ancient Mediterranean and Near Eastern Studies and Archaeology

Butler U, IN B
Creighton U, NE B
U of Illinois at Chicago, IL B
U of Michigan, MI B

Classics

Augustana Coll, SD B
Grand Valley State U, MI B
Pontifical Coll Josephinum, OH B
Rockford Coll, IL B

Classics and Classical Languages Related

Concordia Coll, MN B
Lawrence U, WI B
Saint Louis U, MO B
Wheaton Coll, IL B

Classics and Languages, Literatures and Linguistics

Augustana Coll, IL B
Ball State U, IN B
Beloit Coll, WI B
Bowling Green State U, OH B
Calvin Coll, MI B
Carleton Coll, MN B
Case Western Reserve U, OH B
Coe Coll, IA B
Coll of Saint Benedict, MN B
The Coll of Wooster, OH B
Cornell Coll, IA B
Denison U, OH B
DePauw U, IN B
Earlham Coll, IN B
Franciscan U of Steubenville, OH B
Grinnell Coll, IA B
Gustavus Adolphus Coll, MN B
Hanover Coll, IN B
Hillsdale Coll, MI B
Hope Coll, MI B
Illinois Wesleyan U, IL B
Indiana U Bloomington, IN B
John Carroll U, OH B
Kalamazoo Coll, MI B
Kent State U, OH B
Kenyon Coll, OH B
Knox Coll, IL B
Lawrence U, WI B
Loyola U Chicago, IL B
Macalester Coll, MN B
Marquette U, WI B
Miami U, OH B
Miami U Hamilton, OH B
Monmouth Coll, IL B
North Central Coll, IL B
North Dakota State U, ND B
Northwestern U, IL B
Oberlin Coll, OH B
The Ohio State U, OH B
Ohio U, OH B
Ohio Wesleyan U, OH B
Purdue U, IN B
Rockford Coll, IL B
Saint John's U, MN B
St. Olaf Coll, MN B
Southern Illinois U Carbondale, IL B
Transylvania U, KY B
Truman State U, MO B
The U of Akron, OH B
U of Chicago, IL B
U of Cincinnati, OH B
U of Dallas, TX B
U of Evansville, IN B
U of Illinois at Chicago, IL B
U of Illinois at Urbana–Champaign, IL B
The U of Iowa, IA B
The U of Kansas, KS B
U of Michigan, MI B
U of Missouri–Columbia, MO B
U of Nebraska–Lincoln, NE B
U of North Dakota, ND B
U of Notre Dame, IN B
U of Oklahoma, OK B
The U of South Dakota, SD B
The U of Toledo, OH B
U of Wisconsin–Madison, WI B
U of Wisconsin–Milwaukee, WI B
Valparaiso U, IN B
Wabash Coll, IN B
Washington U in St. Louis, MO B
Wayne State U, MI B
Wright State U, OH B
Xavier U, OH B

Clinical Laboratory Science/ Medical Technology

Anderson U, IN B
Andrews U, MI B
Aquinas Coll, MI B
Augustana Coll, SD B
Ball State U, IN B
Bemidji State U, MN B
Benedictine U, IL B
Bowling Green State U, OH B
Bradley U, IL B
Cameron U, OK B
Carroll U, WI B
Cedarville U, OH B
Central Michigan U, MI B
Coll of Saint Mary, NE B
Coll of the Ozarks, MO B
Concordia Coll, MN B
Defiance Coll, OH B
DePaul U, IL B
DeVry U, Chicago, IL B
Dordt Coll, IA B
Eastern Illinois U, IL B
Eastern Michigan U, MI B
Elmhurst Coll, IL B
Eureka Coll, IL B
Evangel U, MO B
Ferris State U, MI B
Fort Hays State U, KS B
Graceland U, IA B
Grand Valley State U, MI B
Illinois Coll, IL B
Illinois State U, IL B
Indiana State U, IN B
Indiana U Kokomo, IN B
Indiana U–Purdue U Fort Wayne, IN B
Indiana U–Purdue U Indianapolis, IN B
Indiana U South Bend, IN B
Indiana U Southeast, IN B
Indiana Wesleyan U, IN B
Jamestown Coll, ND B
Kansas State U, KS B
Kent State U, OH B
Lake Superior State U, MI B
Lincoln U, MO B
Loras Coll, IA B
Loyola U Chicago, IL B
Madonna U, MI B
Malone U, OH B
Manchester Coll, IN B
Maryville U of Saint Louis, MO B
Mayville State U, ND B
McKendree U, IL B
Miami U, OH B
Miami U Hamilton, OH B
Michigan State U, MI B
Michigan Technological U, MI B
Minnesota State U Mankato, MN B
Minnesota State U Moorhead, MN B
Minot State U, ND B
Missouri Southern State U, MO B
Missouri State U, MO B
Missouri Western State U, MO B
Morningside Coll, IA B
Mount Marty Coll, SD B
Mount Mercy Coll, IA B
Mount Union Coll, OH B
Mount Vernon Nazarene U, OH B
Muskingum Coll, OH B
National-Louis U, IL B
North Dakota State U, ND B
Northeastern State U, OK B
Northern Michigan U, MI B
Northern State U, SD B
North Park U, IL B
Northwest Missouri State U, MO B
Oakland U, MI B
Ohio Northern U, OH B
Oklahoma Christian U, OK B
Oklahoma Panhandle State U, OK B
Olivet Nazarene U, IL B
Oral Roberts U, OK B
Purdue U, IN B
Purdue U Calumet, IN B
Quincy U, IL B
Rockhurst U, MO B
Rush U, IL B
Saginaw Valley State U, MI B
St. Catherine U, MN B
St. Cloud State U, MN B
Saint Joseph's Coll, IN B
Saint Louis U, MO B
Saint Mary-of-the-Woods Coll, IN B
Saint Mary's Coll, IN B
Saint Mary's U of Minnesota, MN B
South Dakota State U, SD B
Southeast Missouri State U, MO B
Southwest Baptist U, MO B
Southwestern Oklahoma State U, OK B
Union Coll, NE B
U of Central Missouri, MO B
U of Central Oklahoma, OK B
U of Cincinnati, OH B
U of Evansville, IN B
The U of Findlay, OH B
U of Illinois at Springfield, IL B
U of Indianapolis, IN B
The U of Iowa, IA B
The U of Kansas, KS B
U of Mary, ND B
U of Michigan, MI B
U of Michigan–Flint, MI B
U of Minnesota, Twin Cities Campus, MN B
U of Nebraska Medical Center, NE B
U of New Orleans, LA B
U of North Dakota, ND B
U of Oklahoma, OK B
U of Rio Grande, OH B
U of St. Francis, IL B
U of Saint Francis, IN B
U of Sioux Falls, SD B
The U of Toledo, OH A,B
U of Wisconsin–La Crosse, WI B
U of Wisconsin–Madison, WI B
U of Wisconsin–Milwaukee, WI B
U of Wisconsin–Oshkosh, WI B
U of Wisconsin–Stevens Point, WI B
Wartburg Coll, IA B
Wayne State U, MI B
Western Illinois U, IL B
Wichita State U, KS B
William Jewell Coll, MO B
Winona State U, MN B
Wright State U, OH B
Xavier U, OH B
Youngstown State U, OH B

A—associate degree; B—bachelor's degree

Clinical/Medical Laboratory Assistant
Coll of Saint Benedict, MN B

Clinical/Medical Laboratory Science and Allied Professions Related
Roosevelt U, IL B
Youngstown State U, OH A

Clinical/Medical Laboratory Technology
Argosy U, Twin Cities, MN B
Baker Coll of Owosso, MI A
Cameron U, OK B
Ferris State U, MI A
Indiana U Northwest, IN A
Indiana U–Purdue U Fort Wayne, IN B
Indiana U South Bend, IN A
Marquette U, WI B
Northern Michigan U, MI A
Northern State U, SD B
Northwest Missouri State U, MO B
Pittsburg State U, KS B
Shawnee State U, OH A
U of Cincinnati, OH A
U of Missouri–Kansas City, MO B
U of Rio Grande, OH A
U of Science and Arts of Oklahoma, OK B
Washburn U, KS B
Winona State U, MN B
Youngstown State U, OH A

Clinical Nutrition
Loyola U Chicago, IL B
U of North Dakota, ND B

Clinical Psychology
U of Michigan–Flint, MI B

Clothing/Textiles
Bluffton U, OH B
Minnesota State U Mankato, MN B
Northwest Missouri State U, MO B
The Ohio State U, OH B
U of Central Oklahoma, OK B
U of Minnesota, Twin Cities Campus, MN B
U of Wisconsin–Madison, WI B

Cognitive Psychology and Psycholinguistics
Lawrence U, WI B
Northwestern U, IL B
The U of Kansas, KS B
Washington U in St. Louis, MO B

Cognitive Science
Case Western Reserve U, OH B
Central Michigan U, MI B
Indiana U Bloomington, IN B
Lawrence U, WI B
U of Evansville, IN B

Commercial and Advertising Art
Anderson U, IN B
Ashland U, OH B
Baker Coll of Auburn Hills, MI A
Baker Coll of Clinton Township, MI A
Baker Coll of Muskegon, MI A
Baker Coll of Owosso, MI A,B
Baker Coll of Port Huron, MI A
Bemidji State U, MN B
Black Hills State U, SD B
Buena Vista U, IA B
Carroll U, WI B
The Cleveland Inst of Art, OH B
Coll for Creative Studies, MI B
Columbus Coll of Art & Design, OH B
Concordia U Chicago, IL B
Concordia U, Nebraska, NE B
Concordia U Wisconsin, WI B
Dominican U, IL B
Dordt Coll, IA B
Drake U, IA B
Ferris State U, MI A,B
Fontbonne U, MO B
Fort Hays State U, KS B
Graceland U, IA B
Huntington U, IN B
Indiana U Bloomington, IN B
Indiana U–Purdue U Fort Wayne, IN A,B
Iowa State U of Science and Technology, IA B
Kent State U, OH B
Marian U, IN B
Marietta Coll, OH B
Miami U, OH B
Millikin U, IL B
Minneapolis Coll of Art and Design, MN B
Minnesota State U Mankato, MN B
Minnesota State U Moorhead, MN B
Morningside Coll, IA B
Mount Mary Coll, WI B
Northeastern State U, OK B
Northern Michigan U, MI A
Northern State U, SD A
Northwest Missouri State U, MO B
Ohio Northern U, OH B
Ohio U, OH B
Oklahoma Christian U, OK B
Oklahoma City U, OK B
Oral Roberts U, OK B
Pittsburg State U, KS B
Robert Morris Coll, IL A
St. Norbert Coll, WI B
Southwest Baptist U, MO B
Southwestern Oklahoma State U, OK B
Trinity Christian Coll, IL B
Truman State U, MO B
Union Coll, NE B
U of Central Missouri, MO B
U of Central Oklahoma, OK B
U of Cincinnati, OH B
U of Dayton, OH B
U of Indianapolis, IN B
U of Minnesota, Duluth, MN B
U of Minnesota, Twin Cities Campus, MN B
U of Saint Francis, IN B
U of Sioux Falls, SD B
U of Wisconsin–Platteville, WI B
U of Wisconsin–Stevens Point, WI B
Wartburg Coll, IA B
Washington U in St. Louis, MO B
Westwood Coll–Chicago Du Page, IL A,B
Wichita State U, KS B
Winona State U, MN B

Commercial Photography
Minnesota State U Moorhead, MN B

Communication and Journalism Related
Benedictine U, IL B
Bowling Green State U, OH B
Cedarville U, OH B
Coll of the Ozarks, MO B
Franklin U, OH B
Friends U, KS B
Hannibal-LaGrange Coll, MO B
Illinois Inst of Technology, IL B
Indiana U Bloomington, IN B
Indiana U Kokomo, IN B
Madonna U, MI A
Malone U, OH B
Milwaukee School of Engineering, WI B
Mount Mercy Coll, IA B
Northern Michigan U, MI B
Ohio Northern U, OH B
Ohio U, OH B
Oklahoma Christian U, OK B
Siena Heights U, MI B
Sterling Coll, KS B
Tiffin U, OH B
U of Evansville, IN B
U of Illinois at Urbana–Champaign, IL B
U of Wisconsin–Green Bay, WI B
Valparaiso U, IN A,B
Washington U in St. Louis, MO B
Webster U, MO B

Communication and Media Related
AIB Coll of Business, IA A
Alma Coll, MI B
Calumet Coll of Saint Joseph, IN B
Crown Coll, MN B
Greenville Coll, IL B
Loyola U Chicago, IL B
Northwestern U, IL B
Southwestern Coll, KS B
Trinity International U, IL B
U of Central Missouri, MO B
U of Evansville, IN B
U of Illinois at Springfield, IL B
Walsh U, OH B
Western Michigan U, MI B

Communication Disorders
Baldwin-Wallace Coll, OH B
Bowling Green State U, OH B
Butler U, IN B
Case Western Reserve U, OH B
Central Michigan U, MI B
Eastern Illinois U, IL B
Kansas State U, KS B
Minnesota State U Mankato, MN B
Minot State U, ND B
Northwestern U, IL B
St. Cloud State U, MN B
Saint Mary's Coll, IN B
Southeast Missouri State U, MO B
Southern Illinois U Carbondale, IL B
Truman State U, MO B
The U of Kansas, KS B
U of Nebraska at Kearney, NE B
U of North Dakota, ND B
The U of South Dakota, SD B
U of Wisconsin–Eau Claire, WI B
Wayne State U, MI B
Western Illinois U, IL B

Communication Disorders Sciences and Services Related
Ohio U, OH B
St. Cloud State U, MN B
U of Missouri–Columbia, MO B
U of Oklahoma Health Sciences Center, OK B

Communication/Speech Communication and Rhetoric
Adrian Coll, MI B
Aquinas Coll, MI B
Augustana Coll, SD B
Aurora U, IL B
Avila U, MO B
Baker Coll of Jackson, MI A
Baker U, KS B
Baldwin-Wallace Coll, OH B
Benedictine U, IL B
Bethany Coll, KS B
Bethany Lutheran Coll, MN B
Bethel Coll, IN B
Bethel U, MN B
Bluffton U, OH B
Bowling Green State U, OH B
Bradley U, IL B
Buena Vista U, IA B
Butler U, IN B
Calumet Coll of Saint Joseph, IN B
Calvin Coll, MI B
Cameron U, OK B
Capital U, OH B
Carroll U, WI B
Cedarville U, OH B
Central Coll, IA B
Central Methodist U, MO B
Central Michigan U, MI B
Clarkson U, NY B
Cleveland State U, OH B
Coll of Mount St. Joseph, OH A,B

The Coll of St. Scholastica, MN B
Coll of the Ozarks, MO B
The Coll of Wooster, OH B
Columbia Coll, MO B
Concordia Coll, MN B
Concordia U Chicago, IL B
Concordia U, Nebraska, NE B
Creighton U, NE B
DePaul U, IL B
Dominican U, IL B
Drury U, MO B
Eastern Michigan U, MI B
Edgewood Coll, WI B
Elmhurst Coll, IL B
Emporia State U, KS B
Ferris State U, MI B
Fontbonne U, MO B
Franciscan U of Steubenville, OH B
Grace Coll, IN B
Grace U, NE B
Grand Valley State U, MI B
Great Lakes Christian Coll, MI B
Hannibal-LaGrange Coll, MO B
Hillsdale Coll, MI B
Hope Coll, MI B
Huntington U, IN B
Illinois State U, IL B
Indiana State U, IN B
Indiana Tech, IN B
Indiana U Bloomington, IN B
Indiana U East, IN B
Indiana U Kokomo, IN B
Indiana U Northwest, IN B
Indiana U–Purdue U Fort Wayne, IN B
Indiana U–Purdue U Indianapolis, IN B
Indiana U Southeast, IN B
Indiana Wesleyan U, IN A,B
Jamestown Coll, ND B
Kansas State U, KS B
Kaplan U–Davenport Campus, IA B
Kuyper Coll, MI B
Lake Forest Coll, IL B
Lawrence Technological U, MI B
Loyola U Chicago, IL B
Luther Coll, IA B
Madonna U, MI A,B
Marian U, WI B
Marian U, IN B
Marietta Coll, OH B
Marquette U, WI B
McPherson Coll, KS B
Miami U, OH B
Miami U Hamilton, OH B
Michigan State U, MI B
Michigan Technological U, MI B
Millikin U, IL B
Missouri Baptist U, MO B
Missouri Southern State U, MO B
Missouri State U, MO B
Moody Bible Inst, IL B
Mount Mary Coll, WI B
Mount Mercy Coll, IA B
Mount Vernon Nazarene U, OH B
Nebraska Wesleyan U, NE B
Northern Michigan U, MI B
North Park U, IL B
Northwestern Coll, MN B
Northwestern U, IL B
Oakland U, MI B
Ohio Dominican U, OH B
Ohio Northern U, OH B
The Ohio State U, OH B
Ohio U, OH B
Ohio U–Chillicothe, OH B
Oklahoma Baptist U, OK B
Olivet Coll, MI B
Olivet Nazarene U, IL B
Oral Roberts U, OK B
Park U, MO B
Pittsburg State U, KS B
Presentation Coll, SD A
Purdue U, IN B
Purdue U Calumet, IN B
Purdue U North Central, IN B
Quincy U, IL B
Ripon Coll, WI B
Rockhurst U, MO B
Roosevelt U, IL B
Saginaw Valley State U, MI B
Saint Louis U, MO B
Saint Mary's Coll, IN B
St. Norbert Coll, WI B
Saint Xavier U, IL B
Southeastern Oklahoma State U, OK B
Southeast Missouri State U, MO B
Southwest Baptist U, MO B
Southwest Minnesota State U, MN B
Spring Arbor U, MI B
Taylor U, IN B
Tiffin U, OH B
Trine U, IN A,B
Trinity Christian Coll, IL B
Truman State U, MO B
The U of Akron, OH B
U of Central Oklahoma, OK B
U of Illinois at Chicago, IL B
U of Illinois at Urbana–Champaign, IL B
U of Indianapolis, IN B
U of Michigan, MI B
U of Michigan–Dearborn, MI B
U of Minnesota, Crookston, MN B
U of Missouri–Columbia, MO B
U of Missouri–Kansas City, MO B
U of Missouri–St. Louis, MO B
U of Nebraska–Lincoln, NE B
U of New Orleans, LA B
U of North Dakota, ND B
U of Northern Iowa, IA B
U of Oklahoma, OK B
U of Rio Grande, OH A,B
U of Saint Francis, IN B
U of Science and Arts of Oklahoma, OK B
U of Sioux Falls, SD B
U of Southern Indiana, IN B
The U of Toledo, OH B
U of Tulsa, OK B
U of Wisconsin–Eau Claire, WI B
U of Wisconsin–La Crosse, WI B
U of Wisconsin–Parkside, WI B
U of Wisconsin–Stevens Point, WI B
U of Wisconsin–Whitewater, WI B
Washburn U, KS B
Washington U in St. Louis, MO B
Wayne State Coll, NE B
Wayne State U, MI B
Western Illinois U, IL B
Western Michigan U, MI B
Wheaton Coll, IL B
Wichita State U, KS B
William Jewell Coll, MO B
Wittenberg U, OH B
Wright State U, OH A,B

Communications Systems Installation and Repair Technology
Ranken Tech Coll, MO A

Communications Technologies and Support Services Related
Saint Mary-of-the-Woods Coll, IN B

Communications Technology
Cedarville U, OH B
Eastern Michigan U, MI B
Lawrence Technological U, MI B
Lewis U, IL B
Saint Mary-of-the-Woods Coll, IN B

Community Health and Preventive Medicine
Bowling Green State U, OH B
Ohio U–Eastern, OH B
U of Illinois at Urbana–Champaign, IL B

Community Health Services Counseling
Bethel U, MN B
Cleveland State U, OH B
Indiana State U, IN B
Indiana U–Purdue U Fort Wayne, IN B
Minnesota State U Moorhead, MN B
Northeastern Illinois U, IL B
Northern Michigan U, MI B
The U of Kansas, KS B
U of Nebraska at Omaha, NE B
U of Nebraska–Lincoln, NE B
U of Northern Iowa, IA B
Youngstown State U, OH B

Community Organization and Advocacy
Bemidji State U, MN B
Central Michigan U, MI B
Cleveland State U, OH B
DePaul U, IL B
Eastern Michigan U, MI B
Northern State U, SD B
Northwestern U, IL B
Rockhurst U, MO B
Roosevelt U, IL B
Siena Heights U, MI B
The U of Findlay, OH A
U of Saint Mary, KS B
The U of Toledo, OH B

Community Psychology
Northwestern U, IL B
Rogers State U, OK B
Southern Nazarene U, OK B
U of Saint Mary, KS B
Wright State U, OH B

Comparative Literature
Beloit Coll, WI B
Benedictine U, IL B
Case Western Reserve U, OH B
The Coll of Wooster, OH B
Earlham Coll, IN B
Hillsdale Coll, MI B
Indiana U Bloomington, IN B
Northwestern U, IL B
Oberlin Coll, OH B
The Ohio State U, OH B
St. Cloud State U, MN B
U of Chicago, IL B
U of Cincinnati, OH B
U of Illinois at Urbana–Champaign, IL B
The U of Iowa, IA B
U of Michigan, MI B
U of Minnesota, Twin Cities Campus, MN B
U of Wisconsin–Madison, WI B
U of Wisconsin–Milwaukee, WI B
Washington U in St. Louis, MO B

Computational Mathematics
Indiana U–Purdue U Fort Wayne, IN B
Marquette U, WI B
Michigan State U, MI B
Michigan Technological U, MI B
U of Illinois at Urbana–Champaign, IL B

Computer and Information Sciences
Andrews U, MI B
Aquinas Coll, MI B
Avila U, MO B
Baker Coll of Allen Park, MI A
Baker Coll of Muskegon, MI B
Ball State U, IN A,B
Bethel Coll, IN B
Bethel U, MN B
Black Hills State U, SD A
Bowling Green State U, OH B
Butler U, IN B
Cameron U, OK B
Carroll U, WI B
Central State U, OH B
Clarkson U, NY B

A—associate degree; B—bachelor's degree

Cleveland State U, OH B
Coll of Mount St. Joseph, OH A,B
Coll of Saint Mary, NE A,B
The Coll of St. Scholastica, MN B
Coll of the Ozarks, MO B
Columbia Coll, MO A,B
Concordia U, Nebraska, NE B
Dakota State U, SD B
Davenport U, Grand Rapids, MI B
Doane Coll, NE B
Drury U, MO B
Eastern Michigan U, MI B
Edgewood Coll, WI B
Emmaus Bible Coll, IA B
Emporia State U, KS B
Franciscan U of Steubenville, OH B
Franklin Coll, IN B
Franklin U, OH A,B
Friends U, KS B
Grace Bible Coll, MI B
Grace U, NE B
Grand Valley State U, MI B
Greenville Coll, IL B
Hannibal-LaGrange Coll, MO B
Illinois Inst of Technology, IL B
Indiana State U, IN B
Indiana U Bloomington, IN B
Indiana U Kokomo, IN B
Indiana U Northwest, IN B
Indiana U–Purdue U Indianapolis, IN B
Indiana U South Bend, IN B
Indiana U Southeast, IN B
Indiana Wesleyan U, IN A,B
ITT Tech Inst, Indianapolis, IN A
Kansas State U, KS B
Knox Coll, IL B
Kuyper Coll, MI B
Lewis U, IL B
Little Priest Tribal Coll, NE A
Loyola U Chicago, IL B
Mayville State U, ND B
Miami U, OH A
Michigan State U, MI B
Midstate Coll, IL A
Minnesota State U Moorhead, MN B
Missouri Baptist U, MO B
Missouri Southern State U, MO B
Missouri Western State U, MO B
Mount Mercy Coll, IA B
Mount Vernon Nazarene U, OH B
Northeastern Illinois U, IL B
Northern Michigan U, MI B
North Park U, IL B
Northwestern U, IL B
Northwood U, MI B
Oakland U, MI B
The Ohio State U, OH B
Oklahoma Baptist U, OK B
Oklahoma Panhandle State U, OK A
Oklahoma State U, OK B
Olivet Coll, MI B
Oral Roberts U, OK B
Park U, MO B
Purdue U, IN B
Purdue U Calumet, IN B
Quincy U, IL B
Rogers State U, OK A
Saginaw Valley State U, MI B
St. Augustine Coll, IL A
St. Catherine U, MN B
Saint Joseph's Coll, IN B
Saint Louis U, MO B
Saint Mary-of-the-Woods Coll, IN B
St. Norbert Coll, WI B
Saint Xavier U, IL B
Sanford-Brown Coll, Fenton, MO A
Siena Heights U, MI B
Simpson Coll, IA B
South Dakota State U, SD B
Southeastern Oklahoma State U, OK B
Southeast Missouri State U, MO B
Southern Nazarene U, OK B
Southwest Baptist U, MO B
Southwestern Oklahoma State U, OK B
Sterling Coll, KS B
Tiffin U, OH B
Transylvania U, KY B
Truman State U, MO B
U of Central Missouri, MO B
U of Charleston, WV A,B
U of Cincinnati, OH A,B
U of Evansville, IN B
U of Illinois at Urbana–Champaign, IL B
The U of Kansas, KS B
U of Mary, ND B
U of Michigan–Dearborn, MI B
U of Michigan–Flint, MI B
U of Missouri–Columbia, MO B
U of Missouri–St. Louis, MO B
U of Nebraska at Kearney, NE B
U of Nebraska–Lincoln, NE B
U of North Dakota, ND B
U of Notre Dame, IN B
U of Phoenix–Kansas City Campus, MO B
U of Phoenix–Metro Detroit Campus, MI B
U of Saint Mary, KS B
U of Science and Arts of Oklahoma, OK B
U of Sioux Falls, SD B
The U of South Dakota, SD B
U of Southern Indiana, IN B
U of Wisconsin–Eau Claire, WI B
U of Wisconsin–La Crosse, WI B
U of Wisconsin–Stevens Point, WI B
U of Wisconsin–Superior, WI B
U of Wisconsin–Whitewater, WI B
Valley City State U, ND B
Viterbo U, WI B
Walsh Coll of Accountancy and Business Administration, MI B
Washburn U, KS B
Washington U in St. Louis, MO B
Wayne State Coll, NE B
Wayne State U, MI B
Western Illinois U, IL B
Western Michigan U, MI B
Wichita State U, KS B
William Jewell Coll, MO B
Winona State U, MN B
Wright State U, OH B

Computer and Information Sciences and Support Services Related

Cleary U, MI A
DePaul U, IL B
Ferris State U, MI B
Indiana U East, IN B
Indiana U–Purdue U Indianapolis, IN B
Mayville State U, ND B
Missouri U of Science and Technology, MO B
Mount Union Coll, OH B
Park U, MO B
Purdue U Calumet, IN B
Purdue U North Central, IN B
Tiffin U, OH B
U of Evansville, IN B
U of Michigan, MI B
U of Michigan–Flint, MI B
U of Northern Iowa, IA B
U of Notre Dame, IN B
Valley City State U, ND B
Washington U in St. Louis, MO B

Computer and Information Sciences Related

Chancellor U, OH B
Eastern Illinois U, IL B
Grace U, NE B
Madonna U, MI A
Miami U Hamilton, OH B
Taylor U, IN B
U of Northern Iowa, IA B
U of Wisconsin–Stout, WI B
Washburn U, KS A

Computer and Information Systems Security

Dakota State U, SD B
Davenport U, Grand Rapids, MI B
DePaul U, IL B
Emporia State U, KS B
Indiana Tech, IN B
ITT Tech Inst, Burr Ridge, IL B
ITT Tech Inst, Mount Prospect, IL B
ITT Tech Inst, Fort Wayne, IN B
ITT Tech Inst, Indianapolis, IN B
ITT Tech Inst, Newburgh, IN B
ITT Tech Inst, South Bend, IN B
ITT Tech Inst, IA B
ITT Tech Inst, KS B
ITT Tech Inst, Canton, MI B
ITT Tech Inst, Grand Rapids, MI B
ITT Tech Inst, Troy, MI B
ITT Tech Inst, MN B
ITT Tech Inst, Arnold, MO B
ITT Tech Inst, Earth City, MO B
ITT Tech Inst, Kansas City, MO B
ITT Tech Inst, NE B
ITT Tech Inst, Oklahoma City, OK B
ITT Tech Inst, Tulsa, OK B
ITT Tech Inst, Green Bay, WI B
ITT Tech Inst, Greenfield, WI B
ITT Tech Inst, Madison, WI B
Loyola U Chicago, IL B
Missouri Tech, MO B
Pittsburg State U, KS B
U of Illinois at Urbana–Champaign, IL B
U of Phoenix–Cleveland Campus, OH B
U of Phoenix–Indianapolis Campus, IN B
U of Phoenix–St. Louis Campus, MO B
U of Phoenix–Springfield Campus, MO B
Westwood Coll–Chicago Du Page, IL B

Computer Engineering

Bradley U, IL B
Capital U, OH B
Case Western Reserve U, OH B
Cedarville U, OH B
Clarkson U, NY B
Cleveland State U, OH B
Dominican U, IL B
Dordt Coll, IA B
Illinois Inst of Technology, IL B
Indiana U–Purdue U Fort Wayne, IN B
Indiana U–Purdue U Indianapolis, IN B
Iowa State U of Science and Technology, IA B
Kansas State U, KS B
Kettering U, MI B
Lawrence Technological U, MI B
Marquette U, WI B
Miami U, OH B
Miami U Hamilton, OH B
Michigan State U, MI B
Michigan Technological U, MI B
Milwaukee School of Engineering, WI B
Minnesota State U Mankato, MN B
Missouri U of Science and Technology, MO B
Missouri Western State U, MO A,B
North Dakota State U, ND B

Northwestern U, IL B
Oakland U, MI B
Ohio Northern U, OH B
The Ohio State U, OH B
Ohio U, OH B
Oklahoma Christian U, OK B
Oklahoma State U, OK B
Olivet Nazarene U, IL B
Oral Roberts U, OK B
Purdue U, IN B
Purdue U Calumet, IN B
Rose-Hulman Inst of Technology, IN B
St. Cloud State U, MN B
Saint Louis U, MO B
Saint Mary's U of Minnesota, MN B
South Dakota School of Mines and Technology, SD B
Southern Illinois U Carbondale, IL B
Southern Illinois U Edwardsville, IL B
Southern Methodist U, TX B
Taylor U, IN B
Trine U, IN B
The U of Akron, OH B
U of Cincinnati, OH B
U of Dayton, OH B
U of Evansville, IN B
U of Illinois at Chicago, IL B
U of Illinois at Urbana–Champaign, IL B
U of Indianapolis, IN B
The U of Kansas, KS B
U of Michigan, MI B
U of Minnesota, Duluth, MN B
U of Missouri–Columbia, MO B
U of Nebraska–Lincoln, NE B
U of Notre Dame, IN B
U of Oklahoma, OK B
The U of Toledo, OH B
U of Wisconsin–Madison, WI B
U of Wisconsin–Stout, WI B
Valparaiso U, IN B
Washington U in St. Louis, MO B
Western Michigan U, MI B
Wichita State U, KS B
Wilberforce U, OH B
Wright State U, OH B

Computer Engineering Related
Ohio Northern U, OH B

Computer Engineering Technology
Baker Coll of Owosso, MI A
DeVry U, Addison, IL B
DeVry U, Chicago, IL B
DeVry U, Tinley Park, IL B
DeVry U, Kansas City, MO B
DeVry U, Columbus, OH B
Eastern Michigan U, MI B
East-West U, IL B
Grantham U, MO A,B
Indiana State U, IN B
Indiana U–Purdue U Fort Wayne, IN B
Indiana U–Purdue U Indianapolis, IN A,B
ITT Tech Inst, Burr Ridge, IL A
ITT Tech Inst, Mount Prospect, IL A
ITT Tech Inst, Orland Park, IL A
ITT Tech Inst, Fort Wayne, IN A
ITT Tech Inst, Indianapolis, IN A
ITT Tech Inst, Newburgh, IN A
ITT Tech Inst, South Bend, IN A
ITT Tech Inst, IA A
ITT Tech Inst, KS A
ITT Tech Inst, Canton, MI A
ITT Tech Inst, Grand Rapids, MI A
ITT Tech Inst, Troy, MI A
ITT Tech Inst, MN A
ITT Tech Inst, Arnold, MO A
ITT Tech Inst, Earth City, MO A
ITT Tech Inst, Kansas City, MO A
ITT Tech Inst, Springfield, MO A
ITT Tech Inst, Oklahoma City, OK A
ITT Tech Inst, Tulsa, OK A
ITT Tech Inst, Green Bay, WI A
ITT Tech Inst, Greenfield, WI A
ITT Tech Inst, Madison, WI A
Lake Superior State U, MI A,B
Minnesota State U Mankato, MN B
Ranken Tech Coll, MO A
Shawnee State U, OH B
U of Cincinnati, OH A
U of Dayton, OH B

Computer Graphics
Baker Coll of Cadillac, MI A
Baker Coll of Flint, MI B
Dakota State U, SD B
DePaul U, IL B
Indiana Tech, IN A
Indiana Wesleyan U, IN B
Lewis U, IL B
Rogers State U, OK B

Computer/Information Technology Services Administration Related
Concordia U, St. Paul, MN B
Dordt Coll, IA B
Eastern Illinois U, IL B
Lindenwood U, MO B
Saint Mary's U of Minnesota, MN B
U of Phoenix–Indianapolis Campus, IN B
Washington U in St. Louis, MO B

Computer Management
AIB Coll of Business, IA A
National-Louis U, IL B
Northwest Missouri State U, MO B
U of Cincinnati, OH B

Computer Programming
Andrews U, MI B
Baker Coll of Muskegon, MI A
Baker Coll of Owosso, MI A,B
Baker Coll of Port Huron, MI A
Black Hills State U, SD A
Dakota State U, SD A
DePaul U, IL B
Dordt Coll, IA B
East-West U, IL B
Friends U, KS B
Grace U, NE B
Iowa Wesleyan Coll, IA B
ITT Tech Inst, Grand Rapids, MI A
Kent State U, OH A,B
Michigan Technological U, MI B
Minnesota State U Mankato, MN B
Missouri Southern State U, MO A
Mount Union Coll, OH B
Northwest Missouri State U, MO B
Purdue U Calumet, IN A
Southwestern Coll, KS B
U of Cincinnati, OH A,B
U of Illinois at Urbana–Champaign, IL B
U of Michigan–Dearborn, MI B
The U of Toledo, OH A,B
Westwood Coll–Chicago Du Page, IL A
Winona State U, MN B
Youngstown State U, OH A,B

Computer Programming (Specific Applications)
DePaul U, IL B
Indiana U East, IN A
Indiana U South Bend, IN A
Indiana U Southeast, IN A
Kent State U, OH A,B
Kent State U, Salem Campus, OH A
The U of Toledo, OH A
Westwood Coll–Chicago Du Page, IL B

Computer Science
Albion Coll, MI B
Alma Coll, MI B
Anderson U, IN B
Andrews U, MI B
Aquinas Coll, MI B
Ashland U, OH B
Augsburg Coll, MN B
Augustana Coll, IL B
Augustana Coll, SD B
Aurora U, IL B
Baker Coll of Allen Park, MI A
Baker Coll of Muskegon, MI B
Baker Coll of Owosso, MI A,B
Baker U, KS B
Baldwin-Wallace Coll, OH B
Beloit Coll, WI B
Bemidji State U, MN B
Benedictine Coll, KS B
Benedictine U, IL B
Bethel Coll, IN A,B
Bethel Coll, KS B
Black Hills State U, SD A
Bluffton U, OH B
Bradley U, IL B
Buena Vista U, IA B
Calumet Coll of Saint Joseph, IN A,B
Calvin Coll, MI B
Cameron U, OK B
Capital U, OH B
Carleton Coll, MN B
Case Western Reserve U, OH B
Cedarville U, OH B
Central Christian Coll of Kansas, KS A
Central Coll, IA B
Central Methodist U, MO A,B
Central Michigan U, MI B
Clarkson U, NY B
Cleveland State U, OH B
Coe Coll, IA B
Coll of Saint Benedict, MN B
Coll of the Ozarks, MO B
The Coll of Wooster, OH B
Colorado Tech U Sioux Falls, SD B
Columbia Coll, MO B
Concordia Coll, MN B
Concordia U Chicago, IL B
Concordia U, Nebraska, NE B
Concordia U Wisconsin, WI B
Cornell Coll, IA B
Creighton U, NE A,B
Denison U, OH B
DePaul U, IL B
DePauw U, IN B
Doane Coll, NE B
Dominican U, IL B
Dordt Coll, IA B
Drake U, IA B
Drury U, MO B
Earlham Coll, IN B
Eastern Michigan U, MI B
East-West U, IL A,B
Elmhurst Coll, IL B
Eureka Coll, IL B
Evangel U, MO B
Fontbonne U, MO B
Franciscan U of Steubenville, OH B
Franklin Coll, IN B
Goshen Coll, IN B
Graceland U, IA B
Grace U, NE B
Grand View U, IA B
Grantham U, MO A,B
Grinnell Coll, IA B
Gustavus Adolphus Coll, MN B
Hanover Coll, IN B
Heidelberg U, OH B
Hillsdale Coll, MI B
Hiram Coll, OH B
Hope Coll, MI B
Huntington U, IN B
Illinois Coll, IL B

A—associate degree; B—bachelor's degree

Illinois Inst of Technology, IL B
Illinois State U, IL B
Illinois Wesleyan U, IL B
Indiana Tech, IN B
Indiana U–Purdue U Fort Wayne, IN A,B
Iowa Wesleyan Coll, IA B
Jamestown Coll, ND B
John Carroll U, OH B
Kalamazoo Coll, MI B
Kansas Wesleyan U, KS A,B
Kent State U, OH B
Kettering U, MI B
Kilian Comm Coll, SD A
Lake Forest Coll, IL B
Lakeland Coll, WI B
Lake Superior State U, MI B
Lawrence Technological U, MI B
Lawrence U, WI B
Lewis U, IL B
Lincoln U, MO A
Lindenwood U, MO B
Loras Coll, IA B
Luther Coll, IA B
Macalester Coll, MN B
Madonna U, MI A,B
Malone U, OH B
Manchester Coll, IN A,B
Marietta Coll, OH B
Marquette U, WI B
Maryville U of Saint Louis, MO B
McKendree U, IL B
McPherson Coll, KS B
Miami U, OH B
Miami U Hamilton, OH B
Michigan Technological U, MI B
MidAmerica Nazarene U, KS B
Minnesota State U Mankato, MN B
Minnesota State U Moorhead, MN B
Minot State U, ND B
Missouri State U, MO B
Missouri U of Science and Technology, MO B
Monmouth Coll, IL B
Morningside Coll, IA B
Mount Marty Coll, SD B
Mount Mary Coll, WI B
Mount Mercy Coll, IA B
Mount Vernon Nazarene U, OH B
Muskingum Coll, OH B
Nebraska Wesleyan U, NE B
North Dakota State U, ND B
Northeastern Illinois U, IL B
Northeastern State U, OK B
North Park U, IL B
Northwestern U, IL B
Northwest Missouri State U, MO B
Oberlin Coll, OH B
Oglala Lakota Coll, SD A
Ohio Northern U, OH B
The Ohio State U, OH B
Ohio U, OH B
Ohio U–Chillicothe, OH A
Ohio U–Lancaster, OH A
Ohio Wesleyan U, OH B
Oklahoma Baptist U, OK B
Oklahoma Christian U, OK B
Oklahoma City U, OK B
Olivet Nazarene U, IL B
Oral Roberts U, OK B
Otterbein Coll, OH B
Park U, MO B
Pittsburg State U, KS B
Purdue U, IN B
Quincy U, IL B
Ripon Coll, WI B
Rochester Comm and Tech Coll, MN A
Rockford Coll, IL B
Roosevelt U, IL B
Rose-Hulman Inst of Technology, IN B
Saginaw Valley State U, MI B
St. Ambrose U, IA B
St. Cloud State U, MN B
Saint John's U, MN B
Saint Mary's U of Minnesota, MN B
St. Olaf Coll, MN B
Saint Xavier U, IL B
Simpson Coll, IA B
Sinte Gleska U, SD B
South Dakota School of Mines and Technology, SD B
Southern Illinois U Carbondale, IL B
Southern Illinois U Edwardsville, IL B
Southern Methodist U, TX B
Southwest Baptist U, MO A,B
Southwestern Coll, KS B
Southwestern Oklahoma State U, OK B
Southwest Minnesota State U, MN B
Spring Arbor U, MI B
Taylor U, IN B
Transylvania U, KY B
Trine U, IN B
Trinity Christian Coll, IL B
Trinity International U, IL B
Union Coll, NE B
The U of Akron, OH B
U of Central Oklahoma, OK B
U of Chicago, IL B
U of Cincinnati, OH B
U of Dayton, OH B
The U of Findlay, OH A,B
U of Illinois at Chicago, IL B
U of Illinois at Springfield, IL B
U of Illinois at Urbana–Champaign, IL B
U of Indianapolis, IN B
The U of Iowa, IA B
U of Michigan, MI B
U of Michigan–Flint, MI B
U of Minnesota, Duluth, MN B
U of Minnesota, Morris, MN B
U of Minnesota, Twin Cities Campus, MN B
U of Missouri–Columbia, MO B
U of Missouri–Kansas City, MO B
U of New Orleans, LA B
U of Northern Iowa, IA B
U of Oklahoma, OK B
U of Rio Grande, OH A,B
U of St. Francis, IL B
U of Sioux Falls, SD B
The U of Toledo, OH B
U of Tulsa, OK B
U of Wisconsin–Green Bay, WI B
U of Wisconsin–Madison, WI B
U of Wisconsin–Milwaukee, WI B
U of Wisconsin–Oshkosh, WI B
U of Wisconsin–Parkside, WI B
U of Wisconsin–Platteville, WI B
U of Wisconsin–Superior, WI B
Valparaiso U, IN B
Walsh U, OH A,B
Wartburg Coll, IA B
Washington U in St. Louis, MO B
Webster U, MO B
Western Michigan U, MI B
Westminster Coll, MO B
Wheaton Coll, IL B
Wilberforce U, OH B
William Jewell Coll, MO B
Wilmington Coll, OH B
Winona State U, MN B
Wittenberg U, OH B
Wright State U, OH B
Xavier U, OH B
Youngstown State U, OH B

Computer Software and Media Applications Related

AIB Coll of Business, IA A
Baldwin-Wallace Coll, OH B
Dakota State U, SD A,B
Dakota Wesleyan U, SD B
ITT Tech Inst, Fort Wayne, IN A
ITT Tech Inst, Indianapolis, IN A
ITT Tech Inst, Newburgh, IN A
ITT Tech Inst, Canton, MI A
ITT Tech Inst, Grand Rapids, MI A
ITT Tech Inst, Troy, MI A
ITT Tech Inst, MN A
ITT Tech Inst, Arnold, MO A
ITT Tech Inst, Earth City, MO A
ITT Tech Inst, NE A
ITT Tech Inst, Green Bay, WI A
ITT Tech Inst, Greenfield, WI A
Kilian Comm Coll, SD A

Computer Software Engineering

Carroll U, WI B
Clarkson U, NY B
DeVry U, Addison, IL B
DeVry U, Tinley Park, IL B
DeVry U, Edina, MN B
Indiana Tech, IN B
ITT Tech Inst, Indianapolis, IN B
ITT Tech Inst, MN B
ITT Tech Inst, Arnold, MO B
ITT Tech Inst, Earth City, MO B
ITT Tech Inst, Oklahoma City, OK B
ITT Tech Inst, Tulsa, OK B
ITT Tech Inst, Green Bay, WI B
ITT Tech Inst, Greenfield, WI B
Michigan Technological U, MI B
Milwaukee School of Engineering, WI B
Missouri Tech, MO A,B
Rose-Hulman Inst of Technology, IN B
South Dakota State U, SD B
U of Illinois at Urbana–Champaign, IL B
U of Minnesota, Crookston, MN B
U of Phoenix–Cleveland Campus, OH B
U of Phoenix–Indianapolis Campus, IN B
U of Phoenix–Metro Detroit Campus, MI B
U of Phoenix–St. Louis Campus, MO B
U of Wisconsin–Platteville, WI B
Westwood Coll–Chicago Du Page, IL A

Computer Software Technology

Brown Mackie Coll–Fort Wayne, IN A
Brown Mackie Coll–Merrillville, IN A
Brown Mackie Coll–Michigan City, IN A
Brown Mackie Coll–South Bend, IN A
ITT Tech Inst, Canton, MI A
ITT Tech Inst, Grand Rapids, MI A
ITT Tech Inst, Troy, MI A
ITT Tech Inst, Oklahoma City, OK A
ITT Tech Inst, Tulsa, OK A

Computer Systems Analysis

Baldwin-Wallace Coll, OH B
Davenport U, Grand Rapids, MI A
DeVry U, Addison, IL B
DeVry U, Chicago, IL B
DeVry U, Tinley Park, IL B
DeVry U, Indianapolis, IN B
DeVry U, Edina, MN B
DeVry U, Kansas City, MO B
DeVry U, Columbus, OH B
DeVry U, OK B
DeVry U, Milwaukee, WI B
Kent State U, OH B
Miami U, OH B
Miami U Hamilton, OH B
St. Ambrose U, IA B
The U of Akron, OH A

U of North Dakota, ND B
The U of Toledo, OH A

Computer Systems Networking and Telecommunications

Baker Coll of Allen Park, MI A
Baker Coll of Flint, MI A
Baldwin-Wallace Coll, OH B
Davenport U, Grand Rapids, MI B
DePaul U, IL B
DeVry U, Addison, IL A,B
DeVry U, Chicago, IL A,B
DeVry U, Tinley Park, IL A,B
DeVry U, Indianapolis, IN A,B
DeVry U, Edina, MN A,B
DeVry U, Kansas City, MO A,B
DeVry U, Columbus, OH A,B
DeVry U, OK A,B
DeVry U Southfield Center, MI A
Illinois State U, IL B
Indiana Tech, IN A,B
ITT Tech Inst, Mount Prospect, IL B
ITT Tech Inst, Fort Wayne, IN B
ITT Tech Inst, Arnold, MO B
ITT Tech Inst, Earth City, MO B
ITT Tech Inst, NE B
Kansas State U, KS B
Michigan Technological U, MI B
Missouri Tech, MO A
Northern Michigan U, MI B
Rasmussen Coll St. Cloud, MN A
Robert Morris Coll, IL A
Roosevelt U, IL B
St. Ambrose U, IA B
The U of Akron, OH A,B
The U of Findlay, OH B
U of Phoenix–St. Louis Campus, MO A
U of Wisconsin–Stout, WI B
Western Illinois U, IL B
Westwood Coll–Chicago Du Page, IL A,B

Computer Teacher Education

Alma Coll, MI B
Baker Coll of Flint, MI A
Buena Vista U, IA B
Central Christian Coll of Kansas, KS A
Concordia U Chicago, IL B
Concordia U, Nebraska, NE B
Dakota State U, SD B
DePaul U, IL B
Dordt Coll, IA B
Eastern Michigan U, MI B
Edgewood Coll, WI B
Michigan Technological U, MI B
Union Coll, NE B
U of Nebraska–Lincoln, NE B
Wright State U, OH B

Computer Technology/Computer Systems Technology

Central Michigan U, MI B
Colorado Tech U Sioux Falls, SD B
Miami U, OH A
Miami U Hamilton, OH A
Southeast Missouri State U, MO A
Southwestern Coll, KS B
Wayne State U, MI B

Computer Typography and Composition Equipment Operation

Baker Coll of Auburn Hills, MI A
Baker Coll of Cadillac, MI A
Baker Coll of Clinton Township, MI A
Baker Coll of Flint, MI A
Baker Coll of Jackson, MI A
Calumet Coll of Saint Joseph, IN A
The U of Toledo, OH A

Conducting

Calvin Coll, MI B
Ohio U, OH B

Construction Engineering

Bradley U, IL B
Clarkson U, NY B
Marquette U, WI B
Michigan Technological U, MI B
North Dakota State U, ND B
Purdue U, IN B
U of Cincinnati, OH B
U of Illinois at Urbana–Champaign, IL B

Construction Engineering Technology

Baker Coll of Owosso, MI A
Bemidji State U, MN B
Bowling Green State U, OH B
Central Michigan U, MI B
Eastern Michigan U, MI B
Ferris State U, MI A
Indiana U–Purdue U Fort Wayne, IN B
Kansas State U, KS B
Lake Superior State U, MI A
Lawrence Technological U, MI A
Minnesota State U Moorhead, MN B
Northern Michigan U, MI B
Oklahoma State U, OK B
Oklahoma State U, Oklahoma City, OK A
Pittsburg State U, KS B
Purdue U, IN B
South Dakota State U, SD B
Southern Illinois U Edwardsville, IL B
The U of Akron, OH A,B
U of Cincinnati, OH A,B
U of Nebraska–Lincoln, NE B
The U of Toledo, OH A,B
U of Wisconsin–Stout, WI B
Wright State U, OH A

Construction Management

Baker Coll of Flint, MI A
Eastern Michigan U, MI B
Ferris State U, MI B
Illinois State U, IL B
ITT Tech Inst, Burr Ridge, IL B
ITT Tech Inst, Mount Prospect, IL B
ITT Tech Inst, Orland Park, IL B
ITT Tech Inst, Fort Wayne, IN B
ITT Tech Inst, Indianapolis, IN B
ITT Tech Inst, Newburgh, IN B
ITT Tech Inst, South Bend, IN B
ITT Tech Inst, IA B
ITT Tech Inst, Canton, MI B
ITT Tech Inst, Grand Rapids, MI B
ITT Tech Inst, Troy, MI B
ITT Tech Inst, Arnold, MO B
ITT Tech Inst, Earth City, MO B
ITT Tech Inst, Kansas City, MO B
ITT Tech Inst, NE B
ITT Tech Inst, Oklahoma City, OK B
ITT Tech Inst, Tulsa, OK B
ITT Tech Inst, Green Bay, WI B
ITT Tech Inst, Greenfield, WI B
ITT Tech Inst, Madison, WI B
Lawrence Technological U, MI B
Michigan State U, MI B
Milwaukee School of Engineering, WI B
Minnesota State U Mankato, MN B
Missouri State U, MO B
North Dakota State U, ND B
The Ohio State U, OH B
Oklahoma State U, Oklahoma City, OK A
Pittsburg State U, KS B
Purdue U, IN B
U of Cincinnati, OH B
U of Minnesota, Twin Cities Campus, MN B
U of Northern Iowa, IA B
U of Oklahoma, OK B
U of Wisconsin–Madison, WI B
U of Wisconsin–Platteville, WI B
Western Illinois U, IL B

Construction Trades

Oklahoma State U, Oklahoma City, OK A

Construction Trades Related

Sinte Gleska U, SD A

Consumer Economics

South Dakota State U, SD B
U of Illinois at Urbana–Champaign, IL B

Consumer Merchandising/Retailing Management

Baker Coll of Owosso, MI A
Bradley U, IL B
Fontbonne U, MO B
Lindenwood U, MO B
Madonna U, MI A,B
Northwest Missouri State U, MO B
U of Central Oklahoma, OK B
The U of Toledo, OH A
Winona State U, MN B

Consumer Services and Advocacy

U of Wisconsin–Madison, WI B

Cooking and Related Culinary Arts

Kendall Coll, IL A,B

Corrections

Baker Coll of Muskegon, MI A
Coll of the Ozarks, MO B
Lake Superior State U, MI A,B
Minnesota State U Mankato, MN B
Oklahoma City U, OK B
Saint Louis U, MO B
Saint Mary's U of Minnesota, MN B
Southeast Missouri State U, MO B
Tiffin U, OH B
The U of Toledo, OH A
Washburn U, KS A,B
Winona State U, MN B
Xavier U, OH A

Corrections Administration

Union Inst & U, OH B

Corrections and Criminal Justice Related

Emporia State U, KS B
Mount Mary Coll, WI B
Northland Coll, WI B
Pittsburg State U, KS B
Rasmussen Coll Eagan, MN A
Rasmussen Coll St. Cloud, MN A
U of Michigan–Flint, MI B
U of Phoenix–St. Louis Campus, MO B
U of Phoenix–West Michigan Campus, MI B
Westwood Coll–Chicago Du Page, IL B

Counseling Psychology

Crossroads Coll, MN B
Grace Coll, IN B
Great Lakes Christian Coll, MI B
Jamestown Coll, ND B
Kilian Comm Coll, SD A
Morningside Coll, IA B
Newman U, KS B

A—associate degree; B—bachelor's degree

Northwestern U, IL B
Oak Hills Christian Coll, MN B
Pittsburg State U, KS B
Saint Xavier U, IL B
Wayne State Coll, NE B

Counselor Education/School Counseling and Guidance

Buena Vista U, IA B
Northwest Missouri State U, MO B
Oglala Lakota Coll, SD A,B
St. Cloud State U, MN B
U of Central Oklahoma, OK B
Wright State U, OH B

Court Reporting

AIB Coll of Business, IA A,B
Midstate Coll, IL A
U of Cincinnati, OH A

Crafts, Folk Art and Artisanry

The Cleveland Inst of Art, OH B
Coll for Creative Studies, MI B
Indiana U–Purdue U Fort Wayne, IN B
Kent State U, OH B
Northern Michigan U, MI A
U of Illinois at Urbana–Champaign, IL B

Creative Writing

Ashland U, OH B
Augustana Coll, IL B
Baldwin-Wallace Coll, OH B
Beloit Coll, WI B
Bethel Coll, IN A
Bluffton U, OH B
Bowling Green State U, OH B
Briar Cliff U, IA B
Butler U, IN B
Capital U, OH B
Carroll U, WI B
Central Michigan U, MI B
Coe Coll, IA B
Denison U, OH B
Drury U, MO B
Eastern Michigan U, MI B
Haskell Indian Nations U, KS A
Hiram Coll, OH B
Indiana Wesleyan U, IN B
Kansas City Art Inst, MO B
Knox Coll, IL B
Loras Coll, IA B
Manchester Coll, IN A
Miami U Hamilton, OH B
Minnesota State U Mankato, MN B
Mount Union Coll, OH B
North Central Coll, IL B
Northland Coll, WI B
North Park U, IL B
Northwestern Coll, MN B
Oberlin Coll, OH B
Ohio Northern U, OH B
Ohio U, OH B
Ohio Wesleyan U, OH B
Oklahoma Christian U, OK B
Pittsburg State U, KS B
Purdue U, IN B
St. Catherine U, MN B
St. Cloud State U, MN B
Saint Joseph's Coll, IN B
Saint Mary's Coll, IN B
Siena Heights U, MI B
Southern Methodist U, TX B
Southwest Minnesota State U, MN B
Stephens Coll, MO B
U of Chicago, IL B
U of Evansville, IN B
The U of Findlay, OH B
U of Michigan, MI B
U of Nebraska at Omaha, NE B
U of Wisconsin–Parkside, WI B
Valparaiso U, IN B
Waldorf Coll, IA B
Washington U in St. Louis, MO B

Criminal Justice/Law Enforcement Administration

Adrian Coll, MI B
Anderson U, IN A,B
Argosy U, Schaumburg, IL B
Argosy U, Twin Cities, MN B
Bacone Coll, OK A
Bemidji State U, MN A,B
Bohecker's Business Coll, OH A
Bradley U, IL B
Briar Cliff U, IA B
Brown Mackie Coll–Fort Wayne, IN A,B
Brown Mackie Coll–Indianapolis, IN A,B
Brown Mackie Coll–Merrillville, IN A,B
Brown Mackie Coll–Michigan City, IN A,B
Brown Mackie Coll–South Bend, IN A,B
Brown Mackie Coll–Tulsa, OK A,B
Bryant & Stratton Coll, Parma, OH A
Bryant & Stratton Coll, WI A,B
Bryant & Stratton Coll—Wauwatosa Campus, WI A,B
Calumet Coll of Saint Joseph, IN A,B
Cedarville U, OH B
Central Christian Coll of Kansas, KS A
Chancellor U, OH A,B
Colorado Tech U North Kansas City, MO A,B
Colorado Tech U Sioux Falls, SD A,B
Columbia Coll, MO A,B
Concordia U, MI B
Concordia U Wisconsin, WI B
Culver-Stockton Coll, MO B
Dakota Wesleyan U, SD A,B
Dana Coll, NE B
Dordt Coll, IA B
Evangel U, MO B
Ferris State U, MI B
Grace Coll, IN B
Graceland U, IA B
Grand Valley State U, MI B
Grand View U, IA B
Grantham U, MO A,B
Greenville Coll, IL B
Gustavus Adolphus Coll, MN B
Hamline U, MN B
Hannibal-LaGrange Coll, MO A,B
Harris-Stowe State U, MO B
Indiana Tech, IN B
Indiana U–Purdue U Fort Wayne, IN A,B
Iowa Wesleyan Coll, IA B
ITT Tech Inst, Burr Ridge, IL B
ITT Tech Inst, Mount Prospect, IL B
ITT Tech Inst, Orland Park, IL B
ITT Tech Inst, Fort Wayne, IN A,B
ITT Tech Inst, Indianapolis, IN B
ITT Tech Inst, Newburgh, IN A,B
ITT Tech Inst, South Bend, IN A,B
ITT Tech Inst, IA B
ITT Tech Inst, Canton, MI A,B
ITT Tech Inst, Grand Rapids, MI A,B
ITT Tech Inst, Troy, MI A,B
ITT Tech Inst, Arnold, MO A,B
ITT Tech Inst, Earth City, MO A,B
ITT Tech Inst, Kansas City, MO A,B
ITT Tech Inst, Springfield, MO B
ITT Tech Inst, NE A
ITT Tech Inst, Oklahoma City, OK A,B
ITT Tech Inst, Tulsa, OK A,B
ITT Tech Inst, Green Bay, WI A,B
ITT Tech Inst, Greenfield, WI A,B
ITT Tech Inst, Madison, WI A,B
Kansas Wesleyan U, KS A,B
Kaplan U–Mason City Campus, IA A
Kilian Comm Coll, SD A
Lake Superior State U, MI A,B
Lewis U, IL B
Lincoln U, MO A,B
Lindenwood U, MO B
MacMurray Coll, IL A,B
Marian U, WI B
McKendree U, IL B
Mid-America Christian U, OK B
MidAmerica Nazarene U, KS B
Millikin U, IL B
Missouri Southern State U, MO B
Mount Mercy Coll, IA B
Mount Vernon Nazarene U, OH B
Muskingum Coll, OH B
Newman U, KS B
Northeastern State U, OK B
Northern Michigan U, MI A
Oglala Lakota Coll, SD A,B
Ohio Dominican U, OH B
Ohio Northern U, OH B
Ohio U, OH B
Ohio U–Chillicothe, OH B
Ohio U–Eastern, OH B
Ohio U–Lancaster, OH B
Ohio U–Southern Campus, OH A,B
Ohio U–Zanesville, OH B
Oklahoma City U, OK B
Olivet Nazarene U, IL B
Rasmussen Coll Eagan, MN A
Rasmussen Coll St. Cloud, MN A
Rogers State U, OK A,B
St. Cloud State U, MN B
Saint Louis U, MO B
Saint Mary's U of Minnesota, MN B
Sanford-Brown Coll, Fenton, MO A,B
Simpson Coll, IA B
Sinte Gleska U, SD A
Southern Illinois U Carbondale, IL B
Southwest Baptist U, MO B
Southwestern Coll, KS B
Southwestern Oklahoma State U, OK B
Southwest Minnesota State U, MN B
Tiffin U, OH A,B
Trine U, IN A,B
Union Inst & U, OH B
U of Central Missouri, MO B
U of Central Oklahoma, OK B
U of Cincinnati, OH A,B
U of Dayton, OH B
The U of Findlay, OH A,B
U of Minnesota, Crookston, MN B
U of Missouri–Kansas City, MO B
U of Oklahoma, OK B
U of Phoenix–Chicago Campus, IL B
U of Phoenix–Cleveland Campus, OH B
U of Phoenix–Indianapolis Campus, IN A,B
U of Phoenix–Kansas City Campus, MO B
U of Phoenix–Metro Detroit Campus, MI B
U of Phoenix–Oklahoma City Campus, OK B
U of Phoenix–St. Louis Campus, MO A
U of Phoenix–Tulsa Campus, OK B
U of Phoenix–West Michigan Campus, MI B
U of Phoenix–Wichita Campus, KS B
U of Phoenix–Wisconsin Campus, WI B
The U of South Dakota, SD B
U of Wisconsin–Milwaukee, WI B
U of Wisconsin–Oshkosh, WI B
U of Wisconsin–Parkside, WI B

U of Wisconsin–Platteville, WI B
Washburn U, KS A,B
Western Illinois U, IL B
Wilmington Coll, OH B
Winona State U, MN B

Criminal Justice/Police Science
Bemidji State U, MN B
Cameron U, OK A
Coll of the Ozarks, MO B
Ferris State U, MI A,B
Lake Superior State U, MI A,B
MacMurray Coll, IL A,B
Miami U, OH A
Minnesota State U Mankato, MN B
Missouri Southern State U, MO A
Northern State U, SD B
Ohio Northern U, OH B
Ohio U, OH A
Ohio U–Chillicothe, OH A
Ohio U–Lancaster, OH A
Oklahoma City U, OK B
Oklahoma State U, Oklahoma City, OK A
Rochester Comm and Tech Coll, MN A
St. Gregory's U, Shawnee, OK B
Truman State U, MO B
The U of Akron, OH A
U of Cincinnati, OH A,B
U of Mary, ND B
The U of Toledo, OH A
U of Wisconsin–Milwaukee, WI B
U of Wisconsin–Superior, WI B
Washburn U, KS A,B
Winona State U, MN B
Wright State U, OH B

Criminal Justice/Safety
American InterContinental U Online, IL B
Augsburg Coll, MN B
Aurora U, IL B
Baldwin-Wallace Coll, OH B
Ball State U, IN A,B
Bethany Coll, KS B
Bethel Coll, IN A,B
Bluffton U, OH B
Bowling Green State U, OH B
Buena Vista U, IA B
Central Christian Coll of Kansas, KS A
Central Methodist U, MO B
Central State U, OH B
Concordia U, St. Paul, MN B
Edgewood Coll, WI B
Fort Hays State U, KS B
Friends U, KS B
Grace Coll, IN B
Grantham U, MO A,B
Illinois State U, IL B
Indiana Tech, IN B
Indiana U Bloomington, IN B
Indiana U East, IN A,B
Indiana U Kokomo, IN A,B
Indiana U Northwest, IN A,B
Indiana U–Purdue U Indianapolis, IN A,B
Indiana U South Bend, IN A,B
Indiana U Southeast, IN B
Indiana Wesleyan U, IN A,B
Jamestown Coll, ND B
Kaplan U–Davenport Campus, IA A,B
Lakeland Coll, WI B
Lewis U, IL B
Loras Coll, IA B
Lourdes Coll, OH A,B
Loyola U Chicago, IL B
Madonna U, MI A,B
Manchester Coll, IN A
Martin U, IN B
Michigan State U, MI B
Minnesota School of Business–Blaine, MN A
Minnesota State U Moorhead, MN B
Minot State U, ND B
Missouri Baptist U, MO B
Missouri Western State U, MO A,B
Mount Marty Coll, SD B
Mount Union Coll, OH B
Mount Vernon Nazarene U, OH B
North Dakota State U, ND B
Northeastern Illinois U, IL B
Northern Michigan U, MI A,B
Northwestern Coll, MN B
Ohio Northern U, OH B
Ohio U, OH B
Olivet Coll, MI B
Quincy U, IL B
Rochester Comm and Tech Coll, MN A
Roosevelt U, IL B
Saginaw Valley State U, MI B
St. Ambrose U, IA B
Saint Joseph's Coll, IN B
Saint Xavier U, IL B
Siena Heights U, MI B
Sinte Gleska U, SD B
Southeastern Oklahoma State U, OK B
Southern Illinois U Edwardsville, IL B
Southwest Minnesota State U, MN B
Truman State U, MO B
The U of Akron, OH B
U of Central Oklahoma, OK B
U of Illinois at Chicago, IL B
U of Illinois at Springfield, IL B
U of Mary, ND B
U of Michigan–Dearborn, MI B
U of Nebraska at Kearney, NE B
U of Nebraska at Omaha, NE B
U of North Dakota, ND B
The U of Toledo, OH B
U of Wisconsin–Eau Claire, WI B
U of Wisconsin–Superior, WI B
Viterbo U, WI B
Washburn U, KS B
Wayne State Coll, NE B
Wayne State U, MI B
Western Michigan U, MI B
Wichita State U, KS B
Xavier U, OH A,B
Youngstown State U, OH A,B

Criminology
Butler U, IN B
Capital U, OH B
Coll of Mount St. Joseph, OH B
Dominican U, IL B
Drury U, MO B
Eastern Michigan U, MI B
Elmhurst Coll, IL B
Indiana State U, IN B
Lindenwood U, MO B
Marquette U, WI B
Maryville U of Saint Louis, MO B
Missouri State U, MO B
Mount Union Coll, OH B
The Ohio State U, OH B
Ohio U, OH B
St. Cloud State U, MN B
U of Minnesota, Duluth, MN B
U of Missouri–Kansas City, MO B
U of Missouri–St. Louis, MO B
U of Northern Iowa, IA B
U of Saint Mary, KS B
Valparaiso U, IN B
Wright State U, OH B

Crop Production
North Dakota State U, ND B
U of Minnesota, Crookston, MN B

Culinary Arts
The Art Inst of Indianapolis, IN A
The Art Inst of Michigan, MI A
The Art Insts International–Kansas City, KS A,B
The Art Insts International Minnesota, MN A
Baker Coll of Muskegon, MI A
The Illinois Inst of Art–Chicago, IL A
Kendall Coll, IL A,B
Robert Morris Coll, IL A
St. Augustine Coll, IL A
The U of Akron, OH A

Cultural Studies
Cornell Coll, IA B
Indiana Wesleyan U, IN A,B
Kent State U, OH B
Minnesota State U Mankato, MN B
Ohio Wesleyan U, OH B
U of Wisconsin–Milwaukee, WI B
Washington U in St. Louis, MO B

Curriculum and Instruction
Ohio U, OH B
U of Saint Mary, KS B
The U of South Dakota, SD B
Wright State U, OH B

Customer Service Management
Rochester Comm and Tech Coll, MN A
Southwest Baptist U, MO B
U of Wisconsin–Stout, WI B

Cytogenetics/Genetics/Clinical Genetics Technology
Northern Michigan U, MI B
Saint Mary's U of Minnesota, MN B

Cytotechnology
Edgewood Coll, WI B
Elmhurst Coll, IL B
Illinois Coll, IL B
Indiana U–Purdue U Indianapolis, IN B
Indiana U South Bend, IN B
Indiana U Southeast, IN B
Marian U, WI B
Michigan Technological U, MI B
Minnesota State U Moorhead, MN B
Northern Michigan U, MI B
Oakland U, MI B
Saint Louis U, MO B
Saint Mary's U of Minnesota, MN B
The U of Kansas, KS B
U of North Dakota, ND B
Winona State U, MN B

Dairy Science
Iowa State U of Science and Technology, IA B
South Dakota State U, SD B

Dance
Alma Coll, MI B
Ball State U, IN B
Butler U, IN B
Cleveland State U, OH B
Denison U, OH B
Eastern Michigan U, MI B
Grand Valley State U, MI B
Gustavus Adolphus Coll, MN B
Hope Coll, MI B
Kent State U, OH B
Kenyon Coll, OH B
Lake Erie Coll, OH B
Lindenwood U, MO B
Missouri State U, MO B
Northwestern U, IL B
Oakland U, MI B
Oberlin Coll, OH B
The Ohio State U, OH B
Ohio U, OH B
Oklahoma City U, OK B
Oral Roberts U, OK B
St. Gregory's U, Shawnee, OK B
St. Olaf Coll, MN B
Southern Methodist U, TX B
Stephens Coll, MO B
The U of Akron, OH B
U of Central Oklahoma, OK B
U of Cincinnati, OH B
U of Illinois at Urbana–Champaign, IL B
The U of Iowa, IA B

A—associate degree; B—bachelor's degree

The U of Kansas, KS B
U of Michigan, MI B
U of Minnesota, Twin Cities Campus, MN B
U of Missouri–Kansas City, MO B
U of Nebraska–Lincoln, NE B
U of Oklahoma, OK B
U of Wisconsin–Milwaukee, WI B
U of Wisconsin–Stevens Point, WI B
Washington U in St. Louis, MO B
Wayne State U, MI B
Webster U, MO B
Western Michigan U, MI B
Wright State U, OH B

Data Entry/Microcomputer Applications
Baker Coll of Allen Park, MI A
The U of Akron, OH A

Data Entry/Microcomputer Applications Related
AIB Coll of Business, IA A
Baker Coll of Allen Park, MI A

Data Processing and Data Processing Technology
Baker Coll of Auburn Hills, MI A
Baker Coll of Cadillac, MI A
Baker Coll of Clinton Township, MI A
Baker Coll of Flint, MI A
Baker Coll of Jackson, MI A
Baker Coll of Muskegon, MI A
Baker Coll of Owosso, MI A
Baker Coll of Port Huron, MI A
Bemidji State U, MN B
Bryant & Stratton Coll, Willoughby Hills, OH A
Dordt Coll, IA A
Miami U, OH A
Minnesota State U Mankato, MN B
Mount Vernon Nazarene U, OH A
Northern State U, SD A
Northwest Missouri State U, MO B
Sinte Gleska U, SD A
U of Cincinnati, OH A
U of Southern Indiana, IN B
The U of Toledo, OH A
Wright State U, OH A
Youngstown State U, OH A

Dental Assisting
Rochester Comm and Tech Coll, MN A
U of Southern Indiana, IN A

Dental Hygiene
Argosy U, Twin Cities, MN A
Baker Coll of Port Huron, MI A
Ferris State U, MI A,B
Indiana U Northwest, IN A
Indiana U–Purdue U Fort Wayne, IN A
Indiana U–Purdue U Indianapolis, IN A,B
Indiana U South Bend, IN A,B
Minnesota State U Mankato, MN A,B
Missouri Southern State U, MO A
The Ohio State U, OH B
The Ohio State U at Lima, OH B
Rochester Comm and Tech Coll, MN A
Shawnee State U, OH A
Southern Illinois U Carbondale, IL B
U of Michigan, MI B
U of Minnesota, Twin Cities Campus, MN B
U of Missouri–Kansas City, MO B
U of Nebraska Medical Center, NE B
U of Oklahoma Health Sciences Center, OK B
U of Southern Indiana, IN A,B
Wichita State U, KS A,B
Youngstown State U, OH A

Dental Laboratory Technology
Indiana U–Purdue U Fort Wayne, IN A

Dental Services and Allied Professions Related
Indiana U–Purdue U Indianapolis, IN B

Design and Applied Arts Related
Ferris State U, MI B
Indiana U Bloomington, IN A
Ohio U, OH B
Robert Morris Coll, IL B
St. Cloud State U, MN B
Taylor U, IN B
U of Illinois at Chicago, IL B
U of Saint Francis, IN B
U of Wisconsin–Stout, WI B
Washburn U, KS B
Westwood Coll–Chicago Du Page, IL B

Design and Visual Communications
Alma Coll, MI B
American InterContinental U Online, IL B
Anderson U, IN B
Art Academy of Cincinnati, OH B
The Art Inst of Michigan, MI B
The Art Insts International Minnesota, MN B
Bethel Coll, IN B
Bowling Green State U, OH B
Drury U, MO B
Ferris State U, MI B
Iowa State U of Science and Technology, IA B
ITT Tech Inst, Fort Wayne, IN A
ITT Tech Inst, Indianapolis, IN A
ITT Tech Inst, Newburgh, IN A
ITT Tech Inst, South Bend, IN A
ITT Tech Inst, IA A
ITT Tech Inst, KS A
ITT Tech Inst, Canton, MI A
ITT Tech Inst, Grand Rapids, MI A
ITT Tech Inst, Troy, MI A
ITT Tech Inst, MN A
ITT Tech Inst, Arnold, MO A
ITT Tech Inst, Earth City, MO A
ITT Tech Inst, Kansas City, MO A
ITT Tech Inst, NE A
ITT Tech Inst, Oklahoma City, OK A
ITT Tech Inst, Tulsa, OK A
ITT Tech Inst, Green Bay, WI A
ITT Tech Inst, Greenfield, WI A
Lawrence Technological U, MI B
Loyola U Chicago, IL B
Missouri State U, MO B
Mount Vernon Nazarene U, OH B
Muskingum Coll, OH B
Northeastern State U, OK B
Ohio Northern U, OH B
The Ohio State U, OH B
Ohio U, OH B
Oral Roberts U, OK B
Purdue U, IN B
Saginaw Valley State U, MI B
St. Ambrose U, IA B
Saint Mary-of-the-Woods Coll, IN B
Southern Illinois U Carbondale, IL B
Spring Arbor U, MI B
Truman State U, MO B
U of Evansville, IN B
The U of Kansas, KS B
U of Michigan–Flint, MI B
U of Notre Dame, IN B
Viterbo U, WI B
Washington U in St. Louis, MO B
Westwood Coll–Chicago Du Page, IL A,B

Desktop Publishing and Digital Imaging Design
Art Academy of Cincinnati, OH B
Ferris State U, MI A

Developmental and Child Psychology
Minnesota State U Mankato, MN B
Northeastern State U, OK B
Northern Michigan U, MI B
Northwest Missouri State U, MO B
The U of Kansas, KS B
U of Minnesota, Twin Cities Campus, MN B
The U of Toledo, OH B
U of Wisconsin–Green Bay, WI B
U of Wisconsin–Madison, WI B

Development Economics and International Development
Calvin Coll, MI B
Taylor U, IN B

Diagnostic Medical Sonography and Ultrasound Technology
Argosy U, Twin Cities, MN A
Bacone Coll, OK A
Baker Coll of Auburn Hills, MI A
Baker Coll of Owosso, MI A
Baker Coll of Port Huron, MI A
Benedictine U, IL B
Ferris State U, MI A
Lewis U, IL B
Mercy Coll of Health Sciences, IA A
Nebraska Methodist Coll, NE A,B
Rush U, IL B
St. Catherine U, MN A
U of Missouri–Columbia, MO B
U of Nebraska Medical Center, NE B
Washburn U, KS B

Diesel Mechanics Technology
Pittsburg State U, KS B

Dietetics
Andrews U, MI B
Ashland U, OH B
Ball State U, IN B
Bowling Green State U, OH B
Bradley U, IL B
Case Western Reserve U, OH B
Central Michigan U, MI B
Coll of Saint Benedict, MN B
Coll of the Ozarks, MO B
Concordia Coll, MN B
Dominican U, IL B
Eastern Michigan U, MI B
Fontbonne U, MO B
Iowa State U of Science and Technology, IA B
Kansas State U, KS B
Miami U Hamilton, OH B
Michigan State U, MI B
Minnesota State U Mankato, MN B
Missouri State U, MO B
Mount Mary Coll, WI B
North Dakota State U, ND B
Northwest Missouri State U, MO B
The Ohio State U, OH B
Olivet Nazarene U, IL B
St. Catherine U, MN B
Saint John's U, MN B
U of Central Missouri, MO B
U of Central Oklahoma, OK B
U of Dayton, OH B
U of Illinois at Chicago, IL B

U of Illinois at Urbana–Champaign, IL B
U of Missouri–Columbia, MO B
U of Nebraska at Kearney, NE B
U of North Dakota, ND B
U of Oklahoma Health Sciences Center, OK B
U of Wisconsin–Madison, WI B
U of Wisconsin–Stevens Point, WI B
U of Wisconsin–Stout, WI B
Viterbo U, WI B
Wayne State U, MI B
Western Michigan U, MI B
Youngstown State U, OH B

Dietetics and Clinical Nutrition Services Related

Madonna U, MI B

Dietetic Technician

Purdue U, IN B
Youngstown State U, OH A

Dietitian Assistant

Youngstown State U, OH A

Digital Communication and Media/Multimedia

Butler U, IN B
Calvin Coll, MI B
Clarkson U, NY B
Dordt Coll, IA B
Huntington U, IN B
Indiana U–Purdue U Indianapolis, IN A,B
Kent State U, OH B
Lindenwood U, MO B
Miami U, OH B
Michigan Technological U, MI B
Minot State U, ND B
Mount Marty Coll, SD B
Mount Mercy Coll, IA B
Muskingum Coll, OH B
Northern Michigan U, MI B
Rochester Comm and Tech Coll, MN A
Tiffin U, OH B
U of Northern Iowa, IA B
U of Phoenix–Kansas City Campus, MO B
U of Phoenix–Metro Detroit Campus, MI B
U of Phoenix–St. Louis Campus, MO B

Directing and Theatrical Production

Bradley U, IL B
Coe Coll, IA B
Drake U, IA B
Ohio U, OH B
U of Illinois at Urbana–Champaign, IL B

Divinity/Ministry

Barclay Coll, KS B
Bethel Coll, IN B
Central Christian Coll of Kansas, KS B
Christian Life Coll, IL A,B
Cincinnati Christian U, OH B
Crown Coll, MN A,B
Faith Baptist Bible Coll and Theological Seminary, IA A,B
Grace U, NE B
Great Lakes Christian Coll, MI A,B
Huntington U, IN B
Kuyper Coll, MI B
Messenger Coll, MO B
Mid-America Christian U, OK B
Moody Bible Inst, IL B
North Central U, MN A,B
Oak Hills Christian Coll, MN B
Ohio Christian U, OH A,B
Oklahoma Baptist U, OK B
Trinity Bible Coll, ND B
Tri-State Bible Coll, OH B
U of Mary, ND B
Viterbo U, WI B

Drafting and Design Technology

Baker Coll of Auburn Hills, MI A
Baker Coll of Clinton Township, MI A
Baker Coll of Owosso, MI A,B
Baker Coll of Port Huron, MI A
Black Hills State U, SD A
Cameron U, OK B
ITT Tech Inst, NE A
Lincoln U, MO A
Oklahoma State U, Oklahoma City, OK A
Robert Morris Coll, IL A
Trine U, IN B
The U of Akron, OH A
U of Cincinnati, OH A
U of Rio Grande, OH A,B
The U of Toledo, OH A
Washburn U, KS A
Wright State U, OH A
Youngstown State U, OH A

Drama and Dance Teacher Education

Bowling Green State U, OH B
Central Christian Coll of Kansas, KS A
Concordia U, Nebraska, NE B
Dordt Coll, IA B
Edgewood Coll, WI B
Hope Coll, MI B
Huntington U, IN B
Minnesota State U Moorhead, MN B
Ohio Wesleyan U, OH B
St. Catherine U, MN B
The U of Akron, OH B
U of Evansville, IN B
The U of Iowa, IA B
The U of South Dakota, SD B
Valparaiso U, IN B
Viterbo U, WI B
Waldorf Coll, IA B
Washington U in St. Louis, MO B
Wayne State Coll, NE B
William Jewell Coll, MO B
Youngstown State U, OH B

Dramatic/Theater Arts

Adrian Coll, MI B
Albion Coll, MI B
Alma Coll, MI B
Anderson U, IN B
Aquinas Coll, MI B
Ashland U, OH B
Augsburg Coll, MN B
Augustana Coll, IL B
Augustana Coll, SD B
Aurora U, IL B
Avila U, MO B
Bacone Coll, OK A
Baker U, KS B
Ball State U, IN B
Beloit Coll, WI B
Bemidji State U, MN B
Benedictine Coll, KS B
Bethany Lutheran Coll, MN B
Bethel Coll, IN B
Bethel U, MN B
Bowling Green State U, OH B
Bradley U, IL B
Briar Cliff U, IA B
Butler U, IN B
Calvin Coll, MI B
Capital U, OH B
Carleton Coll, MN B
Carroll U, WI B
Case Western Reserve U, OH B
Cedarville U, OH B
Central Coll, IA B
Central Methodist U, MO B
Central Michigan U, MI B
Clarke Coll, IA B
Cleveland State U, OH B
Coe Coll, IA B
Coll of Saint Benedict, MN B
Coll of the Ozarks, MO B
The Coll of Wooster, OH B
Concordia Coll, MN B
Concordia U Chicago, IL B
Concordia U, Nebraska, NE B
Concordia U, St. Paul, MN B
Cornell Coll, IA B
Creighton U, NE B
Culver-Stockton Coll, MO B
Dakota Wesleyan U, SD B
Denison U, OH B
DePaul U, IL B
DePauw U, IN B
Doane Coll, NE B
Dominican U, IL B
Dordt Coll, IA B
Drake U, IA B
Drury U, MO B
Earlham Coll, IN B
Eastern Illinois U, IL B
Eastern Michigan U, MI B
Elmhurst Coll, IL B
Emporia State U, KS B
Eureka Coll, IL B
Fontbonne U, MO B
Franciscan U of Steubenville, OH B
Franklin Coll, IN B
Friends U, KS B
Goshen Coll, IN B
Graceland U, IA B
Grand Valley State U, MI B
Grand View U, IA B
Greenville Coll, IL B
Grinnell Coll, IA B
Gustavus Adolphus Coll, MN B
Hamline U, MN B
Hannibal-LaGrange Coll, MO A,B
Hanover Coll, IN B
Heidelberg U, OH B
Hillsdale Coll, MI B
Hiram Coll, OH B
Hope Coll, MI B
Huntington U, IN B
Illinois Coll, IL B
Illinois State U, IL B
Illinois Wesleyan U, IL B
Indiana State U, IN B
Indiana U Bloomington, IN A,B
Indiana U Northwest, IN B
Indiana U–Purdue U Fort Wayne, IN B
Indiana U South Bend, IN B
Iowa State U of Science and Technology, IA B
Jamestown Coll, ND B
Kalamazoo Coll, MI B
Kansas State U, KS B
Kansas Wesleyan U, KS B
Kent State U, OH B
Kenyon Coll, OH B
Knox Coll, IL B
Kuyper Coll, MI B
Lake Erie Coll, OH B
Lake Forest Coll, IL B
Lawrence U, WI B
Lewis U, IL B
Lindenwood U, MO B
Loyola U Chicago, IL B
Luther Coll, IA B
Macalester Coll, MN B
MacMurray Coll, IL B
Manchester Coll, IN B
Marietta Coll, OH B
Marquette U, WI B
McPherson Coll, KS B
Miami U, OH B
Michigan State U, MI B
Millikin U, IL B
Minnesota State U Mankato, MN B
Minnesota State U Moorhead, MN B
Missouri Southern State U, MO B
Missouri State U, MO B
Monmouth Coll, IL B
Morningside Coll, IA B
Mount Marty Coll, SD B
Mount Union Coll, OH B
Mount Vernon Nazarene U, OH B
Muskingum Coll, OH B
National-Louis U, IL B
Nebraska Wesleyan U, NE B
North Central Coll, IL B
North Dakota State U, ND B
Northeastern State U, OK B

A—associate degree; B—bachelor's degree

Northern Michigan U, MI	B
Northern State U, SD	B
North Park U, IL	B
Northwestern Coll, MN	B
Northwestern U, IL	B
Northwest Missouri State U, MO	B
Oakland U, MI	B
Oberlin Coll, OH	B
Ohio Northern U, OH	B
The Ohio State U, OH	B
Ohio U, OH	B
Ohio Wesleyan U, OH	B
Oklahoma Baptist U, OK	B
Oklahoma Christian U, OK	B
Oklahoma City U, OK	B
Oklahoma State U, OK	B
Olivet Coll, MI	B
Oral Roberts U, OK	B
Otterbein Coll, OH	B
Park U, MO	B
Purdue U, IN	B
Ripon Coll, WI	B
Rockford Coll, IL	B
Roosevelt U, IL	B
Saginaw Valley State U, MI	B
St. Ambrose U, IA	B
St. Catherine U, MN	B
St. Cloud State U, MN	B
Saint John's U, MN	B
Saint Joseph's Coll, IN	B
Saint Louis U, MO	B
Saint Mary-of-the-Woods Coll, IN	B
Saint Mary's Coll, IN	B
Saint Mary's U of Minnesota, MN	B
St. Norbert Coll, WI	B
St. Olaf Coll, MN	B
Shawnee State U, OH	B
Siena Heights U, MI	B
Simpson Coll, IA	B
Southeastern Oklahoma State U, OK	B
Southeast Missouri State U, MO	B
Southern Illinois U Carbondale, IL	B
Southern Illinois U Edwardsville, IL	B
Southern Methodist U, TX	B
Southwest Baptist U, MO	B
Southwest Minnesota State U, MN	B
Spring Arbor U, MI	B
Stephens Coll, MO	B
Sterling Coll, KS	B
Taylor U, IN	B
Transylvania U, KY	B
Truman State U, MO	B
The U of Akron, OH	B
U of Central Missouri, MO	B
U of Central Oklahoma, OK	B
U of Cincinnati, OH	B
U of Dallas, TX	B
U of Dayton, OH	B
U of Evansville, IN	B
The U of Findlay, OH	B
U of Illinois at Chicago, IL	B
U of Illinois at Urbana–Champaign, IL	B
U of Indianapolis, IN	B
The U of Iowa, IA	B
The U of Kansas, KS	B
U of Michigan, MI	B
U of Michigan–Flint, MI	B
U of Minnesota, Duluth, MN	B
U of Minnesota, Morris, MN	B
U of Minnesota, Twin Cities Campus, MN	B
U of Missouri–Columbia, MO	B
U of Missouri–Kansas City, MO	B
U of Missouri–St. Louis, MO	B
U of Nebraska at Kearney, NE	B
U of Nebraska at Omaha, NE	B
U of Nebraska–Lincoln, NE	B
U of North Dakota, ND	B
U of Northern Iowa, IA	B
U of Notre Dame, IN	B
U of Oklahoma, OK	B
U of Saint Mary, KS	B
U of Science and Arts of Oklahoma, OK	B
The U of South Dakota, SD	B
U of Southern Indiana, IN	B
The U of Toledo, OH	B
U of Tulsa, OK	B
U of Wisconsin–Eau Claire, WI	B
U of Wisconsin–Green Bay, WI	B
U of Wisconsin–La Crosse, WI	B
U of Wisconsin–Madison, WI	B
U of Wisconsin–Milwaukee, WI	B
U of Wisconsin–Oshkosh, WI	B
U of Wisconsin–Parkside, WI	B
U of Wisconsin–Stevens Point, WI	B
U of Wisconsin–Superior, WI	B
U of Wisconsin–Whitewater, WI	B
Valparaiso U, IN	B
Viterbo U, WI	B
Wabash Coll, IN	B
Waldorf Coll, IA	B
Washburn U, KS	B
Washington U in St. Louis, MO	B
Wayne State Coll, NE	B
Wayne State U, MI	B
Webster U, MO	B
Western Illinois U, IL	B
Wichita State U, KS	B
William Jewell Coll, MO	B
Wilmington Coll, OH	B
Winona State U, MN	B
Wittenberg U, OH	B
Wright State U, OH	B

Dramatic/Theater Arts and Stagecraft Related

Baldwin-Wallace Coll, OH	B
Bowling Green State U, OH	B
DePaul U, IL	B
Drake U, IA	B
Indiana U South Bend, IN	B
Nebraska Wesleyan U, NE	B
North Central Coll, IL	B
Oakland U, MI	B
Ohio U, OH	B
St. Cloud State U, MN	B
Southwest Minnesota State U, MN	B
U of Michigan–Flint, MI	B

Drawing

Aquinas Coll, MI	B
Art Academy of Cincinnati, OH	B
Bethany Coll, KS	B
Bradley U, IL	B
The Cleveland Inst of Art, OH	B
Coll of Visual Arts, MN	B
Columbia Coll, MO	B
Drake U, IA	B
Grace Coll, IN	B
Indiana U–Purdue U Fort Wayne, IN	B
Lewis U, IL	B
Lindenwood U, MO	B
Minneapolis Coll of Art and Design, MN	B
Minnesota State U Mankato, MN	B
Northern Michigan U, MI	B
Northwest Missouri State U, MO	B
Oakland U, MI	B
Ohio U, OH	B
St. Cloud State U, MN	B
Shawnee State U, OH	B
Trinity Christian Coll, IL	B
The U of Iowa, IA	B
U of Michigan, MI	B
U of Missouri–St. Louis, MO	B
The U of Toledo, OH	B
Washington U in St. Louis, MO	B
Winona State U, MN	B
Wright State U, OH	B

Driver and Safety Teacher Education

U of Northern Iowa, IA	B

Early Childhood Education

Alma Coll, MI	B
Bacone Coll, OK	B
Baker Coll of Allen Park, MI	A
Baker Coll of Jackson, MI	A
Baldwin-Wallace Coll, OH	B
Bethel Coll, IN	A
Bradley U, IL	B
Brown Mackie Coll–Michigan City, IN	A
Brown Mackie Coll–South Bend, IN	A
Butler U, IN	B
Capital U, OH	B
Carroll U, WI	B
Cedarville U, OH	B
Central Methodist U, MO	B
Central Michigan U, MI	B
Cleveland State U, OH	B
Coll of Mount St. Joseph, OH	B
Coll of Saint Mary, NE	A,B
Coll of the Ozarks, MO	B
Concordia U, MI	B
Concordia U, Nebraska, NE	B
Concordia U, St. Paul, MN	B
Cornerstone U, MI	B
DePaul U, IL	B
Evangel U, MO	B
Ferris State U, MI	B
Grace Bible Coll, MI	B
Great Lakes Christian Coll, MI	A
Greenville Coll, IL	B
Hannibal-LaGrange Coll, MO	B
Harris-Stowe State U, MO	B
Hillsdale Coll, MI	B
Illinois Coll, IL	B
Illinois State U, IL	B
Indiana U Kokomo, IN	B
Indiana U–Purdue U Fort Wayne, IN	A
Indiana U–Purdue U Indianapolis, IN	A,B
Indiana U South Bend, IN	A
Kendall Coll, IL	B
Lake Superior State U, MI	A,B
Lincoln U, MO	A,B
Loras Coll, IA	B
Loyola U Chicago, IL	B
Madonna U, MI	B
Malone U, OH	B
Maranatha Baptist Bible Coll, WI	B
Marian U, WI	B
Martin U, IN	B
Mayville State U, ND	B
Miami U, OH	B
Miami U Hamilton, OH	B
Millikin U, IL	B
Missouri State U, MO	B
Mount Union Coll, OH	B
Mount Vernon Nazarene U, OH	B
Muskingum Coll, OH	B
Northeastern Illinois U, IL	B
Northeastern State U, OK	B
North Park U, IL	B
Northwestern Coll, MN	B
Ohio Dominican U, OH	B
Ohio Northern U, OH	B
The Ohio State U at Lima, OH	B
The Ohio State U at Marion, OH	B
The Ohio State U–Mansfield Campus, OH	B
The Ohio State U–Newark Campus, OH	B
Ohio U, OH	B
Ohio U–Chillicothe, OH	B
Ohio U–Eastern, OH	B
Ohio U–Lancaster, OH	B
Ohio U–Southern Campus, OH	A,B
Ohio Wesleyan U, OH	B
Oklahoma Baptist U, OK	B
Oklahoma Christian U, OK	B
Oklahoma State U, Oklahoma City, OK	A
Oral Roberts U, OK	B
Park U, MO	B
Pittsburg State U, KS	B
Presentation Coll, SD	A
Purdue U, IN	B

Purdue U North Central, IN B
Ripon Coll, WI B
Roosevelt U, IL B
St. Ambrose U, IA B
St. Augustine Coll, IL A
Shawnee State U, OH B
Sinte Gleska U, SD A,B
South Dakota State U, SD B
Southern Illinois U Carbondale, IL B
Southern Illinois U Edwardsville, IL B
Southern Nazarene U, OK B
Southwest Baptist U, MO B
Southwestern Coll, KS B
Stephens Coll, MO B
Taylor U, IN A
U of Cincinnati, OH A,B
U of Illinois at Urbana–Champaign, IL B
The U of Kansas, KS B
U of Mary, ND B
U of Michigan–Dearborn, MI B
U of Michigan–Flint, MI B
U of Minnesota, Crookston, MN B
U of Missouri–Columbia, MO B
U of Missouri–Kansas City, MO B
U of Missouri–St. Louis, MO B
U of New Orleans, LA B
U of North Dakota, ND B
U of Oklahoma, OK B
U of Science and Arts of Oklahoma, OK B
U of Southern Indiana, IN B
U of Tulsa, OK B
U of Wisconsin–Stout, WI B
U of Wisconsin–Whitewater, WI B
Ursuline Coll, OH B
Waldorf Coll, IA B
Walsh U, OH B
Washburn U, KS A
Wayne State Coll, NE B
Youngstown State U, OH B

East Asian Languages

Indiana U Bloomington, IN B
Miami U, OH B
U of Illinois at Urbana–Champaign, IL B
The U of Kansas, KS B

East Asian Languages Related

Michigan State U, MI B
Northwestern U, IL B
Washington U in St. Louis, MO B

Ecology

Bemidji State U, MN B
Bowling Green State U, OH B
Clarkson U, NY B
Defiance Coll, OH B
Eastern Illinois U, IL B
Iowa State U of Science and Technology, IA B
Kent State U, OH B
Lawrence U, WI B
Manchester Coll, IN B
Michigan Technological U, MI B
Minnesota State U Mankato, MN B
Northern Michigan U, MI B
Northland Coll, WI B
Northwestern U, IL B
Northwest Missouri State U, MO B
Oberlin Coll, OH B
Olivet Nazarene U, IL B
St. Cloud State U, MN B
The U of Akron, OH B
U of Illinois at Urbana–Champaign, IL B
U of Michigan, MI B
U of Michigan–Flint, MI B
U of Minnesota, Twin Cities Campus, MN B
U of Northern Iowa, IA B
U of Rio Grande, OH B
U of Wisconsin–Milwaukee, WI B
Winona State U, MN B

Ecology, Evolution, Systematics and Population Biology Related

The Ohio State U, OH B

E-Commerce

Bacone Coll, OK B
Clarkson U, NY B
DePaul U, IL B
Friends U, KS B
Maryville U of Saint Louis, MO B
U of Phoenix–Chicago Campus, IL B
U of Phoenix–Cleveland Campus, OH B
U of Phoenix–Indianapolis Campus, IN B
U of Phoenix–Kansas City Campus, MO B
U of Phoenix–Metro Detroit Campus, MI B
U of Phoenix–St. Louis Campus, MO B
U of Phoenix–West Michigan Campus, MI B
U of Phoenix–Wisconsin Campus, WI B
Western Michigan U, MI B
Westwood Coll–Chicago Du Page, IL B

Econometrics and Quantitative Economics

Miami U Hamilton, OH B
Southern Methodist U, TX B

Economics

Adrian Coll, MI B
Albion Coll, MI B
Alma Coll, MI B
Andrews U, MI B
Aquinas Coll, MI B
Ashland U, OH B
Augsburg Coll, MN B
Augustana Coll, IL B
Augustana Coll, SD B
Baker U, KS B
Baldwin-Wallace Coll, OH B
Ball State U, IN B
Beloit Coll, WI B
Bemidji State U, MN B
Benedictine Coll, KS B
Benedictine U, IL B
Bethel U, MN B
Bluffton U, OH B
Bowling Green State U, OH B
Bradley U, IL B
Butler U, IN B
Calvin Coll, MI B
Capital U, OH B
Carleton Coll, MN B
Case Western Reserve U, OH B
Central Christian Coll of Kansas, KS A
Central Coll, IA B
Central Methodist U, MO B
Central Michigan U, MI B
Central State U, OH B
Chancellor U, OH B
Clarke Coll, IA B
Cleveland State U, OH B
Coe Coll, IA B
Coll of Saint Benedict, MN B
The Coll of Wooster, OH B
Concordia Coll, MN B
Concordia U Wisconsin, WI B
Cornell Coll, IA B
Creighton U, NE B
Denison U, OH B
DePaul U, IL B
DePauw U, IN B
Doane Coll, NE B
Dominican U, IL B
Drury U, MO B
Earlham Coll, IN B
Eastern Illinois U, IL B
Eastern Michigan U, MI B
Edgewood Coll, WI B
Elmhurst Coll, IL B
Emporia State U, KS B
Fort Hays State U, KS B
Franciscan U of Steubenville, OH B
Franklin Coll, IN B
Graceland U, IA B
Grand Valley State U, MI B
Gustavus Adolphus Coll, MN B
Hamline U, MN B
Hanover Coll, IN B
Heidelberg U, OH B
Hillsdale Coll, MI B
Hiram Coll, OH B
Hope Coll, MI B
Huntington U, IN B
Illinois Coll, IL B
Illinois State U, IL B
Illinois Wesleyan U, IL B
Indiana State U, IN B
Indiana U Bloomington, IN B
Indiana U Northwest, IN B
Indiana U–Purdue U Fort Wayne, IN B
Indiana U–Purdue U Indianapolis, IN B
Indiana U South Bend, IN B
Indiana U Southeast, IN B
Indiana Wesleyan U, IN B
Iowa State U of Science and Technology, IA B
John Carroll U, OH B
Kansas State U, KS B
Kent State U, OH B
Kenyon Coll, OH B
Knox Coll, IL B
Lake Forest Coll, IL B
Lawrence U, WI B
Lewis U, IL B
Lincoln U, MO B
Lindenwood U, MO B
Loras Coll, IA B
Luther Coll, IA B
Macalester Coll, MN B
Manchester Coll, IN B
Marian U, IN B
Marietta Coll, OH B
Marquette U, WI B
McKendree U, IL B
Miami U, OH B
Miami U Hamilton, OH B
Michigan State U, MI B
Michigan Technological U, MI B
Minnesota State U Mankato, MN B
Minnesota State U Moorhead, MN B
Minot State U, ND B
Missouri State U, MO B
Missouri U of Science and Technology, MO B
Missouri Western State U, MO B
Monmouth Coll, IL B
Mount Union Coll, OH B
Muskingum Coll, OH B
Nebraska Wesleyan U, NE B
North Central Coll, IL B
North Dakota State U, ND B
Northeastern Illinois U, IL B
Northern Michigan U, MI B
Northern State U, SD B
North Park U, IL B
Northwestern U, IL B
Northwest Missouri State U, MO B
Oakland U, MI B
Oberlin Coll, OH B
Ohio Dominican U, OH B
The Ohio State U, OH B
Ohio U, OH B
Ohio Wesleyan U, OH B
Oklahoma State U, OK B
Oklahoma State U, Oklahoma City, OK A
Olivet Nazarene U, IL B
Otterbein Coll, OH B
Park U, MO B
Pittsburg State U, KS B
Purdue U Calumet, IN B
Ripon Coll, WI B
Rockford Coll, IL B
Rockhurst U, MO B
Roosevelt U, IL B
Rose-Hulman Inst of Technology, IN B
Saginaw Valley State U, MI B
St. Ambrose U, IA B
St. Catherine U, MN B

A—associate degree; B—bachelor's degree

St. Cloud State U, MN B
Saint John's U, MN B
Saint Joseph's Coll, IN B
Saint Louis U, MO B
Saint Mary's Coll, IN B
St. Norbert Coll, WI B
St. Olaf Coll, MN B
Simpson Coll, IA B
South Dakota State U, SD B
Southeast Missouri State U, MO B
Southern Illinois U Carbondale, IL B
Southern Illinois U Edwardsville, IL B
Southern Methodist U, TX B
Taylor U, IN B
Transylvania U, KY B
Truman State U, MO B
The U of Akron, OH B
U of Central Missouri, MO B
U of Central Oklahoma, OK B
U of Chicago, IL B
U of Cincinnati, OH B
U of Dallas, TX B
U of Dayton, OH B
U of Evansville, IN B
The U of Findlay, OH B
U of Illinois at Chicago, IL B
U of Illinois at Springfield, IL B
U of Illinois at Urbana–Champaign, IL B
The U of Iowa, IA B
The U of Kansas, KS B
U of Michigan, MI B
U of Michigan–Dearborn, MI B
U of Michigan–Flint, MI B
U of Minnesota, Duluth, MN B
U of Minnesota, Morris, MN B
U of Minnesota, Twin Cities Campus, MN B
U of Missouri–Columbia, MO B
U of Missouri–Kansas City, MO B
U of Missouri–St. Louis, MO B
U of Nebraska at Kearney, NE B
U of Nebraska at Omaha, NE B
U of Nebraska–Lincoln, NE B
U of New Orleans, LA B
U of North Dakota, ND B
U of Northern Iowa, IA B
U of Notre Dame, IN B
U of Oklahoma, OK B
U of Rio Grande, OH B
U of Science and Arts of Oklahoma, OK B
The U of South Dakota, SD B
U of Southern Indiana, IN B
The U of Toledo, OH B
U of Tulsa, OK B
U of Wisconsin–Eau Claire, WI B
U of Wisconsin–Green Bay, WI B
U of Wisconsin–La Crosse, WI B
U of Wisconsin–Milwaukee, WI B
U of Wisconsin–Oshkosh, WI B
U of Wisconsin–Parkside, WI B
U of Wisconsin–Platteville, WI B
U of Wisconsin–Stevens Point, WI B
U of Wisconsin–Superior, WI B
U of Wisconsin–Whitewater, WI B
Valparaiso U, IN B
Wabash Coll, IN B
Wartburg Coll, IA B
Washburn U, KS B
Washington U in St. Louis, MO B
Wayne State U, MI B
Webster U, MO B
Western Illinois U, IL B
Western Michigan U, MI B
Westminster Coll, MO B
Wheaton Coll, IL B
Wichita State U, KS B
William Jewell Coll, MO B
Wilmington Coll, OH B
Winona State U, MN B
Wittenberg U, OH B
Wright State U, OH B
Xavier U, OH B
Youngstown State U, OH B

Economics Related

Eastern Michigan U, MI B
The U of Akron, OH B
U of Illinois at Urbana–Champaign, IL B
Valparaiso U, IN B
Wright State U, OH B

Education

Adrian Coll, MI B
Albion Coll, MI B
Alma Coll, MI B
Anderson U, IN B
Andrews U, MI B
Aquinas Coll, MI B
Ashland U, OH B
Augsburg Coll, MN B
Augustana Coll, IL B
Bacone Coll, OK A,B
Baker Coll of Auburn Hills, MI A
Baker Coll of Cadillac, MI A
Baldwin-Wallace Coll, OH B
Ball State U, IN B
Beloit Coll, WI B
Bemidji State U, MN B
Benedictine U, IL B
Bethany Coll, KS B
Bethel Coll, IN B
Bowling Green State U, OH B
Briar Cliff U, IA B
Cameron U, OK B
Carroll U, WI B
Central Methodist U, MO B
Cincinnati Christian U, OH A,B
Clarke Coll, IA B
Cleveland State U, OH B
Coe Coll, IA B
Coll of Saint Benedict, MN B
Coll of Saint Mary, NE B
Coll of the Ozarks, MO B
Concordia Coll, MN B
Concordia U Chicago, IL B
Concordia U, Nebraska, NE B
Concordia U, St. Paul, MN B
Concordia U Wisconsin, WI B
Cornerstone U, MI B
Dakota Wesleyan U, SD B
Dana Coll, NE B
Defiance Coll, OH B
Dordt Coll, IA B
Drury U, MO B
Elmhurst Coll, IL B
Eureka Coll, IL B
Fontbonne U, MO B
Graceland U, IA B
Gustavus Adolphus Coll, MN B
Hamline U, MN B
Hannibal-LaGrange Coll, MO B
Heidelberg U, OH B
Hillsdale Coll, MI B
Hiram Coll, OH B
Huntington U, IN B
Illinois Coll, IL B
Illinois Wesleyan U, IL B
Indiana U–Purdue U Fort Wayne, IN B
Indiana U–Purdue U Indianapolis, IN B
Indiana U South Bend, IN B
Indiana Wesleyan U, IN B
Iowa State U of Science and Technology, IA B
Iowa Wesleyan Coll, IA B
John Carroll U, OH B
Kansas Wesleyan U, KS B
Kendall Coll, IL B
Kent State U, OH A,B
Kent State U, Salem Campus, OH A
Kent State U, Stark Campus, OH A
Knox Coll, IL B
Lake Forest Coll, IL B
Lake Superior State U, MI B
Lindenwood U, MO B
Loras Coll, IA B
Manchester Coll, IN B
Maranatha Baptist Bible Coll, WI B
Marian U, IN B
Marietta Coll, OH B
Marquette U, WI B
Mayville State U, ND B
Minnesota State U Mankato, MN B
Missouri Southern State U, MO B
Morningside Coll, IA B
Mount Marty Coll, SD B
Mount Mary Coll, WI B
Mount Vernon Nazarene U, OH B
Muskingum Coll, OH B
Newman U, KS B
North Central Coll, IL B
Northeastern State U, OK B
Northern Michigan U, MI B
Northern State U, SD B
Northland Coll, WI B
Northwestern U, IL B
Northwest Missouri State U, MO B
Ohio Christian U, OH A,B
Ohio Northern U, OH B
Ohio U, OH B
Ohio U–Lancaster, OH B
Ohio Wesleyan U, OH B
Oklahoma Baptist U, OK B
Oklahoma City U, OK B
Oklahoma State U, OK B
Oral Roberts U, OK B
Otterbein Coll, OH B
Purdue U, IN B
Purdue U Calumet, IN B
Ripon Coll, WI B
Rockford Coll, IL B
Rockhurst U, MO B
St. Ambrose U, IA B
St. Catherine U, MN B
St. Cloud State U, MN B
Saint John's U, MN B
Saint Mary-of-the-Woods Coll, IN B
Saint Mary's Coll, IN B
Shawnee State U, OH B
Sinte Gleska U, SD A
Southeastern Oklahoma State U, OK B
Southeast Missouri State U, MO B
Southern Nazarene U, OK B
Southwestern Oklahoma State U, OK B
Southwest Minnesota State U, MN B
Trine U, IN B
Trinity Christian Coll, IL B
Trinity International U, IL B
Union Coll, NE B
Union Inst & U, OH B
U of Central Missouri, MO B
U of Charleston, WV B
U of Cincinnati, OH B
U of Dallas, TX B
U of Dayton, OH B
U of Evansville, IN B
The U of Findlay, OH B
U of Indianapolis, IN B
U of Michigan–Dearborn, MI B
U of Minnesota, Duluth, MN B
U of Minnesota, Morris, MN B
U of Minnesota, Twin Cities Campus, MN B
U of Missouri–Columbia, MO B
U of Missouri–St. Louis, MO B
U of Rio Grande, OH B
U of Saint Francis, IN B
U of Saint Mary, KS B
U of Sioux Falls, SD B
The U of South Dakota, SD B
U of Southern Indiana, IN B
The U of Toledo, OH B
U of Tulsa, OK B
U of Wisconsin–Green Bay, WI B
U of Wisconsin–Milwaukee, WI B
U of Wisconsin–Oshkosh, WI B
U of Wisconsin–Platteville, WI B
U of Wisconsin–Stevens Point, WI B

U of Wisconsin–Superior, WI B
U of Wisconsin–Whitewater, WI B
Valley City State U, ND B
Viterbo U, WI B
Waldorf Coll, IA B
Walsh U, OH B
Washburn U, KS B
Washington U in St. Louis, MO B
Webster U, MO B
Wilmington Coll, OH B
Winona State U, MN B
Wittenberg U, OH B
Wright State U, OH B
Xavier U, OH B
York Coll, NE B
Youngstown State U, OH B

Educational Administration and Supervision Related
Kendall Coll, IL B

Educational, Instructional, and Curriculum Supervision
Wright State U, OH B

Educational/Instructional Media Design
American InterContinental U Online, IL B
Lindenwood U, MO B
St. Cloud State U, MN B
U of Central Oklahoma, OK B
The U of Toledo, OH B
Western Illinois U, IL B

Educational Leadership and Administration
Cleveland State U, OH B
Kendall Coll, IL B
Lindenwood U, MO B
Northwest Missouri State U, MO B
Ohio U, OH B
Oral Roberts U, OK B
St. Cloud State U, MN B
U of Central Oklahoma, OK B
U of Illinois at Springfield, IL B
U of Wisconsin–Superior, WI B
Wright State U, OH B

Educational Psychology
DePaul U, IL B

Educational System Administration and Superintendency
Dordt Coll, IA B

Education (K–12)
Adrian Coll, MI B
Augustana Coll, SD B
Coll of Saint Mary, NE B
The Coll of St. Scholastica, MN B
Dominican U, IL B
Dordt Coll, IA B
Graceland U, IA B
Grace U, NE B
Hamline U, MN B
Hillsdale Coll, MI B
Illinois Coll, IL B
Indiana Wesleyan U, IN B
John Carroll U, OH B
Lake Erie Coll, OH B
Lindenwood U, MO B
McKendree U, IL B
Ohio Dominican U, OH B
Ohio Wesleyan U, OH B
St. Ambrose U, IA B
St. Cloud State U, MN A,B
Saint Mary-of-the-Woods Coll, IN B
Trinity International U, IL B
U of Minnesota, Morris, MN B
Washington U in St. Louis, MO B

Education (Multiple Levels)
Central State U, OH B
Concordia U Wisconsin, WI B
Dakota Wesleyan U, SD B
Indiana U Bloomington, IN B
Lake Superior State U, MI B
Martin Luther Coll, MN B
Miami U Hamilton, OH B
Ohio Northern U, OH B
Ohio Wesleyan U, OH B
Saint Louis U, MO B
Shawnee State U, OH B
U of Illinois at Urbana–Champaign, IL B
U of Nebraska–Lincoln, NE B
U of Rio Grande, OH B
Waldorf Coll, IA B
William Jewell Coll, MO B
Wright State U, OH B
York Coll, NE B

Education Related
Bowling Green State U, OH B
Cedarville U, OH B
Central State U, OH B
Cleveland State U, OH B
Concordia U, St. Paul, MN B
DePaul U, IL B
Edgewood Coll, WI B
Ferris State U, MI B
Grace Coll, IN B
Kendall Coll, IL B
Madonna U, MI B
Messenger Coll, MO B
Northern Michigan U, MI B
Ohio Northern U, OH B
Park U, MO B
Saginaw Valley State U, MI B
The U of Akron, OH A
Wayne State U, MI B
Wright State U, OH B

Education (Specific Levels and Methods) Related
Bradley U, IL B
Kendall Coll, IL B
St. Cloud State U, MN B
The U of Toledo, OH B
Washington U in St. Louis, MO B
Wright State U, OH B
Xavier U, OH B

Education (Specific Subject Areas) Related
Avila U, MO B
Bowling Green State U, OH B
Bradley U, IL B
Central Michigan U, MI B
DePaul U, IL B
Eastern Michigan U, MI B
Hope Coll, MI B
Indiana U Bloomington, IN B
Madonna U, MI B
Minot State U, ND B
Missouri State U, MO B
Ohio U, OH B
The U of Akron, OH B
U of Central Oklahoma, OK B
U of Michigan–Flint, MI B
U of Nebraska–Lincoln, NE B
U of New Orleans, LA B
The U of Toledo, OH B
U of Wisconsin–Eau Claire, WI B
Wayne State Coll, NE B
Wright State U, OH B

Electrical and Electronic Engineering Technologies Related
Lawrence Technological U, MI A
Miami U Hamilton, OH A
Northern Michigan U, MI B
Southern Illinois U Carbondale, IL B
Youngstown State U, OH A

Electrical and Power Transmission Installation
Oklahoma State U, Oklahoma City, OK A

Electrical, Electronic and Communications Engineering Technology
Baker Coll of Cadillac, MI A
Baker Coll of Owosso, MI A,B
Bowling Green State U, OH B
Cameron U, OK A,B
Central Michigan U, MI B
Cleveland State U, OH B
DeVry U, Addison, IL A,B
DeVry U, Chicago, IL A,B
DeVry U, Tinley Park, IL A,B
DeVry U, Indianapolis, IN A
DeVry U, Edina, MN A
DeVry U, Kansas City, MO A,B
DeVry U, Columbus, OH A,B
Eastern Michigan U, MI B
East-West U, IL B
Ferris State U, MI B
Grantham U, MO A,B
Hamilton Tech Coll, IA A,B
Indiana State U, IN A,B
Indiana U–Purdue U Fort Wayne, IN A,B
Indiana U–Purdue U Indianapolis, IN A,B
ITT Tech Inst, Burr Ridge, IL B
ITT Tech Inst, Mount Prospect, IL B
ITT Tech Inst, Orland Park, IL B
ITT Tech Inst, Fort Wayne, IN B
ITT Tech Inst, Indianapolis, IN B
ITT Tech Inst, South Bend, IN B
ITT Tech Inst, IA B
ITT Tech Inst, Canton, MI B
ITT Tech Inst, Grand Rapids, MI B
ITT Tech Inst, Troy, MI B
ITT Tech Inst, MN B
ITT Tech Inst, Arnold, MO B
ITT Tech Inst, Earth City, MO B
ITT Tech Inst, Kansas City, MO B
ITT Tech Inst, NE B
ITT Tech Inst, Oklahoma City, OK B
ITT Tech Inst, Tulsa, OK B
ITT Tech Inst, Green Bay, WI B
ITT Tech Inst, Greenfield, WI B
ITT Tech Inst, Madison, WI B
Kansas State U, KS B
Lake Superior State U, MI A,B
Lawrence Technological U, MI A
Miami U, OH A
Michigan Technological U, MI A,B
Milwaukee School of Engineering, WI B
Minnesota State U Mankato, MN B
Missouri Western State U, MO A,B
Oglala Lakota Coll, SD A
Ohio U, OH A
Oklahoma State U, OK B
Oklahoma State U, Oklahoma City, OK A
Pittsburg State U, KS A,B
Purdue U Calumet, IN A,B
Purdue U North Central, IN A
Rochester Comm and Tech Coll, MN A
St. Cloud State U, MN B
Saint Louis U, MO B
South Dakota State U, SD B
The U of Akron, OH A,B
U of Central Missouri, MO B
U of Cincinnati, OH A,B
U of Dayton, OH B
The U of Toledo, OH A,B
Wayne State U, MI B
Wright State U, OH A
Youngstown State U, OH A,B

Electrical, Electronics and Communications Engineering
Bradley U, IL B
Calvin Coll, MI B
Case Western Reserve U, OH B
Cedarville U, OH B
Central Michigan U, MI B
Clarkson U, NY B
Cleveland State U, OH B
Dominican U, IL B
Dordt Coll, IA B

A—associate degree; B—bachelor's degree

East-West U, IL B
Illinois Inst of Technology, IL B
Indiana Tech, IN B
Indiana U–Purdue U Fort Wayne, IN B
Indiana U–Purdue U Indianapolis, IN B
Iowa State U of Science and Technology, IA B
Kansas State U, KS B
Kettering U, MI B
Lake Superior State U, MI B
Lawrence Technological U, MI B
Marquette U, WI B
Miami U, OH B
Michigan State U, MI B
Michigan Technological U, MI B
Milwaukee School of Engineering, WI B
Minnesota State U Mankato, MN B
Missouri Tech, MO A,B
Missouri U of Science and Technology, MO B
North Dakota State U, ND B
Northwestern U, IL B
Oakland U, MI B
Ohio Northern U, OH B
The Ohio State U, OH B
Ohio U, OH B
Oklahoma Christian U, OK B
Oklahoma State U, OK B
Oral Roberts U, OK B
Purdue U, IN B
Purdue U Calumet, IN B
Rose-Hulman Inst of Technology, IN B
Saginaw Valley State U, MI B
St. Cloud State U, MN B
Saint Louis U, MO B
South Dakota School of Mines and Technology, SD B
South Dakota State U, SD B
Southern Illinois U Carbondale, IL B
Southern Illinois U Edwardsville, IL B
Southern Methodist U, TX B
Trine U, IN B
The U of Akron, OH B
U of Dayton, OH B
U of Evansville, IN B
U of Illinois at Chicago, IL B
U of Illinois at Urbana–Champaign, IL B
The U of Iowa, IA B
The U of Kansas, KS B
U of Michigan, MI B
U of Michigan–Dearborn, MI B
U of Minnesota, Duluth, MN B
U of Minnesota, Twin Cities Campus, MN B
U of Missouri–Columbia, MO B
U of Missouri–Kansas City, MO B
U of Missouri–St. Louis, MO B
U of Nebraska–Lincoln, NE B
U of New Orleans, LA B
U of North Dakota, ND B
U of Notre Dame, IN B
U of Oklahoma, OK B
The U of Toledo, OH B
U of Tulsa, OK B
U of Wisconsin–Madison, WI B
U of Wisconsin–Milwaukee, WI B
U of Wisconsin–Platteville, WI B
Valparaiso U, IN B
Washington U in St. Louis, MO B
Wayne State U, MI B
Western Michigan U, MI B
Wichita State U, KS B
Wilberforce U, OH B
Wright State U, OH B
Youngstown State U, OH B

Electrical/Electronics Equipment Installation and Repair

Sinte Gleska U, SD A

Electrocardiograph Technology

Argosy U, Twin Cities, MN A
Oklahoma State U, Oklahoma City, OK A

Electromechanical Technology

Bowling Green State U, OH B
Miami U Hamilton, OH B
Michigan Technological U, MI A
Northern Michigan U, MI A
Purdue U Calumet, IN A,B
Shawnee State U, OH A
U of Northern Iowa, IA B
The U of Toledo, OH B
Wayne State U, MI B
Wright State U, OH A

Electroneurodiagnostic/ Electroencephalographic Technology

Rochester Comm and Tech Coll, MN A

Elementary and Middle School Administration/Principalship

Ohio U, OH B

Elementary Education

Adrian Coll, MI B
Albion Coll, MI B
Alma Coll, MI B
Anderson U, IN B
Andrews U, MI B
Aquinas Coll, MI B
Ashland U, OH B
Augsburg Coll, MN B
Augustana Coll, IL B
Augustana Coll, SD B
Aurora U, IL B
Avila U, MO B
Bacone Coll, OK B
Baker U, KS B
Ball State U, IN B
Barclay Coll, KS B
Beloit Coll, WI B
Bemidji State U, MN B
Benedictine Coll, KS B
Benedictine U, IL B
Bethany Coll, KS B
Bethany Lutheran Coll, MN B
Bethel Coll, IN B
Bethel Coll, KS B
Bethel U, MN B
Black Hills State U, SD B
Bluffton U, OH B
Bradley U, IL B
Briar Cliff U, IA B
Buena Vista U, IA B
Butler U, IN B
Calumet Coll of Saint Joseph, IN B
Calvary Bible Coll and Theological Seminary, MO B
Calvin Coll, MI B
Cameron U, OK B
Carroll U, WI B
Central Christian Coll of Kansas, KS A
Central Coll, IA B
Central Methodist U, MO B
Central Michigan U, MI B
Clarke Coll, IA B
Cleveland State U, OH B
Coe Coll, IA B
Coll of Saint Benedict, MN B
Coll of Saint Mary, NE B
The Coll of St. Scholastica, MN B
Coll of the Ozarks, MO B
Concordia Coll, MN B
Concordia U, MI B
Concordia U Chicago, IL B
Concordia U, Nebraska, NE B
Concordia U, St. Paul, MN B
Concordia U Wisconsin, WI B
Cornell Coll, IA B
Cornerstone U, MI B
Creighton U, NE B
Crown Coll, MN B
Culver-Stockton Coll, MO B
Dakota State U, SD B
Dakota Wesleyan U, SD B
Dana Coll, NE B
Defiance Coll, OH B
DePaul U, IL B
DePauw U, IN B
Doane Coll, NE B
Dominican U, IL B
Dordt Coll, IA B
Drake U, IA B
Drury U, MO B
Eastern Illinois U, IL B
Eastern Michigan U, MI B
Edgewood Coll, WI B
Elmhurst Coll, IL B
Emmaus Bible Coll, IA B
Emporia State U, KS B
Eureka Coll, IL B
Evangel U, MO B
Faith Baptist Bible Coll and Theological Seminary, IA B
Ferris State U, MI A,B
Fontbonne U, MO B
Fort Hays State U, KS B
Franciscan U of Steubenville, OH B
Franklin Coll, IN B
Friends U, KS B
Goshen Coll, IN B
Grace Bible Coll, MI B
Grace Coll, IN B
Graceland U, IA B
Grace U, NE B
Grand Valley State U, MI B
Grand View U, IA B
Greenville Coll, IL B
Gustavus Adolphus Coll, MN B
Hamline U, MN B
Hannibal-LaGrange Coll, MO B
Harris-Stowe State U, MO B
Haskell Indian Nations U, KS B
Heidelberg U, OH B
Hillsdale Coll, MI B
Hope Coll, MI B
Huntington U, IN B
Illinois Coll, IL B
Illinois State U, IL B
Illinois Wesleyan U, IL B
Indiana State U, IN B
Indiana U Bloomington, IN B
Indiana U East, IN B
Indiana U Kokomo, IN B
Indiana U Northwest, IN B
Indiana U–Purdue U Fort Wayne, IN B
Indiana U–Purdue U Indianapolis, IN B
Indiana U South Bend, IN B
Indiana U Southeast, IN B
Indiana Wesleyan U, IN B
Iowa State U of Science and Technology, IA B
Iowa Wesleyan Coll, IA B
Jamestown Coll, ND B
John Carroll U, OH B
Kansas State U, KS B
Kansas Wesleyan U, KS B
Kendall Coll, IL B
Kuyper Coll, MI B
Lake Erie Coll, OH B
Lake Forest Coll, IL B
Lakeland Coll, WI B
Lake Superior State U, MI B
Lewis U, IL B
Lincoln U, MO B
Lindenwood U, MO B
Loras Coll, IA B
Loyola U Chicago, IL B
Luther Coll, IA B
MacMurray Coll, IL B
Manchester Coll, IN B
Maranatha Baptist Bible Coll, WI B
Marian U, WI B
Marian U, IN B
Marietta Coll, OH B
Marquette U, WI B
Martin Luther Coll, MN B
Maryville U of Saint Louis, MO B
Mayville State U, ND B
McKendree U, IL B
Michigan State U, MI B
Mid-America Christian U, OK B
MidAmerica Nazarene U, KS B
Millikin U, IL B
Minnesota State U Mankato, MN B

Minnesota State U Moorhead, MN B
Minot State U, ND B
Missouri Baptist U, MO B
Missouri Southern State U, MO B
Missouri State U, MO B
Missouri Western State U, MO B
Monmouth Coll, IL B
Morningside Coll, IA B
Mount Marty Coll, SD B
Mount Mary Coll, WI B
Mount Mercy Coll, IA B
Mount Vernon Nazarene U, OH B
National-Louis U, IL B
Nebraska Wesleyan U, NE B
Newman U, KS B
North Central Coll, IL B
North Central U, MN B
Northeastern Illinois U, IL B
Northeastern State U, OK B
Northern Michigan U, MI B
Northern State U, SD B
North Park U, IL B
Northwestern Coll, MN B
Northwest Missouri State U, MO B
Oakland U, MI B
Oglala Lakota Coll, SD A,B
Ohio Northern U, OH B
Ohio U, OH B
Ohio U–Zanesville, OH B
Ohio Wesleyan U, OH B
Oklahoma Baptist U, OK B
Oklahoma Christian U, OK B
Oklahoma City U, OK B
Oklahoma Panhandle State U, OK B
Oklahoma State U, OK B
Olivet Nazarene U, IL B
Oral Roberts U, OK B
Otterbein Coll, OH B
Park U, MO B
Pittsburg State U, KS B
Purdue U, IN B
Purdue U Calumet, IN B
Purdue U North Central, IN B
Quincy U, IL B
Ripon Coll, WI B
Rockford Coll, IL B
Rockhurst U, MO B
Rogers State U, OK A
Roosevelt U, IL B
Saginaw Valley State U, MI B
St. Ambrose U, IA B
St. Catherine U, MN B
St. Cloud State U, MN B
Saint John's U, MN B
Saint Joseph's Coll, IN B
Saint Mary-of-the-Woods Coll, IN B
Saint Mary's Coll, IN B
Saint Mary's U of Minnesota, MN B
St. Norbert Coll, WI B
Saint Xavier U, IL B
Shawnee State U, OH B
Siena Heights U, MI B
Silver Lake Coll, WI B
Simpson Coll, IA B
Sinte Gleska U, SD B
Southeastern Oklahoma State U, OK B
Southeast Missouri State U, MO B
Southern Illinois U Carbondale, IL B
Southern Illinois U Edwardsville, IL B
Southern Nazarene U, OK B
Southwest Baptist U, MO B
Southwestern Coll, KS B
Southwestern Oklahoma State U, OK B
Southwest Minnesota State U, MN B
Spring Arbor U, MI B
Stephens Coll, MO B
Sterling Coll, KS B
Taylor U, IN B
Temple Baptist Coll, OH B
Transylvania U, KY B
Trine U, IN B
Trinity Bible Coll, ND B
Trinity Christian Coll, IL B
Trinity International U, IL B
Union Coll, NE B
Union Inst & U, OH B
U of Central Missouri, MO B
U of Central Oklahoma, OK B
U of Charleston, WV B
U of Cincinnati, OH B
U of Dallas, TX B
U of Dayton, OH B
U of Evansville, IN B
The U of Findlay, OH B
U of Illinois at Chicago, IL B
U of Illinois at Urbana–Champaign, IL B
U of Indianapolis, IN B
The U of Iowa, IA B
The U of Kansas, KS B
U of Mary, ND B
U of Michigan, MI B
U of Michigan–Dearborn, MI B
U of Michigan–Flint, MI B
U of Minnesota, Duluth, MN B
U of Minnesota, Morris, MN B
U of Minnesota, Twin Cities Campus, MN B
U of Missouri–Columbia, MO B
U of Missouri–Kansas City, MO B
U of Missouri–St. Louis, MO B
U of Nebraska at Kearney, NE B
U of Nebraska–Lincoln, NE B
U of New Orleans, LA B
U of North Dakota, ND B
U of Northern Iowa, IA B
U of Oklahoma, OK B
U of Rio Grande, OH B
U of St. Francis, IL B
U of Saint Francis, IN B
U of Saint Mary, KS B
U of Science and Arts of Oklahoma, OK B
U of Sioux Falls, SD B
The U of South Dakota, SD B
U of Southern Indiana, IN B
The U of Toledo, OH B
U of Tulsa, OK B
U of Wisconsin–Eau Claire, WI B
U of Wisconsin–La Crosse, WI B
U of Wisconsin–Madison, WI B
U of Wisconsin–Milwaukee, WI B
U of Wisconsin–Oshkosh, WI B
U of Wisconsin–Platteville, WI B
U of Wisconsin–Stevens Point, WI B
U of Wisconsin–Superior, WI B
U of Wisconsin–Whitewater, WI B
Valley City State U, ND B
Valparaiso U, IN B
Viterbo U, WI B
Waldorf Coll, IA B
Wartburg Coll, IA B
Washburn U, KS B
Washington U in St. Louis, MO B
Wayne State Coll, NE B
Wayne State U, MI B
Webster U, MO B
Western Illinois U, IL B
Westminster Coll, MO B
Wheaton Coll, IL B
Wichita State U, KS B
William Jewell Coll, MO B
Wilmington Coll, OH B
Winona State U, MN B
Wright State U, OH B
Xavier U, OH B
York Coll, NE B
Youngstown State U, OH B

Emergency Medical Technology (EMT Paramedic)

Baker Coll of Cadillac, MI A
Baker Coll of Clinton Township, MI A
Baker Coll of Muskegon, MI A
Creighton U, NE A,B
Hannibal-LaGrange Coll, MO B
Indiana U–Purdue U Indianapolis, IN A
Indiana U South Bend, IN A
Indiana U Southeast, IN A
Mercy Coll of Health Sciences, IA A
Missouri Western State U, MO A
Oklahoma State U, Oklahoma City, OK A
Rochester Comm and Tech Coll, MN A
Rogers State U, OK A
Sanford-Brown Coll, Fenton, MO A
Shawnee State U, OH A
Southwest Baptist U, MO A
U of Minnesota, Twin Cities Campus, MN B
U of Sioux Falls, SD A,B
The U of Toledo, OH A
Youngstown State U, OH A

Energy Management and Systems Technology

Baker Coll of Flint, MI A
Ferris State U, MI B
U of Cincinnati, OH A
U of Rio Grande, OH A

Engineering

Ball State U, IN B
Beloit Coll, WI B
Bethany Lutheran Coll, MN B
Bethel Coll, IN B
Calvin Coll, MI B
Case Western Reserve U, OH B
Central Christian Coll of Kansas, KS A
Clarkson U, NY B
Cleveland State U, OH B
Concordia U, MI B
Dordt Coll, IA B
Drury U, MO B
Ferris State U, MI A
Grand Valley State U, MI B
Hope Coll, MI B
Indiana U–Purdue U Indianapolis, IN B
Iowa State U of Science and Technology, IA B
Kansas Wesleyan U, KS B
Lake Superior State U, MI A
Miami U, OH B
Michigan State U, MI B
Michigan Technological U, MI B
Milwaukee School of Engineering, WI B
Missouri U of Science and Technology, MO B
North Park U, IL B
Northwestern Coll, MN B
Northwestern U, IL B
Ohio Northern U, OH B
The Ohio State U, OH B
Ohio U, OH B
Oklahoma Christian U, OK B
Olivet Nazarene U, IL B
Oral Roberts U, OK B
Purdue U Calumet, IN B
St. Cloud State U, MN B
Union Coll, NE A
The U of Akron, OH B
U of Cincinnati, OH B
U of Illinois at Urbana–Champaign, IL B
The U of Iowa, IA B
U of Michigan, MI B
U of Oklahoma, OK B
U of Southern Indiana, IN B
The U of Toledo, OH B
U of Wisconsin–Madison, WI B
U of Wisconsin–Milwaukee, WI B
Wartburg Coll, IA B
Washington U in St. Louis, MO B
Winona State U, MN B

A—associate degree; B—bachelor's degree

Wright State U, OH B
Youngstown State U, OH B

Engineering/Industrial Management

Chancellor U, OH B
Eastern Michigan U, MI B
Illinois Inst of Technology, IL B
Lake Superior State U, MI B
Miami U, OH B
Miami U Hamilton, OH B
Missouri State U, MO B
Missouri Tech, MO B
Missouri U of Science and Technology, MO B
Saginaw Valley State U, MI B
Saint Louis U, MO B
South Dakota School of Mines and Technology, SD A,B
South Dakota State U, SD B
U of Illinois at Chicago, IL B
U of Minnesota, Crookston, MN B
U of Wisconsin–Stout, WI B
Western Michigan U, MI B

Engineering Mechanics

Cleveland State U, OH B
Dordt Coll, IA B
Michigan Technological U, MI B
U of Cincinnati, OH B
U of Illinois at Urbana–Champaign, IL B
U of Michigan–Flint, MI B
U of Wisconsin–Madison, WI B

Engineering Physics

Augustana Coll, IL B
Augustana Coll, SD B
Bemidji State U, MN B
Bradley U, IL B
Butler U, IN B
Carroll U, WI B
Case Western Reserve U, OH B
Coll of Saint Benedict, MN B
Eastern Michigan U, MI B
Hope Coll, MI B
John Carroll U, OH B
Kettering U, MI B
Loras Coll, IA B
Miami U, OH B
Miami U Hamilton, OH B
Michigan Technological U, MI B
Morningside Coll, IA B
Oakland U, MI B
The Ohio State U, OH B
Oral Roberts U, OK B
Rose-Hulman Inst of Technology, IN B
St. Ambrose U, IA B
Saint John's U, MN B
Saint Louis U, MO B
Saint Mary's U of Minnesota, MN B
South Dakota State U, SD B
Southeast Missouri State U, MO B
Southwestern Coll, KS B
Southwestern Oklahoma State U, OK B
Taylor U, IN B
U of Illinois at Chicago, IL B
U of Illinois at Urbana–Champaign, IL B
The U of Kansas, KS B
U of Michigan, MI B
U of Nebraska at Omaha, NE B
U of Northern Iowa, IA B
U of Oklahoma, OK B
The U of Toledo, OH B
U of Tulsa, OK B
U of Wisconsin–Madison, WI B
Wright State U, OH B

Engineering Related

Augustana Coll, IL B
Cleveland State U, OH B
Eastern Illinois U, IL B
Iowa State U of Science and Technology, IA B
Loras Coll, IA B
Marquette U, WI B
McNally Smith Coll of Music, MN A,B
Northern Michigan U, MI B
Northwestern U, IL B
Oakland U, MI B
Ohio Northern U, OH B
Ohio U, OH B
Ohio Wesleyan U, OH B
Park U, MO B
Purdue U, IN B
Rose-Hulman Inst of Technology, IN B
U of Michigan–Dearborn, MI B
U of Nebraska–Lincoln, NE B
Wheaton Coll, IL B
Wright State U, OH B

Engineering Science

Benedictine U, IL B
Bethel U, MN B
Cleveland State U, OH B
Iowa State U of Science and Technology, IA B
Manchester Coll, IN B
Muskingum Coll, OH B
Northwestern U, IL B
Ohio Wesleyan U, OH B
U of Cincinnati, OH A,B
U of Mary, ND B
U of Michigan, MI B
U of Michigan–Flint, MI B
Wright State U, OH B

Engineering Technologies Related

Ball State U, IN B
Cameron U, OK A,B
McNally Smith Coll of Music, MN A
Missouri Southern State U, MO A
Ohio U, OH B
Rogers State U, OK A,B

Engineering Technology

Cleveland State U, OH B
Dordt Coll, IA B
Eastern Michigan U, MI B
Grantham U, MO A,B
Kansas State U, KS A
Lake Superior State U, MI A
Lawrence Technological U, MI B
Miami U, OH A,B
Miami U Hamilton, OH B
Michigan Technological U, MI A
Missouri Tech, MO A
Northeastern State U, OK B
Oklahoma State U, Oklahoma City, OK A
Purdue U North Central, IN B
St. Cloud State U, MN A,B
Southeast Missouri State U, MO B
Southern Illinois U Carbondale, IL B
Southwestern Oklahoma State U, OK B
U of Wisconsin–Stout, WI B
Youngstown State U, OH A,B

English

Adrian Coll, MI B
Albion Coll, MI B
Alma Coll, MI B
Anderson U, IN B
Andrews U, MI B
Aquinas Coll, MI B
Ashland U, OH B
Augsburg Coll, MN B
Augustana Coll, IL B
Augustana Coll, SD B
Avila U, MO B
Baker U, KS B
Baldwin-Wallace Coll, OH B
Ball State U, IN B
Beloit Coll, WI B
Bemidji State U, MN B
Benedictine Coll, KS B
Benedictine U, IL B
Bethany Coll, KS B
Bethany Lutheran Coll, MN B
Bethel Coll, IN B
Bethel Coll, KS B
Bethel U, MN B
Black Hills State U, SD B
Bluffton U, OH B
Bowling Green State U, OH B
Bradley U, IL B
Briar Cliff U, IA B
Buena Vista U, IA B
Butler U, IN B
Calumet Coll of Saint Joseph, IN A,B
Calvin Coll, MI B
Cameron U, OK B
Capital U, OH B
Carleton Coll, MN B
Carroll U, WI B
Case Western Reserve U, OH B
Cedarville U, OH B
Central Christian Coll of Kansas, KS B
Central Coll, IA B
Central Methodist U, MO A,B
Central Michigan U, MI B
Central State U, OH B
Clarke Coll, IA B
Cleveland State U, OH B
Coe Coll, IA B
Coll of Mount St. Joseph, OH B
Coll of Saint Benedict, MN B
Coll of Saint Mary, NE B
The Coll of St. Scholastica, MN B
Coll of the Ozarks, MO B
The Coll of Wooster, OH B
Columbia Coll, MO B
Concordia Coll, MN B
Concordia U, MI B
Concordia U Chicago, IL B
Concordia U, Nebraska, NE B
Concordia U, St. Paul, MN B
Concordia U Wisconsin, WI B
Cornell Coll, IA B
Cornerstone U, MI B
Creighton U, NE B
Crown Coll, MN B
Culver-Stockton Coll, MO B
Dakota Wesleyan U, SD B
Dana Coll, NE B
Defiance Coll, OH B
Denison U, OH B
DePaul U, IL B
DePauw U, IN B
Doane Coll, NE B
Dominican U, IL B
Dordt Coll, IA B
Drake U, IA B
Drury U, MO B
Earlham Coll, IN B
Eastern Illinois U, IL B
Eastern Michigan U, MI B
East-West U, IL B
Edgewood Coll, WI B
Elmhurst Coll, IL B
Emporia State U, KS B
Eureka Coll, IL B
Evangel U, MO B
Fontbonne U, MO B
Fort Hays State U, KS B
Franciscan U of Steubenville, OH B
Franklin Coll, IN B
Friends U, KS B
Goshen Coll, IN B
Grace Coll, IN B
Graceland U, IA B
Grand Valley State U, MI B
Grand View U, IA B
Greenville Coll, IL B
Grinnell Coll, IA B
Gustavus Adolphus Coll, MN B
Hamline U, MN B
Hannibal-LaGrange Coll, MO A,B
Hanover Coll, IN B
Heidelberg U, OH B
Hillsdale Coll, MI B
Hiram Coll, OH B
Hope Coll, MI B
Huntington U, IN B
Illinois Coll, IL B
Illinois State U, IL B
Indiana State U, IN B
Indiana U Bloomington, IN B
Indiana U East, IN B
Indiana U Kokomo, IN B
Indiana U Northwest, IN B
Indiana U–Purdue U Fort Wayne, IN A,B

Indiana U–Purdue U Indianapolis, IN B
Indiana U South Bend, IN B
Indiana U Southeast, IN B
Indiana Wesleyan U, IN A,B
Iowa State U of Science and Technology, IA B
Iowa Wesleyan Coll, IA B
Jamestown Coll, ND B
John Carroll U, OH B
Kalamazoo Coll, MI B
Kansas State U, KS B
Kansas Wesleyan U, KS B
Kent State U, OH B
Kent State U, Stark Campus, OH B
Kenyon Coll, OH B
Knox Coll, IL B
Lake Erie Coll, OH B
Lake Forest Coll, IL B
Lakeland Coll, WI B
Lake Superior State U, MI B
Lawrence Technological U, MI B
Lawrence U, WI B
Lewis U, IL B
Lincoln U, MO B
Lindenwood U, MO B
Loras Coll, IA B
Lourdes Coll, OH A,B
Loyola U Chicago, IL B
Luther Coll, IA B
Macalester Coll, MN B
MacMurray Coll, IL B
Madonna U, MI A,B
Malone U, OH B
Manchester Coll, IN A,B
Maranatha Baptist Bible Coll, WI B
Marian U, WI B
Marian U, IN B
Marietta Coll, OH B
Marquette U, WI B
Maryville U of Saint Louis, MO B
Mayville State U, ND B
McKendree U, IL B
McPherson Coll, KS B
Miami U, OH B
Miami U Hamilton, OH B
Michigan State U, MI B
Michigan Technological U, MI B
Mid-America Christian U, OK B
MidAmerica Nazarene U, KS B
Millikin U, IL B
Minnesota State U Mankato, MN B
Minnesota State U Moorhead, MN B
Minot State U, ND B
Missouri Baptist U, MO B
Missouri Southern State U, MO B
Missouri State U, MO B
Missouri U of Science and Technology, MO B
Missouri Western State U, MO B
Monmouth Coll, IL B
Morningside Coll, IA B
Mount Marty Coll, SD B
Mount Mary Coll, WI B
Mount Mercy Coll, IA B
Mount Union Coll, OH B
Mount Vernon Nazarene U, OH B
Muskingum Coll, OH B
National-Louis U, IL B
Nebraska Wesleyan U, NE B
Newman U, KS B
North Central Coll, IL B
North Central U, MN B
North Dakota State U, ND B
Northeastern Illinois U, IL B
Northeastern State U, OK B
Northern Michigan U, MI B
Northern State U, SD B
Northland Coll, WI B
North Park U, IL B
Northwestern Coll, MN B
Northwestern U, IL B
Northwest Missouri State U, MO B
Oakland U, MI B
Oberlin Coll, OH B
Ohio Dominican U, OH B
Ohio Northern U, OH B
The Ohio State U, OH B
The Ohio State U at Lima, OH B
The Ohio State U at Marion, OH B
The Ohio State U–Mansfield Campus, OH B
The Ohio State U–Newark Campus, OH B
Ohio U, OH B
Ohio Wesleyan U, OH B
Oklahoma Christian U, OK B
Oklahoma City U, OK B
Oklahoma Panhandle State U, OK B
Oklahoma State U, OK B
Olivet Coll, MI B
Olivet Nazarene U, IL B
Otterbein Coll, OH B
Park U, MO B
Pittsburg State U, KS B
Pontifical Coll Josephinum, OH B
Presentation Coll, SD A
Purdue U, IN B
Purdue U Calumet, IN B
Purdue U North Central, IN B
Quincy U, IL B
Ripon Coll, WI B
Rockford Coll, IL B
Rockhurst U, MO B
Roosevelt U, IL B
Saginaw Valley State U, MI B
St. Ambrose U, IA B
St. Catherine U, MN B
St. Cloud State U, MN B
St. Gregory's U, Shawnee, OK B
Saint John's U, MN B
Saint Joseph's Coll, IN B
Saint Louis U, MO B
Saint Mary-of-the-Woods Coll, IN B
Saint Mary's U of Minnesota, MN B
St. Norbert Coll, WI B
St. Olaf Coll, MN B
Saint Xavier U, IL B
Shawnee State U, OH B
Siena Heights U, MI B
Silver Lake Coll, WI B
Simpson Coll, IA B
South Dakota State U, SD B
Southeastern Oklahoma State U, OK B
Southeast Missouri State U, MO B
Southern Illinois U Carbondale, IL B
Southern Illinois U Edwardsville, IL B
Southern Methodist U, TX B
Southern Nazarene U, OK B
Southwest Baptist U, MO B
Southwestern Christian U, OK B
Southwestern Coll, KS B
Southwestern Oklahoma State U, OK B
Southwest Minnesota State U, MN B
Spring Arbor U, MI B
Stephens Coll, MO B
Sterling Coll, KS B
Taylor U, IN B
Tiffin U, OH B
Transylvania U, KY B
Trine U, IN B
Trinity Christian Coll, IL B
Trinity International U, IL B
Truman State U, MO B
Union Coll, NE B
The U of Akron, OH B
U of Central Missouri, MO B
U of Central Oklahoma, OK B
U of Chicago, IL B
U of Cincinnati, OH B
U of Dallas, TX B
U of Dayton, OH B
U of Evansville, IN B
The U of Findlay, OH B
U of Illinois at Chicago, IL B
U of Illinois at Springfield, IL B
U of Illinois at Urbana–Champaign, IL B
U of Indianapolis, IN B
The U of Iowa, IA B
The U of Kansas, KS B
U of Mary, ND B
U of Michigan–Dearborn, MI B
U of Michigan–Flint, MI B
U of Minnesota, Duluth, MN B
U of Minnesota, Morris, MN B
U of Minnesota, Twin Cities Campus, MN B
U of Missouri–Columbia, MO B
U of Missouri–Kansas City, MO B
U of Missouri–St. Louis, MO B
U of Nebraska at Kearney, NE B
U of Nebraska at Omaha, NE B
U of Nebraska–Lincoln, NE B
U of New Orleans, LA B
U of North Dakota, ND B
U of Northern Iowa, IA B
U of Notre Dame, IN B
U of Oklahoma, OK B
U of Rio Grande, OH B
U of St. Francis, IL B
U of Saint Francis, IN B
U of Saint Mary, KS B
U of Science and Arts of Oklahoma, OK B
U of Sioux Falls, SD B
The U of South Dakota, SD B
U of Southern Indiana, IN B
The U of Toledo, OH B
U of Tulsa, OK B
U of Wisconsin–Eau Claire, WI B
U of Wisconsin–Green Bay, WI B
U of Wisconsin–La Crosse, WI B
U of Wisconsin–Madison, WI B
U of Wisconsin–Milwaukee, WI B
U of Wisconsin–Oshkosh, WI B
U of Wisconsin–Parkside, WI B
U of Wisconsin–Platteville, WI B
U of Wisconsin–Stevens Point, WI B
U of Wisconsin–Superior, WI B
U of Wisconsin–Whitewater, WI B
Ursuline Coll, OH B
Valley City State U, ND B
Valparaiso U, IN B
Viterbo U, WI B
Wabash Coll, IN B
Waldorf Coll, IA B
Walsh U, OH B
Wartburg Coll, IA B
Washburn U, KS B
Washington U in St. Louis, MO B
Wayne State Coll, NE B
Wayne State U, MI B
Webster U, MO B
Western Illinois U, IL B
Western Michigan U, MI B
Westminster Coll, MO B
Wheaton Coll, IL B
Wichita State U, KS B
William Jewell Coll, MO B
Wilmington Coll, OH B
Winona State U, MN B
Wittenberg U, OH B
Wright State U, OH B
Xavier U, OH A,B
York Coll, NE B
Youngstown State U, OH B

English as a Second/Foreign Language (Teaching)

Aquinas Coll, MI B
Bethel U, MN B

A—associate degree; B—bachelor's degree

Calvin Coll, MI B
Concordia U, Nebraska, NE B
Concordia U, St. Paul, MN B
Concordia U Wisconsin, WI B
Doane Coll, NE B
Goshen Coll, IN B
Northwestern Coll, MN B
Ohio U, OH B
Oklahoma Christian U, OK B
The U of Findlay, OH B
U of Nebraska–Lincoln, NE B
U of Northern Iowa, IA B
U of Wisconsin–Oshkosh, WI B
Wright State U, OH B

English Composition

Aurora U, IL B
DePauw U, IN B
Eastern Michigan U, MI B
Graceland U, IA B
Grand Valley State U, MI B
Indiana U–Purdue U Fort Wayne, IN B
Jamestown Coll, ND B
Lakeland Coll, WI B
Marian U, WI B
Marquette U, WI B
Miami U Hamilton, OH B
Oral Roberts U, OK B
U of Evansville, IN B
U of Illinois at Urbana–Champaign, IL B
U of Michigan–Flint, MI B
Wartburg Coll, IA B
Western Michigan U, MI B
Wilberforce U, OH B

English/French as a Second/ Foreign Language (Teaching) Related

Western Michigan U, MI B

English Language and Literature Related

Dakota State U, SD B
Doane Coll, NE B
Ferris State U, MI B
St. Gregory's U, Shawnee, OK B
Saint Mary-of-the-Woods Coll, IN B
U of Chicago, IL B
U of Michigan, MI B
U of Oklahoma, OK B
Viterbo U, WI B
Washington U in St. Louis, MO B
Webster U, MO B

English/Language Arts Teacher Education

Alma Coll, MI B
Anderson U, IN B
Aquinas Coll, MI B
Bethany Coll, KS B
Bethel Coll, IN B
Bethel U, MN B
Bowling Green State U, OH B
Buena Vista U, IA B
Calumet Coll of Saint Joseph, IN B
Capital U, OH B
Carroll U, WI B
Cedarville U, OH B
Central Michigan U, MI B
Coll of the Ozarks, MO B
Concordia Coll, MN B
Concordia U, MI B
Concordia U Chicago, IL B
Concordia U, Nebraska, NE B
Cornerstone U, MI B
Crown Coll, MN B
Culver-Stockton Coll, MO B
Dakota State U, SD B
Dakota Wesleyan U, SD B
Dana Coll, NE B
DePaul U, IL B
Eastern Michigan U, MI B
Edgewood Coll, WI B
Elmhurst Coll, IL B
Faith Baptist Bible Coll and Theological Seminary, IA B
Ferris State U, MI B
Franklin Coll, IN B
Friends U, KS B
Grace Coll, IN B
Grand Valley State U, MI B
Greenville Coll, IL B
Hannibal-LaGrange Coll, MO B
Hope Coll, MI B
Indiana U Bloomington, IN B
Indiana U Northwest, IN B
Indiana U–Purdue U Fort Wayne, IN B
Indiana U–Purdue U Indianapolis, IN B
Indiana U South Bend, IN B
Indiana U Southeast, IN B
Indiana Wesleyan U, IN B
Jamestown Coll, ND B
Kent State U, OH B
Lincoln U, MO B
Malone U, OH B
Maranatha Baptist Bible Coll, WI B
Marian U, WI B
Marquette U, WI B
Maryville U of Saint Louis, MO B
Mayville State U, ND B
McKendree U, IL B
Miami U, OH B
Miami U Hamilton, OH B
Michigan Technological U, MI B
MidAmerica Nazarene U, KS B
Millikin U, IL B
Minnesota State U Moorhead, MN B
Minot State U, ND B
Missouri State U, MO B
Missouri Western State U, MO B
Mount Marty Coll, SD B
Mount Mary Coll, WI B
Mount Vernon Nazarene U, OH B
Nebraska Wesleyan U, NE B
North Dakota State U, ND B
Northeastern State U, OK B
Northern Michigan U, MI B
Northwestern Coll, MN B
Ohio Northern U, OH B
Oklahoma Baptist U, OK B
Oklahoma Christian U, OK B
Oral Roberts U, OK B
Pittsburg State U, KS B
Saginaw Valley State U, MI B
St. Ambrose U, IA B
St. Catherine U, MN B
St. Gregory's U, Shawnee, OK B
Saint Mary's U of Minnesota, MN B
Saint Xavier U, IL B
Shawnee State U, OH B
Southeastern Oklahoma State U, OK B
Southeast Missouri State U, MO B
Southern Nazarene U, OK B
Southwest Baptist U, MO B
Southwestern Oklahoma State U, OK B
Southwest Minnesota State U, MN B
Taylor U, IN B
Tiffin U, OH B
Trinity Christian Coll, IL B
Union Coll, NE B
The U of Akron, OH B
U of Central Oklahoma, OK B
U of Evansville, IN B
U of Illinois at Chicago, IL B
U of Illinois at Urbana–Champaign, IL B
U of Indianapolis, IN B
U of Mary, ND B
U of Michigan–Flint, MI B
U of Minnesota, Twin Cities Campus, MN B
U of Missouri–St. Louis, MO B
U of Nebraska–Lincoln, NE B
U of New Orleans, LA B
U of Oklahoma, OK B
U of Rio Grande, OH B
U of St. Francis, IL B
U of Saint Francis, IN B
The U of South Dakota, SD B
The U of Toledo, OH B
U of Wisconsin–Superior, WI B
Ursuline Coll, OH B
Valley City State U, ND B
Valparaiso U, IN B
Viterbo U, WI B
Waldorf Coll, IA B
Washington U in St. Louis, MO B
Wayne State Coll, NE B
Wayne State U, MI B
Western Michigan U, MI B
William Jewell Coll, MO B
Wright State U, OH B
York Coll, NE B
Youngstown State U, OH B

English Literature (British and Commonwealth)

Indiana U–Purdue U Fort Wayne, IN B
Marian U, WI B
Saint Mary's Coll, IN B
U of Michigan, MI B
Washington U in St. Louis, MO B

Entomology

Iowa State U of Science and Technology, IA B
Michigan State U, MI B
The Ohio State U, OH B
Oklahoma State U, OK B
Purdue U, IN B
U of Illinois at Urbana–Champaign, IL B
U of Nebraska–Lincoln, NE B
U of Wisconsin–Madison, WI B

Entrepreneurial and Small Business Related

Kendall Coll, IL B
Loyola U Chicago, IL B

Entrepreneurship

Anderson U, IN B
Baker Coll of Flint, MI A
Ball State U, IN B
Bradley U, IL B
Buena Vista U, IA B
Central Michigan U, MI B
Clarkson U, NY B
Eastern Michigan U, MI B
Ferris State U, MI B
Iowa State U of Science and Technology, IA B
Kendall Coll, IL B
Millikin U, IL B
Missouri State U, MO B
Newman U, KS B
Northeastern State U, OK B
Northern Michigan U, MI B
South Dakota State U, SD B
Trine U, IN B
Union Coll, NE B
U of Illinois at Chicago, IL B
U of Illinois at Urbana–Champaign, IL B
U of Indianapolis, IN B
U of New Orleans, LA B
U of North Dakota, ND B
U of Phoenix–Kansas City Campus, MO B
U of Phoenix–Metro Detroit Campus, MI B
U of Southern Indiana, IN B
The U of Toledo, OH B
Washington U in St. Louis, MO B
Wichita State U, KS B
Xavier U, OH B

Environmental Biology

Beloit Coll, WI B
Bethel Coll, IN B
Cedarville U, OH B
Central Methodist U, MO B
Cornerstone U, MI B
Ferris State U, MI B
Friends U, KS B
Greenville Coll, IL B
Heidelberg U, OH B
Iowa Wesleyan Coll, IA B
Michigan State U, MI B
Minnesota State U Mankato, MN B
Ohio U, OH B
Otterbein Coll, OH B
St. Cloud State U, MN B

Saint Mary's U of Minnesota, MN B
Southern Nazarene U, OK B
Taylor U, IN B
U of Charleston, WV B
U of Dayton, OH B
Winona State U, MN B

Environmental Design/ Architecture

Ball State U, IN B
Bowling Green State U, OH B
Kent State U, OH B
Lawrence Technological U, MI B
North Dakota State U, ND B
Olivet Nazarene U, IL B
U of Oklahoma, OK B

Environmental Education

Northland Coll, WI B

Environmental Engineering Technology

Baker Coll of Flint, MI A
Baker Coll of Owosso, MI A
Baker Coll of Port Huron, MI A
Ferris State U, MI B
Lake Superior State U, MI B
Ohio U, OH A
Shawnee State U, OH B
U of Cincinnati, OH A
The U of Toledo, OH A
U of Wisconsin–Whitewater, WI B
Wright State U, OH B

Environmental/Environmental Health Engineering

Clarkson U, NY B
Marquette U, WI B
Michigan Technological U, MI B
Missouri U of Science and Technology, MO B
Northeastern State U, OK B
Northwestern U, IL B
Ohio U, OH A
Ohio U–Chillicothe, OH A
South Dakota School of Mines and Technology, SD B
Southern Methodist U, TX B
Taylor U, IN B
U of Illinois at Urbana–Champaign, IL B
U of Michigan, MI B
U of North Dakota, ND B
U of Notre Dame, IN B
U of Oklahoma, OK B
U of Wisconsin–Madison, WI B
U of Wisconsin–Platteville, WI B

Environmental Health

Bowling Green State U, OH B
Clarkson U, NY B
Illinois State U, IL B
Iowa Wesleyan Coll, IA B
Oakland U, MI B
U of Illinois at Urbana–Champaign, IL B
U of Wisconsin–Eau Claire, WI B
Wright State U, OH B

Environmental Science

Adrian Coll, MI B
Aquinas Coll, MI B
Benedictine U, IL B
Bethel U, MN B
Bradley U, IL B
Briar Cliff U, IA B
Capital U, OH B
Carroll U, WI B
Central Methodist U, MO B
Central Michigan U, MI B
DePaul U, IL B
Drake U, IA B
Drury U, MO B
Eureka Coll, IL B
Haskell Indian Nations U, KS B
Heidelberg U, OH B
Indiana U Bloomington, IN B
Indiana U–Purdue U Indianapolis, IN B
Lindenwood U, MO B
Lourdes Coll, OH B
Loyola U Chicago, IL B
Madonna U, MI B
Marietta Coll, OH B
Martin U, IN B
Maryville U of Saint Louis, MO B
Miami U, OH B
Miami U Hamilton, OH B
Michigan State U, MI B
Michigan Technological U, MI B
Monmouth Coll, IL B
Mount Union Coll, OH B
Muskingum Coll, OH B
Northeastern State U, OK B
Northern Michigan U, MI B
Northwestern U, IL B
The Ohio State U, OH B
Oklahoma State U, OK B
Otterbein Coll, OH B
Saint Louis U, MO B
St. Norbert Coll, WI B
Siena Heights U, MI B
Simpson Coll, IA B
Southwest Minnesota State U, MN B
Taylor U, IN B
U of Charleston, WV B
U of Evansville, IN B
U of Illinois at Urbana–Champaign, IL B
U of Michigan–Dearborn, MI B
U of Michigan–Flint, MI B
U of Nebraska at Omaha, NE B
U of Northern Iowa, IA B
U of Notre Dame, IN B
U of Oklahoma, OK B
U of St. Francis, IL B
U of Wisconsin–Green Bay, WI B
Valparaiso U, IN B
Wayne State U, MI B
Westminster Coll, MO B
Wright State U, OH B
Youngstown State U, OH B

Environmental Studies

Adrian Coll, MI B
Albion Coll, MI B
Aquinas Coll, MI B
Ashland U, OH B
Augustana Coll, IL B
Beloit Coll, WI B
Bemidji State U, MN B
Bethel U, MN B
Black Hills State U, SD B
Calvin Coll, MI B
Case Western Reserve U, OH B
Central Christian Coll of Kansas, KS A
Central Coll, IA B
Central Michigan U, MI B
Clarkson U, NY B
Cleveland State U, OH B
Coe Coll, IA B
Coll of Saint Benedict, MN B
Columbia Coll, MO B
Concordia Coll, MN B
Concordia U Chicago, IL B
Cornell Coll, IA B
Creighton U, NE B
Denison U, OH B
DePauw U, IN B
Doane Coll, NE B
Dominican U, IL B
Dordt Coll, IA B
Drake U, IA B
Drury U, MO B
Earlham Coll, IN B
Elmhurst Coll, IL B
Goshen Coll, IN B
Gustavus Adolphus Coll, MN B
Hamline U, MN B
Heidelberg U, OH B
Hiram Coll, OH B
Hope Coll, MI B
Illinois Coll, IL B
Illinois Wesleyan U, IL B
Iowa State U of Science and Technology, IA B
John Carroll U, OH B
Knox Coll, IL B
Lake Erie Coll, OH B
Lake Forest Coll, IL B
Lake Superior State U, MI B
Lawrence U, WI B
Lewis U, IL B
Loyola U Chicago, IL B
Luther Coll, IA B
Macalester Coll, MN B
Manchester Coll, IN B
Marietta Coll, OH B
Maryville U of Saint Louis, MO B
Miami U, OH B
Miami U Hamilton, OH B
Minnesota State U Mankato, MN B
Muskingum Coll, OH B
Northeastern Illinois U, IL B
Northern State U, SD B
Northland Coll, WI B
Northwestern U, IL B
Oberlin Coll, OH B
Ohio Wesleyan U, OH B
Olivet Coll, MI B
Ripon Coll, WI B
Saint John's U, MN B
St. Olaf Coll, MN B
Southeast Missouri State U, MO B
Southern Methodist U, TX B
Trine U, IN B
U of Chicago, IL B
U of Cincinnati, OH A
U of Dayton, OH B
U of Evansville, IN B
The U of Findlay, OH A,B
U of Indianapolis, IN B
The U of Iowa, IA B
The U of Kansas, KS B
U of Michigan, MI B
U of Michigan–Dearborn, MI B
U of Minnesota, Duluth, MN B
U of Minnesota, Twin Cities Campus, MN B
U of Missouri–Columbia, MO B
U of Nebraska–Lincoln, NE B
U of New Orleans, LA B
U of Saint Francis, IN B
The U of Toledo, OH A,B
U of Tulsa, OK B
U of Wisconsin–Green Bay, WI B
Washington U in St. Louis, MO B
Western Michigan U, MI B
Westminster Coll, MO B
Wheaton Coll, IL B

Equestrian Studies

Lake Erie Coll, OH B
North Dakota State U, ND B
Ohio U, OH A
Ohio U–Southern Campus, OH A
Otterbein Coll, OH B
Saint Mary-of-the-Woods Coll, IN A
Stephens Coll, MO B
Truman State U, MO B
The U of Findlay, OH A,B

Ethics

Drake U, IA B
U of Michigan–Flint, MI B

Ethnic, Cultural Minority, and Gender Studies Related

Bowling Green State U, OH B
Cornell Coll, IA B
Indiana U Bloomington, IN B
Lawrence U, WI B
Miami U Hamilton, OH B
St. Olaf Coll, MN B
U of Illinois at Chicago, IL B
Washington U in St. Louis, MO B

European Studies

Beloit Coll, WI B
Carroll U, WI B
Central Michigan U, MI B
Hillsdale Coll, MI B
Ohio U, OH B

A—associate degree; B—bachelor's degree

Southern Methodist U, TX B
The U of Kansas, KS B
U of Minnesota, Morris, MN B
U of Minnesota, Twin Cities Campus, MN B
U of Missouri–Columbia, MO B
U of Northern Iowa, IA B
The U of Toledo, OH B
Washington U in St. Louis, MO B

European Studies (Central and Eastern)
Indiana U Bloomington, IN B
Kent State U, OH B
U of Chicago, IL B
U of Missouri–Columbia, MO B

European Studies (Western)
Illinois Wesleyan U, IL B
U of Nebraska–Lincoln, NE B

Evolutionary Biology
Case Western Reserve U, OH B

Executive Assistant/Executive Secretary
Baker Coll of Allen Park, MI A
Baker Coll of Flint, MI A
Bohecker's Business Coll, OH A
Davenport U, Grand Rapids, MI A

Exercise Physiology
Baldwin-Wallace Coll, OH B
The Coll of St. Scholastica, MN B
Concordia U Wisconsin, WI B
Miami U Hamilton, OH B
Ohio U–Eastern, OH B
Truman State U, MO B

Experimental Psychology
Northern Michigan U, MI B
Tiffin U, OH B
The U of Toledo, OH B
U of Wisconsin–Madison, WI B

Facilities Planning and Management
Eastern Michigan U, MI B

Family and Community Services
Andrews U, MI B
Baker Coll of Flint, MI A
Central Christian Coll of Kansas, KS A
Iowa State U of Science and Technology, IA B
Michigan State U, MI B
Oklahoma Baptist U, OK B
Oklahoma Christian U, OK B
U of Minnesota, Twin Cities Campus, MN B
U of Northern Iowa, IA B
Youngstown State U, OH B

Family and Consumer Economics Related
Andrews U, MI B
Ashland U, OH B
Iowa State U of Science and Technology, IA B
Minnesota State U Mankato, MN B
Northwest Missouri State U, MO B
The U of Akron, OH B
U of Missouri–Columbia, MO B
U of Nebraska at Kearney, NE B
U of Nebraska–Lincoln, NE B
U of Northern Iowa, IA B
U of Wisconsin–Madison, WI B
U of Wisconsin–Stevens Point, WI B

Family and Consumer Sciences/Home Economics Teacher Education
Ashland U, OH B
Bluffton U, OH B
Central Michigan U, MI B
Coll of the Ozarks, MO B
Concordia U, Nebraska, NE B
Ferris State U, MI B
Fontbonne U, MO B
Iowa State U of Science and Technology, IA B
Kent State U, OH B
Michigan State U, MI B
Minnesota State U Mankato, MN B
Missouri State U, MO B
Mount Vernon Nazarene U, OH B
North Dakota State U, ND B
Northwest Missouri State U, MO B
The Ohio State U, OH B
Pittsburg State U, KS B
St. Catherine U, MN B
Southeast Missouri State U, MO B
The U of Akron, OH B
U of Central Oklahoma, OK B
U of Minnesota, Twin Cities Campus, MN B
U of Wisconsin–Madison, WI B
U of Wisconsin–Stevens Point, WI B
U of Wisconsin–Stout, WI B
Wayne State Coll, NE B
Western Michigan U, MI B
Youngstown State U, OH B

Family and Consumer Sciences/Human Sciences
Ashland U, OH B
Ball State U, IN B
Bluffton U, OH B
Bradley U, IL B
Cameron U, OK B
Coll of the Ozarks, MO B
Eastern Illinois U, IL B
Fontbonne U, MO B
Great Lakes Christian Coll, MI B
Illinois State U, IL B
Indiana State U, IN B
Iowa State U of Science and Technology, IA B
Kent State U, OH B
Madonna U, MI B
Michigan State U, MI B
Minnesota State U Mankato, MN B
Mount Vernon Nazarene U, OH A
Northeastern State U, OK B
Northwest Missouri State U, MO B
Oglala Lakota Coll, SD A
Ohio U, OH B
Olivet Nazarene U, IL B
Pittsburg State U, KS B
Purdue U, IN B
St. Catherine U, MN B
Southeast Missouri State U, MO B
U of Central Missouri, MO B
U of Central Oklahoma, OK B
U of Wisconsin–Madison, WI B
Wayne State Coll, NE B
Western Illinois U, IL B
Youngstown State U, OH B

Family and Consumer Sciences/Human Sciences Business Services Related
U of Illinois at Urbana–Champaign, IL B

Family Practice Nursing/Nurse Practitioner
Grand Valley State U, MI B

Family Resource Management
Bradley U, IL B
Iowa State U of Science and Technology, IA B
The Ohio State U, OH B
Ohio U, OH B
Pittsburg State U, KS B
South Dakota State U, SD B

Family Systems
Anderson U, IN B
Central Michigan U, MI B
Spring Arbor U, MI B
The U of Akron, OH B
Western Michigan U, MI B

Farm and Ranch Management
Iowa State U of Science and Technology, IA B
Northwest Missouri State U, MO B
Oklahoma Panhandle State U, OK A
Purdue U, IN B
The U of Findlay, OH B
U of Illinois at Urbana–Champaign, IL B

Fashion/Apparel Design
The Art Inst of Indianapolis, IN B
Ball State U, IN B
Columbus Coll of Art & Design, OH B
Dominican U, IL B
The Illinois Inst of Art–Chicago, IL A,B
The Illinois Inst of Art–Schaumburg, IL B
Iowa State U of Science and Technology, IA B
Kent State U, OH B
Lindenwood U, MO B
Michigan State U, MI B
Minnesota State U Mankato, MN B
Mount Mary Coll, WI B
Northwest Missouri State U, MO B
St. Catherine U, MN B
Stephens Coll, MO B
U of Cincinnati, OH B
Ursuline Coll, OH B
Washington U in St. Louis, MO B

Fashion Merchandising
The Art Inst of Indianapolis, IN B
The Art Inst of Michigan, MI A
The Art Insts International–Kansas City, KS B
Ashland U, OH B
Bowling Green State U, OH B
Central Michigan U, MI B
Dominican U, IL B
Fontbonne U, MO B
The Illinois Inst of Art–Chicago, IL A,B
The Illinois Inst of Art–Schaumburg, IL B
Kent State U, OH B
Lindenwood U, MO B
Mount Mary Coll, WI B
Northwest Missouri State U, MO B
Olivet Nazarene U, IL B
Pittsburg State U, KS B
St. Catherine U, MN B
Stephens Coll, MO B
U of Central Oklahoma, OK B
U of Illinois at Urbana–Champaign, IL B
U of Wisconsin–Madison, WI B
Ursuline Coll, OH B
Youngstown State U, OH B

Fiber, Textile and Weaving Arts
The Cleveland Inst of Art, OH B
Kansas City Art Inst, MO B
Northwest Missouri State U, MO B
The U of Kansas, KS B
U of Michigan, MI B
U of Wisconsin–Milwaukee, WI B

Film/Cinema Studies
Baldwin-Wallace Coll, OH B
Bowling Green State U, OH B
Calvin Coll, MI B
Carleton Coll, MN B
Denison U, OH B
Eastern Michigan U, MI B
Grand Valley State U, MI B
Huntington U, IN B
Kansas City Art Inst, MO B

Missouri Western State U, MO B
Northwestern U, IL B
The Ohio State U, OH B
Ohio U, OH B
St. Cloud State U, MN B
Southern Methodist U, TX B
Stephens Coll, MO B
U of Chicago, IL B
U of Illinois at Urbana–Champaign, IL B
The U of Iowa, IA B
U of Michigan, MI B
U of Minnesota, Twin Cities Campus, MN B
U of Nebraska–Lincoln, NE B
The U of Toledo, OH B
U of Tulsa, OK B
U of Wisconsin–Milwaukee, WI B
Washington U in St. Louis, MO B
Wayne State U, MI B
Webster U, MO B
Wright State U, OH B

Film/Video and Photographic Arts Related

Columbus Coll of Art & Design, OH B
Spring Arbor U, MI B
U of Illinois at Chicago, IL B

Finance

AIB Coll of Business, IA A
Anderson U, IN B
Argosy U, Chicago, IL B
Argosy U, Schaumburg, IL B
Argosy U, Twin Cities, MN B
Ashland U, OH B
Augsburg Coll, MN B
Augustana Coll, IL B
Aurora U, IL B
Avila U, MO B
Bacone Coll, OK B
Baldwin-Wallace Coll, OH B
Ball State U, IN B
Benedictine U, IL B
Bowling Green State U, OH B
Bradley U, IL B
Butler U, IN B
Carroll U, WI B
Cedarville U, OH B
Central Christian Coll of Kansas, KS A
Central Michigan U, MI B
Chancellor U, OH B
Clarkson U, NY B
Cleary U, MI B
Cleveland State U, OH B
The Coll of St. Scholastica, MN B
Colorado Tech U Sioux Falls, SD B
Columbia Coll, MO B
Concordia U, St. Paul, MN B
Creighton U, NE B
Culver-Stockton Coll, MO B
Dakota State U, SD B
Dakota Wesleyan U, SD B
Davenport U, Grand Rapids, MI B
DePaul U, IL B
Drake U, IA B
Drury U, MO B
Eastern Illinois U, IL B
Eastern Michigan U, MI B
East-West U, IL B
Elmhurst Coll, IL B
Ferris State U, MI B
Fort Hays State U, KS B
Franklin U, OH A,B
Grace Coll, IN B
Grand Valley State U, MI B
Hillsdale Coll, MI B
Illinois Coll, IL B
Illinois State U, IL B
Indiana State U, IN B
Indiana U Bloomington, IN B
Indiana U–Purdue U Fort Wayne, IN B
Indiana Wesleyan U, IN A,B
Iowa State U of Science and Technology, IA B
John Carroll U, OH B
Kansas State U, KS B
Kent State U, OH B
Lake Superior State U, MI B
Lewis U, IL B
Lindenwood U, MO B
Loras Coll, IA B
Loyola U Chicago, IL B
MacMurray Coll, IL B
Manchester Coll, IN B
Marian U, WI B
Marian U, IN B
Marquette U, WI B
McKendree U, IL B
McPherson Coll, KS B
Miami U, OH B
Miami U Hamilton, OH B
Michigan State U, MI B
Michigan Technological U, MI B
Millikin U, IL B
Minnesota State U Mankato, MN B
Minnesota State U Moorhead, MN B
Minot State U, ND B
Missouri State U, MO B
Missouri Western State U, MO B
Mount Vernon Nazarene U, OH B
Newman U, KS B
North Central Coll, IL B
North Dakota State U, ND B
Northeastern Illinois U, IL B
Northeastern State U, OK B
Northern Michigan U, MI B
Northern State U, SD B
North Park U, IL B
Northwestern Coll, MN B
Northwest Missouri State U, MO B
Oakland U, MI B
Ohio Dominican U, OH B
The Ohio State U, OH B
Oklahoma Baptist U, OK B
Oklahoma Christian U, OK B
Oklahoma City U, OK B
Oklahoma State U, OK B
Olivet Coll, MI B
Oral Roberts U, OK B
Otterbein Coll, OH B
Pittsburg State U, KS B
Quincy U, IL B
Rockford Coll, IL B
Roosevelt U, IL B
Saginaw Valley State U, MI B
St. Ambrose U, IA B
St. Cloud State U, MN B
Southeastern Oklahoma State U, OK B
Southeast Missouri State U, MO B
Southern Illinois U Carbondale, IL B
Southern Methodist U, TX B
Southern Nazarene U, OK B
Southwest Baptist U, MO B
Southwestern Oklahoma State U, OK B
Southwest Minnesota State U, MN B
Spring Arbor U, MI B
Taylor U, IN B
Tiffin U, OH B
Trinity Bible Coll, ND B
Truman State U, MO B
U of Central Missouri, MO B
U of Central Oklahoma, OK B
U of Charleston, WV B
U of Cincinnati, OH A,B
U of Dayton, OH B
U of Evansville, IN B
U of Illinois at Chicago, IL B
U of Illinois at Urbana–Champaign, IL B
The U of Iowa, IA B
The U of Kansas, KS B
U of Mary, ND B
U of Michigan–Dearborn, MI B
U of Michigan–Flint, MI B
U of Minnesota, Duluth, MN B
U of Minnesota, Twin Cities Campus, MN B
U of Missouri–Columbia, MO B
U of Missouri–St. Louis, MO B
U of Nebraska at Omaha, NE B
U of Nebraska–Lincoln, NE B
U of New Orleans, LA B
U of North Dakota, ND B
U of Northern Iowa, IA B
U of Notre Dame, IN B
U of Oklahoma, OK B
U of Phoenix–Cleveland Campus, OH A,B
U of Phoenix–Indianapolis Campus, IN B
U of Phoenix–Kansas City Campus, MO B
U of Phoenix–Metro Detroit Campus, MI B
U of Phoenix–Oklahoma City Campus, OK B
U of Phoenix–St. Louis Campus, MO B
U of Phoenix–Springfield Campus, MO B
U of Phoenix–Tulsa Campus, OK B
U of Phoenix–Wisconsin Campus, WI B
U of St. Francis, IL B
The U of South Dakota, SD B
U of Southern Indiana, IN B
The U of Toledo, OH B
U of Tulsa, OK B
U of Wisconsin–Eau Claire, WI B
U of Wisconsin–La Crosse, WI B
U of Wisconsin–Madison, WI B
U of Wisconsin–Milwaukee, WI B
U of Wisconsin–Oshkosh, WI B
U of Wisconsin–Parkside, WI B
U of Wisconsin–Superior, WI B
U of Wisconsin–Whitewater, WI B
Valparaiso U, IN B
Waldorf Coll, IA B
Walsh Coll of Accountancy and Business Administration, MI B
Walsh U, OH A,B
Wartburg Coll, IA B
Washburn U, KS B
Washington U in St. Louis, MO B
Wayne State U, MI B
Western Illinois U, IL B
Western Michigan U, MI B
Wichita State U, KS B
Winona State U, MN B
Wright State U, OH B
Xavier U, OH B
York Coll, NE B
Youngstown State U, OH A,B

Finance and Financial Management Services Related

Grace Bible Coll, MI B
Olivet Coll, MI B
Park U, MO B
Southern Methodist U, TX B

Financial Planning and Services

Bethany Coll, KS B
Central Michigan U, MI B
Cleary U, MI B
Jamestown Coll, ND B
Northern Michigan U, MI B
The Ohio State U at Lima, OH B
Olivet Coll, MI B
Purdue U, IN B
Southern Methodist U, TX B
Trinity Christian Coll, IL B
The U of Akron, OH B
U of Illinois at Urbana–Champaign, IL B
Western Michigan U, MI B

Fine Arts Related

Bowling Green State U, OH B
Columbus Coll of Art & Design, OH B

A—associate degree; B—bachelor's degree

Grand Valley State U, MI B
Northern Michigan U, MI B
Oakland U, MI B
Pittsburg State U, KS B
Rogers State U, OK A,B
Sinte Gleska U, SD A,B

Fine/Studio Arts
Alma Coll, MI B
Anderson U, IN B
Aquinas Coll, MI B
Ashland U, OH B
Augsburg Coll, MN B
Augustana Coll, IL B
Baker U, KS B
Beloit Coll, WI B
Bemidji State U, MN B
Benedictine U, IL B
Bethel Coll, KS B
Bethel U, MN B
Bowling Green State U, OH B
Bradley U, IL B
Calvin Coll, MI B
Carleton Coll, MN B
Carroll U, WI B
Cedarville U, OH B
Central Michigan U, MI B
Clarke Coll, IA B
Coe Coll, IA B
Coll for Creative Studies, MI B
Coll of Mount St. Joseph, OH B
Coll of Saint Benedict, MN B
Coll of the Ozarks, MO B
Coll of Visual Arts, MN B
The Coll of Wooster, OH B
Columbia Coll, MO B
Concordia Coll, MN B
Concordia U, Nebraska, NE B
Concordia U, St. Paul, MN B
Denison U, OH B
DePauw U, IN B
Dominican U, IL B
Drake U, IA B
Drury U, MO B
Ferris State U, MI B
Fontbonne U, MO B
Graceland U, IA B
Grand View U, IA B
Hiram Coll, OH B
Hope Coll, MI B
Illinois State U, IL B
Indiana State U, IN B
Indiana U Bloomington, IN B
Indiana U–Purdue U Fort Wayne, IN B
Indiana U–Purdue U Indianapolis, IN B
Indiana U South Bend, IN B
Indiana U Southeast, IN B
Iowa Wesleyan Coll, IA B
Jamestown Coll, ND B
Kent State U, OH B
Lake Erie Coll, OH B
Lake Forest Coll, IL B
Lawrence U, WI B
Lewis U, IL B
Lincoln U, MO B
Lindenwood U, MO B
Loras Coll, IA B
Loyola U Chicago, IL B
Macalester Coll, MN B
MacMurray Coll, IL B
Madonna U, MI A,B
Malone U, OH B
Manchester Coll, IN A,B
Marian U, WI B
Marian U, IN B
Marietta Coll, OH B
Maryville U of Saint Louis, MO B
Miami U, OH B
Millikin U, IL B
Minneapolis Coll of Art and Design, MN B
Minnesota State U Mankato, MN B
Minnesota State U Moorhead, MN B
Missouri State U, MO B
Morningside Coll, IA B
Mount Union Coll, OH B
Northeastern State U, OK B
Northwestern Coll, MN B
Northwest Missouri State U, MO B
Oakland U, MI B
Oberlin Coll, OH B
Ohio Dominican U, OH B
Ohio Northern U, OH B
The Ohio State U, OH B
Ohio U, OH B
Ohio Wesleyan U, OH B
Oklahoma Baptist U, OK B
Oklahoma City U, OK B
Oral Roberts U, OK B
Park U, MO B
Purdue U, IN B
Saginaw Valley State U, MI B
St. Ambrose U, IA B
St. Catherine U, MN B
St. Cloud State U, MN B
St. Gregory's U, Shawnee, OK A,B
Saint John's U, MN B
Saint Joseph's Coll, IN B
Saint Louis U, MO B
Saint Mary-of-the-Woods Coll, IN B
Saint Mary's U of Minnesota, MN B
Shawnee State U, OH B
Southern Illinois U Carbondale, IL B
Southern Illinois U Edwardsville, IL B
Southern Methodist U, TX B
Truman State U, MO B
Union Coll, NE B
U of Central Missouri, MO B
U of Chicago, IL B
U of Dallas, TX B
U of Dayton, OH B
U of Illinois at Chicago, IL B
U of Illinois at Springfield, IL B
U of Indianapolis, IN B
The U of Kansas, KS B
U of Michigan–Flint, MI B
U of Minnesota, Duluth, MN B
U of Minnesota, Morris, MN B
U of Missouri–Kansas City, MO B
U of Missouri–St. Louis, MO B
U of Nebraska–Lincoln, NE B
U of New Orleans, LA B
U of Northern Iowa, IA B
U of Notre Dame, IN B
U of Oklahoma, OK B
U of Science and Arts of Oklahoma, OK B
The U of Toledo, OH B
U of Tulsa, OK B
U of Wisconsin–Milwaukee, WI B
U of Wisconsin–Oshkosh, WI B
U of Wisconsin–Stevens Point, WI B
U of Wisconsin–Superior, WI B
Ursuline Coll, OH B
Washington U in St. Louis, MO B
Webster U, MO B
Western Illinois U, IL B
Winona State U, MN B
Xavier U, OH B
Youngstown State U, OH B

Fire Protection and Safety Technology
Oklahoma State U, OK B
Oklahoma State U, Oklahoma City, OK A
The U of Akron, OH A
U of Cincinnati, OH B
U of Nebraska–Lincoln, NE A
The U of Toledo, OH A

Fire Protection Related
The U of Akron, OH A,B

Fire Science
Lake Superior State U, MI A,B
Madonna U, MI A,B
Oklahoma State U, Oklahoma City, OK A
U of Cincinnati, OH A,B

Fire Services Administration
Columbia Coll, MO A
Lewis U, IL B
Southern Illinois U Carbondale, IL B

Fish/Game Management
Iowa State U of Science and Technology, IA B
Lake Superior State U, MI B
Northland Coll, WI B
U of Minnesota, Twin Cities Campus, MN B
U of Missouri–Columbia, MO B

Fishing and Fisheries Sciences and Management
The Ohio State U, OH B
Purdue U, IN B
U of Missouri–Columbia, MO B

Flight Instruction
South Dakota State U, SD B
U of North Dakota, ND B

Food/Nutrition
The Ohio State U, OH B

Foods and Nutrition Related
Kent State U, OH B
U of Wisconsin–Stout, WI B

Food Science
Dominican U, IL B
Kansas State U, KS B
Michigan State U, MI B
North Dakota State U, ND B
Northwest Missouri State U, MO B
The Ohio State U, OH B
Oklahoma State U, OK B
Purdue U, IN B
U of Illinois at Urbana–Champaign, IL B
U of Missouri–Columbia, MO B
U of Nebraska–Lincoln, NE B
U of Wisconsin–Madison, WI B

Food Science and Technology Related
North Dakota State U, ND B
U of Illinois at Urbana–Champaign, IL B

Food Services Technology
Iowa State U of Science and Technology, IA B
Washburn U, KS A

Food Service Systems Administration
Central Michigan U, MI B
Dominican U, IL B
Iowa State U of Science and Technology, IA B
Northern Michigan U, MI A
U of Wisconsin–Stout, WI B
Western Michigan U, MI B

Foods, Nutrition, and Wellness
Andrews U, MI B
Ashland U, OH B
Bluffton U, OH B
Bowling Green State U, OH B
Coll of Saint Benedict, MN B
Coll of the Ozarks, MO B
Concordia Coll, MN B
Dominican U, IL B
Indiana State U, IN B
Iowa State U of Science and Technology, IA B
Kent State U, OH B
Madonna U, MI A,B
Miami U, OH B
Minnesota State U Mankato, MN B
Northeastern State U, OK B
Northwest Missouri State U, MO B
The Ohio State U, OH B
Ohio U, OH B
Oklahoma State U, OK B
Pittsburg State U, KS B
Purdue U, IN B
St. Catherine U, MN B
Saint John's U, MN B
Saint Louis U, MO B
South Dakota State U, SD B
Southern Illinois U Carbondale, IL B
U of Central Oklahoma, OK B

U of Cincinnati, OH B
U of Dayton, OH B
U of Minnesota, Twin Cities Campus, MN B
U of Missouri–Columbia, MO B
U of Nebraska–Lincoln, NE B
U of Northern Iowa, IA B
U of Wisconsin–Madison, WI B
Wayne State U, MI B
Youngstown State U, OH B

Food Technology and Processing
U of Illinois at Urbana–Champaign, IL B

Foreign Languages and Literatures
Augustana Coll, SD B
Cameron U, OK B
Central Methodist U, MO B
Eastern Illinois U, IL B
Emporia State U, KS B
Grace Coll, IN B
Graceland U, IA B
Kansas State U, KS B
Knox Coll, IL B
Minnesota State U Moorhead, MN B
Oakland U, MI B
Purdue U, IN B
Purdue U Calumet, IN B
Roosevelt U, IL B
Saint Louis U, MO B
Southern Illinois U Edwardsville, IL B
U of Nebraska at Omaha, NE B
U of North Dakota, ND B
U of Northern Iowa, IA B
Wayne State Coll, NE B
Wayne State U, MI B
Wright State U, OH B
Youngstown State U, OH B

Foreign Languages Related
Indiana State U, IN B
Southern Illinois U Carbondale, IL B
U of Michigan–Flint, MI B
U of Northern Iowa, IA B

Foreign Language Teacher Education
Bowling Green State U, OH B
Carroll U, WI B
Central Methodist U, MO B
Eastern Michigan U, MI B
Grand Valley State U, MI B
Indiana U Bloomington, IN B
Kent State U, OH B
Miami U, OH B
Ohio Dominican U, OH B
Ohio Northern U, OH B
Ohio Wesleyan U, OH B
Oral Roberts U, OK B
Southeast Missouri State U, MO B
U of Illinois at Urbana–Champaign, IL B
U of Minnesota, Twin Cities Campus, MN B
U of Nebraska–Lincoln, NE B
U of Northern Iowa, IA B
U of Oklahoma, OK B
The U of South Dakota, SD B
Valparaiso U, IN B
Wayne State Coll, NE B
William Jewell Coll, MO B
Wright State U, OH B
Youngstown State U, OH B

Forensic Psychology
St. Ambrose U, IA B
Tiffin U, OH B

Forensic Science and Technology
Carroll U, WI B
Cedarville U, OH B
Columbia Coll, MO B
Defiance Coll, OH B
Indiana U–Purdue U Indianapolis, IN B
Lewis U, IL B
Loyola U Chicago, IL B
Madonna U, MI B
Mount Marty Coll, SD B
Olivet Coll, MI B
Quincy U, IL B
Simpson Coll, IA B
Tiffin U, OH B
Trine U, IN B
U of Central Oklahoma, OK B
U of Nebraska–Lincoln, NE B
U of North Dakota, ND B
U of Saint Francis, IN A
Washburn U, KS B
Youngstown State U, OH B

Forest/Forest Resources Management
U of Minnesota, Twin Cities Campus, MN B

Forestry
Coll of Saint Benedict, MN B
Iowa State U of Science and Technology, IA B
Michigan State U, MI B
Michigan Technological U, MI B
Northwest Missouri State U, MO B
The Ohio State U, OH B
Oklahoma State U, OK B
Purdue U, IN B
Southern Illinois U Carbondale, IL B
U of Illinois at Urbana–Champaign, IL B
U of Minnesota, Twin Cities Campus, MN B
U of Missouri–Columbia, MO B
U of Wisconsin–Milwaukee, WI B
U of Wisconsin–Stevens Point, WI B

Forestry Technology
Michigan Technological U, MI A

Forest Sciences and Biology
Coll of Saint Benedict, MN B
Saint John's U, MN B
U of Illinois at Urbana–Champaign, IL B

Franchising
St. Catherine U, MN B

French
Adrian Coll, MI B
Albion Coll, MI B
Alma Coll, MI B
Anderson U, IN B
Andrews U, MI B
Aquinas Coll, MI B
Ashland U, OH B
Augsburg Coll, MN B
Augustana Coll, IL B
Augustana Coll, SD B
Baker U, KS B
Baldwin-Wallace Coll, OH B
Ball State U, IN B
Beloit Coll, WI B
Benedictine Coll, KS B
Bethel U, MN B
Bowling Green State U, OH B
Bradley U, IL B
Butler U, IN B
Calvin Coll, MI B
Capital U, OH B
Carleton Coll, MN B
Case Western Reserve U, OH B
Central Coll, IA B
Central Methodist U, MO B
Central Michigan U, MI B
Cleveland State U, OH B
Coe Coll, IA B
Coll of Saint Benedict, MN B
Coll of the Ozarks, MO B
The Coll of Wooster, OH B
Concordia Coll, MN B
Cornell Coll, IA B
Creighton U, NE B
Denison U, OH B
DePaul U, IL B
DePauw U, IN B
Doane Coll, NE B
Dominican U, IL B
Drury U, MO B
Earlham Coll, IN B
Eastern Michigan U, MI B
Edgewood Coll, WI B
Elmhurst Coll, IL B
Fort Hays State U, KS B
Franciscan U of Steubenville, OH B
Franklin Coll, IN B
Grace Coll, IN B
Grand Valley State U, MI B
Grinnell Coll, IA B
Gustavus Adolphus Coll, MN B
Hamline U, MN B
Hanover Coll, IN B
Hillsdale Coll, MI B
Hiram Coll, OH B
Hope Coll, MI B
Illinois Coll, IL B
Illinois State U, IL B
Illinois Wesleyan U, IL B
Indiana U Bloomington, IN B
Indiana U Northwest, IN B
Indiana U–Purdue U Fort Wayne, IN A,B
Indiana U–Purdue U Indianapolis, IN B
Indiana U South Bend, IN B
Indiana U Southeast, IN B
Iowa State U of Science and Technology, IA B
Jamestown Coll, ND B
John Carroll U, OH B
Kalamazoo Coll, MI B
Kent State U, OH B
Kenyon Coll, OH B
Knox Coll, IL B
Lake Erie Coll, OH B
Lake Forest Coll, IL B
Lawrence U, WI B
Lindenwood U, MO B
Loras Coll, IA B
Loyola U Chicago, IL B
Luther Coll, IA B
Macalester Coll, MN B
Manchester Coll, IN B
Marian U, IN B
Miami U, OH B
Miami U Hamilton, OH B
Michigan State U, MI B
Minnesota State U Mankato, MN B
Minot State U, ND B
Missouri Southern State U, MO B
Missouri State U, MO B
Missouri Western State U, MO B
Monmouth Coll, IL B
Mount Mary Coll, WI B
Mount Union Coll, OH B
Muskingum Coll, OH B
Nebraska Wesleyan U, NE B
North Central Coll, IL B
North Dakota State U, ND B
Northeastern Illinois U, IL B
Northern Michigan U, MI B
Northern State U, SD B
North Park U, IL B
Northwestern U, IL B
Northwest Missouri State U, MO B
Oakland U, MI B
Oberlin Coll, OH B
Ohio Northern U, OH B
The Ohio State U, OH B
Ohio U, OH B
Ohio Wesleyan U, OH B
Oklahoma City U, OK B
Oklahoma State U, OK B
Oral Roberts U, OK B
Otterbein Coll, OH B
Pittsburg State U, KS B
Purdue U, IN B
Purdue U Calumet, IN B
Ripon Coll, WI B
Rockford Coll, IL B
Rockhurst U, MO B
Saginaw Valley State U, MI B
St. Ambrose U, IA B
St. Catherine U, MN B
St. Cloud State U, MN B
Saint John's U, MN B

A—associate degree; B—bachelor's degree

Saint Louis U, MO B
Saint Mary's Coll, IN B
Saint Mary's U of Minnesota, MN B
St. Norbert Coll, WI B
St. Olaf Coll, MN B
Simpson Coll, IA B
South Dakota State U, SD B
Southeast Missouri State U, MO B
Southern Illinois U Carbondale, IL B
Southern Methodist U, TX B
Taylor U, IN B
Transylvania U, KY B
Truman State U, MO B
Union Coll, NE B
The U of Akron, OH B
U of Central Missouri, MO B
U of Central Oklahoma, OK B
U of Chicago, IL B
U of Cincinnati, OH B
U of Dallas, TX B
U of Dayton, OH B
U of Evansville, IN B
U of Illinois at Chicago, IL B
U of Illinois at Urbana–Champaign, IL B
U of Indianapolis, IN B
The U of Iowa, IA B
The U of Kansas, KS B
U of Michigan, MI B
U of Michigan–Dearborn, MI B
U of Michigan–Flint, MI B
U of Minnesota, Morris, MN B
U of Minnesota, Twin Cities Campus, MN B
U of Missouri–Columbia, MO B
U of Missouri–Kansas City, MO B
U of Missouri–St. Louis, MO B
U of Nebraska at Kearney, NE B
U of Nebraska at Omaha, NE B
U of Nebraska–Lincoln, NE B
U of New Orleans, LA B
U of North Dakota, ND B
U of Northern Iowa, IA B
U of Notre Dame, IN B
U of Oklahoma, OK B
The U of South Dakota, SD B
U of Southern Indiana, IN B
The U of Toledo, OH B
U of Tulsa, OK B
U of Wisconsin–Eau Claire, WI B
U of Wisconsin–Green Bay, WI B
U of Wisconsin–La Crosse, WI B
U of Wisconsin–Madison, WI B
U of Wisconsin–Milwaukee, WI B
U of Wisconsin–Oshkosh, WI B
U of Wisconsin–Parkside, WI B
U of Wisconsin–Stevens Point, WI B
U of Wisconsin–Whitewater, WI B
Valparaiso U, IN B
Wabash Coll, IN B
Walsh U, OH B
Wartburg Coll, IA B
Washburn U, KS B
Washington U in St. Louis, MO B
Webster U, MO B
Western Illinois U, IL B
Western Michigan U, MI B
Westminster Coll, MO B
Wheaton Coll, IL B
Wichita State U, KS B
William Jewell Coll, MO B
Winona State U, MN B
Wittenberg U, OH B
Wright State U, OH B
Xavier U, OH A,B
Youngstown State U, OH B

French as a Second/Foreign Language (Teaching)

Saginaw Valley State U, MI B
Western Michigan U, MI B

French Language Teacher Education

Alma Coll, MI B
Anderson U, IN B
Bethel U, MN B
Bowling Green State U, OH B
Central Michigan U, MI B
Coll of the Ozarks, MO B
Concordia Coll, MN B
DePaul U, IL B
Eastern Michigan U, MI B
Edgewood Coll, WI B
Elmhurst Coll, IL B
Franklin Coll, IN B
Grace Coll, IN B
Grand Valley State U, MI B
Hope Coll, MI B
Indiana U Bloomington, IN B
Indiana U–Purdue U Fort Wayne, IN B
Indiana U–Purdue U Indianapolis, IN B
Kent State U, OH B
Lindenwood U, MO B
Miami U, OH B
Miami U Hamilton, OH B
Minot State U, ND B
Missouri State U, MO B
Missouri Western State U, MO B
Mount Mary Coll, WI B
Muskingum Coll, OH B
North Dakota State U, ND B
Northern Michigan U, MI B
Ohio Northern U, OH B
Ohio U, OH B
Ohio Wesleyan U, OH B
Pittsburg State U, KS B
Purdue U, IN B
St. Ambrose U, IA B
St. Catherine U, MN B
Saint Mary's U of Minnesota, MN B
Taylor U, IN B
The U of Akron, OH B
U of Evansville, IN B
U of Illinois at Chicago, IL B
U of Illinois at Urbana–Champaign, IL B
U of Indianapolis, IN B
The U of Iowa, IA B
U of Michigan–Flint, MI B
U of Minnesota, Duluth, MN B
U of Missouri–St. Louis, MO B
U of Nebraska–Lincoln, NE B
The U of South Dakota, SD B
The U of Toledo, OH B
Valparaiso U, IN B
Washington U in St. Louis, MO B
Western Michigan U, MI B
Youngstown State U, OH B

French Studies

Carleton Coll, MN B
Case Western Reserve U, OH B
Coe Coll, IA B
Lake Superior State U, MI B
North Park U, IL B

Funeral Direction/Service

Wayne State U, MI B

Funeral Service and Mortuary Science

Ferris State U, MI A
Lindenwood U, MO B
Southern Illinois U Carbondale, IL B
U of Central Oklahoma, OK B
U of Minnesota, Twin Cities Campus, MN B

General Studies

AIB Coll of Business, IA A
Anderson U, IN A,B
Aquinas Coll, MI B
Bacone Coll, OK A
Ball State U, IN A,B
Barclay Coll, KS A
Black Hills State U, SD A
Calumet Coll of Saint Joseph, IN A,B
Cameron U, OK A
Central Coll, IA B
Cleveland State U, OH B
Coll of Mount St. Joseph, OH A
Colorado Tech U North Kansas City, MO A
Colorado Tech U Sioux Falls, SD A
Concordia U, MI A
Concordia U, St. Paul, MN A,B
Concordia U Wisconsin, WI B
Dakota State U, SD A
DePaul U, IL B
Dordt Coll, IA B
Emporia State U, KS B
Ferris State U, MI A
Franciscan U of Steubenville, OH A
Friends U, KS A
Grantham U, MO A,B
Great Lakes Christian Coll, MI A
Illinois State U, IL B
Indiana Tech, IN A
Indiana U Bloomington, IN A,B
Indiana U East, IN A,B
Indiana U Kokomo, IN A,B
Indiana U Northwest, IN A,B
Indiana U–Purdue U Fort Wayne, IN A,B
Indiana U–Purdue U Indianapolis, IN A,B
Indiana U South Bend, IN A,B
Indiana U Southeast, IN A,B
Indiana Wesleyan U, IN A,B
Kent State U, OH B
Kent State U, Stark Campus, OH B
Loyola U Chicago, IL B
Madonna U, MI B
Mayville State U, ND B
Mercy Coll of Northwest Ohio, OH A
Messenger Coll, MO A
Miami U Hamilton, OH A
Michigan Technological U, MI B
Minot State U, ND B
Mount Marty Coll, SD A,B
Mount Vernon Nazarene U, OH A
National American U, MO A
Northeastern State U, OK B
Northern Michigan U, MI A
Northwestern U, IL B
Oak Hills Christian Coll, MN A
Ohio Dominican U, OH A,B
Ohio Northern U, OH B
The Ohio State U at Lima, OH A
Ohio U, OH B
Ohio Wesleyan U, OH B
Oklahoma Panhandle State U, OK A
Oklahoma State U, OK B
Oklahoma State U, Oklahoma City, OK A
Pittsburg State U, KS B
Presentation Coll, SD A
Rochester Comm and Tech Coll, MN A
Saginaw Valley State U, MI B
St. Augustine Coll, IL A
Shawnee State U, OH A,B
Shimer Coll, IL B
Siena Heights U, MI A,B
Silver Lake Coll, WI A
Sinte Gleska U, SD A
South Dakota School of Mines and Technology, SD A
South Dakota State U, SD A
Southeastern Oklahoma State U, OK B
Southeast Missouri State U, MO B
Southern Nazarene U, OK A
Southwest Baptist U, MO A
Southwestern Christian U, OK A
Southwestern Coll, KS B
Southwest Minnesota State U, MN B
Tiffin U, OH A,B
Trinity Bible Coll, ND B
U of Charleston, WV B
U of Dayton, OH B

U of Illinois at Urbana–Champaign, IL B
U of Mary, ND B
U of Michigan, MI B
U of Michigan–Dearborn, MI B
U of Missouri–Columbia, MO B
U of Missouri–St. Louis, MO B
U of Nebraska at Kearney, NE B
U of New Orleans, LA B
U of North Dakota, ND B
U of Phoenix–Cleveland Campus, OH A
U of Phoenix–Indianapolis Campus, IN A
U of Phoenix–St. Louis Campus, MO A
U of Rio Grande, OH A
The U of South Dakota, SD A
The U of Toledo, OH A,B
U of Wisconsin–Stevens Point, WI B
U of Wisconsin–Superior, WI A
Viterbo U, WI A
York Coll, NE B
Youngstown State U, OH B

Genetics
Iowa State U of Science and Technology, IA B
Ohio Wesleyan U, OH B

Geochemistry
Grand Valley State U, MI B
Western Michigan U, MI B

Geography
Aquinas Coll, MI B
Augustana Coll, IL B
Ball State U, IN B
Bemidji State U, MN B
Bowling Green State U, OH B
Calvin Coll, MI B
Central Michigan U, MI B
Concordia U Chicago, IL B
Concordia U, Nebraska, NE B
DePaul U, IL B
Eastern Illinois U, IL B
Eastern Michigan U, MI B
Elmhurst Coll, IL B
Grand Valley State U, MI B
Gustavus Adolphus Coll, MN B
Illinois State U, IL B
Indiana State U, IN B
Indiana U Bloomington, IN B
Indiana U–Purdue U Indianapolis, IN B
Indiana U Southeast, IN B
Kansas State U, KS B
Kent State U, OH B
Macalester Coll, MN B
Miami U, OH B
Miami U Hamilton, OH B
Michigan State U, MI B
Minnesota State U Mankato, MN B
Missouri State U, MO B
Northeastern Illinois U, IL B
Northeastern State U, OK B
Northern Michigan U, MI B
Northwestern U, IL B
Northwest Missouri State U, MO B
The Ohio State U, OH B
Ohio U, OH B
Ohio Wesleyan U, OH B
Oklahoma State U, OK B
Olivet Nazarene U, IL B
Park U, MO B
Pittsburg State U, KS B
St. Cloud State U, MN B
South Dakota State U, SD B
Southern Illinois U Carbondale, IL B
Southern Illinois U Edwardsville, IL B
Taylor U, IN B
The U of Akron, OH B
U of Central Missouri, MO B
U of Central Oklahoma, OK B
U of Chicago, IL B
U of Cincinnati, OH B
U of Illinois at Urbana–Champaign, IL B
The U of Iowa, IA B
The U of Kansas, KS B
U of Minnesota, Duluth, MN B
U of Minnesota, Twin Cities Campus, MN B
U of Missouri–Columbia, MO B
U of Missouri–Kansas City, MO B
U of Nebraska at Kearney, NE B
U of Nebraska at Omaha, NE B
U of Nebraska–Lincoln, NE B
U of New Orleans, LA B
U of North Dakota, ND B
U of Northern Iowa, IA B
U of Oklahoma, OK B
The U of Toledo, OH B
U of Wisconsin–Eau Claire, WI B
U of Wisconsin–La Crosse, WI B
U of Wisconsin–Madison, WI B
U of Wisconsin–Milwaukee, WI B
U of Wisconsin–Oshkosh, WI B
U of Wisconsin–Parkside, WI B
U of Wisconsin–Stevens Point, WI B
U of Wisconsin–Whitewater, WI B
Valparaiso U, IN B
Wayne State Coll, NE B
Wayne State U, MI B
Western Illinois U, IL B
Western Michigan U, MI B
Wittenberg U, OH B
Wright State U, OH A,B
Youngstown State U, OH B

Geography Related
Central Michigan U, MI B
South Dakota State U, SD B

Geography Teacher Education
Central Michigan U, MI B
Concordia U, Nebraska, NE B
DePaul U, IL B
Grand Valley State U, MI B
Mayville State U, ND B
Northern Michigan U, MI B
Shawnee State U, OH B
Valparaiso U, IN B
Wayne State Coll, NE B
Western Michigan U, MI B

Geological and Earth Sciences/Geosciences Related
Earlham Coll, IN B
Ohio U, OH B
The U of Akron, OH B
U of Illinois at Urbana–Champaign, IL B
U of Michigan, MI B
U of Northern Iowa, IA B
U of Oklahoma, OK B
Valparaiso U, IN B
Wittenberg U, OH B

Geological/Geophysical Engineering
Michigan Technological U, MI B
Missouri U of Science and Technology, MO B
South Dakota School of Mines and Technology, SD B
U of Michigan, MI B
U of Minnesota, Twin Cities Campus, MN B
U of North Dakota, ND B

Geology/Earth Science
Adrian Coll, MI B
Albion Coll, MI B
Ashland U, OH B
Augustana Coll, IL B
Ball State U, IN B
Beloit Coll, WI B
Bemidji State U, MN B
Bowling Green State U, OH B
Calvin Coll, MI B
Carleton Coll, MN B
Case Western Reserve U, OH B
Central Michigan U, MI B
Central State U, OH B
Cleveland State U, OH B
The Coll of Wooster, OH B
Cornell Coll, IA B
Denison U, OH B
DePauw U, IN B
Eastern Illinois U, IL B
Eastern Michigan U, MI B
Emporia State U, KS B
Fort Hays State U, KS B
Grand Valley State U, MI B
Gustavus Adolphus Coll, MN B
Hanover Coll, IN B
Hope Coll, MI B
Illinois State U, IL B
Indiana State U, IN B
Indiana U Bloomington, IN B
Indiana U Northwest, IN B
Indiana U–Purdue U Fort Wayne, IN B
Indiana U–Purdue U Indianapolis, IN B
Iowa State U of Science and Technology, IA B
Kansas State U, KS B
Kent State U, OH B
Lake Superior State U, MI B
Lawrence U, WI B
Macalester Coll, MN B
Marietta Coll, OH B
Miami U, OH B
Miami U Hamilton, OH B
Michigan State U, MI B
Michigan Technological U, MI B
Minnesota State U Mankato, MN B
Minot State U, ND B
Missouri State U, MO B
Missouri U of Science and Technology, MO B
Mount Union Coll, OH B
Muskingum Coll, OH B
North Dakota State U, ND B
Northeastern Illinois U, IL B
Northern Michigan U, MI B
Northland Coll, WI B
Northwestern U, IL B
Northwest Missouri State U, MO B
Oberlin Coll, OH B
The Ohio State U, OH B
Ohio U, OH B
Ohio Wesleyan U, OH B
Oklahoma State U, OK B
Olivet Nazarene U, IL B
Purdue U, IN B
St. Cloud State U, MN B
Saint Louis U, MO B
St. Norbert Coll, WI B
South Dakota School of Mines and Technology, SD B
Southern Illinois U Carbondale, IL B
Southern Methodist U, TX B
Taylor U, IN B
The U of Akron, OH B
U of Central Missouri, MO B
U of Cincinnati, OH B
U of Dayton, OH B
U of Illinois at Chicago, IL B
U of Illinois at Urbana–Champaign, IL B
U of Indianapolis, IN B
The U of Iowa, IA B
The U of Kansas, KS B
U of Michigan, MI B
U of Michigan–Dearborn, MI B
U of Minnesota, Duluth, MN B
U of Minnesota, Morris, MN B
U of Minnesota, Twin Cities Campus, MN B
U of Missouri–Columbia, MO B
U of Missouri–Kansas City, MO B
U of Nebraska at Omaha, NE B
U of Nebraska–Lincoln, NE B
U of New Orleans, LA B
U of North Dakota, ND B
U of Northern Iowa, IA B
U of Oklahoma, OK B

A—associate degree; B—bachelor's degree

The U of South Dakota, SD B
U of Southern Indiana, IN B
The U of Toledo, OH B
U of Tulsa, OK B
U of Wisconsin–Eau Claire, WI B
U of Wisconsin–Green Bay, WI B
U of Wisconsin–Madison, WI B
U of Wisconsin–Milwaukee, WI B
U of Wisconsin–Oshkosh, WI B
U of Wisconsin–Parkside, WI B
U of Wisconsin–Platteville, WI B
Valparaiso U, IN B
Washington U in St. Louis, MO B
Wayne State U, MI B
Western Illinois U, IL B
Western Michigan U, MI B
Wheaton Coll, IL B
Wichita State U, KS B
Winona State U, MN B
Wittenberg U, OH B
Wright State U, OH B
Youngstown State U, OH B

Geophysics and Seismology

Eastern Michigan U, MI B
Hope Coll, MI B
Michigan State U, MI B
Michigan Technological U, MI B
Missouri U of Science and Technology, MO B
Saint Louis U, MO B
Southern Methodist U, TX B
The U of Akron, OH B
U of Chicago, IL B
U of Minnesota, Twin Cities Campus, MN B
U of Oklahoma, OK B
U of Tulsa, OK B
U of Wisconsin–Madison, WI B
Western Michigan U, MI B
Wright State U, OH B

Geotechnical Engineering

U of Illinois at Urbana–Champaign, IL B

German

Adrian Coll, MI B
Albion Coll, MI B
Alma Coll, MI B
Aquinas Coll, MI B
Augsburg Coll, MN B
Augustana Coll, IL B
Augustana Coll, SD B
Baker U, KS B
Baldwin-Wallace Coll, OH B
Ball State U, IN B
Beloit Coll, WI B
Bemidji State U, MN B
Bowling Green State U, OH B
Bradley U, IL B
Butler U, IN B
Calvin Coll, MI B
Carleton Coll, MN B
Case Western Reserve U, OH B
Central Michigan U, MI B
Coe Coll, IA B
Coll of Saint Benedict, MN B
The Coll of Wooster, OH B
Concordia Coll, MN B
Concordia U Wisconsin, WI B
Cornell Coll, IA B
Creighton U, NE B
Denison U, OH B
DePaul U, IL B
DePauw U, IN B
Doane Coll, NE B
Drury U, MO B
Earlham Coll, IN B
Eastern Michigan U, MI B
Elmhurst Coll, IL B
Fort Hays State U, KS B
Franciscan U of Steubenville, OH B
Grace Coll, IN B
Grinnell Coll, IA B
Gustavus Adolphus Coll, MN B
Hamline U, MN B
Hanover Coll, IN B
Heidelberg U, OH B
Hillsdale Coll, MI B
Hope Coll, MI B
Illinois Coll, IL B
Illinois State U, IL B
Illinois Wesleyan U, IL B
Indiana U Bloomington, IN B
Indiana U–Purdue U Fort Wayne, IN A,B
Indiana U–Purdue U Indianapolis, IN B
Indiana U South Bend, IN B
Indiana U Southeast, IN B
Iowa State U of Science and Technology, IA B
Jamestown Coll, ND B
John Carroll U, OH B
Kalamazoo Coll, MI B
Kent State U, OH B
Kenyon Coll, OH B
Knox Coll, IL B
Lake Erie Coll, OH B
Lakeland Coll, WI B
Lawrence U, WI B
Loyola U Chicago, IL B
Luther Coll, IA B
Macalester Coll, MN B
Manchester Coll, IN B
Miami U, OH B
Miami U Hamilton, OH B
Michigan State U, MI B
Minnesota State U Mankato, MN B
Minot State U, ND B
Missouri Southern State U, MO B
Missouri State U, MO B
Mount Union Coll, OH B
Muskingum Coll, OH B
Nebraska Wesleyan U, NE B
North Central Coll, IL B
Northern State U, SD B
Northwestern U, IL B
Oakland U, MI B
Oberlin Coll, OH B
The Ohio State U, OH B
Ohio U, OH B
Ohio Wesleyan U, OH B
Oklahoma City U, OK B
Oklahoma State U, OK B
Oral Roberts U, OK B
Ripon Coll, WI B
St. Ambrose U, IA B
St. Cloud State U, MN B
Saint John's U, MN B
Saint Louis U, MO B
St. Norbert Coll, WI B
St. Olaf Coll, MN B
Simpson Coll, IA B
South Dakota State U, SD B
Southeast Missouri State U, MO B
Southern Illinois U Carbondale, IL B
Southern Methodist U, TX B
Transylvania U, KY B
Truman State U, MO B
Union Coll, NE B
U of Central Missouri, MO B
U of Central Oklahoma, OK B
U of Chicago, IL B
U of Cincinnati, OH B
U of Dallas, TX B
U of Dayton, OH B
U of Evansville, IN B
U of Illinois at Urbana–Champaign, IL B
U of Indianapolis, IN B
The U of Iowa, IA B
U of Michigan, MI B
U of Minnesota, Morris, MN B
U of Minnesota, Twin Cities Campus, MN B
U of Missouri–Columbia, MO B
U of Missouri–Kansas City, MO B
U of Missouri–St. Louis, MO B
U of Nebraska at Kearney, NE B
U of Nebraska at Omaha, NE B
U of Nebraska–Lincoln, NE B
U of North Dakota, ND B
U of Northern Iowa, IA B
U of Notre Dame, IN B
U of Oklahoma, OK B
The U of South Dakota, SD B
U of Southern Indiana, IN B
The U of Toledo, OH B
U of Tulsa, OK B
U of Wisconsin–La Crosse, WI B
U of Wisconsin–Madison, WI B
U of Wisconsin–Milwaukee, WI B
U of Wisconsin–Oshkosh, WI B
U of Wisconsin–Parkside, WI B
U of Wisconsin–Platteville, WI B
U of Wisconsin–Stevens Point, WI B
U of Wisconsin–Whitewater, WI B
Valparaiso U, IN B
Wabash Coll, IN B
Wartburg Coll, IA B
Washburn U, KS B
Washington U in St. Louis, MO B
Wayne State U, MI B
Webster U, MO B
Western Michigan U, MI B
Wheaton Coll, IL B
Winona State U, MN B
Wittenberg U, OH B
Wright State U, OH B
Xavier U, OH A,B
Youngstown State U, OH B

Germanic Languages

Bethel Coll, KS B
Cleveland State U, OH B
Eastern Michigan U, MI B
Grand Valley State U, MI B
The U of Kansas, KS B
U of Wisconsin–Eau Claire, WI B
U of Wisconsin–Green Bay, WI B
Washington U in St. Louis, MO B

Germanic Languages Related

Calvin Coll, MI B
Ohio Northern U, OH B

German Language Teacher Education

Alma Coll, MI B
Central Michigan U, MI B
Concordia Coll, MN B
Concordia U Wisconsin, WI B
DePaul U, IL B
Eastern Michigan U, MI B
Elmhurst Coll, IL B
Grace Coll, IN B
Grand Valley State U, MI B
Hope Coll, MI B
Indiana U Bloomington, IN B
Indiana U–Purdue U Fort Wayne, IN B
Indiana U–Purdue U Indianapolis, IN B
Miami U, OH B
Miami U Hamilton, OH B
Minot State U, ND B
Missouri State U, MO B
Muskingum Coll, OH B
Ohio Northern U, OH B
Ohio U, OH B
Ohio Wesleyan U, OH B
Purdue U, IN B
St. Ambrose U, IA B
U of Evansville, IN B
U of Illinois at Chicago, IL B
U of Illinois at Urbana–Champaign, IL B
The U of Iowa, IA B
U of Minnesota, Duluth, MN B
U of Missouri–St. Louis, MO B
U of Nebraska–Lincoln, NE B
The U of South Dakota, SD B
The U of Toledo, OH B
Valparaiso U, IN B
Washington U in St. Louis, MO B
Western Michigan U, MI B

German Studies
Case Western Reserve U, OH B
Central Coll, IA B
Coe Coll, IA B
The Coll of Wooster, OH B
Purdue U, IN B
U of Illinois at Chicago, IL B

Gerontology
Alma Coll, MI B
Bowling Green State U, OH B
Brown Mackie Coll–Merrillville, IN A
Case Western Reserve U, OH B
Cleveland State U, OH B
Dominican U, IL B
Indiana U Kokomo, IN B
John Carroll U, OH B
Lindenwood U, MO B
Madonna U, MI A,B
Manchester Coll, IN A
Martin U, IN B
Miami U, OH B
Miami U Hamilton, OH B
Minnesota State U Moorhead, MN B
Missouri State U, MO B
National-Louis U, IL B
Ohio Dominican U, OH A
St. Cloud State U, MN B
Siena Heights U, MI A
U of Nebraska at Omaha, NE B
U of Northern Iowa, IA B
The U of Toledo, OH A
Wichita State U, KS B
Youngstown State U, OH B

Graphic and Printing Equipment Operation/ Production
Ferris State U, MI B
Western Illinois U, IL B

Graphic Communications
Carroll U, WI B
Grand View U, IA B
Minnesota State U Moorhead, MN B
Pittsburg State U, KS B
Southern Nazarene U, OK B
U of North Dakota, ND B
U of Northern Iowa, IA B
U of Phoenix–Cleveland Campus, OH A,B
U of Phoenix–Indianapolis Campus, IN A
U of Phoenix–St. Louis Campus, MO A

Graphic Design
Alma Coll, MI B
Art Academy of Cincinnati, OH A
The Art Inst of Indianapolis, IN A,B
The Art Inst of Michigan, MI A
The Art Insts International–Kansas City, KS A,B
The Art Insts International Minnesota, MN A,B
Bradley U, IL B
Briar Cliff U, IA B
Bryant & Stratton Coll–Wauwatosa Campus, WI A
Cedarville U, OH B
Central Michigan U, MI B
The Cleveland Inst of Art, OH B
Coll for Creative Studies, MI B
Coll of Mount St. Joseph, OH A,B
Coll of Visual Arts, MN B
Columbia Coll, MO B
Concordia U Wisconsin, WI B
Creighton U, NE B
Dana Coll, NE B
Dordt Coll, IA B
Drake U, IA B
Edgewood Coll, WI B
Ferris State U, MI A,B
Grace Coll, IN B
Grand View U, IA B
Huntington U, IN B
The Illinois Inst of Art–Chicago, IL A,B
The Illinois Inst of Art–Schaumburg, IL A,B
Indiana U–Purdue U Fort Wayne, IN B
Iowa State U of Science and Technology, IA B
Iowa Wesleyan Coll, IA B
Kansas City Art Inst, MO B
Madonna U, MI A,B
Marian U, WI B
Marietta Coll, OH B
Maryville U of Saint Louis, MO B
Miami U Hamilton, OH B
MidAmerica Nazarene U, KS B
Missouri Coll, MO A
Missouri Western State U, MO B
Mount Mary Coll, WI B
Mount Mercy Coll, IA B
Mount Vernon Nazarene U, OH B
North Central Coll, IL B
Northern Michigan U, MI B
Northwestern Coll, MN B
Ohio Dominican U, OH B
Ohio Northern U, OH B
Oklahoma Baptist U, OK B
Park U, MO B
Quincy U, IL B
Rochester Comm and Tech Coll, MN A
St. Ambrose U, IA B
Saint Mary's U of Minnesota, MN B
Shawnee State U, OH B
South Dakota State U, SD B
Spring Arbor U, MI B
Stephens Coll, MO B
Union Coll, NE A,B
The U of Akron, OH B
U of Evansville, IN B
U of Illinois at Chicago, IL B
U of Illinois at Urbana–Champaign, IL B
The U of Kansas, KS B
U of Michigan, MI B
U of Missouri–St. Louis, MO B
U of North Dakota, ND B
U of Rio Grande, OH B
Ursuline Coll, OH B
Viterbo U, WI B
Washington U in St. Louis, MO B
Wayne State Coll, NE B
Western Michigan U, MI B
Westwood Coll–Chicago Du Page, IL A
Youngstown State U, OH B

Graphic/Printing Equipment
Coll of the Ozarks, MO B

Greenhouse Management
Rochester Comm and Tech Coll, MN A

Hazardous Materials Information Systems Technology
Ohio U, OH A
Ohio U–Chillicothe, OH A

Hazardous Materials Management and Waste Technology
Ohio U, OH A

Health and Medical Administrative Services Related
Kent State U, OH A,B
Missouri Coll, MO A
Missouri Southern State U, MO B
Mount Mercy Coll, IA B
U of Michigan–Flint, MI B
U of Minnesota, Crookston, MN B
Ursuline Coll, OH B

Health and Physical Education
Adrian Coll, MI B
Anderson U, IN B
Baker U, KS B
Baldwin-Wallace Coll, OH B
Bethel Coll, IN B
Bethel Coll, KS B
Bethel U, MN B
Black Hills State U, SD B
Bluffton U, OH B
Cameron U, OK B
Capital U, OH B
Carroll U, WI B
Cedarville U, OH B
Central Christian Coll of Kansas, KS A,B
Central Michigan U, MI B
Coll of the Ozarks, MO B
Concordia Coll, MN B
Concordia U, MI B
Concordia U, Nebraska, NE B
Concordia U Wisconsin, WI B
DePaul U, IL B
Doane Coll, NE B
Dordt Coll, IA B
Eastern Michigan U, MI B
Elmhurst Coll, IL B
Evangel U, MO B
Friends U, KS B
Grace Coll, IN B
Hamline U, MN B
Haskell Indian Nations U, KS A
Iowa State U of Science and Technology, IA B
Lindenwood U, MO B
Loras Coll, IA B
Luther Coll, IA B
Mayville State U, ND B
Miami U, OH B
Minnesota State U Moorhead, MN B
Missouri Western State U, MO B
Mount Vernon Nazarene U, OH A,B
Nebraska Wesleyan U, NE B
Northern Michigan U, MI B
Northwestern Coll, MN B
Ohio Northern U, OH B
The Ohio State U, OH B
Ohio U, OH B
Oklahoma Baptist U, OK B
Oklahoma Panhandle State U, OK B
Olivet Coll, MI B
Oral Roberts U, OK B
Purdue U, IN B
Robert Morris Coll, IL A
St. Ambrose U, IA B
St. Catherine U, MN B
Saint Joseph's Coll, IN B
South Dakota State U, SD B
Southeast Missouri State U, MO B
Southern Illinois U Edwardsville, IL B
Southwest Baptist U, MO B
Southwestern Coll, KS B
Southwest Minnesota State U, MN B
Sterling Coll, KS B
The U of Kansas, KS B
U of Mary, ND B
U of Nebraska at Omaha, NE B
U of New Orleans, LA B
U of Northern Iowa, IA B
U of Oklahoma, OK B
U of Rio Grande, OH B
U of Science and Arts of Oklahoma, OK B
U of Wisconsin–Stevens Point, WI B
U of Wisconsin–Superior, WI B
Valparaiso U, IN B
Walsh U, OH B
Youngstown State U, OH B

Health and Physical Education Related
Avila U, MO B
Bowling Green State U, OH B
Coe Coll, IA B
Concordia U Wisconsin, WI B
Cornell Coll, IA B
Gustavus Adolphus Coll, MN B
Mayville State U, ND B
Missouri Southern State U, MO B

A—associate degree; B—bachelor's degree

Ohio Northern U, OH B
South Dakota State U, SD B
Southern Nazarene U, OK B
U of Central Oklahoma, OK B
U of Minnesota, Twin Cities Campus, MN B
U of Wisconsin–Superior, WI B
Wayne State Coll, NE B

Health Communication

Grand Valley State U, MI B
North Dakota State U, ND B
Ohio U–Eastern, OH B

Health/Health-Care Administration

Argosy U, Chicago, IL B
Argosy U, Schaumburg, IL B
Argosy U, Twin Cities, MN B
Augustana Coll, SD B
Baker Coll of Auburn Hills, MI A,B
Baker Coll of Flint, MI A
Baker Coll of Owosso, MI B
Baker Coll of Port Huron, MI B
Benedictine U, IL B
Black Hills State U, SD B
Bowling Green State U, OH B
Brown Mackie Coll–Fort Wayne, IN A
Brown Mackie Coll–Indianapolis, IN A
Brown Mackie Coll–Merrillville, IN B
Brown Mackie Coll–Michigan City, IN A
Brown Mackie Coll–South Bend, IN A,B
Calumet Coll of Saint Joseph, IN B
Central Michigan U, MI B
Chancellor U, OH B
Colorado Tech U North Kansas City, MO B
Colorado Tech U Sioux Falls, SD B
Concordia Coll, MN B
Concordia U Wisconsin, WI B
Creighton U, NE B
Davenport U, Grand Rapids, MI B
Eastern Michigan U, MI B
Ferris State U, MI B
Franklin U, OH B
Harris-Stowe State U, MO B
Heidelberg U, OH B
Indiana Tech, IN B
Indiana U–Purdue U Fort Wayne, IN B
Indiana U–Purdue U Indianapolis, IN B
Lindenwood U, MO B
Lourdes Coll, OH B
Loyola U Chicago, IL B
Madonna U, MI B
Mercy Coll of Health Sciences, IA B
Mercy Coll of Northwest Ohio, OH B
Midstate Coll, IL B
Minnesota School of Business–Blaine, MN B
Minnesota State U Moorhead, MN B
Mount Mercy Coll, IA B
National-Louis U, IL B
Northeastern State U, OK B
The Ohio State U at Lima, OH B
Ohio U–Eastern, OH B
Oklahoma State U, Oklahoma City, OK A
Park U, MO A
Rasmussen Coll Eagan, MN A
Saint Louis U, MO B
Sanford-Brown Coll, Fenton, MO B
Southern Illinois U Carbondale, IL B
Southwestern Oklahoma State U, OK B
Spring Arbor U, MI B
U of Cincinnati, OH B
U of Evansville, IN B
U of Michigan–Dearborn, MI B
U of Michigan–Flint, MI B
U of Phoenix–Cleveland Campus, OH B
U of Phoenix–Indianapolis Campus, IN B
U of Phoenix–Kansas City Campus, MO B
U of Phoenix–Metro Detroit Campus, MI B
U of Phoenix–Oklahoma City Campus, OK B
U of Phoenix–Tulsa Campus, OK B
U of Phoenix–West Michigan Campus, MI B
U of St. Francis, IL B
U of Saint Francis, IN B
U of Wisconsin–Eau Claire, WI B
U of Wisconsin–Milwaukee, WI B
Ursuline Coll, OH B
Washburn U, KS A
Western Illinois U, IL B
Wichita State U, KS B
Wilberforce U, OH B
Winona State U, MN B
Wright State U, OH B

Health Information/Medical Records Administration

Baker Coll of Auburn Hills, MI A,B
Baker Coll of Cadillac, MI A
Baker Coll of Clinton Township, MI A
Baker Coll of Flint, MI A
Baker Coll of Jackson, MI A
Baker Coll of Port Huron, MI A
The Coll of St. Scholastica, MN B
Dakota State U, SD B
Davenport U, Grand Rapids, MI B
Ferris State U, MI B
Illinois State U, IL B
Indiana U East, IN B
Indiana U–Purdue U Indianapolis, IN B
Indiana U South Bend, IN B
Indiana U Southeast, IN B
The Ohio State U, OH B
Park U, MO A
Rasmussen Coll Eagan, MN A
Rasmussen Coll St. Cloud, MN A
Saint Louis U, MO B
Southwestern Oklahoma State U, OK B
Stephens Coll, MO B
U of Cincinnati, OH A,B
U of Illinois at Chicago, IL B
The U of Kansas, KS B
The U of Toledo, OH B
U of Wisconsin–Milwaukee, WI B

Health Information/Medical Records Technology

Bacone Coll, OK A
Baker Coll of Flint, MI A
Baker Coll of Jackson, MI A
Dakota State U, SD A
Davenport U, Grand Rapids, MI A
DeVry U, Chicago, IL A
DeVry U, Columbus, OH A
Ferris State U, MI A
Franklin U, OH B
Indiana U Northwest, IN A
Indiana U South Bend, IN A
ITT Tech Inst, Indianapolis, IN A
ITT Tech Inst, Oklahoma City, OK A
Mercy Coll of Northwest Ohio, OH A
Midstate Coll, IL A
Missouri Western State U, MO A
Rasmussen Coll Eagan, MN A
Rochester Comm and Tech Coll, MN A
St. Catherine U, MN A
Sanford-Brown Coll, Fenton, MO A
Washburn U, KS A

Health/Medical Preparatory Programs Related

Aurora U, IL B
Avila U, MO B
Benedictine U, IL B
Cedarville U, OH B
Coll of the Ozarks, MO B
Concordia U, Nebraska, NE B
Madonna U, MI B
Maryville U of Saint Louis, MO B
Northern Michigan U, MI B
St. Cloud State U, MN B
Southern Nazarene U, OK B
Union Coll, NE A
The U of Akron, OH B
U of Evansville, IN B
U of Missouri–Columbia, MO B
Wright State U, OH B

Health Occupations Teacher Education

U of Central Oklahoma, OK B

Health Professions Related

Baldwin-Wallace Coll, OH B
Bowling Green State U, OH B
Bradley U, IL B
Cleveland State U, OH B
Missouri Southern State U, MO B
Northeastern State U, OK B
Oakland U, MI B
The Ohio State U, OH B
Ohio U–Southern Campus, OH A
Purdue U, IN B
U of Charleston, WV A,B
U of Northern Iowa, IA B
U of Saint Francis, IN B
U of Southern Indiana, IN B
Washington U in St. Louis, MO B
Wayne State U, MI B
Youngstown State U, OH B

Health Science

Alma Coll, MI B
Benedictine U, IL B
Bradley U, IL B
Coll of the Ozarks, MO B
Graceland U, IA B
Kalamazoo Coll, MI B
Manchester Coll, IN B
Maryville U of Saint Louis, MO B
Minnesota State U Mankato, MN B
Newman U, KS A,B
Northwest Missouri State U, MO B
The Ohio State U, OH B
Truman State U, MO B
Union Coll, NE A
Union Inst & U, OH B
U of Wisconsin–Milwaukee, WI B
Waldorf Coll, IA B
Winona State U, MN B
Youngstown State U, OH B

Health Services Administration

Brown Mackie Coll–Tulsa, OK A,B
Indiana U Northwest, IN B
Indiana U–Purdue U Fort Wayne, IN B
Indiana U–Purdue U Indianapolis, IN B
Indiana U South Bend, IN B
U of Illinois at Urbana–Champaign, IL B
U of Phoenix–Cleveland Campus, OH A
U of Phoenix–Indianapolis Campus, IN A,B
U of Phoenix–Kansas City Campus, MO B
U of Phoenix–Metro Detroit Campus, MI B
U of Phoenix–Oklahoma City Campus, OK B
U of Phoenix–St. Louis Campus, MO A

U of Phoenix–Tulsa Campus, OK B
U of Phoenix–West Michigan Campus, MI B
U of Phoenix–Wichita Campus, KS B
Ursuline Coll, OH B

Health Services/Allied Health/Health Sciences

The Coll of St. Scholastica, MN B
Kent State U, OH B
Little Priest Tribal Coll, NE A
Ohio U–Southern Campus, OH A
Purdue U, IN B
Saginaw Valley State U, MI B
St. Cloud State U, MN B
Truman State U, MO B
U of Michigan–Flint, MI B
U of Minnesota, Crookston, MN B
Ursuline Coll, OH B
Washburn U, KS B
Wheaton Coll, IL B

Health Teacher Education

Alma Coll, MI B
Aquinas Coll, MI B
Ashland U, OH B
Augsburg Coll, MN B
Ball State U, IN B
Bemidji State U, MN B
Bethel U, MN B
Capital U, OH B
Carroll U, WI B
Cedarville U, OH B
Central Christian Coll of Kansas, KS A,B
Central Michigan U, MI B
Coll of the Ozarks, MO B
Concordia Coll, MN B
Concordia U, MI B
Concordia U, Nebraska, NE B
Concordia U, St. Paul, MN B
Defiance Coll, OH B
DePaul U, IL B
Eastern Illinois U, IL B
Ferris State U, MI B
Graceland U, IA B
Grand Valley State U, MI B
Gustavus Adolphus Coll, MN B
Hamline U, MN B
Heidelberg U, OH B
Illinois State U, IL B
Indiana U Bloomington, IN B
Indiana U–Purdue U Indianapolis, IN B
Indiana U Southeast, IN B
Iowa State U of Science and Technology, IA B
Kansas Wesleyan U, KS B
Kent State U, OH B
Malone U, OH B
Manchester Coll, IN B
Mayville State U, ND B
Miami U, OH B
Miami U Hamilton, OH B
Minnesota State U Mankato, MN B
Minnesota State U Moorhead, MN B
Missouri Baptist U, MO B
Mount Union Coll, OH B
Mount Vernon Nazarene U, OH B
Muskingum Coll, OH B
North Dakota State U, ND B
Northeastern State U, OK B
Northern Michigan U, MI B
Northern State U, SD B
Northwest Missouri State U, MO B
Ohio Northern U, OH B
Ohio Wesleyan U, OH B
Oral Roberts U, OK B
Otterbein Coll, OH B
Purdue U, IN B
St. Ambrose U, IA B
St. Cloud State U, MN B
Southeastern Oklahoma State U, OK B
Southern Illinois U Carbondale, IL B
Southern Illinois U Edwardsville, IL B
Southwest Baptist U, MO B
Southwest Minnesota State U, MN B
U of Charleston, WV B
U of Cincinnati, OH B
U of Dayton, OH B
U of Minnesota, Duluth, MN B
U of Nebraska–Lincoln, NE B
U of Northern Iowa, IA B
U of Rio Grande, OH B
U of Saint Francis, IN B
The U of South Dakota, SD B
The U of Toledo, OH B
U of Wisconsin–La Crosse, WI B
Valley City State U, ND B
Waldorf Coll, IA B
Wayne State U, MI B
Western Illinois U, IL B
Western Michigan U, MI B
Wilmington Coll, OH B
Winona State U, MN B
Wright State U, OH B
Youngstown State U, OH B

Heating, Air Conditioning and Refrigeration Technology

Ferris State U, MI A
Northern Michigan U, MI A
U of Cincinnati, OH A

Heating, Air Conditioning, Ventilation and Refrigeration Maintenance Technology

Bohecker's Business Coll, OH A
Ranken Tech Coll, MO A
U of Cincinnati, OH A

Heavy Equipment Maintenance Technology

Ferris State U, MI A,B

Heavy/Industrial Equipment Maintenance Technologies Related

Ranken Tech Coll, MO A

Hebrew

Concordia U Wisconsin, WI B
Laura and Alvin Siegal Coll of Judaic Studies, OH B
The Ohio State U, OH B
U of Illinois at Urbana–Champaign, IL B
U of Michigan, MI B
U of Minnesota, Twin Cities Campus, MN B
U of Wisconsin–Madison, WI B
U of Wisconsin–Milwaukee, WI B
Washington U in St. Louis, MO B

Higher Education/Higher Education Administration

Wright State U, OH B

Hindi

U of Chicago, IL B

Hispanic American, Puerto Rican, and Mexican American/Chicano Studies

Southern Methodist U, TX B
U of Michigan, MI B
U of Minnesota, Twin Cities Campus, MN B
U of Wisconsin–Madison, WI B

Histologic Technician

Indiana U–Purdue U Indianapolis, IN A
Indiana U South Bend, IN A
Northern Michigan U, MI A
The U of Akron, OH A

Histologic Technology/Histotechnologist

Argosy U, Twin Cities, MN A
Michigan Technological U, MI B
Northern Michigan U, MI B
Oakland U, MI B

Historic Preservation and Conservation

Ursuline Coll, OH B

History

Adrian Coll, MI B
Albion Coll, MI B
Alma Coll, MI B
Anderson U, IN B
Andrews U, MI B
Aquinas Coll, MI B
Ashland U, OH B
Augsburg Coll, MN B
Augustana Coll, IL B
Augustana Coll, SD B
Aurora U, IL B
Avila U, MO B
Baker U, KS B
Baldwin-Wallace Coll, OH B
Ball State U, IN B
Beloit Coll, WI B
Bemidji State U, MN B
Benedictine Coll, KS B
Benedictine U, IL B
Bethany Coll, KS B
Bethany Lutheran Coll, MN B
Bethel Coll, IN B
Bethel Coll, KS B
Bethel U, MN B
Black Hills State U, SD B
Bluffton U, OH B
Bowling Green State U, OH B
Bradley U, IL B
Briar Cliff U, IA B
Buena Vista U, IA B
Butler U, IN B
Calvin Coll, MI B
Cameron U, OK B
Capital U, OH B
Carleton Coll, MN B
Carroll U, WI B
Case Western Reserve U, OH B
Cedarville U, OH B
Central Christian Coll of Kansas, KS A,B
Central Coll, IA B
Central Methodist U, MO B
Central Michigan U, MI B
Central State U, OH B
Clarke Coll, IA B
Clarkson U, NY B
Coe Coll, IA B
Coll of Mount St. Joseph, OH B
Coll of Saint Benedict, MN B
The Coll of St. Scholastica, MN B
Coll of the Ozarks, MO B
The Coll of Wooster, OH B
Columbia Coll, MO B
Concordia Coll, MN B
Concordia U, MI B
Concordia U Chicago, IL B
Concordia U, Nebraska, NE B
Concordia U, St. Paul, MN B
Concordia U Wisconsin, WI B
Cornell Coll, IA B
Cornerstone U, MI B
Creighton U, NE B
Crown Coll, MN B
Culver-Stockton Coll, MO B
Dakota Wesleyan U, SD B
Dana Coll, NE B
Defiance Coll, OH B
Denison U, OH B
DePaul U, IL B
DePauw U, IN B
Doane Coll, NE B
Dominican U, IL B
Dordt Coll, IA B
Drake U, IA B
Drury U, MO B
Earlham Coll, IN B
Eastern Illinois U, IL B
Eastern Michigan U, MI B
Edgewood Coll, WI B
Elmhurst Coll, IL B
Emporia State U, KS B
Eureka Coll, IL B
Evangel U, MO B
Ferris State U, MI B
Fontbonne U, MO B
Fort Hays State U, KS B
Franciscan U of Steubenville, OH B

A—associate degree; B—bachelor's degree

Institution	Degree
Franklin Coll, IN	B
Friends U, KS	B
Goshen Coll, IN	B
Grace Coll, IN	B
Graceland U, IA	B
Grand Valley State U, MI	B
Grand View U, IA	B
Great Lakes Christian Coll, MI	B
Greenville Coll, IL	B
Grinnell Coll, IA	B
Gustavus Adolphus Coll, MN	B
Hamline U, MN	B
Hannibal-LaGrange Coll, MO	B
Hanover Coll, IN	B
Heidelberg U, OH	B
Hillsdale Coll, MI	B
Hiram Coll, OH	B
Hope Coll, MI	B
Huntington U, IN	B
Illinois Coll, IL	B
Illinois State U, IL	B
Illinois Wesleyan U, IL	B
Indiana State U, IN	B
Indiana U Bloomington, IN	B
Indiana U Northwest, IN	B
Indiana U–Purdue U Fort Wayne, IN	A,B
Indiana U–Purdue U Indianapolis, IN	B
Indiana U South Bend, IN	B
Indiana U Southeast, IN	B
Indiana Wesleyan U, IN	A,B
Iowa State U of Science and Technology, IA	B
Iowa Wesleyan Coll, IA	B
Jamestown Coll, ND	B
John Carroll U, OH	B
Kalamazoo Coll, MI	B
Kansas State U, KS	B
Kansas Wesleyan U, KS	B
Kent State U, OH	B
Kent State U, Stark Campus, OH	B
Kenyon Coll, OH	B
Knox Coll, IL	B
Lake Forest Coll, IL	B
Lakeland Coll, WI	B
Lake Superior State U, MI	B
Lawrence U, WI	B
Lewis U, IL	B
Lincoln U, MO	B
Lindenwood U, MO	B
Loras Coll, IA	B
Lourdes Coll, OH	A,B
Loyola U Chicago, IL	B
Luther Coll, IA	B
Macalester Coll, MN	B
MacMurray Coll, IL	B
Madonna U, MI	B
Malone U, OH	B
Manchester Coll, IN	B
Marian U, WI	B
Marian U, IN	B
Marietta Coll, OH	B
Marquette U, WI	B
Maryville U of Saint Louis, MO	B
McKendree U, IL	B
McPherson Coll, KS	B
Miami U, OH	B
Miami U Hamilton, OH	B
Michigan State U, MI	B
Michigan Technological U, MI	B
Mid-America Christian U, OK	B
MidAmerica Nazarene U, KS	B
Millikin U, IL	B
Minnesota State U Mankato, MN	B
Minnesota State U Moorhead, MN	B
Minot State U, ND	B
Missouri Baptist U, MO	B
Missouri Southern State U, MO	B
Missouri State U, MO	B
Missouri U of Science and Technology, MO	B
Missouri Western State U, MO	B
Monmouth Coll, IL	B
Morningside Coll, IA	B
Mount Marty Coll, SD	B
Mount Mary Coll, WI	B
Mount Mercy Coll, IA	B
Mount Union Coll, OH	B
Mount Vernon Nazarene U, OH	B
Muskingum Coll, OH	B
Nebraska Wesleyan U, NE	B
Newman U, KS	B
North Central Coll, IL	B
North Dakota State U, ND	B
Northeastern Illinois U, IL	B
Northeastern State U, OK	B
Northern Michigan U, MI	B
Northern State U, SD	B
Northland Coll, WI	B
North Park U, IL	B
Northwestern Coll, MN	B
Northwestern U, IL	B
Northwest Missouri State U, MO	B
Oakland U, MI	B
Oberlin Coll, OH	B
Oglala Lakota Coll, SD	B
Ohio Dominican U, OH	B
Ohio Northern U, OH	B
The Ohio State U, OH	B
The Ohio State U at Lima, OH	B
The Ohio State U at Marion, OH	B
The Ohio State U–Mansfield Campus, OH	B
The Ohio State U–Newark Campus, OH	B
Ohio Wesleyan U, OH	B
Oklahoma Baptist U, OK	B
Oklahoma Christian U, OK	B
Oklahoma City U, OK	B
Oklahoma Panhandle State U, OK	B
Oklahoma State U, OK	B
Oklahoma State U, Oklahoma City, OK	A
Olivet Coll, MI	B
Olivet Nazarene U, IL	B
Oral Roberts U, OK	B
Otterbein Coll, OH	B
Park U, MO	B
Pittsburg State U, KS	B
Pontifical Coll Josephinum, OH	B
Purdue U, IN	B
Purdue U Calumet, IN	B
Quincy U, IL	B
Ripon Coll, WI	B
Rockford Coll, IL	B
Rockhurst U, MO	B
Rogers State U, OK	A
Roosevelt U, IL	B
Saginaw Valley State U, MI	B
St. Ambrose U, IA	B
St. Catherine U, MN	B
St. Cloud State U, MN	B
St. Gregory's U, Shawnee, OK	B
Saint John's U, MN	B
Saint Joseph's Coll, IN	B
Saint Louis U, MO	B
Saint Mary's Coll, IN	B
Saint Mary's U of Minnesota, MN	B
St. Norbert Coll, WI	B
St. Olaf Coll, MN	B
Saint Xavier U, IL	B
Shawnee State U, OH	B
Siena Heights U, MI	B
Silver Lake Coll, WI	B
Simpson Coll, IA	B
South Dakota State U, SD	B
Southeastern Oklahoma State U, OK	B
Southeast Missouri State U, MO	B
Southern Illinois U Carbondale, IL	B
Southern Illinois U Edwardsville, IL	B
Southern Methodist U, TX	B
Southern Nazarene U, OK	B
Southwest Baptist U, MO	B
Southwestern Coll, KS	B
Southwestern Oklahoma State U, OK	B
Southwest Minnesota State U, MN	B
Spring Arbor U, MI	B
Sterling Coll, KS	B
Taylor U, IN	B
Tiffin U, OH	B
Transylvania U, KY	B
Trinity Christian Coll, IL	B
Trinity International U, IL	B
Truman State U, MO	B
Union Coll, NE	B
U of Central Missouri, MO	B
U of Central Oklahoma, OK	B
U of Charleston, WV	B
U of Chicago, IL	B
U of Cincinnati, OH	B
U of Dallas, TX	B
U of Dayton, OH	B
U of Evansville, IN	B
The U of Findlay, OH	B
U of Illinois at Chicago, IL	B
U of Illinois at Springfield, IL	B
U of Illinois at Urbana–Champaign, IL	B
U of Indianapolis, IN	B
The U of Iowa, IA	B
The U of Kansas, KS	B
U of Michigan, MI	B
U of Michigan–Dearborn, MI	B
U of Michigan–Flint, MI	B
U of Minnesota, Duluth, MN	B
U of Minnesota, Morris, MN	B
U of Minnesota, Twin Cities Campus, MN	B
U of Missouri–Columbia, MO	B
U of Missouri–Kansas City, MO	B
U of Missouri–St. Louis, MO	B
U of Nebraska at Kearney, NE	B
U of Nebraska at Omaha, NE	B
U of Nebraska–Lincoln, NE	B
U of New Orleans, LA	B
U of North Dakota, ND	B
U of Northern Iowa, IA	B
U of Notre Dame, IN	B
U of Oklahoma, OK	B
U of Rio Grande, OH	A,B
U of St. Francis, IL	B
U of Saint Francis, IN	B
U of Saint Mary, KS	B
U of Science and Arts of Oklahoma, OK	B
U of Sioux Falls, SD	B
The U of South Dakota, SD	B
U of Southern Indiana, IN	B
The U of Toledo, OH	B
U of Tulsa, OK	B
U of Wisconsin–Eau Claire, WI	B
U of Wisconsin–Green Bay, WI	B
U of Wisconsin–La Crosse, WI	B
U of Wisconsin–Madison, WI	B
U of Wisconsin–Milwaukee, WI	B
U of Wisconsin–Oshkosh, WI	B
U of Wisconsin–Parkside, WI	B
U of Wisconsin–Platteville, WI	B
U of Wisconsin–Stevens Point, WI	B
U of Wisconsin–Superior, WI	B
U of Wisconsin–Whitewater, WI	B
Ursuline Coll, OH	B
Valley City State U, ND	B
Valparaiso U, IN	B
Wabash Coll, IN	B
Waldorf Coll, IA	B
Walsh U, OH	B
Wartburg Coll, IA	B
Washburn U, KS	B
Washington U in St. Louis, MO	B
Wayne State Coll, NE	B
Wayne State U, MI	B
Webster U, MO	B
Western Illinois U, IL	B
Western Michigan U, MI	B
Westminster Coll, MO	B
Wheaton Coll, IL	B
Wichita State U, KS	B

William Jewell Coll, MO B
Wilmington Coll, OH B
Winona State U, MN B
Wittenberg U, OH B
Wright State U, OH A,B
Xavier U, OH A,B
York Coll, NE B
Youngstown State U, OH B

History and Philosophy of Science and Technology

Case Western Reserve U, OH B
U of Wisconsin–Madison, WI B

History Related

Cedarville U, OH B
Grace Coll, IN B
Marquette U, WI B
Saint Mary's U of Minnesota, MN B

History Teacher Education

Alma Coll, MI B
Buena Vista U, IA B
Carroll U, WI B
Central Christian Coll of Kansas, KS A,B
Central Michigan U, MI B
Coll of the Ozarks, MO B
Concordia U, MI B
Concordia U Chicago, IL B
Concordia U, Nebraska, NE B
Concordia U Wisconsin, WI B
Cornerstone U, MI B
Crown Coll, MN B
Culver-Stockton Coll, MO B
Dakota Wesleyan U, SD B
Dana Coll, NE B
DePaul U, IL B
Dordt Coll, IA B
Eastern Michigan U, MI B
Elmhurst Coll, IL B
Evangel U, MO B
Ferris State U, MI B
Grand Valley State U, MI B
Greenville Coll, IL B
Hannibal-LaGrange Coll, MO B
Hope Coll, MI B
Indiana U–Purdue U Fort Wayne, IN B
Jamestown Coll, ND B
Lindenwood U, MO B
Maranatha Baptist Bible Coll, WI B
Maryville U of Saint Louis, MO B
Mayville State U, ND B
McKendree U, IL B
Minot State U, ND B
Missouri State U, MO B
Mount Marty Coll, SD B
Mount Mary Coll, WI B
Mount Vernon Nazarene U, OH B
North Dakota State U, ND B
Northern Michigan U, MI B
Ohio Northern U, OH B
Ohio Wesleyan U, OH B
Saginaw Valley State U, MI B
St. Ambrose U, IA B
Saint Xavier U, IL B
Shawnee State U, OH B
Southwestern Oklahoma State U, OK B
Tiffin U, OH B
Trinity Christian Coll, IL B
Union Coll, NE B
U of Central Oklahoma, OK B
U of Illinois at Chicago, IL B
U of Illinois at Urbana–Champaign, IL B
The U of Iowa, IA B
U of Mary, ND B
U of Michigan–Flint, MI B
U of Nebraska–Lincoln, NE B
U of Rio Grande, OH B
The U of South Dakota, SD B
U of Wisconsin–Superior, WI B
Valley City State U, ND B
Valparaiso U, IN B
Wartburg Coll, IA B
Washington U in St. Louis, MO B
Wayne State Coll, NE B
Western Michigan U, MI B
York Coll, NE B

Horse Husbandry/Equine Science and Management

Oklahoma Panhandle State U, OK B
Rochester Comm and Tech Coll, MN A
Stephens Coll, MO B
Tiffin U, OH B
U of Minnesota, Crookston, MN B

Horticultural Science

Andrews U, MI A
Coll of the Ozarks, MO B
Iowa State U of Science and Technology, IA B
Kansas State U, KS B
Michigan State U, MI B
Missouri State U, MO B
North Dakota State U, ND B
Northwest Missouri State U, MO B
Oklahoma State U, OK B
Oklahoma State U, Oklahoma City, OK A
Purdue U, IN B
Southeast Missouri State U, MO B
Truman State U, MO B
U of Illinois at Urbana–Champaign, IL B
U of Minnesota, Crookston, MN B
U of Nebraska–Lincoln, NE B

Horticulture Science

Oklahoma State U, Oklahoma City, OK A

Hospital and Health-Care Facilities Administration

Avila U, MO B
Black Hills State U, SD B
The U of South Dakota, SD B
The U of Toledo, OH B
Ursuline Coll, OH B
Youngstown State U, OH B

Hospitality Administration

The Art Insts International Minnesota, MN B
Baker Coll of Flint, MI A
Baker Coll of Owosso, MI A
Bowling Green State U, OH B
Central Michigan U, MI B
Coll of the Ozarks, MO B
Eastern Michigan U, MI B
Ferris State U, MI B
Grand Valley State U, MI B
The Illinois Inst of Art–Chicago, IL A
Indiana U–Purdue U Fort Wayne, IN A,B
Kaplan U–Davenport Campus, IA A
Kendall Coll, IL A,B
Lexington Coll, IL A,B
Madonna U, MI B
Missouri State U, MO B
North Dakota State U, ND B
Northern Michigan U, MI B
The Ohio State U, OH B
The Ohio State U at Lima, OH B
Oklahoma State U, OK B
Roosevelt U, IL B
Tiffin U, OH B
Trine U, IN B
The U of Akron, OH A
U of Illinois at Urbana–Champaign, IL B
U of Minnesota, Crookston, MN B
U of Nebraska–Lincoln, NE B
U of New Orleans, LA B
U of Phoenix–Cleveland Campus, OH B
U of Phoenix–Indianapolis Campus, IN B
U of Phoenix–St. Louis Campus, MO B
U of Wisconsin–Stout, WI B
Youngstown State U, OH A,B

Hospitality Administration Related

Indiana U–Purdue U Indianapolis, IN B
Kendall Coll, IL B
Kent State U, OH B
Purdue U, IN A
Purdue U Calumet, IN A
Southern Illinois U Carbondale, IL B

Hospitality and Recreation Marketing

AIB Coll of Business, IA A
Ferris State U, MI A,B
Kendall Coll, IL B
Northwest Missouri State U, MO B

Hotel and Restaurant Management

Coll of the Ozarks, MO B

Hotel/Motel Administration

Ashland U, OH B
Baker Coll of Muskegon, MI A
Baker Coll of Owosso, MI A
Baker Coll of Port Huron, MI A
Central Michigan U, MI B
Ferris State U, MI B
Grand Valley State U, MI B
Iowa State U of Science and Technology, IA B
Kansas State U, KS B
Kendall Coll, IL A,B
Michigan State U, MI B
Purdue U Calumet, IN B
South Dakota State U, SD B
Southwest Minnesota State U, MN B
The U of Akron, OH A,B
U of Central Missouri, MO B
U of Central Oklahoma, OK B
The U of Findlay, OH B
U of Missouri–Columbia, MO B

Housing and Human Environments

Missouri State U, MO B
Ohio U, OH B
Oklahoma State U, OK B
The U of Akron, OH B
U of Missouri–Columbia, MO B
U of Northern Iowa, IA B

Human Development and Family Studies

Antioch U McGregor, OH B
Ashland U, OH B
Bowling Green State U, OH B
Concordia U, MI B
Concordia U, St. Paul, MN B
Indiana State U, IN B
Kansas State U, KS B
Kent State U, OH B
Miami U, OH B
Missouri State U, MO B
National-Louis U, IL B
North Dakota State U, ND B
The Ohio State U, OH B
Ohio U, OH B
Oklahoma State U, OK B
Purdue U, IN B
South Dakota State U, SD B
Southwestern Christian U, OK B
Stephens Coll, MO B
U of Chicago, IL B
U of Illinois at Urbana–Champaign, IL B
U of Missouri–Columbia, MO B
U of Wisconsin–Stout, WI B
Youngstown State U, OH B

Human Development and Family Studies Related

Ball State U, IN B
Kent State U, OH B
Park U, MO B

A—associate degree; B—bachelor's degree

Rasmussen Coll St. Cloud, MN A
The U of Toledo, OH A

Humanities
Alma Coll, MI B
Antioch U McGregor, OH B
Augsburg Coll, MN B
Bemidji State U, MN B
Bradley U, IL B
Clarkson U, NY B
Coll of Saint Benedict, MN B
Coll of Saint Mary, NE B
The Coll of St. Scholastica, MN B
Concordia Coll, MN B
Concordia U Wisconsin, WI B
DePaul U, IL B
Franciscan U of Steubenville, OH B
Hope Coll, MI B
Indiana U East, IN B
Indiana U Kokomo, IN B
John Carroll U, OH B
Kansas State U, KS B
Lawrence Technological U, MI B
Macalester Coll, MN B
Maranatha Baptist Bible Coll, WI B
Michigan State U, MI B
Michigan Technological U, MI A
Minnesota State U Mankato, MN B
Minot State U, ND B
Muskingum Coll, OH B
North Central Coll, IL B
North Dakota State U, ND B
Northwestern U, IL B
Northwest Missouri State U, MO B
The Ohio State U, OH B
Ohio U, OH A
Ohio U–Southern Campus, OH A
Ohio Wesleyan U, OH B
Oklahoma Baptist U, OK B
Oklahoma City U, OK B
Oklahoma State U, Oklahoma City, OK A
Pontifical Coll Josephinum, OH B
Purdue U, IN B
Quincy U, IL B
Rockford Coll, IL B
St. Gregory's U, Shawnee, OK A,B
Saint John's U, MN B
Saint Louis U, MO B
Saint Mary-of-the-Woods Coll, IN B
Saint Mary's Coll, IN B
St. Norbert Coll, WI B
Shawnee State U, OH A
Shimer Coll, IL B
Siena Heights U, MI B
Southeast Missouri State U, MO B
Southern Methodist U, TX B
Trinity International U, IL B
The U of Akron, OH B
U of Chicago, IL B
U of Cincinnati, OH A,B
The U of Findlay, OH A
U of Illinois at Urbana–Champaign, IL B
The U of Kansas, KS B
U of Michigan, MI B
U of Michigan–Dearborn, MI B
U of Northern Iowa, IA B
U of Oklahoma, OK B
U of Rio Grande, OH B
The U of Toledo, OH B
U of Wisconsin–Green Bay, WI B
U of Wisconsin–Parkside, WI B
Ursuline Coll, OH B
Valparaiso U, IN A,B
Waldorf Coll, IA B
Washburn U, KS A
Washington U in St. Louis, MO B
Wright State U, OH B

Human Nutrition
Case Western Reserve U, OH B
Kansas State U, KS B
Kent State U, OH B
The Ohio State U, OH B
U of Illinois at Urbana–Champaign, IL B

Human Resources Development
Oakland U, MI B
The Ohio State U, OH B
Park U, MO A,B
Trinity International U, IL B

Human Resources Management
Antioch U McGregor, OH B
Avila U, MO B
Baker Coll of Owosso, MI A,B
Baldwin-Wallace Coll, OH B
Ball State U, IN B
Black Hills State U, SD B
Bradley U, IL B
Briar Cliff U, IA B
Bryant & Stratton Coll, Willoughby Hills, OH A
Buena Vista U, IA B
Carroll U, WI B
Central Christian Coll of Kansas, KS A
Central Michigan U, MI B
Chancellor U, OH B
Clarkson U, NY B
Cleary U, MI B
Colorado Tech U Sioux Falls, SD B
Concordia U, St. Paul, MN B
Davenport U, Grand Rapids, MI B
DePaul U, IL B
Ferris State U, MI B
Franklin U, OH B
Friends U, KS B
Indiana State U, IN B
Indiana Tech, IN B
Lewis U, IL B
Lindenwood U, MO B
Loras Coll, IA B
Lourdes Coll, OH B
Loyola U Chicago, IL B
Madonna U, MI B
Marian U, WI B
Marian U, IN B
Marietta Coll, OH B
Marquette U, WI B
Michigan State U, MI B
MidAmerica Nazarene U, KS B
Mount Mercy Coll, IA B
North Central Coll, IL B
Northeastern Illinois U, IL B
Northeastern State U, OK B
Oakland U, MI B
The Ohio State U, OH B
Olivet Nazarene U, IL B
Roosevelt U, IL B
St. Cloud State U, MN B
Saint Louis U, MO B
Saint Mary-of-the-Woods Coll, IN B
Silver Lake Coll, WI B
Southwestern Coll, KS B
Spring Arbor U, MI B
Tiffin U, OH B
Trinity Christian Coll, IL B
Trinity International U, IL B
U of Central Missouri, MO B
U of Central Oklahoma, OK B
The U of Findlay, OH A,B
U of Illinois at Urbana–Champaign, IL B
The U of Iowa, IA B
U of Michigan–Dearborn, MI B
U of Michigan–Flint, MI B
U of Minnesota, Duluth, MN B
U of Nebraska at Omaha, NE B
U of North Dakota, ND B
U of St. Francis, IL B
U of Saint Francis, IN A
The U of Toledo, OH B
U of Wisconsin–Milwaukee, WI B
U of Wisconsin–Whitewater, WI B
Ursuline Coll, OH B
Valley City State U, ND B
Washington U in St. Louis, MO B
Western Illinois U, IL B
Western Michigan U, MI B
Wichita State U, KS B
Winona State U, MN B
Wright State U, OH B
Xavier U, OH B
York Coll, NE B
Youngstown State U, OH B

Human Resources Management and Services Related
Bryant & Stratton Coll, Parma, OH A
Bryant & Stratton Coll, WI A
Bryant & Stratton Coll—Wauwatosa Campus, WI A
Grand Valley State U, MI B
Miami U Hamilton, OH B
Park U, MO B
U of Oklahoma, OK B

Human Services
Albion Coll, MI B
Antioch U McGregor, OH B
Baker Coll of Clinton Township, MI A
Baker Coll of Flint, MI A
Baker Coll of Muskegon, MI A
Bethel Coll, IN B
Black Hills State U, SD B
Calumet Coll of Saint Joseph, IN B
Columbia Coll, MO B
Concordia U, St. Paul, MN B
Dakota Wesleyan U, SD B
Doane Coll, NE B
Fontbonne U, MO B
Grace Bible Coll, MI B
Graceland U, IA B
Grand View U, IA B
Hannibal-LaGrange Coll, MO B
Indiana Tech, IN B
Indiana U East, IN A
Indiana U–Purdue U Fort Wayne, IN B
Kendall Coll, IL A,B
Lake Superior State U, MI B
Lindenwood U, MO B
Loyola U Chicago, IL B
Missouri Baptist U, MO B
Mount Marty Coll, SD B
Mount Vernon Nazarene U, OH A
National-Louis U, IL B
Oglala Lakota Coll, SD A,B
Ohio U, OH A
Ohio U–Chillicothe, OH A
Oklahoma State U, Oklahoma City, OK A
Park U, MO B
Quincy U, IL B
Saint Mary-of-the-Woods Coll, IN B
Saint Mary's U of Minnesota, MN B
Siena Heights U, MI B
Southwest Baptist U, MO B
Tiffin U, OH B
Union Inst & U, OH B
U of Cincinnati, OH A
U of Minnesota, Morris, MN B
U of Phoenix–Chicago Campus, IL B
U of Phoenix–Indianapolis Campus, IN B
U of Phoenix–Kansas City Campus, MO B
U of Phoenix–Metro Detroit Campus, MI B
U of Phoenix–Oklahoma City Campus, OK B
U of Phoenix–St. Louis Campus, MO B
U of Phoenix–Springfield Campus, MO B
U of Phoenix–Tulsa Campus, OK B
U of Phoenix–West Michigan Campus, MI B
U of Phoenix–Wisconsin Campus, WI B
U of Saint Francis, IN A

U of Wisconsin–Oshkosh, WI B
Walsh U, OH A,B

Hydrology and Water Resources Science
Heidelberg U, OH B
Lake Superior State U, MI A
Northland Coll, WI B
U of Wisconsin–Madison, WI B
U of Wisconsin–Stevens Point, WI B
Western Michigan U, MI B
Wright State U, OH B

Illustration
Art Academy of Cincinnati, OH B
The Cleveland Inst of Art, OH B
Coll for Creative Studies, MI B
Columbus Coll of Art & Design, OH B
Grace Coll, IN B
Lawrence Technological U, MI B
Lewis U, IL B
Oklahoma State U, Oklahoma City, OK A
The U of Kansas, KS B
Washington U in St. Louis, MO B

Industrial and Organizational Psychology
Clarkson U, NY B
Madonna U, MI B
Maryville U of Saint Louis, MO B
Nebraska Wesleyan U, NE B
Saint Xavier U, IL B
U of Illinois at Urbana–Champaign, IL B
U of Minnesota, Crookston, MN B
Washington U in St. Louis, MO B
Wright State U, OH B

Industrial Arts
Bemidji State U, MN B
Coll of the Ozarks, MO B
Fort Hays State U, KS B
Minnesota State U Mankato, MN B
Northern State U, SD B
Ohio Northern U, OH B
Pittsburg State U, KS B
St. Cloud State U, MN B
Southwestern Oklahoma State U, OK B
U of Cincinnati, OH A
U of Wisconsin–Platteville, WI B

Industrial Design
The Cleveland Inst of Art, OH B
Coll for Creative Studies, MI B
Columbus Coll of Art & Design, OH B
Ferris State U, MI B
Northern Michigan U, MI A
The Ohio State U, OH B
U of Cincinnati, OH B
U of Illinois at Chicago, IL B
U of Illinois at Urbana–Champaign, IL B
The U of Kansas, KS B
U of Michigan, MI B
U of Wisconsin–Platteville, WI B
Western Michigan U, MI B

Industrial Electronics Technology
Ferris State U, MI A
Ranken Tech Coll, MO A

Industrial Engineering
Bradley U, IL B
Cleveland State U, OH B
Indiana Tech, IN A,B
Iowa State U of Science and Technology, IA B
Kansas State U, KS B
Kent State U, OH B
Kettering U, MI B
Lawrence Technological U, MI B
Michigan Technological U, MI B
Milwaukee School of Engineering, WI B
Missouri Southern State U, MO B
Missouri U of Science and Technology, MO B
North Dakota State U, ND B
Northwestern U, IL B
Oakland U, MI B
The Ohio State U, OH B
Ohio U, OH B
Oklahoma State U, OK B
Purdue U, IN B
St. Ambrose U, IA B
St. Cloud State U, MN B
South Dakota School of Mines and Technology, SD B
Southern Illinois U Edwardsville, IL B
U of Cincinnati, OH B
U of Illinois at Chicago, IL B
U of Illinois at Urbana–Champaign, IL B
The U of Iowa, IA B
U of Michigan, MI B
U of Michigan–Dearborn, MI B
U of Minnesota, Duluth, MN B
U of Minnesota, Twin Cities Campus, MN B
U of Missouri–Columbia, MO B
U of Nebraska–Lincoln, NE B
U of Oklahoma, OK B
The U of Toledo, OH A,B
U of Wisconsin–Madison, WI B
U of Wisconsin–Milwaukee, WI B
U of Wisconsin–Platteville, WI B
Wayne State U, MI B
Western Michigan U, MI B
Wichita State U, KS B
Youngstown State U, OH B

Industrial Mechanics and Maintenance Technology
Northern Michigan U, MI A

Industrial Production Technologies Related
Central Michigan U, MI B
Ferris State U, MI A,B
McPherson Coll, KS B
Southwestern Coll, KS B
U of Nebraska–Lincoln, NE A,B
U of Wisconsin–Stout, WI B
Wayne State Coll, NE B
Wayne State U, MI B

Industrial Radiologic Technology
Baker Coll of Owosso, MI A,B
Briar Cliff U, IA B
Concordia U Wisconsin, WI B
Fort Hays State U, KS A
National-Louis U, IL B
U of Cincinnati, OH A

Industrial Safety Technology
Northeastern State U, OK B
South Dakota State U, SD B

Industrial Technology
Baker Coll of Flint, MI B
Baker Coll of Muskegon, MI A
Ball State U, IN B
Bemidji State U, MN B
Black Hills State U, SD B
Bowling Green State U, OH B
Central State U, OH B
Cleveland State U, OH B
Eastern Illinois U, IL B
Eastern Michigan U, MI B
Ferris State U, MI B
Illinois State U, IL B
Indiana State U, IN B
Indiana U–Purdue U Fort Wayne, IN A,B
ITT Tech Inst, Fort Wayne, IN B
ITT Tech Inst, Indianapolis, IN B
ITT Tech Inst, Newburgh, IN B
Kansas State U, KS A
Kent State U, OH A,B
Kent State U, Salem Campus, OH A
Lake Superior State U, MI B
Lawrence Technological U, MI B
Minnesota State U Mankato, MN B
Minnesota State U Moorhead, MN B
Northern Michigan U, MI B
Ohio Northern U, OH B
Ohio U, OH B
Ohio U–Lancaster, OH A
Oklahoma Panhandle State U, OK A,B
Pittsburg State U, KS B
Purdue U, IN B
Purdue U Calumet, IN A
Purdue U North Central, IN A
Southeast Missouri State U, MO B
Southern Illinois U Carbondale, IL B
Southwestern Oklahoma State U, OK B
Trine U, IN A
U of Cincinnati, OH A
U of Dayton, OH B
U of North Dakota, ND B
U of Northern Iowa, IA B
U of Rio Grande, OH A,B
The U of Toledo, OH A,B
U of Wisconsin–Platteville, WI B
Washburn U, KS A
Wayne State U, MI B
Western Illinois U, IL B
Wright State U, OH A

Information Resources Management
Clarkson U, NY B
U of Wisconsin–Eau Claire, WI B
Western Michigan U, MI B

Information Science/Studies
Anderson U, IN B
Andrews U, MI B
Ashland U, OH B
Bacone Coll, OK B
Baker Coll of Clinton Township, MI A
Baker Coll of Owosso, MI A,B
Baker U, KS B
Bemidji State U, MN B
Benedictine U, IL B
Bluffton U, OH B
Bradley U, IL B
Calumet Coll of Saint Joseph, IN A,B
Carroll U, WI B
Central Coll, IA B
Clarke Coll, IA B
Cleary U, MI B
Cleveland State U, OH B
Colorado Tech U North Kansas City, MO B
Colorado Tech U Sioux Falls, SD B
Concordia U Chicago, IL B
Culver-Stockton Coll, MO B
DePaul U, IL B
Doane Coll, NE B
Dominican U, IL B
Eastern Michigan U, MI B
Emporia State U, KS B
Fort Hays State U, KS B
Friends U, KS B
Grand Valley State U, MI B
Grand View U, IA B
Harris-Stowe State U, MO B
Heidelberg U, OH B
Illinois Coll, IL B
Illinois State U, IL B
Indiana U–Purdue U Fort Wayne, IN A,B
Iowa Wesleyan Coll, IA B
Kansas State U, KS B
Kansas Wesleyan U, KS B

A—associate degree; B—bachelor's degree

Lincoln U, MO	B
MacMurray Coll, IL	B
Marietta Coll, OH	B
McKendree U, IL	B
Michigan Technological U, MI	B
Midstate Coll, IL	A
Minnesota State U Mankato, MN	B
Missouri U of Science and Technology, MO	B
Missouri Western State U, MO	B
National American U, MO	A,B
National-Louis U, IL	B
Nebraska Wesleyan U, NE	B
Newman U, KS	A,B
Northwestern U, IL	B
Northwest Missouri State U, MO	B
Ohio Dominican U, OH	B
The Ohio State U, OH	B
Oklahoma Baptist U, OK	B
Oklahoma Christian U, OK	B
Oklahoma State U, Oklahoma City, OK	A
Olivet Nazarene U, IL	B
Rasmussen Coll Eagan, MN	A
St. Ambrose U, IA	B
St. Cloud State U, MN	B
Saint Mary-of-the-Woods Coll, IN	B
Silver Lake Coll, WI	B
Southeastern Oklahoma State U, OK	B
Southern Illinois U Carbondale, IL	B
Southern Methodist U, TX	B
Southern Nazarene U, OK	B
Union Coll, NE	A,B
U of Charleston, WV	B
U of Cincinnati, OH	A,B
U of Dayton, OH	B
U of Illinois at Chicago, IL	B
The U of Iowa, IA	B
U of Mary, ND	B
U of Michigan–Flint, MI	B
U of Nebraska at Omaha, NE	B
U of Oklahoma, OK	B
The U of Toledo, OH	A,B
U of Tulsa, OK	B
U of Wisconsin–Superior, WI	B
Waldorf Coll, IA	B
Wartburg Coll, IA	B
Washington U in St. Louis, MO	B
Wayne State Coll, NE	B
Wayne State U, MI	B
Wilberforce U, OH	B
William Jewell Coll, MO	B
Winona State U, MN	B
Wright State U, OH	B

Information Technology

AIB Coll of Business, IA	A
American InterContinental U Online, IL	B
Bluffton U, OH	B
Brown Mackie Coll–South Bend, IN	A
Brown Mackie Coll–Tulsa, OK	A
Bryant & Stratton Coll, Parma, OH	A
Bryant & Stratton Coll, Willoughby Hills, OH	A
Bryant & Stratton Coll, WI	A
Cameron U, OK	A,B
Central Michigan U, MI	B
Coll of the Ozarks, MO	B
Colorado Tech U Sioux Falls, SD	A,B
Dakota State U, SD	B
DePaul U, IL	B
Ferris State U, MI	A,B
Franklin U, OH	A,B
Grace Coll, IN	B
Illinois Inst of Technology, IL	B
Illinois State U, IL	B
Indiana State U, IN	B
Indiana Tech, IN	A
Indiana U Bloomington, IN	B
Indiana U Kokomo, IN	B
Indiana U–Purdue U Indianapolis, IN	B
Indiana U Southeast, IN	B
Kaplan U–Davenport Campus, IA	A,B
Kaplan U–Mason City Campus, IA	A
Kilian Comm Coll, SD	A
Lawrence Technological U, MI	B
Marian U, WI	B
Marquette U, WI	B
Minnesota School of Business–Blaine, MN	A,B
Missouri Tech, MO	A,B
Mount Marty Coll, SD	B
North Park U, IL	B
Oakland U, MI	B
Oklahoma State U, Oklahoma City, OK	A
Robert Morris Coll, IL	B
Sanford-Brown Coll, Fenton, MO	B
Tiffin U, OH	A,B
U of Missouri–Kansas City, MO	B
U of Phoenix–Chicago Campus, IL	B
U of Phoenix–Cleveland Campus, OH	B
U of Phoenix–Indianapolis Campus, IN	A,B
U of Phoenix–Kansas City Campus, MO	B
U of Phoenix–Metro Detroit Campus, MI	B
U of Phoenix–Oklahoma City Campus, OK	B
U of Phoenix–St. Louis Campus, MO	A,B
U of Phoenix–Springfield Campus, MO	B
U of Phoenix–Tulsa Campus, OK	B
U of Phoenix–West Michigan Campus, MI	B
U of Phoenix–Wichita Campus, KS	B
U of Phoenix–Wisconsin Campus, WI	B
U of Rio Grande, OH	B
U of St. Francis, IL	B
U of Saint Mary, KS	B
U of Tulsa, OK	B
U of Wisconsin–Whitewater, WI	B
Youngstown State U, OH	A,B

Institutional Food Workers

Kendall Coll, IL	A,B

Instrumentation Technology

Ranken Tech Coll, MO	A

Insurance

Bradley U, IL	B
Illinois State U, IL	B
Illinois Wesleyan U, IL	B
Indiana State U, IN	B
Martin U, IN	B
Minnesota State U Mankato, MN	B
Missouri State U, MO	B
Olivet Coll, MI	B
St. Cloud State U, MN	B
U of Cincinnati, OH	A,B
U of Illinois at Urbana–Champaign, IL	B
U of Minnesota, Twin Cities Campus, MN	B
U of Wisconsin–La Crosse, WI	B
U of Wisconsin–Madison, WI	B

Insurance/Risk Management

Illinois Wesleyan U, IL	B
The Ohio State U, OH	B

Intercultural/Multicultural and Diversity Studies

Evangel U, MO	B
North Central U, MN	B
St. Catherine U, MN	B
Trinity Bible Coll, ND	B

Interdisciplinary Studies

Augsburg Coll, MN	B
Beloit Coll, WI	B
Calvin Coll, MI	B
Carleton Coll, MN	B
Cedarville U, OH	B
Central Coll, IA	B
Central Methodist U, MO	A,B
Clarkson U, NY	B
Cleveland State U, OH	B
Coe Coll, IA	B
Coll of the Ozarks, MO	B
The Coll of Wooster, OH	B
Cornell Coll, IA	B
Cornerstone U, MI	B
Dana Coll, NE	B
DePauw U, IN	B
Earlham Coll, IN	B
Elmhurst Coll, IL	B
Franklin U, OH	B
Grinnell Coll, IA	B
Gustavus Adolphus Coll, MN	B
Harris-Stowe State U, MO	B
Hillsdale Coll, MI	B
Hope Coll, MI	B
Illinois Coll, IL	B
Illinois State U, IL	B
Iowa State U of Science and Technology, IA	B
John Carroll U, OH	B
Kalamazoo Coll, MI	B
Kansas City Art Inst, MO	B
Kansas State U, KS	A
Kaplan U–Davenport Campus, IA	A
Kaplan U–Mason City Campus, IA	A
Kuyper Coll, MI	B
Lake Superior State U, MI	B
Luther Coll, IA	B
Manchester Coll, IN	B
Martin Luther Coll, MN	B
Maryville U of Saint Louis, MO	B
McPherson Coll, KS	B
Minneapolis Coll of Art and Design, MN	B
Minnesota State U Moorhead, MN	B
Morningside Coll, IA	B
Nebraska Wesleyan U, NE	B
North Central U, MN	A,B
North Dakota State U, ND	B
Northwestern U, IL	B
Oberlin Coll, OH	B
Ohio U, OH	B
Oklahoma Baptist U, OK	B
Olivet Coll, MI	B
Pittsburg State U, KS	B
Purdue U, IN	B
Ripon Coll, WI	B
St. Cloud State U, MN	B
Saint Mary's Coll, IN	B
Sinte Gleska U, SD	B
South Dakota School of Mines and Technology, SD	B
Stephens Coll, MO	B
Sterling Coll, KS	B
U of Chicago, IL	B
The U of Iowa, IA	B
U of Minnesota, Duluth, MN	B
U of Missouri–Columbia, MO	B
U of Missouri–Kansas City, MO	B
U of Saint Mary, KS	B
U of Wisconsin–Green Bay, WI	B
U of Wisconsin–Milwaukee, WI	B
U of Wisconsin–Parkside, WI	B
Wayne State Coll, NE	B
Webster U, MO	B
Western Illinois U, IL	B

Interior Architecture

Bowling Green State U, OH	B
Central Michigan U, MI	B
Ferris State U, MI	A,B
Indiana State U, IN	B
Lawrence Technological U, MI	B
Miami U, OH	B
U of Missouri–Columbia, MO	B
U of Nebraska–Lincoln, NE	B

Interior Design

Adrian Coll, MI	B

The Art Inst of Indianapolis, IN B
The Art Inst of Michigan, MI B
The Art Insts International–Kansas City, KS B
The Art Insts International Minnesota, MN A,B
Baker Coll of Allen Park, MI A
Baker Coll of Auburn Hills, MI A
Baker Coll of Clinton Township, MI A
Baker Coll of Muskegon, MI A
Baker Coll of Owosso, MI A
Baker Coll of Port Huron, MI A
The Cleveland Inst of Art, OH B
Coll for Creative Studies, MI B
Coll of Mount St. Joseph, OH A,B
Columbus Coll of Art & Design, OH B
Concordia U Wisconsin, WI B
Eastern Michigan U, MI B
The Illinois Inst of Art–Chicago, IL B
The Illinois Inst of Art–Schaumburg, IL B
Indiana U Bloomington, IN B
Indiana U–Purdue U Fort Wayne, IN A,B
Indiana U–Purdue U Indianapolis, IN B
Iowa State U of Science and Technology, IA B
Kansas State U, KS B
Kent State U, OH B
Marian U, IN A
Maryville U of Saint Louis, MO B
McPherson Coll, KS B
Miami U Hamilton, OH B
Michigan State U, MI B
Minnesota State U Mankato, MN B
Mount Mary Coll, WI B
North Dakota State U, ND B
Northwest Missouri State U, MO B
The Ohio State U, OH B
Oklahoma Christian U, OK B
Park U, MO B
Pittsburg State U, KS B
Purdue U, IN B
Robert Morris Coll, IL A
South Dakota State U, SD B
Southern Illinois U Carbondale, IL B
Stephens Coll, MO B
U of Central Missouri, MO B
U of Central Oklahoma, OK B
U of Cincinnati, OH B
The U of Kansas, KS B
U of Minnesota, Twin Cities Campus, MN B
U of Northern Iowa, IA B
U of Oklahoma, OK B
U of Wisconsin–Madison, WI B
U of Wisconsin–Stevens Point, WI B
Ursuline Coll, OH B
Western Michigan U, MI B
Westwood Coll–Chicago Du Page, IL B

Intermedia/Multimedia

Art Academy of Cincinnati, OH B
Calumet Coll of Saint Joseph, IN B
The Cleveland Inst of Art, OH B
Lewis U, IL B
Minneapolis Coll of Art and Design, MN B
Missouri State U, MO B
U of Michigan, MI B
Westwood Coll–Chicago Du Page, IL A,B

International Agriculture

Iowa State U of Science and Technology, IA B
U of Illinois at Urbana–Champaign, IL B
U of Missouri–Columbia, MO B

International Business/Trade/Commerce

Adrian Coll, MI B
Alma Coll, MI B
Anderson U, IN B
Aquinas Coll, MI B
Argosy U, Chicago, IL B
Argosy U, Schaumburg, IL B
Argosy U, Twin Cities, MN B
Augsburg Coll, MN B
Avila U, MO B
Bacone Coll, OK B
Baker U, KS B
Benedictine U, IL B
Bethany Coll, KS B
Bethel Coll, IN B
Bowling Green State U, OH B
Bradley U, IL B
Buena Vista U, IA B
Butler U, IN B
Cedarville U, OH B
Central Coll, IA B
Central Michigan U, MI B
Clarke Coll, IA B
Clarkson U, NY B
The Coll of St. Scholastica, MN B
Coll of the Ozarks, MO B
Columbia Coll, MO B
Concordia Coll, MN B
Cornell Coll, IA B
Creighton U, NE B
Davenport U, Grand Rapids, MI B
Dominican U, IL B
Drake U, IA B
Eastern Michigan U, MI B
Elmhurst Coll, IL B
Ferris State U, MI B
Franklin U, OH B
Grace Coll, IN B
Graceland U, IA B
Grand Valley State U, MI B
Gustavus Adolphus Coll, MN B
Hamline U, MN B
Illinois State U, IL B
Illinois Wesleyan U, IL B
Iowa State U of Science and Technology, IA B
Jamestown Coll, ND B
Kuyper Coll, MI B
Lake Erie Coll, OH B
Lakeland Coll, WI B
Lawrence Technological U, MI B
Lewis U, IL B
Loras Coll, IA B
Loyola U Chicago, IL B
Madonna U, MI B
Marietta Coll, OH B
Marquette U, WI B
McPherson Coll, KS B
MidAmerica Nazarene U, KS B
Millikin U, IL B
Milwaukee School of Engineering, WI B
Minnesota State U Mankato, MN B
Minnesota State U Moorhead, MN B
Minot State U, ND B
Monmouth Coll, IL B
Mount Mercy Coll, IA B
Mount Union Coll, OH B
Mount Vernon Nazarene U, OH B
Muskingum Coll, OH B
National-Louis U, IL B
Nebraska Wesleyan U, NE B
North Central Coll, IL B
Northeastern State U, OK B
Northern State U, SD B
North Park U, IL B
Northwestern Coll, MN B
Northwest Missouri State U, MO B
Ohio Dominican U, OH B
Ohio Northern U, OH B
The Ohio State U, OH B
Ohio Wesleyan U, OH B
Oklahoma Baptist U, OK B
Oklahoma City U, OK B
Oklahoma State U, OK B
Olivet Nazarene U, IL B
Oral Roberts U, OK B
Otterbein Coll, OH B
Pittsburg State U, KS B
Roosevelt U, IL B
Saginaw Valley State U, MI B
St. Ambrose U, IA B
St. Catherine U, MN B
St. Cloud State U, MN B
Saint Mary's U of Minnesota, MN B
St. Norbert Coll, WI B
Saint Xavier U, IL B
Simpson Coll, IA B
Tiffin U, OH B
Trinity International U, IL B
U of Dayton, OH B
U of Evansville, IN B
The U of Findlay, OH B
U of Indianapolis, IN B
U of Michigan–Flint, MI B
U of Minnesota, Twin Cities Campus, MN B
U of Missouri–Columbia, MO B
U of Missouri–St. Louis, MO B
U of Nebraska–Lincoln, NE B
U of Phoenix–Cleveland Campus, OH B
U of Phoenix–Indianapolis Campus, IN B
U of Phoenix–Kansas City Campus, MO B
U of Phoenix–Metro Detroit Campus, MI B
U of Phoenix–Oklahoma City Campus, OK B
U of Phoenix–St. Louis Campus, MO B
U of Phoenix–Tulsa Campus, OK B
U of Phoenix–Wisconsin Campus, WI B
U of Rio Grande, OH B
The U of Toledo, OH B
U of Tulsa, OK B
U of Wisconsin–La Crosse, WI B
Valparaiso U, IN B
Wartburg Coll, IA B
Washington U in St. Louis, MO B
Webster U, MO B
Westminster Coll, MO B
Wichita State U, KS B
William Jewell Coll, MO B
Xavier U, OH B

International Economics

Eastern Michigan U, MI B
John Carroll U, OH B
Lawrence U, WI B
Ohio U, OH B
Rockford Coll, IL B
St. Catherine U, MN B
Valparaiso U, IN B
Washington U in St. Louis, MO B

International Finance

Washington U in St. Louis, MO B

International/Global Studies

Adrian Coll, MI B
Baker U, KS B
Baldwin-Wallace Coll, OH B
Benedictine U, IL B
Case Western Reserve U, OH B
Cedarville U, OH B
Central Coll, IA B
The Coll of St. Scholastica, MN B
Concordia Coll, MN B
Dana Coll, NE B
Doane Coll, NE B
Greenville Coll, IL B
Hanover Coll, IN B
Hope Coll, MI B
Illinois Wesleyan U, IL B
Lewis U, IL B

A—associate degree; B—bachelor's degree

Macalester Coll, MN B
Miami U Hamilton, OH B
Michigan State U, MI B
Minnesota State U Moorhead, MN B
Monmouth Coll, IL B
Nebraska Wesleyan U, NE B
North Dakota State U, ND B
North Park U, IL B
The Ohio State U, OH B
Pittsburg State U, KS B
Rockford Coll, IL B
Saint Mary's U of Minnesota, MN B
South Dakota State U, SD B
Southeast Missouri State U, MO B
Spring Arbor U, MI B
U of Chicago, IL B
U of Illinois at Urbana–Champaign, IL B
U of Nebraska at Omaha, NE B
U of New Orleans, LA B
U of North Dakota, ND B
U of Oklahoma, OK B
U of Wisconsin–Whitewater, WI B
Western Michigan U, MI B

International Marketing

Oklahoma Baptist U, OK B

International Relations and Affairs

Adrian Coll, MI B
Albion Coll, MI B
Aquinas Coll, MI B
Ashland U, OH B
Augsburg Coll, MN B
Augustana Coll, SD B
Beloit Coll, WI B
Benedictine U, IL B
Bethel U, MN B
Bowling Green State U, OH B
Bradley U, IL B
Butler U, IN B
Calvin Coll, MI B
Capital U, OH B
Carleton Coll, MN B
Carroll U, WI B
Case Western Reserve U, OH B
Cedarville U, OH B
Central Michigan U, MI B
Cleveland State U, OH B
The Coll of Wooster, OH B
Cornell Coll, IA B
Creighton U, NE B
Denison U, OH B
DePaul U, IL B
Drake U, IA B
Earlham Coll, IN B
Edgewood Coll, WI B
Graceland U, IA B
Grand Valley State U, MI B
Hamline U, MN B
Heidelberg U, OH B
Hillsdale Coll, MI B
Illinois Coll, IL B
Illinois Wesleyan U, IL B
Indiana U Bloomington, IN B
Indiana U–Purdue U Indianapolis, IN B
Indiana U Southeast, IN B
Iowa State U of Science and Technology, IA B
John Carroll U, OH B
Kent State U, OH B
Kenyon Coll, OH B
Knox Coll, IL B
Lake Forest Coll, IL B
Lawrence U, WI B
Lindenwood U, MO B
Loras Coll, IA B
Loyola U Chicago, IL B
Luther Coll, IA B
McKendree U, IL B
Miami U, OH B
Michigan State U, MI B
Millikin U, IL B
Minnesota State U Mankato, MN B
Missouri Southern State U, MO B
Mount Mary Coll, WI B
Mount Mercy Coll, IA B
Mount Union Coll, OH B
Muskingum Coll, OH B
Northern Michigan U, MI B
Northwestern U, IL B
Oakland U, MI B
Ohio Northern U, OH B
The Ohio State U, OH B
Ohio U, OH B
Ohio Wesleyan U, OH B
Oklahoma Baptist U, OK B
Oral Roberts U, OK B
Otterbein Coll, OH B
Rockhurst U, MO B
Roosevelt U, IL B
Saginaw Valley State U, MI B
St. Catherine U, MN B
St. Cloud State U, MN B
Saint Joseph's Coll, IN B
Saint Louis U, MO B
St. Norbert Coll, WI B
Saint Xavier U, IL B
Shawnee State U, OH B
Simpson Coll, IA B
Southern Methodist U, TX B
Southern Nazarene U, OK B
Taylor U, IN B
Tiffin U, OH B
Union Coll, NE B
The U of Akron, OH B
U of Cincinnati, OH B
U of Dayton, OH B
U of Evansville, IN B
U of Indianapolis, IN B
The U of Kansas, KS B
U of Minnesota, Duluth, MN B
U of Minnesota, Twin Cities Campus, MN B
U of Nebraska at Kearney, NE B
U of Nebraska–Lincoln, NE B
U of Southern Indiana, IN B
The U of Toledo, OH B
U of Wisconsin–Madison, WI B
U of Wisconsin–Milwaukee, WI B
U of Wisconsin–Oshkosh, WI B
U of Wisconsin–Parkside, WI B
U of Wisconsin–Platteville, WI B
U of Wisconsin–Stevens Point, WI B
U of Wisconsin–Superior, WI B
U of Wisconsin–Whitewater, WI B
Valparaiso U, IN B
Wartburg Coll, IA B
Washington U in St. Louis, MO B
Webster U, MO B
Westminster Coll, MO B
Wheaton Coll, IL B
William Jewell Coll, MO B
Winona State U, MN B
Wright State U, OH B
Xavier U, OH B

Investments and Securities

U of Nebraska at Omaha, NE B

Islamic Studies

DePaul U, IL B
East-West U, IL B
The Ohio State U, OH B
Washington U in St. Louis, MO B

Italian

DePaul U, IL B
Dominican U, IL B
Indiana U Bloomington, IN B
Lake Erie Coll, OH B
Loyola U Chicago, IL B
Northwestern U, IL B
The Ohio State U, OH B
Saint Louis U, MO B
Saint Mary's Coll, IN B
Southern Methodist U, TX B
U of Chicago, IL B
U of Illinois at Chicago, IL B
U of Illinois at Urbana–Champaign, IL B
The U of Iowa, IA B
U of Michigan, MI B
U of Minnesota, Twin Cities Campus, MN B
U of Notre Dame, IN B
U of Wisconsin–Madison, WI B
U of Wisconsin–Milwaukee, WI B
Washington U in St. Louis, MO B
Youngstown State U, OH B

Italian Studies

Miami U, OH B

Japanese

Aquinas Coll, MI B
Augustana Coll, IL B
Ball State U, IN B
Eastern Michigan U, MI B
Gustavus Adolphus Coll, MN B
Hope Coll, MI B
Lawrence U, WI B
Macalester Coll, MN B
Mount Union Coll, OH B
North Central Coll, IL B
The Ohio State U, OH B
Purdue U, IN B
U of Chicago, IL B
The U of Findlay, OH B
The U of Iowa, IA B
U of Minnesota, Twin Cities Campus, MN B
U of Notre Dame, IN B
U of Wisconsin–Madison, WI B
Washington U in St. Louis, MO B

Japanese Studies

Adrian Coll, MI B
Case Western Reserve U, OH B
Earlham Coll, IN B
Gustavus Adolphus Coll, MN B
Purdue U, IN B

Jazz/Jazz Studies

Augustana Coll, IL B
Bowling Green State U, OH B
Capital U, OH B
Central State U, OH B
DePaul U, IL B
Drake U, IA B
Hope Coll, MI B
Michigan State U, MI B
North Central Coll, IL B
Northwestern U, IL B
Oberlin Coll, OH B
The Ohio State U, OH B
Roosevelt U, IL B
St. Cloud State U, MN B
The U of Akron, OH B
U of Cincinnati, OH B
U of Illinois at Urbana–Champaign, IL B
The U of Iowa, IA B
U of Michigan, MI B
U of Minnesota, Duluth, MN B
Western Michigan U, MI B

Jewish/Judaic Studies

DePaul U, IL B
Hebrew Theological Coll, IL B
Indiana U Bloomington, IN B
Laura and Alvin Siegal Coll of Judaic Studies, OH B
Oberlin Coll, OH B
The Ohio State U, OH B
U of Chicago, IL B
U of Cincinnati, OH B
U of Michigan, MI B
U of Minnesota, Twin Cities Campus, MN B
Washington U in St. Louis, MO B

Journalism

Adrian Coll, MI B
Andrews U, MI B
Ashland U, OH B
Augustana Coll, SD B
Bacone Coll, OK A
Ball State U, IN B
Bemidji State U, MN B
Bethel Coll, IN A
Bethel U, MN B
Bowling Green State U, OH B
Bradley U, IL B
Butler U, IN B

Carroll U, WI B
Cedarville U, OH B
Central Michigan U, MI B
Central State U, OH B
Cincinnati Christian U, OH B
The Coll of St. Scholastica, MN B
Coll of the Ozarks, MO B
Concordia Coll, MN B
Creighton U, NE B
Doane Coll, NE B
Dominican U, IL B
Dordt Coll, IA B
Drake U, IA B
Eastern Illinois U, IL B
Fort Hays State U, KS B
Franklin Coll, IN B
Goshen Coll, IN B
Grace Coll, IN B
Grand Valley State U, MI B
Grand View U, IA B
Huntington U, IN B
Illinois Inst of Technology, IL B
Illinois State U, IL B
Indiana U Bloomington, IN B
Indiana U–Purdue U Indianapolis, IN B
Indiana U Southeast, IN A,B
Iowa State U of Science and Technology, IA B
Kansas State U, KS B
Kent State U, OH B
Lewis U, IL B
Lincoln U, MO B
Lindenwood U, MO B
Loras Coll, IA B
Loyola U Chicago, IL B
Madonna U, MI A,B
Manchester Coll, IN A
Marietta Coll, OH B
Marquette U, WI B
Miami U, OH B
Miami U Hamilton, OH B
Michigan State U, MI B
Minnesota State U Mankato, MN B
Minnesota State U Moorhead, MN B
Missouri State U, MO B
Mount Mercy Coll, IA B
Mount Vernon Nazarene U, OH B
Muskingum Coll, OH B
North Central Coll, IL B
North Central U, MN A,B
Northeastern State U, OK B
Northwestern Coll, MN B
Northwestern U, IL B
Northwest Missouri State U, MO B
Oakland U, MI B
Ohio Northern U, OH B
The Ohio State U, OH B
Ohio U, OH B
Ohio Wesleyan U, OH B
Oklahoma Baptist U, OK B
Oklahoma Christian U, OK B
Oklahoma City U, OK B
Oklahoma State U, OK B
Olivet Coll, MI B
Olivet Nazarene U, IL B
Otterbein Coll, OH B
Pittsburg State U, KS B
Purdue U, IN B
Roosevelt U, IL B
St. Ambrose U, IA B
St. Catherine U, MN B
St. Cloud State U, MN B
St. Gregory's U, Shawnee, OK B
Saint Mary-of-the-Woods Coll, IN B
Saint Mary's U of Minnesota, MN B
South Dakota State U, SD B
Southern Illinois U Carbondale, IL B
Southern Methodist U, TX B
Tiffin U, OH B
Truman State U, MO B
Union Coll, NE B
U of Central Missouri, MO B
U of Central Oklahoma, OK B
U of Dayton, OH B
The U of Findlay, OH B
U of Illinois at Urbana–Champaign, IL B
The U of Iowa, IA B
The U of Kansas, KS B
U of Michigan–Flint, MI B
U of Minnesota, Twin Cities Campus, MN B
U of Missouri–Columbia, MO B
U of Nebraska at Kearney, NE B
U of Nebraska at Omaha, NE B
U of Oklahoma, OK B
U of Southern Indiana, IN B
The U of Toledo, OH B
U of Wisconsin–Eau Claire, WI B
U of Wisconsin–Madison, WI B
U of Wisconsin–Milwaukee, WI B
U of Wisconsin–Oshkosh, WI B
U of Wisconsin–Superior, WI B
U of Wisconsin–Whitewater, WI B
Valparaiso U, IN B
Waldorf Coll, IA B
Wartburg Coll, IA B
Wayne State U, MI B
Webster U, MO B
Western Illinois U, IL B
Western Michigan U, MI B
Winona State U, MN B
Youngstown State U, OH B

Journalism Related

Benedictine U, IL B
Dana Coll, NE B
Kent State U, OH B
Ohio U, OH B
Roosevelt U, IL B
Southern Nazarene U, OK B
The U of Akron, OH B
U of Nebraska–Lincoln, NE B

Juvenile Corrections

Harris-Stowe State U, MO B

Kindergarten/Preschool Education

Alma Coll, MI B
Ashland U, OH B
Augsburg Coll, MN B
Baker Coll of Clinton Township, MI A
Baker Coll of Muskegon, MI A
Baker Coll of Owosso, MI A
Ball State U, IN B
Black Hills State U, SD B
Bluffton U, OH B
Bowling Green State U, OH B
Butler U, IN B
Central Christian Coll of Kansas, KS A
Central Methodist U, MO B
Cincinnati Christian U, OH B
Clarke Coll, IA B
Concordia U Chicago, IL B
Concordia U, Nebraska, NE B
Concordia U Wisconsin, WI B
Eastern Illinois U, IL B
Elmhurst Coll, IL B
Evangel U, MO B
Fontbonne U, MO B
Fort Hays State U, KS B
Hannibal-LaGrange Coll, MO B
Harris-Stowe State U, MO B
Hillsdale Coll, MI B
Iowa Wesleyan Coll, IA B
John Carroll U, OH B
Kansas Wesleyan U, KS A
Kendall Coll, IL A,B
Kent State U, OH B
Lakeland Coll, WI B
Lindenwood U, MO B
Loras Coll, IA B
Manchester Coll, IN A
Maranatha Baptist Bible Coll, WI A,B
Martin Luther Coll, MN B
Maryville U of Saint Louis, MO B
McPherson Coll, KS B
Minnesota State U Mankato, MN B
Minnesota State U Moorhead, MN B
Missouri Baptist U, MO B
Mount Mary Coll, WI B
Mount Vernon Nazarene U, OH B
National-Louis U, IL B
Northeastern Illinois U, IL B
Northwest Missouri State U, MO B
Oglala Lakota Coll, SD A,B
Ohio Dominican U, OH B
Ohio Northern U, OH B
Ohio U, OH B
Ohio U–Southern Campus, OH A
Ohio Wesleyan U, OH B
Oklahoma Baptist U, OK B
Oklahoma Christian U, OK B
Oklahoma City U, OK B
Olivet Nazarene U, IL B
Purdue U, IN B
St. Catherine U, MN B
St. Cloud State U, MN B
Saint Mary-of-the-Woods Coll, IN B
Saint Xavier U, IL B
Shawnee State U, OH B
Siena Heights U, MI B
Silver Lake Coll, WI B
Southeastern Oklahoma State U, OK B
Southeast Missouri State U, MO B
Southwest Minnesota State U, MN B
Stephens Coll, MO B
U of Central Oklahoma, OK B
U of Cincinnati, OH B
U of Dayton, OH B
U of Illinois at Urbana–Champaign, IL B
U of Minnesota, Duluth, MN B
U of Minnesota, Twin Cities Campus, MN B
U of Missouri–Columbia, MO B
U of Northern Iowa, IA B
U of Rio Grande, OH A
The U of Toledo, OH B
U of Wisconsin–Madison, WI B
U of Wisconsin–Milwaukee, WI B
U of Wisconsin–Oshkosh, WI B
U of Wisconsin–Platteville, WI B
U of Wisconsin–Stevens Point, WI B
Waldorf Coll, IA B
Walsh U, OH B
Wartburg Coll, IA B
Winona State U, MN B
Wright State U, OH B

Kinesiology and Exercise Science

Adrian Coll, MI B
Alma Coll, MI B
Augustana Coll, SD B
Baker U, KS B
Bethany Lutheran Coll, MN B
Bethel Coll, IN B
Bethel U, MN B
Calvin Coll, MI B
Capital U, OH B
Carroll U, WI B
Cedarville U, OH B
Central Christian Coll of Kansas, KS B
Central Coll, IA B
Central Michigan U, MI B
Cleveland State U, OH B
Concordia Coll, MN B
Concordia U Chicago, IL B
Concordia U, Nebraska, NE B
Concordia U, St. Paul, MN B
Cornell Coll, IA B
Cornerstone U, MI B
Creighton U, NE B

A—associate degree; B—bachelor's degree

Dakota State U, SD B
Defiance Coll, OH B
DePauw U, IN B
Dordt Coll, IA B
Drury U, MO B
Elmhurst Coll, IL B
Eureka Coll, IL B
Greenville Coll, IL B
Hamline U, MN B
Hanover Coll, IN B
Hope Coll, MI B
Huntington U, IN B
Illinois State U, IL B
Indiana Wesleyan U, IN B
Iowa Wesleyan Coll, IA B
Kansas State U, KS B
Kent State U, OH B
Kuyper Coll, MI B
Lake Superior State U, MI B
Loras Coll, IA B
Malone U, OH B
Manchester Coll, IN A
Marquette U, WI B
Miami U, OH B
MidAmerica Nazarene U, KS B
Minnesota State U Moorhead, MN B
Mount Union Coll, OH B
Mount Vernon Nazarene U, OH B
Nebraska Wesleyan U, NE B
North Central Coll, IL B
Northeastern State U, OK B
Northern Michigan U, MI B
North Park U, IL B
Northwestern Coll, MN B
Ohio Northern U, OH B
Ohio U, OH B
Oklahoma Baptist U, OK B
Oklahoma City U, OK B
Olivet Nazarene U, IL B
Oral Roberts U, OK B
Purdue U, IN B
Saginaw Valley State U, MI B
St. Cloud State U, MN B
Saint Louis U, MO B
St. Olaf Coll, MN B
Southern Illinois U Carbondale, IL B
Southern Nazarene U, OK B
Spring Arbor U, MI B
Taylor U, IN B
Transylvania U, KY B
Trinity Christian Coll, IL B
Truman State U, MO B
Union Coll, NE B
The U of Akron, OH B
U of Dayton, OH B
U of Evansville, IN B
U of Illinois at Chicago, IL B
U of Illinois at Urbana–Champaign, IL B
U of Indianapolis, IN B
The U of Iowa, IA B
U of Mary, ND B
U of Michigan, MI B
U of Minnesota, Duluth, MN B
U of Nebraska at Omaha, NE B
U of Sioux Falls, SD B
U of Southern Indiana, IN B
The U of Toledo, OH B
U of Tulsa, OK B
U of Wisconsin–Eau Claire, WI B
U of Wisconsin–Superior, WI B
Valparaiso U, IN B
Western Illinois U, IL B
Western Michigan U, MI B
Winona State U, MN B
Youngstown State U, OH B

Korean
The Ohio State U, OH B

Labor and Industrial Relations
Cleveland State U, OH B
Indiana U Bloomington, IN A,B
Indiana U–Purdue U Indianapolis, IN A,B
The U of Iowa, IA B
U of Wisconsin–Madison, WI B
U of Wisconsin–Milwaukee, WI B
Winona State U, MN B
Youngstown State U, OH A

Labor Studies
Eastern Michigan U, MI B
Indiana U Bloomington, IN A,B
Indiana U Kokomo, IN A,B
Indiana U Northwest, IN A,B
Indiana U–Purdue U Fort Wayne, IN A,B
Indiana U–Purdue U Indianapolis, IN B
Indiana U South Bend, IN A,B
Wayne State U, MI B

Landscape Architecture
Ball State U, IN B
Iowa State U of Science and Technology, IA B
Michigan State U, MI B
North Dakota State U, ND B
Northwest Missouri State U, MO B
The Ohio State U, OH B
Oklahoma State U, OK B
Purdue U, IN B
U of Illinois at Urbana–Champaign, IL B
U of Minnesota, Twin Cities Campus, MN B
U of Nebraska–Lincoln, NE B

Landscaping and Groundskeeping
Andrews U, MI B
Oklahoma State U, OK B
South Dakota State U, SD B
U of Nebraska–Lincoln, NE B

Land-Use Planning and Management
Northland Coll, WI B
U of Wisconsin–Platteville, WI B

Language Interpretation and Translation
Oklahoma State U, Oklahoma City, OK A
Southern Nazarene U, OK B

Latin
Augustana Coll, IL B
Bowling Green State U, OH B
Butler U, IN B
Calvin Coll, MI B
Carleton Coll, MN B
The Coll of Wooster, OH B
Concordia Coll, MN B
Cornell Coll, IA B
Creighton U, NE B
DePauw U, IN B
Hope Coll, MI B
John Carroll U, OH B
Kent State U, OH B
Kenyon Coll, OH B
Lawrence U, WI B
Loyola U Chicago, IL B
Miami U Hamilton, OH B
Missouri State U, MO B
Monmouth Coll, IL B
Oberlin Coll, OH B
Ohio U, OH B
Rockford Coll, IL B
St. Olaf Coll, MN B
U of Chicago, IL B
The U of Iowa, IA B
U of Michigan, MI B
U of Minnesota, Twin Cities Campus, MN B
U of Missouri–Columbia, MO B
U of Nebraska–Lincoln, NE B
U of Wisconsin–Milwaukee, WI B
Wabash Coll, IN B
Washington U in St. Louis, MO B
Western Michigan U, MI B
Wichita State U, KS B

Latin American Studies
Ball State U, IN B
Beloit Coll, WI B
Carleton Coll, MN B
Cornell Coll, IA B
Denison U, OH B
DePaul U, IL B
Earlham Coll, IN B
Gustavus Adolphus Coll, MN B
Hamline U, MN B
Illinois Wesleyan U, IL B
Indiana U Bloomington, IN B
Kent State U, OH B
Lake Forest Coll, IL B
Macalester Coll, MN B
Miami U, OH B
Oakland U, MI B
Oberlin Coll, OH B
Ohio U, OH B
Ohio Wesleyan U, OH B
Pontifical Coll Josephinum, OH B
Ripon Coll, WI B
St. Cloud State U, MN B
St. Olaf Coll, MN B
Southern Methodist U, TX B
U of Chicago, IL B
U of Cincinnati, OH B
U of Illinois at Chicago, IL B
U of Illinois at Urbana–Champaign, IL B
The U of Iowa, IA B
The U of Kansas, KS B
U of Michigan, MI B
U of Minnesota, Morris, MN B
U of Minnesota, Twin Cities Campus, MN B
U of Missouri–Columbia, MO B
U of Nebraska at Omaha, NE B
U of Nebraska–Lincoln, NE B
U of Northern Iowa, IA B
The U of Toledo, OH B
U of Wisconsin–Eau Claire, WI B
U of Wisconsin–Milwaukee, WI B
Washington U in St. Louis, MO B

Latin Teacher Education
Hope Coll, MI B
Kent State U, OH B
Miami U, OH B
Miami U Hamilton, OH B
Ohio Wesleyan U, OH B
U of Illinois at Urbana–Champaign, IL B
Western Michigan U, MI B

Law and Legal Studies Related
Bradley U, IL B
U of Nebraska–Lincoln, NE B

Legal Administrative Assistant
Bryant & Stratton Coll, Parma, OH A

Legal Administrative Assistant/Secretary
Baker Coll of Auburn Hills, MI A
Baker Coll of Clinton Township, MI A
Baker Coll of Flint, MI A
Baker Coll of Jackson, MI A
Baker Coll of Muskegon, MI A
Baker Coll of Owosso, MI A
Baker Coll of Port Huron, MI A
Bohecker's Business Coll, OH A
Dordt Coll, IA A
Northwest Missouri State U, MO B
Shawnee State U, OH A
Sinte Gleska U, SD A
U of Cincinnati, OH A
U of Rio Grande, OH A
The U of Toledo, OH A
Washburn U, KS A
Wright State U, OH A
Youngstown State U, OH A

Legal Assistant/Paralegal
Ball State U, IN A
Brown Mackie Coll–Fort Wayne, IN A
Brown Mackie Coll–Merrillville, IN A
Brown Mackie Coll–Michigan City, IN A
Brown Mackie Coll–South Bend, IN A
Calumet Coll of Saint Joseph, IN B
Chancellor U, OH A,B

Coll of Mount St. Joseph, OH A,B
Coll of Saint Mary, NE A
Concordia U Wisconsin, WI B
Davenport U, Grand Rapids, MI A,B
Eastern Michigan U, MI B
Ferris State U, MI A
Grand Valley State U, MI B
Hamline U, MN B
ITT Tech Inst, Fort Wayne, IN A
ITT Tech Inst, Indianapolis, IN A
ITT Tech Inst, Newburgh, IN A
ITT Tech Inst, South Bend, IN A
Kaplan U–Davenport Campus, IA A,B
Kaplan U–Mason City Campus, IA A
Lake Erie Coll, OH B
Lake Superior State U, MI A,B
Madonna U, MI A,B
Maryville U of Saint Louis, MO B
Midstate Coll, IL A
Minnesota State U Moorhead, MN B
Missouri Western State U, MO A
National American U, MO A,B
Oglala Lakota Coll, SD A,B
Robert Morris Coll, IL A
Rogers State U, OK A
Roosevelt U, IL B
Saint Mary-of-the-Woods Coll, IN A
Sanford-Brown Coll, Fenton, MO A
Shawnee State U, OH A
Southern Illinois U Carbondale, IL B
The U of Akron, OH A
U of Cincinnati, OH A
The U of Toledo, OH A
Ursuline Coll, OH B
Winona State U, MN B

Legal Professions and Studies Related

Ball State U, IN B
Bethany Coll, KS B
Loyola U Chicago, IL B
Missouri Southern State U, MO B
U of Evansville, IN B
U of Illinois at Springfield, IL B
U of Nebraska–Lincoln, NE B
U of Tulsa, OK B

Legal Studies

Brown Mackie Coll–Fort Wayne, IN B
Brown Mackie Coll–Indianapolis, IN B
Brown Mackie Coll–Merrillville, IN B
Brown Mackie Coll–Michigan City, IN B
Brown Mackie Coll–South Bend, IN B
Brown Mackie Coll–Tulsa, OK B
Central Christian Coll of Kansas, KS A
Central Michigan U, MI B
Concordia U Chicago, IL B
Franciscan U of Steubenville, OH B
Hamline U, MN B
Kaplan U–Davenport Campus, IA B
Lake Superior State U, MI A,B
Minnesota State U Moorhead, MN B
Northwestern U, IL B
Oberlin Coll, OH B
Park U, MO B
U of Wisconsin–Superior, WI B
Washburn U, KS B
Webster U, MO B
Winona State U, MN B

Legal Support Services Related

Midstate Coll, IL A

Liberal Arts and Sciences and Humanities Related

Ball State U, IN A,B
Central Christian Coll of Kansas, KS B
Ferris State U, MI A
Malone U, OH B
Ohio U, OH B
Purdue U, IN B
Shimer Coll, IL B
Southern Methodist U, TX B
Southwestern Coll, KS B
Taylor U, IN A
The U of Akron, OH B
U of Illinois at Urbana–Champaign, IL B
U of Wisconsin–Green Bay, WI A
U of Wisconsin–La Crosse, WI B
U of Wisconsin–Whitewater, WI B
Walsh U, OH A
Wright State U, OH B

Liberal Arts and Sciences/ Liberal Studies

Alma Coll, MI B
Antioch U McGregor, OH B
Aquinas Coll, MI B
Ashland U, OH A,B
Augsburg Coll, MN B
Augustana Coll, IL B
Augustana Coll, SD B
Ball State U, IN A,B
Bemidji State U, MN A,B
Benedictine Coll, KS B
Bethany Lutheran Coll, MN B
Bethel Coll, IN A,B
Bethel U, MN A
Bowling Green State U, OH B
Bradley U, IL B
Briar Cliff U, IA A
Butler U, IN A,B
Calumet Coll of Saint Joseph, IN A,B
Central Christian Coll of Kansas, KS B
Central Michigan U, MI B
Chancellor U, OH A,B
Clarke Coll, IA A
Clarkson U, NY B
Cleveland State U, OH B
Coe Coll, IA B
Coll of Mount St. Joseph, OH B
Coll of Saint Benedict, MN B
The Coll of St. Scholastica, MN B
Columbia Coll, MO A,B
Concordia U Wisconsin, WI B
Cornell Coll, IA B
Cottey Coll, MO A
Crossroads Coll, MN A,B
Dakota Wesleyan U, SD A
Defiance Coll, OH B
Donnelly Coll, KS A
Eastern Illinois U, IL B
East-West U, IL A
Edgewood Coll, WI A
Eureka Coll, IL B
Fontbonne U, MO B
Fort Hays State U, KS B
Friends U, KS B
Grace Bible Coll, MI A
Graceland U, IA B
Grace U, NE A,B
Grand Valley State U, MI B
Grand View U, IA A,B
Greenville Coll, IL B
Hannibal-LaGrange Coll, MO B
Haskell Indian Nations U, KS A
Illinois Coll, IL B
Illinois Inst of Technology, IL B
Illinois Wesleyan U, IL B
Indiana State U, IN A,B
Indiana U Bloomington, IN A
Indiana U East, IN A
Indiana U Northwest, IN A
Indiana U–Purdue U Indianapolis, IN A
Indiana U South Bend, IN A
Indiana U Southeast, IN A
Iowa State U of Science and Technology, IA B
Iowa Wesleyan Coll, IA B
Kansas Wesleyan U, KS B
Kent State U, OH A,B
Kent State U, Salem Campus, OH A
Kent State U, Stark Campus, OH A
Kilian Comm Coll, SD A
Kuyper Coll, MI A
Lake Superior State U, MI A
Lewis U, IL B
Lindenwood U, MO B
Little Priest Tribal Coll, NE A
Lourdes Coll, OH A
MacMurray Coll, IL B
Marian U, WI B
Marian U, IN A
Marietta Coll, OH B
Martin U, IN B
Maryville U of Saint Louis, MO B
Miami U, OH A
Michigan Technological U, MI B
Mid-America Christian U, OK A
MidAmerica Nazarene U, KS A
Minnesota State U Mankato, MN A,B
Minnesota State U Moorhead, MN A
Missouri Southern State U, MO A
Monmouth Coll, IL B
Mount Marty Coll, SD A,B
Mount Mary Coll, WI B
National-Louis U, IL B
Newman U, KS A,B
North Central Coll, IL B
Northeastern Illinois U, IL B
Northern Michigan U, MI A
Northern State U, SD A
Northwestern Coll, MN A
Northwestern U, IL B
Oakland U, MI B
Oglala Lakota Coll, SD A
Ohio Dominican U, OH B
The Ohio State U at Marion, OH A
The Ohio State U–Mansfield Campus, OH A
The Ohio State U–Newark Campus, OH A
Ohio U, OH A,B
Ohio U–Chillicothe, OH A,B
Ohio U–Eastern, OH A,B
Ohio U–Southern Campus, OH A
Oklahoma Christian U, OK B
Oklahoma City U, OK B
Oklahoma State U, OK B
Olivet Coll, MI B
Olivet Nazarene U, IL B
Oral Roberts U, OK B
Park U, MO B
Purdue U, IN B
Purdue U North Central, IN B
Rochester Comm and Tech Coll, MN A
Rogers State U, OK A,B
Roosevelt U, IL B
St. Augustine Coll, IL A
St. Catherine U, MN A
St. Cloud State U, MN A,B
St. Gregory's U, Shawnee, OK A,B
St. Louis Christian Coll, MO A
Saint Mary-of-the-Woods Coll, IN A
St. Olaf Coll, MN B
Saint Xavier U, IL B
Shimer Coll, IL B
Sinte Gleska U, SD A,B
South Dakota State U, SD B
Southern Illinois U Carbondale, IL B
Southern Illinois U Edwardsville, IL B
Southwestern Coll, KS B

A—associate degree; B—bachelor's degree

Spring Arbor U, MI A
Stephens Coll, MO A
Trine U, IN A
Trinity Bible Coll, ND A
Trinity International U, IL B
Union Inst & U, OH B
The U of Akron, OH A,B
U of Central Oklahoma, OK B
U of Chicago, IL B
U of Cincinnati, OH A,B
U of Evansville, IN B
U of Illinois at Springfield, IL B
U of Illinois at Urbana–Champaign, IL B
The U of Kansas, KS B
U of Michigan–Dearborn, MI B
U of Michigan–Flint, MI B
U of Minnesota, Morris, MN B
U of Missouri–Kansas City, MO B
U of Missouri–St. Louis, MO B
U of Nebraska–Lincoln, NE B
U of Northern Iowa, IA B
U of Notre Dame, IN B
U of Oklahoma, OK B
U of St. Francis, IL B
U of Saint Francis, IN B
U of Saint Mary, KS A
U of Sioux Falls, SD A,B
The U of South Dakota, SD B
U of Southern Indiana, IN B
The U of Toledo, OH A,B
U of Tulsa, OK B
U of Wisconsin–Eau Claire, WI A
U of Wisconsin–Green Bay, WI B
U of Wisconsin–Oshkosh, WI A,B
U of Wisconsin–Platteville, WI A,B
U of Wisconsin–Stevens Point, WI A
U of Wisconsin–Superior, WI A
U of Wisconsin–Whitewater, WI A,B
Viterbo U, WI B
Walsh U, OH B
Washburn U, KS A,B
Washington U in St. Louis, MO B
Webster U, MO B
Western Illinois U, IL B
Wichita State U, KS A,B
Wilmington Coll, OH B
Winona State U, MN B
Wittenberg U, OH B
Wright State U, OH B
Xavier U, OH A,B
York Coll, NE A
Youngstown State U, OH A,B

Library Science
Ball State U, IN B
St. Cloud State U, MN B
U of Nebraska at Omaha, NE B

Linguistic and Comparative Language Studies Related
Iowa State U of Science and Technology, IA B

Linguistics
Central Coll, IA B
Cleveland State U, OH B
Crown Coll, MN B
Eastern Michigan U, MI B
Indiana U Bloomington, IN B
Iowa State U of Science and Technology, IA B
Lawrence U, WI B
Loyola U Chicago, IL B
Macalester Coll, MN B
Miami U, OH B
Miami U Hamilton, OH B
Northeastern Illinois U, IL B
Northwestern U, IL B
Oakland U, MI B
The Ohio State U, OH B
Ohio U, OH B
St. Cloud State U, MN B
Southern Illinois U Carbondale, IL B
Truman State U, MO B
U of Chicago, IL B
U of Cincinnati, OH B
U of Illinois at Urbana–Champaign, IL B
The U of Iowa, IA B
The U of Kansas, KS B
U of Michigan, MI B
U of Minnesota, Twin Cities Campus, MN B
U of Missouri–Columbia, MO B
U of Oklahoma, OK B
The U of Toledo, OH B
U of Wisconsin–Madison, WI B
U of Wisconsin–Milwaukee, WI B
Wayne State U, MI B
Wright State U, OH B

Linguistics of ASL and Other Sign Languages
Kent State U, OH B

Literature
Augustana Coll, IL B
Beloit Coll, WI B
Coe Coll, IA B
Eureka Coll, IL B
Graceland U, IA B
John Carroll U, OH B
Kansas Wesleyan U, KS B
Lake Superior State U, MI B
Manchester Coll, IN A
Minnesota State U Mankato, MN B
Morningside Coll, IA B
North Central U, MN A
North Park U, IL B
Northwest Missouri State U, MO B
The Ohio State U, OH B
Ohio Wesleyan U, OH B
Otterbein Coll, OH B
Pittsburg State U, KS B
Rockford Coll, IL B
St. Catherine U, MN B
Shimer Coll, IL B
U of Cincinnati, OH B
The U of Iowa, IA B
U of Missouri–St. Louis, MO B
The U of Toledo, OH B
U of Wisconsin–Milwaukee, WI B
Washington U in St. Louis, MO B
Webster U, MO B
Wilberforce U, OH B

Logistics and Materials Management
Bowling Green State U, OH B
Central Michigan U, MI B
Clarkson U, NY B
Elmhurst Coll, IL B
Iowa State U of Science and Technology, IA B
Michigan State U, MI B
Missouri State U, MO B
Northeastern State U, OK B
The Ohio State U, OH B
Park U, MO B
The U of Akron, OH A
The U of Findlay, OH B
U of Illinois at Urbana–Champaign, IL B
The U of Kansas, KS B
The U of Toledo, OH A,B
Wayne State U, MI B
Western Illinois U, IL B
Wright State U, OH B

Machine Shop Technology
Missouri Southern State U, MO A

Machine Tool Technology
Northern Michigan U, MI A
Ranken Tech Coll, MO A

Management Information Systems
Augsburg Coll, MN B
Augustana Coll, SD B
Aurora U, IL B
Avila U, MO B
Baker Coll of Flint, MI B
Ball State U, IN B
Bowling Green State U, OH B
Bradley U, IL B
Briar Cliff U, IA B
Buena Vista U, IA B
Butler U, IN B
Calvin Coll, MI B
Cameron U, OK A
Carroll U, WI B
Cedarville U, OH B
Central Michigan U, MI B
Chancellor U, OH B
Clarke Coll, IA B
Clarkson U, NY B
Cleary U, MI B
Colorado Tech U Sioux Falls, SD B
Concordia U, Nebraska, NE B
Cornerstone U, MI B
Creighton U, NE B
Culver-Stockton Coll, MO B
Dana Coll, NE B
DePaul U, IL B
Dordt Coll, IA B
Eastern Illinois U, IL B
Eastern Michigan U, MI B
Edgewood Coll, WI B
Elmhurst Coll, IL B
Eureka Coll, IL B
Franklin U, OH B
Friends U, KS B
Grace Coll, IN B
Graceland U, IA B
Grand View U, IA B
Greenville Coll, IL B
Illinois Coll, IL B
Indiana State U, IN B
Indiana Tech, IN B
Iowa State U of Science and Technology, IA B
Jamestown Coll, ND B
Lake Superior State U, MI A
Lindenwood U, MO B
Loras Coll, IA B
Luther Coll, IA B
MacMurray Coll, IL B
Madonna U, MI B
Maranatha Baptist Bible Coll, WI B
Maryville U of Saint Louis, MO B
Miami U, OH B
Miami U Hamilton, OH A
Michigan Technological U, MI B
Mid-America Christian U, OK B
Milwaukee School of Engineering, WI B
Minot State U, ND B
Missouri State U, MO B
Monmouth Coll, IL B
Morningside Coll, IA B
Mount Mercy Coll, IA B
Mount Vernon Nazarene U, OH B
Newman U, KS B
North Central Coll, IL B
North Dakota State U, ND B
Northeastern State U, OK B
Northern Michigan U, MI B
Northern State U, SD B
Northwestern Coll, MN B
Northwest Missouri State U, MO B
Oakland U, MI B
The Ohio State U, OH B
Ohio U–Southern Campus, OH A
Oklahoma Baptist U, OK B
Oklahoma City U, OK B
Oklahoma State U, OK B
Olivet Nazarene U, IL B
Oral Roberts U, OK B
Park U, MO B
Rockford Coll, IL B
St. Augustine Coll, IL A
St. Catherine U, MN B
Saint Joseph's Coll, IN A,B
Saint Louis U, MO B
Saint Mary's Coll, IN B
Shawnee State U, OH A,B
Southern Illinois U Edwardsville, IL B
Southwestern Coll, KS B
Spring Arbor U, MI B
Trine U, IN B
Truman State U, MO B
U of Central Missouri, MO B
U of Cincinnati, OH B

U of Dayton, OH B
U of Evansville, IN B
U of Illinois at Urbana–Champaign, IL B
The U of Iowa, IA B
The U of Kansas, KS B
U of Mary, ND B
U of Michigan–Dearborn, MI B
U of Minnesota, Crookston, MN B
U of Minnesota, Twin Cities Campus, MN B
U of Missouri–Columbia, MO B
U of Missouri–St. Louis, MO B
U of New Orleans, LA B
U of Northern Iowa, IA B
U of Notre Dame, IN B
U of Oklahoma, OK B
U of Phoenix–Chicago Campus, IL B
U of Phoenix–Cleveland Campus, OH B
U of Phoenix–Indianapolis Campus, IN B
U of Phoenix–Metro Detroit Campus, MI B
U of Phoenix–Oklahoma City Campus, OK B
U of Phoenix–St. Louis Campus, MO B
U of Phoenix–Springfield Campus, MO B
U of Phoenix–Tulsa Campus, OK B
U of Phoenix–West Michigan Campus, MI B
U of Phoenix–Wisconsin Campus, WI B
The U of Toledo, OH B
U of Tulsa, OK B
U of Wisconsin–Green Bay, WI B
U of Wisconsin–La Crosse, WI B
U of Wisconsin–Milwaukee, WI B
U of Wisconsin–Oshkosh, WI B
U of Wisconsin–Whitewater, WI B
Ursuline Coll, OH B
Viterbo U, WI B
Walsh U, OH B
Wayne State U, MI B
Western Illinois U, IL B
Westminster Coll, MO B
Wichita State U, KS B
Winona State U, MN B
Wright State U, OH A,B
Xavier U, OH B
Youngstown State U, OH B

Management Information Systems and Services Related

Bowling Green State U, OH B
Buena Vista U, IA B
Indiana U–Purdue U Indianapolis, IN A
Purdue U, IN B
Purdue U North Central, IN A
Rasmussen Coll Eagan, MN A
Rasmussen Coll St. Cloud, MN A
Rogers State U, OK B

Management Science

Aurora U, IL B
Central Methodist U, MO B
Columbia Coll, MO B
DePaul U, IL B
Eastern Illinois U, IL B
Friends U, KS B
Grace Bible Coll, MI B
Grand Valley State U, MI B
Lourdes Coll, OH B
Madonna U, MI B
Mid-America Christian U, OK B
Minnesota State U Mankato, MN B
National American U, MO A,B
North Park U, IL B
Ohio Northern U, OH B
Oklahoma Baptist U, OK B
Olivet Nazarene U, IL B
Oral Roberts U, OK B
Quincy U, IL B
Roosevelt U, IL B
St. Ambrose U, IA B
St. Gregory's U, Shawnee, OK B
Saint Louis U, MO B
Southeastern Oklahoma State U, OK B
Southern Illinois U Carbondale, IL B
Southern Methodist U, TX B
Southwestern Coll, KS B
Trinity Bible Coll, ND B
Trinity International U, IL B
U of Illinois at Chicago, IL B
U of Illinois at Urbana–Champaign, IL B
The U of Iowa, IA B
U of Mary, ND B
U of Minnesota, Morris, MN B
U of Missouri–St. Louis, MO B
U of Nebraska–Lincoln, NE B
U of Oklahoma, OK B
U of Phoenix–Chicago Campus, IL B
U of Phoenix–Cleveland Campus, OH B
U of Phoenix–Kansas City Campus, MO B
U of Phoenix–Metro Detroit Campus, MI B
U of Phoenix–Oklahoma City Campus, OK B
U of Phoenix–St. Louis Campus, MO B
U of Phoenix–Tulsa Campus, OK B
U of Phoenix–West Michigan Campus, MI B
U of Phoenix–Wisconsin Campus, WI B
U of St. Francis, IL B
Valparaiso U, IN B
Western Michigan U, MI B
Wright State U, OH B

Management Sciences and Quantitative Methods Related

Indiana State U, IN B
Ohio Northern U, OH B
Southwest Minnesota State U, MN B
The U of Iowa, IA B
The U of Toledo, OH B
Valparaiso U, IN B

Manufacturing Engineering

Bradley U, IL B
Central Michigan U, MI B
Central State U, OH B
Clarkson U, NY B
Miami U, OH B
North Dakota State U, ND B
Northwestern U, IL B
Southern Illinois U Edwardsville, IL B
U of Illinois at Urbana–Champaign, IL B
U of Michigan–Dearborn, MI B
U of Wisconsin–Stout, WI B
Wichita State U, KS B

Manufacturing Technology

Bradley U, IL B
Central Michigan U, MI B
Eastern Michigan U, MI B
Ferris State U, MI B
Indiana State U, IN B
Lawrence Technological U, MI A
Missouri Western State U, MO A
Northern Michigan U, MI B
Pittsburg State U, KS B
Purdue U, IN B
South Dakota State U, SD B
Southwestern Coll, KS B
The U of Akron, OH A,B
U of Northern Iowa, IA B
Wayne State U, MI B
Western Illinois U, IL B

Marine Biology

Michigan Technological U, MI B

Marine Biology and Biological Oceanography

Bemidji State U, MN B
Bowling Green State U, OH B
Southwestern Coll, KS B

Marketing/Marketing Management

AIB Coll of Business, IA A
Alma Coll, MI B
Anderson U, IN B
Andrews U, MI B
Argosy U, Chicago, IL B
Argosy U, Schaumburg, IL B
Argosy U, Twin Cities, MN B
Ashland U, OH B
Augsburg Coll, MN B
Augustana Coll, IL B
Aurora U, IL B
Avila U, MO B
Bacone Coll, OK B
Baker Coll of Allen Park, MI A
Baker Coll of Auburn Hills, MI A,B
Baker Coll of Cadillac, MI A
Baker Coll of Clinton Township, MI A
Baker Coll of Owosso, MI A,B
Baldwin-Wallace Coll, OH B
Ball State U, IN B
Benedictine U, IL B
Black Hills State U, SD B
Bohecker's Business Coll, OH A
Bradley U, IL B
Buena Vista U, IA B
Butler U, IN B
Capital U, OH B
Carroll U, WI B
Cedarville U, OH B
Central Christian Coll of Kansas, KS A
Central Michigan U, MI B
Chancellor U, OH A,B
Clarke Coll, IA B
Clarkson U, NY B
Cleary U, MI B
Cleveland State U, OH B
The Coll of St. Scholastica, MN B
Coll of the Ozarks, MO B
Colorado Tech U North Kansas City, MO B
Colorado Tech U Sioux Falls, SD B
Columbia Coll, MO B
Concordia U, St. Paul, MN B
Concordia U Wisconsin, WI B
Cornerstone U, MI B
Creighton U, NE B
Crown Coll, MN A
Dakota State U, SD B
Dakota Wesleyan U, SD B
Davenport U, Grand Rapids, MI A,B
DePaul U, IL B
Drake U, IA B
Drury U, MO B
Eastern Illinois U, IL B
Eastern Michigan U, MI B
Elmhurst Coll, IL B
Emporia State U, KS B
Evangel U, MO B
Ferris State U, MI B
Fontbonne U, MO B
Fort Hays State U, KS B
Franklin U, OH B
Friends U, KS B
Grace Bible Coll, MI B
Grace Coll, IN B
Grand Valley State U, MI B
Greenville Coll, IL B
Hannibal-LaGrange Coll, MO B
Harris-Stowe State U, MO B
Hillsdale Coll, MI B
Illinois State U, IL B
Indiana State U, IN B
Indiana Tech, IN B
Indiana U–Purdue U Fort Wayne, IN B
Indiana Wesleyan U, IN B

A—associate degree; B—bachelor's degree

Iowa State U of Science and Technology, IA B
Jamestown Coll, ND B
John Carroll U, OH B
Kansas State U, KS B
Kendall Coll, IL B
Kent State U, OH B
Lakeland Coll, WI B
Lewis U, IL B
Lincoln U, MO B
Lindenwood U, MO B
Loras Coll, IA B
Lourdes Coll, OH B
Loyola U Chicago, IL B
MacMurray Coll, IL B
Madonna U, MI B
Manchester Coll, IN B
Maranatha Baptist Bible Coll, WI B
Marian U, WI B
Marian U, IN B
Marietta Coll, OH B
Marquette U, WI B
Maryville U of Saint Louis, MO B
McKendree U, IL B
Miami U, OH A,B
Miami U Hamilton, OH A
Michigan State U, MI B
Michigan Technological U, MI B
Mid-America Christian U, OK B
MidAmerica Nazarene U, KS B
Millikin U, IL B
Minnesota State U Mankato, MN B
Minnesota State U Moorhead, MN B
Minot State U, ND B
Missouri Baptist U, MO B
Missouri State U, MO B
Missouri Western State U, MO B
Morningside Coll, IA B
Mount Mary Coll, WI B
Mount Mercy Coll, IA B
Mount Vernon Nazarene U, OH B
Newman U, KS B
North Central Coll, IL B
North Dakota State U, ND B
Northeastern Illinois U, IL B
Northeastern State U, OK B
Northern Michigan U, MI B
Northern State U, SD B
North Park U, IL B
Northwestern Coll, MN B
Northwest Missouri State U, MO B
Northwood U, MI B
Oakland U, MI B
The Ohio State U, OH B
Oklahoma Baptist U, OK B
Oklahoma Christian U, OK B
Oklahoma City U, OK B
Oklahoma State U, OK B
Olivet Coll, MI B
Olivet Nazarene U, IL B
Oral Roberts U, OK B
Otterbein Coll, OH B
Park U, MO B
Pittsburg State U, KS B
Purdue U, IN B
Quincy U, IL B
Rockford Coll, IL B
Roosevelt U, IL B
Saginaw Valley State U, MI B
St. Ambrose U, IA B
St. Catherine U, MN B
St. Cloud State U, MN B
St. Gregory's U, Shawnee, OK B
Saint Louis U, MO B
Saint Mary-of-the-Woods Coll, IN B
Saint Mary's Coll, IN B
Saint Mary's U of Minnesota, MN B
Simpson Coll, IA B
Southeastern Oklahoma State U, OK B
Southeast Missouri State U, MO B
Southern Illinois U Carbondale, IL B
Southern Methodist U, TX B
Southern Nazarene U, OK B
Southwest Baptist U, MO B
Southwestern Oklahoma State U, OK B
Southwest Minnesota State U, MN A,B
Stephens Coll, MO B
Taylor U, IN B
Tiffin U, OH B
Trine U, IN B
Trinity Christian Coll, IL B
Trinity International U, IL B
Truman State U, MO B
The U of Akron, OH A,B
U of Central Missouri, MO B
U of Central Oklahoma, OK B
U of Charleston, WV B
U of Cincinnati, OH A,B
U of Dayton, OH B
U of Evansville, IN B
The U of Findlay, OH B
U of Illinois at Chicago, IL B
U of Illinois at Urbana–Champaign, IL B
U of Indianapolis, IN B
The U of Iowa, IA B
The U of Kansas, KS B
U of Mary, ND B
U of Michigan–Dearborn, MI B
U of Michigan–Flint, MI B
U of Minnesota, Duluth, MN B
U of Minnesota, Twin Cities Campus, MN B
U of Missouri–Columbia, MO B
U of Missouri–St. Louis, MO B
U of Nebraska at Omaha, NE B
U of Nebraska–Lincoln, NE B
U of New Orleans, LA B
U of North Dakota, ND B
U of Northern Iowa, IA B
U of Notre Dame, IN B
U of Oklahoma, OK B
U of Phoenix–Chicago Campus, IL B
U of Phoenix–Cleveland Campus, OH B
U of Phoenix–Indianapolis Campus, IN B
U of Phoenix–Kansas City Campus, MO B
U of Phoenix–Metro Detroit Campus, MI B
U of Phoenix–Oklahoma City Campus, OK B
U of Phoenix–St. Louis Campus, MO B
U of Phoenix–Springfield Campus, MO B
U of Phoenix–Tulsa Campus, OK B
U of Phoenix–West Michigan Campus, MI B
U of Phoenix–Wisconsin Campus, WI B
U of Rio Grande, OH B
U of St. Francis, IL B
The U of South Dakota, SD B
U of Southern Indiana, IN B
The U of Toledo, OH B
U of Tulsa, OK B
U of Wisconsin–Eau Claire, WI B
U of Wisconsin–La Crosse, WI B
U of Wisconsin–Milwaukee, WI B
U of Wisconsin–Oshkosh, WI B
U of Wisconsin–Superior, WI B
U of Wisconsin–Whitewater, WI B
Ursuline Coll, OH B
Valparaiso U, IN B
Viterbo U, WI B
Waldorf Coll, IA B
Walsh Coll of Accountancy and Business Administration, MI B
Walsh U, OH A
Wartburg Coll, IA B
Washburn U, KS B
Washington U in St. Louis, MO B
Wayne State U, MI B
Webster U, MO B
Western Illinois U, IL B
Western Michigan U, MI B
Westwood Coll–Chicago Du Page, IL B
Wichita State U, KS B
Wilberforce U, OH B
Wilmington Coll, OH B
Winona State U, MN B
Wright State U, OH A,B
Xavier U, OH B
Youngstown State U, OH A,B

Marketing Related

Bowling Green State U, OH B
Franklin U, OH B
Miami U Hamilton, OH B
The U of Akron, OH B
The U of Iowa, IA B
Washington U in St. Louis, MO B
Western Michigan U, MI B

Marketing Research

Ashland U, OH B
Baker Coll of Jackson, MI B
U of Illinois at Urbana–Champaign, IL B
The U of Toledo, OH B

Marriage and Family Therapy/Counseling

Grace U, NE B
Oklahoma Baptist U, OK B

Massage Therapy

Brown Mackie Coll–Michigan City, IN A
Davenport U, Grand Rapids, MI A
Mercy Coll of Northwest Ohio, OH A
Minnesota School of Business–Blaine, MN A

Mass Communication/Media

Albion Coll, MI B
Anderson U, IN B
Andrews U, MI B
Ashland U, OH B
Augsburg Coll, MN B
Augustana Coll, IL B
Baker U, KS B
Baldwin-Wallace Coll, OH B
Beloit Coll, WI B
Bemidji State U, MN B
Benedictine Coll, KS B
Bethel Coll, KS B
Bethel U, MN B
Black Hills State U, SD A,B
Briar Cliff U, IA B
Buena Vista U, IA B
Calvary Bible Coll and Theological Seminary, MO B
Calvin Coll, MI B
Cedarville U, OH B
Clarke Coll, IA B
Coll of the Ozarks, MO B
The Coll of Wooster, OH B
Concordia Coll, MN B
Concordia U, Nebraska, NE B
Concordia U, St. Paul, MN B
Concordia U Wisconsin, WI B
Cornerstone U, MI B
Culver-Stockton Coll, MO B
Defiance Coll, OH B
Denison U, OH B
DePauw U, IN B
Dominican U, IL B
Dordt Coll, IA B
Drake U, IA B
Eureka Coll, IL B
Fort Hays State U, KS B
Goshen Coll, IN B
Grand View U, IA B
Greenville Coll, IL B
Gustavus Adolphus Coll, MN B
Hamline U, MN B
Hanover Coll, IN B
Haskell Indian Nations U, KS A
Heidelberg U, OH B
Hiram Coll, OH B
Huntington U, IN B
Illinois Coll, IL B
Illinois State U, IL B

Indiana U–Purdue U Fort Wayne, IN B
Indiana U South Bend, IN B
Iowa State U of Science and Technology, IA B
Iowa Wesleyan Coll, IA B
John Carroll U, OH B
Kansas Wesleyan U, KS B
Kent State U, OH B
Kuyper Coll, MI B
Lewis U, IL B
Lindenwood U, MO B
Loras Coll, IA B
Manchester Coll, IN B
Marian U, IN B
Maryville U of Saint Louis, MO B
McKendree U, IL B
Miami U, OH B
Miami U Hamilton, OH B
MidAmerica Nazarene U, KS B
Minnesota State U Mankato, MN B
Minnesota State U Moorhead, MN B
Missouri State U, MO B
Morningside Coll, IA B
Newman U, KS B
North Central U, MN A,B
North Park U, IL B
Northwest Missouri State U, MO B
Oglala Lakota Coll, SD A
Oklahoma Baptist U, OK B
Oklahoma Christian U, OK B
Oklahoma City U, OK B
Olivet Nazarene U, IL B
St. Ambrose U, IA B
St. Catherine U, MN B
St. Cloud State U, MN B
Saint Joseph's Coll, IN B
Saint Mary-of-the-Woods Coll, IN B
Simpson Coll, IA B
Southern Illinois U Edwardsville, IL B
Southwestern Oklahoma State U, OK B
Stephens Coll, MO B
Taylor U, IN B
Tiffin U, OH B
Truman State U, MO B
U of Cincinnati, OH B
U of Dayton, OH B
U of Illinois at Urbana–Champaign, IL B
The U of Iowa, IA B
U of Mary, ND B
U of Minnesota, Twin Cities Campus, MN B
U of Missouri–Columbia, MO B
U of Missouri–Kansas City, MO B
U of Missouri–St. Louis, MO B
U of Nebraska at Kearney, NE B
U of Rio Grande, OH A,B
U of St. Francis, IL B
U of Sioux Falls, SD B
The U of South Dakota, SD B
The U of Toledo, OH B
U of Wisconsin–Eau Claire, WI B
U of Wisconsin–Madison, WI B
U of Wisconsin–Milwaukee, WI B
U of Wisconsin–Oshkosh, WI B
U of Wisconsin–Platteville, WI B
U of Wisconsin–Superior, WI B
Valley City State U, ND B
Valparaiso U, IN B
Waldorf Coll, IA B
Wartburg Coll, IA B
Washburn U, KS B
Wayne State Coll, NE B
Wilberforce U, OH B
Wilmington Coll, OH B
Winona State U, MN B
Wright State U, OH B

Materials Engineering

Case Western Reserve U, OH B
Clarkson U, NY B
Illinois Inst of Technology, IL B
Iowa State U of Science and Technology, IA B
Michigan Technological U, MI B
Northwestern U, IL B
The Ohio State U, OH B
Purdue U, IN B
U of Illinois at Urbana–Champaign, IL B
U of Michigan, MI B
U of Minnesota, Twin Cities Campus, MN B
U of Wisconsin–Milwaukee, WI B
Winona State U, MN B
Wright State U, OH B

Materials Science

Case Western Reserve U, OH B
Clarkson U, NY B
Michigan State U, MI B
Northwestern U, IL B
The Ohio State U, OH B
U of Illinois at Urbana–Champaign, IL B
U of Michigan, MI B
U of Minnesota, Twin Cities Campus, MN B

Maternal and Child Health

Union Inst & U, OH B

Mathematics

Adrian Coll, MI B
Albion Coll, MI B
Alma Coll, MI B
Anderson U, IN B
Andrews U, MI B
Aquinas Coll, MI B
Ashland U, OH B
Augsburg Coll, MN B
Augustana Coll, IL B
Augustana Coll, SD B
Aurora U, IL B
Avila U, MO B
Baker U, KS B
Baldwin-Wallace Coll, OH B
Ball State U, IN B
Beloit Coll, WI B
Bemidji State U, MN B
Benedictine Coll, KS B
Benedictine U, IL B
Bethany Coll, KS B
Bethany Lutheran Coll, MN B
Bethel Coll, IN B
Bethel Coll, KS B
Bethel U, MN B
Black Hills State U, SD B
Bluffton U, OH B
Bowling Green State U, OH B
Bradley U, IL B
Briar Cliff U, IA B
Buena Vista U, IA B
Butler U, IN B
Calvin Coll, MI B
Cameron U, OK B
Capital U, OH B
Carleton Coll, MN B
Carroll U, WI B
Case Western Reserve U, OH B
Cedarville U, OH B
Central Christian Coll of Kansas, KS A
Central Coll, IA B
Central Methodist U, MO B
Central Michigan U, MI B
Central State U, OH B
Clarke Coll, IA B
Clarkson U, NY B
Cleveland State U, OH B
Coe Coll, IA B
Coll of Mount St. Joseph, OH B
Coll of Saint Benedict, MN B
Coll of Saint Mary, NE B
The Coll of St. Scholastica, MN B
Coll of the Ozarks, MO B
The Coll of Wooster, OH B
Columbia Coll, MO B
Concordia Coll, MN B
Concordia U, MI B
Concordia U Chicago, IL B
Concordia U, Nebraska, NE B
Concordia U, St. Paul, MN B
Concordia U Wisconsin, WI B
Cornell Coll, IA B
Creighton U, NE A,B
Culver-Stockton Coll, MO B
Dakota Wesleyan U, SD B
Dana Coll, NE B
Defiance Coll, OH B
Denison U, OH B
DePaul U, IL B
DePauw U, IN B
Doane Coll, NE B
Dominican U, IL B
Dordt Coll, IA B
Drake U, IA B
Drury U, MO B
Earlham Coll, IN B
Eastern Illinois U, IL B
Eastern Michigan U, MI B
East-West U, IL B
Edgewood Coll, WI B
Elmhurst Coll, IL B
Emporia State U, KS B
Eureka Coll, IL B
Evangel U, MO B
Ferris State U, MI B
Fontbonne U, MO B
Fort Hays State U, KS B
Franciscan U of Steubenville, OH B
Franklin Coll, IN B
Friends U, KS B
Goshen Coll, IN B
Grace Coll, IN B
Graceland U, IA B
Grand Valley State U, MI B
Greenville Coll, IL B
Grinnell Coll, IA B
Gustavus Adolphus Coll, MN B
Hamline U, MN B
Hannibal-LaGrange Coll, MO B
Hanover Coll, IN B
Heidelberg U, OH B
Hillsdale Coll, MI B
Hiram Coll, OH B
Hope Coll, MI B
Huntington U, IN B
Illinois Coll, IL B
Illinois State U, IL B
Illinois Wesleyan U, IL B
Indiana State U, IN B
Indiana U Bloomington, IN B
Indiana U Kokomo, IN B
Indiana U Northwest, IN B
Indiana U–Purdue U Fort Wayne, IN A,B
Indiana U–Purdue U Indianapolis, IN B
Indiana U South Bend, IN B
Indiana U Southeast, IN B
Indiana Wesleyan U, IN A,B
Iowa State U of Science and Technology, IA B
Iowa Wesleyan Coll, IA B
Jamestown Coll, ND B
John Carroll U, OH B
Kalamazoo Coll, MI B
Kansas State U, KS B
Kansas Wesleyan U, KS B
Kent State U, OH B
Kenyon Coll, OH B
Knox Coll, IL B
Lake Erie Coll, OH B
Lake Forest Coll, IL B
Lakeland Coll, WI B
Lake Superior State U, MI B
Lawrence Technological U, MI B
Lawrence U, WI B
Lewis U, IL B
Lincoln U, MO B
Lindenwood U, MO B
Loras Coll, IA B
Loyola U Chicago, IL B
Luther Coll, IA B
Macalester Coll, MN B
MacMurray Coll, IL B
Madonna U, MI B
Malone U, OH B
Manchester Coll, IN B

A—associate degree; B—bachelor's degree

Marian U, WI B
Marian U, IN B
Marietta Coll, OH B
Marquette U, WI B
Maryville U of Saint Louis, MO B
Mayville State U, ND B
McKendree U, IL B
McPherson Coll, KS B
Miami U, OH B
Miami U Hamilton, OH B
Michigan State U, MI B
Michigan Technological U, MI B
Mid-America Christian U, OK B
MidAmerica Nazarene U, KS B
Minnesota State U Mankato, MN B
Minnesota State U Moorhead, MN B
Minot State U, ND B
Missouri Baptist U, MO B
Missouri Southern State U, MO B
Missouri State U, MO B
Missouri Western State U, MO B
Monmouth Coll, IL B
Morningside Coll, IA B
Mount Marty Coll, SD B
Mount Mary Coll, WI B
Mount Mercy Coll, IA B
Mount Union Coll, OH B
Mount Vernon Nazarene U, OH B
Muskingum Coll, OH B
National-Louis U, IL B
Nebraska Wesleyan U, NE B
Newman U, KS B
North Central Coll, IL B
North Dakota State U, ND B
Northeastern Illinois U, IL B
Northeastern State U, OK B
Northern Michigan U, MI B
Northern State U, SD B
Northland Coll, WI B
North Park U, IL B
Northwestern Coll, MN B
Northwestern U, IL B
Northwest Missouri State U, MO B
Oakland U, MI B
Oberlin Coll, OH B
Ohio Dominican U, OH B
Ohio Northern U, OH B
The Ohio State U, OH B
Ohio U, OH B
Ohio Wesleyan U, OH B
Oklahoma Baptist U, OK B
Oklahoma Christian U, OK B
Oklahoma City U, OK B
Oklahoma Panhandle State U, OK B
Oklahoma State U, OK B
Olivet Coll, MI B
Olivet Nazarene U, IL B
Oral Roberts U, OK B
Otterbein Coll, OH B
Park U, MO B
Pittsburg State U, KS B
Purdue U, IN B
Purdue U Calumet, IN B
Purdue U North Central, IN A
Quincy U, IL B
Ripon Coll, WI B
Rockford Coll, IL B
Rockhurst U, MO B
Roosevelt U, IL B
Rose-Hulman Inst of Technology, IN B
Saginaw Valley State U, MI B
St. Ambrose U, IA B
St. Catherine U, MN B
St. Cloud State U, MN B
St. Gregory's U, Shawnee, OK B
Saint John's U, MN B
Saint Joseph's Coll, IN B
Saint Louis U, MO B
Saint Mary-of-the-Woods Coll, IN B
Saint Mary's Coll, IN B
Saint Mary's U of Minnesota, MN B
St. Norbert Coll, WI B
St. Olaf Coll, MN B
Saint Xavier U, IL B
Shawnee State U, OH B
Siena Heights U, MI B
Silver Lake Coll, WI B
Simpson Coll, IA B
South Dakota School of Mines and Technology, SD B
South Dakota State U, SD B
Southeastern Oklahoma State U, OK B
Southeast Missouri State U, MO B
Southern Illinois U Carbondale, IL B
Southern Illinois U Edwardsville, IL B
Southern Methodist U, TX B
Southern Nazarene U, OK B
Southwest Baptist U, MO B
Southwestern Coll, KS B
Southwestern Oklahoma State U, OK B
Southwest Minnesota State U, MN B
Spring Arbor U, MI B
Sterling Coll, KS B
Taylor U, IN B
Transylvania U, KY B
Trine U, IN A,B
Trinity Christian Coll, IL B
Trinity International U, IL B
Truman State U, MO B
Union Coll, NE B
The U of Akron, OH B
U of Central Missouri, MO B
U of Central Oklahoma, OK B
U of Chicago, IL B
U of Cincinnati, OH B
U of Dallas, TX B
U of Dayton, OH B
U of Evansville, IN B
The U of Findlay, OH B
U of Illinois at Chicago, IL B
U of Illinois at Springfield, IL B
U of Illinois at Urbana–Champaign, IL B
U of Indianapolis, IN B
The U of Iowa, IA B
The U of Kansas, KS B
U of Mary, ND B
U of Michigan, MI B
U of Michigan–Dearborn, MI B
U of Michigan–Flint, MI B
U of Minnesota, Duluth, MN B
U of Minnesota, Morris, MN B
U of Minnesota, Twin Cities Campus, MN B
U of Missouri–Columbia, MO B
U of Missouri–Kansas City, MO B
U of Missouri–St. Louis, MO B
U of Nebraska at Kearney, NE B
U of Nebraska at Omaha, NE B
U of Nebraska–Lincoln, NE B
U of New Orleans, LA B
U of North Dakota, ND B
U of Northern Iowa, IA B
U of Notre Dame, IN B
U of Oklahoma, OK B
U of Rio Grande, OH A,B
U of St. Francis, IL B
U of Saint Francis, IN B
U of Saint Mary, KS B
U of Science and Arts of Oklahoma, OK B
U of Sioux Falls, SD B
The U of South Dakota, SD B
U of Southern Indiana, IN B
The U of Toledo, OH B
U of Tulsa, OK B
U of Wisconsin–Eau Claire, WI B
U of Wisconsin–Green Bay, WI B
U of Wisconsin–La Crosse, WI B
U of Wisconsin–Madison, WI B
U of Wisconsin–Milwaukee, WI B
U of Wisconsin–Oshkosh, WI B
U of Wisconsin–Parkside, WI B
U of Wisconsin–Platteville, WI B
U of Wisconsin–Stevens Point, WI B
U of Wisconsin–Superior, WI B
U of Wisconsin–Whitewater, WI B
Ursuline Coll, OH B
Valley City State U, ND B
Valparaiso U, IN B
Viterbo U, WI B
Wabash Coll, IN B
Walsh U, OH B
Wartburg Coll, IA B
Washburn U, KS B
Washington U in St. Louis, MO B
Wayne State Coll, NE B
Wayne State U, MI B
Webster U, MO B
Western Illinois U, IL B
Western Michigan U, MI B
Westminster Coll, MO B
Wheaton Coll, IL B
Wichita State U, KS B
William Jewell Coll, MO B
Wilmington Coll, OH B
Winona State U, MN B
Wittenberg U, OH B
Wright State U, OH B
Xavier U, OH B
Youngstown State U, OH B

Mathematics and Computer Science

Anderson U, IN B
Augustana Coll, IL B
Bethel Coll, IN B
Central Coll, IA B
Central Michigan U, MI B
Coll of Saint Benedict, MN B
DePaul U, IL B
Eastern Illinois U, IL B
Friends U, KS B
Indiana U–Purdue U Fort Wayne, IN B
Lake Superior State U, MI B
Lawrence Technological U, MI B
Lawrence U, WI B
Loyola U Chicago, IL B
Saint John's U, MN B
Saint Mary's Coll, IN B
Saint Mary's U of Minnesota, MN B
U of Illinois at Chicago, IL B
U of Illinois at Urbana–Champaign, IL B
U of St. Francis, IL B
Washington U in St. Louis, MO B

Mathematics and Statistics Related

Anderson U, IN B
Dakota State U, SD B
Miami U Hamilton, OH B
Taylor U, IN B

Mathematics Related

Hillsdale Coll, MI B
Ohio Northern U, OH B

Mathematics Teacher Education

Alma Coll, MI B
Anderson U, IN B
Bethany Coll, KS B
Bethel Coll, IN B
Bethel U, MN B
Black Hills State U, SD B
Bowling Green State U, OH B
Buena Vista U, IA B
Capital U, OH B
Carroll U, WI B
Cedarville U, OH B
Central Christian Coll of Kansas, KS A
Central Michigan U, MI B
Coll of the Ozarks, MO B
Concordia Coll, MN B
Concordia U, MI B
Concordia U Chicago, IL B
Concordia U, Nebraska, NE B
Concordia U, St. Paul, MN B
Cornerstone U, MI B

Culver-Stockton Coll, MO B
Dakota State U, SD B
Dakota Wesleyan U, SD B
Dana Coll, NE B
DePaul U, IL B
Eastern Michigan U, MI B
Edgewood Coll, WI B
Elmhurst Coll, IL B
Ferris State U, MI B
Franklin Coll, IN B
Friends U, KS B
Grace Coll, IN B
Grand Valley State U, MI B
Greenville Coll, IL B
Gustavus Adolphus Coll, MN B
Hannibal-LaGrange Coll, MO B
Hope Coll, MI B
Indiana U Bloomington, IN B
Indiana U Northwest, IN B
Indiana U–Purdue U Fort Wayne, IN B
Indiana U South Bend, IN B
Indiana U Southeast, IN B
Indiana Wesleyan U, IN B
Jamestown Coll, ND B
Lincoln U, MO B
Lindenwood U, MO B
Loyola U Chicago, IL B
Madonna U, MI B
Maranatha Baptist Bible Coll, WI B
Marian U, WI B
Marquette U, WI B
Maryville U of Saint Louis, MO B
Mayville State U, ND B
McKendree U, IL B
Miami U, OH B
Miami U Hamilton, OH B
Michigan Technological U, MI B
MidAmerica Nazarene U, KS B
Millikin U, IL B
Minnesota State U Moorhead, MN B
Minot State U, ND B
Missouri State U, MO B
Mount Marty Coll, SD B
Mount Mary Coll, WI B
Mount Vernon Nazarene U, OH B
North Dakota State U, ND B
Northeastern State U, OK B
Northern Michigan U, MI B
Northwestern Coll, MN B
Northwestern U, IL B
Ohio Dominican U, OH B
Ohio Northern U, OH B
Ohio U, OH B
Ohio Wesleyan U, OH B
Oklahoma Baptist U, OK B
Oklahoma Christian U, OK B
Oral Roberts U, OK B
Pittsburg State U, KS B
Purdue U, IN B
Saginaw Valley State U, MI B
St. Ambrose U, IA B
St. Catherine U, MN B
St. Gregory's U, Shawnee, OK B
Saint Mary's U of Minnesota, MN B
Saint Xavier U, IL B
Shawnee State U, OH B
Southeastern Oklahoma State U, OK B
Southeast Missouri State U, MO B
Southern Nazarene U, OK B
Southwest Baptist U, MO B
Southwest Minnesota State U, MN B
Taylor U, IN B
Trine U, IN B
Trinity Christian Coll, IL B
Union Coll, NE B
The U of Akron, OH B
U of Central Oklahoma, OK B
U of Evansville, IN B
U of Illinois at Chicago, IL B
U of Illinois at Urbana–Champaign, IL B
U of Indianapolis, IN B
The U of Iowa, IA B
U of Mary, ND B
U of Michigan–Dearborn, MI B
U of Michigan–Flint, MI B
U of Minnesota, Duluth, MN B
U of Minnesota, Twin Cities Campus, MN B
U of Missouri–Columbia, MO B
U of Missouri–St. Louis, MO B
U of Nebraska–Lincoln, NE B
U of New Orleans, LA B
U of North Dakota, ND B
U of Northern Iowa, IA B
U of Oklahoma, OK B
U of Rio Grande, OH B
U of St. Francis, IL B
U of Saint Francis, IN B
The U of South Dakota, SD B
The U of Toledo, OH B
U of Tulsa, OK B
U of Wisconsin–Superior, WI B
Ursuline Coll, OH B
Valley City State U, ND B
Valparaiso U, IN B
Viterbo U, WI B
Walsh U, OH B
Wartburg Coll, IA B
Washington U in St. Louis, MO B
Wayne State Coll, NE B
Wayne State U, MI B
Western Michigan U, MI B
Wright State U, OH B
York Coll, NE B
Youngstown State U, OH B

Mechanical Design Technology

Lincoln U, MO B

Mechanical Drafting and CAD/CADD

Baker Coll of Flint, MI A
Cameron U, OK A
Eastern Michigan U, MI B
Indiana U–Purdue U Indianapolis, IN A
Purdue U, IN B
Purdue U Calumet, IN A,B

Mechanical Engineering

Andrews U, MI B
Baker Coll of Flint, MI B
Bradley U, IL B
Calvin Coll, MI B
Case Western Reserve U, OH B
Cedarville U, OH B
Central Michigan U, MI B
Clarkson U, NY B
Cleveland State U, OH B
Dordt Coll, IA B
Illinois Inst of Technology, IL B
Indiana Tech, IN B
Indiana U–Purdue U Fort Wayne, IN B
Indiana U–Purdue U Indianapolis, IN B
Iowa State U of Science and Technology, IA B
Kansas State U, KS B
Kettering U, MI B
Lake Superior State U, MI B
Lawrence Technological U, MI B
Marquette U, WI B
Miami U, OH B
Michigan State U, MI B
Michigan Technological U, MI B
Milwaukee School of Engineering, WI B
Minnesota State U Mankato, MN B
Missouri U of Science and Technology, MO B
North Dakota State U, ND B
Northwestern U, IL B
Oakland U, MI B
Ohio Northern U, OH B
The Ohio State U, OH B
Ohio U, OH B
Oklahoma Christian U, OK B
Oklahoma State U, OK B
Oral Roberts U, OK B
Purdue U, IN B
Purdue U Calumet, IN B
Purdue U North Central, IN B
Rose-Hulman Inst of Technology, IN B
Saginaw Valley State U, MI B
St. Cloud State U, MN B
Saint Louis U, MO B
South Dakota School of Mines and Technology, SD B
South Dakota State U, SD B
Southern Illinois U Carbondale, IL B
Southern Illinois U Edwardsville, IL B
Southern Methodist U, TX B
Trine U, IN B
The U of Akron, OH B
U of Cincinnati, OH B
U of Dayton, OH B
U of Evansville, IN B
U of Illinois at Chicago, IL B
U of Illinois at Urbana–Champaign, IL B
U of Indianapolis, IN B
The U of Iowa, IA B
The U of Kansas, KS B
U of Michigan, MI B
U of Michigan–Dearborn, MI B
U of Minnesota, Twin Cities Campus, MN B
U of Missouri–Columbia, MO B
U of Missouri–Kansas City, MO B
U of Missouri–St. Louis, MO B
U of Nebraska–Lincoln, NE B
U of New Orleans, LA B
U of North Dakota, ND B
U of Notre Dame, IN B
U of Oklahoma, OK B
The U of Toledo, OH B
U of Tulsa, OK B
U of Wisconsin–Madison, WI B
U of Wisconsin–Milwaukee, WI B
U of Wisconsin–Platteville, WI B
Valparaiso U, IN B
Washington U in St. Louis, MO B
Wayne State U, MI B
Western Michigan U, MI B
Wichita State U, KS B
Winona State U, MN B
Wright State U, OH B
Youngstown State U, OH B

Mechanical Engineering/ Mechanical Technology

Baker Coll of Flint, MI A
Bowling Green State U, OH B
Central Michigan U, MI B
Eastern Michigan U, MI B
Ferris State U, MI A,B
Indiana U–Purdue U Fort Wayne, IN A,B
Indiana U–Purdue U Indianapolis, IN A,B
Lake Superior State U, MI A,B
Lawrence Technological U, MI A
Miami U, OH A
Miami U Hamilton, OH A,B
Michigan Technological U, MI A,B
Milwaukee School of Engineering, WI B
Northern Michigan U, MI B
Ohio U, OH B
Oklahoma State U, OK B
Pittsburg State U, KS B
Purdue U, IN B
Rochester Comm and Tech Coll, MN A
The U of Akron, OH A,B
U of Cincinnati, OH A,B
U of Dayton, OH B
U of Rio Grande, OH A,B
The U of Toledo, OH A,B
Wayne State U, MI B
Youngstown State U, OH A,B

A—associate degree; B—bachelor's degree

Mechanical Engineering Technologies Related
Cleveland State U, OH B
Indiana State U, IN B
Purdue U, IN B
Purdue U Calumet, IN A
Purdue U North Central, IN A,B

Medical Administrative Assistant
Bryant & Stratton Coll, Willoughby Hills, OH A
Minnesota School of Business–Blaine, MN A
Sinte Gleska U, SD A

Medical Administrative Assistant and Medical Secretary
Baker Coll of Auburn Hills, MI A,B
Baker Coll of Cadillac, MI A
Baker Coll of Clinton Township, MI A
Baker Coll of Flint, MI A
Baker Coll of Jackson, MI A
Baker Coll of Muskegon, MI A
Baker Coll of Owosso, MI A
Baker Coll of Port Huron, MI A
Bohecker's Business Coll, OH A
Bryant & Stratton Coll, Parma, OH A
Bryant & Stratton Coll, WI A
Northern Michigan U, MI A
Ohio U–Lancaster, OH A
Rochester Comm and Tech Coll, MN A
U of Cincinnati, OH B
U of Rio Grande, OH A
Wright State U, OH A

Medical/Clinical Assistant
Argosy U, Twin Cities, MN A
Baker Coll of Allen Park, MI A
Baker Coll of Auburn Hills, MI A
Baker Coll of Cadillac, MI A
Baker Coll of Clinton Township, MI A
Baker Coll of Flint, MI A
Baker Coll of Jackson, MI A
Baker Coll of Muskegon, MI A
Baker Coll of Owosso, MI A
Baker Coll of Port Huron, MI A
Bohecker's Business Coll, OH A
Brown Mackie Coll–Fort Wayne, IN A
Brown Mackie Coll–Indianapolis, IN A
Brown Mackie Coll–Merrillville, IN A
Brown Mackie Coll–Michigan City, IN A
Brown Mackie Coll–South Bend, IN A
Brown Mackie Coll–Tulsa, OK A
Bryant & Stratton Coll, Parma, OH A
Bryant & Stratton Coll, Willoughby Hills, OH A
Bryant & Stratton Coll, WI A
Colorado Tech U North Kansas City, MO A
Colorado Tech U Sioux Falls, SD A
Davenport U, Grand Rapids, MI A
Kaplan U–Davenport Campus, IA A
Kaplan U–Mason City Campus, IA A
Midstate Coll, IL A
Ohio U, OH A
Palmer Coll of Chiropractic, IA A
Presentation Coll, SD A
Rasmussen Coll St. Cloud, MN A
Robert Morris Coll, IL A
Sanford-Brown Coll, Fenton, MO A
The U of Akron, OH A
The U of Toledo, OH A
Youngstown State U, OH A

Medical Dietician
The Ohio State U, OH B

Medical/Health Management and Clinical Assistant
Davenport U, Grand Rapids, MI B

Medical Illustration
Alma Coll, MI B
The Cleveland Inst of Art, OH B
Iowa State U of Science and Technology, IA B

Medical Insurance Coding
Baker Coll of Allen Park, MI A
Kilian Comm Coll, SD A
Missouri Coll, MO A

Medical Insurance/Medical Billing
Baker Coll of Allen Park, MI A

Medical Laboratory Technology
Argosy U, Twin Cities, MN A
Evangel U, MO A

Medical Microbiology and Bacteriology
Bowling Green State U, OH B
Miami U, OH B
Michigan Technological U, MI B
Minnesota State U Mankato, MN B
Ohio U, OH B
Ohio Wesleyan U, OH B
St. Cloud State U, MN B
U of Cincinnati, OH B
U of Minnesota, Twin Cities Campus, MN B
U of Wisconsin–La Crosse, WI B
U of Wisconsin–Madison, WI B
U of Wisconsin–Oshkosh, WI B

Medical Office Assistant
Bryant & Stratton Coll—Wauwatosa Campus, WI A
Concordia U Wisconsin, WI B
Mercy Coll of Health Sciences, IA A
Metro Business Coll, Cape Girardeau, MO A

Medical Office Computer Specialist
Baker Coll of Allen Park, MI A

Medical Office Management
Brown Mackie Coll–Merrillville, IN A
Brown Mackie Coll–Michigan City, IN A
Kaplan U–Davenport Campus, IA A
Kilian Comm Coll, SD A
Missouri Coll, MO A
Presentation Coll, SD A
The U of Akron, OH A

Medical Pharmacology and Pharmaceutical Sciences
The Ohio State U, OH B
South Dakota State U, SD B
U of Michigan, MI B

Medical Radiologic Technology
Argosy U, Twin Cities, MN A
Avila U, MO B
Bacone Coll, OK A
Ball State U, IN A,B
Carroll U, WI B
Colorado Tech U North Kansas City, MO A,B
Ferris State U, MI A
Grand Valley State U, MI B
Indiana U East, IN B
Indiana U Kokomo, IN B
Indiana U–Purdue U Indianapolis, IN A,B
Indiana U South Bend, IN A
Indiana U Southeast, IN B
Kent State U, Salem Campus, OH A,B
Mercy Coll of Health Sciences, IA A
Mercy Coll of Northwest Ohio, OH A
Minot State U, ND B
Missouri Southern State U, MO A,B
Mount Marty Coll, SD B
North Central Coll, IL B
Oakland U, MI B
Roosevelt U, IL B
St. Catherine U, MN A
Saint Louis U, MO B
Shawnee State U, OH A
Southern Illinois U Carbondale, IL B
The U of Akron, OH A
U of Michigan–Flint, MI B
U of Missouri–Columbia, MO B
U of Nebraska Medical Center, NE B
U of St. Francis, IL B
U of Saint Francis, IN A
U of Sioux Falls, SD B
U of Southern Indiana, IN A
U of Wisconsin–La Crosse, WI B
Wayne State U, MI B

Medical Staff Services Technology
Mount Vernon Nazarene U, OH B

Medical Transcription
Baker Coll of Flint, MI A
Baker Coll of Jackson, MI A
Kaplan U–Davenport Campus, IA A
Presentation Coll, SD A
Rasmussen Coll Eagan, MN A
Rasmussen Coll St. Cloud, MN A

Medicinal and Pharmaceutical Chemistry
Ohio Northern U, OH B
Pittsburg State U, KS B
U of Michigan, MI B

Medicinal/Pharmaceutical Chemistry
Michigan Technological U, MI B

Medieval and Renaissance Studies
Cornell Coll, IA B
Hanover Coll, IN B
The Ohio State U, OH B
Ohio Wesleyan U, OH B
Southern Methodist U, TX B
U of Chicago, IL B
The U of Iowa, IA B
U of Michigan, MI B
U of Nebraska–Lincoln, NE B
U of Notre Dame, IN B
The U of Toledo, OH B
Washington U in St. Louis, MO B

Mental and Social Health Services and Allied Professions Related
Franklin U, OH B
Sinte Gleska U, SD A,B
The U of Toledo, OH B
Wright State U, OH B

Mental Health/Rehabilitation
Kansas Wesleyan U, KS B
Lake Superior State U, MI A
Newman U, KS B
St. Cloud State U, MN B
The U of Toledo, OH A

Merchandising
Michigan State U, MI B
The U of Akron, OH A

Merchandising, Sales, and Marketing Operations Related (General)
Eastern Michigan U, MI B
Washington U in St. Louis, MO B

Merchandising, Sales, and Marketing Operations Related (Specialized)
Eastern Michigan U, MI B

Metal and Jewelry Arts
The Cleveland Inst of Art, OH B
Ferris State U, MI B
Kent State U, OH B
Northern Michigan U, MI B
Northwest Missouri State U, MO B
The U of Iowa, IA B
The U of Kansas, KS B
U of Michigan, MI B
U of Wisconsin–Milwaukee, WI B

Metallurgical Engineering
Cleveland State U, OH B
Michigan Technological U, MI B
Missouri U of Science and Technology, MO B
South Dakota School of Mines and Technology, SD B
U of Cincinnati, OH B
U of Illinois at Urbana–Champaign, IL B
U of Wisconsin–Madison, WI B

Metallurgical Technology
U of Cincinnati, OH B

Meteorology
Central Michigan U, MI B
Purdue U, IN B
U of Oklahoma, OK B
Western Illinois U, IL B

Microbiological Sciences and Immunology Related
Wright State U, OH B

Microbiology
Iowa State U of Science and Technology, IA B
Kansas State U, KS B
Miami U Hamilton, OH B
Michigan State U, MI B
Michigan Technological U, MI B
North Dakota State U, ND B
Northern Michigan U, MI B
The Ohio State U, OH B
Oklahoma State U, OK B
Purdue U, IN B
South Dakota State U, SD B
Southern Illinois U Carbondale, IL B
The U of Akron, OH B
U of Illinois at Urbana–Champaign, IL B
The U of Kansas, KS B
U of Michigan–Dearborn, MI B
U of Northern Iowa, IA B
U of Oklahoma, OK B

Microbiology/Bacteriology
U of Wisconsin–La Crosse, WI B

Middle/Near Eastern and Semitic Languages Related
U of Michigan, MI B
Wayne State U, MI B

Middle School Education
Ashland U, OH B
Avila U, MO B
Baker U, KS B
Baldwin-Wallace Coll, OH B
Bethel Coll, IN B
Black Hills State U, SD B
Bluffton U, OH B
Bowling Green State U, OH B
Butler U, IN B
Capital U, OH B
Carroll U, WI B
Cedarville U, OH B
Central Methodist U, MO B
Central State U, OH B
Clarke Coll, IA B
Cleveland State U, OH B
Coll of Mount St. Joseph, OH B
Coll of the Ozarks, MO B
Concordia U, Nebraska, NE B
Concordia U, St. Paul, MN B
Concordia U Wisconsin, WI B
Dakota Wesleyan U, SD B
Eastern Illinois U, IL B
Evangel U, MO B
Fontbonne U, MO B
Grace U, NE B
Grand Valley State U, MI B
Harris-Stowe State U, MO B
Huntington U, IN B
Indiana Wesleyan U, IN B
Kent State U, OH B
Kent State U, Stark Campus, OH B
Lakeland Coll, WI B
Lake Superior State U, MI B
Lincoln U, MO B
Lindenwood U, MO B
Lourdes Coll, OH B
Malone U, OH B
Marian U, WI B
Marquette U, WI B
Maryville U of Saint Louis, MO B
McKendree U, IL B
Miami U, OH B
MidAmerica Nazarene U, KS B
Minnesota State U Moorhead, MN B
Missouri Baptist U, MO B
Missouri State U, MO B
Mount Mercy Coll, IA B
Mount Union Coll, OH B
Mount Vernon Nazarene U, OH B
Muskingum Coll, OH B
Nebraska Wesleyan U, NE B
Northwest Missouri State U, MO B
Ohio Christian U, OH B
Ohio Dominican U, OH B
Ohio Northern U, OH B
The Ohio State U, OH B
The Ohio State U at Lima, OH B
The Ohio State U at Marion, OH B
The Ohio State U–Mansfield Campus, OH B
The Ohio State U–Newark Campus, OH B
Ohio U, OH B
Ohio U–Chillicothe, OH B
Ohio U–Eastern, OH B
Ohio U–Lancaster, OH B
Ohio Wesleyan U, OH B
Otterbein Coll, OH B
St. Cloud State U, MN B
Shawnee State U, OH B
Sinte Gleska U, SD B
Southeast Missouri State U, MO B
Southwest Baptist U, MO B
Transylvania U, KY B
Trinity Christian Coll, IL B
The U of Akron, OH B
U of Central Missouri, MO B
The U of Kansas, KS B
U of Minnesota, Duluth, MN B
U of Missouri–Columbia, MO B
U of Missouri–Kansas City, MO B
U of Nebraska–Lincoln, NE B
U of New Orleans, LA B
U of North Dakota, ND B
U of Northern Iowa, IA B
U of Sioux Falls, SD B
The U of South Dakota, SD B
U of Wisconsin–Platteville, WI B
Ursuline Coll, OH B
Valparaiso U, IN B
Waldorf Coll, IA B
Walsh U, OH B
Washington U in St. Louis, MO B
Wayne State Coll, NE B
Westminster Coll, MO B
William Jewell Coll, MO B
Winona State U, MN B
Wright State U, OH B
Xavier U, OH B
York Coll, NE B
Youngstown State U, OH B

Military Technologies
Wright State U, OH B

Mining and Mineral Engineering
Missouri U of Science and Technology, MO B
South Dakota School of Mines and Technology, SD B
Southern Illinois U Carbondale, IL B
U of Wisconsin–Madison, WI B

Missionary Studies and Missiology
Allegheny Wesleyan Coll, OH B
Bethel Coll, IN B
Calvary Bible Coll and Theological Seminary, MO B
Cedarville U, OH B
Central Bible Coll, MO B
Central Christian Coll of Kansas, KS A,B
Concordia U, St. Paul, MN B
Concordia U Wisconsin, WI B
Crossroads Coll, MN B
Crown Coll, MN B
Dordt Coll, IA B
Emmaus Bible Coll, IA B
Faith Baptist Bible Coll and Theological Seminary, IA A,B
Grace Bible Coll, MI B
Grace U, NE B
Hannibal-LaGrange Coll, MO A
Huntington U, IN B
Kuyper Coll, MI B
Manhattan Christian Coll, KS A,B
Maranatha Baptist Bible Coll, WI B
Messenger Coll, MO B
MidAmerica Nazarene U, KS B
Moody Bible Inst, IL B
North Central U, MN A,B
Northwestern Coll, MN B
Ohio Christian U, OH A,B
Oklahoma Christian U, OK B
Olivet Nazarene U, IL B
Oral Roberts U, OK B
Southern Nazarene U, OK B
Southwest Baptist U, MO B
Spring Arbor U, MI B

Modern Greek
Butler U, IN B
Calvin Coll, MI B
Concordia U Wisconsin, WI B
Cornell Coll, IA B
John Carroll U, OH B
Oberlin Coll, OH B
The Ohio State U, OH B
Saint Louis U, MO B
U of Michigan, MI B
U of Minnesota, Twin Cities Campus, MN B
U of Wisconsin–Madison, WI B
U of Wisconsin–Milwaukee, WI B
Wabash Coll, IN B
Wright State U, OH B

Modern Languages
Albion Coll, MI B
Alma Coll, MI B
Beloit Coll, WI B
Bemidji State U, MN B
Cornell Coll, IA B
Kenyon Coll, OH B
Lake Erie Coll, OH B
Minnesota State U Mankato, MN B
U of Chicago, IL B
Walsh U, OH B
Washington U in St. Louis, MO B
Wilmington Coll, OH B
Wright State U, OH B

A—associate degree; B—bachelor's degree

Molecular Biochemistry

Michigan Technological U, MI B

Molecular Biology

Baker U, KS B
Beloit Coll, WI B
Benedictine U, IL B
Clarkson U, NY B
Coe Coll, IA B
The Coll of Wooster, OH B
Kenyon Coll, OH B
Lawrence Technological U, MI B
Marquette U, WI B
Millikin U, IL B
Missouri State U, MO B
Muskingum Coll, OH B
Northwestern U, IL B
Ohio Northern U, OH B
Otterbein Coll, OH B
Purdue U, IN B
The U of Kansas, KS B
U of Michigan–Flint, MI B
U of Minnesota, Duluth, MN B
U of Wisconsin–Eau Claire, WI B
U of Wisconsin–Madison, WI B
U of Wisconsin–Parkside, WI B
William Jewell Coll, MO B

Molecular Genetics

The Ohio State U, OH B

Montessori Teacher Education

Oklahoma City U, OK B
Siena Heights U, MI B
Xavier U, OH B

Multi/Interdisciplinary Studies Related

Anderson U, IN B
Baldwin-Wallace Coll, OH B
Bethel U, MN B
Bluffton U, OH B
Bowling Green State U, OH B
Buena Vista U, IA B
Cameron U, OK B
Capital U, OH B
Cleveland State U, OH B
Coll of the Ozarks, MO B
The Coll of Wooster, OH B
Cornell Coll, IA B
Cornerstone U, MI B
DePauw U, IN B
Earlham Coll, IN B
Eastern Illinois U, IL B
Eastern Michigan U, MI B
Edgewood Coll, WI B
Emporia State U, KS B
Grace Bible Coll, MI B
Grantham U, MO A,B
Greenville Coll, IL B
Hope Coll, MI B
Illinois Wesleyan U, IL B
Indiana U–Purdue U Indianapolis, IN B
Indiana U Southeast, IN B
Iowa State U of Science and Technology, IA B
Kent State U, OH B
Knox Coll, IL B
Lourdes Coll, OH B
Marian U, WI B
Marquette U, WI B
Miami U, OH A
Miami U Hamilton, OH B
Millikin U, IL B
Missouri Baptist U, MO B
Missouri Western State U, MO B
North Central Coll, IL B
Northeastern State U, OK B
Northwestern Coll, MN B
Northwestern U, IL B
Ohio U, OH A
Ohio U–Southern Campus, OH B
Ohio Wesleyan U, OH B
Otterbein Coll, OH B
Park U, MO B
Rogers State U, OK B
St. Ambrose U, IA B
St. Cloud State U, MN B
Saint Mary's U of Minnesota, MN B
St. Olaf Coll, MN B
Southeast Missouri State U, MO B
Southern Illinois U Carbondale, IL B
Southern Methodist U, TX B
Truman State U, MO B
The U of Akron, OH B
U of Evansville, IN B
U of Michigan, MI B
U of Michigan–Dearborn, MI B
U of Michigan–Flint, MI B
U of Minnesota, Crookston, MN B
U of Nebraska at Omaha, NE B
U of North Dakota, ND B
U of Oklahoma, OK B
U of St. Francis, IL B
U of Saint Mary, KS B
The U of Toledo, OH A,B
U of Wisconsin–Superior, WI B
Ursuline Coll, OH B
Valparaiso U, IN B
Viterbo U, WI B
Washington U in St. Louis, MO B
Wayne State U, MI B
Wheaton Coll, IL B
Wright State U, OH B

Museum Studies

Beloit Coll, WI B
The U of Iowa, IA B
Walsh U, OH B

Music

Adrian Coll, MI B
Albion Coll, MI B
Alma Coll, MI B
Andrews U, MI B
Aquinas Coll, MI B
Ashland U, OH B
Augsburg Coll, MN B
Augustana Coll, IL B
Augustana Coll, SD B
Avila U, MO B
Baker U, KS B
Baldwin-Wallace Coll, OH B
Ball State U, IN B
Beloit Coll, WI B
Bemidji State U, MN B
Benedictine Coll, KS B
Benedictine U, IL B
Bethany Coll, KS B
Bethany Lutheran Coll, MN B
Bethel Coll, IN A,B
Bethel U, MN B
Black Hills State U, SD B
Bluffton U, OH B
Bowling Green State U, OH B
Bradley U, IL B
Briar Cliff U, IA B
Butler U, IN B
Calvin Coll, MI B
Cameron U, OK B
Capital U, OH B
Carleton Coll, MN B
Carroll U, WI B
Case Western Reserve U, OH B
Cedarville U, OH B
Central Christian Coll of Kansas, KS B
Central Coll, IA B
Central Methodist U, MO B
Central Michigan U, MI B
Clarke Coll, IA B
Cleveland State U, OH B
Coe Coll, IA B
Coll of Mount St. Joseph, OH B
Coll of Saint Benedict, MN B
Coll of the Ozarks, MO B
The Coll of Wooster, OH B
Concordia Coll, MN B
Concordia U, MI B
Concordia U Chicago, IL B
Concordia U, Nebraska, NE B
Concordia U, St. Paul, MN B
Concordia U Wisconsin, WI B
Cornell Coll, IA B
Cornerstone U, MI B
Creighton U, NE B
Crossroads Coll, MN B
Culver-Stockton Coll, MO B
Dakota Wesleyan U, SD B
Dana Coll, NE B
Denison U, OH B
DePauw U, IN B
Doane Coll, NE B
Dordt Coll, IA B
Drake U, IA B
Drury U, MO B
Earlham Coll, IN B
Eastern Illinois U, IL B
Eastern Michigan U, MI B
Edgewood Coll, WI B
Elmhurst Coll, IL B
Emporia State U, KS B
Eureka Coll, IL B
Evangel U, MO B
Fort Hays State U, KS B
Friends U, KS B
Grace Bible Coll, MI B
Graceland U, IA B
Grace U, NE A,B
Grand Valley State U, MI B
Grand View U, IA B
Greenville Coll, IL B
Grinnell Coll, IA B
Gustavus Adolphus Coll, MN B
Hamline U, MN B
Hannibal-LaGrange Coll, MO B
Hanover Coll, IN B
Heidelberg U, OH B
Hillsdale Coll, MI B
Hiram Coll, OH B
Hope Coll, MI B
Huntington U, IN B
Illinois Coll, IL B
Illinois State U, IL B
Illinois Wesleyan U, IL B
Indiana State U, IN B
Indiana U Bloomington, IN B
Indiana U–Purdue U Fort Wayne, IN B
Indiana U Southeast, IN B
Indiana Wesleyan U, IN A,B
Iowa State U of Science and Technology, IA B
Iowa Wesleyan Coll, IA B
Jamestown Coll, ND B
Kalamazoo Coll, MI B
Kansas State U, KS B
Kent State U, OH B
Kenyon Coll, OH B
Knox Coll, IL B
Lake Erie Coll, OH B
Lake Forest Coll, IL B
Lakeland Coll, WI B
Lawrence U, WI B
Lewis U, IL B
Lindenwood U, MO B
Loras Coll, IA B
Loyola U Chicago, IL B
Luther Coll, IA B
Macalester Coll, MN B
MacMurray Coll, IL B
Madonna U, MI B
Malone U, OH B
Manchester Coll, IN B
Maranatha Baptist Bible Coll, WI B
Marian U, WI B
Marian U, IN B
Marietta Coll, OH B
McKendree U, IL B
McPherson Coll, KS B
Messenger Coll, MO B
Miami U, OH B
Miami U Hamilton, OH B
Michigan State U, MI B
Mid-America Christian U, OK B
Millikin U, IL B
Minnesota State U Mankato, MN B
Minnesota State U Moorhead, MN B
Minot State U, ND B
Missouri State U, MO B
Missouri Western State U, MO B
Monmouth Coll, IL B
Morningside Coll, IA B
Mount Marty Coll, SD B
Mount Mary Coll, WI B
Mount Mercy Coll, IA B
Mount Union Coll, OH B
Mount Vernon Nazarene U, OH A,B
Muskingum Coll, OH B

Nebraska Wesleyan U, NE B
North Central Coll, IL B
North Central U, MN A,B
North Dakota State U, ND B
Northeastern Illinois U, IL B
Northeastern State U, OK B
Northern Michigan U, MI B
Northern State U, SD B
Northland Coll, WI B
North Park U, IL B
Northwestern Coll, MN B
Northwestern U, IL B
Northwest Missouri State U, MO B
Oakland U, MI B
Oberlin Coll, OH B
Ohio Northern U, OH B
The Ohio State U, OH B
Ohio U, OH B
Ohio Wesleyan U, OH B
Oklahoma Baptist U, OK B
Oklahoma Christian U, OK B
Oklahoma City U, OK B
Oklahoma Panhandle State U, OK B
Oklahoma State U, OK B
Olivet Coll, MI B
Olivet Nazarene U, IL B
Oral Roberts U, OK B
Otterbein Coll, OH B
Park U, MO B
Purdue U, IN B
Quincy U, IL B
Ripon Coll, WI B
Rockford Coll, IL B
Saginaw Valley State U, MI B
St. Ambrose U, IA B
St. Catherine U, MN B
St. Cloud State U, MN B
Saint John's U, MN B
Saint Louis U, MO B
Saint Mary-of-the-Woods Coll, IN B
Saint Mary's Coll, IN B
Saint Mary's U of Minnesota, MN B
St. Norbert Coll, WI B
St. Olaf Coll, MN B
Saint Xavier U, IL B
Shawnee State U, OH A
Silver Lake Coll, WI B
Simpson Coll, IA B
South Dakota State U, SD B
Southeastern Oklahoma State U, OK B
Southeast Missouri State U, MO B
Southern Illinois U Carbondale, IL B
Southern Illinois U Edwardsville, IL B
Southern Methodist U, TX B
Southern Nazarene U, OK B
Southwest Baptist U, MO B
Southwestern Coll, KS B
Southwestern Oklahoma State U, OK B
Southwest Minnesota State U, MN B
Spring Arbor U, MI B
Sterling Coll, KS B
Taylor U, IN B
Trinity Christian Coll, IL B
Trinity International U, IL B
Truman State U, MO B
Union Coll, NE B
The U of Akron, OH B
U of Central Missouri, MO B
U of Central Oklahoma, OK B
U of Chicago, IL B
U of Cincinnati, OH B
U of Dayton, OH B
U of Evansville, IN B
U of Illinois at Chicago, IL B
U of Illinois at Urbana–Champaign, IL B
U of Indianapolis, IN B
The U of Iowa, IA B
The U of Kansas, KS B
U of Michigan, MI B
U of Michigan–Flint, MI B
U of Minnesota, Duluth, MN B
U of Minnesota, Morris, MN B
U of Minnesota, Twin Cities Campus, MN B
U of Missouri–Columbia, MO B
U of Missouri–Kansas City, MO B
U of Missouri–St. Louis, MO B
U of Nebraska at Kearney, NE B
U of Nebraska at Omaha, NE B
U of Nebraska–Lincoln, NE B
U of New Orleans, LA B
U of North Dakota, ND B
U of Northern Iowa, IA B
U of Notre Dame, IN B
U of Oklahoma, OK B
U of Rio Grande, OH A,B
U of St. Francis, IL B
U of Science and Arts of Oklahoma, OK B
U of Sioux Falls, SD B
The U of South Dakota, SD B
The U of Toledo, OH B
U of Tulsa, OK B
U of Wisconsin–Eau Claire, WI B
U of Wisconsin–Green Bay, WI B
U of Wisconsin–La Crosse, WI B
U of Wisconsin–Madison, WI B
U of Wisconsin–Milwaukee, WI B
U of Wisconsin–Oshkosh, WI B
U of Wisconsin–Parkside, WI B
U of Wisconsin–Platteville, WI B
U of Wisconsin–Stevens Point, WI B
U of Wisconsin–Superior, WI B
U of Wisconsin–Whitewater, WI B
Valley City State U, ND B
Valparaiso U, IN B
Viterbo U, WI B
Wabash Coll, IN B
Wartburg Coll, IA B
Washburn U, KS B
Washington U in St. Louis, MO B
Wayne State Coll, NE B
Wayne State U, MI B
Webster U, MO B
Western Illinois U, IL B
Western Michigan U, MI B
Wheaton Coll, IL B
Wichita State U, KS B
Wilberforce U, OH B
William Jewell Coll, MO B
Winona State U, MN B
Wittenberg U, OH B
Wright State U, OH B
Xavier U, OH B
York Coll, NE B
Youngstown State U, OH B

Musical Instrument Fabrication and Repair

Indiana U Bloomington, IN A

Music History, Literature, and Theory

Baldwin-Wallace Coll, OH B
Bowling Green State U, OH B
Butler U, IN B
Calvin Coll, MI B
Central Christian Coll of Kansas, KS A
The Coll of Wooster, OH B
Indiana U Bloomington, IN B
Northwestern U, IL B
Oberlin Coll, OH B
The Ohio State U, OH B
Ohio U, OH B
Otterbein Coll, OH B
St. Cloud State U, MN B
Saint Joseph's Coll, IN B
Trinity International U, IL B
U of Chicago, IL B
U of Cincinnati, OH B
U of Illinois at Urbana–Champaign, IL B
U of Michigan, MI B
U of Wisconsin–Milwaukee, WI B
Washington U in St. Louis, MO B
Wheaton Coll, IL B
Wright State U, OH B
Youngstown State U, OH B

Music Management and Merchandising

Anderson U, IN B
Bradley U, IL B
Butler U, IN B
Capital U, OH B
Coll of the Ozarks, MO B
DePaul U, IL B
DePauw U, IN B
Drake U, IA B
Elmhurst Coll, IL B
Ferris State U, MI A,B
Greenville Coll, IL B
Heidelberg U, OH B
Huntington U, IN B
Lewis U, IL B
Marian U, WI B
McNally Smith Coll of Music, MN A,B
Minnesota State U Mankato, MN B
Minnesota State U Moorhead, MN B
North Central U, MN B
Northwest Missouri State U, MO B
Ohio Northern U, OH B
Ohio U, OH B
Oklahoma City U, OK B
Otterbein Coll, OH B
Saint Joseph's Coll, IN B
Saint Mary's U of Minnesota, MN B
South Dakota State U, SD B
Southern Nazarene U, OK B
Southwestern Oklahoma State U, OK B
Southwest Minnesota State U, MN B
U of Evansville, IN B
Valparaiso U, IN B
Waldorf Coll, IA B
Winona State U, MN B

Musicology and Ethnomusicology

Baldwin-Wallace Coll, OH B
Northwestern U, IL B
The U of Kansas, KS B

Music Pedagogy

Cedarville U, OH B
Lawrence U, WI B
Maranatha Baptist Bible Coll, WI B
Michigan State U, MI B
St. Cloud State U, MN B
Spring Arbor U, MI B
Trinity International U, IL B
U of Oklahoma, OK B
Viterbo U, WI B

Music Performance

Alma Coll, MI B
Anderson U, IN B
Aquinas Coll, MI B
Augustana Coll, IL B
Avila U, MO B
Baldwin-Wallace Coll, OH B
Bethel Coll, IN B
Bethel U, MN B
Black Hills State U, SD B
Bowling Green State U, OH B
Bradley U, IL B
Buena Vista U, IA B
Butler U, IN B
Calvin Coll, MI B
Capital U, OH B
Cedarville U, OH B
Central Christian Coll of Kansas, KS A,B
Central Methodist U, MO B
Central State U, OH B
Coe Coll, IA B
The Coll of St. Scholastica, MN B
The Coll of Wooster, OH B
Concordia Coll, MN B
Cornerstone U, MI B

A—associate degree; B—bachelor's degree

DePaul U, IL B
DePauw U, IN B
Dordt Coll, IA B
Drake U, IA B
Drury U, MO B
Eastern Michigan U, MI B
Friends U, KS B
Grace Coll, IN B
Gustavus Adolphus Coll, MN B
Hope Coll, MI B
Illinois State U, IL B
Illinois Wesleyan U, IL B
Indiana State U, IN B
Indiana U Bloomington, IN B
Indiana U South Bend, IN B
Jamestown Coll, ND B
Kent State U, OH B
Lawrence U, WI B
Madonna U, MI B
Maranatha Baptist Bible Coll, WI B
McNally Smith Coll of Music, MN A,B
Miami U, OH B
Michigan State U, MI B
Millikin U, IL B
Missouri Baptist U, MO B
Missouri Southern State U, MO B
Missouri State U, MO B
Mount Union Coll, OH B
Mount Vernon Nazarene U, OH B
Nebraska Wesleyan U, NE B
North Central U, MN B
Northwestern Coll, MN B
Northwestern U, IL B
Oakland U, MI B
Ohio Northern U, OH B
The Ohio State U, OH B
Ohio U, OH B
Ohio Wesleyan U, OH B
Oklahoma Baptist U, OK B
Olivet Nazarene U, IL B
Oral Roberts U, OK B
Otterbein Coll, OH B
Pittsburg State U, KS B
Rockford Coll, IL B
Roosevelt U, IL B
St. Cloud State U, MN B
Saint Mary-of-the-Woods Coll, IN B
Saint Mary's U of Minnesota, MN B
St. Olaf Coll, MN B
Saint Xavier U, IL B
Simpson Coll, IA B
Southeastern Oklahoma State U, OK B
Southern Methodist U, TX B
Southern Nazarene U, OK B
Southwestern Christian U, OK B
Transylvania U, KY B
Trinity Christian Coll, IL B
Truman State U, MO B
Union Coll, NE B
U of Evansville, IN B
U of Illinois at Urbana–Champaign, IL B
U of Indianapolis, IN B
The U of Kansas, KS B
U of Mary, ND B
U of Michigan–Flint, MI B
U of Missouri–Kansas City, MO B
U of Missouri–St. Louis, MO B
U of Nebraska at Omaha, NE B
U of North Dakota, ND B
U of Northern Iowa, IA B
U of St. Francis, IL B
U of Tulsa, OK B
U of Wisconsin–Superior, WI B
Valparaiso U, IN B
Viterbo U, WI B
Waldorf Coll, IA B
Wartburg Coll, IA B
Washburn U, KS B
Webster U, MO B
Western Illinois U, IL B
Western Michigan U, MI B
Wheaton Coll, IL B
William Jewell Coll, MO B
Wright State U, OH B
Youngstown State U, OH B

Music Related

Bethel Coll, KS B
Bowling Green State U, OH B
Calvary Bible Coll and Theological Seminary, MO B
Capital U, OH B
Central Michigan U, MI B
Coll of the Ozarks, MO B
DePaul U, IL B
Greenville Coll, IL B
Illinois Wesleyan U, IL B
Indiana U Bloomington, IN B
Indiana U South Bend, IN B
Northwestern U, IL B
Ohio Northern U, OH B
Roosevelt U, IL B
Saint Mary's U of Minnesota, MN B
St. Olaf Coll, MN B
Transylvania U, KY B
Trinity International U, IL A
The U of Akron, OH B
U of Michigan, MI B
U of Saint Francis, IN B
U of Tulsa, OK B
Western Illinois U, IL B
Wheaton Coll, IL B

Music Teacher Education

Adrian Coll, MI B
Alma Coll, MI B
Anderson U, IN B
Andrews U, MI B
Aquinas Coll, MI B
Ashland U, OH B
Augsburg Coll, MN B
Augustana Coll, IL B
Augustana Coll, SD B
Baker U, KS B
Baldwin-Wallace Coll, OH B
Beloit Coll, WI B
Bemidji State U, MN B
Benedictine Coll, KS B
Bethany Coll, KS B
Bethel Coll, IN B
Bethel U, MN B
Bluffton U, OH B
Bowling Green State U, OH B
Bradley U, IL B
Buena Vista U, IA B
Butler U, IN B
Calvary Bible Coll and Theological Seminary, MO B
Calvin Coll, MI B
Capital U, OH B
Carroll U, WI B
Case Western Reserve U, OH B
Cedarville U, OH B
Central Christian Coll of Kansas, KS A,B
Central Coll, IA B
Central Methodist U, MO B
Central Michigan U, MI B
Clarke Coll, IA B
Coe Coll, IA B
Coll of the Ozarks, MO B
The Coll of Wooster, OH B
Concordia Coll, MN B
Concordia U, MI B
Concordia U Chicago, IL B
Concordia U, Nebraska, NE B
Concordia U, St. Paul, MN B
Concordia U Wisconsin, WI B
Cornell Coll, IA B
Cornerstone U, MI B
Crown Coll, MN B
Culver-Stockton Coll, MO B
Dakota Wesleyan U, SD B
Dana Coll, NE B
DePaul U, IL B
DePauw U, IN B
Dordt Coll, IA B
Drake U, IA B
Drury U, MO B
Eastern Michigan U, MI B
Edgewood Coll, WI B
Elmhurst Coll, IL B
Emporia State U, KS B
Eureka Coll, IL B
Evangel U, MO B
Faith Baptist Bible Coll and Theological Seminary, IA B
Fort Hays State U, KS B
Friends U, KS B
Grace Bible Coll, MI B
Grace Coll, IN B
Graceland U, IA B
Grace U, NE B
Grand Valley State U, MI B
Greenville Coll, IL B
Gustavus Adolphus Coll, MN B
Hamline U, MN B
Hannibal-LaGrange Coll, MO B
Heidelberg U, OH B
Hope Coll, MI B
Huntington U, IN B
Illinois State U, IL B
Illinois Wesleyan U, IL B
Indiana U Bloomington, IN B
Indiana U–Purdue U Fort Wayne, IN B
Indiana U South Bend, IN B
Indiana Wesleyan U, IN B
Iowa State U of Science and Technology, IA B
Iowa Wesleyan Coll, IA B
Jamestown Coll, ND B
Kansas State U, KS B
Kent State U, OH B
Lakeland Coll, WI B
Lawrence U, WI B
Lincoln U, MO B
Lindenwood U, MO B
MacMurray Coll, IL B
Malone U, OH B
Manchester Coll, IN B
Maranatha Baptist Bible Coll, WI B
Marian U, WI B
Marian U, IN B
McKendree U, IL B
Miami U, OH B
Miami U Hamilton, OH B
Michigan State U, MI B
Mid-America Christian U, OK B
MidAmerica Nazarene U, KS B
Millikin U, IL B
Minnesota State U Mankato, MN B
Minnesota State U Moorhead, MN B
Minot State U, ND B
Missouri Baptist U, MO B
Missouri State U, MO B
Missouri Western State U, MO B
Morningside Coll, IA B
Mount Marty Coll, SD B
Mount Mary Coll, WI B
Mount Mercy Coll, IA B
Mount Union Coll, OH B
Mount Vernon Nazarene U, OH B
Muskingum Coll, OH B
Nebraska Wesleyan U, NE B
North Central Coll, IL B
North Dakota State U, ND B
Northeastern State U, OK B
Northern Michigan U, MI B
Northern State U, SD B
North Park U, IL B
Northwestern Coll, MN B
Northwestern U, IL B
Northwest Missouri State U, MO B
Oakland U, MI B
Oberlin Coll, OH B
Ohio Christian U, OH B
Ohio Northern U, OH B
The Ohio State U, OH B
Ohio U, OH B
Ohio Wesleyan U, OH B
Oklahoma Baptist U, OK B
Oklahoma Christian U, OK B
Oklahoma City U, OK B
Oklahoma State U, OK B
Olivet Coll, MI B
Olivet Nazarene U, IL B
Oral Roberts U, OK B
Otterbein Coll, OH B
Pittsburg State U, KS B
Quincy U, IL B
Ripon Coll, WI B
Roosevelt U, IL B
Saginaw Valley State U, MI B
St. Ambrose U, IA B
St. Catherine U, MN B
St. Cloud State U, MN B

Saint Mary-of-the-Woods Coll, IN B
Saint Mary's Coll, IN B
Saint Mary's U of Minnesota, MN B
St. Norbert Coll, WI B
St. Olaf Coll, MN B
Saint Xavier U, IL B
Silver Lake Coll, WI B
Simpson Coll, IA B
South Dakota State U, SD B
Southeastern Oklahoma State U, OK B
Southeast Missouri State U, MO B
Southern Methodist U, TX B
Southern Nazarene U, OK B
Southwest Baptist U, MO B
Southwestern Coll, KS B
Southwestern Oklahoma State U, OK B
Southwest Minnesota State U, MN B
Spring Arbor U, MI B
Sterling Coll, KS B
Taylor U, IN B
Transylvania U, KY B
Trinity Christian Coll, IL B
Trinity International U, IL B
Union Coll, NE A,B
The U of Akron, OH B
U of Central Missouri, MO B
U of Central Oklahoma, OK B
U of Charleston, WV B
U of Cincinnati, OH B
U of Dayton, OH B
U of Evansville, IN B
U of Illinois at Urbana–Champaign, IL B
U of Indianapolis, IN B
The U of Iowa, IA B
The U of Kansas, KS B
U of Mary, ND B
U of Michigan, MI B
U of Michigan–Flint, MI B
U of Minnesota, Duluth, MN B
U of Minnesota, Twin Cities Campus, MN B
U of Missouri–Columbia, MO B
U of Missouri–Kansas City, MO B
U of Missouri–St. Louis, MO B
U of Nebraska at Omaha, NE B
U of Nebraska–Lincoln, NE B
U of North Dakota, ND B
U of Northern Iowa, IA B
U of Oklahoma, OK B
U of Rio Grande, OH B
U of St. Francis, IL B
U of Sioux Falls, SD B
The U of South Dakota, SD B
The U of Toledo, OH B
U of Tulsa, OK B
U of Wisconsin–Madison, WI B
U of Wisconsin–Milwaukee, WI B
U of Wisconsin–Oshkosh, WI B
U of Wisconsin–Stevens Point, WI B
U of Wisconsin–Superior, WI B
U of Wisconsin–Whitewater, WI B
Valley City State U, ND B
Valparaiso U, IN B
Viterbo U, WI B
Waldorf Coll, IA B
Wartburg Coll, IA B
Washburn U, KS B
Wayne State Coll, NE B
Webster U, MO B
Western Michigan U, MI B
Wheaton Coll, IL B
Wichita State U, KS B
William Jewell Coll, MO B
Wilmington Coll, OH B
Winona State U, MN B
Wright State U, OH B
Xavier U, OH B
York Coll, NE B
Youngstown State U, OH B

Music Theory and Composition

Baldwin-Wallace Coll, OH B
Bowling Green State U, OH B
Bradley U, IL B
Butler U, IN B
Calvin Coll, MI B
Capital U, OH B
Cedarville U, OH B
Central Michigan U, MI B
Coe Coll, IA B
The Coll of Wooster, OH B
Concordia Coll, MN B
DePaul U, IL B
DePauw U, IN B
Drury U, MO B
Grace U, NE B
Hope Coll, MI B
Huntington U, IN B
Illinois Wesleyan U, IL B
Indiana Wesleyan U, IN B
Lawrence U, WI B
McNally Smith Coll of Music, MN B
Michigan State U, MI B
Minnesota State U Moorhead, MN B
Northwestern Coll, MN B
Northwestern U, IL B
Oberlin Coll, OH B
The Ohio State U, OH B
Ohio U, OH B
Oklahoma Baptist U, OK B
Oklahoma City U, OK B
Olivet Nazarene U, IL B
Oral Roberts U, OK B
Rochester Comm and Tech Coll, MN A
Roosevelt U, IL B
St. Cloud State U, MN B
St. Olaf Coll, MN B
Southern Methodist U, TX B
Trinity International U, IL B
U of Central Missouri, MO B
U of Illinois at Urbana–Champaign, IL B
The U of Kansas, KS B
U of Michigan, MI B
U of Missouri–Kansas City, MO B
U of Nebraska at Omaha, NE B
U of Northern Iowa, IA B
U of Tulsa, OK B
Valparaiso U, IN B
Wartburg Coll, IA B
Washington U in St. Louis, MO B
Webster U, MO B
Western Michigan U, MI B
Wheaton Coll, IL B
William Jewell Coll, MO B
Wright State U, OH B
Youngstown State U, OH B

Music Therapy

Augsburg Coll, MN B
Baldwin-Wallace Coll, OH B
The Coll of Wooster, OH B
Eastern Michigan U, MI B
Indiana U–Purdue U Fort Wayne, IN B
Maryville U of Saint Louis, MO B
Michigan State U, MI B
Saint Mary-of-the-Woods Coll, IN B
Southern Methodist U, TX B
Southwestern Oklahoma State U, OK B
U of Dayton, OH B
U of Evansville, IN B
The U of Iowa, IA B
The U of Kansas, KS B
U of Minnesota, Twin Cities Campus, MN B
U of North Dakota, ND B
U of Wisconsin–Milwaukee, WI B
U of Wisconsin–Oshkosh, WI B
Wartburg Coll, IA B
Western Michigan U, MI B

Natural Resources and Conservation Related

Mount Mercy Coll, IA B
St. Gregory's U, Shawnee, OK B

Natural Resources/ Conservation

Ball State U, IN B
Carroll U, WI B
Central Michigan U, MI B
Grand Valley State U, MI B
Gustavus Adolphus Coll, MN B
Haskell Indian Nations U, KS A
Kent State U, OH B
Mount Vernon Nazarene U, OH B
Muskingum Coll, OH B
Northern Michigan U, MI B
Northland Coll, WI B
Northwest Missouri State U, MO B
Purdue U, IN B
Southeastern Oklahoma State U, OK B
U of Illinois at Urbana–Champaign, IL B
U of Michigan–Flint, MI B
U of Minnesota, Crookston, MN B
U of Missouri–Columbia, MO B
U of Nebraska–Lincoln, NE B
U of Wisconsin–Milwaukee, WI B
U of Wisconsin–Stevens Point, WI B
Washington U in St. Louis, MO B
Winona State U, MN B

Natural Resources/ Conservation Related

U of Illinois at Urbana–Champaign, IL B

Natural Resources Management

U of Illinois at Urbana–Champaign, IL B

Natural Resources Management and Policy

Bacone Coll, OK A
Bowling Green State U, OH B
Fort Hays State U, KS B
Huntington U, IN B
Iowa State U of Science and Technology, IA B
Lake Superior State U, MI A
North Dakota State U, ND B
Northland Coll, WI B
Oglala Lakota Coll, SD A
Sinte Gleska U, SD A
South Dakota State U, SD B
U of Illinois at Urbana–Champaign, IL B
U of Minnesota, Twin Cities Campus, MN B
U of Nebraska–Lincoln, NE B
U of Wisconsin–Stevens Point, WI B

Natural Sciences

Augsburg Coll, MN B
Bemidji State U, MN B
Benedictine Coll, KS B
Bethel Coll, KS B
Calvin Coll, MI B
Cameron U, OK B
Case Western Reserve U, OH B
Central Christian Coll of Kansas, KS B
Central Coll, IA B
Coll of Mount St. Joseph, OH B
Coll of Saint Benedict, MN B
Coll of Saint Mary, NE B
The Coll of St. Scholastica, MN B
Concordia U Chicago, IL B
Concordia U, Nebraska, NE B
Defiance Coll, OH B
Doane Coll, NE B
Dordt Coll, IA B

A—associate degree; B—bachelor's degree

Edgewood Coll, WI B
Haskell Indian Nations U, KS A
Indiana U East, IN A,B
Iowa Wesleyan Coll, IA B
Kansas State U, KS B
Lourdes Coll, OH A
Madonna U, MI A,B
McPherson Coll, KS B
Minnesota State U Mankato, MN B
Missouri Western State U, MO B
Oklahoma Baptist U, OK B
Park U, MO B
St. Cloud State U, MN B
Saint John's U, MN B
Shawnee State U, OH A,B
Shimer Coll, IL B
Siena Heights U, MI B
Taylor U, IN B
U of Cincinnati, OH A,B
U of Nebraska at Omaha, NE B
U of Science and Arts of Oklahoma, OK B
The U of Toledo, OH A,B
U of Wisconsin–Stevens Point, WI B
Viterbo U, WI B
Washburn U, KS A
Washington U in St. Louis, MO B
Winona State U, MN B
Xavier U, OH B
York Coll, NE B

Naval Architecture and Marine Engineering
U of Michigan, MI B
U of New Orleans, LA B

Near and Middle Eastern Studies
Indiana U Bloomington, IN B
Oberlin Coll, OH B
U of Chicago, IL B
U of Michigan, MI B
U of Minnesota, Twin Cities Campus, MN B
The U of Toledo, OH B
Washington U in St. Louis, MO B

Neurobiology and Neurophysiology
Andrews U, MI B

Neuroscience
Baldwin-Wallace Coll, OH B
Bowling Green State U, OH B
Central Michigan U, MI B
The Coll of Wooster, OH B
Dominican U, IL B
Drake U, IA B
Hiram Coll, OH B
Indiana U Bloomington, IN B
John Carroll U, OH B
Kenyon Coll, OH B
Knox Coll, IL B
Lawrence U, WI B
Macalester Coll, MN B
Mount Union Coll, OH B
Muskingum Coll, OH B
Northwestern U, IL B
Oberlin Coll, OH B
Ohio Wesleyan U, OH B
U of Evansville, IN B
U of Illinois at Chicago, IL B
U of Michigan, MI B
U of Minnesota, Twin Cities Campus, MN B
Washington U in St. Louis, MO B

Nonprofit Management
Clarkson U, NY B
Franklin U, OH B
Friends U, KS B
Indiana Tech, IN B
Lakeland Coll, WI B
Manchester Coll, IN B
North Park U, IL B
Southwestern Christian U, OK B
Southwest Minnesota State U, MN B
Tiffin U, OH B
Trinity International U, IL B
Washburn U, KS B

Norwegian
St. Olaf Coll, MN B

Nuclear Engineering
Kansas State U, KS B
Missouri U of Science and Technology, MO B
Purdue U, IN B
U of Cincinnati, OH B
U of Illinois at Urbana–Champaign, IL B
U of Michigan, MI B
U of Wisconsin–Madison, WI B

Nuclear Medical Technology
Ball State U, IN A
Benedictine U, IL B
Ferris State U, MI A,B
Indiana U–Purdue U Indianapolis, IN B
Indiana U South Bend, IN B
Indiana U Southeast, IN B
Lewis U, IL B
Loras Coll, IA B
Mercy Coll of Health Sciences, IA A
North Central Coll, IL B
Oakland U, MI B
Roosevelt U, IL B
St. Cloud State U, MN B
Saint Louis U, MO B
Saint Mary's U of Minnesota, MN B
U of Cincinnati, OH B
The U of Findlay, OH A,B
The U of Iowa, IA B
U of Missouri–Columbia, MO B
U of Nebraska Medical Center, NE B
U of Oklahoma Health Sciences Center, OK B
U of St. Francis, IL B

Nursing Administration
Central Methodist U, MO B
Clarkson Coll, NE B
Huntington U, IN B
Nebraska Wesleyan U, NE B
U of Phoenix–Indianapolis Campus, IN B

Nursing Assistant/Aide and Patient Care Assistant
Central Christian Coll of Kansas, KS A

Nursing (Licensed Practical/Vocational Nurse Training)
Central Christian Coll of Kansas, KS A
Grace U, NE A
Ohio U–Southern Campus, OH A
Sinte Gleska U, SD A
The U of Akron, OH B

Nursing (Registered Nurse Training)
Allen Coll, IA B
Anderson U, IN B
Andrews U, MI B
Augsburg Coll, MN B
Augustana Coll, SD B
Aurora U, IL B
Bacone Coll, OK A,B
Baker Coll of Clinton Township, MI A
Baker Coll of Flint, MI A
Baker Coll of Muskegon, MI A
Baker Coll of Owosso, MI A
Baker U, KS B
Ball State U, IN A,B
Bellin Coll of Nursing, WI B
Bemidji State U, MN B
Benedictine U, IL B
Bethel Coll, IN A,B
Bethel Coll, KS B
Bethel U, MN B
Blessing-Rieman Coll of Nursing, IL B
Bowling Green State U, OH B
Bradley U, IL B
Briar Cliff U, IA B
Bryant & Stratton Coll, Parma, OH A
Bryant & Stratton Coll, Willoughby Hills, OH A
Bryant & Stratton Coll—Wauwatosa Campus, WI A
Calvin Coll, MI B
Capital U, OH B
Carroll U, WI B
Case Western Reserve U, OH B
Cedarville U, OH B
Central Christian Coll of Kansas, KS A
Central Methodist U, MO B
Chamberlain Coll of Nursing, MO A,B
Clarkson Coll, NE B
Cleveland State U, OH B
Coe Coll, IA B
Coll of Mount St. Joseph, OH B
Coll of Saint Benedict, MN B
Coll of Saint Mary, NE A,B
The Coll of St. Scholastica, MN B
Coll of the Ozarks, MO B
Columbia Coll, MO A
Columbia Coll of Nursing, WI B
Concordia Coll, MN B
Concordia U Chicago, IL B
Concordia U Wisconsin, WI B
Creighton U, NE B
Crown Coll, MN B
Culver-Stockton Coll, MO B
Dakota Wesleyan U, SD A
Davenport U, Grand Rapids, MI B
Defiance Coll, OH B
DePaul U, IL B
Dordt Coll, IA B
Eastern Illinois U, IL B
Eastern Michigan U, MI B
Edgewood Coll, WI B
Elmhurst Coll, IL B
Emporia State U, KS B
Ferris State U, MI A,B
Fort Hays State U, KS B
Franciscan U of Steubenville, OH B
Goldfarb School of Nursing at Barnes-Jewish Coll, MO B
Goshen Coll, IN B
Graceland U, IA B
Grace U, NE B
Grand Valley State U, MI B
Grand View U, IA B
Gustavus Adolphus Coll, MN B
Hannibal-LaGrange Coll, MO A,B
Hiram Coll, OH B
Hope Coll, MI B
Illinois State U, IL B
Illinois Wesleyan U, IL B
Indiana State U, IN B
Indiana U Bloomington, IN B
Indiana U East, IN A,B
Indiana U Kokomo, IN A,B
Indiana U Northwest, IN A,B
Indiana U–Purdue U Fort Wayne, IN A,B
Indiana U–Purdue U Indianapolis, IN A,B
Indiana U South Bend, IN B
Indiana U Southeast, IN B
Indiana Wesleyan U, IN B
Iowa Wesleyan Coll, IA B
ITT Tech Inst, Fort Wayne, IN A
ITT Tech Inst, Indianapolis, IN A
ITT Tech Inst, Oklahoma City, OK A
Jamestown Coll, ND B
Kansas Wesleyan U, KS A,B
Kent State U, OH A,B
Kent State U, Stark Campus, OH B
Kuyper Coll, MI B
Lake Superior State U, MI B
Lewis U, IL B
Lincoln U, MO A,B
Lourdes Coll, OH B
Loyola U Chicago, IL B
Luther Coll, IA B
MacMurray Coll, IL B
Madonna U, MI B
Malone U, OH B

Maranatha Baptist Bible Coll, WI B
Marian U, WI B
Marian U, IN A,B
Marquette U, WI B
Maryville U of Saint Louis, MO B
McKendree U, IL B
Medcenter One Coll of Nursing, ND B
MedCentral Coll of Nursing, OH B
Mercy Coll of Health Sciences, IA A
Mercy Coll of Northwest Ohio, OH A,B
Miami U, OH A,B
Michigan State U, MI B
MidAmerica Nazarene U, KS B
Millikin U, IL B
Milwaukee School of Engineering, WI B
Minnesota State U Mankato, MN B
Minnesota State U Moorhead, MN B
Minot State U, ND B
Missouri Southern State U, MO B
Missouri State U, MO B
Missouri Western State U, MO B
Morningside Coll, IA B
Mount Marty Coll, SD B
Mount Mary Coll, WI B
Mount Mercy Coll, IA B
Mount Vernon Nazarene U, OH B
Muskingum Coll, OH B
National American U, MO A,B
Nebraska Methodist Coll, NE B
Newman U, KS B
North Dakota State U, ND B
Northeastern State U, OK B
Northern Michigan U, MI B
Northland Coll, WI B
North Park U, IL B
Oakland U, MI B
Oglala Lakota Coll, SD A
The Ohio State U, OH B
The Ohio State U at Lima, OH B
The Ohio State U at Marion, OH B
Ohio U–Chillicothe, OH A,B
Ohio U–Eastern, OH B
Ohio U–Lancaster, OH B
Ohio U–Southern Campus, OH A,B
Oklahoma Baptist U, OK B
Oklahoma Christian U, OK B
Oklahoma City U, OK B
Oklahoma State U, Oklahoma City, OK A
Olivet Nazarene U, IL B
Oral Roberts U, OK B
Otterbein Coll, OH B
Park U, MO A
Pittsburg State U, KS B
Presentation Coll, SD A,B
Purdue U, IN B
Purdue U North Central, IN A,B
Quincy U, IL B
Research Coll of Nursing, MO B
Rochester Comm and Tech Coll, MN A
Rockford Coll, IL B
Rockhurst U, MO B
Rogers State U, OK A,B
Rush U, IL B
Saginaw Valley State U, MI B
St. Ambrose U, IA B
St. Catherine U, MN B
St. Cloud State U, MN B
Saint Francis Medical Center Coll of Nursing, IL B
Saint John's U, MN B
Saint Joseph's Coll, IN B
Saint Louis U, MO B
Saint Mary's Coll, IN B
St. Olaf Coll, MN B
Saint Xavier U, IL B
Shawnee State U, OH A,B
South Dakota State U, SD B
Southeast Missouri State U, MO B
Southern Illinois U Edwardsville, IL B
Southern Nazarene U, OK B
Southwest Baptist U, MO A,B
Southwestern Coll, KS B
Southwestern Oklahoma State U, OK B
Trinity Christian Coll, IL B
Truman State U, MO B
Union Coll, NE B
U of Central Missouri, MO B
U of Central Oklahoma, OK B
U of Charleston, WV A,B
U of Cincinnati, OH A,B
U of Evansville, IN B
U of Illinois at Chicago, IL B
The U of Iowa, IA B
U of Mary, ND B
U of Michigan, MI B
U of Michigan–Flint, MI B
U of Minnesota, Twin Cities Campus, MN B
U of Missouri–Columbia, MO B
U of Missouri–Kansas City, MO B
U of Missouri–St. Louis, MO B
U of Nebraska Medical Center, NE B
U of North Dakota, ND B
U of Oklahoma Health Sciences Center, OK B
U of Phoenix–Cleveland Campus, OH B
U of Phoenix–Indianapolis Campus, IN B
U of Phoenix–Kansas City Campus, MO B
U of Phoenix–Metro Detroit Campus, MI B
U of Phoenix–Oklahoma City Campus, OK B
U of Phoenix–St. Louis Campus, MO B
U of Phoenix–Tulsa Campus, OK B
U of Phoenix–West Michigan Campus, MI B
U of Rio Grande, OH A
U of St. Francis, IL B
U of Saint Francis, IN B
U of Saint Mary, KS B
The U of South Dakota, SD A
U of Southern Indiana, IN A,B
The U of Toledo, OH A,B
U of Tulsa, OK B
U of Wisconsin–Eau Claire, WI B
U of Wisconsin–Green Bay, WI B
U of Wisconsin–Madison, WI B
U of Wisconsin–Milwaukee, WI B
U of Wisconsin–Oshkosh, WI B
U of Wisconsin–Parkside, WI B
Ursuline Coll, OH B
Valparaiso U, IN B
Viterbo U, WI B
Walsh U, OH B
Washburn U, KS B
Webster U, MO B
Western Illinois U, IL B
Western Michigan U, MI B
West Suburban Coll of Nursing, IL B
William Jewell Coll, MO B
Winona State U, MN B
Wright State U, OH B
Youngstown State U, OH B

Nursing Related

Avila U, MO B
Madonna U, MI A,B
Minot State U, ND B
U of Saint Francis, IN B
The U of Toledo, OH B
Wheaton Coll, IL B
Wright State U, OH B

Nursing Science

Clarke Coll, IA B
Clarkson Coll, NE B
Mercy Coll of Health Sciences, IA B
Missouri Baptist U, MO B
The Ohio State U, OH B
The U of Kansas, KS B
U of Phoenix–Metro Detroit Campus, MI B
Wayne State U, MI B
Wichita State U, KS B
Xavier U, OH B

Nutrition Sciences

Benedictine U, IL B
Case Western Reserve U, OH B
Coll of Saint Benedict, MN B
Elmhurst Coll, IL B
Purdue U, IN B
U of Southern Indiana, IN B

Occupational Health and Industrial Hygiene

Clarkson U, NY B
Grand Valley State U, MI B
Oakland U, MI B
Purdue U, IN B

Occupational Safety and Health Technology

Grand Valley State U, MI B
Indiana State U, IN B
Indiana U Bloomington, IN A
Indiana U Southeast, IN A
Oklahoma State U, Oklahoma City, OK A
Southeastern Oklahoma State U, OK B
Southwest Baptist U, MO B
U of Central Missouri, MO B
U of Central Oklahoma, OK B
U of Cincinnati, OH A
U of North Dakota, ND B
U of Wisconsin–Whitewater, WI B
Wright State U, OH A

Occupational Therapist Assistant

Baker Coll of Muskegon, MI A
Brown Mackie Coll–Fort Wayne, IN A
Brown Mackie Coll–Indianapolis, IN A
Brown Mackie Coll–Merrillville, IN A
Brown Mackie Coll–South Bend, IN A
St. Catherine U, MN A
U of Southern Indiana, IN A

Occupational Therapy

Augustana Coll, IL B
Baker Coll of Flint, MI B
Calvin Coll, MI B
Cleveland State U, OH B
Coll of Saint Benedict, MN B
Concordia U Wisconsin, WI B
Drury U, MO B
Eastern Michigan U, MI B
Elmhurst Coll, IL B
Eureka Coll, IL B
Grand Valley State U, MI B
Hamline U, MN B
Illinois Coll, IL B
Indiana U–Purdue U Indianapolis, IN B
Maryville U of Saint Louis, MO B
McKendree U, IL B
Mount Mary Coll, WI B
North Park U, IL B
St. Catherine U, MN B
Saint John's U, MN B
Shawnee State U, OH A,B
Stephens Coll, MO B
The U of Findlay, OH B
U of Minnesota, Twin Cities Campus, MN B
U of Missouri–Columbia, MO B
U of Southern Indiana, IN B
U of Wisconsin–Madison, WI B
U of Wisconsin–Milwaukee, WI B

A—associate degree; B—bachelor's degree

Wartburg Coll, IA B
Western Michigan U, MI B
Xavier U, OH B

Oceanography (Chemical and Physical)

Central Michigan U, MI B
U of Michigan, MI B

Office Management

Baker Coll of Jackson, MI A
Ball State U, IN B
Brown Mackie Coll–Tulsa, OK A
Dakota State U, SD A
Eastern Michigan U, MI B
Indiana State U, IN B
Lake Superior State U, MI A
Loyola U Chicago, IL B
Maranatha Baptist Bible Coll, WI B
Mayville State U, ND B
Miami U, OH A
Miami U Hamilton, OH B
Mount Vernon Nazarene U, OH A,B
Olivet Nazarene U, IL B
Park U, MO A
Shawnee State U, OH A
Southeast Missouri State U, MO B
Southwest Baptist U, MO B
U of Central Missouri, MO B
U of Southern Indiana, IN B
Valley City State U, ND B
Washburn U, KS A
Wright State U, OH B

Office Occupations and Clerical Services

Ohio U–Southern Campus, OH A
Rasmussen Coll St. Cloud, MN A
Sinte Gleska U, SD A
Wright State U, OH A

Operations Management

Ball State U, IN B
Central Michigan U, MI B
Clarkson U, NY B
Ferris State U, MI B
Franklin U, OH B
Friends U, KS B
Indiana U–Purdue U Fort Wayne, IN A,B
Indiana U–Purdue U Indianapolis, IN A,B
Iowa State U of Science and Technology, IA B
Kent State U, OH B
Loyola U Chicago, IL B
Marian U, WI B
Miami U, OH B
Michigan State U, MI B
Michigan Technological U, MI B
Missouri Baptist U, MO B
Northeastern State U, OK B
Oakland U, MI B
The Ohio State U, OH B
Purdue U, IN B
Purdue U North Central, IN B
Saginaw Valley State U, MI B
Trine U, IN B
The U of Akron, OH B
U of Illinois at Urbana–Champaign, IL B
U of Indianapolis, IN B
U of Michigan–Flint, MI B
U of Nebraska at Kearney, NE B
U of North Dakota, ND B
U of Phoenix–Indianapolis Campus, IN B
U of Phoenix–St. Louis Campus, MO B
The U of Toledo, OH B
U of Wisconsin–Stout, WI B
U of Wisconsin–Whitewater, WI B
Washington U in St. Louis, MO B
Wright State U, OH B

Operations Research

U of Cincinnati, OH B
U of Illinois at Urbana–Champaign, IL B

Ophthalmic Laboratory Technology

Indiana U Bloomington, IN A

Optical Sciences

Saginaw Valley State U, MI B

Optometric Technician

Indiana U Bloomington, IN A
St. Cloud State U, MN A

Organizational Behavior

Anderson U, IN B
Argosy U, Chicago, IL B
Argosy U, Schaumburg, IL B
Argosy U, Twin Cities, MN B
Benedictine U, IL B
Bluffton U, OH B
Calvary Bible Coll and Theological Seminary, MO B
Carroll U, WI B
The Coll of St. Scholastica, MN B
Denison U, OH B
DePaul U, IL B
Greenville Coll, IL B
Loyola U Chicago, IL B
Northwestern U, IL B
Oral Roberts U, OK B
Roosevelt U, IL B
St. Ambrose U, IA B
Saint Louis U, MO B
U of Illinois at Urbana–Champaign, IL B
U of Michigan, MI B
U of Michigan–Flint, MI B
U of Phoenix–Cleveland Campus, OH B
U of Phoenix–Indianapolis Campus, IN B
U of St. Francis, IL B
The U of Toledo, OH B
U of Tulsa, OK B
Wayne State U, MI B

Organizational Communication

Aquinas Coll, MI B
Buena Vista U, IA B
Capital U, OH B
Carroll U, WI B
Cedarville U, OH B
Central Michigan U, MI B
Creighton U, NE A
Dana Coll, NE B
Franklin U, OH B
Indiana U–Purdue U Fort Wayne, IN B
Marian U, WI B
McKendree U, IL B
Mount Union Coll, OH B
North Central Coll, IL B
Ohio Northern U, OH B
Ohio U–Eastern, OH B
Ohio U–Lancaster, OH B
Rockhurst U, MO B
Roosevelt U, IL B
The U of Akron, OH B
U of Illinois at Urbana–Champaign, IL B
U of Michigan–Flint, MI B
U of Northern Iowa, IA B
Valparaiso U, IN B
Western Michigan U, MI B
Wright State U, OH B

Ornamental Horticulture

Ferris State U, MI A
Iowa State U of Science and Technology, IA B
U of Illinois at Urbana–Champaign, IL B
U of Wisconsin–Platteville, WI B

Orthotics/Prosthetics

Baker Coll of Flint, MI A

Painting

Aquinas Coll, MI B
Art Academy of Cincinnati, OH B
Bethany Coll, KS B
Bradley U, IL B
The Cleveland Inst of Art, OH B
Coe Coll, IA B
Columbia Coll, MO B
Drake U, IA B
Ferris State U, MI B
Grace Coll, IN B
Indiana U–Purdue U Fort Wayne, IN B
Indiana Wesleyan U, IN B
Kansas City Art Inst, MO B
Lewis U, IL B
Minneapolis Coll of Art and Design, MN B
Minnesota State U Moorhead, MN B
Oakland U, MI B
Ohio Northern U, OH B
Ohio U, OH B
Pittsburg State U, KS B
St. Cloud State U, MN B
Shawnee State U, OH B
Trinity Christian Coll, IL B
U of Dallas, TX B
U of Illinois at Urbana–Champaign, IL B
The U of Iowa, IA B
The U of Kansas, KS B
U of Missouri–St. Louis, MO B
Washington U in St. Louis, MO B

Paralegal/Legal Assistant

Brown Mackie Coll–Indianapolis, IN A
Brown Mackie Coll–Tulsa, OK A
Bryant & Stratton Coll—Wauwatosa Campus, WI A
Minnesota School of Business–Blaine, MN A,B
Newman U, KS A

Parks, Recreation and Leisure

Ashland U, OH B
Aurora U, IL B
Bemidji State U, MN B
Bethany Coll, KS B
Black Hills State U, SD B
Bluffton U, OH B
Bowling Green State U, OH B
Calvin Coll, MI B
Central Michigan U, MI B
Central State U, OH B
Dordt Coll, IA B
Emporia State U, KS B
Evangel U, MO B
Graceland U, IA B
Greenville Coll, IL B
Huntington U, IN B
Indiana U Bloomington, IN B
Lake Superior State U, MI B
Minnesota State U Mankato, MN B
Missouri State U, MO B
North Dakota State U, ND B
Northern Michigan U, MI B
Northwest Missouri State U, MO B
The Ohio State U, OH B
Ohio U, OH B
Oklahoma Baptist U, OK B
Oklahoma State U, OK B
Pittsburg State U, KS B
Presentation Coll, SD B
Southeastern Oklahoma State U, OK B
Southeast Missouri State U, MO B
Southern Illinois U Carbondale, IL B
Southwest Baptist U, MO B
Southwestern Oklahoma State U, OK B
Spring Arbor U, MI B
U of Central Missouri, MO B
U of Illinois at Urbana–Champaign, IL B
The U of Iowa, IA B
U of Minnesota, Duluth, MN B
U of Missouri–Columbia, MO B
U of Nebraska at Kearney, NE B
U of Nebraska at Omaha, NE B
U of Northern Iowa, IA B
The U of South Dakota, SD B
The U of Toledo, OH B
U of Wisconsin–Madison, WI B

U of Wisconsin–Milwaukee, WI B
Western Michigan U, MI B
William Jewell Coll, MO B
Winona State U, MN B

Parks, Recreation and Leisure Facilities Management
Carroll U, WI B
Central Michigan U, MI B
Coll of the Ozarks, MO B
Eastern Illinois U, IL B
Eastern Michigan U, MI B
Ferris State U, MI B
Hannibal-LaGrange Coll, MO B
Illinois State U, IL B
Indiana State U, IN B
Indiana Tech, IN A,B
Indiana Wesleyan U, IN B
Kansas State U, KS B
Kent State U, OH B
Lake Superior State U, MI B
Michigan State U, MI B
Minnesota State U Mankato, MN B
Missouri Western State U, MO B
Mount Marty Coll, SD B
Ohio U, OH B
Oral Roberts U, OK B
South Dakota State U, SD B
Trine U, IN B
U of Minnesota, Twin Cities Campus, MN B
U of North Dakota, ND B
U of St. Francis, IL B
U of Wisconsin–La Crosse, WI B
Western Illinois U, IL B
Winona State U, MN B

Parks, Recreation, and Leisure Related
Franklin Coll, IN B
Indiana U Southeast, IN A
Southern Nazarene U, OK A
Trinity Christian Coll, IL B
The U of Toledo, OH B

Pastoral Counseling and Specialized Ministries Related
Calvary Bible Coll and Theological Seminary, MO B
Greenville Coll, IL B
Madonna U, MI B
Malone U, OH B
Mid-America Christian U, OK B
Northwestern Coll, MN B
Oak Hills Christian Coll, MN B
Trinity International U, IL B

Pastoral Studies/Counseling
Barclay Coll, KS B
Bethel Coll, IN B
Calvary Bible Coll and Theological Seminary, MO B
Cedarville U, OH B
Central Bible Coll, MO B
Central Christian Coll of Kansas, KS B
Coll of Mount St. Joseph, OH B
Concordia U Chicago, IL B
Concordia U, Nebraska, NE B
Concordia U Wisconsin, WI B
Cornerstone U, MI B
Crown Coll, MN B
Faith Baptist Bible Coll and Theological Seminary, IA B
Grace Bible Coll, MI B
Grace U, NE B
Greenville Coll, IL B
Indiana Wesleyan U, IN A,B
Kuyper Coll, MI B
Lindenwood U, MO B
Manhattan Christian Coll, KS B
Maranatha Baptist Bible Coll, WI B
Marian U, IN A,B
Messenger Coll, MO B
Moody Bible Inst, IL B
Mount Vernon Nazarene U, OH B
Newman U, KS B
North Central U, MN A,B
Oak Hills Christian Coll, MN B
Olivet Nazarene U, IL B
Oral Roberts U, OK B
St. Gregory's U, Shawnee, OK B
Saint Joseph's Coll, IN B
Southwest Baptist U, MO B
Southwestern Coll, KS B
Spring Arbor U, MI B
Union Coll, NE B
U of Saint Mary, KS B
Walsh U, OH B

Pathologist Assistant
Wayne State U, MI B

Peace Studies and Conflict Resolution
Bethel U, MN B
Coll of Saint Benedict, MN B
DePauw U, IN B
Earlham Coll, IN B
Goshen Coll, IN B
Hamline U, MN B
Kent State U, OH B
Manchester Coll, IN B
Ohio Dominican U, OH B
Saint John's U, MN B
U of Missouri–Columbia, MO B
U of Wisconsin–Milwaukee, WI B
U of Wisconsin–Superior, WI B

Petroleum Engineering
Marietta Coll, OH B
Missouri U of Science and Technology, MO B
The U of Kansas, KS B
U of Oklahoma, OK B
U of Tulsa, OK B

Pharmacology
U of Cincinnati, OH B
U of Wisconsin–Madison, WI B

Pharmacology and Toxicology
Wright State U, OH B

Pharmacy
Butler U, IN B
Drake U, IA B
Illinois Inst of Technology, IL B
Ohio Northern U, OH B
The Ohio State U, OH B
Purdue U, IN B
St. Louis Coll of Pharmacy, MO B
South Dakota State U, SD B
Southwestern Oklahoma State U, OK B
U of Cincinnati, OH B
The U of Iowa, IA B
The U of Kansas, KS B
U of Missouri–Kansas City, MO B
The U of Toledo, OH B
U of Wisconsin–Madison, WI B

Pharmacy Administration/ Pharmaceutics
Drake U, IA B
U of Michigan, MI B

Pharmacy, Pharmaceutical Sciences, and Administration Related
North Dakota State U, ND B
Ohio Northern U, OH B
The U of Toledo, OH B

Pharmacy Technician
Baker Coll of Flint, MI A
Baker Coll of Jackson, MI A
Baker Coll of Muskegon, MI A
Madonna U, MI A
National American U, MO A
Rasmussen Coll Eagan, MN A
Rasmussen Coll St. Cloud, MN A

Philosophy
Adrian Coll, MI B
Albion Coll, MI B
Alma Coll, MI B
Anderson U, IN B
Aquinas Coll, MI B
Ashland U, OH B
Augsburg Coll, MN B
Augustana Coll, IL B
Augustana Coll, SD B
Baker U, KS B
Baldwin-Wallace Coll, OH B
Ball State U, IN B
Beloit Coll, WI B
Bemidji State U, MN B
Benedictine Coll, KS B
Benedictine U, IL B
Bethany Coll, KS B
Bethel Coll, IN B
Bethel U, MN B
Bowling Green State U, OH B
Bradley U, IL B
Butler U, IN B
Calvin Coll, MI B
Capital U, OH B
Carleton Coll, MN B
Case Western Reserve U, OH B
Cedarville U, OH B
Central Coll, IA B
Central Methodist U, MO B
Central Michigan U, MI B
Clarke Coll, IA B
Cleveland State U, OH B
Coe Coll, IA B
Coll of Saint Benedict, MN B
Coll of the Ozarks, MO B
The Coll of Wooster, OH B
Concordia Coll, MN B
Concordia U, MI B
Concordia U Chicago, IL B
Cornell Coll, IA B
Creighton U, NE B
Dakota Wesleyan U, SD B
Denison U, OH B
DePaul U, IL B
DePauw U, IN B
Divine Word Coll, IA B
Doane Coll, NE B
Dominican U, IL B
Dordt Coll, IA B
Drake U, IA B
Drury U, MO B
Earlham Coll, IN B
Eastern Illinois U, IL B
Eastern Michigan U, MI B
Elmhurst Coll, IL B
Eureka Coll, IL B
Fort Hays State U, KS B
Franciscan U of Steubenville, OH B
Franklin Coll, IN B
Friends U, KS B
Grand Valley State U, MI B
Greenville Coll, IL B
Grinnell Coll, IA B
Gustavus Adolphus Coll, MN B
Hamline U, MN B
Hanover Coll, IN B
Heidelberg U, OH B
Hillsdale Coll, MI B
Hiram Coll, OH B
Hope Coll, MI B
Huntington U, IN B
Illinois Coll, IL B
Illinois State U, IL B
Illinois Wesleyan U, IL B
Indiana State U, IN B
Indiana U Bloomington, IN B
Indiana U Northwest, IN B
Indiana U–Purdue U Fort Wayne, IN B
Indiana U–Purdue U Indianapolis, IN B
Indiana U South Bend, IN B
Indiana U Southeast, IN B
Indiana Wesleyan U, IN B
Iowa State U of Science and Technology, IA B
John Carroll U, OH B
Kalamazoo Coll, MI B
Kansas State U, KS B
Kent State U, OH B
Kenyon Coll, OH B
Knox Coll, IL B
Lake Forest Coll, IL B
Lawrence U, WI B

A—associate degree; B—bachelor's degree

Lewis U, IL B
Loras Coll, IA B
Loyola U Chicago, IL B
Luther Coll, IA B
Macalester Coll, MN B
MacMurray Coll, IL B
Madonna U, MI B
Malone U, OH B
Manchester Coll, IN B
Marian U, IN B
Marietta Coll, OH B
Marquette U, WI B
McKendree U, IL B
McPherson Coll, KS B
Miami U, OH B
Miami U Hamilton, OH B
Michigan State U, MI B
Millikin U, IL B
Minnesota State U Mankato, MN B
Minnesota State U Moorhead, MN B
Missouri State U, MO B
Missouri U of Science and Technology, MO B
Monmouth Coll, IL B
Morningside Coll, IA B
Mount Mary Coll, WI B
Mount Mercy Coll, IA B
Mount Union Coll, OH B
Mount Vernon Nazarene U, OH B
Muskingum Coll, OH B
Nebraska Wesleyan U, NE B
North Central Coll, IL B
North Dakota State U, ND B
Northeastern Illinois U, IL B
Northern Michigan U, MI B
North Park U, IL B
Northwestern U, IL B
Northwest Missouri State U, MO B
Oakland U, MI B
Oberlin Coll, OH B
Ohio Dominican U, OH B
Ohio Northern U, OH B
The Ohio State U, OH B
Ohio U, OH B
Ohio Wesleyan U, OH B
Oklahoma Baptist U, OK B
Oklahoma City U, OK B
Oklahoma State U, OK B
Olivet Nazarene U, IL B
Otterbein Coll, OH B
Pontifical Coll Josephinum, OH B
Purdue U, IN B
Purdue U Calumet, IN B
Quincy U, IL B
Ripon Coll, WI B
Rockford Coll, IL B
Rockhurst U, MO B
Roosevelt U, IL B
St. Ambrose U, IA B
St. Catherine U, MN B
St. Cloud State U, MN B
St. Gregory's U, Shawnee, OK B
Saint John's U, MN B
Saint Joseph's Coll, IN B
Saint Louis U, MO B
Saint Mary's Coll, IN B
Saint Mary's U of Minnesota, MN B
St. Norbert Coll, WI B
St. Olaf Coll, MN B
Saint Xavier U, IL B
Siena Heights U, MI B
Simpson Coll, IA B
Southeast Missouri State U, MO B
Southern Illinois U Carbondale, IL B
Southern Illinois U Edwardsville, IL B
Southern Methodist U, TX B
Southern Nazarene U, OK B
Southwest Minnesota State U, MN B
Spring Arbor U, MI B
Taylor U, IN B
Transylvania U, KY B
Trinity Christian Coll, IL B
Trinity International U, IL B
Truman State U, MO B
The U of Akron, OH B
U of Central Oklahoma, OK B
U of Chicago, IL B
U of Cincinnati, OH B
U of Dallas, TX B
U of Dayton, OH B
U of Evansville, IN B
The U of Findlay, OH B
U of Illinois at Chicago, IL B
U of Illinois at Springfield, IL B
U of Illinois at Urbana–Champaign, IL B
U of Indianapolis, IN B
The U of Iowa, IA B
The U of Kansas, KS B
U of Michigan, MI B
U of Michigan–Dearborn, MI B
U of Michigan–Flint, MI B
U of Minnesota, Duluth, MN B
U of Minnesota, Morris, MN B
U of Minnesota, Twin Cities Campus, MN B
U of Missouri–Columbia, MO B
U of Missouri–Kansas City, MO B
U of Missouri–St. Louis, MO B
U of Nebraska at Omaha, NE B
U of Nebraska–Lincoln, NE B
U of New Orleans, LA B
U of North Dakota, ND B
U of Northern Iowa, IA B
U of Notre Dame, IN B
U of Oklahoma, OK B
U of Saint Francis, IN B
U of Sioux Falls, SD B
The U of South Dakota, SD B
U of Southern Indiana, IN B
The U of Toledo, OH B
U of Tulsa, OK B
U of Wisconsin–Eau Claire, WI B
U of Wisconsin–Green Bay, WI B
U of Wisconsin–La Crosse, WI B
U of Wisconsin–Madison, WI B
U of Wisconsin–Milwaukee, WI B
U of Wisconsin–Oshkosh, WI B
U of Wisconsin–Parkside, WI B
U of Wisconsin–Platteville, WI B
U of Wisconsin–Stevens Point, WI B
Ursuline Coll, OH B
Valparaiso U, IN B
Wabash Coll, IN B
Walsh U, OH B
Wartburg Coll, IA B
Washburn U, KS B
Washington U in St. Louis, MO B
Wayne State U, MI B
Webster U, MO B
Western Illinois U, IL B
Western Michigan U, MI B
Westminster Coll, MO B
Wheaton Coll, IL B
Wichita State U, KS B
William Jewell Coll, MO B
Wilmington Coll, OH B
Wittenberg U, OH B
Wright State U, OH B
Xavier U, OH B
Youngstown State U, OH B

Philosophy and Religious Studies Related

Buena Vista U, IA B
Butler U, IN B
Columbia Coll, MO B
Graceland U, IA B
Iowa Wesleyan Coll, IA B
Maryville U of Saint Louis, MO B
Saint Joseph's Coll, IN B
Southwestern Coll, KS B
Sterling Coll, KS B
U of Notre Dame, IN B
Viterbo U, WI B
Washington U in St. Louis, MO B

Philosophy Related

Lewis U, IL B
Ohio Northern U, OH B

Photographic and Film/Video Technology

Kent State U, OH B
Ohio U, OH B

Photography

Aquinas Coll, MI B
Art Academy of Cincinnati, OH B
The Art Inst of Indianapolis, IN A,B
The Art Insts International Minnesota, MN B
Bradley U, IL B
Carroll U, WI B
Central Christian Coll of Kansas, KS A
The Cleveland Inst of Art, OH B
Coe Coll, IA B
Coll for Creative Studies, MI B
Coll of Visual Arts, MN B
Columbia Coll, MO B
Dominican U, IL B
Ferris State U, MI B
Grand Valley State U, MI B
The Illinois Inst of Art–Schaumburg, IL B
Indiana U–Purdue U Fort Wayne, IN B
Indiana Wesleyan U, IN B
Kansas City Art Inst, MO B
Minneapolis Coll of Art and Design, MN B
Morningside Coll, IA B
Northern Michigan U, MI B
Oakland U, MI B
Purdue U, IN B
Shawnee State U, OH B
Trinity Christian Coll, IL B
The U of Akron, OH B
U of Central Missouri, MO B
U of Central Oklahoma, OK B
U of Dayton, OH B
U of Illinois at Chicago, IL B
U of Illinois at Urbana–Champaign, IL B
The U of Iowa, IA B
U of Michigan, MI B
U of Missouri–St. Louis, MO B
Washington U in St. Louis, MO B
Webster U, MO B
Wright State U, OH B
Youngstown State U, OH B

Photojournalism

Bradley U, IL B
Central Michigan U, MI B
Pittsburg State U, KS B
U of Missouri–Columbia, MO B

Physical and Theoretical Chemistry

Michigan State U, MI B

Physical Education Teaching and Coaching

Albion Coll, MI B
Alma Coll, MI B
Anderson U, IN B
Aquinas Coll, MI B
Ashland U, OH B
Augsburg Coll, MN B
Augustana Coll, IL B
Augustana Coll, SD B
Aurora U, IL B
Bacone Coll, OK B
Ball State U, IN B
Bemidji State U, MN B
Benedictine Coll, KS B
Bethany Coll, KS B
Bethel Coll, IN B
Bethel U, MN B
Bowling Green State U, OH B
Briar Cliff U, IA B
Buena Vista U, IA B
Calvin Coll, MI B
Cameron U, OK B
Capital U, OH B
Carroll U, WI B
Cedarville U, OH B

Central Christian Coll of Kansas, KS A,B
Central Methodist U, MO B
Central Michigan U, MI B
Clarke Coll, IA B
Cleveland State U, OH B
Coe Coll, IA B
Coll of the Ozarks, MO B
Concordia Coll, MN B
Concordia U, MI B
Concordia U Chicago, IL B
Concordia U, Nebraska, NE B
Concordia U, St. Paul, MN B
Concordia U Wisconsin, WI B
Cornell Coll, IA B
Cornerstone U, MI B
Crown Coll, MN B
Culver-Stockton Coll, MO B
Dakota State U, SD B
Dakota Wesleyan U, SD B
Defiance Coll, OH B
Denison U, OH B
DePaul U, IL B
DePauw U, IN B
Doane Coll, NE B
Dordt Coll, IA B
Eastern Illinois U, IL B
Eastern Michigan U, MI B
Elmhurst Coll, IL B
Eureka Coll, IL B
Evangel U, MO B
Fort Hays State U, KS B
Franklin Coll, IN B
Friends U, KS B
Goshen Coll, IN B
Grace Coll, IN B
Graceland U, IA B
Grand Valley State U, MI B
Greenville Coll, IL B
Gustavus Adolphus Coll, MN B
Hamline U, MN B
Hannibal-LaGrange Coll, MO B
Hanover Coll, IN B
Heidelberg U, OH B
Hillsdale Coll, MI B
Hope Coll, MI B
Huntington U, IN B
Illinois Coll, IL B
Illinois State U, IL B
Indiana State U, IN B
Indiana Tech, IN B
Indiana U Bloomington, IN B
Indiana U–Purdue U Indianapolis, IN B
Indiana Wesleyan U, IN B
Iowa Wesleyan Coll, IA B
Jamestown Coll, ND B
John Carroll U, OH B
Kansas Wesleyan U, KS B
Kent State U, OH B
Lincoln U, MO B
Lindenwood U, MO B
Loras Coll, IA B
Luther Coll, IA B
MacMurray Coll, IL B
Malone U, OH B
Manchester Coll, IN B
Maranatha Baptist Bible Coll, WI B
Marian U, IN B
Mayville State U, ND B
McKendree U, IL B
McPherson Coll, KS B
Miami U, OH B
Miami U Hamilton, OH B
Michigan State U, MI B
MidAmerica Nazarene U, KS B
Millikin U, IL B
Minnesota State U Mankato, MN B
Minnesota State U Moorhead, MN B
Minot State U, ND B
Missouri Baptist U, MO B
Missouri State U, MO B
Monmouth Coll, IL B
Mount Union Coll, OH B
Mount Vernon Nazarene U, OH B
Muskingum Coll, OH B
Nebraska Wesleyan U, NE B
North Central Coll, IL B
North Dakota State U, ND B
Northeastern Illinois U, IL B
Northeastern State U, OK B
Northern Michigan U, MI B
Northern State U, SD B
North Park U, IL B
Northwestern Coll, MN B
Northwest Missouri State U, MO B
Ohio Northern U, OH B
The Ohio State U, OH B
Ohio U, OH B
Ohio Wesleyan U, OH B
Oklahoma Baptist U, OK B
Oklahoma Christian U, OK B
Oklahoma City U, OK B
Oklahoma State U, OK B
Olivet Nazarene U, IL B
Oral Roberts U, OK B
Otterbein Coll, OH B
Pittsburg State U, KS B
Purdue U, IN B
Quincy U, IL B
Ripon Coll, WI B
Rockford Coll, IL B
Saginaw Valley State U, MI B
St. Ambrose U, IA B
St. Catherine U, MN B
St. Cloud State U, MN B
Saint Joseph's Coll, IN B
Simpson Coll, IA B
Southeastern Oklahoma State U, OK B
Southeast Missouri State U, MO B
Southern Nazarene U, OK B
Southwest Baptist U, MO B
Southwestern Oklahoma State U, OK B
Southwest Minnesota State U, MN B
Spring Arbor U, MI B
Sterling Coll, KS B
Taylor U, IN B
Transylvania U, KY B
Trine U, IN B
Trinity Bible Coll, ND B
Trinity Christian Coll, IL B
Trinity International U, IL B
Union Coll, NE B
Union Inst & U, OH B
The U of Akron, OH B
U of Central Missouri, MO B
U of Central Oklahoma, OK B
U of Cincinnati, OH B
U of Dayton, OH B
U of Evansville, IN B
The U of Findlay, OH B
U of Illinois at Urbana–Champaign, IL B
U of Indianapolis, IN B
The U of Kansas, KS B
U of Mary, ND B
U of Michigan, MI B
U of Minnesota, Duluth, MN B
U of Minnesota, Twin Cities Campus, MN B
U of Missouri–St. Louis, MO B
U of Nebraska at Kearney, NE B
U of Nebraska–Lincoln, NE B
U of New Orleans, LA B
U of North Dakota, ND B
U of Northern Iowa, IA B
U of Rio Grande, OH A,B
The U of South Dakota, SD B
U of Southern Indiana, IN B
The U of Toledo, OH B
U of Wisconsin–La Crosse, WI B
U of Wisconsin–Madison, WI B
U of Wisconsin–Oshkosh, WI B
U of Wisconsin–Stevens Point, WI B
U of Wisconsin–Superior, WI B
U of Wisconsin–Whitewater, WI B
Valley City State U, ND B
Valparaiso U, IN B
Waldorf Coll, IA B
Walsh U, OH B
Wartburg Coll, IA B
Washburn U, KS B
Wayne State Coll, NE B
Wayne State U, MI B
Western Michigan U, MI B
Westminster Coll, MO B
Wichita State U, KS B
William Jewell Coll, MO B
Wilmington Coll, OH B
Winona State U, MN B
Wright State U, OH B
York Coll, NE B
Youngstown State U, OH B

Physical Sciences

Bemidji State U, MN B
Black Hills State U, SD B
Calvin Coll, MI B
Coe Coll, IA B
Concordia U, MI B
Concordia U Chicago, IL B
Concordia U, Nebraska, NE B
Dakota State U, SD B
Defiance Coll, OH B
Doane Coll, NE B
Emporia State U, KS B
Fort Hays State U, KS B
Grace Coll, IN B
Graceland U, IA B
Grand View U, IA B
Kansas State U, KS B
Loras Coll, IA B
Michigan State U, MI B
Michigan Technological U, MI B
Minnesota State U Mankato, MN B
Minot State U, ND B
Northwest Missouri State U, MO B
Olivet Nazarene U, IL B
Otterbein Coll, OH B
Ripon Coll, WI B
St. Cloud State U, MN B
Shawnee State U, OH B
Southern Nazarene U, OK B
Trine U, IN B
U of Dayton, OH B
U of North Dakota, ND B
U of Rio Grande, OH B
The U of Toledo, OH B
U of Wisconsin–La Crosse, WI B
U of Wisconsin–Superior, WI B
Winona State U, MN B

Physical Sciences Related

Baldwin-Wallace Coll, OH B
The Coll of St. Scholastica, MN B
Eastern Michigan U, MI B
Ohio U, OH B
U of Saint Francis, IN B
Wayne State U, MI B

Physical Science Technologies Related

Missouri State U, MO B

Physical Therapist Assistant

Baker Coll of Flint, MI A
Baker Coll of Muskegon, MI A
Brown Mackie Coll–Fort Wayne, IN A
Brown Mackie Coll–South Bend, IN A
Mercy Coll of Health Sciences, IA A
Missouri Western State U, MO A
St. Catherine U, MN A
Southern Illinois U Carbondale, IL A
U of Evansville, IN A
U of Indianapolis, IN A
U of Saint Francis, IN A
Washburn U, KS A

Physical Therapy

Andrews U, MI B
Clarke Coll, IA B
Clarkson Coll, NE A
Cleveland State U, OH B
Coll of Saint Benedict, MN B
Concordia U Wisconsin, WI B
Elmhurst Coll, IL B
Grand Valley State U, MI B
Gustavus Adolphus Coll, MN B
Indiana U Southeast, IN B
Marquette U, WI B

A—associate degree; B—bachelor's degree

Maryville U of Saint Louis, MO B
Mount Vernon Nazarene U, OH B
Muskingum Coll, OH B
North Park U, IL B
Pittsburg State U, KS B
St. Cloud State U, MN B
Saint John's U, MN B
Saint Louis U, MO B
Saint Mary's U of Minnesota, MN B
Shawnee State U, OH A
U of Cincinnati, OH A
The U of Findlay, OH B
U of Minnesota, Morris, MN B
U of Minnesota, Twin Cities Campus, MN B
U of North Dakota, ND B
The U of Toledo, OH B
U of Wisconsin–Milwaukee, WI B
Winona State U, MN B

Physician Assistant

Augsburg Coll, MN B
Bryant & Stratton Coll—Wauwatosa Campus, WI A
Butler U, IN B
Central Christian Coll of Kansas, KS A
Elmhurst Coll, IL B
Grand Valley State U, MI B
Marquette U, WI B
Southern Illinois U Carbondale, IL B
Union Coll, NE B
The U of Findlay, OH B
U of Saint Francis, IN B
U of Wisconsin–Madison, WI B
Wichita State U, KS B

Physics

Adrian Coll, MI B
Albion Coll, MI B
Alma Coll, MI B
Anderson U, IN B
Andrews U, MI B
Aquinas Coll, MI B
Ashland U, OH B
Augsburg Coll, MN B
Augustana Coll, IL B
Augustana Coll, SD B
Baker U, KS B
Baldwin-Wallace Coll, OH B
Ball State U, IN B
Beloit Coll, WI B
Bemidji State U, MN B
Benedictine Coll, KS B
Benedictine U, IL B
Bethel Coll, IN B
Bethel Coll, KS B
Bethel U, MN B
Bluffton U, OH B
Bowling Green State U, OH B
Bradley U, IL B
Buena Vista U, IA B
Butler U, IN B
Calvin Coll, MI B
Cameron U, OK B
Carleton Coll, MN B
Cedarville U, OH B
Central Coll, IA B
Central Methodist U, MO B
Central Michigan U, MI B
Clarkson U, NY B
Cleveland State U, OH B
Coe Coll, IA B
Coll of Saint Benedict, MN B
The Coll of Wooster, OH B
Concordia Coll, MN B
Concordia U, MI B
Cornell Coll, IA B
Creighton U, NE B
Denison U, OH B
DePaul U, IL B
DePauw U, IN B
Doane Coll, NE B
Dordt Coll, IA B
Drake U, IA B
Drury U, MO B
Earlham Coll, IN B
Eastern Illinois U, IL B
Eastern Michigan U, MI B
Elmhurst Coll, IL B
Emporia State U, KS B
Fort Hays State U, KS B
Goshen Coll, IN B
Grand Valley State U, MI B
Greenville Coll, IL B
Grinnell Coll, IA B
Gustavus Adolphus Coll, MN B
Hamline U, MN B
Hanover Coll, IN B
Heidelberg U, OH B
Hillsdale Coll, MI B
Hiram Coll, OH B
Hope Coll, MI B
Illinois Coll, IL B
Illinois Inst of Technology, IL B
Illinois State U, IL B
Illinois Wesleyan U, IL B
Indiana State U, IN B
Indiana U Bloomington, IN B
Indiana U–Purdue U Fort Wayne, IN B
Indiana U–Purdue U Indianapolis, IN B
Indiana U South Bend, IN B
Iowa State U of Science and Technology, IA B
John Carroll U, OH B
Kalamazoo Coll, MI B
Kansas State U, KS B
Kansas Wesleyan U, KS B
Kent State U, OH B
Kenyon Coll, OH B
Kettering U, MI B
Knox Coll, IL B
Lake Forest Coll, IL B
Lawrence Technological U, MI B
Lawrence U, WI B
Lewis U, IL B
Lincoln U, MO B
Loras Coll, IA B
Loyola U Chicago, IL B
Luther Coll, IA B
Macalester Coll, MN B
MacMurray Coll, IL B
Manchester Coll, IN B
Marietta Coll, OH B
Marquette U, WI B
Miami U, OH B
Miami U Hamilton, OH B
Michigan State U, MI B
Michigan Technological U, MI B
Millikin U, IL B
Minnesota State U Mankato, MN B
Minnesota State U Moorhead, MN B
Minot State U, ND B
Missouri Southern State U, MO B
Missouri State U, MO B
Missouri U of Science and Technology, MO B
Monmouth Coll, IL B
Morningside Coll, IA B
Mount Union Coll, OH B
Mount Vernon Nazarene U, OH B
Muskingum Coll, OH B
Nebraska Wesleyan U, NE B
North Central Coll, IL B
North Dakota State U, ND B
Northeastern Illinois U, IL B
Northern Michigan U, MI B
North Park U, IL B
Northwestern U, IL B
Northwest Missouri State U, MO B
Oakland U, MI B
Oberlin Coll, OH B
Ohio Northern U, OH B
The Ohio State U, OH B
Ohio U, OH B
Ohio Wesleyan U, OH B
Oklahoma Baptist U, OK B
Oklahoma City U, OK B
Oklahoma State U, OK B
Oklahoma State U, Oklahoma City, OK A
Oral Roberts U, OK B
Otterbein Coll, OH B
Pittsburg State U, KS B
Purdue U, IN B
Purdue U Calumet, IN B
Purdue U North Central, IN A
Rockhurst U, MO B
Rogers State U, OK A
Rose-Hulman Inst of Technology, IN B
Saginaw Valley State U, MI B
St. Ambrose U, IA B
St. Catherine U, MN B
St. Cloud State U, MN B
Saint John's U, MN B
Saint Louis U, MO B
St. Norbert Coll, WI B
St. Olaf Coll, MN B
Simpson Coll, IA B
South Dakota School of Mines and Technology, SD B
South Dakota State U, SD B
Southeast Missouri State U, MO B
Southern Illinois U Carbondale, IL B
Southern Illinois U Edwardsville, IL B
Southern Methodist U, TX B
Southern Nazarene U, OK B
Southwestern Coll, KS B
Southwestern Oklahoma State U, OK B
Spring Arbor U, MI B
Taylor U, IN B
Transylvania U, KY B
Truman State U, MO B
Union Coll, NE B
The U of Akron, OH B
U of Central Missouri, MO B
U of Central Oklahoma, OK B
U of Chicago, IL B
U of Cincinnati, OH B
U of Dallas, TX B
U of Dayton, OH B
U of Evansville, IN B
U of Illinois at Chicago, IL B
U of Illinois at Urbana–Champaign, IL B
U of Indianapolis, IN B
The U of Iowa, IA B
The U of Kansas, KS B
U of Michigan, MI B
U of Michigan–Dearborn, MI B
U of Michigan–Flint, MI B
U of Minnesota, Duluth, MN B
U of Minnesota, Morris, MN B
U of Minnesota, Twin Cities Campus, MN B
U of Missouri–Columbia, MO B
U of Missouri–Kansas City, MO B
U of Missouri–St. Louis, MO B
U of Nebraska at Kearney, NE B
U of Nebraska at Omaha, NE B
U of Nebraska–Lincoln, NE B
U of New Orleans, LA B
U of North Dakota, ND B
U of Notre Dame, IN B
U of Oklahoma, OK B
U of Science and Arts of Oklahoma, OK B
The U of South Dakota, SD B
The U of Toledo, OH B
U of Tulsa, OK B
U of Wisconsin–Eau Claire, WI B
U of Wisconsin–La Crosse, WI B
U of Wisconsin–Milwaukee, WI B
U of Wisconsin–Oshkosh, WI B
U of Wisconsin–Parkside, WI B
U of Wisconsin–Stevens Point, WI B
U of Wisconsin–Whitewater, WI B
Valparaiso U, IN B
Wabash Coll, IN B
Wartburg Coll, IA B
Washburn U, KS B
Washington U in St. Louis, MO B
Wayne State U, MI B
Western Illinois U, IL B
Western Michigan U, MI B
Westminster Coll, MO B
Wheaton Coll, IL B
Wichita State U, KS B

William Jewell Coll, MO B
Winona State U, MN B
Wittenberg U, OH B
Xavier U, OH B
Youngstown State U, OH B

Physics Related
The Coll of Wooster, OH B
Lawrence Technological U, MI B
Ohio Northern U, OH B
Ohio U, OH B
Spring Arbor U, MI B
U of Northern Iowa, IA B
U of Notre Dame, IN B
Wright State U, OH B

Physics Teacher Education
Alma Coll, MI B
Bethel U, MN B
Buena Vista U, IA B
Cedarville U, OH B
Central Methodist U, MO B
Central Michigan U, MI B
Concordia Coll, MN B
Concordia U, MI B
Concordia U, Nebraska, NE B
DePaul U, IL B
Eastern Michigan U, MI B
Elmhurst Coll, IL B
Grand Valley State U, MI B
Greenville Coll, IL B
Gustavus Adolphus Coll, MN B
Hope Coll, MI B
Indiana U Bloomington, IN B
Indiana U–Purdue U Fort Wayne, IN B
Indiana U South Bend, IN B
Lincoln U, MO B
Miami U, OH B
Miami U Hamilton, OH B
Minnesota State U Moorhead, MN B
Minot State U, ND B
Missouri State U, MO B
Mount Vernon Nazarene U, OH B
North Dakota State U, ND B
Northeastern State U, OK B
Northern Michigan U, MI B
Ohio Dominican U, OH B
Ohio Northern U, OH B
Ohio Wesleyan U, OH B
Pittsburg State U, KS B
Purdue U, IN B
Saginaw Valley State U, MI B
St. Ambrose U, IA B
Saint Mary's U of Minnesota, MN B
Shawnee State U, OH B
Union Coll, NE B
U of Central Missouri, MO B
U of Evansville, IN B
U of Illinois at Chicago, IL B
U of Illinois at Urbana–Champaign, IL B
U of Michigan–Flint, MI B
U of Missouri–Columbia, MO B
U of Missouri–St. Louis, MO B
U of Nebraska–Lincoln, NE B
U of Rio Grande, OH B
The U of South Dakota, SD B
Valparaiso U, IN B
Washington U in St. Louis, MO B
Western Michigan U, MI B
William Jewell Coll, MO B
Xavier U, OH B

Physiological Psychology/ Psychobiology
Earlham Coll, IN B
Oberlin Coll, OH B
Ripon Coll, WI B
York Coll, NE B

Physiology
Michigan State U, MI B
Northern Michigan U, MI B
Oklahoma Baptist U, OK B
Oklahoma State U, OK B
Southern Illinois U Carbondale, IL B
U of Illinois at Urbana–Champaign, IL B

Piano and Organ
Andrews U, MI B
Augustana Coll, IL B
Baldwin-Wallace Coll, OH B
Bethel Coll, IN B
Bowling Green State U, OH B
Butler U, IN B
Calvary Bible Coll and Theological Seminary, MO B
Calvin Coll, MI B
Capital U, OH B
Cincinnati Christian U, OH B
Concordia U Chicago, IL B
Concordia U, Nebraska, NE B
Dordt Coll, IA B
Drake U, IA B
Grace U, NE B
Hannibal-LaGrange Coll, MO B
Heidelberg U, OH B
Hope Coll, MI B
Huntington U, IN B
Illinois Wesleyan U, IL B
Indiana U–Purdue U Fort Wayne, IN B
Kent State U, OH B
Lawrence U, WI B
Maranatha Baptist Bible Coll, WI B
Millikin U, IL B
Minnesota State U Mankato, MN B
Minnesota State U Moorhead, MN B
Northwestern Coll, MN B
Northwestern U, IL B
Northwest Missouri State U, MO B
Oakland U, MI B
Oberlin Coll, OH B
The Ohio State U, OH B
Ohio U, OH B
Oklahoma City U, OK B
Oral Roberts U, OK B
Otterbein Coll, OH B
Roosevelt U, IL B
St. Cloud State U, MN B
Southern Methodist U, TX B
Southwestern Oklahoma State U, OK B
Spring Arbor U, MI B
Trinity Christian Coll, IL B
Truman State U, MO B
U of Central Oklahoma, OK B
U of Cincinnati, OH B
The U of Iowa, IA B
The U of Kansas, KS B
U of Nebraska at Omaha, NE B
U of Tulsa, OK B
Valparaiso U, IN B

Plant Genetics
Purdue U, IN B

Plant Molecular Biology
Pittsburg State U, KS B
U of Illinois at Urbana–Champaign, IL B

Plant Pathology/ Phytopathology
Michigan State U, MI B

Plant Physiology
Pittsburg State U, KS B

Plant Protection and Integrated Pest Management
Iowa State U of Science and Technology, IA B
U of Illinois at Urbana–Champaign, IL B
U of Nebraska–Lincoln, NE B

Plant Sciences
The Ohio State U, OH B
Southeast Missouri State U, MO B
Southern Illinois U Carbondale, IL B
U of Minnesota, Twin Cities Campus, MN B
U of Missouri–Columbia, MO B

Plastics Engineering Technology
Eastern Michigan U, MI B
Ferris State U, MI A,B
Pittsburg State U, KS B
Shawnee State U, OH A,B
Western Michigan U, MI B

Playwriting and Screenwriting
DePaul U, IL B
Ohio U, OH B

Plumbing Technology
Sinte Gleska U, SD A

Polish
U of Illinois at Chicago, IL B
U of Michigan, MI B

Political Communication
Cedarville U, OH B
Nebraska Wesleyan U, NE B

Political Science and Government
Albion Coll, MI B
Alma Coll, MI B
Anderson U, IN B
Andrews U, MI B
Aquinas Coll, MI B
Ashland U, OH B
Augsburg Coll, MN B
Augustana Coll, IL B
Augustana Coll, SD B
Aurora U, IL B
Avila U, MO B
Baker U, KS B
Baldwin-Wallace Coll, OH B
Ball State U, IN B
Beloit Coll, WI B
Bemidji State U, MN B
Benedictine Coll, KS B
Benedictine U, IL B
Bethany Coll, KS B
Bethel U, MN B
Black Hills State U, SD B
Bowling Green State U, OH B
Bradley U, IL B
Briar Cliff U, IA B
Buena Vista U, IA B
Butler U, IN B
Calumet Coll of Saint Joseph, IN B
Calvin Coll, MI B
Cameron U, OK B
Capital U, OH B
Carleton Coll, MN B
Carroll U, WI B
Case Western Reserve U, OH B
Cedarville U, OH B
Central Coll, IA B
Central Methodist U, MO B
Central Michigan U, MI B
Central State U, OH B
Clarkson U, NY B
Cleveland State U, OH B
Coe Coll, IA B
Coll of Saint Benedict, MN B
Coll of the Ozarks, MO B
The Coll of Wooster, OH B
Columbia Coll, MO B
Concordia Coll, MN B
Concordia U Chicago, IL B
Cornell Coll, IA B
Creighton U, NE B
Culver-Stockton Coll, MO B
Denison U, OH B
DePaul U, IL B
DePauw U, IN B
Doane Coll, NE B
Dominican U, IL B
Dordt Coll, IA B
Drake U, IA B
Drury U, MO B
Earlham Coll, IN B
Eastern Illinois U, IL B
Eastern Michigan U, MI B
Edgewood Coll, WI B
Elmhurst Coll, IL B
Emporia State U, KS B
Eureka Coll, IL B
Evangel U, MO B
Ferris State U, MI B
Fort Hays State U, KS B
Franciscan U of Steubenville, OH B
Franklin Coll, IN B
Friends U, KS B

A—associate degree; B—bachelor's degree

Grand Valley State U, MI	B
Grand View U, IA	B
Greenville Coll, IL	B
Grinnell Coll, IA	B
Gustavus Adolphus Coll, MN	B
Hamline U, MN	B
Hanover Coll, IN	B
Heidelberg U, OH	B
Hillsdale Coll, MI	B
Hiram Coll, OH	B
Hope Coll, MI	B
Huntington U, IN	B
Illinois Coll, IL	B
Illinois Inst of Technology, IL	B
Illinois State U, IL	B
Illinois Wesleyan U, IL	B
Indiana State U, IN	B
Indiana U Bloomington, IN	B
Indiana U East, IN	B
Indiana U Northwest, IN	B
Indiana U–Purdue U Fort Wayne, IN	A,B
Indiana U–Purdue U Indianapolis, IN	B
Indiana U South Bend, IN	B
Indiana U Southeast, IN	B
Indiana Wesleyan U, IN	A,B
Iowa State U of Science and Technology, IA	B
John Carroll U, OH	B
Kalamazoo Coll, MI	B
Kansas State U, KS	B
Kent State U, OH	B
Kenyon Coll, OH	B
Knox Coll, IL	B
Lake Forest Coll, IL	B
Lake Superior State U, MI	B
Lawrence U, WI	B
Lewis U, IL	B
Lincoln U, MO	B
Lindenwood U, MO	B
Loras Coll, IA	B
Loyola U Chicago, IL	B
Luther Coll, IA	B
Macalester Coll, MN	B
MacMurray Coll, IL	B
Malone U, OH	B
Manchester Coll, IN	B
Marian U, WI	B
Marian U, IN	B
Marietta Coll, OH	B
Marquette U, WI	B
Maryville U of Saint Louis, MO	B
McKendree U, IL	B
Miami U, OH	B
Miami U Hamilton, OH	B
Michigan State U, MI	B
Millikin U, IL	B
Minnesota State U Mankato, MN	B
Minnesota State U Moorhead, MN	B
Missouri Southern State U, MO	B
Missouri State U, MO	B
Missouri Western State U, MO	B
Monmouth Coll, IL	B
Morningside Coll, IA	B
Mount Mercy Coll, IA	B
Mount Union Coll, OH	B
Muskingum Coll, OH	B
Nebraska Wesleyan U, NE	B
North Central Coll, IL	B
North Dakota State U, ND	B
Northeastern Illinois U, IL	B
Northeastern State U, OK	B
Northern Michigan U, MI	B
Northern State U, SD	B
North Park U, IL	B
Northwestern U, IL	B
Northwest Missouri State U, MO	B
Oakland U, MI	B
Oberlin Coll, OH	B
Ohio Dominican U, OH	B
Ohio Northern U, OH	B
The Ohio State U, OH	B
Ohio U, OH	B
Ohio Wesleyan U, OH	B
Oklahoma Baptist U, OK	B
Oklahoma City U, OK	B
Oklahoma State U, OK	B
Olivet Nazarene U, IL	B
Oral Roberts U, OK	B
Otterbein Coll, OH	B
Park U, MO	B
Pittsburg State U, KS	B
Purdue U, IN	B
Purdue U Calumet, IN	B
Quincy U, IL	B
Ripon Coll, WI	B
Rockford Coll, IL	B
Rockhurst U, MO	B
Roosevelt U, IL	B
Saginaw Valley State U, MI	B
St. Ambrose U, IA	B
St. Catherine U, MN	B
St. Cloud State U, MN	B
St. Gregory's U, Shawnee, OK	B
Saint John's U, MN	B
Saint Joseph's Coll, IN	B
Saint Louis U, MO	B
Saint Mary's Coll, IN	B
St. Norbert Coll, WI	B
St. Olaf Coll, MN	B
Saint Xavier U, IL	B
Simpson Coll, IA	B
South Dakota State U, SD	B
Southeastern Oklahoma State U, OK	B
Southeast Missouri State U, MO	B
Southern Illinois U Carbondale, IL	B
Southern Illinois U Edwardsville, IL	B
Southern Methodist U, TX	B
Southwest Baptist U, MO	B
Southwestern Oklahoma State U, OK	B
Southwest Minnesota State U, MN	B
Spring Arbor U, MI	B
Taylor U, IN	B
Transylvania U, KY	B
Truman State U, MO	B
U of Central Missouri, MO	B
U of Central Oklahoma, OK	B
U of Chicago, IL	B
U of Cincinnati, OH	B
U of Dallas, TX	B
U of Dayton, OH	B
U of Evansville, IN	B
The U of Findlay, OH	B
U of Illinois at Chicago, IL	B
U of Illinois at Springfield, IL	B
U of Illinois at Urbana–Champaign, IL	B
U of Indianapolis, IN	B
The U of Iowa, IA	B
The U of Kansas, KS	B
U of Michigan, MI	B
U of Michigan–Dearborn, MI	B
U of Michigan–Flint, MI	B
U of Minnesota, Duluth, MN	B
U of Minnesota, Morris, MN	B
U of Minnesota, Twin Cities Campus, MN	B
U of Missouri–Columbia, MO	B
U of Missouri–Kansas City, MO	B
U of Missouri–St. Louis, MO	B
U of Nebraska at Kearney, NE	B
U of Nebraska at Omaha, NE	B
U of Nebraska–Lincoln, NE	B
U of New Orleans, LA	B
U of North Dakota, ND	B
U of Northern Iowa, IA	B
U of Notre Dame, IN	B
U of Oklahoma, OK	B
U of Rio Grande, OH	B
U of St. Francis, IL	B
U of Saint Mary, KS	B
U of Science and Arts of Oklahoma, OK	B
U of Sioux Falls, SD	B
The U of South Dakota, SD	B
U of Southern Indiana, IN	B
The U of Toledo, OH	A,B
U of Tulsa, OK	B
U of Wisconsin–Eau Claire, WI	B
U of Wisconsin–Green Bay, WI	B
U of Wisconsin–La Crosse, WI	B
U of Wisconsin–Madison, WI	B
U of Wisconsin–Milwaukee, WI	B
U of Wisconsin–Oshkosh, WI	B
U of Wisconsin–Parkside, WI	B
U of Wisconsin–Platteville, WI	B
U of Wisconsin–Stevens Point, WI	B
U of Wisconsin–Superior, WI	B
U of Wisconsin–Whitewater, WI	B
Valparaiso U, IN	B
Wabash Coll, IN	B
Walsh U, OH	B
Wartburg Coll, IA	B
Washburn U, KS	B
Washington U in St. Louis, MO	B
Wayne State Coll, NE	B
Wayne State U, MI	B
Webster U, MO	B
Western Illinois U, IL	B
Western Michigan U, MI	B
Westminster Coll, MO	B
Wheaton Coll, IL	B
Wichita State U, KS	B
Wilberforce U, OH	B
William Jewell Coll, MO	B
Wilmington Coll, OH	B
Winona State U, MN	B
Wittenberg U, OH	B
Wright State U, OH	B
Xavier U, OH	A,B
Youngstown State U, OH	B

Political Science and Government Related

Buena Vista U, IA	B
Capital U, OH	B
Saint Mary's U of Minnesota, MN	B
U of Northern Iowa, IA	B
U of Saint Francis, IN	B

Polymer Chemistry

Pittsburg State U, KS	B
The U of Akron, OH	B
U of Wisconsin–Stevens Point, WI	B
Winona State U, MN	B

Polymer/Plastics Engineering

Case Western Reserve U, OH	B
The U of Akron, OH	B
U of Illinois at Urbana–Champaign, IL	B
U of Wisconsin–Stout, WI	B
Winona State U, MN	B

Portuguese

Indiana U Bloomington, IN	B
The Ohio State U, OH	B
U of Illinois at Urbana–Champaign, IL	B
The U of Iowa, IA	B
U of Minnesota, Twin Cities Campus, MN	B
U of Wisconsin–Madison, WI	B

Pre-Dentistry Studies

Alma Coll, MI	B
Anderson U, IN	B
Ashland U, OH	B
Augsburg Coll, MN	B
Augustana Coll, IL	B
Augustana Coll, SD	B
Ball State U, IN	B
Beloit Coll, WI	B
Calvin Coll, MI	B
Carroll U, WI	B
Cedarville U, OH	B
Central Christian Coll of Kansas, KS	B
Clarkson U, NY	B
Coe Coll, IA	B
Coll of Saint Benedict, MN	B
Coll of Saint Mary, NE	B
Concordia Coll, MN	B
Concordia U Chicago, IL	B
Concordia U, Nebraska, NE	B
Concordia U Wisconsin, WI	A
Cornerstone U, MI	B
Defiance Coll, OH	B

Dominican U, IL B
Dordt Coll, IA B
Drake U, IA B
Drury U, MO B
Elmhurst Coll, IL B
Eureka Coll, IL B
Evangel U, MO B
Graceland U, IA B
Grand Valley State U, MI B
Gustavus Adolphus Coll, MN B
Hamline U, MN B
Heidelberg U, OH B
Hillsdale Coll, MI B
Huntington U, IN B
Illinois Coll, IL B
Indiana U–Purdue U Fort Wayne, IN B
Indiana Wesleyan U, IN B
Iowa State U of Science and Technology, IA B
Iowa Wesleyan Coll, IA B
John Carroll U, OH B
Kansas Wesleyan U, KS B
Kent State U, OH B
Lake Erie Coll, OH B
Lake Superior State U, MI B
Lawrence U, WI B
Lewis U, IL B
Lindenwood U, MO B
MacMurray Coll, IL B
Manchester Coll, IN B
Marian U, IN B
Marquette U, WI B
Maryville U of Saint Louis, MO B
Mayville State U, ND B
McKendree U, IL B
Michigan Technological U, MI B
Millikin U, IL B
Minnesota State U Mankato, MN B
Minnesota State U Moorhead, MN B
Missouri U of Science and Technology, MO B
Morningside Coll, IA B
Mount Mary Coll, WI B
Mount Mercy Coll, IA B
Mount Vernon Nazarene U, OH B
Muskingum Coll, OH B
Newman U, KS B
North Central Coll, IL B
Northern Michigan U, MI B
Northern State U, SD B
North Park U, IL B
Northwest Missouri State U, MO B
Ohio Northern U, OH B
The Ohio State U, OH B
Ohio Wesleyan U, OH B
Oklahoma City U, OK B
Otterbein Coll, OH B
Pittsburg State U, KS B
Purdue U, IN B
Purdue U Calumet, IN B
Ripon Coll, WI B
Rockford Coll, IL B
St. Catherine U, MN B
St. Cloud State U, MN B
St. Gregory's U, Shawnee, OK B
Saint John's U, MN B
Saint Mary-of-the-Woods Coll, IN B
Simpson Coll, IA B
Southwestern Oklahoma State U, OK B
Southwest Minnesota State U, MN B
Trinity Christian Coll, IL B
Truman State U, MO B
U of Central Missouri, MO B
U of Dallas, TX B
U of Dayton, OH B
U of Evansville, IN B
U of Illinois at Chicago, IL B
U of Indianapolis, IN B
The U of Iowa, IA B
U of Minnesota, Duluth, MN B
U of Minnesota, Morris, MN B
U of Minnesota, Twin Cities Campus, MN B
U of Missouri–St. Louis, MO B
U of Nebraska–Lincoln, NE B
U of Rio Grande, OH B
U of St. Francis, IL B
U of Sioux Falls, SD B
The U of Toledo, OH B
U of Wisconsin–Milwaukee, WI B
U of Wisconsin–Oshkosh, WI B
U of Wisconsin–Parkside, WI B
Valley City State U, ND B
Walsh U, OH B
Washburn U, KS B
Washington U in St. Louis, MO B
Wilmington Coll, OH B
Winona State U, MN B
Wright State U, OH B
Youngstown State U, OH B

Pre-Engineering

Drake U, IA B
Ferris State U, MI A
Lewis U, IL B
Lincoln U, MO A
Marian U, IN A
Maryville U of Saint Louis, MO B
Minnesota State U Mankato, MN A
Newman U, KS A,B
Northern State U, SD A
Oklahoma State U, Oklahoma City, OK A
Pittsburg State U, KS B
Shawnee State U, OH A
Siena Heights U, MI A
Simpson Coll, IA B
Valley City State U, ND B

Pre-Law

Maryville U of Saint Louis, MO B

Pre-Law Studies

Adrian Coll, MI B
Albion Coll, MI B
Alma Coll, MI B
Anderson U, IN B
Andrews U, MI B
Aquinas Coll, MI B
Ashland U, OH B
Augsburg Coll, MN B
Augustana Coll, IL B
Augustana Coll, SD B
Beloit Coll, WI B
Bemidji State U, MN B
Bethel Coll, IN B
Bowling Green State U, OH B
Calumet Coll of Saint Joseph, IN A,B
Calvin Coll, MI B
Cedarville U, OH B
Central Christian Coll of Kansas, KS B
Clarkson U, NY B
Coe Coll, IA B
Coll of Saint Benedict, MN B
Coll of Saint Mary, NE B
Coll of the Ozarks, MO B
Concordia Coll, MN B
Concordia U, MI B
Concordia U Chicago, IL B
Concordia U, Nebraska, NE B
Concordia U Wisconsin, WI B
Creighton U, NE B
Crown Coll, MN B
Defiance Coll, OH B
Dominican U, IL B
Dordt Coll, IA B
Drake U, IA B
Drury U, MO B
Elmhurst Coll, IL B
Eureka Coll, IL B
Evangel U, MO B
Ferris State U, MI A
Fontbonne U, MO B
Fort Hays State U, KS B
Graceland U, IA B
Grand View U, IA B
Gustavus Adolphus Coll, MN B
Hamline U, MN B
Hannibal-LaGrange Coll, MO B
Heidelberg U, OH B
Huntington U, IN B
Illinois Coll, IL B
Indiana Wesleyan U, IN B
Iowa State U of Science and Technology, IA B
Iowa Wesleyan Coll, IA B
John Carroll U, OH B
Kansas Wesleyan U, KS B
Lake Erie Coll, OH B
Lake Superior State U, MI B
Lawrence U, WI B
Lewis U, IL B
Lindenwood U, MO B
MacMurray Coll, IL B
Manchester Coll, IN B
Marian U, IN B
Marquette U, WI B
Mayville State U, ND B
McKendree U, IL B
Michigan Technological U, MI B
Millikin U, IL B
Minnesota State U Mankato, MN B
Minnesota State U Moorhead, MN B
Missouri U of Science and Technology, MO B
Morningside Coll, IA B
Mount Mary Coll, WI B
Mount Mercy Coll, IA B
Mount Vernon Nazarene U, OH B
Muskingum Coll, OH B
Newman U, KS B
North Central Coll, IL B
Northern Michigan U, MI B
Northern State U, SD B
North Park U, IL B
Northwest Missouri State U, MO B
Ohio Northern U, OH B
Ohio U, OH B
Ohio Wesleyan U, OH B
Oklahoma Christian U, OK B
Oklahoma City U, OK B
Otterbein Coll, OH B
Pittsburg State U, KS B
Purdue U Calumet, IN B
Ripon Coll, WI B
Rockford Coll, IL B
St. Catherine U, MN B
St. Cloud State U, MN B
St. Gregory's U, Shawnee, OK B
Saint John's U, MN B
Saint Mary-of-the-Woods Coll, IN B
Shawnee State U, OH B
Siena Heights U, MI B
Simpson Coll, IA B
Southwestern Oklahoma State U, OK B
Southwest Minnesota State U, MN B
Stephens Coll, MO B
Trine U, IN B
Truman State U, MO B
U of Cincinnati, OH B
U of Dallas, TX B
U of Dayton, OH B
The U of Findlay, OH B
U of Illinois at Urbana–Champaign, IL B
U of Indianapolis, IN B
The U of Iowa, IA B
U of Minnesota, Duluth, MN B
U of Minnesota, Morris, MN B
U of Minnesota, Twin Cities Campus, MN B
U of Missouri–St. Louis, MO B
U of Rio Grande, OH B
U of Sioux Falls, SD B
The U of Toledo, OH B
U of Wisconsin–Milwaukee, WI B
U of Wisconsin–Oshkosh, WI B
U of Wisconsin–Parkside, WI B
U of Wisconsin–Superior, WI B
Valley City State U, ND B
Wabash Coll, IN B
Washburn U, KS B
Westminster Coll, MO B
Wilmington Coll, OH B

A—associate degree; B—bachelor's degree

Winona State U, MN B
Wright State U, OH B
Youngstown State U, OH B

Premedical Studies

Adrian Coll, MI B
Albion Coll, MI B
Alma Coll, MI B
Anderson U, IN B
Andrews U, MI B
Ashland U, OH B
Augsburg Coll, MN B
Augustana Coll, IL B
Augustana Coll, SD B
Ball State U, IN B
Beloit Coll, WI B
Bemidji State U, MN B
Bethel Coll, IN B
Bluffton U, OH B
Calvin Coll, MI B
Carroll U, WI B
Cedarville U, OH B
Central Christian Coll of Kansas, KS B
Clarkson U, NY B
Coe Coll, IA B
Coll of Saint Benedict, MN B
Coll of Saint Mary, NE B
Coll of the Ozarks, MO B
Concordia Coll, MN B
Concordia U, MI B
Concordia U Chicago, IL B
Concordia U, Nebraska, NE B
Concordia U Wisconsin, WI A
Cornerstone U, MI B
Defiance Coll, OH B
Dominican U, IL B
Dordt Coll, IA B
Drake U, IA B
Drury U, MO B
Earlham Coll, IN B
Elmhurst Coll, IL B
Eureka Coll, IL B
Evangel U, MO B
Graceland U, IA B
Grand Valley State U, MI B
Gustavus Adolphus Coll, MN B
Hamline U, MN B
Heidelberg U, OH B
Hillsdale Coll, MI B
Huntington U, IN B
Illinois Coll, IL B
Indiana U–Purdue U Fort Wayne, IN B
Indiana Wesleyan U, IN B
Iowa State U of Science and Technology, IA B
Iowa Wesleyan Coll, IA B
John Carroll U, OH B
Kansas Wesleyan U, KS B
Kent State U, OH B
Lake Erie Coll, OH B
Lawrence U, WI B
Lewis U, IL B
Lindenwood U, MO B
MacMurray Coll, IL B
Manchester Coll, IN B
Marian U, IN B
Marquette U, WI B
Maryville U of Saint Louis, MO B
Mayville State U, ND B
McKendree U, IL B
Michigan Technological U, MI B
Millikin U, IL B
Minnesota State U Mankato, MN B
Minnesota State U Moorhead, MN B
Missouri U of Science and Technology, MO B
Morningside Coll, IA B
Mount Mary Coll, WI B
Mount Mercy Coll, IA B
Mount Vernon Nazarene U, OH B
Muskingum Coll, OH B
Newman U, KS B
North Central Coll, IL B
Northern Michigan U, MI B
Northern State U, SD B
North Park U, IL B
Northwestern U, IL B
Northwest Missouri State U, MO B
Ohio Northern U, OH B
Ohio Wesleyan U, OH B
Oklahoma City U, OK B
Otterbein Coll, OH B
Pittsburg State U, KS B
Purdue U, IN B
Purdue U Calumet, IN B
Ripon Coll, WI B
Rochester Comm and Tech Coll, MN A
Rockford Coll, IL B
St. Catherine U, MN B
St. Cloud State U, MN B
St. Gregory's U, Shawnee, OK B
Saint John's U, MN B
Saint Mary-of-the-Woods Coll, IN B
Shawnee State U, OH B
Simpson Coll, IA B
Southwestern Oklahoma State U, OK B
Southwest Minnesota State U, MN B
Trine U, IN B
Trinity Christian Coll, IL B
Trinity International U, IL B
Truman State U, MO B
U of Central Missouri, MO B
U of Cincinnati, OH B
U of Dallas, TX B
U of Dayton, OH B
U of Evansville, IN B
The U of Findlay, OH B
U of Indianapolis, IN B
The U of Iowa, IA B
U of Minnesota, Duluth, MN B
U of Minnesota, Morris, MN B
U of Minnesota, Twin Cities Campus, MN B
U of Missouri–St. Louis, MO B
U of Nebraska–Lincoln, NE B
U of Notre Dame, IN B
U of Rio Grande, OH B
U of St. Francis, IL B
U of Sioux Falls, SD B
The U of Toledo, OH B
U of Wisconsin–Milwaukee, WI B
U of Wisconsin–Oshkosh, WI B
U of Wisconsin–Parkside, WI B
Valley City State U, ND B
Wabash Coll, IN B
Walsh U, OH B
Washburn U, KS B
Washington U in St. Louis, MO B
Wilmington Coll, OH B
Winona State U, MN B
Wright State U, OH B
Youngstown State U, OH B

Prenursing Studies

Cleveland State U, OH B
Concordia U, MI B
Concordia U, Nebraska, NE B
Concordia U Wisconsin, WI A
Dordt Coll, IA B
Lindenwood U, MO B
Missouri U of Science and Technology, MO B
Oklahoma City U, OK B
Oklahoma State U, Oklahoma City, OK A
St. Gregory's U, Shawnee, OK B
Trinity International U, IL A

Pre-Pharmacy Studies

Ashland U, OH B
Benedictine U, IL B
Carroll U, WI B
Central Christian Coll of Kansas, KS B
Coll of Saint Benedict, MN B
Coll of the Ozarks, MO B
Concordia U, Nebraska, NE B
Dordt Coll, IA B
Drury U, MO B
Elmhurst Coll, IL B
Ferris State U, MI A
Iowa Wesleyan Coll, IA B
Lewis U, IL B
Madonna U, MI A
Mayville State U, ND B
Michigan Technological U, MI B
Millikin U, IL B
Mount Vernon Nazarene U, OH B
Muskingum Coll, OH B
Northern Michigan U, MI B
Oklahoma City U, OK B
Pittsburg State U, KS B
St. Cloud State U, MN B
St. Gregory's U, Shawnee, OK B
Saint John's U, MN B
Saint Mary-of-the-Woods Coll, IN B
Simpson Coll, IA B
Truman State U, MO B
U of Central Missouri, MO B
U of Charleston, WV B
U of Evansville, IN B
The U of Iowa, IA B
U of Minnesota, Duluth, MN B
U of Minnesota, Morris, MN B
U of Missouri–St. Louis, MO B
U of Nebraska–Lincoln, NE B
U of Saint Francis, IN B
U of Wisconsin–Parkside, WI B
Valley City State U, ND B
Washburn U, KS B
Washington U in St. Louis, MO B
Wright State U, OH B
Youngstown State U, OH B

Pre-Theology/Pre-Ministerial Studies

Adrian Coll, MI B
Alma Coll, MI B
Ashland U, OH B
Central Christian Coll of Kansas, KS B
Coll of Saint Benedict, MN B
Concordia Coll, MN B
Concordia U, MI B
Concordia U Chicago, IL B
Concordia U, Nebraska, NE B
Cornerstone U, MI B
Crossroads Coll, MN B
Emmaus Bible Coll, IA B
Grace U, NE B
Kuyper Coll, MI B
Loras Coll, IA B
Manchester Coll, IN A
Martin Luther Coll, MN B
Minnesota State U Mankato, MN B
Northwestern Coll, MN B
Ohio Northern U, OH B
Ohio Wesleyan U, OH B
Saint John's U, MN B
Simpson Coll, IA B
Trinity Christian Coll, IL B
Trinity International U, IL B
U of Dallas, TX B
U of Indianapolis, IN B
U of Rio Grande, OH B
Washburn U, KS B

Pre-Veterinary Studies

Adrian Coll, MI B
Albion Coll, MI B
Alma Coll, MI B
Anderson U, IN B
Andrews U, MI B
Ashland U, OH B
Augsburg Coll, MN B
Augustana Coll, IL B
Augustana Coll, SD B
Bemidji State U, MN B
Calvin Coll, MI B
Carroll U, WI B
Cedarville U, OH B
Central Christian Coll of Kansas, KS B
Clarkson U, NY B
Coe Coll, IA B
Coll of Saint Benedict, MN B
Coll of Saint Mary, NE B
Coll of the Ozarks, MO B
Concordia Coll, MN B
Concordia U, Nebraska, NE B
Cornerstone U, MI B
Defiance Coll, OH B
Dominican U, IL B
Dordt Coll, IA B
Drake U, IA B
Drury U, MO B

Elmhurst Coll, IL B
Eureka Coll, IL B
Evangel U, MO B
Grand Valley State U, MI B
Gustavus Adolphus Coll, MN B
Hamline U, MN B
Heidelberg U, OH B
Hillsdale Coll, MI B
Huntington U, IN B
Illinois Coll, IL B
Indiana U–Purdue U Fort Wayne, IN B
Indiana Wesleyan U, IN B
Iowa State U of Science and Technology, IA B
Iowa Wesleyan Coll, IA B
John Carroll U, OH B
Kansas Wesleyan U, KS B
Lake Erie Coll, OH B
Lawrence U, WI B
Lewis U, IL B
Lindenwood U, MO B
MacMurray Coll, IL B
Manchester Coll, IN B
Marian U, IN B
Mayville State U, ND B
McKendree U, IL B
Michigan Technological U, MI B
Millikin U, IL B
Minnesota State U Mankato, MN B
Minnesota State U Moorhead, MN B
Missouri U of Science and Technology, MO B
Morningside Coll, IA B
Mount Mary Coll, WI B
Mount Mercy Coll, IA B
Mount Vernon Nazarene U, OH B
Muskingum Coll, OH B
Newman U, KS B
North Central Coll, IL B
Northern Michigan U, MI B
North Park U, IL B
Northwest Missouri State U, MO B
Ohio Northern U, OH B
Ohio Wesleyan U, OH B
Oklahoma City U, OK B
Otterbein Coll, OH B
Pittsburg State U, KS B
Purdue U Calumet, IN B
Ripon Coll, WI B
Rockford Coll, IL B
St. Catherine U, MN B
St. Cloud State U, MN B
Saint John's U, MN B
Saint Mary-of-the-Woods Coll, IN B
Shawnee State U, OH A
Simpson Coll, IA B
Southwestern Oklahoma State U, OK B
Southwest Minnesota State U, MN B
Trine U, IN B
Trinity Christian Coll, IL B
Truman State U, MO B
U of Central Missouri, MO B
U of Cincinnati, OH B
U of Evansville, IN B
The U of Findlay, OH B
U of Illinois at Urbana–Champaign, IL B
U of Indianapolis, IN B
The U of Iowa, IA B
U of Minnesota, Crookston, MN B
U of Minnesota, Duluth, MN B
U of Minnesota, Morris, MN B
U of Minnesota, Twin Cities Campus, MN B
U of Missouri–St. Louis, MO B
U of Nebraska–Lincoln, NE B
U of Rio Grande, OH B
U of St. Francis, IL B
U of Sioux Falls, SD B
The U of Toledo, OH B
U of Wisconsin–Oshkosh, WI B
U of Wisconsin–Parkside, WI B
Valley City State U, ND B
Wabash Coll, IN B
Walsh U, OH B
Washburn U, KS B
Washington U in St. Louis, MO B
Wilmington Coll, OH B
Winona State U, MN B
Wright State U, OH B
Youngstown State U, OH B

Printing Management
Carroll U, WI B
Ferris State U, MI B
U of Central Missouri, MO B
U of Wisconsin–Stout, WI B

Printmaking
Aquinas Coll, MI B
Art Academy of Cincinnati, OH B
Bradley U, IL B
The Cleveland Inst of Art, OH B
Coll of Visual Arts, MN B
Columbia Coll, MO B
Drake U, IA B
Indiana U–Purdue U Fort Wayne, IN B
Indiana Wesleyan U, IN B
Kansas City Art Inst, MO B
Kent State U, OH B
Minneapolis Coll of Art and Design, MN B
Minnesota State U Moorhead, MN B
Northern Michigan U, MI B
Ohio Northern U, OH B
Ohio U, OH B
St. Cloud State U, MN B
Trinity Christian Coll, IL B
U of Dallas, TX B
The U of Iowa, IA B
The U of Kansas, KS B
U of Michigan, MI B
U of Missouri–St. Louis, MO B
Washington U in St. Louis, MO B

Professional Studies
Bemidji State U, MN B
Briar Cliff U, IA B
Kent State U, OH B
Ohio Christian U, OH A,B
Saint Mary-of-the-Woods Coll, IN B

Psychiatric/Mental Health Services Technology
Franciscan U of Steubenville, OH B
Indiana U–Purdue U Fort Wayne, IN B
Lake Superior State U, MI A
Rochester Comm and Tech Coll, MN A
The U of Toledo, OH A

Psychoanalysis and Psychotherapy
St. Cloud State U, MN A

Psychology
Adrian Coll, MI B
Albion Coll, MI B
Alma Coll, MI B
Anderson U, IN B
Andrews U, MI B
Aquinas Coll, MI B
Argosy U, Chicago, IL B
Argosy U, Schaumburg, IL B
Argosy U, Twin Cities, MN B
Ashland U, OH B
Augsburg Coll, MN B
Augustana Coll, IL B
Augustana Coll, SD B
Aurora U, IL B
Avila U, MO B
Baker U, KS B
Baldwin-Wallace Coll, OH B
Ball State U, IN B
Barclay Coll, KS B
Beloit Coll, WI B
Bemidji State U, MN B
Benedictine Coll, KS B
Benedictine U, IL B
Bethany Coll, KS B
Bethany Lutheran Coll, MN B
Bethel Coll, IN B
Bethel Coll, KS B
Bethel U, MN B
Black Hills State U, SD B
Bluffton U, OH B
Bowling Green State U, OH B
Bradley U, IL B
Briar Cliff U, IA B
Buena Vista U, IA B
Butler U, IN B
Calumet Coll of Saint Joseph, IN B
Calvin Coll, MI B
Cameron U, OK B
Capital U, OH B
Carleton Coll, MN B
Carroll U, WI B
Case Western Reserve U, OH B
Cedarville U, OH B
Central Christian Coll of Kansas, KS B
Central Coll, IA B
Central Methodist U, MO A,B
Central Michigan U, MI B
Central State U, OH B
Cincinnati Christian U, OH B
Clarke Coll, IA B
Clarkson U, NY B
Cleveland State U, OH B
Coe Coll, IA B
Coll of Mount St. Joseph, OH B
Coll of Saint Benedict, MN B
Coll of Saint Mary, NE B
The Coll of St. Scholastica, MN B
Coll of the Ozarks, MO B
The Coll of Wooster, OH B
Columbia Coll, MO B
Concordia Coll, MN B
Concordia U, MI B
Concordia U Chicago, IL B
Concordia U, Nebraska, NE B
Concordia U, St. Paul, MN B
Concordia U Wisconsin, WI B
Cornell Coll, IA B
Cornerstone U, MI B
Creighton U, NE B
Culver-Stockton Coll, MO B
Dakota Wesleyan U, SD B
Dana Coll, NE B
Defiance Coll, OH B
Denison U, OH B
DePaul U, IL B
DePauw U, IN B
Doane Coll, NE B
Dominican U, IL B
Dordt Coll, IA B
Drake U, IA B
Drury U, MO B
Earlham Coll, IN B
Eastern Illinois U, IL B
Eastern Michigan U, MI B
Edgewood Coll, WI B
Elmhurst Coll, IL B
Emporia State U, KS B
Eureka Coll, IL B
Evangel U, MO B
Ferris State U, MI A,B
Fontbonne U, MO B
Fort Hays State U, KS B
Franciscan U of Steubenville, OH B
Franklin Coll, IN B
Friends U, KS B
Goshen Coll, IN B
Grace Coll, IN B
Graceland U, IA B
Grace U, NE B
Grand Valley State U, MI B
Grand View U, IA B
Greenville Coll, IL B
Grinnell Coll, IA B
Gustavus Adolphus Coll, MN B
Hamline U, MN B
Hannibal-LaGrange Coll, MO B
Hanover Coll, IN B
Heidelberg U, OH B
Hillsdale Coll, MI B
Hiram Coll, OH B
Hope Coll, MI B
Huntington U, IN B

A—associate degree; B—bachelor's degree

Illinois Coll, IL B
Illinois Inst of Technology, IL B
Illinois State U, IL B
Illinois Wesleyan U, IL B
Indiana State U, IN B
Indiana Tech, IN B
Indiana U Bloomington, IN B
Indiana U East, IN B
Indiana U Kokomo, IN B
Indiana U Northwest, IN B
Indiana U–Purdue U Fort Wayne, IN A,B
Indiana U–Purdue U Indianapolis, IN B
Indiana U South Bend, IN B
Indiana U Southeast, IN B
Indiana Wesleyan U, IN B
Iowa State U of Science and Technology, IA B
Iowa Wesleyan Coll, IA B
Jamestown Coll, ND B
John Carroll U, OH B
Kalamazoo Coll, MI B
Kansas State U, KS B
Kansas Wesleyan U, KS B
Kent State U, OH B
Kent State U, Stark Campus, OH B
Kenyon Coll, OH B
Knox Coll, IL B
Lake Erie Coll, OH B
Lake Forest Coll, IL B
Lakeland Coll, WI B
Lake Superior State U, MI B
Lawrence Technological U, MI B
Lawrence U, WI B
Lewis U, IL B
Lincoln U, MO B
Lindenwood U, MO B
Loras Coll, IA B
Lourdes Coll, OH B
Loyola U Chicago, IL B
Luther Coll, IA B
Macalester Coll, MN B
MacMurray Coll, IL B
Madonna U, MI B
Malone U, OH B
Manchester Coll, IN B
Marian U, WI B
Marian U, IN A,B
Marietta Coll, OH B
Marquette U, WI B
Martin U, IN B
Maryville U of Saint Louis, MO B
McKendree U, IL B
McPherson Coll, KS B
Miami U, OH B
Miami U Hamilton, OH B
Michigan State U, MI B
Michigan Technological U, MI B
MidAmerica Nazarene U, KS B
Millikin U, IL B
Minnesota State U Mankato, MN B
Minnesota State U Moorhead, MN B
Minot State U, ND B
Missouri Baptist U, MO B
Missouri State U, MO B
Missouri U of Science and Technology, MO B
Missouri Western State U, MO B
Monmouth Coll, IL B
Morningside Coll, IA B
Mount Marty Coll, SD B
Mount Mary Coll, WI B
Mount Mercy Coll, IA B
Mount Union Coll, OH B
Mount Vernon Nazarene U, OH B
Muskingum Coll, OH B
National-Louis U, IL B
Nebraska Wesleyan U, NE B
Newman U, KS B
North Central Coll, IL B
North Central U, MN A,B
North Dakota State U, ND B
Northeastern Illinois U, IL B
Northeastern State U, OK B
Northern Michigan U, MI B
Northern State U, SD B
North Park U, IL B
Northwestern Coll, MN B
Northwestern U, IL B
Northwest Missouri State U, MO B
Oakland U, MI B
Oberlin Coll, OH B
Ohio Christian U, OH B
Ohio Dominican U, OH B
Ohio Northern U, OH B
The Ohio State U, OH B
The Ohio State U at Lima, OH B
The Ohio State U at Marion, OH B
The Ohio State U–Mansfield Campus, OH B
The Ohio State U–Newark Campus, OH B
Ohio U, OH B
Ohio Wesleyan U, OH B
Oklahoma Baptist U, OK B
Oklahoma Christian U, OK B
Oklahoma City U, OK B
Oklahoma Panhandle State U, OK B
Oklahoma State U, OK B
Oklahoma State U, Oklahoma City, OK A
Olivet Coll, MI B
Olivet Nazarene U, IL B
Oral Roberts U, OK B
Otterbein Coll, OH B
Park U, MO B
Pittsburg State U, KS B
Purdue U, IN B
Purdue U Calumet, IN B
Quincy U, IL B
Ripon Coll, WI B
Rockford Coll, IL B
Rockhurst U, MO B
Roosevelt U, IL B
Saginaw Valley State U, MI B
St. Ambrose U, IA B
St. Catherine U, MN B
St. Cloud State U, MN B
St. Gregory's U, Shawnee, OK B
Saint John's U, MN B
Saint Joseph's Coll, IN B
Saint Louis U, MO B
Saint Mary-of-the-Woods Coll, IN B
Saint Mary's Coll, IN B
Saint Mary's U of Minnesota, MN B
St. Norbert Coll, WI B
St. Olaf Coll, MN B
Saint Xavier U, IL B
Shawnee State U, OH B
Siena Heights U, MI A,B
Silver Lake Coll, WI B
Simpson Coll, IA B
South Dakota State U, SD B
Southeastern Oklahoma State U, OK B
Southeast Missouri State U, MO B
Southern Illinois U Carbondale, IL B
Southern Illinois U Edwardsville, IL B
Southern Methodist U, TX B
Southern Nazarene U, OK B
Southwest Baptist U, MO B
Southwestern Coll, KS B
Southwestern Oklahoma State U, OK B
Southwest Minnesota State U, MN B
Spring Arbor U, MI B
Stephens Coll, MO B
Taylor U, IN B
Tiffin U, OH B
Transylvania U, KY B
Trine U, IN B
Trinity Christian Coll, IL B
Trinity International U, IL B
Truman State U, MO B
Union Coll, NE B
Union Inst & U, OH B
The U of Akron, OH B
U of Central Missouri, MO B
U of Central Oklahoma, OK B
U of Charleston, WV B
U of Chicago, IL B
U of Cincinnati, OH B
U of Dallas, TX B
U of Dayton, OH B
U of Evansville, IN B
The U of Findlay, OH B
U of Illinois at Chicago, IL B
U of Illinois at Springfield, IL B
U of Illinois at Urbana–Champaign, IL B
U of Indianapolis, IN B
The U of Iowa, IA B
The U of Kansas, KS B
U of Mary, ND B
U of Michigan, MI B
U of Michigan–Dearborn, MI B
U of Michigan–Flint, MI B
U of Minnesota, Duluth, MN B
U of Minnesota, Morris, MN B
U of Minnesota, Twin Cities Campus, MN B
U of Missouri–Columbia, MO B
U of Missouri–Kansas City, MO B
U of Missouri–St. Louis, MO B
U of Nebraska at Kearney, NE B
U of Nebraska at Omaha, NE B
U of Nebraska–Lincoln, NE B
U of New Orleans, LA B
U of North Dakota, ND B
U of Northern Iowa, IA B
U of Notre Dame, IN B
U of Oklahoma, OK B
U of Phoenix–Cleveland Campus, OH B
U of Phoenix–Indianapolis Campus, IN B
U of Phoenix–Oklahoma City Campus, OK B
U of Phoenix–St. Louis Campus, MO B
U of Phoenix–Springfield Campus, MO B
U of Phoenix–Tulsa Campus, OK B
U of Rio Grande, OH A
U of St. Francis, IL B
U of Saint Francis, IN B
U of Saint Mary, KS B
U of Science and Arts of Oklahoma, OK B
U of Sioux Falls, SD B
The U of South Dakota, SD B
U of Southern Indiana, IN B
The U of Toledo, OH B
U of Tulsa, OK B
U of Wisconsin–Eau Claire, WI B
U of Wisconsin–Green Bay, WI B
U of Wisconsin–La Crosse, WI B
U of Wisconsin–Madison, WI B
U of Wisconsin–Milwaukee, WI B
U of Wisconsin–Oshkosh, WI B
U of Wisconsin–Parkside, WI B
U of Wisconsin–Platteville, WI B
U of Wisconsin–Stevens Point, WI B
U of Wisconsin–Stout, WI B
U of Wisconsin–Superior, WI B
U of Wisconsin–Whitewater, WI B
Ursuline Coll, OH B
Valley City State U, ND B
Valparaiso U, IN B
Viterbo U, WI B
Wabash Coll, IN B
Waldorf Coll, IA B
Walsh U, OH B
Wartburg Coll, IA B
Washburn U, KS B
Washington U in St. Louis, MO B
Wayne State Coll, NE B
Wayne State U, MI B
Webster U, MO B
Western Illinois U, IL B
Western Michigan U, MI B
Westminster Coll, MO B

Wheaton Coll, IL B
Wichita State U, KS B
Wilberforce U, OH B
William Jewell Coll, MO B
Wilmington Coll, OH B
Winona State U, MN B
Wittenberg U, OH B
Wright State U, OH A,B
Xavier U, OH A,B
York Coll, NE B
Youngstown State U, OH B

Psychology Related

Buena Vista U, IA B
Cedarville U, OH B
Loyola U Chicago, IL B
Madonna U, MI B
Mayville State U, ND B
Ohio Northern U, OH B
U of Michigan, MI B
U of Michigan–Flint, MI B
The U of Toledo, OH B

Psychology Teacher Education

Alma Coll, MI B
Carroll U, WI B
Central Christian Coll of Kansas, KS A
Concordia U, MI B
Ohio Wesleyan U, OH B
Pittsburg State U, KS B
St. Ambrose U, IA B
Shawnee State U, OH B
U of Michigan–Flint, MI B
U of Missouri–St. Louis, MO B
Valparaiso U, IN B
Wayne State Coll, NE B
York Coll, NE B

Psychometrics and Quantitative Psychology

North Dakota State U, ND B

Public Administration

Augustana Coll, IL B
Bowling Green State U, OH B
Buena Vista U, IA B
Calvin Coll, MI B
Capital U, OH B
Cedarville U, OH B
Central Methodist U, MO A,B
Chancellor U, OH A,B
Cleveland State U, OH B
Doane Coll, NE B
Eastern Michigan U, MI B
Evangel U, MO B
Ferris State U, MI B
Franklin U, OH B
Grand Valley State U, MI B
Hamline U, MN B
Harris-Stowe State U, MO B
Heidelberg U, OH B
Indiana U Bloomington, IN A,B
Indiana U East, IN B
Indiana U Kokomo, IN B
Indiana U Northwest, IN A,B
Indiana U–Purdue U Fort Wayne, IN A,B
Indiana U–Purdue U Indianapolis, IN A,B
Indiana U South Bend, IN B
Iowa State U of Science and Technology, IA B
John Carroll U, OH B
Lewis U, IL B
Lincoln U, MO B
Loyola U Chicago, IL B
Miami U, OH B
Miami U Hamilton, OH B
Michigan State U, MI B
Minnesota State U Mankato, MN B
Missouri State U, MO B
Northern Michigan U, MI B
Northern State U, SD B
Northland Coll, WI B
Northwest Missouri State U, MO B
Oakland U, MI B
Ohio Wesleyan U, OH B
Park U, MO B
Roosevelt U, IL B
Saginaw Valley State U, MI B
St. Ambrose U, IA B
St. Cloud State U, MN B
Siena Heights U, MI B
Southwest Minnesota State U, MN B
Union Inst & U, OH B
The U of Kansas, KS B
U of Michigan–Flint, MI B
U of Missouri–St. Louis, MO B
U of North Dakota, ND B
U of Northern Iowa, IA B
U of Oklahoma, OK B
U of Phoenix–Cleveland Campus, OH B
U of Phoenix–Indianapolis Campus, IN B
U of Phoenix–Kansas City Campus, MO B
U of Phoenix–Metro Detroit Campus, MI B
U of Phoenix–St. Louis Campus, MO B
U of Wisconsin–Green Bay, WI B
U of Wisconsin–La Crosse, WI B
U of Wisconsin–Stevens Point, WI B
U of Wisconsin–Whitewater, WI B
Washburn U, KS B
Wayne State U, MI B
Winona State U, MN B
Wright State U, OH B

Public Administration and Social Service Professions Related

Eastern Michigan U, MI B
Northeastern Illinois U, IL B
Ohio U, OH B
Oklahoma State U, Oklahoma City, OK A
The U of Akron, OH A
U of Phoenix–Kansas City Campus, MO B
U of Phoenix–West Michigan Campus, MI B

Public/Applied History and Archival Administration

North Dakota State U, ND B
Western Michigan U, MI B

Public Health

Alma Coll, MI B
Indiana U Bloomington, IN B
Maryville U of Saint Louis, MO B
Minnesota State U Mankato, MN B
Truman State U, MO B
U of Cincinnati, OH B
U of Minnesota, Twin Cities Campus, MN B
Winona State U, MN B

Public Health/Community Nursing

Capital U, OH B
Wright State U, OH B

Public Health Education and Promotion

Central Michigan U, MI B
Malone U, OH B
Oklahoma State U, OK B
U of Michigan–Flint, MI B
The U of Toledo, OH B
U of Wisconsin–La Crosse, WI B

Public Health Related

Indiana U Bloomington, IN B
Indiana U–Purdue U Indianapolis, IN B
U of Illinois at Urbana–Champaign, IL B

Public Policy Analysis

Albion Coll, MI B
DePaul U, IL B
Indiana U Bloomington, IN A,B
Indiana U–Purdue U Fort Wayne, IN B
Muskingum Coll, OH B
Northwestern U, IL B
Olivet Nazarene U, IL B
St. Cloud State U, MN B
Southern Methodist U, TX B
U of Charleston, WV B
U of Chicago, IL B
U of Cincinnati, OH B
The U of Toledo, OH B
U of Wisconsin–Whitewater, WI B

Public Relations

Southern Methodist U, TX B

Public Relations, Advertising, and Applied Communication Related

Buena Vista U, IA B
Carroll U, WI B
The Coll of St. Scholastica, MN B
Marietta Coll, OH B
Pittsburg State U, KS B
Saint Mary's U of Minnesota, MN B
Spring Arbor U, MI B
Western Michigan U, MI B

Public Relations/Image Management

Andrews U, MI B
Avila U, MO B
Baldwin-Wallace Coll, OH B
Bowling Green State U, OH B
Bradley U, IL B
Capital U, OH B
Carroll U, WI B
Central Michigan U, MI B
Clarke Coll, IA B
Cleveland State U, OH B
Coe Coll, IA B
Coll of the Ozarks, MO B
Concordia Coll, MN B
Drake U, IA B
Drury U, MO B
Eastern Michigan U, MI B
Ferris State U, MI B
Fort Hays State U, KS B
Goshen Coll, IN B
Greenville Coll, IL B
Heidelberg U, OH B
Huntington U, IN B
Illinois State U, IL B
Kent State U, OH B
Lewis U, IL B
Lindenwood U, MO B
Loras Coll, IA B
Marquette U, WI B
McKendree U, IL B
McPherson Coll, KS B
Miami U, OH B
MidAmerica Nazarene U, KS B
Minnesota State U Mankato, MN B
Minnesota State U Moorhead, MN B
Monmouth Coll, IL B
Mount Mary Coll, WI B
Mount Mercy Coll, IA B
Mount Vernon Nazarene U, OH B
North Dakota State U, ND B
Northeastern State U, OK B
Northern Michigan U, MI B
Northwestern Coll, MN B
Northwest Missouri State U, MO B
Ohio Dominican U, OH B
Ohio U, OH B
Ohio U–Zanesville, OH B
Oklahoma Christian U, OK B
Oklahoma City U, OK B
Otterbein Coll, OH B
Purdue U, IN B
Purdue U Calumet, IN B
Roosevelt U, IL B
St. Ambrose U, IA B
St. Cloud State U, MN B
Southern Methodist U, TX B
Stephens Coll, MO B
Tiffin U, OH B
Union Coll, NE B
The U of Akron, OH B
U of Central Missouri, MO B
U of Central Oklahoma, OK B
U of Dayton, OH B
The U of Findlay, OH B
U of Mary, ND B
U of Northern Iowa, IA B

A—associate degree; B—bachelor's degree

U of Rio Grande, OH B
U of Southern Indiana, IN B
U of Wisconsin–Madison, WI B
Ursuline Coll, OH B
Valparaiso U, IN B
Wartburg Coll, IA B
Wayne State U, MI B
Webster U, MO B
Winona State U, MN B
Xavier U, OH A,B

Publishing
Graceland U, IA B
Saint Mary's U of Minnesota, MN B
U of Missouri–Columbia, MO B

Purchasing, Procurement/ Acquisitions and Contracts Management
Central Michigan U, MI B
Miami U Hamilton, OH A
Saint Louis U, MO B
Southwestern Coll, KS B
U of Illinois at Urbana–Champaign, IL B
Wright State U, OH B

Quality Control and Safety Technologies Related
Madonna U, MI A,B

Quality Control Technology
Baker Coll of Cadillac, MI A
Baker Coll of Flint, MI A
Baker Coll of Muskegon, MI A
Bowling Green State U, OH B
Ferris State U, MI B
U of Cincinnati, OH A
Winona State U, MN B

Radiation Protection/Health Physics Technology
Indiana U East, IN B
Indiana U Northwest, IN A
Indiana U–Purdue U Indianapolis, IN B
Indiana U South Bend, IN A,B
Indiana U Southeast, IN A,B
Lewis U, IL B

Radio and Television
Bemidji State U, MN B
Bradley U, IL B
Butler U, IN B
Cedarville U, OH B
Central State U, OH B
Concordia Coll, MN B
Drake U, IA B
Evangel U, MO B
Fort Hays State U, KS B
Grand Valley State U, MI B
Grand View U, IA B
Kent State U, OH B
Lawrence Technological U, MI A
Lindenwood U, MO B
Marietta Coll, OH B
Minot State U, ND B
North Central Coll, IL B
Northwestern Coll, MN A,B
Northwestern U, IL B
Northwest Missouri State U, MO B
Ohio Northern U, OH B
Ohio U, OH A,B
Ohio U–Zanesville, OH A
Oklahoma Christian U, OK B
Oklahoma City U, OK B
Otterbein Coll, OH B
Pittsburg State U, KS B
St. Ambrose U, IA B
St. Cloud State U, MN B
Southern Illinois U Carbondale, IL B
Southwest Minnesota State U, MN B
Stephens Coll, MO B
The U of Akron, OH B
U of Central Missouri, MO B
U of Central Oklahoma, OK B
U of Cincinnati, OH B
U of Dayton, OH B
U of Missouri–Columbia, MO B
U of Northern Iowa, IA B
U of Sioux Falls, SD B
U of Southern Indiana, IN B
U of Wisconsin–Madison, WI B
U of Wisconsin–Oshkosh, WI B
U of Wisconsin–Superior, WI B
Valparaiso U, IN B
Wayne State U, MI B
Webster U, MO B
Western Illinois U, IL B
Winona State U, MN B
Xavier U, OH A,B
Youngstown State U, OH B

Radio and Television Broadcasting Technology
Eastern Michigan U, MI B
Ferris State U, MI B
Lewis U, IL B
Ohio U, OH B
Ohio U–Southern Campus, OH A
Pittsburg State U, KS B

Radiologic Technology/ Science
Allen Coll, IA A
Argosy U, Twin Cities, MN A
Baker Coll of Clinton Township, MI A
Baker Coll of Muskegon, MI A
Clarkson Coll, NE A
Friends U, KS B
Indiana U East, IN A
Indiana U Northwest, IN A,B
Indiana U–Purdue U Fort Wayne, IN A
Indiana U–Purdue U Indianapolis, IN A
Indiana U South Bend, IN A,B
Indiana U Southeast, IN A,B
Jamestown Coll, ND B
Kent State U, OH B
Marian U, WI B
Missouri State U, MO B
Nebraska Methodist Coll, NE A
Newman U, KS A
North Dakota State U, ND B
Northern Michigan U, MI A
Oakland U, MI B
The Ohio State U, OH B
Oklahoma State U, Oklahoma City, OK A
Presentation Coll, SD A,B
Rochester Comm and Tech Coll, MN A
Sanford-Brown Coll, Fenton, MO A
U of Charleston, WV B
U of Mary, ND B
U of Missouri–Columbia, MO B
U of Nebraska Medical Center, NE B
U of Oklahoma Health Sciences Center, OK B
U of Rio Grande, OH A
U of St. Francis, IL B
Washburn U, KS A

Radio, Television, and Digital Communication Related
Central Michigan U, MI B
Drake U, IA B
Madonna U, MI A,B
North Dakota State U, ND B
Rogers State U, OK B
The U of Akron, OH B

Range Science and Management
Fort Hays State U, KS B
North Dakota State U, ND B
South Dakota State U, SD B
U of Nebraska–Lincoln, NE B

Reading Teacher Education
Aquinas Coll, MI B
Dordt Coll, IA B
Eastern Michigan U, MI B
Grand Valley State U, MI B
Northwest Missouri State U, MO B
Ohio U, OH B
St. Cloud State U, MN B
U of Central Missouri, MO B
U of Central Oklahoma, OK B
U of Nebraska–Lincoln, NE B
U of Northern Iowa, IA B
U of Wisconsin–Superior, WI B
Winona State U, MN B
Wright State U, OH B
York Coll, NE B

Real Estate
Central Michigan U, MI B
DePaul U, IL B
Miami U, OH A
Miami U Hamilton, OH A
Minnesota State U Mankato, MN B
The Ohio State U, OH B
St. Cloud State U, MN B
U of Central Oklahoma, OK B
U of Cincinnati, OH A,B
U of Illinois at Urbana–Champaign, IL B
U of Missouri–Columbia, MO B
U of Nebraska at Omaha, NE B
U of Northern Iowa, IA B
U of Wisconsin–Madison, WI B
U of Wisconsin–Milwaukee, WI B

Receptionist
Baker Coll of Allen Park, MI A

Recording Arts Technology
Butler U, IN B
The Illinois Inst of Art–Schaumburg, IL B
Indiana U Bloomington, IN A,B
Malone U, OH B

Regional Studies
Washington U in St. Louis, MO B

Rehabilitation and Therapeutic Professions Related
Southern Illinois U Carbondale, IL B
U of Wisconsin–La Crosse, WI B

Rehabilitation Therapy
Baker Coll of Muskegon, MI B
Wilberforce U, OH B

Religious Education
Allegheny Wesleyan Coll, OH B
Andrews U, MI B
Aquinas Coll, MI B
Ashland U, OH B
Barclay Coll, KS B
Calvary Bible Coll and Theological Seminary, MO A,B
Cedarville U, OH B
Central Bible Coll, MO A,B
Cincinnati Christian U, OH A,B
Coll of Mount St. Joseph, OH B
Coll of Saint Benedict, MN B
Concordia U, MI B
Concordia U Chicago, IL B
Concordia U, Nebraska, NE B
Concordia U, St. Paul, MN B
Crossroads Coll, MN B
Crown Coll, MN B
Defiance Coll, OH B
Edgewood Coll, WI B
Faith Baptist Bible Coll and Theological Seminary, IA B
Franciscan U of Steubenville, OH B
Grace U, NE B
Great Lakes Christian Coll, MI B
Hannibal-LaGrange Coll, MO B
Indiana Wesleyan U, IN A,B
John Carroll U, OH B
Kansas Wesleyan U, KS B
Kuyper Coll, MI A,B
Loyola U Chicago, IL B
Malone U, OH B
Manhattan Christian Coll, KS A,B
Maranatha Baptist Bible Coll, WI B
Marian U, IN B
Messenger Coll, MO B

- MidAmerica Nazarene U, KS B
- Missouri Baptist U, MO B
- Moody Bible Inst, IL B
- Mount Mary Coll, WI B
- Mount Vernon Nazarene U, OH B
- Oak Hills Christian Coll, MN B
- Oklahoma Christian U, OK B
- Oklahoma City U, OK B
- Olivet Nazarene U, IL B
- Oral Roberts U, OK B
- Saint John's U, MN B
- St. Louis Christian Coll, MO B
- Saint Mary's U of Minnesota, MN B
- Southern Nazarene U, OK B
- Southwest Baptist U, MO B
- Southwestern Christian U, OK B
- Sterling Coll, KS B
- Temple Baptist Coll, OH B
- Trinity Christian Coll, IL B
- Tri-State Bible Coll, OH B
- Union Coll, NE B
- U of Dayton, OH B
- Wheaton Coll, IL B
- York Coll, NE B

Religious/Sacred Music

- Anderson U, IN B
- Aquinas Coll, MI A,B
- Augustana Coll, IL B
- Barclay Coll, KS B
- Bethany Lutheran Coll, MN B
- Bethel Coll, IN B
- Bethel U, MN B
- Calvary Bible Coll and Theological Seminary, MO B
- Calvin Coll, MI B
- Cedarville U, OH B
- Central Bible Coll, MO A,B
- Central Christian Coll of Kansas, KS B
- Cincinnati Christian U, OH A,B
- Coll of the Ozarks, MO B
- Concordia U, MI B
- Concordia U Chicago, IL B
- Concordia U, Nebraska, NE B
- Concordia U, St. Paul, MN B
- Crossroads Coll, MN B
- Drake U, IA B
- Evangel U, MO B
- Faith Baptist Bible Coll and Theological Seminary, IA B
- Franciscan U of Steubenville, OH B
- Grace U, NE B
- Great Lakes Christian Coll, MI B
- Gustavus Adolphus Coll, MN B
- Hannibal-LaGrange Coll, MO B
- Huntington U, IN B
- Indiana Wesleyan U, IN A,B
- Kuyper Coll, MI B
- Madonna U, MI B
- Malone U, OH B
- Manhattan Christian Coll, KS A,B
- Maranatha Baptist Bible Coll, WI B
- Messenger Coll, MO B
- Mid-America Christian U, OK B
- MidAmerica Nazarene U, KS A,B
- Missouri Baptist U, MO B
- Moody Bible Inst, IL B
- Mount Vernon Nazarene U, OH A,B
- North Central U, MN A,B
- North Park U, IL B
- Ohio Christian U, OH A,B
- Oklahoma Baptist U, OK B
- Oklahoma City U, OK B
- Olivet Nazarene U, IL B
- Oral Roberts U, OK B
- St. Louis Christian Coll, MO B
- Southern Nazarene U, OK B
- Southwestern Christian U, OK B
- Southwestern Oklahoma State U, OK B
- Trinity International U, IL B
- Valparaiso U, IN B
- Wartburg Coll, IA B
- William Jewell Coll, MO B

Religious Studies

- Adrian Coll, MI B
- Albion Coll, MI B
- Alma Coll, MI B
- Anderson U, IN B
- Andrews U, MI B
- Aquinas Coll, MI B
- Ashland U, OH B
- Augsburg Coll, MN B
- Augustana Coll, IL B
- Augustana Coll, SD B
- Avila U, MO B
- Baker U, KS B
- Baldwin-Wallace Coll, OH B
- Ball State U, IN B
- Beloit Coll, WI B
- Bemidji State U, MN B
- Benedictine Coll, KS B
- Bethany Coll, KS B
- Bethany Lutheran Coll, MN B
- Bethel Coll, KS B
- Bluffton U, OH B
- Bradley U, IL B
- Butler U, IN B
- Calumet Coll of Saint Joseph, IN A,B
- Calvin Coll, MI B
- Capital U, OH B
- Carleton Coll, MN B
- Carroll U, WI B
- Case Western Reserve U, OH B
- Central Bible Coll, MO B
- Central Christian Coll of Kansas, KS A,B
- Central Coll, IA B
- Central Methodist U, MO B
- Central Michigan U, MI B
- Clarke Coll, IA B
- Cleveland State U, OH B
- Coe Coll, IA B
- Coll of Mount St. Joseph, OH B
- The Coll of St. Scholastica, MN B
- Coll of the Ozarks, MO B
- The Coll of Wooster, OH B
- Concordia Coll, MN B
- Concordia U, MI B
- Concordia U Wisconsin, WI B
- Cornell Coll, IA B
- Culver-Stockton Coll, MO B
- Dakota Wesleyan U, SD B
- Dana Coll, NE B
- Defiance Coll, OH B
- Denison U, OH B
- DePaul U, IL B
- DePauw U, IN B
- Doane Coll, NE B
- Dordt Coll, IA B
- Drake U, IA B
- Drury U, MO B
- Earlham Coll, IN B
- Edgewood Coll, WI B
- Eureka Coll, IL B
- Fontbonne U, MO B
- Franklin Coll, IN B
- Friends U, KS B
- Grace Bible Coll, MI A
- Graceland U, IA B
- Grand View U, IA B
- Greenville Coll, IL B
- Grinnell Coll, IA B
- Gustavus Adolphus Coll, MN B
- Hamline U, MN B
- Heidelberg U, OH B
- Hillsdale Coll, MI B
- Hiram Coll, OH B
- Hope Coll, MI B
- Huntington U, IN B
- Illinois Coll, IL B
- Illinois Wesleyan U, IL B
- Indiana U Bloomington, IN B
- Indiana U East, IN B
- Indiana U–Purdue U Indianapolis, IN B
- Iowa State U of Science and Technology, IA B
- Jamestown Coll, ND B
- John Carroll U, OH B
- Kalamazoo Coll, MI B
- Kansas Wesleyan U, KS B
- Kenyon Coll, OH B
- Lakeland Coll, WI B
- Laura and Alvin Siegal Coll of Judaic Studies, OH B
- Lawrence U, WI B
- Lewis U, IL B
- Lindenwood U, MO B
- Loras Coll, IA B
- Lourdes Coll, OH A,B
- Luther Coll, IA B
- Macalester Coll, MN B
- MacMurray Coll, IL B
- Madonna U, MI A,B
- Manchester Coll, IN A,B
- Manhattan Christian Coll, KS B
- Maranatha Baptist Bible Coll, WI A,B
- Martin U, IN B
- McKendree U, IL B
- Messenger Coll, MO B
- Miami U, OH B
- Michigan State U, MI B
- MidAmerica Nazarene U, KS B
- Missouri Baptist U, MO A,B
- Missouri State U, MO B
- Monmouth Coll, IL B
- Morningside Coll, IA B
- Mount Marty Coll, SD A,B
- Mount Mary Coll, WI B
- Mount Mercy Coll, IA B
- Mount Union Coll, OH B
- Mount Vernon Nazarene U, OH A,B
- Muskingum Coll, OH B
- Nebraska Wesleyan U, NE B
- North Central Coll, IL B
- North Central U, MN B
- Northland Coll, WI B
- Northwestern U, IL B
- Oberlin Coll, OH B
- Ohio Northern U, OH B
- Ohio Wesleyan U, OH B
- Oklahoma Baptist U, OK B
- Oklahoma Christian U, OK B
- Oklahoma City U, OK B
- Olivet Nazarene U, IL B
- Otterbein Coll, OH B
- Presentation Coll, SD A
- Purdue U, IN B
- Ripon Coll, WI B
- Saint Mary-of-the-Woods Coll, IN B
- Saint Mary's Coll, IN B
- St. Norbert Coll, WI B
- St. Olaf Coll, MN B
- Saint Xavier U, IL B
- Siena Heights U, MI B
- Simpson Coll, IA B
- Southern Methodist U, TX B
- Southwest Baptist U, MO B
- Southwestern Christian U, OK B
- Spring Arbor U, MI B
- Transylvania U, KY B
- Trinity Christian Coll, IL B
- Truman State U, MO B
- Union Coll, NE B
- U of Chicago, IL B
- U of Dayton, OH B
- The U of Findlay, OH A,B
- U of Illinois at Urbana–Champaign, IL B
- U of Indianapolis, IN B
- The U of Iowa, IA B
- The U of Kansas, KS B
- U of Mary, ND B
- U of Michigan, MI B
- U of Minnesota, Twin Cities Campus, MN B
- U of Missouri–Columbia, MO B
- U of Nebraska at Omaha, NE B
- U of North Dakota, ND B
- U of Northern Iowa, IA B
- U of Oklahoma, OK B
- U of Saint Francis, IN B
- The U of Toledo, OH B
- U of Tulsa, OK B
- U of Wisconsin–Eau Claire, WI B

A—associate degree; B—bachelor's degree

U of Wisconsin–Milwaukee, WI B
U of Wisconsin–Oshkosh, WI B
Viterbo U, WI B
Wabash Coll, IN B
Walsh U, OH B
Wartburg Coll, IA B
Washburn U, KS B
Washington U in St. Louis, MO B
Webster U, MO B
Western Michigan U, MI B
Westminster Coll, MO B
William Jewell Coll, MO B
Wilmington Coll, OH B
Wittenberg U, OH B
Wright State U, OH B
York Coll, NE B
Youngstown State U, OH B

Religious Studies Related
Ohio Northern U, OH B
Ursuline Coll, OH B

Resort Management
Lakeland Coll, WI B

Respiratory Care Therapy
Ball State U, IN A,B
Cameron U, OK A
Dakota State U, SD A,B
Ferris State U, MI A
Hannibal-LaGrange Coll, MO B
Indiana U East, IN B
Indiana U Northwest, IN A
Indiana U–Purdue U Indianapolis, IN A,B
Indiana U South Bend, IN A,B
Indiana U Southeast, IN B
Missouri State U, MO B
National-Louis U, IL B
Nebraska Methodist Coll, NE A,B
Newman U, KS A
North Dakota State U, ND B
The Ohio State U, OH B
St. Augustine Coll, IL A
St. Catherine U, MN B
Sanford-Brown Coll, Fenton, MO A
Shawnee State U, OH A
The U of Akron, OH A,B
U of Indianapolis, IN B
The U of Kansas, KS B
U of Mary, ND B
U of Missouri–Columbia, MO B
U of Southern Indiana, IN A
The U of Toledo, OH A
Washburn U, KS A
Youngstown State U, OH B

Respiratory Therapy Technician
Northern Michigan U, MI A

Restaurant, Culinary, and Catering Management
The Art Inst of Indianapolis, IN B
The Art Inst of Michigan, MI B
The Art Insts International Minnesota, MN B
Ferris State U, MI A
The Illinois Inst of Art–Chicago, IL B
Kendall Coll, IL B
U of Illinois at Urbana–Champaign, IL B

Restaurant/Food Services Management
Coll of the Ozarks, MO B
Kendall Coll, IL B
The Ohio State U, OH B
Southwest Minnesota State U, MN B
The U of Akron, OH A
U of Missouri–Columbia, MO B

Retailing
Central Michigan U, MI B
Rochester Comm and Tech Coll, MN A
U of Central Oklahoma, OK B

Retail Management
The Art Inst of Indianapolis, IN B
The Art Insts International Minnesota, MN B
U of Phoenix–Cleveland Campus, OH B
U of Phoenix–Indianapolis Campus, IN B
U of Phoenix–Kansas City Campus, MO B
U of Phoenix–Metro Detroit Campus, MI B
U of Phoenix–Oklahoma City Campus, OK B
U of Phoenix–St. Louis Campus, MO B
U of Phoenix–Springfield Campus, MO B
U of Phoenix–Tulsa Campus, OK B

Robotics Technology
Indiana State U, IN B
Indiana U–Purdue U Indianapolis, IN A,B
Lake Superior State U, MI B
Purdue U, IN A,B
U of Rio Grande, OH A,B

Romance Languages
Beloit Coll, WI B
Cameron U, OK B
Carleton Coll, MN B
DePauw U, IN B
Northwest Missouri State U, MO B
Oberlin Coll, OH B
Ripon Coll, WI B
Rockford Coll, IL B
Truman State U, MO B
U of Chicago, IL B
U of Cincinnati, OH B
U of Illinois at Chicago, IL B
U of Michigan, MI B
U of Notre Dame, IN B
Washington U in St. Louis, MO B

Romance Languages Related
U of Michigan–Flint, MI B

Russian
Beloit Coll, WI B
Bowling Green State U, OH B
Carleton Coll, MN B
Cornell Coll, IA B
Grinnell Coll, IA B
Gustavus Adolphus Coll, MN B
Kent State U, OH B
Lawrence U, WI B
Macalester Coll, MN B
Miami U, OH B
Miami U Hamilton, OH B
Michigan State U, MI B
Oberlin Coll, OH B
The Ohio State U, OH B
Ohio U, OH B
Oklahoma State U, OK B
Purdue U, IN B
Saint Louis U, MO B
St. Olaf Coll, MN B
Truman State U, MO B
U of Chicago, IL B
U of Illinois at Chicago, IL B
U of Illinois at Urbana–Champaign, IL B
The U of Iowa, IA B
U of Michigan, MI B
U of Minnesota, Twin Cities Campus, MN B
U of Missouri–Columbia, MO B
U of Nebraska–Lincoln, NE B
U of Northern Iowa, IA B
U of Notre Dame, IN B
U of Oklahoma, OK B
U of Wisconsin–Madison, WI B
U of Wisconsin–Milwaukee, WI B
Washington U in St. Louis, MO B

Russian Studies
Beloit Coll, WI B
Carleton Coll, MN B
The Coll of Wooster, OH B
Concordia Coll, MN B
DePauw U, IN B
Grand Valley State U, MI B
Gustavus Adolphus Coll, MN B
Hamline U, MN B
Iowa State U of Science and Technology, IA B
Kent State U, OH B
Lawrence U, WI B
Luther Coll, IA B
Oberlin Coll, OH B
St. Olaf Coll, MN B
U of Chicago, IL B
U of Illinois at Urbana–Champaign, IL B
The U of Kansas, KS B
U of Michigan, MI B
U of Minnesota, Twin Cities Campus, MN B
U of Missouri–Columbia, MO B
U of Northern Iowa, IA B
U of Tulsa, OK B
U of Wisconsin–Milwaukee, WI B
Washington U in St. Louis, MO B
Wittenberg U, OH B

Safety/Security Technology
Ohio U, OH A
U of Central Oklahoma, OK B
U of Cincinnati, OH A

Sales and Marketing/Marketing and Distribution Teacher Education
Bowling Green State U, OH B
Central Christian Coll of Kansas, KS A
Kent State U, OH B
U of Nebraska–Lincoln, NE B
U of Wisconsin–Stout, WI B
Wright State U, OH B

Sales, Distribution and Marketing
Baker Coll of Flint, MI A
Baker Coll of Jackson, MI A
Black Hills State U, SD B
McKendree U, IL B
Minnesota School of Business–Blaine, MN A
St. Cloud State U, MN A
Trinity Christian Coll, IL B
The U of Akron, OH B
U of Central Oklahoma, OK B
The U of Findlay, OH A,B
U of Illinois at Urbana–Champaign, IL B
U of Wisconsin–Stout, WI B
U of Wisconsin–Superior, WI B
Wichita State U, KS B

Sanskrit and Classical Indian Languages
U of Chicago, IL B

Scandinavian Languages
Augsburg Coll, MN B
Augustana Coll, IL B
Concordia Coll, MN B
Gustavus Adolphus Coll, MN B
North Park U, IL B
U of Minnesota, Twin Cities Campus, MN B
U of North Dakota, ND B
U of Wisconsin–Madison, WI B

Scandinavian Studies
Gustavus Adolphus Coll, MN B
Luther Coll, IA B
North Park U, IL B

School Librarian/School Library Media
The Coll of St. Scholastica, MN B

School Psychology
Fort Hays State U, KS B

Science Teacher Education
Adrian Coll, MI B
Alma Coll, MI B
Anderson U, IN B
Andrews U, MI B
Aquinas Coll, MI B
Ashland U, OH B
Augustana Coll, IL B
Ball State U, IN B

Beloit Coll, WI B
Bemidji State U, MN B
Bethel Coll, IN B
Black Hills State U, SD B
Bowling Green State U, OH B
Buena Vista U, IA B
Calumet Coll of Saint Joseph, IN B
Calvin Coll, MI B
Capital U, OH B
Carroll U, WI B
Cedarville U, OH B
Central Christian Coll of Kansas, KS A
Central Methodist U, MO B
Central Michigan U, MI B
Coe Coll, IA B
Coll of Saint Mary, NE B
Coll of the Ozarks, MO B
Concordia Coll, MN B
Concordia U, MI B
Concordia U Chicago, IL B
Concordia U, Nebraska, NE B
Concordia U Wisconsin, WI B
Cornerstone U, MI B
Culver-Stockton Coll, MO B
Dakota Wesleyan U, SD B
Dana Coll, NE B
Defiance Coll, OH B
Dordt Coll, IA B
Eastern Illinois U, IL B
Eastern Michigan U, MI B
Edgewood Coll, WI B
Evangel U, MO B
Fort Hays State U, KS B
Grace Coll, IN B
Graceland U, IA B
Grand Valley State U, MI B
Hamline U, MN B
Hannibal-LaGrange Coll, MO B
Heidelberg U, OH B
Hope Coll, MI B
Huntington U, IN B
Indiana State U, IN B
Indiana U Bloomington, IN B
Indiana U–Purdue U Fort Wayne, IN B
Indiana U South Bend, IN B
Indiana Wesleyan U, IN B
Kent State U, OH B
Lakeland Coll, WI B
Lindenwood U, MO B
Madonna U, MI B
Malone U, OH B
Manchester Coll, IN B
Maranatha Baptist Bible Coll, WI B
Marian U, WI B
Marquette U, WI B
Miami U, OH B
Miami U Hamilton, OH B
Michigan Technological U, MI B
Minnesota State U Mankato, MN B
Minnesota State U Moorhead, MN B
Minot State U, ND B
Missouri Baptist U, MO B
Missouri State U, MO B
Morningside Coll, IA B
Mount Mercy Coll, IA B
Mount Vernon Nazarene U, OH B
Nebraska Wesleyan U, NE B
North Dakota State U, ND B
Northeastern State U, OK B
Northern Michigan U, MI B
Northwest Missouri State U, MO B
Ohio Dominican U, OH B
Ohio Northern U, OH B
Ohio U, OH B
Oklahoma Baptist U, OK B
Oklahoma Christian U, OK B
Oklahoma City U, OK B
Olivet Nazarene U, IL B
Oral Roberts U, OK B
Otterbein Coll, OH B
Purdue U, IN B
St. Ambrose U, IA B
St. Cloud State U, MN B
Shawnee State U, OH B
Southeastern Oklahoma State U, OK B
Southeast Missouri State U, MO B
Southern Illinois U Edwardsville, IL B
Southern Nazarene U, OK B
Southwest Baptist U, MO B
Southwestern Oklahoma State U, OK B
Taylor U, IN B
Trine U, IN B
Trinity Christian Coll, IL B
The U of Akron, OH B
U of Central Oklahoma, OK B
U of Charleston, WV B
U of Cincinnati, OH A
U of Dayton, OH B
U of Evansville, IN B
The U of Findlay, OH B
U of Illinois at Urbana–Champaign, IL B
U of Indianapolis, IN B
The U of Iowa, IA B
U of Michigan–Dearborn, MI B
U of Michigan–Flint, MI B
U of Minnesota, Duluth, MN B
U of Minnesota, Twin Cities Campus, MN B
U of Missouri–Columbia, MO B
U of Nebraska–Lincoln, NE B
U of North Dakota, ND B
U of Northern Iowa, IA B
U of Notre Dame, IN B
U of Oklahoma, OK B
U of Rio Grande, OH B
U of St. Francis, IL B
U of Saint Francis, IN B
U of Sioux Falls, SD B
The U of South Dakota, SD B
The U of Toledo, OH B
U of Wisconsin–Eau Claire, WI B
U of Wisconsin–Madison, WI B
U of Wisconsin–Platteville, WI B
U of Wisconsin–Superior, WI B
U of Wisconsin–Whitewater, WI B
Ursuline Coll, OH B
Valley City State U, ND B
Valparaiso U, IN B
Viterbo U, WI B
Walsh U, OH B
Washington U in St. Louis, MO B
Wayne State Coll, NE B
Wayne State U, MI B
Western Michigan U, MI B
Wichita State U, KS B
Wilmington Coll, OH B
Winona State U, MN B
Wright State U, OH B
Xavier U, OH B
York Coll, NE B
Youngstown State U, OH B

Science Technologies Related

Madonna U, MI A,B
U of Wisconsin–Stout, WI B

Science, Technology and Society

Butler U, IN B
Cleveland State U, OH B
Coll of the Ozarks, MO B
Michigan State U, MI B
Northwestern U, IL B
Washington U in St. Louis, MO B

Sculpture

Aquinas Coll, MI B
Art Academy of Cincinnati, OH B
Bethany Coll, KS B
Bradley U, IL B
The Cleveland Inst of Art, OH B
Coll of Visual Arts, MN B
Drake U, IA B
Ferris State U, MI B
Indiana U–Purdue U Fort Wayne, IN B
Kansas City Art Inst, MO B
Kent State U, OH B
Minneapolis Coll of Art and Design, MN B
Minnesota State U Mankato, MN B
Minnesota State U Moorhead, MN B
Northern Michigan U, MI B
Northwest Missouri State U, MO B
Ohio Northern U, OH B
Ohio U, OH B
St. Cloud State U, MN B
Trinity Christian Coll, IL B
U of Dallas, TX B
U of Illinois at Urbana–Champaign, IL B
The U of Iowa, IA B
The U of Kansas, KS B
U of Michigan, MI B
U of Wisconsin–Milwaukee, WI B
Washington U in St. Louis, MO B
Western Michigan U, MI B

Secondary Education

Adrian Coll, MI B
Albion Coll, MI B
Alma Coll, MI B
Andrews U, MI B
Aquinas Coll, MI B
Ashland U, OH B
Augsburg Coll, MN B
Augustana Coll, IL B
Augustana Coll, SD B
Baker U, KS B
Beloit Coll, WI B
Bemidji State U, MN B
Benedictine Coll, KS B
Benedictine U, IL B
Bethel Coll, IN B
Black Hills State U, SD B
Briar Cliff U, IA B
Butler U, IN B
Calumet Coll of Saint Joseph, IN B
Calvary Bible Coll and Theological Seminary, MO B
Calvin Coll, MI B
Cameron U, OK B
Central Christian Coll of Kansas, KS A,B
Central Methodist U, MO B
Central State U, OH B
Clarke Coll, IA B
Coe Coll, IA B
Coll of Saint Benedict, MN B
Coll of Saint Mary, NE B
Coll of the Ozarks, MO B
Concordia Coll, MN B
Concordia U, MI B
Concordia U Chicago, IL B
Concordia U, Nebraska, NE B
Concordia U, St. Paul, MN B
Concordia U Wisconsin, WI B
Cornell Coll, IA B
Cornerstone U, MI B
Dakota Wesleyan U, SD B
Dana Coll, NE B
Defiance Coll, OH B
DePaul U, IL B
Dordt Coll, IA B
Drake U, IA B
Drury U, MO B
Elmhurst Coll, IL B
Emporia State U, KS B
Evangel U, MO B
Ferris State U, MI A
Fontbonne U, MO B
Grace Bible Coll, MI B
Graceland U, IA B
Grace U, NE B
Grand Valley State U, MI B
Gustavus Adolphus Coll, MN B
Hamline U, MN B
Hannibal-LaGrange Coll, MO B
Harris-Stowe State U, MO B
Heidelberg U, OH B
Hillsdale Coll, MI B
Hope Coll, MI B
Huntington U, IN B

A—associate degree; B—bachelor's degree

Illinois Coll, IL B
Indiana U Bloomington, IN B
Indiana U East, IN B
Indiana U Kokomo, IN B
Indiana U Northwest, IN B
Indiana U–Purdue U Fort Wayne, IN B
Indiana U–Purdue U Indianapolis, IN B
Indiana U South Bend, IN B
Indiana U Southeast, IN B
Indiana Wesleyan U, IN B
Iowa State U of Science and Technology, IA B
Iowa Wesleyan Coll, IA B
John Carroll U, OH B
Kansas State U, KS B
Kuyper Coll, MI B
Lake Forest Coll, IL B
Lakeland Coll, WI B
Lake Superior State U, MI B
Lawrence U, WI B
Lindenwood U, MO B
Loras Coll, IA B
Lourdes Coll, OH B
Loyola U Chicago, IL B
MacMurray Coll, IL B
Madonna U, MI B
Manchester Coll, IN B
Maranatha Baptist Bible Coll, WI B
Marian U, WI B
Marian U, IN B
Marietta Coll, OH B
Marquette U, WI B
Maryville U of Saint Louis, MO B
McKendree U, IL B
Miami U, OH B
Michigan Technological U, MI B
Mid-America Christian U, OK B
MidAmerica Nazarene U, KS B
Minnesota State U Mankato, MN B
Minnesota State U Moorhead, MN B
Missouri Southern State U, MO B
Missouri U of Science and Technology, MO B
Morningside Coll, IA B
Mount Marty Coll, SD B
Mount Mary Coll, WI B
Mount Mercy Coll, IA B
Mount Vernon Nazarene U, OH B
Newman U, KS B
North Central Coll, IL B
North Central U, MN B
Northeastern State U, OK B
Northern Michigan U, MI B
Northern State U, SD B
North Park U, IL B
Northwestern U, IL B
Northwest Missouri State U, MO B
Ohio Dominican U, OH B
Ohio Northern U, OH B
Ohio U, OH B
Ohio Wesleyan U, OH B
Oklahoma Christian U, OK B
Oklahoma City U, OK B
Oklahoma State U, OK B
Otterbein Coll, OH B
Purdue U, IN B
Purdue U Calumet, IN B
Purdue U North Central, IN B
Ripon Coll, WI B
Rockford Coll, IL B
Rockhurst U, MO B
Rogers State U, OK A
St. Ambrose U, IA B
St. Catherine U, MN B
St. Cloud State U, MN B
Saint John's U, MN B
Saint Joseph's Coll, IN B
Saint Mary-of-the-Woods Coll, IN B
Shawnee State U, OH B
Siena Heights U, MI B
Simpson Coll, IA B
Sinte Gleska U, SD B
Southeastern Oklahoma State U, OK B
Southwestern Oklahoma State U, OK B
Spring Arbor U, MI B
Trine U, IN B
Trinity Bible Coll, ND B
Trinity Christian Coll, IL B
Trinity International U, IL B
Union Coll, NE B
Union Inst & U, OH B
U of Central Missouri, MO B
U of Central Oklahoma, OK B
U of Cincinnati, OH B
U of Dallas, TX B
U of Dayton, OH B
The U of Findlay, OH B
U of Illinois at Urbana–Champaign, IL B
U of Indianapolis, IN B
The U of Iowa, IA B
The U of Kansas, KS B
U of Michigan, MI B
U of Michigan–Dearborn, MI B
U of Minnesota, Morris, MN B
U of Missouri–Columbia, MO B
U of Missouri–Kansas City, MO B
U of Missouri–St. Louis, MO B
U of Nebraska at Omaha, NE B
U of Rio Grande, OH B
U of Sioux Falls, SD B
The U of South Dakota, SD B
The U of Toledo, OH B
U of Wisconsin–Madison, WI B
U of Wisconsin–Milwaukee, WI B
U of Wisconsin–Oshkosh, WI B
U of Wisconsin–Platteville, WI B
U of Wisconsin–Stevens Point, WI B
U of Wisconsin–Whitewater, WI B
Valley City State U, ND B
Valparaiso U, IN B
Walsh U, OH B
Wartburg Coll, IA B
Washburn U, KS B
Washington U in St. Louis, MO B
Westminster Coll, MO B
Wheaton Coll, IL B
Wichita State U, KS B
William Jewell Coll, MO B
Wilmington Coll, OH B
Winona State U, MN B
Wright State U, OH B
York Coll, NE B
Youngstown State U, OH B

Securities Services Administration
Davenport U, Grand Rapids, MI B
Southwestern Coll, KS B

Security and Loss Prevention
Northern Michigan U, MI B

Security and Protective Services Related
Concordia U, MI B
Eastern Michigan U, MI B
Lewis U, IL B
Madonna U, MI B
North Dakota State U, ND B
Ohio U, OH A
St. Ambrose U, IA B
Tiffin U, OH B
U of Phoenix–Cleveland Campus, OH B
U of Phoenix–Indianapolis Campus, IN B
U of Phoenix–Kansas City Campus, MO B
U of Phoenix–Metro Detroit Campus, MI B
U of Phoenix–St. Louis Campus, MO B
U of Phoenix–Springfield Campus, MO B
Washburn U, KS B
Western Illinois U, IL B

Selling Skills and Sales
Bradley U, IL B
The U of Akron, OH A

Sign Language Interpretation and Translation
Augustana Coll, SD B
Bethel Coll, IN A,B
Cincinnati Christian U, OH A
Goshen Coll, IN B
Indiana U–Purdue U Indianapolis, IN B
MacMurray Coll, IL B
North Central U, MN A,B
Oklahoma State U, Oklahoma City, OK A
Quincy U, IL B
St. Catherine U, MN A

Slavic Languages
Indiana U Bloomington, IN B
Northwestern U, IL B
U of Chicago, IL B
U of Illinois at Chicago, IL B
U of Illinois at Urbana–Champaign, IL B
The U of Kansas, KS B
U of Wisconsin–Madison, WI B
U of Wisconsin–Milwaukee, WI B
Wayne State U, MI B

Slavic Studies
Lawrence U, WI B
Northwestern U, IL B
Oakland U, MI B

Small Business Administration
Avila U, MO B
Bradley U, IL B
Carroll U, WI B
Kendall Coll, IL B
Missouri Coll, MO A
North Central Coll, IL B
Northern Michigan U, MI B
The U of Akron, OH A
U of Nebraska at Omaha, NE B

Social and Philosophical Foundations of Education
Northwestern U, IL B
Washington U in St. Louis, MO B

Social Psychology
Central Christian Coll of Kansas, KS A
Grand Valley State U, MI B
Lawrence U, WI B
Maryville U of Saint Louis, MO B
U of Wisconsin–Superior, WI B

Social Sciences
Adrian Coll, MI B
Alma Coll, MI B
Andrews U, MI B
Aquinas Coll, MI B
Ashland U, OH B
Augsburg Coll, MN B
Ball State U, IN B
Bemidji State U, MN B
Benedictine Coll, KS B
Benedictine U, IL B
Bethany Lutheran Coll, MN B
Bethel Coll, IN B
Bethel U, MN B
Black Hills State U, SD B
Bluffton U, OH B
Buena Vista U, IA B
Calvin Coll, MI B
Central Christian Coll of Kansas, KS B
Central Coll, IA B
Central Michigan U, MI B
Chancellor U, OH B
Clarkson U, NY B
Cleveland State U, OH B
Coll of Saint Benedict, MN B
Coll of Saint Mary, NE B
The Coll of St. Scholastica, MN B
Concordia U, MI B
Concordia U, Nebraska, NE B
Crown Coll, MN A
Dana Coll, NE B
Defiance Coll, OH B
DePaul U, IL B
Divine Word Coll, IA A,B

Doane Coll, NE	B
Dominican U, IL	B
Dordt Coll, IA	B
Eastern Michigan U, MI	B
East-West U, IL	B
Edgewood Coll, WI	B
Emporia State U, KS	B
Fontbonne U, MO	B
Graceland U, IA	B
Grand Valley State U, MI	B
Gustavus Adolphus Coll, MN	B
Hamline U, MN	B
Hope Coll, MI	B
Indiana Wesleyan U, IN	A,B
Kansas State U, KS	B
Kansas Wesleyan U, KS	B
Kent State U, OH	B
Lake Erie Coll, OH	B
Lake Superior State U, MI	B
Mayville State U, ND	B
McKendree U, IL	B
Michigan State U, MI	B
Michigan Technological U, MI	B
Mid-America Christian U, OK	B
Minnesota State U Mankato, MN	B
Minot State U, ND	B
Missouri Baptist U, MO	B
Mount Vernon Nazarene U, OH	B
National-Louis U, IL	B
North Central Coll, IL	B
North Dakota State U, ND	B
Northland Coll, WI	B
Northwest Missouri State U, MO	B
Ohio U, OH	A,B
Ohio U–Zanesville, OH	A
Oklahoma Baptist U, OK	B
Oklahoma Panhandle State U, OK	B
Olivet Coll, MI	B
Olivet Nazarene U, IL	B
Purdue U, IN	B
Rockford Coll, IL	B
Rogers State U, OK	B
Roosevelt U, IL	B
St. Catherine U, MN	B
St. Cloud State U, MN	B
St. Gregory's U, Shawnee, OK	B
Saint John's U, MN	B
Saint Mary-of-the-Woods Coll, IN	B
Saint Mary's U of Minnesota, MN	B
Saint Xavier U, IL	B
Shawnee State U, OH	A,B
Shimer Coll, IL	B
Siena Heights U, MI	B
Southern Illinois U Carbondale, IL	B
Southern Methodist U, TX	B
Spring Arbor U, MI	B
Trine U, IN	A,B
Trinity International U, IL	B
Union Coll, NE	B
The U of Akron, OH	B
U of Chicago, IL	B
U of Cincinnati, OH	A,B
The U of Findlay, OH	A,B
U of Mary, ND	B
U of Michigan, MI	B
U of Michigan–Dearborn, MI	B
U of Michigan–Flint, MI	B
U of Minnesota, Morris, MN	B
U of North Dakota, ND	B
U of Rio Grande, OH	B
U of Sioux Falls, SD	A
U of Southern Indiana, IN	A,B
The U of Toledo, OH	A
U of Wisconsin–La Crosse, WI	B
U of Wisconsin–Madison, WI	B
U of Wisconsin–Platteville, WI	B
U of Wisconsin–Stevens Point, WI	B
U of Wisconsin–Superior, WI	B
U of Wisconsin–Whitewater, WI	B
Valley City State U, ND	B
Valparaiso U, IN	A,B
Viterbo U, WI	B
Washington U in St. Louis, MO	B
Wayne State Coll, NE	B
Webster U, MO	B
Western Michigan U, MI	B
Wilmington Coll, OH	B
Winona State U, MN	B
Youngstown State U, OH	B

Social Sciences Related

Central Michigan U, MI	B
Cleveland State U, OH	B
Eastern Michigan U, MI	B
Indiana U Bloomington, IN	B
Indiana U Kokomo, IN	B
Northwestern U, IL	B
Transylvania U, KY	B
The U of Akron, OH	B
U of Illinois at Springfield, IL	B
U of Wisconsin–Green Bay, WI	B
Washington U in St. Louis, MO	B

Social Science Teacher Education

Alma Coll, MI	B
Buena Vista U, IA	B
Carroll U, WI	B
Central Christian Coll of Kansas, KS	A
Central Methodist U, MO	B
Concordia U Chicago, IL	B
Concordia U, Nebraska, NE	B
Cornerstone U, MI	B
Dana Coll, NE	B
DePaul U, IL	B
Dordt Coll, IA	B
Eastern Illinois U, IL	B
Eastern Michigan U, MI	B
Emporia State U, KS	B
Ferris State U, MI	B
Friends U, KS	B
Grace U, NE	B
Lindenwood U, MO	B
Marquette U, WI	B
Mayville State U, ND	B
McKendree U, IL	B
Michigan State U, MI	B
Millikin U, IL	B
Minot State U, ND	B
Nebraska Wesleyan U, NE	B
St. Ambrose U, IA	B
Saint Mary's U of Minnesota, MN	B
Southwest Baptist U, MO	B
Southwestern Oklahoma State U, OK	B
Union Coll, NE	B
U of Evansville, IN	B
U of Illinois at Urbana–Champaign, IL	B
U of Mary, ND	B
U of Minnesota, Twin Cities Campus, MN	B
U of Nebraska–Lincoln, NE	B
U of North Dakota, ND	B
U of Northern Iowa, IA	B
U of Rio Grande, OH	B
The U of South Dakota, SD	B
U of Wisconsin–Superior, WI	B
Valley City State U, ND	B
Valparaiso U, IN	B
Wartburg Coll, IA	B
Washington U in St. Louis, MO	B
Wayne State Coll, NE	B
Western Michigan U, MI	B
York Coll, NE	B
Youngstown State U, OH	B

Social Studies Teacher Education

Alma Coll, MI	B
Anderson U, IN	B
Aquinas Coll, MI	B
Augustana Coll, SD	B
Bethany Coll, KS	B
Bethel Coll, IN	B
Bethel U, MN	B
Bowling Green State U, OH	B
Calumet Coll of Saint Joseph, IN	B
Capital U, OH	B
Carroll U, WI	B
Cedarville U, OH	B
Central Christian Coll of Kansas, KS	A,B
Central Michigan U, MI	B
Concordia Coll, MN	B
Concordia U, MI	B
Concordia U, St. Paul, MN	B
Cornerstone U, MI	B
Crown Coll, MN	B
Dakota Wesleyan U, SD	B
Dordt Coll, IA	B
Eastern Michigan U, MI	B
Ferris State U, MI	B
Franklin Coll, IN	B
Grace Coll, IN	B
Grand Valley State U, MI	B
Gustavus Adolphus Coll, MN	B
Hope Coll, MI	B
Illinois State U, IL	B
Indiana State U, IN	B
Indiana U Bloomington, IN	B
Indiana U Northwest, IN	B
Indiana U–Purdue U Fort Wayne, IN	B
Indiana U–Purdue U Indianapolis, IN	B
Indiana U South Bend, IN	B
Indiana U Southeast, IN	B
Indiana Wesleyan U, IN	B
Kent State U, OH	B
Madonna U, MI	B
Malone U, OH	B
Maranatha Baptist Bible Coll, WI	B
Marian U, WI	B
Miami U, OH	B
Miami U Hamilton, OH	B
MidAmerica Nazarene U, KS	B
Minnesota State U Mankato, MN	B
Minnesota State U Moorhead, MN	B
Mount Vernon Nazarene U, OH	B
North Dakota State U, ND	B
Northeastern State U, OK	B
Northern Michigan U, MI	B
Northwestern Coll, MN	B
Ohio Dominican U, OH	B
Ohio Northern U, OH	B
Ohio U, OH	B
Ohio Wesleyan U, OH	B
Oklahoma Baptist U, OK	B
Oklahoma Christian U, OK	B
Oral Roberts U, OK	B
Pittsburg State U, KS	B
Purdue U, IN	B
St. Catherine U, MN	B
St. Gregory's U, Shawnee, OK	B
St. Olaf Coll, MN	B
Shawnee State U, OH	B
Siena Heights U, MI	B
Southeastern Oklahoma State U, OK	B
Southeast Missouri State U, MO	B
Southern Nazarene U, OK	B
Taylor U, IN	B
Trine U, IN	B
The U of Akron, OH	B
U of Central Oklahoma, OK	B
U of Charleston, WV	B
U of Evansville, IN	B
U of Illinois at Urbana–Champaign, IL	B
U of Indianapolis, IN	B
The U of Iowa, IA	B
U of Michigan–Dearborn, MI	B
U of Michigan–Flint, MI	B
U of Minnesota, Duluth, MN	B
U of Missouri–Columbia, MO	B
U of Missouri–St. Louis, MO	B
U of New Orleans, LA	B
U of Northern Iowa, IA	B
U of Oklahoma, OK	B
U of St. Francis, IL	B
U of Saint Francis, IN	B
The U of Toledo, OH	B
U of Wisconsin–Eau Claire, WI	B

A—associate degree; B—bachelor's degree

U of Wisconsin–Superior, WI B
Ursuline Coll, OH B
Viterbo U, WI B
Waldorf Coll, IA B
Washington U in St. Louis, MO B
Wayne State U, MI B
Wheaton Coll, IL B
Wright State U, OH B
York Coll, NE B
Youngstown State U, OH B

Social Work

Adrian Coll, MI B
Anderson U, IN B
Andrews U, MI B
Ashland U, OH B
Augsburg Coll, MN B
Augustana Coll, SD B
Aurora U, IL B
Avila U, MO B
Ball State U, IN B
Bemidji State U, MN B
Bethany Coll, KS B
Bethel Coll, KS B
Bethel U, MN B
Bluffton U, OH B
Bowling Green State U, OH B
Bradley U, IL B
Briar Cliff U, IA B
Buena Vista U, IA B
Calvin Coll, MI B
Capital U, OH B
Cedarville U, OH B
Central Christian Coll of Kansas, KS A
Central Michigan U, MI B
Central State U, OH B
Clarke Coll, IA B
Cleveland State U, OH B
Coll of Mount St. Joseph, OH B
Coll of Saint Benedict, MN B
The Coll of St. Scholastica, MN B
Coll of the Ozarks, MO B
Concordia Coll, MN B
Concordia U Chicago, IL B
Concordia U Wisconsin, WI B
Cornerstone U, MI B
Creighton U, NE B
Dana Coll, NE B
Defiance Coll, OH B
Dordt Coll, IA B
Eastern Michigan U, MI B
Evangel U, MO B
Ferris State U, MI A,B
Fort Hays State U, KS B
Franciscan U of Steubenville, OH B
Goshen Coll, IN B
Grace Coll, IN B
Graceland U, IA B
Grand Valley State U, MI B
Greenville Coll, IL B
Haskell Indian Nations U, KS A
Hope Coll, MI B
Huntington U, IN B
Illinois State U, IL B
Indiana State U, IN B
Indiana U Bloomington, IN B
Indiana U East, IN B
Indiana U–Purdue U Indianapolis, IN B
Indiana Wesleyan U, IN B
Kansas State U, KS B
Kent State U, OH B
Kilian Comm Coll, SD A
Kuyper Coll, MI B
Lewis U, IL B
Lindenwood U, MO B
Loras Coll, IA B
Lourdes Coll, OH B
Loyola U Chicago, IL B
Luther Coll, IA B
MacMurray Coll, IL B
Madonna U, MI B
Malone U, OH B
Manchester Coll, IN B
Marian U, WI B
Marquette U, WI B
McKendree U, IL B
Miami U, OH B
Michigan State U, MI B
Millikin U, IL B
Minnesota State U Mankato, MN B
Minnesota State U Moorhead, MN B
Minot State U, ND B
Missouri State U, MO B
Missouri Western State U, MO B
Mount Mary Coll, WI B
Mount Mercy Coll, IA B
Mount Vernon Nazarene U, OH B
Nebraska Wesleyan U, NE B
North Central U, MN B
Northeastern Illinois U, IL B
Northeastern State U, OK B
Northern Michigan U, MI B
Northern State U, SD A
Oakland U, MI B
Oglala Lakota Coll, SD A,B
Ohio Dominican U, OH B
The Ohio State U, OH B
Ohio U, OH B
Olivet Nazarene U, IL B
Oral Roberts U, OK B
Pittsburg State U, KS B
Presentation Coll, SD B
Purdue U, IN B
Rockford Coll, IL B
Saginaw Valley State U, MI B
St. Augustine Coll, IL B
St. Catherine U, MN B
St. Cloud State U, MN B
Saint John's U, MN B
Saint Joseph's Coll, IN B
Saint Louis U, MO B
Saint Mary's Coll, IN B
St. Olaf Coll, MN B
Siena Heights U, MI B
Southeast Missouri State U, MO B
Southern Illinois U Carbondale, IL B
Southern Illinois U Edwardsville, IL B
Southwestern Oklahoma State U, OK B
Southwest Minnesota State U, MN B
Spring Arbor U, MI B
Taylor U, IN B
Trinity Christian Coll, IL B
Union Coll, NE B
Union Inst & U, OH B
The U of Akron, OH B
U of Central Missouri, MO B
U of Cincinnati, OH A,B
The U of Findlay, OH B
U of Illinois at Chicago, IL B
U of Illinois at Springfield, IL B
U of Indianapolis, IN B
The U of Iowa, IA B
The U of Kansas, KS B
U of Mary, ND B
U of Michigan–Flint, MI B
U of Missouri–Columbia, MO B
U of Missouri–St. Louis, MO B
U of Nebraska at Kearney, NE B
U of North Dakota, ND B
U of Northern Iowa, IA B
U of Oklahoma, OK B
U of Rio Grande, OH A,B
U of St. Francis, IL B
U of Saint Francis, IN B
U of Sioux Falls, SD B
The U of South Dakota, SD B
U of Southern Indiana, IN B
The U of Toledo, OH A,B
U of Wisconsin–Eau Claire, WI B
U of Wisconsin–Green Bay, WI B
U of Wisconsin–Madison, WI B
U of Wisconsin–Milwaukee, WI B
U of Wisconsin–Oshkosh, WI B
U of Wisconsin–Superior, WI B
U of Wisconsin–Whitewater, WI B
Ursuline Coll, OH B
Valparaiso U, IN B
Viterbo U, WI B
Wartburg Coll, IA B
Washburn U, KS B
Wayne State U, MI B
Western Illinois U, IL B
Western Michigan U, MI B
Wichita State U, KS B
Wilberforce U, OH B
Wilmington Coll, OH B
Winona State U, MN B
Wright State U, OH A,B
Xavier U, OH B
Youngstown State U, OH A,B

Social Work Related

Miami U Hamilton, OH B
The U of Akron, OH A

Sociobiology

Beloit Coll, WI B

Sociology

Adrian Coll, MI B
Albion Coll, MI B
Alma Coll, MI B
Anderson U, IN B
Andrews U, MI B
Aquinas Coll, MI B
Ashland U, OH B
Augsburg Coll, MN B
Augustana Coll, IL B
Augustana Coll, SD B
Aurora U, IL B
Avila U, MO B
Bacone Coll, OK A
Baker U, KS B
Baldwin-Wallace Coll, OH B
Ball State U, IN B
Beloit Coll, WI B
Bemidji State U, MN B
Benedictine Coll, KS B
Benedictine U, IL B
Bethany Coll, KS B
Bethany Lutheran Coll, MN B
Bethel Coll, IN B
Black Hills State U, SD B
Bluffton U, OH B
Bowling Green State U, OH B
Bradley U, IL B
Buena Vista U, IA B
Butler U, IN B
Calvin Coll, MI B
Cameron U, OK B
Capital U, OH B
Carleton Coll, MN B
Carroll U, WI B
Case Western Reserve U, OH B
Cedarville U, OH B
Central Christian Coll of Kansas, KS A,B
Central Coll, IA B
Central Methodist U, MO B
Central Michigan U, MI B
Central State U, OH B
Clarkson U, NY B
Cleveland State U, OH B
Coe Coll, IA B
Coll of Mount St. Joseph, OH B
Coll of Saint Benedict, MN B
Coll of the Ozarks, MO B
The Coll of Wooster, OH B
Columbia Coll, MO B
Concordia Coll, MN B
Concordia U, MI B
Concordia U Chicago, IL B
Concordia U, Nebraska, NE B
Concordia U, St. Paul, MN B
Cornell Coll, IA B
Creighton U, NE B
Dakota Wesleyan U, SD B
Denison U, OH B
DePaul U, IL B
DePauw U, IN B
Doane Coll, NE B
Dominican U, IL B
Dordt Coll, IA B
Drake U, IA B
Drury U, MO B
Earlham Coll, IN B
Eastern Illinois U, IL B
Eastern Michigan U, MI B
East-West U, IL B
Edgewood Coll, WI B
Elmhurst Coll, IL B
Emporia State U, KS B

Eureka Coll, IL B
Evangel U, MO B
Ferris State U, MI B
Fontbonne U, MO B
Fort Hays State U, KS B
Franciscan U of Steubenville, OH B
Franklin Coll, IN B
Friends U, KS B
Goshen Coll, IN B
Grace Coll, IN B
Graceland U, IA B
Grand Valley State U, MI B
Grand View U, IA A
Greenville Coll, IL B
Grinnell Coll, IA B
Gustavus Adolphus Coll, MN B
Hamline U, MN B
Hannibal-LaGrange Coll, MO B
Hanover Coll, IN B
Hillsdale Coll, MI B
Hiram Coll, OH B
Hope Coll, MI B
Huntington U, IN B
Illinois Coll, IL B
Illinois State U, IL B
Illinois Wesleyan U, IL B
Indiana U Bloomington, IN B
Indiana U East, IN B
Indiana U Kokomo, IN B
Indiana U Northwest, IN B
Indiana U–Purdue U Fort Wayne, IN B
Indiana U–Purdue U Indianapolis, IN B
Indiana U South Bend, IN B
Indiana U Southeast, IN B
Indiana Wesleyan U, IN B
Iowa State U of Science and Technology, IA B
John Carroll U, OH B
Kalamazoo Coll, MI B
Kansas State U, KS B
Kansas Wesleyan U, KS B
Kent State U, OH B
Kenyon Coll, OH B
Knox Coll, IL B
Lake Erie Coll, OH B
Lake Forest Coll, IL B
Lakeland Coll, WI B
Lake Superior State U, MI B
Lewis U, IL B
Lincoln U, MO B
Lindenwood U, MO B
Loras Coll, IA B
Lourdes Coll, OH A,B
Loyola U Chicago, IL B
Luther Coll, IA B
Macalester Coll, MN B
Madonna U, MI B
Manchester Coll, IN B
Marian U, IN B
Marquette U, WI B
Martin U, IN B
Maryville U of Saint Louis, MO B
McKendree U, IL B
McPherson Coll, KS B
Miami U, OH B
Miami U Hamilton, OH B
Michigan State U, MI B
MidAmerica Nazarene U, KS B
Millikin U, IL B
Minnesota State U Mankato, MN B
Minnesota State U Moorhead, MN B
Minot State U, ND B
Missouri Southern State U, MO B
Missouri State U, MO B
Monmouth Coll, IL B
Mount Mercy Coll, IA B
Mount Union Coll, OH B
Mount Vernon Nazarene U, OH B
Muskingum Coll, OH B
Nebraska Wesleyan U, NE B
Newman U, KS B
North Central Coll, IL B
North Dakota State U, ND B
Northeastern Illinois U, IL B
Northeastern State U, OK B
Northern Michigan U, MI B
Northern State U, SD B
Northland Coll, WI B
North Park U, IL B
Northwestern U, IL B
Northwest Missouri State U, MO B
Oakland U, MI B
Oberlin Coll, OH B
Ohio Dominican U, OH B
Ohio Northern U, OH B
The Ohio State U, OH B
Ohio U, OH B
Ohio Wesleyan U, OH B
Oklahoma Baptist U, OK B
Oklahoma City U, OK B
Oklahoma State U, OK B
Olivet Coll, MI B
Olivet Nazarene U, IL B
Otterbein Coll, OH B
Park U, MO B
Pittsburg State U, KS B
Purdue U, IN B
Purdue U Calumet, IN B
Ripon Coll, WI B
Rockford Coll, IL B
Roosevelt U, IL B
Saginaw Valley State U, MI B
St. Ambrose U, IA B
St. Catherine U, MN B
St. Cloud State U, MN B
St. Gregory's U, Shawnee, OK B
Saint John's U, MN B
Saint Joseph's Coll, IN B
Saint Louis U, MO B
Saint Mary's Coll, IN B
Saint Mary's U of Minnesota, MN B
St. Norbert Coll, WI B
St. Olaf Coll, MN B
Saint Xavier U, IL B
Shawnee State U, OH B
Simpson Coll, IA B
South Dakota State U, SD B
Southeastern Oklahoma State U, OK B
Southern Illinois U Carbondale, IL B
Southern Illinois U Edwardsville, IL B
Southern Methodist U, TX B
Southern Nazarene U, OK B
Southwest Baptist U, MO B
Southwest Minnesota State U, MN B
Spring Arbor U, MI B
Taylor U, IN B
Transylvania U, KY B
Trinity Christian Coll, IL B
Truman State U, MO B
The U of Akron, OH B
U of Central Missouri, MO B
U of Central Oklahoma, OK B
U of Chicago, IL B
U of Cincinnati, OH B
U of Dayton, OH B
U of Evansville, IN B
The U of Findlay, OH B
U of Illinois at Chicago, IL B
U of Illinois at Urbana–Champaign, IL B
U of Indianapolis, IN B
The U of Iowa, IA B
The U of Kansas, KS B
U of Michigan, MI B
U of Michigan–Dearborn, MI B
U of Michigan–Flint, MI B
U of Minnesota, Duluth, MN B
U of Minnesota, Morris, MN B
U of Minnesota, Twin Cities Campus, MN B
U of Missouri–Columbia, MO B
U of Missouri–Kansas City, MO B
U of Missouri–St. Louis, MO B
U of Nebraska at Kearney, NE B
U of Nebraska at Omaha, NE B
U of Nebraska–Lincoln, NE B
U of New Orleans, LA B
U of North Dakota, ND B
U of Northern Iowa, IA B
U of Notre Dame, IN B
U of Oklahoma, OK B
U of Rio Grande, OH A,B
U of Saint Francis, IN B
U of Saint Mary, KS B
U of Science and Arts of Oklahoma, OK B
U of Sioux Falls, SD B
The U of South Dakota, SD B
U of Southern Indiana, IN B
The U of Toledo, OH B
U of Tulsa, OK B
U of Wisconsin–Eau Claire, WI B
U of Wisconsin–La Crosse, WI B
U of Wisconsin–Madison, WI B
U of Wisconsin–Milwaukee, WI B
U of Wisconsin–Oshkosh, WI B
U of Wisconsin–Parkside, WI B
U of Wisconsin–Stevens Point, WI B
U of Wisconsin–Superior, WI B
U of Wisconsin–Whitewater, WI B
Ursuline Coll, OH B
Valparaiso U, IN B
Viterbo U, WI B
Walsh U, OH B
Wartburg Coll, IA B
Washburn U, KS B
Wayne State Coll, NE B
Wayne State U, MI B
Western Illinois U, IL B
Western Michigan U, MI B
Westminster Coll, MO B
Wheaton Coll, IL B
Wichita State U, KS B
Wilberforce U, OH B
Winona State U, MN B
Wittenberg U, OH B
Wright State U, OH A,B
Xavier U, OH A,B
Youngstown State U, OH B

Soil Conservation

U of Wisconsin–Stevens Point, WI B

Soil Science and Agronomy

Michigan State U, MI B
North Dakota State U, ND B
Oklahoma State U, OK B
U of Minnesota, Twin Cities Campus, MN B
U of Nebraska–Lincoln, NE B

South Asian Languages

Northwestern U, IL B
U of Chicago, IL B

Spanish

Adrian Coll, MI B
Albion Coll, MI B
Alma Coll, MI B
Anderson U, IN B
Andrews U, MI B
Aquinas Coll, MI B
Ashland U, OH B
Augsburg Coll, MN B
Augustana Coll, IL B
Augustana Coll, SD B
Aurora U, IL B
Baker U, KS B
Baldwin-Wallace Coll, OH B
Ball State U, IN B
Beloit Coll, WI B
Bemidji State U, MN B
Benedictine Coll, KS B
Benedictine U, IL B
Bethel Coll, IN B
Bethel Coll, KS B
Bethel U, MN B
Black Hills State U, SD B
Bluffton U, OH B
Bowling Green State U, OH B
Bradley U, IL B
Briar Cliff U, IA B
Buena Vista U, IA B
Butler U, IN B
Calvin Coll, MI B
Capital U, OH B
Carleton Coll, MN B

A—associate degree; B—bachelor's degree

Carroll U, WI B
Case Western Reserve U, OH B
Cedarville U, OH B
Central Coll, IA B
Central Methodist U, MO B
Central Michigan U, MI B
Clarke Coll, IA B
Cleveland State U, OH B
Coe Coll, IA B
Coll of Saint Benedict, MN B
Coll of the Ozarks, MO B
The Coll of Wooster, OH B
Concordia Coll, MN B
Concordia U, Nebraska, NE B
Concordia U Wisconsin, WI B
Cornell Coll, IA B
Cornerstone U, MI B
Creighton U, NE B
Dakota Wesleyan U, SD B
Dana Coll, NE B
Denison U, OH B
DePaul U, IL B
DePauw U, IN B
Doane Coll, NE B
Dominican U, IL B
Dordt Coll, IA B
Drury U, MO B
Earlham Coll, IN B
Eastern Michigan U, MI B
Edgewood Coll, WI B
Elmhurst Coll, IL B
Evangel U, MO B
Fort Hays State U, KS B
Franciscan U of Steubenville, OH B
Franklin Coll, IN B
Friends U, KS B
Goshen Coll, IN B
Grace Coll, IN B
Graceland U, IA B
Grand Valley State U, MI B
Greenville Coll, IL B
Grinnell Coll, IA B
Gustavus Adolphus Coll, MN B
Hamline U, MN B
Hanover Coll, IN B
Heidelberg U, OH B
Hillsdale Coll, MI B
Hiram Coll, OH B
Hope Coll, MI B
Huntington U, IN B
Illinois Coll, IL B
Illinois State U, IL B
Illinois Wesleyan U, IL B
Indiana U Bloomington, IN B
Indiana U Northwest, IN B
Indiana U–Purdue U Fort Wayne, IN A,B
Indiana U–Purdue U Indianapolis, IN B
Indiana U South Bend, IN B
Indiana U Southeast, IN B
Indiana Wesleyan U, IN B
Iowa State U of Science and Technology, IA B
Jamestown Coll, ND B
John Carroll U, OH B
Kalamazoo Coll, MI B
Kansas Wesleyan U, KS B
Kent State U, OH B
Kenyon Coll, OH B
Knox Coll, IL B
Lake Erie Coll, OH B
Lake Forest Coll, IL B
Lakeland Coll, WI B
Lawrence U, WI B
Lincoln U, MO B
Lindenwood U, MO B
Loras Coll, IA B
Loyola U Chicago, IL B
Luther Coll, IA B
Macalester Coll, MN B
MacMurray Coll, IL B
Madonna U, MI B
Malone U, OH B
Manchester Coll, IN B
Marian U, WI B
Marian U, IN B
Marietta Coll, OH B
Marquette U, WI B
McPherson Coll, KS B
Miami U, OH B
Miami U Hamilton, OH B
Michigan State U, MI B
MidAmerica Nazarene U, KS B
Millikin U, IL B
Minnesota State U Mankato, MN B
Minnesota State U Moorhead, MN B
Minot State U, ND B
Missouri Southern State U, MO B
Missouri State U, MO B
Missouri Western State U, MO B
Monmouth Coll, IL B
Morningside Coll, IA B
Mount Mary Coll, WI B
Mount Union Coll, OH B
Mount Vernon Nazarene U, OH B
Muskingum Coll, OH B
Nebraska Wesleyan U, NE B
North Central Coll, IL B
North Dakota State U, ND B
Northeastern Illinois U, IL B
Northeastern State U, OK B
Northern Michigan U, MI B
Northern State U, SD B
North Park U, IL B
Northwestern Coll, MN B
Northwestern U, IL B
Northwest Missouri State U, MO B
Oakland U, MI B
Oberlin Coll, OH B
Ohio Northern U, OH B
The Ohio State U, OH B
Ohio U, OH B
Ohio Wesleyan U, OH B
Oklahoma Baptist U, OK B
Oklahoma Christian U, OK B
Oklahoma City U, OK B
Oklahoma Panhandle State U, OK B
Oklahoma State U, OK B
Olivet Nazarene U, IL B
Oral Roberts U, OK B
Otterbein Coll, OH B
Park U, MO B
Pittsburg State U, KS B
Purdue U, IN B
Ripon Coll, WI B
Rockford Coll, IL B
Rockhurst U, MO B
Roosevelt U, IL B
Saginaw Valley State U, MI B
St. Ambrose U, IA B
St. Catherine U, MN B
St. Cloud State U, MN B
Saint John's U, MN B
Saint Louis U, MO B
Saint Mary's Coll, IN B
Saint Mary's U of Minnesota, MN B
St. Norbert Coll, WI B
St. Olaf Coll, MN B
Saint Xavier U, IL B
Siena Heights U, MI B
Simpson Coll, IA B
South Dakota State U, SD B
Southeastern Oklahoma State U, OK B
Southeast Missouri State U, MO B
Southern Illinois U Carbondale, IL B
Southern Methodist U, TX B
Southern Nazarene U, OK B
Southwest Baptist U, MO B
Southwest Minnesota State U, MN B
Spring Arbor U, MI B
Taylor U, IN B
Transylvania U, KY B
Trinity Christian Coll, IL B
Truman State U, MO B
Union Coll, NE B
The U of Akron, OH B
U of Central Missouri, MO B
U of Central Oklahoma, OK B
U of Chicago, IL B
U of Cincinnati, OH B
U of Dallas, TX B
U of Dayton, OH B
U of Evansville, IN B
The U of Findlay, OH B
U of Illinois at Chicago, IL B
U of Illinois at Urbana–Champaign, IL B
U of Indianapolis, IN B
The U of Iowa, IA B
The U of Kansas, KS B
U of Michigan, MI B
U of Michigan–Dearborn, MI B
U of Michigan–Flint, MI B
U of Minnesota, Duluth, MN B
U of Minnesota, Morris, MN B
U of Minnesota, Twin Cities Campus, MN B
U of Missouri–Columbia, MO B
U of Missouri–Kansas City, MO B
U of Missouri–St. Louis, MO B
U of Nebraska at Kearney, NE B
U of Nebraska at Omaha, NE B
U of Nebraska–Lincoln, NE B
U of New Orleans, LA B
U of North Dakota, ND B
U of Northern Iowa, IA B
U of Notre Dame, IN B
U of Oklahoma, OK B
The U of South Dakota, SD B
U of Southern Indiana, IN B
The U of Toledo, OH B
U of Tulsa, OK B
U of Wisconsin–Eau Claire, WI B
U of Wisconsin–Green Bay, WI B
U of Wisconsin–La Crosse, WI B
U of Wisconsin–Madison, WI B
U of Wisconsin–Milwaukee, WI B
U of Wisconsin–Oshkosh, WI B
U of Wisconsin–Parkside, WI B
U of Wisconsin–Platteville, WI B
U of Wisconsin–Stevens Point, WI B
U of Wisconsin–Whitewater, WI B
Valley City State U, ND B
Valparaiso U, IN B
Viterbo U, WI B
Wabash Coll, IN B
Walsh U, OH B
Wartburg Coll, IA B
Washburn U, KS B
Washington U in St. Louis, MO B
Wayne State Coll, NE B
Webster U, MO B
Western Illinois U, IL B
Western Michigan U, MI B
Westminster Coll, MO B
Wheaton Coll, IL B
Wichita State U, KS B
William Jewell Coll, MO B
Wilmington Coll, OH B
Winona State U, MN B
Wittenberg U, OH B
Wright State U, OH B
Xavier U, OH A,B
Youngstown State U, OH B

Spanish and Iberian Studies

Coe Coll, IA B

Spanish Language Teacher Education

Alma Coll, MI B
Anderson U, IN B
Bethel Coll, IN B
Bethel U, MN B
Buena Vista U, IA B
Carroll U, WI B
Cedarville U, OH B
Central Michigan U, MI B
Coll of Saint Mary, NE B
Concordia Coll, MN B
Concordia U, Nebraska, NE B
Concordia U Wisconsin, WI B
Dana Coll, NE B
DePaul U, IL B
Dordt Coll, IA B
Edgewood Coll, WI B
Elmhurst Coll, IL B
Evangel U, MO B
Franklin Coll, IN B
Friends U, KS B

Grace Coll, IN B
Grand Valley State U, MI B
Greenville Coll, IL B
Hope Coll, MI B
Indiana U Bloomington, IN B
Indiana U Northwest, IN B
Indiana U–Purdue U Fort Wayne, IN B
Indiana U–Purdue U Indianapolis, IN B
Indiana U South Bend, IN B
Kent State U, OH B
Lindenwood U, MO B
Malone U, OH B
Marian U, WI B
Miami U, OH B
Miami U Hamilton, OH B
MidAmerica Nazarene U, KS B
Minnesota State U Moorhead, MN B
Minot State U, ND B
Missouri State U, MO B
Missouri Western State U, MO B
Mount Mary Coll, WI B
Mount Vernon Nazarene U, OH B
Muskingum Coll, OH B
North Dakota State U, ND B
Northeastern State U, OK B
Northern Michigan U, MI B
Ohio Northern U, OH B
Ohio U, OH B
Ohio Wesleyan U, OH B
Oklahoma Baptist U, OK B
Oral Roberts U, OK B
Pittsburg State U, KS B
Purdue U, IN B
Saginaw Valley State U, MI B
St. Ambrose U, IA B
St. Catherine U, MN B
Saint Mary's U of Minnesota, MN B
Saint Xavier U, IL B
Southeastern Oklahoma State U, OK B
Southwest Minnesota State U, MN B
Taylor U, IN B
The U of Akron, OH B
U of Evansville, IN B
U of Illinois at Chicago, IL B
U of Illinois at Urbana–Champaign, IL B
U of Indianapolis, IN B
The U of Iowa, IA B
U of Michigan–Flint, MI B
U of Minnesota, Duluth, MN B
U of Missouri–St. Louis, MO B
U of Nebraska–Lincoln, NE B
The U of South Dakota, SD B
The U of Toledo, OH B
Valley City State U, ND B
Valparaiso U, IN B
Viterbo U, WI B
Washington U in St. Louis, MO B
Western Michigan U, MI B
William Jewell Coll, MO B
Youngstown State U, OH B

Special Education

Ashland U, OH B
Augustana Coll, SD B
Aurora U, IL B
Avila U, MO B
Benedictine Coll, KS B
Benedictine U, IL B
Black Hills State U, SD B
Bowling Green State U, OH B
Buena Vista U, IA B
Calvin Coll, MI B
Capital U, OH B
Cedarville U, OH B
Central State U, OH B
Cleveland State U, OH B
Coll of Mount St. Joseph, OH B
Coll of Saint Mary, NE B
Concordia U, Nebraska, NE B
Culver-Stockton Coll, MO B
Dakota State U, SD B
Dakota Wesleyan U, SD B
Dana Coll, NE B
DePaul U, IL B
Doane Coll, NE B
Eastern Illinois U, IL B
Eastern Michigan U, MI B
Elmhurst Coll, IL B
Eureka Coll, IL B
Evangel U, MO B
Fontbonne U, MO B
Goshen Coll, IN B
Grace Coll, IN B
Grand Valley State U, MI B
Greenville Coll, IL B
Heidelberg U, OH B
Huntington U, IN B
Illinois State U, IL B
Indiana State U, IN B
Indiana U Bloomington, IN B
Indiana U South Bend, IN B
Indiana U Southeast, IN B
Indiana Wesleyan U, IN B
Iowa Wesleyan Coll, IA B
John Carroll U, OH B
Kansas Wesleyan U, KS B
Kent State U, OH B
Lewis U, IL B
Lincoln U, MO B
Lindenwood U, MO B
Loyola U Chicago, IL B
MacMurray Coll, IL B
Manchester Coll, IN B
Marian U, IN B
McPherson Coll, KS B
Miami U, OH B
Miami U Hamilton, OH B
Michigan State U, MI B
Minnesota State U Moorhead, MN B
Missouri State U, MO B
Morningside Coll, IA B
Mount Marty Coll, SD B
Mount Union Coll, OH B
Mount Vernon Nazarene U, OH B
Muskingum Coll, OH B
Nebraska Wesleyan U, NE B
Northeastern Illinois U, IL B
Northeastern State U, OK B
Northern Michigan U, MI B
Northern State U, SD B
Northwest Missouri State U, MO B
Oglala Lakota Coll, SD B
Ohio Dominican U, OH B
The Ohio State U, OH B
Ohio U, OH B
Oklahoma Baptist U, OK B
Oral Roberts U, OK B
Quincy U, IL B
Rockford Coll, IL B
Roosevelt U, IL B
Saginaw Valley State U, MI B
St. Cloud State U, MN B
Saint Mary-of-the-Woods Coll, IN B
Shawnee State U, OH B
Sinte Gleska U, SD A,B
Southeast Missouri State U, MO B
Southern Illinois U Carbondale, IL B
Southern Illinois U Edwardsville, IL B
Southwestern Oklahoma State U, OK B
Southwest Minnesota State U, MN B
Spring Arbor U, MI B
Trinity Christian Coll, IL B
The U of Akron, OH B
U of Central Missouri, MO B
U of Central Oklahoma, OK B
U of Cincinnati, OH B
U of Dayton, OH B
U of Evansville, IN B
The U of Findlay, OH B
U of Illinois at Urbana–Champaign, IL B
U of Minnesota, Duluth, MN B
U of Missouri–St. Louis, MO B
U of Nebraska at Kearney, NE B
U of Nebraska at Omaha, NE B
U of Northern Iowa, IA B
U of Oklahoma, OK B
U of St. Francis, IL B
U of Saint Francis, IN B
The U of South Dakota, SD B
The U of Toledo, OH B
U of Wisconsin–Eau Claire, WI B
U of Wisconsin–Madison, WI B
U of Wisconsin–Milwaukee, WI B
U of Wisconsin–Oshkosh, WI B
U of Wisconsin–Superior, WI B
U of Wisconsin–Whitewater, WI B
Ursuline Coll, OH B
Walsh U, OH B
Wayne State Coll, NE B
Wayne State U, MI B
Western Illinois U, IL B
Winona State U, MN B
Xavier U, OH B
York Coll, NE B
Youngstown State U, OH B

Special Education (Administration)

Wright State U, OH B

Special Education (Early Childhood)

Purdue U, IN B
U of Illinois at Urbana–Champaign, IL B
U of Northern Iowa, IA B

Special Education (Emotionally Disturbed)

Augsburg Coll, MN B
Central Michigan U, MI B
Eastern Michigan U, MI B
Grand Valley State U, MI B
Hope Coll, MI B
Loras Coll, IA B
Minnesota State U Moorhead, MN B
Olivet Coll, MI B
Trinity Christian Coll, IL B
The U of Toledo, OH B
Wright State U, OH B

Special Education (Gifted and Talented)

Grand Valley State U, MI B
Wright State U, OH B

Special Education (Hearing Impaired)

Augustana Coll, SD B
Bowling Green State U, OH B
Eastern Michigan U, MI B
Grand Valley State U, MI B
MacMurray Coll, IL B
Minot State U, ND B
Ohio U–Chillicothe, OH A
U of Nebraska–Lincoln, NE B
U of Science and Arts of Oklahoma, OK B
The U of Toledo, OH B
U of Tulsa, OK B

Special Education (Mentally Retarded)

Bradley U, IL B
Central Michigan U, MI B
Eastern Michigan U, MI B
Grand Valley State U, MI B
Loras Coll, IA B
Minnesota State U Moorhead, MN B
Minot State U, ND B
Northern Michigan U, MI B
Silver Lake Coll, WI B
Trinity Christian Coll, IL B
U of Mary, ND B
U of Northern Iowa, IA B
U of Rio Grande, OH B
U of Wisconsin–Stout, WI B
Western Michigan U, MI B
Wright State U, OH B

Special Education (Multiply Disabled)

Ball State U, IN B
Grand Valley State U, MI B
Ohio U, OH B
U of Illinois at Urbana–Champaign, IL B
U of Northern Iowa, IA B

A—associate degree; B—bachelor's degree

The U of Toledo, OH B
Wright State U, OH B

Special Education (Orthopedic and Other Physical Health Impairments)

Eastern Michigan U, MI B
Grand Valley State U, MI B
Wright State U, OH B

Special Education Related

Minot State U, ND A,B
Southeastern Oklahoma State U, OK B
U of Missouri–Columbia, MO B
U of Nebraska–Lincoln, NE B
U of Southern Indiana, IN B
The U of Toledo, OH B
Wright State U, OH B

Special Education (Specific Learning Disabilities)

Aquinas Coll, MI B
Baldwin-Wallace Coll, OH B
Bradley U, IL B
Eastern Michigan U, MI B
Hope Coll, MI B
Malone U, OH B
Minnesota State U Moorhead, MN B
Northeastern State U, OK B
Northwestern U, IL B
Silver Lake Coll, WI B
Trinity Christian Coll, IL B
U of Rio Grande, OH B
The U of Toledo, OH B
Wright State U, OH B

Special Education (Speech or Language Impaired)

Eastern Michigan U, MI B
Minot State U, ND B
U of Nebraska at Omaha, NE B
The U of Toledo, OH B
Wayne State U, MI B

Special Education (Vision Impaired)

Eastern Michigan U, MI B
The U of Toledo, OH B
Western Michigan U, MI B

Special Products Marketing

Dominican U, IL B
Iowa State U of Science and Technology, IA B

Speech and Rhetoric

Ashland U, OH B
Augsburg Coll, MN B
Augustana Coll, IL B
Ball State U, IN B
Bemidji State U, MN B
Black Hills State U, SD B
Bowling Green State U, OH B
Butler U, IN B
Calvin Coll, MI B
Coe Coll, IA B
Coll of Saint Benedict, MN B
Coll of the Ozarks, MO B
Concordia Coll, MN B
Concordia U, Nebraska, NE B
Cornell Coll, IA B
Cornerstone U, MI B
Creighton U, NE B
Denison U, OH B
Drake U, IA B
Eastern Illinois U, IL B
Evangel U, MO B
Ferris State U, MI A,B
Graceland U, IA B
Greenville Coll, IL B
Gustavus Adolphus Coll, MN B
Hannibal-LaGrange Coll, MO B
Illinois Coll, IL B
Illinois State U, IL B
Indiana U Bloomington, IN B
Indiana U South Bend, IN B
Iowa State U of Science and Technology, IA B
Kansas Wesleyan U, KS B
Kent State U, OH B
Lewis U, IL B
Madonna U, MI B
Manchester Coll, IN B
Marietta Coll, OH B
McKendree U, IL B
Miami U, OH B
Minnesota State U Mankato, MN B
Minnesota State U Moorhead, MN B
Minot State U, ND B
Monmouth Coll, IL B
Mount Mercy Coll, IA B
Nebraska Wesleyan U, NE B
North Central Coll, IL B
Northeastern Illinois U, IL B
Northeastern State U, OK B
Northern State U, SD B
North Park U, IL B
Northwestern U, IL B
Northwest Missouri State U, MO B
Ohio U, OH B
Oklahoma Baptist U, OK B
Oklahoma Christian U, OK B
Oklahoma City U, OK B
Olivet Nazarene U, IL B
St. Catherine U, MN B
St. Cloud State U, MN B
Saint John's U, MN B
South Dakota State U, SD B
Southeast Missouri State U, MO B
Southern Illinois U Carbondale, IL B
Southern Illinois U Edwardsville, IL B
Southern Nazarene U, OK B
Truman State U, MO B
U of Central Missouri, MO B
U of Illinois at Urbana–Champaign, IL B
The U of Iowa, IA B
The U of Kansas, KS B
U of Minnesota, Morris, MN B
U of Nebraska at Kearney, NE B
U of Nebraska at Omaha, NE B
U of Northern Iowa, IA B
U of Sioux Falls, SD B
U of Wisconsin–Platteville, WI B
U of Wisconsin–Superior, WI B
U of Wisconsin–Whitewater, WI B
Wabash Coll, IN B
William Jewell Coll, MO B
Winona State U, MN B
Youngstown State U, OH B

Speech-Language Pathology

Augustana Coll, IL B
Baker Coll of Muskegon, MI A
Ball State U, IN B
Eastern Michigan U, MI B
Miami U, OH B
Miami U Hamilton, OH B
Northern Michigan U, MI B
Northwestern U, IL B
Oklahoma State U, OK B
Purdue U, IN B
Rockhurst U, MO B
St. Cloud State U, MN B
Saint Xavier U, IL B
U of Central Missouri, MO B
U of Nebraska–Lincoln, NE B
U of Northern Iowa, IA B
U of Oklahoma Health Sciences Center, OK B
U of Science and Arts of Oklahoma, OK B
The U of Toledo, OH B
U of Wisconsin–Whitewater, WI B

Speech Teacher Education

Anderson U, IN B
Buena Vista U, IA B
Capital U, OH B
Central Christian Coll of Kansas, KS A
Central Michigan U, MI B
Concordia U, MI B
Concordia U Chicago, IL B
Concordia U, Nebraska, NE B
Culver-Stockton Coll, MO B
Dordt Coll, IA B
Evangel U, MO B
Indiana U Bloomington, IN B
Indiana U–Purdue U Fort Wayne, IN B
Indiana U–Purdue U Indianapolis, IN B
Miami U, OH B
Minnesota State U Moorhead, MN B
Northeastern State U, OK B
Olivet Coll, MI B
St. Ambrose U, IA B
St. Catherine U, MN B
Southeast Missouri State U, MO B
Southern Nazarene U, OK B
Southwest Baptist U, MO B
Southwest Minnesota State U, MN B
Taylor U, IN B
U of Indianapolis, IN B
The U of Iowa, IA B
U of Michigan–Flint, MI B
U of Northern Iowa, IA B
U of Rio Grande, OH B
The U of South Dakota, SD B
Wayne State Coll, NE B
William Jewell Coll, MO B
York Coll, NE B

Speech/Theater Education

Augustana Coll, SD B
Bemidji State U, MN B
Culver-Stockton Coll, MO B
Graceland U, IA B
Hamline U, MN B
McKendree U, IL B
Missouri Western State U, MO B
Oklahoma City U, OK B
Saginaw Valley State U, MI B
St. Ambrose U, IA B
St. Cloud State U, MN B
Southwest Minnesota State U, MN B
U of Minnesota, Morris, MN B
Wartburg Coll, IA B
York Coll, NE B

Speech Therapy

Augustana Coll, IL B
Fontbonne U, MO B
Indiana U Bloomington, IN B
Northwestern U, IL B
St. Cloud State U, MN B
U of Oklahoma Health Sciences Center, OK B
The U of Toledo, OH B
U of Wisconsin–Madison, WI B

Sport and Fitness Administration/Management

Augustana Coll, SD B
Baker U, KS B
Baldwin-Wallace Coll, OH B
Bemidji State U, MN B
Bethany Coll, KS B
Bethel Coll, IN B
Black Hills State U, SD B
Bluffton U, OH B
Bowling Green State U, OH B
Buena Vista U, IA B
Calvin Coll, MI B
Cedarville U, OH B
Central Christian Coll of Kansas, KS B
Central Methodist U, MO B
Central Michigan U, MI B
Clarke Coll, IA B
Cleveland State U, OH B
Coll of Mount St. Joseph, OH B
Concordia U, Nebraska, NE B
Concordia U Wisconsin, WI B
Crown Coll, MN B
Culver-Stockton Coll, MO B
Dana Coll, NE B
Davenport U, Grand Rapids, MI B
Defiance Coll, OH B
Drury U, MO B
Elmhurst Coll, IL B
Fontbonne U, MO B
Friends U, KS B
Grace Coll, IN B
Greenville Coll, IL B
Indiana Tech, IN B
Indiana U Bloomington, IN B
Indiana Wesleyan U, IN B
Iowa Wesleyan Coll, IA B

Lake Superior State U, MI A
Lewis U, IL B
Lindenwood U, MO B
Loras Coll, IA B
MacMurray Coll, IL B
Madonna U, MI B
Malone U, OH B
Marian U, WI B
Marian U, IN B
Maryville U of Saint Louis, MO B
Miami U, OH B
MidAmerica Nazarene U, KS B
Millikin U, IL B
Minnesota State U Mankato, MN B
Minnesota State U Moorhead, MN B
Minot State U, ND B
Missouri Baptist U, MO B
Mount Union Coll, OH B
Mount Vernon Nazarene U, OH A
Nebraska Wesleyan U, NE B
North Central Coll, IL B
North Central U, MN B
North Dakota State U, ND B
Northern Michigan U, MI B
Northern State U, SD B
Northwest Missouri State U, MO B
Northwood U, MI B
Ohio Dominican U, OH B
Ohio Northern U, OH B
Ohio U, OH B
Oklahoma Baptist U, OK B
Oklahoma Christian U, OK B
Olivet Coll, MI B
Olivet Nazarene U, IL B
Otterbein Coll, OH B
Quincy U, IL B
Rockhurst U, MO B
Rogers State U, OK B
St. Ambrose U, IA B
Saint Joseph's Coll, IN B
Shawnee State U, OH B
Siena Heights U, MI B
Simpson Coll, IA B
Southeast Missouri State U, MO B
Southern Nazarene U, OK B
Southwest Baptist U, MO B
Southwestern Coll, KS B
Spring Arbor U, MI B
Taylor U, IN B
Tiffin U, OH B
Trine U, IN B
Union Coll, NE B
The U of Akron, OH B
U of Dayton, OH B
U of Evansville, IN B
U of Illinois at Urbana–Champaign, IL B
U of Indianapolis, IN B
The U of Iowa, IA B
U of Mary, ND B
U of Michigan, MI B
U of Minnesota, Crookston, MN B
U of Nebraska at Kearney, NE B
U of Saint Mary, KS B
U of Tulsa, OK B
U of Wisconsin–Parkside, WI B
Valparaiso U, IN B
Wartburg Coll, IA B
Wayne State Coll, NE B
Wichita State U, KS B
Wilmington Coll, OH B
Winona State U, MN B
Xavier U, OH B
York Coll, NE B

Statistics

Bowling Green State U, OH B
Case Western Reserve U, OH B
Central Michigan U, MI B
Clarkson U, NY B
DePaul U, IL B
Eastern Michigan U, MI B
Grace Coll, IN B
Grand Valley State U, MI B
Indiana U Bloomington, IN B
Indiana U–Purdue U Fort Wayne, IN B
Iowa State U of Science and Technology, IA B
Kansas State U, KS B
Loyola U Chicago, IL B
Luther Coll, IA B
Marquette U, WI B
Miami U, OH B
Miami U Hamilton, OH B
Michigan State U, MI B
Michigan Technological U, MI B
North Dakota State U, ND B
Northwestern U, IL B
Oakland U, MI B
Ohio Northern U, OH B
Ohio Wesleyan U, OH B
Oklahoma State U, OK B
Purdue U, IN B
St. Cloud State U, MN B
Southern Methodist U, TX B
The U of Akron, OH B
U of Chicago, IL B
U of Illinois at Chicago, IL B
U of Illinois at Urbana–Champaign, IL B
The U of Iowa, IA B
U of Michigan, MI B
U of Minnesota, Duluth, MN B
U of Minnesota, Morris, MN B
U of Missouri–Columbia, MO B
U of Missouri–Kansas City, MO B
U of Nebraska at Kearney, NE B
U of Wisconsin–Madison, WI B
U of Wisconsin–Milwaukee, WI B
Washington U in St. Louis, MO B
Western Michigan U, MI B
Winona State U, MN B
Wright State U, OH B

Statistics Related

Ohio Northern U, OH B

Stringed Instruments

The U of Kansas, KS B

Structural Engineering

Clarkson U, NY B
U of Illinois at Urbana–Champaign, IL B
The U of Toledo, OH B
Western Michigan U, MI B

Substance Abuse/Addiction Counseling

Argosy U, Chicago, IL B
Argosy U, Schaumburg, IL B
Argosy U, Twin Cities, MN B
Calumet Coll of Saint Joseph, IN B
Dominican U, IL B
Indiana U–Purdue U Fort Wayne, IN B
Indiana Wesleyan U, IN A,B
Kansas Wesleyan U, KS B
Martin U, IN B
Minot State U, ND B
National-Louis U, IL B
Newman U, KS A,B
North Central U, MN B
Ohio Christian U, OH B
Oklahoma State U, Oklahoma City, OK A
St. Augustine Coll, IL A
St. Catherine U, MN B
St. Cloud State U, MN B
Sinte Gleska U, SD B
Tiffin U, OH B
The U of Akron, OH A
U of Mary, ND B
The U of South Dakota, SD B
The U of Toledo, OH A
Washburn U, KS A,B

Surgical Technology

Baker Coll of Clinton Township, MI A
Baker Coll of Flint, MI A
Baker Coll of Jackson, MI A
Baker Coll of Muskegon, MI A
Brown Mackie Coll–Fort Wayne, IN A
Brown Mackie Coll–Merrillville, IN A
Brown Mackie Coll–Michigan City, IN A
Colorado Tech U North Kansas City, MO A
Mercy Coll of Health Sciences, IA A
Northern Michigan U, MI A
Presentation Coll, SD A
Robert Morris Coll, IL A
Rochester Comm and Tech Coll, MN A
The U of Akron, OH A
U of Saint Francis, IN A
Washburn U, KS A

Surveying Engineering

Purdue U, IN B

Survey Technology

Ferris State U, MI A,B
Michigan Technological U, MI B
Oklahoma State U, Oklahoma City, OK A
Purdue U, IN B
The U of Akron, OH A,B
U of Wisconsin–Madison, WI B

Swedish

Augustana Coll, IL B

System Administration

Dordt Coll, IA B
Michigan Technological U, MI B
Missouri Coll, MO A
Rochester Comm and Tech Coll, MN A

System, Networking, and LAN/WAN Management

Baker Coll of Auburn Hills, MI A
ITT Tech Inst, Burr Ridge, IL A
ITT Tech Inst, Mount Prospect, IL A
ITT Tech Inst, Orland Park, IL A
ITT Tech Inst, Fort Wayne, IN A
ITT Tech Inst, Indianapolis, IN A
ITT Tech Inst, Newburgh, IN A
ITT Tech Inst, South Bend, IN A
ITT Tech Inst, IA A
ITT Tech Inst, KS A
ITT Tech Inst, Canton, MI A
ITT Tech Inst, Troy, MI A
ITT Tech Inst, MN A
ITT Tech Inst, Arnold, MO A
ITT Tech Inst, Earth City, MO A
ITT Tech Inst, Kansas City, MO A
ITT Tech Inst, Springfield, MO A
ITT Tech Inst, NE A
ITT Tech Inst, Oklahoma City, OK A
ITT Tech Inst, Tulsa, OK A
ITT Tech Inst, Green Bay, WI A
ITT Tech Inst, Greenfield, WI A
ITT Tech Inst, Madison, WI A
Southern Nazarene U, OK B
U of Northern Iowa, IA B
U of Phoenix–Cleveland Campus, OH A
U of Phoenix–Indianapolis Campus, IN A
Westwood Coll–Chicago Du Page, IL B

Systems Engineering

Case Western Reserve U, OH B
Ohio U, OH B
Washington U in St. Louis, MO B
Wright State U, OH B

A—associate degree; B—bachelor's degree

Systems Science and Theory
Washington U in St. Louis, MO B
Wright State U, OH B

Talmudic Studies
Telshe Yeshiva–Chicago, IL B
Yeshiva Gedolah of Greater Detroit, MI B

Tamil
U of Chicago, IL B

Taxation
Fontbonne U, MO B
Grand Valley State U, MI B

Teacher Assistant/Aide
Dordt Coll, IA A
Rochester Comm and Tech Coll, MN A
Tiffin U, OH A
U of Phoenix–Cleveland Campus, OH A
U of Phoenix–Indianapolis Campus, IN A
U of Phoenix–St. Louis Campus, MO A
Valparaiso U, IN A

Technical and Business Writing
Bowling Green State U, OH B
Cedarville U, OH B
Clarkson U, NY B
Eastern Michigan U, MI B
Ferris State U, MI A,B
Indiana U–Purdue U Fort Wayne, IN B
Iowa State U of Science and Technology, IA B
Madonna U, MI B
Miami U Hamilton, OH B
Michigan Technological U, MI B
Missouri State U, MO B
Mount Mary Coll, WI B
Northwestern Coll, MN B
Ohio Northern U, OH B
Oklahoma State U, Oklahoma City, OK A
Pittsburg State U, KS B
Spring Arbor U, MI B
U of Wisconsin–Stout, WI B
Valparaiso U, IN B
Webster U, MO B
Youngstown State U, OH B

Technical Teacher Education
Bowling Green State U, OH B
Eastern Illinois U, IL B
Ferris State U, MI B
The Ohio State U, OH B
Oklahoma State U, OK B
Pittsburg State U, KS B
South Dakota State U, SD B
The U of Akron, OH B
U of Illinois at Urbana–Champaign, IL B
U of Missouri–Columbia, MO B
U of Nebraska at Kearney, NE B
U of Wisconsin–Stout, WI B
Valley City State U, ND B
Wayne State U, MI B
Wright State U, OH B

Technology/Industrial Arts Teacher Education
Ball State U, IN B
Bemidji State U, MN B
Central Michigan U, MI B
Coll of the Ozarks, MO B
Concordia U, Nebraska, NE B
Eastern Michigan U, MI B
Illinois State U, IL B
Kent State U, OH B
Lindenwood U, MO B
Michigan Technological U, MI B
Northern Michigan U, MI B
The Ohio State U, OH B
Purdue U, IN B
St. Cloud State U, MN B
Southeast Missouri State U, MO B
Southwestern Oklahoma State U, OK B
U of Nebraska–Lincoln, NE B
U of Northern Iowa, IA B
U of Wisconsin–Stout, WI B
Valley City State U, ND B
Viterbo U, WI B
Wayne State Coll, NE B
Western Michigan U, MI B

Telecommunications
Ball State U, IN B
Michigan State U, MI B
Ohio U, OH B
U of Wisconsin–Platteville, WI B
Winona State U, MN B

Telecommunications Technology
Ferris State U, MI B

Theater Design and Technology
Bowling Green State U, OH B
Central Michigan U, MI B
Coe Coll, IA B
Coll of the Ozarks, MO B
DePaul U, IL B
Doane Coll, NE B
Huntington U, IN B
Illinois Wesleyan U, IL B
Indiana U Bloomington, IN A
Michigan Technological U, MI B
Millikin U, IL B
Oakland U, MI B
Ohio U, OH B
Oklahoma City U, OK B
Oral Roberts U, OK B
The U of Kansas, KS B
U of Michigan, MI B
U of Michigan–Flint, MI B
U of Rio Grande, OH A
Webster U, MO B
Wright State U, OH B

Theater Literature, History and Criticism
Buena Vista U, IA B
DePaul U, IL B
Northwestern U, IL B
Ohio U, OH B
U of Illinois at Urbana–Champaign, IL B
Washington U in St. Louis, MO B

Theater/Theater Arts Management
Cedarville U, OH B
Eastern Michigan U, MI B
Haskell Indian Nations U, KS A
Miami U Hamilton, OH B
Ohio Northern U, OH B
Ohio U, OH B
Pittsburg State U, KS B
St. Cloud State U, MN B
U of Evansville, IN B

Theological and Ministerial Studies Related
Bacone Coll, OK A
Creighton U, NE A
Huntington U, IN B
Manhattan Christian Coll, KS A,B
Messenger Coll, MO B
Northwestern Coll, MN B
U of Saint Francis, IN B

Theology
Anderson U, IN B
Andrews U, MI B
Augsburg Coll, MN B
Benedictine U, IL B
Briar Cliff U, IA A,B
Calumet Coll of Saint Joseph, IN B
Calvin Coll, MI B
Cedarville U, OH B
Central Bible Coll, MO B
Central Christian Coll of Kansas, KS A
Coll of Saint Benedict, MN B
Coll of Saint Mary, NE B
Concordia U Chicago, IL B
Concordia U, Nebraska, NE B
Concordia U, St. Paul, MN B
Concordia U Wisconsin, WI B
Creighton U, NE A,B
Crossroads Coll, MN B
Crown Coll, MN B
Dakota Wesleyan U, SD B
Dominican U, IL B
Dordt Coll, IA B
Elmhurst Coll, IL B
Franciscan U of Steubenville, OH A,B
Friends U, KS B
Grace Bible Coll, MI B
Hanover Coll, IN B
Huntington U, IN B
Indiana Wesleyan U, IN B
Kuyper Coll, MI B
Lake Forest Coll, IL B
Loyola U Chicago, IL B
Madonna U, MI B
Manhattan Christian Coll, KS B
Marian U, IN A,B
Martin Luther Coll, MN B
MidAmerica Nazarene U, KS B
Missouri Baptist U, MO A
Moody Bible Inst, IL B
Mount Vernon Nazarene U, OH B
Newman U, KS B
Ohio Dominican U, OH A,B
Olivet Nazarene U, IL B
Oral Roberts U, OK B
Quincy U, IL B
Rockhurst U, MO B
St. Ambrose U, IA B
St. Catherine U, MN B
St. Gregory's U, Shawnee, OK B
Saint John's U, MN B
St. Louis Christian Coll, MO B
Saint Louis U, MO B
Saint Mary-of-the-Woods Coll, IN B
Saint Mary's U of Minnesota, MN B
Silver Lake Coll, WI B
Southwest Baptist U, MO B
Southwestern Christian U, OK B
Spring Arbor U, MI B
Trinity Christian Coll, IL B
Union Coll, NE B
U of Dallas, TX B
U of Evansville, IN B
U of Mary, ND B
U of Notre Dame, IN B
U of St. Francis, IL B
U of Saint Francis, IN B
U of Saint Mary, KS B
Valparaiso U, IN B
Walsh U, OH B
Xavier U, OH A,B

Theology and Religious Vocations Related
Cedarville U, OH B
Crossroads Coll, MN B
Hope Coll, MI B
Marquette U, WI B
Missouri Baptist U, MO B
Southern Nazarene U, OK B

Therapeutic Recreation
Ashland U, OH B
Calvin Coll, MI B
Central Michigan U, MI B
Eastern Michigan U, MI B
Grand Valley State U, MI B
Indiana Tech, IN B
Minnesota State U Mankato, MN B
Northwest Missouri State U, MO B
Pittsburg State U, KS B
St. Cloud State U, MN B
Southwestern Oklahoma State U, OK B
The U of Akron, OH B
The U of Iowa, IA B
U of Nebraska at Kearney, NE B
U of Wisconsin–La Crosse, WI B
U of Wisconsin–Milwaukee, WI B
Winona State U, MN B

Tibetan
U of Chicago, IL B

Tool and Die Technology
Ferris State U, MI A

Tourism and Travel Services Management
AIB Coll of Business, IA A
Baker Coll of Flint, MI A
Baker Coll of Muskegon, MI A
Black Hills State U, SD A,B
Bowling Green State U, OH B
Indiana U–Purdue U Indianapolis, IN B
Northeastern State U, OK B
Ohio U, OH A
Purdue U, IN B
St. Cloud State U, MN B
The U of Akron, OH A
Western Michigan U, MI B

Tourism and Travel Services Marketing
AIB Coll of Business, IA A
Ohio U, OH A
Ohio U–Southern Campus, OH A
U of Central Missouri, MO B
Western Michigan U, MI B

Tourism Promotion
AIB Coll of Business, IA A
Bowling Green State U, OH B
St. Cloud State U, MN A

Toxicology
Ashland U, OH B
Clarkson U, NY B
Eastern Michigan U, MI B
Minnesota State U Mankato, MN B
U of Wisconsin–Madison, WI B

Trade and Industrial Teacher Education
Bemidji State U, MN B
Carroll U, WI B
Cincinnati Christian U, OH A
Concordia U, Nebraska, NE B
Indiana State U, IN B
Iowa State U of Science and Technology, IA B
Kent State U, OH B
Southern Illinois U Carbondale, IL B
U of Central Oklahoma, OK B
U of Nebraska–Lincoln, NE B
The U of Toledo, OH B
Wright State U, OH B

Transportation Management
U of Wisconsin–Superior, WI B

Transportation Technology
Baker Coll of Flint, MI A
U of Cincinnati, OH A,B
The U of Toledo, OH A

Turf and Turfgrass Management
North Dakota State U, ND B
The Ohio State U, OH B
Oklahoma State U, Oklahoma City, OK A
Rochester Comm and Tech Coll, MN A
U of Minnesota, Crookston, MN B
U of Nebraska–Lincoln, NE B

Turkish
U of Chicago, IL B

Urban Education and Leadership
Harris-Stowe State U, MO B
U of Missouri–Kansas City, MO B

Urban Forestry
U of Illinois at Urbana–Champaign, IL B

Urban Studies/Affairs
Aquinas Coll, MI B
Augsburg Coll, MN B
Ball State U, IN B
Butler U, IN B
Calvary Bible Coll and Theological Seminary, MO B
Cleveland State U, OH B
The Coll of Wooster, OH B
DePaul U, IL B
Elmhurst Coll, IL B
Hamline U, MN B
Harris-Stowe State U, MO B
MidAmerica Nazarene U, KS B
Minnesota State U Mankato, MN B
Mount Mercy Coll, IA B
North Central U, MN B
Northeastern Illinois U, IL B
Northwestern U, IL B
Ohio Wesleyan U, OH B
St. Cloud State U, MN B
Saint Louis U, MO B
U of Cincinnati, OH B
U of Illinois at Chicago, IL B
U of Minnesota, Duluth, MN B
U of Minnesota, Twin Cities Campus, MN B
U of Missouri–Kansas City, MO B
U of New Orleans, LA B
The U of Toledo, OH B
U of Wisconsin–Green Bay, WI B
U of Wisconsin–Madison, WI B
U of Wisconsin–Milwaukee, WI B
U of Wisconsin–Oshkosh, WI B
Washington U in St. Louis, MO B
Wayne State U, MI B
Wright State U, OH B

Urdu
U of Chicago, IL B

Vehicle/Equipment Operation
Baker Coll of Flint, MI A

Vehicle Maintenance and Repair Technologies Related
McPherson Coll, KS A

Veterinary/Animal Health Technology
Baker Coll of Cadillac, MI A
Baker Coll of Jackson, MI A
Baker Coll of Muskegon, MI A
Baker Coll of Port Huron, MI A
Michigan State U, MI B
North Dakota State U, ND B
Purdue U, IN A,B
Rochester Comm and Tech Coll, MN A
U of Nebraska–Lincoln, NE B

Veterinary Technology
Argosy U, Twin Cities, MN A
Brown Mackie Coll–Michigan City, IN A
Brown Mackie Coll–South Bend, IN A
Michigan State U, MI B
Minnesota School of Business–Blaine, MN A
Oklahoma State U, Oklahoma City, OK A

Violin, Viola, Guitar and Other Stringed Instruments
Augustana Coll, IL B
Butler U, IN B
Heidelberg U, OH B
Hope Coll, MI B
Lawrence U, WI B
Northwestern Coll, MN B
Northwestern U, IL B
Northwest Missouri State U, MO B
Oberlin Coll, OH B
Oklahoma City U, OK B
Otterbein Coll, OH B
Roosevelt U, IL B
St. Cloud State U, MN B
U of Central Oklahoma, OK B
U of Cincinnati, OH B
The U of Iowa, IA B
The U of Kansas, KS B
U of Nebraska at Omaha, NE B
U of Wisconsin–Milwaukee, WI B

Visual and Performing Arts
Edgewood Coll, WI B
Iowa State U of Science and Technology, IA B
Loras Coll, IA B
Missouri State U, MO B
Northwestern U, IL B
Ohio Northern U, OH B
Ohio U, OH B
Purdue U, IN B
Rogers State U, OK B
St. Gregory's U, Shawnee, OK B
South Dakota State U, SD B
Southeast Missouri State U, MO B
Truman State U, MO B
U of Oklahoma, OK B
U of Rio Grande, OH B
U of St. Francis, IL B
U of Saint Mary, KS B
U of Wisconsin–La Crosse, WI B
U of Wisconsin–Superior, WI B
Viterbo U, WI B
Wichita State U, KS B

Visual and Performing Arts Related
Baldwin-Wallace Coll, OH B
Cameron U, OK B
Coll of Visual Arts, MN B
Dana Coll, NE B
Illinois State U, IL B
Illinois Wesleyan U, IL B
Indiana U Bloomington, IN B
Millikin U, IL B
Ohio Northern U, OH B
St. Cloud State U, MN B
Spring Arbor U, MI B
U of Wisconsin–Green Bay, WI B

Vocational Rehabilitation Counseling
Emporia State U, KS B
Maryville U of Saint Louis, MO B
U of Illinois at Urbana–Champaign, IL B
U of North Dakota, ND B
U of Wisconsin–Stout, WI B
Wright State U, OH B

Voice and Opera
Andrews U, MI B
Augustana Coll, IL B
Baldwin-Wallace Coll, OH B
Bethel Coll, IN B
Black Hills State U, SD B
Bowling Green State U, OH B
Butler U, IN B
Calvary Bible Coll and Theological Seminary, MO B
Calvin Coll, MI B
Capital U, OH B
Cincinnati Christian U, OH B
Concordia Coll, MN B
Concordia U Chicago, IL B
Concordia U, Nebraska, NE B
Dordt Coll, IA B
Drake U, IA B
Grace U, NE B
Hannibal-LaGrange Coll, MO B
Heidelberg U, OH B
Hope Coll, MI B
Huntington U, IN B
Illinois Wesleyan U, IL B
Indiana U–Purdue U Fort Wayne, IN B
Lawrence U, WI B
MidAmerica Nazarene U, KS B
Millikin U, IL B
Minnesota State U Mankato, MN B
Minnesota State U Moorhead, MN B
Northern State U, SD B
Northwestern Coll, MN B
Northwestern U, IL B
Northwest Missouri State U, MO B
Oakland U, MI B
Oberlin Coll, OH B
The Ohio State U, OH B

A—associate degree; B—bachelor's degree

Ohio U, OH B
Oklahoma Baptist U, OK B
Oklahoma Christian U, OK B
Oklahoma City U, OK B
Oral Roberts U, OK B
Otterbein Coll, OH B
Roosevelt U, IL B
St. Cloud State U, MN B
Southern Methodist U, TX B
Southwestern Oklahoma State U, OK B
Truman State U, MO B
U of Central Oklahoma, OK B
U of Cincinnati, OH B
U of Illinois at Urbana–Champaign, IL B
The U of Iowa, IA B
The U of Kansas, KS B
U of Nebraska at Omaha, NE B
U of Tulsa, OK B
U of Wisconsin–Milwaukee, WI B
Valparaiso U, IN B
Washington U in St. Louis, MO B
Winona State U, MN B

Waldorf/Steiner Teacher Education

U of Michigan–Flint, MI B

Water Quality and Wastewater Treatment Management and Recycling Technology

Lake Superior State U, MI A
Wright State U, OH A

Water Resources Engineering

Central State U, OH B
U of Illinois at Urbana–Champaign, IL B

Water, Wetlands, and Marine Resources Management

Bowling Green State U, OH B

Web/Multimedia Management and Webmaster

Grace U, NE B
ITT Tech Inst, Indianapolis, IN A
ITT Tech Inst, Canton, MI A
ITT Tech Inst, Grand Rapids, MI A
ITT Tech Inst, Troy, MI A
ITT Tech Inst, Arnold, MO A
ITT Tech Inst, Earth City, MO A
ITT Tech Inst, Green Bay, WI A
U of St. Francis, IL B
Westwood Coll–Chicago Du Page, IL B

Web Page, Digital/Multimedia and Information Resources Design

The Art Inst of Indianapolis, IN B
The Art Inst of Michigan, MI A,B
The Art Insts International–Kansas City, KS B
The Art Insts International Minnesota, MN A,B
Baker Coll of Allen Park, MI A
The Cleveland Inst of Art, OH B
Dakota State U, SD B
Dana Coll, NE B
DePaul U, IL B
DeVry U, Addison, IL A,B
DeVry U, Chicago, IL A,B
DeVry U, Tinley Park, IL A,B
DeVry U, Indianapolis, IN A,B
DeVry U, Edina, MN A,B
DeVry U, Kansas City, MO A,B
DeVry U, Columbus, OH A
DeVry U, OK A,B
DeVry U Southfield Center, MI A
Franklin U, OH B
The Illinois Inst of Art–Chicago, IL A,B
The Illinois Inst of Art–Schaumburg, IL A,B
Indiana Tech, IN A,B
ITT Tech Inst, Burr Ridge, IL A
ITT Tech Inst, Mount Prospect, IL A
ITT Tech Inst, Orland Park, IL A
ITT Tech Inst, Fort Wayne, IN A
ITT Tech Inst, Indianapolis, IN A
ITT Tech Inst, Newburgh, IN A
ITT Tech Inst, Canton, MI A
ITT Tech Inst, Grand Rapids, MI A
ITT Tech Inst, Troy, MI A
ITT Tech Inst, MN A
ITT Tech Inst, Arnold, MO A
ITT Tech Inst, Earth City, MO A
ITT Tech Inst, NE A
ITT Tech Inst, Tulsa, OK A
ITT Tech Inst, Green Bay, WI A
ITT Tech Inst, Greenfield, WI A
Mount Union Coll, OH B
Oklahoma State U, Oklahoma City, OK A
Rasmussen Coll St. Cloud, MN A
Rochester Comm and Tech Coll, MN A
Silver Lake Coll, WI B
U of Wisconsin–Stevens Point, WI B

Welding Technology

Ferris State U, MI A,B
The Ohio State U, OH B
The U of Toledo, OH A

Wildlife and Wildlands Science and Management

Coll of the Ozarks, MO B
Dakota Wesleyan U, SD B
Fort Hays State U, KS B
Lake Superior State U, MI B
Michigan Technological U, MI B
Missouri State U, MO B
Northland Coll, WI B
Northwest Missouri State U, MO B
The Ohio State U, OH B
Purdue U, IN B
South Dakota State U, SD B
U of Illinois at Urbana–Champaign, IL B
U of Missouri–Columbia, MO B
U of Wisconsin–Stevens Point, WI B
Winona State U, MN B

Wildlife Biology

Baker U, KS B
Central Christian Coll of Kansas, KS A
Friends U, KS B
Kansas State U, KS B
Northeastern State U, OK B
Northwest Missouri State U, MO B
Ohio U, OH B
St. Cloud State U, MN B
U of Michigan–Flint, MI B
Winona State U, MN B

Wind/Percussion Instruments

Augustana Coll, IL B
Butler U, IN B
Concordia U Chicago, IL B
Lawrence U, WI B
Minnesota State U Mankato, MN B
Minnesota State U Moorhead, MN B
Northwestern U, IL B
Northwest Missouri State U, MO B
Oberlin Coll, OH B
Oklahoma Christian U, OK B
Oklahoma City U, OK B
Otterbein Coll, OH B
Southwestern Oklahoma State U, OK B
U of Central Oklahoma, OK B
U of Cincinnati, OH B
The U of Iowa, IA B
The U of Kansas, KS B
U of Wisconsin–Milwaukee, WI B

Women's Studies

Albion Coll, MI B
Augsburg Coll, MN B
Augustana Coll, IL B
Ball State U, IN B
Beloit Coll, WI B
Bowling Green State U, OH B
Carleton Coll, MN B
Case Western Reserve U, OH B
Central Michigan U, MI B
Coll of Saint Benedict, MN B
The Coll of Wooster, OH B
Cornell Coll, IA B
Denison U, OH B
DePaul U, IL B
DePauw U, IN B
Earlham Coll, IN B
Eastern Michigan U, MI B
Grand Valley State U, MI B
Gustavus Adolphus Coll, MN B
Hamline U, MN B
Illinois Wesleyan U, IL B
Indiana U–Purdue U Fort Wayne, IN A,B
Indiana U South Bend, IN B
Iowa State U of Science and Technology, IA B
Kansas State U, KS B
Kenyon Coll, OH B
Knox Coll, IL B
Loyola U Chicago, IL B
Luther Coll, IA B
Macalester Coll, MN B
Marquette U, WI B
Miami U, OH B
Minnesota State U Mankato, MN B
Nebraska Wesleyan U, NE B
North Dakota State U, ND B
Northeastern Illinois U, IL B
Northwestern U, IL B
Oakland U, MI B
Oberlin Coll, OH B
The Ohio State U, OH B
Ohio Wesleyan U, OH B
Purdue U, IN B
St. Catherine U, MN B
Saint Louis U, MO B
St. Olaf Coll, MN B
U of Illinois at Urbana–Champaign, IL B
The U of Iowa, IA B
The U of Kansas, KS B
U of Michigan, MI B
U of Michigan–Dearborn, MI B
U of Minnesota, Duluth, MN B
U of Minnesota, Morris, MN B
U of Minnesota, Twin Cities Campus, MN B
U of Nebraska at Omaha, NE B
U of Nebraska–Lincoln, NE B
U of New Orleans, LA B
U of Oklahoma, OK B
The U of Toledo, OH B
U of Wisconsin–Eau Claire, WI B
U of Wisconsin–Madison, WI B
U of Wisconsin–Milwaukee, WI B
U of Wisconsin–Whitewater, WI B
Washington U in St. Louis, MO B
Western Illinois U, IL B
Western Michigan U, MI B
Wichita State U, KS B
Wright State U, OH B

Wood Science and Wood Products/Pulp and Paper Technology

Miami U, OH B
Pittsburg State U, KS A,B
U of Minnesota, Twin Cities Campus, MN B
U of Wisconsin–Stevens Point, WI B

Word Processing

Baker Coll of Allen Park, MI A

Work and Family Studies

Miami U Hamilton, OH B
Ursuline Coll, OH B

Youth Ministry

Anderson U, IN B
Andrews U, MI B
Benedictine Coll, KS B
Bethel Coll, IN B
Bethel U, MN B
Bluffton U, OH B
Calvary Bible Coll and Theological Seminary, MO B
Cedarville U, OH B
Central Christian Coll of Kansas, KS B
Concordia U Wisconsin, WI B
Crossroads Coll, MN B
Dordt Coll, IA B
Grace Bible Coll, MI B
Grace Coll, IN B
Grace U, NE B
Great Lakes Christian Coll, MI B
Greenville Coll, IL B
Kuyper Coll, MI B
Malone U, OH B
Manhattan Christian Coll, KS B
Maranatha Baptist Bible Coll, WI B
Messenger Coll, MO B
Mount Vernon Nazarene U, OH A,B
North Central U, MN B
North Park U, IL B
Northwestern Coll, MN B
Oak Hills Christian Coll, MN B
Ohio Christian U, OH B
Olivet Nazarene U, IL B
Saint Mary's U of Minnesota, MN B
Southern Nazarene U, OK B
Spring Arbor U, MI B
Trinity Bible Coll, ND B
Trinity International U, IL B
U of Indianapolis, IN B
U of Sioux Falls, SD B

Zoology/Animal Biology

Andrews U, MI B
Central Christian Coll of Kansas, KS A
Eastern Illinois U, IL B
Kent State U, OH B
Malone U, OH B
Miami U, OH B
Miami U Hamilton, OH B
Michigan State U, MI B
North Dakota State U, ND B
Northern Michigan U, MI B
Northwest Missouri State U, MO B
The Ohio State U, OH B
Ohio U, OH B
Ohio Wesleyan U, OH B
Oklahoma State U, OK B
Olivet Nazarene U, IL B
Purdue U, IN B
Southeastern Oklahoma State U, OK B
Southern Illinois U Carbondale, IL B
The U of Akron, OH B
U of Oklahoma, OK B
U of Wisconsin–Madison, WI B
U of Wisconsin–Milwaukee, WI B
Winona State U, MN B

A—associate degree; B—bachelor's degree

Athletic Programs and Scholarships

Archery

Case Western Reserve U, OH M, W
Kenyon Coll, OH M, W
North Dakota State U, ND M, W

Badminton

Carleton Coll, MN M, W
The Coll of Wooster, OH M, W
Saint Louis U, MO M, W

Baseball

Adrian Coll, MI M
Albion Coll, MI M
Alma Coll, MI M
Anderson U, IN M
Aquinas Coll, MI M(s)
Ashland U, OH M(s)
Augsburg Coll, MN M
Augustana Coll, IL M
Augustana Coll, SD M(s)
Aurora U, IL M
Avila U, MO M(s)
Baker U, KS M(s)
Baldwin-Wallace Coll, OH M
Ball State U, IN M(s)
Beloit Coll, WI M
Bemidji State U, MN M(s)
Benedictine Coll, KS M(s)
Benedictine U, IL M
Bethany Coll, KS M(s)
Bethany Lutheran Coll, MN M
Bethel Coll, IN M(s)
Bethel U, MN M
Blessing-Rieman Coll of Nursing, IL M(s), W(s)
Bluffton U, OH M
Bowling Green State U, OH M(s)
Bradley U, IL M(s)
Briar Cliff U, IA M(s)
Buena Vista U, IA M
Butler U, IN M(s)
Calumet Coll of Saint Joseph, IN M
Calvin Coll, MI M
Cameron U, OK M(s)
Capital U, OH M
Carleton Coll, MN M
Carroll U, WI M
Case Western Reserve U, OH M
Cedarville U, OH M(s)
Central Christian Coll of Kansas, KS M(s)
Central Coll, IA M
Central Methodist U, MO M(s)
Central Michigan U, MI M(s)
Cincinnati Christian U, OH M
Clarke Coll, IA M(s)
Clarkson U, NY M
Cleveland State U, OH M(s)
Coe Coll, IA M
Coll of Mount St. Joseph, OH M
The Coll of St. Scholastica, MN M
Coll of the Ozarks, MO M(s)
The Coll of Wooster, OH M
Concordia Coll, MN M
Concordia U, MI M(s)
Concordia U Chicago, IL M
Concordia U, Nebraska, NE M(s)
Concordia U, St. Paul, MN M(s)
Concordia U Wisconsin, WI M
Cornell Coll, IA M
Creighton U, NE M(s)
Crossroads Coll, MN M
Crown Coll, MN M
Culver-Stockton Coll, MO M(s)
Dakota State U, SD M(s)
Dakota Wesleyan U, SD M(s)
Dana Coll, NE M(s)
Defiance Coll, OH M
Denison U, OH M
DePauw U, IN M
Doane Coll, NE M(s)
Dominican U, IL M
Dordt Coll, IA M(s)
Drury U, MO M(s)
Earlham Coll, IN M
Eastern Illinois U, IL M(s)
Eastern Michigan U, MI M(s)
Edgewood Coll, WI M
Elmhurst Coll, IL M
Emporia State U, KS M(s)
Eureka Coll, IL M
Evangel U, MO M(s)
Fontbonne U, MO M
Fort Hays State U, KS M(s)
Franciscan U of Steubenville, OH M
Franklin Coll, IN M
Friends U, KS M(s)
Goshen Coll, IN M(s)
Grace Coll, IN M(s)
Graceland U, IA M(s)
Grand Valley State U, MI M(s)
Grand View U, IA M(s)
Greenville Coll, IL M
Grinnell Coll, IA M
Gustavus Adolphus Coll, MN M
Hamline U, MN M
Hannibal-LaGrange Coll, MO M(s)
Hanover Coll, IN M
Harris-Stowe State U, MO M(s)
Heidelberg U, OH M
Hillsdale Coll, MI M
Hiram Coll, OH M
Hope Coll, MI M
Huntington U, IN M(s)
Illinois Coll, IL M
Illinois Inst of Technology, IL M(s)
Illinois State U, IL M(s)
Illinois Wesleyan U, IL M
Indiana State U, IN M(s)
Indiana Tech, IN M(s)
Indiana U Bloomington, IN M(s)
Indiana U Northwest, IN M
Indiana U–Purdue U Fort Wayne, IN M(s)
Indiana U Southeast, IN M
Indiana Wesleyan U, IN M(s)
Iowa Wesleyan Coll, IA M(s)
Jamestown Coll, ND M(s)
John Carroll U, OH M
Kalamazoo Coll, MI M
Kansas State U, KS M(s)
Kansas Wesleyan U, KS M(s)
Kent State U, OH M(s)
Kenyon Coll, OH M
Knox Coll, IL M
Lake Erie Coll, OH M
Lake Forest Coll, IL M
Lakeland Coll, WI M
Lawrence U, WI M
Lewis U, IL M(s)
Lincoln U, MO M(s)
Lindenwood U, MO M(s)
Loras Coll, IA M
Luther Coll, IA M
Macalester Coll, MN M
MacMurray Coll, IL M
Madonna U, MI M(s)
Malone U, OH M(s)
Manchester Coll, IN M
Manhattan Christian Coll, KS M
Maranatha Baptist Bible Coll, WI M
Marian U, WI M
Marian U, IN M(s)
Marietta Coll, OH M
Marquette U, WI M
Martin Luther Coll, MN M
Maryville U of Saint Louis, MO M
Mayville State U, ND M(s)
McKendree U, IL M(s)
Miami U, OH M(s), W
Miami U Hamilton, OH M
Michigan State U, MI M(s)
Mid-America Christian U, OK M
MidAmerica Nazarene U, KS M(s)
Millikin U, IL M
Milwaukee School of Engineering, WI M
Minnesota State U Mankato, MN M(s)
Minot State U, ND M(s)
Missouri Baptist U, MO M(s)
Missouri Southern State U, MO M(s)
Missouri State U, MO M(s)
Missouri U of Science and Technology, MO M(s)
Missouri Western State U, MO M(s)
Monmouth Coll, IL M
Morningside Coll, IA M(s)
Mount Marty Coll, SD M(s)
Mount Mercy Coll, IA M(s)
Mount Union Coll, OH M

M—for men; W—for women; (s)—scholarship offered

Mount Vernon Nazarene U, OH M(s)
Muskingum Coll, OH M
Nebraska Wesleyan U, NE M
Newman U, KS M(s)
North Central Coll, IL M
North Central U, MN M
North Dakota State U, ND M(s)
Northeastern State U, OK M(s)
Northern State U, SD M
Northland Coll, WI M
North Park U, IL M
Northwestern Coll, MN M
Northwestern U, IL M(s)
Northwest Missouri State U, MO M(s)
Northwood U, MI M(s)
Oakland U, MI M(s)
Oberlin Coll, OH M
Ohio Christian U, OH M
Ohio Dominican U, OH M(s)
Ohio Northern U, OH M
The Ohio State U, OH M(s)
The Ohio State U at Lima, OH M
Ohio U, OH M(s)
Ohio U–Zanesville, OH M
Ohio Wesleyan U, OH M
Oklahoma Baptist U, OK M(s)
Oklahoma Christian U, OK M(s)
Oklahoma City U, OK M(s)
Oklahoma Panhandle State U, OK M(s)
Oklahoma State U, OK M(s)
Olivet Coll, MI M
Olivet Nazarene U, IL M(s)
Oral Roberts U, OK M(s)
Otterbein Coll, OH M
Park U, MO M(s)
Pittsburg State U, KS M(s)
Presentation Coll, SD M
Purdue U, IN M(s)
Purdue U North Central, IN M(s)
Quincy U, IL M(s)
Research Coll of Nursing, MO M(s)
Ripon Coll, WI M
Robert Morris Coll, IL M(s)
Rochester Comm and Tech Coll, MN M
Rockford Coll, IL M
Rockhurst U, MO M(s)
Rogers State U, OK M
Rose-Hulman Inst of Technology, IN M
Saginaw Valley State U, MI M(s)
St. Ambrose U, IA M(s)
St. Cloud State U, MN M(s)
St. Gregory's U, Shawnee, OK M(s)
Saint John's U, MN M
Saint Joseph's Coll, IN M(s)
St. Louis Christian Coll, MO M
Saint Louis U, MO M(s)
Saint Mary's U of Minnesota, MN M
St. Norbert Coll, WI M
St. Olaf Coll, MN M
Saint Xavier U, IL M(s)
Shawnee State U, OH M(s)
Siena Heights U, MI M(s)
Simpson Coll, IA M
South Dakota State U, SD M(s)
Southeastern Oklahoma State U, OK M(s)
Southeast Missouri State U, MO M(s)
Southern Illinois U Carbondale, IL M(s)
Southern Illinois U Edwardsville, IL M(s)
Southern Methodist U, TX M
Southern Nazarene U, OK M(s)
Southwest Baptist U, MO M(s)
Southwestern Oklahoma State U, OK M(s)
Southwest Minnesota State U, MN M(s)
Spring Arbor U, MI M(s)
Sterling Coll, KS M(s)
Taylor U, IN M(s)
Tiffin U, OH M(s)
Transylvania U, KY M
Trine U, IN M
Trinity Bible Coll, ND M
Trinity Christian Coll, IL M(s)
Trinity International U, IL M(s)
Truman State U, MO M(s)
The U of Akron, OH M(s)
U of Central Missouri, MO M(s)
U of Central Oklahoma, OK M(s)
U of Charleston, WV M(s)
U of Chicago, IL M
U of Cincinnati, OH M
U of Dallas, TX M
U of Dayton, OH M(s)
U of Evansville, IN M(s)
The U of Findlay, OH M(s)
U of Illinois at Chicago, IL M(s)
U of Illinois at Urbana–Champaign, IL M(s)
U of Indianapolis, IN M(s)
The U of Iowa, IA M(s)
The U of Kansas, KS M(s)
U of Mary, ND M(s)
U of Michigan, MI M(s)
U of Minnesota, Crookston, MN M(s)
U of Minnesota, Duluth, MN M(s)
U of Minnesota, Morris, MN M
U of Minnesota, Twin Cities Campus, MN M(s)
U of Missouri–Columbia, MO M(s)
U of Missouri–St. Louis, MO M(s)
U of Nebraska at Kearney, NE M(s)
U of Nebraska at Omaha, NE M(s)
U of Nebraska–Lincoln, NE M(s)
U of New Orleans, LA M(s)
U of North Dakota, ND M(s)
U of Northern Iowa, IA M(s)
U of Notre Dame, IN M(s)
U of Oklahoma, OK M(s)
U of Rio Grande, OH M(s)
U of St. Francis, IL M(s)
U of Saint Francis, IN M(s)
U of Saint Mary, KS M(s)
U of Science and Arts of Oklahoma, OK M(s)
U of Sioux Falls, SD M(s)
U of Southern Indiana, IN M(s)
The U of Toledo, OH M(s)
U of Wisconsin–La Crosse, WI M
U of Wisconsin–Milwaukee, WI M
U of Wisconsin–Oshkosh, WI M
U of Wisconsin–Parkside, WI M(s)
U of Wisconsin–Platteville, WI M
U of Wisconsin–Stevens Point, WI M
U of Wisconsin–Stout, WI M
U of Wisconsin–Superior, WI M
U of Wisconsin–Whitewater, WI M
Valley City State U, ND M(s)
Valparaiso U, IN M(s)
Viterbo U, WI M(s)
Wabash Coll, IN M
Waldorf Coll, IA M(s)
Walsh U, OH M(s)
Wartburg Coll, IA M
Washburn U, KS M(s)
Washington U in St. Louis, MO M
Wayne State Coll, NE M(s)
Wayne State U, MI M(s)
Webster U, MO M
Western Illinois U, IL M(s)
Western Michigan U, MI M(s)
Westminster Coll, MO M
Wheaton Coll, IL M
Wichita State U, KS M(s)
William Jewell Coll, MO M(s)
Wilmington Coll, OH M
Winona State U, MN M(s)
Wittenberg U, OH M
Wright State U, OH M(s)
Xavier U, OH M(s)
York Coll, NE M(s)
Youngstown State U, OH M(s)

Basketball

Adrian Coll, MI M, W
AIB Coll of Business, IA W(s)
Albion Coll, MI M, W
Alma Coll, MI M, W
Anderson U, IN M, W
Aquinas Coll, MI M(s), W(s)
Ashland U, OH M(s), W(s)
Augsburg Coll, MN M, W
Augustana Coll, IL M, W
Augustana Coll, SD M(s), W(s)
Aurora U, IL M, W
Avila U, MO M(s), W(s)
Baker U, KS M(s), W(s)
Baldwin-Wallace Coll, OH M, W
Ball State U, IN M(s), W(s)
Barclay Coll, KS M, W
Beloit Coll, WI M, W
Bemidji State U, MN M(s), W(s)
Benedictine Coll, KS M(s), W(s)
Benedictine U, IL M, W
Bethany Coll, KS M(s), W(s)
Bethany Lutheran Coll, MN M, W
Bethel Coll, IN M(s), W(s)
Bethel Coll, KS M(s), W(s)
Bethel U, MN M, W
Black Hills State U, SD M(s), W(s)
Blessing-Rieman Coll of Nursing, IL M(s), W(s)
Bluffton U, OH M, W
Bowling Green State U, OH M(s), W(s)
Bradley U, IL M(s), W(s)
Briar Cliff U, IA M(s), W(s)
Buena Vista U, IA M, W
Butler U, IN M(s), W(s)
Calumet Coll of Saint Joseph, IN M, W
Calvary Bible Coll and Theological Seminary, MO M, W
Calvin Coll, MI M, W
Cameron U, OK M(s), W(s)
Capital U, OH M, W
Carleton Coll, MN M, W
Carroll U, WI M, W
Case Western Reserve U, OH M, W
Cedarville U, OH M(s), W(s)
Central Christian Coll of Kansas, KS M(s), W(s)
Central Coll, IA M, W
Central Methodist U, MO M(s), W(s)
Central Michigan U, MI M(s), W(s)
Central State U, OH M(s), W(s)

M—for men; W—for women; (s)—scholarship offered

Institution	Programs
Cincinnati Christian U, OH	M(s), W
Clarke Coll, IA	M(s), W(s)
Clarkson U, NY	M, W
Cleveland State U, OH	M(s), W(s)
Coe Coll, IA	M, W
Coll of Mount St. Joseph, OH	M, W
Coll of Saint Benedict, MN	W
Coll of Saint Mary, NE	W(s)
The Coll of St. Scholastica, MN	M, W
Coll of the Ozarks, MO	M(s), W(s)
The Coll of Wooster, OH	M, W
Columbia Coll, MO	M(s), W(s)
Concordia Coll, MN	M, W
Concordia U, MI	M(s), W(s)
Concordia U Chicago, IL	M, W
Concordia U, Nebraska, NE	M(s), W(s)
Concordia U, St. Paul, MN	M(s), W(s)
Concordia U Wisconsin, WI	M, W
Cornell Coll, IA	M, W
Cornerstone U, MI	M(s), W(s)
Cottey Coll, MO	W(s)
Creighton U, NE	M(s), W(s)
Crossroads Coll, MN	M, W
Crown Coll, MN	M, W
Culver-Stockton Coll, MO	M(s), W(s)
Dakota State U, SD	M(s), W(s)
Dakota Wesleyan U, SD	M(s), W(s)
Dana Coll, NE	M(s), W(s)
Davenport U, Grand Rapids, MI	M(s), W(s)
Defiance Coll, OH	M, W
Denison U, OH	M, W
DePaul U, IL	M(s), W(s)
DePauw U, IN	M, W
Doane Coll, NE	M(s), W(s)
Dominican U, IL	M, W
Dordt Coll, IA	M(s), W(s)
Drake U, IA	M(s), W(s)
Drury U, MO	M(s), W(s)
Earlham Coll, IN	M, W
Eastern Illinois U, IL	M(s), W(s)
Eastern Michigan U, MI	M(s), W(s)
East-West U, IL	M
Edgewood Coll, WI	M, W
Elmhurst Coll, IL	M, W
Emmaus Bible Coll, IA	M, W
Emporia State U, KS	M(s), W(s)
Eureka Coll, IL	M, W
Evangel U, MO	M(s), W(s)
Faith Baptist Bible Coll and Theological Seminary, IA	M, W
Ferris State U, MI	M(s), W(s)
Fontbonne U, MO	M, W
Fort Hays State U, KS	M(s), W(s)
Franciscan U of Steubenville, OH	M, W
Franklin Coll, IN	M, W
Friends U, KS	M(s), W(s)
Goshen Coll, IN	M(s), W(s)
Grace Bible Coll, MI	M, W
Grace Coll, IN	M(s), W(s)
Graceland U, IA	M(s), W(s)
Grace U, NE	M, W
Grand Valley State U, MI	M(s), W(s)
Grand View U, IA	M(s), W(s)
Great Lakes Christian Coll, MI	M, W
Greenville Coll, IL	M, W
Grinnell Coll, IA	M, W
Gustavus Adolphus Coll, MN	M, W
Hamline U, MN	M, W
Hannibal-LaGrange Coll, MO	M(s), W(s)
Hanover Coll, IN	M, W
Harris-Stowe State U, MO	M(s), W(s)
Haskell Indian Nations U, KS	M, W
Heidelberg U, OH	M, W
Hillsdale Coll, MI	M, W
Hiram Coll, OH	M, W
Hope Coll, MI	M, W
Huntington U, IN	M(s), W(s)
Illinois Inst of Technology, IL	M(s), W(s)
Illinois State U, IL	M(s), W(s)
Illinois Wesleyan U, IL	M, W
Indiana State U, IN	M(s), W(s)
Indiana Tech, IN	M(s), W(s)
Indiana U Bloomington, IN	M(s), W(s)
Indiana U East, IN	M
Indiana U Northwest, IN	M, W
Indiana U–Purdue U Fort Wayne, IN	M(s), W(s)
Indiana U–Purdue U Indianapolis, IN	M(s), W(s)
Indiana U South Bend, IN	M(s), W(s)
Indiana U Southeast, IN	M(s), W(s)
Indiana Wesleyan U, IN	M(s), W(s)
Iowa State U of Science and Technology, IA	M(s), W(s)
Iowa Wesleyan Coll, IA	M(s), W(s)
Jamestown Coll, ND	M(s), W(s)
John Carroll U, OH	M, W
Kalamazoo Coll, MI	M, W
Kansas State U, KS	M(s), W(s)
Kansas Wesleyan U, KS	M(s), W(s)
Kent State U, OH	M(s), W(s)
Kenyon Coll, OH	M, W
Knox Coll, IL	M, W
Kuyper Coll, MI	M, W
Lake Erie Coll, OH	M, W
Lake Forest Coll, IL	M, W
Lakeland Coll, WI	M, W
Lake Superior State U, MI	M(s), W(s)
Lawrence U, WI	M, W
Lewis U, IL	M(s), W(s)
Lincoln U, MO	M(s), W(s)
Lindenwood U, MO	M(s), W(s)
Logan U–Coll of Chiropractic, MO	M, W
Loras Coll, IA	M, W
Loyola U Chicago, IL	M(s), W(s)
Luther Coll, IA	M, W
Macalester Coll, MN	M, W
MacMurray Coll, IL	M, W
Madonna U, MI	M(s), W(s)
Malone U, OH	M(s), W(s)
Manchester Coll, IN	M, W
Manhattan Christian Coll, KS	M, W
Maranatha Baptist Bible Coll, WI	M, W
Marian U, WI	M, W
Marian U, IN	M(s), W(s)
Marietta Coll, OH	M, W
Marquette U, WI	M(s), W(s)
Martin Luther Coll, MN	M, W
Maryville U of Saint Louis, MO	M, W
Mayville State U, ND	M(s), W(s)
McKendree U, IL	M(s), W(s)
McPherson Coll, KS	M, W
Miami U, OH	M(s), W(s)
Miami U Hamilton, OH	M, W
Michigan State U, MI	M(s), W(s)
Michigan Technological U, MI	M(s), W(s)
Mid-America Christian U, OK	M, W
MidAmerica Nazarene U, KS	M(s), W(s)
Millikin U, IL	M, W
Milwaukee School of Engineering, WI	M, W
Minnesota State U Mankato, MN	M(s), W(s)
Minnesota State U Moorhead, MN	M(s), W(s)
Minot State U, ND	M(s), W(s)
Missouri Baptist U, MO	M(s), W(s)
Missouri Southern State U, MO	M(s), W(s)
Missouri State U, MO	M(s), W(s)
Missouri U of Science and Technology, MO	M(s), W(s)
Missouri Western State U, MO	M(s), W(s)
Monmouth Coll, IL	M, W
Moody Bible Inst, IL	M, W
Morningside Coll, IA	M(s), W(s)
Mount Marty Coll, SD	M(s), W(s)
Mount Mary Coll, WI	W
Mount Mercy Coll, IA	M(s), W(s)
Mount Union Coll, OH	M, W
Mount Vernon Nazarene U, OH	M(s), W(s)
Muskingum Coll, OH	M, W
Nebraska Wesleyan U, NE	M, W
Newman U, KS	M(s), W(s)
North Central Coll, IL	M, W
North Central U, MN	M, W
North Dakota State U, ND	M(s), W(s)
Northeastern State U, OK	M(s), W(s)
Northern Michigan U, MI	M(s), W(s)
Northern State U, SD	M(s), W(s)
Northland Coll, WI	M, W
North Park U, IL	M, W
Northwestern Coll, MN	M, W
Northwestern U, IL	M(s), W(s)
Northwest Missouri State U, MO	M(s), W(s)
Northwood U, MI	M(s), W(s)
Oak Hills Christian Coll, MN	M
Oakland U, MI	M(s), W(s)
Oberlin Coll, OH	M, W
Ohio Christian U, OH	M, W
Ohio Dominican U, OH	M(s), W(s)
Ohio Northern U, OH	M, W
The Ohio State U, OH	M(s), W(s)
The Ohio State U at Lima, OH	M, W
Ohio U, OH	M(s), W(s)
Ohio U–Eastern, OH	M, W
Ohio U–Zanesville, OH	M, W
Ohio Wesleyan U, OH	M, W
Oklahoma Baptist U, OK	M(s), W(s)
Oklahoma Christian U, OK	M(s), W(s)
Oklahoma City U, OK	M(s), W(s)
Oklahoma Panhandle State U, OK	M(s), W(s)
Oklahoma State U, OK	M(s), W(s)
Olivet Coll, MI	M, W
Olivet Nazarene U, IL	M(s), W(s)
Oral Roberts U, OK	M(s), W(s)
Otterbein Coll, OH	M, W
Park U, MO	M(s), W(s)
Pittsburg State U, KS	M(s), W(s)
Presentation Coll, SD	M, W
Purdue U, IN	M(s), W(s)
Purdue U Calumet, IN	M(s), W(s)
Purdue U North Central, IN	M(s)
Quincy U, IL	M(s), W(s)
Research Coll of Nursing, MO	M(s), W(s)
Ripon Coll, WI	M, W
Robert Morris Coll, IL	M(s), W(s)
Rochester Comm and Tech Coll, MN	M, W
Rockford Coll, IL	M, W
Rockhurst U, MO	M(s), W(s)
Rogers State U, OK	M, W
Rose-Hulman Inst of Technology, IN	M, W
Saginaw Valley State U, MI	M(s), W(s)
St. Ambrose U, IA	M(s), W(s)
St. Catherine U, MN	W
St. Cloud State U, MN	M(s), W(s)
St. Gregory's U, Shawnee, OK	M(s), W(s)

Saint John's U, MN	M
Saint Joseph's Coll, IN	M(s), W(s)
St. Louis Christian Coll, MO	M
St. Louis Coll of Pharmacy, MO	M, W
Saint Louis U, MO	M(s), W(s)
Saint Mary-of-the-Woods Coll, IN	W(s)
Saint Mary's Coll, IN	W
Saint Mary's U of Minnesota, MN	M, W
St. Norbert Coll, WI	M, W
St. Olaf Coll, MN	M, W
Saint Xavier U, IL	M(s)
Shawnee State U, OH	M(s), W(s)
Siena Heights U, MI	M(s), W(s)
Silver Lake Coll, WI	M(s), W(s)
Simpson Coll, IA	M, W
South Dakota School of Mines and Technology, SD	M(s), W(s)
South Dakota State U, SD	M(s), W(s)
Southeastern Oklahoma State U, OK	M(s), W(s)
Southeast Missouri State U, MO	M(s), W(s)
Southern Illinois U Carbondale, IL	M(s), W(s)
Southern Illinois U Edwardsville, IL	M(s), W(s)
Southern Methodist U, TX	M(s), W(s)
Southern Nazarene U, OK	M(s), W(s)
Southwest Baptist U, MO	M(s), W(s)
Southwestern Christian U, OK	M
Southwestern Coll, KS	M(s), W(s)
Southwestern Oklahoma State U, OK	M(s), W(s)
Southwest Minnesota State U, MN	M(s), W(s)
Spring Arbor U, MI	M(s), W(s)
Stephens Coll, MO	W(s)
Sterling Coll, KS	M(s), W(s)
Taylor U, IN	M(s), W(s)
Temple Baptist Coll, OH	M, W
Tiffin U, OH	M(s), W(s)
Transylvania U, KY	M, W
Trine U, IN	M, W
Trinity Bible Coll, ND	M, W
Trinity Christian Coll, IL	M(s), W(s)
Trinity International U, IL	M(s), W(s)
Truman State U, MO	M(s), W(s)
Union Coll, NE	M, W
The U of Akron, OH	M(s), W(s)
U of Central Missouri, MO	M(s), W(s)
U of Central Oklahoma, OK	M(s), W(s)
U of Charleston, WV	M(s), W(s)
U of Chicago, IL	M, W
U of Cincinnati, OH	M(s), W(s)
U of Dallas, TX	M, W
U of Dayton, OH	M(s), W(s)
U of Evansville, IN	M(s), W(s)
The U of Findlay, OH	M(s), W(s)
U of Illinois at Chicago, IL	M(s), W(s)
U of Illinois at Springfield, IL	M(s), W(s)
U of Illinois at Urbana–Champaign, IL	M(s), W(s)
U of Indianapolis, IN	M(s), W(s)
The U of Iowa, IA	M(s), W(s)
The U of Kansas, KS	M(s), W(s)
U of Mary, ND	M(s), W(s)
U of Michigan, MI	M(s), W(s)
U of Michigan–Dearborn, MI	M(s), W(s)
U of Minnesota, Crookston, MN	M(s), W(s)
U of Minnesota, Duluth, MN	M(s), W(s)
U of Minnesota, Morris, MN	M, W
U of Minnesota, Twin Cities Campus, MN	M(s), W(s)
U of Missouri–Columbia, MO	M(s), W(s)
U of Missouri–Kansas City, MO	M(s), W(s)
U of Missouri–St. Louis, MO	M(s), W(s)
U of Nebraska at Kearney, NE	M(s), W(s)
U of Nebraska at Omaha, NE	M(s), W(s)
U of Nebraska–Lincoln, NE	M(s), W(s)
U of New Orleans, LA	M(s), W(s)
U of North Dakota, ND	M(s), W(s)
U of Northern Iowa, IA	M(s), W(s)
U of Notre Dame, IN	M(s), W(s)
U of Oklahoma, OK	M(s), W(s)
U of Rio Grande, OH	M(s), W(s)
U of St. Francis, IL	M(s), W(s)
U of Saint Francis, IN	M(s), W(s)
U of Saint Mary, KS	M(s), W(s)
U of Science and Arts of Oklahoma, OK	M(s), W(s)
U of Sioux Falls, SD	M(s), W(s)
The U of South Dakota, SD	M(s), W(s)
U of Southern Indiana, IN	M(s), W(s)
The U of Toledo, OH	M(s), W(s)
U of Tulsa, OK	M(s), W(s)
U of Wisconsin–Eau Claire, WI	M, W
U of Wisconsin–Green Bay, WI	M(s), W(s)
U of Wisconsin–La Crosse, WI	M, W
U of Wisconsin–Madison, WI	M(s), W(s)
U of Wisconsin–Milwaukee, WI	M(s), W(s)
U of Wisconsin–Oshkosh, WI	M, W
U of Wisconsin–Parkside, WI	M(s), W(s)
U of Wisconsin–Platteville, WI	M, W
U of Wisconsin–Stevens Point, WI	M, W
U of Wisconsin–Stout, WI	M, W
U of Wisconsin–Superior, WI	M, W
U of Wisconsin–Whitewater, WI	M, W
Ursuline Coll, OH	W(s)
Valley City State U, ND	M(s), W(s)
Valparaiso U, IN	M(s), W(s)
Viterbo U, WI	M(s), W(s)
Wabash Coll, IN	M
Waldorf Coll, IA	M(s), W(s)
Walsh U, OH	M(s), W(s)
Wartburg Coll, IA	M, W
Washburn U, KS	M(s), W(s)
Washington U in St. Louis, MO	M, W
Wayne State Coll, NE	M(s), W(s)
Wayne State U, MI	M(s), W(s)
Webster U, MO	M, W
Western Illinois U, IL	M(s), W(s)
Western Michigan U, MI	M(s), W(s)
Westminster Coll, MO	M, W
Wheaton Coll, IL	M, W
Wichita State U, KS	M(s), W(s)
Wilberforce U, OH	M, W
William Jewell Coll, MO	M(s), W(s)
Wilmington Coll, OH	M, W
Winona State U, MN	M(s), W(s)
Wittenberg U, OH	M, W
Wright State U, OH	M(s), W(s)
Xavier U, OH	M(s), W(s)
York Coll, NE	M(s), W(s)
Youngstown State U, OH	M(s), W(s)

Bowling

Adrian Coll, MI	W
Baker U, KS	W(s)
Ball State U, IN	M, W
Calumet Coll of Saint Joseph, IN	M, W
Davenport U, Grand Rapids, MI	M, W
Elmhurst Coll, IL	W
Fontbonne U, MO	W
Lindenwood U, MO	M(s), W(s)
McKendree U, IL	M(s), W(s)
Minnesota State U Mankato, MN	W
Missouri Baptist U, MO	M(s), W
Missouri State U, MO	M, W
Newman U, KS	M(s), W(s)
North Dakota State U, ND	M, W
Robert Morris Coll, IL	M(s), W(s)
Saginaw Valley State U, MI	M(s)
St. Ambrose U, IA	M(s), W(s)
St. Cloud State U, MN	M, W
Saint Louis U, MO	M, W
South Dakota State U, SD	M, W
U of Central Missouri, MO	M, W
U of Nebraska–Lincoln, NE	W(s)
U of Wisconsin–Platteville, WI	M, W
U of Wisconsin–Whitewater, WI	M, W
Viterbo U, WI	M(s), W(s)
Wichita State U, KS	M, W
Winona State U, MN	M, W

Cheerleading

AIB Coll of Business, IA	M(s), W(s)
Albion Coll, MI	M, W
Augustana Coll, IL	M, W
Augustana Coll, SD	W
Avila U, MO	W(s)
Baker U, KS	M(s), W(s)
Barclay Coll, KS	M, W
Benedictine Coll, KS	M(s), W(s)
Bethel Coll, IN	M(s), W(s)
Bradley U, IL	M, W
Calvary Bible Coll and Theological Seminary, MO	W
Case Western Reserve U, OH	M, W
Central Christian Coll of Kansas, KS	M(s), W(s)
Central State U, OH	M(s), W(s)
Clarke Coll, IA	W
Coe Coll, IA	W
Coll of Mount St. Joseph, OH	W
Coll of the Ozarks, MO	M, W
The Coll of Wooster, OH	W
Concordia Coll, MN	W
Concordia U Chicago, IL	M, W
Culver-Stockton Coll, MO	M(s), W(s)
Dakota State U, SD	M, W
Dakota Wesleyan U, SD	M(s), W(s)
DePauw U, IN	M, W
Drake U, IA	M(s), W(s)
Drury U, MO	M(s), W(s)
Earlham Coll, IN	W
Emporia State U, KS	M(s), W(s)
Fontbonne U, MO	W
Grace Coll, IN	M(s), W(s)
Grand Valley State U, MI	M, W
Hannibal-LaGrange Coll, MO	M(s), W(s)
Harris-Stowe State U, MO	M(s), W(s)
Haskell Indian Nations U, KS	M, W
Hiram Coll, OH	M, W
Hope Coll, MI	M, W
Illinois Coll, IL	W
Illinois Wesleyan U, IL	M, W
Indiana Tech, IN	M(s), W(s)
Indiana U East, IN	W
Indiana Wesleyan U, IN	M(s), W(s)
John Carroll U, OH	W
Kansas Wesleyan U, KS	M(s), W(s)
Lake Forest Coll, IL	M, W
Lewis U, IL	M(s), W(s)
Lindenwood U, MO	M(s), W(s)
Loyola U Chicago, IL	M, W
MacMurray Coll, IL	M, W
Malone U, OH	M, W
Manchester Coll, IN	M, W

M—for men; W—for women; (s)—scholarship offered

Marian U, IN M(s), W(s)
Marietta Coll, OH W
Marquette U, WI M, W
McKendree U, IL M(s), W(s)
Miami U Hamilton, OH W
Michigan State U, MI M, W
MidAmerica Nazarene U, KS M(s), W(s)
Millikin U, IL M, W
Milwaukee School of Engineering, WI M, W
Minnesota State U Mankato, MN M, W
Minot State U, ND W
Mount Union Coll, OH W
Nebraska Wesleyan U, NE W
North Central Coll, IL W
North Dakota State U, ND M, W
Northern Michigan U, MI M, W
Northwestern U, IL M, W
Northwest Missouri State U, MO M(s), W(s)
Northwood U, MI M(s), W(s)
Oberlin Coll, OH W
Ohio Dominican U, OH M, W
The Ohio State U, OH M, W
Ohio U, OH M, W
Oklahoma City U, OK M(s), W(s)
Oklahoma Panhandle State U, OK W(s)
Olivet Nazarene U, IL M(s), W(s)
Otterbein Coll, OH M, W
Purdue U North Central, IN M, W
Quincy U, IL M, W
Ripon Coll, WI M, W
Rogers State U, OK M, W
Rose-Hulman Inst of Technology, IN M, W
Saginaw Valley State U, MI M, W
St. Ambrose U, IA M(s), W(s)
St. Cloud State U, MN M, W
St. Gregory's U, Shawnee, OK M, W
Saint Joseph's Coll, IN M(s), W(s)
Simpson Coll, IA M, W
South Dakota State U, SD M, W
Southeast Missouri State U, MO M(s), W(s)
Southern Illinois U Carbondale, IL M, W
Southern Methodist U, TX M(s), W(s)
Southern Nazarene U, OK M(s), W(s)
Southwest Baptist U, MO M, W
Southwestern Coll, KS M(s), W(s)
Southwestern Oklahoma State U, OK M, W
Sterling Coll, KS W(s)
Tiffin U, OH M(s), W(s)
Transylvania U, KY M, W
Truman State U, MO M, W
The U of Akron, OH M, W
U of Charleston, WV W(s)
U of Cincinnati, OH M, W
U of Dayton, OH M, W
U of Illinois at Springfield, IL W
U of Illinois at Urbana–Champaign, IL M, W
U of Michigan, MI M(s), W(s)
U of Minnesota, Duluth, MN W
U of Missouri–Columbia, MO M, W
U of Missouri–Kansas City, MO W
U of Oklahoma, OK M(s), W(s)
U of St. Francis, IL W(s)
U of Saint Francis, IN M(s), W(s)
U of Science and Arts of Oklahoma, OK M(s), W(s)
U of Sioux Falls, SD W(s)
U of Southern Indiana, IN M, W
U of Wisconsin–La Crosse, WI M, W
U of Wisconsin–Madison, WI M, W
U of Wisconsin–Platteville, WI M, W
U of Wisconsin–Superior, WI M, W
U of Wisconsin–Whitewater, WI M, W
Waldorf Coll, IA W(s)
Walsh U, OH W
Wartburg Coll, IA W
Washburn U, KS M(s), W(s)
Wheaton Coll, IL W
Wichita State U, KS M, W
William Jewell Coll, MO M(s), W(s)
Xavier U, OH M, W

Crew

Beloit Coll, WI M, W
Butler U, IN M, W
Calvin Coll, MI M, W
Carleton Coll, MN M, W
Case Western Reserve U, OH M, W
Coll of Saint Benedict, MN W
Creighton U, NE W(s)
Denison U, OH M
DePauw U, IN M, W
Drake U, IA W
Eastern Michigan U, MI W(s)
Grand Valley State U, MI M, W
Indiana U Bloomington, IN W(s)
John Carroll U, OH M, W
Kansas State U, KS W(s)
Lawrence U, WI M, W
Macalester Coll, MN M, W
Marietta Coll, OH M, W
Marquette U, WI M, W
Michigan State U, MI W(s)
Milwaukee School of Engineering, WI M
Northern Michigan U, MI M, W
Oklahoma City U, OK M, W
St. Cloud State U, MN M, W
Saint John's U, MN M
Saint Louis U, MO M, W
Southern Methodist U, TX W(s)
U of Charleston, WV M(s), W(s)
U of Cincinnati, OH M, W
U of Dayton, OH W
The U of Iowa, IA M, W(s)
The U of Kansas, KS W(s)
U of Michigan, MI M(s), W(s)
U of Minnesota, Duluth, MN M, W
U of Nebraska–Lincoln, NE M, W
U of Notre Dame, IN W(s)
U of Oklahoma, OK W(s)
U of Tulsa, OK W(s)
Wabash Coll, IN M
Washington U in St. Louis, MO M, W
Wheaton Coll, IL M, W
Wichita State U, KS M, W
Wittenberg U, OH M, W
Xavier U, OH M, W

Cross-Country Running

Adrian Coll, MI M, W
Albion Coll, MI M, W
Alma Coll, MI M, W
Anderson U, IN M, W
Aquinas Coll, MI M(s), W(s)
Ashland U, OH M(s), W(s)
Augsburg Coll, MN M, W
Augustana Coll, IL M, W
Augustana Coll, SD M(s), W(s)
Aurora U, IL M, W
Baker U, KS M(s), W(s)
Baldwin-Wallace Coll, OH M, W
Ball State U, IN M(s), W(s)
Beloit Coll, WI M, W
Bemidji State U, MN W
Benedictine Coll, KS M(s), W(s)
Benedictine U, IL M, W
Bethany Coll, KS M(s), W(s)
Bethany Lutheran Coll, MN M, W
Bethel Coll, IN M(s), W(s)
Bethel Coll, KS M(s), W(s)
Bethel U, MN M, W
Black Hills State U, SD M(s), W(s)
Bluffton U, OH M, W
Bowling Green State U, OH M(s), W(s)
Bradley U, IL M(s), W(s)
Briar Cliff U, IA M(s), W(s)
Buena Vista U, IA M, W
Butler U, IN M(s), W(s)
Calumet Coll of Saint Joseph, IN M, W
Calvin Coll, MI M, W
Cameron U, OK M(s)
Capital U, OH M, W
Carleton Coll, MN M, W
Carroll U, WI M, W
Case Western Reserve U, OH M, W
Cedarville U, OH M(s), W(s)
Central Coll, IA M, W
Central Methodist U, MO M(s), W(s)
Central Michigan U, MI M(s), W(s)
Central State U, OH M(s), W(s)
Cincinnati Christian U, OH M, W
Clarke Coll, IA M(s), W(s)
Clarkson U, NY M, W
Cleveland State U, OH W(s)
Coe Coll, IA M, W
Coll of Mount St. Joseph, OH M, W
Coll of Saint Benedict, MN W
Coll of Saint Mary, NE W(s)
The Coll of St. Scholastica, MN M, W
The Coll of Wooster, OH M, W
Concordia Coll, MN M, W
Concordia U, MI M(s), W(s)
Concordia U Chicago, IL M, W
Concordia U, Nebraska, NE M(s), W(s)
Concordia U, St. Paul, MN M(s), W(s)
Concordia U Wisconsin, WI M, W
Cornell Coll, IA M, W
Cornerstone U, MI M(s), W(s)
Creighton U, NE M(s), W(s)
Crown Coll, MN M, W
Culver-Stockton Coll, MO M(s), W(s)
Dakota State U, SD M(s), W(s)
Dakota Wesleyan U, SD M(s), W(s)
Dana Coll, NE M(s), W(s)
Davenport U, Grand Rapids, MI M(s), W(s)
Defiance Coll, OH M, W
Denison U, OH M, W
DePaul U, IL M(s), W(s)
DePauw U, IN M, W
Doane Coll, NE M(s), W(s)
Dominican U, IL M, W
Dordt Coll, IA M(s), W(s)
Drake U, IA M(s), W(s)
Drury U, MO M(s), W(s)
Earlham Coll, IN M, W
Eastern Illinois U, IL M(s), W(s)
Eastern Michigan U, MI M(s), W(s)
Edgewood Coll, WI M, W
Elmhurst Coll, IL M, W
Emporia State U, KS M(s), W(s)
Evangel U, MO M(s), W(s)
Ferris State U, MI M(s), W(s)
Fontbonne U, MO M, W

Fort Hays State U, KS	M(s), W(s)
Franciscan U of Steubenville, OH	M, W
Franklin Coll, IN	M, W
Friends U, KS	M(s), W(s)
Goshen Coll, IN	M(s), W(s)
Grace Coll, IN	M(s), W(s)
Graceland U, IA	M(s), W(s)
Grand Valley State U, MI	M(s), W(s)
Grand View U, IA	M(s), W(s)
Greenville Coll, IL	M, W
Grinnell Coll, IA	M, W
Gustavus Adolphus Coll, MN	M, W
Hamline U, MN	M, W
Hannibal-LaGrange Coll, MO	M(s), W(s)
Hanover Coll, IN	M, W
Haskell Indian Nations U, KS	M, W
Heidelberg U, OH	M, W
Hiram Coll, OH	M, W
Hope Coll, MI	M, W
Huntington U, IN	M(s), W(s)
Illinois Coll, IL	M, W
Illinois Inst of Technology, IL	M(s), W(s)
Illinois State U, IL	M(s), W(s)
Illinois Wesleyan U, IL	M, W
Indiana State U, IN	M(s), W(s)
Indiana Tech, IN	M(s), W(s)
Indiana U Bloomington, IN	M(s), W(s)
Indiana U–Purdue U Fort Wayne, IN	M(s), W(s)
Indiana U–Purdue U Indianapolis, IN	M(s), W(s)
Indiana Wesleyan U, IN	M(s), W(s)
Iowa State U of Science and Technology, IA	M(s), W(s)
Iowa Wesleyan Coll, IA	M, W
Jamestown Coll, ND	M(s), W(s)
John Carroll U, OH	M, W
Kalamazoo Coll, MI	M, W
Kansas State U, KS	M(s), W(s)
Kansas Wesleyan U, KS	M(s), W(s)
Kent State U, OH	M(s), W(s)
Kenyon Coll, OH	M, W
Knox Coll, IL	M, W
Lake Erie Coll, OH	M, W
Lake Forest Coll, IL	M, W
Lakeland Coll, WI	M, W
Lake Superior State U, MI	M(s), W(s)
Lawrence U, WI	M, W
Lewis U, IL	M(s), W(s)
Lincoln U, MO	W(s)
Lindenwood U, MO	M(s), W(s)
Loras Coll, IA	M, W
Loyola U Chicago, IL	M(s), W(s)
Luther Coll, IA	M, W
Macalester Coll, MN	M, W
Madonna U, MI	M(s), W(s)
Malone U, OH	M(s), W(s)
Manchester Coll, IN	M, W
Maranatha Baptist Bible Coll, WI	M, W
Marian U, WI	M, W
Marian U, IN	M(s), W(s)
Marietta Coll, OH	M, W
Marquette U, WI	M(s), W(s)
Martin Luther Coll, MN	M, W
Maryville U of Saint Louis, MO	M, W
McKendree U, IL	M(s), W(s)
McPherson Coll, KS	M
Miami U, OH	M(s), W(s)
Michigan State U, MI	M(s), W(s)
Michigan Technological U, MI	M, W
MidAmerica Nazarene U, KS	M(s), W(s)
Millikin U, IL	M, W
Milwaukee School of Engineering, WI	M, W
Minnesota State U Mankato, MN	M(s), W(s)
Minnesota State U Moorhead, MN	M, W
Minot State U, ND	M(s), W(s)
Missouri Baptist U, MO	M(s), W(s)
Missouri Southern State U, MO	M(s), W(s)
Missouri State U, MO	W(s)
Missouri U of Science and Technology, MO	M(s), W(s)
Monmouth Coll, IL	M, W
Morningside Coll, IA	M(s), W(s)
Mount Marty Coll, SD	M(s), W(s)
Mount Mary Coll, WI	W
Mount Mercy Coll, IA	M(s), W(s)
Mount Union Coll, OH	M, W
Mount Vernon Nazarene U, OH	M(s), W(s)
Muskingum Coll, OH	M, W
Nebraska Wesleyan U, NE	M, W
Newman U, KS	M(s), W(s)
North Central Coll, IL	M, W
North Central U, MN	M, W
North Dakota State U, ND	M(s), W(s)
Northern Michigan U, MI	W(s)
Northern State U, SD	M(s), W(s)
Northland Coll, WI	M, W
North Park U, IL	M, W
Northwestern Coll, MN	M, W
Northwestern U, IL	W(s)
Northwest Missouri State U, MO	M(s), W(s)
Northwood U, MI	M(s), W(s)
Oakland U, MI	M(s), W(s)
Oberlin Coll, OH	M, W
Ohio Dominican U, OH	M, W
Ohio Northern U, OH	M, W
The Ohio State U, OH	M(s), W(s)
Ohio U, OH	M(s), W(s)
Ohio Wesleyan U, OH	M, W
Oklahoma Baptist U, OK	M(s), W(s)
Oklahoma Christian U, OK	M(s), W(s)
Oklahoma Panhandle State U, OK	M(s), W(s)
Oklahoma State U, OK	M(s), W(s)
Olivet Coll, MI	M, W
Olivet Nazarene U, IL	M(s), W(s)
Oral Roberts U, OK	M(s), W(s)
Otterbein Coll, OH	M, W
Park U, MO	M(s), W(s)
Pittsburg State U, KS	M(s), W(s)
Presentation Coll, SD	M, W
Purdue U, IN	M(s), W(s)
Ripon Coll, WI	M, W
Robert Morris Coll, IL	M(s), W(s)
Rose-Hulman Inst of Technology, IN	M, W
Saginaw Valley State U, MI	M(s), W(s)
St. Ambrose U, IA	M(s), W(s)
St. Catherine U, MN	W
St. Cloud State U, MN	M(s), W
Saint John's U, MN	M
Saint Joseph's Coll, IN	M(s), W(s)
St. Louis Coll of Pharmacy, MO	M, W
Saint Louis U, MO	M(s), W(s)
Saint Mary's Coll, IN	W
Saint Mary's U of Minnesota, MN	M, W
St. Norbert Coll, WI	M, W
St. Olaf Coll, MN	M, W
Saint Xavier U, IL	W(s)
Shawnee State U, OH	M(s), W(s)
Siena Heights U, MI	M(s), W(s)
Silver Lake Coll, WI	M(s), W(s)
Simpson Coll, IA	M, W
South Dakota School of Mines and Technology, SD	M(s), W(s)
South Dakota State U, SD	M(s), W(s)
Southeastern Oklahoma State U, OK	W(s)
Southeast Missouri State U, MO	M(s), W(s)
Southern Illinois U Carbondale, IL	M(s), W(s)
Southern Illinois U Edwardsville, IL	M(s), W(s)
Southern Methodist U, TX	W(s)
Southern Nazarene U, OK	M(s), W(s)
Southwest Baptist U, MO	M(s), W(s)
Southwestern Coll, KS	M(s), W(s)
Southwestern Oklahoma State U, OK	W(s)
Spring Arbor U, MI	M(s), W(s)
Stephens Coll, MO	W(s)
Sterling Coll, KS	M(s), W(s)
Taylor U, IN	M(s), W(s)
Tiffin U, OH	M(s), W(s)
Transylvania U, KY	M, W
Trine U, IN	M, W
Trinity Christian Coll, IL	M(s), W(s)
Truman State U, MO	M(s), W(s)
The U of Akron, OH	M(s), W(s)
U of Central Missouri, MO	M(s), W(s)
U of Central Oklahoma, OK	M(s), W(s)
U of Charleston, WV	M(s), W(s)
U of Chicago, IL	M, W
U of Cincinnati, OH	M(s), W(s)
U of Dallas, TX	M, W
U of Dayton, OH	M(s), W(s)
U of Evansville, IN	M(s), W(s)
The U of Findlay, OH	M(s), W(s)
U of Illinois at Chicago, IL	M(s), W(s)
U of Illinois at Urbana–Champaign, IL	M(s), W(s)
U of Indianapolis, IN	M(s), W(s)
The U of Iowa, IA	M(s), W(s)
The U of Kansas, KS	M(s), W(s)
U of Mary, ND	M(s), W(s)
U of Michigan, MI	M(s), W(s)
U of Minnesota, Duluth, MN	M(s), W(s)
U of Minnesota, Morris, MN	M, W
U of Minnesota, Twin Cities Campus, MN	M(s), W(s)
U of Missouri–Columbia, MO	M(s), W(s)
U of Missouri–Kansas City, MO	M(s), W(s)
U of Nebraska at Kearney, NE	M(s), W(s)
U of Nebraska at Omaha, NE	W(s)
U of Nebraska–Lincoln, NE	M(s), W(s)
U of North Dakota, ND	M, W
U of Northern Iowa, IA	M(s), W(s)
U of Notre Dame, IN	M(s), W(s)
U of Oklahoma, OK	M(s), W(s)
U of Rio Grande, OH	M(s), W(s)
U of St. Francis, IL	M(s), W(s)
U of Saint Francis, IN	M(s), W(s)
U of Sioux Falls, SD	M(s), W(s)
The U of South Dakota, SD	M(s), W(s)
U of Southern Indiana, IN	M(s), W(s)
The U of Toledo, OH	M(s), W(s)
U of Tulsa, OK	M(s), W(s)
U of Wisconsin–Eau Claire, WI	M, W
U of Wisconsin–Green Bay, WI	M(s), W(s)
U of Wisconsin–La Crosse, WI	M, W
U of Wisconsin–Madison, WI	M(s), W(s)
U of Wisconsin–Milwaukee, WI	M(s), W(s)
U of Wisconsin–Oshkosh, WI	M, W
U of Wisconsin–Parkside, WI	M(s), W(s)
U of Wisconsin–Platteville, WI	M, W

M—for men; W—for women; (s)—scholarship offered

U of Wisconsin–Stevens Point, WI M, W
U of Wisconsin–Stout, WI M, W
U of Wisconsin–Superior, WI M, W
U of Wisconsin–Whitewater, WI M, W
Ursuline Coll, OH W(s)
Valparaiso U, IN M(s), W(s)
Viterbo U, WI M(s), W(s)
Wabash Coll, IN M
Walsh U, OH M(s), W(s)
Wartburg Coll, IA M, W
Washington U in St. Louis, MO M, W
Wayne State Coll, NE M(s), W(s)
Wayne State U, MI M(s), W(s)
Webster U, MO W
Western Illinois U, IL M(s), W(s)
Western Michigan U, MI W(s)
Wheaton Coll, IL M, W
Wichita State U, KS M(s), W(s)
Wilberforce U, OH M, W
William Jewell Coll, MO M(s), W(s)
Wilmington Coll, OH M, W
Winona State U, MN M, W(s)
Wittenberg U, OH M, W
Wright State U, OH M(s), W(s)
Xavier U, OH M(s), W(s)
Youngstown State U, OH M(s), W(s)

Equestrian Sports

Albion Coll, MI M, W
Ball State U, IN M, W
Carleton Coll, MN M, W
The Coll of Wooster, OH W
Denison U, OH M, W
Earlham Coll, IN W
Hillsdale Coll, MI W
Hiram Coll, OH M, W
Kenyon Coll, OH M, W
Miami U, OH M, W
Michigan State U, MI M, W
Missouri State U, MO M, W
Oberlin Coll, OH M, W
Ohio U, OH M, W
Ohio Wesleyan U, OH M, W
Oklahoma Panhandle State U, OK W(s)
Oklahoma State U, OK W(s)
Otterbein Coll, OH M, W
St. Cloud State U, MN M, W
Saint Louis U, MO M, W
Saint Mary-of-the-Woods Coll, IN W(s)
Saint Mary's Coll, IN W
South Dakota State U, SD W
Southern Methodist U, TX W(s)
Southwestern Oklahoma State U, OK M(s), W(s)
Tiffin U, OH M(s), W(s)
Truman State U, MO M, W
U of Minnesota, Crookston, MN W
Washington U in St. Louis, MO M, W
Xavier U, OH M, W

Fencing

Beloit Coll, WI M, W
Bradley U, IL M, W
Carleton Coll, MN M, W
Case Western Reserve U, OH M, W
Cleveland State U, OH M(s), W(s)
Kenyon Coll, OH M, W
Lake Forest Coll, IL M, W
Lawrence U, WI M, W
Macalester Coll, MN M, W
Marquette U, WI M, W
Miami U, OH M, W
Michigan Technological U, MI M, W
Northwestern U, IL W(s)
Oberlin Coll, OH M, W
The Ohio State U, OH M(s), W(s)
Southern Methodist U, TX M, W
U of Nebraska–Lincoln, NE M, W
U of Notre Dame, IN M(s), W(s)
Washington U in St. Louis, MO M, W
Wayne State U, MI M(s), W(s)
Winona State U, MN M, W
Xavier U, OH M, W

Field Hockey

Ball State U, IN W(s)
Carleton Coll, MN W
Central Michigan U, MI W(s)
The Coll of Wooster, OH W
Denison U, OH W
DePauw U, IN W
Earlham Coll, IN W
Fontbonne U, MO W
Indiana U Bloomington, IN W
John Carroll U, OH W
Kent State U, OH W(s)
Kenyon Coll, OH W
Lindenwood U, MO W(s)
Miami U, OH M, W(s)
Michigan State U, MI W(s)
Missouri State U, MO W(s)
Northwestern U, IL W(s)
Oberlin Coll, OH W
The Ohio State U, OH W(s)
Ohio U, OH W(s)
Ohio Wesleyan U, OH W
Saint Louis U, MO W(s)
Saint Mary's Coll, IN W
Transylvania U, KY W
The U of Iowa, IA W(s)
U of Michigan, MI W(s)
Washington U in St. Louis, MO W
Wittenberg U, OH W
Xavier U, OH M, W

Football

Adrian Coll, MI M
Albion Coll, MI M
Alma Coll, MI M
Anderson U, IN M
Ashland U, OH M(s)
Augsburg Coll, MN M
Augustana Coll, IL M
Augustana Coll, SD M(s)
Aurora U, IL M
Avila U, MO M(s)
Baker U, KS M(s)
Baldwin-Wallace Coll, OH M
Ball State U, IN M(s)
Beloit Coll, WI M
Bemidji State U, MN M(s)
Benedictine Coll, KS M(s)
Benedictine U, IL M
Bethany Coll, KS M(s)
Bethel Coll, KS M(s)
Bethel U, MN M
Black Hills State U, SD M(s)
Blessing-Rieman Coll of Nursing, IL M(s)
Bluffton U, OH M
Bowling Green State U, OH M(s)
Briar Cliff U, IA M(s)
Buena Vista U, IA M
Butler U, IN M
Capital U, OH M
Carleton Coll, MN M
Carroll U, WI M
Case Western Reserve U, OH M
Central Coll, IA M
Central Methodist U, MO M(s)
Central Michigan U, MI M(s)
Coe Coll, IA M
Coll of Mount St. Joseph, OH M
The Coll of St. Scholastica, MN M
The Coll of Wooster, OH M
Concordia Coll, MN M
Concordia U Chicago, IL M
Concordia U, Nebraska, NE M(s)
Concordia U, St. Paul, MN M(s)
Concordia U Wisconsin, WI M
Cornell Coll, IA M
Crown Coll, MN M
Culver-Stockton Coll, MO M(s)
Dakota State U, SD M(s)
Dakota Wesleyan U, SD M(s)
Dana Coll, NE M(s)
Defiance Coll, OH M
Denison U, OH M
DePauw U, IN M
Doane Coll, NE M(s)
Dordt Coll, IA M(s)
Drake U, IA M
Earlham Coll, IN M
Eastern Illinois U, IL M(s)
Eastern Michigan U, MI M(s)
Elmhurst Coll, IL M
Emporia State U, KS M(s)
Eureka Coll, IL M
Evangel U, MO M(s)
Ferris State U, MI M(s)
Fort Hays State U, KS M(s)
Franklin Coll, IN M
Friends U, KS M(s)
Graceland U, IA M(s)
Grand Valley State U, MI M(s)
Grand View U, IA M(s)
Greenville Coll, IL M
Grinnell Coll, IA M
Gustavus Adolphus Coll, MN M
Hamline U, MN M
Hanover Coll, IN M
Haskell Indian Nations U, KS M
Heidelberg U, OH M
Hillsdale Coll, MI M(s)
Hiram Coll, OH M
Hope Coll, MI M
Illinois Coll, IL M
Illinois State U, IL M(s)
Illinois Wesleyan U, IL M
Indiana State U, IN M(s)
Indiana U Bloomington, IN M(s)
Iowa State U of Science and Technology, IA M(s)
Iowa Wesleyan Coll, IA M(s)
Jamestown Coll, ND M(s)
John Carroll U, OH M
Kalamazoo Coll, MI M
Kansas State U, KS M(s)
Kansas Wesleyan U, KS M(s)
Kent State U, OH M(s)
Kenyon Coll, OH M
Knox Coll, IL M
Lake Erie Coll, OH M
Lake Forest Coll, IL M
Lakeland Coll, WI M
Lawrence U, WI M
Lincoln U, MO M(s)
Lindenwood U, MO M(s)
Loras Coll, IA M

Luther Coll, IA M
Macalester Coll, MN M
MacMurray Coll, IL M
Malone U, OH M(s)
Manchester Coll, IN M
Maranatha Baptist Bible Coll, WI M
Marian U, IN M(s)
Marietta Coll, OH M
Marquette U, WI M
Martin Luther Coll, MN M
Mayville State U, ND M(s)
McKendree U, IL M(s)
McPherson Coll, KS M
Miami U, OH M(s)
Michigan State U, MI M(s)
Michigan Technological U, MI M(s)
MidAmerica Nazarene U, KS M(s)
Millikin U, IL M
Minnesota State U Mankato, MN M(s)
Minnesota State U Moorhead, MN M(s)
Minot State U, ND M(s)
Missouri Southern State U, MO M(s)
Missouri State U, MO M(s)
Missouri U of Science and Technology, MO M(s)
Missouri Western State U, MO M(s)
Monmouth Coll, IL M
Morningside Coll, IA M(s)
Mount Union Coll, OH M
Muskingum Coll, OH M
Nebraska Wesleyan U, NE M
North Central Coll, IL M
North Dakota State U, ND M(s)
Northeastern State U, OK M(s)
Northern Michigan U, MI M(s)
Northern State U, SD M(s)
North Park U, IL M
Northwestern Coll, MN M
Northwestern U, IL M(s)
Northwest Missouri State U, MO M(s)
Northwood U, MI M(s)
Oberlin Coll, OH M
Ohio Dominican U, OH M(s)
Ohio Northern U, OH M
The Ohio State U, OH M(s)
Ohio U, OH M(s)
Ohio Wesleyan U, OH M
Oklahoma Panhandle State U, OK M(s)
Oklahoma State U, OK M(s)
Olivet Coll, MI M
Olivet Nazarene U, IL M(s)
Otterbein Coll, OH M
Pittsburg State U, KS M(s)
Purdue U, IN M(s)
Quincy U, IL M(s)
Ripon Coll, WI M
Rochester Comm and Tech Coll, MN M
Rockford Coll, IL M
Rose-Hulman Inst of Technology, IN M
Saginaw Valley State U, MI M(s)
St. Ambrose U, IA M(s)
St. Cloud State U, MN M(s)
Saint John's U, MN M
Saint Joseph's Coll, IN M(s)
St. Norbert Coll, WI M
St. Olaf Coll, MN M
Saint Xavier U, IL M(s)
Simpson Coll, IA M
South Dakota School of Mines and Technology, SD M(s)
South Dakota State U, SD M(s)
Southeastern Oklahoma State U, OK M(s)
Southeast Missouri State U, MO M(s)
Southern Illinois U Carbondale, IL M(s)
Southern Methodist U, TX M(s)
Southern Nazarene U, OK M(s)
Southwest Baptist U, MO M(s)
Southwestern Coll, KS M(s)
Southwestern Oklahoma State U, OK M(s)
Southwest Minnesota State U, MN M(s)
Sterling Coll, KS M(s)
Taylor U, IN M(s)
Tiffin U, OH M(s)
Trine U, IN M
Trinity Bible Coll, ND M
Trinity International U, IL M(s)
Truman State U, MO M(s)
The U of Akron, OH M(s)
U of Central Missouri, MO M(s)
U of Central Oklahoma, OK M(s)
U of Charleston, WV M(s)
U of Chicago, IL M
U of Cincinnati, OH M(s)
U of Dayton, OH M
The U of Findlay, OH M(s)
U of Illinois at Urbana–Champaign, IL M(s)
U of Indianapolis, IN M(s)
The U of Iowa, IA M(s)
The U of Kansas, KS M(s)
U of Mary, ND M(s)
U of Michigan, MI M(s)
U of Minnesota, Crookston, MN M(s)
U of Minnesota, Duluth, MN M(s)
U of Minnesota, Morris, MN M
U of Minnesota, Twin Cities Campus, MN M(s)
U of Missouri–Columbia, MO M(s)
U of Nebraska at Kearney, NE M(s)
U of Nebraska at Omaha, NE M(s)
U of Nebraska–Lincoln, NE M(s)
U of North Dakota, ND M(s)
U of Northern Iowa, IA M(s)
U of Notre Dame, IN M(s)
U of Oklahoma, OK M(s)
U of St. Francis, IL M(s)
U of Saint Francis, IN M(s)
U of Saint Mary, KS M(s)
U of Sioux Falls, SD M(s)
The U of South Dakota, SD M(s)
The U of Toledo, OH M(s)
U of Tulsa, OK M(s)
U of Wisconsin–Eau Claire, WI M
U of Wisconsin–La Crosse, WI M
U of Wisconsin–Madison, WI M(s)
U of Wisconsin–Oshkosh, WI M
U of Wisconsin–Platteville, WI M
U of Wisconsin–Stevens Point, WI M
U of Wisconsin–Stout, WI M
U of Wisconsin–Whitewater, WI M
Valley City State U, ND M(s)
Valparaiso U, IN M
Wabash Coll, IN M
Waldorf Coll, IA M(s)
Walsh U, OH M(s)
Wartburg Coll, IA M
Washburn U, KS M(s)
Washington U in St. Louis, MO M
Wayne State Coll, NE M(s)
Wayne State U, MI M(s)
Western Illinois U, IL M(s)
Western Michigan U, MI M(s)
Westminster Coll, MO M
Wheaton Coll, IL M
William Jewell Coll, MO M(s)
Wilmington Coll, OH M
Winona State U, MN M(s)
Wittenberg U, OH M
Xavier U, OH M
Youngstown State U, OH M(s)

Golf

Adrian Coll, MI M, W
AIB Coll of Business, IA M(s), W(s)
Albion Coll, MI M, W
Alma Coll, MI M, W
Anderson U, IN M, W
Aquinas Coll, MI M(s), W(s)
Ashland U, OH M(s), W(s)
Augsburg Coll, MN M, W
Augustana Coll, IL M, W
Augustana Coll, SD M, W(s)
Aurora U, IL M, W
Avila U, MO W(s)
Baker U, KS M(s), W(s)
Baldwin-Wallace Coll, OH M, W
Ball State U, IN M(s)
Beloit Coll, WI M, W
Bemidji State U, MN M, W
Benedictine Coll, KS M(s), W(s)
Benedictine U, IL M, W
Bethany Coll, KS M(s)
Bethany Lutheran Coll, MN M, W
Bethel Coll, IN M(s), W(s)
Bethel Coll, KS M(s), W(s)
Bethel U, MN M, W
Black Hills State U, SD W
Bowling Green State U, OH M(s), W(s)
Bradley U, IL M(s), W(s)
Briar Cliff U, IA M(s), W(s)
Buena Vista U, IA M, W
Butler U, IN M(s), W(s)
Calumet Coll of Saint Joseph, IN M, W
Calvin Coll, MI M, W
Cameron U, OK M(s), W(s)
Capital U, OH M, W
Carleton Coll, MN M, W
Carroll U, WI M, W
Cedarville U, OH M(s)
Central Christian Coll of Kansas, KS M(s), W(s)
Central Coll, IA M, W
Central State U, OH M(s), W(s)
Cincinnati Christian U, OH M
Clarke Coll, IA M(s), W(s)
Clarkson U, NY M
Cleveland State U, OH M(s)
Coe Coll, IA M, W
Coll of Mount St. Joseph, OH M, W
Coll of Saint Benedict, MN W
The Coll of Wooster, OH M, W
Concordia Coll, MN M, W
Concordia U, MI M(s), W(s)
Concordia U Chicago, IL M
Concordia U, Nebraska, NE M(s), W(s)
Concordia U, St. Paul, MN M(s), W(s)
Concordia U Wisconsin, WI M, W
Cornell Coll, IA M, W
Cornerstone U, MI M(s), W

M—for men; W—for women; (s)—scholarship offered

Creighton U, NE M(s), W(s)
Crossroads Coll, MN M, W
Crown Coll, MN M
Culver-Stockton Coll, MO M(s), W(s)
Dakota Wesleyan U, SD M(s), W(s)
Dana Coll, NE W(s)
Davenport U, Grand Rapids, MI M(s), W(s)
Defiance Coll, OH M, W
Denison U, OH M
DePaul U, IL M(s)
DePauw U, IN M, W
Doane Coll, NE M(s), W(s)
Dominican U, IL M
Dordt Coll, IA M(s)
Drake U, IA M(s), W
Drury U, MO M(s), W(s)
Eastern Illinois U, IL M(s), W(s)
Eastern Michigan U, MI M(s), W(s)
Edgewood Coll, WI M, W
Elmhurst Coll, IL M, W
Eureka Coll, IL M
Evangel U, MO M(s), W(s)
Ferris State U, MI M(s), W(s)
Fontbonne U, MO M, W
Fort Hays State U, KS M(s)
Franklin Coll, IN M, W
Friends U, KS M(s)
Goshen Coll, IN M(s)
Grace Coll, IN M(s)
Graceland U, IA M(s), W(s)
Grand Valley State U, MI M(s), W(s)
Grand View U, IA M(s), W(s)
Grinnell Coll, IA M, W
Gustavus Adolphus Coll, MN M, W
Hannibal-LaGrange Coll, MO M(s)
Hanover Coll, IN M, W
Haskell Indian Nations U, KS M
Heidelberg U, OH M, W
Hiram Coll, OH M, W
Hope Coll, MI M, W
Huntington U, IN M(s)
Illinois Coll, IL M, W
Illinois State U, IL M(s), W(s)
Illinois Wesleyan U, IL M, W
Indiana State U, IN W(s)
Indiana Tech, IN M(s), W(s)
Indiana U Bloomington, IN M(s), W(s)
Indiana U East, IN M
Indiana U Northwest, IN M, W
Indiana U–Purdue U Fort Wayne, IN M(s), W(s)
Indiana U–Purdue U Indianapolis, IN M(s), W
Indiana Wesleyan U, IN M(s)
Iowa State U of Science and Technology, IA M(s), W(s)
Iowa Wesleyan Coll, IA M(s), W(s)
Jamestown Coll, ND M(s), W(s)
John Carroll U, OH M, W
Kalamazoo Coll, MI M, W
Kansas State U, KS M(s), W(s)
Kansas Wesleyan U, KS M(s), W(s)
Kent State U, OH M(s), W(s)
Kenyon Coll, OH M
Knox Coll, IL M, W
Lake Erie Coll, OH M, W
Lake Forest Coll, IL M, W
Lakeland Coll, WI M, W
Lawrence U, WI M
Lewis U, IL M(s), W(s)
Lincoln U, MO M(s), W(s)
Lindenwood U, MO M(s), W(s)
Logan U–Coll of Chiropractic, MO M
Loras Coll, IA M, W
Loyola U Chicago, IL M(s), W(s)
Luther Coll, IA M, W
Macalester Coll, MN M, W
MacMurray Coll, IL M, W
Madonna U, MI M(s), W(s)
Malone U, OH M(s), W(s)
Manchester Coll, IN M, W
Marian U, WI M, W
Marian U, IN M(s), W(s)
Marquette U, WI M(s)
Martin Luther Coll, MN M
Maryville U of Saint Louis, MO M, W
McKendree U, IL M(s), W(s)
Miami U, OH M(s)
Miami U Hamilton, OH M
Michigan State U, MI M(s), W(s)
Mid-America Christian U, OK M
Millikin U, IL M, W
Milwaukee School of Engineering, WI M, W
Minnesota State U Mankato, MN M(s), W(s)
Minnesota State U Moorhead, MN M, W
Minot State U, ND M, W
Missouri Baptist U, MO M(s), W
Missouri Southern State U, MO M(s)
Missouri State U, MO M(s), W(s)
Missouri Western State U, MO M(s), W
Monmouth Coll, IL M, W
Morningside Coll, IA M(s), W(s)
Mount Mercy Coll, IA M(s), W(s)
Mount Union Coll, OH M, W
Mount Vernon Nazarene U, OH M(s)
Muskingum Coll, OH M, W
Nebraska Wesleyan U, NE M, W
Newman U, KS M(s), W(s)
North Central Coll, IL M, W
North Central U, MN M
North Dakota State U, ND M, W(s)
Northeastern State U, OK M(s), W(s)
Northern Michigan U, MI M(s)
Northern State U, SD M, W(s)
North Park U, IL M, W
Northwestern Coll, MN M
Northwestern U, IL M(s), W(s)
Northwest Missouri State U, MO W(s)
Northwood U, MI M(s), W(s)
Oakland U, MI M(s), W(s)
Oberlin Coll, OH M, W
Ohio Christian U, OH M
Ohio Dominican U, OH M(s), W(s)
Ohio Northern U, OH M, W
The Ohio State U, OH M(s), W(s)
The Ohio State U at Lima, OH M
Ohio U, OH M(s), W(s)
Ohio U–Zanesville, OH M, W
Ohio Wesleyan U, OH M
Oklahoma Baptist U, OK M(s), W(s)
Oklahoma Christian U, OK M(s)
Oklahoma City U, OK M(s), W(s)
Oklahoma Panhandle State U, OK M(s), W(s)
Oklahoma State U, OK M(s), W(s)
Olivet Coll, MI M, W
Olivet Nazarene U, IL M(s)
Oral Roberts U, OK M(s), W(s)
Otterbein Coll, OH M, W
Park U, MO W
Pittsburg State U, KS M(s)
Presentation Coll, SD M, W
Purdue U, IN M(s), W(s)
Quincy U, IL M(s), W(s)
Research Coll of Nursing, MO M(s), W(s)
Ripon Coll, WI M, W
Robert Morris Coll, IL M(s), W(s)
Rochester Comm and Tech Coll, MN M, W
Rockford Coll, IL M, W
Rockhurst U, MO M(s), W(s)
Rose-Hulman Inst of Technology, IN M, W
Saginaw Valley State U, MI M(s)
St. Ambrose U, IA M(s), W(s)
St. Cloud State U, MN M, W(s)
Saint John's U, MN M
Saint Joseph's Coll, IN M(s), W(s)
Saint Louis U, MO M, W
Saint Mary's Coll, IN W
Saint Mary's U of Minnesota, MN M, W
St. Norbert Coll, WI M, W
St. Olaf Coll, MN M, W
Saint Xavier U, IL M(s)
Shawnee State U, OH M(s)
Siena Heights U, MI M(s), W(s)
Silver Lake Coll, WI M(s), W(s)
Simpson Coll, IA M, W
South Dakota School of Mines and Technology, SD M, W
South Dakota State U, SD M(s), W(s)
Southern Illinois U Carbondale, IL M(s), W(s)
Southern Illinois U Edwardsville, IL M(s), W(s)
Southern Methodist U, TX M(s), W(s)
Southern Nazarene U, OK M(s), W(s)
Southwest Baptist U, MO M(s)
Southwestern Christian U, OK M
Southwestern Coll, KS M(s), W(s)
Southwestern Oklahoma State U, OK M(s), W(s)
Southwest Minnesota State U, MN W(s)
Spring Arbor U, MI M(s)
Sterling Coll, KS M, W
Taylor U, IN M(s)
Tiffin U, OH M(s), W(s)
Transylvania U, KY M, W
Trine U, IN M, W
Trinity Bible Coll, ND M
Truman State U, MO M(s), W(s)
The U of Akron, OH M(s), W(s)
U of Central Missouri, MO M(s)
U of Central Oklahoma, OK M(s), W(s)
U of Charleston, WV M(s)
U of Cincinnati, OH M(s)
U of Dallas, TX M
U of Dayton, OH M(s), W(s)
U of Evansville, IN M(s), W(s)
The U of Findlay, OH M(s), W(s)
U of Illinois at Springfield, IL M(s), W(s)
U of Illinois at Urbana–Champaign, IL M(s), W(s)
U of Indianapolis, IN M(s), W(s)
The U of Iowa, IA M(s), W(s)
The U of Kansas, KS M(s), W(s)
U of Mary, ND M(s), W(s)
U of Michigan, MI M(s), W(s)
U of Minnesota, Crookston, MN M, W
U of Minnesota, Morris, MN M, W
U of Minnesota, Twin Cities Campus, MN M(s), W(s)
U of Missouri–Columbia, MO M(s), W(s)
U of Missouri–Kansas City, MO M(s), W(s)
U of Missouri–St. Louis, MO M(s), W(s)
U of Nebraska at Kearney, NE M(s), W(s)
U of Nebraska at Omaha, NE W
U of Nebraska–Lincoln, NE M(s), W(s)

U of New Orleans, LA	M(s)
U of North Dakota, ND	M, W
U of Northern Iowa, IA	M(s), W(s)
U of Notre Dame, IN	M(s), W(s)
U of Oklahoma, OK	M(s), W(s)
U of St. Francis, IL	M(s), W(s)
U of Saint Francis, IN	M(s), W
U of Sioux Falls, SD	M(s), W(s)
The U of South Dakota, SD	M(s), W(s)
U of Southern Indiana, IN	M(s), W(s)
The U of Toledo, OH	M(s), W(s)
U of Tulsa, OK	M(s), W(s)
U of Wisconsin–Eau Claire, WI	M, W
U of Wisconsin–Green Bay, WI	M(s), W(s)
U of Wisconsin–Madison, WI	M(s), W(s)
U of Wisconsin–Oshkosh, WI	W
U of Wisconsin–Parkside, WI	M(s)
U of Wisconsin–Platteville, WI	W
U of Wisconsin–Stevens Point, WI	W
U of Wisconsin–Superior, WI	W
U of Wisconsin–Whitewater, WI	W
Ursuline Coll, OH	W(s)
Viterbo U, WI	M(s), W(s)
Wabash Coll, IN	M
Waldorf Coll, IA	M(s), W(s)
Walsh U, OH	M(s), W(s)
Wartburg Coll, IA	M, W
Washburn U, KS	M(s)
Washington U in St. Louis, MO	M, W
Wayne State Coll, NE	M(s), W(s)
Wayne State U, MI	M(s)
Webster U, MO	M
Western Illinois U, IL	M(s), W
Western Michigan U, MI	W(s)
Westminster Coll, MO	M, W
Wheaton Coll, IL	M, W
Wichita State U, KS	M(s), W(s)
William Jewell Coll, MO	M(s), W(s)
Wilmington Coll, OH	M, W
Winona State U, MN	M(s), W(s)
Wittenberg U, OH	M, W
Wright State U, OH	M(s)
Xavier U, OH	M(s), W(s)
Youngstown State U, OH	M(s), W

Gymnastics

Ball State U, IN	W(s)
Bowling Green State U, OH	W(s)
Carleton Coll, MN	W
Central Michigan U, MI	W(s)
Eastern Michigan U, MI	W(s)
Gustavus Adolphus Coll, MN	W
Hamline U, MN	W
Illinois State U, IL	W(s)
Iowa State U of Science and Technology, IA	W(s)
Kent State U, OH	W(s)
Miami U, OH	M, W
Michigan State U, MI	W(s)
The Ohio State U, OH	M(s), W(s)
Saint Mary's Coll, IN	W
Southeast Missouri State U, MO	W(s)
U of Illinois at Chicago, IL	M(s), W(s)
U of Illinois at Urbana–Champaign, IL	M(s), W(s)
The U of Iowa, IA	M(s), W(s)
U of Michigan, MI	M(s), W(s)
U of Minnesota, Twin Cities Campus, MN	M(s), W(s)
U of Missouri–Columbia, MO	W(s)
U of Nebraska–Lincoln, NE	M(s), W(s)
U of Oklahoma, OK	M(s), W(s)
U of Wisconsin–Eau Claire, WI	W
U of Wisconsin–La Crosse, WI	W
U of Wisconsin–Oshkosh, WI	W
U of Wisconsin–Stout, WI	W
U of Wisconsin–Whitewater, WI	W
Washington U in St. Louis, MO	M, W
Western Michigan U, MI	W(s)
Winona State U, MN	W(s)
Xavier U, OH	M, W

Ice Hockey

Adrian Coll, MI	M, W
Augsburg Coll, MN	M, W
Beloit Coll, WI	M, W
Bemidji State U, MN	M(s), W(s)
Bethel U, MN	M, W
Bowling Green State U, OH	M(s)
Bradley U, IL	M
Butler U, IN	M
Calvin Coll, MI	M
Carleton Coll, MN	M, W
Case Western Reserve U, OH	M, W
Clarkson U, NY	M(s), W(s)
Coll of Saint Benedict, MN	W
The Coll of St. Scholastica, MN	M
Concordia Coll, MN	M, W
Davenport U, Grand Rapids, MI	M(s)
Denison U, OH	M
Dordt Coll, IA	M(s)
Ferris State U, MI	M(s)
Grand Valley State U, MI	M
Gustavus Adolphus Coll, MN	M, W
Hamline U, MN	M, W
Hillsdale Coll, MI	M
Hope Coll, MI	M
John Carroll U, OH	M
Kenyon Coll, OH	M, W
Kettering U, MI	M
Lake Forest Coll, IL	M, W
Lake Superior State U, MI	M(s)
Lawrence U, WI	M, W
Lindenwood U, MO	M, W
Loras Coll, IA	M
Macalester Coll, MN	M, W
Marian U, WI	M, W
McKendree U, IL	M
Miami U, OH	M(s), W
Michigan State U, MI	M(s), W
Michigan Technological U, MI	M(s), W
Milwaukee School of Engineering, WI	M
Minnesota State U Mankato, MN	M(s), W(s)
Minot State U, ND	M
Missouri State U, MO	M
North Dakota State U, ND	M
Northern Michigan U, MI	M(s), W
Northland Coll, WI	M
Northwestern Coll, MN	M
Oakland U, MI	M
Oberlin Coll, OH	M, W
The Ohio State U, OH	M(s), W(s)
Ohio U, OH	M
Ohio Wesleyan U, OH	M, W
Otterbein Coll, OH	W
Robert Morris Coll, IL	M, W
Saginaw Valley State U, MI	M
St. Catherine U, MN	W
St. Cloud State U, MN	M(s), W(s)
Saint John's U, MN	M
Saint Louis U, MO	M
Saint Mary's U of Minnesota, MN	M, W
St. Norbert Coll, WI	M
St. Olaf Coll, MN	M, W
South Dakota State U, SD	M, W
Southern Methodist U, TX	M
U of Cincinnati, OH	M
The U of Findlay, OH	M, W
The U of Iowa, IA	M
The U of Kansas, KS	M
U of Michigan, MI	M(s)
U of Michigan–Dearborn, MI	M
U of Minnesota, Crookston, MN	M
U of Minnesota, Duluth, MN	M(s), W(s)
U of Minnesota, Twin Cities Campus, MN	M(s), W(s)
U of Missouri–St. Louis, MO	M
U of Nebraska at Omaha, NE	M(s)
U of North Dakota, ND	M(s), W(s)
U of Notre Dame, IN	M(s)
U of Southern Indiana, IN	M
U of Wisconsin–Eau Claire, WI	M, W
U of Wisconsin–Madison, WI	M(s), W(s)
U of Wisconsin–Platteville, WI	M, W
U of Wisconsin–Stevens Point, WI	M, W
U of Wisconsin–Stout, WI	M, W
U of Wisconsin–Superior, WI	M, W
U of Wisconsin–Whitewater, WI	M, W
Washington U in St. Louis, MO	M
Wayne State U, MI	W(s)
Western Michigan U, MI	M(s)
Wheaton Coll, IL	M
Wichita State U, KS	M, W
Winona State U, MN	M
Xavier U, OH	M, W

Lacrosse

Adrian Coll, MI	M, W
Aquinas Coll, MI	M(s), W
Augustana Coll, IL	M
Ball State U, IN	M, W
Beloit Coll, WI	M, W
Calvin Coll, MI	M, W
Carleton Coll, MN	M, W
Clarkson U, NY	M, W
Coll of Mount St. Joseph, OH	M, W
Coll of Saint Benedict, MN	W
The Coll of Wooster, OH	M, W
Davenport U, Grand Rapids, MI	M(s), W(s)
Denison U, OH	M, W
Dordt Coll, IA	M
Earlham Coll, IN	M, W
Fontbonne U, MO	M, W
Gustavus Adolphus Coll, MN	M
Hamline U, MN	W
Hillsdale Coll, MI	M
Hope Coll, MI	M, W
Illinois Wesleyan U, IL	M
John Carroll U, OH	M, W
Kenyon Coll, OH	M, W
Kettering U, MI	M
Lake Erie Coll, OH	M, W
Lake Forest Coll, IL	M
Lindenwood U, MO	M(s), W(s)
Marietta Coll, OH	M
Marquette U, WI	M
Miami U, OH	M, W
Michigan State U, MI	M, W
Missouri Baptist U, MO	M(s), W(s)
Missouri State U, MO	M
North Central Coll, IL	W
North Dakota State U, ND	M

M—for men; W—for women; (s)—scholarship offered

Northern Michigan U, MI M
Northwestern U, IL W(s)
Oberlin Coll, OH M, W
The Ohio State U, OH M(s), W(s)
Ohio U, OH W
Ohio Wesleyan U, OH M, W
Otterbein Coll, OH M
Robert Morris Coll, IL W
Saginaw Valley State U, MI M, W
Saint John's U, MN M
Saint Louis U, MO M, W
Siena Heights U, MI M(s)
Southern Methodist U, TX M
Trine U, IN M, W
Truman State U, MO W
U of Cincinnati, OH W(s)
U of Dallas, TX W
The U of Iowa, IA M, W
U of Michigan–Dearborn, MI M
U of Minnesota, Duluth, MN M(s), W
U of Notre Dame, IN M(s), W(s)
U of Wisconsin–Platteville, WI M, W
U of Wisconsin–Whitewater, WI M
Wabash Coll, IN M
Washington U in St. Louis, MO M, W
Wheaton Coll, IL M, W
Wittenberg U, OH M, W
Xavier U, OH M, W

Racquetball
Michigan State U, MI M, W
Michigan Technological U, MI M, W
Missouri State U, MO M, W
Saint Louis U, MO M, W
Wichita State U, KS M, W
Xavier U, OH M, W

Riflery
Coll of Saint Benedict, MN W
Denison U, OH M, W
Hillsdale Coll, MI M, W
Lindenwood U, MO M(s), W(s)
Michigan Technological U, MI M, W
North Dakota State U, ND M, W
The Ohio State U, OH M, W
Rose-Hulman Inst of Technology, IN M, W
Saint John's U, MN M
The U of Akron, OH M, W(s)
U of Missouri–Kansas City, MO M(s), W(s)
U of Nebraska–Lincoln, NE W(s)
U of Wisconsin–Oshkosh, WI M, W

Rock Climbing
Ball State U, IN M, W
Calvin Coll, MI M, W
Lake Forest Coll, IL M, W
Macalester Coll, MN W
Northeastern State U, OK M, W
Ohio U, OH M, W
St. Cloud State U, MN M, W
U of Central Missouri, MO M, W
U of Minnesota, Duluth, MN M, W

Rugby
Ball State U, IN M, W
Butler U, IN M
Calvin Coll, MI M
Carleton Coll, MN M, W
Coll of Saint Benedict, MN W
The Coll of Wooster, OH M, W
Denison U, OH M, W
DePauw U, IN M
Earlham Coll, IN W
Eastern Illinois U, IL M, W(s)
Franciscan U of Steubenville, OH M
Grand Valley State U, MI M, W
Gustavus Adolphus Coll, MN M, W
Hiram Coll, OH M, W
John Carroll U, OH M, W
Kenyon Coll, OH M, W
Lake Forest Coll, IL M, W
Loras Coll, IA M
Macalester Coll, MN M, W
Marquette U, WI M, W
Miami U, OH M, W
Michigan State U, MI M, W
North Dakota State U, ND M, W
Northern Michigan U, MI M, W
Oberlin Coll, OH M, W
Ohio Wesleyan U, OH M, W
Palmer Coll of Chiropractic, IA M, W
Ripon Coll, WI M, W
Saint John's U, MN M
Saint Louis U, MO M
South Dakota State U, SD M, W
Southern Methodist U, TX M, W
Truman State U, MO M, W
U of Cincinnati, OH M
The U of Iowa, IA M, W
The U of Kansas, KS M, W
U of Michigan–Dearborn, MI M
U of Minnesota, Duluth, MN M, W
U of Southern Indiana, IN M
U of Wisconsin–Platteville, WI M, W
U of Wisconsin–Whitewater, WI M, W
Wabash Coll, IN M
Washington U in St. Louis, MO M, W
Wayne State Coll, NE M, W
Wichita State U, KS M
Winona State U, MN M, W
Wittenberg U, OH M, W
Xavier U, OH M, W

Sailing
Carleton Coll, MN M, W
Denison U, OH M, W
Grand Valley State U, MI M, W
Hiram Coll, OH M, W
Hope Coll, MI M, W
John Carroll U, OH M, W
Kenyon Coll, OH M, W
Lake Forest Coll, IL M, W
Miami U, OH M, W
Michigan State U, MI M, W
Ohio Wesleyan U, OH M, W
The U of Iowa, IA M, W
U of Wisconsin–Madison, WI M, W
Wabash Coll, IN M
Washington U in St. Louis, MO M, W

Skiing (Cross-Country)
Carleton Coll, MN M, W
Clarkson U, NY M, W
Coll of Saint Benedict, MN W
Concordia Coll, MN M, W
Gustavus Adolphus Coll, MN M, W
John Carroll U, OH M, W
Macalester Coll, MN M, W
Michigan State U, MI M, W
Michigan Technological U, MI M, W
Northern Michigan U, MI M(s), W(s)
St. Cloud State U, MN M, W(s)
Saint John's U, MN M
St. Olaf Coll, MN M, W
U of Minnesota, Duluth, MN M, W
U of Wisconsin–Green Bay, WI M(s), W(s)

Skiing (Downhill)
Carleton Coll, MN M, W
Clarkson U, NY M, W
Denison U, OH M, W
Grand Valley State U, MI M, W
John Carroll U, OH M, W
Loras Coll, IA M
Marquette U, WI M, W
Michigan State U, MI M, W
Michigan Technological U, MI M, W
Northern Michigan U, MI M, W
St. Cloud State U, MN M, W
Saint Mary's Coll, IN W
St. Olaf Coll, MN M, W
U of Minnesota, Duluth, MN M, W
Winona State U, MN M, W

Soccer
Adrian Coll, MI M, W
Albion Coll, MI M, W
Alma Coll, MI M, W
Anderson U, IN M, W
Aquinas Coll, MI M(s), W(s)
Ashland U, OH M(s), W(s)
Augsburg Coll, MN M, W
Augustana Coll, IL M, W
Augustana Coll, SD W(s)
Aurora U, IL M, W
Avila U, MO M(s), W(s)
Baker U, KS M(s), W(s)
Baldwin-Wallace Coll, OH M, W
Ball State U, IN M, W
Barclay Coll, KS M
Beloit Coll, WI M, W
Bemidji State U, MN W(s)
Benedictine Coll, KS M(s), W(s)
Benedictine U, IL M, W
Bethany Coll, KS M(s), W(s)
Bethany Lutheran Coll, MN M, W
Bethel Coll, IN M(s), W(s)
Bethel Coll, KS M(s), W(s)
Bethel U, MN M, W
Blessing-Rieman Coll of Nursing, IL M(s), W(s)
Bluffton U, OH M, W
Bowling Green State U, OH M(s), W(s)
Bradley U, IL M(s), W
Briar Cliff U, IA M(s), W(s)
Buena Vista U, IA M, W
Butler U, IN M(s), W(s)
Calumet Coll of Saint Joseph, IN M, W
Calvary Bible Coll and Theological Seminary, MO M
Calvin Coll, MI M, W
Capital U, OH M, W
Carleton Coll, MN M, W
Carroll U, WI M, W
Case Western Reserve U, OH M, W
Cedarville U, OH M(s), W(s)
Central Christian Coll of Kansas, KS M(s), W(s)
Central Coll, IA M, W
Central Methodist U, MO M(s), W(s)
Central Michigan U, MI W(s)
Cincinnati Christian U, OH M(s), W
Clarke Coll, IA M(s), W(s)
Clarkson U, NY M, W
Cleveland State U, OH M(s)
Coe Coll, IA M, W
Coll of Mount St. Joseph, OH M, W
Coll of Saint Benedict, MN W
Coll of Saint Mary, NE W(s)
The Coll of St. Scholastica, MN M, W
The Coll of Wooster, OH M, W

Columbia Coll, MO	M(s)
Concordia Coll, MN	M, W
Concordia U, MI	M(s), W(s)
Concordia U Chicago, IL	M, W
Concordia U, Nebraska, NE	M(s), W(s)
Concordia U, St. Paul, MN	W(s)
Concordia U Wisconsin, WI	M, W
Cornell Coll, IA	M, W
Cornerstone U, MI	M(s), W(s)
Creighton U, NE	M(s), W(s)
Crown Coll, MN	M, W
Culver-Stockton Coll, MO	M(s), W(s)
Dana Coll, NE	M(s), W(s)
Davenport U, Grand Rapids, MI	M(s), W(s)
Defiance Coll, OH	M, W
Denison U, OH	M, W
DePaul U, IL	M(s), W(s)
DePauw U, IN	M, W
Doane Coll, NE	M(s), W(s)
Dominican U, IL	M, W
Dordt Coll, IA	M(s), W(s)
Drake U, IA	M(s), W(s)
Drury U, MO	M(s), W(s)
Earlham Coll, IN	M, W
Eastern Illinois U, IL	M(s), W(s)
Eastern Michigan U, MI	W(s)
Edgewood Coll, WI	M, W
Elmhurst Coll, IL	M, W
Emporia State U, KS	W(s)
Faith Baptist Bible Coll and Theological Seminary, IA	M, W
Ferris State U, MI	M(s), W(s)
Fontbonne U, MO	M, W
Franciscan U of Steubenville, OH	M, W
Franklin Coll, IN	M, W
Friends U, KS	M(s), W(s)
Goshen Coll, IN	M(s), W(s)
Grace Bible Coll, MI	M
Grace Coll, IN	M(s), W(s)
Graceland U, IA	M(s), W(s)
Grace U, NE	M
Grand Valley State U, MI	M, W(s)
Grand View U, IA	M(s), W(s)
Great Lakes Christian Coll, MI	M
Greenville Coll, IL	M, W
Grinnell Coll, IA	M, W
Gustavus Adolphus Coll, MN	M, W
Hamline U, MN	M, W
Hannibal-LaGrange Coll, MO	M(s), W(s)
Hanover Coll, IN	M, W
Harris-Stowe State U, MO	M(s), W(s)
Heidelberg U, OH	M, W
Hillsdale Coll, MI	W
Hiram Coll, OH	M, W
Hope Coll, MI	M, W
Huntington U, IN	M(s), W(s)
Illinois Coll, IL	M, W
Illinois Inst of Technology, IL	M(s), W(s)
Illinois State U, IL	W(s)
Illinois Wesleyan U, IL	M, W
Indiana State U, IN	W(s)
Indiana Tech, IN	M(s), W(s)
Indiana U Bloomington, IN	M(s), W(s)
Indiana U–Purdue U Fort Wayne, IN	M(s), W(s)
Indiana U–Purdue U Indianapolis, IN	M(s), W(s)
Indiana Wesleyan U, IN	M(s), W(s)
Iowa State U of Science and Technology, IA	W(s)
Iowa Wesleyan Coll, IA	M(s), W(s)
Jamestown Coll, ND	M(s), W(s)
John Carroll U, OH	M, W
Kalamazoo Coll, MI	M, W
Kansas Wesleyan U, KS	M(s), W(s)
Kent State U, OH	W(s)
Kenyon Coll, OH	M, W
Kettering U, MI	M
Knox Coll, IL	M, W
Lake Erie Coll, OH	M, W
Lake Forest Coll, IL	M, W
Lakeland Coll, WI	M, W
Lawrence U, WI	M, W
Lewis U, IL	M(s), W(s)
Lindenwood U, MO	M(s), W(s)
Logan U–Coll of Chiropractic, MO	M
Loras Coll, IA	M, W
Loyola U Chicago, IL	M(s), W(s)
Luther Coll, IA	M, W
Macalester Coll, MN	M, W
MacMurray Coll, IL	M, W
Madonna U, MI	M(s), W(s)
Malone U, OH	M(s), W(s)
Manchester Coll, IN	M, W
Manhattan Christian Coll, KS	M, W
Maranatha Baptist Bible Coll, WI	M, W
Marian U, WI	M, W
Marian U, IN	M(s), W(s)
Marietta Coll, OH	M, W
Marquette U, WI	M(s), W(s)
Martin Luther Coll, MN	M, W
Maryville U of Saint Louis, MO	M, W
McKendree U, IL	M(s), W(s)
McPherson Coll, KS	M, W
Miami U, OH	M, W(s)
Michigan State U, MI	M(s), W(s)
Michigan Technological U, MI	M, W
Mid-America Christian U, OK	M, W
MidAmerica Nazarene U, KS	M(s), W(s)
Millikin U, IL	M, W
Milwaukee School of Engineering, WI	M, W
Minnesota State U Mankato, MN	W(s)
Minnesota State U Moorhead, MN	W(s)
Missouri Baptist U, MO	M(s), W(s)
Missouri Southern State U, MO	M(s), W(s)
Missouri State U, MO	M(s), W(s)
Missouri U of Science and Technology, MO	M(s), W(s)
Missouri Western State U, MO	W
Monmouth Coll, IL	M, W
Moody Bible Inst, IL	M
Morningside Coll, IA	M(s), W(s)
Mount Marty Coll, SD	M(s), W(s)
Mount Mary Coll, WI	W
Mount Mercy Coll, IA	M(s), W(s)
Mount Union Coll, OH	M, W
Mount Vernon Nazarene U, OH	M(s), W(s)
Muskingum Coll, OH	M, W
Nebraska Wesleyan U, NE	M, W
Newman U, KS	M(s), W(s)
North Central Coll, IL	M, W
North Central U, MN	M, W
North Dakota State U, ND	M, W(s)
Northeastern State U, OK	M(s), W(s)
Northern Michigan U, MI	M, W(s)
Northern State U, SD	W(s)
Northland Coll, WI	M, W
North Park U, IL	M, W
Northwestern Coll, MN	M, W
Northwestern U, IL	M(s), W(s)
Northwest Missouri State U, MO	W(s)
Northwood U, MI	M(s), W(s)
Oakland U, MI	M(s), W(s)
Oberlin Coll, OH	M, W
Ohio Christian U, OH	M
Ohio Dominican U, OH	M(s), W(s)
Ohio Northern U, OH	M, W
The Ohio State U, OH	M(s), W(s)
Ohio U, OH	M, W(s)
Ohio Wesleyan U, OH	M, W
Oklahoma Baptist U, OK	M, W
Oklahoma Christian U, OK	M(s), W(s)
Oklahoma City U, OK	M(s), W(s)
Oklahoma Panhandle State U, OK	M, W
Oklahoma State U, OK	W(s)
Olivet Coll, MI	M, W
Olivet Nazarene U, IL	M(s), W(s)
Oral Roberts U, OK	M(s), W(s)
Otterbein Coll, OH	M, W
Park U, MO	M(s), W(s)
Presentation Coll, SD	M, W
Purdue U, IN	W(s)
Quincy U, IL	M(s), W(s)
Research Coll of Nursing, MO	M(s), W(s)
Ripon Coll, WI	M, W
Robert Morris Coll, IL	M(s), W(s)
Rochester Comm and Tech Coll, MN	W
Rockford Coll, IL	M, W
Rockhurst U, MO	M(s), W(s)
Rogers State U, OK	M, W
Rose-Hulman Inst of Technology, IN	M, W
Saginaw Valley State U, MI	M(s), W(s)
St. Ambrose U, IA	M(s), W(s)
St. Catherine U, MN	W
St. Cloud State U, MN	M, W(s)
St. Gregory's U, Shawnee, OK	M(s), W(s)
Saint John's U, MN	M
Saint Joseph's Coll, IN	M(s), W(s)
Saint Louis U, MO	M(s), W(s)
Saint Mary-of-the-Woods Coll, IN	W(s)
Saint Mary's Coll, IN	W
Saint Mary's U of Minnesota, MN	M, W
St. Norbert Coll, WI	M, W
St. Olaf Coll, MN	M, W
Saint Xavier U, IL	M(s), W(s)
Shawnee State U, OH	M(s), W(s)
Siena Heights U, MI	M(s), W(s)
Simpson Coll, IA	M, W
South Dakota State U, SD	M, W(s)
Southeast Missouri State U, MO	W(s)
Southern Illinois U Edwardsville, IL	M(s), W(s)
Southern Methodist U, TX	M(s), W(s)
Southern Nazarene U, OK	M(s), W(s)
Southwest Baptist U, MO	M, W(s)
Southwestern Christian U, OK	M
Southwestern Coll, KS	M(s), W(s)
Southwestern Oklahoma State U, OK	W(s)
Southwest Minnesota State U, MN	W(s)
Spring Arbor U, MI	M(s), W(s)
Sterling Coll, KS	M(s), W(s)
Taylor U, IN	M(s), W(s)
Tiffin U, OH	M(s), W(s)
Transylvania U, KY	M, W
Trine U, IN	M, W
Trinity Christian Coll, IL	M(s), W(s)
Trinity International U, IL	M(s), W(s)
Truman State U, MO	M(s), W(s)
The U of Akron, OH	M(s), W(s)
U of Central Missouri, MO	M, W(s)

M—for men; W—for women; (s)—scholarship offered

U of Central Oklahoma, OK W(s)
U of Charleston, WV M(s), W(s)
U of Chicago, IL M, W
U of Cincinnati, OH M(s), W(s)
U of Dallas, TX M, W
U of Dayton, OH M(s), W(s)
U of Evansville, IN M(s), W(s)
The U of Findlay, OH M(s), W(s)
U of Illinois at Chicago, IL M(s)
U of Illinois at Springfield, IL M(s), W(s)
U of Illinois at Urbana–Champaign, IL W(s)
U of Indianapolis, IN M(s), W(s)
The U of Iowa, IA M, W(s)
The U of Kansas, KS W(s)
U of Mary, ND M(s), W(s)
U of Michigan, MI M(s), W(s)
U of Michigan–Dearborn, MI M, W
U of Minnesota, Crookston, MN W(s)
U of Minnesota, Duluth, MN M, W(s)
U of Minnesota, Morris, MN M, W
U of Minnesota, Twin Cities Campus, MN W(s)
U of Missouri–Columbia, MO W(s)
U of Missouri–Kansas City, MO M(s)
U of Missouri–St. Louis, MO M(s), W(s)
U of Nebraska at Omaha, NE W
U of Nebraska–Lincoln, NE W(s)
U of North Dakota, ND W
U of Northern Iowa, IA W(s)
U of Notre Dame, IN M(s), W(s)
U of Oklahoma, OK W(s)
U of Rio Grande, OH M(s), W
U of St. Francis, IL M(s), W(s)
U of Saint Francis, IN M(s), W(s)
U of Saint Mary, KS M(s), W(s)
U of Science and Arts of Oklahoma, OK M(s), W(s)
U of Sioux Falls, SD M(s), W(s)
The U of South Dakota, SD W(s)
U of Southern Indiana, IN M(s), W(s)
The U of Toledo, OH W(s)
U of Tulsa, OK M(s), W(s)
U of Wisconsin–Eau Claire, WI W
U of Wisconsin–Green Bay, WI M(s), W(s)
U of Wisconsin–La Crosse, WI W
U of Wisconsin–Madison, WI M(s), W(s)
U of Wisconsin–Milwaukee, WI M(s), W(s)
U of Wisconsin–Oshkosh, WI M, W
U of Wisconsin–Parkside, WI M(s), W(s)
U of Wisconsin–Platteville, WI M, W
U of Wisconsin–Stevens Point, WI W
U of Wisconsin–Stout, WI M, W
U of Wisconsin–Superior, WI M, W
U of Wisconsin–Whitewater, WI M, W
Ursuline Coll, OH W(s)
Valparaiso U, IN M(s), W(s)
Viterbo U, WI M(s), W(s)
Wabash Coll, IN M
Waldorf Coll, IA M(s), W(s)
Walsh U, OH M(s), W(s)
Wartburg Coll, IA M, W
Washburn U, KS W(s)
Washington U in St. Louis, MO M, W
Wayne State Coll, NE M, W(s)
Webster U, MO M, W
Western Illinois U, IL M(s), W(s)
Western Michigan U, MI M(s), W(s)
Westminster Coll, MO M, W
Wheaton Coll, IL M, W
Wichita State U, KS M, W
William Jewell Coll, MO M(s), W(s)
Wilmington Coll, OH M, W
Winona State U, MN M, W(s)
Wittenberg U, OH M, W
Wright State U, OH M(s), W(s)
Xavier U, OH M(s), W(s)
York Coll, NE M(s), W(s)
Youngstown State U, OH W

Softball

Adrian Coll, MI W
Albion Coll, MI W
Alma Coll, MI W
Anderson U, IN W
Aquinas Coll, MI W(s)
Ashland U, OH M, W(s)
Augsburg Coll, MN W
Augustana Coll, IL W
Augustana Coll, SD W(s)
Aurora U, IL W
Avila U, MO W(s)
Baker U, KS W(s)
Baldwin-Wallace Coll, OH W
Ball State U, IN W(s)
Beloit Coll, WI W
Bemidji State U, MN W(s)
Benedictine Coll, KS W(s)
Benedictine U, IL W
Bethany Coll, KS W(s)
Bethany Lutheran Coll, MN W
Bethel Coll, IN W(s)
Bethel U, MN W
Bluffton U, OH W
Bowling Green State U, OH W(s)
Bradley U, IL W(s)
Briar Cliff U, IA W(s)
Buena Vista U, IA W
Butler U, IN W(s)
Calumet Coll of Saint Joseph, IN W
Calvin Coll, MI W
Cameron U, OK W(s)
Capital U, OH W
Carleton Coll, MN W
Case Western Reserve U, OH W
Cedarville U, OH W(s)
Central Christian Coll of Kansas, KS W(s)
Central Coll, IA W
Central Methodist U, MO W(s)
Central Michigan U, MI W(s)
Clarke Coll, IA W(s)
Cleveland State U, OH W(s)
Coe Coll, IA W
Coll of Mount St. Joseph, OH W
Coll of Saint Benedict, MN W
Coll of Saint Mary, NE W(s)
The Coll of St. Scholastica, MN W
The Coll of Wooster, OH W
Columbia Coll, MO W(s)
Concordia Coll, MN W
Concordia U, MI W(s)
Concordia U Chicago, IL W
Concordia U, Nebraska, NE W(s)
Concordia U, St. Paul, MN W(s)
Concordia U Wisconsin, WI W
Cornell Coll, IA W
Cornerstone U, MI W(s)
Cottey Coll, MO W(s)
Creighton U, NE W(s)
Crossroads Coll, MN W
Crown Coll, MN W
Culver-Stockton Coll, MO W(s)
Dakota State U, SD W(s)
Dakota Wesleyan U, SD W(s)
Dana Coll, NE W(s)
Defiance Coll, OH W
Denison U, OH W
DePaul U, IL W(s)
DePauw U, IN W
Doane Coll, NE W(s)
Dominican U, IL W
Dordt Coll, IA W(s)
Drake U, IA W(s)
Drury U, MO W(s)
Eastern Illinois U, IL W(s)
Eastern Michigan U, MI W(s)
Edgewood Coll, WI W
Elmhurst Coll, IL W
Emporia State U, KS W(s)
Eureka Coll, IL W
Evangel U, MO W(s)
Ferris State U, MI W(s)
Fontbonne U, MO W
Fort Hays State U, KS W
Franciscan U of Steubenville, OH W
Franklin Coll, IN W
Friends U, KS W(s)
Goshen Coll, IN W(s)
Grace Coll, IN W(s)
Graceland U, IA W(s)
Grand Valley State U, MI W(s)
Grand View U, IA W(s)
Greenville Coll, IL W
Grinnell Coll, IA W
Gustavus Adolphus Coll, MN W
Hamline U, MN W
Hannibal-LaGrange Coll, MO W(s)
Hanover Coll, IN W
Harris-Stowe State U, MO W(s)
Haskell Indian Nations U, KS W
Heidelberg U, OH W
Hillsdale Coll, MI W(s)
Hiram Coll, OH W
Hope Coll, MI W
Huntington U, IN W(s)
Illinois Coll, IL W
Illinois State U, IL W(s)
Illinois Wesleyan U, IL W
Indiana State U, IN W(s)
Indiana Tech, IN W(s)
Indiana U Bloomington, IN W(s)
Indiana U–Purdue U Fort Wayne, IN W(s)
Indiana U–Purdue U Indianapolis, IN W(s)
Indiana U Southeast, IN W
Indiana Wesleyan U, IN W(s)
Iowa State U of Science and Technology, IA W(s)
Iowa Wesleyan Coll, IA W(s)
Jamestown Coll, ND W(s)
John Carroll U, OH W
Kalamazoo Coll, MI W
Kansas Wesleyan U, KS W(s)
Kent State U, OH W(s)
Kenyon Coll, OH W
Knox Coll, IL W
Lake Erie Coll, OH W
Lake Forest Coll, IL W
Lakeland Coll, WI W
Lake Superior State U, MI W(s)
Lawrence U, WI W
Lewis U, IL W(s)
Lincoln U, MO W(s)
Lindenwood U, MO W(s)
Loras Coll, IA W

Loyola U Chicago, IL	W
Luther Coll, IA	W
Macalester Coll, MN	W
MacMurray Coll, IL	W
Madonna U, MI	W(s)
Malone U, OH	W(s)
Manchester Coll, IN	W
Maranatha Baptist Bible Coll, WI	W
Marian U, WI	W
Marian U, IN	W(s)
Marietta Coll, OH	W
Marquette U, WI	W
Martin Luther Coll, MN	W
Maryville U of Saint Louis, MO	W
Mayville State U, ND	W(s)
McKendree U, IL	W(s)
McPherson Coll, KS	W
Miami U, OH	M, W(s)
Miami U Hamilton, OH	W
Michigan State U, MI	W
Mid-America Christian U, OK	W
MidAmerica Nazarene U, KS	W(s)
Millikin U, IL	W
Milwaukee School of Engineering, WI	W
Minnesota State U Mankato, MN	W(s)
Minnesota State U Moorhead, MN	W(s)
Minot State U, ND	W(s)
Missouri Baptist U, MO	W(s)
Missouri Southern State U, MO	W(s)
Missouri State U, MO	W(s)
Missouri U of Science and Technology, MO	W(s)
Missouri Western State U, MO	W(s)
Monmouth Coll, IL	W
Morningside Coll, IA	W(s)
Mount Marty Coll, SD	W(s)
Mount Mary Coll, WI	W
Mount Mercy Coll, IA	W(s)
Mount Union Coll, OH	W
Mount Vernon Nazarene U, OH	W(s)
Muskingum Coll, OH	W
Nebraska Wesleyan U, NE	W
Newman U, KS	W(s)
North Central Coll, IL	W
North Central U, MN	W
North Dakota State U, ND	W(s)
Northeastern State U, OK	W(s)
Northern State U, SD	W(s)
Northland Coll, WI	W
North Park U, IL	W
Northwestern Coll, MN	W
Northwestern U, IL	W(s)
Northwest Missouri State U, MO	W(s)
Northwood U, MI	W(s)
Oakland U, MI	W(s)
Oberlin Coll, OH	W
Ohio Christian U, OH	W
Ohio Dominican U, OH	W(s)
Ohio Northern U, OH	W
The Ohio State U, OH	W(s)
Ohio U, OH	W(s)
Ohio U–Zanesville, OH	W
Ohio Wesleyan U, OH	W
Oklahoma Baptist U, OK	W(s)
Oklahoma Christian U, OK	W(s)
Oklahoma City U, OK	W(s)
Oklahoma Panhandle State U, OK	W(s)
Oklahoma State U, OK	W(s)
Olivet Coll, MI	W
Olivet Nazarene U, IL	W(s)
Otterbein Coll, OH	W
Park U, MO	W(s)
Pittsburg State U, KS	W(s)
Presentation Coll, SD	W
Purdue U, IN	W(s)
Purdue U North Central, IN	W(s)
Quincy U, IL	W(s)
Research Coll of Nursing, MO	W(s)
Ripon Coll, WI	W
Robert Morris Coll, IL	W(s)
Rochester Comm and Tech Coll, MN	W
Rockford Coll, IL	W
Rockhurst U, MO	W(s)
Rogers State U, OK	W
Rose-Hulman Inst of Technology, IN	W
Saginaw Valley State U, MI	W(s)
St. Ambrose U, IA	W(s)
St. Catherine U, MN	W
St. Cloud State U, MN	W(s)
St. Gregory's U, Shawnee, OK	W(s)
Saint Joseph's Coll, IN	W(s)
Saint Louis U, MO	W(s)
Saint Mary-of-the-Woods Coll, IN	W(s)
Saint Mary's Coll, IN	W
Saint Mary's U of Minnesota, MN	W
St. Norbert Coll, WI	W
St. Olaf Coll, MN	W
Saint Xavier U, IL	W(s)
Shawnee State U, OH	W
Siena Heights U, MI	W(s)
Simpson Coll, IA	W
South Dakota State U, SD	W(s)
Southeastern Oklahoma State U, OK	W(s)
Southeast Missouri State U, MO	W(s)
Southern Illinois U Carbondale, IL	W(s)
Southern Illinois U Edwardsville, IL	W(s)
Southern Nazarene U, OK	W(s)
Southwest Baptist U, MO	W(s)
Southwestern Coll, KS	W(s)
Southwestern Oklahoma State U, OK	W(s)
Southwest Minnesota State U, MN	W(s)
Spring Arbor U, MI	W(s)
Stephens Coll, MO	W(s)
Sterling Coll, KS	W(s)
Taylor U, IN	W(s)
Tiffin U, OH	W(s)
Transylvania U, KY	W
Trine U, IN	W
Trinity Christian Coll, IL	W(s)
Trinity International U, IL	W(s)
Truman State U, MO	W(s)
The U of Akron, OH	W(s)
U of Central Missouri, MO	W(s)
U of Central Oklahoma, OK	W(s)
U of Charleston, WV	W(s)
U of Chicago, IL	W
U of Dallas, TX	W
U of Dayton, OH	W(s)
U of Evansville, IN	W(s)
The U of Findlay, OH	W(s)
U of Illinois at Chicago, IL	W(s)
U of Illinois at Springfield, IL	W(s)
U of Illinois at Urbana–Champaign, IL	W(s)
U of Indianapolis, IN	W(s)
The U of Iowa, IA	W(s)
The U of Kansas, KS	W(s)
U of Mary, ND	W(s)
U of Michigan, MI	W(s)
U of Michigan–Dearborn, MI	M(s)
U of Minnesota, Crookston, MN	W(s)
U of Minnesota, Duluth, MN	W(s)
U of Minnesota, Morris, MN	W
U of Minnesota, Twin Cities Campus, MN	W(s)
U of Missouri–Columbia, MO	W(s)
U of Missouri–Kansas City, MO	W(s)
U of Missouri–St. Louis, MO	W(s)
U of Nebraska at Kearney, NE	W(s)
U of Nebraska at Omaha, NE	W(s)
U of Nebraska–Lincoln, NE	W(s)
U of North Dakota, ND	W(s)
U of Northern Iowa, IA	W(s)
U of Notre Dame, IN	W(s)
U of Oklahoma, OK	W(s)
U of Rio Grande, OH	W(s)
U of St. Francis, IL	W(s)
U of Saint Francis, IN	W(s)
U of Saint Mary, KS	W(s)
U of Science and Arts of Oklahoma, OK	W(s)
U of Sioux Falls, SD	W(s)
The U of South Dakota, SD	W(s)
U of Southern Indiana, IN	W(s)
The U of Toledo, OH	W(s)
U of Tulsa, OK	W(s)
U of Wisconsin–Eau Claire, WI	W
U of Wisconsin–Green Bay, WI	W(s)
U of Wisconsin–La Crosse, WI	W
U of Wisconsin–Madison, WI	W(s)
U of Wisconsin–Oshkosh, WI	W
U of Wisconsin–Parkside, WI	W(s)
U of Wisconsin–Platteville, WI	W
U of Wisconsin–Stevens Point, WI	W
U of Wisconsin–Stout, WI	W
U of Wisconsin–Superior, WI	W
U of Wisconsin–Whitewater, WI	W
Ursuline Coll, OH	W(s)
Valley City State U, ND	W(s)
Valparaiso U, IN	W(s)
Viterbo U, WI	W(s)
Waldorf Coll, IA	W(s)
Walsh U, OH	W(s)
Wartburg Coll, IA	W
Washburn U, KS	W(s)
Washington U in St. Louis, MO	W
Wayne State Coll, NE	W(s)
Wayne State U, MI	W(s)
Webster U, MO	W
Western Illinois U, IL	W(s)
Western Michigan U, MI	W(s)
Westminster Coll, MO	M, W
Wheaton Coll, IL	W
Wichita State U, KS	W(s)
William Jewell Coll, MO	W(s)
Wilmington Coll, OH	W
Winona State U, MN	W(s)
Wittenberg U, OH	W
Wright State U, OH	W(s)
Xavier U, OH	M, W
York Coll, NE	W(s)
Youngstown State U, OH	W(s)

Squash

Denison U, OH	M, W
Kenyon Coll, OH	M, W
Michigan Technological U, MI	M, W

M—for men; W—for women; (s)—scholarship offered

Swimming and Diving

Albion Coll, MI M, W
Alma Coll, MI M, W
Ashland U, OH M(s), W(s)
Augsburg Coll, MN W
Augustana Coll, IL M, W
Baldwin-Wallace Coll, OH M, W
Ball State U, IN M(s), W(s)
Beloit Coll, WI M, W
Benedictine U, IL M, W
Bowling Green State U, OH W(s)
Butler U, IN W
Calvin Coll, MI M, W
Carleton Coll, MN M, W
Carroll U, WI M, W
Case Western Reserve U, OH M, W
Clarkson U, NY M, W
Cleveland State U, OH M(s), W(s)
Coe Coll, IA M, W
Coll of Saint Benedict, MN W
Coll of Saint Mary, NE W(s)
The Coll of Wooster, OH M, W
Concordia Coll, MN W
Denison U, OH M, W
DePauw U, IN M, W
Drury U, MO M(s), W(s)
Eastern Illinois U, IL M(s), W(s)
Eastern Michigan U, MI M(s), W(s)
Eureka Coll, IL M, W
Grand Valley State U, MI M(s), W(s)
Grinnell Coll, IA M, W
Gustavus Adolphus Coll, MN M, W
Hamline U, MN M, W
Hannibal-LaGrange Coll, MO M(s), W(s)
Hillsdale Coll, MI W(s)
Hiram Coll, OH M, W
Hope Coll, MI M, W
Illinois Coll, IL M, W
Illinois Inst of Technology, IL M(s), W(s)
Illinois State U, IL W(s)
Illinois Wesleyan U, IL M, W
Indiana U Bloomington, IN M(s), W(s)
Indiana U–Purdue U Indianapolis, IN M(s), W(s)
Iowa State U of Science and Technology, IA M(s), W(s)
John Carroll U, OH M, W
Kalamazoo Coll, MI M, W
Kenyon Coll, OH M, W
Knox Coll, IL M, W
Lake Forest Coll, IL M, W
Lawrence U, WI M, W
Lewis U, IL M(s), W(s)
Lindenwood U, MO M(s), W(s)
Loras Coll, IA M, W
Luther Coll, IA M, W
Macalester Coll, MN M, W
MacMurray Coll, IL M, W
Malone U, OH M(s), W(s)
Marquette U, WI M, W
Miami U, OH M(s), W(s)
Michigan State U, MI M(s), W(s)
Michigan Technological U, MI M, W
Millikin U, IL M, W
Minnesota State U Mankato, MN M(s), W(s)
Minnesota State U Moorhead, MN W
Missouri State U, MO M(s), W(s)
Missouri U of Science and Technology, MO M(s)
Monmouth Coll, IL M, W
Morningside Coll, IA M(s), W(s)
Mount Union Coll, OH M, W
North Central Coll, IL M, W
Northern Michigan U, MI W(s)
Northern State U, SD W(s)
Northwestern U, IL M(s), W(s)
Oakland U, MI M(s), W(s)
Oberlin Coll, OH M, W
Ohio Northern U, OH M, W
The Ohio State U, OH M(s), W(s)
Ohio U, OH W(s)
Ohio Wesleyan U, OH M, W
Olivet Coll, MI M, W
Purdue U, IN M(s), W(s)
Ripon Coll, WI M, W
Robert Morris Coll, IL W(s)
Rose-Hulman Inst of Technology, IN M, W
St. Catherine U, MN W
St. Cloud State U, MN M(s), W(s)
Saint John's U, MN M
Saint Louis U, MO M(s), W(s)
Saint Mary's Coll, IN W
Saint Mary's U of Minnesota, MN M, W
St. Norbert Coll, WI W
St. Olaf Coll, MN M, W
Simpson Coll, IA M, W
South Dakota State U, SD M(s), W(s)
Southern Illinois U Carbondale, IL M(s), W(s)
Southern Methodist U, TX M(s), W(s)
Stephens Coll, MO W(s)
Transylvania U, KY M, W
Truman State U, MO M(s), W(s)
The U of Akron, OH W(s)
U of Charleston, WV M(s), W(s)
U of Chicago, IL M, W
U of Cincinnati, OH M(s), W(s)
U of Evansville, IN M(s), W(s)
The U of Findlay, OH M(s), W(s)
U of Illinois at Chicago, IL M(s), W(s)
U of Illinois at Urbana–Champaign, IL W(s)
U of Indianapolis, IN M(s), W(s)
The U of Iowa, IA M(s), W(s)
The U of Kansas, KS W(s)
U of Michigan, MI M(s), W(s)
U of Minnesota, Duluth, MN M, W
U of Minnesota, Morris, MN W
U of Minnesota, Twin Cities Campus, MN M(s), W(s)
U of Missouri–Columbia, MO M(s), W(s)
U of Nebraska at Kearney, NE W(s)
U of Nebraska at Omaha, NE W
U of Nebraska–Lincoln, NE W(s)
U of New Orleans, LA M(s), W(s)
U of North Dakota, ND M, W(s)
U of Northern Iowa, IA W(s)
U of Notre Dame, IN M(s), W(s)
The U of South Dakota, SD M(s), W(s)
The U of Toledo, OH W(s)
U of Wisconsin–Eau Claire, WI M, W
U of Wisconsin–Green Bay, WI M(s), W(s)
U of Wisconsin–La Crosse, WI M, W
U of Wisconsin–Madison, WI M(s), W(s)
U of Wisconsin–Milwaukee, WI M(s), W(s)
U of Wisconsin–Oshkosh, WI M, W
U of Wisconsin–Stevens Point, WI M, W
U of Wisconsin–Whitewater, WI M, W
Valparaiso U, IN M(s), W(s)
Wabash Coll, IN M
Washington U in St. Louis, MO M, W
Wayne State U, MI M(s), W(s)
Webster U, MO M, W
Western Illinois U, IL M(s), W(s)
Wheaton Coll, IL M, W
Wichita State U, KS M, W
Wilmington Coll, OH M, W
Wittenberg U, OH M, W
Wright State U, OH M(s), W(s)
Xavier U, OH M(s), W(s)
Youngstown State U, OH W

Table Tennis

Bradley U, IL M, W
Hiram Coll, OH M, W
Lake Forest Coll, IL M, W
Lindenwood U, MO M(s), W(s)
Michigan Technological U, MI M, W
Saint Louis U, MO M, W
The U of Iowa, IA M, W
U of Missouri–St. Louis, MO M, W
Washington U in St. Louis, MO M, W

Tennis

Adrian Coll, MI M, W
Albion Coll, MI M, W
Alma Coll, MI M, W
Anderson U, IN M, W
Aquinas Coll, MI M(s), W(s)
Ashland U, OH M, W
Augustana Coll, IL M, W
Augustana Coll, SD M, W(s)
Aurora U, IL M, W
Baker U, KS M(s), W(s)
Baldwin-Wallace Coll, OH M, W
Ball State U, IN M(s), W(s)
Barclay Coll, KS M, W
Beloit Coll, WI M, W
Bemidji State U, MN W(s)
Benedictine U, IL W
Bethany Coll, KS M(s), W(s)
Bethany Lutheran Coll, MN M, W
Bethel Coll, IN M(s), W(s)
Bethel Coll, KS M(s), W(s)
Bethel U, MN M, W
Bluffton U, OH M, W
Bowling Green State U, OH W(s)
Bradley U, IL M(s), W(s)
Briar Cliff U, IA M(s), W(s)
Buena Vista U, IA M, W
Butler U, IN M(s), W(s)
Calumet Coll of Saint Joseph, IN M, W
Calvin Coll, MI M, W
Cameron U, OK M(s), W(s)
Capital U, OH M, W
Carleton Coll, MN M, W
Carroll U, WI M, W
Case Western Reserve U, OH M, W
Cedarville U, OH M(s), W(s)
Central Christian Coll of Kansas, KS M(s), W(s)
Central Coll, IA M, W
Central State U, OH M(s), W(s)
Clarke Coll, IA W(s)
Cleveland State U, OH W(s)
Coe Coll, IA M, W
Coll of Mount St. Joseph, OH M, W
Coll of Saint Benedict, MN W
The Coll of St. Scholastica, MN M, W
The Coll of Wooster, OH M, W
Concordia Coll, MN M, W
Concordia U Chicago, IL M, W
Concordia U, Nebraska, NE M(s), W(s)
Concordia U Wisconsin, WI M, W
Cornell Coll, IA M, W
Creighton U, NE M(s), W(s)
Crossroads Coll, MN M, W
Defiance Coll, OH M, W

College	Tennis
Denison U, OH	M, W
DePaul U, IL	M(s), W(s)
DePauw U, IN	M, W
Doane Coll, NE	M, W
Dominican U, IL	M, W
Dordt Coll, IA	M(s), W(s)
Drake U, IA	M(s), W(s)
Drury U, MO	M(s), W(s)
Earlham Coll, IN	M, W
Eastern Illinois U, IL	M(s), W(s)
Eastern Michigan U, MI	W(s)
Edgewood Coll, WI	W
Elmhurst Coll, IL	M, W
Emporia State U, KS	M(s), W(s)
Eureka Coll, IL	M, W
Evangel U, MO	M(s), W(s)
Ferris State U, MI	M(s), W(s)
Fontbonne U, MO	M, W
Fort Hays State U, KS	W(s)
Franklin Coll, IN	M, W
Friends U, KS	M(s), W(s)
Goshen Coll, IN	M(s), W(s)
Grace Coll, IN	M(s), W(s)
Graceland U, IA	M(s), W(s)
Grand Valley State U, MI	M(s), W(s)
Greenville Coll, IL	M, W
Grinnell Coll, IA	M, W
Gustavus Adolphus Coll, MN	M, W
Hamline U, MN	M, W
Hanover Coll, IN	M, W
Heidelberg U, OH	M, W
Hiram Coll, OH	M, W
Hope Coll, MI	M, W
Huntington U, IN	M(s), W(s)
Illinois Coll, IL	M, W
Illinois State U, IL	M(s), W(s)
Illinois Wesleyan U, IL	M, W
Indiana State U, IN	M(s), W(s)
Indiana U Bloomington, IN	M(s), W(s)
Indiana U–Purdue U Fort Wayne, IN	M(s), W(s)
Indiana U–Purdue U Indianapolis, IN	M(s), W(s)
Indiana U Southeast, IN	M, W
Indiana Wesleyan U, IN	M(s), W(s)
Iowa State U of Science and Technology, IA	W(s)
John Carroll U, OH	M, W
Kalamazoo Coll, MI	M, W
Kansas State U, KS	W(s)
Kansas Wesleyan U, KS	M(s), W(s)
Kenyon Coll, OH	M, W
Knox Coll, IL	M, W
Lake Erie Coll, OH	M, W
Lake Forest Coll, IL	M, W
Lakeland Coll, WI	M, W
Lake Superior State U, MI	M(s), W(s)
Lawrence U, WI	M, W
Lewis U, IL	M(s), W(s)
Lincoln U, MO	W(s)
Lindenwood U, MO	M(s), W(s)
Logan U–Coll of Chiropractic, MO	M
Loras Coll, IA	M, W
Luther Coll, IA	M, W
Macalester Coll, MN	M, W
Malone U, OH	M(s), W(s)
Manchester Coll, IN	M, W
Marian U, WI	M, W
Marian U, IN	M(s), W(s)
Marietta Coll, OH	M, W
Marquette U, WI	M(s), W(s)
Martin Luther Coll, MN	M, W
Maryville U of Saint Louis, MO	M, W
McKendree U, IL	M(s), W(s)
McPherson Coll, KS	M, W
Miami U, OH	M, W(s)
Miami U Hamilton, OH	M, W
Michigan State U, MI	M(s), W(s)
Michigan Technological U, MI	M, W(s)
Millikin U, IL	W
Milwaukee School of Engineering, WI	M, W
Minnesota State U Mankato, MN	M(s), W(s)
Minnesota State U Moorhead, MN	W
Missouri Baptist U, MO	M(s), W(s)
Missouri Southern State U, MO	W(s)
Missouri Western State U, MO	W(s)
Monmouth Coll, IL	M, W
Morningside Coll, IA	M(s), W(s)
Mount Mary Coll, WI	W
Mount Union Coll, OH	M, W
Muskingum Coll, OH	M, W
Nebraska Wesleyan U, NE	M, W
Newman U, KS	M(s), W(s)
North Central Coll, IL	M, W
North Central U, MN	M, W
Northeastern State U, OK	W(s)
Northern State U, SD	M, W(s)
Northwestern Coll, MN	M, W
Northwestern U, IL	M(s), W(s)
Northwest Missouri State U, MO	M(s), W(s)
Northwood U, MI	M(s), W(s)
Oakland U, MI	W(s)
Oberlin Coll, OH	M, W
Ohio Dominican U, OH	M(s), W(s)
Ohio Northern U, OH	M, W
The Ohio State U, OH	M(s), W(s)
Ohio U–Zanesville, OH	M, W
Ohio Wesleyan U, OH	M, W
Oklahoma Baptist U, OK	M(s), W(s)
Oklahoma Christian U, OK	M(s), W(s)
Oklahoma State U, OK	M(s), W(s)
Olivet Coll, MI	W
Olivet Nazarene U, IL	M(s), W(s)
Oral Roberts U, OK	M(s), W(s)
Otterbein Coll, OH	M, W
Purdue U, IN	M(s), W(s)
Quincy U, IL	M(s), W(s)
Research Coll of Nursing, MO	M(s), W(s)
Ripon Coll, WI	M, W
Robert Morris Coll, IL	W(s)
Rockford Coll, IL	M, W
Rockhurst U, MO	M(s), W(s)
Rose-Hulman Inst of Technology, IN	M, W
Saginaw Valley State U, MI	W(s)
St. Ambrose U, IA	M(s), W(s)
St. Catherine U, MN	W
St. Cloud State U, MN	M(s), W(s)
Saint John's U, MN	M
Saint Joseph's Coll, IN	M(s), W(s)
Saint Louis U, MO	M(s), W(s)
Saint Mary's Coll, IN	W
Saint Mary's U of Minnesota, MN	M, W
St. Norbert Coll, WI	M, W
St. Olaf Coll, MN	M, W
Shawnee State U, OH	W(s)
Simpson Coll, IA	M, W
South Dakota School of Mines and Technology, SD	M
South Dakota State U, SD	M(s), W(s)
Southeastern Oklahoma State U, OK	M(s), W(s)
Southeast Missouri State U, MO	W(s)
Southern Illinois U Carbondale, IL	M(s), W(s)
Southern Illinois U Edwardsville, IL	M(s), W(s)
Southern Methodist U, TX	M(s), W(s)
Southern Nazarene U, OK	M(s), W(s)
Southwest Baptist U, MO	M(s), W(s)
Southwestern Coll, KS	M(s), W(s)
Southwest Minnesota State U, MN	W(s)
Spring Arbor U, MI	M(s), W(s)
Stephens Coll, MO	W(s)
Taylor U, IN	M(s), W(s)
Tiffin U, OH	M(s), W(s)
Transylvania U, KY	M, W
Trine U, IN	M, W
Truman State U, MO	M(s), W(s)
The U of Akron, OH	W(s)
U of Central Oklahoma, OK	M(s), W(s)
U of Charleston, WV	M(s), W(s)
U of Chicago, IL	M, W
U of Cincinnati, OH	M(s), W(s)
U of Dallas, TX	W
U of Dayton, OH	M(s), W(s)
U of Evansville, IN	W(s)
The U of Findlay, OH	M(s), W(s)
U of Illinois at Chicago, IL	M(s), W(s)
U of Illinois at Springfield, IL	M(s), W(s)
U of Illinois at Urbana–Champaign, IL	M(s), W(s)
U of Indianapolis, IN	M(s), W(s)
The U of Iowa, IA	M(s), W(s)
The U of Kansas, KS	W(s)
U of Mary, ND	M(s), W(s)
U of Michigan, MI	M(s), W(s)
U of Minnesota, Crookston, MN	W(s)
U of Minnesota, Duluth, MN	W(s)
U of Minnesota, Morris, MN	M, W
U of Minnesota, Twin Cities Campus, MN	M(s), W(s)
U of Missouri–Columbia, MO	W(s)
U of Missouri–Kansas City, MO	M(s), W(s)
U of Missouri–St. Louis, MO	M(s), W(s)
U of Nebraska at Kearney, NE	M(s), W(s)
U of Nebraska at Omaha, NE	W
U of Nebraska–Lincoln, NE	M(s), W(s)
U of New Orleans, LA	M(s), W(s)
U of North Dakota, ND	W
U of Northern Iowa, IA	W(s)
U of Notre Dame, IN	M(s), W(s)
U of Oklahoma, OK	M(s), W(s)
U of St. Francis, IL	M(s), W(s)
U of Saint Francis, IN	W(s)
U of Sioux Falls, SD	M(s), W(s)
The U of South Dakota, SD	W(s)
U of Southern Indiana, IN	M(s), W(s)
The U of Toledo, OH	M(s), W(s)
U of Tulsa, OK	M(s), W(s)
U of Wisconsin–Eau Claire, WI	M, W
U of Wisconsin–Green Bay, WI	M(s), W(s)
U of Wisconsin–La Crosse, WI	M, W
U of Wisconsin–Madison, WI	M(s), W(s)
U of Wisconsin–Milwaukee, WI	M(s), W(s)
U of Wisconsin–Oshkosh, WI	M, W
U of Wisconsin–Stevens Point, WI	W
U of Wisconsin–Stout, WI	W
U of Wisconsin–Whitewater, WI	M, W
Ursuline Coll, OH	W(s)
Valparaiso U, IN	M(s), W(s)
Wabash Coll, IN	M
Walsh U, OH	M(s), W(s)

M—for men; W—for women; (s)—scholarship offered

Wartburg Coll, IA	M, W
Washburn U, KS	M(s), W(s)
Washington U in St. Louis, MO	M, W
Wayne State U, MI	M(s), W(s)
Webster U, MO	M, W
Western Illinois U, IL	M(s), W(s)
Western Michigan U, MI	M(s), W(s)
Westminster Coll, MO	M, W
Wheaton Coll, IL	M, W
Wichita State U, KS	M(s), W(s)
William Jewell Coll, MO	M(s), W(s)
Wilmington Coll, OH	M, W
Winona State U, MN	M(s), W(s)
Wittenberg U, OH	M, W
Wright State U, OH	M(s), W(s)
Xavier U, OH	M(s), W(s)
Youngstown State U, OH	M(s), W(s)

Track and Field

Adrian Coll, MI	M, W
Albion Coll, MI	M, W
Alma Coll, MI	M, W
Anderson U, IN	M, W
Aquinas Coll, MI	M(s), W(s)
Ashland U, OH	M(s), W(s)
Augsburg Coll, MN	M, W
Augustana Coll, IL	M, W
Augustana Coll, SD	M(s), W(s)
Aurora U, IL	M, W
Baker U, KS	M(s), W(s)
Baldwin-Wallace Coll, OH	M, W
Ball State U, IN	M(s), W(s)
Beloit Coll, WI	M, W
Bemidji State U, MN	M(s), W(s)
Benedictine Coll, KS	M(s), W(s)
Benedictine U, IL	M, W
Bethany Coll, KS	M(s), W(s)
Bethel Coll, IN	M(s), W(s)
Bethel Coll, KS	M(s), W(s)
Bethel U, MN	M, W
Black Hills State U, SD	M(s), W(s)
Bluffton U, OH	M, W
Bowling Green State U, OH	W(s)
Bradley U, IL	W(s)
Briar Cliff U, IA	M(s), W(s)
Buena Vista U, IA	M, W
Butler U, IN	M, W
Calumet Coll of Saint Joseph, IN	M, W
Calvin Coll, MI	M, W
Capital U, OH	M, W
Carleton Coll, MN	M, W
Carroll U, WI	M, W
Case Western Reserve U, OH	M, W
Cedarville U, OH	M(s), W(s)
Central Coll, IA	M, W
Central Methodist U, MO	M(s), W(s)
Central Michigan U, MI	M(s), W(s)
Central State U, OH	M(s), W(s)
Clarke Coll, IA	M(s), W(s)
Cleveland State U, OH	W(s)
Coe Coll, IA	M, W
Coll of Mount St. Joseph, OH	M, W
Coll of Saint Benedict, MN	W
The Coll of St. Scholastica, MN	M, W
The Coll of Wooster, OH	M, W
Concordia Coll, MN	M, W
Concordia U Chicago, IL	M, W
Concordia U, Nebraska, NE	M(s), W(s)
Concordia U, St. Paul, MN	M(s), W(s)
Concordia U Wisconsin, WI	M, W
Cornell Coll, IA	M, W
Cornerstone U, MI	M(s), W(s)
Culver-Stockton Coll, MO	M(s), W(s)
Dakota State U, SD	M(s), W(s)
Dakota Wesleyan U, SD	M(s), W(s)
Dana Coll, NE	M(s), W(s)
Davenport U, Grand Rapids, MI	M(s), W(s)
Defiance Coll, OH	M, W
Denison U, OH	M, W
DePaul U, IL	M(s), W(s)
DePauw U, IN	M, W
Doane Coll, NE	M(s), W(s)
Dordt Coll, IA	M(s), W(s)
Drake U, IA	M(s), W(s)
Drury U, MO	M, W
Earlham Coll, IN	M, W
Eastern Illinois U, IL	M(s), W(s)
Eastern Michigan U, MI	M(s), W(s)
Edgewood Coll, WI	M, W
Elmhurst Coll, IL	M, W
Emporia State U, KS	M(s), W(s)
Evangel U, MO	M(s), W(s)
Ferris State U, MI	M(s), W(s)
Fontbonne U, MO	M, W
Fort Hays State U, KS	M(s), W(s)
Franciscan U of Steubenville, OH	M, W
Franklin Coll, IN	M, W
Friends U, KS	M(s), W(s)
Goshen Coll, IN	M(s), W(s)
Grace Coll, IN	M(s), W(s)
Graceland U, IA	M(s), W(s)
Grand Valley State U, MI	M(s), W(s)
Grand View U, IA	M(s), W(s)
Greenville Coll, IL	M, W
Grinnell Coll, IA	M, W
Gustavus Adolphus Coll, MN	M, W
Hamline U, MN	M, W
Hannibal-LaGrange Coll, MO	M(s), W(s)
Hanover Coll, IN	M, W
Haskell Indian Nations U, KS	M, W
Heidelberg U, OH	M, W
Hillsdale Coll, MI	M(s), W(s)
Hiram Coll, OH	M, W
Hope Coll, MI	M, W
Huntington U, IN	M(s), W(s)
Illinois Coll, IL	M, W
Illinois State U, IL	M(s), W(s)
Illinois Wesleyan U, IL	M, W
Indiana State U, IN	M(s), W(s)
Indiana Tech, IN	M(s), W(s)
Indiana U Bloomington, IN	M(s), W(s)
Indiana U–Purdue U Fort Wayne, IN	W(s)
Indiana Wesleyan U, IN	M(s), W(s)
Iowa State U of Science and Technology, IA	M(s), W(s)
Iowa Wesleyan Coll, IA	M(s), W(s)
Jamestown Coll, ND	M(s), W(s)
John Carroll U, OH	M, W
Kansas State U, KS	M(s), W(s)
Kansas Wesleyan U, KS	M(s), W(s)
Kent State U, OH	M(s), W(s)
Kenyon Coll, OH	M, W
Knox Coll, IL	M, W
Lake Erie Coll, OH	M, W
Lake Forest Coll, IL	M, W
Lake Superior State U, MI	M(s), W(s)
Lawrence U, WI	M, W
Lewis U, IL	M(s), W(s)
Lincoln U, MO	M(s), W(s)
Lindenwood U, MO	M(s), W(s)
Loras Coll, IA	M, W
Loyola U Chicago, IL	M(s), W(s)
Luther Coll, IA	M, W
Macalester Coll, MN	M, W
Malone U, OH	M(s), W(s)
Manchester Coll, IN	M, W
Marian U, IN	M(s), W(s)
Marietta Coll, OH	M, W
Marquette U, WI	M(s), W(s)
Martin Luther Coll, MN	M, W
McKendree U, IL	M(s), W(s)
McPherson Coll, KS	M
Miami U, OH	M(s), W(s)
Michigan State U, MI	M(s), W(s)
Michigan Technological U, MI	M, W
MidAmerica Nazarene U, KS	M(s), W(s)
Millikin U, IL	M, W
Milwaukee School of Engineering, WI	M, W
Minnesota State U Mankato, MN	M(s), W(s)
Minnesota State U Moorhead, MN	M(s), W(s)
Minot State U, ND	M(s), W(s)
Missouri Baptist U, MO	M(s), W(s)
Missouri Southern State U, MO	M(s), W(s)
Missouri State U, MO	W(s)
Missouri U of Science and Technology, MO	M(s), W(s)
Monmouth Coll, IL	M, W
Morningside Coll, IA	M(s), W(s)
Mount Marty Coll, SD	M(s), W(s)
Mount Mercy Coll, IA	M(s), W(s)
Mount Union Coll, OH	M, W
Muskingum Coll, OH	M, W
Nebraska Wesleyan U, NE	M, W
North Central Coll, IL	M, W
North Central U, MN	M, W
North Dakota State U, ND	M(s), W(s)
Northern Michigan U, MI	M, W(s)
Northern State U, SD	M(s), W(s)
North Park U, IL	M, W
Northwestern Coll, MN	M, W
Northwest Missouri State U, MO	M(s), W(s)
Northwood U, MI	M(s), W(s)
Oakland U, MI	M, W
Oberlin Coll, OH	M, W
Ohio Northern U, OH	M, W
The Ohio State U, OH	M(s), W(s)
Ohio U, OH	W(s)
Ohio Wesleyan U, OH	M, W
Oklahoma Baptist U, OK	M(s), W(s)
Oklahoma Christian U, OK	M(s), W(s)
Oklahoma City U, OK	M(s), W(s)
Oklahoma State U, OK	M(s), W(s)
Olivet Coll, MI	M, W
Olivet Nazarene U, IL	M(s), W(s)
Oral Roberts U, OK	M(s), W(s)
Otterbein Coll, OH	M, W
Park U, MO	M(s), W(s)
Pittsburg State U, KS	M(s), W(s)
Purdue U, IN	M(s), W(s)
Ripon Coll, WI	M, W
Robert Morris Coll, IL	W(s)
Rose-Hulman Inst of Technology, IN	M, W
Saginaw Valley State U, MI	M(s), W(s)
St. Ambrose U, IA	M(s), W(s)
St. Catherine U, MN	W
St. Cloud State U, MN	M(s), W(s)
Saint John's U, MN	M
Saint Joseph's Coll, IN	M(s), W(s)
Saint Louis U, MO	M(s), W(s)
Saint Mary's U of Minnesota, MN	M, W
St. Norbert Coll, WI	M, W
St. Olaf Coll, MN	M, W
Siena Heights U, MI	M(s), W(s)

Simpson Coll, IA M, W
South Dakota School of Mines and Technology, SD M(s), W(s)
South Dakota State U, SD M(s), W(s)
Southeast Missouri State U, MO M(s), W(s)
Southern Illinois U Carbondale, IL M(s), W(s)
Southern Illinois U Edwardsville, IL M(s), W(s)
Southern Methodist U, TX W
Southern Nazarene U, OK M(s), W(s)
Southwest Baptist U, MO M(s), W(s)
Southwestern Christian U, OK M, W
Southwestern Coll, KS M(s), W(s)
Spring Arbor U, MI M(s), W(s)
Sterling Coll, KS M(s), W(s)
Taylor U, IN M(s), W(s)
Tiffin U, OH M(s), W(s)
Transylvania U, KY M, W
Trine U, IN M, W
Trinity Bible Coll, ND M, W
Trinity Christian Coll, IL M(s), W(s)
Trinity International U, IL M, W
Truman State U, MO M(s), W(s)
The U of Akron, OH M(s), W(s)
U of Central Missouri, MO M(s), W(s)
U of Charleston, WV M(s), W(s)
U of Chicago, IL M, W
U of Cincinnati, OH M(s), W
U of Dallas, TX M, W
U of Dayton, OH W(s)
The U of Findlay, OH M(s), W(s)
U of Illinois at Chicago, IL M(s), W(s)
U of Illinois at Urbana–Champaign, IL M(s), W(s)
U of Indianapolis, IN M(s), W(s)
The U of Iowa, IA M(s), W(s)
The U of Kansas, KS M(s), W(s)
U of Mary, ND M(s), W(s)
U of Michigan, MI M(s), W(s)
U of Minnesota, Duluth, MN M(s), W(s)
U of Minnesota, Morris, MN M, W
U of Minnesota, Twin Cities Campus, MN M(s), W(s)
U of Missouri–Columbia, MO M(s), W(s)
U of Missouri–Kansas City, MO M(s), W(s)
U of Nebraska at Kearney, NE M(s), W(s)
U of Nebraska–Lincoln, NE M(s), W(s)
U of North Dakota, ND M(s), W(s)
U of Northern Iowa, IA M(s), W(s)
U of Notre Dame, IN M(s), W(s)
U of Oklahoma, OK M(s), W(s)
U of Rio Grande, OH M(s), W(s)
U of St. Francis, IL M(s), W(s)
U of Saint Francis, IN M(s), W(s)
U of Sioux Falls, SD M(s), W(s)
The U of South Dakota, SD M(s), W(s)
The U of Toledo, OH W(s)
U of Tulsa, OK M(s), W(s)
U of Wisconsin–Eau Claire, WI M, W
U of Wisconsin–La Crosse, WI M, W
U of Wisconsin–Madison, WI M(s), W(s)
U of Wisconsin–Milwaukee, WI M(s), W(s)
U of Wisconsin–Oshkosh, WI M, W
U of Wisconsin–Parkside, WI M(s), W(s)
U of Wisconsin–Platteville, WI M, W
U of Wisconsin–Stevens Point, WI M, W
U of Wisconsin–Stout, WI M, W
U of Wisconsin–Superior, WI M, W
U of Wisconsin–Whitewater, WI M, W
Ursuline Coll, OH W(s)
Valparaiso U, IN M(s), W(s)
Wabash Coll, IN M
Walsh U, OH M(s), W(s)
Wartburg Coll, IA M, W
Washington U in St. Louis, MO M, W
Wayne State Coll, NE M(s), W(s)
Western Illinois U, IL M(s), W(s)
Western Michigan U, MI W(s)
Wheaton Coll, IL M, W
Wichita State U, KS M(s), W(s)
William Jewell Coll, MO M(s), W(s)
Wilmington Coll, OH M, W
Winona State U, MN W(s)
Wittenberg U, OH M, W
Wright State U, OH W(s)
Xavier U, OH M(s), W(s)
Youngstown State U, OH M(s), W(s)

Ultimate Frisbee

Augustana Coll, IL M, W
Calvin Coll, MI M, W
Carleton Coll, MN M, W
Case Western Reserve U, OH M, W
Coll of Saint Benedict, MN W
The Coll of Wooster, OH M, W
Earlham Coll, IN M, W
Faith Baptist Bible Coll and Theological Seminary, IA M(s), W(s)
Gustavus Adolphus Coll, MN M, W
Hiram Coll, OH M, W
Illinois Wesleyan U, IL M, W
John Carroll U, OH M
Kenyon Coll, OH M, W
Lake Forest Coll, IL M, W
Lawrence U, WI M, W
Macalester Coll, MN M, W
Miami U, OH M, W
Missouri State U, MO M, W
Oberlin Coll, OH M, W
Ohio U–Zanesville, OH M(s), W(s)
Ohio Wesleyan U, OH M, W
St. Cloud State U, MN M, W
Saint John's U, MN M
St. Louis Christian Coll, MO M(s), W(s)
Saint Louis U, MO M, W
Saint Mary's Coll, IN W
Truman State U, MO M, W
U of Cincinnati, OH M
The U of Iowa, IA M, W
The U of Kansas, KS M, W
U of Michigan–Dearborn, MI M
U of Michigan–Flint, MI M, W
U of Minnesota, Duluth, MN M, W
U of Wisconsin–Madison, WI M, W
U of Wisconsin–Platteville, WI M, W
Washington U in St. Louis, MO M, W
Xavier U, OH M, W

Volleyball

Adrian Coll, MI W
Albion Coll, MI M, W
Alma Coll, MI W
Anderson U, IN W
Aquinas Coll, MI W(s)
Ashland U, OH W(s)
Augsburg Coll, MN W
Augustana Coll, IL M, W
Augustana Coll, SD W(s)
Aurora U, IL W
Avila U, MO W(s)
Baker U, KS W(s)
Baldwin-Wallace Coll, OH W
Ball State U, IN M(s), W(s)
Barclay Coll, KS W
Beloit Coll, WI W
Bemidji State U, MN W(s)
Benedictine Coll, KS W(s)
Benedictine U, IL W
Bethany Coll, KS W(s)
Bethany Lutheran Coll, MN W
Bethel Coll, IN W(s)
Bethel Coll, KS W(s)
Bethel U, MN M, W
Black Hills State U, SD W(s)
Blessing-Rieman Coll of Nursing, IL M(s), W(s)
Bluffton U, OH W
Bowling Green State U, OH M, W(s)
Bradley U, IL W(s)
Briar Cliff U, IA W(s)
Buena Vista U, IA W
Butler U, IN W(s)
Calumet Coll of Saint Joseph, IN W
Calvary Bible Coll and Theological Seminary, MO W
Calvin Coll, MI M, W
Cameron U, OK W(s)
Capital U, OH W
Carleton Coll, MN M, W
Carroll U, WI W
Case Western Reserve U, OH M, W
Cedarville U, OH W(s)
Central Christian Coll of Kansas, KS W(s)
Central Coll, IA W
Central Methodist U, MO W(s)
Central Michigan U, MI W(s)
Central State U, OH W(s)
Cincinnati Christian U, OH W
Clarke Coll, IA M(s), W(s)
Clarkson U, NY M, W
Cleveland State U, OH W(s)
Coe Coll, IA W
Coll of Mount St. Joseph, OH W
Coll of Saint Benedict, MN W
Coll of Saint Mary, NE W(s)
The Coll of St. Scholastica, MN W
Coll of the Ozarks, MO W(s)
The Coll of Wooster, OH M, W
Columbia Coll, MO W(s)
Concordia Coll, MN M, W
Concordia U, MI W(s)
Concordia U Chicago, IL W
Concordia U, Nebraska, NE W(s)
Concordia U, St. Paul, MN W(s)
Concordia U Wisconsin, WI W
Cornell Coll, IA M, W
Cornerstone U, MI W(s)
Cottey Coll, MO W(s)
Creighton U, NE W(s)
Crossroads Coll, MN M, W
Crown Coll, MN W
Culver-Stockton Coll, MO W(s)
Dakota State U, SD W(s)
Dakota Wesleyan U, SD W(s)
Dana Coll, NE W(s)
Davenport U, Grand Rapids, MI W(s)
Defiance Coll, OH W
Denison U, OH W
DePaul U, IL W(s)
DePauw U, IN W
Doane Coll, NE W(s)
Dominican U, IL M, W
Dordt Coll, IA W(s)
Drake U, IA W(s)
Drury U, MO W(s)
Earlham Coll, IN M, W

M—for men; W—for women; (s)—scholarship offered

Eastern Illinois U, IL	W(s)
Eastern Michigan U, MI	W(s)
Edgewood Coll, WI	W
Elmhurst Coll, IL	W
Emporia State U, KS	W(s)
Eureka Coll, IL	W
Evangel U, MO	W(s)
Faith Baptist Bible Coll and Theological Seminary, IA	M(s), W(s)
Ferris State U, MI	W(s)
Fontbonne U, MO	M, W
Fort Hays State U, KS	W(s)
Franciscan U of Steubenville, OH	W
Franklin Coll, IN	W
Friends U, KS	W(s)
Goshen Coll, IN	W(s)
Grace Bible Coll, MI	W
Grace Coll, IN	W(s)
Graceland U, IA	M(s), W(s)
Grace U, NE	W
Grand Valley State U, MI	M, W(s)
Grand View U, IA	W(s)
Great Lakes Christian Coll, MI	W
Greenville Coll, IL	W
Grinnell Coll, IA	W
Gustavus Adolphus Coll, MN	M, W
Hamline U, MN	W
Hannibal-LaGrange Coll, MO	M(s), W(s)
Hanover Coll, IN	W
Harris-Stowe State U, MO	W(s)
Haskell Indian Nations U, KS	W
Heidelberg U, OH	M, W
Hillsdale Coll, MI	W(s)
Hiram Coll, OH	M, W
Hope Coll, MI	W
Huntington U, IN	W(s)
Illinois Coll, IL	W
Illinois Inst of Technology, IL	W(s)
Illinois State U, IL	W(s)
Illinois Wesleyan U, IL	M, W
Indiana State U, IN	W(s)
Indiana Tech, IN	W(s)
Indiana U Bloomington, IN	W(s)
Indiana U East, IN	W
Indiana U Northwest, IN	W
Indiana U–Purdue U Fort Wayne, IN	M(s), W(s)
Indiana U–Purdue U Indianapolis, IN	W(s)
Indiana U Southeast, IN	W(s)
Indiana Wesleyan U, IN	W(s)
Iowa State U of Science and Technology, IA	W(s)
Iowa Wesleyan Coll, IA	W(s)
Jamestown Coll, ND	W(s)
John Carroll U, OH	M, W
Kalamazoo Coll, MI	W
Kansas State U, KS	W(s)
Kansas Wesleyan U, KS	W(s)
Kent State U, OH	W(s)
Kenyon Coll, OH	W
Kettering U, MI	M
Knox Coll, IL	W
Lake Erie Coll, OH	W
Lake Forest Coll, IL	W
Lakeland Coll, WI	M, W
Lake Superior State U, MI	W(s)
Lawrence U, WI	M, W
Lewis U, IL	M(s), W(s)
Lindenwood U, MO	M(s), W(s)
Loras Coll, IA	M, W
Loyola U Chicago, IL	M(s), W(s)
Luther Coll, IA	W
Macalester Coll, MN	M, W
MacMurray Coll, IL	W
Madonna U, MI	W(s)
Malone U, OH	W(s)
Manchester Coll, IN	W
Manhattan Christian Coll, KS	W
Maranatha Baptist Bible Coll, WI	W
Marian U, WI	W
Marian U, IN	W(s)
Marietta Coll, OH	W
Marquette U, WI	M, W(s)
Martin Luther Coll, MN	W
Maryville U of Saint Louis, MO	W
Mayville State U, ND	W(s)
McKendree U, IL	W(s)
McPherson Coll, KS	W
Miami U, OH	M, W(s)
Miami U Hamilton, OH	W
Michigan State U, MI	M, W(s)
Michigan Technological U, MI	W(s)
Mid-America Christian U, OK	W
MidAmerica Nazarene U, KS	W(s)
Millikin U, IL	W
Milwaukee School of Engineering, WI	M, W
Minnesota State U Mankato, MN	W(s)
Minnesota State U Moorhead, MN	W(s)
Minot State U, ND	W(s)
Missouri Baptist U, MO	M(s), W(s)
Missouri Southern State U, MO	W(s)
Missouri State U, MO	M, W(s)
Missouri U of Science and Technology, MO	W(s)
Missouri Western State U, MO	W(s)
Monmouth Coll, IL	W
Moody Bible Inst, IL	M, W
Morningside Coll, IA	W(s)
Mount Marty Coll, SD	W(s)
Mount Mary Coll, WI	W
Mount Mercy Coll, IA	W(s)
Mount Union Coll, OH	W
Mount Vernon Nazarene U, OH	W(s)
Muskingum Coll, OH	W
Nebraska Wesleyan U, NE	W
Newman U, KS	W(s)
North Central Coll, IL	W
North Central U, MN	W
North Dakota State U, ND	M, W(s)
Northern Michigan U, MI	W(s)
Northern State U, SD	W(s)
Northland Coll, WI	W
North Park U, IL	W
Northwestern Coll, MN	M, W
Northwestern U, IL	W(s)
Northwest Missouri State U, MO	W(s)
Northwood U, MI	W(s)
Oak Hills Christian Coll, MN	W
Oakland U, MI	W(s)
Oberlin Coll, OH	M, W
Ohio Christian U, OH	W
Ohio Dominican U, OH	W(s)
Ohio Northern U, OH	M, W
The Ohio State U, OH	M(s), W(s)
The Ohio State U at Lima, OH	M, W
Ohio U, OH	M, W(s)
Ohio U–Eastern, OH	W
Ohio U–Zanesville, OH	M(s), W(s)
Ohio Wesleyan U, OH	M, W
Oklahoma Panhandle State U, OK	W(s)
Olivet Coll, MI	W
Olivet Nazarene U, IL	W(s)
Oral Roberts U, OK	W(s)
Otterbein Coll, OH	W
Park U, MO	M(s), W(s)
Pittsburg State U, KS	W(s)
Presentation Coll, SD	W
Purdue U, IN	W(s)
Purdue U North Central, IN	M(s)
Quincy U, IL	M(s), W(s)
Research Coll of Nursing, MO	W(s)
Ripon Coll, WI	W
Robert Morris Coll, IL	W(s)
Rochester Comm and Tech Coll, MN	W
Rockford Coll, IL	M, W
Rockhurst U, MO	W(s)
Rose-Hulman Inst of Technology, IN	W
Saginaw Valley State U, MI	W(s)
St. Ambrose U, IA	M(s), W(s)
St. Catherine U, MN	W
St. Cloud State U, MN	M, W(s)
St. Gregory's U, Shawnee, OK	W(s)
Saint John's U, MN	M
Saint Joseph's Coll, IN	W(s)
St. Louis Christian Coll, MO	M(s), W(s)
St. Louis Coll of Pharmacy, MO	W
Saint Louis U, MO	M, W(s)
Saint Mary's Coll, IN	W
Saint Mary's U of Minnesota, MN	W
St. Norbert Coll, WI	W
St. Olaf Coll, MN	W
Saint Xavier U, IL	W(s)
Shawnee State U, OH	W(s)
Siena Heights U, MI	M(s), W(s)
Simpson Coll, IA	W
South Dakota School of Mines and Technology, SD	W(s)
South Dakota State U, SD	W(s)
Southeastern Oklahoma State U, OK	W(s)
Southeast Missouri State U, MO	W(s)
Southern Illinois U Carbondale, IL	W(s)
Southern Illinois U Edwardsville, IL	W(s)
Southern Methodist U, TX	W(s)
Southern Nazarene U, OK	W(s)
Southwest Baptist U, MO	W(s)
Southwestern Christian U, OK	W
Southwestern Coll, KS	W(s)
Southwest Minnesota State U, MN	W(s)
Spring Arbor U, MI	W(s)
Stephens Coll, MO	W(s)
Sterling Coll, KS	W(s)
Taylor U, IN	W(s)
Tiffin U, OH	W(s)
Transylvania U, KY	W
Trine U, IN	W
Trinity Bible Coll, ND	W
Trinity Christian Coll, IL	W(s)
Trinity International U, IL	W(s)
Truman State U, MO	M, W(s)
Union Coll, NE	W
The U of Akron, OH	W(s)
U of Central Missouri, MO	W(s)
U of Central Oklahoma, OK	W(s)
U of Charleston, WV	W(s)
U of Chicago, IL	W
U of Cincinnati, OH	W(s)
U of Dallas, TX	W
U of Dayton, OH	W(s)
U of Evansville, IN	W(s)
The U of Findlay, OH	W(s)
U of Illinois at Chicago, IL	W(s)

U of Illinois at Springfield, IL W(s)
U of Illinois at Urbana–Champaign, IL W(s)
U of Indianapolis, IN W(s)
The U of Iowa, IA M, W(s)
The U of Kansas, KS W(s)
U of Mary, ND W(s)
U of Michigan, MI W(s)
U of Michigan–Dearborn, MI W(s)
U of Minnesota, Crookston, MN W(s)
U of Minnesota, Duluth, MN M, W(s)
U of Minnesota, Morris, MN W
U of Minnesota, Twin Cities Campus, MN W(s)
U of Missouri–Columbia, MO W(s)
U of Missouri–Kansas City, MO W(s)
U of Missouri–St. Louis, MO W(s)
U of Nebraska at Kearney, NE W(s)
U of Nebraska at Omaha, NE W(s)
U of Nebraska–Lincoln, NE W(s)
U of New Orleans, LA W(s)
U of North Dakota, ND W(s)
U of Northern Iowa, IA W(s)
U of Notre Dame, IN W(s)
U of Oklahoma, OK W(s)
U of Rio Grande, OH W(s)
U of St. Francis, IL W(s)
U of Saint Francis, IN W(s)
U of Saint Mary, KS W(s)
U of Sioux Falls, SD W(s)
The U of South Dakota, SD W(s)
U of Southern Indiana, IN W(s)
The U of Toledo, OH W(s)
U of Tulsa, OK W(s)
U of Wisconsin–Eau Claire, WI W
U of Wisconsin–Green Bay, WI W(s)
U of Wisconsin–La Crosse, WI W
U of Wisconsin–Madison, WI W(s)
U of Wisconsin–Milwaukee, WI M, W(s)
U of Wisconsin–Oshkosh, WI W
U of Wisconsin–Parkside, WI W(s)
U of Wisconsin–Platteville, WI M, W
U of Wisconsin–Stevens Point, WI W
U of Wisconsin–Stout, WI M, W
U of Wisconsin–Superior, WI W
U of Wisconsin–Whitewater, WI M, W
Ursuline Coll, OH W(s)
Valley City State U, ND W(s)
Valparaiso U, IN W(s)
Viterbo U, WI W(s)
Waldorf Coll, IA W(s)
Walsh U, OH W(s)
Wartburg Coll, IA W
Washburn U, KS W(s)
Washington U in St. Louis, MO M, W
Wayne State Coll, NE W(s)
Wayne State U, MI W(s)
Webster U, MO W
Western Illinois U, IL W(s)
Western Michigan U, MI W(s)
Westminster Coll, MO W
Wheaton Coll, IL M, W
Wichita State U, KS M, W(s)
William Jewell Coll, MO W(s)
Wilmington Coll, OH W
Winona State U, MN M, W(s)
Wittenberg U, OH M, W
Wright State U, OH W(s)
Xavier U, OH M, W(s)
York Coll, NE W
Youngstown State U, OH W(s)

Water Polo

Ball State U, IN M, W
Carleton Coll, MN M, W
Grand Valley State U, MI M, W
Illinois Wesleyan U, IL M
Indiana U Bloomington, IN W(s)
Lake Forest Coll, IL M, W
Lindenwood U, MO M(s), W(s)
Loras Coll, IA M
Macalester Coll, MN M, W
Miami U, OH M, W
Michigan State U, MI M, W
Michigan Technological U, MI M, W
Oberlin Coll, OH M, W
Ohio U, OH M, W
Saint John's U, MN M
Saint Louis U, MO M
Saint Mary's Coll, IN W
The U of Findlay, OH M, W
U of Michigan, MI M(s), W(s)
U of Wisconsin–Madison, WI M, W
Wabash Coll, IN M
Washington U in St. Louis, MO M, W
Wheaton Coll, IL W
Xavier U, OH M, W

Weight Lifting

Bowling Green State U, OH M, W
Miami U, OH M, W
Ohio U, OH M
Truman State U, MO M, W
U of Wisconsin–La Crosse, WI M, W
U of Wisconsin–Whitewater, WI M

Wrestling

Ashland U, OH M(s)
Augsburg Coll, MN M
Augustana Coll, IL M
Augustana Coll, SD M(s)
Baker U, KS M(s)
Baldwin-Wallace Coll, OH M
Ball State U, IN M
Bethel Coll, IN M(s)
Briar Cliff U, IA M(s)
Buena Vista U, IA M
Case Western Reserve U, OH M
Central Coll, IA M
Central Michigan U, MI M(s)
Cleveland State U, OH M(s)
Coe Coll, IA M
Coll of Mount St. Joseph, OH M
Concordia Coll, MN M
Concordia U, Nebraska, NE M(s)
Concordia U Wisconsin, WI M
Cornell Coll, IA M
Dakota Wesleyan U, SD M(s)
Dana Coll, NE M(s)
Eastern Michigan U, MI M(s)
Elmhurst Coll, IL M
Fort Hays State U, KS M(s)
Grand Valley State U, MI M
Grand View U, IA M
Hannibal-LaGrange Coll, MO M(s)
Heidelberg U, OH M
Indiana U Bloomington, IN M(s)
Iowa State U of Science and Technology, IA M(s)
Jamestown Coll, ND M(s), W(s)
John Carroll U, OH M
Kent State U, OH M(s)
Knox Coll, IL M
Lakeland Coll, WI M
Lawrence U, WI M
Lindenwood U, MO M(s)
Loras Coll, IA M
Luther Coll, IA M
Manchester Coll, IN M
Maranatha Baptist Bible Coll, WI M
Marietta Coll, OH M, W
McKendree U, IL M(s)
Miami U, OH M, W
Michigan State U, MI M(s)
Milwaukee School of Engineering, WI M
Minnesota State U Mankato, MN M(s)
Minnesota State U Moorhead, MN M(s)
Missouri Baptist U, MO M(s)
Missouri State U, MO M
Morningside Coll, IA M(s)
Mount Union Coll, OH M
Muskingum Coll, OH M
Newman U, KS M(s)
North Central Coll, IL M
North Dakota State U, ND M(s)
Northern State U, SD M(s)
Northwestern U, IL M(s)
Ohio Northern U, OH M
The Ohio State U, OH M(s)
Ohio U, OH M(s)
Oklahoma City U, OK M(s), W(s)
Oklahoma State U, OK M(s)
Olivet Coll, MI M
Oral Roberts U, OK M
Purdue U, IN M(s)
Rochester Comm and Tech Coll, MN M
Rose-Hulman Inst of Technology, IN M
St. Cloud State U, MN M(s)
Saint John's U, MN M
St. Olaf Coll, MN M
Simpson Coll, IA M
South Dakota State U, SD M(s)
Southern Illinois U Edwardsville, IL M(s)
Southern Methodist U, TX M
Southwest Minnesota State U, MN M(s)
Trine U, IN M
Trinity Bible Coll, ND M
Truman State U, MO M(s)
U of Central Missouri, MO M(s)
U of Central Oklahoma, OK M(s)
U of Chicago, IL M
U of Cincinnati, OH M
U of Dallas, TX M
The U of Findlay, OH M(s)
U of Illinois at Urbana–Champaign, IL M(s)
U of Indianapolis, IN M(s)
The U of Iowa, IA M(s)
U of Mary, ND M(s)
U of Michigan, MI M(s)
U of Minnesota, Twin Cities Campus, MN M(s)
U of Missouri–Columbia, MO M(s)
U of Nebraska at Kearney, NE M(s)
U of Nebraska at Omaha, NE M(s)
U of Nebraska–Lincoln, NE M(s)
U of Northern Iowa, IA M(s)
U of Oklahoma, OK M(s)
U of Southern Indiana, IN M
U of Wisconsin–Eau Claire, WI M
U of Wisconsin–La Crosse, WI M
U of Wisconsin–Madison, WI M(s)

M—for men; W—for women; (s)—scholarship offered

U of Wisconsin–Oshkosh, WI	M
U of Wisconsin–Parkside, WI	M(s)
U of Wisconsin–Platteville, WI	M
U of Wisconsin–Stevens Point, WI	M
U of Wisconsin–Whitewater, WI	M
Wabash Coll, IN	M
Waldorf Coll, IA	M(s)
Wartburg Coll, IA	M
Wayne State Coll, NE	M
Wheaton Coll, IL	M
Wichita State U, KS	M
Wilmington Coll, OH	M
Winona State U, MN	M
York Coll, NE	M

ROTC Programs

Institution	Program
Allen Coll, IA	A(c)
Alma Coll, MI	A(c)
Augsburg Coll, MN	A(c), N(c), AF(c)
Aurora U, IL	A(c)
Avila U, MO	A(c)
Baker U, KS	A(c), AF(c)
Baldwin-Wallace Coll, OH	AF(c)
Ball State U, IN	A
Bellin Coll of Nursing, WI	A(c)
Benedictine Coll, KS	A
Benedictine U, IL	A(c)
Bethany Lutheran Coll, MN	A(c)
Bethel Coll, IN	A(c), AF(c)
Bethel U, MN	A(c), AF(c)
Black Hills State U, SD	A
Bowling Green State U, OH	A, AF
Bradley U, IL	A(c)
Butler U, IN	A, AF(c)
Calvary Bible Coll and Theological Seminary, MO	A(c)
Calvin Coll, MI	A(c)
Cameron U, OK	A
Capital U, OH	A, AF(c)
Carroll U, WI	A(c), AF(c)
Case Western Reserve U, OH	A(c), AF(c)
Cedarville U, OH	A(c), AF(c)
Central Methodist U, MO	A(c), AF(c)
Central Michigan U, MI	A
Central State U, OH	A
Chamberlain Coll of Nursing, MO	A(c)
Clarke Coll, IA	A(c)
Clarkson Coll, NE	A(c), AF(c)
Clarkson U, NY	A, AF
Cleveland State U, OH	A(c), N(c), AF(c)
Coe Coll, IA	A(c), AF(c)
Coll of Mount St. Joseph, OH	A(c), AF(c)
Coll of Saint Benedict, MN	A(c)
Coll of Saint Mary, NE	A(c), AF(c)
The Coll of St. Scholastica, MN	AF(c)
Coll of the Ozarks, MO	A
Colorado Tech U Sioux Falls, SD	A(c)
Columbia Coll, MO	A(c), N(c), AF(c)
Concordia Coll, MN	A(c), AF(c)
Concordia U, MI	A(c), AF(c)
Concordia U, Nebraska, NE	A(c), AF(c)
Concordia U, St. Paul, MN	A(c), N(c), AF(c)
Cornerstone U, MI	A(c)
Creighton U, NE	A, AF(c)
Dakota State U, SD	A, AF(c)
Dana Coll, NE	A(c), AF(c)
Denison U, OH	A(c)
DePaul U, IL	A(c)
DePauw U, IN	A(c), AF(c)
DeVry U, Columbus, OH	A(c)
Doane Coll, NE	A(c), AF(c)
Drake U, IA	A, AF(c)
Drury U, MO	A(c)
Eastern Illinois U, IL	A
Eastern Michigan U, MI	A, N(c), AF(c)
Elmhurst Coll, IL	A(c), AF(c)
Evangel U, MO	A
Ferris State U, MI	A(c)
Fontbonne U, MO	A(c), AF(c)
Franciscan U of Steubenville, OH	A(c)
Franklin Coll, IN	A(c)
Franklin U, OH	A(c), AF(c)
Grace Bible Coll, MI	A(c)
Grace U, NE	A(c), AF(c)
Grand View U, IA	A(c), AF(c)
Gustavus Adolphus Coll, MN	A(c)
Hamline U, MN	AF(c)
Harris-Stowe State U, MO	AF(c)
Haskell Indian Nations U, KS	AF(c)
Heidelberg U, OH	A(c), AF(c)
Hope Coll, MI	A(c)
Illinois Inst of Technology, IL	A, N, AF
Illinois State U, IL	A
Illinois Wesleyan U, IL	A(c)
Indiana State U, IN	A, AF
Indiana U Bloomington, IN	A, AF
Indiana U Kokomo, IN	A(c)
Indiana U Northwest, IN	A
Indiana U–Purdue U Indianapolis, IN	A, N(c), AF(c)
Indiana U South Bend, IN	A(c), N(c), AF(c)
Indiana U Southeast, IN	A, N
Indiana Wesleyan U, IN	A(c)
Iowa State U of Science and Technology, IA	A, N, AF
John Carroll U, OH	A
Kalamazoo Coll, MI	A(c)
Kansas State U, KS	A, AF
Kent State U, OH	A, AF
Kent State U, Salem Campus, OH	A(c), AF(c)
Kent State U, Stark Campus, OH	A(c), AF(c)
Lawrence Technological U, MI	A(c), N(c), AF(c)
Lewis U, IL	A(c), AF(c)
Lincoln U, MO	A, N(c), AF(c)
Lindenwood U, MO	A, AF(c)
Loras Coll, IA	A(c)
Lourdes Coll, OH	A(c), AF(c)
Loyola U Chicago, IL	A(c), N(c), AF(c)
Macalester Coll, MN	N(c), AF(c)
Malone U, OH	A(c), AF(c)
Manhattan Christian Coll, KS	A(c), AF(c)
Maranatha Baptist Bible Coll, WI	A
Marian U, WI	A
Marian U, IN	A(c)
Marquette U, WI	A, N, AF
Maryville U of Saint Louis, MO	A(c)
Mayville State U, ND	A(c), AF(c)
McKendree U, IL	A(c), AF(c)
Miami U, OH	A(c), N, AF
Miami U Hamilton, OH	N(c), AF(c)
Michigan State U, MI	A, AF
Michigan Technological U, MI	A, AF
MidAmerica Nazarene U, KS	A(c), AF(c)
Milwaukee School of Engineering, WI	A(c), N(c), AF(c)
Minnesota State U Mankato, MN	A
Minnesota State U Moorhead, MN	A(c), AF(c)
Missouri Baptist U, MO	A(c)
Missouri State U, MO	A
Missouri U of Science and Technology, MO	A, N(c), AF
Missouri Western State U, MO	A
Monmouth Coll, IL	A(c)
Morningside Coll, IA	A(c)
Mount Marty Coll, SD	A(c)
Mount Mary Coll, WI	A(c)
Mount Union Coll, OH	A(c), AF(c)
Nebraska Methodist Coll, NE	A(c), AF(c)
Nebraska Wesleyan U, NE	A(c), AF(c)
North Central Coll, IL	A(c), AF(c)
North Central U, MN	A(c), AF(c)
North Dakota State U, ND	A, AF
Northeastern Illinois U, IL	A(c), AF(c)
Northeastern State U, OK	A
Northern Michigan U, MI	A
Northwestern Coll, MN	A(c), AF(c)
Northwestern U, IL	A(c), N, AF(c)
Northwest Missouri State U, MO	A
Oakland U, MI	AF(c)
Ohio Dominican U, OH	A(c)
Ohio Northern U, OH	A(c), AF(c)
The Ohio State U, OH	A, N, AF
The Ohio State U at Lima, OH	A(c), N(c), AF(c)
The Ohio State U at Marion, OH	A(c), N(c), AF(c)
The Ohio State U–Mansfield Campus, OH	A(c), N(c), AF(c)
The Ohio State U–Newark Campus, OH	A(c), N(c), AF(c)
Ohio U, OH	A, AF
Ohio U–Chillicothe, OH	A(c), AF(c)
Ohio U–Lancaster, OH	A(c), AF(c)
Ohio Wesleyan U, OH	A(c), AF(c)
Oklahoma Baptist U, OK	AF(c)
Oklahoma Christian U, OK	A(c), AF(c)
Oklahoma City U, OK	A(c), AF(c)
Oklahoma State U, OK	A, AF
Olivet Nazarene U, IL	A
Oral Roberts U, OK	AF(c)
Otterbein Coll, OH	A(c), AF(c)
Park U, MO	A
Pittsburg State U, KS	A
Purdue U, IN	A, N, AF
Research Coll of Nursing, MO	A(c)
Ripon Coll, WI	A
Robert Morris Coll, IL	A(c)
Rockford Coll, IL	A(c)
Rockhurst U, MO	A(c)
Rogers State U, OK	AF(c)
Rose-Hulman Inst of Technology, IN	A, AF
St. Catherine U, MN	A(c), AF(c)
St. Cloud State U, MN	A
St. Gregory's U, Shawnee, OK	AF(c)
Saint John's U, MN	A
St. Louis Coll of Pharmacy, MO	A(c), AF(c)
Saint Louis U, MO	A(c), AF
Saint Mary-of-the-Woods Coll, IN	A(c), AF(c)
Saint Mary's Coll, IN	A(c), N(c), AF(c)
Saint Mary's U of Minnesota, MN	A(c)
St. Norbert Coll, WI	A
Saint Xavier U, IL	AF(c)
South Dakota School of Mines and Technology, SD	A
South Dakota State U, SD	A, AF
Southeast Missouri State U, MO	AF
Southern Illinois U Carbondale, IL	A, AF
Southern Illinois U Edwardsville, IL	A, AF
Southern Methodist U, TX	A, AF(c)

A—Army; N—Navy; AF—Air Force; (c)—available through a cooperating host institution

Southern Nazarene U, OK A(c), AF(c)
Southwest Baptist U, MO A(c)
Spring Arbor U, MI A, AF(c)
Stephens Coll, MO A(c), AF(c)
Tiffin U, OH A(c), AF(c)
Transylvania U, KY A(c), AF(c)
Truman State U, MO A
The U of Akron, OH A, AF(c)
U of Central Missouri, MO A, AF(c)
U of Central Oklahoma, OK A
U of Charleston, WV A
U of Chicago, IL A(c), AF(c)
U of Cincinnati, OH A, AF
U of Dallas, TX A(c), AF(c)
U of Dayton, OH A, AF(c)
The U of Findlay, OH A(c), AF(c)
U of Illinois at Chicago, IL A, N(c), AF(c)
U of Illinois at Urbana–Champaign, IL A, N, AF
U of Indianapolis, IN A(c)
The U of Iowa, IA A, AF
The U of Kansas, KS A, N, AF
U of Michigan, MI A, AF
U of Michigan–Dearborn, MI A(c), N(c), AF(c)
U of Minnesota, Crookston, MN AF(c)
U of Minnesota, Duluth, MN AF
U of Minnesota, Twin Cities Campus, MN A, N, AF
U of Missouri–Columbia, MO A, N, AF
U of Missouri–Kansas City, MO A, AF(c)
U of Missouri–St. Louis, MO A(c), AF(c)
U of Nebraska at Omaha, NE A(c), AF
U of Nebraska–Lincoln, NE A, N, AF
U of Nebraska Medical Center, NE A(c), AF(c)
U of New Orleans, LA A(c), N(c), AF(c)
U of North Dakota, ND A, AF
U of Northern Iowa, IA A
U of Notre Dame, IN A, N, AF
U of Oklahoma, OK A, N, AF
U of Oklahoma Health Sciences Center, OK A(c), AF(c)
U of Rio Grande, OH A(c)
U of Saint Mary, KS A(c), AF(c)
The U of South Dakota, SD A
U of Southern Indiana, IN A
The U of Toledo, OH A, AF(c)
U of Tulsa, OK AF(c)
U of Wisconsin–Green Bay, WI A(c)
U of Wisconsin–La Crosse, WI A
U of Wisconsin–Madison, WI A, N, AF
U of Wisconsin–Milwaukee, WI A(c), AF(c)
U of Wisconsin–Oshkosh, WI A
U of Wisconsin–Parkside, WI A(c)
U of Wisconsin–Platteville, WI A(c)
U of Wisconsin–Stevens Point, WI A
U of Wisconsin–Superior, WI AF(c)
U of Wisconsin–Whitewater, WI A, AF
Ursuline Coll, OH A(c)
Valparaiso U, IN AF(c)
Viterbo U, WI A(c)
Washburn U, KS A, N(c), AF(c)
Washington U in St. Louis, MO A, AF(c)
Wayne State Coll, NE A
Wayne State U, MI AF(c)
Webster U, MO A(c), AF(c)
Western Illinois U, IL A
Western Michigan U, MI A
Westminster Coll, MO A(c), AF(c)
Wheaton Coll, IL A
Wilberforce U, OH A(c), AF(c)
Winona State U, MN A(c)
Wittenberg U, OH A(c), AF(c)
Wright State U, OH A, AF
Xavier U, OH A, AF(c)
York Coll, NE A(c), N(c), AF(c)
Youngstown State U, OH A, AF(c)

Alphabetical Listing of Colleges and Universities

In this index, the page locations of the **Profiles** are printed in regular type, **Profiles** with **Special Messages to Students** in *italics*, and **Close-Ups** in **bold type**.

Alphabetical Listing of Colleges and Universities

Notes

Notes

Notes

Notes

Notes

Notes

Peterson's
Book Satisfaction Survey

Give Us Your Feedback

Thank you for choosing Peterson's as your source for personalized solutions for your education and career achievement. Please take a few minutes to answer the following questions. Your answers will go a long way in helping us to produce the most user-friendly and comprehensive resources to meet your individual needs.

When completed, please tear out this page and mail it to us at:

Publishing Department
Peterson's, a Nelnet company
2000 Lenox Drive
Lawrenceville, NJ 08648

You can also complete this survey online at **www.petersons.com/booksurvey.**

1. What is the ISBN of the book you have purchased? (The ISBN can be found on the book's back cover in the lower right-hand corner.) ______________

2. Where did you purchase this book?

❑ Retailer, such as Barnes & Noble
❑ Online reseller, such as Amazon.com
❑ Petersons.com
❑ Other (please specify) ______________

3. If you purchased this book on Petersons.com, please rate the following aspects of your online purchasing experience on a scale of 4 to 1 (4 = Excellent and 1 = Poor).

	4	3	2	1
Comprehensiveness of Peterson's Online Bookstore page	❑	❑	❑	❑
Overall online customer experience	❑	❑	❑	❑

4. Which category best describes you?

❑ High school student
❑ Parent of high school student
❑ College student
❑ Graduate/professional student
❑ Returning adult student
❑ Teacher
❑ Counselor
❑ Working professional/military
❑ Other (please specify) ______________

5. Rate your overall satisfaction with this book.

Extremely Satisfied	Satisfied	Not Satisfied
❑	❑	❑

6. Rate each of the following aspects of this book on a scale of 4 to 1 (4 = Excellent and 1 = Poor).

	4	3	2	1
Comprehensiveness of the information	❑	❑	❑	❑
Accuracy of the information	❑	❑	❑	❑
Usability	❑	❑	❑	❑
Cover design	❑	❑	❑	❑
Book layout	❑	❑	❑	❑
Special features *(e.g., CD, flashcards, charts, etc.)*	❑	❑	❑	❑
Value for the money	❑	❑	❑	❑

7. This book was recommended by:

❑ Guidance counselor
❑ Parent/guardian
❑ Family member/relative
❑ Friend
❑ Teacher
❑ Not recommended by anyone—I found the book on my own
❑ Other (please specify) ____________________

8. Would you recommend this book to others?

Yes	Not Sure	No
❑	❑	❑

9. Please provide any additional comments.

____

____

____

____

____

Remember, you can tear out this page and mail it to us at:

Publishing Department
Peterson's, a Nelnet company
2000 Lenox Drive
Lawrenceville, NJ 08648

or you can complete the survey online at **www.petersons.com/booksurvey.**

Your feedback is important to us at Peterson's, and we thank you for your time!

If you would like us to keep in touch with you about new products and services, please include your e-mail address here: ____________________